THE
NORTON/GROVE
DICTIONARY OF
WOMEN
COMPOSERS

THE NORTON/GROVE DICTIONARY OF WOMEN COMPOSERS

EDITED BY
Julie Anne Sadie & Rhian Samuel

W·W·NORTON & COMPANY
NEW YORK   LONDON

The New Grove is a registered trademark in the United States,
of Macmillan Publishers Limited, London.

Macmillan Publishers Limited, London and its associated
companies are the proprietors of the trademarks *Grove's*,
The New Grove, and *The New Grove Dictionary of Music and
Musicians* throughout the world.

The New Grove ® Dictionary of Women Composers
edited by Julie Anne Sadie and Rhian Samuel, 1994

First published in the United Kingdom by
The Macmillan Press Ltd, London and Basingstoke

ISBN 0-333-515986

First American edition published 1994 by
W.W. Norton & Company, Inc.,
500 Fifth Avenue, New York, NY 10110
W.W. Norton & Company Ltd
10 Coptic Street, London WC1A 1PU

ISBN 0-393-03487-9

1 2 3 4 5 6 7 8 9 0

Typeset by Florencetype Ltd, Kewstoke, Avon
Printed in the United States of America

Contents

Foreword   vii
Preface   ix
Acknowledgments   xix
Chronology   xx
General Abbreviations   xxxiii
Bibliographical Abbreviations   xxxvii
Library Sigla   xl
Editorial Conventions in this Dictionary   xliii

The Dictionary A–Z   1

Illustration Acknowledgments   517
List of Contributors   519
Index   523

Editors
Julie Anne Sadie
Rhian Samuel

Illustrations Editor
Elisabeth Agate

Series Editor
Stanley Sadie

Foreword

The New Grove Dictionary of Women Composers is the last of the subject dictionaries related to the 20-volume *New Grove Dictionary of Music and Musicians* (1980). Here the relationship between the new dictionary and the parent one is particularly slender. While *The New Grove* gave extensive coverage to musical instruments, to American music and to opera (to name the topics of our principal subject dictionaries), its treatment of women composers was relatively modest. In the intellectual climate of the 1970s, the criteria governing the inclusion of women composers – those same criteria of supposed merit and prominence as governed the inclusion of men composers – seemed perfectly adequate; the increase since then in our awareness of women's contribution, and, more particularly, of the failure of earlier historians (not excluding historians of contemporary music) to acknowledge it, to give it a sufficient context and to identify any specific elements of its character, justifies the present volume. By the time *The New Grove Dictionary of American Music* (1986) came to be compiled – its list of headwords was drawn up almost a decade later than that of *The New Grove* – attitudes were changing, and in any case the nature of American society dictated that women had for longer enjoyed greater opportunity than they had in most other countries. Our editors could therefore take advantage of a more up-to-date starting-point for their work on composers of the USA.

Of the two editors, Julie Anne Sadie took primary responsibility for earlier composers and Rhian Samuel for more modern ones, with an overlap in the early twentieth century.

The question under which name an entry is located, when a person has borne more than one, arises particularly in the case of a dictionary of women. There has been no rigid policy of entering a woman under her maiden name in preference to her married name, or vice-versa; rather, the traditional *Grove* policy has been followed – of placing an entry where most people are likely to seek it first. We apologize to those whose expectations may be disappointed but have done our best to help them by supplying ample cross-references.

Like other *Grove* dictionaries, *The New Grove Dictionary of Women Composers* is a record of achievement, not of promise; and it is not a directory. Few composers born as late as the end of the 1950s are entered; the cut-off date in general is 1955.

It may be objected that women composers ought not form the topic of a specific dictionary, as they do not form a class apart, in the sense that (for example) French composers, or Renaissance composers, or composers of piano music, might do. Such an objection should be resisted. Women composers have – or, rightly or wrongly, have generally been taken to have – the same objectives as the men alongside whom they have worked and have been trained. The aim of this dictionary is not to establish or to acknowledge any supposed separation between the sexes (although it may help to establish whether such separation exists and if so what form it may take); rather, it is to repair a deficiency in existing reference materials on the subject, and by applying the tried *Grove* procedures involving information-gathering, from scholars and critics of substance and authority, evaluation and sorting, to provide a useful tool for those who wish to look more deeply into what is in its own right a significant and worthwhile area of study. Perhaps it will prove its value most clearly and effectively if it quickly becomes out of date because of the research, criticism and discussion it may provoke, not to mention fresh composition. I look forward to the need for a second edition.

London, Summer 1994   STANLEY SADIE

Preface

1: Women Composers in Musical Lexicography

Julie Anne Sadie

It is commonly supposed that dictionaries of women composers are a relatively recent innovation. In fact, the first was compiled in 1902 and, remarkably, contains more than 750 entries. Otto Ebel published *Women Composers: a Biographical Handbook of Women's Work in Music* in Brooklyn, New York, and then, eight years later in Paris, as *Les femmes compositeurs de musique*. Also in 1902 Adolph Wilhartitz published in Los Angeles a 16-page booklet of *Some Facts About Women in Music*, listing European and American composers of opera and other theatre music. The following year, Arthur Elson published in Boston a companion volume of sorts, *Woman's Work in Music*. The subtitle admirably sums up its contents: 'being an account of her influence on the art, in ancient as well as modern times; a summary of her musical compositions, in the different countries of the civilized world; and an estimate of their rank in comparison with those of man.' He covers the ground in twelve chapters, which proceed in chronological order and reveal a considerable command of the history of women musicians, including with them an appendix arranged by country. Elson's view sweeps aside that of his New England predecessor, George P. Upton, who wrote in *Woman in Music* (Boston, 1880) that women were not in general intellectually capable of grasping the intricacies of music composition. The precedents for this remarkable flurry of activity would seem to be little more than a handful of articles in American and French periodicals containing vignettes of individual women composers; the American articles concentrate on prominent contemporaries while the French already begin isolating and surveying their national heritage.[1]

After an unconscionable hiatus, a number of lexicographic books on women composers and their music began appearing in the 1970s, many of them compiled by women. Some attempt to embrace the field[2] while others limit their scope to a period, place or genre;[3] but together they have made possible the undertaking of historical surveys.[4] By far the largest effort undertaken by an individual on behalf of women composers remains that of Aaron I. Cohen: his two-volume *International Encyclopedia of Women Composers* (New York, 1981), now in its second edition (1987), proved an essential point of reference, when carefully used, in compiling *The New Grove Dictionary of Women Composers*. Cohen, like Ebel, is an enthusiast, whose work, if derivative and less than critical, flew in the face of convention and sowed the seeds we nurture and cultivate today.

Women composers have from the beginning figured in biographical dictionaries of music. In 1732 Evrard Titon du Tillet in Paris (*Le Parnasse françois*) and Johann Gottfried Walther in Leipzig (*Musicalisches Lexicon*) produced the earliest dictionaries to include biographies of musicians. Each included an entry on Elisabeth-Claude Jacquet de la Guerre, who had died only three years earlier, Titon du Tillet additionally assigning her one of only three coveted places immediately below Jean-Baptiste Lully on his projected monument to the literary and musical glories of the *louisquatorzien* era. Walther's *Lexicon* is wider in scope and attempts to cover musicians from all over Europe, so although only one woman composer is to be found in Titon, half a dozen (Sappho and Barbara Strozzi among them) appear in Walther. Sir John Hawkins incorporated short biographical sketches in *A General History of the Science and Practice of Music* (London, 1776), which include Jacquet de la Guerre, Strozzi and Esther Elizabeth Velkiers (who was blind) as composers. Jean-Benjamin de La Borde did much the

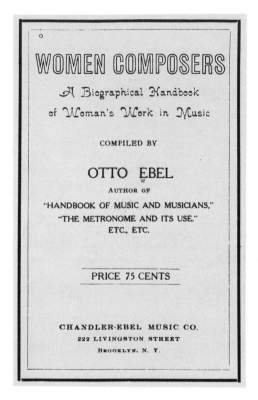

same in his four-volume *Essai sur la musique ancienne et moderne* (Paris, 1780), though he subdivided the dictionary element into four complete alphabets, corresponding to the different periods of musical history under consideration; yet, while surveying literally dozens of Italian *cantatrices*, La Borde acknowledges only three French women as composers: Jacquet de la Guerre, Mlle Duval and Mme la Marquise de la Mezangère (whom he describes as merely an 'habile compositrice').

Ernst Ludwig Gerber enlarged Walther's *Lexicon* in his *Historisch-biographisches Lexicon der Tonkünstler* (Leipzig, 1790–92), but included less than a dozen women who are known to have been composers, three of them *virtuose* of his own time: Maddalena Laura Lombardini Sirmen, Anne Louise Boyvin d'Hardancourt Brillon de Jouy and Maria Theresia von Paradis (another blind musician). With assistance from Ernst Chladni and Johann Friedrich Reichardt (whose wife Juliane and daughter Louise were composers and appear in the dictionary), Gerber revised and substantially augmented his lexicon to incorporate more than two dozen women composers – including, for the first time as a composer in a dictionary, Francesca Caccini (her music is noted in Charles Burney's history 23 years earlier) – in his four-volume *Neues historisch-biographisches Lexicon der Tonkünstler* (1812–14).

In the meantime, Alexandre-Etienne Choron and François Fayolle, relying substantially on Gerber's lexicon, published their *Dictionnaire des musiciens* (Paris, 1810–11, 2/1817); it contains much the same number of women composers, but the selection is slightly different. Choron and Fayolle omitted Marianna von Auenbrugger and Juliane Reichardt in favour of such diverse figures as 'Anne de-Boulen' (Anne Boleyn is the only woman not certainly a composer to be admitted to *The New Grove Dictionary of Women Composers*), Isabella Colbran, Sophie Gail and Corona Schröter. Believing British musicians in general to have fared badly in the continental dictionaries of Gerber and Choron and Fayolle, John H. Sainsbury published anonymously *A Dictionary of Musicians* (London, 1824), including entries on more than 30 women known to have composed, among them Jane Mary Guest.

François-Joseph Fétis, in his monumental *Biographie universelle des musiciens et bibliographie générale de la musique* (eight volumes; Brussels, 1835–44, 2/1860–65), was the first to write at length about women composers and their music (quantities of which he claimed to have heard), appending work-lists to some of the more than 50 entries on them appearing in the first edition. Italian women composers fare nearly as well as French in *Biographie universelle*, German and English less well. Fétis's anecdotal account of the meeting in Venice of Benedetto Marcello and his composer-wife Rosanna Scalfi on the Grand Canal brings sentiment to their relationship; while his assessment of the quality of a woman's music is always written with a certain deference, his remarks on Clara Schumann's stage manner at the piano reveal a harsher side to his critical acumen. *Biographie universelle* was updated by Arthur Pougin in a supplement (1878–80), nearly doubling the number of women composers. Concurrently with the first volumes of Fétis's *Biographie universelle*, the first of the six volumes of Gustav Schilling's *Encyclopädie der gesammten musikalischen Wissenschaften oder Universal Lexikon der Tonkunst* (1835–8) began appearing in Stuttgart. The 38 women composers in Schilling's first edition include Delphine von Schauroth (a friend of Felix and, later, Fanny Mendelssohn).

Between 1878 and 1889, George Grove prepared the first *Dictionary of Music and Musicians (A.D. 1450–1887)* and issued it in London in fascicles making up four volumes. Of 36 women composers discussed, only 29 are dignified with entries of their own. Grove wrote at least eight of these himself – notably those on Fanny Mendelssohn and Clara Schumann – and invited half a dozen women to serve on the editorial board, of whom Florence Ashton Marshall (herself a composer) wrote entries on Lombardini Sirmen and Pauline Viardot, and Mrs Walter Carr wrote on Hortense de Beauharnais. The last important general biographical dictionary of music before Ebel's *Women Composers* appeared in 1902 was edited by the music publisher Carlo Schmidl, whose *Dizionario universale dei musicisti* (Milan, 1887–9) contains nearly 90 entries on women composers, mostly 19th-

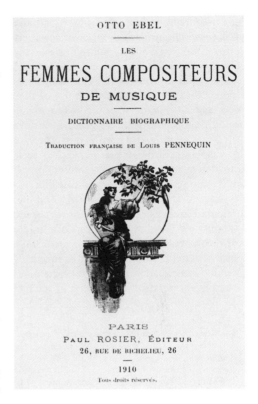

OTTO EBEL

LES

FEMMES COMPOSITEURS
DE MUSIQUE

DICTIONNAIRE BIOGRAPHIQUE

TRADUCTION FRANÇAISE DE LOUIS PENNEQUIN

PARIS
PAUL ROSIER, ÉDITEUR
26, RUE DE RICHELIEU, 26
—
1910
Tous droits réservés.

century. Despite Fanny Mendelssohn's famous surname and the beauty of her music, she is given relatively short shrift by Fétis (under 'Hensel') and later by Grove, only to be relegated by Schmidl to a passing reference in her brother's entry.

Because historically women composers were often the daughters,[5] sisters,[6] wives[7] or lovers[8] as well as the pupils of famous men composers, the number of women represented in these earlier dictionaries can be substantially augmented by reckoning in those hidden in the entries of their 'menfolk'. Many women composers appear simply as performers, with no hint of their creative output; the incompleteness of these profiles, together with their inaccessibility, has not only inhibited proper recognition of the range of their musical achievements but has led to a general lack of awareness of women composers. The often long and complicated forms in which their names have been transmitted, their use of titles and married names (sometimes more than one), and the penchant of composers of both sexes for masquerading under pseudonyms of either sex, further add to the difficulties of establishing details of their lives and works, whether in dictionaries, archives or catalogues. The index and system of cross-references we have used are intended to enumerate and regularize the forms in which their names appear; the index should prove a useful tool, independent of the dictionary, which can be employed in other contexts to gather information about women composers and their music as well as the institutions with which they have been associated. The extent to which women composers have always participated in acknowledged circles of men composers has yet to be fully appreciated. The editors have provided a separate chronology of the achievements of women composers (pp. xx–xxxii), extracted from the dictionary, to help speed the process of assimilation.

If the works of most women composers have been neglected, the fault lies in part with musicians themselves. In the past, most of those who directed performances were themselves composers. That they were also mostly men, who had of professional necessity to perform primarily their own most recent compositions, provides one reason why music of the same era by women composers was rarely sought or performed in public. However, a small (but enlightened) number of conductors and performers have always been willing to perform women's operas, symphonies, concertos, quartets and sonatas; and since the 16th century there have been printers and publishers willing to produce editions of their music. It is difficult to understand the hesitancy to explore and promote music composed by women that persists today. If much of the music of women of the past has been lost or become relatively inaccessible, a remarkable amount has survived and is retrievable. We hope that the discussion of specific works and the inclusion of work-lists, with information about sources and editions, in *The New Grove Dictionary of Women Composers* will fire the determination of performers to seek out, perform and popularize their music. Knowledge about women composers of the past remains shallow, a state of affairs that has sorely hampered the editors of this dictionary but one that can be rectified. When more studies of the music of individual composers, modern editions of their works and better integrated studies of the social context of music-making have been produced, a truer, more even-handed view of the history of music will emerge. Only then will the larger musical world of performers, publishers, recording companies and audiences begin to accept the music of women composers on its merit. *The New Grove Dictionary of Women Composers* is intended to help all of these to take the next step and to ensure that women composers will be better, more fairly represented in the future.

---

[1] M. Bourges: 'Des femmes compositeurs', *Revue et Gazette musicale*, xiv (1847), 305– 7, 313–15; continued by A. de la Fage, 323–25; Eugénie de Solenière: *Les femmes compositeurs* (Paris, 1895); R. Hughes: 'Woman Composers', *The Century Magazine*, lv (1898), 768–79 and 'The Women Composers', *Contemporary American Composers* (Boston, 1900), 432–41. John Towers, *Women in Music* (Winchester, Virginia, 1897) lists more than 1000 European and American musicians, many of whom were living composers of vocal music.

[2] These include Don L. Hixon and Don Hennesse's *Women in Music: a Bio-bibliography* (Metuchen, NJ, 1975), Susan Stern's *Women Composers: a Handbook* (Metuchen, NJ, 1978), Karl Zelenka's *Komponierende Frauen* (Cologne, 1980), Eva Rieger's *Frau, Musik und Männerherrschaft* (Frankfurt, 1981) and Eva Weissweiler's *Komponistinnen aus 500 Jahren* (Frankfurt, 1981) and Patricia Adkins Chiti's *Donne in musica* (Rome, 1982).

[3] These include J. Smith's *Directory of American Women Composers* (Chicago, 1970), M.D. Green's *Study of the Lives and Works of Black Women Composers in America* (Ann Arbor, 1975), A. Laurence's *Women of Note: 1,000 Women Composers Born before 1900* (New York, 1978), Adrienne Fried Block and Carol Neuls-Bates's *Women in American Music: a Bibliography of Music and Literature* (Westport, CT, 1979), Jane Weiner LePage's three-volume series *Women Composers, Conductors and Musicians of the Twentieth Century* (New York and London, 1980–89), Judith Tick's *American Women Composers before 1870* (Ann Arbor, 1983), and Gene Claghorn's *Women Composers and Hymnists: a Concise Biographical Dictionary* (Metuchen, NJ, 1984).

[4] These include the collection of essays edited by Jane Bowers and Judith Tick entitled *Women Making Music: the Western Art Tradition, 1150–1950* (Urbana and Chicago, 1986), James R. Briscoe's *Historical Anthology of Music by Women* (Bloomington and Indianapolis, 1987) and Karin Pendle's *Women and Music: a History* (Bloomington and Indianapolis, 1991).

[5] For example, Francesca Caccini, Lucile Grétry and Juliane Reichardt (Benda).

[6] Franziska Lebrun (Danzi) and the Dussek sisters, Olivia and Veronika.

[7] Isabella Colbran Rossini, Clara Schumann, Alma Mahler and Elsa Respighi.

[8] Charles Gounod's Georgina Weldon, to name but one.

2: Women's Music: A Twentieth-Century Perspective

Rhian Samuel

This dictionary includes entries on nearly 900 women composers writing in the Western classical (notation-based) tradition. The confines of this tradition are not as narrow as might first appear: it encompasses composers from Chile to China and draws upon influences from jazz to folk to pop music; in fact many younger composers are difficult to categorize as their language is often a fusion of idioms without any noticeable hierarchy. The definition is used as a guide, not a limitation, reflecting the tendency of so many composers in this century to look beyond parochial boundaries.

The move to unearth women artists, in music as in any other art, is not a neutral act, any more than is their previous neglect. Indeed, the present exercise has involved the revision of many aspects of music criticism, including issues of artistic achievement, acknowledgment and even merit.[1] For instance, in the past, to compose, let alone to be heard, a woman has needed to conquer social restriction and taboo. While her domestic life has often limited practical opportunities for composing, even when she has managed to find the time and space for this activity,[2] she has been far less able than her male peers to enjoy valuable interaction with orchestras and opera companies and to develop her technique (a situation which bears many parallels to that of women painters, barred in the 19th century from life-drawing classes). Her success in these larger media, particularly before the present day, should therefore be seen as doubly significant. And success there has been, onwards from Cécile Chaminade (1857–1944), Ethel Smyth (1858–1944) and Amy Beach (1867–1944) at the turn of the century. Yet many women, pragmatically, have preferred to turn to smaller forms, which in the eyes of critics had been less prestigious; the songs of Liza Lehmann (1862–1918) and Maude Valérie White (1855–1937), to cite two, show a technical skill equal to any man's.[3] Even though circumstances may have improved, women have continued this tradition, excelling spectacularly in popular song forms (witness, for instance, May Brahe's 'Bless This House', 1927–32, and Consuelo Velásquez's 'Besame mucho', 1941). In more 'serious' music in general, and in that of the early 20th century in particular, great emphasis has been placed on innovation; yet the response of a woman composer to a male-dominated world has frequently been subversive or revisionary rather than pioneering.[4] A woman's 'achievement', therefore, is often of a different order from a man's.

Despite these obstacles to success, women composers from Elisabeth-Claude Jacquet de la Guerre (1665–1729) to Lili Boulanger (1893–1918) have been acknowledged enthusiastically by their audiences and peers – in their own lifetimes. But posthumously their reputations have sunk into oblivion among the concert-going public. Very recently, however, there has been a sea-change with regard to public acknowledgment: recordings have suddenly become available, anthologies have begun to include women's music and some major organizations are beginning to show an interest in performing it; this dictionary itself reflects the trend. Publicly forgotten women composers are becoming 'established' again: Rebecca Clarke (1886–1979), whose Viola Sonata now seems to be entering the canon, is a clear case in point. But the notion of 'establishment', by which the success of many a man composer has been measured in the past, can clearly be seen as an unreliable yardstick for the success of women composers.[5]

Some critics assert that women's music has not survived because it is simply not good enough. The issue of 'quality' in music can provide a convenient means of dismissing women's music, both heard and unheard, particularly when the critic overlooks such vital issues as the fact that aesthetic judgments are never absolute and that criteria for musical quality are inextricably linked to the established repertoire in a spiral that constantly bypasses women composers.[6] The issue is further clouded by a cultural antipathy towards the concept of the female creative artist which has flourished from the 18th century onwards. Perhaps it is no coincidence that until almost the mid-20th century most musicologists and critics (as in every other artistic field) were male.[7]

There may be another significant reason for such opinions, however, which concerns the very nature of musical discourse. What if a woman composer should speak differently from a man? Should she not then be evaluated differently? The fact of sociological conditioning certainly encourages us to consider the likelihood of a 'gendered voice' for both men and women.[8] And given the physicality and sensuousness of music itself, is it beyond the realms of possibility that even biology might have some influence on musical utterance too?[9] Some critics emphatically deny its existence; but given that a *comparative* study of the male and female repertories is the only condition, by definition, that would reveal the existence of such a voice (and its male counterpart), and that no large-scale, detailed study of women's music to rival that already afforded men's has yet taken place, surely no soundly based judgment on this issue can at present be offered.

A separate female identity and an intrinsic female voice: neither concept was promoted by women composers in the early part of the century. Mabel Wheeler Daniels (1877–1971) was perhaps typical in that she eschewed the labels 'feminist' and even 'woman composer', yet worked for women's suffrage, as did Helen Hopekirk (1856–1945). Ethel Smyth was something of an exception: more militant than most about her music, she complained loudly about the sexual discrimination she suffered; she served a spell in Holloway Prison in 1912 and wrote the suffragettes' anthem, *March of the Women*. She was also probably the most widely performed and critically acclaimed woman composer of her age. In 1927, for instance, the critic and lexicographer, H. C. Colles, commenting on the plot and other aspects of *The Wreckers* (1904), wrote:

> all these points are among the most remarkable things in modern opera, and it is difficult to point to a work of any nationality since Wagner that has a more direct appeal to the emotions, or that is more skilfully planned and carried out.[10]

Despite this fulsome praise, however, Colles is typical of the time in believing that the successful, creative woman becomes an honorary male. He remarks in the same article

> This work [the Mass in D] definitely placed the composer among the most eminent composers of her time, and easily at the head of all those of her own sex. The most striking thing about it was the entire absence of the qualities that are usually associated with feminine productions; throughout, it was virile, masterly in construction and workmanship, and particularly remarkable for the excellence and rich colouring of the orchestration.

In this he echoes the sentiments of the anonymous American reviewer in 1903, who, in complimenting Smyth on her opera *Der Wald*, added that 'the gifted Englishwoman has successfully emancipated herself from her sex'.[11]

In the light of such remarks we might view the general reluctance of Smyth's female contemporaries to be identified as 'women composers' as quite rational, and Smyth's own predilection in later years (long after the suffragette episode) for smoking a pipe and wearing manly tweeds as something of a wily public-relations move.

Also in the light of these remarks we might now regard the use of such catch-words as 'feminine' or 'virile' with some distrust. The former term, when applied to men's music, generally serves to indicate an emotional breadth (the composer can be both masculine and feminine);[12] yet the same cannot be said of Colles's use of the term 'virile' with regard to Smyth: this term, unmarred by 'femininity', proves a compliment in its own right. Further, the term 'feminine' applied to a woman's music (as in 'feminine productions') may simply serve to remind us of the composer's sex — and therefore of her artistic status. Are, then, Florent Schmitt's description of *Transparancies* (1931) by Jeanne Leleu (1898–1979) as a 'marvel of freshness, finesse and feminine grace'[13] and Maurice Ravel's characterization of Germaine Tailleferre's music as 'full of feminine charm'[14] really the innocent expressions of admiration they seem at first glance (particularly when we note that they are the comments of one composer about another)? Unfortunately such terms have continued to be critically applied throughout the 20th century.

Following in Smyth's footsteps, women composers have lately become more radical. While a small minority still refuses to be classed as 'women composers', there is a growing sense of obligation among the rest to speak specifically as women: for instance, vast numbers employ texts which refer to women or take a woman's point of view. Wry comment on the state of women is indicated by titles such as Sorrel Hays's *Exploitation* (1981), written for the first International Congress on Women in Music, and Jennifer Fowler's *And Ever Shall Be* (1989, a BBC-commissioned chamber cycle which sets four traditional verses). The 'alternative perspective' is indicated by the title of Ruth Schonthal's piano piece, *Self-Portrait of the Artist as an Older Woman* (1991), and Elizabeth Vercoe's series, *Herstory I, II* and *III* (1975–86), while Adriana Hölszky's opera, *Bremer Freiheit* (1987, text by Thomas Körner, after R. W. Fassbinder), 'can be seen as a female counterpart to Bartók's Bluebeard' (Detlef Gojowy) and even García Lorca acquires a feminist slant in Nicola LeFanu's opera *Blood Wedding* (1992).

Women composers' overt concern with a female identity has recently prompted a more significant development: their own affirmation of the concept of an innate woman's voice. In a 1981 survey, several women were found to 'evince womanly pride in being linked with female traits'; the New Zealand composer Annea Lockwood observed, ' "Sounding like a woman" is taking on other connotations . . . at least among women. It implies that vague term, a sense of wholeness in the work, a strongly centered work. A positive term'.[15] The assertion of the existence of innate attributes previously unacknowledged is a significant step towards the emancipation of any previously oppressed group, and thus it is with women composers.[16] This may be the primary significance of the 'innate voice': a concept mainly for composers themselves, referring to the wellspring of women's music – its fundamental inspiration.

However, listeners too must be allowed a quest for its identification. Such a quest would at best be long and arduous, but a first step might be a survey of women's music. Should this reveal trends which differ in any significant way from the trends in men's music of the same periods, we might be brought a little closer to a recognition of the female voice. To this end, let us look broadly at women's music in the 20th century.[17]

In the past hundred years, Western classical music, previously Eurocentric and notation-based, has undergone an enormous expansion from which women composers have undoubtedly benefitted. But their contribution has also been substantial. The medium now includes not only traditional orchestral instruments, but also folk instruments (perhaps the most notable example by a woman composer being Sofiya Gubaydulina's use of the bayan in *Seven Last Words*, 1982) and newly invented ones (for instance, Lucia Dlugoszewski's 'timbre piano', Laurie Anderson's tape-bow violin and Annea Lockwood's 'glass concert' of objects to be struck, rubbed, shaken and even snapped). The exploration of the vocal medium inspired by Arnold Schoenberg's *Pierrot lunaire* (1912) reached an apex in the mid-century, not least because of the improvisatory explorations of Joan La Barbara (*b* 1947) and Cathy Berberian (1925–83), composer of *Stripsody* (1966) and Luciano Berio's acknowledged muse. Probably the most profound expansion of the medium has been through electronics: Else Pade at Danish Radio in 1954, Bebe Barron in the USA, co-author of the music for *Forbidden Planet* in 1956, Daphne Oram, one of the initiators of the BBC Radiophonic Workshop in 1958, and Ruth White, who created her own studio in Los Angeles in 1964, have all been pioneers in this field.

The range of materials has also expanded, a change placed in high relief by the strong emphasis on absolute music in the early part of the century. Abstract modernism was espoused by

Ruth Crawford (1901–53); her celebrated String Quartet (1931) is an outstanding example of the style. For Elisabeth Lutyens (1906–83), serialism meant working stubbornly against the English mainstream, while for Barbara Pentland (b 1912), in Canada, exposure to Anton Webern's music in 1955 prompted adoption of 12-note procedures and a reinvigoration of her concern with the Germanic symphonic principle of organic growth. Other women composers, including Germaine Tailleferre (1892–1983), Louise Talma (b 1906), Grażyna Bacewicz (1909–69), Elizabeth Maconchy (b 1907) and Miriam Gideon (b 1906), refused to adopt rigorous pre-compositional systems; they were to varying degrees sympathetic to Stravinskian neo-classicism (actively promoted by the teachings of Nadia Boulanger in Paris), which, despite its referential basis, also tends to absolute music.

An interest in folk music has flourished throughout this century; many women composers have collected folk materials. (That Ruth Crawford abandoned composing for many years to become a folklorist is particularly significant in this context.) Not only in the West have women undertaken such activities: in 1959 Wang Qiang (b 1935) began 20 years of research in Inner Mongolia, Yunnan, Fujian and Hainan Island; Chen Yi (b 1953) undertook similar research activity 20 years later. Countless women composers have incorporated their own culture's folk materials into their music, from Jórunn Viðar (b 1918), in Iceland, to Gillian Whitehead (b 1941), part Maori, who has written a series of works on Maori themes, and Florence Price (1887–1953), the symphonic composer, who incorporated African-American elements into classical forms. Some have sought publicly to reconcile the techniques of folk music and composition: Eleonora Eksanishvili (b 1919), for instance, published her ideas on developing creative abilities through Georgian folksong in 1970, but many others have also looked beyond their own culture. Lily Strickland (1887–1958), looking further afield, drew inspiration from Indian music, like Olivier Messiaen, but she also turned to the African-American music she heard on her grandparents' estate and, like Catherine Urner (1891–1942), to Native American music. The South African Priaulx Rainier (1903–86), though never consciously using African techniques, was influenced by the language and music of the Zulu. Somewhat later, the Australian Peggy Glanville-Hicks (1912–90) drew on Hindu sources for her first opera *The Transposed Heads* (1953). Helen Gifford (b 1935), Elaine Barkin (b 1932) and Barbara Benary (b 1946), among many others, have found Balinese and Javanese music a rich trove, while Katherine Hoover (b 1937) and Ruth Lomon (b 1930), in the steps of Urner and Strickland, borrowed Native American myths and ceremonies for their inspiration.

Cultural influences have travelled in both directions. Lili'uokalani, Queen of Hawaii (1838–1917), composed Hawaiian songs including the famous 'Aloha 'oe', but also played Western instruments and wrote a three-act comic opera (incomplete), while the works of Lee Young-ja (b 1936), from Korea, and the Japanese Kimi Sato (b 1949), the first non-French recipient of the Prix de Rome, reveal their French training. The Korean Younghi Pagh-Paan (b 1945), living in Germany, actively strives to fuse avant-garde and Japanese techniques; Haruna Miyake (b 1942) seeks to create art which differs from European but which Westerners would not perceive as Asian.

'Musical eclecticism', a term used here with no pejorative connotations, is the assembling of many disparate materials within a single piece. The materials may, like the famous third movement of Berio's Sinfonia (1968), all be drawn from art music, but they can also be culturally diverse, like the verbal texts of the whole work. The Australian Florence Ewart (1864–1949), in a body of music written entirely before World War II, not only quotes from Verdi, Bizet and Puccini but also includes Greek classical references, Native American melodies, Corsican folksongs and an Indian *rektah*. In the 1950s the Russian song composer Alexandra Pakhmutova (b 1929) juxtaposed art song, folksong, Soviet songs, military music and Western pop music and in later works has extended her range to include operatic arioso, lovesongs, disco and rock music. The trend continues: the American Sheila Silver (b 1946) turns to classical Greek, Roman and Indian mythology, American jazz and Jewish chant; the Canadian Alexina Louie (b 1949) includes gamelan sounds, references to Gustav Mahler and

J. S. Bach and also attempts to blur the boundaries between electronic and human music. Eclecticism involves subject matter too: Judith Weir (*b* 1954) draws on a wealth of inspiration from an early Icelandic saga, the Bayeux tapestry, Chinese Yuan dramas, Serbian folksong texts and the Spanish epic *El Cid* as well as her own Scottish musical tradition.

Of all the various trends of the late 20th century, this reconciliation of styles and cultures seems to have found particular favour among women composers.[18] Should this tendency eventually prove to be more pronounced among women than men, the resultant image of the woman composer as Conciliator, or Reaper (of marginalized concerns) seems entirely appropriate, given her parallel social role of Wife/Mother.

A persistent complaint concerning the difficulty of isolating a woman's voice is the lack of a female tradition of composition; indeed, it has often been claimed that the tradition is entirely male. But women's influence is more pervasive than has been recognized. While women in general have learnt their art from men, the debts owed by men to women are also documented in this dictionary. The relationship between female student and male teacher has often proved mutually beneficial, particularly when the teacher is a composer. According to Jiří Macek and Anna Šerých, Bohuslav Martinů and Vitězslava Kaprálová (1915–40) consulted each other while composing pieces for similar forces, and Elise Kirk cites Charles Koechlin's acknowledgment of the influence of his student, Catherine Urner, on his modal-contrapuntal style. Ludmila Kovnatskaya recounts that Dmitry Shostakovich so admired the music of his student Galina Ustvol'skaya that he incorporated some of it into his own.

The results are sometimes less fortuitous for the student; when the teacher is male, the relationship may lead to marriage and a silencing – at least temporarily – of her muse. Ruth Crawford is the most celebrated 20th-century example;[19] but there are several others, including Nadezhda Rimskaya-Korsakova. Rebecca Clarke postponed such a fate by leaving the Royal Academy of Music when her harmony teacher, Percy Miles, proposed to her, but, according to Stephen Banfield, fell mute for a long period in the 1930s when a clandestine affair sapped her energy for composing, and virtually stopped again when she eventually married at 58.

Though women composers have generally been taught by men, Nadia Boulanger (1887–1979), the composers' teacher *par excellence*, guided the early careers of numerous women; so, in the next generation, did Miriam Gideon and Louise Talma among others. A few contemporary women composers, such as Irina Elcheva (*b* 1926), Nicola LeFanu (*b* 1947) and Tona Scherchen (*b* 1938), have even inherited a compositional tradition directly from their mothers. As female composers proliferate, so will female composer-teachers. Assuming that this trend continues (aided, we hope, by enterprises such as this dictionary) the as-yet elusive female legacy, now being pursued by historians and critics alike, may eventually be recognized and appreciated.

---

1 I am grateful to Naomi Segal, Curtis Price and Laurence Dreyfus for their insights and forbearance in discussing these issues with me. The opinions are my own.

2 This is a principal theme of Virginia Woolf's *A Room of One's Own* (London, 1929), a book which has provided inspiration for many modern women artists.

3 For a more detailed discussion of this issue, see Derek Scott, 'The Sexual Politics of Victorian Musical Aesthetics', *JRMA*, cxix (1994), 91–114. Marcia Citron, in *Gender and the Musical Canon* (Cambridge, 1993), 108, discusses a parallel issue, the similarly denigrated genre of 'salon music', to which many women composers contributed at the turn of the century.

4 See, for instance, Citron's analysis of the first movement of Chaminade's Piano Sonata (ibid., pp.145–59).

5 This notion continues to flourish: in a British television documentary about women composers, *To Mention but a Few* (28 June 1994), Andrew Kurowski, producer of new music for BBC Radio 3, explained that, when choosing music for broadcast, he looked at both the work's quality and 'the standing of the composer'.

6 For instance, Smyth's *Sleepless Dreams* (1912), a rarely performed work for chorus and orchestra, begins in a rich, late Romantic style, but momentarily, towards the end, breaks into a heavy, modernist ostinato passage. 'Stylistically inconsistent!' cry her critics; 'Smythian', we reply.

7 See Christine Battersby, *Gender and Genius: Towards a Feminist Aesthetics* (London, 1989), 3–4. Battersby argues that the notion of genius has excluded the female, presenting an impressive (and depressing) list of influential writers who have tended towards this belief, from Coleridge, Schopenhauer, Jung, Nietzsche, John Ruskin, Gerard Manley Hopkins and Otto Weininger on to Anthony Burgess. Scott (p.99) claims that the notion of the sublime has been similarly exclusive.

8 As in other aesthetic fields, critics are divided on the crucial question of a female voice. Battersby (p.154) believes in its existence; Susan McClary, on the other hand, in her pioneering work of musical feminist criticism, *Feminine Endings* (Minneapolis, 1991), 131, is sceptical. Citron (pp.69, 151) alerts the reader to the difficulties of identifying such a voice due to the lack of a female *stylistic* tradition (a subtly different concept) thus far and (p.176) cites several writers who believe that a pure female mode currently does not exist because women are socialized into male culture. All these conclusions seem to have been reached without any major study of the repertoire.

9 Citron (p.159) and Battersby (p.154) disagree with the notion; the concern of both, however, is with the reception of women's music as opposed to its creation.

10 'Smyth, Dame Ethel Mary', *Grove's Dictionary of Music and Musicians* (3/1927).

11 *Musical Courier*, xlvi/1 (18 March 1903), 12, quoted in Citron, p.68.

12 It is occasionally used pejoratively, as by Ives of Mozart.

13 See David Cox's entry on Leleu in this dictionary.

14 In an interview with André Révész, *ABC de Madrid* (1 May 1924), 26. (I am grateful to Professor Robert Orledge for bringing this to my attention.)

15 Published in *Perspectives of New Music* (1981) and cited in Citron, pp.161–2.

16 McClary's lack of faith in the concept of an innate female voice is nowhere more evident than when she urges women composers actively (and artificially) to construct one, by choosing 'alternate models' from those of our inherited male culture, and engaging in deconstruction of its images (p.131). I discuss her advice to women composers in 'Feminist Musicology; Endings or Beginnings', in *Women: a Cultural Review*, iii/1 (Summer 1992), 65–9; Georgina Born responds in the same issue (pp.81–2).

17 This particular survey of course would need to be followed by more detailed surveys and to culminate, ultimately, in a comparison of men's and women's music at various periods. These subsequent steps are unfortunately outside the scope of the present study.

18 This seems perhaps to resonate with some of McClary's comments. When she asks what a women composer may do to establish her own, gendered voice, she considers the 'time-honored strategy [of minorities] of creating a stylistic synthesis' of components from the mainstream and elements of 'their own readily recognized idiom' (p.114). But, she maintains, this is not possible for women because there is 'no traditional woman's voice'.

19 J. Michele Edwards, however, claims more complicated reasons for the compositional hiatus (cited in Citron, p.93).

Acknowledgments

During the five years of this project we have been helped by numerous people. First, of course, we are grateful to our authors (listed on pp.519–22), in particular for their many valuable suggestions and for their ready responses to our queries. We are much indebted to our correspondents in many countries who were asked to make their recommendations, on composers, past and present, who might be included, and those who should write on them; it is impossible to acknowledge everyone who has helped but we would particularly like to mention Judith Tick, Christine Ammer, J. Michele Edwards and Catherine Parsons Smith (for the USA), Gaynor Jones (Canada), Yang Yandi (China), John Thomson (New Zealand), Keith Howard (Korea), Robert Stevenson (Latin America) and also Irati Antonio (Brazil), and for European coverage Rosario Marciano (Austria), Markéta Hallová and Anna Šerých (Czech Republic), Françoise Andrieux (France), Eva Rieger, Detlef Gojowy, Birgitta Schmid and Roswitha Sperber (Germany), Stefan Barandoni, Paula Damiani, Matteo Sansone, Robert Kendrick and Suzanne Cusick (Italy), Helen Metzelaar (the Netherlands), Barbara Zwolska-Stęszewska and Zofia Chechlińska (Poland), Viorel Cosma (Romania), Malcolm H. Brown, Ludmila Kovnatskaya and Olga Manulkina (Russia), Inge Bruland, Kari Michelsen and Eva Öhrström (the Scandinavian countries), Xoán M. Carriera and Emilio Casares Alonso (Spain) and Chris Walton (Switzerland), as well as many contributors from the United Kingdom, among whom we would particularly mention Olive Baldwin and Thelma Wilson for their help on earlier composers and Nigel Burton, Sophie Fuller, John Gardner and Derek Scott on the Victorians and beyond. We are also happy to acknowledge the help supplied by many Music Information Centres.

Elisabeth Agate's imaginative and sensitive work as picture editor has added a happy visual dimension to the dictionary. She in turn wishes to thank Oliver Davies (of the Royal College of Music) and Richard Macnutt for their untiring and generous help.

We are particularly grateful for the immense labour and constant watchfulness supplied by the team of Grove editors, especially Audrey Twine, Ingalo Thomson and Madeleine Laddell, and to Caroline Perkins for her ever-dependable administrative grasp. Margot Levy and Stanley Sadie were our taskmasters: we thank Margot for her unfailing interest and Stanley for coming to the rescue in various crises.

J.A.S., R.S.

Chronology

7th century BC — Sappho composes monody and choral poetry.

early 8th century AD — Xosroviduxt and Sahakduxt, Armenian hermits, compose hymns.

9th century — Kassia composes Byzantine chants.

1151 — Hildegard of Bingen finishes all (or part) of her morality play incorporating 82 melodies, *Ordo virtutum*, at Rupertsberg.

mid to late 12th century — Troubadours: Alamanda, Azalais de Porcairages, Beatriz de Dia, Maria de Ventadorn and Tibors.

13th century — Troubadours: Castelloza and Garsenda.

Trouvères: Blanche of Castile, Maroie de Dregnau de Lille and Duchess of Lorraine; Dame Margot and Dame Maroie.

1568 — Maddalena Casulana publishes her first collection of madrigals in Venice.

1585 — Paola Massarenghi's madrigal 'Quando spiega l'insegn'al sommo padre' is included in Arcangelo Gherardini's *Primo libro de' madrigali a cinque voci*.

1593 — Raffaella Aleotti takes over the direction of the *concerto grande* at the Augustinian convent of S Vito, Ferrara, and publishes a collection of *Sacrae cantiones*, in Venice; Vittoria Aleotti publishes *Ghirlanda de madrigali a quattro voci*, also in Venice.

1607 — Francesca Caccini composes the music for a *torneo La stiava* by Michelangelo Buonarroti, given at the Florentine Carnival; further Carnival music for Buonarroti in 1610, 1611, 1614 and 1619, and, in 1615, music to Ferdinando Saracinelli's *Il ballo delle Zingane*.

1609 — Caterina Assandra publishes her *Motetti*, op.2, in Milan.

1610 — Settimia Caccini contributes some of her own part in Buonarroti's *Mascherate delle ninfe della Senna*.

1611 — Lucia Quinciani becomes the first woman to publish a monody: her setting of G. B. Guarini's 'Udite lagrimosi spirti d'Averno, udite' is included in Marc'Antonio Negri's second book of *Affetti amorosi*, Venice.

1613 — Claudia Sessa publishes two sacred monodies in *Canoro pianto di Maria Vergine* in Milan.

1618 — F. Caccini publishes *Il primo libro delle musiche* (monodies) in Florence.

1619 — Sulpitia Cesis publishes her eight-part *Motetti spirituali* in Modena.

1622 — F. Caccini collaborates with G. B. da Gagliano on setting Jacopo Cicognini's *Il martirio di S Agata* for the Florentine Carnival.

Alba Trissina's four motets are included in Leone Leoni's *Sacri fiori*.

1623 — Lucrezia Orsina Vizzana publishes a collection of continuo motets for one and two voices, in Venice.

Andreana Basile and F. Caccini improvise on poetry in a competition held in Mantua in November.

1625 — F. Caccini composes an opera, *La liberazione di Ruggiero dall' isola d'Alcina*, in Florence (also given in Warsaw, 1628); the following year she is commissioned by Prince Władisław of Poland to compose *Rinaldo innamorato*.

1629 — Francesca Campana publishes *Arie a 1, 2, e 3 voci*, op.1, in Rome.

1630 — Claudia Rusca publishes a collection of *Sacri concerti* in Milan.

1640 — Chiara Margarita Cozzolani publishes *Primavera di fiori musicali*, op.1, for 1–4 voices and continuo, in Milan.

1642 — Cozzolani's *Concerti sacri*, op.2, are published in Venice, followed by the *Scherzi di sacra melodia*, op.3 (1648), and *Salmi à otto*, op.3 [sic] (1650).

1644 — Barbara Strozzi publishes *Il primo libro de madrigali* in Venice.

1651 — Strozzi's *Cantate, ariette e duetti*, op.2. Three years later she publishes *Cantate e ariette*, op.3, in Venice.

Sophie Elisabeth, Duchess of Brunswick-Lüneburg, publishes, in Wolfenbüttel, her first collection of hymn melodies, *Vinetum evangelicum*. In 1653 she composes an entertainment, *Glückwünschende Gedancken* for one voice and three instruments, to celebrate her husband's birthday.

1655 — Strozzi's *Sacri musicali affetti, libro I*, op.5, are published in Venice; her 'Quis dabit mihi' is included in B. Marcesso's *Sacra corona, motetti a due e tre voci di diversi eccelentissimi autori moderni* (1656).

Lady Mary Dering is the composer of three songs included in Henry Lawes's *Select Ayres and Dialogues*, dedicated to her and published in London.

1657   Strozzi's *Ariette a voce sola*, op.6, is followed by *Diporti di Euterpe, overo Cantate e ariette a voce sola*, op.7 (1659).

1659   Cornelia Calegari publishes *Motetti à voce sola* in Bergamo.

1664   Strozzi publishes *Arie a voce sola*, op.8, in Venice.

1665   Isabella Leonarda publishes her first book of motets, op.2, in Milan.

Marieta Morosina Priuli dedicates to the Habsburg Dowager Empress Eleonora her four-part *Balletti e correnti*, published in Venice.

1667   Sophie Elisabeth's second collection of hymn melodies, *ChristFürstliches Davids-Harpfen-Spiel*, is published in Nuremberg.

1684   Rosa Giacinta Badalla publishes a collection of *Motetti a voce sola* in Milan.

1685   Elisabeth-Claude Jacquet de la Guerre composes music for a ballet, *Les jeux à l'honneur de la victoire*, in Paris.

1687   Jacquet de la Guerre publishes her first book of *pièces de clavecin* in Paris.

1689   Angiola Teresa Moratori Scanabecchi's oratorio, *Il martirio di S Colomba*, is performed at the Oratorio of S Filippo Neri, Bologna.

1691   Mlle de Ménétou publishes a *recueil d'airs* in Paris.

1692   Amalia Catharina, Countess of Erbach, publishes *Andächtige Sing-Lust*, a collection of Pietist songs, in Hildburghausen.

1693   Isabella Leonarda publishes solo and ensemble sonatas, op.16, in Bologna.

1694   Jacquet de la Guerre's opera, *Cephale et Procris*, is performed in Paris by the Académie Royale de Musique; a short score is published.

Moratori Scanabecchi's *Li giochi di Sansone* is performed at S Filippo Neri, Bologna; *L'Esterre* is performed the following year.

c1695   Jacquet de la Guerre composes trio sonatas, which remain unpublished, in Paris.

1696   Moratori Scanabecchi's *Cristo morto* is performed at the oratory of the Arciconfraternità di S Maria della Morte, Bologna.

1703   Maria Anna de Raschenau's oratorio *Le sacre visioni di Santa Teresa* is performed in Vienna.

1705   Caterina Benedicta Grazianini's oratorio *S Gemignano vescovo e protettore di Modena* is performed in Vienna.

1707   Camilla de Rossi is commissioned by Joseph I to compose an oratorio, *Santa Beatrice d'Este*.

Jacquet de la Guerre publishes a book of *Sonates pour le viollon et pour le clavecin* in Paris.

1708   Rossi composes *Il sacrifizio di Abramo* (an oratorio in which she uses chalumeaux) in Vienna.

Jacquet de la Guerre publishes her first book of cantatas on sacred subjects, in Paris; the second appears in 1711.

1713   Maria Margherita Grimani's oratorios *Pallade e Marte* and *La visitazione di Elisabetta* are performed in Vienna; in 1715 *La decollazione di S Giovanni Battista* is given.

1715   'Mrs. Philarmonica' publishes trio sonatas in London.

Jacquet de la Guerre publishes a third book of cantatas in Paris.

1721   Jacquet de la Guerre's *Te Deum* is sung in Paris, marking the recovery of Louis XV from smallpox.

1736   Mlle Duval's *ballet-héroïque Les Génies, ou Les caractères de l'Amour* is performed at the Paris Opéra.

Julie Pinel publishes a collection of *airs* in Paris; a second collection appears the following year.

1740   Wilhelmina's opera, *Argenore*, is given before the court at Bayreuth.

Michielina Della Pietà composes a Litany for the Feast of the Nativity, to be performed at the Ospedale della Pietà, Venice; the following year she composes a setting of the hymn *Pange lingua* for Corpus Christi.

Elisabeth de Haulteterre's *Premier livre de sonates* for violin and continuo is published in Paris.

1744   Haulteterre publishes a *Concerto à cinq* in Paris.

1747   Maria Teresa Agnesi's opera *Il restauro d'Arcadia* is given at the Regio Ducal Teatro, Milan.

1748   Elisabetta de Gambarini publishes two collections of *Lessons for the Harpsichord* in London; op.2 is dedicated to the Prince of Wales.

1750   Queen María Barbara composes an orchestrally accompanied *Salve regina* which is performed by members of the Spanish royal chapel at the Salesian monastery she founded in Madrid.

c1752   Hélène-Louise Demars publishes three *cantatilles* in Paris.

1754   Maria Antonia Walpurgis (Electress of Saxony) takes a leading role in her opera, *Il trionfo della fedeltà*, at the Dresden court; it is later published by Breitkopf in Leipzig.

1755   Mlle Guerin's *Opera de Daphnis et d'Amalthée* is given at Amiens.

1756   Anna Lucia Boni dedicates her op.1 flute sonatas to her employer, Frederick the Great.

1760   Maria Antonia Walpurgis's opera *Talestri, regina delle amazoni* is given at Nymphenburg and published by Breitkopf in Leipzig.

1768   Maddalena Laura Lombardini Sirmen performs her own violin concerto at the Concert Spirituel, Paris.

1771   Lombardini Sirmen performs her own concertos at the King's Theatre, at Covent Garden, and in the Bach-Abel concert series, London.

1773   Marianne von Martínez is made an honorary member of the Bologna Accademia Filarmonica.

1774   Maria Rosa Coccia's composing skills are acclaimed by the examiners of the Roman Accademia di S Cecilia and she is accorded membership in the Bologna Accademia Filarmonica.

1776   Anna Amalia, Duchess of Saxe-Weimar, composes a Singspiel, *Erwin und Elmire*, which is performed in Weimar.

Marie Emmanuelle Bayon (Mme Louis) is the composer of *Fleur d'épine*, an *opéra-comique* given at the Théâtre Italien, Paris.

Mlle Duverger (Marie Elizabeth Cléry) publishes an *air* for soprano, harp and bass in the *Mercure de France*.

Maria Barthélemon publishes a collection of six sonatas for accompanied keyboard in London.

1777   Anne Louise Boyvin d'Hardancourt Brillon de Jouy, a Parisian friend of Benjamin Franklin, composes a *Marche des insurgents* to celebrate the American victory at Saratoga.

1778   Anna Amalia, Duchess of Saxe-Weimar, composes a divertimento, *Das Jahrmarktsfest zu Plundersweilern*, which is performed at Weimar.

Mme Ravissa publishes a collection of keyboard sonatas, op.1, in Paris.

1780   Franziska Lebrun publishes two collections of violin sonatas, opp.1–2, in London.

Harriett Abrams is thought to have published her *8 Italian and English Canzonets* in London.

Adelheid Maria Eichner publishes *12 Lieder mit Melodien fürs Clavier* in Potsdam.

c1781   Marianna von Auenbrugger publishes a *Sonata per il Clavicembalo o Forte piano* in Vienna.

1781   Henriette Adélaïde Villard de Beaumesnil's one-act opera, *Anacréon*, is given at the Brunoy residence of the Comte de Provence.

Elizabeth, Margravine of Anspach, contributes (along with Samuel Arnold and Tommaso Giordani) incidental music to her afterpiece, *The Silver Tankard*, performed at the Haymarket Theatre, London.

1783   Jane Mary Guest publishes six keyboard sonatas with violin or flute accompaniment, op.1, in London.

Jane Savage publishes *Six Easy Lessons*, op.2, for keyboard, in London.

1784   Beaumesnil's acte de ballet, *Tibule et Délie, ou Les Saturnales*, is given at the Paris Opéra.

Julie Candeille performs one of her piano concertos at the Concert Spirituel, Paris.

1785   Marie Elizabeth Cléry publishes sonatas for harp or piano with violin accompaniment, op.1, in Paris and a *Recueil d'airs* arranged for harp with flute or violin accompaniment, op.2, in Versailles.

Maria Hester Park publishes keyboard sonatas with violin accompaniment in London.

1786   Maria Theresia von Paradis publishes *12 Lieder auf ihrer Reise in Musik gesetzt*, in Leipzig.

Lucile Grétry's comedy, *Le mariage d'Antonio* (on which she collaborated with her father), is given in Paris.

Caroline Wuiet composes the *opéra comique L'heureuse erreur* as a possible sequel to A.-E.-M. Grétry's and Desforges' *L'épreuve villageoise* but abandoned after rehearsals at the Comédie-Italienne, Paris; Wuiet's *L'heureux stratagème, ou Le vol supposé* is staged at the Théâtre des Beaujolais.

Corona Elisabeth Wilhelmine Schröter publishes her first collection of lieder in Weimar; she publishes a second collection in 1794.

1790   Josepha Barbara von Auernhammer publishes six German lieder in Vienna.

Cléry publishes *Le soldat patriote au champ de Mars* in Paris.

Savage publishes a collection of keyboard rondos and a cantata, *Strephan and Flavia*, opp.3 and 4, about this time in London.

1791   Paradis's melodrama *Ariadne und Bacchus* is given at the Schlosstheater, Laxenburg.

Cecilia Maria Barthélemon publishes a collection of keyboard sonatas, op.1, in London.

Abrams organizes the Ladies' Concerts in London.

1792   Candeille makes her début as playwright and theatre composer in *Catherine, ou La belle fermière* at the Théâtre Français; she takes the title role, singing and playing in 154 performances.

Beaumesnil's *opéra comique Plaire, c'est commander* is given at the Théâtre Montansier, Paris.

Paradis's Singspiel *Der Schulkandidat* is given at the Marinellitheater, Vienna.

Maria Theresia Ahlefeldt's opera-ballet *Telemak paa Calypsos Øe* is given at the Kongelige Teater, Copenhagen; the vocal score is published a year later.

C. M. Barthélemon publishes two accompanied keyboard sonatas, op.2, in London; she dedicates her harpsichord sonata, op.3, to Haydn.

1794   Mary Ann Pownall becomes one of the first women to publish songs in the United States.

c1795   Hélène de Nervo de Montgeroult, a professor at the newly founded Paris

Conservatoire, publishes *Trois sonates pour le forte-piano* and a *Cours complet pour l'enseignement du forte-piano* in Paris.

Katerina Maier publishes a set of three keyboard sonatas in St Petersburg.

Park publishes her keyboard concerto in London.

1795   C. M. Barthélemon publishes an accompanied keyboard sonata, op.4, and a choral work, *The Capture of the Cape of Good Hope*, in London.

M. Barthélemon publishes *Three Hymns, and Three Anthems Composed for the Asylum, & Magdalen Chapels*, op.3, and *An Ode on the Late Providential Preservation of our Most Gracious Sovereign*, op.5, in London.

1797   Paradis's *Rinaldo und Alcina* is given at the Estates Theatre, Prague.

1798   Ann Valentine publishes her accompanied keyboard sonatas, op.1, in London.

1799   Elizabeth, Margravine of Anspach, is composer of *The Princess of Georgia*, an opera given at Covent Garden, London.

Maria F. Parke publishes *3 Grand Sonatas*, op.1, for piano, in London.

1800   Paradis publishes a piano trio in Vienna.

Louise Reichardt collaborates with her father (J. F. Reichardt) on *12 deutsche Lieder*, published in Zerbst.

1801   Margarethe Danzi's three sonatas for piano and violin, op.1, are published posthumously in Munich.

1805   Mlle Le Sénéchal de Kerkado's one-act comedy, *La méprise volontaire, ou La double leçon* is given at the Opéra-Comique, Paris.

L. Reichardt publishes *12 deutsche und italiänische romantische Gesänge* in Berlin.

1806   Sophia Maria Westenholz publishes *12 deutsche Lieder*, op.4, in Berlin.

1807   Maria Brizzi Giorgi composes military music which is performed for Napoleon when he passes through Bologna.

1811   L. Reichardt publishes *12 Gesänge* in Hamburg.

Park publishes about this time a *Divertimento* for accompanied piano, in London.

1813   Sophie Gail's one-act operas *Les deux jaloux* and *Mlle de Launay à la Bastille* are staged by the Opéra-Comique at the Théâtre Feydeau, Paris.

1814   Gail's *Angéla, ou L'atelier de Jean Cousin* is given at the Théâtre Feydeau, Paris.

1816   Amalie (Princess of Saxony) composes a comic opera, *Le nozze funeste*, in Dresden.

Maria Aghate Szymanowska publishes vocal music with Polish texts in Warsaw.

1818   Gail's *La Sérénade*, with its scandalous libretto, is given at the Théâtre Feydeau, Paris.

1819   Marianna Bottini composes in memory of her mother a *Stabat mater* and a *Messa da Requiem* (for which in 1820 she is admitted

to the Bolognese Accademia Filarmonica as 'Maestra compositrice onoraria'); she also composes a *Te Deum*.

Fanny Mendelssohn composes a lied honouring her father's birthday.

L. Reichardt publishes *12 Gesänge* and *6 Lieder* in Hamburg.

1820   Szymanowska publishes a *Divertimento* for violin and piano and a *Sérénade* for cello and piano in Leipzig.

Mendelssohn becomes a pupil at the Berlin Singakademie.

1822   Bottini composes a Mass and an opera, *Elena e Gerardo*.

1823   Sophie Bawr contributes the volume on the *Histoire de la musique* to the *Encyclopédie des dames*, published in Paris.

1830   Carolina Uccelli writes both words and music for a sacred opera, *Saul*, given at the Teatro della Pergola, Florence.

Louise-Geneviève de La Hye teaches harmony at the Paris Conservatoire to a class of young women.

Gertrude van den Bergh is elected an honorary member of the Netherlands Maatschappij tot Bevordering der Toonkunst.

1831   Mendelssohn composes her *Oratorium nach den Bildern der Bibel* in Berlin.

Clara Schumann publishes her *Polonaises*, op.1, in Leipzig.

1833   The Sheridan sisters, Helen Blackwood and Caroline Norton, collaborate on *A Set of ten Songs and two Duets*, published in London.

1835   La Hye's dramatic choral work *Le songe de la religieuse* is performed at the Hôtel de Ville, Paris.

1836   Loïsa Puget's one-act operetta, *Le mauvais oeil*, is premièred at the Opéra-Comique, Paris.

Maria Malibran's *Dernières pensées musicales* are published posthumously in Paris and, a year later, in London.

1837   Schumann publishes her piano concerto in A minor in Leipzig and is appointed *k.k. Kammervirtuosin* to the Austrian court.

1838   Alicia Ann Scott's song 'Annie Laurie' is published in the third volume of *The Vocal Melodies of Scotland*.

1839   Louise Farrenc composes her Piano Quintet in A minor, op.30 (Paris, 1842).

Elizabeth Masson becomes the first treasurer of the Royal Society of Female Musicians.

1840   Farrenc composes her Piano Quintet in E major, op.31.

1842   Emilie Zumsteeg publishes six lieder, op.6.

Adelaide Orsola Appignani becomes an honorary member of the Roman Accademia di S Cecilia.

1843   Bettina Brentano publishes a collection of lieder in Leipzig.

Caroline Orger performs her Piano Concerto at the Hanover Square Rooms, London; with Charlotte Sainton-Dolby she gave her Piano Trio at a concert at the same venue the following year.

1844   Schumann is named an honorary member of the St Petersburg Philharmonic Society.

1846   Mendelssohn composes her Piano Trio, op.11, and publishes *Sechs Lieder*, op.1, in Berlin.

Schumann composes her Piano Trio, op.17; the following year Breitkopf & Härtel publish it in Leipzig.

Kate Loder composes a string quartet.

1847   Mendelssohn composes a song, 'Bergeslust', the day before she dies, in Berlin; her *Gartenlieder*, op.3, are published posthumously.

1849   Felicita Casella's Portuguese opera *Haydée* is given in Oporto and, four years later in revised form, at the Teatro Dona Maria, Lisbon.

Farrenc composes her Nonet, op.38.

Fredrikke Egeberg publishes collections of sacred and secular songs in Christiania and, in 1850, collections of songs and piano pieces (*6 Songs without Words*) in Christiania.

1852   Emilie Mayer composes her Sinfonia no.6 in B minor (later published in a version for piano, four hands) in Berlin.

1853   Norton publishes her drawing room ballad 'Juanita' in London.

1855   Ann Mounsey's oratorio *The Nativity* is performed at St Martin's Hall, London.

1856   Tekla Bądarzewska-Baranowska publishes *Modlitwa dziewicy* ('The Maiden's Prayer') in Warsaw.

1857   Carlotta Ferrari's *dramma lirico Ugo* is performed at the Teatro di S Radegonda, Milan.

1859   Marie Grandval's operetta *Le sou de Lise* is performed at the Théâtre des Bouffes-Parisiens and published under her pseudonym 'Caroline Blangy' in Paris.

Constance Faunt Le Roy Runcie founds one of the first women's clubs in the United States, the Minerva Society, in New Harmony, Indiana.

1861   Alice Mary Smith composes her first piano quartet.

1863   Grandval's *opéra comique Les fiancés de Rosa* is performed at the Théâtre Lyrique, Paris.

A. M. Smith's Symphony in C minor is performed in London.

Filipina Brzezińska-Szymanowska's patriotic song *Nie opuszczaj nas* ('Do Not Leave Us') is popular during the Polish uprising against Russia.

1864   Grandval's *La comtesse Eva* is performed in Baden-Baden.

A 'Select Catalogue of Mrs E. A. Parkhurst's Compositions' is issued by her New York publisher, Horace Waters.

1865   Casella's opera *Cristoforo Colombo* is given at the Théâtre Impérial, Nice.

1866   C. Ferrari's *dramma lirico Sofia* is performed at the Teatro Sociale, Lodi.

Susan McFarland Parkhurst composes the song *Father's a Drunkard and Mother is Dead*, which she and her daughter perform at concerts and temperance meetings in New York.

Johanne Amalie Fenger publishes a collection of *6 Danske sange* in Copenhagen.

1867   Ingeborg Bronsart's three-act opera *Die Göttin von Sais, oder Linas und Liane* is performed at the Kronprinzliches Palais, Berlin.

A. M. Smith is elected Female Professional Associate of the Philharmonic Society, London.

Mary Ann Virginia Gabriel's operetta *Widows Bewitched* is given at the Gallery of Illustration, London.

1868   Grandval's *La pénitente* is performed by the Opéra-Comique at the Salle Favart, Paris.

Schumann joins Agnes Zimmermann in Zimmermann's Andante and Variations for two pianos at St James's Hall, London.

Martha von Sabinin abandons her career as a pianist and composer at the Russian court to serve as a nurse on the front during the Crimean War.

1869   Grandval's opera *Piccolino* is performed at the Théâtre Italien, Paris.

Puget's operetta *La veilleuse, ou Les nuits de milady* is performed at the Théâtre du Gymnase, Paris.

Lili'uokalani's *Nani nā pua* is possibly the first Hawaiian song to be published on the American mainland.

1870   Schumann publishes cadenzas for two Beethoven piano concertos in Leipzig.

1871   C. Ferrari's *Eleonora d'Arborea* is given at the Teatro Civico, Cagliari.

1872   A. M. Smith's clarinet concerto is performed at the Norwich Festival.

1873   Bronsart's second opera, *Jery und Bätely*, has its première in Weimar and is taken on tour to more than ten other German cities.

Ella Georgiyevna Adayevskaya composes an opera, *Neprigozhaya* ('The Homely Girl')/ *Doch' boyarina* ('The Boyar's Daughter').

Gabriel's cantata *Evangeline* is premièred at the Brighton Festival.

1874   Soledad Bengoechea de Cármena's zarzuelas *Flor de los cielos* and *El gran día* are given at the Teatro Jovellanos, Madrid.

1875   Sophia Dellaporta's patriotic *Recueil musical* (Leipzig, 1877) wins a prize at the Third Greek Composers' Competition in Athens.

1876 Appignani's melodrama *Clara di Clevers* is given at the Teatro Nazionale, Bologna.

Sainton-Dolby composes her cantata *The Legend of St Dorothea* in London.

Annie Fortescue Harrison composes *In the Gloaming*.

1877 Adayevskaya's opera, *Zarya svobodi* ('The Dawn of Freedom'), dedicated to Alexander II, is banned by the Russian censors.

Luísa Leonardo's *Grande marcha triunfal* is performed by the Pasdeloup orchestra under Albert Lavignac at the Herz Hall, Paris.

Luise Adolpha Le Beau composes a Piano Trio, op.15.

Marie Jaëll publishes her *Valses à quatre mains* in Paris.

1878 Clara Angela Macirone's part-song *Sir Knight* is the first music heard by Queen Victoria over the telephone.

1879 Jaëll publishes the symphonic poem *Ossiane* in Paris.

Maude Valérie White is the first woman to win the Mendelssohn Scholarship at the RAM, London.

Elfrida Andrée is made a member of the Swedish Kungliga Musikaliska Akademien.

1880 Grandval wins the Concours Rossini for her oratorio *La fille de Jaïre*, first performed in 1881 at the Paris Conservatoire.

Ethel Smyth composes a Prelude and Fugue in F sharp minor and a String Quartet in D minor.

1881 Augusta Holmès' dramatic symphony *Les Argonautes* is performed in Paris.

Cécile Chaminade publishes two piano trios, op.11, in Paris.

Adayevskaya composes a *Greek Sonata* for clarinet and piano, using quarter tones.

1882 A. M. Smith's ode, *The Passions*, is performed at the Hereford Festival.

Chaminade's *opéra comique La Sévillane* is privately performed in Paris.

Josephine Lang is commemorated by the publication of a collection of lieder by Breitkopf & Härtel in Leipzig.

1883 Sophie Menter is awarded honorary membership of the Philharmonic Society of London.

1884 A. M. Smith is made Hon. RAM in London.

Valborg Aulin composes her string quartet in F.

1885 Valentina Semyonovna Serova's opera *Uriel Acosta* is performed at the Bol'shoy Theatre, Moscow.

Mayer is made an honorary member of the Philharmonic Society of Munich.

1887 Le Beau composes her Piano Concerto, op.37.

Margaret Ruthven Lang has five songs included in a Boston recital by Myron W. Whitney, launching her professional career.

1888 Chaminade publishes her *symphonie dramatique Les amazones*, op.26, about this time in Paris; her *ballet symphonique Callirhoë* is performed in Marseilles.

Dora Bright becomes the first woman to win the Lucas Medal for composition at the RAM, London, and the following year performs her Piano Concerto in A minor under Reinecke in Dresden, Cologne and Leipzig.

1889 Holmès composes a symphonic *Ode triomphale*, to mark the centenary of the French Revolution.

Rosalind Frances Ellicott undertakes a commission from the Gloucester Three Choirs Festival to compose a cantata, *Elysium*.

Aulin composes a second string quartet in E minor, op.17.

Helena Munktell's ballad, *Isjungfrun*, for baritone and orchestra, is performed at Salle Pleyel, Paris.

Amy Elsie Horrocks wins the Sterndale Bennett Prize at the RAM, London.

1890 Smyth's Serenade and her overture to *Antony and Cleopatra* are performed at Crystal Palace, London.

Amy Marcy Beach composes her Mass in E flat; it is performed in Boston in 1892.

Eva Dell'Acqua's *La ruse de Pierrette* is given, with the composer in the title role, in Brussels.

1891 Smyth completes her Mass in D.

R. Ethel Harraden's operetta *His Last Chance* is given at the Gaiety Theatre and published in London.

1892 Eugénie-Emilie Juliette Folville's opera *Atala* has its first performance in Lille.

Grandval's *Mazeppa* is given at the Grand Théâtre Municipal, Bordeaux.

Luisa Casagemas's opera *Schiava e regina* (composed *c*1880) wins a prize in connection with the World's Columbian Exposition, Chicago.

Alice Tegnér publishes her first book of songs for children *Sjung med oss, Mamma!* ('Sing with us, Mother!').

1893 Beach composes her *Festival Jubilate*, op.17, for the dedication of the Women's Building of the World's Columbian Exposition, Chicago.

M. R. Lang's *Dramatic Overture*, op.12, is performed by the Boston Symphony Orchestra under Arthur Nikisch and her overture *Witichis*, op.10, is performed at the World's Columbian Exposition, Chicago.

Casagemas's symphonic *Crepúsculo* is performed by the Orquesta Catalana de Conciertos in Barcelona.

Cecilia Arizti's Trio, the first chamber work written by a Cuban woman, is played at Anselmo López's salon-concert.

1894   Emma Roberto Steiner conducts a concert of her own works at Chickering Hall, New York.

Le Beau composes her Symphony in F major, op.41, about this time; her opera *Hadumoth* (1888–91) is performed in Baden-Baden.

Gisella Delle Grazie's opera *Atala* is given at the Teatro Balbo, Turin.

1895   Delle Grazie's opera *La trecciaiuola di Firenze* is given at the Teatro Filodrammatico, Trieste.

Harraden's operetta *The Taboo* is given at the Trafalgar Square Theatre, London.

1896   Beach's 'Gaelic' symphony is performed by the Boston SO; she also composes her Violin Sonata in A minor.

Liza Lehmann publishes a song cycle, *In a Persian Garden*, in London.

Maude Nugent composes the waltz ballad *Sweet Rosie O'Grady*.

1897   Josefina Brdlíková publishes two volumes of piano music, *Album skladeb klavírních*, in Prague as well as a further volume of *Waltz Aphorisms* for piano, four hands.

Cornélie van Oosterzee is made a Knight of the Order of Oranje-Nassau.

1898   Catharina van Rennes conducts her *Oranje-Nassau-Cantate* with a choir of 1800 children and an orchestra at the coronation of Queen Wilhelmina.

Oosterzee composes a choral cantata for the opening ceremony of the National Exhibition on Women's Work in The Hague.

Mary Wurm founds and conducts a women's orchestra in Berlin.

1899   Serova's opera *Il'ya Muromets* is given at the Solodovnikov Theatre, Moscow.

Tekla Griebel Wandall's opera *Skøn Karen* (1894) is performed at the Kongelige Teater, Copenhagen.

Edith Swepstone's tone poem *Daramona* is performed by Dan Godfrey and the Bournemouth Municipal Orchestra, the first of her 14 orchestral works played by the orchestra in 24 performances.

Horrocks publishes her narrative *scena* with piano trio, *The Lady of Shalott*, in London.

1901   M. R. Lang's *Ballade*, op.36, is premièred by the Baltimore SO at the Women in Music Grand Concert in Baltimore.

1902   Smyth's second opera, *Der Wald*, is given in Berlin and at Covent Garden, London; the following year it became the first opera by a woman to be performed at the Metropolitan Opera House, New York.

Mabel Wheeler Daniels is the first woman to enter Ludwig Thuille's score-reading class at the Munich conservatory.

1903   Roberta Geddes-Harvey's opera *La terre bonne* (or *The Land of the Maple Leaf*) is given at the Royal Opera House, Guelph, Ontario.

Ethel Barns's Second Violin Sonata is performed by Joseph Joachim on tour in Germany.

1904   Jane Vieu's operetta *Arlette* is premièred at the Théâtre Royal des Galeries St Hubert, Brussels.

Pauline Viardot composes an *opéra comique*, *Cendrillon*.

1905   Elisabeth Kuyper is the first woman to win the Mendelssohn State Composition Prize in Berlin.

1906   Smyth's third opera, *Les naufrageurs* (1902–4), is given in German as *Strandrecht* at the Neuestheater, Leipzig, and in Prague.

Ida Georgina Moberg conducts a programme of her orchestral music, including an overture, symphony and choral work, in Helsinki.

1907   Beach composes her Piano Quintet in F sharp minor.

Rebecca Clarke becomes the first woman to study composition with Charles Villiers Stanford at the RCM.

Florence Maud Ewart composes her *Ode to Australia* for the Exhibition of Women's Works in Melbourne, where Marian Arkwright's Suite for Strings is also performed.

1908   Kuyper becomes the first woman to teach theory and composition at the Berlin Hochschule für Musik.

Nadia Boulanger causes controversy by submitting an instrumental (rather than vocal) fugue for her preliminary submissions for the Prix de Rome at the Paris Conservatoire.

Ethel Scarborough appears as soloist in her Piano Concerto with Dan Godfrey and the Bournemouth Municipal Orchestra.

1909   Smyth's opera *The Wreckers*, a translation of *Les naufrageurs*, is performed under Thomas Beecham at His Majesty's Theatre, London.

Gabrielle Ferrari's *drame lyrique Le Cobzar* is given at Monte Carlo; when revived in Paris in 1912 it becomes the subject of fierce debate between pro- and anti-feminist writers.

Mary Carr Moore organizes an American Music Center in Seattle.

1910   Smyth is awarded the honorary DMus by the University of Durham.

Adela Maddison's opera *Der Talisman* is given at the Stadttheater, Leipzig.

Barns's *Concertstück* for violin and orchestra is performed at the Queen's Hall Promenade Concerts, London.

Alma Mahler publishes *Fünf Lieder* in Vienna.

Carrie Bond composes the song, 'A Perfect Day', which is to sell over eight million sheet music copies and five million records.

Kuyper founds the Berlin Tonkünstlerinnen-Orchester.

Johanna Senfter wins the Arthur Nikisch prize for composition in Leipzig.

1911   The Society of Women Musicians is founded in London with Lehmann as its first president; Katharine Emily Eggar proclaims 'We believe in a great future for Women Composers'.

Smyth's 'March of the Women' becomes the anthem of the Women's Social and Political Union.

M. C. Moore completes her opera *Narcissa* which she conducts in Seattle (1912), San Francisco (1925) and Los Angeles (1945); in 1930 *Narcissa* wins the David Bispham Memorial Medal.

1912   Smyth serves two months in Holloway Prison, London.

Poldowski's *Nocturnes* for orchestra is performed at the Queen's Hall Promenade Concerts, London.

M. C. Moore's opera *Narcissa* is presented in Seattle with the composer conducting.

Chiquinha Gonzaga's three-act operetta *Forrobadó* begins a run of over 1500 performances in Rio de Janeiro.

1913   Smyth composes her comedy *The Boatswain's Mate*.

Chaminade is admitted to the Légion d'Honneur.

Lili Boulanger becomes the first woman to win the Prix de Rome, with *Faust et Hélène*.

1914   Hilda Sehested's opera *Agnete og Havmanden* is accepted at the Kongelige Teater, Copenhagen, but never staged.

1915   Maria Rodrigo's opera *Becqueriana* is performed at the Teatro de la Zarzuela, Madrid.

Vincenza Garelli della Morea's operetta *Incantesimo* is given at the Teatro Garibaldi, Padua.

1916   Garelli della Morea's *Il viaggio dei Perrichon* is given at the Teatro Alfieri, Turin.

1917   Signe Lund becomes a founder member of the Norwegian Association of Composers.

1918   Nancy Dalberg's three symphonic works are conducted by Carl Nielsen at a composition evening in Copenhagen.

Louisa Emily (Emma) Lomax is appointed a professor of composition at the RAM, London.

Clarke's *Morpheus* (1917) is performed at Carnegie Hall, New York.

Fannie Charles Dillon gives a concert of her piano music to the Beethoven Society, New York.

Ethel Hier wins the first of her 14 fellowships at the MacDowell Colony, Peterborough, New Hampshire.

Dora Pejačević's Symphony in F sharp minor is performed in Vienna (two movements); two years later it is given in Dresden.

L. Boulanger's opera *La Princesse Maleine* is left unfinished at her death.

1919   Clarke's Viola Sonata wins second place in the Coolidge Competition, after initially tying for first place with Bloch's Viola Suite.

Dorothy Howell's symphonic poem *Lamia* is performed at the London Promenade Concerts, conducted by Henry Wood.

Smyth publishes her first autobiographical book, *Impressions that Remained*, in London.

Mana Zucca performs her Piano Concerto with the Los Angeles SO.

1920   Ina Boyle receives a Carnegie Award for *The Magic Harp*, and the work is performed in London.

Marguerite Canal wins the Prix de Rome with *Don Juan*.

Priaulx Rainier wins the Cape University Scholarship as a violin student to study at the RAM, London.

Germaine Tailleferre is the only female member of the newly-formed Les Six.

E. R. Steiner conducts a concert of her own works at the Metropolitan Opera House, New York.

1921   Marion Bauer co-founds the American Music Guild.

Beach is a fellow at the MacDowell Colony.

Howell's *Phantasy* for violin and piano wins the Cobbett Prize at the RAM.

1922   Mary Howe earns her diploma in composition at the Peabody Conservatory.

Smyth is created DBE, the first woman composer to be so honoured.

Kuyper founds the London Women's Symphony Orchestra and presents with them her *Das Lied von der Seele* for orchestra, seven soloists and dance; she founds the American Women's Symphony Orchestra in New York City in 1924.

1923   Marion Bauer, on her second visit to Paris, is probably the first American student taught by Nadia Boulanger.

Smyth's *Fête galante* is given at the Repertory Theatre, Birmingham.

1924   Garelli della Morea's *Le nozze di Leporello* is given at the Teatro Sociale, Brescia.

1925   The Festival of American Women Composers takes place in Washington, DC.

Amy Beach, Mary Howe, Gena Branscombe and Ethel Hier found the Society of American Women Composers, and Beach serves as its first president.

Smyth's comedy *Entente cordiale* is performed at the RCM, London, and, the next year, at the Royal Theatre, Bristol.

Freda Swain's *The Harp of Aengus* is performed at Queen's Hall, London.

1926 Smyth is awarded the honorary DMus at Oxford University.

Ruth Crawford joins the board of Henry Cowell's New Music Society.

1927 Berta Bock's opera *Die Pfingstkrone* is performed throughout Transylvania and in 1931 in the USA.

Crawford's Violin Sonata is performed in New York at a League of Composers concert consisting of music by six 'Young Americans' (including Aaron Copland and Marc Blitzstein).

Frida Kern is the first woman to graduate in composition and conducting from the Akademie für Musik in Vienna.

May Brahe first writes 'Bless this House'.

1928 Crawford becomes a founder member of the Chicago chapter of the International Society for Contemporary Music.

Andrée Bonhomme's *Drie Schetsen* are performed by the Maastricht city orchestra at a concert in which she plays a Mozart piano concerto.

Mary Lucas's *Rhapsody* is played by the Bournemouth Municipal Orchestra.

Imogen Holst wins the Cobbett Prize for composition at the RCM, London.

Grete von Zieritz receives the Mendelssohn Prize for composition and the Schubert Grant, given by the Columbia Phonograph Co. of New York.

1929 Beach completes her String Quartet, op.89, in Rome.

Marta Canales wins first prize at the Latin-American Exhibition, Seville, for her work as a composer.

Lucas's *Fugue* is performed by the Bournemouth Municipal Orchestra.

Elsa Barraine wins the Prix de Rome with *La vierge guerrière*.

Barbara Pentland arrives in Paris from Canada to study composition with Cécile Gauthiez.

1930 Crawford becomes the first woman to be awarded a Guggenheim Fellowship in composition.

Elizabeth Maconchy's suite *The Land* is played at the London Promenade Concerts.

Grace Williams goes to Vienna on a travelling scholarship to study with Egon Wellesz.

Holst wins an Octavia travelling scholarship at the RCM.

1931 Crawford completes her string quartet.

First of the Macnaghten-Lemare concerts, given in London; the programme includes works by Holst and Elisabeth Lutyens.

Peggy Glanville-Hicks goes to London from Australia to study with Vaughan Williams at the RCM.

Verdina Shlonsky's *Poème hébraïque* wins a French government competition for women composers.

1932 Yvonne Desportes wins the Prix de Rome with *Le Pardon*.

Florence Price wins first prize at the Wanamaker competition for her Symphony in E minor.

1933 Howe studies for a short time with Nadia Boulanger in Paris.

Marcelle de Manziarly gives the first performance of her Piano Concerto at the 1933 ISCM Festival with the Concertgebouw under Casella.

1934 Margaret Bonds becomes the first African-American soloist to appear with the Chicago SO in a performance of Florence Price's Piano Concerto at the Chicago world's fair.

1935 Ethel Leginska's one-act opera *Gale* is given its first performance by the Chicago City Opera, conducted by the composer.

1936 Swain founds the British Music Movement.

Barbara Giuranna's Adagio and Allegro for nine instruments is performed at the Venice Biennale.

1937 Mildred Couper's *Dirge* appears in Cowell's New Music Edition.

Ernestina Lecuona Casado becomes a founder member of the Orquesta Feminina de Concierto, Cuba.

1938 Glanville-Hicks's Choral Suite is performed under Adrian Boult and Vítězslava Kaprálová conducts the BBC SO in her *Military Sinfonietta*, both at the ISCM Festival, London.

Lucas's *Variations on a Theme of Purcell* is performed by the New York Philharmonic Society at Saratoga Springs and by the Boyd Neel Orchestra in London.

Pauline Hall becomes president of Ny Musikk in Norway, retaining this position until 1960.

1939 Hier's *Asolo Bells* is played at the Festival of American Music at the Eastman School of Music; six years later it is played by the Cincinnati SO, and in 1953 (as part of Three Orchestral Pieces) wins a Composers Press publication award.

Lutyens writes her Chamber Concerto no.1, using her own version of the 12-note method.

1940   Joan Trimble wins the Cobbett Prize at the RCM for her *Phantasy Trio*.

Johanna Bordewijk-Roepman's *Les illuminations* is performed by the Rotterdam PO under Eduard Flipse.

1942   Violet Archer studies composition with Béla Bartók in New York; her *Britannia* overture is broadcast to the troops in Europe.

Gonzalo Gisela Hernández becomes a founder member of the Grupo de Renovación Musical (1942–8) in Cuba.

1943   Berthe di Vito-Delvaux wins the Prix de Rome of Belgium.

1944   Kathleen Richards serves as Smyth's musical executor.

Hernández receives the National Composition Prize of Cuba for her *Suite coral* (1942); it is performed in Mexico and published in Uruguay.

1946   Henriëtte Hilda Bosmans's *Doodenmarsch* is performed by the Concertgebouw Orchestra under Boult.

1947   Doreen Carwithen is the first composer chosen from the RAM for the J. Arthur Rank Apprenticeship Scheme to study film music.

1948   Alice Parker becomes the principal arranger for the Robert Shaw Chorale (until 1967).

1949   Adrienne Clostre wins the Prix de Rome with *La résurrection de Lazare*.

Grażyna Bacewicz wins the first prize for her Piano Concerto at the International Chopin Competition for Composers, Warsaw.

1950   Eunice Catunda's *Homenagem a Schoenberg* is performed at the ISCM Festival.

Dorothea Franchi wins the Tertis Prize at the RCM, London, for her Rhapsody for Viola and Orchestra.

Glanville-Hicks becomes director of the New York Composers' Forum and in the next ten years helps organize a series of concerts of new American music.

1952   Glanville-Hicks's *Letters from Morocco* is performed under Leopold Stokowski at the Museum of Modern Art, New York.

1953   Maconchy's overture *Proud Thames* wins the London County Council's prize of the Coronation Year.

Lucia Dlugoszewski becomes composer-in-residence for the Erick Hawkins Dance Company, New York, a position she holds for 11 years.

1954   Glanville-Hicks's opera *The Transposed Heads* is given by the Louisville Orchestra; subsequent performances are given in New York (1958) and Sydney (1970).

1956   Pentland, influenced by her visit to Darmstadt, writes her Concerto for Piano and Strings using serial techniques.

Bebe and Louis Barron present the score to *Forbidden Planet*, one of the first electronic scores for a commercial film and an influential work in the development of electronic music.

Teresa Procaccini wins the Viotti competition.

Lucrecia Kasilag is elected chairman of the League of Filipino Composers.

1957   Avril Coleridge-Taylor writes the *Ceremonial March* to celebrate Ghana's independence.

1958   Daphne Oram is one of the initiators of the BBC Radiophonic Workshop.

1959   Maconchy becomes the first woman chairman of the Composers' Guild of Great Britain.

Alicia Terzian receives the Gold Medal from the Buenos Aires Conservatorio Nacional.

Jacqueline Fontyn wins the Prix de Rome.

1960   Bacewicz wins the first orchestral prize for Music for Strings, Trumpets and Percussion at UNESCO's International Rostrum of Composers in Paris.

1961   In Tokyo, Mieko Shiomi with two colleagues forms Group-Ongaku, an experimental ensemble focussing on improvisation, tape music and 'events'.

1962   Louise Talma's *The Alcestiad* (1958) is the first opera by an American woman to be produced at a major European opera house, at Frankfurt.

Gaziza Zhubanova becomes chairman of the Kazakh Composers' Union, a position she retains until 1968.

Krystyna Moszumańska-Nazar wins a prize for her *Music for Strings* at Buenos Aires.

Thea Musgrave's *The Phoenix and the Turtle* is commissioned for the BBC Proms.

1963   Esther Ballou's *Capriccio* for violin and piano is the first work by an American woman composer to be given its first performance at the White House, Washington, DC.

1964   Beatriz Fereyra joins Pierre Schaeffer's Groupe de Recherches Musicales at ORTF, Paris.

1964   Fontyn wins the Queen Elisabeth of Belgium prize for composition.

1965   Jeanne Behrend receives the Order of the Southern Cross for services to Brazilian music.

Teresa Rampazzi founds, with Enio Chioggio, the group Nuove Proposte Sonore in Padua.

Thérèse Brenet wins the Prix de Rome.

Bacewicz wins the gold medal of the Queen Elisabeth of Belgium International Composition Competition in Brussels for her Seventh Violin Concerto.

1966   Irma Ravinale is appointed to the chair of composition at the Conservatorio di Musica S Cecilia, Rome.

Monic Cecconi-Botella wins the Prix de Rome.

Nini Bulterijs wins the Queen Elisabeth of Belgium International Composition Competition with her Symphony (1965).

Grace Williams's *The Parlour* is given by the Welsh National Opera at the New Theatre, Cardiff.

1967   Giuranna wins the international prize of the City of Trieste with her second Concerto for Orchestra.

Maryanne Amacher creates *City-Links* (live environmental sounds transmitted by mixing facilities).

1968   Ruth Anderson founds and becomes the first director of the electronic music studio at Hunter College, City University of New York.

Edith Lejet wins the Prix de Rome.

Dorothy Rudd Moore helps found the Society of Black Composers.

Gitta Steiner co-founds the Composers Group for International Performance, New York.

1969   Barbara Kolb is the first American woman to win the Prix de Rome.

Micheline Saint-Marcoux, Joanna Bruzdowicz and four others found the Groupe International de Musique Electro-Acoustique, in Paris, which tours in Europe, Canada and South America until 1973.

Meredith Monk's theatre piece *Juice* is first given at the Guggenheim Museum, New York.

Joan Tower founds and becomes the pianist for the Da Capo Chamber Players, the New York ensemble for which she also composes.

Mary Lou Williams's *Music for Peace* is commissioned by the Vatican; in 1971, revised as *Mary Lou's Mass*, it is choreographed by Alvin Ailey and widely performed.

Lutyens is made a CBE.

1970   Carin Malmlöf-Forssling is elected to the Society of Swedish Composers.

Peggy Stuart-Coolidge is the first American to have a programme of her music presented by the USSR Union of Composers, Moscow; she also receives the medal of the Soviet Union of Workers in Art.

Ludmila Ulehla becomes chairperson of the Composition Department at the Manhattan School of Music, New York.

Françoise Barrière founds the Groupe de Musique Experimentale de Bourges (GMEB) with Christian Clozier.

Annea Lockwood creates *Piano Transplants*, 'sound sculptures' recording the decay and transformation of pianos.

1971   Melanie Daiken's opera *Mayakovsky and the Sun*, commissioned by the Edinburgh

Festival, is performed there by Music Theatre Ensemble under Alexander Goehr.

Jennifer Fowler shares the Radcliffe Award of Great Britain.

1972   Bonds's *Credo* is performed (one month after her death) by the Los Angeles PO under Zubin Mehta.

1973   Nicola LeFanu's *The Hidden Landscape* has its première at the London Proms.

Libby Larsen and Stephen Paulus establish the Minnesota Composers Forum.

Diane Thome is the first woman to receive the PhD in composition at Princeton University.

1974   Nicole Lachartre founds the Association pour la Collaboration des Interprètes et des Compositeurs.

Talma is the first woman composer to be elected to the National Institute of Arts and Letters, followed in 1975 by Miriam Gideon.

S.-C. Eckhardt-Gramatté is the first composer to receive the Diplôme d'honneur of the Canadian Conference of the Arts.

Musgrave's chamber opera *The Voice of Ariadne* is commissioned by the Royal Opera House for the Aldeburgh Festival; in 1977 the composer conducts performances with the New York City Opera.

Betsy Jolas is awarded the French Grand Prix National de la Musique.

1975   Nancy Van de Vate founds the International League of Women Composers.

Lycia de Biase Bidart of Brazil receives a prize at the Concorso Internationale de Musica G. B. Viotti, for her piano sonata.

Ellen Taaffe Zwilich is the first woman to receive the DMA in composition from the Juilliard School, New York.

Alison Bauld wins a Gulbenkian Dance Award for composition.

Pozzi Escot's *Sands* (1965) is performed by the New York Philharmonic.

1976   Fontyn's Violin Concerto is commissioned for performance at the Queen Elisabeth of Belgium International Competition.

Maconchy becomes president of the SPNM.

Musgrave conducts the Philadelphia Orchestra in a performance of her Concerto for Orchestra.

Laurie Spiegel is artist-in-residence at the WNET Experimental Television Laboratory, New York.

1977   The International Congress on Women in Music is founded by Jeannie Pool.

Gisèle Barreau receives the Koussevitsky Prize for *Tlalec* and, a year later, the SACEM Prix Enesco.

Dorothy Buchanan becomes the first 'composer-in-schools' in Christchurch, New Zealand.

Maconchy is made a CBE.

Judith Bingham receives the BBC Young Composer Award.

Dlugoszewski become the first woman to win the Koussevitzky International Recording Award, for *Fire Fragile Flight*.

Ann Southam and Diana McIntosh found the Winnipeg-based Music Inter Alia, which presents and commissions new works and (from 1981–2) holds an annual competition.

Musgrave's opera *Mary Queen of Scots*, commissioned by Scottish Opera, is first performed at the Edinburgh Festival with the composer conducting; in 1981 it is given by the New York City Opera.

Spiegel's *Realization of Kepler's Harmony of the Planets* is included as the first item in the 'Sounds of Earth' recording on the Voyager spacecraft.

Pauline Oliveros wins the Beethovenpreis der Stadt Bonn for *Bonn Feier*.

1978   Terzian founds the group, Encountros Internacionales de Música Contemporánea, and a year later receives the award of Chevalier de l'ordre de palmes academiques from the French Government.

Vivienne Olive wins the City of Stuttgart Prize for *Tomba di Bruno*.

1979   Tona Scherchen receives the Koussevitsky Prize.

The Internationaler Arbeitskreis Frau und Musik is founded.

Musgrave's opera *A Christmas Carol* is given by Virginia Opera in Norfolk.

1980   The International Congress on Women in Music, devoted to the mounting of biennial conferences, holds its first meeting in New York.

Kvinder i Musik (Women in Music) is founded in Denmark.

Southam is elected first president of the Association of Canadian Women Composers (1980–88).

Younghi Pagh-Paan wins first prize at the UNESCO International Rostrum of Composers, Paris, with *SORI* for full orchestra.

1981   Sorrel Hays composes *Exploitation* for the first International Congress on Women in Music.

1982   The second International Congress on Women in Music is held in Los Angeles.

Gillian Bibby becomes president of the Composers Association of New Zealand.

1983   Zwilich is the first woman to win the Pulitzer Prize with her Symphony no.1, first performed in 1982 by the American Composers Orchestra under Gunther Schuller.

Laurie Anderson's four-part *United States* is performed at the Brooklyn Academy of Music, New York; it is later recorded and published as a book.

Priaulx Rainier becomes the first Lady Liveryman of the Worshipful Company of Musicians.

Giuranna is made an *accademico di S Cecilia* in Rome.

Synne Skouen writes the music for the radio production of *Måkespisere* ('The Gull Eaters') which wins the Prix Italia.

Larsen becomes a composer-in-residence with the Minnesota Orchestra.

1984   The third International Congress on Women in Music is held in Mexico City and Paris.

Wendy Carlos's hundreds of near-perfect replicas of instrumental voices are used in the first digitally synthesized orchestra, heard on the album *Digital Moonscapes*.

Ursula Mamlok's *When Summer Sang* is chosen to represent the USA at the 1984 UNESCO International Rostrum of Composers.

Tat'yana Chudova is awarded the Lenin Komsomol Prize.

Ruth Zechlin becomes the first woman full professor of composition in Germany, at the Hanns Eisler Hochschule für Musik, East Berlin.

Kimi Sato wins the Prix de Rome on Olivier Messiaen's recommendation.

Musgrave's opera *Harriet, the Woman Called Moses* is commissioned jointly by the Royal Opera House, Covent Garden, and the Virginia Opera Association.

Jolas's *D'un opéra de poupée en sept musiques* (1984) is performed at IRCAM, Paris.

1985   Barron becomes the first secretary of the Society for Electro-Acoustic Music in the USA.

Ivana Stefanović founds the Sound Workshop of Radio Belgrade.

Women's Music Festival '/85 takes place in Boston.

Oliveros is honoured with a restrospective at the John F. Kennedy Center for the Performing Arts, Washington, DC.

Qü Xixian is elected vice-chairman of the Chinese Musicians' Association.

1986   The fourth International Congress on Women in Music is held at Atlanta, Georgia.

Marta Ptaszyńska wins second place at the UNESCO International Rostrum of Composers, Paris, with *La novella d'inverno*.

Sofiya Gubaydulina composes her 12-movement *Stimmen . . . Verstummen . . .*, one of whose movements is a conductor's solo.

Alexina Louie is named Composer of the Year by the Canadian Music Council.

1987 Maconchy is made a DBE.

Kolb wins the Kennedy Center Friedheim Award with *Millefoglie*.

LeFanu's essay 'Master Musicians: an Impregnable Taboo?' draws attention to the neglect of the music of women composers in the UK.

Anne Lauber becomes director of the Canadian Music Centre.

1988 The fifth International Congress on Women in Music is held at Bremen and Heidelberg.

Women in Music is founded in London.

Kaija Saariaho wins the Prix Italia for the radiophonic composition *Stilleben*.

Tower wins the Kennedy Center Friedheim Award with *Silver Ladders*, which in 1990 wins the Grawemeyer Award .

Cecilie Ore wins the first prize for young composers and second prize overall at the International Rostrum for Electroacoustic Music in Stockholm with *Etapper*.

Bauld's opera *Nell* has its première in the London International Opera Festival.

1989 Minna Keal's Symphony is performed and broadcast at the BBC Proms.

Ravinale is appointed director of the Conservatorio di Musica S Cecilia, Rome.

1990 At its sixth conference, in New York, the International Congress on Women in Music merges with the International League of Women Composers. The library is moved to the International Institute for the Study of Women in Music at California State University, Northridge.

M. L. Williams becomes the first woman instrumentalist to be admitted to the *Down Beat* Hall of Fame.

Zechlin becomes vice-president of the Akademie der Künste, Berlin.

Jolas's *Schliemann* is given in concert form at the opening of the Opéra Bastille, Paris.

Judith Weir's opera *The Vanishing Bridegroom* is given by Scottish Opera at the Theatre Royal, Glasgow.

1991 The seventh International Congress on Women in Music, organized by Stichting Vrouw en Muziek, is held at Utrecht.

Shulamit Ran's Symphony (1990), commissioned by the Philadelphia Orchestra, wins the Pulitzer Prize.

Monk is commissioned by Houston Grand Opera to compose *Atlas*.

Eve de Castro-Robinson is appointed composer-in-residence with the Auckland PO.

Renata Kunkel wins third prize in the first Lutosławski Composers' Competition, Warsaw.

Erika Fox's opera *The Dancer, Hotoke* is performed as part of The Garden Venture project, London.

Lam Bun-ching wins the Prix de Rome.

Anne Boyd is appointed Professor of Music at the University of Sydney.

The first Music and Gender Conference in the UK takes place at King's College, London.

Escot becomes president of the International Society of Hildegard von Bingen Studies.

1992 The eighth International Congress on Women in Music, organized by Mujeres en la Música of Spain, is held at Bilbao.

Musgrave completes her opera *Simon Bolívar,* commissioned jointly by the Los Angeles Music Center Opera and Scottish Opera.

1993 The ninth International Congress on Women in Music is held at Fairbanks, Alaska.

Hays completes *The Glass Woman*, an opera on six renowned women collectors commemorated by their own museums.

Nicola LeFanu is appointed Professor of Music at King's College, London, and, the following year, Professor and Head of Department at the University of York.

1994 Weir's opera *Blond Eckbert* is given by English National Opera at the Coliseum, London.

General Abbreviations

A	alto [voice]		Bulg.	Bulgarian
a	alto [instrument]		bur.	buried
AB	Bachelor of Arts		BVM	Blessed Virgin Mary
ABC	Australian Broadcasting Commission			
ACA	American Composers Alliance		C	contralto
acc.	accompaniment, accompanied by		c	circa [about]
AD	anno Domini		CA	California (USA)
add, addl	additional		carn.	Carnival
add, addn	addition		CBC	Canadian Broadcasting Corporation
ad lib	ad libitum		CBE	Commander of the Order of the
AIDS	Acquired Immune Deficiency Syndrome			British Empire
AK	Alaska (USA)		CBS	Columbia Broadcasting System (USA)
AL	Alabama (USA)		CBSO	City of Birmingham Symphony
AMC	American Music Center			Orchestra
amp	amplified		CD	compact disc
anon.	anonymous(ly)		CeBeDeM	Centre Belge de Documentation
ant	antiphon			Musicale
appx	appendix		cel	celesta
AR	Arkansas (USA)		CFE	Composers Facsimile Edition
ARAM	Associate of the Royal Academy of		chap.	chapter
	Music, London		Chin.	Chinese
ARCM	Associate of the Royal College of		choreog.	choreography, choreographer,
	Music, London			choreographed by
arr.	arrangement, arranged by/for		cimb	cimbalom
ASCAP	American Society of Composers,		cl	clarinet
	Authors and Publishers		clvd	clavichord
attrib.	attribution, attributed to		CO	Colorado (USA)
Aug	August		Co.	Company; County
aut.	autumn		col(s).	column(s)
AZ	Arizona (USA)		collab.	in collaboration with
			comp.	composed, composed by
B	bass [voice]		conc.	concerto
b	bass [instrument]		cond.	conductor, conducted by
b	born		CPEMC	Columbia-Princeton Electronic
BA	Bachelor of Arts			Music Center
bap.	baptized		CRI	Composers Recordings Inc.
Bar	baritone [voice]		CT	Connecticut (USA)
bar	baritone [instrument]		Ct	countertenor
B–Bar	bass–baritone		CUNY	City University of New York
BBC	British Broadcasting Corporation		Cz.	Czech
BC	British Columbia (Canada)			
BC	before Christ		D	Deutsch catalogue [Schubert]
bc	basso continuo		d	died
Bd.	Band [volume]		DAAD	Deutscher Akademischer
BEd	Bachelor of Education			Austauschdienst
Berks.	Berkshire (GB)		Dan.	Danish
Berwicks.	Berwickshire (GB)		db	double bass
BFA	Bachelor of Fine Arts		DBE	Dame Commander of the Order of
bk(s)	book(s)			the British Empire
BM	British Museum; Bachelor of Music		dbn	double bassoon
BME	Bachelor of Music Education		DC	District of Columbia (USA)
BMI	Broadcast Music Inc. (USA)		DE	Delaware (USA)
BMus	Bachelor of Music		Dec	December
BS	Bachelor of Science		ded.	dedication, dedicated to
bn	bassoon		Derbys.	Derbyshire (GB)
Bros.	Brothers		dir.	director, directed by
Bucks.	Buckinghamshire (GB)		diss.	dissertation

DMA	Doctor of Musical Arts
DMus	Doctor of Music
DPhil	Doctor of Philosophy
DSM	Doctor of Sacred Music
ed.	editor, edited (by)
edn(s)	edition(s)
e.g.	exempli gratia [for example]
el	electric
el-ac	electroacoustic
elec	electronic(s)
EMI	Electrical and Musical Industries
Eng.	English
eng hn	english horn
ENO	English National Opera
ens	ensemble
esp.	especially
etc.	et cetera [and so on]
ex., exx.	example, examples
f, ff	following page, following pages
f., ff.	folio, folios
f	forte
facs.	facsimile
Feb	February
ff	fortissimo
fff	fortississimo
fig.	figure [illustration]
FL	Florida (USA)
fl	flute
fl	floruit [she/he flourished]
Fr.	French
frag(s).	fragment(s)
FRAM	Fellow of the Royal Academy of Music, London
FRCM	Fellow of the Royal College of Music, London
GA	Georgia (USA)
GB	Great Britain
GEDOK	Gemeinschaft Deutscher Organizationen von Künstlerinnen und Kunstfreundinnen (Mannheim)
Ger.	German
Gk.	Greek
Glam.	Glamorgan (GB)
glock	glockenspiel
Glos., Gloucs.	Gloucestershire (GB)
GSM	Guildhall School of Music and Drama, London
gui	guitar
H	Hoboken catalogue [Haydn]
Hants.	Hampshire (GB)
Heb.	Hebrew
Herts.	Hertfordshire (GB)
HI	Hawaii (USA)
hn	horn
Hon.	Honorary; Honourable
hpd	harpsichord
Hunts.	Huntingdonshire (GB)
IA	Iowa (USA)
ibid	ibidem [in the same place]
ID	Idaho (USA)

i.e.	id est [that is]
IL	Illinois (USA)
ILWC	International League of Women Composers
IN	Indiana (USA)
Inc.	Incorporated
inc.	incomplete
incid.	incidental
incl.	includes, including
inst(s)	instrument(s), instrumental
IRCAM	Institut de Recherche et de Coordination Acoustique/Musique (France)
ISCM	International Society for Contemporary Music
ISME	International Society of Music Educators
It.	Italian
Jan	January
Jap.	Japanese
Jb	Jahrbuch [yearbook]
Jg.	Jahrgang [year of publication/volume]
jr	junior
K	Kirkpatrick catalogue [D. Scarlatti]; Köchel catalogue [Mozart; no. after / is from 6th edn]
kbd	keyboard
KS	Kansas (USA)
KY	Kentucky (USA)
£	libra, librae [pound, pounds sterling]
LA	Louisiana (USA)
Lancs.	Lancashire (GB)
Lat.	Latin
Leics.	Leicestershire (GB)
LH	left hand
lib	libretto
Lincs.	Lincolnshire (GB)
LLD	Doctor of Laws
LPO	London Philharmonic Orchestra
LSO	London Symphony Orchestra
MA	Master of Arts
MA	Massachusetts (USA)
mand	mandolin
mar	marimba
MBE	Member of the Order of the British Empire
MD	Maryland (USA)
ME	Maine (USA)
Mez	mezzo-soprano
MFA	Master of Fine Arts
mf	mezzo-forte
MI	Michigan (USA)
MIDI	musical instrument digital interface
MIT	Massachusetts Institute of Technology
Mlle	Mademoiselle
MM	Master of Music
MMA	Master of Musical Arts
Mme	Madame
MMus	Master of Music
MN	Minnesota (USA)

MO	Missouri (USA)	p., pp.	page, pages
Mon.	Monmouthshire (GB)	*p*	piano
movt(s)	movement(s)	PA	Pennsylvania (USA)
mp	mezzo–piano	perc	percussion
MS	Mississippi (USA)	perf.	performance, performed (by)
MS(S)	manuscript(s); Master of Science	pf	piano
MSc	Master of Science(s)	PhD	Doctor of Philosophy
MSM	Master of Sacred Music	pic	piccolo
MT	Montana (USA)	pl(s).	plate(s)
Mt	Mount	PO	Philharmonic Orchestra
MusB, MusBac	Bachelor of Music	Pol.	Polish
MusD, MusDoc	Doctor of Music	posth.	posthumous
MusM	Master of Music	*pp*	pianissimo
		ppp	pianississimo
n.	note, footnote	pr.	printed
nar	narrator	prol	prologue
NATS	National Association of Teachers of Singing (USA)	Ps	Psalm
		pseud.	pseudonym
NBC	National Broadcasting Company (USA)	pt(s)	part(s)
		pubd	published
NC	North Carolina (USA)	pubn	publication
ND	North Dakota (USA)	PWM	Polskie Wydawnictwo Muzyczne
n.d.	no date		
NE	Nebraska (USA)	QC	Queen's Counsel
NEA	National Endowment for the Arts (USA)	qnt	quintet
		qt	quartet
NH	New Hampshire (USA)		
NJ	New Jersey (USA)	R	[in signature] editorial revision
NM	New Mexico (USA)	R	photographic reprint
no.	number	r	recto
Nor.	Norwegian	RAI	Radio Audizioni Italiana
Northants.	Northamptonshire (GB)	RAM	Royal Academy of Music, London
Notts.	Nottinghamshire (GB)	RCM	Royal College of Music, London
Nov	November	rec	recorder
n.p.	no place	recit.	recitative
nr	near	reorchd	reorchestrated
NRK	Norsk Rikskringkasting (Norwegian Broadcasting Corporation)	repr.	reprinted
		resp	respond
		Rev.	Reverend
NSW	New South Wales (Australia)	rev.	revision, revised (by/for)
NV	Nevada (USA)	RH	right hand
NY	New York State (USA)	RI	Rhode Island (USA)
		RISM	Répertoire International des Sources Musicales
ob	oboe		
obbl	obbligato	RMCM	Royal Manchester College of Music
OBE	Officer of the Order of the British Empire	RNCM	Royal Northern College of Music, Manchester
Oct	October	Rom.	Romanian
OH	Ohio (USA)	RPO	Royal Philharmonic Orchestra (GB)
OK	Oklahoma (USA)	RSFSR	Russian Soviet Federated Socialist Republic
OM	Order of Merit		
Ont.	Ontario (Canada)	RTF	Radiodiffusion-Télévision Française
op., opp.	opus, opera	Russ.	Russian
opt.	optional		
OR	Oregon (USA)	S	San, Santa, Santo, São [Saint]; soprano [voice]
orch	orchestra, orchestral		
orchd	orchestrated (by)	S.	south, southern
org	organ	$	dollars
orig.	original(ly)	s	soprano [instrument]
ORTF	Office de Radiodiffusion-Télévision Française	SACEM	Société d'Auteurs, Compositeurs et Editeurs de Musique (France)
OUP	Oxford University Press	Sask.	Saskatchewan (Canada)
ov(s).	overture(s)	sax	saxophone
Oxon.	Oxfordshire	SC	South Carolina (USA)

SD	South Dakota (USA)	U.	University
Sept	September	UCLA	University of California at Los Angeles
seq	sequence		(USA)
ser.	series	UK	United Kingdom of Great Britain
sing.	singular		and Northern Ireland
SO	Symphony Orchestra	unacc.	unaccompanied
SOCAN	Society of Composers, Authors and	UNESCO	United Nations Educational, Scientific
	Music Publishers of Canada		and Cultural Organization
spkr	speaker	unorchd	unorchestrated
Spl	Singspiel	unperf.	unperformed
SPNM	Society for the Promotion of New	unpubd	unpublished
	Music (GB)	US	United States [adjective]
spr.	spring	USA	United States of America
sq	square	USSR	Union of Soviet Socialist Republics
SS	Saints	UT	Utah (USA)
SSR	Soviet Socialist Republic		
St	Saint, Sint, Szent	v, vv	voice, voices
Ste	Sainte	*v*	verso
Staffs.	Staffordshire (GB)	VA	Virginia (USA)
str	string(s)	va	viola
sum.	summer	vc	cello
SUNY	State University of New York	vib	vibraphone
suppl.	supplement, supplementary	vle	violone
Swed.	Swedish	vn	violin
sym.	symphony, symphonic	vol(s).	volume(s)
synth	synthesizer	vs	vocal score
		VT	Vermont (USA)
T	te~nor [voice]	W.	west, western
t	tenor [instrument]	WA	Washington (USA)
timp	timpani	Warwicks.	Warwickshire (GB)
TN	Tennessee (USA)	WI	Wisconsin (USA)
tpt	trumpet	Wilts.	Wiltshire (GB)
Tr	treble [voice]	wint.	winter
tr˙	tract; treble [instrument]	Worcs.	Worcestershire (GB)
trad.	traditional	WV	West Virginia (USA)
trans.	translation, translated by	ww	woodwind
transcr(s).	transcription(s), transcribed by/for	WY	Wyoming (USA)
trbn	trombone		
TV	television	xyl	xylophone
TX	Texas (USA)		
		Yorks.	Yorkshire (GB)

Bibliographical Abbreviations

The bibliographical abbreviations used in this dictionary are listed below. For reference works and collected editions, places and dates of publication are shown; dates only are given for periodicals. Fuller bibliographical information for musical reference works, editions and periodicals up to 1979 may be found in the appropriate entries on *The New Grove Dictionary of Music and Musicians*. In this list, and throughout the dictionary, italic type is used for periodicals and books, including reference works, and roman type for editions, musical series etc.

In bibliographies, a dagger (†) is placed after a reference-work abbreviation when the subject is discussed only within an entry on another member of the same family or in a family entry.

ACAB	*American Composers Alliance Bulletin* (1952–65)	*CC*	B. Morton and P. Collins, eds.: *Contemporary Composers* (Chicago and London, 1992)
AcM	*Acta musicologica* (1928/9–)		
ADB	*Allgemeine deutsche Biographie* (Leipzig, 1875–1912)	*Choron-FayolleD (2)*	A.-E. Choron and F. J. M. Fayolle: *Dictionnaire historique des musiciens* (Paris, 1810–11, 2/1817)
AMe (AMeS)	*Algemene muziekencyclopedie* (and suppl.) (Antwerp and Amsterdam, 1957–63; suppl., 1972)	*CMc*	*Current Musicology* (1965–)
		CohenE	A. I. Cohen: *International Encyclopedia of Women Composers* (New York, 1981, 2/1987)
AMw	*Archiv für Musikwissenschaft* (1918/19–)		
AMZ	*Allgemeine musikalische Zeitung* (1798/9–1882)	*ČSHS*	*Československý hudební slovník* (Prague, 1963–5)
AMz	*Allgemeine Musik-Zeitung* (1874–1943)	*ČSS*	A. Martínková: *Čeští skladatelé současnosti* [Czech Contemporary Composers] (Prague, 1985)
Anderson 2	E. R. Anderson: *Contemporary American Composers: a Biographical Dictionary* (Boston, 2/1982)		
AnMc	*Analecta musicologica* [some vols. in series Studien zur italienisch-deutschen Musikgeschichte] (Cologne, 1963–)	*DBF*	*Dictionnaire de biographie française* (Paris, 1933–)
		DEUMM	*Dizionario enciclopedico universale della musica e dei musicisti* (Turin, 1985–8)
AnnM	*Annales musicologiques* (1953–77)	*DNB*	*Dictionary of National Biography* (London, 1885–1901, suppls.)
Baker6(–8)	*Baker's Biographical Dictionary of Musicians* (New York, 6/1978, 7/1984, 8/1992)	*DTB*	Denkmäler der Tonkunst in Bayern (Leipzig, 1900–31, 2/1962–); new ser. (Wiesbaden, 1967–)
BDA	P. H. Highfill jr, K. A. Burnim and E. A. Langhans: *A Biographical Dictionary of Actors, Actresses, Musicians, Dancers, Managers & Other Stage Personnel in London, 1660–1800* (Carbondale and Edwardsville, IL, 1973–)	*DTÖ*	Denkmäler der Tonkunst in Österreich (Vienna, Leipzig and Graz, 1894–)
		EitnerQ	R. Eitner: *Biographisch-bibliographisches Quellen-Lexikon* (Leipzig, 1900–04, 2/1959–60)
BMw	*Beiträge zur Musikwissenschaft* (1959–)	*EMc*	*Early Music* (1973–)
BPiM	*The Black Perspective in Music* (1973–)	*EMC 2*	*Encyclopedia of Music in Canada* (Toronto, 2/1990)
BurneyGN	C. Burney: *The Present State of Music in Germany, the Netherlands, and United Provinces* (London, 1773, 2/1775); ed. P. A. Scholes, *Dr Burney's Musical Tours in Europe*, ii (London, 1959)	*ES*	S. and F. D'Amico, eds.: *Enciclopedia dello spettacolo* (Rome and Florence, 1954–62; suppls. 1963 and 1966, index 1968)
BurneyH	C. Burney: *A General History of Music from the Earliest Ages to the Present* (London, 1776–89) [p. nos. refer to edn of 1935]	*EwenD*	D. Ewen: *American Composers: a Biographical Dictionary* (New York, 1982)
		FétisB (FétisBS)	F.-J. Fétis: *Biographie universelle des musiciens* (and suppl.) (Brussels, 2/1860–65; suppl. 1878–80)
CBY	*Current Biography Yearbook* (New York, 1940–)		

FlorimoN   F. Florimo: *La scuola musicale di Napoli e i suoi conservatorii* (Naples, 1880–83)

Fuller-LeFanuRM   S. Fuller and N. LeFanu: *Reclaiming the Muse,* Contemporary Music Review, xi (1994)

GänzlBMT   K. Gänzl: *The British Musical Theatre,* i: *1865–1914,* ii: *1915–1984* (London, 1986)

GerberL   E. L. Gerber: *Historisch-biographisches Lexikon der Tonkünstler* (Leipzig, 1790–92)

GerberNL   E. L. Gerber: *Neues historisch-biographisches Lexikon der Tonkünstler* (Leipzig, 1812–14)

Grove1(–5)   G. Grove, ed.: *A Dictionary of Music and Musicians* (London, 1878–90; 2/1904–10 ed. J. A. Fuller Maitland, 3/1927–8 and 4/1940 ed. H. C. Colles, 5/1954 ed. E. Blom with suppl. 1961, all as *Grove's Dictionary of Music and Musicians*)

Grove6   S. Sadie, ed.: *The New Grove Dictionary of Music and Musicians* (London, 1980)

GroveAM   H. W. Hitchcock and S. Sadie, eds.: *The New Grove Dictionary of American Music* (New York, 1986)

GroveI   S. Sadie, ed.: *The New Grove Dictionary of Musical Instruments* (London, 1984)

GroveJ   B. Kernfeld, ed.: *The New Grove Dictionary of Jazz* (London, 1988)

GroveO   S. Sadie, ed.: *The New Grove Dictionary of Opera* (London, 1992)

HawkinsH   J. Hawkins: *A General History of the Science and Practice of Music* (London, 1776) [p. nos. refer to edn of 1853]

HiFi/MusAm   *High Fidelity/Musical America* (1965–87)

HRo   *Hudební rozhledy* (1948/9–)

IMSCR   *International Musicological Society Congress Report* (1930–)

JAMS   *Journal of the American Musicological Society* (1949–)

JbMP   *Jahrbuch der Musikbibliothek Peters* (1895–1941)

JIFMC   *Journal of the International Folk Music Council* (Cambridge, 1949–68)

JMT   *Journal of Music Theory* (1957–)

KompA–Z   A. Olivier and K. Weingartz-Perschel: *Komponistinnen von A–Z* (Düsseldorf, 1988)

LaborD   *Diccionario de la música Labor* (Barcelona, 1954)

LePageWC   J. LePage: *Women Composers, Conductors and Musicians of the Twentieth Century* (Metuchen, NJ, 1981–8) [3 vols.]

LipowskyBL   F. J. Lipowsky: *Baierisches Musik-Lexikon* (Munich, 1811)

LS   *The London Stage, 1660–1800* (Carbondale, IL, 1960–68, index 1979)

MB   *Musica britannica* (London, 1951–)

ME   *Muzïkal'naya entsiklopediya* (Moscow, 1973–82)

MEMM   A. E. Wier, ed.: *The Macmillan Encyclopedia of Music and Musicians* (London, 1938)

Mf   *Die Musikforschung* (1948–)

MGG   F. Blume, ed.: *Die Musik in Geschichte und Gegenwart* (Kassel and Basle, 1949–68; suppl., 1973–9, index 1986)

MJb   *Mozart-Jahrbuch des Zentralinstituts für Mozartforschung* (1951–)

ML   *Music and Letters* (1920–)

MMg   *Monatshefte für Musikgeschichte* (1869–1905)

MMR   *The Monthly Musical Record* (1871–1960)

MO   *Musical Opinion* (1877/8–)

MQ   *The Musical Quarterly* (1915–)

MSD   Musicological Studies and Documents (Rome, 1951–)

MT   *The Musical Times* (1844/5–)

MusAm   *Musical America* (1898–1964, 1987–92)

MZ   *Muzikološki zbornik* (1965–)

NA   *Note d'archivio per la storia musicale* (1924–7, 1930–43)

NAW   *Notable American Women* (Cambridge, MA, 1971; suppl. 1980)

NDB   *Neue deutsche Biographie* (Berlin, 1953–)

NRMI   *Nuova rivista musicale italiana* (1967–)

NZM   *Neue Zeitschrift für Musik* (1834–1943, 1950–74, 1979)

OM   *Opus musicum* (1969–)

ÖMz   *Österreichische Musikzeitschrift* (1946–)

ON   *Opera News* (New York, 1936/7–)

PazdirekH   B. Pazdírek: *Universal-Handbuch der Musikliteratur aller Zeiten und Völker* (Vienna, 1904–10)

PL   *Patrologiae cursus completus,* i: Series latina (Paris, 1844–64)

PNM   *Perspectives of New Music* (1962/3–)

PSB   *Polskich słownik biograficzny* (Kraków, 1935)

RaM   *La rassegna musicale* (1928–43, 1947–62)

RdM	Revue de musicologie (1917/19–)
ReM	La revue musicale (1920–40, 1946–)
RHCM	Revue d'histoire et de critique musicales (1901); La revue musicale (1902–11)
RiemannL 11, 12	H. Riemann: Musik-Lexikon (Leipzig, 1882, 11/1929 rev. A. Einstein, 12/1959–75 rev. W. Gurlitt, H. H. Eggebrecht and C. Dahlhaus)
RIM	Rivista italiana di musicologia (1966–)
RISM	Répertoire international des sources musicales (Munich and Duisburg, 1960–; Kassel, 1971–)
RMFC	Recherches sur la musique française classique (1960–)
RMI	Rivista musicale italiana (1894–1932, 1936–43, 1946–55)
RRMBE	Recent Researches in the Music of the Baroque Era (New Haven, CT, and Madison, WI, 1964–)
RRMCE	Recent Researches in the Music of the Classical Era (Madison, WI, 1975–)
SainsburyD	J. S. Sainsbury: A Dictionary of Musicians (London, 1824, 2/1827)
SartoriB	C. Sartori: Bibliografia della musica strumentale italiana stampata in Italia fino al 1700 (Florence, 1952–68)
SBL	Svenska biografiskt leksikon (Stockholm, 1918–)
SchillingE (SchillingES)	G. Schilling: Encyclopädie der gesammten musikalischen Wissenschaften oder Universal-Lexicon der Tonkunst (Stuttgart, 1835–8, suppl. 1841–2)
SchmidlD (SchmidlDS)	C. Schmidl: Dizionario universale dei musicisti (and suppl.) (Milan, 1887–90, 2/1928–9, suppl. 1938)
SCMA	Smith College Music Archives (Northampton, MA, 1935–)
SIMG	Sammelbände der Internationalen Musik-Gesellschaft (1899/1900–1913/14)
SMP	Słownik muzyków polskich (Kraków, 1964–7)

SMw	Studien zur Musikwissenschaft (1913–16, 1918–34, 1955–6, 1960–66, 1977–)
SMz	Schweizerische Musikzeitung/Revue musicale suisse (1861–)
SouthernB	E. Southern: Biographical Dictionary of Afro-American and African Musicians (Westport, CT, 1982)
SovM	Sovetskaya muzïka (1933–41, 1946–)
StiegerO	F. Stieger: Opern-Lexikon (Tutzing, 1975–83)
TVNM	Tijdschrift van de Vereniging voor Nederlandse muziekgeschiedenis (1885–)
VogelB	E. Vogel: Bibliothek der gedruckten weltlichen Vocalmusik Italiens, aus den Jahren 1500 bis 1700 (Berlin, 1892); rev. A. Einstein (Hildesheim, 1962); rev. F. Lesure and C. Sartori, as Bibliografia della musica italiana vocale profana pubblicata dal 1500 al 1700 (Geneva, 1978)
WaltherML	J. G. Walther: Musicalisches Lexicon oder Musicalische Bibliothek (Leipzig, 1732)
WAM	A. F. Block and C. Neuls-Bates: Women in American Music: a Bibliography of Music and Literature (Westport, CT, 1979)
WCBH	O. Ebel: Women Composers: a Biographical Handbook of Woman's Work in Music (Brooklyn, NY, 1902, 3/1913)
WurzbachL	C. von Wurzbach: Biographisches Lexikon des Kaiserthums Oesterreich (Vienna, 1856–91)
ZfM	Zeitschrift für Musik (1920–55)
ZMw	Zeitschrift für Musikwissenschaft (1918/19–1935)

Library Sigla

The system of library sigla in this dictionary follows that used in its publications (Series A) by Répertoire International des Sources Musicales, Kassel, by arrangement. Below are listed the sigla to be found; some are additional to those in the published RISM lists but have been established in consultation with the RISM organization. Some original RISM sigla that have now been changed are retained here.

In the dictionary, sigla are always printed in *italic*. In any listing of sources a national sigillum applies without repetition until it is contradicted.

Within each national list below, entries are alphabetized by sigillum, first by capital letters (showing the city or town) and then by lower-case ones (showing the institution or collection).

A: AUSTRIA
LIm	Linz, Oberösterreichisches Landesmuseum
Wgm	Vienna, Gesellschaft der Musikfreunde
Wm	——, Minoritenkonvent
Wn	——, Österreichische Nationalbibliothek, Musiksammlung
Wst	——, Stadtbibliothek, Mussiksammlung

AUS: AUSTRALIA
Msl	Melbourne, State Library of Victoria

B: BELGIUM
Bc	Brussels, Conservatoire Royal de Musique
Lc	Liège, Conservatoire Royal de Musique

CH: SWITZERLAND
BEsu	Berne, Stadt- und Universitätsbibliothek; Bürgerbibliothek

CS: CZECHOSLOVAKIA
Bm	Brno, Ústav Dějin Hudby Moravského Musea, Hudebněhistorické Oddělení
Pnm	Prague, Národní Muzeum, Hudební Oddělení

CU: CUBA
Hn	Havana, Biblioteca Nacional

D: GERMANY
B	see *Bsb*
Bds	see *Bsb*
Bim	Berlin, Staatliches Institut für Musikforschung, Stiftung Preussischer Kulturbesitz
Bsb	——, Staatsbibliothek zu Berlin, Preussischer Kulturbesitz: formerly Staatsbibliothek Preussischer Kulturbesitz (*B*) and Deutsche Staatsbibliothek (*Bds*)
Bsp	——, Sprachkonvikt
Dlb	Dresden, Sächsische Landesbibliothek
DEl	Dessau, Stadtbibliothek (formerly Universitäts- und Landesbibliothek)
DÜk	Düsseldorf, Goethe-Museum
Hs	Hamburg, Staats- und Universitätsbibliothek Carl von Ossietzky
KA	Karlsruhe, Badische Landesbibliothek
Mbn	Munich, Bayerisches Nationalmuseum
Mbs	——, Bayerische Staatsbibliothek
Rtt	Regensburg, Fürst Thurn und Taxis Hofbibliothek
SWl	Schwerin, Wissenschaftliche Allgemeinbibliothek (formerly Mecklenburgische Landesbibliothek)

W	Wolfenbüttel, Herzog-August-Bibliothek
WIl	Wiesbaden, Hessische Landesbibliothek
WRdn	Weimar, Deutsches Nationaltheater
WRgs	——, Goethe-Schiller-Archiv
WRl	——, Staatsarchiv (formerly Landeshauptarchiv)
WRtl	——, Thüringische Landesbibliothek, Musiksammlung [in *WRz*]
WRz	——, Zentralbibliothek der deutschen Klassik
Zsch	Zwickau, Robert-Schumann-Haus

DK: DENMARK
Kk	Copenhagen, Det Kongelige Bibliotek

E: SPAIN
Mc	Madrid, Conservatorio Superior de Música
Mn	——, Biblioteca Nacional

EIRE: IRELAND
Dtc	Dublin, Trinity College

F: FRANCE
AS	Arras, Bibliothèque Municipale
Pa	Paris, Bibliothèque de l'Arsenal
Pc	——, Fonds du Conservatoire National de Musique [in *Pn*]
Pn	——, Bibliothèque Nationale
Po	——, Bibliothèque-Musée de l'Opéra
V	Versailles, Bibliothèque Municipale

GB: GREAT BRITAIN
AB	Aberystwyth, National Library of Wales
ALb	Aldeburgh, Britten-Pears Library
Cfm	Cambridge, Fitzwilliam Museum
Cp	——, Peterhouse
Cpl	——, Pendlebury Library of Music
CDu	Cardiff, University of Wales College of Cardiff (formerly University College of Wales and Monmouthshire)
DRu	Durham, University Library
Ge	Glasgow, Euing Music Library
Lbl	London, British Library (formerly *Lbm*, British Museum)
Lcm	——, Royal College of Music
Lfm	——, Faber Music
Lmic	——, British Music Information Centre
Lue	——, Universal Edition
Ob	Oxford, Bodleian Library
Och	——, Christ Church

GR: GREECE
Aleotsakos	Athens, George Leotsakos, private collection

H: HUNGARY

Bn   Budapest, Országos Széchényi Könyvtára

I: ITALY

AN   Ancona, Biblioteca Comunale Benincasa
Bc   Bologna, Civico Museo Bibliografico Musicale
Bca   ——, Biblioteca Comunale dell'Archiginnasio
Fc   Florence, Conservatorio di Musica Luigi
          Cherubini
Fn   ——, Biblioteca Nazionale Centrale
FEc   Ferrara, Biblioteca Comunale Ariostea
Gl   Genoa, Conservatorio di Musica Nicolò
          Paganini
Li   Lucca, Istituto Musicale Luigi Boccherini (incl.
          Bottini Collection)
Ma   Milan, Biblioteca Ambrosiana
Mb   ——, Biblioteca Nazionale Braidense
Mc   ——, Conversatorio di Musica Giuseppe
          Verdi
Nc   Naples, Conservatorio di Musica S Pietro a
          Majella
Os   Ostiglia, Fondazione Greggiati
Ria   Rome, Istituto di Archeologia e Storia
          dell'Arte
Rsc   ——, Conservatorio di Musica S Cecilia
Rvat   ——, Biblioteca Apostolica Vaticana
Sc   Siena, Biblioteca Comunale degli Intronati
TRa   Trent, Archivio di Stato
Vc   Venice, Conservatorio di Musica Benedetto
          Marcello
Vmc   ——, Museo Civico Correr
Vnm   ——, Biblioteca Nazionale Marciana
VIb   Vicenza, Biblioteca Civica Bertoliana

NZ: NEW ZEALAND

Wt   Wellington, Alexander Turnbull Library

PL: POLAND

Kj   Kraków, Biblioteka Jagiellońska

RU: RUSSIA

SPsc   St Petersburg, Gosudarstvennaya Ordena
          Trudovogo Krasnogo Znameni Publichnaya
          Biblioteka imeni M. E. Saltïkova-Shchedrina

S: SWEDEN

L   Lund, Universitetsbiblioteket
Sic   Stockholm, Informationscentral för Svensk
          Musik
Skma   ——, Statens Musiksamlingar: formerly
          Kungliga Musikaliska Akademiens Bibliotek
Sm   ——, Musikhistoriska Museet [in Skma]
Smf   ——, Stiftelsen Musikkulturens Främjande

US: UNITED STATES OF AMERICA

AA   Ann Arbor, University of Michigan, Music
          Library
AUS   Austin, University of Texas
Bc   Boston, New England Conservatory of Music
Bp   ——, Public Library, Music Department
BE   Berkeley, University of California, Music Library
Cn   Chicago, Newberry Library
KC   Kansas City, University of Missouri, Kansas City
          Conservatory of Music
LAu   Los Angeles, University of California, Walter H.
          Rubsamen Music Library
LOu   Louisville, University, School of Music Library
NH   New Haven (CT), Yale University, School of
          Music Library
NYcu   New York, Columbia University, Music Library
NYp   ——, Public Library at Lincoln Center, Library
          and Museum of the Performing Arts
PHf   Philadelphia, Free Library of Philadelphia
PHps   ——, American Philosophical Society
PHu   ——, University of Pennsylvania Libraries (Otto
          E. Albrecht Music Library; Van Pelt Library;
          Rare Book Collection)
Wc   Washington, DC, Library of Congress, Music
          Division

Editorial Conventions in this Dictionary

The editorial principles governing this dictionary are the same as those of *The New Grove Dictionary of Music and Musicians* (1980). For a full account of these the reader is referred to the Introduction to that work, printed in Vol. 1, pp.xi–xx. It may however be useful to outline certain basic procedures.

Abbreviations in general use are listed on pp.xxxiii–xxxvi; bibliographical abbreviations (periodicals, reference works, editions, etc.) are listed separately on pp.xxxvii–xxxix.

Alphabetization of headings, or in alphabetically organized lists, is based on the principle that words are read continuously, ignoring spaces, hyphens, accents, diacriticals, bracketed matter etc. up to the first commas; the same principle applies afresh thereafter. 'Mc' and 'M' are listed as if 'Mac', 'St' as 'Saint'.

Bibliographies are arranged chronologically, by order of year of first publication, alphabetically by author within years and alphabetically by first main word within authors.

Cross-references are shown in small capitals, with a large capital at the beginning of the first word of the entry referred to; thus 'she was a colleague of MARY JONES SMITH' would indicate that the entry on Mary Jones Smith is to be found under 'Smith, Mary Jones' (not 'Jones Smith, Mary').

Headwords show the entrant's name in its full form, with parentheses marking off names or parts of names not generally used. Bracketed material may show variant spellings, maiden or married names, nicknames or pseudonyms.

Signatures are shown at the foot of each article. Where an article is the work of more than one author, the authors are listed in alphabetical order. Where an article by an author, A, who is no longer active or available, is revised by B, the signature takes the form A/B; A/R signifies an editorial revision.

Work-lists are normally arranged chronologically (within section, where divided). Italic symbols used in them (such as *F-Pn* or *US-Wc*) refer to the libraries in which source material is held and are explained on pp.xl–xli; each national sigillum stands until contradicted.

THE
NORTON/GROVE
DICTIONARY OF
WOMEN
COMPOSERS

A

A'Beckett, Mary Anne (*b* London, 1817; *d* London, 11 Dec 1863). English composer. She was the eldest daughter of Joseph Glossop, a friend of George IV; she married Gilbert Abbott A'Beckett, a magistrate and humorous writer. Apart from a dozen songs and two waltzes for piano A'Beckett composed three operas. *The Young Pretender* (three songs were published); *Agnes Sorrel*, an 'operatic farce' (based on the story of Agnès Sorel, mistress of Charles VII of France), which was the first production at John Braham's St James's Theatre, London (August 1835); and *Little Red Riding Hood*, produced at the Surrey Gardens Theatre, London, in August 1842. She declined invitations to conduct them herself.

JOHN R. GARDNER

WORKS
selective list

Orch: Vespers in a Convent Garden, sym. suite, 1956; 13 Variations, 2 pf, orch, 1957; Valle de los caidos, rhapsody, 1964; Sym. 'The Trilogy of Man', 1971; Sym. 'Guerilla', 1972; Dalawang Pusong Dakila [Two Great Hearts], 1975; Pag-ibig sa Tinubuang Bayan [Love for the Native Land], choral sym., 1979; Sym. no.3 'Hold High the Torch', 1981

Choral: Advent Cantata, 1957; The Conversion of King Humabon, cantata, 1967; Redemption Oratorio, 1969; masses, other pieces

Solo vocal: Pamuhatbuhat [Faith Healing], Bar, wind, native perc, str, 1973; Larawan ng Isang Babae [Woman's Portrait], S, orch; Buhay [Life], S, orch; sacred songs

Inst: 3 str qts, 1949–54; Academic Festival Qt, 1966; Pf Qnt, 1966; Octet, wind, str, 1970; Maranaw Trail, 2 mar, pf, perc, 1971; Octet, brass, perc, 1972; Strings on the Dignity of Man, 1979; Dithyrambic Strings for the General, 1982; The Absent Baritone, 1985

LUCRECIA R. KASILAG

Abejo, Rosalina (*b* Tagoloan, Oriental Misamis, 13 July 1922; *d* Fremont, CA, 5 June 1991). Filipina composer and conductor. She studied at Lourdes College, St Scholastica's College and the Philippine Women's University (MM 1957). Later she attended the Labunski School of Composition in Ohio, the Eastman School, and the Catholic University of America, Washington, DC. She was a nun of the Order of the Virgin Mary until 1976, and taught composition and conducted fund-raising concerts, receiving the Republic Culture Heritage Award (1967) and the Philippines Independence Day Award. She moved to the USA in 1977 and joined the International Sisters for Christian Community in 1979. She taught at Kansas University and St Pius Seminary in Kentucky before moving to Fremont, California. In 1980 she was elected president of the Philippine Foundation of Performing Arts in America. She composed over 300 works; her style is marked by neo-classical and impressionist features, with quartal harmonies, added-note chords, pentatonic and modal scales.

Abrams, Harriett (*b* *c*1758; *d* *c*1822). English composer and soprano. She made her stage début in October 1775 as the little gypsy in *May Day*, a piece designed for her by David Garrick with music by her teacher Thomas Arne. However, she had limited success as a stage personality and in 1780 left Drury Lane to become a principal singer at fashionable London concerts and provincial festivals. She appeared in the Handel Commemoration concerts in 1784, when Charles Burney praised the sweetness and taste of her singing, in the concerts of Ancient Music until 1789 and in seasons organized by Venanzio Rauzzini and J. P. Salomon. At her benefit concerts in 1792, 1794 and 1795 Haydn presided at the piano. According to W. T. Parke, in the 1791–2 season she organized the Ladies' Concerts, held in the private houses of their aristocratic lady directors.

Her published works were all vocal. M. G. ('Monk') Lewis wrote of how 'the celebrated Miss Abrams' made the first and most successful setting of his *Crazy Jane* and sang it

1

herself at fashionable parties. She must also have taken part in the performance of her own two- and three-part songs. Her younger sisters, Eliza and the contralto Theodosia, often sang with her; three other sisters sang and two brothers were string players.

WORKS
all published in London

8 Italian and English Canzonets, 1, 2vv (?1780); 2nd set of Italian and English Canzonets (?1785); Collection of Scotch Songs, harmonized for 2, 3vv (*c*1790); Collection of Songs (1803), ded. to the Queen

More than a dozen songs, mainly sentimental ballads, pubd separately

BIBLIOGRAPHY

BDA; *Choron-FayolleD*; *GerberL*; *GerberNL*; *LS*; *SainsburyD*; *SchillingE*

C. Burney: *An Account of the Musical Performances . . . in Commemoration of Handel* (London, 1785)

R. Edgcumbe [Mount Edgcumbe]: *Musical Reminiscences* (London, 1824, 4/1834)

W. T. Parke: *Musical Memoirs* (London, 1830)

[M. Baron-Wilson]: *The Life and Correspondence of M. G. Lewis* (London, 1839)

OLIVE BALDWIN, THELMA WILSON

Adam de Aróstegui, María de las Mercedes (*b* Camagüey, Cuba, 24 Sept 1873; *d* Madrid, 20 October 1957). Cuban composer resident in Spain. After moving to Spain with her family at the age of nine, she began her musical training under Joaquín Zuazagoitia in Santiago de Compostela, continuing at the Conservatorio Real, Madrid, where she studied piano (receiving first prize in 1888), harmony, composition, ensemble playing and organ. Later, in Paris, she was a member of Louis Diémer's piano class and Jules Massenet's instrumentation and composition classes; she also studied with Vincent d'Indy. Her music was performed in Paris, and in Spain she gave recitals and took part in chamber concerts with Pablo Casals. Although resident in Europe, she nevertheless maintained professional and personal links with Cuba and several of her works were performed there, notably by the Havana SO and Havana PO, including, in 1933, the *Serenata española*, *La peregrinación de Childe Harold* (composed 1898–9), the *Poema sinfónico* (composed 1914) and *En el campo de Waterloo*; her only opera, *La vida es sueño*, based on Pedro Calderón de la Barca's play, was also given in Havana during the 1930s, her most prolific period. Orchestral works were pre-eminent in her output and include *La infancia*, *Danzas cubanas*, *Serenata andaluza*, and the *Ballade guerrière écossaise* to a text by Sir Walter Scott; she also wrote songs

and a piece for voice and cello *A une femme*. During her time in Paris she published an essay 'La ética y la estética en la obra musical'.

ALICIA VALDÉS CANTERO

Adayevskaya [née Schultz], **Ella Georgiyevna** (*b* St Petersburg, 10/22 Feb 1846; *d* Bonn, 26 July 1926). Russian composer, ethnomusicologist and pianist. The name Adayevskaya is a pseudonym derived from the notes of the kettledrum (A, D, A) in Mikhail Glinka's *Ruslan and Lyudmila*. At the age of eight she started piano lessons with Adolf Henselt, continued with Anton Rubinstein and Alexander Dreyschock at the St Petersburg Conservatory (1862–6), and later gave concerts in Russia and Europe. She also studied composition at the conservatory with N. I. Zaremba and A. S. Famintsïn and about 1870 began composing choruses for the Imperial Chapel Choir. Two operas followed, *Neprigozhaya* ('The Homely Girl')/ *Doch' boyarina* ('The Boyar's Daughter', 1873) and *Zarya svobodï* ('The Dawn of Freedom', 1877), the latter dedicated to Alexander II but rejected by the censor for its scene of peasant uprising. A comic opera *Solomonida Saburova* remained in manuscript. A *Greek Sonata* (1881), for clarinet and piano, using quarter tones, was inspired by Adayevskaya's research into the music of ancient Greece, the Greek church and Slavonic folksong. About 1891 she settled in Venice, then (1911) moved with her friend Baroness von Loë to Germany and joined the liberal-minded artistic circle around the poet Carmen Sylva (Elisabeth, Queen of Romania). Folk music research eventually dominated Adayevskaya's musical pursuits, resulting in a substantial output of publications and a secure reputation among the pioneers of modern ethnomusicology.

WORKS
selective list

Operas: Neprigozhaya [The Homely Girl]/Doch' boyarina] [The Boyar's Daughter] (1), 1873; Zarya svobodï [The Dawn of Freedom] (4), 1877; Solomonida Saburova

Vocal: Yolka [The Fir Tree], cantata, ?1870; songs

Inst: Svadebnïy khor [Wedding Chorus], ov., ?1870; Greek Sonata (Fantasia), cl, pf, 1881; pf pieces

BIBLIOGRAPHY

ME, *RiemannL* 12 and suppl. ('Adaiewsky')

G. B. Bernandt and I. M. Yampol'sky: *Kto pisal o muzïke* [Writers on Music] (Moscow, 1971–89)

H. G. [Gaidoz]: 'Mlle E. de Schoultz-Adaievsky', *Mélusine*, xi (1912), 213–16

M. Ivanov-Boretsky: 'Shul'ts-Adayevskaya', *Muzïkal'noye obrazovaniye*, i/5–6 (1926), 144 [obituary]

E. Kraack: 'Ella von Schultz-Adaiewsky', *ZfM*, xciii (1926), 624–6 [obituary]
Obituary, *RMI*, xxxiii (1926), 500–01

MALCOLM HAMRICK BROWN

Agata. *See* DELLA PIETÀ, AGATA.

Agnesi, Maria Teresa (*b* Milan, 17 Oct 1720; *d* Milan, 19 Jan 1795). Italian composer, harpsichordist, singer and librettist. As a girl she performed in her home while her elder sister Maria Gaetana (1718–99; she became a distinguished mathematician) lectured and debated in Latin. Charles de Brosses, who heard them on 16 July 1739 and was highly impressed, reported that Maria Teresa performed harpsichord pieces by Rameau and both sang and played compositions of her own invention. Her first theatrical work, *Il restauro d'Arcadia*, was successfully presented in Milan's ducal theatre in 1747. At about this time she dedicated collections of her own arias and instrumental pieces to the rulers of Saxony and Austria; according to Simonetti the Empress Maria Theresa sang from a collection of arias that Agnesi had given her. She married Pier Antonio Pinottini on 13 June 1752 but had no children. Her next opera, *Ciro in Armenia*, produced at the Regio Ducal Teatro in 1753, was to her own libretto. In 1766 her *Insubria consolata* was performed in Milan to honour the engagement of Beatrice d'Este and the

Archduke Ferdinand. Her portrait hangs in the theatre museum of La Scala; other portraits are reproduced in the encyclopedia *Storia di Milano* (vols. xii, xiv).

Agnesi's works have yet to be studied in the context of mid-century Milanese styles. Her semi-public career as a theatrical composer was made possible by the changes in women's status taking place in Austrian Lombardy, with a notable decline in female monasticization and the emergence of public roles for women. Her talents seem to have found a warmer reception in Vienna and Dresden than in her native city, to judge by the elegant copies of *La Sofonisba*, *Il re pastore* and the arias that were produced for these courts. Her operas represent the centre of her output. Stylistically, they show a progression from relative simplicity (*Ciro in Armenia*) to a far more ambitious and virtuoso writing in the later works. *Il re pastore* and *Ulisse* feature lengthy ritornellos and use da capo form almost exclusively; several of the arias in *Il re pastore* and in *La Sofonisba* are miniature two-part scenas. The latter opera includes some of Agnesi's most powerful writing; Sophonisba's last aria before dying, 'Già s'appressa il fatal momento', is a particularly moving and dramatic close to an *opera seria*. The entire work is suitable to the cult of the classical heroine as cultivated at Maria Theresa's court. Agnesi's instrumental music, less sharply characterized, is sometimes technically challenging, in a generic north-Italian style.

WORKS

DRAMATIC

Il restauro d'Arcadia (cantata pastorale, G. Riviera), Milan, Regio Ducal Teatro, 1747, lost
Ciro in Armenia (dramma serio, 3, ? Agnesi), Milan, Regio Ducal Teatro, 26 Dec 1753, Act 3 frags. *I-Mc* (not identical with anon. Milanese lib of the opera for carn. 1754 in *Mb*, *US-Wc* etc.)
La Sofonisba (dramma eroico, 3, G. F. Zanetti), Naples, 1765, *A-Wgm*, *Wn*
L'insubria consolata (componimento drammatico, 2, ? Agnesi), Milan, Regio Ducal Teatro, 1766, ? lost or ? in *F-Pc*, lib *I-Mb*
Nitocri (dramma serio, 3, A. Zeno), Venice, 1771, Act 2 frags. *Mc*
Il re pastore (dramma serio, 3, P. Metastasio), ?1756, *A-Wn*
Ulisse in Campania (serenata, 2, ? Agnesi), *I-Nc*

OTHER WORKS

12 arias, S, 2 vn, va, bc, *D-Dlb*
Aria en Murki: Still, stille Mann!, 2vv, kbd, *Dlb*
4 concs. (F, F, F, D), hpd, 2 vn, b, *A-Wgm*, *Wn*, *B-Bc*, *D-Dlb* (str pts. missing in *A-Wn*, *D-Dlb*), 1 cited in 1766 Breitkopf catalogue
Sonata, G, kbd, *KA*, cited in 1767 Breitkopf catalogue
Allegro ou Presto, kbd, B, *Dlb*
Allemande militare & Menuetto grazioso, kbd (with

Maria Teresa Agnesi: portrait by an unknown artist, 18th century

special stops), *H-Bn*; ed. F. Brodszky, *Thesaurus Musicus*, xvii (1962)

Lost: conc., E♭, hpd, cited in 1766 Breitkopf catalogue; sonata, G, kbd, cited in 1767 Breitkopf catalogue; ? Airs divers, 1v, harp

BIBLIOGRAPHY

Choron-FayolleD; *FétisB*; *GerberL*; *Grove1* (Mrs W. Carr); *MGG* (S. Simonetti); *SainsburyD*; *SchmidlD*

G. M. Mazzuchelli: *Gli scrittori d'Italia*, i (Brescia, 1753), 198–9

C. de Brosses: *Lettres historiques et critiques sur l'Italie* (Paris, 1798–9; It. trans., 1957)

M. G. Agnesi: Letters (MS, *I-Ma*)

L. Anzoletti: *Maria Gaetana Agnesi* (Milan, 1900)

G. Seregni: 'La cultura Milanese nel settecento', *Storia di Milano*, xii (1959), 567–640

G. Barblan: 'Il teatro musicale in Milano: il settecento', *Storia di Milano*, xii (1959), 965–96

B. S. Brook, ed.: *The Breitkopf Thematic Catalogues, 1762–87* (New York, 1966)

C. de Jong: *The Life and Keyboard Works of Maria Teresa d'Agnesi* (diss., U. of Minnesota, 1978)

R. L. Kendrick: *Maria Teresa Agnesi: an Introduction to her Works* (forthcoming)

SVEN HANSELL, ROBERT L. KENDRICK

Agolli, Lejla (*b* Korçë, 4 Oct 1950). Albanian composer. She studied composition and orchestration with Tish Daija at the Tirana Conservatory, part of the Superior Institute of Fine Arts (1968–73). Since 1974 she has taught solfège, harmony and formal analysis at the Jordan Misja Art Lyceum, Tirana, Albania's oldest secondary music school, where for the past few years she has encouraged composition by means of an experimental programme for 12- and 13-year-olds. Agolli is an outstanding figure in the younger generation of Albanian composers. Her works include two cantatas, a three-movement Symphony in C♯ minor (1973), two piano concertos (1973, 1984) and two violin concertos, as well as several other occasional works for violin and orchestra and two *Albums* for violin and piano, consisting of ten pieces each. As the Second Violin Concerto (1983) clearly shows, her music combines original melodic invention with subtle rhythmic differentiations and exhibits a tendency to thwart initial implications through its elegant and intelligent design.

GEORGE LEOTSAKOS

Agudela, Graciela (*b* Mexico City, 7 Dec 1945). Mexican pianist and composer. She studied the piano at the Universidad Nacional Autónoma de México and composition in the workshop of the Conservatorio Nacional de Música under Héctor Quintanar and Mario Lavista. Her extensive output reveals a diversity of techniques and styles without formal adherence to compositional schools or avant-garde trends, but with an emphasis on the search for expressive freedom. Avant-garde techniques, however, are sometimes used to enhance the colour and integrity of her music, as in *Navegantes del crepúsculo* ('Voyagers of the Twilight', 1993), a trio in four movements for clarinet, bassoon and piano, which she describes as 'a fantasy of abstract lyricism'. In *Arabesco* for solo recorder, the music explores the technical potential of the instrument and the performer, including the simultaneous use of two recorders, the contrapuntal exposition of the theme through multiphonics and nimble alternation between voice and instrument.

BIBLIOGRAPHY

G. Béhague: *Sonidas de las Americas Festival*, New York, 30 Jan–6 Feb 1994, pp.21, 26–7 [American Composers' Orchestra; programme booklet]

Ahlefeldt, Countess **Maria Theresia** (*b* Regensburg, 28 Feb 1755; *d* Prague, 20 Dec 1810). Danish composer of German birth. The daughter of Count Alexander of Thurn and Taxis, she was born into a flourishing cultural environment. In 1780 she married the Danish count Ferdinand Ahlefeldt (1747–1815). They lived for a number of years at the court of Ansbach, where Maria Theresia was active in operatic circles. The couple moved to Dresden in 1798 and finally, in 1800, to Prague.

While still in Regensburg she had composed a *Symphonie* in F and at Ansbach wrote the libretto, and possibly the music, for the comic opera *La folie, ou Quel conte!* In 1792 Count Ahlefeldt was made *Hofmarskal* (Lord Chamberlain) and director of the Kongelige Teater in Copenhagen, where Maria Theresia gained the opportunity to compose an opera-ballet, *Telemak paa Calypsos Øe*, with choreography by Vincenzo Galeotti (1792); 37 performances were given up to 1812. Her music is characterized by well-formed and sensitive melody in a simple harmonic and compositional frame, influenced by French *opéra comique* tradition. She was praised by her contemporaries for her orchestration.

WORKS

STAGE

Telemak paa Calypsos Øe (opera-ballet, 4, C. Pram), Copenhagen, Royal Theatre, 28 Dec 1792; vs (Copenhagen, 1793), full score, 1805, *DK-Kk*

Veddemaalet (intermezzo, 1, P. H. Haste), 1793, *Kk*

La folie, ou Quel conte! (comic opera, 2, Ahlefeldt), music lost (? by Ahlefeldt); lib in *Nouveau théâtre*, ed. E. Asimont, i (Anspach, 1789)

OTHER WORKS

Klage, 1v, fl, kbd, in I. F. Zehelein: *Vermischte Gedichte* (Bayreuth, 1790); L'harmonie, cantata, 2 S, B, orch, 1792, vs *D-Dlb*; Vaer laenge, laenge lykkelig, 1v, chorus, 1792, music lost; Romance de Nina, 1v, 2 vn, 2 hn, b, full score *Dlb*; Symphonie, F, *Rtt*

BIBLIOGRAPHY

FétisB; *SchillingE*; *SchmidlD*

M. Magnussen: *Komponisten Maria Theresia Ahlefeldt – og andre kvinder i dansk musikliv ca 1750–1800* (diss., Copenhagen U., 1990)

INGE BRULAND

Ahrens, Sieglinde (*b* Berlin, 19 Feb 1936). German composer and organist. She had her first music lessons from her father, Joseph Ahrens, with whom she continued organ studies at the Berlin Hochschule für Musik, where her composition teacher was Boris Blacher. Subsequently she studied with Messiaen and Milhaud at the Paris Conservatoire. She made her début as an organist in 1947 and from then until 1957 played at the Salvatorkirche, Berlin. In 1962 she was appointed to teach at the Folkwang-Hochschule, Essen, becoming professor of organ in 1970. She has made concert tours in Germany, France and the Netherlands and won numerous awards, including the Förderungspreis (the arts prize of North Rhine-Westphalia; 1964). Ahrens, in her relatively small output, shows herself to be more concerned with personal expression than with technical innovation or with an 'avant garde' expansion of musical material. A certain affinity with the work of Peter Eben is evident, something both composers have acknowledged. Her works for solo organ include Three Pieces (Deprecatio, Interludium and Elegie), Fantasia, Rhapsody, a suite and the meditation *In fletu solatium*. Some chamber works also feature the organ, for example the Sonata for violin and organ and Three Songs for bass and organ; other chamber works include Five Pieces for string trio. Her writings include *Das Orgelwerk Olivier Messiaens*, in collaboration with Hans-Dieter Möller and Almut Rössler (Duisburg, 1976), and a translation into German of Messiaen's *Technique de mon langage musicale* (1965).

JOHN MORGAN, ROSWITHA SPERBER

Akers, Doris (Mae) (*b* Brookfield, MO, 21 May 1923). American gospel singer, pianist and composer. She began piano lessons when she was five and by the age of ten was playing for her church choir. She started to compose while still in her teens. Later she moved to California and formed the Simmons-Akers Singers, with whom she remained until the mid-1950s. Thereafter she served as music director for various white congregations, composing and performing in a style more closely associated with white gospel. She has therefore been only modestly successful in black gospel circles, although many of her compositions are standards among black singers, including *Lead me, guide me* (1953), *You can't beat God giving* (1957), *Sweet, sweet spirit* (1972) and *Lord, don't move the mountain* (1972). Her songs have been recorded by George Beverly Shea and Mahalia Jackson and were sung by the Stamps Quartet in the documentary film about Elvis Presley, *Elvis on Tour* (1972).

BIBLIOGRAPHY

H. C. Boyer: 'An Overview: Gospel Music Comes of Age', *Black World*, xxiii/1 (1973), 42, 79

I. V. Jackson: *Afro-American Religious Music: a Bibliography and Catalogue of Gospel Music* (Westport, CT, 1979)

HORACE CLARENCE BOYER

Akiyoshi, Toshiko (*b* Darien, Manchuria, 12 Dec 1929). Japanese composer, pianist and band leader. Much of her compositional style developed while working in Tokyo as a jazz pianist and through listening to jazz performers, especially Bud Powell, but also Duke Ellington and Charles Mingus. By the mid-1950s Akiyoshi was recognized as the leading jazz pianist in Japan. In 1956 she took up a scholarship at the Berklee College of Music, Boston, where she remained for the following three years.

In the 1960s in New York and Tokyo she played with the Toshiko-Mariano Quartet with her first husband, saxophonist Charlie Mariano, and appeared with Japanese symphony orchestras. She made a critically successful Town Hall solo début in 1967. Her marriage to saxophonist-flautist Lew Tabackin (1969) initiated formation of the Akiyoshi-Tabackin Big Band (1973, Los Angeles; it was re-formed in New York in 1982) as a vehicle for her arrangements. Akiyoshi and her ensemble have been nominated for Grammy awards and have won outright other awards in *Down Beat*, *Stereo Review* and Japan's *Swing Journal*. By the early 1970s she was enriching her music with traditional Japanese elements: shakuhachi-style flute solos, *tsuzumi* drums and *biwa*, and noh vocal recitations. Her extended works reflect her philosophical and social concerns (*Kogun*, *Tales of a Courtesan*, *Minimata* and *Two Faces of a Nation*).

J. McManus: 'Women Jazz Composers and Arrangers', *The Musical Woman: an International Perspective*, i: *1983*, ed. J. L. Zaimont and others (Westport, CT, 1984), 197–208

L. Koplewitz: 'Toshiko Akiyoshi: Jazz Composer, Arranger, Pianist, and Conductor', *The Musical Woman: an International Perspective*, ii: *1984–5*, ed. J. L. Zaimont and others (New York, 1987), 256–79 [incl. bibliography and discography]

L. Feather: 'Blind Test: Toshiko Akiyoshi', *Down Beat*, lvi/9 (1989), 96

K. Whitehead: 'Toshiko Akiyoshi', *Down Beat*, lviii/12 (1991), 72–3

B. Hochkeppel: 'Tasteful Sounds: the Toshiko-Tabackin Big Band', *The Instrumentalist*, xxxviii/April (1984), 21–6

J. MICHELE EDWARDS

Alamanda (*fl* late 12th century). Troubadour. She exchanged a *tenso* with Giraut (or Guiraut) de Bornelh, *S'ieus quier cosselh bel ami Alamanda* (PC 242.69). The music survives in one manuscript (*F-Pn* f.f. 22543, f.8r; ed. in H. van der Werf: *The Extant Troubadour Melodies*, Rochester, NY, 1984).

BIBLIOGRAPHY
M. Bogin: *The Women Troubadours* (New York, 1976), 102–5, 170

MARIA V. COLDWELL

WORKS
selective list

Orch: My Elegy, 1958 [album, 1984]; Silhouette, 1958; Double Exposure, 1970; Fool, 1970; Tuning Up,1973

Big band: Between Me and Myself, c1954; Kogun, band, tsuzumi drum, 1974 [album, 1974]; American Ballad, 1974; Notorious Tourist from the East, 1974; Warning!, 1976; Minimata, band, child's v, noh vocalist, 1976; Sumie, band, 5 fl, 1976; Farewell (To Mingus), 1980 [album, 1980]; 2 Faces of a Nation, 1983; Kourokan, 1991; Children of the Universe, 1991

Other Albums: Long Yellow Road, 1974; Toshiko Akiyoshi-Lew Tabackin Big Band Live at Newport '77, 1977; European Memoirs, 1982; The Toshiko Akiyoshi-Lew Tabackin Big Band, 1991

Film scores and theatre music

Principal publisher: Kendor

BIBLIOGRAPHY
GroveJ (J. B. Robinson)
N. Dean: 'Toshiko Akiyoshi', *Metronome*, xxii/April (1956), 23
L. Feather: 'Toshiko Akiyoshi: the Leader of the Band', *Ms*, vii/5 (1978), 34–5, 40
C. Gans: 'T.A.L.T. Conference: a Conversation with Toshiko Akiyoshi and Lew Tabackin', *Jazz Forum* (1980), Feb
P. Rothbart: 'Toshiko Akiyoshi: Arranging on a Steady Ascent', *Down Beat*, xlvii/8 (1980), 14–15, 62
A. Swan: 'Jazz with Oriental Spice', *Newsweek* (14 July 1980)

Alberga, Eleanor (*b* Kingston, Jamaica, 30 Sept 1949). Jamaican composer. She came to London in 1970 on a scholarship to the RAM, where she studied singing and piano; although she had composed as a child, she did not undertake formal composition study. Nevertheless her music is informed by her classical training and also reflects the diversity of her background, which includes dancing with an authentic African dance company and singing Jamaican folksongs. She began to compose seriously while working as a pianist with the London Contemporary Dance Theatre and much of her music is for piano, for example: *Jamaican Medley* (1983), *Whose Own* (prepared piano and sound processor, 1988) and *Hill and Gully Ride* (two pianos, eight hands, 1990). Commissions from the 1990 Chard Festival of Women in Music and the European Women's Orchestra have produced the orchestral works *Sun Warrior* (1990) and *Jupiter's Fairground* (1991). *Dancing with the Shadow* was written for Lontano in 1991.

WORKS
selective list

Orch: Mobile I, 1983; Sun Warrior, 1990; Jupiter's Fairground, 1991

Chamber: Resolution, ob, gui, 1982; Clouds, pf qnt, 1984; Mobile II, cl, sax, pf, str qt, 1988; Animal Banter, fl, gui, db, 1989; The Edge, fl, vc, kbd, sitar, 1991; Dancing with the Shadow, fl, cl, vn, vc, perc, 1991

Pf: Jamaican Medley, 1983; Ice Flow, 1985; It's Time, 1986; Stone Dream, prepared pf, tape, 1986; Suite, 2 pf 4 hands, 1986; F. Y. S., 1988; Whose Own, prepared pf + sound processor, 1988; Hill and Gully Ride, 2 pf 8 hands, 1990

Film score: Escape from Kampala, 1991

BIBLIOGRAPHY

Fuller-LeFanuRM

TONI CALAM

Alden, Sonia. See EWART, FLORENCE MAUD.

Aldridge, Amanda Ira [Amanda Christina Elizabeth; Ring, Montague] (*b* London, 16 March 1866; *d* London, 5 March 1956). English composer, singer and teacher. An important member of London's black community, Amanda Ira Aldridge was the daughter of the famous tragic actor Ira Aldridge. In 1883 she won a scholarship to the RCM. A pupil of Jenny Lind, her successful career as a contralto was ended by damage to her throat caused by laryngitis. She then established a distinguished career as a teacher, with pupils that included Marian Anderson and Paul Robeson.

Aldridge started publishing her compositions in her thirties, using the pseudonym Montague Ring. Her surviving works are in a popular style with strong rhythmic appeal. She published over 25 songs, often with words by African-American poets, such as 'Where the Paw-Paw Grows' (words by H. E. Downing, 1907) and 'Summah is de Lovin' Time' (P. L. Dunbar, 1925). Her best-known work, *Three African Dances*, for piano, uses themes with West African origins.

BIBLIOGRAPHY

H. Marshall and M. Stock: *Ira Aldridge: the Negro Tragedian* (London, 1958)

J. Green: 'Afro-American Symphony: Popular Black Concert Hall Performers 1900–40', *Black Music in Britain: Essays on the Afro-Asian Contribution to Popular Music*, ed. P. Oliver (Milton Keynes, 1990)

SOPHIE FULLER

Aleotti, Raffaella (*b* Ferrara, *c*1570; *d* after 1646). Italian composer and organist, elder sister of Vittoria Aleotti (Carruthers-Clement believes that Raffaella and Vittoria were the same person, because Vittoria is not listed in the father's will). She studied singing, keyboard performance and composition with Alessandro Milleville and Ercole Pasquini, both of whom had been hired as private tutors by her father (the Ferrarese court architect Giovanni Battista Aleotti) because she had inherited musical gifts from her mother and because she aspired to convent life. In about 1590 she took vows at the Augustinian convent of S Vito, Ferrara, and in about 1593 she became director of the main ensemble there, the 'concerto grande'. Vividly described by Bottrigari and Artusi (and universally praised), the ensemble consisted of 23 singers and instrumentalists, and included harpsichord, lutes, viols, flutes, cornetts and trombones in its instrumentation. A collection of her motets for five, seven, eight and nine voices and instruments was published by Amadino in 1593. Its dedication to Ippolito Bentivoglio is thought by Bowers to imply that she would willingly have left S Vito to enter Bentivoglio's service. Her motets show a thorough mastery of contrapuntal technique, rhythmic vitality and sensitivity to the meaning of the texts.

Aleotti last appears in a document of S Vito on 2 August 1640, but according to Gasparo Sardi she was still alive in 1646.

WORKS

Sacrae cantiones quinque, septem, octo et decem vocibus decantande (Venice, 1593); excerpts ed. C. A. Carruthers-Clement, *Nine Centuries of Music by Women* (New York, 1983): Angelus ad pastores ait; Ascendens Christus in altum; Facta est cum Angelo

BIBLIOGRAPHY

FétisB; GerberNL; SainsburyD; SchillingE; SchmidlD

Elenco delle monache che furono in S Vita agostinianae (MS, *I-FEc* Antolini 56)

E. Bottrigari: *Il desiderio* (Venice, 1594), 48–50; Eng. trans., MSD ix (1962)

G. M. Artusi: *L'Artusi, overo Delle imperfettioni della moderna musica* (Venice, 1600), 1

M. Guarini: *Compendio historico dell'origine, accrescimento, e prerogative delle chiese, e luoghi pii della città, e diocesi di Ferrara* (Ferrara, 1621)

G. Sardi and A. Faustini: *Libro delle historie ferrarese* (Ferrara, 1646)

L. N. Cittadella: 'Memorie intorno alle vita alle opere dell'architetto G. B. Aleotti Argentano', *Dell'interrimento del Po di Ferrara* (Ferrara, 1847), 5–57

C. A. [Carruthers-]Clement: *The Madrigals and Motets of Vittoria (Raphaella) Aleotti* (diss., Kent State U., 1982)

J. Bowers: 'The Emergence of Women Composers in Italy, 1566–1700', *Women Making Music: the Western Art Tradition, 1150–1950*, ed. J. Bowers and J. Tick (Urbana and Chicago, 1986), 116–67

ADRIANO CAVICCHI, SUZANNE G. CUSICK

Aleotti, Vittoria (*b* Ferrara, *c*1573; *d* after 1620). Italian composer, younger sister of Raffaella Aleotti (Carruthers-Clement believes that Vittoria and Raffaella were the same person, because Vittoria is not listed in the father's will). She apparently received her first musical training by overhearing her sister's lessons with Alessandro Milleville and Ercole Pasquini. According to their father (the court architect Giovanni Battista Aleotti, who dedicated Vittoria's anthology *Ghirlanda de madrigali a quattro voci* of 1593 to his patron Ippolito Bentivoglio), by the age of six Vittoria could play the harpsichord. Pasquini probably urged that Vittoria be brought up in the Augustinian convent of S Vito, Ferrara, already the home of her sister Raffaella. At 14 Vittoria chose to take vows as a nun of the convent.

All of Aleotti's surviving madrigals are set to poetry by G. B. Guarini, whom her father had asked to provide her with texts. They represent a range of late 16th-century styles, from simple canzonettas to serious efforts at exploiting dissonance to express images of amorous longing or distress. Occasional awkward handlings of imitation or of text declamation suggest that the madrigals of *Ghirlanda* were still student works.

WORKS

Di pallide viole, madrigal, 5vv, pubd in *Giardino de musici ferraresi* (Venice, 1591⁹)
Ghirlanda de madrigali a quattro voci (Venice, 1593); 2 ed. C. A. Carruthers-Clement, *Nine Centuries of Music by Women* (New York, 1983): Baciai per haver vita; Hor che la vaga aurora

BIBLIOGRAPHY

FétisB; *GerberNL*; *SainsburyD*; *SchillingE*; *SchmidlD*; *WaltherML*

For further bibliography see ALEOTTI, RAFFAELLA.

ADRIANO CAVICCHI, SUZANNE G. CUSICK

Alessandra, Caterina. *See* ASSANDRA, CATERINA.

Alexander (Pollack), Leni (*b* Breslau [now Wrocław], 8 June 1924). Chilean composer and educator of German origin. She emigrated to Chile in 1939 and adopted Chilean nationality in 1951. She studied with Frè Focke (1949–53) in Chile and with René Leibowitz and Olivier Messiaen in France in 1954. Through several significant educational projects she has contributed to a better public understanding of contemporary music in Chile; she has also promoted Chilean musical culture in Europe. Her works have won international prizes and she has received commissions from patrons and organizations in Europe and the USA. Her music, modernist in style and sometimes using sounds generated by unconventional means, includes two ballets, *Las tres caras de la luna* (1966) and . . . *a false alarm on the nightbell once answered cannot be made good, not ever*

(1977–8), and several works for full orchestra, including *Cinco epigramas* (1952), *Equinoccio* (1962), *Aulicio* (1968) and . . . *ils sont perdus dans l'espace étoilé* (1975). She has also written works for chamber orchestra and chamber ensemble, sometimes with solo voice, for example *Maramoh* (mezzo and seven instruments; 1972) and *Par quoi? A quoi? Pour quoi?* (mezzo, children's voices, instrumental ensemble and electronic sounds; 1971). Works for percussion include *Sous le quotidien, décelez l'inexplicable* (two pianos and two percussionists; 1979) and *Menetekel* (two percussionists; 1990).

BIBLIOGRAPHY

L. M. Montero: 'La revista musical chilena y los compositores nacionales del presente siglio: una bibliografía', *Revista musical chilena*, no.163 (1985), 3–69, esp.14

RAQUEL BUSTOS VALDERRAMA

Alexandra (Moraru), Liana (*b* Bucharest, 27 May 1947). Romanian composer and teacher. She studied composition at the Bucharest Conservatory (1965–71) with Tudor Ciortea and Tiberiu Olah. Later she attended the International Seminar in Weimar (1973) and the Darmstadt summer courses (1974, 1978, 1980). She was appointed Reader at the Bucharest Academy (chair of instrumentation, form and composition), and she also became a member of the Frau und Musik organization, Berlin. She has been awarded many prizes, both national (including the Uniunea Compozitorilor and the Academia Română) and international (Weber, Gaudeamus, Fanny Mendelssohn and GEDOK competitions). Her musical technique is of a high order, particularly in virtuoso orchestration. She combines derived rows with a non-serial harmonic language built on both the folk modes of Romania and the laws of consonance.

WORKS
selective list
STAGE

Crăiasa zăpezii [The Snow Queen], op.21 (opera, 1, L. Alexandra, after H. C. Andersen), concert perf., Bucharest, 18 May 1980; stage, Bucharest, 18 Nov 1982
Mica sirenă [The Little Siren], op.25 (ballet, 1, A. Boldur, after Andersen), Bucharest, 22 Nov 1983
În labyrint [In the Labyrinth] (opera, 2, G. Arion), concert perf., Bucharest, 1987; stage, Timişoara, 1988

OTHER WORKS

Orch: 7 syms.: no.1, op.1, 1971, no.2, op.16, 1978, no.3 'Diacronii-armonii pentru pacea lumii', op.24, 1981, no.4, op.28, 1984, no.5, 1985, no.6, 1989, no.7, 1993; Cl Conc., op.6, 1974; Rezonanţe, op.7, pf, orch, 1974; Concertante music, op.10, 5 solo insts, orch, 1975; 2 imagini [2 Images], op.20, 1978; Concerto, op.23, va, fl, chamber orch, 1980; Ierusalim, sym. poem, 1991

Chamber and solo inst: Music, op.2, cl, harp, perc, 1972; Sonata, op.3, fl, 1973; Secvenţă lirică, op.4, cl, tpt, pf, 1974; Sonata, op.11, cl, 1976; Colaje, op.12, wind qnt, 1977; Incantaţii II [Incantations II], op.17 no.2, cl, vn, va, vc, pf, 1978; Consonanţe I–V, op.18: no.1, 4 trbn, 1978, no.2, cl, pf/cel, 1979, no.3, org, 1979, no.4, cl, tape, 1981, no.5, org, 1980; Imagini întrerupte, op.26, wind qnt, 1983; Quasi cadenza, op.27, vn, 1983

Vocal: Către pace [Towards Peace], op.8 (N. Stănescu), mixed chorus, perc, tape, 1974; 2 cîntece împotriva morţii, op.9 (E. Jebeleanu), mixed chorus, perc, 1975; De dor şi de bucurie, op.13 (trad.), S, str orch, 1977, Ţară, pămînt, ţară idee, op. 14 (Stănescu), cantata, mixed chorus, orch, 1977; Laudă, op.15, cantata, mixed chorus, orch, 1977; Incantaţii I [Incantations I], op.17 no.1, Mez, fl, hpd, perc, 1978; 2 imagini [2 Images] op.19 (trad.), children's chorus, orch, 1978; Soarele şi luna [Sun and Moon], op.23 (trad.), ballad, mixed chorus, 1981

BIBLIOGRAPHY

CohenE

V. Cosma: Muzicieni din România (Bucharest, 1989)

VIOREL COSMA

Ali-Zadeh, Franghiz (b Baku, 29 May 1947). Azerbaijan composer and pianist. At the Baku Conservatory she studied piano with U. Khalilov (1970) and then composition with Kara Karayev (1972), whom she assisted during her postgraduate studies (1973–6). She subsequently taught at the Conservatory. In 1980 she won the prize of the Azerbaijan Composers' Union. In her music Ali-Zadeh resourcefully employs a wide range of devices, continuing the innovations of composers such as Witold Lutosławski and John Cage; the well-springs of her work however are her own national heritage and the music of the Second Viennese School. In her interpretation of these traditions she has, not surprisingly, been influenced by Kara Karayev. Ali-Zadeh attempts to 'translate' Schoenberg's technique into the language of the Azerbaijan mugam: she inverts 12-note melodic motifs to form a chain of variants similar to mugam monody. Another distinctive feature of her music is the way in which it alternates between delicate lyricism and tense, dynamic expression.

WORKS

Stage: Legenda o belom vsadnike [The Legend about White Horseman] (rock-opera, 1, folk texts), 1985

Orch: Pf Conc., 1972; Symphony, 1976; Conc., chamber orch, 1986

Choral: Pesni o Rodine [Songs about the Motherland] (oratorio, N. Khaeri), 3vv, chorus, orch, 1978; Oda [Ode] (D. Nasib), chorus, orch, 1980

Other vocal: 3 akvareli [3 Aquarelles] (N. Rafibeili), 1v, fl, prepared pf, 1987; Iz yaponskoy poezii [From Japanese Poetry] (I. Takuboku), 1v, fl, vib/cel, 1990

Inst: Pf Sonata no.1, 1970; Str Qt, 1974; K 'Pesnyam ob umershikh detyakh' [To the Kindertotenlieder], cl, vn, perc, 1977; Gabil-sajagy [In the Style of Gabil], vc, prepared pf, 1979; Fantasia, org, 1982; Dilogy I, str qt, 1988; Dilogy II, str qt, wind qnt, 1989, Music, pf, 1989; Pf Sonata no.2, 1990; Peresecheniya [Crossings], chamber ens, 1992

BIBLIOGRAPHY

L. Karagicheva: 'Vstrechi s Ali-Zadeh' [Meetings with Ali-Zadeh], SovM (1990), no.11, pp.22–6

OLGA MANULKINA

Allen, Judith Shatin. See SHATIN, JUDITH.

Allik, Kristi (Anne) (b Toronto, 6 Feb 1952). Canadian composer and teacher, of Estonian descent. She studied at Toronto University with John Weinzweig, Oskar Morawetz and Lothar Klein (BMus 1975), then in the USA, at Princeton (MFA 1977) and the University of Southern California (DMA 1982), with James Hopkins, Frederick Leseman and Milton Babbitt. She has taught at the universities of Victoria, 1980–81, and Western Ontario, 1982–7, and in 1988 was appointed to Queen's University, Kingston, Ontario, where she co-founded with David Keane the Computer Laboratory for Applications in Music (CLAM). Even in her early works, when writing for conventional ensembles, Allik was always intrigued by unusual timbres; after 1982 she has composed purely electroacoustic and integrated media works, some of which reflect her active interest in theatre, and she has also written an opera. Her music has been performed in North America and Europe and ranges in style from serialist and minimalist to works in which timbres function like tonal centres; some pieces reflect her Estonian cultural heritage.

WORKS

selective list

Multi-media (with visuals by R. Mulder): Electronic Zen Garden, perc, el-ac tape, theatre set, 1984; Rondeau, el-ac tape, 1985; Cometose, el-ac tape, 1986; Integra, el-ac tape, 1986; Rhythm and Culture (L. Allen), performer, live elec, el-ac tape, 1986; Alambic Rhythms, el-ac tape, 1987; Till Rust do us Part, el-ac tape, live sound effects, 1988; Vitamin B-52, interactive sound, video, 1989

Other multi-media and music theatre: Loom Sword River (opera, 3, P. Such), solo vv, chorus, chamber orch, 1982; Of All the People (Such), solo vv, chamber ens, 1983; Skyharp, interactive sound sculpture, audio-visual installation, 1991

Elec and el-ac chamber: Woods of Tontla, fl, cl, vn, db, harp, elec tape, 1976; Meditation, vn, vc, el-ac tape, 1984; Silicon Sidewinder, 2 perc, vc, el-ac tape, 1985; Rhapsody, cl, el-ac tape, 1986; Integra, sax, elec, 1987; Xanthe, cl, elec, 1988

Inst and choral: Qt for Winds and Percussion, fl, bn, 2 perc, 1973; Pf Piece, 1974; Fragments, pf, 1976; Trio, fl, vn, cl, 1977; Pf Trio, 1979; L.A. '79, fl, 2 tpt, hn, trbn, 2 perc, Rhodes pf, el db, 1980; Lend me your Harp, chorus, chamber orch, 1981; North Star South Wind, pf, 1983; Zone Two, chamber orch, 1984; Rohan, vc, chamber orch, 1988; Trio, cl, pf, 1v, 1989

GAYNOR G. JONES

Allitsen [Bumpus], **(Mary) Frances** (*b* London, 30 Dec 1848; *d* London, 30 Sept 1912). English composer. She was the daughter of the bookseller John Bumpus and sister of John and Edward Bumpus, the music distributors; 'Allitsen' was a pseudonym. She had a natural gift for melody but 'had no technical knowledge' until she studied at the GSM. She made a late singing début in 1882, but devoted herself largely to composition. Her songs were immensely popular, particularly those in a patriotic vein, and were presented to the public by the leading singers of the day; Hayden Coffin and Clara Butt were her special favourites. Her settings of Heinrich Heine and her four songs on Chinese poems (1910) from *A Lute of Jade* are on a higher level. She also experimented with other musical forms, including song cycles (*Seven Psychological Studies*, 1906; *Moods and Tenses*, 1905) and dramatic cantatas (*Cleopatra*, 1904, for Clara Butt; *For the Queen*, 1911). *For the Queen*, a full-scale musical drama in two scenes, indicates her growing interest in theatrical presentations. n 1912 her two-act romantic opera *Bindra the Minstrel* was published, but it remained unperformed. The detailed diary of her dealings with music publishers in the last years of her life, with her melancholy personal comments (*GB-Lbl*), provides interesting and useful information about the publishing business.

DUNCAN CHISHOLM

Alotin, Yardena (*b* Tel-Aviv, 19 Oct 1930). Israeli composer. She studied at the Tel-Aviv Music Teachers' College (1948–50) and at the Israel Academy of Music (1950–52), where her principal teachers were Oedoen Partos (composition) and Ilona Vincze-Kraus (piano). Her works for unaccompanied choir include Cantata (1956), dedicated to the memory of her teacher Leo Kestenberg and performed in 1960 both in Israel and at the international festival of sacred music in Perugia, and *Shir Hag* ('Festive Song') (1984), which was commissioned by the

Frances Allitsen

Tel-Aviv Foundation for Literature and Art to mark the 75th anniversary of that city. Both works are settings of biblical texts; they are challenging to sing and exploit rhythmic ostinatos, a feature typical of Alotin's music. Other compositions include *Al Golah Dvuyah* ('A Painful Exile') for mezzo-soprano and orchestra (1958), a setting of the composer's own text, and a Cello Sonata, written in 1976 while Alotin was composer-in-residence at Bar-Ilan University.

A pianist and piano teacher, she has also written youth and educational music. Her flute piece *Yefei Nof* (1978), composed for James Galway and performed by him many times, mainly as an encore, has become established in the international flute repertory.

Principal publishers: Israeli Music Institute, Mifalei Tarbut Vehinuch, Schirmer

WILLIAM Y. ELIAS

Alsted, Birgitte (*b* Odense, 15 June 1942). Danish composer. Educated at the Kongelige Danske Musikkonservatorium in Copenhagen as a violinist, she became a member of the Conservatory study circle of contemporary music, which encouraged her development as a composer. Since producing her first work in 1971 she has devoted herself to composing, but at the same time she derives inspiration from working as a freelance violinist and teacher, where her main concern is encouraging creativity in children. All her activities, not least her theatrical projects, reveal an experimental approach. She has co-operated very successfully with the actor, producer and writer Brigitte Kolerus to create fascinating and thought-provoking performance-pieces, usually with a feminist stance, such as *Frokost i det grønne* ('Lunch in the Open Air') and *Drømmespil* ('Dream-play'). She was one of the founders of Kvinder i Musik (Women in Music) in 1980 and has worked to promote the performance of music by women.

WORKS

Stage: 12 toner i Zoologisk Have [12 Tones in the Zoo], 1974; Smedierne i Granada [The Smiths in Granada], 1975; Timileskoven, 1980; Antigone, 1983; Turning Point (ballet), 1985; Frokost i det grønne [Lunch in the Open Air], 1985; Drømmespil [Dreamplay], 1988; Piji (ballet), 1990

Orch, chamber and solo inst: Opbrud [Departure], orch, 1988; Vi lærer at producere uden kærlighed [We Learn to Produce without Love], chamber ens, 1970; Str Qt, C and D, 1977; Gentagne gange [Over and over Again], pf, 1979–82; Facing Moon – Facing Changing, pf, 1983; Kære allesammen [Dear Everybody], pf, 1984; To sange til døden [2 Songs to Death], accordion, 1990

Vocal: Tredie tilstand [Third Condition], S, Mez, Bar, SATB, 1979; Solen og jeg [The Sun and I], children's chorus, inst ens, 1981; Solen på møddingen [The Sun on the Dungheap], Bar, chamber ens, 1981; På afstand af bølgen [Distant from the Wave], S, pf, 1984–5; This Is It, Mez, pf

Tape: Heksekedel [Witches' Cauldron], 1984; Vaekst [Growth], slides, vn, 1989; Lyst [Lust], dancer, S, accordion

BIBLIOGRAPHY

E. Dabrowska: 'Birgitte Alsted: komponist, et interview', KIM-NYT, ii/6 (1985), 10–23
I. Bruland: 'Fire danske kvindelige komponister fra det 20. århundrede' [Four Danish Women Composers of the 20th Century], Kvinders former, ed. I. Bruland, I. Busk-Jensen and T. Ørum (Copenhagen, 1986), 33–59
B. Larsson: 'Birgitte Alsted: tonsättare' (unpubd article, Göteborg, 1987)

INGE BRULAND

Amacher, Maryanne (*b* Kates, PA, 25 Feb 1943). American composer, performer and mixed-media artist. She studied composition with George Rochberg at the University of Pennsylvania (BFA 1964) and with Karlheinz Stockhausen. She later studied computer science at the universities of Pennsylvania and Illinois. Her music has been greatly influenced by science and has been devoted to exploring the psychoacoustical effects of sound. In 1967 Amacher began creating a series of projects called *City-Links* for which microphones were installed at distant locations (cities, or places within a city); the live sounds were then transmitted to mixing facilities at her studio or at a performance space. The effect was to 'displace' the listener by setting up an unaccustomed sound environment. Amacher continued this work as a Fellow at the Massachusetts Institute of Technology (1972–6) and at Radcliffe College, Harvard University (1978–9). While at MIT, Amacher set up a system for the transmission of sounds directly to her office and home from a nearby pier in Boston for an extended period of time. Her observations showed that living in the sound environment of a distant site (in this case the pier) could have a great effect on everyday patterns of working, talking, sleeping and dreaming, thus proving that people's lives are greatly determined by the sounds around them. Amacher also used the results of her sound experiments in collaborations with John Cage and with the choreographer Merce Cunningham. In the series *Music for Sound-Joined Rooms* (1980–82) she created a unique form of avant-garde theatre music by using the rooms of a building to tell a story.

WORKS
selective list

City-Links, perf. New York, Buffalo, Chicago, Paris and elsewhere, mixed media, 1967–79; Lecture on the Weather, mixed media, 1975, collab. Cage; Remainder, dance music [for M. Cunningham: Torse], tape, elec, 1976; Close Up [acc. to Cage: Empty Words], tape, elec, 1979; Music for Sound-Joined Rooms, mixed media, 1980–82; other elec and mixed-media works

BIBLIOGRAPHY

T. Johnson: 'Maryanne Amacher: Acoustics Joins Electronics', Village Voice (15 Dec 1975)
T. Hight: 'The Arts: Music', Omni, iv/2 (1981), 32, 142–6

CHARLES PASSY

Amalia Catharina, Countess of Erbach (*b* Arolsen, 8 Aug 1640; *d* Cuylenburg [now Culemborg], 4 Jan 1697). German poet and composer. She was the daughter of Count Philipp Theodor von Waldeck; her mother was born Countess of Nassau. She appears to have spent her youth at Arolsen, the seat of the Waldeck family. In 1664 she married Count Georg Ludwig von Erbach, and then settled at Michelstadt, near Erbach, Odenwald. She was typical of the numerous princesses of the years around 1700 who inclined to Pietism and gave expression to it in verse. She published *Andächtige Sing-Lust, das ist i. Morgen-, ii. Abend-, iii. Tage-, iv. Beth-, v. Buss-, vi. Klag- und Trost-, vii. Lob- und Dank-, viii. Lehrlieder* (Hildburghausen, 1692). The place of publication is explained by its being the residence of one of her sisters, who was the wife of the Duke Ernst of Saxe-Hildburghausen and to whom she dedicated her book. It is therefore possible that it was written under Middle German influence. Moreover, the Princesses of Reuss and Schwarzburg, who lived nearby, were ardent disciples of Pietism. Amalia Catharina's publication is a collection of songs for household devotion. It contains 67 poems, some of which are provided with melodies with figured bass. This music (which is not given by Zahn) is certainly by Amalia Catharina herself and is an important contribution to the development of the German sacred continuo song.

BIBLIOGRAPHY

Choron-FayolleD; SchillingE; WaltherML
G. Simon: Die Geschichte der Dynasten und Grafen zu Erbach und ihres Landes (Frankfurt, 1858)
J. Zahn: Die Melodien der deutschen evangelischen Kirchenlieder, vi (Gütersloh, 1893)

WALTER BLANKENBURG

Amalie, Princess of Saxony [Marie Auguste Friederike Amalie] (*b* Dresden, 10 Aug 1794; *d* Dresden, 18 Sept 1870). German writer and composer. The sister of King John of Saxony, she was taught the piano by Joseph Schuster, singing by Vincenzo Rastrelli and Johann Miksch, and music theory by Franz Anton Schubert and Carl Maria von Weber. Weber found her 'highly talented'. She spent her whole life in the castle of Pillnitz, Dresden. Princess Amalie was stimulated by the cultivation of Italian opera in Dresden and composed a number of operas (under the name Amalie Serena), which were performed during family celebrations and within the court circle. Some of her operas were performed in the Pillnitz theatre. Her operas are modelled on *opéra comique* and *opera buffa*. Her strength lies in her comic operas; she illustrates the characters with originality and humour. The instrumentation is simple, but the instrumental colouring is related to the characters and the various situations. After 1835 she stopped composing and wrote comedies, using the pseudonym Amalie Heiter.

WORKS

Operas: Una donna; Le tre cinture; Le nozze funeste, 1816; Il prigioniere; L'Americana, 1820; Elvira, 1821; Elisa ed Ernesto, 1823; La fedeltà alla prova, 1826; Vecchiezza e gioventù, 1828; Der Kanonenschuss, 1828; Il figlio pentito, 1831; Il marchesino, 1834; Die Siegesfahne, 1834; La casa disabitata, 1835
Other works: sacred music, incl. Stabat mater, cantatas; songs; melodramas; str qt; Variations, pf

BIBLIOGRAPHY

M. Boerner-Sandrini: Erinnerungen einer alten Dresdenerin (Dresden, 1873)
M. Fürstenau: Die musikalischen Beschäftigungen der Prinzessin Amalie (Dresden, 1874)
R. Waldmüller: Aus den Memoiren einer Fürstentachter (Dresden, 1883)

EVA RIEGER

Ancona, Solange (*b* Paris, 14 Aug 1943). French composer. She had piano lessons when very young, then entered the Paris Conservatoire. In Olivier Messiaen's class, she was awarded first prize for analysis (1964) and composition (1970), and in Georges Hugon's class, first prize for harmony. She participated in courses given by Pierre Boulez, Bruno Maderna, Karlheinz Stockhausen and Henri Pousseur in Basle, Darmstadt and Cologne (1965–6), and received her first grounding in electroacoustic music with Jean-Étienne Marie at the Schola Cantorum in Paris (1968–9). The human voice in all its variety and a fascination for spirals, mirrors, colour spectra and metamorphoses are elements that have played a part in influencing the structure of her works, in play with time in slow motion.

WORKS
selective list

Maïamoï, 5vv, inst ens, 1967; Chtaslîvi, inst ens, tape, 1971; Slantzó III (after Dante: Paradiso), S, orch, 1975; All'eterno dal tempo, org, 1982; Preludio, 2 va, 1989

JEAN-NOËL VON DER WEID

Anderson, Avril (*b* Southsea, 10 June 1953). English composer. She studied at Winchester Art College (1970–72) and at the RCM (1972–6), where her composition teachers included Humphrey Searle and John Lambert. In 1977 scholarships enabled her to study in the USA at the New England Conservatory; she also took lessons from David Del Tredici in New York. She returned to England and spent the next year at Sussex University, where her composition teacher was Jonathan Harvey. In 1987, with her husband, the director and composer David Sutton-Anderson, she founded the contemporary music group Sounds Positive. Her music, mostly for small forces, is strongly rhythmic; it features the repetition of short melodic cells and superimposed ostinatos and a bold, clean, innovative manipulation of texture. Solo vocal works include *Black Eyes in an Orange Sky*, for soprano and piano (1979), *Private Energy*, for soprano, flute, oboe, clarinet, trumpet and piano (1983), and *Où allons nous?* for soprano and orchestra (1976); other important works include *Mono-status* for three clarinets (1975), *Edward II*, a one-act opera (1978), and *Dynamics of Matter* for piano (1989).

BIBLIOGRAPHY

Fuller-LeFanuRM

MARIE FITZPATRICK

Anderson, Beth [Barbara Elizabeth] (*b* Lexington, KY, 3 Jan 1950). American composer. She studied at the University of Kentucky, the University of California, Davis (BA 1971), where she was a pupil of Larry Austin, John Cage and Richard Swift; and at Mills College, Oakland (MFA 1973, MA 1974), with Robert Ashley and Terry Riley. In 1974 she completed the oratorio *Joan* as a commission for the Cabrillo Music Festival. Active as a writer and editor, Anderson was co-editor of *Ear*, 1973–9, as well as one of its principal contributors, and after moving to New York in 1975 founded *Ear Magazine*; her criticism has also appeared in the *Soho Weekly News*, *Heresies* and *Intermedia*. She has devoted herself increasingly to solo performance (piano, voice); she also teaches college music courses and accompanies dancers, for instance at the Martha Graham School of Dance and the American Dance Studio.

By the early 1970s Anderson had composed graphic scores (*Music for Charlemagne Palestine*), text-sound pieces (*Torero Piece*), and tape works (*Tulip Clause*). In the late 1970s, her music became more regular in rhythm, more popular in orientation and overtly 'romantic'. As a composer she often adopts a principled arbitrariness in determining pitches by code transfer, from letters of texts or from numbers (Anderson is a practising astrologist); she has also shown consistent interest in feminist imagery and history and a fondness for music as theatrical entertainment.

WORKS

selective list

Stage: Queen Christina (opera, Anderson), 1973; Soap Tuning (theatre piece, Anderson), 1976; Zen Piece (theatre piece, Anderson), 1976; Nirvana Manor (musical, J. Morely), 1981; Elizabeth Rex: or the well-bred Mother goes to Camp (musical, J. Kreston), 1983; The Fat Opera (musical, Kreston), 1991

Orch: Ov., band, 1981; Revelation, 1981, rev. chamber orch as Revel, 1984; Suite, wind, perc, 1981

Inst: Lullaby of the Eighth Ancestor, fl, pf, 1979–80; Preparation for the Dominant: Outrunning the Inevitable, fl/vn/ocarina, 1979; Dream (Trio: Dream), pf, fl, vc, 1980; Skater's Suite, 4 insts,

1980, arr. pf as Skate Suite; Pennyroyal Swale, str qt, 1985; Rosemary Swale, str qt, 1986; Brass Swale, brass qt, 1989; Saturday/Sunday Swale, brass qnt, 1991; 3 other works

Pf: Quilt Music, 1982; Manos inquietas, pts. 1–3, 1982; Taking Sides, 1983; Belgian Tango, 1984

Tape: Tulip Clause, chamber ens, tape, 1973; Tower of Power, org, tape, 1973; Good-Bye Bridget Bardot or Hello Charlotte Moorman, vc, tape, 1974; They Did It, pf, tape, 1975–6; Ode, 1976; Joan, 1977; German Swale, 1990; several other works

Mixed-media: Music for Charlemagne Palestine, graphic score, 2 str insts, 2 lighting technicians, 1973; Peachy Keen-O, org, el gui, vib, perc, vv, dancers, light, tape, 1973; Morning View & Maiden Spring, spkr, slides, light, tape, 1978; 1 other work

Vocal (texts by Anderson unless otherwise stated): Joan, oratorio, 1974; Incline Thine ear to me, chant, 1975; Black/White, chant, 1976; text-sound pieces, incl. Torero Piece, 2vv, 1973; The People Rumble Louder, 1v, 1975; I Can't Stand It, 1v, perc, 1976; Yes Sir Ree, 1v, 1978; many songs, incl. A Day, 1967; WomanRite, 1972; Music for Myself, 1973; Beauty Runs Faster, 1978; In Six, 1979; Knots (R. D. Laing), 1981

Other: Hallophone, musical environment, 1973; 1 film score, 1980

Principal publisher: ACA

CHARLES SHERE

Anderson, Laurie (*b* Chicago, 5 June 1947). American performance artist and composer. She was trained as a violinist and, after moving to New York in 1966, as a painter and sculptor at Barnard College and Columbia University; later she studied privately with the minimalist painter Sol LeWitt. In the early 1970s she taught art history and wrote art criticism, as well as exhibiting sound-object sculpture, graphic collages, illustrated books and super-8 films. Influenced by the confessional performance artist Vito Acconci and by the whole burgeoning performance art movement of the time, she made her first performance piece, *Automotive*, an outdoor concert for car horns, in 1972. In 1974, she began making her own instruments, most notably modifying the violin (the first had an internal speaker).

Anderson's work reached maturity at the end of the 1970s with *Americans on the Move*; this piece eventually became incorporated into *United States*, Parts I–IV, given its première in its complete form in 1983 at the Brooklyn Academy of Music. Dubbed an opera, it lasted seven hours, was performed over a two-night period, and was a compilation of almost everything she had produced over the four-year period; it was later issued both on record and as a book. By this time she had made many tours of Europe and her performances, conceived for intimate gallery spaces, were given in opera houses and rock-concert theatres. This was the result of the unexpected commercial success of her 'song' from *United States*, 'O Superman (for Massenet)' which in 1981 reached number two in the British pop charts. After signing a contract with Warner Bros., she released *Big Science* and *Mister Heartbreak*, two recordings that won her a progressive-rock audience. Her emphasis on the visual coincided exactly with a fad in rock for video vignettes.

By the early 1980s she had become the best-known American performance artist, and her popularity reached its peak in 1986, the year she directed *Home of the Brave*, a feature film of one of her performances, toured internationally with a large pop band and even appeared in an American Express television commercial. Finding herself overwhelmed and exhausted by the ambitiousness and the logistics of such undertakings, Anderson returned to a more intimate style in succeeding pieces, *Talk Normal* (1987),

Empty Places (1989), *Voices from the Beyond* (1991) and *Halcion Days: Stories from the Nerve Bible* (1992). In these pieces she appeared alone or with a few backing musicians; however, she continued to enrich her musical and visual resources with ever-evolving technology.

Anderson's pieces are mixed-media collages, solo operas built up from a sequence of 'stories', usually told in the first person, either recited or sung; the often simple sung melodies (and sometimes the recitations) employ deft, sophisticated art-rock accompaniments. Perhaps the most significant of her innovations in instrument design is the tape-bow violin, created in 1977, which consists of a violin with a tape playback head mounted on the bridge and a bow that has prerecorded lengths of audio tape instead of hair; drawing the bow across the head, the performer activates the tape, controlling the speed, intensity, and direction of the playback. Anderson often electronically

Laurie Anderson

transposes her voice into the male range to create the alter-ego figure of authority, and she surrealistically turns her body into a booming percussion instrument with the use of contact-microphones. With each new performance she adds different and more advanced computer graphics.

Although she began as a poet (William Burroughs is a prime influence) and visual artist, illustrating her performances with sophisticated lighting, film, slides and props, she grew more accomplished as a musician in the 1980s, writing for orchestra and dance and scoring films. She took formal voice lessons, which resulted in a more expressive singing style in her later performance works. The childlike nature of her earlier songs was appropriate for the droll, hip humour of that period and it was from that that much of her initial popularity derived. But in the later works, her whimsical futuristic bemusement has turned into darker, less romantic visions of the future.

WORKS
selective list

Performances: Automotive, 1972; Duets on Ice, 1972; As:If, 1975; For Instants, for Instants, 1976; Some Songs, 1977; Songs for Lines, Songs for Waves, 1977; That's Not the Way I Heard it, 1977; Like a Stream, 1978; Americans on the Move, 1978; Suspended Sentences, 1979; United States, Parts I–IV, 1983; Mister Heartbreak, 1984; Natural History, 1986; Talk Normal, 1987; Empty Places, 1989; Voices from the Beyond, 1991; Halcion Days: Stories from the Nerve Bible, 1992

Orch: Like a Stream, 1979; It's Cold Outside, 1982

Dance: Set and Reset, 1984

Film Scores: Swimming to Cambodia, 1987; Monster in a Box, 1991

Recordings (all Warner Bros.): Big Science, 1982; Mister Heartbreak, 1984; Home of the Brave, 1986; Strange Angels, 1989

BIBLIOGRAPHY
CBY 1983

L. Anderson: *Words in Reverse* (Buffalo, NY, 1979)

J. Kardon, ed.: *Laurie Anderson: Works from 1969 to 1983* (Philadelphia, 1983)

J. Rockwell: 'Women Composers, Performance Art and the Perils of Fashion: Laurie Anderson', *All American Music: Composition in the Late Twentieth Century* (New York, 1983), 123–32

L. Anderson: *United States* (New York, 1984)

——: *Home of the Brave* (New York, 1986)

M. Sumner, K. Burch and M. Sumner, eds.: *The Guests Go to Supper* (Oakland, CA, 1986)

H. Sayre: *The Object of Performance: the American Avant-Garde since 1970* (Chicago, 1989)

L. Anderson: *Postcard Book* (New York, 1990)

——: *Empty Places* (New York, 1991)

S. McClary: *Feminine Endings: Music, Gender and Sexuality* (Minneapolis, 1991), 132–47

J. Howell: *Laurie Anderson* (New York, 1992)

JOHN ROCKWELL, MARK SWED

Anderson, Ruth (*b* Kalispell, MT, 21 March 1928). American composer, flautist, orchestrator and teacher. At the University of Washington she received the BA in flute (1949) and was the first woman to receive the MA in composition (1951). She then studied at Columbia University (electronic music, CPEMC) and Princeton University (composition), where she was one of the first four women admitted, and she took private lessons with Nadia Boulanger, Darius Milhaud (composition), John Wummer and Jean-Pierre Rampal (flute). She worked as a flautist and freelance arranger and orchestrator for many years before settling at Hunter College, where she was professor of composition and theory (1966–88) and director of the electronic music studio (designed by her in 1968), the first operative studio within the City University of New York. Among her many awards are two Fulbright scholarships in Paris (1958–60), MacDowell Colony and Yaddo residencies (1966–73) and numerous grants.

Anderson's early compositions are lyrical and colouristic, using instrumental, electronic and vocal media in traditional forms. Her later text, computer, ad hoc electronic interactive and performance pieces, games and installations, derive from a holistic concept of music, reflecting her work in psychoacoustics and electroacoustic design and her study of Zen Buddhism. In *Centering* (1979), the reactions of four observers generate rising and falling pitches by means of GSRs (galvanic skin resistance oscillators) attached to their fingers as they respond to a dancer's changes of energy. The dancer, in turn, reacts spontaneously to the changing pitch arcs, creating a double biofeedback process.

WORKS

Many early works for vv, pf, str, chamber orch, str and pf with fl, tape, withdrawn; numerous arrs, orchestrations

Tape (concrete, analogue, digital): The Pregnant Dream (M. Swenson), 1968; ES II, 1969; DUMP, collage, 1970; SUM (State of the Union Message), collage, 1973; Conversations, 1974; I come out of your sleep (L. Bogan), 1979; Resolutions, 1984; several others

Text pieces: Naming, 1975; A Long Sound, 1976; Sound Portraits I–II, 1977; Silent Sound, 1978; Greetings from the Right Hemisphere, 1979; Communications, 1980; Hearing as Though . . . I–VI, 1990–91

Performance: Centering, dancer, 4 observers, interactive live biofeedback electronics, 1979

Installations and electronic games: Sound Environment, 1975; Time and Tempo, 1984; others

Other: Fugue, pf/str, 1948; The Merchant's Song (P. Coombs), A, pf, 1951; 2 Pieces, str, 1957; 2 Movts, str, 1958

Principal publishers: American Composers Edition, Schirmer, Warner Bros.

BARBARA A. PETERSEN

Andrée, Elfrida (*b* Visby, 19 Feb 1841; *d* Göteborg, 11 Jan 1929). Swedish composer, conductor and organist. She was the first woman organist and telegraphist in Sweden, the first to compose chamber and orchestral music and the first to conduct a symphony orchestra. In 1879 she became a member of the Swedish Kungliga Musikaliska Akademien. Andrée and her sister (who was later the famous opera singer Fredrika Stenhammar), were first taught music by their father. In 1855 Elfrida went to Stockholm and two years later passed her examination as the first woman organist in Sweden. In 1860 she studied composition with Ludvig Norman and in 1870 with Niels Gade in Copenhagen. She used her influence to bring about the revision of a law enabling women to hold the office of organist, and in 1861 was employed as an organist in Stockholm. In 1867 she moved to Göteborg, where she was organist at the cathedral until she died. She performed frequently and conducted performances of her works for choir and orchestra. In 1897 she took charge of the so-called Labour Concerts, for which she organized about 800 concerts. A typical feminist, her motto was 'the education of womankind'.

Andrée composed more than a hundred works, in the style of contemporary Scandinavian composers influenced by the Leipzig school, above all Mendelssohn and Schumann. Her chamber and symphonic music are closely related to that of Norman and Gade. The influence of Mendelssohn and also the French Romantic organ school is evident in her first Organ Symphony. Her music was performed mostly in Göteborg. *Snöfrid* (1879), a ballad for soloists, mixed choir and orchestra, was performed several times at the turn of the century, and the Organ Symphony has always been highly esteemed by organists. During the 1980s new interest in her music arose, and her chamber music is widely performed in Scandinavia.

WORKS
selective list
MSS in S-Skma; complete catalogue in S-Sm

Fritiofs saga (opera, S. Lagerlöf), unperf.; lib (Göteborg, 1899)
Orch: 2 syms., C, 1869, a, 1893; ov., D, 1873 (later rev.); 2 suites from Fritiofs saga

Elfrida Andrée at the organ of Göteborg Cathedral

Chamber: Pf Qnt, e (Stockholm, 1865); Pf Qt, a, 1865; 2 str qts, A, 1861, d, 1887; 2 pf trios, c, 1860, g (Stockholm, 1887); 2 vn sonatas, Bb, n.d., Eb, 1872; 2 romanser, vn, pf (Stockholm, 1884); 3 romanser, vn, pf (no.2, 1872)
Pf solo: Sonata, A, op.3 (Copenhagen, 1873); Tonbilder, op.4 (Copenhagen, 1875); 5 smärre tonbilder, op.7 (Stockholm, 1880)
Organ: 2 org syms., no.1, b (London, 1892), no.2, Eb, with brass insts, c1892 [arr. of vn sonata, Eb]; Andante, G, and Larghetto, c (Slite, 1975); arrs. of Swedish chorales
Choral: Snöfrid (V. Rydberg), soloists, mixed choir, orch, 1879, vs (Stockholm, 1884); Ur Drömlif (Rydberg), a cappella (Göteborg, 1882); Svensk mässa [Swedish Mass], no.1, 1902, vs (Copenhagen, 1907); Svensk mässa no.2, 1903
Songs: I Templet, 1v, pf/org (Stockholm, 1871, repr., 1929); Skogsrået, 1v, pf (Rydberg) (Göteborg, 1878); 3 sånger med piano, op.8 (Oslo, 1881); other songs and arrs. of folksongs

BIBLIOGRAPHY
SchmidlD
E. M. Stuart: *Elfrida Andrée* (Stockholm, 1925)
E. Stenhammar, ed.: *Fredrika Stenhammar: Brev* [Letters of Fredrika Stenhammar] (Uppsala, 1958)
A. Lönn: *Elfrida Andrée: Presentation av ett nytt källmaterial* [A Presentation of New Source Material] (Stockholm, 1965)
M. Larson: *Elfrida Andrée: Sveriges första kvinnliga organist* [Sweden's First Woman Organist] (Katrineholm, 1971)
E. Öhrström: *Borgerliga kvinnors musicerande i 1800-talets Sverige* [Middle-Class Women Playing Music in 19th-Century Sweden] (Göteborg, 1987)

EVA ÖHRSTRÖM

Anna Amalia, Duchess of Saxe-Weimar: portrait (1770) by Johann Ernst Heinsius

Anna Amalia (i), Princess of Prussia (*b* Berlin, 9 Nov 1723; *d* Berlin, 30 March 1787). German patron of music, amateur musician and composer. The youngest sister of Frederick the Great, she first studied music under Frederick himself and the Berlin cathedral organist Gottlieb Hayne. Though her talent was inferior to her brother's, she reached a high level of accomplishment as a keyboard player, and was fairly proficient as a violinist and flautist. The soirées in her royal apartments were attended by the artists and intelligentsia of Berlin and Europe, and her library, established in about 1735, reflected both a breadth of general education and a highly professional musical training.

She did not begin studying composition in earnest until her mid-30s. J. P. Kirnberger became her Kapellmeister in 1758, and under his tutelage she was able to display a remarkable knowledge of counterpoint. She composed a setting of C. W. Ramler's *Der Tod Jesu* before C. H. Graun did, with such success that Kirnberger later published part of it in his *Kunst des reinen Satzes* as a model for professionals. She also produced a few sonatas, marches, chorales, arias and songs. The musical part of her library (the Amalien-Bibliothek) contains only one small bundle of works by her; it is unlikely that much more ever existed (a few attractive instrumental pieces were edited by G. Lenzewski, Berlin, 1927–8). Like Frederick, she allowed her musical taste to become reactionary; the instinct that made her such an apt student of counterpoint and of the old masters prevented her from seeing much virtue in newer styles. In a letter to Kirnberger about *Iphigénie en Tauride* she expressed a particularly unfavourable opinion of Gluck, whom she found greatly inferior to Graun and J. A. Hasse; however, she gave support to C. P. E. Bach and a few other progressive musicians.

Amalia's real significance to music, however, lies in her music library, a collection of incalculable value. It is particularly rich in 18th-century music – that of J. S. Bach above all. She willed her library to the Joachimsthalschen Gymnasium in Berlin. In 1914 the musical portion was transferred on permanent loan to the Royal Library in Berlin, remaining intact and under its own name there. The Blechschmidt catalogue, listing all musical items ever belonging to the library (680 items) regardless of their present availability, is the most complete to date.

BIBLIOGRAPHY

Choron-FayolleD; FétisB; GerberL; GerberNL; Grove1 (F. Gehring); SainsburyD; SchillingE; SchmidlD

C. Sachs: 'Prinzessin Amalie von Preussen als Musikerin', Hohenzollern-Jb 1910, 181

R. Eitner: Katalog der Musikalien-Sammlung des Joachimsthalschen Gymnasium zu Berlin (Berlin, 1884); repr. in MMg, xvi, suppl.

F. Bose: 'Anna Amalie von Preussen und Johann Philipp Kirnberger', Mf, x (1957), 129–35

E. R. Blechschmidt: Die Amalienbibliothek (Berlin, 1965)

E. E. Löhr: Das Werk der Prinzessin von Preussen, Anna Amalie, im mentalitätsgeschichtlichen und biographischen Kontext (diss., U. of Freiburg im Breisgau, in preparation)

EUGENE HELM

Anna Amalia [Amalie] **(ii),** Duchess of Saxe-Weimar (b Wolfenbüttel, 24 Oct 1739; d Weimar, 10 April 1807). German patron, amateur musician and composer. She was the daughter of Duke Karl I of Brunswick and a niece of Frederick the Great. As a child she was given a good musical education. At the age of 16 she married the 18-year-old Duke Ernst August Konstantin of Saxe-Weimar; after his death two years later until the accession of her eldest son Duke Karl August on 3 September 1775 she conducted the regency. She continued to take lessons in composition and keyboard playing from the leading musician in Weimar at that time, Ernst Wilhelm Wolf (later the court Kapellmeister), and gathered round her a group of scholars, poets and musicians. In this 'court of the muses', as Wilhelm Bode called it, whose members included C. M. Wieland, J. G. Herder and eventually Goethe, Anna Amalia herself played a significant part in bringing together the poetry of 'Weimar Classicism' and the music of the time. J. A. Hiller's most successful Singspiel, Die Jagd (dedicated to the duchess), received its first performance in Weimar in 1770, and Weimar was also the scene of the première (28 May 1773) of the 'first German opera', Anton Schweitzer's setting of Wieland's Alceste. After the destruction of the theatre by fire in 1774, Anna Amalia continued the tradition of the Singspiel with performances in the amateur court theatre of her own compositions to texts by Goethe. Her Singspiel Erwin und Elmire (1776), without being eclectic in effect, reveals an intimate familiarity with the German Singspiel of Hiller and the contemporary Italian opera remarkable for an amateur, and shows thorough technical competence and spontaneous inventiveness. The majority of pieces, apart from occasional folklike songs, belong stylistically to the Empfindsamkeit, in the manner of Hiller and Schweitzer, combining features of song and of arioso. But Anna Amalia's significance lies mainly in the decisive influence exerted by her artistic convictions on German intellectual life at the period of its flowering in Weimar. Her collection of about 2000 volumes, acquired mainly during her visit to Italy, is now in the Zentralbibliothek der Deutschen Klassik, Weimar.

For illustration see p. 17.

WORKS

MSS in D-WRl

Erwin und Elmire (Singspiel, J. W. von Goethe), Weimar, 24 May 1776; vocal score, ed. M. Friedlaender (Leipzig, 1921)

Das Jahrmarktsfest zu Plundersweilern (Goethe), Weimar, 20 Oct 1778

Divertimento, pf, cl, va, vc (Weimar, n.d.)

Other works are of doubtful attribution

BIBLIOGRAPHY

Choron-FayolleD; FétisB; GerberL; Grove1 (F. Gehring); MGG (A. A. Abert) SainsburyD; SchillingE; SchmidlD

W. Bode: Amalie, Herzogin von Weimar (Berlin, 1908)

H. Abert: Goethe und die Musik (Stuttgart, 1922)

A. Krille: Beiträge zur Geschichte der Musikerziehung und Musikübung der deutschen Frau (Berlin, 1938)

R. Münnich: 'Aus der Musikationsammlung der Weimarer Landesbibliothek, besonders dem Nachlass der Anna Amalia', Aus der Geschichte der Landesbibliothek zu Weimar und ihrer Sammlungen, Festschrift zur Feier ihres 250jährigen Bestehens (Jena, 1941)

O. Heuschele: Herzogin Anna Amalia (Munich, 1947)

ANNA AMALIE ABERT

Anselmi, Lucia Contini. See CONTINI ANSELMI, LUCIA.

Anspach [Ansbach], **Elizabeth,** Margravine of [Craven, Elizabeth] (b London, 17 Dec 1750; d Naples, bur. 13 Jan 1828). English composer and playwright. She was the daughter of the Earl of Berkeley and at 16 married William Craven, later Earl of Craven, by whom she had seven children. Beautiful, lively and indiscreet, she loved amateur theatricals and music. Her first play, The Sleep-Walker (1778), was published by Walpole at Strawberry Hill and her comedy The Miniature Picture received an indifferent performance at Drury Lane in 1780. She provided music, as did Samuel Arnold and Tommaso Giordani, for her afterpiece The Silver Tankard. This had some success in July 1781 at the Haymarket Theatre, but a week earlier an adaptation of her Christmas entertainment The Baron, with music by Arnold, had been a flop.

In 1783 she and her husband separated; she then travelled extensively, publishing a book on her trip through the Crimea to Constantinople. She settled in Anspach with the Margrave, Christian Frederick (1736–1806), and wrote French plays and arranged productions for the court theatre, which had a good orchestra. They married immediately after Craven's death in 1791 and settled in England. Her private theatricals at Brandenburg House, their London home, dazzled and scandalized polite society. She flung herself into acting, singing, writing and composing. The casts were stiffened by a few professionals and in 1799 she allowed her opera *The Princess of Georgia* to be performed at Covent Garden for the benefit of the actor Fawcett. The published text shows that she composed six of the airs and that at Brandenburg House she sang the good fairy Nainda. None of her music survives apart from a two-part arrangement of her setting of *O mistress mine*, published about 1795. Her *Memoirs* were published in London in 1826.

BIBLIOGRAPHY

DNB (E. D. Cook); *LS*

A. M. Broadley and L. Melville: *The Beautiful Lady Craven* (London, 1914)

R. Fiske: *English Theatre Music in the Eighteenth Century* (London, 1973, 2/1986)

OLIVE BALDWIN, THELMA WILSON

Aorena, Mme. *See* LILI'UOKALANI.

Appeldoorn, Dina (*b* Rotterdam, 24 Dec 1884; *d* The Hague, 5 Dec 1938). Dutch composer and pianist. She studied with F. E. A. Koeberg and Johan Wagenaar. She began her career as a piano teacher in The Hague, but gradually turned to composition. Her choral works, including *Het Zwervers'Lied*

Elizabeth Anspach (Elizabeth Craven): portrait (c1776) attributed to Thomas Beach

(1936), were performed by the male-voice choir Die Haghe Sanghers and some of her orchestral works were given their premières by the Utrecht city orchestra (notably her symphony 'De Nordzee' in 1925) and the Rotterdam PO. Her output includes two symphonies, the symphonic poem *Pêcheurs d'Islande* (1912), an impressionist Pastorale for alto saxophone and orchestra (1934), chamber music, the three-act children's operetta *Duinsprookje* (1927) and many songs.

HELEN METZELAAR

Appignani, Adelaide Orsola [Aspri, Orsola] (*b* Rome, *c*1807; *d* Rome, 30 Sept 1884). Italian composer, singer and conductor. After her father's death, her mother married the violinist Andrea Aspri and Appignani adopted her stepfather's surname and used Orsola as her first name. She studied with Valentino Fioravanti. On 6 January 1833 she sang Smeton in a performance of Donizetti's *Anna Bolena*, given by the Roman Accademia Filarmonica at Palazzo Lancellotti. Already a member of that academy, she was offered honorary membership of the Accademia di S Cecilia, Rome, on 13 September 1842. As a conductor she was active in Rome and Florence (1839). She was also a singing teacher and had among her pupils the tenor Settimio Malvezzi. She married Count Girolamo Cenci-Bolognetti. Her *melodramma Clara di Clevers* was first performed at the Teatro Nazionale, Bologna, in 1876, on the inauguration of its change of name from Teatro di Via Nosadella.

WORKS

DRAMATIC

Le avventure di una giornata (melodramma, 2) Rome, Teatro Valle, 13 May 1827
I riti indiani, 1834, unperf.
Francesca da Rimini, 1835, unperf.
I pirati (melodramma, 2, G. E. Bidera), Rome, Teatro Alibert, spr. 1843
Clara di Clevers (melodramma, 2), Bologna, Teatro Nazionale, spr. 1876

OTHER WORKS

Inst: Sinfonia, Rome, 28 Nov 1834; pf pieces
Vocal: La redenzione di Roma, cantata, 1871

BIBLIOGRAPHY

SchmidlD
Catalogo dei maestri compositori dei professori di musica e dei soci di onore della Congregazione e Accademia di S Cecilia di Roma residente nel collegio di S Carlo a Catinari (Rome, 1845), 31
G. Radiciotti: *Teatro e musica in Roma nel secondo quarto di secolo XIX* (Rome, 1905)
A. Cametti: *L'Accademia filarmonica romana dal 1821 al 1860* (Rome, 1924), 19, 54
P. Adkins Chiti: *Donne in musica* (Rome, 1982)
A. Bonaventura: 'Le donne italiane e la musica', *RMI*, xxxii (1925), 519–34

MATTEO SANSONE

Archer (Balestreri), **Violet** (*b* Montreal, 24 April 1913). Canadian composer and pianist. She legally adopted the name Archer in 1940. Her formative years were spent in Italy and her earliest memories are of Italian music. She studied piano and organ at McGill Conservatory and composition at McGill University, Montreal (BMus 1936), and in the USA at Yale University (BMus 1948, MMus 1949); her teachers included Claude Champagne, Douglas Clarke, Béla Bartók (1942, New York) and Paul Hindemith (1947–9). She played percussion in the Montreal Women's SO from 1940 to 1947, taught theory and the piano and worked as an accompanist. With the performance of her *Scherzo sinfonico* by the Montreal SO in 1940 and the choice by Sir Adrian Boult of her *Britannia: a Joyful Overture* (1941) for broadcast by the BBC in 1942 (the work was relayed to the troops in Europe), her career as a composer was launched; her choral and orchestral work *The Bell* won the Woods-Chandler prize at Yale in 1949. She was percussionist in the New Haven SO from 1947 to 1949, also teaching in summer schools at the University of Alberta, 1948–9, and she travelled to Europe in 1950, performing her music in England. She was composer-in-residence at North Texas State College from 1950 to 1953 (and also studied musicology there with Otto Kinkeldey, 1952–3), taught at Cornell University in 1952 and at the University of Oklahoma, 1953–61. She moved to the University of Alberta in 1962, where, after her retirement as emeritus professor, she continued as a part-time lecturer; she has also remained active as a teacher of composition to young people.

Archer's music is on the one hand dissonantly contrapuntal yet on the other refreshingly folksy. Early modality gave way to a more chromatic style, with a period during the 1950s in which the influence of Hindemith and Gebrauchsmusik is strongly evident. Although she taught 12-note technique to her students in the USA, she has not used it in her own music, and it is mainly in her variation technique or in a short-lived expressionistic phase in the mid-1960s that her study of Arnold Schoenberg is discernible. Her works are generally characterized by economical, almost lean, textures, skilful manipulation of form, and counterpoint. She

Violet Archer

has explored new sonorities using parallelism and folk tunes, while rejecting serialism and chance music. Her open-minded approach to new sounds is reflected in her use in the 1970s of electronic music.

Archer was awarded the honorary DMus by McGill University in 1971 and by the University of Windsor in 1986, and the LLD by the University of Calgary in 1989. Her many distinctions include the Creative and Performance Award of Edmonton in 1972, induction into Edmonton's Cultural Hall of Fame in 1987, membership of the Order of Canada in 1983 and the Canadian Music Council's Composer of the Year award in 1984. There was a three-day Violet Archer Festival in Edmonton in October 1985.

WORKS
selective list

Music-theatre: Sganarelle (comedy opera, 1, Archer, after Molière, trans. T. S. Eliot), 9 solo vv, 2 perc, pf/str, 1973; The Meal (opera, 1, R. H. Wilson), T, Bar, 1983

Orch: Poem, 1940; Scherzo sinfonico, 1940; Britannia: a Joyful Overture, 1941; Fantasia concertante, fl, ob, cl, str, 1941; Fantasy, cl, str, 1942; Cl Concertino, 1946, rev. 1956; Fantasy on a Ground, 1946, rev. 1956; Sym., 1946; Fanfare and Passacaglia, 1948–9; Pf Conc. no.1, 1956; Divertimento, 1957; Vn Conc., 1959; 3 Sketches, 1961; Prelude: Incantation, 1964; Sinfonietta, 1968; Sinfonia, 1969; Little Suite, str orch, 1970; Divertimento, pf, str, 1985; Evocations, 2 pf, orch,

1987; Improvisation on a Name, chamber orch, 1987; 4 Dialogues, gui, chamber orch, 1990

Chamber and solo inst: Str Qt no.1, 1940; Sonata, fl, cl, pf, 1944; Qt, fl, ob, cl, bn, 1945; Fantasy, vn, pf, 1946; 2 Pieces, fl, 1947; Divertimento no.1, ob, cl, bn, 1949; Str Qt no.2, 1949; Fantasy in the Form of a Passacaglia, chamber ens, 1951; Str Trio no.1, 1953; Pf Trio no.1, 1954; Prelude and Allegro, vn, pf, 1954; 3 Duets, 2 vn, 1955; Vc Sonata, 1956; Vn Sonata no.1, 1956; Pf Trio no.2, 1957; Divertimento no.2, ob, vn, vc, 1957; Str Trio no.2, 1961; Divertimento, brass qnt, 1963; Introduction, Dance and Finale, tpt, hn, trbn, tuba, harp/pf, perc, 1963; Hn Sonata, 1965; Cl Sonata, 1970; Dance, vn, vc, 1970; 3 Little Studies, vn, pf, 1970; Suite, 4 vn, 1971; Sonata, a sax, pf, 1972; Ob Sonata, 1973; Little Suite, tpt, pf, 1975; Simple Tune, rec, pf, 1975; Sonata, va, vc, pf, 1976; Suite, solo fl, 1976; Ob Sonatina, 1977; Bn Sonatina, 1978; Cl Sonatina, 1978; Fantasy on 'Blanche comme la neige', gui, 1978; Divertimento, sax qt, 1979; 4 Duets, vn, pf, 1979; Bn Sonata, 1980; Capriccio, vc, pf, 1981; 12 Miniatures, vn, pf, 1981; Soliloquies, cl, 1981; Sonata, vc, 1981; Str Qt no.3, 1981; Statements, fl, 1982; Celebration, brass qnt, 1983; Ikpakhuag, vn, vc, pf, 1984; 6 Miniatures, vc, 1984; 6 Miniatures, db, 1984; 6 Miniatures, va, pf, 1984; Signatures, a fl, 1984; Ivavati, brass qnt, 1985; Moods, cl, a sax, 1985; The Dancing Kitten, vn, pf, 1986; 6 Miniatures, str brass, pf, 1986; Improvisation, snare drum, 1990; Prelude and Dance, timp, 1990; One Fifth on Four, xyl, cel, pf, cl, vc, 1991

Kbd: Org Sonatina, 1944; Pf Sonata, 1945, rev. as Pf Sonata no.1, 1957; Pf sonatinas no.1, 1945, no.2, 1946; 6 Preludes, pf, 1947; 3 Sketches, 2 pf, 1947; Suite, pf, 1947; Theme and Variations on 'Là haut', pf, 1952: 10 Folk Songs, pf 4 hands, 1953; 11 Short Pieces, pf, 1960; Chorale Improvisation on 'O Worship the King', org, 1967; Improvisations, pf, 1968; Pf Sonatina no.3, 1973; 4 Bagatelles, pf, 1977; Prelude and Fantasy on 'Winchester New', org, 1978; Festive Fantasy, org, 1979; Pf Sonata no.2, 1979; Variations on 'Aberystwyth', org, 1984; 4 Miniatures, accordion, 1988

Choral: Lamentations of Jeremy (Bible), SATB, orch, 1947; The Bell (J. Donne), SATB, orch, 1949; Landscapes (T. S. Eliot), unacc. SATB, 1950; 3 French Canadian Folk Songs, unacc. SATB, 1953; Proud Horses (Sampley), unacc. SATB, 1953; 2 Songs (A. Bass), SSA, ob, pf, 1955; Apocalypse (Bible, *Revelation*, iv–v), S, SATB, brass, timp, 1958; Introit and Choral Prayer (liturgical, G. R. Campbell), SATB, org, 1962; Sing, the Muse, choral cycle (J. Marston, W. Shakespeare, W. Drummond, W. Raleigh), unacc. SATB, 1964; Cantata sacra (medieval texts), S, A, T, Bar, B, orch, 1966; Centennial Springtime, unison vv, pf, 1967; I will lift up mine eyes (Ps cxxi), SATB, org, 1967; O sing unto the Lord (Ps xcvi), SA, 2 tpt/org, 1968; Psalmody (Pss cxxx, xlvi, ciii, cxlviii), Bar, SATB, 1978; The Cat and the Moon (W. B. Yeats), SATB, pf, 1983; Reflections (D. Carter), unacc. SSAATB, 1983

Vocal: 2 Songs (W. Blake), S, cl, 1958, rev. for Mez, 1987; Moon Songs (Vachel-Lindsay), Mez, pf, 1976; Northern Landscape (A. J. M. Smith), Mez, pf, 1978; A Sprig of Flowers (Kuan Han Ch'ing), T, fl, pf, 1979; Primeval (Native American songs,

trans. F. Densmore and J. A. Neihardt), T, pf, 1980; The Owl Queen, S/T, pf, 1989; Surly, Burly Shirley (S. Ottman), S/T, pf, 1989; Northern Journey, Bar, pf, 1990
Many other works incl.: Episodes, elec tape, 1973; Someone Cares, film score, 1976; Whatsoever Things Are True, film score, 1980

BIBLIOGRAPHY
CC (M. Matthews); EMC 2 (E. Keillor, H. Kallman)
C. Foreman: 'Violet Archer – Sonata no.2: "All Great Music Is Variations"', Composers West, iii/March (1980), 4–5
H. D. Huiner: The Choral Music of Violet Archer (diss., U. of Iowa, 1980)
G. Hicks: 'Our Cultural Heritage: Violet Archer', Encore (1982), Jan, 6–10
P. McCoppin: 'Violet Archer at 70: at Last, a Freedom to Compose', Music Scene, no.332 (1983), 7–9
J . Brown: 'An Interview with Canadian Composer Violet Archer', Prairie Sounds, iv/wint. (1985), 3–8
R. Weber: 'A Western Voice with Historical Ties', Music, ix/1 (1986), 14–16
G. A. Proctor: 'Notes on Violet Archer', Musical Canada: Words and Music Honouring Helmut Kallmann, ed. J. Beckwith and F. A. Hall (Toronto, 1988), 188–202
J. Reid: 'An Interview with Dr Violet Archer', Prairie Sounds (1989), Sept, 5–9; (1990), Jan, 9–10; (1990), April, 7–8
L. Hartig: Violet Archer: a Bio-Bibliography (Westport, CT, 1991)
GAYNOR G. JONES

Aretz (de Ramón y Rivera), Isabel (b Buenos Aires, 13 April 1913). Venezuelan folklorist, ethnomusicologist and composer of Argentine birth. She married the Venezuelan folklorist Luis Felipe Ramón y Rivera. She studied the piano under Rafael González (1923–31) and composition with Athos Palma (1928–33) at the Conservatorio Nacional de Música, Buenos Aires, orchestration with Heitor Villa-Lobos in Brazil (1937), anthropology with José Imbelloni, ethnography with Enrique Palavecino, and folklore and musicology with Carlos Vega (1938–44) at the Museo de Ciencias Naturales in Buenos Aires. Her work as a researcher and a teacher from the 1940s onwards has made her a leading authority on South American folk and traditional music.

As a composer, Aretz has naturally turned to the indigenous and Afro-Hispanic folk traditions that she knows so well. Her earlier orchestral pieces Puneñas (1937) and Serie infantil (1939) evoke highland Andean culture and Argentine folk culture respectively. Likewise, Serie criolla (1949) relies on the folk genres of the cueca, vidala and triunfo. In the late 1950s and early 1960s she wrote three short ballets, Ahónaya (1958), Movimiento de percusión (1960) and Páramo (1961), that also recreate most effectively expressive aspects of indigenous culture.

Aretz believes in combining indigenous sources with modern composition techniques. In Birimbao (1968), for four timpani and tape, the amplified sounds of the birimbao (jew's harp) of the Venezuelan Guajiro Indians are heard alongside a simulation of talking drums, which creates a ritualistic character. Similarly, in the cantata-ballet Yekuana (1971), for eight solo voices, orchestra and tape, recorded birdsongs make up the tape interludes, while the text refers to Yekuana Indian mythology. Afro-Venezuelan melodies and rhythms inspired the cantata Simiente (1964), based on the text 'Los negros' from Juan Liscano's Nuevo Mundo Orinoco. Aretz's more recent works show a further, more abstract involvement with native sources. Kwaltaya (1980), for soprano and tape, described as an 'ethnodrama in three scenes', was inspired by Venezuelan Indian, Haitian and creole world-views; the taped music consists of a collage-combination of the most varied Caribbean musical traditions. Her Hombre al cosmos, for piano and tape (1993) was given its première in New York by North/South Consonance.

WORKS
selective list

Ballet: El llamado de la tierra, 1952; Ahónaya, 1958; Movimiento de percusión, 1960; Páramo, 1961

Orch: Puneñas, 1937; Serie infantil, str, 1939; 2 acuarelas, str, 1940; Serie criolla, small orch, 1949; Segunda serie criolla, str, 1950; Constelación espectral, 1982

Vocal orch: Poema araucano, S, small orch, 1950; Soneto de la fe en Cristo, S, str, 1954; Tocuyana, ballet suite, vv, orch, 1957; Simiente (cantata, J. Liscano), nar, S, Mez, T, B, orch, 1964; Yekuana (cantata-ballet, D. Barandiaran), 8 solo vv, orch, tape, 1971; Argentina hasta la muerte, nar, chamber orch, 2 tapes, 1975; Gritos de una ciudad, 2 nar, small orch, tape, 1979; Padre libertador (oratorio, E. Blanco, A. Baeza Flores, P. Neruda), nar, solo vv, chorus, tape, 1982

Chamber: Altiplano, 1v, fl, pf, 1937; Tres en sonata, vn, va, pf, 1965; Birimbao, 4 timp, tape, 1968

Vocal: Primera serie criolla (M. Silvano de Régoli), 1v, pf, 1937–40; 3 cantos indios, 1v, pf, 1960; 5 fulías sobre melodías folklóricas venezolanas, 1v, pf, 1965; Kwaltaya (ethnodrama, 3 scenes), S, tape, 1980

Kbd (pf unless otherwise stated): Sonata, 1931; De mi infancia, 1935; Por la senda de Kh'asana, 1935; Segunda serie criolla, 1942; 3 preludios negros, 1954; Comentarios musicales a 3 poemas de Andrés Eloy Blanco, 1961; Sonata 1965, 1965; Suite para clave, hpd, 1967; Hombre al cosmos (3 encuentros siderales), pf, tape, 1993

Principal publisher: Ricordi Americana

BIBLIOGRAPHY
Composers of the Americas, xvii (Washington DC, 1971), 27–32
R. Stevenson: 'Isabel Aretz, Composer: a Birthday Tribute', *Inter-American Music Review*, v/2 (1983), 3–7

GERARD BÉHAGUE

Arho, Anneli (*b* Helsinki, 12 April 1951). Finnish composer. She studied composition, theory (diploma 1989) and ear training at the Sibelius Academy, and composition with Jukka Tiensuu both at the Academy and privately. She continued her studies in Freiburg (1977–9) with Klaus Huber and Brian Ferneyhough. In 1979 she was appointed to teach at the Sibelius Academy. Her output is small but every work has a distinctive identity. Both *Once Upon a Time* (1979), for wind quintet, and *Les temps emboités* (1987), for three cellos, reveal her interest in the philosophy of time. Among her other works are *Answer*, for mezzo-soprano, horn and string quartet (1978), *Minos'* for harpsichord (1978), and *Par comparaison*, for three cellos with or without pantomime (1981).

KIMMO KORHONEN

Arizti (Sobrino), Cecilia (*b* Havana, 28 Oct 1856; *d* Havana, 30 June 1930). Cuban composer, pianist and teacher. She studied first of all with her father, the pianist and composer Fernando Arizti, and continued more formally with Francisco Fuente and Nicolás Ruiz Espadero. In 1887 a number of her piano works, including *Danza*, *Mazurka* and *Reverie*, were published in New York. She taught the piano privately and at Peyrellade's Conservatorio de Música, Havana, and gave recitals in Cuba and, in 1896, in New York; she also wrote a manual of piano technique. In addition to several piano works, her compositions include violin pieces, two works for small band, and a piano trio (1893, the first chamber work to have been written by a Cuban woman); written in a traditional harmonic language, they are marked by melodic beauty and careful formal construction. Her piano writing shows the influence of Chopin. In 1959 the Biblioteca Nacional José Marti in Cuba began publishing a series of her piano works. Her manuscripts are conserved in the Biblioteca Nacional and the Museo Nacional de la Música, Havana.

BIBLIOGRAPHY
J. Calero and L. Valdés Quesada: *Cuba musical* (Havana, 1929)
E. Pérez Sanjuro: *Historia de la música cubana* (Miami, 1986)
M. Barnet: *Autógrafos cubanos* (Havana, 1989)
A. Valdés: *Mujeres notables en la música colonial cubana* (Havana, 1992)

ALICIA VALDÉS CANTERO

Arkwright, Marian (Ursula) (*b* Norwich, 25 Jan 1863; *d* Highclere, nr Newbury, 23 March 1922). English composer. She studied music at Durham University (MusB 1895, MusD 1913). Her symphonic suite *Winds of the World* won a prize offered by the magazine *The Gentlewoman* for an orchestral work by a woman, and her Suite for strings was written for the Australian Exhibition of Women's Work at Melbourne in 1907. She was a leading figure in the Rural Music Schools movement.

Arkwright's music is heavily influenced by the composers of the so-called English Renaissance, especially C. V. Stanford, from whom features of Brahms's vocabulary are derived at second-hand. Although austere, her style is thoroughly English, and frequently anticipates that of Ralph Vaughan Williams. Her vocal writing is particularly idiomatic: the classical simplicity of the 'Recordare' (for four-part female chorus), in the Requiem, goes some way to redeem an otherwise disappointing work. Her pieces for children, however, of which *The Dragon of Wantley* is the best, evince a sense of fun which makes their music immediately attractive.

WORKS
printed works published in London
unless otherwise stated

Stage: The Water-Babies (operetta, C. Kingsley)
Orch: Winds of the World, sym. suite; Suite, str, 1907
Chamber: 12 Duets, 2 vn, vc and pf ad lib (1896); 6 Duets, 2 vn, vc and pf ad lib (1896); 4 Duets, 2 vn, vc and pf ad lib (1896); 2 Concert Pieces, va, pf (1908); pieces for ww
Vocal: Come, pretty wag (M. Peerson), partsong, 2vv (1897); In midst of woods (J. Munday), partsong, 2vv (1913); Requiem Mass, S, Bar, chorus 8vv, orch (1914); The Dragon of Wantley, ballad, children's chorus 3vv, pf (1915); The lark now leaves his watery nest (W. Davenant), S, Mez (York, 1924); The last rhyme of true Thomas, chorus, str; ? songs
Arr. of Mozart: Kyrie, d, vs (1902)

BIBLIOGRAPHY
CohenE; *Grove5* (E. Blom); *MGG* (A. D. Walker)
British Music Society Annual (1920), 80, 140–41
A. E. Hull, ed.: *Dictionary of Modern Music and Musicians* (London, 1924)

NIGEL BURTON

Armer, Elinor (*b* Oakland, CA, 6 Oct 1939). American composer and pianist. She studied composition at Mills College (BA 1961), the University of California, Berkeley (1966–8), and California State University,

San Francisco (MA 1972). Her teachers included Darius Milhaud and Leon Kirchner (composition), and Alexander Libermann (piano). In 1976 she was appointed to teach at San Francisco Conservatory of Music, where she is head of the composition department. Writing with a rich harmonic vocabulary and colourful scoring, Armer has developed an individualistic style. Her compositions are often programmatic or include text; theatrical elements bring pieces to life. She is collaborating with the author Ursula K. Le Guin on an imaginative series entitled *Uses of Music in Uttermost Parts* about an archipelago of islands each of which experiences music in an unusual manner, for example as food, sexual attractant or geological phenomena.

WORKS
selective list

Orch and orch with nar: Pearl, 1986; The Great Instrument of the Geggerets (U. K. Le Guin), nar, orch, 1989 [Uses of Music in Uttermost Parts no.3]

Inst and inst with nar: Thaw, pf, 1974; Recollections and Revel, vc, pf, 1978; Str Qt, 1983; The Seasons of Oling (Le Guin), nar, va, vc, pf, perc, 1987 [Uses of Music no.2]; Open and Shut (Le Guin), reader, ob/eng hn, cl/b cl, vn, vc, db, 1991 [Uses of Music no.5]; Sailing among the Pheromones, gui, mar, harp, tape, 1991 [Uses of Music no.6]

Vocal: Spin, Earth (J. R. Baughan), mixed vv, pf/org, 1970; Lockerbones/Airbones (Le Guin), Mez, fl, vn, pf, perc, 1983; Eating with the Hoi (Le Guin), S, nar, chorus, perc, 1986 [Uses of Music no.1]; A Season of Grief (A. Tennyson and W. Bynner), low v, pf, 1987; Anithaca (Le Guin), girls' vv, 1990 [Uses of Music no.4]; Island Earth (Le Guin), chorus, orch, 1993 [Uses of Music no.8]

Principal publishers: Elkus, Fallen Leaf, Lawson-Gould, MMB, Peters

Elinor Armer

Claude Arrieu

BIBLIOGRAPHY

P. Moor: 'Bay Area Women's Philharmonic: Armer "The Great Instrument of the Geggerets" ', *MusAm*, cix/6 (1989), 48–9

'A Conversation with Vivian Fine: Two Composers Talk Shop', *Strings*, v/5 (1991), 73–8

J. MICHELE EDWARDS

Arnim, Bettina von. *See* BRENTANO, BETTINA.

Arrieu, Claude (*b* Paris, 30 Nov 1903; *d* Paris, 7 March 1990). French composer. She studied at the Paris Conservatoire with Noël Gallon, Georges Caussade, Marguerite Long, Jean Roger-Ducasse and Paul Dukas, taking a *premier prix* for composition in 1932. Her subsequent career was in teaching and in French radio (1946), where she worked as a producer and as assistant head of the sound-effects department. A prolific composer, she retained in her music the ease of flow and elegance of structure that typified Parisian neo-classicism, while avoiding the often concomitant frivolity. Her technical mastery allowed her to use strict formal rules not as constraints but as supports for a spontaneous expression marked by vivacity, clarity of expression and a natural melodic vein. Arrieu's musical style places her in a direct line of composers descending from Emmanuel Chabrier, yet her harmonic manner is individual and she took a discriminating interest in later innovations: she was, for example, one of the first to work with Pierre Schaeffer, though she did not use electronic means in any of her own concert works. Her radio score *Frédéric Général* won a Prix Italia in 1949.

WORKS
selective list
STAGE

Noé (imagerie musicale, 3, A. Obey), 1932–4; Strasbourg, Opéra, 29 Jan 1950
Cadet-Roussel (opéra bouffe, 5, A. de La Tourrasse, after J. Limozin), 1938–9; Marseilles, Opéra, 2 Oct 1953
Fête Galante (ballet, B. Kochno), 1947; Berne, 1947
Les deux rendez-vous (opéra-comique, 1, P. Bertin, after G. de Nerval), 1948; RTF, 22 June 1951
Le chapeau à musique (opérette enfantine, 2, Tourrasse and P. Dumaine), 1953; RTF, 1953
La princesse de Babylone (opéra bouffe, 3, P. Dominique, after Voltaire), 1953–5; Rheims, Opéra, 3 March 1960
La cabine téléphonique (opéra bouffe, 1, M. Vaucaire), 1958; RTF, 15 March 1959
Cymbeline (2, J. Tournier and M. Jacquemont, after W. Shakespeare), 1958–63; Quimper, 1971
Commedia umana (ballet, after Boccaccio), 1960; Nervi, 1960
Balthazar, ou Le mort-vivant (opéra bouffe, 1, Dominique), 1966, unperf.
La statue (ballet, J. Provins), 1968
Un clavier pour un autre (opéra bouffe, 1, J. Tardieu), 1969–70; Avignon, Opéra, 3 April 1971
Barberine (3, after A. de Musset), 1972, inc.
Les amours de Don Perlimpin et Belise en son jardin (imagerie lyrique, 4 tableaux, after F. García Lorca), Tours, Grand Théâtre, 1 March 1980
Many scores for the theatre, cinema and broadcasting

OTHER WORKS

Vocal orch: Cantate des sept poèmes d'amour en guerre (P. Eluard), S, Bar, orch, RTF, 1946; Mystère de Noël (L. Masson), 10 solo vv, chorus, orch, RTF, 1951
Orch: concs. for pf, 1932, vn, 1938, 2 pf, 1938, fl, 1946, vn, 1949, tpt, 1965; Partita, 1934; Petite suite, 1945; Suite, str, 1959; Variations classiques, str, 1970; many other pieces, most of them short
Chamber: Trio d'anches, ob, cl, bn, 1936; Sonatine, fl, pf, 1943; Histoires de Paris, str qt, db, perc, 1947; Vn Sonata, 1948; Wind Qnt, 1955; Pf Trio, 1957; Fantaisie lyrique, ondes martenot, pf, 1959; 5 mouvements, 4 cl, 1964; Cl Qt no.l, 1964; 2 pièces, str qnt, harp, hn, perc; Wind Dixtuor, 1967; Capriccio, cl, pf, 1970; Suite, ob, cl, bn, 1980; Suite, fl, ob, cl, bn, 1980; Cl Qt no.2, 1984; Impromptu II, ob, pf, 1985; many other pieces
Songs: Chansons bas (S. Mallarmé), 1933; Poèmes de Louise de Vilmorin, 1944; many other settings of poems by F. Jammes, L. Aragon, J. Cocteau and J. Tardieu
Radiophonic works incl. La coquille à planètes (P. Schaeffer), RTF, 1943–4; pf and unacc. choral works

Principal publishers: Amphion, Billaudot, Editions Français de Musique, Heugel, Leduc, Ricordi
FRANÇOISE ANDRIEUX

Asachi [née Teyber], **Elena** [Asaky, Héléne; Tayber; Teyber, Eleonora] (*b* Vienna, 30 Oct 1789; *d* Iaşi, 9 May 1877). Romanian composer, pianist and singer. She began musical studies in Dresden with her father, Anton Teyber, and continued in Vienna (1822–4) under the guidance of the opera singer Domenico Donzelli. She was subsequently appointed professor of music at Iaşi Conservatory, where she was also prominent as a pianist and composer (1827–63); she gave recitals and accompanied Romanian and foreign musicians on tours throughout Moldavia. She adapted the music of Vincenzo Bellini, D. F. E. Auber, Saverio Mercadante, Gaspare Spontini, Giuseppe Verdi and others for a series of Romanian plays. She was married to the writer Gheorghe Asachi, with whom she collaborated on various didactic publications.

WORKS
selective list

Fête pastorale des bergers moldaves (pastoral-vaudeville, G. Asachi), 1834; Iaşi, 10 April 1837
Contrabantul [The Smuggler] (comedy-vaudeville, 2), Iaşi, 20 Dec 1837
Ţiganii [The Gypsies] (vaudeville with songs, G. Asachi), Iaşi, 24 Jan 1856

Songs: Ballade moldave (G. Asachi) (Iaşi, 1834); Sie starb, sagst du (G. Asachi, trans. E. Asachi) (1837); Song of Society (G. Asachi) (Iaşi, 1849)

BIBLIOGRAPHY

T. Burada: *Elena Asachi* (Iaşi, 1887)
V. Cosma: 'Die Tonsetzerin und Klavierspielerin E. A.', *Tribuna României*, no.290 (15 April 1985)
—— : *Muzicieni din România* [Musicians from Romania] (Bucharest, 1989)
VIOREL COSMA

Aspri, Orsola. *See* APPIGNANI, ADELAIDE ORSOLA.

Assandra [Alessandra]**, Caterina** (*b* Pavia; *fl* 1609–18). Italian composer. A nun at the Convent of S Agata at Lomello, near Milan, she was one of a number of north Italian composers who published motets for a few voices and organ continuo in the new concertato style. Her op.1 has not survived; her *Motetti* op.2 (Milan, 1609) consists of two-and three-part motets with continuo following the model of Lodovico Viadana's *Cento concerti ecclesiastici* of 1602; vocal lines are melismatic, there is much imitation between the voices in duets, and where one voice is a bass it has a more ornate part than the continuo bass. The sequential approach to harmony, apparent for example in the works of Viadana and in Monteverdi's madrigals, can also be seen in Assandra's motets. The publication includes a canzona and litany by her teacher, Benedetto Re, *maestro di cappella* at Pavia Cathedral; she in turn contributed one motet each to his sacred publications of 1611 and 1618, and two of her 1609 motets were reprinted in German anthologies (*RISM* 1616², 1622²).

BIBLIOGRAPHY

FétisB; SchmidlD

J. L. A. Roche: *North Italian Liturgical Music in the Early 17th Century* (diss., U. of Cambridge, 1968)

——: *North Italian Church Music in the Age of Monteverdi* (Oxford, 1984)

J. Bowers and J. Tick, eds.: *Women Making Music: the Western Art Tradition, 1150–1950* (Urbana and Chicago, 1986), 130

C. Gianturco: 'Caterina Assandra, suora compositrice', *La musica sacra in Lombardia nella prima meta del seicento* (Como, 1987), 115–27

JEROME ROCHE

Athanasiu-Gardeev, Esmeralda (*b* Galaţi, 1834; *d* Bucharest, 1917) Romanian composer and pianist. She studied in Bucharest, then in Paris with Julius Schulhoff (piano and composition) and in St Petersburg with Anton Rubinstein (composition). She was married briefly to Vasile Hermeziu, then to the Russian General Gardeev, who introduced her to European aristocratic circles (many of her works are dedicated to King Charles I of Romania and members of the aristocracy) and, in particular, to the salons of George Sand, Nicolò Rubini, Sophie Menter, Camillo Sivori, Vasile Alecsandri, Grigore Ventura, Dumitru Kiriac-Georgescu, Anton Rubinstein and others. At the end of the Romanian War of Independence (1877–8), she settled in Bucharest, teaching the piano, singing and the lute. Her music was inspired by Romanian folklore, which in turn influenced Rubinstein (*The Demon* and *Sulamith*) – her *Rumänisches Charakterstück* op.44 is dedicated to him.

WORKS

selective list

Pf: Marş român [Romanian March], op.1; Alboum collectif, 4 bks: op.18, op.30, op.31, op.32; Rumänisches Charakterstück, op.44; 2 mazurkas; Myosotis, Souvenir de Odessa; Polca capricioasa; Romanţă fără cuvinte [Wordless Romance]; Scherzo

Choral: Imn [Hymn], mixed chorus

Songs: 3 Lieder, op.33 (J. von Eichendorff, O. Roquette, A. Wernherr); Collection de chansons, 7 bks, opp.35–41: op.35 (F. von Schiller, H. Heine), op.36 (Heine), op.37 (J. W. von Goethe), op.38 (Heine, Goethe, N. Lenau), op.39 (V. Alecsandri, D. Bolintineanu), op.40 (J.-J. Rousseau, E. Gardeev, V. Alecsandri), op.41 (V. Alecsandri); Si tu m'aimais, op.46 (E. Gardeyev)

Principal publishers: J. André, C. Gebauer, Lyra Română, C. Wolf

BIBLIOGRAPHY

O. L. Cosma: *Hronicul muzicii româneşti* [Romanian Music Chronicle], vii (1986); viii (1988)

VIOREL COSMA

Auenbrugger [D'Auenbrugg], **Marianna von** (*fl* Vienna; *d* 1786). Austrian keyboard player and composer. The daughter of Leopold von Auenbrugger, a well-known Austrian physician who wrote the German libretto for Antonio Salieri's comic opera *Der Rauchfangkehrer*, she studied composition with Salieri and published her only known work together with two of his odes. Marianna and her sister Katharina, both distinguished keyboard players, were known to Haydn and to the Mozart family. Haydn dedicated six of his piano sonatas to them (HXVI: 35–9 and 20). In a letter of 25 February 1780 to his publisher Artaria, Haydn wrote that, 'the approval of the *Demoiselles* von Auenbrugger . . . is most important to me, for their way of playing and genuine insight into music equal those of the greatest masters. Both deserve to be known throughout Europe through the public newspapers'. Leopold Mozart, in a letter to his wife (12 August 1773), also refers to 'the daughter of Dr Auenbrugger . . . who . . . play[s] extraordinarily well and [is] thoroughly musical'. Her *Sonata per il Clavicembalo o Forte piano* was published in Vienna by Artaria in about 1781. It is a three-movement Classical sonata of great charm and feeling.

BIBLIOGRAPHY

GerberL

W. S. Newman: *The Sonata in the Classic Era* (Chapel Hill, 1963)

S. Stern: *Women Composers: a Handbook* (Metuchen, NJ, 1978)

J. Meggett: *Keyboard Music by Women Composers* (Westport, CT, 1981)

S. Glickman, ed.: *Marianna D'Auenbrugg: Sonata per il Clavicembalo o Forte piano* (Bryn Mawr, PA, 1990)

SYLVIA GLICKMAN

Auernhammer, Josepha Barbara von (*b* Vienna, 25 Sept 1756; *d* Vienna, 30 Jan 1820). Austrian pianist and composer. She was a pupil of Leopold Kozeluch and (apparently) Georg Friedrich Richter. When Mozart decided to stay in Vienna and take pupils, she and Therese von Trattner became Mozart's favourite pupils. Mozart dedicated his piano and violin sonatas K296 and 376–80 to her, and composed the sonata for two pianos K448 for both of them. (It was Christoph Torricella, Mozart's editor, who inscribed Auernhammer's name on the variations for piano on 'Ah, vous dirais je, maman' K265.) Mozart and Auernhammer performed together on a number of occasions between the end of 1781 and the beginning of 1785. She was one of Mozart's first editors (Artaria designated her the supervisor of Mozart's sonatas and 'Variierte Arietten'). She was evidently exceptionally ugly, prompting Mozart to write on 22 August 1781 that 'her face could inspire "a portrait of the devil"' and on 27 June 1784 that, 'the rascal is frightful but she plays enchantingly'. When her father died in March 1782, Mozart took her to Baroness Waldstätten, who gave her a home and the security to continue her work. In 1786 she married Johann Bessenig (1752–1837), a civil servant with whom she had a daughter, Marianna, who sang. They later appeared together in concerts. She composed mainly piano music, especially variations, which reveal a comprehensive knowledge of piano technique and refined use of the instrument.

WORKS
printed works published in Vienna
unless otherwise stated

Kbd variations: 6 on Nel cor più non mi sento [G. Paisiello: La Molinara] (Speyer, 1790); 6 on Der Vogelfänger bin ich ja [Mozart: Die Zauberflöte] (Offenbach, 1792; 1793); 8 on contredanse [S. Viganò: La figlia mal custodita] (1794); 6 on La stessa, la stessissima [A. Salieri] (1799); 6 variazioni per il pianoforte (1801); 6 on march [Cherubini: Les deux journées] (1803); 6 variations sur un thème hongrois (1810); 10 on theme from ballet Les folies amoureuses (n.d.); 10 variations dédiées a Madame de Brown, op.63 (n.d.)

Other works incl. 6 German lieder (1790), 2 kbd sonatas, vn sonata, 6 minuets for kbd

BIBLIOGRAPHY
SainsburyD
O, E, Deutsch: 'Ein Fräulein will Mozart heiraten', *National-Zeitung Basel: Sonntagsbeilage* (1 May 1938; 4 July 1938)
—— : 'Das Fräulein von Auernhammer', *MJb 1958*, 12–17
H. W. Hamann: 'Mozarts Schülerkreis', *MJb 1962–3*, 115–39
A. Weinmann: *Giovanni Cappi bis A. O. Witzendorf, Beiträge zur Geschichte des Alt-Wiener Musikverlages*, 2nd ser., xi (Vienna, 1967), 157
R. Angermüller: 'An die Auernhammer bitte kein Kompliment', *Mitteilungen der Internationalen Stiftung Mozarteum*, xxx/3–4 (1982), 8–14
ROSARIO MARCIANO,
JORGE SANCHEZ-CHIONG

Aulin, (Laura) Valborg

(*b* Gävle, 9 Jan 1860; *d* Örebro, 13 March 1928). Swedish composer, pianist and teacher, she was the sister of the violinist, composer and conductor Tor Aulin. In 1873 she began harmony lessons with Albert Rubenson and later studied at the Stockholm Kungliga Musikaliska Akademien (1877–82), where her teachers included Rubenson and Ludvig Norman. After being awarded the Jenny Lind grant she studied in Paris (1885–7) with E. Bourgain and Benjamin Godard (and possibly with Jules Massenet and Ernest Guiraud), and briefly with Niels Gade in Copenhagen. Many of her compositions are songs and salon pieces for the piano, which show the influence of Chopin and national Romantic traditions. She taught the piano and music theory in Stockholm and (after 1903) in Örebro.

WORKS
Orch: Suite, op.15, 1886
Vocal: Herr Olof, ballad, T, chorus, orch, op.3, 1880; Julsång, chorus 8vv, op.23; Två körer, unacc. mixed chorus, op.24, 1898; Procul este (C. D. Wirsén), S, chorus, str orch, harp, op.28, 1886; Tre damkörer, women's choir, pf, 1895; Veni sancte spiritus, mixed chorus, pf, op.31, 1898; 11 songs, 1v, pf, 1881–1900
Chamber: 2 str qts, F, 1884, e, op.17, 1889; pieces for vn, pf
Kbd (for pf unless otherwise stated): 5 tondikter, op.7, 1882; 7 pieces, op.8, 1884; Sonata, f, op.14, 1885; Valse élégiaque, 1892; Albumblad, op.29, 1898; Fantasistycken, op.30, 1898; Meditation, org

Principal publishers: Elkan & Schildknecht

BIBLIOGRAPHY
SBL (O. Morales)
E. Öhrström: *Borgerliga kvinnors musicerande i 1800-talets Sverige* (diss., U. of Göteborg, 1987), 145–55, 198–9
ROLF HAGLUND

Florence Aylward

Aylward, Florence (*b* Brede, Sussex, 10 March 1862; *d* St Leonards, Sussex, 14 Oct 1950). A daughter of Rev. Augustus Aylward and Mary (née Frewen), she was not related to the musical Aylwards of the West Country. She attended a school in Norwood while studying the organ privately with Dr John Abram of St Leonards and the piano with Theodore Treakell. She then studied at the GSM with Henry Gadsby. Aylward married Harold A. Kinder in 1881 and was widowed in 1940. She published nearly 150 songs between 1879 and 1931, most of them sentimental in character but considered fine; several specify organ accompaniment with cello obbligato. *Beloved, it is morn* was her most popular song; an immediate favourite with both amateurs and professionals when it was published in 1886, it helped to revitalize the John Boosey's London Ballad Concerts.

For illustration see p. 27.

JOHN R. GARDNER

Azalais de Porcairages (*fl* mid-12th century). Troubadour. According to her *vida*, Azalais was from the region of Montpellier, and the lover of Gui Guerrejat, brother of Guillaume VII of Montpellier. Only one of her poems, without music, is extant.

BIBLIOGRAPHY

M. Bogin: *The Women Troubadours* (New York, 1976), 94–7, 166–7

MARIA V. COLDWELL

B

Baader-Nobs, Heidi (*b* Delémont, 5 Dec 1940). Swiss composer. After training as a teacher, she studied composition and music theory at the Basle Musik-Akademie with Robert Suter and Jacques Wildberger. Her first compositions employed dodecaphonic and serial techniques. She interrupted her composing career for several years in order to devote herself to her family. After 1976 she turned away from serialism and developed an interest in graphic scores. She has described her later works as acoustic realizations of visual ideas.

WORKS
selective list

Orch and inst: Musique, vn, str orch, 1969; Str Qt, 1980; Variations sur un thème connu, children's str ens, 1980; Musique de fête, orch, 1981; Duo, solo vc, 1986; Session, ens, 1987–8; Contrevenant, vc, 9 str, 1989–90; Bifurcation, tuba, pf, 1991; Spires, vn, 1993

Vocal: 5 pièces, S, fl, cl, vib, harp, 1967; 5 histoires brèves, vv, 1968; Lamento y protesto, 16vv, 1984–5

CHRIS WALTON

Bacewicz, Grażyna (*b* Łódź, 5 Feb 1909; *d* Warsaw, 17 Jan 1969). Polish composer, violinist, pianist and writer. After early instrumental and theory studies in Łódź, Bacewicz attended the Warsaw Conservatory, where she studied composition with Kazimierz Sikorski, violin with Józef Jarzębski and piano with Józef Turczyński (she also studied philosophy at Warsaw University). She graduated in composition and violin in 1932, furthering her studies in Paris in 1932 and 1933 with Nadia Boulanger and the violinist André Touret. After a brief period teaching in Łódź, she returned to Paris to study with Carl Flesch in 1934. At the request of the conductor Grzegorz Fitelberg, Bacewicz was principal violinist of the Polish Radio Orchestra (1936–8) and she performed as a soloist in several European countries before returning to Poland two months before World War II. She continued as a concert violinist after the war until the mid-1950s. Her prowess as a pianist should not be ignored: she was, for example, a notable interpreter of her own Second Piano Sonata.

Among her other activities, Bacewicz was an accomplished writer of short stories, novels and autobiographical anecdotes. Among the awards she received for her music were the top prize at the International Chopin Competition for Composers in Warsaw (1949), for her Piano Concerto; first prize at the International Composers' Competition in Liège (1951), for her String Quartet no.4; first prize in the orchestral section at UNESCO's International Rostrum of Composers in Paris (1960), for her *Music for Strings, Trumpets and Percussion*; and the Gold Medal at the Queen Elisabeth International Music Competition in Brussels (1965) for her Violin Concerto no.7, as well as various State awards from 1949 onwards.

Bacewicz made her most lasting mark on 20th-century music as a composer rather than as a performer or teacher (she taught composition rarely, but notably at the Warsaw Conservatory during the last three years of her life). She had an uncommonly vibrant yet modest personality and was much admired and loved by her fellow Poles during her lifetime.

Bacewicz's career as a composer may be seen to divide into three broad spans, of which the first (1932–44) is largely preparatory to the second (1945–59), with the third (1960–69) a more distinct entity. The first period shows the development and refinement of Bacewicz's neo-classical persona. Although only a few of these early works have been published, her music's salient characteristics of clarity, wit and brevity are already evident in the Wind Quintet, a piece that also shows signs of Bacewicz following Szymanowski's example in the incorporation of folk elements. Her works from the time of World War II show a greater muscularity and unrelenting activity, with a daring disregard for traditional classical structures, as in the Sonata no.1 for solo violin. The Overture is a characteristic example of Bacewicz's unerring instinct for propelling music towards a final goal.

After the war, Bacewicz's music became increasingly personal, sloughing off any remaining Parisian *chic* and becoming distinctively resilient. Occasionally she indulged in pastiche (the Sonata da camera), but her stronger music is reminiscent of Szymanowski (the Violin Concerto no.3 and, later, the Piano Sonata no.2 and Violin Concerto no.5). These and other outstanding works such as the String Quartet no.3 and the Concerto for String Orchestra have mostly maintained their place in the international repertory. As with many of her contemporaries, she used folk materials (both directly and indirectly) during the period of intense *socrealizm* (1949–54), in large forms (the Piano Concerto) and in encore pieces for her recitals. Her output during the height of Stalinist cultural dogma is, however, remarkably free of mass songs or other pieces with a 'message'. The three symphonies are the most grandiose works, although their scoring is at times refreshingly restrained. The chamber music reveals a tougher, more challenging musical idiom, most notably in the fourth and fifth quartets: the former is structurally loose-limbed and the latter highly integrated in its motivic design and adventurous for the time in its non–diatonic harmonic language. This innovatory streak in Bacewicz's musical personality is carried through into the Partita, especially in its intermezzo. By the mid-1950s Bacewicz had already moved far from conventional notions of neo-classicism.

In the late 1950s Bacewicz, like her contemporaries, had to face up to the sudden explosion of younger composers and avant-garde influences from abroad. Unlike some of her contemporaries, she grasped the nettle, even though it was not always with absolute conviction. In some works, such as the String Quartet no.6, there are passages of outright 12-note writing. But she soon settled down to her own brand of chromaticism and dynamic gestures that veer from the routine (Cello Concerto no.2) to the highly imaginative (*Pensieri notturni*). At times, Bacewicz appears to have experienced some difficulty in putting pen to paper, although in 1965 she composed no less than seven large-scale works. It is not easy to judge the many cross-references and large-scale self-borrowings in the works dating from 1965 to 1967: were these perhaps signs of uncertainty about where she was heading in this new musical world? Her evident attachment to

the intermezzo from the Partita gave rise to citations from that movement's opening bars in later works (e.g. the Viola Concerto); such quotations form part of a highly successful patchworking technique that Bacewicz developed during the 1960s. There is even the suggestion in the Viola Concerto that Bacewicz, like some of her younger compatriots, was returning to folk material.

Bacewicz's position in Polish postwar music is undeniable: hers was an individual and independent voice; she was more innovative than she is often given credit for; and she carried the torch for the many Polish women composers who followed her example. Even though she may have lost her sure-footedness in the mid-1960s, this should not detract from a musical achievement that is being recognized outside Poland as one of the most remarkable of the mid-20th century.

WORKS
selective list

STAGE

Z chłopa król [The Peasant King] (ballet, A. M. Swinarski, after P. Baryka), 1953–4; Poznań, 1954
Przygoda króla Artura [The Adventure of King Arthur] (comic opera for radio, E. Fischer), 1959; Polish Radio, 1959; televised 1960
Esik w Ostendzie [Esik in Ostend] (comic ballet, L. Terpilowski, after T. Boy-Żeleński), 1964; Poznań, 1964
Pożądanie [Desire] (ballet, 2, M. Bibrowski, after Picasso: *Désir attrapé par la queue*), 1968–9, inc.; Warsaw, 1973
Also incid. music for 7 plays.

ORCHESTRAL

Syms.: Sym., 1933, lost; Sym., 1938, lost; Sym. no.1, 1945; Sym., str, 1946; Sym. no.2, 1951; Sym. no.3, 1952; Sym. no.4, 1953
Vn concs.: no.1, 1937; no.2, 1945; no.3, 1948; no.4, 1951; no.5, 1954; no.6, 1957; no.7, 1965
Other concs.: Conc., str, 1948; Pf Conc., 1949; Vc conc. no.1, 1951; Conc. for Orch, 1962; Vc Conc. no.2, 1963; Conc., 2 pf, 1966; Va Conc., 1968
Other concert works: Sinfonietta, chamber orch, 1929; Suite, str, 1931; Sinfonietta, 1932; 3 karykatury, 1932; Pochód radości [Procession of Joy], 1933; Sinfonietta, str, 1935; Ov., 1943; Introdukcja i kaprys, 1947; Rapsodia polska, vn, orch, 1949; Uwertura polska, 1954; Partita [arr. Partita, vn, pf], 1955; Wariacje, 1957; Music for Strings, Trumpets and Percussion, 1958; Pensieri notturni, chamber orch, 1961; Divertimento, str, 1965; Musica sinfonica, 1965; Contradizione, chamber orch, 1966; In una parte, 1967
Pieces for radio: Mazur [Mazurka], 1944; Pod strzechą [Under the Thatch], 1945; Suite, str, 1946; Ze starej muzyki [From Old Music], 1946; Polish Dance no.2, 1948; Szkice ludowe [Folk Sketches], 1948; Groteska, 1949; Waltz, 1949; Krakowiak, 1950; Serenada, 1950; Suita tańców polskich, 1950; Wiwat, cl, str, 1950; Oberek noworoczny, 1952; others

CHAMBER

Str qts: no.1, 1938; no.2, 1943; no.3, 1947; no.4, 1951; no.5, 1955; no.6, 1960; no.7, 1965
Other works: Wind Qnt, 1932; Trio, ob, vn, vc, 1935; Sonata, ob, pf, 1936; Łatwè utwory [Easy Pieces], cl, pf, 1948; Trio, ob, cl, bn, 1948; Oberek no.1, cl, pf, 1949; Qt, 4 vn, 1949; Kaprys polski, cl, 1952; 2 pf qnts, 1952, 1965; Qt, 4 vc, 1964; Inkrustacje [Incrustations], hn, ens, 1965; Trio, ob, harp, perc, 1965

VIOLIN

With pf: Partita, 1930; Kaprys no.1, 1932; Witraż [Stained Glass], 1932; Andante i allegro, 1934; Kaprys no.2, 1934; Pieśń litewska [Lithuanian Song], 1934; Theme and Variations, 1934; Legenda, 1945; Sonata no.1 'da camera', 1945, 4th movt (Andante sostenuto) arr. vn/vc, org, 1945; Kaprys, 1946; Sonatas, no.2, 1946, no.3, 1947; Taniec polski, 1948; Melodia, 1949; Oberek no.1, 1949; Sonata, no.4, 1949; Taniec antyczny [Antique Dance], 1950; Sonata no.5, 1951; Taniec mazowiecki, 1951; Kołysanka [Lullaby], 1952; Oberek no.2, 1952; Taniec słowiański, 1952; Humoresque, 1953; Partita [no.2], 1955
Solo: Sonata, 1929; Sonata no.1, 1941; Kaprys polski, 1949; Kaprys no.2, 1952; Sonata no.2, 1958; 4 kaprysy, 1968
2 vn: Suite, 1943; Łatwe duety [Easy Duets], 1945
Easy pieces for vn, pf: Concertino, 1945; Łatwe utwory, 1946, 1949

KEYBOARD

Pf: Theme with Variations, 1924; Preludium, 1928; Allegro, 1929; Sonata, 1930; Toccata, 1932; 3 pièces caracteristiques, 1932; Sonatina, 1933; Suita dziecięca [Children's Suite], 1933; Scherzo, 1934; Sonata (Sonata 1935), 1935; 3 groteski, 1935; 3 preludia, 1941; Krakowiak koncertowy, 1949; Sonata no.1, 1949; Etiuda tercjowa [Study in 3rds], 1952; Sonata no.2, 1953; Sonatina no.2, 1955; 10 etiud koncertowych, 1956; Mały tryptyk [Little Triptych], 1965
Org: Esquisse, 1966

VOCAL

With orch: De profundis, solo vv, chorus, orch, 1932; 3 Songs (10th-century Arabic, trans. L. Staff), T, orch/pf, 1938; Kantata olimpijska (Pindar), chorus, orch, 1948; Kantata na 600-lecie Uniwersytetu Jagiellońskiego (S. Wyspiański: Akropolis), chorus, orch, 1964
Songs (1v, pf): Trzy róze [Three Roses] (Arabic, trans. Staff), 1934; Mów do mnie, miły [Speak to me, Dear] (R. Tagore, trans. J. Kasprowicz), 1936; Oto jest noc [Here is the Night] (K. I. Gałczyński), 1947; Smuga cienia [Trail of Shadow] (W. Broniewski), 1949; Rozstanie [Parting] (Tagore, trans. Kasprowicz), 1949; Usta i pełnia [Lips and Fullness] (Gałczyński), 1949; Boli mnie głowa [My Head Aches] (Bacewicz), 1955; Dzwon i dzwonki [Bells and Little Bells] (A. Mickiewicz), 1955; Nad wodą wielką i czystą [Over the Wide, Clear Water] (Mickiewicz), 1955; Sroczka [Little Magpie] (trad.), 1956

Principal publisher: Polskie Wydawnictwo Muzyczne

BIBLIOGRAPHY

A. Malawski: 'Uwertura Bacewiczówny', Ruch muzyczny (1947), no.17, p.19
H. Swolkień: 'III koncert skrzypcowy Grażyny Bacewicz', Ruch muzyczny (1949), nos.11–12
S. Łobaczewska: 'IV sonata na fortepian i skrzypce Grażyny Bacewicz', Muzyka, iii/11 (1952), 22
J. M. Chomiński: 'Koncert na orkiestrę smyczkową Grażyny Bacewicz', Muzyka, vi/5–6 (1955), 20; Studia muzykologiczne (1956), no.5, p.385
A. Helman: 'Problem stylizacji muzyki dawnej w 'Sonacie da camera' Grażyny Bacewicz' [The Problem of Early Musical Idioms in 'Sonata da camera'], Studia muzykologiczne (1956), no.5, p.367
T. A. Zieliński: 'VI kwartet Grażyny Bacewicz', Ruch muzyczny, iv/18 (1960), 6
K. Biegański: 'Jeszcze raz o 'VI kwartecie' Grażyny Bacewicz' [6th Quartet Revisited], Ruch muzyczny, iv/21 (1960), 7
E. Derewecka: 'Opery radiowe', ibid, 12–13
W. Hordyński: 'Grażyna Bacewicz', Życie literackie (1960), no.42
M. Gorczycka: '"Pensieri notturni"', Ruch muzyczny, v/21 (1961), 9–10
T. A. Zieliński: 'Walor szlachetnego rzemiosła (o twórczości G. Bacewicz)' [The Value of Noble Craftsmanship (in the Work of G. Bacewicz)], Ruch muzyczny, v/8 (1961), 1–2
J. Kański: 'II koncert wiolonczelowy Grażyny Bacewicz', Ruch muzyczny, vii/22 (1963), 20
S. Kisielewski: Grażyna Bacewicz i jej czasy [Grażyna Bacewicz and Her Times] (Kraków, 1963)
H. Schiller: 'Ze studiów nad muzyką Grażyny Bacewicz', Muzyka, ix/3–4 (1964), 3–15
S. Kisielewski: '"Musica sinfonica" Grażyny Bacewicz', Ruch muzyczny, ix/17 (1965), 7–8
T. Marek: 'Grażyna Bacewicz', Polish Music (1969), no.1, p.3
Ruch muzyczny, xiii/7 (1969) [Bacewicz issue]
T. A. Zieliński: 'Ostatnie utwory Grażyny Bacewicz' [Bacewicz's Last Works], Ruch muzyczny, xvi/12 (1972), 3–6
B. Cisowska: '"Pożądanie" – ostatnie dzieło G. Bacewicz' ['Desire' – Bacewicz's Last Work], Ruch muzyczny, xvii/13 (1973), 3–5
T. A. Zieliński: 'Grażyna Bacewicz (1913 [sic]–1969)', Polish Perspectives (1974), no.10, pp.20–26
S. Kisielewski: 'Grażyna Bacewicz 1913 [sic]–1969', Polish Music (1975), no.2, pp.11–15
G. Bacewicz: 'Z notatek osobistych, listów i wypowiedzi' [From Personal Notes, Letters and Statements], Ruch muzyczny, xxvi/4 (1982), 4–5
J. Rosen: Grażyna Bacewicz: Her Life and Works (Los Angeles, 1984)
A. Thomas: Grażyna Bacewicz: Chamber and Orchestral Music (Los Angeles, 1985)
J. Wenzlaff: 'Technik ist Wertvoll', Annäherungen an sieben Komponistinnen, ed. R. Matthei and B. Sonntag, v (Kassel, 1989), 6–13

ADRIAN THOMAS

Bach, Maria (b Vienna, 1 March 1896; d Vienna, 26 Feb 1978). Austrian pianist and composer. Her ancestors, Catholic members of the famous Bach dynasty, came to Austria during Martin Luther's time. Her mother was a well-known singer, her father an amateur violinist, and she was brought up in an artistic milieu. She studied the violin (with Arnold Rosé) and the piano from an early age, presenting her first successful piano recital when she was ten. Although she decided to become a concert pianist, her *Flohtanz* for piano (1917) was so successful that she took up composition seriously, studying with Joseph Marx. In 1962 she received the first prize in the Buenos Aires International Composers' Competition.

Bach belongs to the tradition of the late Romantic period as exemplified by E. W. Korngold, Alexander Zemlinsky and Franz Schreker. In her later years she took up painting and writing poetry, composing music for her own poems. Her large output includes much vocal music with orchestra and smaller forces.

WORKS
selective list

Stage: Silhouetten, ballet, orch, 1939
Vocal orch (all song cycles): 4 Narrenlieder (after J. Bierbaum), Bar/T, orch, 1921; Japanischer Frühling (15 songs, trad. Jap. lyrics), S/T, orch, 1930; 4 Lieder des Hafis (trad. Persian texts), T/S, vc, orch/ pf, 1940; 6 Marienlieder (trad. German texts), S, str orch, 1944, rev. 1v, pf, 1944–5; 3 Orchesterlieder, S, orch, 1944; 2 Orchesterlieder, S, str, 1949; Das Marienleben (R. M. Rilke), S, Bar, str orch, 1952; 5 Orchesterlieder, S/T, 2 hn, str, 1952
Choral (for SATB): 7 Japanische Lieder (trad. Jap. texts), 1932; Draussen im weiten Krieg (C. Morgenstern), 1945; 4 Volkslieder (trad. Chinese texts), 1952
Other vocal (for 1v, pf): 6 Lieder (A. Wildgans, F. Hebbel, Hartlieb, G. Falke, Bierbaum, F. Werfel), 1925–8; 18 Lieder (Rilke), 1925–6; 5 Sonette (E. Barrett-Browning), 1940; 5 Lieder (song cycle, A. Lambe), 1959
Inst: Flohtanz, pf, 1917; Sonata, vc, 1922; Sonata, vc, pf, 1924; Pf Qnt, 1930; Str Qt no.1, 1935; Str Qnt, 1936; Str Qt no.2, 1937; Wilde Myrthe (T. Lanjus), C, (cl, vc, pf)/str, 1952; Stücke: Caravelle, Glockenspiel, Holztanz, pf, 1957

ROSARIO MARCIANO

Badalla, Rosa Giacinta (*b* c1660; *d* Milan, c1715). Italian composer. She is recorded in the lists of the Benedictine monastery of S Radegonda in Milan from about 1678, and must have professed final vows by that year. Her only printed collection, *Motetti a voce sola* (1684), is remarkable among Milanese solo motet books of the time for its patent vocal virtuosity, motivic originality and self-assured compositional technique, particularly when Badalla, in her preface, noted her youth and inexperience. The collection consists of so-called para-liturgical sanctoral, Marian and Eucharistic texts in clear sectional forms. Of her two surviving secular cantatas (a further testimony to the practice of secular music inside S Radegonda's walls), *Vuò cercando* is a succession of short da capo arias interspersed with recitative, while *O fronde care* (for which Badalla also wrote the

text) is a more extended piece with short melismas, repetitive bass patterns and instrumental *sinfonie*.

WORKS

Motetti a voce sola, S, bc (Venice, 1684); 1 ed. in R. L. Kendrick: '*Le Sirene Celesti': Generations, Gender and Genres in Seicento Milanese Nuns' Music* (diss., New York U., 1993)
Vuò cercando, A, bc, *GB-Lbl*; ed. ibid
O fronde care, A, 2 vn/tpt, 2 rec, bc, *F-Pn*

ROBERT L. KENDRICK

Bądarzewska-Baranowska, Tekla (*b* Warsaw, 1834; *d* Warsaw, 29 Sept 1861). Polish composer. An amateur, with no musical training, she is known chiefly for *Modlitwa dziewicy* ('The Maiden's Prayer'). This piece, which won world-wide popularity, was originally published in Warsaw in 1856; later the music appeared as a supplement to the *Revue et gazette musicale* (Paris, 1859), entitled *La prière d'une vierge*, and was issued by more than 80 publishers in France, Germany, Italy, England, Australia and the USA. Arrangements were produced for piano (four or eight hands) and other instruments, and for voice. *The Maiden's Prayer* is of no artistic merit, being a salon composition of a type common in the 19th century. Other works of a similar nature failed to repeat its success.

BIBLIOGRAPHY

FétisBS; *PazdirekH* [incl. list of works]; *SchmidlD*; *SMP*

ZOFIA CHECHLIŃSKA

Badian, Maya (*b* Bucharest, 18 April 1945). Romanian composer. She studied at the Bucharest Conservatory (1962–8) with Tiberiu Olah (composition), Aurel Stroe (orchestration), Zeno Vancea (counterpoint) and Tudor Ciortea (form). Her music daringly exploits Romanian folk archetypes in a modern musical language of experimental sounds and sound combinations. In particular she has tried to widen the timbral range of wind instruments, for which she has composed solo and ensemble works; they include *Capriccio* (bassoon), *Harmonies* (flute), *Incantation* (clarinet), *Monodies* (oboe), *Profiles* (trombone), *Movimento* (wind quintet) and a trio for oboe, clarinet and bassoon. She has produced a considerable body of orchestral music, including *Symphonic Diptych* (1976), *Spre inalt* ('On high', for soprano and orchestra, 1979), concertos for guitar (1981), marimba and vibraphone (1984) and for four timpani (1985), and a Concertino for piano (1977), as well as string solo and chamber music (*Monologue*, violin;

Dances, trio, 1971; *Accents*, quartet, 1973), a piano sonata and other piano works, lieder, and songs for children.

BIBLIOGRAPHY

CohenE

VIOREL COSMA

Baeva, Vera (*b* Burgas, 18 March 1930). Bulgarian composer and pianist. After graduating in 1953 from the Sofia State Academy of Music, where she was a pupil of Dimiter Nenov, she worked as conductor of the chorus at Radio Sofia. In 1986 she became lecturer in interpretation in the vocal department of the Sofia State Academy of Music and since 1993 has taught chamber music at the 'Open Society' Foundation. Her reputation as a pianist extends beyond Bulgaria to the rest of Europe. Baeva's compositions, distinguished by their melodic richness and clear formal structure, consist mostly of chamber, instrumental and vocal music.

WORKS
selective list

Inst: 5 Impressions, pf, 1973; 2 Preludes, vc, 1984; Nostalgichno, chamber orch, 1986; Sonata, pf 4 hands, 1988; Sonata Do-Re, pf 4 hands, 1988; Tristezza, vn sonata, 1990

Vocal: 4 Songs, female vv, fl, pf, 1975; Perperuda [Butterfly], female vv, chamber orch, 1989; Dance around the Fire of the God Tangra, male vv, chamber orch, 1991

Principal publishers: Nauka i Izkustvo, Muzïka

MAGDALENA MANOLOVA

Bailey, Judith Margaret (*b* Camborne, 18 July 1941). English composer and conductor. She studied the clarinet, piano, conducting and composition at the RAM from 1959 to 1963. In 1971 she became a freelance composer, conductor and lecturer. Many of her large-scale works, such as the orchestral tone poem *Trencrom* (1978), the two symphonies (1981 and 1982), the overture *Penwith* (1986), *Fiesta* (1988) and the Concerto for clarinet and strings (1988), were first performed by her own ensembles (she conducts the Southampton Concert Orchestra and the Petersfield Orchestra). *Seascape* (1985), for female voices, woodwind trio and string orchestra, was commissioned by the Petersfield Festival in 1983. Bailey has also written much chamber music, especially for wind instruments. A major inspiration for all her work is her Cornish background.

BIBLIOGRAPHY

Fuller-LeFanuRM

SOPHIE FULLER

Bakke, Ruth (*b* Bergen, 2 Aug 1947). Norwegian composer and organist. She was educated first at the Bergen Musikkonservatorium and at Oslo University; she studied thereafter at Texas Lutheran College, the University of Redlands, California, and Washington State University, from which she received the Master's degree in 1972. In 1973 she was appointed organist at the Storetveit Church in Bergen. In her music she uses a free tonality, frequently including tone clusters and sometimes employing improvisation techniques; timbre and rhythm are central elements. Bakke's output ranges from *Chromocumuli* ('Colour Clouds', 1972) for symphony orchestra and *Rumus* (1977) for chamber orchestra to her *Trollsuite* (1981) for string quartet, *Noncense* (1990) for solo voice and *Suite ACD* (1992) for Renaissance instruments. There are many compositions for organ: the solo works include a sonata (1970) and *Sphaerae* (1992); for organ with other instruments she has composed *Into the Light* (with violin, 1982), *Meditation* (with horn, 1986), *Psalm 2000* (with tuba, 1993) and *Bønn* (with soprano and guitar, 1976). She has also written music for synthesizer, and unaccompanied choral works.

KARI MICHELSEN

Baldacci, Giovanna Bruna (*b* Pistoia, 19 Nov 1886; *d* ? after 1910). Italian composer, pianist and poet. At the Istituto Musicale in Florence she studied the piano, and composition with Francesco Cilea and Moretti. As a concert pianist she performed in Italy and Switzerland. She was also a contributor to literary and musical journals and taught choral singing in state schools. Her compositions include choruses for children (*I mesi dell'anno*), songs and piano pieces. In 1910 she won the first prize with a *Madrigale* ('in the old style', for three voices and piano) in a competition launched by the Italian Lyceum.

BIBLIOGRAPHY

SchmidlD

A. de Angelis: *L'Italia musicale d'oggi: Dizionario dei musicisti* (Rome, 1918, 3/1928)
A. Bonaventura: 'Le donne italiane e la musica', *RMI*, xxxii (1925), 519–34

FRANCESCA PERRUCCIO SICA

Ballou, Esther (Williamson) (*b* Elmira, NY, 17 July 1915; *d* Chichester, England, 12 March 1973). American composer, pianist and educationist. She studied the piano and the organ as a child and graduated from Bennington College, Vermont (1937), Mills College (1938) and the Juilliard School (1943); at Bennington she took composition lessons from Otto Luening, and at Juilliard from Bernard Wagenaar and privately from Wallingford Riegger. While in California she composed ballets for Louise Kloepper and José Limón and toured nationally as a pianist with various dance companies. From 1955 she taught at the American University, Washington, DC. During her subsequent career as an educationist she put forward experimental methods for theory teaching at college level. Her music, according to her own description, 'tends towards classicism in that it stresses clarity of design and directness of expression'. In 1963 she became the first American woman composer to have a work (the Capriccio for violin and piano) given its first performance at the White House, and in 1964 she received the honorary doctorate from Hood College, Maryland. Her manuscripts, which include a pedagogical text, *Creative Explorations of Musical Elements* (1971), are in the Special Collections of the American University Library, Washington, DC.

WORKS
selective list

Orch: Suite, chamber orch, 1939; Blues, 1944; Pf Conc. no.1, 1945; Prelude and Allegro, pf, str, 1951; Concertino, ob, str, 1953; Adagio, bn, str, 1960; In memoriam, ob, str, 1960; Gui Conc., 1964; Pf Conc. no.2, 1964

Choral: Bag of Tricks (I. Orgel), SSAA, 1956; The Beatitudes, SATB, org, 1957; A Babe is Born (15th century), SATB, 1959; May the words of my mouth (Bible), SATB, 1965; I will lift up mine eyes, S, SATB, org, 1965; O the sun comes up-up-up in the opening sky (E. E. Cummings), SSA, 1966; Hear Us!, SATB, brass, perc, 1967

Other vocal: 4 Songs (A. E. Housman), S, vc, pf, 1937; What if a much of a which of a wind (Cummings), S, Bar, B, wind qnt, 1959; Street Scenes (H. Champers), S, pf, 1960; 5-4-3 (Cummings), Mez, va, harp, 1966

Chamber: Impertinence, cl, pf, 1936; In Blues Tempo, cl, pf, 1937; Nocturne, str qt, 1937; Pf Trio, 1955, rev. 1957; Divertimento, str qt, 1958; Vn Sonata, 1959; A Passing Word, fl, vc, pf, ob, 1960; Capriccio, vn, pf, 1963; Prism, str trio, 1969; Romanzo, vn, pf, 1969

Kbd: Dance Suite, pf, 1937; 2 pf sonatinas, 1941, 1964; 2 sonatas, 2 pf, 1943, 1958; Beguine, pf, 8 hands, 1950, arr. 2 pf, 1957, arr. orch, 1960; Music for the Theatre, 2 pf, 1952; Pf Sonata, 1955; Rondino, hpd, 1961; Impromptu, org, 1968

Principal publisher: ACA

BIBLIOGRAPHY
R. D. Ringenwald: *The Music of Esther Williamson Ballou: an Analytical Study* (diss., American U., Washington, DC, 1960)

E. W. Ballou: 'Theory with a Thrust', *Music Educators Journal*, lv (1968–9), Sept, 56; Jan, 55
J. R. Heintze: *Esther Williamson Ballou: a Bio-Bibliography* (New York, 1987)

JAMES R. HEINTZE

Barberis, Mansi (*b* Iaşi, 12 March 1899; *d* Bucharest, 10 Oct 1986). Romanian composer and teacher. She studied music at the Iaşi Conservatory (1918–22), in Berlin (1922–3) and in Paris (1926–7), where she was a pupil of Vincent d'Indy (conducting) and Noël Gallon (composition). She returned to Romania to teach singing and the violin in Iaşi and Bucharest. Her compositions include several operas based on Moldavian folklore, incidental music for the theatre, orchestral, chamber and choral music, and more than a hundred songs. The folklike melodies and nationalist themes of her operas and the romantic ballad style of her orchestral pieces brought her considerable recognition in Romania. A volume of her recollections, *Din zori pînă în amurg* ('From Dawn to Dusk'), was published in Bucharest in 1989.

WORKS
selective list
OPERAS

Prinţesa îndepărtată [The Distant Princess] (3, M. Codreanu, after E. Rostand), 1946, inc.; rev. 1971 as Domniţa din depărtări [The Princess Far Away] (3, M. Barberis), Iaşi, 9 May 1976

Apus de soare [Sunset] (3, G. Teodorescu, after B. Ştefănescu-Delavrancea), 1958; Bucharest, 30 Dec 1967; rev. 1968

Kera Duduca, 1963 (television opera, 3, A. Ionescu-Arbore, after N. Filimon: *Ciocoii vechi şi noi* [The Old and New Boyars]), 1963; rev., 1970, Romanian TV, 26 July 1970

Căruţa cu paiaţe [The Cart with Clowns] (3 acts and 2 tableaux, Ionescu-Arbore, after M. Ştefănescu), 1981; Iaşi, 10 May 1982

OTHER WORKS

Orch: Viziuni [Visions], sym. poem, 1934; Suite no.1 'Pastorala', 1936; Sym. no.1, 1941; Suite no.2 'Trei momente descriptive', 1951; Pf Conc., D, 1954; Suită festivă, 1959; Sym. Variations, 1970; Piesă concertantă, cl, orch, 1972; Piesă de concert, va, orch, 1981

Vocal: Kyrie eleison, mixed chorus 8vv, 1924; Călin (M. Eminescu), 4 solo vv, orch, 1947; La ţară [In the Country] (O. Cazimir), chorus 2vv, pf, 1948; Concert în luncă [Concert in the River Meadow] (V. Alecsandri), S, orch, 1954; Zmeoaica (ballad, St O. Iosif), S, T, orch, 1969; Pintea cel Viteaz [Pintea the Brave] (cantata, D. Stanca), B, mixed chorus, orch, 1974; *c*100 songs

Chamber: Vn Sonata, 1957; Capriciu, harp, 1965; Str Qt, 1976; other pieces: vn, pf, 1936, 1949, bn, pf, 1981; pieces for solo pf

BIBLIOGRAPHY
V. Cosma: *Muzicieni din România* (Bucharest, 1989)

VIOREL COSMA

Barbosa, Cacilda Campos Borges (*b* Rio de Janeiro, 18 May 1914). Brazilian composer, pianist and conductor. At the age of 14 she entered the Instituto Nacional de Música, Rio de Janeiro, where her teachers included Francisco Braga (composition) and Ernst Widmer. For many years she worked with Heitor Villa-Lobos at the Superintendência de Educação Musical e Artística (SEMA), where she founded and directed a youth orchestra. She was director of the Villa-Lobos Institute, taught at the Escola Popular de Educação Musical and directed several choral and orchestral ensembles; she also published some piano-teaching materials. Barbosa was one of the pioneers of electronic music in Brazil.

WORKS
selective list

Inst: Uirapiranga (ballet), 1955; Chibraseando, 20 perc, 1973
Vocal: Segunda missa brasileira, 1968; Cota zero, chorus, fl, perc, vib, db, 1969; Missa em fugas, 1971; Pé-de-vento, children's chorus, 1974; Procissão da chuva, children's chorus

IRATI ANTONIO

Barkin [neé Radoff], **Elaine** (*b* Bronx, NY, 15 Dec 1932). American composer, writer and performer. After gaining the BA (1954) from Queens College, CUNY, she studied composition with Irving Fine, Harold Shapero and Arthur Berger at Brandeis University (MFA 1956, PhD 1971) and with Boris Blacher at the Berlin Hochschule für Musik (1956–7). She taught at various colleges and universities before joining the composition and theory faculty at UCLA in 1974. For three decades she has been involved with *Perspectives of New Music*, in an editorial and advisory capacity, and as a frequent contributor; she has also written extensively on 20th-century music for other journals.

In about 1978 Barkin turned from using 12-note and serial techniques to explore compositional processes involving collaboration, interactive performance and improvisation. In notes written about her 1989 piece for bassett horn and tape, . . . *out of the air* . . . , she outlined her aesthetic: 'to foster the potentials of collaborative participation . . . to relinquish authority albeit not responsibility; and to minimize my role as proprietary instruction-giver by supplying an adaptable stimulus for activity, directly inspired by, and having arisen out of the head of, the same person for whom it has been conceived'. Her search for non-competitive and non-hierarchical musical environments has led to her interest in Javanese and Balinese gamelan. She has been involved with gamelan as a player and composer since 1987 and during three study trips to Bali she compiled interviews, led improvisation workshops and produced video tapes of audience reactions at new music concerts.

Barkin's 'texts' – whether for print medium, live performance or tape collage – often blur the distinction between text and music or between essay and poetry. Some works also merge theoretical commentary with the creative process in the form of poetic-graphic explications of music by other composers. Barkin's compositions disclose extensive verbal and gestural interplay, and later works integrate timbral and conceptual influences from gamelan. Through improvisation and collective work that is not necessarily intended for public display, she seeks to redefine the relationship of performer and audience.

WORKS
selective list

Stage: (incl. text-pieces and tape collages): De amore (chamber mini-opera, after A. Capellanus and 12th–20th-century love texts), 4 female and 4 male spkr-singers, va, gui, harp, db, slide projector, 1980; Media Speak, 9 spkrs, sax, slide projector, 1981; . . . to piety more prone . . . , 4 female spkrs, tape collage of spkrs and singers incl. I. Cox, Ma Rainey, B. Smith, E. Waters, 1983, rev. 1985; Anonymous was a Woman (tape collage for dancers), 1984; On the Way to Becoming (tape collage, E. Barkin), 1985; Past is Part of (tape collage, Barkin), 1985; To whom it may Concern 2 (tape collage, B. Boretz and others), 1989; (Continuous), minimum 5 players, 1991
Orch: Essay, 1957; Plus ça change, str orch, 3 perc incl. mar, vib, xyl, 1971, also version for tape, arr. S. Beck, 1987
Chamber and solo inst: Refrains, fl, cl, vn, va, vc, cel, 1967; 6 Compositions, pf, 1968; Str Qt, 1969; Mixed Modes, b cl, vn, va, vc, pf, 1975; Inward & Outward Bound, fl + pic, cl + b cl, bn, hn, trbn, tuba, vn, va, vc, db, 2 perc incl. vib, mar, timp, 1975; Plein chant, a fl, 1977; . . . in its surrendering . . . , tuba, 1980; Rhapsodies, pic + fl, cl + a fl, 1986; [Be] Coming Together Apart, vn, mar, 1987; Encore, Javanese gamelan, 1988; . . . out of the air . . . , basset hn, tape, 1989; Legong Dreams, ob, 1990; Exploring the Rigors of in between, fl, hn, vn, va, vc, 1991; Gamelange, harp, mixed gamelan, 1992
Vocal: 2 Dickinson Choruses, SATB, 1977; . . . the suple suitor . . . (E. Dickinson), Mez, fl, ob, vc, vib + bells, hpd + pf, 1978; . . . the sky . . . (E. E. Cummings), SSA, pf, 1978

Principal publishers: ACA, Association for the Promotion of New Music, Mobart

BIBLIOGRAPHY

CohenE
H. W. Jacobi: *Contemporary American Composers* (Paradise, CA, 1975), 9–10

E. Cory: 'Barkin's String Quartet', *MQ*, lxii (1976), 616–20

E. Barkin: 'Questionnaire [about being a woman composer in the US]', *PNM*, xix/2 (1980–81), 460–62; continued as 'In Response', xx/2 (1981–2), 288–329

C. Ammer: *Unsung: a History of Women in American Music* (Westport, CT, 1980), 240

J. L. Zaimont and others, eds.: *The Musical Woman: an International Perspective* i (Westport, CT, 1984); ii–iii (New York, 1987–91); passim

N. L. Neukirch: 'Elaine Barkin – Professor of Music at UCLA: In-clusive instead of Ex-clusive', *KIM-NYT*, vi (1989)

J. Rahn: 'New Research Paradigms', *Music Theory Spectrum*, xi/1 (1989), 84–94

J. M. Edwards: 'North America since 1920', *Women and Music: a History*, ed. K. Pendle (Bloomington, IN, 1991), 211–57, esp. 241

C. Boge: 'Pedagogically Speaking: Poetic Analysis as Part of Analysis Pedagogy', *In Theory Only*, xii/3–4 (1992), 47–67

J. M. Frey: 'Elaine Barkin: Active Participant', *PNM*, xxxi/2 (1992–3), 252–63

J. MICHELE EDWARDS

Barnard [née Pye], **Charlotte Alington** [Claribel] (*b* Louth, Lincs., 23 Dec 1830; *d* Dover, 30 Jan 1869). English poet and ballad composer. She studied the piano and composition with W. H. Holmes and others, mostly after her marriage in 1854 and her move to London in 1857. She also studied singing with some of the leading artists who introduced her songs, including Euphrosyne Parepa and Charlotte Sainton-Dolby. From about 1858 she published songs under the pseudonym 'Claribel', her first great success being *Janet's Choice* (1859); she also published two volumes of verse. In all she composed the music and wrote most of the words for about a hundred published sentimental ballads, children's songs and hymns, and was the foremost composer of popular ballads in England during her lifetime. Her works include *Jamie* (1860), the children's song *Won't you tell me why, Robin?* (1861), *Five O'Clock in the Morning* (1862) and *Take back the Heart* (1864), probably the most popular of her works in the USA. The lessons she took towards the end of her life to improve her compositional technique are reflected in an increased subtlety in *Come back to Erin* (1866). This remains the most popular of her songs in Britain, where it is often thought of as an Irish folksong.

BIBLIOGRAPHY

DNB (W. B. Squire); *FétisBS*

J. D. Brown and S. S. Stratton: *British Musical Biography* (Birmingham, 1897) [incl. summary list of works]

S. Spaeth: *A History of Popular Music in America* (New York, 1948), 143

P. M. Smith: *The Story of Claribel* (Lincoln, 1965)

ANDREW LAMB, DEANE L. ROOT

Barnett, Alice (Ray) (*b* Lewiston, IL, 26 May 1886; *d* San Diego, 28 Aug 1975). American composer, teacher and patron. She studied with Rudolf Ganz and Felix Borowski at the Chicago Musical College (BM 1906) and with Heniot Levy and Adolf Weidig at the American Conservatory, Chicago; she also studied composition in Chicago with Wilhelm Middleschulte and in Berlin with Hugo Kaun (1909–10). From 1917 to 1926 she taught music at the San Diego High School. A respected and influential leader of musical life in San Diego, she helped to found the San Diego Opera Guild and the San Diego Civic SO (of which she was chairwoman for 14 years). Barnett wrote some 60 art songs, 49 of which were published by G. Schirmer and Summy between 1906 and 1932. They display a lyrical gift, sure tonal sense and, despite her German training, strong French harmonic influence. They are often exotic and colourful, especially *Chanson of the Bells of Oseney* (1924) and the Browning cycle *In a Gondola* (1920), which is also dramatic; others of her songs are *Panels from a Chinese Screen* (1924), *Harbor Lights* (1927) and *Nirvana* (1932). She also wrote instrumental music, including a piano trio (1920) and *Effective Violin Solos* (1924). Although Barnett stopped composing in the late 1930s, she maintained her musical activities in San Diego. Her manuscripts and papers are at the San Diego Historical Society.

BIBLIOGRAPHY

WAM

W. T. Upton: 'Some Recent Representative American Song-Composers', *MQ*, xi (1925), 383–417, esp. 398–417

——: *Art-Song in America* (Boston, 1930), 214–24 [incl. music exx.]

ADRIENNE FRIED BLOCK

Barns, Ethel (*b* London, 1880; *d* Maidenhead, 31 Dec 1948). English composer, violinist and pianist. She studied at the RAM with Emile Sauret (violin), Ebenezer Prout (composition) and Frederick Westlake (piano), and made her début at the Crystal Palace in 1896, probably playing the violin. She toured in England and the USA and in 1899 married the baritone Charles Phillips. Her Second Violin Sonata was played by Joseph Joachim in Germany in 1903; her *Concertstück* for violin and orchestra was given at the Queen's

Ethel Barns

Hall Promenade Concerts in 1910; and her *Fantaisie trio* was frequently performed by Sauret. Barns's intimate knowledge of the potential of the violin resulted in music satisfying for beginners and virtuosos alike. Her music is emotionally highly charged in the manner of Tchaikovsky and Grieg, and her best works (such as the *Fantaisie trio* and the *Concertstück*) are those in which her rhapsodic style – she was somewhat restricted by sonata form – had room to expand. Her piano pieces exhibit the same strength of personality, but her songs are effusive and sentimental.

WORKS
printed works published in London

Orch: Concertstück, vn, orch, ?1908, arr. vn, pf, 1908; L'escarpolette, str, arr. vn, pf (1907); Vn Conc.

Chamber (for vn, pf, unless otherwise stated): Romance (1891); Polonaise (1892); Mazurka (1894); Valse caprice (1894); Tarantella (1895); Chanson gracieuse (1904); Sonata no.2, A, op.9 (1904); [43] Compositions pour violon et piano, 1907–28 (c1928; all previously pubd separately); Sonata no.4, g, op.24 (1911); Fantaisie trio, 2 vn, pf, op.26 (1912); 2 Compositions (1913); Crépuscule (1913); Idylle, vc, pf (1913); Aubade (1917); Carina (1917); Pierrette (1917); 3 sonatas, 2 trios, all unpubd

Pf: 4 Sketches (1899); 2 Dances (1907); Prelude (1908); Valse gracieuse (1908); Humoreske (1910); [3] Scènes villageoises (1911); An Impression (1912); Cri du coeur (1916); Monkey Land (Scherzo) (1916); 4 Landscapes (1919)

Songs: A Fancy (1892); Waiting for Thee (M. Collins) (1892); Two Songs: Berceuse (J. E. Woolacott), 'Twas ever thus (K. E. Smith) (1901); Remembrance (N. Fielding) (1903); Remember or Forget (C. Rossetti) (1904); A Ransom (H. Simpson) (1907); Sleep, Weary Heart (J. J. Elliot) (1911); Dewdrops (Simpson) (1912); For Thee (G. Hubi-Newcombe) (1914); I Long to Live (F. G. Bowles) (1914); Soul of Mine (T. Hooley) (1914); A Talisman (P. J. O'Reilly) (1914); Out on Deep Waters (E. Lockton) (1918); 5 others (n.d.); arrs. of Susani (14th-century carol) (1903), Lullaby (C. M. Scott) (1918)

BIBLIOGRAPHY
CohenE; Grove5 (W. W. Cobbett); MEMM; PazdirekH; RiemannL 12; SchmidlD
W. W. Cobbett, ed.: *Cyclopedic Survey of Chamber Music* (London, 2/1963)
J. Creighton: *Discopaedia of the Violin, 1889–1971* (Toronto, 1974)

NIGEL BURTON

Baroni, Leonora (*b* Mantua, Dec 1611; *d* Rome, 6 April 1670). Italian singer, theorbist and composer. The daughter (and presumably pupil) of the *virtuosa* and composer Andreana Basile, Baroni became one of the most admired singers of the 17th century. By 1630 she had won acclaim singing with her mother in Naples, Genoa and Florence. In 1633 they settled in Rome. Baroni frequented the salons at the Palazzo Barberini and on 27 May 1640 she married Francesco Barberini's secretary, Giulio Cesare Castellani. In February 1644 Baroni accepted a generous stipend at the court of Anne of Austria, Regent of France, but returned to Rome in April 1645 and was active as a chamber singer there until shortly before her death. In praising her singing, the French traveller André Maugars remarked that Baroni's depth of musical understanding was so great that she even composed. His is the only known reference to her as a composer; no works attributed to her are known.

BIBLIOGRAPHY
GerberNL; SainsburyD; SchillingE; SchmidlD; WaltherML
V. Costazuti, ed.: *Applausi poetici alle glorie della Signora Leonora Baroni* (Rome, 1639, 2/1641)
A. Maugars: *Response faite a un curieux sur le sentiment de la musique d'Italie, escrite a Rome le premier octobre 1639* (Paris, 1640); ed. E. Thoinan (Paris, 1865); Eng. trans. in J. S. Shedlock: 'Andre Maugars', *Studies in Music*, ed. R. Grey (London, 1901), 215–32

SUZANNE G. CUSICK

Baroni-Cavalcabò [von Webenau; von Britto], **Julia** [Giuglia] (*b* Lemberg [now L'viv], 16 or 22 Oct 1813; *d* Graz, 2 July 1887). Austrian pianist and composer of Italian descent. She was a pupil of Mozart's younger son, Franz Xaver Wolfgang (1791–1844), with whom she studied until 1836 (the year he moved from Lemberg). In 1835 she travelled with him to Leipzig; there she met Robert Schumann, who dedicated his *Humoreske* op.20 to her. She married in 1839 and, as Frau von Webenau, settled in Vienna. She and her sister-in-law, Josephine Baroni-Cavalcabò (née Countess Castiglione), were active members of an important cultural Viennese circle. She began publishing her songs and 'Charakter-Stücke' for piano in 1830. Most of them were published during her lifetime and many contemporary articles, as well as analyses, were written. Of her piano fantasy op.25 *L'adieu et le retour*, Robert Schumann remarked that 'she knows how to plan and perfect a piece of music; she gives us choice harmonies, often elegant and tender; her melodies are deep-felt, though often echoing the Italian softness'.

WORKS

Pf: Variations on 'Là ci darem la mano', op.1; 3 caprices, f, op.2, op.12, op.18; 2 sonatas, E♭, op.3, E; 2 fantasies, c, op.4, op.19; Introduction et Rondo, B♭, op.5; Allegro di bravura, op.8; Zwist und Sühne, op.15; L'adieu et le retour, op.25; Au bord du lac, op.26; 2 morceaux, op.28; Barcarolle, op.29; La chasse, MS, 1854

Lieder: Die Grabes-Rose, bar, op.6; Lebewohl! (Schöne Wiege meiner Leiden), op.9; 3 Deutsche Lieder, op.10; Der Ungenannte, op.11; Er segelt sanft, op.17; Abschied von Liebchen, op.20; Warum?, op.22; 2 Lieder, op.24; Der Bescheiden, Treue Liebe, op.30; Dein Bild; Reiterlied, Bar

BIBLIOGRAPHY

FétisB; *PazdirekH*; *SchmidlD*

G. W. Fink: Reviews, *AMZ*, xxxiv (1831); xli (1838)

A. Elson: *Woman's Work in Music* (Boston, 1903, 2/1931)

M. Kreisig, ed.: *Gesammelte Schriften über Musik und Musiker von Robert Schumann* (Leipzig, 5/1914)

F. Jansen, ed.: *Robert Schumanns Briefe: neue Folge* (Leipzig, 2/1904), 111–2, 138–40 [letters of 9 Feb 1838, 10 Oct 1838]

P. Rehberg and W. Rehberg: *Robert Schumann* (Zürich and Stuttgart, 1954)

R. Münster: *Komponistinnen aus 3 Jhdt* (Munich, 1977)

ROSARIO MARCIANO

Barradas, (María del) Carmen (Pérez) (*b* Montevideo, 18 March 1888; *d* Montevideo, 12 May 1963). Uruguayan composer and pianist. Studying under Antonio Franck, she began composing very young; later she entered the Conservatorio Musical La Lira to study with Aurora and Vicente Pablo and Martín López. In 1914 she settled in Spain and began to develop a new and revolutionary system of musical notation based on graphic designs similar to those that came into use 50 years later, shocking Spanish and

French musicians and critics. Using that system she composed *Fabricación* (1922), a piano work that reproduced the sound of a factory working at full blast. This work, *Aserradero* and *Taller mecánico*, which she performed in Madrid and Barcelona, placed her as a true pioneer of modern music. Returning to Montevideo, around 1928, she began teaching choral singing at the Normal Institute and continued her composition career principally with piano pieces and children's songs.

BIBLIOGRAPHY

S. Salgado: *Breve historia de la música culta en el Uruguay* (Montevideo, 1971, 2/1980)

SUSANA SALGADO

Barraine, Elsa (*b* 13 Feb 1910). French composer. The daughter of musical parents, she studied at the Paris Conservatoire with Paul Dukas for composition, Jean Gallon for harmony (*premier prix* 1925), Georges Caussade for fugue and A. C. Estyle for accompaniment (*premiers prix* for both in 1927). In 1929 she won the Prix de Rome with a cantata *La vierge guerrière*. Barraine worked for French radio (RTF) from 1936 to 1940 as a pianist, sound recordist and as head of singing, and after the war as a sound mixer; she left in 1948. She continued to compose and in 1953 became a professor at the Conservatoire, where she taught classes in sight-reading and analysis.

Profoundly sensitive to the enormous upheavals of her time, Barraine was unable to dissociate her creative processes from her personal, humanist, political and social preoccupations. The violent, sometimes brutal nature of her writing reflects the tragic emotional world of her works, yet despite this expressive tension, her musical language remains tonal, residing within strict formal frameworks. An exception to this is her *Musique rituelle* (1966–7), inspired by the Tibetan Book of the Dead, in which she uses serialism, creating the music's form from its rhythmic material. Barraine must be considered one of the most outstanding French women composers since Lili Boulanger.

WORKS

selective list

Dramatic: Printemps de la liberté (incid. music, J. Grémillon), 1948; La chanson du mal-aimé (ballet, after G. Apollinaire), 1950; Claudine à l'école (ballet, Colette), 1950

Orch: Sym., 1931; Pogromes, 1933; Sym., 1938; Variations sur 'Le fleuve rouge', 1945; Suite astrologique, small orch, 1945; Hommage à Prokofiev, hpd, orch, 1953; 3 ridicules, 1955; Les jongleurs, 1959; Les tziganes, 1959

Vocal: Avis (P. Eluard), chorus, orch, 1944; Poésie ininterrompue (cantata, Eluard), 3 solo vv, orch,

1948; L'homme sur terre (Eluard), chorus, orch, 1949; La nativité (L. Masson), solo vv, chorus, orch, 1951; Les cinq plaies (M. Manoll), solo vv, chorus, orch, 1952; Les paysans (A. Frenaud), 4 solo vv, chamber orch, 1958; De premier mai en premier mai (Eluard), 4 mixed vv, chorus, unacc., 1977

Chamber: Wind Qnt, 1931; Improvisation, sax, pf, 1947; Variations, perc, pf, 1950; Atmosphère, ob, 10 str, 1966; Musique rituelle (Bardo Thödol), org, gongs, xylorimba, 1966–7

Kbd: Hommage à Paul Dukas, 1936; Marche du printemps sans amour, 1946; Fantaisie, hpd, 1961

Film music, incl. Pattes blanches (J. Grémillon), 1948; Le sabotier du Val de Loire (J. Demy), 1956

Principal publishers: Costallat, Durand, Salabert, Schott

BIBLIOGRAPHY
A. Carré: *Souvenirs de théâtre* (Paris, 1950)
FRANÇOISE ANDRIEUX, PAUL GRIFFITHS

Barreau, Gisèle (*b* Cuëron, 28 Feb 1948). French composer. She studied at the Paris Conservatoire with Olivier Messiaen, Betsy Jolas and André Boucourechliev, then with the Groupe de Recherches Musicales. She received the Edgard Varèse scholarship (USA) and became Morton Feldman's assistant at SUNY, Buffalo; she has also served as composer-in-residence at the MacDowell Colony (USA) and at the Villa Medici, Rome. She was awarded the Koussevitzky Prize for *Tlaloc* in 1977, the SACEM Prix Enesco in 1978 and Prix Chapelier-Clergue in 1988, and the prize of the Ministère pour les Droits de la Femme in 1986 for her *Aires pour Marion*. Barreau's aesthetic conveys a constant concern for 'affect' and heightened emotion. Her writing shows particular sensitivity to the shaping of sound and, in a great number of works, she endeavours to make the text an integral part of the total sound material.

WORKS

Orch and inst: Océanes, 2 orch, 1976; Submarines, 2 pf, perc, 1977; Tlaloc, 2 perc, 1977; Piano-Piano, 2 fl, eng hn, 2 cl, dbn, tpt, hn, trbn, str qnt, 3 perc, 2 amp pf, 1981; Sterne, orch,1983; Little Rain, 2 perc, 1988; Inside, fl, cl, ob, tpt, 2 hn, pf, perc, 1989; Ostinato, 1/2 tpt, 1989; Qt, cl, str, 1991

Vocal: Rituel, men's chorus, ob, eng hn, 2 trbn, perc, 1974; Profils, female vv, fl, clvd, 2 perc, 1975; Cendres (St J. Perse), 8vv, 2 fl, 2 tuba, 3 perc, 1978; Clameurs (Perse), 2 choruses, orch, 1978; Aires pour Marion, 12vv, 6 perc, 1980

MARIE NOËLLE MASSON

Barrell [née Gedye], **Joyce Howard** (*b* Salisbury, 26 Nov 1917; *d* Ipswich, 6 Dec 1989). English composer. She studied harmony, composition and the piano with Benjamin Burrows, violin with his sister Grace and piano accompaniment with Harold Craxton. In 1945 she married the composer Bernard Barrell and in 1946 they settled in Suffolk. She worked as a guitar teacher and piano accompanist from 1958 to 1985. From 1939 until her death she composed prolifically, particularly chamber music and music for children, writing judiciously for a diversity of instruments. Her works include several pieces for string quartet (opp.15, 21, 32 and 77); six songs for children entitled *What am I?* op.68, for chorus and piano (1983); *Serenade* op.92, for saxophones (1989); and *Nightmare* op.93 (words by Stephen Coates), for soprano, clarinet and piano (1989). Her principal publishers are Anglian, MSM, Oecumuse/Barry Brunton, Thames, Schauer and May, and Wise Owl. Some material is held at the British Music Information Centre in London.

BIBLIOGRAPHY
CohenE
M. Dawney: Obituary, *MO*, cxiii (1989–90), 112
MARIE FITZPATRICK

Barrière, Françoise (*b* Paris, 12 June 1944). French composer. She studied the piano at the Versailles Conservatoire and composition at the Paris Conservatoire; she also studied at the Service de la Recherche de l'ORTF and at the Ecole Pratique des Hautes Etudes (ethnomusicology). She is committed to the development and dissemination of electroacoustic music, and to discussion of this music and its place in contemporary artistic creation. In 1970 she founded with Christian Clozier the Groupe de Musique Expérimentale de Bourges (GMEB), which is known for its creation of electroacoustic instruments for broadcasting or performance ('Gmebaphone'), and for beginners ('Gmebogosse'). Her works have been played widely and broadcast throughout the world since 1970, when her *Ode à la terre marine* for tape was composed. Barrière writes for both electroacoustic and mixed media. Her music combines technological development, as for example the mixing techniques of *Aujourd'hui* (1975), which are placed at the service of the compositional process, with a deep humanity, evident in the personal reminiscences of *Musique pour le temps de Noël* and *Par temps calme et ensoleillé*. Of *Aujourd'hui* she wrote that she was inspired by the 'overwhelming solitude of the individual in our modern society'.

WORKS
selective list; for tape unless otherwise stated

Ode à la terre marine, 1970; Cordes-ci, cordes-ça, vn, hurdy-gurdy, tape, 1971; Variations hydrophilusiennes, 1971; Java Rosa, 1972; Au paradis des assassins, 1973; Ritratto di Giovane, pf, tape, 1972–3;

Aujourd'hui, 1975; Chant à la mémoire des Aurignaciens, 1977; Musique pour le temps de Noël, sax, va, vc, perc, tape, 1979; Mémoires enfuies, 1980

Scènes des voyages d'Ulysse, 1981; Par temps calme et ensoleillé I, pf, tape, 1983; Par temps calme et ensoleillé II, vc, tape, 1985–9; Chant de consonnes, 1987; Le tombeau de Robespierre, 1989; L'envers des mots, 1990; Conversations enfantines, 1991; Nos petits monstres musiciens, child actor-musician, tape, 1992

PIERRE SABY

Barron, Bebe [née Charlotte Wind] (*b* Minneapolis, 16 June 1927). American composer. She and her husband Louis Barron (*b* Minneapolis, 23 April 1920; *d* Los Angeles, 1 Nov 1989) were pioneers in the field of electroacoustic music. She received the MA in political science from the University of Minnesota, where she studied composition with Roque Cordero, and she also spent a year studying composition and ethnomusicology at the University of Mexico. In 1948 she moved to New York and, while working as a researcher for *Time-Life*, studied composition with Wallingford Riegger and Henry Cowell. That same year the Barrons were married and began their experiments with taped electronic sounds; in 1949 in New York they established one of the earliest electroacoustic music studios. When they collaborated on a composition, Louis designed and built the electronic circuits for sound generation while Bebe searched the taped material for its musical potential and proposed the application of particular processing and compositional techniques. In 1956 the Barrons composed the music for *Forbidden Planet*, one of the first electronic scores written for a commercial film, and an influential work in the development of electronic music. In 1962 the Barrons moved to Los Angeles; they divorced in 1970. Bebe became the first Secretary of the Society for Electro-Acoustic Music in the United States in 1985 and also served on the Board of Directors.

WORKS
all electroacoustic, composed with Louis Barron

Dramatic: Legend (American Mime Theatre), 1955; Ballet (P. Feigay), 1958; incid. music for 4 plays, 1957–62

Tape: Heavenly Menagerie, 1951–2; For an Electronic Nervous System, 1954; Music of Tomorrow, 1960; Spaceboy, 1971; The Circe Circuit, 1982; Elegy for a Dying Planet, 1982

Film scores: Bells of Atlantis (I. Hugo), 1952; Miramagic (W. Lewisohn), 1954; Forbidden Planet (F. M. Wilcox), 1956; Jazz of Lights (Hugo), 1956; Bridges (S. Clarke), 1959; Crystal Growing (Western Electric), 1959; The Computer Age (IBM), 1968; Spaceboy (R. Druks), 1973 [arr. of 1971 tape piece]; More than Human (A. Singer), 1974; Cannabis (Computer Graphics), 1975

BIBLIOGRAPHY

P. Glanville-Hicks: 'Tapesichord: the Music of Whistle and Bang', *Vogue* (July 1953), 80–81, 108

L. Barron and B. Barron: 'Forbidden Planet', *Film Music*, xv/5 (1956), 18

C. Harmon: 'Music of the Future', *Time*, lxviii/1 (2 July 1956), 36

E. Wallace: 'Ah, the Sweet Mystery of Noise', *New York World-Telegram* (6 May 1956)

P. Manvell and J. Huntley: *Technique of Film Music* (New York, 1957), 166

A. Nin: *The Diary of Anaïs Nin*, v–vii (New York, 1974–80)

S. Rubin: 'Retrospect: Forbidden Planet', *Cinefantastique*, iv/ l (1975), 4–13

F. Clarke and S. Rubin: 'Making Forbidden Planet', *Cinefantastique*, vii/2–3 (1979), 42–54

D. Shary: *Heyday* (Boston, 1979), 290–91

B Schrader: *Introduction to Electro-Acoustic Music* (Englewood Cliffs, NJ, 1982), 78–9

V. Vale and A. Juno: *Incredibly Strange Music No.2* (San Francisco, 1994) 194–202

BARRY SCHRADER

Barthélemon, Cecilia Maria (*b* 1769/70; *d* after 1840). English composer and singer, daughter of Maria Barthélemon. She went with her parents on their continental tour (1776–7) and sang before the King of Naples and Marie Antoinette. She appeared with her parents in England from 1778, as a singer and as a pianist. She does not appear to have had an independent performing career or to have composed after her marriage to Captain E. P. Henslowe (not W. H. Henslowe; see the memoir *Francis Barthelemon*, London, 1896). Haydn was a friend of the Barthélemons; Cecilia dedicated her keyboard sonata op.3 to him and was a subscriber (listed as 'Mrs Ed. Henslow') to *The Creation*.

WORKS
all published in London

Inst: 3 Sonatas, pf/hpd, op.1 (1791), no.2 with vn acc.; 2 Sonatas, pf/hpd, vn/fl, vc acc., op.2 (1792); Sonata, pf/hpd, op.3 (1794); Sonata, pf/hpd, vn acc., op.4 (1795)

Vocal: The Capture of the Cape of Good Hope, pf/hpd, S (1795)

For bibliography *see* BARTHÉLEMON, MARIA.

OLIVE BALDWIN, THELMA WILSON

Barthélemon [née Young], **Maria** [Polly; Mary] (*b* London, *c*1749; *d* London, 20 Sept 1799). English composer and singer. She was the youngest of the six female members of the Young family who were celebrated singers. Her aunt Cecilia Young was the wife of Thomas Arne and Maria (known as 'Polly') went with the Arnes to Dublin where she sang 'perfectly in Time and Tune' in Arne's *Eliza* at the age of six. In 1758 Mrs Delany wrote 'the race of Youngs are *born* songsters and musicians' after hearing the child Polly accompanying on the harpsichord. She returned to London in 1762 and sang in English stage works, Italian operas and concerts. After marrying the violinist and composer François Hippolyte Barthélemon in 1766 she almost always appeared with him, in London and Ireland and on a visit to the Continent (1776–7). Her compositions reflect her performing career and her charitable interests.

WORKS
all published in London

Inst: 6 Sonatas, hpd/pf, vn acc. (1776)

Vocal: 6 English and Italian Songs, op.2 (1786); The Weaver's Prayer, song (?1790); 3 Hymns and 3 Anthems, op.3 (1795); An Ode on the Late Providential Preservation of our Most Gracious Sovereign, op.5 (1795)

BIBLIOGRAPHY
BDA; *BurneyH*

F. H. Barthélemon: *Jefte in Masfa* [incl. a memoir by C. M. Barthélemon] (London, 1827)

M. Delany: *Autobiography and Correspondence of Mary Granville, Mrs Delany*, ed. Lady Llanover (London, 1861–2)

C. Higham: *Francis Barthelemon* (London, 1896)

H. C. R. Landon, ed.: *The Collected Correspondence and London Notebooks of Joseph Haydn* (London, 1959)

H. C. R. Landon: *Haydn in England 1791–1795* (London, 1976)

B. Boydell: *A Dublin Musical Calendar 1700–1760* (Dublin, 1988)

OLIVE BALDWIN, THELMA WILSON

Bartholomew, Ann Mounsey. *See* MOUNSEY, ANN.

Basile, Andreana (*b* Posillipo, nr Naples, *c*1580; *d* Rome, *c*1640). Italian singer, instrumentalist and composer. She was known as 'la bella Adriana', for the beauty of her singing. By 1603 she was a singer of renown in Naples, and had married Muzio Baroni. Vicenzo Gonzaga, Duke of Mantua, heard her sing in Naples in 1603; she agreed to come to his court only after extracting promises that various family members would also be in his service and that she would be formally in the service of the Duchess rather than the Duke (to guarantee her reputation for sexual virtue). She left Naples for Mantua on 23 May 1610 and remained in service there until 1624. In 1630 she sang with her daughter Leonora Baroni and in 1633 she settled in Rome with Leonora and her other daughter.

Monteverdi thought Basile the most capable singer of her generation; in a letter of 9 December 1616, referring to the Mantuan preparations for *Le nozze di Tetide*, he asserts that Basile (along with her sisters) would be capable of composing her own music for the part she was to play. Although no music of Basile's survives, she is known to have improvised on poetry given to her, notably in competition with Francesca Caccini in November 1623. Her artistry was lavishly praised by contemporary poets.

BIBLIOGRAPHY
GerberNL; *SainsburyD*; *SchillingE*; *SchmidlD*; *WaltherML*

D. Bombarda: *Teatro delle glorie della S.ra. Adriana Basile* (Venice, 1623; repr., Naples, 1628)

A. M. Crinò: 'Virtuose di canto e poeti a Roma e a Firenze nella prima metà del seicento', *Studi secenteschi*, i (1960), 175

E. Rosand: 'Barbara Strozzi: the Composer's Voice', *JAMS*, xxxi (1978), 241–81

J. Bowers: 'The Emergence of Women Composers in Italy, 1566–1700', *Women Making Music: the Western Art Tradition, 1150–1950*, ed. J. Bowers and J. Tick (Urbana and Chicago, 1986), 116–67

J. Chater: 'Musical Patronage in Rome at the Turn of the Seventeenth Century: the Case of Cardinal Montaldo', *Studi musicali*, xvi/2 (1987), 179–227

SUZANNE G. CUSICK

Bate, Peggy. *See* GLANVILLE-HICKS, PEGGY.

Bauer, Marion Eugénie (*b* Walla Walla, WA, 15 Aug 1882; *d* South Hadley, MA, 9 Aug 1955). American composer, teacher and writer on music. She pursued a musical education through private study in New York, Paris (1906–7, 1923–6) and Berlin (1910–11) with Emilie Frances Bauer (her older sister as well as a respected music critic and occasional composer), Henry Holden Huss, Eugene Heffley and Walter Henry Rothwell; with Raoul Pugno, Nadia Boulanger (probably as her first American pupil), Louis Campbell-Tipton and, later, André Gédalge; and with John Paul Ertel. Beginning in 1919, she spent many enriching summers at the MacDowell Colony, where she met several other important women composers including Amy Beach, Mabel Daniels, Mary Howe, Miriam Gideon and Ruth Crawford, whose MacDowell Colony diaries for summer 1929 and winter 1930 bear witness to feelings of affinity and a mutually supportive relationship with Bauer. She taught music history and composition at New York University (1926–51) and at Juilliard (1940–44) and lectured widely elsewhere. Colouristic harmony, programmatic titles and through-

Marion Bauer

composed forms predominate in her works. In some she blurred functional tonality through extended harmonies and diatonic dissonance, yet her writing remained melodic in focus and was grounded in tertian harmony and periodic rhythm.

During her lifetime she was recognized through performances of and publicity about her works, but changing tastes shifted assessment from a 'radical member of the musical left wing' in the 1920s to a middle-of-the-road impressionist by the 40s (Howard, 192). Open to various styles, she strongly supported American music and modern composers as is evident from her co-founding of the American Music Guild (1921), her membership of the Society of American Women Composers and her participation in many other American musical organizations. Her acceptance in male circles was perhaps due to her having studied in France, which by the early 1920s was the centre for musical activity, her influence as a music critic and her intellectual approach to new music, demonstrated in such writings as *Twentieth Century Music* (New York, 1933, 2/1947).

WORKS
selective list

INSTRUMENTAL

Orch: A Lament on an African Theme, op.20a, str, 1927 [orig. for str qt, op.20]; Sun Splendor, ?1936 [orch of pf work, ?1929]; Sym. Suite, op.34, str,

1940; Pf Conc. 'American Youth', op.36, 1943, arr. 2 pf, 1946; Sym. no.1, op.45, 1947–50; Prelude and Fugue, op.43, fl, str, 1948/9

Chamber: Up the Ocklawaha, op.6, vn, pf, 1913; Vn Sonata no.1, op.14, 1921/2; Str Qt, 1925; Fantasia quasi una sonata, op.18, vn, pf, 1928; Sonata, op.22, va/cl, pf, 1932; Suite (Duo), op.25, ob, cl, 1932; Concertino, op.32b, ob, cl, str qt/str orch, 1939/1943; Trio Sonata no.1, op.40, fl, vc, pf, 1944; 5 Pieces (Patterns), op.41, str qt, 1946–9 [orig. for pf], no.2 arr. double ww qnt, db, 1948; Aquarelle, op39/2[a], double ww qnt, 2 db, 1948 [orig. for pf]; Trio Sonata no.2, fl, vc, pf, 1951; Ww Qnt, op.48, fl, ob, cl, bn, hn

Kbd (pf solo unless otherwise stated): From New Hampshire Woods, op.12, 1921 [no.2, Indian Pipes, orchd M. Bernstein, 1927–8; 3 Preludettes, 1921; 6 Preludes, op.15, 1922; Turbulence, op.17/2, 1924; A Fancy, 1927; Sun Splendor, ?1929, arr. 2 pf, ?1930; 4 Pf Pieces, op.21, 1930; Dance Sonata, op.24, 1932; Meditation and Toccata, org, 1951

Other inst: Prometheus Bound (incid. music, Aeschylus), 2 fl, 2 pf, 1930; Pan and Syrinx, op.31 (choreog. sketch for film), fl, ob, cl, pf, vn, va, vc, 1937

VOCAL

Wenn ich rufe an dich, Herr, mein Gott, op.3 (Ps 28), S, women's chorus, org/pf, 1903; Coyote Song (J. S. Reed), Bar, pf, 1912; The Red Man's Requiem (E. F. Bauer), 1v, pf, 1912; Fair Daffodils (R. Herrick), women's chorus, kbd, 1914; Orientale (E. Arnold), S, orch, 1914, orchd 1932/1934; The Lay of the Four Winds, op.8 (C. Y. Rice), men's chorus, pf, 1915; Four Poems, op.16 (J. G. Fletcher), high v, pf, 1916/1924; A Parable (The Blade of Grass) (S. Crane), 1v, pf, 1922

Here at High Morning, op.27 (M. Lewis), men's chorus, 1931; Faun Song, A, chamber orch, 1934; 4 Songs (Suite), S, str qt, 1935/6; The Thinker, op.35, mixed chorus, 1938; China, op.38 (B. Todrin), mixed chorus, orch/pf, 1944; At the New Year, op.42 (K. Patchen), mixed chorus, pf, 1947; Death Spreads his Gentle Wings (E. P. Crain), mixed chorus, 1949/1951; A Foreigner Comes to Earth on Boston Common (H. Gregory), S, T, mixed chorus, 1951

Principal publishers: Composers Facsimile Edition/ ACA, G. Schirmer, A. P. Schmidt

BIBLIOGRAPHY

EwenD; *KompA-Z*; *NAW* (C. Ammer); *WAM*

J. T. Howard: *Our Contemporary Composers* (New York, 1941), 192–3

C. Reis: *Composers in America: Biographical Sketches* (New York, 1947 [4th edn of *American Composers*])

M. Goss: *Modern Music Makers* (New York, 1952), 126–40

C. Ammer: *Unsung: a History of Women in American Music* (Westport, CT, 1980), esp. 123–7

J. M. Meggett: *Keyboard Music by Women Composers: a Catalogue and Bibliography* (Westport, CT, 1981)

A. I. Cohen: *International Discography of Women Composers* (Westport, CT, 1984)

J. L. Zaimont and others, eds.: *The Musical Woman: an International Perspective*, i (Westport, CT, 1984); ii–iii (New York, 1987–91) [incl. A. F. Block: 'Arthur P. Schmidt, Music Publisher and Champion of American Women Composers', ii, 145–76, esp. 146, 163, 167–72]

J. M. Edwards: 'North America since 1920', *Women in Music: a History*, ed. K. Pendle (Bloomington, IN, 1991), 211–57, esp. 211–12

J. MICHELE EDWARDS

Bauld, Alison (Margaret) (*b* Sydney, 7 May 1944). Australian composer. She showed early promise as a pianist but studied drama at the National Institute of Dramatic Art (1961–2) and worked briefly as an actress before entering Sydney University to read English and Music (BMus 1968). In 1969 she was awarded a two-year Moss Travelling Scholarship to London, where she studied with Elisabeth Lutyens and Hans Keller. Having settled in England, she gained the PhD from York University in 1974 and the following year received a Gulbenkian Dance Award for composition. She was Musical Director of the Laban Centre, London, 1975–8, and in 1978 was composer-in-residence at the New South Wales Conservatorium. She has fulfilled numerous commissions and in 1980 received a bursary from the Arts Council of Great Britain.

Bauld's knowledge of theatre (she has lectured on theatre history at York University) informs many of her works, perhaps most noticeably in her studies of Shakespearean heroines: *Banquo's Buried*, *Cry, Cock-a-Doodle-Doo* and *The Witches' Song*. She favours writing for the voice and often sets her own texts, producing works with a particularly integrated dramatic content, such as her opera *Nell*; this was first performed at the Donmar Warehouse as part of the 1988 London International Opera Festival. She has devoted the early 1990s to preparing a series of original keyboard tutors, *Play Your Way*, which use newly composed material.

WORKS
selective list

Stage: On the Afternoon of the Pigsty (Bauld), female spkr, a melodica, pf, perc, 1971; Nell (ballad opera, Bauld), S, Mez, T, Bar, chorus, fl, ob, cl, a melodica, bn, perc, pf, 2 vn, va, vc, db, 1988

Chamber and inst: Concert (pf, tape)/2 pf, 1974; The Busker's Story, a sax, bn, tpt, vn, db, 1978; Monody, fl, 1985, rev. as Copy Cats, vn, vc, pf, 1985; My Own Island, cl, pf, 1989; Play Your Way, pf, 1992 [3 vols.]

Vocal: Withdrawal I and II, S, nar, vn, vc, pf, vib, perc, tape, 1968–70; In a Dead Brown Land, S, T, chorus, fl, pic, a melodica, vn, vc, pipes, drums, 1971, rev. 1974; Humpty Dumpty (Bauld), T, fl, gui, 1972; Dear Emily (Bauld), S, harp/kbd, 1973; Mad Moll (Bauld), S, 1973; One Pearl (Bauld), S/Ct, str qt, 1973, rev. as One Pearl II, S, a fl, str orch, 1976; Van Diemen's Land (Bauld), SATB, 1976; I Loved Miss Watson, S, pf, tape, 1977; Banquo's Buried (W. Shakespeare), S, pf, 1982;

Richard III (after Shakespeare), 1v, str qt, 1985; Once Upon a Time (Bauld), 5 solo vv, 3 children's vv (opt.), chamber orch, 1986; Cry, Cock-a-Doodle-Doo, S, pf, 1989; Exult, children's chorus, org, brass qt (opt.), 1990; The Witches' Song, S, 1990

Principal publisher: Novello

BIBLIOGRAPHY

Fuller-LeFanuRM

P. Griffiths: 'Alison Bauld', *MT*, cxvii (1976), 903–4

A. Bauld: 'Sounding a Personal Note', *MT*, cxxix (1988), 339–40

TONI CALAM, THÉRÈSE RADIC

Bawr, (Alexandrine-)Sophie (Goury de Champgrand), Mme **de** [Comtesse de Saint-Simon, Baronne de Bawr; M. François] (*b* Paris, 8 Oct 1773; *d* Paris, 31 Dec 1860). French composer and author. Though born out of wedlock to a marquis and an opera singer, she was recognized and reared by both parents and given a good education. In her early years she took lessons from the singer Pierre Garat and the composers A.-E.-M. Grétry and Nicolas Roze and sang her own songs in salons (she was also an accomplished pianist). She was further encouraged in composition by Adrien Boieldieu and the singer Jean Elleviou and may have been friendly with the singer-composer Sophie Gail. During her long life, she published, mainly as Mme de Bawr (she sometimes used the name M. François), a number of touching and harmonically expert songs, wrote successful history books, novels, stories, one-act plays, *mélodrames* (plays with music she composed), as well as an opera that apparently was never performed. Some of her writings were translated into German or Spanish. An early feminist, she argued in her writings that the position of women in society, and especially in the arts, needed to be improved.

She was briefly married (1801–2) to the social theorist Claude Henri de Rouvroy, Comte de Saint-Simon (1760–1825); Grétry and the dramatist Alexandre Duval were witnesses at the wedding. (Some accounts mention, apparently erroneously, a previous marriage.) She ran a salon for Saint-Simon so that he might meet prominent musicians and writers. She illegally retained the title 'Comtesse' after marrying the young Russian Baron de Bawr in about 1809; however, de Bawr soon died (in about 1810) after being hit by a heavy cart in the road. Left penniless, Mme de Bawr turned to a more systematic professional musical career that lasted decades. During the Bourbon Restoration, she was granted a pension by Louis XVIII.

For the *Encyclopédie des dames* she wrote the volume *Histoire de la musique* (Paris, 1823) and she published her memoirs, *Mes souvenirs* (Paris, 1853).

WORKS
selective list

Stage: Les chevaliers du lion (mélodrame, 3, Bawr), lib (Paris, 1804), ?music lost; Léon, ou Le château de Montaldi (opera, 3, Bawr), Paris, Théâtre de l'Ambigu-Comique, 22 Oct 1811, lost
Songs (romances, for 1v, pf, harp or gui): D'aimer besoin puissant (Viot), after 1800; J'étais heureux (Paris, after 1800); A la mémoire d'un être chéri (O, toi qui ne peux plus m'entendre) (Bawr), in *Le souvenir des ménestrels*, no.20 (1814), pp.78–9

BIBLIOGRAPHY

FétisB; *FétisBS*; *DBF*; *MGG* suppl. (R. Cotte); *SchmidlD*
C. Gardeton: *Annales de la musique . . . pour l'an 1819* (Paris, 1819), 11
——: *Bibliographie musicale de la France et de l'étranger* (Paris, 1822)
J. C. F. Hoefer: *Nouvelle biographie générale* (Paris, 1859)
E. Gagne [E. Moreau]: *Mme de Bawr: étude sur sa vie et ses oeuvres* (Paris, 1861)
J. Janin: Obituary, *Journal des débats* (14 Jan 1861)
H. Gougelot: *Catalogue des romances parues sous la Révolution et l'Empire* (Melun, 1937–43), i, 174
——: *La romance française sous la Révolution et l'Empire* (Melun, 1938–43), i, 147
R. P. Locke: *Music, Musicians, and the Saint-Simonians* (Chicago and London, 1986), 25–6

RALPH P. LOCKE

Bayon, Marie Emmanuelle (*b* Marcei, Orne, 1746; *d* Aubevoye, Eure, 19 March 1825). French pianist and composer. She published six keyboard sonatas, three with violin accompaniment (1769); a two-act *opéra-comique Fleur d'épine* (performed in Paris at the Théâtre Italien, 1776); and arrangements of the overture and selected *airs* and *ariettes*. She was a member of the 1767 salon of Mme de Genlis, who discusses Bayon's music in her *Mémoires* (Paris, 1825). She married the architect Victor Louis in 1770, presided over a distinguished salon in Bordeaux, then in Paris, and brought the fortepiano into vogue in France.

BIBLIOGRAPHY

Choron-FayolleD; *GerberL*; *SainsburyD*
D. Hayes: Introduction to *M. E. Bayon: Six sonates* (New York, 1990)
——: 'Marie-Emmanuelle Bayon, later Madame Louis, and Music in Late Eighteenth-Century France', *College Music Symposium*, xxx (1990), 14–33

DEBORAH HAYES

Beach [née Cheney], **Amy Marcy** [Mrs H. H. A. Beach] (*b* Henniker, NH, 5 Sept 1867; *d* New York, 27 Dec 1944). Composer and pianist. She was the first American woman to succeed as a composer of large-scale art music and was celebrated during her lifetime as the foremost woman composer of the USA. A descendant of a distinguished New England family, she was the only child of Charles Abbott Cheney, a paper manufacturer and importer, and Clara Imogene (Marcy) Cheney, a talented amateur singer and pianist. At the age of one she could sing 40 tunes accurately and always in the same key; before the age of two she improvised alto lines against her mother's soprano melodies; at three she taught herself to read; and at four she mentally composed her first piano pieces and later played them, and could play hymns by ear in four-part harmony. The Cheneys moved to Chelsea, Massachusetts, about 1871. Amy's mother agreed to teach her the piano when she was six, and at seven she gave her first public recitals, playing works by Handel, Beethoven and Chopin, and her own pieces. In 1875 the family moved to Boston, where her parents were advised that she could enter a European conservatory; but they decided on local training, engaging Ernst Perabo and later Carl Baermann as piano teachers. In composition, Wilhelm Gericke prescribed a course of independent study using the masters as models. She had one year of harmony and counterpoint with Junius W. Hill, then taught herself orchestration and fugue, translating treatises by Hector Berlioz and François-Auguste Gevaert. Her development as a pianist was monitored by a circle including Percy Goetschius, H. W. Longfellow, Oliver Wendell Holmes, William Mason, and Henry Harris Aubrey Beach (1843–1910), a physician who lectured on anatomy at Harvard and was an amateur singer; she was to marry him in 1885.

At her successful début in Boston (24 October 1883) she played Chopin's Rondo in E♭ and Moscheles's G minor Concerto, conducted by Adolf Neuendorff; at her début with the Boston SO (28 March 1885), the first of several appearances with that orchestra, she played Chopin's F minor Concerto with Gericke conducting. After her marriage to Dr Beach, and in respect of his wishes, she curtailed her performances, donating the fees to charity, and concentrated on composition.

Beach's first published work was *The Rainy Day*, a setting of Longfellow's poem, composed in 1880 and issued in 1883. Her major works during the period 1885–1910 include the Mass in E♭ op.5, *Eilende Wolken* op.18, the Symphony op.32 and the

Amy Marcy Beach

poser and the critic Ferdinand Pfohl called Beach a 'virtuoso pianist' who had, as a composer, 'a musical nature tinged with genius'.

At the outbreak of World War I Beach returned to the USA, with 30 concerts already scheduled in the East and Midwest, and in 1915 moved to New York. Thereafter she spent winters on tour and summers practising and composing in Hillsboro, New Hampshire; in Centerville on Cape Cod, Massachusetts, where she owned land purchased with the proceeds of her song *Ecstasy* op.19 no.2; and, from 1921, as a fellow at the MacDowell Colony. She made several trips abroad, including one to Rome (1929), where she finished her String Quartet op.89. In 1942, to celebrate Beach's 75th birthday, Elena de Sayn, a violinist and critic from Washington, DC, organized two retrospective concerts of her music.

A highly disciplined composer, capable of producing large-scale works in a few days, Beach was also energetic in the promotion of her compositions, arranging for performances as soon as works were completed. As a pianist, she had a virtuoso technique and an extraordinary memory. She was interested in philosophy and science, and was fluent in German and French. Deeply religious, she later became virtual composer-in-residence at St Bartholomew's Protestant Episcopal Church, New York. She was generous, using her status as dean of American women composers to further the careers of many young musicians. She served as leader of several organizations including the Music Teachers National Association and the Music Educators National Conference, and was co-founder in 1925 and the first president of the Society of American Women Composers. Her will assigned her royalties to the MacDowell Colony.

Beach's earliest works demonstrate her ability to create a long line and her sensitivity to relationships between music and text. Song is at the core of her style – she used some of her songs as themes in her instrumental works (e.g. the Symphony, the Piano Concerto op.45 and the Piano Trio op.150) – but her remarkable ear for harmony and harmonic colour also is apparent from the beginning. Like the early Romantics, Beach emphasized modal degrees and used mixed modes. Her perfect pitch and association of keys with colours and by extension with moods resulted in the expressive use of modulation (e.g. the song *Die vier Brüder* from op.1).

Piano Concerto op.45 – all introduced by such ensembles as the Boston Handel and Haydn Society, the Boston SO, and the Symphony Society of New York. Among her commissioned works were the *Festival Jubilate* op.17, written for the dedication (1 May 1893) of the Women's Building of the World's Columbian Exposition, Chicago, and the *Song of Welcome* op.42, for the Trans-Mississippi Exposition, Omaha (1898); others were the *Panama Hymn* op.74, for the international Panama Pacific Exposition in San Francisco (1915), and the Theme and Variations for Flute and String Quartet op.80, for the San Francisco Chamber Music Society. Beach performed in annual solo recitals and introduced her works, playing with orchestral, choral, and chamber groups.

After her husband's death, Beach went to Europe (sailing on 5 September 1911), determined to establish a reputation there as both performer and composer and to promote the sale of her own works. Beginning in autumn 1912 she gave recitals in German cities, playing her concerto, sonata and quintet, and accompanying her songs; several German orchestras played her symphony. The reviews were favourable: one journal stated that Beach was the leading American com-

Her mature style, characterized by increasing chromaticism, use of long-held and overlapping appoggiaturas, 7th- and augmented-6th chords, modulation by 3rds, and avoidance of the dominant, shows her debt to the late Romantics, as well to the use of Scottish and Irish folk music. Some of Beach's late works, while remaining tonal, move away from triadic harmony by means of linear textures and increased dissonance, beginning with the String Quartet of 1929, in which she quotes Inuit melodies as themes.

Beach first made her reputation as a composer of art songs. But it was her large-scale works beginning with the Mass and the Symphony that won her acceptance first by her Boston colleagues then nationally and internationally. Her most popular works in addition to the songs were the Symphony, which had dozens of performances by leading orchestras, the Violin Sonata, the Piano Quintet, the Theme and Variations for flute quintet, the *Hermit Thrush* pieces for piano and, among the secular choral works, *The Chambered Nautilus*. Her sacred works, in particular the anthem *Let this mind be in you* and *The Canticle of the Sun*, remained in the repertory of church choirs for years after her death when her other works were no longer heard. Many of her works have returned to the concert stage and about a third of a total of 300 have been recorded.

WORKS
*printed works published in Boston
unless otherwise stated*
fs – full score   os – organ score
ps – piano score

Sources: An extensive collection of MSS, correspondence, printed music, scrapbooks and photographs is in the University of New Hampshire, Durham, NH; further MSS, printed editions and correspondence are in *US-Wc*; orchestral scores are in *Bc* and *PHf*; a smaller collection of printed music and MSS, including juvenilia, is in *KC*.

Editions:
Amy Beach: Piano Music, Women Composers Series, x (New York, 1982) [WC x]
Amy Marcy Beach: Twenty-Eight Songs (Huntsville, TX, 1985) [BS]
Amy Beach: Twenty-Three Songs, Women Composers Series, xxv (New York, 1992) [WC xxv]
Collection of Piano Music, ed. S. Glickman (Bryn Mawr, PA, 1994) [G]
Amy Beach: Five Pieces for Violin and Piano, ed. S. Plant (Bryn Mawr, PA, 1994) [P]

op.

OPERA
149   Cabildo (1, N. B. Stephens), solo vv, chorus, speaker, vn, vc, pf, 1932, *US-KC*; Athens, GA, 27 Feb 1945

ORCHESTRAL, VOCAL ORCHESTRAL
18   Eilende Wolken, Segler die Lüfte (F. von Schiller), A, orch, 1892, vs (1892); New York, 2 Dec 1892
22   Bal masque, New York, 12 Dec 1893 [see also KEYBOARD]
32   Sym. 'Gaelic', e, 1894–6, fs (1897); Boston, 30 Oct 1896
45   Pf Conc., c♯, 1899; Boston, 6 April 1900; arr. 2 pf (1900)
53   Jephthah's Daughter (Mollevaut, after *Judges* xi.38; It. trans., I. Martinez; Eng. trans., A. M. Beach), S, orch, vs (1903)

CHAMBER
23   Romance, vn, pf (1893), P; Boston, 22 Jan 1893
34   Vn Sonata, a, 1896 (1899), ed. in Women Composers, ser. xix (New York, 1986); Boston, 4 Jan 1897
40/1–3   Three Compositions, vn, pf (1898), P: La captive, Berceuse, Mazurka; Boston, 2 April 1898; arr. vc (1903)
55   Invocation, vn, pf/org, vc obbl (1904), P
67   Pf Qnt, f♯, 1907 (1909/R1979); Boston, 27 Feb 1908
80   Theme and Variations, fl, str qt, 1916 (New York, 1920), ed. J. Graziano, *American Chamber Music*, Three Centuries of American Music, viii (n.p., 1991); San Francisco, 28 Sept 1916
—   Caprice, The Water Sprites, fl, vc, pf, 1921, KC
89   Str Qt, 1 movt, 1929, Wc, ed. A.F. Block, Music of the United States of America, iii (Madison, WI, 1994); Washington DC, 28 Nov 1942
90   Pastorale, fl, vc, pf, 1921, KC
125   Lento espressivo, vn, pf, MS in U. of New Hampshire, Durham
150   Pf Trio, 1938 (New York, 1939); New York, 15 Jan 1939
151   Pastorale, ww qnt (New York, 1942)

KEYBOARD
piano unless otherwise stated
3   Cadenza to Beethoven: Pf Conc. no.3, op.37, 1st movt (1888); Boston, 28 April 1888
4   Valse-caprice (1889), WC x; Boston, 21 March 1889
6   Ballad (1894), WC x, G; Boston, 27 Feb 1891
15/1–4   Four Sketches (1892), WC x: In Autumn, G; Phantoms, G; Dreaming, G; Fireflies, G; nos.1 and 3, Boston, 29 Nov 1892
22   Bal masque (1894)
25   Children's Carnival (1894)
28/1–3   Trois morceaux caractéristiques (1894), WC x, G: Barcarolle, Minuet italien, Danse des fleurs
36/1–5   Children's Album (1897): Minuet, Gavotte, Waltz, March, Polka
47   Summer Dreams, pf 4 hands (1901)
54/1–2   Scottish Legend, Gavotte fantastique (1903), G; Boston, 25 Nov 1904
60   Variations on Balkan Themes, 1904 (1906), arr. orch 1906, rev. (1936), arr. 2 pf (1937); Boston, 8 Feb 1905
64/1–4   Eskimos: Four Characteristic Pieces (1907), rev. (1943): Arctic Night, The Returning Hunter, Exiles, With Dog Teams
65   Suite: Les rêves de Columbine (1907), G; Boston, 11 Feb 1908

70   Iverniana, 2 pf, 1910, lost; Boston, 10 Feb
       1910
81   Prelude and Fugue (New York, 1918), WC x;
       Boston, 16 Dec 1914
83   From Blackbird Hills (1922)
87   Fantasia fugata (Philadelphia, 1923), WC x;
       Boston, 4 April 1922
91   The Fair Hills of Eire, pf/org (1922); New
       London, NH, 8 Oct 1921; rev. as Prelude
       on an Old Folk Tune, org (New York,
       1943)
92/1–2 The Hermit Thrush at Eve, The Hermit
       Thrush at Morn (1922); New London, NH,
       8 Oct 1921
97/1–5 From Grandmother's Garden (1922), G:
       Morning Glories, Heartsease, Mignonette,
       Rosemary and Rue, Honeysuckle
102/   Pf Compositions (1924): Farewell Summer,
1–2   Dancing Leaves
104   Suite for Two Pianos Founded upon Old
       Irish Melodies (Cincinnati, 1924); Paris, 25
       Oct 1924
106   Old Chapel by Moonlight (Cincinnati, 1924)
107   Nocturne (Cincinnati, 1924), WC x
108   A Cradle Song of the Lonely Mother (1924),
       WC x
111   From Olden Times
114   By the Still Waters (St Louis, 1925);
       Washington DC, 7 March 1925
116   Tyrolean Valse-fantaisie (1926), WC x;
       Pittsburgh, 1 Dec 1915
119   From Six to Twelve (1927)
—   A Bit of Cairo (Philadelphia, 1928)
128/   Three Pf Pieces (Philadelphia, 1932),
1–3   WC x: Scherzino, Young Birches, A
       Humming Bird
130   Out of the Depths (1932)
148   Five Improvisations (New York, 1938)

SACRED CHORAL
4vv and organ, unless otherwise stated

5   Mass, Eb, 4vv, orch, 1890, os (1890); Boston,
       7 Feb 1892
7   O praise the Lord, all ye nations (Ps cxvii)
       (1891); Boston, 7 Feb 1891
8/1–3 Choral Responses (1891): Nunc dimittis
       (*Luke* ii.29), With prayer and supplication
       (*Philippians* iv.6–7), Peace I leave with you
       (*John* iv.27)
17   Festival Jubilate (Ps c), D, 7vv, orch, 1891, ps
       (1892); Chicago, 1 May 1893
24   Bethlehem (G. C. Hugg) (1893)
27   Alleluia, Christ is risen (after M. Weisse, C.
       F. Gellert, T. Scott, T. Gibbons) (1895);
       arr. with vn obbl (1904)
33   Teach me thy way (Ps lxxxvi.11–12), 1895,
       KC
38   Peace on earth (E. H. Sears) (1897)
50   Help us, O God (Pss lxxix.9, 5; xlv.6;
       xliv.26), 5vv (1903)
52   A Hymn of Freedom: America (S. F. Smith),
       4vv, org/pf (1903); rev. with text O Lord
       our God arise (1944)
63   Service in A, S, A, T, B, 4vv, org: Te Deum,
       Benedictus (1905); Jubilate Deo,
       Magnificat, Nunc dimittis (1906)
74   All hail the power of Jesus' name (E.
       Perronet), 4vv, org/pf (New York, 1915)
76   Thou knowest, Lord (J. Borthwick), T, B,
       4vv, org (New York, 1915)

78/1–4 Canticles (New York, 1916): Bonum est,
       confiteri (Ps xcii.1–4), S, 4vv, org, Deus
       misereatur (Ps lxvii), Cantate Domino (Ps
       xcviii), Benedic, anima mea (Ps ciii)
84   Te Deum, f, T, male chorus 3vv, org (Phila-
       delphia, 1922)
95   Constant Christmas (P. Brooks), S, A, 4vv,
       org (Philadelphia, 1922)
96   The Lord is my shepherd (Ps xxiii), female
       chorus 3vv, org (Philadelphia, 1923)
98   I will lift up mine eyes (Ps cxxi), 4vv (Phila-
       delphia, 1923)
103/   Benedictus es, Domine, Benedictus (*Luke*
1–2   i.67–81), B, 4vv, org (1924)
105   Let this mind be in you (*Philippians* ii.5–11),
       S, B, 4vv, org (Cincinnati, 1924)
109   Lord of the worlds above (I. Watts), S, T, B,
       4vv, org (1925)
115   Around the manger (R. Davis), 4vv, org/pf
       (1925); rev. female chorus 3vv, org/pf
       (1925); rev. female chorus 4vv, org/pf
       (1929) [see also SONGS]
121   Benedicite omnia opera Domini (*Daniel*
       iii.56–8) (1928)
122   Communion Responses: Kyrie, Gloria tibi,
       Sursum corda, Sanctus, Agnus Dei, Gloria,
       S, A, T, B, 4vv, org (1928)
123   The Canticle of the Sun (St Francis), S, Mez,
       T, B, 4vv, orch, os (1928); New York, 9
       Dec 1928
125/2 Evening Hymn: The shadows of the evening
       hours (A. Procter), S, A, 4vv (1936) [arr. of
       song]
132   Christ in the universe (A. Meynell), A, T,
       4vv, orch, os (New York, 1931); New
       York, 17 April 1932
133   God is our stronghold (E. Wordsworth), S,
       4vv, org
139   Hearken unto me (*Isaiah* li. 1, 3; xliii.1–3;
       xl.28, 31), S, A, T, B, 4vv, orch, os (1934)
140   We who sing have walked in glory (A. S.
       Bridgman) (1934); New York, 13 Jan 1935
141   O Lord, God of Israel (1 *Kings* viii.23, 27–30,
       34), S, A, B, 4vv, 1941
—   Hymn: O God of love, O King of peace (H.
       W. Baker), 4vv, 1941 (New York, 1942)
146   Lord of all being (O. W. Holmes) (New
       York, 1938)
147   I will give thanks (Ps cxi), S, 4vv, org (1939)
—   Pax nobiscum (E. Marlatt), female chorus
       3vv/male chorus 3vv/4vv, org (New York,
       1944)

SECULAR CHORAL

9   The Little Brown Bee (M. Eytinge), female
       chorus 4vv (1891)
16   The Minstrel and the King: Rudolph von
       Hapsburg (F. von Schiller), T, B, male
       chorus 4vv, orch, ps (1890)
26/4   Wouldn't that be queer (E. J. Cooley), female
       chorus 3vv, pf (1919) [arr. of song]
30   The Rose of Avon-Town (C. Mischka), S, A,
       female chorus 4vv, orch, ps (1896);
       Brooklyn, NY, 22 April 1896
31/1–3 Three Flower Songs (M. Deland), female
       chorus 4vv, pf (1896): The Clover, The
       Yellow Daisy, The Bluebell
37/3   Fairy Lullaby (W. Shakespeare), female chor-
       us 4vv (1907) [arr. of song]
39/1–3 Three Shakespeare Choruses, female chorus

4vv, pf (1897): Over hill, over dale; Come unto these yellow sands; Through the house give glimmering light

42 Song of Welcome (H. M. Blossom), 4vv, orch, os (1898); Omaha, NE, 1 June 1898

43/4 Far Awa' (R. Burns), female chorus 3vv, pf (1918) [arr. of song]

44/1–2 The year's at the spring (R. Browning), female chorus 4vv, pf (1909); Ah, love, but a day (Browning), female chorus 4vv, pf (1927) [arr. of songs]

46 Sylvania: a Wedding Cantata (F. W. Bancroft, after W. Bloem), S, S, A, T, B, 8vv, orch, os (1901); Boston, 7 April 1905

49 A Song of Liberty (F. L. Stanton), 4vv, orch, 1902, ps (1902); arr. male chorus 4vv, pf (1917)

51/3 Juni (E. Jensen), 4vv, pf (1931), female chorus 3vv (1931) [arr. of song]

56/4 Shena Van (W. Black), female chorus 3vv/male chorus 4vv (1917) [arr. of song]

57/1–3 Only a Song (A. L. Hughes), One Summer Day (Hughes), female chorus 4vv (1904); Indian Lullaby, female chorus 4vv (n.p., 1895)

59 The Sea-Fairies (A. Tennyson), S, A, female chorus 2vv, orch, 1904, ps (1904)

66 The Chambered Nautilus (Holmes), S, A, female chorus 4vv, orch, org ad lib, ps (1907), ed. A. F. Block (Bryn Mawr PA, 1994); Boston, 25 April 1908

74 Panama Hymn (W. P. Stafford), 4vv, orch; arr. 4vv, org/pf (New York, 1915)

75/1, 3 The Candy Lion (A. F. Brown), Dolladine (W. B. Rands), female chorus 4vv (New York, 1915)

82 Dusk in June (S. Teasdale), female chorus 4vv (New York, 1917)

86 May Eve, 4vv, pf, 1921 (New York, 1933)

94 Three School Songs, 4vv (n.p., 1933)

101 Peter Pan (J. Andrews), female chorus 3vv, pf (Philadelphia, 1923)

110 The Greenwood (W. L. Bowles), 4vv (1925)

118/ The Moonboat, 4vv (New York, 1929); Who
1–2 has seen the wind (C. G. Rossetti), 4vv (New York, 1930)

126/ Sea Fever (J. Masefield), The Last Prayer,
1–2 male chorus 4vv, pf (1931)

127 When the last sea is sailed (Masefield), male chorus 4vv (1931)

129 Drowsy Dream Town (R. Norwood), S, female chorus 3vv, pf (1932)

144 This morning very early (P. L. Hills), female chorus 3vv, pf (1937)

SONGS

1v, pf, unless otherwise stated

1/1–4 Four Songs: With violets (K. Vannah) (1885), BS; Die vier Brüder (F. von Schiller) (1887); Jeune fille et jeune fleur (F. R. Chateaubriand) (1887); Ariette (P. B. Shelley) (1886), WC xxv

2/1–3 Three Songs: Twilight (A. M. Beach) (1887); When far from her (H. H. A. Beach) (1889); Empress of night (H. H. A. Beach) (1891), BS

10/1–3 Songs of the Sea (1890): A Canadian Boat Song (T. Moore), S, B, pf; The Night Sea (H. P. Spofford), S, S, pf; Sea Song (W. E. Channing), S, S, pf

11/1–3 Three Songs (W. E. Henley), BS: Dark is the night (1890); The Western Wind (1889); The Blackbird (1889)

12/1–3 Three Songs (R. Burns) (1887): Wilt thou be my dearie?, BS; Ye banks and braes o' bonnie doon, BS; My luve is like a red, red rose

13 Hymn of Trust (O. W. Holmes) (1891); rev. with vn obbl (1901), BS

14/1–4 Four Songs, 1890 (1891), BS: The Summer Wind (W. Learned); Le secret (J. de Resseguier); Sweetheart, sigh no more (T. B. Aldrich), WC xxv; The Thrush (E. R. Sill); nos.2–3 rev. (1901)

19/1–3 Three Songs (1893): For me the jasmine buds unfold (F. E. Coates), BS; Ecstasy (A. M. Beach), 1v, pf, vn obbl, BS, WC xxv; Golden Gates; no.2, Boston, 29 Nov 1892

20 Across the World: Villanelle (E. M. Thomas) (1894)

21/1–3 Three Songs (1893), WC xxv: Chanson d'amour (V. Hugo); Extase (Hugo); Elle et moi (F. Bovet)

26/1–4 Four Songs (1894): My Star (C. Fabbri), WC xxv; Just for this (Fabbri), BS; Spring (Fabbri); Wouldn't that be queer (E. J. Cooley); no.4 arr. chorus

29/1–4 Four Songs, 1894 (1895): Within thy heart (A. M. Beach), BS, WC xxv; The Wandering Knight (anon., Eng. trans., J. G. Lockhart), BS; Sleep, little darling (Spofford); Haste, O beloved (W. A. Sparrow)

35/1–4 Four Songs, 1896 (1897): Nachts (C. F. Scherenberg); Allein! (H. Heine); Nähe des Geliebten (J. W. von Goethe) WC xxv; Forget-me-not (H. H. A. Beach), BS

37/1–3 Three Shakespeare Songs (1897), BS: O mistress mine, BS; Take, O take those lips away; Fairy Lullaby; no.3 arr. chorus

41/1–3 Three Songs (1898): Anita (Fabbri); Thy beauty (Spofford); Forgotten (Fabbri), WC xxv

43/1–5 Five Burns Songs (1899): Dearie, WC xxv; Scottish Cradle Song; Oh were my love yon lilac fair!, BS, WC xxv; Far awa', BS, WC xxv; My lassie; no.3 arr. S, S, pf (1918), no.4 arr. chorus

44/1–3 Three [R.] Browning Songs (1900), WC xxv: The year's at the spring; Ah, love but a day; I send my heart up to thee; no.2 arr. S, T, pf (1917), arr. with vn obbl (1920); nos. 1–2 arr. chorus

48/1–4 Four Songs (1902): Come, ah come (H. H. A. Beach); Good Morning (A. H. Lockhart), BS; Good Night (Lockhart), BS; Canzonetta (A. Sylvestre)

51/1–4 Four Songs (1903): Ich sagete nicht (E. Wissman); Wir drei (H. Eschelbach), WC xxv; Juni (E. Jansen), BS, WC xxv; Je demande à l'oiseau (Sylvestre); no.3 arr. chorus

56/1–4 Four Songs, 1904 (1904): Autumn Song (H. H. A. Beach); Go not too far (F. E. Coates); I know not how to find the spring (Coates); Shena Van (W. Black), WC xxv; no.4 arr. with vn obbl (1919), arr. chorus

61 Give me not love (Coates), S, T, pf (1905)

62 When soul is joined to soul (E. B. Browning) (1905)

68 After (Coates) (1909)

69/1–2   Two Mother Songs: Baby (G. MacDonald)
(Springfield, OH, 1908); Hush, baby dear
(A. L. Hughes) (1908)
71/1–3   Three Songs (1910): A Prelude (A. M.
Beach); O sweet content (T. Dekker), WC
xxv; An Old Love-Story (B. L. Stathem)
72/1–2   Two Songs (New York, 1914): Ein altes
Gebet, Boston, 18 Nov 1914; Deine
Blumen (L. Zacharias)
73/1–2   Two Songs (Zacharias) (New York, 1914),
Boston, 18 Nov 1914: Grossmütterchen;
Der Totenkranz
75/1–2   A Thanksgiving Fable; Prayer of a Tired
Child; (New York, 1914)
76/1–2   Two Songs (New York, 1914), Boston, 18
Nov 1914: Separation (J. L. Stoddard); The
Lotos Isles (Tennyson)
77/1–2   Two Songs (New York, 1916): I
(C. Fanning); Wind o' the Westland
(D. Burnett), WC xxv
78/1–3   Three Songs (New York, 1917):
Meadowlarks (I. Coolbrith); Night Song at
Amalfi (Teasdale); In Blossom Time
(Coolbrith)
—   A Song for Little May (E. H. Miller), 1922,
KC
—   The Arrow and the Song (H. W.
Longfellow), 1922, KC
—   Clouds (F. D. Sherman), 1922, KC
85   In the Twilight (Longfellow) (1922)
88   Spirit Divine (A. Read), S, T, org (Philadel-
phia, 1922)
93   Message (Teasdale) (Philadelphia, 1922)
99/1–4   Four Songs (Philadelphia, 1923): When
Mama Sings (A. M. Beach); Little Brown-
Eyed Laddie (A. D. O. Greenwood); The
Moonpath (K. Adams); The Artless Maid
(L. Barili)
100/   Two Songs (1924): A Mirage (B. Ochsner);
1–2   Stella viatoris (J. H. Nettleton), S, vn, vc, pf
112   Jesus my Saviour (A. Elliott) (Philadelphia,
1925)
113   Mine be the lips (L. Speyer) (1921), WC xxv
115   Around the Manger (Davis), 1v, pf/org
(1925) [see also CHORAL]
117/   Three Songs (M. Lee) (Cincinnati, 1925): The
1–3   Singer; The Host; Song in the Hills
120   Rendezvous (Speyer), with vn obbl (1928)
—   Mignonnette (n.p.), 1929)
124   Springtime (S. M. Heywood) (New York,
1929)
125/   Two Sacred Songs: Spirit of Mercy (anon.)
1–2   (1930); Evening Hymn: The shadows of the
evening hours (A. Procter) (1934); no.2 arr.
chorus
131   Dark Garden (Speyer) (1932)
135   To one I love (1932)
136   Fire and Flame (A. A. Moody), 1932 (1933)
137/   Baby (S. R. Quick); May Flowers (Moody);
1–2   1932 (1933)
142   I sought the Lord (anon.), 1v, org (1937)
143   I shall be brave (Adams) (1932)
145   Dreams
152   Though I Take the Wings of Morning (R. N.
Spencer), 1v, org/pf (New York, 1941)
—   The heart that melts, KC
—   The Icicle Lesson, KC
—   If women will not be inclined, KC
—   Time has wings and swiftly flies, KC

—   Whither (W. Müller) [after Chopin: Trois
nouvelles études, no.3], KC

OTHER WORKS

—   Arr.: Beethoven: Pf Conc. no.1, 2nd movt,
pf 4 hands, 1887
—   St John the Baptist (St Matthew, St Luke), lib,
1889, KC
—   Arr.: Berlioz: Les Troyens, Act 1 scene iii,
1v, pf, 1896
49   Transcr. of R. Strauss: Ständchen, pf (1902);
Brooklyn, NY, 18 March 1902
—   Arr.: On a hill: Negro melody (trad.), 1v, pf
(1929)

JUVENILIA

Air and Variations, pf, 1877, KC; Mamma's Waltz,
pf, 1877, KC; Menuetto, pf, 1877, KC; Romanza,
pf, 1877, KC; Petite valse, pf, 1878, KC; The Rainy
Day (Longfellow), 1v, pf, 1880 (1883), KC; Allegro
appassionato, KC; Moderato, pf
4 Chorales: Come ye faithful (J. Hupton); Come to
me (C. Elliott); O Lord, how happy should we be
(J. Anstice); To heav'n I lift my waiting eyes, 4vv,
1882, KC

For index to vocal works see GroveAM

Principal publishers: Ditson, Presser, G. Schirmer,
Schmidt

WRITINGS

'Cristofori redivivus', Music, xvi/May (1899), 1–5
'Why I Chose my Profession: the Autobiography of a
Woman Composer', Mother's Magazine, xi/Feb
(1914), 7–8
'The Outlook for the Young American Composer',
The Etude, xxxiii/Jan (1915), 1
'Music's Ten Commandments as given for Young
Composers', Los Angeles Examiner (28 June 1915)
'Common Sense in Pianoforte Touch and Technic',
The Etude, xxxiv/Oct (1916), 701–2
'Work out your own Salvation', The Etude, xxxvi/Jan
(1918), 11–12
'To the Girl who wants to Compose', The Etude,
xxxv/Nov (1918), 695
'Emotion Versus Intellect in Music', Studies in Musical
Education, History, and Aesthetics, Proceedings of the
Music Teachers National Association, ser. xxvi
(Oberlin, OH, 1932), 17–19
'The Twenty-fifth Anniversary of a Vision', ibid, ser.
xxvii (Oberlin, OH, 1933), 45–8
'The Mission of the Present Day Composer', Triangle
of Mu Phi Epsilon, xxxvi/Feb (1942), 71–2
'The "How" of Creative Composition', The Etude,
lxi/March (1943), 151, 208–9
'The World Cries out for Harmony', The Etude
(1944), Jan

BIBLIOGRAPHY

EwenD; NAW; SchmidlD
L. C. Elson: The History of American Music (New
York, 1904; enlarged 2/1915; enlarged by A. Elson,
3/1925), 294–305
P. Goetschius: Mrs H. H. A. Beach (Boston, 1906)
[incl. analytical sketch of Sym. op.32 and list of
works]
'Mrs H. H. A. Beach', Musikliterarische Blätter, i
(Vienna, 1904), 1
G. Cowen: 'Mrs H. H. A. Beach, the Celebrated
Composer', Musical Courier, no.60 (8 June 1910),
14–15

'Mrs. Beach's Compositions', *Musical Courier*, no.70 (24 March 1915), 37

H. Brower: *Piano Mastery* (New York, 1917), 179–87

B. C. Tuthill: 'Mrs H. H. A. Beach', *MQ*, xxvi (1940), 297–310

E. L. Merrill: *Mrs H. H. A. Beach: Her Life and Music* (diss., U. of Rochester, 1963)

M. G. Eden: *Anna Hyatt Huntington, Sculptor, and Mrs H. H. A. Beach, Composer* (diss., Syracuse U., 1977) [incl. list of works]

A. F. Block: *Introduction to Amy Beach: Quintet in f♯ op.67* (New York, 1979)

C. Ammer: *Unsung: a History of Women in American Music* (Westport, CT, 1980)

A. F. Block: 'Why Amy Beach Succeeded as a Composer: the Early Years', *CMc*, no.36 (1983), 41–59

M. S. Miles: *The Solo Piano Works of Mrs. H. H. A. Beach* (diss., Peabody Institute, Johns Hopkins U., 1985)

A. F. Block: 'Arthur P. Schmidt, Publisher and Champion of Women Composers', *The Musical Woman: an International Perspective*, ii, *1984–5*, ed. J. L. Zaimont and others (Westport, CT, 1987), 145–76

L. Petteys: '*Cabildo* by Amy Marcy Beach', *Opera Journal*, xxii/1 (1989), 10–20

A. F. Block: 'Dvořák, Beach and American Music', *A Celebration of American Music: Words and Music in Honor of H. Wiley Hitchcock* (Ann Arbor, 1990), 256–80

——: 'Amy Beach's Music on Native American Themes', *American Music*, viii/sum. (1990), 141–66

J. E. Brown: *The Chamber Works of Amy Marcy Cheney Beach* (diss., U. of Maryland, 1993)

ADRIENNE FRIED BLOCK

Beamish, Sally (*b* London, 26 Aug 1956). English composer and viola player. Her early interest in composition was nurtured by occasional lessons with Alan Richardson and Lennox Berkeley, but at the RNCM she concentrated on performance and after graduating worked principally as a professional violist. She has played with a variety of groups specializing in contemporary music, including the London Sinfonietta and Lontano; this experience has been valuable to her development as a composer. A bursary from the Arts Council of Great Britain in 1989 has led her to concentrate almost exclusively on composing. She has been commissioned to write works for several orchestras, including the Academy of St Martin-in-the-Fields and the Iceland SO. In 1991 she was composer-in-residence with the Scottish Chamber Orchestra.

WORKS

Orch: Variation on a theme of Lennox Berkeley, 1983

Chamber and solo inst: Vn Sonata, 1976; Sonatina, vn, 1977; Little Suite, va, 1978; Entre chien et loup, pf, 1978; Adagio and Allegro, vn, pf RH, 1981; Habkreis, va, pf, 1982; Lullaby for Owain, pf, 1985; Variations, hn, pf, 1985; Variations, va, pf, 1986; Dances and Nocturnes, vn, db, pf, 1986; Introduction and Rondo Capriccioso, vn, pf, 1987; Capriccio, bn, pf, 1988; Commedia, fl, cl, vn, vc, pf, 1990; Winter Trees, vn, pf, 1990; Songs and Blessings, ob, bn, vn, va, pf, 1991; The Wedding at Cana, str sextet, 1991; Piobaireachd, vn, vc, pf, 1991

Vocal: I see his blood upon the rose (hymn-tune, Plunkett), 1982; Three ladies met in a garden (anthem, Beamish), children's vv, org, 1982; Mr and Mrs Discobbollus (E. Lear), nar, cl, pf, vn, va, vc/db, 1983; Sonnet (W. Shakespeare), S, fl, ob d'amore, pf, 1986; No, I'm not afraid, (6 poems, I. Ratushinskaya), spkr, ob, hp, str, 1988; Tuscan Lullaby (anon), S, 2 cl, va, vc, db, 1989; 3 Winter Songs (E. Dickinson), S, vn, 1989; 7 Songs (Dickinson), girls' chorus, 1990; Oracle Beach (D. Pownall), Mez, pf trio, 1991; The Lost Pibroch, harp, str, 5 school groups, bagpipes, wind, fiddles, perc, 1991

BIBLIOGRAPHY

Fuller-LeFanuRM

M. Miller: 'New Consciousness', *MT*, cxxxii (1991), 205

TONI CALAM

Beat, Janet (Eveline) (*b* Streetly, Staffs., 17 Dec 1937). British composer and teacher. She studied at Birmingham University between 1956 and 1968 (BMus 1960, MA 1968) and with Alexander Goehr. During the 1960s she worked as a freelance horn player and as a music lecturer at colleges of education; in 1972 she was appointed lecturer at the Royal Scottish Academy of Music and Drama. She was a founder member of the Scottish Society of Composers and the Scottish Electro-Acoustic Music Society and in 1988 formed the contemporary music ensemble Soundstrata. As a composer, she has acknowledged the influence of Bartók, Stockhausen and oriental music, and she was a pioneer of British electronic music. She combines natural and artificially generated or mediated sound, often using tape, as in *Fêtes pour Claude*, and also creates purely electronic works (for example *Dancing on Moonbeams*, 1980, and the ballet *A Vision of the Unseen* no.2, 1988). Electronic music has greatly affected her attitudes to timbre, rhythm and the use of montage effects. For example, even in a non-electronic work such as *Mestra*, she is concerned with exploring timbre to the utmost possible degree, involving not only the flute's sound, but also the noise made by the instrument's mechanism and the player's breathing.

She has written about her *Cross Currents and Reflections* in *Stretto* (iv/1, 1985, pp.1–4), and has also worked on Baroque music, with an essay on Monteverdi's opera orchestra (*The Monteverdi Companion*, 1968) and editions of works by Giacomo Carissimi and Handel.

WORKS
selective list

Elec: Apollo and Marsyas, cl, tape, 1973; .The Gossamer Web, dance drama, S, pf, perc, tape, 1975; Hunting Horns are Memories, hn, tape, 1977; Piangam, pf, tape, 1978–9; Dancing on Moonbeams, tape, 1980; Ongaku, hpd, tape, 1981; Cross Currents and Reflections, vol.1, pf, vol.2 [to be played with vol.1], pf, el pf, synth, tape, 1981–2; A Willow Swept by Rain, gui, tape, 1982; Journey of a Letter, ballet, tape, 1986; Echoes from Bali, computer, synth, 1987; A Vision of the Unseen, 1988: no.1, inst trio, tape, no.2, tape; Aztec Myth, Mez, tape, 1988; A Springtime Pillow Book, Mez, fl + a fl, synth (DX7), computer-controlled synths/tape, 1989–90; Mandala, computer-controlled synths, fl, synth (WX7), Tibetan monastery bells, 1990; Memories of Java, gĕnder panĕrus [metallophone], sampler, tape, 1990; The Song of the Silkie, vc, kbd, 1991; Fêtes pour Claude: 3 Homages to Debussy, Mez, fl, pf, tape, 1992

Chamber and solo inst: Le tombeau de Claude, fl, ob, harp, 1973; After Reading 'Lessons of the War', vn, pf, 1976; Landscapes, T, ob, 1976–7; Mestra, fl + pic + a fl + b fl, 1980–81; Nomoi aulodiki, S, 3 cl, 1984; Pf Sonata no.1, 1985–7; Fireworks in Steel, tpt, 1987; Cat's Cradle for the Nemuri-Neko, female v, clarsach, 1991; Scherzo notturno, str qt, 1992

Principal publishers: Bastet, Furore
Some material in *GB-Lmic*

BIBLIOGRAPHY

CC (K. Mathieson); *CohenE*; *Fuller-LeFanuRM* (N. J. Pearce)
J. Purser: 'Scottish Women Composers', *Chapman*, no.27–8 (1980), 62–4
P. Adkins-Chiti: 'Musiciste famose: compositrici d'oggi', *Strumenti & musica* (1986), April
A. Mackay: 'Soundstrata', *Music Current*, no.17 (1990)

MARIE FITZPATRICK

Beath, Betty [Elizabeth] **(Mary)** (*b* nr Bundaberg, Queensland, 19 Nov 1932). Australian composer. She studied at the Sydney Conservatorium with Frank Hutchens and at the Queensland Conservatorium, where she was later appointed lecturer and accompanist (1969). She represented women composers of Australia at the 3rd International Congress on Women in Music, Mexico City (1984) and was on the executive board of the International League of Women Composers (1986–7, 1988–9). In 1987 she was resident composer at North Adams State College, Massachusetts.

During the 1970s she spent some time in Indonesia with her husband, the writer and illustrator David Cox, studying the cultures of Bali and Java, and her compositions show the influence of these cultures. Her output includes stage works for children's voices to librettos by Cox, and a large number of vocal chamber works; the cycle *Songs from the Beasts' Choir* (1978) has been one of her most successful compositions.

WORKS
selective list

STAGE

The Strange Adventures of Marco Polo (opera, 1, D. Cox), Queensland, 1973; rev. 1976 as Marco Polo
Francis (Cox, after St Francis of Assissi), Brisbane, 17 Oct 1974
Balyet (opera, 3, P. Wrightson), 1990–
Music dramas for children (texts by Cox; all performed in Brisbane): Abigail and the Bushranger, 17 Oct 1974; Abigail and the Rainmaker, 15 Oct 1976; The Raja who Married an Angel, 21 Oct 1979, rev. 1982; Abigail and the Mythical Beast, 1985

OTHER WORKS

Inst: Piccolo Victory (Images of Colonial Australia), fl + pic, hpd/pf, vc, rhythm sticks, 1982; Trio, fl, vc, hpd, 1982; Black on White, pf LH, ruler, 1983; Brisbane Waters, b cl, opt. taped didjeridu, 1986; Asmaradana, pf, 1988; Music for Gillian, a fl, pf, 1988; Contrasts, pf, 1990
Vocal: Francis (D. Cox), T, pf, 1973; In this Garden (Cox), medium v, chamber orch, 1973; Riddles, medium v, chamber orch, 1974; Indonesian Triptych (H. Aveling, M. Goenawan), medium v, pf, 1977; Songs from the Beasts' Choir (C. Bernos de Gasztold, trans. R. Godden), medium v, pf, 1978; Poems from the Chinese (trans. K. Rexroth), S, cl, vc, 1979; Nawang Wulan (S. Sastrowardojo), medium v, pf, 1980; 3 Psalms [xxiii, cxxi, cl], high v, fl, harp, 1981; Yungamurra (P. Wrightson), S, (fl, vc)/pf, 1984; Ninya (Wrightson), S, choir, fl, bn, vc, db, pf, perc, 1985; In the Carnarvon Ranges (Cox), S, A, fl, pf, rhythm sticks, 1987; Points in a Journey (St Francis, T. Traherne and others), S, fl, pf, 1987; River Songs (J. Woodhouse), S, pf, 1990–91

BIBLIOGRAPHY

CC (J. Dawson); *Fuller-LeFanuRM*

GRAHAM HAIR,
GRETA MARY HAIR

Beatriz de Dia (*fl* late 12th century). Troubadour. The 'Comtessa' de Dia is described in her *vida* as the wife of Guillem of Poitiers and the lover of the famous troubadour Raimbaut d'Orange. Of five extant poems ascribed to her, only one survives with music, *A chantar m'er de so qu'eu no volria* (Pillet and Carstens, 46.2; *F-Pn* f.f. 844, f.204r). The song is a *canso* of five strophes plus a *tornada*, each strophe having the musical form *ABABCDB*. In *A chantar* Beatriz berates her unfaithful lover and reminds him of her considerable virtues.

BIBLIOGRAPHY

O. Schultz-Gora: *Die provenzalische Dichterinnen* (Leipzig, 1888), 8, 17ff

Hortense Eugénie de Beauharnais: portrait (1815) by Richard Fleury

J. Chevallier: 'La comtesse de Die', *Bulletin de la Société départementale d'archéologie et de statistique de la Drôme*, xxvii (1893), 183
S. Santy: *La comtesse de Die: sa vie, ses oeuvres complètes* (Paris, 1893), [text edn]
G. Kussler-Ratyé: 'Les chansons de la comtesse de Die', *Archivum romanicum*, i (1917), 161
A. Pillet and H. Carstens: *Bibliographie der Troubadours* (Halle, 1933)
M. Bogin: *The Women Troubadours* (New York, 1976), 82–91, 163–4 [text edns and Engl. trans.]
I. Fernandez de la Cuesta: *Las cançons dels trobadors* (Toulouse, 1979) [music edn]
C. Neuls-Bates, ed.: *Women in Music: an Anthology of Source Readings from the Middle Ages to the Present* (New York, 1982), 21–4
H. Van der Werf: *The Extant Troubadour Melodies* (Rochester, NY, 1984) [music edn]
M. V. Coldwell: 'Jougleresses and Trobairitz: Secular Musicians in Medieval France', *Women Making Music: the Western Art Tradition 1150–1950*, ed. J. Bowers and J. Tick (Urbana and Chicago, 1986), 39–61, esp. 48–50 [music edn]
MARIA V. COLDWELL, IAN R. PARKER

Beauharnais, Hortense Eugénie de (*b* Paris, 10 April 1783; *d* Arenenberg, 5 Oct 1837). French composer and artist. She was the daughter of the Viscount Alexandre de Beauharnais (guillotined in 1794) and Marie-Joseph-Rose Tascher de la Pagerie (the future Empress Josephine); she was 13 when her mother married Napoleon Bonaparte and 18 when, on 4 January 1802, she married

Louis Bonaparte (King of Holland, 1806–10). Her third son, Louis Napoleon (*b* 21 April 1808), became Napoleon III. She acquired her sobriquet 'la reine Hortense' when her husband abdicated the Dutch throne, naming her regent; a fourth son, Charles de Flahaut, was born in 1811. Louis XVIII made her Duchess of Saint-Leu after the fall of Paris in March 1814 and her mother's death at Malmaison in May. She lived in exile (in Switzerland, Germany, Italy and London), composing *tristes romances*, until her son assumed power.

Hortense sang (she was a pupil of Barnaba Bonesi), played the piano (studying with Daniel Steibelt, Théodore Mozin and Hyacinthe Jadin) and the harp (M.-P. Dalvimare) as well as the lyre, and composed *romances* to pseudo-medieval texts, of which some 150 survive. She was assisted by friends and music masters at court, including Dalvimare, J.-F.-N. Carbonel and C.-H. Plantade, who provided accompaniments. One song, *Partant pour la Syrie* (text by Alexandre de Laborde), was a rallying cry for *bonapartistes* during the Restoration; it continued to be widely sung during the 1809 war and, under Napoleon III, became a national hymn. Though Hortense claimed to have composed it at Malmaison while her mother played *tric-trac*, Pougin and others believed it was composed by L.-F.-P. Drouet, flautist at the Bonaparte court in The Hague. J. N. Hummel composed piano variations on both *Partant pour la Syrie* and *La sentinelle* (which had been popular during the war with Spain); in 1818, Schubert dedicated his variations on her *Bon Chevalier* (which he would have known from an 1817 Leipzig edition) to Beethoven.

Her first publication of songs appeared in 1813, beautifully bound and lavishly illustrated with engravings of her watercolours portraying medieval knights and idyllic countrysides. A second album of eight *romances* appeared in pocket format in about 1814–15. During the next decade she published a further collection, dedicated to her brother, Prince Eugène (*d* 1824), illustrated with lithographs. Her 1828 collection of a further 12 was sold for the benefit of the Greeks. In 1853 Heugel published a deluxe edition of 12 more, launched with a charity concert at Salle Herz. A nearly complete edition, of 144 songs, appeared in 1867.

Hortense performed her *romances*, and those of her contemporaries such as Pauline Duchambge, in a simple declamatory style at intimate gatherings at her homes at Saint-Leu

'Le beau Dunois' ('Partant pour la Syrie'), with its associated engraving (below) from Hortense de Beauharnais' first book of 'Romances' (London: Dobbs, 1813)

(1804–14), The Hague (1806–10), Malmaison (1814–15), Kónstanz (1815–17), Augsburg (1817–25), Rome (Villa Paolina, 1826–31) and Arenenberg (1831–7). Her memoirs were published by her son in 1837. Her music library is conserved at the Napoleon Museum at Arenenberg and some of her furniture at Malmaison; her drawings and paintings are divided between the two. Many portraits (and self-portraits) were made of her; that by Richard Fleury (1815; Bibliothèque Thiers, Paris) represents her best. An exhibition of her life and works was mounted at Malmaison in 1993.

BIBLIOGRAPHY

FétisB; Grove1 (Mrs. W. Carr); SchmidlD

L. Cochelet: Mémoires sur la reine Hortense et la famille impériale (Paris, 1836–8)

F. Halévy: 'L'album de la reine Hortense', Revue et gazette musicale de Paris, x (1853), 145–7

A. Pougin: '"Partant pour la Syrie", histoire d'un pseudo-chant national', Chronique musicale, iv/23 (1 June 1874), 193–203

J. Hanoteau, ed.: Mémoires, lettres et papiers de Valérie Mazuyer, dame d'honneur de la reine Hortense (Paris, 1937)

D. Baumann: 'Die Musiksammlung der Königin Hortense auf Arenenberg', Librarium [Journal de la société suisse de bibliophilie], ii (1985), 110–37

La Reine Hortense: une femme artiste 27 May–27 Sept 1993 (Malmaison, 1993) [exhibition catalogue]

JULIE ANNE SADIE

Beaumesnil, Henriette Adélaïde Villard de (b Paris, 30 or 31 Aug 1748; d Paris, 1813). French singer and composer. Having specialized from the age of seven in soubrette roles in comedies, she made a successful début at the Paris Opéra on 27 November 1766, replacing Sophie Arnould in the title role of Silvie (P.-M. Berton and J.-C. Trial). Although she sang in many premières and revivals until her retirement in 1781, creating with Rosalie Levasseur the role of Iphigenia in Gluck's Iphigénie en Tauride (1779), her talents were overshadowed by those of Arnould and Levasseur.

Anacréon, a one-act opera and her first composition, received a private performance at the Brunoy residence of the Comte de Provence on 5 December 1781. Beaumesnil then achieved public success with her acte de ballet Tibulle et Délie, ou Les Saturnales (after L. Fuzelier: Les fêtes grecques et romaines), which was given at the Paris Opéra on 15 March 1784 after a court première the previous month (MS F-Po), and with the two-act opéra comique Plaire, c'est commander (libretto by Marquis de La Salle), which was given at the Théâtre Montansier, Paris, on 12 May 1792. An oratorio, Les Israélites pour-

suivis par Pharaon, was performed at the Concert Spirituel on 8 December 1784. She is further remembered for her part in a 'duel au pistolet' with the dancer Mlle Théodore.

BIBLIOGRAPHY

Choron-FayolleD; FétisB; GerberL; SainsburyD; SchillingE

H. Audiffret: 'Beaumesnil, Henrietta-Adélaïde Villard', Biographie universelle, ed. L. Michaud (Paris, 1843–65), iii, 407–8

V. Fournel: Curiosités théâtrales anciennes et modernes (Paris, 1859), 259

F. M. Grimm: Correspondance littéraire, philosophique et critique (Paris, 1813); complete edn, ed. M. Tourneux (Paris, 1877–82), vii, 200–01

E. Campardon: L'Académie royale de musique au XVIIIe siècle (Paris, 1884), i, 49–57

J. Gourret: Dictionnaire des cantatrices de l'Opéra de Paris (Paris, 1987), 23–4

ELISABETH COOK

Beckett, Mary Anne A'. See A'BECKETT, MARY ANNE.

Béclard d'Harcourt [née Béclard], **Marguerite** (b Paris, 24 Feb 1884; d Paris, 2 Aug 1964). French composer and ethnomusicologist. She studied composition at the Schola Cantorum under Abel Decaux, Vincent d'Indy and Maurice Emmanuel – an education that revealed the enormous resources of modality and which gave her an extensive knowledge of Gregorian chant, of ancient Greece and of folksong. After her marriage to the ethnologist Raoul d'Harcourt, she accompanied him on voyages to South America and they later published La musique des Incas et ses survivances (Paris, 1925). Alone she edited books of Indian and Canadian songs.

WORKS
selective list

Operas: Raïmi ou fête du soleil, 1925; Dierdane, 1937–41

Orch and chamber: Str Qt, 1930; 3 mouvements symphoniques, 1932; Sonatine, fl, pf, 1946; Sym. no.2 'Les Saisons', 1951; Conc. grosso, str, 1956

Songs: La flûte de jade (F. Toussaint), 1924; L'amour par terre (P. Verlaine), 1927; 2 poèmes (P. Valéry), 1927; 3 sonnets de la renaissance française, 1930; Les enfants de l'enclos, 1934; 2 pièces (J. du Bellay), 1v, vn, 1936; Madrigal (P. de Ronsard), 1940

ANNE GIRARDOT

Beecroft, Norma (Marian) (b Oshawa, Ont., 11 April 1934). Canadian composer and broadcaster. She studied at the Toronto Conservatory from 1950, beginning composition lessons with John Weinzweig in 1952. Later she studied with Lukas Foss and Aaron Copland at Tanglewood (1958), Goffredo Petrassi and Bruno Maderna in Europe

(1959–62), Myron Schaeffer at the University of Toronto (1962–3) and with Mario Davidovsky at the Columbia-Princeton Electronic Music Center (1964). After her early, neo-classical student works her style changed, moving through a variety of techniques including serialism, improvisation and collage. Although after the 1950s her primary interest became electroacoustic music, she has continued to combine technology with instruments (for example in *From Dreams of Brass*, 1963–4, for large orchestra and tape, and in chamber works), while following technological trends. In the mid-1980s she began to use digital sound sources. Her aim is 'the quality of the sound result' and she acknowledges the influence of Debussy in her choice and blending of timbres. Beecroft worked for many years as a producer, programme organizer and commentator for the CBC and became music director for the classical music station CJRT-fm. In 1971 in Toronto she was a co-founder of the New Music Concerts, of which for 20 years she was president and general manager.

WORKS
selective list

Dramatic: Undersea Fantasy (puppet show), 2-track tape, 1967; Hedda (ballet, after H. Ibsen: *Hedda Gabler*), orch, tape, 1982–3; The Dissipation of Purely Sound (radiophonic opera, 3 simultaneous sections), tape, 1988

Orch: Fantasy for Strings, 1958; 2 Movements, 1958; Improvvisazioni concerti no.1, fl, orch, 1961; Pièce concertante no.1, 1966; Improvvisazioni concerti, no.2, orch, 1971, no.3, fl, 2 timp, orch, 1973; Jeu de Bach, 1985; Hemispherics, 1990; Jeu IV 'Mozart', fortepiano + cel, orch, 2-track tape, 1991

Vocal: The Hollow Men (T. S. Eliot), unacc. chorus, 1956; From Dreams of Brass, nar, male chorus, orch, tape, 1963–4; Elegy (L. Cohen), S, fl, 1967; Two Went to Sleep (L. Cohen), S, fl, perc, tape, 1967; The Living Flame of Love (N. Beecroft, after St John of the Cross), unacc. male chorus, 1967; 3 Impressions from Sweetgrass (W. Keon), male chorus, pf, perc, 1973; Rasas II (various texts), C, fl, harp, gui, el org/pf, 2 perc, 2-track tape, 1973, rev. 1975; Rasas III, S, 4 musicians, 2-track tape, 1974

Chamber: Contrasts, ob, va, xylorimba, perc, harp, vib, 1961; 3 pezzi brevi, fl, harp/gui/pf, 1961; Rasas I, fl, harp, vn, va, vc, perc, pf, 1968; 11 & 7 for 5+, brass qnt, tape, 1975; Piece for Bob, fl, 2-track tape, 1975; Collage '76, solo fl, fl, ob, hn, vc, db, pf, harp, 3 perc, tape, 1976; Consequences for Five, 3 brass, pf, synth, tape, 1977; Collage '78, bn, pf, 2 perc, tape, 1978; Quaprice, hn, perc, tape, 1979; Cantorum vitae, fl, vc, 2 pf, perc, tape, 1980; Troissants, solo va, 2 perc, tape, 1982; Jeu II, fl, va, 6-track tape, live digital processing, 1985; Images, wind qnt, 1986; Jeu III, va, tape, 1987; Accordion Play, accordion, 2 perc, 1989

El-ac: Evocations: Images of Canada, digital synth MIDI controlled, digitally mixed, 1991

GAYNOR G. JONES

Behrend, Jeanne (*b* Philadelphia, 11 May 1911; *d* Philadelphia, 20 March 1988). American pianist, composer, musicologist and teacher. She graduated from the Curtis Institute (1934), where she studied with Josef Hofmann (piano) and Rosario Scalero (composition). In 1936 she was awarded the Joseph Bearns Prize from Columbia University for her piano suite *A Child's Day* and song cycle on poems by Sara Teasdale. Increasingly frustrated by the indifference of publishers and the scarcity of performances of her works, she began to champion American composers, past and present, in piano recitals and recordings, and after 1944 she virtually ceased to compose. Recommended for sponsorship by Heitor Villa-Lobos, she undertook a US State Department tour of South America (1945–6), and later founded and directed the Philadelphia Festival of Western Hemisphere Music (1959–60), which opened with her last composition, *Festival Fanfare: Prelude to the National Anthem*.

In 1965 the Brazilian government awarded her the Order of the Southern Cross for services to Brazilian music. She taught the piano at several prestigious institutions before joining the piano faculty of the Philadelphia College of Performing Arts in 1969. A dedicated supporter of the Louis Moreau Gottschalk revival, she edited Gottschalk's *Notes of a Pianist* (New York, 1964) and a selection of his piano music. Behrend's manuscripts, including several songs that she considered to be her best works, are in the Free Library, Philadelphia.

WORKS
selective list

Orch and chamber: Str Qt, op.8, 1937–40; From Dawn to Dusk, orch, 1939 [version of pf suite]; Lamentation, va, pf, 1944; Festival Fanfare: Prelude to the National Anthem, orch, 1959

Vocal: Song cycle (S. Teasdale), 1932–43; Easter Hymn (A. E. Housman), women's chorus, orch, 1940; Fantasy on Shostakovich's 'Song of the United Nations', S, women's chorus, 2 pf, 1942; other songs

Pf: Quiet Piece, 1932; Dance into Space, 1932; From Dawn until Dusk: a Child's Day, op.6, suite, 1934; Sonata, op.7, 1935; Sonatina (Sonata), 1935–42

BIBLIOGRAPHY

E. A. Hostetter: *Jeanne Behrend: Pioneer Performer of American Music, Pianist, Teacher, Musicologist, and Composer* (diss., Arizona State U., 1990)

JOHN G. DOYLE
(with ELIZABETH A. HOSTETTER)

Beijerman-Walraven, Jeanne (*b* Semarang, Indonesia, 14 June 1878; *d* Arnhem, 20

Autograph of part of Antonia Bembo's cantata spirituale 'Martirio de Santa Regina' from the 'Produzioni armoniche' (c1697)

Sept 1969). Dutch composer. She studied harmony and composition privately with F. E. A. Koeberg at The Hague. Her first compositions belong to the late Romantic tradition, showing the influence of Mahler, Bruckner and Franck. However, she soon developed her own style, characterized by the alternation of bold, muscular gestures with more delicate effects, and later turned to a more contemporary Schoenbergian, atonal language. Her mature works are strongly expressionist, often based on the development of a single motif with short violent drives towards a climax. Her output spans half a century but is limited because of her many revisions. Orchestral works include *Concertouverture* (1910), *Orkeststuk* (1921) and *Feestlied* (1926); among her chamber and instrumental works are a String Quartet (1912), Three Lieder for voice and piano (text by M.-A. Carême, 1952), and Two Pieces (1929) and *Andante expressivo* (1950) for piano. Her principal publishers are Broekmans & Van Poppel and Donemus.

HELEN METZELAAR

Belleville, Anna Caroline de. *See* OURY, ANNA CAROLINE.

Bembo, Antonia (*b* Venice, *c*1643; *d* Paris, before 1715). Italian composer and singer, active in Paris during the latter part of Louis XIV's reign. She was the only child of Giacomo Padovani, a doctor, and Diana Daresco Megalin. In 1654 she was studying with Francesco Cavalli. She married a nobleman, Lorenzo Bembo, in 1659; they had three children, Andrea, Giacomo and Diana. Before 1676 Antonia Bembo left Venice in the company of an as yet unidentified person who took her to Paris, where she remained. Documents discovered in 1992 in Venice corroborate the 'autobiography' provided by the dedications of her six volumes of manuscript music, in the Bibliothèque Nationale, Paris. Bembo wrote that she sang for Louis XIV, who awarded her a pension, enabling her to live in the community of the Petite Union Chrétienne des Dames de Saint Chaumont in the Parisian parish of Notre Dame de Bonne Nouvelle. Bembo's music can be dated from 1697 to after 1707 and includes sacred and secular vocal compositions, which she dedicated to Louis XIV and other members of the royal family. The first set, *Produzioni armoniche*, is a collection of 41 chamber pieces on Italian, French and Latin texts. Three of the Italian texts are attributed to Aurelia Fedeli (*c*1615–1704), an Italian poet and actress in Paris. Most of these arias and cantatas are for soprano and continuo. Bembo's Venetian musical training is reflected here in vocal virtuosity, madrigalisms, long melismas and expressive dissonance. Book 2 is dedicated to Maria Adelaide of Savoy, Duchess of Burgundy, on the occasion of the birth of the first Duke of

Brittany in 1704. It contains a three-voice *Te Deum* and a five-voice Italian serenata ('un picciolo divertimento'), revealing a firm grasp of musical structure, melodic control and harmonic modulation. The characteristics of Bembo's books 3–5 testify to the many years that she lived in France. Her music is somewhat similar to that of her Italian expatriate contemporaries, Paolo Lorenzani and Theobaldo di Gatti, who also adopted French styles in the pieces that they wrote in Paris and Versailles. The third volume contains two motets, a five-voice setting of the *Te Deum* (a *grand motet* in the style of J.-B. Lully and M.-R. de Lalande) and a three-voice setting of Psalm xix. The 1707 opera *Ercole amante* is the only manuscript bearing a date. Bembo set Francesco Buti's libretto, as used by Cavalli in 1662; there is no evidence that it was ever performed. Though similar to contemporary Italian operas, Bembo's work attests to its French provenance in the chorus, *ouverture* and instrumental dance forms. The culture of Bembo's adoptive country is particularly evident in her last book, *Les sept Pseaumes de David*. Here she composed music for the seven penitential psalms in French paraphrases from the *Essay de pseaumes* (1694, repr. 1715) of Elisabeth Sophie Chéron, a Parisian painter, engraver, poet and musician. Bembo's *Sept Pseaumes* mark a return to vocal chamber music but now in the French idiom, where she shows her command of gallic prosody with numerous metric changes.

BIBLIOGRAPHY

Y. Rokseth: 'Antonia Bembo, Composer to Louis XIV', *MQ*, xxiii (1937), 147–69

M. Laini: *Le 'Produzioni armoniche' di Antonia Bembo* (diss., U. of Pavia, 1987)

C. A. Fontijn: *Antonia Bembo: 'Les goûts réunis', Royal Patronage, and the Role of the Woman Composer during the Reign of Louis XIV* (diss., Duke U., Durham, NC, 1994)

CLAIRE A. FONTIJN, MARINELLA LAINI

Benary, Barbara (*b* Bay Shore, NY, 7 April 1946). American composer. After studying at Sarah Lawrence College (BA 1968) and Wesleyan University (MA 1971, PhD 1973), she taught ethnomusicology at Rutgers University, New Jersey (1973–80). She was a Woodrow Wilson Fellow in 1972–3 and took up a Residency at the Yellow Springs Institute in 1985. She has received, in addition to many Meet the Composer awards (since 1979), a Consortium Commission (1981–2) and an Opera/Music Theatre grant (1993) from the NEA. Benary plays the Western and Karnatic violin as well as Chinese and Bulgarian string instruments. In 1976 she created the Gamelan Son of Lion Ensemble, which aims to reproduce the form and sound of a traditional Javanese village gamelan. She has written many works for this ensemble, several of which are recorded on the Smithsonian Folkways and New Wilderness labels. Some of her gamelan compositions are in the style of traditional Javanese court music, while others integrate techniques of process music and minimalism with traditional Javanese vocal and instrumental styles. The *Braid* compositions present varying treatments of a 14–note sequence within interlocking rhythmic structures. Benary has also written music for dance and theatre, including incidental music for the 1981 New York Shakespeare Festival's production of *The Tempest*.

WORKS
selective list

Music-theatre and incid. music: 3 Sisters who are not Sisters (G. Stein), 1967; The Only Jealousy of Emer (W. B. Yeats), 1970; The Gauntlet, or The Moon's on Fire (J. Braswell), 1976; Sanguine (Braswell), 1976; The Interior Castle (Braswell), 1979; The Tempest (incid. music, W. Shakespeare), 1981

Chamber: No Friends in an Auction, 1976; In Time Enough, 1978; Moon Cat Chant, 1980; Singing Braid, 1980; Exchanges, 1981; 4 × 4, mallet perc qt, 1987; Tintinnalogia, vn, pf, perc, 1993

Gamelan: The Moon Gang Goes East, 1974; Braid, 1975; Gong Fanfare, 1978; Sleeping Braid (B. Benary), female v, gamelan, 1979; Backtracking Braid, 1979; Counterbraid, 1979; Dragon Toes, 1979; The Zen Story (K. Maue), female v, gamelan, 1979; In Scrolls of Leaves (anon.), 2 female vv, gamelan, 1980; O'Rourke in New York, 1980; Gamelan NEA, 1982, collab. P. Corner, D. Goode, P. Griggs; The Falls of Richmond, 1982; Hot-Rolled Steel, 1984; Gending Kental-Kental, 1984; Eliahu, 1986; Vancouver, 1987; Yudishthra's Quartet, computer, gamelan, 1989; Sharon (for Karen), 1991; Sambal, 1992; Slendro Steel, 1993

Other: System Pieces [sourcebook of pieces for vocal and percussion improvisation], 1972; Gong of Java (Javanese shadow-puppet play), 1978; Night Thunks (dance score), 1980; Exlasega, sym. band, 1981; A New Pantheon (dance score), 1981; Night Shadow (dance score), 1982; Karna (shadow-puppet opera), 1993

Principal publisher: Frog Peak Music (Hanover, NH)

BIBLIOGRAPHY

CohenE

T. Johnson: 'Barbara Benary Brings Java to Jersey', *Village Voice* (17 July 1976)

Zummo: 'Benary Builds Gamelan', *Soho Weekly News* (19 May 1977)

J. Rockwell: 'Recordings: the Gentle Magic of Javanese Gamelan', *New Music Times* (12 Aug 1979)

R. Johnson, ed.: *Scores: an Anthology of New Music* (New York, 1981)

T. Johnson: 'Composers in Collaboration', *Village Voice* (1 June 1982)
D. Goode: 'Barbary Benary', *Music Works* (1993), sum.

SARA JOBIN, STEPHEN RUPPENTHAL

Benati, Chiara (*b* Bologna, 18 July 1956). Italian composer. She graduated from the Bologna Conservatory, where she studied the piano, conducting and composition; her teachers included Paolo Renosto and Cesare Augusto Grandi. She continued her conducting studies with Piero Bellugi and Franco Ferrara. Her output includes orchestral and chamber works, for which she has received both national and international prizes, including an award in the Camillo Togni competition in Brescia. Among her several works for guitar are *Non solo . . . (Imagines des sphères)*, *Nel tempo della memoria* (both 1986), *Dediche* (1991), commissioned by Oscar Ghiglia, and a Concerto for Guitar and Strings (1990). In 1991 she wrote a set of *Variazioni su una sequenza di Maderna* for solo harp. She works in collaboration with the most prominent Italian and foreign artists, and also teaches harmony and counterpoint at the Conservatory in Bologna.

PAOLA DAMIANI

Benda, Juliane. *See* REICHARDT, JULIANE.

Benda, Maria Carolina. *See* WOLF, MARIA CAROLINA.

Bengoecha de Cármena, Soledad (*b* Madrid, 21 March 1849; *d* Madrid, 1893). Spanish composer. She studied the piano, harmony and instrumentation with Arriola, Jesús Monasterio and Ledesma. During her childhood she took part in the concerts organized by her father at home. The first performance of her Mass (1867) was received with enormous enthusiasm. The Madrid critics wrote (in *El artista*, 30 May and 7 June, and *Revista y gaceta musical*, 2 and 9 June) that the beauty of its texture was reminiscent of Renaissance Spanish polyphony. In 1874 her zarzuelas *Flor de los cielos* and *El gran día* were produced in the Teatro Jovellanos, Madrid. The zarzuela *A la fuerza ahorcan* (1876) was performed only twice, despite praise for the music from the critic of *La opera española* (8 and 15 March). Her finest works were the overture *Sybille*, composed in Paris in 1873 (première 1875), and the *Marcha triunfal*, both performed at the Sociedad de Conciertos, Madrid. Her musical style combines elements of German music and Italian opera.

She was a founder member of the Asociación Artístico-Musical de Socorros Mutuos.

WORKS

Stage (all zarzuelas, first perf. in Madrid): Flor de los cielos (1, N. Serra), 5 April 1874; El gran día (1, Serra), 5 April 1874; A la fuerza ahorcan (3, P. Vizcaino), 6 March 1876

Orch: Sybille, ov., 1873; Capricho, orchd F. Espino; Geneviève, melody; Marcha triunfal

Sacred: Misa [Mass], 1867; Ave verum, T/S, C, chorus, 1881; O salutaris hostia, S, C (Madrid, 1881); Salve, S, chorus, pf/harp, 1883; Benedictus; 2 salutaciones a la Virgen, S, chorus, harp; Salve coreada

Other vocal: Les larmes, S, pf, 1873; Balada (Serra), 1v, pf; Serenata (R. Zapzter de Otal), 1v, harmonie-flûte, pf

Pf: Scherzo (Madrid, 1868); Gran vals de concierto (Madrid, 1869); Capricho, scherzo (Madrid, 1872); Marcha triunfal (Madrid, 1883); Mazurca, 1893

BIBLIOGRAPHY
LaborD
F. Pedrell: *Diccionario biográfico y bibliográfico de músicos y escritores de música* (Barcelona, 1894–7)

RAMON SOBRINO SANCHEZ

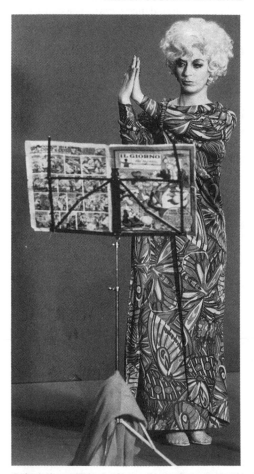

Cathy Berberian performing 'Stripsody' (1966)

Berberian, Cathy [Catherine Anahid] (*b* Attleboro, MA, 4 July 1925; *d* Rome, 6 March 1983). American singer and composer. After studying mime, writing and opera at the Universities of New York and Columbia, she took singing lessons with Giorgina del Vigo at the Verdi Conservatory in Milan. As a singer she specialized in avant-garde music, combining virtuoso performance skills with extended vocal techniques and a strong dramatic ability. Her marriage to the composer Luciano Berio, which lasted from 1950 to 1966, was a productive musical partnership as they fostered and built on each other's theatrical interests. Her vocal skills influenced many of his compositions, notably *Chamber Music*, *Circles*, *Visage*, *Sequenza III*, *Prière* and *Recital I (for Cathy)*, and also inspired works by John Cage, Igor Stravinsky, Sylvano Bussotti, Henri Pousseur, Bruno Maderna, Hans Werner Henze and others. *Stripsody* (1966), perhaps Berberian's best-known original composition, also written for her own voice, deals with comic strips as cultural discourse; it is a witty collage of onomatopoeic words and scenes from various comics, and includes material based on Charles Schulz's cartoon 'Peanuts'. Among her other works are the piano piece *Morsicat(h)y* (1971) and two more compositions for solo voice: *Awake and ReadJoyce* and *Anathema con VarieAzioni* (both 1972). Her music is published by Peters and Universal.

BIBLIOGRAPHY

KompA–Z

N. Soames: 'Profile on Cathy Berberian', *MO*, xcix (1975–6), 210–11

—— : 'Cathy Berberian, *Music and Musicians*, xxvi/6 (1978), 8, 10, 12

Obituary, *New York Times* (8 March 1983)

J. M. Edwards: 'North America since 1920', *Women and Music: a History*, ed. K. Pendle (Bloomington, IN, 1991), 226–7

J. MICHELE EDWARDS

Bergh, Gertrude van den (bap. Cologne, 21 Jan 1793; *d* The Hague, 10 Sept 1840). Netherlands pianist and composer. Van den Bergh studied the piano with Ferdinand Ries and composition with J. A. F. Burgmüller in Cologne. Her first composition, a sonata for piano, was published by J. J. Hummel when she was nine years old. By 1813 she had moved to The Hague, where she spent the rest of her short life. She was regarded as one of the top pianists of Europe and was especially renowned for her interpretation of Beethoven. She was also one of the earliest 'revivalists' of J. S. Bach's music in the Netherlands. She was the first Dutch woman to publish an instruction manual on the fundamentals of music theory, *Principes de musique* (*c*1830). Besides composing and conducting a number of choirs, she supported herself by teaching members of the Dutch royal family. Her sweetly romantic *Lied für Pianoforte* was probably the earliest 'Song without Words' to be written in the Netherlands. She also composed virtuoso works, such as the *Rondeau pour le pianoforte* op.3 (*c*1820–21). Many works, including her string quartet and preludes and fugues, are lost. In 1830 she was made an honorary member of the Maatschappij tot Bevordering der Toonkunst (Association for the Promotion of Music); the next woman member elected was Clara Schumann in 1854.

BIBLIOGRAPHY

H. Metzelaar: 'Gertrude van den Bergh', *Zes vrouwelijke componisten* (Zutphen, 1991), 21–51

HELEN METZELAAR

Berl, Christine (*b* New York, 22 July 1943). American composer. She received her early training from her father, Paul Berl, who for more than 22 years was Victoria de Los Angeles's accompanist. She studied the piano at the Mannes College of Music (1961–4) and composition at Queens College (MA 1970), where her teachers included Hugo Weisgall and George Perle, and later studied privately with Henry Weinberg and Yehudi Wyner. From 1974 she taught composition at the Mannes College. Her acknowledged output, which dates from 1974, is small, but some works have been given by internationally acclaimed performers. Emanuel Ax gave her *Elegy* for piano at the first Ravinia Fall Festival in 1988, and in 1989 Frederica von Stade gave the première of *Dark Summer*, which was commissioned by the Chamber Music Society of Lincoln Center. In the following year Peter Serkin commissioned and performed *Lord of the Dance* for solo piano, a work that draws its inspiration from Hindu sources. Berl has received several grants, including one for *The Violent Bear it Away* (1988) for orchestra and mixed chorus, which was commissioned and first performed by the Bay Area Women's Philharmonic. David Goldman has written (programme note, Kaufmann Concert Hall, New York, 13 Oct 1990) that her work can be situated in the tradition of Debussy and Bartók, where diatonic harmony never quite disappears; she seeks to reconcile an adventurous, post-tonal musical language with the long-range harmonic breadth of the music of the past.

WORKS

Vocal: And how that a Life was but a Flower (H. Weinfield: *The Book of Sir Tristram*), unacc. chorus, 1979; Ab la dolchor (Weinfield), cantata, S, chorus, orch, 1979, reorchd Mez, vn, cl, pf, 1990; The Violent Bear it Away (after F. O'Connor), chorus, orch, 1988, reorchd 2 pf, orch, 1990; Dark Summer (L. Bogan), Mez, str trio, pf, 1989

Chamber: In memoriam (2 movts, incl. Elegy), pf, 1974; 3 pieces, ens, 1975; Sonata quasi una fantasia, vc, pf, 1987; Lord of the Dance, pf, 1990; Ballade, vc, pf, 1990

Berroa, Catalina (*b* Trinidad, Cuba, 28 Feb 1849; *d* Trinidad, 23 Nov 1911). Cuban composer and instrumentalist. After studying with local teachers in Trinidad, she became organist and choir director at Santísima Trinidad and organist at San Francisco de Asís. In 1879 she organized a trio in which she played the cello, Manuel Jiménez (her nephew) the violin and Ana Luisa Vivanco the piano. She formed her own musical academy at Trinidad, and played the violin in the local Teatro Brunet (inaugurated in December 1840).

Berroa composed songs for voice and guitar (including 'La Josefa', 'Tu delirio', 'Condenado' and 'La Súplica') which show the influence of the music of both European and African immigrants to Cuba, *guarachas*, hymns, waltzes and sacred vocal works with piano and organ accompaniment; none was published.

BIBLIOGRAPHY

H. Orovio: *Diccionario de la música cubana* (Havana, 1981), 45–6

A. Valdés: *Caracterización de mujeres notables en la música colonial cubana* (Havana, 1992)

ROBERT STEVENSON,
ALICIA VALDÉS CANTERO

Bertin, Louise(-Angélique) (*b* Les Roches, 15 Jan 1805; *d* Paris, 26 April 1877). French composer. She was the daughter of Louis Bertin and sister of Armand Bertin, successive proprietors and editors of the influential *Journal des débats*. She was brought up in an artistic and literary milieu, and her energies were channelled into painting and poetry as well as music. She had singing lessons from F.-J. Fétis, who directed a private performance in 1825 of her first opera, *Guy Mannering*, following the current fashion for Sir Walter Scott's novels, with a libretto written by herself. In 1827 *Le loup-garou*, to a libretto by Eugène Scribe, was produced at

Louise Bertin: engraving after a lost drawing (c1830) by Jean-Auguste-Dominique Ingres

the Opéra-Comique. But this one-act opera of intrigue, with its Rossinian music, was less characteristic of her lofty aspirations than the two larger operas that followed: *Fausto* in 1831, in which a marked originality of style was observed, and *La Esmeralda*, produced at the Opéra in 1836, to a libretto by Victor Hugo based on his own *Notre-Dame de Paris*. Despite the prestige of Hugo and the Bertins, or more probably because of it, and falling very much under the shadow of the success of *Les Huguenots*, the opera was not a success. Berlioz, critic of the *Débats*, gave Louise Bertin much assistance in the preparation of the production, although this did not extend, as some maintained, to composing the music for her. He acknowledged only that he suggested an improved end to Quasimodo's aria in Act 4. He held a high opinion of certain parts of the opera and criticized it for its extreme irregularity of phrasing and heavy orchestration, both evidence of the music's boldness for contemporary ears. Her style had developed very quickly in a short period.

The failure of *La Esmeralda* turned Bertin away from opera, and her music thereafter, mainly a series of cantatas, was played only in private. She published two volumes of poetry, *Glanes* in 1842 and *Nouvelles glanes* in 1876. Throughout her career she had to contend with the prejudice against women which forced her sometimes to conceal her identity as a composer, and also against partial paralysis, from which she suffered from birth.

WORKS
printed works published in Paris

OPERAS

Guy Mannering (opéra comique, 3, L. Bertin after W. Scott), Bièvres, 25 Aug 1825, *US-Bp*

Le loup-garou (opéra comique, 1, E. Scribe and E. Mazères), Paris, Opéra-Comique, 10 March 1827 (1827)

Fausto (opera semiseria, 4, after J. W. von Goethe), Paris, Théâtre Italien, 7 March 1831, vs (1831)

La Esmeralda (5, V. Hugo after his *Notre-Dame de Paris*), Paris, Opéra (in 4 acts), 14 Nov 1836, vs ed. F. Liszt (*c*1836)

OTHER WORKS

Pf Trio (n.d.); 6 ballades (1842); 5 chamber syms., unpubd; Prière avec choeurs, unpubd

12 unpubd cantatas: Hymne à Apollon, Jean le Parricide, La chasse et la guerre, Le départ du Comte, Le plus beau présent des dieux, Le retour d'Agamemnon, Les chasseurs, Les enfants des fées, Les esprits, Les Juifs, Ronde de jeunes filles, Vanité

BIBLIOGRAPHY

FétisB; *FétisBS*; *Grove1*; *SchmidlD*

H. Berlioz: 'La Esmeralda', *Revue et gazette musicale de Paris*, iii (20 Nov 1836), 409

H. Blaze de Bury: 'La musique des femmes: Mlle Louise Bertin', *Revue des deux mondes*, 4th ser., viii (1836), 611–25

F. Halévy: *Derniers souvenirs et portraits* (Paris, 1863)

H. Berlioz: *Mémoires* (Paris, 1870; Eng. trans., 1969, 2/1977)

M. Brenet: 'Quatre femmes musiciennes, 3: Mlle Bertin', *L'art*, 2nd ser., iv/4 (1894), 177–83

M. Daubresse: 'Quelques compositrices françaises', *Guide musical*, liii (1907), 695–8

D. Boneau: *Louise Bertin and Opera in Paris in the 1820s and 1830s* (diss., U. of Chicago, 1989)

HUGH MACDONALD

Bibby, Gillian (*b* Lower Hutt, 31 Aug 1945). New Zealand composer, pianist, writer and teacher. She grew up in a musical family and began piano lessons at the age of seven. She graduated from the University of Otago, first in English and then in piano and composition (BMus 1968) and musicology (MA 1969). A New Zealand University Grants Committee scholarship took her to Victoria University in Wellington where she studied electronic music under Douglas Lilburn, gaining a diploma (1970). She subsequently studied in Berlin and Cologne (1971–5) with Aloys Kontarsky, Wilhelm Hecker, Karlheinz Stockhausen and Mauricio Kagel, being awarded the Kranichstein Prize in new music (1974) and a Boswil Artistic Residency in Switzerland (1975). She married the singer Roger Wilson, returned to New Zealand as Mozart Fellow (1976–7), and after diverse experience in teaching, editing *Canzona* (journal of the Composers' Association of New Zealand, whose President she was from 1982 to 1984) and writing for radio, she began teaching young

Design by Charles Cambon for Act 1 of Louise Bertin's opera 'La Esmeralda' in the original production at the Paris Opéra in 1836

children the piano and composition. She has given training in the Suzuki Method and in 1992 was awarded a Churchill Fellowship for this purpose. She contributes regularly to New Zealand publications, continues concert performances, makes recordings and fulfils commissions. Bibby's music is forcefully direct, often experimental, and diverse in its allegiances: it has at times shown the influence of John Cage, minimalism, Olivier Messiaen, Pierre Boulez, György Ligeti and Henri Pousseur and sometimes reflects her love-hate relationship with the music of Stockhausen. In her later compositions she has moved from atonality and dissonance to a more tonal-pantonal language.

WORKS
selective list

Stage: Sanctuary of Spirits (children's opera, A. Campell) 1970; Lest you be my enemy (ballet), tape, 1976; Fanfares for Rackets (incid. music), 2 tapes, 1977; Marama Music (music-theatre), 2vv, chamber ens, 1978

Inst and tape: Anacrosmos I, a fl, b cl, tpt, 1971; Anacrosmos II, fl, cl, b cl, 1972; Musik für drei Hörer, chamber ens, 1972; Musik für drei und einige Hörer, chamber ens, electronics, 1972; Tropus, org, 1972; Amongst, chamber orch, 1973; Beneidenswert, 1974; Incident I, chamber ens, 1974; Incident II, chamber ens, 1974; Aie!, a Conversation Piece, tape, 1975; 5 Miniatures, pf, 1975; Space, org, 4 Renaissance trbn, zink, 1975; Fire Music, exotic insts, 1977; Synthesis, tape, 1977; 11 Characters in Search of a Composer, military band, perc, 1987

Vocal: Musik für eine Aula, 7vv, chamber ens, 1974; You Can't Kiss the Tummy of a Caged Lion (L. V. Bibby and others), S, S, S, chamber ens, 1978; In Memoriam (Bibby), 8vv, org, perc, 1979; The Beasts (Middle English), Bar, pf, 1973, rev. 1981

J. M. THOMSON

Bidart, Lycia de Biase (*b* Vitória, Espírito Santo, 18 Feb 1910). Brazilian pianist and composer. She began her studies with Neusa França (piano) and continued them with Giovanni Giannetti (harmony, composition, counterpoint and fugue) in Rio de Janeiro; she also studied the piano with Magda Tagliaferro. She made her début as a pianist in 1930 in Rio de Janeiro. From 1941 to 1945 she was artistic director of the Curso Santa Rosa de Lima. She has written extensively for the piano and has produced much chamber and orchestral music. In 1975 she was awarded a prize in the Viotti international competition, Italy, for her Sonata fantasia no.1: 'Sonata ao mar' (1961). A catalogue of her works was published in 1978 by the Ministério das Relações Exteriores in Brazil.

WORKS
selective list

Stage: A noiva do mar (opera), 1939; Som e cor (ballet), 1971; Simbolismo e vivência do Jardim Botânico do Rio de Janeiro (ballet), 1976

Orch and solo inst: Prelúdios nos.1–3, orch, 1931–67; Anchieta, sym. poem, 1934; Noite, pf, 1961; Sonata fantasia no.1 'Sonata ao mar', pf, 1961; Interlúdio cantabile, pf, 1969; Adagio improviso, orch, 1971; Cantos ameríndios brasileiros, orch, 1973; Albatroz, chamber ens, 1974; Série Brasília, chamber ens, 1975; Estudos, pf, 1976

Vocal: Ave Maria, 1v, pf, 1927; Canaan, sym. poem, chorus, orch, 1932; Tríptico, vv, pf, 1947; Convite tribal, chorus, 1973; Canto de louvação, chorus, 1974; Brauna, chorus, 1975

IRATI ANTONIO

Bigot (de Morogues) [née Kiené], **Marie** (*b* Colmar, 3 March 1786; *d* Paris, 16 Sept 1820). Alsatian pianist and composer. At the age of five she moved with her parents to Neuchâtel, Switzerland, where her mother gave her early piano lessons. In 1804 she married Paul Bigot, librarian to Count Razumovsky in Vienna, and thus gained introductions to Haydn, Salieri and Beethoven. On 20 February 1805 she played to Haydn, who exclaimed 'Oh! my dear child, it is not I who wrote that music, it is you!'. In May 1805 she played at the opening concert of the Augarten, encouraged by Beethoven, and Nohl recorded that she played the 'Appassionata' Sonata at sight from the autograph, which Beethoven later gave her. In 1809 the Bigots moved to Paris, where Marie came in contact with Luigi Cherubini, Pierre Baillot and many others. Her husband was captured during the Russian campaign of 1812, and the remaining years of her life were devoted to teaching; one of her pupils was the young Felix Mendelssohn. She published some minor piano works in Vienna and Paris, including a set of Etudes and a *Rondeau*; Fétis regarded 12 *Valses* attributed to her as of doubtful authenticity.

BIBLIOGRAPHY
FétisB; SchmidlD

Miel: 'Marie Bigot', *Revue musicale*, vii (1833), no.40, p.316

L. Nohl: *Beethoven's Leben* (Vienna, 1864–77), ii, 246

M. Daubresse: 'Quelques compositrices françaises', *Guide musical*, liii (1907), 675–8

J. Beahrs: 'The Immortal Beloved Revisited', *Beethoven Newsletter*, i/2 (1986), 17, 22–4

HUGH MACDONALD

Billington [née Weichsell], **Elizabeth** (*b* London, ?1765–8; *d* nr Venice, 25 Aug 1818). English soprano and composer. She was the daughter of Carl Weichsell, a German-born oboist and clarinet player; her

Elizabeth Billington as
St Cecilia: portrait (1786–9)
by Joshua Reynolds

mother was a well-known singer and a pupil of J. C. Bach. Elizabeth also had singing lessons with J. C. Bach and piano lessons with J. S. Schroeter. She appeared in public at an early age as a pianist, together with her violinist brother, Charles. She composed *Three Lessons for the Harpsichord or Piano Forte*, published in about 1775 as by 'a Child eight Years of Age', and as her op.2, in 1778, *Six Sonatas for the Piano Forte or Harpsichord*, 'in the Eleventh Year of her Age'. No further compositions are known.

After the death of Bach she studied with James Billington, a double bass player and singing teacher whom she married in 1783. She went on to a highly successful career as a singer, principally in London but also in Italy (1794–1801), where she had gone following the publication of James Ridgway's scurrilous *Memoirs of Mrs Billington*, and where she also married her second husband, Felissent or Felican.

BIBLIOGRAPHY
Choron-FayolleD; *FétisB*; *GerberL*; *Grove1* (W. H. Husk); *SchillingE*; *SchmidlD*; *WaltherML*
MOLLIE SANDS

Bingham, Judith (*b* Nottingham, 21 June 1952). She studied composition with Alan Bush and singing with Eric Fenby at the RAM, where she won the Principal's Prize for Composition in 1971. She later continued her composition studies with Hans Keller. In 1977 she won the BBC Young Composer Award with a work that numbers among many she has since withdrawn. Her work as a composer is combined with a career as a freelance singer, and this clearly informs her vocal works (though she writes with similar skill in other genres). In 1983 she became a member of the BBC Singers, for whom she has sung regularly and also written several pieces, including *A Hymn before Sunrise in the Vale of Chamounix* (1982), *A Winter Walk at Noon* (1987) and *Irish Tenebrae* (1990). Although a large proportion of her output is devoted to choral and vocal music, at the end of the 1980s she began to write for brass band. In her music an aural lucidity masks an underlying intellectual refinement. She has received many commissions and her works have been widely performed and broadcast.

WORKS
selective list

Orch and inst: Into the Wilderness, org, 1982; Scenes from Nature, hpd, 1983; Brazil, brass band, 1988; Chartres, orch, 1988; Christmas Past, Christmas Present, pf, 1989; Dove Cottage by Moonlight, 2 pf, 1989; The Stars above, the Earth below, brass band, 1991; Four Minute Mile, brass band, 1991
Vocal: A Hymn before Sunrise in the Vale of Chamounix, 16vv, 1982; Just before Dawn (Bible, C. Kingsley), SSAA, 1985, rev. 1990; A Winter Walk at Noon (E. Thomas, W. Cowper, E. Bronte, W. Wordsworth), 28vv, 1987; A Cold Spell (J. Clare, anon., G. M. Hopkins, G. K. Chesterton, J. Masefield), SATB, 1987; Where Light and Shade Repose (J. Betjeman, W. H. Auden, Wordsworth), SATB, 1989; Tu creasti domine (H. Belloc), SATB, org, 1989; Irish Tenebrae (W. B. Yeats, S. Heeney, G. Craig, Cormac, Lavin, T. Parnell), S, male vv, vn, org, perc, 1990; I have a secret to tell (Cormac), male vv, bell, 1990; Alba (E. Pound), T, pf, 1991; Unpredictable but Providential (Bingham), SATB, 1991; The Uttermost (C. Marlowe), T, chorus, orch, 1992

Principal publishers: Maecenas Music, Novello

BIBLIOGRAPHY
Fuller-LeFanuRM

TONI CALAM

Birnstein, Renate (*b* Hamburg, 17 Nov 1946). German composer. She had violin and piano lessons from an early age and in 1966 entered the Staatliche Hochschule für Musik, Hamburg, where she studied music theory and composition with Diether de la Motte and György Ligeti. From 1973 to 1980 she taught music theory at the Hochschule für Musik in Lübeck and from 1979 at the Hamburg Hochschule, where in 1988 she became a professor. She has received many prizes and grants, including a three month stay at the Boswil Künstlerhaus in Switzerland and a year at the Villa Massimo, Rome. Birnstein's output includes orchestral, choral and chamber music. Her rigorously structural, crystalline and linear thought processes were originally stamped by the music of Anton Webern, but it was Steve Reich's minimalism, first encountered by her in 1972, that provided new inspiration at a time of disenchantment with the Darmstadt School. Her choral piece *In terra* (1978), is an example of how she used a kind of 'pattern technique' based on small motivic units to produce her own minimalist style. In the 1980s she wrote a number of multi-layered compositions, including the Sextet (1981) for six orchestral ensembles and the Octet (1984).

WORKS
selective list

Orch: Imaginations, 1972; Scatola, 1978–9; 5 Pieces, str, 1979–80; Sextet, 6 orch ens, 1981; Intrada, str, 1987
Chamber: 4 Pieces, cl, trbn, vc, 1971; Ribambelle, cl, perc, 1972; Ossia, qnt, fl, cl, S, vn, vc, 1974; Idem, sextet, fl, a fl, cl, vn, va, vc, 1974; Inter pares, qnt, fl, vn, vc, vib, pf, 1975; Peram, trio, fl, gui, vib, 1976; Variations, vn, va, vc, 1977; Duo concertante, vc, b cl, 1980; Str Qnt, 1982; Piano Music II, cl, pf, 1977–84; Trio in 12 pts, fl, vn, vc, 1984; Octet, fl, cl, trbn, vn, va, vc, perc, 1984; Str Qt, 1986; Schattenspiele, b fl, basset-hn, 1986; Septet, fl, cl, vn, va, vc, db, pf, 1988
Solo inst: Heptagon, pf, 1976; Quasi fantasia, gui, 1983; Wie ein Kondukt, b fl, 1985; Kassiopeias Lied, cl, 1989; Kurwenal, vc, 1990
Choral: In terra, 24vv, 1978; Ich rufe an mit meiner Stimme, sacred conc., SATB, vn, org, 1980–81

ROSWITHA SPERBER

Bitgood [Wiersma], **Roberta** (*b* New London, CT, 15 Jan 1908). American composer, organist and choral director. After graduation from Connecticut College for Women (BA 1928), she studied theory and organ at the Guilmant Organ School (1930), attended Columbia University (MA 1932) and was the first woman to take the doctorate at the School of Sacred Music, Union Theological Seminary (MSM 1935; DSM 1945). Her principal composition teachers included Lawrence Erb, Howard Murphy, Edwin Stringham (1933–5), T. Tertius Noble (1943–5) and Wayne Bohrnsted (1957–60). During her career as organist and director of music she held positions in Protestant churches and temples in New York, New Jersey, California and Michigan. After her official retirement and return to Connecticut in 1976, she continued to work as an organist and church musician. She was the first woman president of the American Guild of Organists (1975–81). As a composer she has focussed exclusively on church music, writing many anthems for young people and giving special attention to literature feasible for small church choirs. Her style is triadic, using seventh chords, and the harmonic motion and partwriting of her vocal music are influenced by organ playing. *Ye Works of the Lord* (commissioned in 1993 for a jubilee celebration in her honour in New London) includes typical changes of tonality.

WORKS
selective list

Edition: *The Roberta Bitgood Organ Album* (New York, 1991) [B]

Choral: Give me a Faith (C. L. Reynolds), S, Bar, mixed chorus, org, 1945, arr. 1v, pf (New York, 1962); Job (cantata, Bible, D. ben Judah, trans. N. Mann and M. Landsberg), S, 2 T, Bar, mixed chorus, org, 1945; Wise Men Seeking Jesus, S, mixed chorus, fl, org, 1960, arr. unison chorus; Joseph (cantata, Bible, N. Selnecker), T, Bar, 2 nar, mixed chorus, org, 1962 (New York, 1966); Let there be Light (cantata, M. L. Kerr), children's SA chorus, org, 1965; Ye Works of the Lord (Bible, W. Blake), mixed chorus, org, 1993
Other vocal: The Greatest of These is Love (Bible, *1 Corinthians* xiii), 1v, pf/org, 1934, arr. SSA/mixed chorus, arr. (S, A)/(T, B); Be Still and Know that I am God (Bible), 1v, pf/org, 1940, arr. mixed chorus
Organ: Chorale Prelude on 'Jewels', 1942, B; Chorale Prelude on 'Siloam', 1952, B; Chorale Prelude on 'God Himself is with Us', 1953, B; At Eventide [arr. of 'Am Abend, da es kühle war' from Bach: St Matthew Passion], 1957, B; On an Ancient Alleluia, 1962 (New York, 1962), B; Offertories from Afar (7 pieces based on folk melodies) (New York, 1964); Meditation on 'Kingsfold', 1976

Principal publishers: Choristers Guild, Flammer, H. W. Gray, Sacred Music Press, Westminster

BIBLIOGRAPHY
Anderson 2; *WAM*
J. M. Meggett: *Keyboard Music by Women Composers: a Catalog and Bibliography* (Westport, CT, 1981)
G. Claghorn: *Women Composers and Hymnists* (Metuchen, NJ, 1984), 19
E. Liberman: 'She never Lost Touch', *The Day* [New London, CT] (29 April 1993)
'Roberta Bitgood Jubilee 1993', *American Organist*, xxvii/3 (1993),10
J. MICHELE EDWARDS

Blackwood [née Sheridan], **Helen (Selina)** [Lady Dufferin; Hay, Helen, Countess of Gifford] (*b* 1807; *d* Highgate, 13 June 1867). English composer. She was a granddaughter of Richard Brinsley Sheridan, statesman and dramatist, and Elizabeth Sheridan (née Linley), celebrated English soprano. She collaborated with her sister,

Caroline Norton, on a publication entitled *A Set of ten Songs and two Duets . . . by two Sisters* (London, 1833). She moved to Ireland when her first husband became Baron Dufferin in 1839. In such songs as *Terence's Farewell* (London, 1848), which make use of traditional airs, she cast the text in a quasi-Irish vernacular.

BIBLIOGRAPHY
D. Scott: *The Singing Bourgeois* (Milton Keynes, 1989)
DEREK B. SCOTT

Leopoldine Blahetka: lithograph

Blahetka, (Marie) [Maria] **Leopoldine** (*b* Guntramsdorf, nr Vienna, 15 Nov 1810/11; *d* Boulogne, 12 Jan 1887). Austrian pianist and composer. She was the daughter of the journalist and teacher Joseph L. Blahetka and his wife (née Traeg), a brilliant player of the *harmonika* and Leopoldine's first music teacher. She went on to study the piano with Carl Czerny, Frédéric Kalkbrenner, Ignaz Moscheles and Catherina Cibbini-Kozeluch, and composition with Hieronymus Payer and Simon Sechter.

On 1 March 1818 she was presented as the special attraction at a concert that included the première of Schubert's second Overture in the Italian Style D591, at the Hotel zum Römischen Kaiser in Vienna. From then on she was permanently installed in the Viennese Biedermeier musical world, a member of the circle of Schubert's friends and a regular guest at Leopold von Sonnleithner's Hauskonzerte (which Schubert also attended). There are reports of a concert on 21 March 1824 with a work by Schubert performed by 'Miss Blahetka'. In October 1818 Josef Doppler had written to Schubert that, 'Mr Blahetka asks you kindly to compose for his daughter a brilliant Rondo, or whatever you desire, which she shall play this winter. It should be a piece for piano and orchestra.' She enjoyed a career as a concert pianist, touring Germany (1825–6), the Netherlands, Bohemia, England and France.

In 1829 she met Chopin, who was visiting Vienna; he wrote to his friend Tytus Woyciechowski of the beautiful young pianist. In August 1828 Chopin described his farewell from Vienna as 'really touching because Miss Blahetka gave me a composition of hers with a personal dedication as a present'. Chopin and Blahetka did not meet again, although when he learnt of her Polish tour, he offered to perform two-piano music with her in a concert in Warsaw.

From 1834 until 1840 she remained in Vienna, then settled in Boulogne. She gradually gave up performing and concentrated on teaching and composing. Her output includes more than 70 works, most of which were published during her lifetime.

WORKS

Opera: Die Räuber und der Sänger
Orch: Variations brillantes, pf, orch, op.14; Variations brillantes sur un thème hongrois, pf, orch/str qt, op.18; Concertstück, pf, orch/str qt, op.25; Souvenir d'Angleterre, fantaisie, pf, orch/str qt, op.38
Chamber: Pf Trio, op.5; Variations concertantes, vn, pf, op.10; Grande polonaise concertante, vc, pf, op.11; Vn Sonata, op.15; Pf Qt no.1, A, op.43; Pf Qt no.2, E♭, op.44
Pf solo: 14 sets of variations incl. opp.2, 4, 6, 20, 26–9, 33, 39, 63; Grande polonaise, op.9; Polonaise, op.19; 6 valses favorites de Vienne, op.35; 3 rondeaux élégantes, op.37; 2 fantaisies, opp.38, 40; 2 nocturnes, op.46; Quadrille des Patineurs, op.56; Nocturne no.4, op.62; other pieces
Vocal: Rastlose Liebe (J. W. von Goethe), 1v, pf, op.32; Ave Maria, 1v, pf/org, op.57; Pater noster, 4vv, pf/org, op.58; Fragment du poëme 'Maud' (A. Tennyson), 1v, pf, op.64; 6 deutsche Lieder, 1v, pf (without op. no., n.d.); La fille de Golconde (J. Méry), 1v, pf (Paris, 1835); How oft in the moonshine (F. von Matthison: Abendwehmuth) (London, 1848)

BIBLIOGRAPHY

FétisB; GerberL; Grove1 (F. Gehring); PazdirekH; SchillingE; SchmidlD; WurzbachL
A. Weinmann: Verzeichnis der Musikalien des Verlages Johann Traeg (Vienna, 1966, enlarged 2/1973)
L. H. Ledeen: Introduction to Leopoldine Blahetka: Music for Piano (Bryn Mawr, PA, 1992) [incl. edn of variations, a polonaise and a fantaisie]
ROSARIO MARCIANO,
JORGE SANCHEZ-CHIONG

Blanche of Castile (b 1188; d 1252). Spanish-French trouvère, a daughter of Alfonso VIII of Castile. She was the wife of Louis VIII of France and Regent of France during the minority of her son Louis IX, and during his Crusade (1248–52). Blanche was wooed by a powerful nobleman, Count Thibaut de Champagne, the King of Navarre, one of the most renowned trouvères. In one fragmentary manuscript (F-Pn f.f., nouvelles acq. 21677) a chanson is ascribed to 'Roïne Blance'. The song Amours, u trop tart me sui pris is a prayer to the Virgin Mary in four strophes; the last two lines of each strophe constitute a musical and textual refrain.

BIBLIOGRAPHY

F. Gennrich: Rondeaux, Virelais und Balladen, ii (Göttingen, 1927), 125–6 [music edn]
J. Maillard: Anthologie de chants de trouvères (Paris, 1967), 63–4 [music edn]
R. Pernoud: La reine Blanche (Paris, 1972; Eng. trans., 1975, as Blanche of Castile)
F. Gies and J. Gies: Women in the Middle Ages (New York, 1978), 97–119
M. V. Coldwell: 'Jougleresses and Trobairitz: Secular Musicians in Medieval France', Women Making Music: the Western Art Tradition, 1150–1950, ed. J. Bowers and J. Tick (Urbana and Chicago, 1986), 39–61, esp. 50, 53 [music of Amours, u trop tart me sui pris]; see also pp.3–4
MARIA V. COLDWELL

Bland [née Romanzini], **Maria Theresa** (b c1769; d London, 15 Jan 1838). English composer and soprano of Italian-Jewish descent. She was on stage as a child and became one of the most popular singers of her day, appearing at Drury Lane from 1786 to 1822. Storace created roles for her in nearly all his operas. Mount Edgcumbe noted her 'pure Italian taste' when she sang with the Italian opera company in the 1798–9 season, but she was particularly admired for the sweet simplicity of her ballad singing. She composed her own pieces in this style, notably ''Twas in the solemn midnight hour', which she performed in the comedy Sighs (1799) and which had several editions in London and Dublin (print in GB-Lbl). She also set The Rose of Aberdeen, Lorenzo (prints of both in Ob), Stay Dear Youth (Lbl), Crazy Jane (ALb), The Fisherman and the River Queen (which she sang at Drury Lane in 1800) and The Banks of Allen Water (Lbl) – the last three with words by M. G. ('Monk') Lewis – and wrote a popular march performed by the Duke of York's Band.

BIBLIOGRAPHY

BDA; LS

R. Edgcumbe [Mount Edgcumbe]: *Musical Reminiscences* (London, 1824, 4/1834)

W. Oxberry: 'Memoir of Mrs Bland', *Dramatic Biography*, i (1825), 161–7

M. Kelly: *Reminiscences* (London, 1826, 2/1826); ed. R. Fiske (London, 1975)

OLIVE BALDWIN, THELMA WILSON

Blangy, Caroline. *See* GRANDVAL, MARIE.

Blaustein, Susan Morton (*b* Palo Alto, CA, 22 March 1953). American composer. She studied the piano and composition with Karl Kohn at Pomona College (BA 1975), and composition with Henri Pousseur at the Liège Conservatory in Belgium, with Seymour Shifrin at Brandeis University and with Jacob Druckman and Betsy Jolas at Yale (MM 1979, MMA 1980, DMA in composition 1986), where she subsequently lectured. She was a Junior Fellow at Harvard and an Assistant Professor of Music at Columbia University (1985–90). She has been commissioned by the Schoenberg Institute, the Koussevitsky Foundation and the Fromm Foundation, and she received a Guggenheim Fellowship in 1988. She has also received awards from the American Academy of Arts and Letters, the NEA, and the League of Composers – ISCM. Her music is freely atonal with a lyric element.

WORKS
selective list

Orch and chamber: Commedia, 8 players, 1980; Str Qt no.1, ricercare, 1981; Sextet, fl, cl, pf, vn, vc, perc, 1983; Conc., vc, chamber orch, 1984

Pf: La espoza de Don Garcia; Fantasia, 1980

Vocal: The Moon has Nothing to be Excited about, canzona, 1977; The Moon has Nothing to be Sad about, 6 poems (S. Plath); 2 Madrigals (T. Tasso), v, perc, ens, 1979; To Orpheus (R. M. Rilke), 4 sonnets, SATB, 1982; Song of Songs, Mez, T, orch, 1985

Principal publisher: BMI

SARA JOBIN

Bley [née Borg], Carla (*b* Oakland, CA, 11 May 1938). American composer, bandleader and keyboard player. She learned the fundamentals of music from her father, a church musician, but is otherwise self-taught. At the age of 17 she moved to New York, where she worked intermittently as a pianist and cigarette girl, writing jazz tunes for musicians such as George Russell, Jimmy Giuffre,

and her husband at the time, Paul Bley. In 1964, with her second husband, Mike Mantler, she formed the Jazz Composers Guild Orchestra, known from 1965 as the Jazz Composer's Orchestra. She first came to public notice with *A Genuine Tong Funeral* (1967), a cycle of pieces recorded with the Gary Burton Quartet, and with her compositions and arrangements for Charlie Haden's *Liberation Music Orchestra* (1969). In 1971 she completed her eclectic 'jazz opera', *Escalator over the Hill*, which was extraordinarily well received by the international jazz press and led to several composing grants. During the 1970s and 80s Bley continued to compose and to lead her own ten-piece touring band. In the mid-1980s she began to favour smaller ensembles, working principally with a sextet; she made an album *Sextet* and wrote *Coppertone* to a commission from the Lincoln Center Chamber Music Society. Other works of this period include *Continuoso*, a fanfare for the Houston SO, and some piano pieces, *Romantic Notions*, for Ursula Oppens. But she also worked with larger groups, touring Europe with a 15-piece band, and she founded the Big Carla Bley Band in 1989 and wrote her own big band orchestrations for the Berlin Contemporary Jazz Orchestra (*All Fall Down*, 1989). She taught at the College of William and Mary, Williamsburg, Virginia in 1990, and later toured, notably in Scotland, Italy and Finland, working with the Very Big Carla Bley Band (an 18-piece group) and other large bands (her works of the early 1990s include *Birds of Paradise*, for violin and band); she also collaborated with the bass player Steve Swallow, touring with him in Europe and Japan, writing music for their recordings (*Duets*, *Go Together*).

Not exceptional as a keyboard player, Bley is outstanding as a jazz composer, with a very wide range of styles. Much of her best work is infused with a spirit of parody and sardonic humour. Among her compositions are *3/4* for piano and orchestra, which has been performed by musicians as varied as Keith Jarrett, Ursula Oppens and Frederic Rzewski, and the soundtrack for the film *Mortelle randonnée* (1985).

BIBLIOGRAPHY

*Grove*J (J. B. Robinson)

M. Cuscuna: 'Carla Bley's New Opera: Worth the Toil and Trouble', *Down Beat*, xxxix/6 (1972), 16–17

G. Buhles: 'Die Jazzkomponistin Carla Bley: Kurzbiographie, Werkanalyse, Würdigung', *Jazzforschung*, viii (1976), 11

H. Mandel: 'Carla Bley: Independent Ringleader', *Down Beat*, xlv/11 (1978), 18–19, 38–40, 40–45

B. Primack: 'Carla Bley: First Lady of the Avant-garde', *Contemporary Keyboard*, v/2 (1979), 9–11
L. Dahl: *Stormy Weather: the Music and Lives of a Century of Jazzwomen* (London, Melbourne and New York, 1984)
D. Palmer: 'My Dinner with Carla', *Down Beat*, li/8 (1984), 24–6

J. BRADFORD ROBINSON/R

Bliss, Mrs J. Worthington. *See* LINDSAY, MARIA.

Blomfield Holt, Patricia (*b* Lindsay, Ont., 15 Sept 1910). Canadian composer. She studied with Norman Wilks, Hayunga Carman, Norah De Kresz and Healey Willan at the Toronto Conservatory of Music from 1929 to 1939, later returning to teach there (now the Royal Conservatory) from 1954 to 1984. Her works, which have been performed in North America, Russia and Europe, are tonally conservative and well-crafted. The Suite no.1 for violin and piano was co-winner, for the best Canadian composition, in the second annual Vogt Society competition in 1939. She is best known as a chamber music and vocal composer, but among her few orchestral works is the *Legend of the North Woods* (1985), an evocation of a lake depicted in Canadian painter J. R. Seauvy's picture of an unspoilt early Indian scene in the lake country, where the composer had spent many summers.

WORKS
selective list

Incid. music: Sister Beatrice, 1936
Orch: Pastorale, 1940; Short Sketch on a Theme, 1940; Legend of the North Woods, 1985; To the Distant Shore, 1988
Chamber: Pastorale and Finale, vn, pf, 1935; Suite no.1, vn, pf, 1936; Lyric pieces nos.1–2, vc, pf, 1937; Str Qt no.1, 1937, rev. 1985; Suite no.2, vn/va, pf, 1939; Str Qt no.2, 1956, rev. 1985, 1987; Metamorphosis, va, pf, 1985; Set of Two, fl, pf, 1987; Vc Sonata, 1987; Invocations, fl, vc, harp, 1989
Vocal: Songs of Early Canada, Bar harp, hn, str, 1950; Songs of my Country (D. C. Scott, S. Moodie, M. Pickthall), B/A, harp, hn, str, 1950; 3 Songs of Contemplation (E. J. Pratt, M. Adeney, A. Lowell), 1v, pf, 1970; The Birds (H. Belloc), 1971; A Lake Memory (W. W. Campbell, low v, pf, 1979; Magnificat, SATB unacc. 1986; Polar Chrysalis: 10 Haiku Poems (C. Pratt), Mez, pf, vc, hn, perc, 1988
Also piano pieces and piano teaching material

GAYNOR G. JONES

Bo, Sonia (*b* Lecco, 27 March 1960). Italian composer. After studying the piano, choral music and choral conducting, she took composition lessons with Renato Dionisi and Azio Corghi at the Milan Conservatory,

graduating in 1985. From then until 1988 she studied with Franco Donatoni at the Accademia di S Cecilia, Rome. In 1985 she was awarded first prize in the Fondazione Guido D'Arezzo international competition for her *Frammenti da Jacopone* for female choir, and in the same year her *Da una lettura di Husserl* won the competition promoted by the European Cultural Foundation for European Music Year. She has received several other important awards in Italy and elsewhere and her works are performed in Italy's principal venues. She teaches composition at the Piacenza Conservatory.

WORKS
selective list

Da una lettura di Husserl, conc., chamber orch, 1984; Frammenti da Jacopone, female chorus, 1985; Come un'allegoria, S, cl, vc, pf, 1986; Lauda, spkr, chorus, orch, 1987; D'Iride, chamber ens, 1988; 2 bagatelle, fl, gui, 1988; Polittico, 5 songs, chamber ens, 1991–2

PAOLA DAMIANI

Bock [née Spech], **Berta (Johanna Amalie)** (*b* Sibiu [Ger. Hermannstadt], 15 March 1857; *d* Sibiu, 4 April 1945). Romanian composer and pianist of German (Saxon) origin. Benefiting from the musical environment and tradition of her family (her grandfather Wilhelm Conrad, Baron von Conradsheim, founded the Hermannstädter Musikverein in Sibiu), she studied the piano and theory as a child with Berta Spech and the conductor Hermann Bönicke, then singing with Rosa Pfaff. While performing in concerts and recitals in Transylvania, Austria and Germany, she participated in the artistic soirées organized by Bishop Georg Daniel Teutsch in Sibiu. Saxon folklore in Transylvania provided the inspiration for her opera *Die Pfingstkrone* (1927), which was performed throughout Transylvania, and in 1931 in Cleveland, Ohio. The melodies of the lieder have a simplicity characteristic of Saxon folk music and the modal harmony gives the songs an exceptional originality.

WORKS
selective list

Stage: Klein Elschens Traum, op.3, (pantomime-ballet, 1, E. Sigerus), 1906, Sibiu, 1907; Das erste Veilchen, op.4 (pantomime-ballet, 1, Sigerus), Sibiu, 1910; Die Pfingstkrone, op.16 (opera, 3, A. Schuller), Sibiu, 26 April 1927
Songs: 5 Lieder, op.5 (Leipzig, n.d.); 4 Lieder, op.6 (Leipzig, n.d.); 4 Lieder, op.7 (Leipzig, n.d.); Das verlassene Mägdlein, op.8 (Leipzig, n.d.); Über den Bergen, op.9 (Leipzig, n.d.); 5 Lieder, op.9a (Berlin, n.d.); 2 songs, male chorus, op.12; 6 Lieder op.13; 2 Duets, S, S, op.25; 2 Songs in ballad style, op.14

BIBLIOGRAPHY
H. Tobie: 'Berta Bock: ein Leben für die Musik', *Karpatenrundschau*, nos.21 and 22 (1974)

VIOREL COSMA

Bocquet, Mlle **(Anne** or **Marguerite)** (*b* ?Paris, early 17th century; *d* Paris, after 1660). French lutenist and composer. She played 'miraculously' on the lute, according to Mlle de Scudéry, whose confidante she was and with whom from 1653 to 1659 she held a famous salon inspired by that of the Hôtel de Rambouillet. Here she was in touch with various artists and some of the founders of the Académie Française – J.-F. Sarazin, Valentin Conrart, Paul Pellisson and Jean Chapelain among them. She very probably composed the music in a manuscript (at *F-Pn*) containing 17 *Préludes marquant les cadences* and a *Prélude sur tous les tons* for the lute, which constitute a thorough exploration of various tonalities, taking the chromatic possibilities of the lute as their starting-point. Other lute pieces, which bear the name Bocquet and must be attributed to her, are found in French, German and English manuscripts of the second half of the 17th century. (All this music appears in M. Rollin and A. Souris, eds.: *Oeuvres des Bocquet*, Paris, 1972.)

MONIQUE ROLLIN

Bodorová, Sylvie (*b* České Budějovice, 31 Dec 1954). Czech composer. She was a piano and composition pupil at the conservatory in Bratislava, before studying at the Janáček Academy of Music in Brno (1974–9), under Ctirad Kohoutek, and at the Academy of Musical Arts in Prague. Further work with Franco Donatoni at the composition course at Siena (1981) ensued. She devotes herself exclusively to composing and has won prizes within Czechoslovakia. Her style is characterized by structural simplicity and lyrical sonority. In later works blocks of sound are juxtaposed and layered.

WORKS
selective list

Orch: Concertino doppio con eco, 2 vn, vc, str orch, 1977; Passion Plays, va, orch, 1982; Pontem video, org, perc, str, 1983; Jubiloso, chamber orch, 1984; 3 canzoni da suonare, gui, str, 1985; Slunečná suita [Sun Suite], 1986; Messagio, vn conc., 1989; Detva, chamber orch, 1990; Magikon, ob, str, 1990; Panamody, fl, str, 1992

Vocal: Výstraha [Warning] (Bodorová), S, B, bn, str qt, 1974; Jihočeske madrigaly [South Bohemian Madrigals], chorus, 1975; Bohemian Songs for the Linha Singers, 1977; Jahodová noc [Strawberry Night] (V. Binorová), reciter, S, fl, hn, vn, harp,

1979; Canto di Lode, vv, orch, 1980; Zápas s andělem [Struggle with the Angel] (J. Seifert), male v, str orch, 1982; Kale Bala, Mez, cl, va, pf, 1984

Inst: Metamorphoses terrae, fl, ob, vc, pf, 1975; Vůně léta [Summer Scent]: Miniattaca, fl, pf, 1976; Musica slovacca, fl, 1977; Balticke miniatury [Baltic Miniatures], gui, 1979; Gil'a Roma!, va, 1980; Musica dedicata per due Boemi, b cl, pf, 1980; Saluti da Siena, cl, 1981; Musica per due, org, 1982; Models, pf trio, 1983; Anvils, b cl, pf, str qnt, 1984; Dignitas homini, str qt, 1987; Sine dolore, vl, vc, 1989; Dža more, va, 1990; Sostar mange, gui, 1990; Trio, ob, cl, vn, 1991; Ventimiglia, tpt, 6 perc, 1992; Una volta prima vera (Vn Sonata), 1992

Educational music and works for children, incl. Little Pool, ballet-opera, 1976

Principal publishers: Classic, Czech Music Fund, Panton

BIBLIOGRAPHY
ČSS

ANNA ŠERÝCH

Boetzelaer [née van Aerssen], **Josina (van den)** (*b* The Hague, 3 Jan 1733; *d* IJsselstein, 3 Sept 1797). Netherlands composer. Boetzelaer is one of the few 18th-century Netherlands women composers whose music survives. She was a baroness and until her marriage to Carl van den Boetzelaer in 1768 served as a lady of the court, first to Princess Anna of Hanover, wife of the Stadtholder William IV, and later to their daughter, Princess Caroline. She studied music with F. P. Ricci, who was also employed by the House of Orange. Three published works survive: a set of ariettas for voice and continuo and two collections of arias with orchestral accompaniment (opp.2 and 4). Written in early 18th-century Italian opera style, her arias are well-balanced, pleasing pieces in a light, elegant style.

BIBLIOGRAPHY
H. Metzelaar: 'An Unknown 18th-Century Dutch Woman Composer: Josina Boetzelaer (1793–1797)', *TVNM*, xl/2 (1990), 3–56

HELEN METZELAAR

Bofill Levi, Ana (*b* Barcelona, 25 April 1944). Spanish architect and composer. She began piano and theory studies with Jordi Albareda in 1950, continuing with J. Cercós, Xavier Montsalvatge and Josep Mestres-Quadreny. She worked on electronic and acoustic music at the Laboratorio Phonos in Barcelona with Gabriel Brnčic, and studied composition with Luigi Nono, Juan Guinjoán and C. Aharonian. In 1974 she qualified as an architect. She continued to be active simultaneously in music and architecture and published several works in both fields, including a translation of Iannis Xenakis's

Musique-architecture into Catalan (Barcelona, 1983). In 1985 she won a scholarship to work in Paris at the Centre d'Études de Mathématique et Automates Musicales with Xenakis.

Her music is largely serialist and, like that of Xenakis, imparts a strong sense of abstract constructivism. The premières of *Urfaust* (1983, composed in collaboration with J. M. Berenguer) and *Fills d'un Déu Menor* (1984) were given in Barcelona by the Adriá Gual company, directed by Ricard Salvat.

WORKS
selective list

Chamber and solo inst: Esclat, fl, ob, cl, pf, perc, 2 vn, va, vc, 1971; Poema, pf, 1974 (Barcelona, 1980); Espai sonor, perc, 2 tapes, 1976; Qt, gui, pf, hpd, perc, 1976; Suite, hpd, 1977; Septet de set sous, fl, cl, gui, pf, perc, vn, va, 1978; Suite de Tamanrassat, gui, 1978; Trio, pf, vn, tape, 1981
Vocal: Enigma (M. Antònia Salvà), 1v, pf, 1981; Cancíon de primavera (M. Cinta Montagut), 1v, gui, 1983; Mezquita (Cinta Montagut), 1v, pf, 1984
Other works: Urfaust (J. W. von Goethe), scenography, tape, Barcelona, 3 June 1983, collab. J. M. Berenguer; Fills d'un Déu Menor (M. Medoff), tape, Barcelona, 1984

BIBLIOGRAPHY
68 compositors catalans (Barcelona, 1980) [pubn of the Associació Catalana de Compositors]
ALICIA CASARES-ALONSO

Bokanowski, Michèle (*b* Cannes, 9 Aug 1943). French composer. After studying composition and analysis with Michel Puig (1965–9), she undertook a period of training from 1970 to 1972 with the Groupe de Recherches Musicales of the ORTF in Paris under the direction of Pierre Schaeffer, and at the same time studied computer music with Patrick Greussay at the University of Paris at Vincennes. She then became part of a group, again under the aegis of the Groupe de Recherches Musicales, researching into sound synthesis by computer. From 1972 onwards, her output has been essentially electroacoustic: tape and voice, tape and instruments, *musique concrète*, etc. The original sound-worlds she creates through her use of greatly varied and refined sonorities are a notable feature of her music. She employs the principle of random repetition, sometimes adopting natural sound models as a basis, as for example in *Tabou* (1983–4). She has also composed much film music; Michel Chion, commenting upon her husband Patrick Bokanowski's film *L'Ange* (1982), wrote that Michèle's music is 'never a commentary' but very much 'takes an active part in the film's space, pulse and song'.

WORKS
selective list

Stage: Salomé, parabole du désir (ballet), insts, tape, 1985; Hamlet (incid. music, W. Shakespeare), tape, 1986; Ishtar et Tammuz, duo d'amour (ballet), tape, 1986; L'éclipse de la balle (incid. music, A. Calveyra), tape, 1987
El-ac: Kore, 8 solo vv, tape, 1972; Pour un pianiste, prepared pf, tape, 1973–4; 3 chambres d'inquiétude, musique concrète, 1976; Suite pour l'ange, musique concrète, vn, va, vc, 1980; Tabou, musique concrète, 1983–4; Près du silence, lute, tape, 1984; Phone Variations, musique concrète, 1986–8
Inst: Sonata, 4 insts, 1968; Xeud, fl, perc, 1970
Film: La femme qui se poudre (P. Bokanowski), 1972; Déjeuner du matin (P. Bokanowski), 1975; L'Ange (P. Bokanowski), 1982; Solo (video-dance, R. Cahen), 1989; La plage (P. Bokanowski), 1991; Au bord du lac (P. Bokanowski), 1993

PIERRE SABY

Boleyn, Anne (*b* ?Blickling, Norfolk, *c*1501; *d* London, 19 May 1536). Second wife of Henry VIII, King of England. Though often said to be a composer, she is not in fact known to have written any music. Her cosmopolitan education introduced her to French court music, and she was taught to sing and play the lute. She may also have studied with the organist Henry Bredemers. Through her courtship with Henry VIII, and after their marriage in 1533, she is likely to have encouraged the performance of Continental repertories at the Tudor court. A manuscript containing French motets and chansons (*GB-Lcm* 1070), copied in France, is associated with her. A poem attributed to her, *Defyled is my name*, was set by Robert Johnson.

BIBLIOGRAPHY
Choron-FayolleD ('Anne de Boleyn'); HawkinsH
E. E. Lowinsky: 'A Music Book for Anne Boleyn', *Florilegium historiale: Essays Presented to Wallace K. Ferguson* (Toronto, 1971), 161–235
E. W. Ives: *Anne Boleyn* (Oxford, 1986)
JOHN MILSOM

Bond [Jacobs-Bond], **Carrie** (*b* Janesville, WI, 11 Aug 1862; *d* Hollywood, CA, 28 Dec 1946). American composer and publisher. She showed early talent for improvising songs to her own words and in painting. Her only formal study was with local teachers and at 18 she married E. J. Smith, by whom she had one child, Fred Jacobs Smith. They separated in 1887 and in 1889 she married Frank Lewis Bond. She published her first songs, *Is my Dolly Dead?* and *Mother's Cradle Song* in 1894. Frustrated by difficulties encountered in getting further songs published after the death of her second husband in 1895, and displaying the enterprising spirit that characterized the rest of her life, she formed her own publishing company, Carrie Jacobs-Bond & Son. By performing her songs (which required distinctively improvisational delivery mixing speech and song), she cultivated influential contacts. The baritone David Bispham sang a recital exclusively of Bond songs in Chicago in 1901, and friends arranged for her to perform for President Roosevelt at the White House. She published about 175 songs, of which two were highly successful. *I Love you Truly* (1901) sold over a million copies, and *A Perfect Day* (1910) sold eight million copies of sheet music and over five million records. She designed her own music covers, and the wild rose was a prominent image in words and decoration. Her publishing company moved eight times in Chicago to accommodate the growing business, and in 1920 she moved her business to Hollywood. In 1927 she published her autobiography *The Roads of Melody*; in 1928 she stopped composing for a time after her son's suicide. A book of her poetry and philosophical commentary, *The End of the Road*, was published in 1940 and her last song, *Because of the Light*, was copyrighted in 1944 when she was 82. Bond believed that 'the multitude needs music – perhaps even more than the cultured few'.

Victoria Bond

WORKS
selective list;
most works published in Chicago

Songs (texts by Bond unless otherwise stated): 7 Songs as Unpretentious as the Wild Rose (1901); California, the Land of Blossoms (1902); 2 Songs for Contralto: His Lullaby (B. Healy), Longing (1907); Love and Sorrow (P. L. Dunbar) (1908); A Perfect Day (1910); Half Minute Songs (1910–11); A Cottage in God's Garden (1917); Roses are in Bloom (1926); Because of the Light (F. Carlton) (1944)

Arrs. (tunes transcr. M. Gillen and O. Chalifoux): Negro Spirituals of the South (1918); Old Melodies of the South (1918)

Pf: The Chimney Swallows (1897); Memories of Versailles (1898); Reverie (1902); Betty's Music Box (1917)

Principal publisher: Boston Music Co.

BIBLIOGRAPHY

C. Jacobs Bond: 'Music Composition as a Field for Women', *The Etude*, xxxviii (1920), 583–4
Obituary, *New York Times* (29 Dec 1946)
P. R. Bruce: *From Rags to Roses: the Life and Times of Carrie Jacobs Bond, an American Composer* (thesis, Wesleyan U., 1980)
M. Good: *Carrie Jacobs Bond: Her Life and Times* (thesis, Butler U., 1984)

PAMELA FOX

Bond, Victoria (*b* Los Angeles, CA, 6 May 1945). American conductor and composer. She studied composition, with Ingolf Dahl, and singing at the University of Southern California before attending the Juilliard School, where she studied composition with Roger Sessions and Vincent Persichetti and conducting with Jean Morel, Sixten Ehrling, and Herbert von Karajan (MMA 1975, DMA 1977); she was the first woman to be awarded the doctorate in conducting at Juilliard. She made her American début at Alice Tully Hall, New York, in 1973. After graduating from the Juilliard School, she was an Exxon/Arts Endowment conductor with the Pittsburgh SO and music director of both the Pittsburgh Youth Orchestra and the New Amsterdam SO (1978–80). She made her European début with the Radio Telefís Orchestra, Dublin, in 1982, her Chinese début with the Shanghai SO in 1993, and has appeared with a number of American orchestras, including the Houston SO and the Buffalo PO. She was music director of the Bel Canto Opera in New York, 1983–8, and was responsible for the programming and conducting of the Albany SO's youth concerts, 1984–7. In 1986 she became director of the Roanoke SO, Virginia, and was subsequently named artistic director of Opera Roanoke.

Although better known as a conductor, Bond devotes equal time to composition and has had many of her works published – mainly chamber music and ballets. In Los Angeles she composed and arranged music for the Universal and Metro-media film studios and worked on a Jacques Cousteau documentary. Major works include two ballet scores choreographed by Lynn Taylor Corbett, *Equinox* (1977, commissioned by the Pennsylvania Ballet) and *Other Selves* (1979, commissioned by the Jacob's Pillow Dance Festival), and two works for narrator and orchestra, *The Frog Prince* (1983–4) and *What's the Point of Counterpoint?* (1984–5). *Urban Bird*, for alto saxophone and orchestra, was first performed by The Women's Philharmonic, San Francisco, in 1993; a programmatic work, it quotes two jazz classics, Charlie Parker's 'Au privave' and John Coltrane's 'Blue Trane'.

WORKS
selective list
DRAMATIC

Equinox (ballet), New York, 1977

Great Galloping Gottschalk (ballet), 1981; Miami, 1986

The Frog Prince (musical fairy-tale, after J. L. Grimm and W. C . Grimm), Albany, NY, 1984

What's the Point of Counterpoint? (musical fable), nar, orch, Albany, NY, 1985

Everyone is Good for Something (musical for young audiences), Louisville, KY, 1986

Gulliver (opera, 3, after J. Swift: *Gulliver's Travels*), Louisville, KY, 17 March 1988, withdrawn; rev. as Travels (opera, 2), c1994

Molly ManyBloom (monodrama), S, str qt, New York, 16 June 1991

OTHER WORKS

Orch: Elegy, 1971; 4 Fragments, 1972; Sonata for Orch, 1972; Ringing, 1986; Black Light, conc., jazz pianist, orch, 1988; Urban Bird, conc., a sax, orch, 1993

Inst: Qt, cl, vn, va, vc, 1967; Trio, hn, tpt, trbn, 1969; Can(n)ons, cl, vn, 1970; Recitative, eng hn, str qt, 1970; Ménage à trois, a fl, b cl, a sax, 1971; Vc Sonata, 1971; C-A-G-E-D, str qnt, 1972; Conversation Piece, va, vib, 1975; Pf Trio, 1979; Sandburg Suite, pf, 1980; White on Black, conc., sax qt, concert band, 1983; Batucada, pf, 1985; Notes from Underground, a sax, pf, 1985; Old New Borrowed Blues (Variations on Flow my Tears), perc, hpd, db, vib, 1986; Hot Air, ww qnt, 1991; Dreams of Flying, str qt, 1994

Vocal: Aria (V. Bond), S, str qt, 1970; Suite aux troubadours, S, inst ens, 1970; Peter Quince at the Clavier (W. Stevens), S, pf, 1978; Margaret (G. M. Hopkins), S, fl, vn, vc, pf, 1984; Scat (II), S, tpt, 1984

Principal publishers: Alexander Broude, Theodore Presser, G. Schirmer, Seesaw

BIBLIOGRAPHY

LePageWC, i

C. Apone: 'Victoria Bond: Composer, Conductor', *HiFi/MusAm*, xxix/4 (1979), 28–35

H. Dudar: 'Bloomsday Music', *Wall Street Journal* (5 July 1991)

J. Hoffman: 'In Concert: Victoria Bond's Baton Revives Symphony', *Wall Street Journal* (9 June 1987)

SAM DI BONAVENTURA, BARBARA JEPSON

Bonds [née Majors]**, Margaret Allison** [Jeannette] (*b* Chicago, 3 March 1913; *d* Los Angeles, 26 April 1972). American composer, pianist and teacher. The daughter of a pioneering black physician, Dr Monroe Alpheus Majors, and his second wife, Estelle C. Bonds, an organist and music teacher, she began her musical studies with her mother, whose home was a gathering place for young black writers, artists and musicians, including the composers Will Marion Cook and Florence Price. Bonds showed early promise, composing her first work, *Marquette Street Blues*, at the age of five. While in high school she studied the piano and composition with Price and later with William Dawson; she received the BM and MM degrees from Northwestern University (1933, 1934). She moved to New York in 1939 and in 1940 married Lawrence Richardson, though she retained the surname 'Bonds' (her mother's maiden name) throughout her life. At the Juilliard Graduate School she studied the piano with Djane Herz and composition with Robert Starer. Other teachers included Roy Harris, Emerson Harper and Walter Gossett.

Bonds first came to public notice in 1932 when she won the Wanamaker prize for her song *Sea Ghost*. In 1933 she became the first black soloist to appear with the Chicago SO, in a performance of Price's Piano Concerto at the World's Fair. During the 1930s Bonds opened the Allied Arts Academy for ballet and music in Chicago, and was active as a solo and duo pianist in Canada and the USA. In New York she taught and served as music director for music theatre institutions, and organized a chamber society to foster the work of black musicians and composers. She also established a sight-singing programme at Mount Calvary Baptist Church in Harlem. Later, she taught at the Inner City Institute and worked with the Inner City Repertory Theater in Los Angeles.

Bonds's output consists largely of vocal music. Her best-known works are spirituals for solo voice with or without chorus, but she also wrote large music-theatre works, notably *Shakespeare in Harlem, Romey and*

Julie and *U.S.A.* As a popular-song writer she collaborated with Andy Razaf, Joe Davis and Harold Dickinson; the best-known of their works are *Peachtree Street* and *Spring will be so sad*. Her works for orchestra and for piano are programmatic and reflect her strong sense of ethnic identity in their use of spiritual materials, jazz harmonies and social themes (e.g. *Montgomery Variations*, dedicated to Martin Luther King and written at the time of the march on Montgomery in 1965). Her last major work, *Credo*, was first performed a month after her death by the Los Angeles PO under Zubin Mehta. Some of her arrangements of spirituals were commissioned and recorded by Leontyne Price during the 1960s.

WORKS
Stage: Shakespeare in Harlem (L. Hughes), Westport, CT, 1959; Romey and Julie (R. Dunmore); U.S.A. (J. Dos Passos); The Migration, ballet, perf. 1964; Wings over Broadway (ballet); 4 other music-theatre works

Orch: 4 works, incl. Montgomery Variations, 1965

Choral: The Ballad of the Brown King (L. Hughes), solo vv, chorus, orch, 1954; Mass, d, chorus, org, perf. 1959 [only Kyrie is extant; reconstructed score in Thomas, 1983]; Fields of Wonder (Hughes), song cycle, male chorus, pf, perf. 1964; Credo (W. E. B. Dubois) Bar, chorus, orch, perf. 1972; many other sacred and secular works

Songs: 42, incl. Sea Ghost, 1932; The Negro Speaks of Rivers (L. Hughes), 1941; To a Brown Girl, Dead (Hughes), 1956; 3 Dream Portraits (Hughes), 1959; The Pasture (R. Frost), 1958; Stopping by the woods on a snowy evening (Frost), 1963

Popular songs: 14, incl. Peachtree Street, collab. A. Razaf, J. Davis, 1939; Spring will be so sad when she comes this year, collab. H. Dickinson, 1940; Georgia, collab. Razaf, Davis, c1939

Spirituals (all or most arrs.): 5 Spirituals, perf. 1942 (1964); Ezekiel saw the wheel, 1v, pf (1959), arr. orch, 1968; I got a home in that rock, 1v, orch/pf (1959), rev. 1968; Sing aho, 1v, pf (1960); Go tell it on the mountain, 1v/chorus, pf (1962); This little light of mine, S, chorus, orch; Standin' in the need of prayer (1v, pf)/(S, chorus); He's got the whole world in his hands, 1v, pf (1963); Ev'ry time I feel the spirit, 1v, pf (1970); I wish I knew how it would feel to be free, S, chorus, orch; Sinner, please don't let this harvest pass (1v, pf)/(S, mixed chorus); 6 others

Pf: 4 works, incl. Spiritual Suite, Troubled Water, 1967

Principal publishers: Beekman Music, Dorsey, Sam Fox, W.C. Handy, Mutual Music Society, Ricordi

BIBLIOGRAPHY
SouthernB

H. J. Yuhasz: 'Black Composers and their Piano Music Part I', *American Music Teacher*, xix/4 (1970), 24–6

C. C. Harris, jr.: 'Three Schools of Black Choral Composers and Arrangers 1900–1970', *Choral Journal*, xiv/8 (1974), 11–18

M. D. Green: *A Study of the Lives and Works of Five Black Women Composers in America* (diss., U. of Oklahoma, 1975)

L. Berry: *Biographical Dictionary of Black Musicians and Music Educators* (Guthrie, OK, 1978)

C. Ammer: *Unsung: a History of Women in American Music* (Westport, CT, 1980)

A. Tischler: *Fifteen Black American Composers with a Bibliography of their Works* (Detroit, 1981) [incl. list of works]

W. W. Coker: 'The Black Composer Speaks: an Implied Aesthetic', *Black Music Research Journal*, ii (1981–2), 94–105

F. Berry: *Langston Hughes: Before and Beyond Harlem* (Westport, CT, 1983)

M. D. Green: *Black Women Composers: a Genesis* (Boston, 1983)

A. J. Thomas: *A Study of the Selected Masses of Twentieth-Century Black Composers: Margaret Bonds, Robert Ray, George Walker and David Baker* (diss., U. of Illinois, 1983)

—— : 'A Brief Analysis of Masses by Black Composers: Baker, Bonds, Ray, and Walker', *Choral Journal*, xxvii/5 (1986), 7–12

J. MacAuslan and K. Aspen: 'Noteworthy Women: Three Black Women Composers – Price, Bonds, and Perry', *Hot Wire: the Journal of Women's Music and Culture*, v/3 (1989), 12–13

R. L. Brown: 'Florence B. Price and Margaret Bonds: the Chicago Years', *Black Music Research Bulletin*, xii/2 (1990), 11–14

H. Walker-Hill: 'Black Women Composers in Chicago: then and now', *Black Music Research Journal*, xii/1 (1992), 1–23

BARBARA GARVEY JACKSON

Bonhomme, Andrée M. C. (*b* Maastricht, 1 Dec 1905; *d* Brunssum, 1 March 1982). Dutch composer and pianist. She studied the piano at the Maastricht Muzieklyceum and composition with Henri Hermans. She made her début with the Maastricht city orchestra in 1928, both as a soloist in a Mozart piano concerto and as a composer with her *Drie schetsen* for chamber orchestra. In 1932 she was appointed teacher of theory and piano at the Heerlen music school. Attracted by musical developments in Paris, she visited Darius Milhaud every summer from about 1928 until 1940 to discuss her compositions. After World War II Bonhomme was put in charge of a programme that prepared music students in Heerlen for their state examinations. Her music, most of it unpublished, is in a French impressionist style with occasional use of polytonality.

WORKS
selective list

Orch: 3 schetsen, chamber orch, 1928; Xantis, ballet music, 1935–40; Triptique, 1958

Chamber: Vn Sonata, c1923; Pièce en forme de sonate, op.86, 1943; Erotic, vn, pf, 1953; Prélude et fugue, str qt, 1955

Vocal and choral: La flûte de Jade (Li Tai Po), S, orch, 1931; Dansons la gigue (P. Verlaine), T, mixed chorus, orch, *c*1945; Shéhérazade (T. Klingsor), Bar, orch, 1945; De waterlelie (F. van Eeden), 1v, pf, 1953; Lied (T. Gautier), 1v, pf, 1953; La tourterelle de Rolande (A. Samain), 1v, pf, 1953; Le tombeau d'Antar, T, male chorus, pf, fl, perc, 6 brass insts, 1953; 4 mélodies (Klingsor), T, orch, 1956

BIBLIOGRAPHY

H. van Dijk: ' "Ik heb het altijd zelf weten op te knappen": de Limburgse componiste Andrée Bonhomme (1905–1982)' [I was Always able to deal with Matters myself], *Harmonie en perspectief*, ed. A. Annegarn and others (Deventer, 1988), 85–96

HELEN METZELAAR

Boni [Bon, Bonn], **Anna Lucia** (*b* ?1738/9). Italian composer. She was the daughter of the Bolognese artist Girolamo Boni and the singer Rosa Ruvinetti. On 8 March 1743, Boni was admitted at the age of four to the music school (*coro*) of the Ospedale della Pietà in Venice; that she had a surname indicates that she was not a foundling, as were most of the Pietà wards, but a tuition-paying pupil (*figlia di spese*). She studied with the *maestra di viola*, Candida dalla Pietà (who herself had been admitted into the *coro* in 1707). Anna Boni's earliest published music dates from 1756 when she held the new post of 'chamber music virtuosa' at the court of Frederick the Great of Prussia, to whom she dedicated her six op.1 flute sonatas, published in Nuremberg.

BIBLIOGRAPHY

GerberL; *GerberNL*

G. Rostirolla: 'L'organizzazione musicale nell' Ospedale veneziano della Pietà al tempo di Vivaldi', *NRMI*, xiii (1979), 168–95, esp. 191 n.77

J. L. Baldauf-Berdes: *Women Musicians of Venice: Musical Foundations, 1525–1855* (Oxford, 1993)

JANE L. BERDES

Bonis, Mélanie (Hélène) [Mel-Bonis] (*b* Paris, 21 Jan 1858; *d* Sarcelles, Seine-et-Oise, 18 March 1937). French composer. She used the pseudonym Mel-Bonis. Born into a middle-class family, Bonis began piano lessons at an early age and made remarkable progress. A family friend, Professor Maury of the Paris Conservatoire, introduced her to César Franck in 1876. The following year she was admitted to the Conservatoire, where she studied harmony with Ernest Guiraud and the organ with Franck. She won second prize in harmony and accompaniment in 1879, and first prize in harmony a year later. Claude Debussy and Gabriel Pierné were also students during her years there.

Bonis married Albert Domange in 1883, and for about ten years devoted herself to

raising a family. She began composing regularly in about 1894, writing more than 300 compositions, most of which were published. Among her works are 20 chamber pieces, 150 works for piano solo, 27 choral pieces, and organ music, songs and orchestral works. Her music was warmly praised by Camille Saint-Saëns, Célestin Joubert, and Pierné. Already unwell, she suffered acutely the death in 1932 of her younger son; she died five years later. Her children assembled a memoir from her notebooks and published it as *Souvenirs et réflexions* (Paris, n.d.).

WORKS

selective list; printed works published in Paris

Orch and chamber: Suite . . . en forme de valses, orch (1898), also arr. pf; Fl Sonata (1904); Pf Qt, B (1905); Vc Sonata (1905); Soir et matin, pf trio (1907); Vn Sonata (1923); Suite, vn, pf (1926); Pf Qt, D, op.72 (1927); Scènes de la fôret, fl, hn/va, pf (*c*1930); Suite, fl, vn, pf (n.d.); Elève-toi mon âme, vc, pf; Méditation, vc, pf or solo pf; Septet, 2 cl, str, pf; Sérénade, vn/vc, pf; Sextet, wind insts; Suite orientale, pf trio

Pf: L'escarpolette, waltz, 1898; Orientale, waltz, 1898; Prélude, 1901; Le moustique, 1905; Pavane, 4 hands, 1906; Pavane, 1909; Phoebè, 1909; Salomé, 1909; Sarabande, 1909; Viviane, 1909; Desdemona, 1913; Miocheries, 1928; [14] Scènes enfantines, 1928; La cathédrale blessée, 1929; Les gitans, 4

Mélanie Bonis in 1907

hands; Scherzo, 2 pf; Suite . . . en forme de valses; Ballabile, pf solo/4 hands; Interlude et bacchanale, 4 hands; Variations, 2 pf
Songs (1v, pf, unless otherwise stated): La mer; Pourriez-vous pas me dire; Reproche tendre; Sorrente; Sur la plage (A. L. Hettich), 1v, pf/gui; Suzanne!; Veille de Noël; Villanelle (Hettich), 1v, pf/gui
Other vocal: Cantique de Jean Racine, T, vocal qt/S, org, harp ad lib (n.d.); Epithalame, 2-part women's chorus; Madrigal, 1v, chorus 2vv/women's chorus 3vv; Le moulin, 2 solo vv/chorus; O salutaris, 1v, org; Prière, SATB; Prière de Noël, SATB; Regina coeli, 2 solo vv, pf/harmonium/org, vc ad lib; Le ruisseau, 2 solo vv/women's chorus 2vv

Principal publishers: A. Leduc, E. Demets, L. Grus

BIBLIOGRAPHY
Baker8; CohenE; PazdirekH
N. Dufourcq: 'Mélanie Domange Bonis (1858–1937) dite Mel Bonis', L'orgue, no.185 (1983), 1–5
JUDY S. TSOU

Boorn-Coclet, Henriette van den (b Liège, 15 Jan 1866; d Liège, 6 March 1945). Belgian composer. She was a pupil of Jean-Théodore Radoux and Sylvain Dupuis at the Liège Conservatory, where she took the *premier prix* in solfège (1887), harmony (1882) and fugue (1884), and a silver medal (1886) in chamber music (piano and strings). She taught at the conservatory from 1892 to 1931. Her compositions are carefully written and are in the late 19th-century neo-romantic style.

WORKS
selective list
Orch: Andante symphonique (1894); Symphonie, F (1904); Renouveau, poème symphonique (1913); Symphonie wallonne, D (1923); Vers l'infini, vc, orch, B-Bc
Other inst: Sonata, vn, pf (1907); Sérénade, vc, pf, Bc; Tarentelle, pf, Bc
Vocal: Cantate Callirhoe (1895); choruses for female vv; motets; mélodies

BIBLIOGRAPHY
'Archives du Conservatoire royal de musique de Liège', Conservatoire de musique de Liège: centième anniversaire de sa fondation, 1826–1926 (Liège, n.d.), 17
PHILIPPE GILSON

Bordewijk-Roepman, Johanna (b Rotterdam, 4 Aug 1892; d The Hague, 8 Oct 1971). Dutch composer. After pursuing studies in English, she began to compose at the age of 25. Except for some lessons in orchestration with Eduard Flipse (1936–7), she was self-taught as a composer.

Bordewijk-Roepman's first major success was in 1940 with a performance of *Les illuminations* (based on three Rimbaud poems) by the Rotterdams Philharmonisch Orkest under Flipse. Her works were regularly performed during the 1940s and 50s and she received numerous government commissions, as well as a government prize for the Piano Sonata (1943).

Eclectic in style, Bordewijk-Roepman's works are mostly based on Classical formal principles and show a concern for solid construction and logical development. She wrote ten orchestral works and many pieces for men's chorus. Some of her choral works acknowledge the influence of Debussy, although others employ a close-harmony style. She was married to a well-known writer, Frans Bordewijk, who contributed texts for two works, the one-act opera *Rotonde* (1943) and the oratorio *Plato's Dood* (1949). The latter work was first performed in 1990 by students at the University of Amsterdam.

WORKS
selective list
Orch and inst: Les illuminations (A Rimbaud), 3 pièces symphoniques, S [2nd piece], orch, 1940; Pf Conc. no.1, 1940; Sym. no.1, 1942; Epiloog, orch, 1943; Pf Sonata, 1943; Triptiek, carillon, 1951
Dramatic and vocal: Rotonde (opera, 1, F. Bordewijk), 1943; Plato's Dood (static oratorio, Bordewijk), 1949; 5 tempelzangen, 1v, pf, 1950; De heilige cirkel, male chorus, 1950

Principal publishers: Alsbach, Donemus

BIBLIOGRAPHY
W. Paap: 'Johanna Bordewijk-Roepman', Mensch en melodie, i (1946), 101–06
MADDIE STARREVELD-BARTELS/
HELEN METZELAAR

Borroff, Edith (b New York, 2 Aug 1925). American composer, musicologist and teacher. Daughter of the composer and pianist Marie Bergersen, she demonstrated an early talent for piano and composition. She entered Oberlin College Conservatory in 1943, but later transferred to the American Conservatory, Chicago (BMus 1946, MM 1948, composition) where her principal teacher was Irwin Fischer. Unheard as a composer, she became a musicologist (PhD, University of Michigan, 1958) and pursued a teaching career; from 1973–92, she taught at SUNY, Binghamton. She had made major contributions to musicology by the time her compositions attracted interest in the 1970s.

Borroff has been commissioned frequently by both instrumentalists and singers. Rather than adopting a particular aesthetic, she concerns herself primarily with nurturing communication between the composer, performer(s) and audience. She has drawn on a variety of styles, sometimes in the same work, producing a highly serious and expressive body of works through a sensibility marked by formal control, wit and musicianly restraint.

WORKS
selective list

Stage: Spring over Brooklyn (musical), 1954; Pygmalion (incid. music, G. B. Shaw), S, chamber choir, ww qnt, 2 perc, perf. 1955; La folle de Chaillot (J. Giraudoux), S, pf, perc, perf. 1962, lost; The Sun and the Wind (opera, 3 scenes, Borroff), perf. 1977

Chamber: Str Qt, 1941; Vc Sonata, 1943; Str Qt 'Grand Rondo', 1944; Str Qt, e, 1945; Cl Qnt, 1948; Vorspiel, In dulci jubilo, 2 fl, 2 hn, pf, 1951; Hn Sonata, 1953; Sonatina giocosa, va, pf, 1953, rev. version, vn, pf, 1980; Variations and Theme, ob, pf, 1956; Ions: 14 Pieces in the Form of a Sonnet, fl, pf, 1968; Str Qt 'Chance Encounter' (Romp or Rehearsal?), 1974; Game Pieces, suite, ww qnt, 1980; Pf Trio, 1983; Gui Sonata, 1984; Suite: 8 canons, 6 perc, 1984; Mottoes, 8 sax, 1989; 5 Pieces, va, pf, 1989; 32 Variations in the Form of a Sonata, cl, pf, 1992; Vc Sonata, 1993

Also pf pieces; organ music, incl. Passacaglia, 1946; choral works, incl. Light in Dark Places (19th-century black women), 1988; songs

MSS in *US-Cn*

BIBLIOGRAPHY

A. Franco: *A Study of Selected Piano Chamber Works by Twentieth Century American Woman Composers* (diss., Columbia U., 1985)

J. Regier: *The Organ Works of Edith Borroff: an Introduction* (diss., U. of Oklahoma, 1993)

R. Seletsky: *The Woodwind Quintet: a General Introduction and Selective Analysis* (thesis, SUNY, Binghamton, 1993)

CATHERINE PARSONS SMITH

Bosmans, Henriëtte Hilda (*b* Amsterdam, 6 Dec 1895; *d* Amsterdam, 2 July 1952). Dutch pianist and composer. She was the daughter of Henri Bosmans, principal cellist of the Concertgebouw Orchestra, and Sarah Benedicts, a concert pianist and teacher at the Amsterdam Conservatory. She studied the piano with her mother, graduating with honours at the age of 17. As a concert pianist she performed with leading orchestras, gave many recitals and broadcasts in the Netherlands and elsewhere and was also active as an accompanist.

She began composing when she was 15, producing many works for cello, including a sonata, two concertos and a *Poème* for cello and orchestra. In the early 1920s she studied orchestration with Cornelis Dopper and, later, composition with Willem Pijper (1927–30). She was soon considered the most talented Dutch woman composer of her

time. Her early compositions had a traditional German Romantic character, but after her studies with Pijper she wrote in a more compact style, incorporating modernisms such as bitonality and metrical changes. Yet certain characteristics, such as the use of 'Debussian' open parallel chords based on fourths and fifths, remained constant through her entire output.

Owing to personal circumstances and World War II, Bosmans stopped composing between 1936 and 1945. At the end of this hiatus, her *Doodenmarsch* was first performed by the Concertgebouw Orchestra under Adrian Boult. In the years 1948–50 she corresponded regularly with Benjamin Britten, whose Piano Concerto she performed, and she accompanied Peter Pears's recitals in the Netherlands. Increasingly she turned towards composing songs, many in French, setting poems by Paul Fort, Jacques Prévert, Paul Eluard and André Verdet, among others, and performing them with the French singer Noëmie Perugia. After the war she also regularly contributed articles on music to various newspapers. She is one of the few Dutch women composers who has not been forgotten after her death, and the best of her works have lost none of their vitality.

WORKS
selective list

Orch: Vc Conc. no.2, 1924; Poème, vc, orch, 1926; Pf Concertino, 1928; Concertstuk, fl, chamber orch, 1929; Concertstuk, vn, orch, 1934; Belsazer, A, orch, 1936; Doodenmarsch, nar, orch, 1946

Chamber and inst: 6 préludes, pf, 1918; Pf Trio, 1921; Str Qt, 1928

Songs: Der Kaiser, 1927; Liebestrunken, 1927; Schmied Schmerz, 1927; Im Mondenglanz ruht das Meer, 1933; Recueil, 10 songs, 1933–51; Die heiligen drei Könige, 1935; The Artist's Secret, 1948; Verzen uit Maria Lecina, 1949; On frappe, 1950; Aurore, 1950; Chanson, 1951; On ne sait rien, 1951; Das macht den Menschen glücklich, 1951

Principal publishers: Broekmans & Van Poppel, Donemus

BIBLIOGRAPHY

W. Paap: 'De componiste Henriëtte Bosmans', *Mensch en melodie*, iii (1947), 72–6

N. van der Elst: 'Henriëtte Bosmans als liedercomponiste', *Mens en melodie*, vii (1952), 173–97

E. Looyestijn: 'Henriëtte Bosmans', *Zes vrouwelijke componisten*, ed. H. Metzelaar (Zutphen, 1991), 119–63

MADDIE STARREVELD-BARTELS/
HELEN METZELAAR

Botet Dubois, María Enma (*b* Matanzas, 10 Aug 1903). Cuban composer and teacher. She studied with Hubert de Blanck and

Joaquín Nin in Havana and has devoted her life to teaching the piano, first at the Hubert de Blanck and then at the Amadeo Roldán conservatories in Havana; many of her pupils have become important figures in Cuban music education. Apart from a few songs and arrangements, she has composed exclusively for the piano, writing in genres such as the *son*, *guaracha*, *criolla*, *guajira*, *pregón* as well as the bolera, habanera and rumba; some of her works, in particular the *Suite cubana* for piano, are used in teaching centres in Cuba. Her music has simple melodies and harmonies and there is liberal use of five beats to a bar and of syncopation – typical rhythmic elements of Cuban music. Included in her considerable output are *Rositas* (1954), *Nocturno guajiro* (1955), *Guaracha humoristica* (1967), *Habanera lenta* (1968), *Pequeño son* (1972) for left hand, *Micro-suite* (1974–5) and *Dancita de ayer no.1* (1980).

ALICIA VALDÉS CANTERO

Bottini [née Motroni Andreozzi], **Marianna** (*b* Lucca, 7 Nov 1802; *d* Lucca, 25 Jan 1858). Italian composer and harp teacher. Her parents were the nobleman Sebastiano Motroni Andreozzi and his wife Eleonora Flekestein. She studied the piano and counterpoint with Domenico Quilici. On 19 December 1820 she was admitted to the Accademia Filarmonica in Bologna as 'Maestra compositrice onoraria' on account of a *Stabat mater* and a *Messa da Requiem* written in 1819 in memory of her mother. In 1823 she married Lorenzo Bottini, a marquis and prominent figure in Luccan political life. Most of her output dates from her early years, from the ages of 13 to 20. It includes arias, duets, *romanze* and other pieces composed for the refined salons of the Luccan nobility, and contrapuntal sacred works. She was the only woman to provide compositions for the traditional Luccan festival in honour of St Cecilia in 1822, 1825, 1828, 1832, 1834 and 1840. Her manuscripts are in the Istituto Musicale Luigi Boccherini, Lucca (Bottini Collection).

WORKS

all unpublished; MSS in I-Li

Opera: Elena e Gerardo (2), 1822, unperf.
Cantatas: In sacri cantici, 3vv, wind insts, bc, 1819; Briseide (C. Moscheni), 3vv, chorus, orch, 1820; Cantiamo, cantiamo, 5vv, orch
Other vocal: Motet, 1v, orch, 1818; Qui tollis, 1v, chorus, orch, 1818; Messa da requiem, 4vv, orch, 1819; Motet, 1v, orch, 1819; Quoniam, 1v, orch, 1819; Qui tollis, 1v, orch, 1819; Stabat mater, 3vv, 1819; Te Deum, 3vv, 1819; Stabat mater, 3vv, 1820; Mass, 4vv, orch, 1822; Motet, 1v, orch, 1822;

Magnificat, 4vv, orch, after 1823; Miserere, 3vv, bc, 1824; Crucifixus, 2vv, bc; Dixit dominus, 5vv, orch; Domine ad adjuvandum, 4vv, orch; other works for v/vv and insts, incl. 3 arias, 1 duet, 2 notturni, 4 romanze, 2 canzonette
Orch: Cl Conc.; Pf Conc.; 2 syms.; 1 ov.
Other inst: Qt, cl, hn, pf, harp; Trio, vn, bn, pf; Duet, pf, harp; Il mulinaro (ballo); other works for pf, harp and other insts, incl. 10 contradanze inglesi, 9 monferrine, 39 quadrilles, 15 sets of variations, 18 waltzes; 26 other works, incl. studies

BIBLIOGRAPHY

FétisBS; *SchmidlD*
D. A. Ceru: *Cenni storici sull'insegnamento della musica in Lucca e dei maestri compositori* (Lucca, 1871), 84–6
L. Nerici: *Storia della musica in Lucca* (Lucca, 1880), 323–4, 355–71
M. Cappelletti: *Donne illustri lucchesi* (Lucca, 1903), 25–6
G. Sforza: *Ricordi e biografie lucchesi* (Lucca, 1918), 208–9
P. Pecchiai: *Biblioteche e archivi della città di Pisa* (Parma, 1935), 67–73
E. Lazzereschi: *Inventario del R. Archivio di Stato in Lucca*, v (Péscia, 1946), 17–21
D. Sansone: *Il 'Fondo Bottini' dell'Istituto Boccherini di Lucca: catalogo delle edizioni a stampa delle opere di teoria musicale, armonia e contrappunto e della musica per organo, complessi strumentali e strumenti soli non tastati* (thesis, U. of Pisa, 1989–90)
M. S. La Pusata: *Marianna Bottini (1802–1858), compositrice lucchese: biografia e catalogo tematico delle sue musiche* (thesis, U. of Pisa, 1989–90)
—— 'Una compositrice lucchese da scoprire: la Marchesa Marianna M. A. Bottini', *I tesori della musica lucchese*, ed. M. P. Fazzi (Lucca, 1990), 49–56
D. Sansone: 'La biblioteca di Marianna Bottini', *I tesori della musica lucchese*, ed. M. S. La Pusata (Lucca, 1990), 57–69

MARIA SABRINA LA PUSATA

Boulanger, (Marie-Juliette Olga) Lili (*b* Paris, 21 Aug 1893; *d* Mézy, 15 March 1918). French composer. She enjoyed a cultured upbringing (her father Ernest won the Prix de Rome in 1835 and wrote operas) and her sister Nadia guided the early development of her precocious musical career. In 1895, bronchial pneumonia left her immune system permanently damaged and she remained prey to Crohn's disease throughout her life. As a result, she was only able to work sporadically and led a cosseted existence heavily protected by her mother. In December 1909 she resolved to concentrate her energies on composition and winning the Prix de Rome, studying harmony and counterpoint with Georges Caussade before she officially entered the Paris Conservatoire in January 1912 (as a composition student of Paul Vidal). In July 1913, she became the first woman to win the Prix de Rome with her cantata *Faust et Hélène*, after which her achievements became headline news and she

Lili Boulanger

signed a publishing contract with Ricordi. She spent little more than six months at the Villa Medici in 1914 and 1916, interrupting her studies to help the war effort by founding and organizing the Comité Franco-Américain du Conservatoire National, whose aim was to keep musicians in touch and help their families. In February 1916 she secured Maurice Maeterlinck's permission to set *La Princesse Maleine*, as her contract with Ricordi included the composition of two full-length operas. She nearly finished this opera, identifying closely with its fragile, isolated heroine and her tragic destiny, but only one complete scene survives. An appendectomy performed in July 1917 brought her only temporary relief and by early 1918 she was so weak that she had to dictate her *Pie Jesu* from her bed.

Throughout her brief life, Lili Boulanger was a fervent but open-minded Catholic who will be best remembered for her choral music (both sacred and secular) and in particular for her psalm settings, such as the powerfully intense *Du fond de l'abîme* (Psalm cxxx, 1910–17), whose solemnity, grandeur, vivid contrasts and technical mastery seem unlikely to have emerged from one so frail. However, Lili remained firmly in control of her creative destiny and all the evidence suggests that she wrote quickly and surely whenever she was able to, with spirit, vision and profundity. She also wrote imaginative chamber music and songs (being particularly attracted to the poetry of Maeterlinck and Francis Jammes), and in her *Vieille prière bouddhique* (1914–17) she successfully incorporated a degree of

exoticism. Her music is characterized by its inner contrapuntal strength and ardent lyricism and her harmonic language, with its occasional references to Debussy, is advanced for its time. Above all, her sensitive handling of large choral and orchestral forces continue to compel admiration.

WORKS
printed works published in Paris

STAGE
La Princesse Maleine (opera, M. Maeterlinck), 1912–18, inc.

CHORAL
Ps cxxix 'Ils m'ont assez opprimé', Bar, male chorus, orch, 1910–16 (1921)

Ps cxxx 'Du fond de l'abîme', A, T, chorus, org, orch, 1910–17 (1925)

Sous bois (P. Gille), chorus, orch, 1911

Les sirènes (C. Grandmougin), Mez, chorus, pf, 1911 (1919)

Le soir, chorus, pf/orch, 1912

Hymne au soleil (C. Delavigne), A, chorus, pf/orch, 1912 (1919)

La tempête [Pendant la tempête] (T. Gautier), chorus, pf, 1912

La source (Leconte de Lisle), chorus, orch, 1912

Pour les funérailles d'un soldat (A. de Musset), Bar, chorus, orch, 1912–13, vs with Eng. trans. by F. Martens (1918), full score (1919)

Soir sur la plaine (A. Samain), S, T, chorus, orch, 1913 (1918)

Vieille prière bouddhique, T, chorus, orch, 1914–17, vs (1921), full score (1925)

Ps xxiv 'La terre appartient à l'Eternel', T, chorus, org, orch, 1916 (1924)

OTHER VOCAL
Reflets (M. Maeterlinck), v, pf/orch, 1911 (1919)

Renouveau (A. Silvestre), 4 solo vv, pf/orch, 1911–13 (1919)

Attente (Maeterlinck), v, pf, 1912 (1919)

Le retour (G. Delaquys), v, pf, 1912 (1918) [orig. version: La nef légère]

Faust et Hélène, cantata (E. Adenis, after J. W. von

Goethe), Mez, T, Bar, orch, 1913, vs (1913), full score (1921)

Clairières dans le ciel, cycle of 13 songs (F. Jammes), T, pf [nos.1, 5–7, 10–13 orchd], 1913–14 (1919, rev. N. Boulanger, 1970)

Dans l'immense tristesse (B. Galéron de Calone), v, pf, 1916 (1919)

Pie Jesu, S, str qt, harp, org, 1918 (1922, reduced for v, org, 1924)

INSTRUMENTAL

Nocturne (orig. Pièce courte), vn/fl, pf/orch, 1911 (1918)

Prélude, B, pf, 1911

Prélude, Db, pf, 1911

Morceau de piano: Thème et variations, pf, 1911–14

2 fugues for the Concours d'essai (Prix de Rome), 4 pts, 1912, 1913

D'un jardin clair, pf, 1914 (1918)

D'un vieux jardin, pf, 1914 (1918)

Cortège, (vn/fl, pf) or pf solo, 1914 (1919)

D'un matin de printemps, (vn/fl, pf) or orch, 1917–18 (1922)

D'un soir triste, (str trio/vc, pf) or orch, 1917–18

LOST OR DESTROYED

Valse, E, pf, 1905–6, inc.

La lettre de mort (E. Manuel), v, pf, 1906

Pss cxxxi, cxxxvii, solo vv, orch, 1907

Ave Maria, v, org, 1908

Pss i, cxix, chorus, orch, 1909

1 Corinthians xiii, chorus, orch, 1909

Apocalypse, solo vv, chorus, orch, 1909, inc.

5 études, pf, 1909

Maîa (F. Beisser), S, T, B, pf, 1911

Soleils de septembre, chorus, orch, 1911

Frédégonde (C. Morel), S, T, B, pf, 1911–12, inc.

Soir d'été, chorus, pf, 1912

2 études, pf, 4 hands, 1912

Alyssa, cantata, 1913

Pièce, vc, pf, 1914

Pièce, ob, pf, 1914

Pièce, tpt, small orch, 1915

Poème symphonique, orch, 1915–16, inc.

Sicilienne, small orch, 1916

Marche gaîe, small orch, 1916

Marche funèbre, small orch, 1916

Sonate, vn, pf, 1912–16, inc.

Les pauvres (E. Verhaeren), v, pf, undated, inc.

Ps cxxvi, chorus, orch, undated, inc.

Principal publishers: Durand, Ricordi

BIBLIOGRAPHY

M. Piré: En recueillement (Paris, 1920)

C. Mauclair: 'La vie et l'oeuvre de Lili Boulanger', ReM, ii/10 (1921), 147–55

J. Méry: 'Lili Boulanger', Rives d'Azur, clxvii (1924), 891–3

P. Landormy: 'Lili Boulanger', MQ, xvi (1930), 510–15

H.-E. Reeser: 'Lili Boulanger', De Muziek, vii (1933), 210–21, 264–79

E. Lebeau: Lili Boulanger (Paris, 1968) [F-Pn exhibition catalogue]

C. Palmer: 'Lili Boulanger, 1893–1918', MT, cix (1968), 227–8

L. Rosenstiel: The Life and Works of Lili Boulanger (Rutherford, 1978)

D. Peacock Sezic: Women Composers: the Lost Tradition Found (New York, 1988), 139–46

A. Fauser: 'Die Musik hinter der Legende: Lili Boulangers Liederzyklus Clairières dans le ciel', NZM, Jg.151, no.11 (1990), 9–14

K. Pendle, ed.: Women and Music: a History (Bloomington, IN, 1991), 130–33

C. Nies and R. Aulenkamp-Moeller, eds.: Lili Boulanger 1893–1918 (Kassel, 1993) [Catalogue for 3rd International Festival on Women Composers]

O. Mattis: 'Lili Boulanger: polytoniste', Lili Boulanger-Tage Bremen 1993. Zum 100. Geburtstag der Komponistin, ed. K. Mosler (Bremen, 1993), 48–51

A. Fauser: 'Eine verlorene Prinzessin der Avantgarde? Zum Schaffen von Lili Boulanger', Neue Zürcher Zeitung, no.191 (21 Aug 1993)

ROBERT ORLEDGE

(work-list with ANNEGRET FAUSER)

Nadia Boulanger

Boulanger, Nadia (Juliette) (b Paris, 16 Sept 1887; d Paris, 22 Oct 1979). French teacher and composer, sister of Lili Boulanger. Her father, Ernest Boulanger (1815–1900), and her grandfather both taught at the Paris Conservatoire; her mother had been one of her father's students. Nadia herself entered the Conservatoire at the age of ten, studying harmony with Paul Antonin Vidal, organ with Louis Vierne and Alexander Guilmant, and composition with Charles-Marie Widor and Gabriel Fauré. She first caused controversy in France with her 1908 Prix de Rome preliminary submissions by including an instrumental fugue (rather than the required vocal fugue), but was placed second in the competition with her work *La sirène*. She was deeply affected by the premature death of her sister (and pupil) Lili in 1918, whom she believed to be more talented than herself. After 1919 Boulanger was no longer openly active as a composer: although she may have continued to compose after that, in public she vehemently denied any such suggestion. The remainder of her life was devoted to conducting – she was the first woman to conduct a symphony orchestra at a Royal Philharmonic Society concert in London in 1937 – and teaching, a profession in which she was acknowledged as perhaps the most influential musical practitioner of the 20th century. She taught mostly in France and the USA, and numbered among her pupils Lennox Berkeley, Elliott Carter, Aaron Copland, Jean Françaix, Roy Harris, Thea Musgrave and Walter Piston.

Boulanger's known works, including the *Rhapsodie variée* for piano and orchestra (?1912), written for Raoul Pugno and performed to some acclaim in Germany, display virtuoso tendencies she later denigrated in others. Influences of Debussy and especially Fauré are also evident. She is reputed to have been at work with Raoul Pugno on an opera at the time of his death in 1914. The opening of her private papers at the Bibliothèque Nationale in the year 2009 may confirm the existence of other compositions.

WORKS
Orch: Rhapsodie variée, pf, orch, ?1912
Choral: Fugue choeur, 1907; A l'hirondelle, 1908; Fugue choeur, 1909; La sirène, cantata, 1908; La Roussalka, cantata, soloists, orch, 1909
Vocal: Les heures claires (E. Verhaeren), 1910, collab. R. Pugno; Mélodies, 1910; La ville morte, ?1911; Soir d'hiver, 1916
Inst: Fugue, str qt, 1908; 3 Pièces, vc, pf, 1915; Pièce sur des airs populaires flamands, 1918; Vers la vie nouvelle, 1919

Principal publishers: Hamelle, Heugel, Ricordi

BIBLIOGRAPHY
Grove6, GroveAM
R. Orr: 'A Note on Nadia Boulanger', MT, cxx (1979), 999
B. Monsaingeon: *Mademoiselle: entretiens avec Nadia Boulanger* (Luynes, 1980; Eng. trans., 1985)
L. Rosenstiel: *Nadia Boulanger: a Life in Music* (New York, 1982)
J. Spycket: *Nadia Boulanger* (Lausanne, 1987)
                    VIVIAN PERLIS, LÉONIE ROSENSTIEL

Bowater, Helen (*b* Wellington, 16 Nov 1952). New Zealand composer. One of a musical family, she studied the violin and piano with Gwyneth Brown who gave her a comprehensive and imaginative musical foundation. From 1977 she began to sing with vocal ensembles and choirs such as Cantoris. In 1982 she graduated (BMus) from the School of Music at Victoria University, Wellington, where she developed a special interest in ethnomusicology (which included playing and singing with the gamelan) and in early and contemporary music. In 1984 she joined Jack Body's composition class for six months, writing *Raindance* and, after her father's death, *Black Rain*. In 1991 she was awarded a substantial QEII Arts Council grant. Her experiments in electroacoustic music led to the montage *Witch's Mine* (1991). She became resident composer at the Nelson School of Music in 1992 and the following year Mozart Fellow at the University of Otago. She enjoys writing for solo instruments, ensembles and orchestras, and favours music-theatre and multi-media works.

WORKS
selective list
Orch: Magma, 1992
Vocal: Raindance, S, 2 cl, pf, drum, bull roarer, 1985; Black Rain, S, vc, 1985; Skeleton Souvenirs, S, S, mixed media, 1987; He does not Come, S, mixed media, 1988; Songs of Mourning, Bar, str qt, 1989; Naja naja naja, S, S, B, ob, cl, tpt, vc, perc, amplifier, 1989; Cantiga de Amigo de Jogral, Mendinho, S/T, chorus, 1991; Dancing to my Tune (D. Glover), choir, 2vn; Makara Late Winter (R. Cook), M, pf
Inst: Zingaro: a Caprice for Sam Konise, vn, el vn, 1988; Little Bit, pf, 1989; Stay Awake Ananda, 5 perc, 1990; The Bodhi Tree, str qt, 1991; Ixion's Wheel, cl, pf
Misc: The Chafing of the Stump, mixed media, 1987, collab. D. Bowater; The Frivolous Cake, 6 performers, 1990; Witch's Mine, tape, 1991

BIBLIOGRAPHY
N. Sanders: 'Climactic Calm: Helen Bowater and her Music', *Music in New Zealand*, xv (1991–2), 16–19
                                        J. M. THOMSON

Bowditch, Janet. *See* FURZE, JESSIE.

Boyd, Anne (Elizabeth) (*b* Sydney, 10 April 1946). Australian composer. She studied at the NSW Conservatorium, with Peter Sculthorpe at the University of Sydney (BA 1969), where she won the Frank Albert Prize, and, through the award of a Commonwealth Overseas Scholarship, with Wilfrid Mellers and Bernard Rands at York University, England (DPhil 1972). She was subsequently appointed lecturer in music at the University of Sussex. From 1977 to 1980 she lived at Pearl Beach, north of Sydney, devoting herself exclusively to

Anne Boyd with a Chinese sheng, 1993

composition. She has particular interests in the musical cultures of Asia and the Pacific, and in music education. In 1981 she was appointed Reader and founding head of the music department at the University of Hong Kong, and in 1991 became professor of music at the University of Sydney. She holds the rare distinction for a foreigner of being admitted to the Hong Kong Composers' Guild and of lecturing on her own work at the Shanghai Conservatory. Her compositional style is sparse, disciplined and cogent, placing contemporary techniques at the service of a personal and individual manner.

WORKS
all early works withdrawn

STAGE
As Far as Crawls the Toad (theatre piece), 5 young perc players, 1970, rev. 1972; The Rose Garden (theatre piece), Mez, chorus, ens, 1972; The Little Mermaid (children's opera) 1977–8; The Beginning of the Day (children's opera), 1980

ORCHESTRAL
The Voice of the Phoenix, 1971; Black Sun, 1989; Conc. for Flute and Strings, 1992; Grathawai, 1993

CHAMBER AND INSTRUMENTAL
Str Qt no.1, 'Tu Dai Oan' (The Fourth Generation), 1968, rev. 1971; The Metamorphosis of the Solitary

Female Phoenix, wind qnt, pf, perc, 1971; As It Leaves the Bell, pf, harp, perc, 1973; Str Qt no.2, 1973; Angklung, pf, 1974; Bencharong, str ens, 1976; Goldfish through Summer Rain, fl, pf, 1978; Angklung 2, vn, 1980; The Book of Bells, pf, 1980; Red Sun, Chill Wind, fl, pf, 1980; Cloudy Mountain, fl, pf, 1981; Songs from Telegraph Bay (J. Kemp and J. Spencer), unspecified insts, 1984; Kakan, a fl, mar, pf, 1984; Wind across Bamboo, wind qnt, 1984; Bali Moods no.1, fl, pf, 1987; Str Qt no.3, 1991

CHORAL AND VOCAL
As I Crossed a Bridge of Dreams, 12vv, 1975; Summer Nights, Ct, harp, str, perc, 1976; As All Waters Flow, 5 female vv, ens, 1976; The Death of Captain Cook (oratorio, D. Kim), 1978; My Name is Tain (cycle, Kim), S, fl, va, harp, perc, 1979; Coal River, (choral sym., Kim), Bar, children's vv, SATB, brass band, orch, 1979; Cycle of Love (cycle, Kim), Ct/C, a fl, vc, pf, 1981; The Last of his Tribe (H. Kendall), SSA, 1979; Song of Rain (C. J. Dennis), children's choir, 1986

BIBLIOGRAPHY
Fuller-LeFanuRM; LePageWC, iii

THÉRÈSE RADIC

Boyle, Ina [Selina] (*b* Enniskerry, Co. Wicklow, 8 March 1889; *d* Enniskerry, 10 March 1967). Irish composer. As well as studying the violin and cello, she took composition lessons with George Hewson and Charles Kitson in Dublin and, by correspondence, with Charles Wood, a cousin. In 1920 her *Soldiers at Peace* was performed with great success and *The Magic Harp* received a Carnegie Award. The latter was published and performed in London, as were some partsongs and choral works. In 1928 she studied with Ralph Vaughan Williams in London. Although his influence can be heard in her music, her own musical personality, predominantly quiet and serious, is always evident. Her inspiration was usually poetry. Boyle led a quiet, isolated life in Ireland and although she wrote prolifically, it was with little opportunity for performance.

WORKS
selective list

Stage: Virgilian Suite (ballet), 1930–31; The Dance of Death (masque for dancing, after H. Holbein woodcuts), 1935–6; The Vision of Er (mimed drama/ballet, after Plato), 1938–9; Maudlin of Paplewick (opera, after B. Jonson: *The Sad Shepherd*), 1964–6
Orch: The Magic Harp, 1919; Colin Clout, 1921; Glencree (In the Wicklow Hills), sym., 1924–7; The Dream of the Rood, sym., 1929–30; Overture, 1933/4; Wild Geese, 1942
Vocal orch: Soldiers at Peace, chorus, orch, 1916; Hellas (Gk. epitaphs, trans. J. W. Mackail), S, chorus, orch, 1941; The Prophet (A. S. Pushkin, trans. M. Baring), Bar, orch, 1945; From the Darkness,

sym. (E. Sitwell), C, orch, 1946–51; No Coward
Soul is Mine (E. Brontë), S, str, 1953
Songs, chamber and unacc. choral music

Principal publishers: Chester, Novello, Stainer & Bell
MSS in *EIRE-Dtc*

BIBLIOGRAPHY
E. Maconchy: *Ina Boyle: an Appreciation with a Select
List of her Music* (Dublin, 1974)
SARAH M. BURN

Brahe, May [Mary] **Hannah** (*b* Melbourne,
6 Nov 1884; *d* Sydney, 14 Aug 1956).
Australian composer. She studied in Melbourne with Alicia Rebottaro and Mona
McBurney. The majority of her 290 published songs were composed in England,
where she lived from 1912 to 1939, and published by Allans, Enoch and Boosey. Her
most enduringly popular songs (and two of
her three musicals) were written in collaboration with Helen Taylor, notably 'I Passed
by Your Window' (1916) and 'Bless This
House' (1927–32). She wrote under nine
pseudonyms, namely Stanley Dickson
('Thanks Be to God'), Mervyn Banks,
Donald Crichton, Alison Dodd, Stanton
Douglas, Eric Faulkner, Wilbur B. Fox,
Henry Lovell and George Pointer. Her discography lists some 270 performances of 51
compositions, recorded by many great performers. It is however dominated by three
songs: 'I Passed by your Window', 'Down
Here', and especially 'Bless This House',
which continues to figure prominently in
world record catalogues and appears to have
attained the status of an evergreen. Brahe
also wrote two operettas for children and
four piano pieces. The Grainger Museum at
the University of Melbourne has a May
Brahe collection containing manuscript and
published scores, newspaper clippings, correspondence and transcripts of interviews.

BIBLIOGRAPHY
M. Colligan: 'May Brahe: Composer Australian', *Lip*
(1978–9), 114–5
——: 'Mary Hannah Brahe', *Australian Dictionary of
Biography*, ed. J. Ritchie and C. Cuerneen, vii (Mel-
bourne, 1979)
K. Dreyfus and P. Burgis: 'May Brahe Composition
Discography', *Australian Record and Music Review*,
xv Oct (1992), 12–20; xvi Jan (1993), 23
KAY DREYFUS

Brand-Vrabely, Stephanie. *See* WURM-
BRAND-STUPPACH, STEPHANIE.

Branscombe, Gena (*b* Picton, Ont., 4 Nov
1881; *d* New York, 26 July 1977). American
composer and conductor. She studied at the

Gena Branscombe

Chicago Musical College with Rudolph
Ganz (piano) and Felix Borowski (composition), twice winning the gold medal for
composition (1901, 1902). After a year of
further study in Germany, which included
lessons with Engelbert Humperdinck, she
moved in 1910 to New York and in the 1920s
studied conducting with Chalmers Clifton
and Albert Stoessel. She was active in
women's arts organizations and as a choral
conductor, notably of the Branscombe
Choral (1933–54), a women's chorus for
which she composed and arranged many
works and commissioned works by other
women composers.

A tireless advocate of American music and
especially of women composers, she was
awarded the annual prize of the League of
American Pen Women for the best work
produced by a woman composer (*Pilgrims of
Destiny*, 1928, concerning the pilgrim
fathers). Many of her songs and other choral
works were also inspired by historical
events, notably the choral cycle *Youth of the
World*, the unfinished opera *The Bells of
Circumstance* (set in early Quebec) and
Coventry's Choir. Textual expression is of
prime importance in her works and is
achieved through an emphasis on late-
Romantic, richly textured harmony.
Branscombe's most important orchestral

work is *Quebec Suite*, drawn from *The Bells of Circumstance*.

WORKS
*texts of vocal works by Branscombe
unless otherwise stated*

Vocal, orch: The Bells of Circumstance (opera), 1920s, inc.; Dancer of Fjaard, SSA, orch, 1926; Pilgrims of Destiny, S, B, chorus, 1928; Quebec Suite, T, orch, 1930; Youth of the World, SSA, chamber orch, 1932; c35 works, mostly choral arrs.
Songs, 1v, pf, unless otherwise stated: Serenade (R. Browning), 1905; Autumn Wind, 1911; A Lute of Jade (Chin. poets), song cycle, 1911; The Sun Dial (K. Banning), song cycle, 1913; I bring you heartsease, 1915; Three Unimproving Songs for Enthusiastic Children, 1922; Hail ye tyme of holiedayes (Banning), 1924; Wreathe the holly, SSAA, pf, 1938; Coventry's Choir, SSAA, pf, 1944; Bridesmaid's Song, SSAA, pf, 1956; A Joyful Litany, SSAA, pf, 1967; c100 others; c70 choral arrs.
Chamber, inst: Concertstück, pf, 1906; Sonata, vn, pf, 1920; Procession, tpt, pf, 1930; Pacific Sketches, hn, pf, 1956; American Suite, hn, pf, 1959; c20 ens works; c30 pf works; c15 vn pieces

Principal publisher: Arthur P. Schmidt

BIBLIOGRAPHY
L. A. E. Marlow: *Gena Branscombe (1881–1977)* (diss., U. of Texas, 1980)

LAURINE ELKINS-MARLOW

Brdlíková [née Mourková], **Josefina** (*b* Prague, 20 March 1843; *d* Prague, 21 April 1910). Czech composer. She studied music first with members of her family, the music historian V. V. Zelený and J. Mourek, choirmaster at Mariastern in Lusatia. She continued her studies in Prague with Zikmund Kolešovský, and later with Jindřich Kàan. Her high soprano voice and remarkable erudition made her an idol of Prague society. Her songs, which have melodic charm and simple harmony, were inspired by the poetry of her friends Jaroslav Vrchlický and Eliška Krásnohorská. In addition to six volumes of songs she composed piano music, including *Album skladeb klavírních* ('Album of Piano Pieces'), in two volumes (Prague, 1897), and *Aforismy valčíkové* ('Waltz Aphorisms'), for four hands (Prague, 1897). Her aim was to demonstrate women's creativity in the new Czech society. The writer Sofie Podlipská was particularly inspired by her.

BIBLIOGRAPHY
ČSS
A. Pražák: *Královny, kněžny a velké ženy české* [Queens, Princesses and Important Czech Women] (Prague, 1940)
A. Šerých: 'Po přeslici' [On the Distaff Side], *OM*, xx/2 (1988), 61–4, xvii
——: *J. Brdlíková: a Biography* (Prague, forthcoming)

ANNA ŠERÝCH

Brenet, Thérèse (*b* Paris, 22 Oct 1935). French composer. She studied at the Paris Conservatoire, where she obtained first prizes in harmony, counterpoint, fugue and composition. She won the Prix de Rome in 1965 and has received several other international awards; she became a professor at the Conservatoire in 1970. Her output is important and eclectic, relying on an atonal musical language into which are integrated aleatory techniques and microtonal intervals. She is sensitive to instrumental timbres created by bold superimpositions, and her notable use of the celtic harp bears witness to her continuing interest in the exploration of sonorities. She is particularly drawn to writing for the voice.

WORKS
selective list

Orch: Conc. 'pour un poème inconnu', pf, str orch, ondes martenot, 1965; 6 pièces brèves, 1967; Sidérales, 1971; Hapax, 4 songs for orch (after F. W. Nietzsche: *Nocturne*), 1978; Moires, 6 ondes martenot, str orch, 1984: Vibration, celtic harp, str orch, 1984; Fragor, poem in 6 movts, 2 pf, orch; see also vocal works
Vocal: Aube morte (after Lautréamont [I. L. Ducasse]: *Les chants de Maldoror*), poème lyrique, Bar, orch, 1964; Clamavit (Bible, *Job*), reciter, S, chorus, orch, 1965, It. version, 1968; Hommage à Signorelli (after P.-J. Jouve: *La résurrection des morts*), S, pf, ondes martenot, 2 perc, 1967; 7 poèmes chinois (F. Toussaint: *La flûte de jade*), Bar, chamber orch, 1967; Le chant des mondes (Evren dile geldi) (Celaleddin Rumi: *Masnavi*), sym. poem, reciter, pf, orch, 1972; Incandescence, Bar, sax, pf, 1985; Les mains (M. Saint-Lô: *Mains du temps*), S, 3 reciters, 4 S, 4 A, 4 tpt, 4 perc, 4 vc; Calligramme, S/A [arr. of work for sax]
Chamber and inst: Inter silentia, tpt, pf, 1970; 6 pièces, tpt, pf/org, 1973; Pantomime, fl, 1974; Tétrapyle, 4 movts, sax qt, pf, 1979; Caprice d'une chatte anglaise, 2 gui, 1980; Ce que pensent les étoiles, 4 perc, 1981; Accordance, ob, celtic harp, 1982; Calligramme, sax, 1982, also arr. S/A; Cristaux, mand, celtic harp, 1983; Suite fantasque, celtic harp, 1983; Océanides, pf LH, 1986; Plus souple que l'eau, ondes martenot, perc, 1986; Vision flamboyante, vn, pf

DANIEL KAWKA

Brentano [von Arnim], **Bettina** [Elisabeth] (*b* Frankfurt, 4 April 1785; *d* Berlin, 20 Jan 1859). German poet, composer, singer and sculptor. The daughter of a French mother and an Italian father, Brentano was one of the most versatile and flamboyant figures of the early 19th century. Her brother Clemens (1778–1842) was a famous writer, as was her husband, Achim von Arnim (1781–1831), whom she married in 1811. She was on close terms with many of the leading figures in the world of politics and the arts. She met

Bettina Brentano (seated right of centre) listening to a quartet recital at her Berlin home: watercolour (c1855) by Carl Johann Arnold (Joseph Joachim plays first violin; Graf Flemming, cello; and probably Woldemar Bargiel, second violin)

Goethe in 1807 and tried to interest him in music of her Romantic taste. She later recounted their romance in a fanciful manner in *Goethes Briefwechsel mit einem Kinde* (Berlin, 1835, 7/1929). A great admirer and close friend of Beethoven, Bettina had musical talent both as a singer (at the Berlin Singakademie, 1810–12) and as a composer. In 1843 she published in Leipzig a collection of lieder, 7 *Gesangstücke mit Pianoforte dédié à Spontini*, three of which use texts by Goethe. One of these, *O schaudre nicht*, was republished in *Goethes Gedichte in Kompositionen von Zeitgenossen* (Weimar, 1896), edited by Max Friedlaender, who noted that Brentano probably composed only the vocal line, while the harmonies of the piano accompaniment were written by musicians of her circle. The melody is occasionally tonally awkward, and inclinations towards new keys occur suddenly without proper preparation.

Brentano's collection of letters, written in a fresh and direct style, provide a vivid picture of the life, personalities and attitudes of the time. Her versatility, intellect and enthusiasm reveal one of the most accomplished women of German Romanticism.

BIBLIOGRAPHY

'Mancherlei', *AMZ*, xxxvii (1835), 366–7

A. F. Schindler: *Beethoven in Paris: ein Nachtrag zur Biographie Beethoven's* (Münster, 1842) [incl. 3 letters to Bettina]

H. Deiters, ed.: *Die Briefe Beethoven's an Bettina von Arnim* (Leipzig, 1882)

M. Carriere: *Bettina von Arnim* (Breslau, 1887)

W. Oehlke: *Bettina von Arnims Briefromane* (Berlin, 1905)

A. Leitzmann: 'Beethoven und Bettina', *Deutsche Revue*, xliii/1 (1918), 109

R. Rolland: *Goethe et Beethoven* (Paris, 1930; Eng. trans., 1931)

O. Mallon: 'Bibliographische Bemerkungen zu Bettina von Arnims sämtlichen Werken', *Zeitschrift für deutsche Philologie*, lvi (1931), 446–65

I. Seidel: *Bettina* (Stuttgart, 1944)

H. J. Moser: *Goethe und die Musik* (Leipzig, 1949)

R. Cardinal: *German Romantics in Context* (London, 1975)

A. Willison: *Women, Poetry and Song: Composer-Authors in German Romanticism* (diss., Indiana U., in preparation)

MARCIA J. CITRON

Bright, Dora (Estella) (*b* Sheffield, 16 Aug 1863; *d* London, 16 Nov 1951). English composer and pianist. She attended the RAM from 1881 to 1888, studying the piano with Walter Macfarren and composition with Ebenezer Prout. She won the Potter Exhibition in 1884 and in 1888 was the first woman to win the Lucas Medal for composition. She began her recital career in January 1889, and in the autumn of that year successfully performed her Piano Concerto in A minor, conducted by Carl Reinecke at Dresden, Cologne and Leipzig; it was subsequently given under August Manns's direction at the Crystal Palace concerts (28 March 1891). On 11 May 1892 she became the first woman to have one of her compositions performed by the Philharmonic Society, when she played her specially commissioned *Fantasia* in G. That same year she gave the first-ever recital of English keyboard music, entitled 'From Byrd to Cowen', and married Captain Knatchbull, of Bath. She then turned increasingly to composition, writing a large number of ballets for the dancer Adeline Genée, whose talents her music particularly suited.

Bright's music developed consistently throughout her career and she forged a personal style of great individuality. The early piano pieces rely too heavily, perhaps, on simple ternary form and the idioms of Felix Mendelssohn and William Sterndale Bennett, but she was always capable of springing a surprise, as in the final bravura section of the Allegro from the *Two Sketches* (1884). The Macfarren Variations (1894) point the way to her later ability to conceive effectively related miniatures: her ballet music shows how successful she was in this respect. Her piano writing is always idiomatically conceived, yet her most effective use of the instrument is found within the context of wider combinations (due, no doubt, to her early experience of composing for piano and orchestra). Her finest pieces demonstrate an exceptional capacity for musical 'conversation', as in the dialogue between the instruments in the Scherzino and Finale from the Suite for violin and piano (1891). The most progressive movement in the Suite is the Scotch Air and Variations, which employs bold modality (variation 3) and rich Quilter-like harmony (variation 4). All these positive qualities find full expression in her songs, which respond subtly to the poems' emotional nuances – notably in the last of the *Jungle Book Songs* (1903), in which Toomai's mother lulls his baby brother to sleep as she sings of Shiva the Preserver.

WORKS
all printed works published in London

DRAMATIC

Operas: The Portrait (D. Bright), 1 chansonette (1911); Quong Lung's Shadow; 1 other opera

Ballets: The Dryad (pastoral fantasy), pf score (1909); La Camargo (miniature ballet), pf score, excerpts (1912); 10 other ballets and mime plays

INSTRUMENTAL

Orch: Pf Conc. no.1, a, 1888; Air with Variations, 1890; Fantasia, G, pf, orch, 1892; Pf Conc. no.2, d, 1892; Suite of 18th-Century Dances, pf, orch; Suite, fl, orch; Suite of Russian Dances; Variations on an Original Theme of Sir George Alexander Macfarren, pf, orch, also arr. 2 pf; Vienna

Chamber: Romance and Seguidilla, fl, pf (1891); Suite, vn, pf (1891); Qt, D, pf, str, 1893; 2 Pieces, vc, pf/vn, pf, 1934 (no.1 = Meyerbeer: Das Fischermädchen, arr. Bright); Berceuse, fl, pf; Liebeslied, fl, pf; Suite, fl, pf; Tarantella, fl, pf

Pf (solo unless otherwise indicated): 2 Sketches (1884); 3 Duos, 2 pf, 1886; Romanza and Scherzetto (1889); Variations on an Original Theme of Sir George Alexander Macfarren, 2 pf (1894); 3 Pieces (1895)

VOCAL

Choral: Messmates (H. Newbolt), Bar, male chorus, 1907

Songs: Whither? (H. W. Longfellow) (1882); 12 Songs (R. Herrick, W. Shakespeare and others) (1889); The Ballad of the Red Deer (F. H.), 1903; 6 Songs from the Jungle Book (R. Kipling), 1903; To Daffodils (Herrick), 1903; Colinette (chansonette from her opera The Portrait) (1911); I know a lady sweet and kind (Herrick), 1913; The Donkey (G. K. Chesterton), 1936; There sits a bird; To Blossom; To Music; Who is Sylvia? (Shakespeare)

ARRANGEMENTS

Vocal: The Orchard Rhymes (with E. M. Boyce), school songs, 1917

Inst: J. Strauss ii: Neu Wien, pf, 1924; Siciliano and Gigue from Arne: Sonata no.4, pf (1948)

BIBLIOGRAPHY

CohenE; Grove5 (H. C. Colles); *PazdirekH; RiemannL 12; WCBH*

J. D. Brown and S. S. Stratton: *British Musical Biography* (Birmingham, 1897)

J. Towers, ed.: *Dictionary-Catalogue of Operas and Operettas* (Morgantown, WV, 1910)

L. Ronald, ed.: *Who's Who in Music* (London, 1935)

O. Thompson, ed.: *The International Cyclopedia of Music and Musicians* (London, 4/1942)

W. W. Cobbett, ed.: *Cyclopedic Survey of Chamber Music* (London, 2/1963)

NIGEL BURTON

Title-page of Dora Bright's Six Songs from 'The Jungle Book' (London: Elkin, 1903)

Brillon de Jouy, Anne Louise Boyvin d'Hardancourt (*b* Paris, 13 Dec 1744; *d* Villers-sur-Mer, Calvados, 5 Dec 1824). French harpsichordist, pianist and composer. Both her father and her husband were

Autograph of part of the keyboard Sonata in A minor by Anne Louise Brillon de Jouy, showing the end of the Andante molto con espressione, and beginning of the Allegro con moto

financial officers for the crown, and her wealth allowed her to maintain salons in the Marais district of Paris and down the Seine at Passy. She was the musical star of these *soirées*, which Benjamin Franklin dubbed his 'opera' during his years in Passy (1777–85). The violinist André-Noël Pagin was a member of her entourage, and Johann Schobert, Luigi Boccherini, Ernst Eichner and Henri-Joseph Rigel all dedicated sonatas to her (opp.6, 5, 3 and 7 respectively); Rigel commented on her receptiveness to talented musicians and the enthusiasm engendered by her own performances. In 1770, Charles Burney reported that

she had not acquired her reputation in music without meriting it. She plays with great ease, taste and feeling – is an excellent sightswoman. . . . She likewise composes and she was so obliging as to play several of her own pieces both on the harpsichord and piano forte accompanied with the violin by M. Pagin.

She possessed an English piano sent by J. C. Bach, a German piano and a harpsichord, and she specified this instrumentation in two keyboard trios.

The surviving library of her own music and scores by other composers is the only such collection associated with a French harpsichordist, almost all of it from the 1760s to the early 80s. In addition, Franklin preserved her voluminous correspondence. The music documents the transition from harpsichord to piano in France, demonstrating that although the differences between the two instruments were appreciated by performers and listeners they were not yet exploited by composers. Her compositions have the charm of *galant* simplicity, and although there are occasional technical lapses, she displays both taste and originality. Her signature tune was a *Marche des insurgents*, written to celebrate the American victory at Saratoga (1777).

WORKS

most MSS in US-PHps;
catalogue in Gustafson 1987, revised 1994

44 acc. kbd sonatas; 6 multiple kbd sonatas; Sonata, harp, pf; Marche des insurgents, orch; 36 vocal works, incl. romances

BIBLIOGRAPHY

Choron-FayolleD; *FétisB*; *GerberL*; *SainsburyD*

L. de La Laurencie: 'Benjamin Franklin and the Claveciniste Brillon de Jouy', *MQ*, ix (1923), 245–59

C.-A. Lopez: *Mon Cher Papa, Benjamin Franklin and the Ladies of Paris* (New Haven, CT, 1966; rev. 1990 as *Le sceptre et la foudre: Benjamin Franklin à Paris*)

The Papers of Benjamin Franklin, xxiii– (New Haven, CT, 1983–)

B. Gustafson: 'The Music of Madame Brillon: a Unified Collection from Benjamin Franklin's Circle', *Notes*, xliii (1986–7), 522–43

B. Gustafson and D. Fuller: *A Catalogue of French Harpsichord Music, 1699–1780* (Oxford, 1990)

B. Gustafson: 'Madame Brillon et son salon' (forthcoming)

BRUCE GUSTAFSON

Britain, Radie (*b* Silverton, TX, 17 March 1903). American composer. After graduating in piano from the American Conservatory, Chicago (BM 1924), she went to Europe, where she studied composition and theory in Munich with Albert Noelte and organ in Paris with Marcel Dupré. She returned from Europe in 1926 and continued to work with Noelte, then at the Chicago Conservatory, and subsequently spent two seasons at the MacDowell Colony. She also studied the piano with Leopold Godowsky and organ with Pietro Yon. From 1930 to 1934 she taught harmony and composition at the Girvin Institute of Music, Chicago, and from 1934 to 1939 was on the faculty of the Chicago Conservatory; she taught piano and composition privately in Hollywood from 1940 to 1960. Over 50 of her compositions have received national or international awards, including *Epic Poem* (1927), *Light* (1935) and *Cosmic Mist Symphony* (1962); in 1945 she became the first woman to receive the Juilliard Publication Award, for *Heroic Poem*. She wrote *Composer's Corner* (1978) and three other books.

Although she experimented with atonal and serial techniques in some of her later works, Britain's primary concerns have been lyric expression and the creation of atmosphere in music. Many of her programmatic or pictorial works are inspired by American geography and scenery, especially that of her native Southwest. She has written: 'I wish to feel in American music the conquest of the pioneer, the determined man of the soil, the gigantic beauty of a sunset, the nobility of the Rockies, the wonder of the Grand Canyon, the serenity of the hidden violet and the purity of the wild flower'.

WORKS

Dramatic: Ubiquity (musical drama, L. Luther), 1937; Happyland (operetta, A. Greenfield), 1946; Carillon (opera, R. Hughs), 1952; The Spider and the Butterfly (children's operetta, 3, L. P. Hasselberg), 1953; Kuthara (chamber opera, 3, Luther), 1960; 5 ballets, 1929–64, incl. Wheel of Life, 1933, Lady in the Dark, 1960, Western Testament, 1964

Orch and choral: Sym. Intermezzo, 1928, arr. 5 insts, 1976; Heroic Poem, 1929; Rhapsody, pf, orch, 1933; Light, 1935; Drouth, 1939, arr. pf, 1939; Ontonagon Sketches, 1939; Suite, str, 1940;

Phantasy, ob, orch, 1942, arr. fl, pf, 1962; We Believe, 1942; Serenata sorrentina, small orch, 1946, arr. pf, 1946; Cactus Rhapsody, orch, 1953, arr. 2 pf, 1965, rev. orch, 1974; Nisan (K. Hammond), SSAA, pf, str, 1961, arr. SATB, pf, 1961; Cosmic Mist Sym., 1962; Brothers of the Clouds, male vv, orch, 1964, arr. SATB, pf; Anwar Sadat (In Memory), orch, 1982; many other works

Chamber and solo inst: Epic Poem, str qt, 1927; Str Qt, 1934; Prison (Lament), str qt, 1935; Pastorale, 2 pf, 1935, arr. orch, 1939, arr. ob, harp, hpd, 1967, arr. fl, harp, 1977; The Chateau, pf, harp, 1938; Chipmunks, ww, 1940, arr. ww, harp, perc, 1940; Serenade, vn, pf, 1944; Barcarola, vn, pf, 1948, arr. S, 8 vc, 1958; Pf Sonata, 1958; In the Beginning, 4 hn, 1962; The Famous 12, pf, 1965, arr. 12 insts as Les fameux douze, 1966; Recessional, 4 trbn, 1969; Phantasie, ww trio, 1975; Adoration, brass qt, 1976; Translunar Cycle, vc, pf, 1980; Ode to NASA, brass qnt, 1981; Soul of the Sea, vc, pf, 1984; many other works

Vocal: Many choruses, incl. Drums of Africa (Jenkins), 1934; Noontide (F. Nietzsche), 1935; Harvest Heritage (Britain), 1963; over 50 songs; several song cycles

Principal publishers: Clayton Summy, C. Fischer, Green, Henroico, Kjos, Ricordi, Wilmark

MSS in Amarillo Public Library, Amarillo, TX; *US-AUS*; Wyoming U. Library, Laramie, WY; *LAu*; Moldenhauer Archives, Spokane, WA; *Wc*

BIBLIOGRAPHY

C. Reis: *Composers in America: Biographical Sketches* (New York, 1947 [4th edn of American Composers])

M. Goss: *Modern Music Makers* (New York, 1952)

J. L. Zaimont and K. Famera: *Contemporary Concert Music by Women* (Westport, CT, 1981)

KATHERINE K. PRESTON

Britto, Julia von. *See* BARONI-CAVALCABÒ, JULIA.

Brizzi Giorgi, Maria (*b* Bologna, 7 Aug 1775; *d* Bologna, 26 Dec 1822). Italian organist, pianist and composer. She belonged to a well-known Italian musical family in Bologna. She began to perform in public at a very early age, arousing admiration everywhere. She was particularly noted for her ability to improvise. Because of her exceptional gifts the Sisters of St Bartholemew in Ancona requested her services as organist and choral director, posts she held from 1787 until 1790. Returning to Bologna, she continued her musical studies, concentrating particularly on counterpoint. She composed occasional music, vocal and instrumental, the latter mainly for the piano. In 1793 she married Luigi Giorgi and presided over a salon. As a pianist she was admired for her technical and expressive abilities; she travelled in Austria and Germany, where she was heard by Haydn, Clementi and Leopold Kozeluch, who dedicated works to her. When Napoleon passed through Bologna in 1807, military music composed by Brizzi was performed.

She was a dedicated teacher and a member of the Accademia Filarmonica in Bologna. Giordani (in his *Elogio funebre* for Brizzi) related that shortly before her death (following the birth of a child) she got up from her bed and improvised at the piano on a theme by Giovanni Paisiello, begging her sister Teresa (also a pianist) to preserve her last composition for posterity.

BIBLIOGRAPHY

SchmidlD

P. Giordani: *Elogio funebre di Maria Brizzi Giorgi nelle solenni esequie a lei fatte* (Bologna, 1813)

S. Muzzi: *Notizie di quattro donne eccellenti nella dottrina dell'armonia e della sociale convivenza* (Bologna, 1864)

STEFANO BARANDONI

Bronsart [née Starck], **Ingeborg (Lena) von** (*b* St Petersburg, 12/24 Aug 1840; *d* Munich, 17 June 1913). German composer and pianist of Swedish parentage. She already showed remarkable pianistic and compositional talent before the age of eight. After studies with Adolf Henselt in St Petersburg (1855–7), she moved in early 1858 to Weimar to complete her training with Liszt, who came to esteem her as both pianist and composer. In the winter of 1858 she embarked upon a successful, decade-long career as a travelling virtuoso. She was often accompanied by the conductor and pianist – and Liszt pupil – Hans Bronsart von Schellendorf (1830–1913), whom she had married in 1861. Ingeborg was required to forsake her career as a pianist as a result of her husband's appointments as Intendant at the court theatres in Hanover (1867–87) and Weimar (1887–95). She then devoted herself to composition, primarily of songs and operas. Bronsart achieved her greatest successes with the *Kaiser-Wilhelm-Marsch* of 1871 (performed at the opening of the Women's Exhibit at the 1893 Columbian Exposition in Chicago) and the Singspiel *Jery und Bätely* (1873), which was performed with acclaim in more than ten German cities. The opera *Hiarne* was also favourably received at its première in Berlin in 1891. After the couple's retirement to Munich in 1895, Ingeborg composed the opera *Die Sühne*, which was produced in Dessau in 1909.

Bronsart's compositional output embraces the major genres of the time, except for the symphony and oratorio. Regardless of genre, her music displays vocally derived melodies, traditional forms and mildly chromatic

harmonies; it is generally characterized by technical mastery. For the piano music and some of the songs, Liszt served as the model, whereas Wagner's works exerted an influence upon her last two operas (she herself vehemently denied any indebtedness to Wagner's musical style). Her more successful works, including the opera *Jery und Bätely* and the *Zwölf Kinderreime* op.17, incorporate elements derived from folk music. The other operas suffer from poor librettos. The sensitive declamation of Bronsart's vocal music anticipates the style of Richard Strauss's songs and operas. Unfortunately, much of the early piano music and more than thirty songs were never published.

WORKS

STAGE

* – autograph score

Die Göttin von Sais, oder Linas und Liane (idyllische Oper, 3, Meyer), Berlin, Kronprinzliches Palais, 1867, lost; lib (Berlin, 1866)

Jery und Bätely (Operette, 1, J. W. von Goethe), Weimar, Hoftheater, 26 April 1873, D-B, Mbn, WRdn, US-NYp*; (Leipzig, 1876)

Hiarne (prol, 3, H. von Bronsart and F. von Bodenstedt), *c*1870–90; Berlin, Königlichestheater, 14 Feb 1891, D-WRdn*; lib (Weimar, 1896)

Die Sühne (Tragödie, 1, after T. Körner), Dessau, Hoftheater, 12 April 1909, DEl*; vs (Berlin, 1910)

OTHER WORKS

Orch: Pf Conc., f, by 1863; Kaiser-Wilhelm-Marsch (Berlin, 1872)

Chamber: Romanze, a, vn, pf (Weimar, 1873); Notturno, vc, pf, op.13 (Leipzig, 1879); Elegie, vc, pf, op.14 (Leipzig, 1879); Romanze, Bb, vc, pf, op.15 (Leipzig, 1879); Phantasie, vn, pf, op.21 (Leipzig, 1891)

Pf: 3 études, Nocturne, Tarantella, all pubd (St Petersburg, 1855); Fuge über die Namen Maria und Martha, Sonata, Variations on themes by Bach, toccatas, other fugues and variations, all by 1859; Kaiser-Wilhelm-Marsch (Berlin, 1871); 4 Clavierstücke (Mainz, 1874): Valse-Caprice, Impromptu, 2 Wiegenlieder; Phantasie, op.18 (Leipzig, 1891)

Vocal (for 1v, pf, unless otherwise stated): Die Loreley (H. Heine) (Mainz, 1865); Und ob der holde Tag vergangen (Sturm), 1870, Mbn*; 3 Lieder (Dunker, Neubauer, Zeise) (Mainz, 1871); Hurrah Germania! (F. Freiligrath), male vv (Hanover, 1871); 3 Lieder (Heine, O. Roquette) (Hanover, 1872); Kennst du die rothe Rose?, solo v, male vv, mixed vv (Weimar, 1873); 5 Lieder (Goethe, A. Platen, F. Rückert) (Oldenburg, 1878); 6 Lieder (from *Lieder des Mirza Schaffy*), op.8 (Leipzig, 1879); Hafisa, 3 Lieder (from *Lieder des Mirza Schaffy*), op. 9 (Leipzig, 1879); 6 Gedichte (Bodenstedt), op.10 (Leipzig, 1879); 5 Weihnachtslieder, op.11 (Oldenburg, 1880); 5 Gedichte, op.12 (Oldenburg, 1880); 5 Gedichte (E. von Wildenbruch), op.16 (Breslau [Wrocław], 1882); 12 Kinderreime (after K. Groth: *Vaer de Gaern*), op.17 (Leipzig, 1882); 6 Gedichte (Groth and others), op.20 (Leipzig, 1891); 3 Gedichte (P. Cornelius), op.22 (Leipzig, 1891); 3 Lieder (Goethe, N. Lenau), op.23 (Berlin, 1892); Im Lenz (P. Heyse), 1898, *Mbn**; Rappelle-toi! (A. de Musset), op.24 (Leipzig, 1902); 3 Lieder (Bodenstedt, Goethe, Heine), op.25 (Leipzig, 1902); Abschied (F. Dahn), op.26 (Leipzig, 1902); Osterlied (Platen), mixed vv (Leipzig, 1903); Lieder (ded. to La Mara), 1910; Verwandlung (Heyse), 1910, *Mbn**

BIBLIOGRAPHY

CohenE; *FétisBS*; *Grove1* (W. Barclay Squire); *KompA-Z*; *NDB* (G. Schmidt; 'Bronsart v. Schellendorf'); *SchmidlD*

H. Mendel and A. Reissmann: 'Bronsart', *Musikalisches Conversations-Lexikon*, ii (Berlin, 1872), 193

R. Pohl: 'Die 14. Tonkünstler-Versammlung des Allgemeinen Deutschen Musikvereins', *NZM*, xliv (1877), 233–4 [*Jery und Bätely*]

E. Polko: 'Ingeborg von Bronsart: biographisches Skizzenblatt', *Neue Musik-Zeitung*, ix (1888), 142–3

'Sangkönig Hiarne', *NZM*, lvii (1890), 37–9

P. Simon: 'Hiarne', ibid, 553–5

—— : 'Die erste Aufführung der Oper Hiarne von Frau Ingeborg von Bronsart im Königl. Opernhause zu Berlin', *NZM*, lviii (1891), 87

G. Crusen: 'Ingeborg von Bronsart's Hiarne im Königlichen Hoftheater zu Hannover', *NZM*, lix (1892), 85–6

W. Asmus: 'Ingeborg von Bronsart', *NZM*, lxv (1898), 193–5

La Mara [M. Lipsius]: 'Ingeborg von Bronsart', *Die Frauen im Tonleben der Gegenwart*, Musikalische Studienköpfe, v (Leipzig, 1902), 35–53

E. Hamann: 'Kritische Rundschau: Dessau', *Neue Musik-Zeitung*, xxx (1909), 326 [*Die Sühne*]

A. Spanuth: '*Die Sühne*', *Signale*, lxvii (1909), 550–52

A. Morsch: 'Ingeborg von Bronsart', *Gesangspädagogische Blätter*, iv (1910), 100–02

A. Kohut: 'Erinnerungen an Bronsart, mit ungedruckten Briefen desselben', *Deutsche Musiker Zeitung*, xliv/48, 50 (1913)

F. Stieger: 'Opernkomponistinnen', *Die Musik*, xiii (1913–14), 270–72

Autographen-Sammlung aus dem Nachlass des Komponisten und Intendanten Hans Bronsart von Schellendorf (Berlin, 1919)

E. Weissweiler: *Komponistinnen aus 500 Jahren* (Frankfurt, 1981), 297

E. Öhrström: *Borgerliga kvinnors musicerande i 1800-talets Sverige* [Bourgeois Women Musicians in 19th-Century Sweden] (diss., U. of Göteborg, 1987), 202

JAMES A. DEAVILLE

Browne (Garrett), Augusta (*b* Dublin, 1820; *d* Washington, DC, 11 Jan 1882). Irish-American composer and writer on music. Her family had moved to the USA by 1830, and during the 1840s and 1850s she was organist at the First Presbyterian Church in Brooklyn, New York. She was described as a 'professor of music' on her compositions published in New York and Boston between 1842 and 1855. One of the most prolific women composers in the USA before 1870, she wrote mainly drawing-room songs and salon piano pieces; Moore, in one of the few published acknowledgments of an American woman composer before 1900, attributes 'over 200' compositions to her and describes her as 'a composer of note'. Her songs are often in modified *ABA* form; the best known include *The Chieftain's Halls* (1844) and *The Warlike Dead in Mexico* (1848). She made use of English and Irish musical sources (for example, John Braham's *The Death of Nelson* was a model for *The Warlike Dead*, and Thomas Moore's *A Selection of Irish Melodies* supplied the themes for *The Hibernian Bouquet* variations), and she resisted any vernacular American styles, describing them as 'taste-corrupting'. Browne was confused in her own lifetime with another composer: Cheney describes her (in *The American Singing Book*, Boston, 1879) as best known for *The Pilgrim Fathers*, a work actually written by HARRIET BROWNE. Augusta Browne became a prominent author in the late 1840s, writing two books and contributing articles on musical taste to various magazines, including the *Columbian Lady's and Gentleman's Magazine* and the *Musical World and New York Musical Times*. In her article 'A Woman on Women' (*Knickerbocker Monthly*, lxi/1, 1863, p.10) she asserted the right of women to a thorough musical education.

WORKS
selective list; printed works published in New York unless otherwise stated

Vocal: The Family Meeting (C. Sprague) (1842); Grand Vesper Chorus (R. Heber) (1842); The Chieftain's Halls (Boston, 1844); A Song for New England (H. W. Elsworth) (1844); The Volunteer's War Song (Mrs. Balmanno) (1846); The Reply of the Messenger Bird (E. Young) (Philadelphia, 1848); The Warlike Dead in Mexico (Balmanno) (1848); Song of Mercy (J. Bunyan) (1851)

Pf: The Caledonian Bouquet, variations (1841); The French Bouquet, variations, op.31 (1841); The American Bouquet, variations (Philadelphia, 1844); The De Meyer Grand Waltz (1846); The Hibernian Bouquet, variations (1840s); The Mexican Volunteer's Quickstep (*c*1850); Angels Whisper, variations (Philadelphia, 1850s); The Merry Mountain Horn, variations (Philadelphia, 1850s); The Ethereal Grand Waltz (n.d.)

BIBLIOGRAPHY

J. Moore: *Appendix to the Encyclopedia of Music* (Boston, 1875)

C. Ammer: *Unsung: a History of Women in American Music* (Westport, CT, 1980)

J. Tick: *American Women Composers before 1870* (Ann Arbor, 1983)

JUDITH TICK

Browne [Hughes], Harriet (Mary) (*b*? Liverpool, *c*1790; *d* 1858). English composer. A sister of the well-known popular poet

Felicia Hemans (1793–1835), she composed songs and duets, principally to her sister's words, many of which were immensely successful during the 1830s and 40s on both sides of the Atlantic. A collection of 12 appeared about 1830; but they circulated chiefly in larger anthologies and in single editions, and some of them were reprinted numerous times: the ballad *The Landing of the Pilgrim Fathers* ('The breaking waves dash high', 1835) ran to at least 46 editions, while others comparably successful were the duet *The Messenger Bird* (1835), *The Captive Knight* (from the 1820s) and the *Tyrolese Evening Hymn* (1827, more than 60 editions). Many were arranged for school choirs, for quartet and with other types of accompaniment.

BIBLIOGRAPHY

GroveAM ('Hemans, Felicia'; J. Tick)

Brusa, Elisabetta (*b* Milan, 3 April 1954). Italian composer. She studied composition with Bruno Bettinelli and Azio Corghi at the Milan Conservatory, graduating in 1980, and attended summer courses at Dartington, England, 1978–85 (concurrently studying privately with Hans Keller), and Tanglewood, USA, 1983. She teaches composition at the Milan Conservatory. Her *Belsize* String Quartet (1980) won first prize at the International String Quartet Competition of the Contemporary Music Forum in Washington, DC, in 1982; later awards include a Fromm Foundation scholarship, a Fulbright travel bursary and three fellowships to the MacDowell Colony, where she wrote a symphony (1988–90). This is the first of a series of several works for full orchestra that includes *La triade* (1992), *Firelights* (1993) and *Requiescat* (1994). The *Belsize* Quartet, dedicated to Keller, is a carefully crafted, two-movement contrapuntal work in which bold melodic gestures intermingle with stuttering repeated pedal notes; towards the end, heavily ornamented lines fly against each other above the reintroduced pedal to produce a sense of texture that briefly overwhelms both melody and rhythm. This momentary feature becomes the language of later works: *La triade*, for example, whose programme is a dark fable by Aesop, is utterly texture-based. It is fashioned from the superposition of discrete layers of orchestral sonority formed from separate instrumental groupings (wind, strings etc.); the layers themselves sometimes build and graphically die away in Berio-esque manner. Brusa's works are published by Sonzogno, Curci and Edipan.

Joanna Bruzdowicz

BIBLIOGRAPHY

P. Adkins Chiti: *Almanacco delle virtuose, primedonne, compositrici e musiciste d'Italia: dall'A.D. 177 ai nostri giorni* (Rome, 1991)
D. Bertoldi and R. Cresti: *Nuova storia della musica* (Florence, 1992)
F. Pagano, ed.: *Autoanalisi dei compositori italiani contemporanei* (Naples, 1992)

RHIAN SAMUEL

Bruzdowicz, Joanna (*b* Warsaw, 19 May 1943). Polish composer. She studied composition with Kazimierz Sikorski at the State Higher School of Music in Warsaw, graduating in 1966. She was awarded a French government scholarship and studied in Paris (1968–70) with Olivier Messiaen, Nadia Boulanger and Pierre Schaeffer. In 1969 she was a co-founder of the Groupe International de Musique Electroacoustique there. In 1975 she moved to Belgium, where she has combined composing with a wide range of other artistic interests. She is active as a critic and as a broadcaster, promoting new music in programmes for French, Belgian and German radio, and directs composition courses at Aix-en-Provence, in the USA (MIT, UCLA and Yale University) and at the University of Montreal. She also promotes Polish music in Belgium and was the founder and first president (1983) of the Belgian Chopin and Szymanowski Society. She is a member of the electronic studios of the Institute for Psychoacoustics and Electronic Music of Ghent University and those of Belgian radio and television.

Bruzdowicz's large output is diverse and her music is performed worldwide. Though she uses all modern techniques and media, they are never employed for ostentatious effects or radical experiments but are subtly integrated into the fabric of the music. She and her husband Jürgen Tittel have written together a number of television film scripts, with music by Bruzdowicz.

WORKS
selective list

STAGE

Kolonia karna [The Penal Colony] (musical drama, 1, J. Simonides, after F. Kafka), 1968; Tours, Grand Théâtre, 12 Feb 1972

Trojanki [Les Troyennes] (musical tragedy, 17 scenes, J. Luccioni, after Euripides), Paris, Théâtre Gérard Philippe, 29 March 1973

Mały Książe [Le petit prince] (ballet, 28 scenes, after A. de Saint-Exupéry), 1976

Bramy raju [The Gates of Paradise] (musical drama, 1, J. Lisowski and J. Bruzdowicz, after J. Andrzejewski), 1982; Warsaw, Wielki Theatre, 15 Nov 1987

Clafouti's Star (musical for children), Brussels, Théâtre du Résidence, 1988

Tides and Waves (opera-musical, Bruzdowicz, H. Fuers-Garcia, J. Tittel), Barcelona, 1992

Maisonneuve (opera-musical, L. Gareau-Du Bois), Montreal, Sept 1992

OTHER WORKS

Orch: Sym., 1974; 3 concs.: pf, 1974, vn, 1975, db, 1982; 4 Seasons' Greetings, solo insts, str orch, 1988–9

Vocal: Urbi et Orbi (cantata, H. Hess, J. Tittel), T, children's choir, 2 tpt, org, 1985; La espero, cantata, S, Bar, ens, 1990

Chamber and inst (incl. insts with tape): Erotiques, pf, 1966; Stigma, vc, 1969; Episode, pf, 13 str, 1973; Mater polonica, org, 1973; An der schönen blauen Donau, 2 pf, tape, 1974; Einklang, hpd, org, 1975; Sonate d'octobre, pf, 1978; Tre contra tre, fl, ob, va, 3 perc, 1979; Trio dei Due Mondi, vn, vc, pf, 1980; Dum spiro spero, fl, tape, 1981; Dreams and Drums, perc, 1982; 2 str qts, no.1 'La vita', 1983, no.2 'Cantus aeternus', 1988; Aurora borealis, hpd, org, 1988; Sonata no.1 'Il ritorno', vn, 1990

Film scores (elec): Sans toit, ni loi (dir. A. Varda), 1985; Stahlkammer Zürich (J. Bruzdowicz, J. Tittel), 36 films, 1985–91; Jacquot de Nantes (dir. Varda), 1991

Principal publishers: Choudens, PWM

BARBARA ZWOLSKA-STĘSZEWSKA

Brzezińska-Szymanowska, Filipina (*b* Warsaw, 1 Jan 1800; *d* Warsaw, 11 Nov 1886). Polish composer and amateur pianist. She studied the piano in Warsaw with Charles Mayer, a pupil of John Field. She was also influenced by the playing of Maria Szymanowska, her sister-in-law. Brzezińska-Szymanowska composed songs and works for organ as well as for piano; most of them were published in Warsaw. Her music is constructed very simply in terms of texture, phrase structure and harmony, and, with its sentimental, cantabile melodies, was well suited to amateurs. The

'The Gates of Paradise', scene from the original production of Joanna Bruzdowicz's opera at the Wielki Theatre, Warsaw, in 1987

piano works are typical salon pieces, with conventional figuration, and include dances (mazurkas, waltzes, contredanses), fantasias, nocturnes and programmatic pieces. Her songs, mainly religious, were composed later – one of them, *Nie opuszczaj nas* ('Do Not Leave Us'), was popular during the 1863 uprising against Russia – and they were still being published in song collections at the beginning of the 20th century.

BIBLIOGRAPHY

PazdirekH; *SMP*

ZOFIA CHECHLIŃSKA

Buchanan, Dorothy Quita (*b* Christchurch, 28 Sept 1945). New Zealand composer and teacher. The second of six daughters, she grew up in an intensely musical environment, both parents being pianists and all sisters singers and instrumentalists. She graduated from the University of Canterbury in 1967. In 1973 she founded the influential Christchurch music workshops, and later formed and directed the Centre Sound choral group. She gained a teaching diploma in 1976 and the following year became the first 'composer-in-schools'. Her work as a teacher has led to a 'school' of young Christchurch composers. She also plays a leading role as a lecturer, writer, adjudicator and musical director.

A prolific composer, she has been influenced above all by landscape. She has worked closely with painters and poets, and has set texts by leading New Zealand poets such as Ian Wedde and Ruth Gilbert as well as the writings of Janet Frame and Margaret Mahy. Of her *Five Vignettes of Women*, for flute and female chorus (1987), Elizabeth Kerr wrote in the *New Zealand Listener* (23 May 1987) 'this moving work is unashamedly romantic . . . The idiom is a simple tonal one, with the gentle and imaginative melodic, harmonic and rhythmic surprises often found in Buchanan's music'. In 1984 she became composer-in-residence at the New Zealand Film Archives in Wellington, where her work includes composing scores for classic silent films.

WORKS

selective list

Orch: Missa de angelis: Pro Anno Infantum, 1979; Sinfonietta in 5 Movements, 1989; Duo concertante, vn, vc, orch, 1991

Stage and film: Lincoln County Incident (film score), 1976; The Tempest (theatre music), 1983; Oedipus (theatre music), 1983; The Adventures of Algy (score for silent film), fl, vc, pf, 1984; Queen of Rivers (film score), cl; Greenleaf (opera), T, T, Bar, Bar, fl, vib, perc, windchimes, 1985

Vocal: Motet to the Virgin, SSA, 1966; 3 Jacques Prévert settings, T, B, vn, pf, nar, 1969; 5 Witchy Poo Songs, 1v, pf/(fl, ob, cl, bn, vc), 1976; Shaduf (I. Wedde), SSAATTBB, 1977; The Lord's my shepherd, chorus, orch, pf, 1978; Magnificat, S, Mez, A, T, B, SSA, fl, 2 tpt, 5 tbn, 1981; The Birds Began to Sing (J. Frame), S, A, T, B, SSA, 1983; 26 Songs (TVNZ Margaret Mahy Series), chamber ens, 1983; Mary Magdalene and the Birds (F. Adcock), Mez, cl, 1989; The Clio Legacy (W. Ihimaera), S, nar, women's chorus, Maori women's group, orch, 1991; Fragments and Letters (Buchanan), 1v, cl, vc, 1992

Chamber: Song without Words, pf duet, 1980; 7 Interpretations (on the painting of Rosemary Campbell), chamber ens, 1979; Echoes and Reflections, cl, gui, vn, vc, 1993

BIBLIOGRAPHY

Fuller-LeFanuRM

J. Commons: 'A Conversation with Dorothy Buchanan', *New Zealand Opera News* (1989), July, 6–8

P. Norman: 'Dorothy Buchanan', *Canzona*, iv/12 (1982), 16–26

J. M. THOMSON

Bulterijs, Nini (*b* Temse, 20 Nov 1929; *d* Wilrijk, 12 Dec 1989). Belgian composer. At the Antwerp Conservatory she studied with Jozef D'Hooghe (piano) and Yvonne Van den Berghe (harmony); later she studied composition with Jean Louel, conductor of the Belgian National Orchestra. For her graduation at the Chapelle Musicale Reine Elisabeth, where her composition teacher was Jean Absil, she wrote a motet for choir and orchestra, a string quartet and a cantata *De triomf van het bloed*. Placed second in the 1963 Belgian Prix de Rome contest, for which she composed the cantata *Arion*, and in the 1966 Queen Elisabeth International Composition Competition, for her Symphony, she won the Emile Doehaerd Prize in 1969 for a piano trio and also received the Pro Civitate prize. She twice represented Belgium at the International Festival of Contemporary Music in Warsaw (1962, 1974). Bulterijs taught at the music schools of Hamme, Vilvoorde and Mechelen, and in 1970 became a professor at the Lemmens Institute at Louvain. She also taught at the Antwerp Conservatory from 1962 (professor of counterpoint and fugue from 1971), retiring in 1988. Her works, rhythmically complex and texturally dense, have a dodecaphonic basis.

WORKS

selective list

Inst: Sonata, 2 vn, pf, 1960; Sym. Movements, 1960; Pf Conc., 1961; Pf Trio, 1962; Conc., 2 vn, orch, 1964; Sym., 1965; Vn Conc., 1968; Rondo, vn, pf, 1972

Vocal: Arion (cantata, B. Decorte), solo vv, chorus, orch, 1963; De terugkeer van de krijgsgevangene, cantata, 1963; De triomf van het bloed (cantata, K. Jonckheere),

BIBLIOGRAPHY

C. Mertens: *Hedendaagse muziek in België* (Brussels, 1967), 54–5, 65

CORNEEL MERTENS/MARIE CORNAZ

Bumpus, Frances. *See* ALLITSEN, FRANCES.

Burrell, Diana (*b* Norwich, 25 Oct 1948). English composer. She studied music at Cambridge University (BA 1971). She taught at Sutton High School, Surrey, and then worked as a freelance viola player before concentrating on composition. Her first work to attract critical attention was the striking *Missa Sancte Endeliente* (1980) for five soloists, chorus and orchestra. Her works have been commissioned by a wide range of leading contemporary music groups and performers, orchestras, festivals and public bodies; for example, *Arched Forms with Bells*, for organ, was a BBC Promenade Concerts commission for 1990, and *Resurrection* a work for the Bournemouth Sinfonietta, 1993. She has also composed music for dance and for television.

Burrell has said that her works begin with the idea of a visual form and that she composes her music as 'architectural shapes on paper'. She has developed a clear, bold musical language that is always concerned to communicate directly with the audience. *Landscape* (1988), for orchestra, creates a primeval urban landscape, using the unusual sounds of steel pans, scrap metal and tenor recorders to forge a personal vision. A work such as *Barrow* (1991), for chamber ensemble, which grew from a dream of a primitive ritual at an ancient burial mound perfectly demonstrates, with its haunting drumming, the dramatic and almost mystical qualities of her music.

WORKS
selective list

Dramatic: Dalliance of Eagles (elec ballet), 1986; The Albatross (opera, Burrell, after S. Hill), 1987; Sequence, vc, tape, 1993

Orch: Praeludium, 1983; Io!, 3 tpt, 3 trbn, str, 1984; Archangel, 2 ob, eng hn, 3 tpt, str, wind, 1987; Landscape, 1988; Landscape with Procession, 1988; Scene with Birds, 1989; Das Meer, das so gross und weit ist, da wimmelt's ohne Zahl, grosse und kleine Tiere, str, 1992; Resurrection, chamber orch, 1992; Anima, str, 1993; Va Conc., 1994

Vocal: Pavan (B. Jonson), S, Bar, va, vc, pf, 1979; Missa Sancte Endeliente (liturgy in Cornish and Lat., trad. hymn), S, C, Ct, T, Bar, chorus, orch, 1980; Io evoe! (ancient Gallic and Native Am. texts), chorus, 3 tpt, 3 trbn, str, 1984; Angelus, S, vc, db, perc, 1986; Creators of the Stars of Night (trad. hymn), chorus, eng hn, org, 1989; Hymn to Wisdom (J. Morley), chorus, 1989; Lights and Shadows (trad. spells), children's choir, chorus, recs, brass insts, perc, str, 1989; Night Songs (Burrell, P. Verlaine), S, chorus, orch, 1991; You Spotted Snakes (W. Shakespeare), children's choir, fl, cl, vn, va, 1991; Invocation for Justice (Carmina gaedelica, ed. A. Carmichael), S, cl, va, 1992; Come Holy Ghost (trad. Whitsuntide hymn), double choir, org, 1993; Heil'ger Geist in's Himmels Throne (trad. Lutheran chorale), chorus, perc, org, 1993; Tachograph (S. Armitage), Bar, pf, 1993

Chamber and solo inst: Concertante, 6 vn, 2 va, 2 vc, db, 1985; Heron, vc, pf, 1988; Shadow, 2 va, 4 vc, db, cel, 1988; Untitled Composition, cl, vc, opt. pf, 1988; Lament, bn/cl, opt. perc, 1988; Arched Forms with Bells, org, 1990; Wind Qnt, 1990; Aria, vn, 1991; Barrow, hn, bn, vc + drums, el gui + drums, pf, 1991; Lucifer, vn, tpt, 1991; Bright Herald of the Morning, cl, pf, 1992; Gulls and Angels, str qt, 1994

BIBLIOGRAPHY

Fuller-LeFanuRM
E. Kelly: 'A Sense of Structure', *Classical Music* (23 May 1987), 43
D. Burrell: 'Accepting Androgyny', *Contact*, no.32 (1988), spr., 52–3

SOPHIE FULLER

Bydwealth, Emily. *See* ZUBELDIA, EMILIANA DE.

C

Caccini [Raffaelli; Signorini; Signorini-Malaspina], **Francesca** ('La Cecchina') (*b* Florence, 18 Sept 1587; *d* after June 1638). Italian composer and singer, the first woman known to have composed opera and probably the most prolific woman composer of her time.

As the daughter, sister, wife and mother of singers, she was immersed in the musical culture of her time from earliest childhood. Her father, Giulio Caccini, was one of the creators of the 'new music' dominated by solo singing which marked the beginning of the Baroque era. She received a literary education as well as training in singing and composition; she is also known to have written poetry and played the keyboard, guitar and harp. She is assumed to have been one of the 'donne di Giulio Romano' (Giulio Caccini) who performed in Jacopo Peri's *Euridice* and her father's *Il rapimento di Cefalo* in 1600. 'Le donne di Giulio Romano' apparently consisted of Francesca, her sister Settimia, her step-mother Margherita della Scala, and occasional pupils of Giulio Caccini, as well as himself and his son Pompeo, dominating the polychoral singing of the Offices during Holy Week and the performance of *intermedi*. Giulio and Grand Duchess Christine of Lorraine went to some lengths to ensure that his daughters' physical and artistic maturity did not break up the group, but Settimia's departure for Lucca and Mantua in 1611 ended the ensemble. It was replaced by a group described in court diaries as 'la sig.a Francesca e le sue figliuole' (Francesca and her pupils), who continued to perform chamber music for women's voices until the late 1620s.

The Caccini family travelled to France to sing for the king and queen in the winter of 1604–5. There Francesca received her first independent job offer, from Marie de' Medici, as a salaried court singer with a dowry of 1000 scudi. Letters from Giulio suggest that Grand Duke Ferdinand I of Florence refused to release Francesca from his service. Francesca returned with the family to Italy in June 1605, spending July to November at Modena, where she taught the Princess Giulia d'Este. In 1606, Giulio tried to negotiate a position for Francesca with Princess Margherita della Somaglia-Peretti, sister-in-law of Cardinal Montalto and of Virginio Orsini in Rome. This offer, too, included a salary and a dowry, along with the assumption that a suitable husband would be found. But by March 1607 negotiations were broken off and seven months later Francesca instead took up a post at the Florentine court, having been promised in marriage to the court singer Giovanni Battista Signorini; by the 1620s she was the highest-paid musician at court. Caccini and Signorini were married in S Maria Maggiore in Florence on 15 November 1607. With her dowry of 1000 scudi Signorini bought in 1610 two adjoining houses in the via Valfonda near S Maria Novella, where they lived until his death; their only child, Margherita (*b* 9 Feb 1622), became a nun and a singer. Although Francesca signed her letters with her married name, she remained 'la figliuola di Giulio Romano' or 'Francesca Caccini' in the Medici court records.

For the 1607 Florentine Carnival, Francesca composed her first music for the stage, a *torneo La stiava*, a setting for castrato voices of the poetry of the family friend and court poet Michelangelo Buonarroti *il giovane*. The court diarist, Cesare Tinghi, described it as having 'una musica stupenda'. (It was repeated in 1626, but none of the music has survived.) Letters of Giulio Caccini imply that Francesca composed the parts by first singing to the poetry, then writing out what she had sung, giving the parts to her father to correct. Giulio considered the commission to be addressed to his household rather than to Francesca personally, a conception which may account for the anonymity of her contribution to this and subsequent Buonarroti entertainments.

While improvising and composing chamber music for herself and her pupils over the next ten years, Francesca also contributed

Francesca Caccini: cameo portrait by an unknown artist

incidental music to the 1611 Carnival entertainment *La mascherata delle ninfe di Senna*; Buonarroti's *commedia rusticale La Tancia* (1611) and his *balletto Il passatempo* (1614); and Ferdinando Saracinelli's *balletto Il ballo delle Zingane* (1615). Her court duties included singing the Office for Holy Week services, and at receptions given by the archduchess, and instructing the princesses, ladies-in-waiting and at least one nun in singing. In spring 1616 she was among the retinue of Cardinal Carlo de' Medici travelling to Rome, where she was cast as La Bellezza and Venus (opposite Signorini as Adonis) in the Peri-Cicognini *commedia Adone* (proposed for performance at Cardinal Montalto's Bologna household). In 1617, she and Signorini toured Genoa, Savona and Milan, her virtuosity winning the praise of Gabriello Chiabrera.

In August 1618 Caccini published some of her compositions as *Il primo libro delle musiche*, thus ensuring the preservation of her work for posterity. It is one of the largest and most varied collections of early monody. The collection's most striking feature is its organization: the table of contents directs the user's attention first to the poetic forms set; secondly to the variety of possible uses of the romanesca; thirdly to genres defined as much by context as by textual form (motets, hymns, canzonettas); and lastly to singing both imitatively and homophonically in

ensemble with a bass. 19 works set sacred texts (seven of them in Latin), while 17 are secular; four are duets for soprano and bass. Virtually all the songs in the *Primo libro* are constructed as strophic variations, even the sonnets and madrigals. In the canzonettas and romanesca arias, Caccini scrupulously observes the integrity of poetic lines and reserves ornaments for accented words, internal caesuras or penultimate syllables. As emotional intensity increases, she inserts rests to break a poetic line into syntactical units, or to create phrases out of syntactical units which run between two lines (as for example in *Che fai, misero core*, a spiritual sonnet contemplating the wounds of Christ). Her careful transcription of vocal ornaments is notable: much more lavishly used in secular than in sacred works, their appearance in variation forms show how they could be used to create progressively more elaborate structures. The notation of rhythm and the placement of syllables is unusually finicky, often displacing syllables to an extremely short upbeat and rendering the variety of Italian speech rhythms with rare precision and grace, as well as representing swift changes in intensity.

During Carnival 1619, her setting of Buonarroti's satirical comedy *La fiera* was performed at court, where it caused a scandal because of its portrayal of women in unseemly conditions (pregnancy and labour) and its affirmation of capitalist, republican values over the values of the principate (Varese). In winter 1622, she collaborated with G. B. da Gagliano in setting Jacopo Cicognini's *Il martirio di S Agata*, apparently contributing the parts of S Agata and Eternità. Giulio Caccini spent the winter and spring of 1623–4 in Rome, again in the entourage of Carlo de' Medici. In November he and the poet G. B. Marino involved her and the singer-composer Andreana Basile in a lengthy comparison of their abilities: Marino declared Caccini to have the deeper musical knowledge, Basile the better voice and agility with *passaggi*. Members of Marino's Accademici degli Umoristici published poems honouring both women. Caccini also sang for Pope Urban VIII on 3 February 1624. By early December 1624, her one surviving opera, *La liberazione di Ruggiero dall'isola d'Alcina*, was in rehearsal in Florence; it was performed on 3 February 1625 at the Villa Poggio Imperiale in the Carnival festivities marking the visit of Prince Władisław of Poland. Commissioned by the Regent Archduchess Maria

Title-page of 'La liberazione di Ruggiero dall'isola d'Alcina' (Florence: Pietro Cecconcelli, 1625) by Francesca Caccini

Maddalena, *La liberazione* allegorically explores women's relationship to the wielding of power through a plot that contrasts a good, androgynous sorceress with an evil, sexually alluring one. Caccini's music for the good sorceress consists of through-composed *stile recitativo*, using the 'natural' hexachord; the music for the evil sorceress consists of ever looser variations on her opening recitative (reminiscent of the strophic variations in Caccini's *Primo libro*), using the 'soft' hexachord. (This usage may show the influence of the political theory of her court colleague, the proto-feminist writer Cristoforo Bronzini.) As a whole, the score is rich and varied in its use of genres: canzonettas for three sopranos (evoking the sound of the 'concerto delle donne') and elaborately ornamented strophic arias frame the lovers' original happiness; unornamented *stile recitativo* is used for the serious exchanges among principal characters; and five-part

madrigal style is used for the choruses of enchanted plants both before and after their liberation. The work has been revived in Cologne (1983), Ferrara (1987), Stockholm (1990) and Minneapolis (1991) and recorded in Japan (1990).

Signorini died in December 1626. Francesca left the Medici payroll in May 1627 and on 4 October 1627 married the Lucchese aristocrat and patron Tomaso Raffaelli. During the three years of their marriage, Francesca may have been involved as a composer with theatrical performances sponsored by Raffaelli's Accademia degli Oscuri. Raffaelli's death in April 1630 left Francesca a wealthy landowner and the mother of a son, Tomaso, born in autumn 1628. After nearly three years of quarantine in Lucca during the plague, in spring 1633 she returned to the Medici payroll and from late 1633 to late 1637 her name appears regularly in the records of the grand duchesses' court. Contemporary letters indicate that she and her daughter Margherita performed as chamber singers during those years, and that she composed and directed entertainments for the young grand duchess. In January 1637 she refused to allow Margherita to sing on stage in a *commedia* at the grand duke's command, arguing that such an appearance could compromise the 15-year-old's chances of an honourable convent placement or marriage contract, would tarnish the social position of her son and break the terms of Raffaelli's will. Documents in Lucca reveal that Caccini was still in Florence in June 1638; she had probably died by February 1645, when guardianship of her son passed to his uncle Girolamo Raffaelli.

In her own time, Francesca Caccini evoked mixed reactions. One contemporary memoir remembers her as 'fiera e irrequeta' (proud and restless), involved in a years-long feud with the court poet Andrea Salvadori over his alleged seduction of female singers. Correspondents of Buonarroti seeking the loan of her music for productions of his plays refer to her as 'always gracious and generous'. Her abilities as a singer, teacher and composer are universally remembered as remarkable.

WORKS

DRAMATIC

La stiava (torneo, M. Buonarroti *il giovane*), Pisa, 26 Feb 1607, music lost

La mascherata delle ninfe di Senna (balletto, O. Rinuccini), Florence, Palazzo Pitti, 14 Feb 1611, collab. J. Peri, M. da Gagliano, V. Archilei and S. Caccini; revived 1613 [1 recit. and trio for women's vv by F. Caccini, lost]

La Tancia (incid. music to commedia rusticale, Buonarroti), Florence, Palazzo Pitti, 25 May 1611, revived, Monasterio di S Miniato, May 1619; La pastorella mia from Act 2.v in Il primo libro delle musiche, p.58, all other music lost

Il passatempo (incid. music to balletto, Buonarroti), Florence, Palazzo Pitti, 11 Feb 1614, part revived, Rome, Casa Barberini, 1624; Chi desia di saper che cos'è Amore from Act 1 in Il primo libro, p.90; Egloga pastorale Tirsi e Filli from Act 2.i in Rome, Biblioteca Universitaria, Ms. 279, *ff.* 61–9; Io veggio i campi verdeggiar fecondi, balletto from Act 3, in Il primo libro, p.56; all other music lost

Il ballo delle Zingane (balletto, F. Saracinelli), Palazzo Pitti, 24 Feb 1615, music lost

La fiera (intermedi and incid. music, Buonarroti), Florence, Palazzo Pitti, 11 Feb 1619; choruses of Romei and Malfranzesi revived, Pesaro, carn. 1622; music lost

Il martirio di S Agata (J. Cicognini), Florence, Compagnia di S Giorgio in Costa, 23 Jan 1622, collab. G. B. da Gagliano [roles of S Agata and Eternità and ensembles for 'women' (male vv by Caccini, music lost]

La liberazione di Ruggiero dall'isola d'Alcina

(commedia in musica, prol., 4 scenes, Saracinelli), Florence, Villa Poggio Imperiale, 3 Feb 1625, revived, Warsaw, 1628 (Florence, 1625), ed. D. Silbert, SCMA, vii (1945)

Rinaldo innamorato, ? one of 2 works commissioned 1626 by Prince Władisław of Poland, MS, formerly owned by G. Baini, lost

OTHER VOCAL

Il primo libro delle musiche, 1–2vv, bc (Florence, 1618/*R*1986), 1 in *I-Bc* Q.49; 1 in *Fn* Magl. XIX.66, f.156; 1 in Rome, Biblioteca Universitaria, Ms. 279, ff.61–9; Dove io credea, 1621[14]; 7 transcr. in Raney (1971)

Ch'io sia fedele, 1629[9]

BIBLIOGRAPHY

FétisB; *GerberNL*; *Grove1*[†]; *SainsburyD*; *SchillingE*[†]; *SchmidlD*

L. Parigi: *Il Parigi: dialogo terzo* (Florence, 1618), 19

G. T. Maja Materdona: *Per le virtuose donne Francesca Signorini Malespina e Adriana Basile, musiche famose* (Rome, 1624)

A. Brunelli: *Prima parte delli fioretti spirituali* (Venice, 1626), 3r

S. Bonini: *Prima parte de' discorsi e regole sopra la musica* (MS, 1649–50), ed., abridged in A. Solerti, *Le origini del melodramma* (Turin, 1903), 129–42, esp.136

P. della Valle: *Della musica dell'età nostra* (1640), ed. in A. Solerti, *Le origini del melodramma* (Turin, 1903), 166

A. de la Fage: 'La prima compositrice di opera in musica, e la sua opera', *Gazzetta musicale di Milano*, vi (1847), 323

—— : *Essais de diphthérographie musicale* (Paris, 1864), 174

A. Ambros: *Geschichte der Musik* (Leipzig, 1881), iv, 295

A. Ademollo: *La bell'Adriana ed altre virtuose del suo tempo alla corte di Mantova* (Città di Castello, 1888)

G. Baccini: *Notizie di alcuni commedie sacre rappresentate in Firenze nel secolo XVII* (Florence, 1889)

R. Rolland: *Histoire de l'opéra en Europe avant Lully et Scarlatti* (Paris, 1895), 114–15

O. Chilesotti: 'La liberazione di Ruggiero dall'isola d'Alcina di Francesca Caccini', *Gazzetta musicale di Milano* (1896), 32

H. Goldschmidt: *Studien zur Geschichte der italienische Oper in 17. Jahrhundert* (Leipzig, 1901), 29

A. Solerti: *Musica, ballo e drammatica alla corte medicea 1600–1637* (Florence, 1905)

A. Bonaventura: 'Un ritratto della Cecchina', *Cultura musicale*, no.6 (1922), 7

F. Boyer: 'Giulio Caccini à la cour d'Henri IV', *ReM*, vii/9 (1925–6), 241–50

—— : 'Les Orsini et les musiciens d'Italie au début du XVII[c] siècle', *Mélanges de philologie, d'histoire et de littérature offerts à Henri Hachette* (Paris, 1934), 301

M. G. Masera: 'Alcune lettere inedite di Francesca Caccini', *RaM*, xiii (1940), 173–82

—— : *Michelangelo Buonarotti il giovane* (Turin, 1941)

—— : 'Una musicista fiorentina del seicento: Francesca Caccini', *RaM*, xiv (1941), 181–207, 237–51; xv (1942), 249–66

M. Gliński: *La prima stagione lirica italiana all'estero* (Siena, 1943)

D. Silbert: 'Francesca Caccini, called La Cecchina', *MQ*, xxxii (1946), 50–62

A. M. Crino: 'Virtuose di canto e poeti a Roma e a

Firenze nella prima metà del seicento', *Studi secenteschi*, i (1960), 175

C. Raney: *Francesca Caccini, Musician to the Medici, and her Primo Libro (1618)* (diss., New York U., 1971)

R. Weaver and N. Weaver: *A Chronology of Music in the Florentine Theater 1590–1750* (Detroit, 1978)

A. Newcomb: *The Madrigal at Ferrara, 1579–1597* (Princeton, 1980)

C. Varese: 'Scene, linguaggio e ideologia nella *Fiera* di Michelangelo Buonarotti il giovane', *Rassegna della letteratura italiana*, lxxxv (1981), 459

U. Limentani: 'Introduzione', *La Fiera di Michelangelo Buonarotti il Giovane: redazione originaria (1619)* (Florence, 1985), 7

J. Bowers: 'The Emergence of Women Composers in Italy, 1566–1700', *Women Making Music: the Western Art Tradition, 1150–1950*, ed. J. Bowers and J. Tick (Urbana and Chicago, 1986), 116–67

J. W. Hill: 'Frescobaldi's *Arie* and the Musical Circle around Cardinal Montalto', *Frescobaldi Studies*, ed. A. Silbiger (Durham, NC, 1987), 157–94, esp.191

E. Rosand: ' "Senza necessità del canto dell'autore": Printed Singing Lessons in Seventeenth-Century Italy', *IMSCR, xiv Bologna 1987*, ii, 214–25

T. Carter: *Jacopo Peri, 1561–1633: His Life and Works* (New York, 1989)

S. G. Cusick: 'Of Women, Music and Power: a Model from Seicento Florence', *Musicology and Difference*, ed. R. Solie (Berkeley, 1993), 281–304

—— : ' "Thinking from Women's Lives": Francesca Caccini after 1627', *MQ*, lxxvii (1993), 484–507

K. A. Harness: *Amazon of God . . .* (thesis, U. of Illinois, 1994)

SUZANNE G. CUSICK

Caccini, Settimia ['La Flora'] (*b* Florence, 6 Oct 1591; *d* after 1661). Italian singer and composer. The daughter of the composer and singer Giulio Caccini and the singer Lucia Caccini, and sister of the composer Francesca Caccini, Settimia may have made her first public appearance at the première (1600) of her father's opera *Il rapimento di Cefalo*, or of his setting of Ottavio Rinuccini's *Euridice* (1602). Until 1611 she seems mostly to have sung with her father's family consort: for Henri IV and Marie de' Medici of France (1604–5); in Carnival and Holy Week entertainments at the Medici court in Florence; in the *intermedi* to Michelangelo Buonarroti's *Il giudizio di Paride* (1608); and in the *Mascherate delle ninfe della Senna* (Carnival 1610–11), for which she wrote some of her own part. In December 1608, the Mantuan court offered her a position as a singer (the terms of her employment included the finding of a suitable husband for her). Ademollo and others claimed that the Medici refused to release her; at any rate, Giulio Caccini declined the offer. A similar offer in 1609 from Enzo Bentivoglio in Rome also came to naught. Ultimately, Settimia married the Lucchese singer and composer Alessandro Ghivizzani,

who received a dowry of 600 scudi from the Medici court. Both became salaried musicians at court in 1609.

However, they left without giving notice in October 1611 and in 1613 were recruited by Duke Ferdinando Gonzaga in Lucca to sing at the court in Mantua, where they remained for six years. They then returned to Lucca and in 1622 settled in Parma, in the service of Cardinal Farnese. Settimia is believed to have argued strongly for Monteverdi's participation in the festivities there for the wedding of Odoardo Farnese and Margherita de' Medici in 1628, and she sang Aurora in his *torneo* for the occasion, *Mercurio e Marte*. After Ghivizzani's death in 1632, she returned to Florence, where she remained on the payroll until 1661.

Settimia's music for *Mascheràte delle ninfe della Senna* does not survive. As many as seven songs in two closely related manuscripts compiled at Florence (*I-Bc* Q.49 and *CS-Pnm* II. La.2, formerly in the Lobkowitz library of Roudnice) may be hers: some attributed to her in one source are attributed either to Ghivizzani or to an otherwise unknown 'Parma' in the other. All show a gift for graceful melody, an adroit use of fleeting chromatic alterations to suggest an equally fleeting change of affect in the text, a fondness for rhythmic play between vocal line and continuo, and clear tonal motion in the bass. Unlike her sister Francesca's known solo songs, none of Settimia's possible works exploit written-out *passaggi*; instead, several require the singer to hold notes for many bars above a rapidly moving, often sequential bass line. All the works attributed to Settimia are strophic songs, set to conventionally amorous texts.

WORKS

all for 1v, continuo
MSS in *CS-Pnm* II. La.2, *I-Bc* Q.49

Cantan gl'augelli innamorati, *I-Bc*
Gia sperai, non spero hor più, *CS-Pnm*; ed. in Haas
Si miei tormenti, *I-Bc, CS-Pnm*

Doubtful: Due luci ridenti [attrib. S. Caccini in *I-Bc*, attrib. Ghivizzani in *CS-Pnm*]; Gioite al mio gioir [anon. in *I-Bc*, attrib. S. Caccini in *CS-Pnm*]; Io già ti fu fedele [anon. in *I-Bc*, attrib. S. Caccini in *CS-Pnm*]; Lascerò di seguir [attrib. S. Caccini in *I-Bc*, attrib. 'Parma' in *CS-Pnm*]

BIBLIOGRAPHY

SchmidlD†

M. Buttigli: *Descrittione dell'apparato fatto per onorare la prima e solenne entrata in Parma della serenissima principessa Margherita di Toscana* (Parma, 1629)

Descrizione delle feste fatte in Firenze per le reali nozze di Serenissimo Gran Duca Ferdinando II e Vittoria della Rovere (Florence, 1637), 34

A. Ademollo: *La bell'Adriana ed altre virtuose del suo tempo alla corte di Mantova* (Città del Castello, 1888)

A. Solerti: *Musica, ballo e drammatica alla corte medicea, 1600–1637* (Florence, 1905)

P. Nettl: 'Über ein handschriftliches Sammelwerke von Gesängen italienischen Frühmonodie', *ZMw*, ii (1919–20), 83

R. Haas: *Die Musik des Barock* (Potsdam, 1928), 45, 49 [incl. edn of *Gia sperai*]

N. Fortune: 'A Florentine Manuscript and its Place in Italian Song', *AcM*, xxiii (1951), 124

A. Newcomb: 'Girolamo Frescobaldi, 1608–1615: a Documentary Study in which Information also appears concerning Giulio and Settimia Caccini, the brothers Piccininni, Stefano Landi, and Ippolita Recupita', *AnnM*, vii (1964–77), 111–58

F. Hammond: 'Musicians at the Medici Court in the Mid-17th Century', *AnMc*, no.14 (1974), 157, 159

R. Giazotto: *Le due patrie di Giulio Caccini, musico mediceo (1551–1618): nuovi contributi anagrafici e d'archivio sulla vita e la sua famiglia* (Florence, 1984)

J. Bowers: 'The Emergence of Women Composers in Italy, 1566–1700', *Women Making Music: the Western Art Tradition, 1150–1950*, ed. J. Bowers and J. Tick (Urbana and Chicago, 1986), 116–67

SUZANNE G. CUSICK

Calame, Geneviève (*b* Geneva, 30 Dec 1946; *d* ?Geneva, 8 Oct 1993). Swiss composer. She studied the piano in Geneva, then with Guido Agosti in Rome. In 1971 she began to study composition with Jacques Guyonnet and later attended courses by Pierre Boulez and Henri Pousseur. In 1975 she was appointed to teach audio-visual studies at the École Supérieure d'Art Visuel in Geneva. Her works, both instrumental and audio-visual, have been performed throughout Europe and the Americas. Her fascination for instrumental timbres, often explored over a slow-moving harmonic background (as in *Sur la margelle du monde*), led her to incorporate non-European instruments in otherwise conventional ensembles, as in *Vent solaire*, for shakuhachi (Japanese flute) and orchestra.

WORKS

Orch (chamber orch unless otherwise stated): StEpHAnE mAllArmE, ou Un coup de dés jamais n'abolira le hasard . . ., 1977; Les aubes d'Onomadore, orch, African insts, 1977; L'homme-miroir, wind insts, perc, elec, 1979; Je lui dis . . ., 1980; Calligrammes, 1983–4; Océanides, 1986; Sur la margelle du monde, 1987; Vent solaire, shakuhachi, orch, 1990; see also vocal works

Vocal: Différentielle verticale, S, orch, 1974; Alpha futur, S ad lib, orch, 1976; Mandala, 7 tpt/7vv, 1978

Other inst: Mantiq-al Tayr, fl, contrabass fl, elec, 1973; Lude, harp, 1975; Iral, désert de métal, 4 tpt, 4 trbn, 1975; Oniria, pf, tape, 1981; Le livre de Tchen, 3 perc, mime ad lib, 1988; Incantation, org, 1989; Dragon de lumière, chamber ens, 1991; Le chant des sables, vc, pf, perc, 1992

Audio-visual: Le chant remémoré, 1975; Geometry

I–III, 1976; Labyrinthes fluides, 1976; Et l'oeil rêve . . ., 1977; Tableaux video, 1977

CHRIS WALTON

Calegari, Cornelia [Maria Cattarina] (*b* Bergamo, 1644; *d* Milan, after 1675). Italian composer. She was well known as a singer in her native city; after her parents failed to place her in a monastery for women there, she took final vows at the Benedictine house of S Margarita in Milan on 19 April 1661. Her religious name was Maria Cattarina. Armellini's account of her early death is at least partly inaccurate, since she is listed at this monastery into the 1670s. Calvi mentions that her *Motetti à voce sola* was printed in Bergamo in 1659; no trace of this collection survives, nor of the madrigals (for one and two voices), six-voice Masses and Vespers that Calvi reports she had composed. The disappearance of her music may have resulted from her conflicts with S Margarita over her spiritual dowry as well as from Archbishop Alfonso Litta's musical restrictions at the monastery in the 1660s.

BIBLIOGRAPHY

FétisB; *GerberNL*; *SainsburyD*; *SchillingE*; *SchmidlD*; *WaltherML*

D. Calvi: *Scena letteraria de gli scrittori bergamaschi* (Bergamo, 1664), after p.61

M. Armellini: *Biblioteca Benedictino Casinensis* (Assisi, 1731–2), pt ii, 93

G. S. Mayr: *Biografie di scrittori e artisti musicali bergamaschi nativi od oriundi* (Bologna, 1875), 143–5

J. Bowers: 'The Emergence of Women Composers in Italy, 1566–1700', *Women Making Music: the Western Art Tradition, 1150–1950*, ed. J. Bowers and J. Tick (Urbana and Chicago, 1986), 116–61, esp.118

R. L. Kendrick: 'Le Sirene Celesti': Generations, Gender and Genres in Seicento Milanese Nuns' Music (diss., New York U., 1993), 205–6

ROBERT L. KENDRICK

Calosso, Eugenia (*b* Turin, 21 April 1878; *d* ? after 1914). Italian composer and conductor. She studied composition in Turin with Giovanni Cravero. She started her career as a conductor at San Remo (Casino Municipale) and continued until 1914, on concert tours both in Italy and elsewhere in Europe, including Basle, Berlin, Brussels, Cologne, London and Paris. Her compositions include the opera *Vespero* (to a libretto by Ernesto Ragazzoni), orchestral suites, madrigals for three and four voices, about 50 lieder, and pieces for violin and piano and for solo piano.

BIBLIOGRAPHY

SchmidlD

A. de Angelis: *L'Italia musicale d'oggi: Dizionario dei musicisti* (Rome, 1918, 3/1928)

LAURA PISTOLESI

Cameu (de Cordoville), Helza (*b* Rio de Janeiro, 28 March 1903). Brazilian pianist, composer and musicologist. She studied the piano first with Alberto Nepomuceno and later with João Nunes at the Instituto Nacional de Música, where she was also taught theory by Alfredo Richard. She continued her studies with Agnello França (harmony), Oscar Lorenzo Fernândez (composition) and Francisco Braga (counterpoint and fugue). She also learnt the violin, cello and singing. Cameu completed the composition course at the Conservatório Brasileiro de Música in 1936, but her first compositions date from 1928.

In 1944 her *Quadro sinfônico* won first prize in a competition organized by the Orquestra Sinfônica Brasileira. She has devoted much of her energy to the study of indigenous music, having published a book, *Introdução ao estudo da música indígena brasileira* (Rio de Janeiro, 1977), and several articles on the subject. Her works often include direct quotations from this repertory. She is a member of the Academia Brasileira de Música.

WORKS

Orch, vocal orch: Pf Conc., 1936; Modinha, 1v, orch, 1937; Quadro sinfônico, 1939; Yara; Ouro Preto; Líricas, 1v, orch, 1941; Serestas nos.1–2, chamber orch, 1942

Chamber: Cantilena, vn, pf, 1928; Meditação, vc, pf, 1928; Scherzetto, vn, pf, 1928; Suite no.1, str trio, 1935; Suite no.2, str qt, 1935; Str Qt, 1937; Vc Sonata, 1942; Cidade nova, ob, bn; Poema, vn, pf, 1959

Pf: 3 prelúdios; 6 estudos; 7 variações sobre um Minueto de Bach; pieces for children

Solo v, pf: Saudade, 1928; Eterna incógnita, 1928; A torre morta do ocaso, 1933; Solidão, 1934; Morena cor de canela, 1934; Ao mar, 1941; Amar, 1942; Tarde, 1943; Silêncio, 1943; Vila branca, 1945; Noitinha, 1945; Trovas, 1946; Acalanto; Querer ver esta menina, 1948

BIBLIOGRAPHY

Enciclopédia da música brasileira (São Paulo, 1977), i, 133

M. V. R. Veiga: *Toward a Brazilian Ethnomusicology: Amerindian Phases* (diss., U. of California, Los Angeles, 1981)

IRATI ANTONIO, CRISTINA MAGALDI

Campana, Francesca (*b* Rome; *d* probably in Rome, July 1665). Italian composer, singer and instrumentalist. In a letter of 3 December 1633 Fulvio Testi commended her to Duke Francesco I of Modena as a master of her art – she composed and played the spinet – and one of the two finest female singers in Rome ('though the most sensitive detect a little

hoarseness in her voice'). She was probably the Francesca, daughter of Andrea Campana of Rome, who became the wife of the composer Giovan Carlo Rossi (possibly after 1633, since Testi mentions no husband) and thus sister-in-law of Luigi Rossi. Her extant music includes two pieces published in 1629 (*RISM* 1629[1]) – a florid setting for solo voice of the canzonet *Pargoletta vezzosetta* and a continuo madrigal for two voices, *Donna, se 'l mio servir* – and *Arie a 1, 2, e 3 voci* op.1 (Rome, 1629). As its title implies, this latter volume consists largely of strophic songs; most of them are in triple or in alternating triple and duple time, and some include virtuoso passages. The volume opens with a sonnet setting for solo voice, *Semplicetto augellin*, and closes with a madrigal, *Occhi belli*, apparently for three solo voices (two sopranos and bass). It is an attractive work, competently written, with some expressive chromaticism.

BIBLIOGRAPHY

A. Cametti: 'Alcuni documenti inediti su la vita di Luigi Rossi compositore di musica (1597–1653)', *SIMG*, xiv (1912–13), 23–4

H. Prunières: *L'opéra italien en France avant Lulli* (Paris, 1913), 319

A. Ghislanzoni: *Luigi Rossi: biografia e analisi delle composizioni* (Milan, 1954), 167–8

M. L. Doglio, ed.: *Fulvio Testi: Lettere* (Bari, 1967), i, 495–6

J. Whenham: *Duet and Dialogue in the Age of Monteverdi* (Ann Arbor, 1982), i, 173; ii, 122–3

J. Bowers: 'The Emergence of Women Composers in Italy, 1566–1700', *Women Making Music: the Western Art Tradition, 1150–1950*, ed. J. Bowers and J. Tick (Urbana and Chicago, 1986), 116–61, esp.118

JOHN WHENHAM

Campos, Lina Pires de (*b* São Paulo, 18 June 1918). Brazilian composer, pianist and teacher. The daughter of an Italian luthier, Angelo Del Vecchio, she studied the piano with Léo Peracchi and music theory with Furio Franceschini, Caldeira Filho and Oswaldo Lacerda. It was not until 1958 that she took up composition, which she studied with Camargo Guarnieri. As a music educator she worked first as Magda Tagliaferro's assistant before establishing her own piano school.

Most of her works, which are published by Irmãos Vitale, are for piano, guitar or voice and they include, for piano, *Acalanto* (1959), *Ponteio* no.1 (1959) and no.2 (1976), and five *Peças infantis* (1962); for voice and piano, *Toada, Embolada* (both 1961) and *Confissão* (1975); and for solo guitar, *Prelúdios* (1975) and *Ponteio e toccatina* (1977). A catalogue of her works was published by the

Ministério das Relações Exteriores (Brasília, 1977).

IRATI ANTONIO

Canal, Marguerite (*b* Toulouse, 29 Jan 1890; *d* Cépet, nr Toulouse, 27 Jan 1978). French composer. She was born into a musical family and excelled at the Paris Conservatoire, taking *premiers prix* in harmony (1911), piano accompaniment (1912) and fugue (1915), and winning the Prix de Rome in 1920 with *Don Juan*. She was the first woman to conduct orchestral concerts in France (Palais de Glace, 1917–18), and in 1919 she was appointed to teach solfège for singers at the Conservatoire. That post she had to leave for the Villa Medici, but she returned to the appointment from 1932 until her retirement.

Canal's music is intimately bound up with her personal emotional life. For instance, her beautiful Violin Sonata, a work in the tradition of Franck and Fauré, evokes the life of a young woman. Her songs, too, reveal her feelings and experience, particularly the cycle *Amours tristes* to her own poems. Many songs show her passion for children (she never had a child); others, especially those to words by Paul Fort, reflect her love of Brittany and the sea. Most of her early works were published by her husband Maxime Jamin; after her divorce she published less. She also left several works unfinished, mainly because she devoted more time to her pupils than to her works and after her retirement suffered from ill-health. The orchestration of the opera *Tlass Atka* remains incomplete and an intended revision of the Requiem never materialized.

WORKS
selective list; printed works published in Paris

Opera: Tlass Atka (Le pays blanc) (4, P. Maudru, F. Gauthier, after J. London), begun ?1922

Vocal orch: La tête de Kenwarc'h (Leconte de Lisle), 1v, orch, 1914; Requiem, solo vv, chorus, orch, 1921, unpubd; Don Juan, scène dramatique, vs (1922)

Songs: Un grand sommeil noir (P. Verlaine) (1919); Ici-bas tous les lilas meurent (R. F. A. Sully-Prudhomme) (1920); 6 chansons écossaises (de Lisle) (1920–21); Les roses de Saadi (M. D. Valmore) (1921); Douceur du soir (G. Rodenbach) (1921); Au jardin de l'infante (A. V. Samain), 4 nos. (1921); La flûte de jade (Toussaint), 7 nos. (1924); 3 chants extraits du Cantique des cantiques (1928); Le bonheur est dans le pré (P. Fort) (1928); Sagesse (Verlaine), 6 nos. (1931); 7 poèmes (C. P. Baudelaire), 3 nos. (1940); L'amour marin (Fort), 2 nos. (1947); many unpubd

Inst: Vn Sonata, 1922; Esquisses mediterranéennes, pf (1930)

Principal publishers: Jamin, Lemoine

MICHEL POUPET

Canales (Pizarro), Marta (*b* Santiago, 17 July 1893; *d* Santiago, 6 Dec 1986). Chilean conductor and composer. She studied with Luigi Stefano Giarda and began conducting and composing at her family home where musical gatherings attracted many connoisseurs. In 1933 and again in 1947 she formed a women's choir devoted to the performance of sacred polyphony. Her own music, mostly sacred choral, is influenced by that of the Renaissance and Baroque; but she handles harmony, the most important aspect of her musical language, with absolute freedom, subordinating it only to the needs of the text. Her works for chorus and orchestra include *Misa de navidad* (1919), *Misa eucarística* (1922) and *Marta y María* (1929). Among her unaccompanied choral works are her *Madrigales Teresianos* (1933) and *Misa gregoriana* (1937). She was awarded first prize at the Latin-American Exhibition, Seville, 1929–30, for her work as a composer.

BIBLIOGRAPHY
V. Salas Viu: *La creación musical en Chile* (Santiago, 1951), 177–8
R. Bustos: 'Marta Canales Pizarro', *Revista musical chilena*, no.157 (1982), 40–64

RAQUEL BUSTOS VALDERRAMA

Canat de Chizy, Edith (*b* Lyons, 26 March 1950). French composer. After studying art, archaeology and philosophy at the Sorbonne, she entered the Paris Conservatoire and between 1978 and 1984 obtained *premiers prix* in harmony, fugue, counterpoint, analysis, orchestration, instrumentation and composition. She was a pupil of Ivo Malec and worked with Guy Reibel in the field of electroacoustics. She has taught the violin, and in 1986 became director of a conservatory in Paris. Her works, propelled by a dialectic of contrasts (darkness/light, crying out/calming down, etc.) reveal a predominant interest in colour and timbre. Though her creative processes are rooted in tradition, Canat de Chizy is always anxious to produce works that are original and spontaneous; above all, she attempts to realize in her music a poetic world in sound.

WORKS
selective list

Orch: Yell, 1985; De noche, 1991; Siloel, str, 1992

Chamber, inst: Sextet, 2 vn, 2 va, 2 vc, 1982; Luceat, 10 solo vn, 1983; Tlaloc, perc, 1984; Black-Light, ob, va, db, pf, 1986; Kyoran, fl, cl, vn, vc, perc,

1987; Suites, 2 gui, 1987; Appels, ob, vn, vc, hpd, perc, 1988; Hallel, str trio, 1991

Vocal: Livre d'heures, S, S, A, A, ens, 1984; Llama, unacc. chorus, 1986; Canciones, 12 solo vv, 1992

Principal publisher: Jobert

FRANÇOISE ANDRIEUX

Candeille, (Amélie) [Emilie] **Julie** [Simons, Julie] (*b* Paris, 31 July 1767; *d* Paris, 4 Feb 1834). French instrumentalist, singer, actress, composer, librettist and author. Her father, the composer and singer Pierre Joseph Candeille, was her principal teacher. By 1780 she had appeared before the king and in public as a singer, pianist and harpist. At 14 she was engaged as a singer at the Opéra and one year later took the title role in Gluck's *Iphigénie en Aulide*. In 1783 she sang Sangaride in Niccolò Piccinni's *Atys*. In August that year she made her fortepiano début at the Concert Spirituel, performing a concerto by Muzio Clementi, in which 'she demonstrated a most brilliant and assured technique', according to the *Journal de Paris*. She appeared again four months later and, the following March, performed one of her own concertos, noted at the time by the *Mercure de France*.

Not content simply to be a musician, Candeille took up acting. She made her début at the Comédie Française in September 1785, attempting Racinian roles, before discovering she was better suited to comedy, both as author and as actress. After five years at the Comédie (where her beauty inspired jealousy) and on tour in the provinces, she joined the Théâtre Français. She made a sensation as the star performer, playwright and composer in her début there in December 1792: Candeille sang and accompanied herself on the piano and harp in 154 performances of her *Catherine, ou La belle fermière*. The *Journal de Paris* warmly praised *Catherine* and it was frequently revived over the next 35 years, its text and music published first in Paris, then in translation in Amsterdam (1796).

Less successful was her one-act comedy, *Bathilde* (1793), in spite of the piano duet she performed on stage with the actor Baptiste l'aîné. According to the *Journal des spectacles*, she was hissed in the title role of *La jeune hôtesse* (1794), for which she composed the music. Her fall from public favour may have been in part politically motivated, for she was known to be the mistress of two notable victims of the guillotine: the Girondist orator Pierre-Victorin Vergniaud (*d* 31 October 1793) and the dramatist Philippe-François-Nazaire Fabre d'Eglantine (*d* 5 April 1794).

In 1794 she married (3 November) Louis-Nicolas Delaroche, a military doctor, and produced *Le commissionnaire* at the Théâtre de l'Egalité (subsequently parodied by B.-J. Marsollier and N.-M. Dalayrac in *Le détenus, ou Cange, commissionnaire de Lazare* at the Théâtre Favart in 1794). *La bayadère* opened under her name in January 1795 at the Théâtre de la République, but was the subject

Julie Candeille in the title role of her 'Catherine, ou La belle fermière' (1792): engraving by Prud'hon

of a snide review in the *Journal de Paris National*, which declared the comedy had met with 'such a mixture of applause and murmuring that it would be impossible to give an accurate account' of it; Candeille replied in an open letter with passion and eloquence. Her most ambitious stage work was the 1807 two-act *opéra comique Ida, ou L'orpheline de Berlin*, based on the life of her sister harpist and writer, Mme de Genlis. Nevertheless, it was probably performed no more than half a dozen times, having elicited critical reviews from the *Journal de l'Empire* and the *Journal de Paris*.

Candeille's theatre music was restricted to songs and, while Mme de Genlis later wrote sympathetically of her gifts as the composer of 'many pieces that did honour to a great composer', her piano works are essentially salon music. She composed throughout her life, dedicating some of the piano pieces to other distinguished women musicians, including Hélène de Montgeroult and Pauline Duchambge.

Candeille met Jean Simons, a rich, Belgian coach builder, in Brussels and married him on 11 February 1798 (following her divorce from Delaroche a year earlier). However, they separated in 1802 and she returned to Paris, where she lived at 39 rue Caumartin, giving piano lessons and publishing music, essays, memoirs and several substantial historical novels. She sought political asylum in England during the 100 Days, appearing in concerts with J. B. Cramer, G. B. Viotti and C. P. Lafont in London, but returned to Paris in 1816, having been granted a pension of 2000 francs by Louis XVIII. In 1822 she married the painter Hilaire-Henri Périé de Senovert and they settled in Nîmes. After his death in 1833 she returned to Paris for the last time, dying of apoplexy early the following year.

WORKS

all printed works published in Paris

STAGE

words and music by Candeille unless otherwise stated

Le couvent ou Les fruits du caractère (1, P. Laujon), Paris, Théâtre de la Nation, 16 April 1790

Catherine, ou La belle fermière (comédie, 3), Paris, Théâtre de la République, 27 Nov 1792 (1793), excerpts arr. and pubd separately

Bathilde, ou Le duc (comédie), Paris, Théâtre de la République, 16 Sept 1793

La jeune hôtesse (comédie, 3, Carbon-Flins [C.-M.-L.-E. Carbon de Flins des Oliviers]), Paris, Théâtre Français, 1794

Le commissionnaire (comédie, 2), Paris, Théâtre de l'Egalité, 27 Nov 1794

Ida, ou L'orpheline de Berlin (opéra comique, 2), Paris, Opéra-Comique, Salle Feydeau, 15 May 1807

Louise, ou La réconciliation (comédie, 5), Paris, Comédie Française, 14 Dec 1808

OTHER WORKS

Vocal: Rose d'amour, le chant nocturne et 4 autre romances nouvelles, pf acc., op.10 (after 1802); Arsenne, ou L'épître dédicatoire, 3 romances et une chansonnette, op.11; Morceau de musique funèbre en l'honneur de Grétry, 1813; Cantique des parisiens, 1–3vv, pf (1814); other chansons and romances, some pubd in contemporary journals

Orch: Conc., pf/hpd, orch/str qt, op.2 (1787); Symphonie concertante, pf, cl, bn, hn, orch, 1786, lost; Conc., pf, fl, hn, orch, 1789, lost

Pf: 3 sonates, vn ad lib, op.1 (1786); Duo, 2 pf, op.3, 1793, in Journal de pièces de clavecin, no.123 (1794); 2 sonates, op.4, lost; Grande sonate, op.5 (1798), lost; Grande sonate, op.6, lost; 2 grandes sonates, pf/hpd, op.8 (n.d.); Nouvelle fantaisie facile et brillante, op.13; Duo, 2 pf (n.d.); 7 variations sur la hymne de la nativité, Chéme Portugaia (n.d.); other fantasias and variations mentioned by Fétis, mostly lost

BIBLIOGRAPHY

Choron-FayolleD; ES (R. Averini and A. Sorel-Nitzberg); FétisB; GerberL; SainsburyD; SchillingE; SchmidlD

Mercure de France (4 Jan 1783), 35; (29 May 1784), 220; (29 Oct 1785), 231

A. J. Candeille: Notice biographique sur Anne-Louise Girodet et Amélie-Julie Candeille, pour mettre en tête de leur correspondance secrète (MS, F-Pn)

A. Ricord: Les fastes de la Comédie-Française (Paris, 1821–2)

E. de Goncourt and J. de Goncourt: Histoire de la Société Française pendant le Directoire (Paris, 1855)

P. A. Larousse: Grand dictionnaire universel du XIXe siècle (Paris, 1867)

A. Pougin: 'Une charmeuse: Julie Candeille', Le ménestrel, xlix (1883), 356, 365, 372, 380, 388, 403, 413

H. Lyonnet: Dictionnaire des comédiens français (Paris, 1904 and many later impressions)

L. Aillaud: 'Julie Candeille', Chronique mondaine, littéraire et artistique (Nîmes, 27 Oct 1923, 12 Jan 1924) [incl. memoirs]

C. Jourdin: Essai historique sur Estaires . . . augmenté d'une étude sur la famille des musiciens estairois Candeille (Paris, 1958)

C. Pierre: Histoire du Concert Spirituel 1725–1790 (Paris, 1975)

J. A. Sadie: 'Musiciennes of the Ancien Régime', Women Making Music: the Western Art Tradition, 1150–1950, ed. J. Bowers and J. Tick (Urbana and Chicago, 1986), 191–223

JULIAN RUSHTON, JULIE ANNE SADIE

Capdeville, Constança (*b* Barcelona, 16 March 1937). Portuguese composer, teacher and performer. She studied the piano, composition, and early music at the Lisbon Conservatório Nacional, where she won the composition prize in 1962 with the organ work *Variaçöes sobre o nome de Stravinsky*. She was appointed to the composition faculty of the musicology department of the Universidade Nova and of the Escola Superior de Música in Lisbon. She is a pianist and percussionist and also participates in 'scenic music' performances. Her compositions include stage and film music, chamber and orchestral works and solo pieces. They have been performed at major European festivals, including Royan, Warsaw, Zagreb and the Gulbenkian. She founded and is an active member of the group Colecviva, which introduced music theatre into Portugal.

Her early pieces, for example the Trombone Sonata and *Diferenças sobre um intervalo* (her first serial composition), reflect a strong attraction to novel techniques and alternative languages. In the mid-1960s Capdeville initiated fruitful contact with Stockhausen, Stravinsky, Vinko Globokar and others, and for some time afterwards was preoccupied with sound research, laying particular emphasis on timbre (e.g. *Momento I*, 1972–4). At the end of the 1970s, inspired by the work of Pina Bauch and Merce Cunningham, she turned to the production of multi-media music-theatre performances. Later works demonstrate a command over a wide range of materials and an imaginative approach to a variety of styles and techniques.

WORKS
selective list

DRAMATIC

Music theatre: Schubertiade, 1980; Uma hora com Igor Stravinsky, 1980; Vamos satiar I, II, III (on music and texts by E. Satie), 1981–5; Don't Juan, 1985; Fe . . . de . . . ri . . . co . . . (50 aniversário da morte de F. García Lorca), 1987; The Cage (on texts and music of J. Cage), 1988; Para um Stabat mater, 1988; Erik Satie, com toda a gente, 1989; Wom, wom Cathy (To Cathy Berberian), 1990

Ballet: Ritual One, 1973; Libera me, 1979; Dimitriana, 1979; Lúdica, 1980; Viva Picasso!, 1982; Só Longe Daqui, 1983; Zooalógica, 1984; As Troianas, 1985; Fado, 1990, collab. C. Zingaro

Scenic music: Quinze rolos de moedas de prata (Chin. trad.), 1979; Almada Dia Claro (A. Negreiros), 1984; Conversa entre um contrabaixo e uma inquietação (M. Cintra), 1988; La prose du transsibérien et de la petite Jeanne de France (B. Cendrars), 1988; Silêncio, depois (S. Beckett), 1990

Film scores: Cerro Maior (dir. L. Filipe Costa), 1979; Solo de violino (dir. M. Rüttler), 1990

Incid. music: Molly Bloom (J. Joyce), 1981; A casa de Bernarda Alba (F. García Lorca), 1983; Filhos de um Deus Menor (M. Medoff), 1984; Pilades (P. P. Pasolini), 1986

OTHER WORKS

Orch: Aria, ob, str orch; Música para 15 executantes, str orch, before 1960; Diferenças sobre um intervalo, 1967; . . . Et maintenant, écoute la lumière, 1990

Chamber: Sonatina, fl, ob, trbn, pf, before 1960; Sonata concertante, trbn, pf, 1963; Momento I, fl, harp, perc, vn, va, vc, 1972, rev. 1974; Mise-en-requiem, fl, harp, vn, va, vc, pf, perc, tape, 1979; In sommo pacis (One for Nothing), ob, va, db, pf, 1980; Amen para uma ausência, (ob, va, db, pf)/(solo v, db, inst ens), 1986; Valse, valsa, vals: Keuschheits Waltz, db, pf, 1987 [also arr. pf solo]; Di lontan fa specchio il mare (Joly Braga Santos, in Memoriam), inst ens, 1989; 1+1+1+1, 4 db, 1989

Solo inst: Caixinha de música, pf, Maman, j'ai vu dans la lune . . . , pf, Humble danse des petites canards, pf, all before 1960; Variações sobre o nome de Stravinsky, org, 1962; In, pf, 1969; Valse, valsa, vals: Keuschheits Waltz, pf, 1987; Border Line, t sax, 1988

Vocal: O natal do Anjinho Dorminhoco (E. de Lemos), cantata for children, vv, recs, perc, 1965; . . . Vocem meam, 1v, 4 timp, 1985

Mixed media: Libera me, choir, pf, perc, tape, lights, 1979; Memoriae, quasi una fantasia I, 2 db (1 player), pf (2 players), 7–15vv, tape, lights; Esboços para um Stabat mater, fl, tpt, gui, harp, vn, va, vc,

pf, perc, tape, lights, dancer, 1981; Double, low v, pf, vc, tape, lights, 1982; Avec Picasso, ce matin, pf, tape, lights, 1984; Um quadrado em redor de Simbad, fl, pf, vib, actor, dancer, light, 1986

GABRIELA CRUZ

Capuis, Matilde (*b* Naples, 1 Jan 1913). Italian composer and pianist. She studied the piano and composition in Venice and in Florence (where she graduated from the Conservatory), completing her composition studies by taking part in the Accademia Chigiana master classes in Siena. She had a long performing career in Italy and abroad in a duo with the cellist U. A. Scabia. She also taught solfeggio at the Turin Conservatory. For her own compositions she has been awarded the Premio Quartetto Veneziano (1948), and first prize in the Concorso Internazionale in Genoa (1952) and in the Rubinstein International Competition for Women Composers in Buenos Aires (1962). She is a member of Frauenmusik, Zürich. Her works include a Symphony in G minor, *Leggenda per la Notte di Natale* for strings, a Violin Sonata in G minor, a Cello Sonata in C minor and *Fiaba Armoniosa* for piano.

PAOLA DAMIANI

Cardenas, de, Countess. *See* GARELLI DELLA MOREA DE CARDENAS, VINCENZA.

Carlos, Wendy [Walter] (*b* Pawtucket, RI, 14 Nov 1939). American composer. An early experimenter in electronic music, Carlos – a transsexual, known until 1979 as Walter Carlos – worked with Ron Nelson at Brown University (AB 1962), then studied composition with Otto Luening, Vladimir Ussachevsky and Jack Beeson at Columbia University (MA 1965). From 1964 she served as an adviser to Robert Moog in modifying and perfecting the Moog synthesizer. In collaboration with the producer Rachel Elkind-Tourre, she developed a method for creating electronic versions of orchestral sounds. The synthesizer gained recognition as a musical instrument and became the standard for electronic realizations owing to the enormous popularity of Carlos's recording *Switched-on Bach* (1968), which was made on a Moog synthesizer; more than a million copies of the album were sold. Her virtuosity as a performer on the synthesizer and creativity as an arranger are convincingly displayed in her later albums, which include original compositions such as *Timesteps* (1970, used in the score for the film *A Clockwork Orange*, 1971) and *Pompous Circumstances* (1974–5). The popularity of these recordings led to experimentation in the merging of orchestral and synthesizer sounds, a technique which was successfully used in the film score *TRON* (1982). Aided by advanced technology, Carlos electronically produced hundreds of near-perfect replicas of instrumental voices. These were used in the first digitally synthesized orchestra for the album *Digital Moonscapes* (1984). *Secrets of Synthesis* (1987) is Carlos's history of 'electronic orchestration' from analogue synthesizer to alternative tunings (such as unequal temperament). In *Switched-on Bach 2000* (1992) she used the latest computer and electronic technology for a 'state-of-the-art' realization of her classic work.

WORKS
selective list

Stage: Noah (opera), 1964–5

Elec, orch: Timesteps, synth, 1970; A Clockwork Orange, film score, synth, 1971; Sonic Seasonings, synth, tape, 1971; Pompous Circumstances, synth/orch, 1974–5; The Shining, film score, synth, tape, orch, 1978–80; Variations on Dies irae, orch, 1980; TRON, film score, synth, orch, 1981–2

Chamber: 3 studies, fl, pf, tape, 1963–5; Vc Sonata, 1965–6; Str Qt, 1991; other works, ens, pf, synth, tape

Principal publisher: Tempi

BIBLIOGRAPHY

D. Milano: 'Wendy Carlos' and 'The Notation used by Wendy Carlos', *Contemporary Keyboard*, v/12 (1979), 32 [incl. discography], 38

R. Moog: 'Wendy Carlos: New Directions for a Synthesizer Pioneer' and 'The Soundtrack of TRON', *Keyboard*, viii/11 (1982), 51–2, 53

D. Milano: 'Wendy Carlos and the LSI Philharmonic Orchestra', *Keyboard*, x/2 (1984), 26

—— : 'Defying Conventions, Discovering New Worlds', *Keyboard*, xii/11 (1986), 50

Freff: 'Tuning into Wendy Carlos', *Electronic Musician*, ii/11 (1986), 30

P. Potyen: 'Survey of Music Software', *Mix*, xiii/1 (1989), 66

D. Milano: 'Wendy Carlos Revisits Switched-on Bach', *Keyboard*, xviii/8 (1992), 88

JUDITH ROSEN

Carmichael, Mary Grant (*b* Birkenhead, 1851; *d* London, 17 March 1935). British composer. At the RAM she studied the piano with Walter Bache, Oscar Beringer and Fritz Hartvigson, and composition with Ebenezer Prout. She appeared as an accompanist at the Monday Popular Concerts (1884–5) but was more widely known as a composer of songs and piano pieces.

Carmichael may have been of Irish parentage: that would account for her many successful settings of Irish texts, in an Irish idiom, and her most ambitious work, the Mass in E♭ (1900), for male voices, was written in a fully Roman Catholic style. The former are charming: *The Rose of Kenmare* and *The white blossom's off the bog*, from the Album of Six Songs (1890) to words by A. P. Graves, are similar to C. V. Stanford's Irish settings, yet closer to genuine folksong. Moreover, they possess a haunting touch of individuality which is unmistakably Irish. The Mass, however, is another matter, even though Wier (*MEMM*) states that it was 'her most successful work'. Like many composers with a light, felicitous touch, Carmichael is apt to become dull when attempting to be serious, though no-one can deny her knowledge of Mozart, Louis Spohr and Luigi Cherubini, who all figure briefly. The Credo is the one movement free of banal prolixity; even so, one would give the whole of the Mass for a song like *Kitty Bawn* (from the Album of Six Songs) or the enchanting early *Humoreske* (1876) for piano.

WORKS
selective list; printed works published in London

Operetta: The Frozen Heart, or The Snow Queen (1, M. C. Gillington, after H. Andersen), Tr vv (1898)

Sacred vocal: The Children's Sacred Wreath (12 Sacred Songs) (1889); Mass, E♭, male vv (1900)

Partsongs: A Canticle to Apollo (R. Herrick), SSAA (1879); To Meadows (Herrick), SSAA (1879); A Single Star in the Rosy Sky (W. Davies) (1884); Melusine (Carmichael, after E. Geibel), SSAA (1885); Evening Song (A. B. Atkinson), SATB (1887); 7 Two-Part Songs (A. J. Daryl) (?1911)

Vocal duets (with pf): 6 Shakespeare Songs (1885); Fly Away (R. S. Hichens), S, C (1888); At Daybreak (Gillington), S, T (1889); Song of the Mill (Hichens), S, C (1889); Love's Light Summer Cloud (T. Moore), S, T (1898)

Songs: 3 Lyrics from Heine's Book of Songs (Eng. text), 2 sets (1876, 1878); 2 Songs (W. Blake) (1876); 3 Songs from the German (Geibel) (1883); Singsong (27 Nursery Rhymes) (C. Rossetti) (1884); The Stream, song cycle (1887); A Child's Garden of Verse (R. L. Stevenson), 12 songs (1888); 4 Songs (Blake, M. Collins, Herrick, W. Shakespeare) (1889); 4 Songs of the Stuarts (1889); Album of 6 Songs (A. P. Graves) (1890); Sunbeams (10 Songs for Children) (F. E. Weatherly) (1891); 3 Songs (T. B. Aldrich, E. Meyers, Mrs D. O' Sullivan), 1898; 2 Songs (R. Bridges, A. Symons), 1900; 14 Nature Songs for Children (L. S. Bransby and others) (1907); 4 Songs (Blake, A. Cary, A. L. Head), 1917; c50 other songs; arrs. of songs by T. Arne, W. Boyce, W. Shield and others, Irish folksongs etc.

Pf: Humoreske (1876); 2 Sketches from Florence (1876); 2 Mazurkas (1878); 5 Waltzes (Duftende

Blumen), 4 hands (1878); Barcarole (1883); In the Twilight, op.11 (1885); 3 Characteristic Pieces (Stray Leaves from Winchelsea) (1898)

BIBLIOGRAPHY

Baker6; CohenE; MEMM; PazdirekH; WCBH

J. D. Brown and S. S. Stratton: British Musical Biography (Birmingham, 1897)

O. Thompson, ed.: The International Cyclopedia of Music and Musicians (London, 10/1975)

S. Stern: Women Composers: a Handbook (Metuchen, NJ, 1978)

NIGEL BURTON

Carr-Boyd, Ann (Kirsten) (b Sydney, 13 July 1938). Australian composer. She studied at the University of Sydney, where she was the first music graduate (BA 1960, MA 1963), and in London with Peter Racine Fricker and Alexander Goehr. She taught at the University of Sydney, 1967–73. Her output includes a large body of chamber and keyboard works, and pieces commissioned by educational organizations. An idiosyncratic feature of her work is a number of pieces for mandolins in small and large groups, commissioned by the Sydney Mandolins. Her music demonstrates an eclectic style including elements as diverse as 12-note serialism and ragtime. She is also well known as a writer and broadcaster.

Teresa Carreño

WORKS
selective list

Orch: Sym., 1964; Theme and Variations, chamber orch, 1965; Textures and Variations, chamber orch, 1972; Gold, 1976; Festival, 1980

Other inst: 2 str qts, 1964, 1966; Duets, pf, 1967; 2 Themes and Variations, double wind qnt, 1967; 10 Duets, pf, 1970; Lullaby for Nuck, hpd, 1972; Combinations, pf trio, 1973; Nadir, vn, 1973; Patterns, str qt, org, 1973; Woodford Bay, fantasy, org, 1974; Music for Narjade, vc, 1975; Look at the Stars, 14 pieces, pf, 1978; Fandango, mand ens, 1982; Music for Sunday, fl, vn, hpd, 1982; Suite for Veronique, hpd, 1982; Australian Baroque, mand ens, 1984; Dance Suite, ww qnt, 1984; Suite veronese, hpd, 1985; Theme and Variations, org, 1989; Fantasy, org, mands, chamber ens, 1990

Vocal: Dixit Dominus (Ps cx), mixed chorus, str qt, db, pf, 1971; The Boomerang Chocolate Cake, S, hpd, 1974; Couperin, op.16, spkr, org, hpd, perc, 1974; 3 leçons, S, hpd, chimes, 1974; 3 Songs of Love (E. E. Cummings), S, pf/hpd, 1974; Folksongs 76 (7 songs from Canada, France, Greece, Mongolia), 1v, ens, 1976; Home Thoughts from Abroad (J. Delbridge), Mez, ens, 1987

BIBLIOGRAPHY

CohenE; Fuller-LeFanuRM

GRAHAM HAIR, GRETA MARY HAIR

Carreño (García de Sena y Toro), (María) Teresa (Gertrudis de Jesús) (b Caracas, 22 Dec 1853; d New York, 12 June 1917). Venezuelan pianist and composer. Her father, Manuel Antonio (a lawyer and finance minister as well as an organist), was the son of the composer, and director of music of Caracas Cathedral, Cayetano Carreño; her mother belonged to an ancient and aristocratic family, closely linked to Simón Bolívar, 'the Liberator'. Teresa was highly gifted musically and at the age of six is said to have learnt by heart, within five days, Sigismond Thalberg's piano transcription of Norma. By this time she had already composed polkas and waltzes.

In 1862 the family emigrated to the USA and made New York their home. There, the young Carreño met Louis Moreau Gottschalk, 'the King of the Piano', and was deeply impressed by his manner of playing; after listening to her, he agreed to teach her whenever he was in New York (she is said to have fainted while listening to his playing and to have learnt his Jerusalem and Le bananier in only six days). She successfully toured many North American cities and Cuba, and in October 1863 played for Abraham Lincoln at the White House.

In 1866 the Carreño family travelled to Europe. In Paris, she met Rossini, who was taken by her youth, beauty and talents. He introduced her to the Paris salons, where she met Liszt through his daughter, Blandine Oliver. Liszt offered to take her as a pupil, but her father's affairs did not permit this, so Liszt could do no more than advise her not to become a mere imitator of other performers. She followed his advice, and in later years her combination of poetic feeling with impassioned power placed her in the first rank of the world's pianists.

Carreño married the violinist Emile Sauret in 1872 or 1873 and bore two children; he abandoned her in 1875. The following year, she married a singer, Giovanni Tagliapetra; this liaison lasted 12 years and there were three more children. During this time she twice visited Venezuela, at the invitation of the president, after an absence of 23 years. The second of these visits ended tragically with the failure of an Italian opera season in which her husband sang. This financial disaster swallowed up their savings from the previous season. When the conductor left the company, Carreño herself took the baton and carried the season through for two more weeks. Caracas society was outraged that the aristocratic Carreño appeared in public playing the piano and had also appeared as a singer in the USA; worst of all, she had divorced, and remarried a 'vulgar person'.

Once back in North America, friends convinced her that she should leave Tagliapetra and go to Germany, where they felt she would be better appreciated. Having no money, she accepted a loan from a sponsor and admirer, N. K. Fairbank, and, in summer 1889, left with two of her children for Europe. On 18 November she performed at the Berlin Singakademie, overnight becoming one of the leading pianists of the day. In 1891 she met the composer and pianist Eugen d'Albert; they married and had two daughters, but separated in 1895. Between 1895 and 1917 Carreño toured worldwide, and in 1902 married once more, to her former brother-in-law Arturo Tagliapetra.

In 1895 she composed a string quartet, but apart from a waltz dedicated to her daughter Teresita, and two hymns written for her visits to Venezuela (one in honour of Simón Bolívar that is often mistaken for the Venezuelan National Anthem, and another in honour of the ruling president), almost all her works are for piano and written between the ages of six and 15. Her creative style was from the first marked by virtuosity. Influenced by Gottschalk, she used folk melodies, both Latin and North American. European rhythms, particularly the Viennese waltz, also left their mark on her style, which was well attuned to dance. Her early compositions exhibit every technical difficulty imaginable: passages of octaves, perilous leaps and, her favourite, trills. Her output includes descriptive pieces, dance tunes, fantasies, choral works and a Serenade for strings (which remained unpublished).

After Carreño's death in New York, her ashes were taken to Caracas in 1938 and placed in the Central Cemetery; on 9 December 1977 the Venezuelan government ordered her remains to be interred in the National Pantheon. The Weber piano specially built for her in New York for the Venezuelan tour of 1885, together with the rest of her belongings, are on display in the Teresa Carreño Museum in Caracas.

WORKS

Edition: *Obras de Teresa Carreño*, Ediciones del Ministerio de Educación (Caracas, 1974)

Pf: Vals Gottschalk, op.1; Caprice-Polka, op.2; Corbeille des fleurs, waltz, op.9; Polka de concert, op.13; Fantaisie on 'Norma', op.14; Ballade, op.15; Plainte, Elégie no.1, op.17; Partie, Elégie no.2, op.18; Fantaisie on 'L'Africaine', op.24; Le printemps, waltz, op.25; Un bal en rêve, op.26; Une revue à Prague, fantaisie, op.27; Un rêve en mer, méditation, op.28; 6 études de concert [no.1: Le ruisseau], op.29; Mazurka de salon, op.30; Scherzo-Caprice, op.31; 2 esquisses italiennes: Venise (Rêverie-barcarolle), op.33, Florence (Cantilène), op.34; Intermezzo scherzoso, op.34; Le sommeil de l'enfant, berceuse, op.35; Scherzino, op.36; Highland (Souvenir de l'Escosse), op.38; La fausse note, fantaisie-valse, op.39; Staccato-Capriccietto, op.40; Marche funèbre (1866); Kleiner Walzer (Teresita) (1883/4); Saludo a Caracas (1885); Vals Gayo

Other works: Himno a Bolívar, chorus, orch, 1883 or 1885; Himno a El ilustre Americano, chorus, orch, 1886; Str Qt, b, 1895; Serenade, str orch, 1895

BIBLIOGRAPHY

FétisBS; *SchmidlD*

H. Ehrlich: *Berühmte Klavierspieler der Vergangenheit und der Gegenwart* (Leipzig, 1893, 2/1898)

M. von Bülow, ed.: *Hans von Bülow: Briefe und Schriften* (Leipzig, 1896–1908)

R. M. Breithaupt: *Die natürliche Klaviertechnik* (Leipzig, 1905–6)

M. Milinowski: *Teresa Carreño: by the Grace of God* (New Haven, CT, 1940)

R. Marciano: *Un ensayo sobre su personalidad* (Caracas, 1966)

—— : *Teresa Carreño: compositora y pedagoga* (Caracas, 1971)

—— : *Biografía escolar* (Caracas, 1975)

—— : *Protocolo y resurrección de un piano* (Caracas, 1975)

—— : *Teresa Carreño als Komponistin und Pedagogin* (Kassel, 1990)

B. Mann: 'The Carreño Collection at Vassar College', *Notes*, xlvii (1990–91), 1064–83

ROSARIO MARCIANO

Carvalho, Dinorá (Gontijo) de (*b* Uberaba, Minas Gerais, 1 June 1904; *d* São Paulo, 28 Feb 1980). Brazilian composer, pianist and conductor. She studied at the São Paulo Conservatory with Lamberto

Baldi (composition), Martin Braunwieser (harmony) and Ernst Mehlich (conducting). She also studied the piano, both at the conservatory and later in Paris with Isidore Philipp; while in Europe she undertook a concert tour, principally through Italy, and on her return home in 1926 toured Brazil. She founded and directed the Orquestra Feminina of São Paulo, the first ensemble of its kind in Latin America. Among her awards were the Associação Paulista de Críticos de Arte prizes for 1969, 1971 and 1975. She was the first woman to be elected to the Academia Brasileira de Música. Her compositions are primarily nationalist in character; they include ballets, theatre music, works for orchestra, chorus and chamber ensemble, songs and many piano pieces. A catalogue of her works was published by the Ministério das Relações Exteriores (Brazil, 1977).

WORKS
selective list

Stage: Noite de São Paulo (fantasia), 1936; Escravos (ballet), 1946; O girassol ambicioso (ballet), 1952

Orch and chamber ens: Serenata da saudade, orch, 1933; Festa na vila, orch, 1936; Fantasia-Conc., pf, orch, 1937; Danças brasileiras, pf, chamber orch, perc, 1940; Contrastes, pf, chamber orch, perc, 1969; Pf Conc. no.2, 1972

Choral: Acalanto, 1933; Caramurus da Bahia, 1936; Procissão de cinzas em Pernambuco, 1936; Angorô, 1966; Credo, 1966; Missa de profundis, chorus, orch, perc, 1975

Pf: Meditação, 1930; 11 peças infantis, 1940; Valsa no.1, 1944; Festa do Santo Rei, 1949; Sonatina no.1, 1949; Suite, 1968; Sonata no.1, 1975

BIBLIOGRAPHY
Enciclopédia da música brasileira (São Paulo, 1977), i, 163–4
IRATI ANTONIO, JOHN M. SCHECHTER

Carwithen, Doreen (*b* Haddenham, Bucks., 15 Nov 1922). English composer. She learnt the cello with Peers Coetmore (1938–41) before entering the RAM in 1941 where her first study was piano. After winning all composition prizes at the Academy she became a sub-professor of composition there from 1946 to 1948. From 1946 to 1961 she also lectured in music at Furzedown College, London. She came to notice with her first orchestral work, an overture suggested by John Masefield's novel *Odtaa*, which was performed by the LPO under Adrian Boult in 1947 and later broadcast. A second overture, *Bishop Rock* (1952), and a Concerto for Piano and Strings (1946–8) confirmed her promise. She was the first composer chosen from the RAM for the J. Arthur Rank Apprenticeship Scheme in 1947 to study film music and she wrote music for over 30 films,

including the official film of the Coronation and two films in which music took the place of dialogue: *The Stranger Left No Card* (1952) and *On the Twelfth Day* (1954). Among her chamber works are *Five Diversions* for wind quintet (1953), three string quartets, a violin sonata and a piano sonatina (1951). In 1961 she became amanuensis and literary secretary to the composer William Alwyn, whom she later married.

LEWIS FOREMAN

Casagemas (y Coll), Luisa (*b* Barcelona, 13 Dec 1863; *d* ? after 1894). Spanish composer. She studied harmony and composition with Francisco Sánchez Gavañach, singing with Giovannina Bardelli, and violin with Agustín Torelló. She began composing early, but the first public performance of her music was in 1893, when *Crepúsculo* was given by the Orquesta Catalana de Conciertos. Between the ages of 16 and 18 she composed an opera, *Schiava e regina*, which was awarded a prize in 1892 in connection with the World's Columbian Exposition in Chicago. It was to have been performed at the Liceu theatre in Barcelona in 1893, but was abandoned after an anarchist attack on the Liceu on 7 November of that year. The royal family arranged for the first performance of excerpts from it in the royal palace, Madrid, in 1894, and some numbers were published in arrangements for voice and piano. Also in Madrid, the novelist Emilia Pardo Bazán introduced her to her friends at a soirée performance of *Schiava e regina*: Casagemas performed passages on the piano, among them the Dance of the Spirits, the tenor *romanza* and the Persian March. She also sang other pieces, including her setting of a *letrilla* by Eusebio Blasco.

Pedrell (*Diccionario*) mentions 110 pieces for voice and piano (19 of which were published), 12 piano solos (five published), 17 pieces for various instruments (one published), and a four-act opera, *I briganti*; *Monserrat* is numbered op.227.

WORKS
selective list

Stage: Schiava e regina (3, J. Barret), *c*1880; I briganti (4)

Orch: Crepúsculo

Sacred: Ave María, antiphon, 1v; Monserrat op.227

Songs (for 1v, pf unless otherwise stated): Album de piezas para canto y piano, *E-Mc*; Il lamento della Chisa; Montserrat (N. Llopis), *Mn*; O dolce bacio, 1v, orch; Tu mi salvasti, amor;

Pf: Aires de Cataluña; Crepúsculo; Gran fantasía sobre la ópera Los amantes de Teruel

BIBLIOGRAPHY
F. Pedrell: 'Las mujeres compositoras', *Ilustración musical española*, no.144, p.3

'Luisa Casagemas', *Ilustración musical española*, no.144, p.74

F. Pedrell: *Diccionario biográfico y bibliográfico de músicos y escritores de música españoles . . . antiguos y modernos* (Barcelona, 1894–7) [incl. list of works]

EMILIO CASARES RODICIO

Casella, Felicita [née Lacombe, Félicie] (*b* ?Bourges, *c*1820; *d* after 1865). Italian composer and singer of French birth. She was a sister of the composer and pianist Louis Lacombe; by 1849 she was married to the Italian composer and cellist Cesare Casella with whom she went to Oporto. Her Portuguese opera *Haydée* (or *Haidée*; libretto by Luiz Felipe Leite after Alexandre Dumas' *Le Comte de Monte Cristo*) was given in Oporto in 1849 and, in revised form, at the Teatro Dona Maria in Lisbon on 16 June 1853, when she sang the principal role. Her second opera, *Cristoforo Colombo* (libretto by Felice Romani), was given at the Théâtre Impérial in Nice in 1865. Among her other works are romances, a *Marcia funebre* (for Maria II) for piano and an *Ave verum* for voice and piano; some of her works were issued by Ricordi.

BIBLIOGRAPHY

FétisBS

Castegnaro, Lola [Lolita] (*b* San José, Costa Rica, 16 May 1900; *d* Mexico City, Sept 1979). Costa Rican composer, conductor and singing teacher. Her first teacher was her father, the Italian-born composer Alvise Castegnaro who had emigrated to Costa Rica in 1893; she later studied singing and piano at the Milan Conservatory. After a period writing music in Paris, she returned to Costa Rica in 1941 and during the next four years gave radio broadcasts. She successfully conducted seasons of opera and was guest conductor of the National SO. In 1945 she moved to Mexico, where she remained, establishing her reputation as a composer, pianist and singing teacher; she also worked as a journalist and wrote a short biography of her father (in *Revista musical* [Costa Rica], i/7–8, 1944). Her output includes works in popular Latin-American genres and other light music, more substantial compositions such as the operetta *Mirka* and a suite for orchestra, and songs.

BIBLIOGRAPHY

J. R. Araya: *Vida musical de Costa Rica* (San José, 1942)

F. Z. Bernal: *La música en Costa Rica* (San José, 1978)

J. L. ACEVEDO VARGAS

Castelloza (*fl* early 13th century). Troubadour. A noblewoman from the

Auvergne, she was the wife of Turc de Mairona. Three of her poems are extant, but without music.

BIBLIOGRAPHY

M. Bogin: *The Women Troubadours* (New York, 1976), 118–29, 175

MARIA V. COLDWELL

Castro-Robinson, Eve de (*b* London, 9 Nov 1956). New Zealand composer. She grew up in a musical household and at the age of five went to New Zealand with her family. After a variety of occupations, she began studies at the University of Auckland (BMus 1985, MMus 1987 and DMus, in composition, 1991), where her principal teachers were John Rimmer and John Elmsly. She was composer-in-residence with the Auckland PO in 1991. In 1992 Radio New Zealand selected her Triple Clarinet Concerto (for Eb, Bb and bass clarinet) as their entry in the International UNESCO Rostrum in Paris.

The Karlheinz Company has performed a number of her works in Auckland, where she has organized concerts of new music (1985–7). Richard Bolley (*Music in New Zealand*, xii, aut. 1991, pp.18–22) was impressed by her 'colour, vitality and incisiveness . . . There quickly emerges also a deliciously knowing sense of humour. And, not surprisingly, all these qualities are found in her music . . . [it] is often dense and complex, rhythmically and texturally rigorous and, most pronounced of all, it inclines towards abstract expressionism'.

WORKS

Orch: Peregrinations, pf, orch, 1987, rev. 1990; Aurora, fanfare, orch, 1990; Triple Cl Conc., 3 cl, orch, 1991

Chamber and solo inst: Stringencies, 11 solo str, 1986; Conundrums, perc + painter, 1987; Undercurrents, cl, 1987; A Resonance of Emerald, t sax, tpt, trbn, hpd, pf, perc, va, vc, db, 1988, rev. 1990; 5 Responses, 6 women's vv, mixed ens, 1989; Countercurrents, t sax, 1989; Split the Lark, vn, pf, 1991; Noah's Ark, pic, fl, cl, a sax, 2 tpt, 2 trbn, 2 perc, 1991; Tumbling Strains, vn, vc, 1992; Tingling Strings, pf, 1993

J. M. THOMSON

Casulana [Mezari], **Maddalena** (*b* ?Casole d'Elsa, nr Siena, *c*1544; *fl* Vicenza, 1566–83). Italian composer, lutenist and singer. The name seems to indicate an origin in Casole d'Elsa; Piccolomini claims her for Siena but knows little about her. Nothing is known to tie her to any place except Vicenza – as early as 1569 she was described as 'Vicentina'.

Her three books of madrigals are the first by a woman composer to be printed. They contain 66 madrigals, of which five previously appeared in anthologies; another is uniquely found in an anthology. *Primo libro de madrigali a quattro voci* (Venice, 1568) was dedicated to Isabella de' Medici Orsina (a noted patron and musical amateur),

not only to give witness to my devotion to Your Excellency, but also to show to the world (to the degree that it is granted to me in this profession of music) the foolish error of men, who so greatly believe themselves to be the masters of high intellectual gifts that [these gifts] cannot, it seems to them, be equally common among women.

This spirited manifesto shows Casulana to be a woman of pride and confidence. She was already a well-known composer and had set an epithalamium *Nil mage iucundum*, in five parts, for a royal wedding in Munich earlier in 1568. Also in that year Antonio Molino, the Venetian merchant, actor and whimsical writer, dedicated to Casulana his *Dilettevoli madrigali a quattro, libro primo*, products, he said, of old age, written after studying music with her. It includes settings of three poems written in Casulana's praise, one in dialect.

In 1569 the Vicentine poet Giambattista Maganza published a canzone in dialect dedicated to 'Signora Madalena Casulana Vicentina'. In May 1570 Casulana dedicated her *Secondo libro de' madrigali a quattro voci* to Don Antonio Londonio, a highly placed official in Milan whose wife, Isabella, was a noted singer. For the next 12 years nothing is known of her. Giambattista Crispolti describes a banquet in Perugia in 1582, after which 'La Casolana famosa . . . cantò al liuto di musica divinamente'. In August 1582 the publisher Angelo Gardano dedicated to 'la Signora Madalena Casulana di Mezarii' his edition of Monte's *Primo libro de madrigali a tre voci*, imploring Casulana to favour him with some compositions in this now neglected genre. 'Di Mezarii', probably her married name, appears on the title-page of her next and last surviving book of music, *Di Madalena Mezari detta Casulana Vicentina, Il primo libro de madrigali a cinque voci*. On 18 January 1583 Casulana performed at a meeting of the Accademia Olimpica in Vicenza, which at one time owned a portrait of her.

Casulana's madrigals show her to have been an original musical thinker, with a very personal style, but they suffer from a tendency to make each madrigal a catalogue of word-painting devices. Her texts include poems of her own and by Petrarch, Caro, Tansillo, Sannazaro, Serafino Aquilano, Vincenzo Quirino, Bernardo Tasso and G. B. Strozzi.

Flaws in the music probably result from the lack of an able and demanding teacher. Points of imitation are few and poorly handled: undistinguished themes are imitated at too close an interval to contrast with the generally homophonic texture. There is a tendency to overuse chromatic alteration and aimless harmonic juxtapositions. Mannerisms include excessive crossing of voices, awkward ranges, much use of second inversions and too frequent parallel 5ths and octaves. These weaknesses, however, are often eclipsed by original and stunning effects. Textures, sometimes monotonous and cramped, at other times provide effective contrast, as in passages with a dramatic opposition between high and low registers, or passages in the style of *falsobordone*. Harmonic effects are often striking. Sometimes a long line is created: in one the line rises slowly and dramatically, as well as chromatically, to the climax. Casulana's use of dissonance is generally masterful and modern. Her music is also liberally sprinkled with dominant 7th chords, approached and resolved in the normal way, at a time when this chord can hardly be found in the music of composers such as Rore, Willaert or Lassus. She also uses 'secondary dominants' (as they are now known) with confidence and skill.

WORKS

Edition: B. Pescerelli, ed.: *I madrigali di Maddalena Casulana* (Florence, 1979)

Il primo libro de madrigali, 4vv (Venice, 1568; repr., Brescia, 1583)

Il secondo libro de madrigali, 4vv (Venice, 1570)

Il primo libro de madrigali, 5vv (Venice, 1583)

Works in: 1566[2], 1567[16], 1586[12]

Wedding piece: 5vv, perf. Munich, 1568, music lost

Madrigali spirituali, books 1 and 2, 4vv (Venice, ?1591), lost

BIBLIOGRAPHY

FétisB; *GerberNL*; *SainsburyD*; *SchmidlD*; *WaltherML*

M. Troiano: *Dialoghi* (Venice, 1569), ff.123*v*–124

La terza parte de le rime di Magagnò, Menon e Begotto (Venice, 1569), ff.177–81

N. Tagliaferro: *L'esercitio de Nicolò Taglia Ferro* (MS, Naples, Biblioteca dei Gerolamini, SM. XXVIII.1.66), f.83*r*

G. Piccolomini: *Siena illustre per antichità* (MS, *I-Sc*, C II 23), ff.239*r*, 240*r*

I-Vlb Accademia Olimpica, busta I, libro A, p.77

A. Borsetti: *Supplemento al compendio historico del Signor D. Marc'Antonio Guarini Ferrarese* (Ferrara, 1670), 196–7

A. Fabretti, ed.: *Cronache della città di Perugia*, iv (Turin, 1892), 79

F. Waldner: 'Zwei Inventarien aus dem XVI. und XVII. Jahrhundert über hintergelassene Musikinstrumente und Musikalien am Innsbrucker Hofe', *SMw*, iv (1916), 128–47, esp. 131 n.41, n.43, n.44

G. Thibault: 'Deux catalogues de libraires musicaux:

Vincenti et Gardane (Venise 1591)', *RdM*, x (1929), 179

A. Einstein: *The Italian Madrigal* (Princeton, 1949), ii, 527

A. Newcomb: *The Madrigal at Ferrara 1579–1597* (Princeton, 1980), i, 218–19

THOMAS W. BRIDGES

Catunda, Eunice (*b* Rio de Janeiro, 14 March 1915). Brazilian pianist and composer. She studied the piano with Oscar Guanabarino and Marieta Lion, and composition with Furio Franceschini and Camargo Guarnieri. H. J. Koellreutter instructed her in the use of 12-note technique, and she was also a conducting student of Hermann Scherchen, who performed her *Quatro cantos à morte* in 1949. An excellent pianist and an original composer, she has combined folk elements with 12-note writing in her *Homenagem a Schoenberg*, which was performed at the 1950 ISCM Festival. Her *Negrinho do pastoreio* is a cantata for three voices, guitar, flute and percussion. She has taught composition at the Rio de Janeiro conservatory and musicology at the University of Brasília.

WORKS
selective list

Choral: Negrinho do pastoreio, cantata, 3vv, fl, gui, perc, 1946; Cantata do soldado morto, chorus, small orch, 1965

Orch: 4 cantos à morte, 1948; A negrinha e Iemanjá, chorus, orch, 1955; Pf conc., 1955

Inst: Homenagem a Schoenberg, cl, va, vc, pf, 1949; Serestas, 4 sax, 1956; 2 serestas, gui, 1972

Pf: Momento de Lorca, 1957; 4 momentos de Rilke, 1958; Sonata de louvação, 1960; Sonata fúnebre, 1970

IRATI ANTONIO, JOHN M. SCHECHTER

Č'ebotaryan, Gayane (Movses) (*b* Rostov-on-Don, 8 Nov 1918). Armenian composer and musicologist. A graduate of the Leningrad Conservatory, she studied composition with K'. K'ušnaryan and piano with Khalfin. In 1947 she began teaching at the Erevan Conservatory, where she set up a special course to research into the polyphonic aspects of Armenian music; her work on polyphony in the music of Aram Khachaturian was published in 1969. She was made an Honoured Art Worker of the Armenian SSR in 1965 and appointed professor of composition in 1977. Although her work incorporates certain national characteristics, both melodic and rhythmic, it also manifests elements of the classic Russian tradition. Č'ebotaryan's music is melodious, striving for simplicity and clarity of expression. A mood of restrained melancholy, however, is pervasive in many of her compositions.

WORKS
selective list

Hayastan [Armenia], cantata, 1947

Orch: Tonakatarut'yun [Festivity], 1950; Pf Conc., 1980

Inst: Pf Sonata, 1943; Str Trio, 1948; Pf Preludes, 1948; Polifonik albom patanekut'yan hamar [Polyphonic Album for Youth], pf, 1972; Posvyashchenia [Dedication], pf, 1972; Str Qts, 1978, 1990; 12 Pieces on Popular Themes, pf, 1991

Songs, choral works, folksong arrs.

Principal publishers: Haypethrat, Sovetskïy Kompozitor

BIBLIOGRAPHY

A. T'adevosyan, ed.: *Sovetakan Hayastani eraštut'yunĕ* [The Music of Soviet Armenia] (Erevan, 1973), 258, 397–403

E. Gilina: *Gayane Chebotaryan* (Erevan, 1979)

ŞAHAN ARZRUNI

Cecchi, Gabriella (*b* Riccò del Golfo, La Spezia, 3 Nov 1944). Italian composer. She began to study music at the age of 16 and graduated as a pianist from the Istituto Musicale, Lucca, in 1970. Before devoting herself to composition, she took courses in Renaissance music and music education; she was a member of a polyphonic choir for two years and taught in schools. From 1974 to 1977 she studied harmony and counterpoint at the conservatory in Genoa, then attended Franco Donatoni's courses at the Accademia Chigiana in Siena, where she was awarded a diploma of merit (1982) for composition. She also studied with Brian Ferneyhough, Francesco Pennisi and Fabio Vacchi. She is active as performer, organizer and teacher, and works on magazines and newspapers. She won the 'Athena' prize for music in 1988.

Cecchi has progressed from her earlier studies and rigorous compositional experiments towards a freer, more pliant style of writing; her works are nevertheless always complex in structure, sometimes to the point where they are linked by a tight network of references: fragments of pre-existing compositions are used to generate new works, as in the case of *Riverberi*, which is constructed from a quotation from *Mutazioni*. Her compositions are performed at major festivals in Italy and elsewhere.

WORKS
selective list

A specchio, 2 fl, 1977; Solo, fl, 1980; Kite, chamber orch, 1981; In proiezione, orch, 1986; Mutazioni, cl, pf, 1986; 5 carte da gioco, reciter, mime, pf, 1987; Riverberi, vn, hpd, 1988; Riferimento, reciter, pf, 1989; X 1, 'operina' for children, 1989; Parvula, 10 fl, 1990

PAOLA DAMIANI

Cecconi-Botella, Monic (*b* Courbevoie, 30 Sept 1936). French composer. She studied at the Paris Conservatoire with Maurice Duruflé (harmony) and Jean Rivier (composition), and in 1966 received the Prix de Rome. From 1973 to 1975, as well as continuing to compose, she organized the concerts of modern music given by the ensemble L'Itinéraire. From 1978 she taught composition and musical analysis, becoming a professor at the Paris Conservatoire in 1982. She is particularly drawn to the operatic idiom; here her vocal writing owes much to the lyric tradition, while her orchestral writing is charged with dramatic tension. In *Imaginaires* (1968), for percussion and dancer, a series of explorations of the combination of the visual and auditory arts, she has combined this love of the theatre with a strong pictorial sensibility. Conceiving music as sound-mass, she uses *musique concrète* to widen her colour spectrum further, but in this rich and vibrant musical universe humour too has a place; this is achieved by compositional subtleties which, despite her true stylistic independence, link her to identifiable traditions in French music.

WORKS
selective list
Dramatic: Il était une fois l'été (opéra-film), S, chamber orch, tape, 1976; Scoop: état de siège en Pologne (mini-opéra, Cecconi-Botella), 3 solo vv, 2 cl, b cl, 3 vc, 1982; Noctuaile (R. David), 8 female vv, chamber orch, 1983; La femme de l'ogre (opéra-conte, P. Fleutiaux), 4 solo vv, chorus, children's chorus, chamber orch, 1986–8; Il signait Vincent (opéra-passion, J. Unal), 7 solo vv, 2 actors, choir, orch, 1987–90; Opéraclown (opera for and by children, R. Pillot), 4 solo vv, 2 actors, children's choirs, 11 insts, 1992; Le triangle de cristal (opera for and by children, F. Arquetout), 3 solo vv, 2 actors, inst ens, 1992
Vocal: Chansons du jour et de la nuit (P. Soupault), S, pf, 1963; Chercher le silence (Soupault), S, vn, vc, pf, 1964; 3 mélodies (Charles d'Orléans, Rutebeuf), S, pf, 1964; 3 méditations pour le temps de Pâques (Soupault), S, pf, 1965; Vocale, S, 3 perc, 1969; Instants, Mez, cl, str orch, 1970; Conte glacé (J. Sternberg), reciter + hpd, 1976; Bestiaire inimaginaire (David), haute-contre/Mez, pf, 1984
Inst: Ellipseis, pf, 1967; Imaginaires, 6 perc, dancer, 1968; Correspondances, orch, 1968–9; Imaginables, 4 perc, 1969; Alpha, 4 perc, 6 gui, 1970–71; D'ailleurs, 2 ondes martenot, perc, el gui, 1972; Nova, chamber orch, 1972; Silences, ob, cl, sax, bn, 1972; Hommage à . . . , 3 qts: ob, cl, sax, bn, and 2 str qts, db, 1974; URP, chamber orch, 1974;

Impromptu, ob, hpd, 1976; Castafioritures, ondes martenot, 1982; Argile, perc, str ens, 1991–2

Principal publishers: Editions Françaises, Leduc, Rideau Rouge

FRANÇOISE ANDRIEUX

Cenova, Julia (*b* Sofia, 30 July 1948). Bulgarian composer and pianist. She graduated in 1972 from the Sofia State Academy of Music, where her teachers were Pancho Vladigerov (composition) and Bogomil Starshinov (piano), and in 1980 returned there as lecturer in jazz and popular music. As a pianist she performs both classical music and light music (in piano bars). Her own compositions, many of which are chamber works, are very free and full of large-scale intellectual invention. They draw on such varied sources as Bulgarian classical and folk traditions, jazz and contemporary classical music. A laconic sense of humour is particularly evident in her children's musicals and in her film and television scores. Many of her latest works concern contemporary issues of music theatre.

WORKS
selective list
Orch: Sym., pf, orch, 1972; Movts, 1981; Festive Music, 1985; Fresco, female folk chorus, orch, 1992
Inst: 3 Pieces with Epilogue, va, pf, 1978; Step and Ragtime, 1984; Introduction and Epilogue, fl, harp, 1985; Cantus firmus a due, 1987; Music in the Pause, pf, va, db, tape, 1988; Music for 3, or Music for Mice, fl, cl, bn, 1986
Vocal: 5 Songs, unacc. chamber choir, 1978; Indian Songs, A, 1980; Monday to Friday, jazz cycle, 1v, db, 1984; Sinking into the Poles, 7vv, 1990

Principal publisher: Muzika

MAGDALENA MANOLOVA

Centa della Morea. *See* GARELLI DELLA MOREA DE CARDENAS, VINCENZA.

Cesis, Sulpitia (*fl* 1619). Italian composer. She was a nun at the convent of S Agostino, Modena, and is known only by her volume of eight-part *Motetti spirituali* (Modena, 1619).

BIBLIOGRAPHY
L. F. Valdrighi: 'Continuazione delle annotazioni bio-bibliografiche intorno a musicisti modenesi e degli stati già estensi', *Atti e memorie delle RR. Deputazioni di storia patria per le provincie dell'Emilia*, new ser., vii/1 (1881), 56

Chaminade, Cécile (Louise Stéphanie) (*b* Paris, 8 Aug 1857; *d* Monte Carlo, 13 April 1944). French composer and pianist. While it is striking that nearly all of Chaminade's approximately 400 compositions were published, even more striking is the sharp decline in her reputation as the 20th century progressed. This is partly attributable to modernism and a general disparagement of late-Romantic French music, but it is also due to the socio-aesthetic conditions affecting women and their music.

Cécile Chaminade

The third of four surviving children, Chaminade received her earliest musical instruction from her mother, a pianist and singer, her first pieces date from the mid-1860s. Because of paternal opposition to her enrolling at the Paris Conservatoire, she studied privately with members of its faculty: Félix Le Couppey, Antoine Marmontel, M.-G.-A. Savard and Benjamin Godard. In the early 1880s Chaminade began to compose in earnest, and works such as the first piano trio op.11 (1880) and the *Suite d'orchestre* op.20 (1881) were well received. She essayed an *opéra comique*, *La Sévillane*, which had a private performance (23 February 1882). Other major works of the decade were the *ballet symphonique Callirhoë* op.37, performed at Marseilles on 16 March 1888; the popular *Concertstück* op.40 for piano and orchestra, which was given its première at Antwerp on 18 April 1888; and *Les amazones*, a *symphonie dramatique*, given on the same

day. After 1890, with the notable exception of the Concertino op.107, commissioned by the Conservatoire (1902), and her only piano sonata (op.21, 1895), Chaminade composed mainly character pieces and *mélodies*. Though the narrower focus may have been due to financial, aesthetic, or discriminatory considerations, this music became very popular, especially in England and the USA; and Chaminade helped to promote sales through extensive concert tours. From 1892 she performed regularly in England and became a welcome guest of Queen Victoria and others.

Meanwhile, enthusiasm grew in the USA, largely through the many Chaminade clubs formed around 1900, and in autumn 1908 she finally agreed to make the arduous journey there. She appeared in 12 cities, from Boston to St Louis, and the tour was a financial success; critical evaluation, however, was mixed.

Prestigious awards began to come her way, culminating in admission to the Légion d'Honneur in 1913 – the first time it was granted to a female composer. Nonetheless, the award was belated and ironic considering that she had been largely ignored in France for some 20 years. In August 1901 Chaminade married Louis-Mathieu Carbonel, an elderly Marseilles music publisher, in what may have been a platonic arrangement; he died in 1907 and she never remarried. While her compositional activity eventually subsided because of World War I and deteriorating health, Chaminade made several recordings, many of them piano rolls, between 1901 and 1914. In later years she was tended by her niece, Antoinette Lorel, who attempted to promote Chaminade's music after her death in 1944.

Chaminade was well aware of the social and personal difficulties facing a woman composer, and she suggested that perseverance and special circumstances are needed to overcome them (*Washington Post*, 1 November 1908). Her output is noteworthy among women composers for its quantity, its high percentage of published works and for the fact that a large portion – notably piano works and *mélodies* – was apparently composed expressly for publication and its attendant sales (Enoch was the main publisher). Chaminade composed almost 200 piano works, most of them character pieces (e.g. *Scarf Dance*, 1888), and more than 125 *mélodies* (e.g. *L'anneau d'argent*, 1891); these two genres formed the basis of her popularity. Stylistically, her music is tuneful and

Title-page, designed by Barbandy, of 'Aux dieux sylvains', op.100 (Paris: Enoch, 1900), for female choir, by Cécile Chaminade

accessible, with memorable melodies, clear textures and mildly chromatic harmonies. Its emphasis on wit and colour is typically French. Many works seem inspired by dance, for example *Scarf Dance* and *La lisonjera*. Of her larger works, the one-movement *Concertstück* recalls aspects of Wagner and Liszt, while the three-movement Piano Sonata shows the formal and expressive experimentation that was typical of the genre by the late 19th century (see Citron 1993 for a feminist analysis of the first movement). The *mélodies* are idiomatic for the voice and well-suited expressively and poetically to the ambience of the *salon* or the recital hall, the likely sites for such works. The Concertino has remained a staple of the flute repertory; while it is a large-scale work and thus represents a relatively small part of her output, the piece still provides a sense of the elegance and attractiveness of Chaminade's music.

WORKS

selective list; printed works published in Paris unless otherwise stated

For a complete list see Citron 1993 and Tardif.

La Sévillane (opéra comique), private perf., 23 Feb 1882
Suite d'orchestre, op.20 (1881)
Les amazones, symphonie dramatique (O. Grandmougin), op.26, vv, orch; vs (*c*1888)
Callirhoë (ballet symphonique), E. Rougier), Marseilles, 16 March 1888; orch suite, op.37, *c*1890
Concertstück, op.40, pf, orch (*c*1893)
Concertino, op.107, fl, orch (*c*1902)
Chamber works incl. 2 pf trios, op.11 (1881), op.34 (1887); 3 morceaux, op.31, vn, pf (Breslau, *c*1885); Chanson (Sérénade) espagnole, op.150, vn, pf (1903) [transcr. of mélodie; transcr. F. Kreisler (1925)]
*c*200 works for pf, incl. 2 Mazurkas, [op.1] (1869); Sonata, c, op.21 (1895); Libellules, op.24 (1881); Etude symphonique, op.28 (1890); Sérénade, op.29 (1884); 6 études de concert, op.35 (1886); Scarf Dance (1888) [from op.37]; La lisonjera, op.50 (Milan, *c*1890); Valse carnavalesque, op.73, 2 pf (1894); 3 danses anciennes, op.95 (1899); Caprice

humoristique, op.113 (1904); Contes bleus, op.122 (1906); Etude humoristique, op.138 (1910); Berceuse du petit soldat blessé, op.156 (1919) c125 mélodies, 1v, pf, incl. L'heure du mystère (P. Barbier) (c1878); Ritournelle (F. Coppée) (1886); L'anneau d'argent (R. Gérard) (1891); Tu me dirais (Gérard) (1891); Si j'étais jardinier (R. Milès) (1893); Viatique (E. Manuel) (1895); Fleur du matin (C. Fuster) (1896); Mon coeur chante (Fuster) (1896); Nuit d'été (Fuster) (1896); Au pays bleu (Fuster) (1898); Reste (R. Myriel) (1899); Ecrin (R. Niverd) (1902); Amour invisible (1905); Les heureuses (1909); Le village (1915); L'anneau du soldat (Gérard) (1916)

BIBLIOGRAPHY

SchmidlD
R. Hughes: 'Women Composers', Century Magazine, lv (1898), 768–79
C. Chaminade: 'How to Sing and Play my Compositions', The Ladies Home Journal, no.22 (1905), Nov, 19
—— : 'How to Play my Best Known Pieces', The Etude, xxvi (1908), 759–60
P. Barillon-Bauché: Augusta Holmès et la femme compositeur (Paris, 1912)
M. J. Citron: Cécile Chaminade: a Bio-Bibliography (Westport, CT, 1988)
—— : 'Women Composers and Musicians in Europe, 1880 to 1918', Women and Music: a History, ed. K. Pendle (Bloomington, IN, 1991), 123–41
—— : Gender and the Musical Canon (Cambridge, 1993)
C. Tardif: Portrait de Cécile Chaminade (Montreal, 1993)

MARCIA J. CITRON

Champgrand, Sophie de. See BAWR, SOPHIE DE.

Chance, Nancy Laird (b Cincinnati, 19 March 1931). American composer and pianist. She studied theory and composition with Vladimir Ussachevsky, Otto Luening and Chou Wen-chung at Columbia University. She received the ASCAP/Nissim prize for orchestral composition twice (1981, Liturgy; 1984, Odysseus), as well as two awards from the NEA and three fellowships from the MacDowell Colony. Her commissioned works include Planasthai (Cleveland Orchestra, 1991), In Paradisium (Florilegium Chamber Choir, 1987) and the Woodwind Quintet (Quintet of the Americas, 1983), and her works have also been performed by the Philadelphia Orchestra, the St Louis SO, the Da Capo Chamber Players and other contemporary chamber ensembles in New York. The New York Times (June 1985), writing of Rhapsodia, described her music as 'densely plotted series of aural clusters . . . gnarled sounds that expand and contract with a violent poetry'. Several of her works have been recorded on Opus One.

WORKS
selective list

Orch: Liturgy, 1979; Odysseus, suite, 1983; Planasthai, 1991
Other inst (for chamber ens unless otherwise stated): Darksong, 1972; Edensong, 1973; Daysongs, 1974; Ritual Sounds, 1975; Ceremonial, 1976; Declamation and Song, 1977; Duos II, ob, eng hn, 1978; Duos III, vn, vc, 1980; Exultation and Lament, a sax, timp, 1980; Solemnities, 1981; Ww Qnt, 1983; Rhapsodia, 1984; Str Qt no.1, 1984–5; Elegy, str orch, 1986; Heat and Silence, 1989
Choral (with orch unless otherwise stated): Domine, Dominus, motet, double chorus unacc., 1964; Odysseus, 1981–3; In Paradisium, 1986–7, chamber version, 1987; Last Images, chorus, chamber orch, synth, 1988; Pie Jesu, Libera me, Hosanna and Benedictus, 1990
Other vocal: 3 Rilke Songs, S, fl, eng hn, vc, 1966; Duos I, S, fl, 1975; Say the Good Words, 1v, synth, 1989

CYNTHIA GREEN LIBBY

Charbonnier, Janine (b Paris, 8 June 1926). French composer and pianist. After studying the piano at the Paris Conservatoire, she committed herself initially to teaching and performing. Her first compositions date from the 1960s and show the influence of her collaboration with Pierre Barbaud and his Groupe de Musique Algorithmique in Paris. Her systematized compositional method, based on mathematical principles, governs not only the form of her works (for example in Générateur I et II and Raison inverse) but also their basic musical materials (Galiens, Réseaux aériens, Hommage à Vera Molnar). Rhythm and timbre are the essential elements of the resulting discourse.

WORKS
selective list

MUSIC THEATRE

Réseaux aériens (M. Butor), actors, pf, hpd, 1962; Conditionnement (Butor), actors, chamber ens, 1968; Montagnes rocheuses (Butor), 1v, actor, tpt, trbn, tape, 1972; Circus (after M. Roche), 1v, actors, cl, tpt, trbn, 2 perc, db, tape, 1973

ENSEMBLE

Générateur I et II 'Hommage à Blaise Pascal', fl, cl, b cl, hn, tpt, trbn, mar, 2 perc, pf, vn, db, 1962; Trajets 'Hommage à J. L. Borges', 2 vn, va, vc, db, ondes martenot, 1964; 01 Hommage à Leibniz, cl, b cl, tpt, trbn, 2 perc, pf, db, ondes martenot, 1966; 01 10 Hommage à Leibniz, 2 tpt, 2 trbn, 2 perc, pf, 2 vn, va, vc, db, ondes martenot, 1970; Filtres, chamber orch, perc, 1972; Raison inverse 'Hommage à Newton', 2 vn, va, vc, db, trbn, perc, 1977; 240 jours météo, trbn, db, perc, 1982; Galiens 'Hommage à Evariste Galois', chamber orch, 1983

OTHER WORKS

Homotopies, tpt, tape, 1970; Hommage à Vera Molnar, perc, 1980

Principal publishers: Editions de la Radio, Editions
Françaises

FRANÇOISE ANDRIEUX

Chazal, Mrs. *See* GAMBARINI, ELISABETTA
DE.

Chebotaryan,   Gayane.   *See*
Č'EBOTARYAN, GAYANE.

Chefaliady-Taban, Maria (*b* Iaşi, 4 Nov
1863; *d* Bucharest, 11 June 1932). Romanian
composer, pianist and teacher. She studied at
the Iaşi Conservatory (1881–3) with Anetta
Boscoff (piano) and Enrico Mezetti (theory
and solfège), then at the Akademie für Musik
und Darstellende Kunst in Vienna (1883–5)
with Joseph Dachs (piano), Adolf Prosnitz
(theory and solfège), the younger Joseph
Hellmesberger (chamber music) and Josef
Gänsbacher (singing, choir). She made her
début as a pianist in Iaşi (11 Nov 1880),
playing Bach, Beethoven, Schumann and
Grieg. She taught at the Humpel Girls'
Institute in Iaşi and in Bucharest; her
students included Adelina Kneisel, Julieta
Missir, Aurelia Protopopescu and Mircea
Ştefănescu. Her music is romantic in style,
influenced by folk elements in works such as
Hora cărturarului Urechia ('Scholar Urechia's
Ring Dance').

WORKS
selective list
Inst: Rêverie poétique, pf (1890); Myosotis Mazurka,
pf (Vienna, 1896); Le lys, pf (Vienna, 1896); Aveu
du coeur, vn, pf (Bucharest, 1899); Avancez soldats,
march, pf (Leipzig, 1899); Marche turque, pf (1899);
Caresses des vagues, pf (1900)
Choral: Pînă cînd? [Since When?] (V. A. Urechia)
chorus, pf (1901); Hora cărturarului Urechia
[Scholar Urechia's Ring Dance] (Urechia), chorus
5vv, pf (Leipzig, 1901); Imnul studenţilor universit-
ari români [Romanian Students' Anthem] (N.
Burlănescu-Alin), chorus 5vv, pf (1901); Marş
eroic: Mărăşeşti şi Oituz [Heroic March: Mărăşeşti
and Oituz], chorus 2vv, pf (1917)
Songs: Atit de fragedă [So Tender] (M. Eminescu),
romance, 1v, pf (1900); Balada nebunului [Fool's
Ballad] (H. Lecca), 1v, pf; Nu mă inţelegi [You
don't Understand me] (Eminescu), 1v, pf (1905);
O, rămîi [Oh, don't Go] (Eminescu), 1v, pf (1905)

BIBLIOGRAPHY
V. Cosma: 'O reprezentantă a şcolii noastre pianistice
din trecut' [A Representative of our Past Piano
School], *Muzica*, xiv/7 (1964)

VIOREL COSMA

Chen Yi (*b* Guangzhou, 4 April 1953).
Chinese composer and violinist. She began
to learn the violin and piano at the age of
three; because of the Cultural Revolution she
was forced to practise in secret and was sent
to work in the countryside for two years,
gaining a deep understanding of her country
and its people. From 1970 to 1978 she was
leader of the orchestra and resident composer
for the Beijing Opera Troupe in Guangzhou.
She went on to study composition with Wu
Zuqiang and Alexander Goehr at the Beijing
Central Conservatory (BA 1983, MA 1986).
From 1979 to 1986 she carried out field research into the folk music of seven Chinese
provinces, then moved to New York to
study composition with Chou Wen-chung
and Mario Davidovsky at Columbia
University (DMA 1993). Chen Yi was in the
vanguard of the 'New Wave' of Chinese
composers who came of age in the 1980s.
Two of her compositions won first prizes in
national Chinese competitions: the String
Quartet in 1982 and the piano piece *Duo Ye*
(1984) in 1985. It was the rhythmic strength
and spirit of the latter work that established
her reputation; it has been widely performed
in both its original and orchestrated versions.
Her *Duo Ye* no.2 (1987) was commissioned
by the Central PO of Beijing for American
and European tours; she has also received
commissions from the Brooklyn PO,
Women's Philharmonic and Hong Kong
Chinese Orchestra and appointments as
composer-in-residence to several organizations. Although she has settled in New
York, Chen Yi has described her music as
having 'Chinese blood', and in it she strives
to fuse Eastern and Western elements.

WORKS
Orch: Xian shi [String Poem], va, orch, 1983; Duo
Ye, chamber orch, 1985 [arr. of pf work]; Sprout
(Meng), str, 1986; Sym. no.1, 1986; Music for Two
Wind and Perc Ensembles, 1986; Duo Ye no.2,
1987; Ov., Chin. orch, 1989; Ov. no.2, Chin. orch,
1990; Pf Conc., 1992; Pipa Rhyme, pipa, chamber
orch, 1993; Sym. no.2, 1993; Ge Xu (Antiphony),
chamber orch, 1994; Shuo, str orch, 1994
Choral: 3 Poems from the Song Dynasty, SATB,
1985
Chamber and inst: Str Qt, 1982; Ww Qnt, 1987; As in
a Dream, S, vn, vc, 1988; Near Distance, fl + a fl, cl
+ b cl, vn, vc, pf, perc, 1988; The Tide, Chin. insts,
1988; The Points, pipa, 1991; Suite, Chin. inst qnt,
1991; Sparkle, fl + pic, Eb cl, 2 perc, pf, vn, vc, db,
1992; Monologue (Impressions on 'The True Story
of Ah Q'), cl, 1993
Pf solo: Variations on the Theme of Awariguli, 1979;
Duo ye, 1984; Yu diao, 1985; Guessing, 1989; Small
Beijing Gong, 1993
Principal publisher: Presser

BIBLIOGRAPHY
CC (Zhou Long)
Yao Guanrong: 'Xian shi, the Viola Concerto of Chen
Yi', *People's Music* [China] (1985), no.1 [in Chin.]
M. Eisenmann: 'Chinas musikalische Spitzenkrafte',
Bild (2 Feb 1986)

Zhu Shirui: *The Formation and .Development of Polyphonic Thought in Chinese Music* (thesis, Central Conservatory, Beijing, 1986) [in Chin.]

G. Lee: *Chen Yi: a Study of a Young Chinese Composer* (thesis, Yale School of Music, 1990)

Vai Meng Lei: *Duo Ye for Piano Solo* (diss., U. of Illinois, Urbana, 1990)

J. C. Lee: 'The Birth of a Composition: The Points', *Artspiral*, vi/sum. (1992), 20–22

Meng Weiyan: 'Woman Composer Chen Yi Seeks Chinese Spirit', *World Journal* (18 Oct 1992)

Zhou Jinmin: *New Wave Music in China* (diss., U. of Maryland, 1993)

JOYCE LINDORFF

Chrétien, Hedwige (Gennaro-) (*b* 1859; *d* 1944). French composer and teacher. She studied with Ernest Guiraud at the Paris Conservatoire, where she won first prize in both harmony and fugue in 1881 and later became a professor. Little else is known of her life. She composed about 150 works, including 50 songs, 50 piano pieces, two one-act comic operas, a very successful ballet, and several chamber and orchestral works. Although the subject matter of her texts is often traditional, such as love, patriotism and troubadours, the musical idiom is clearly 20th century: most works are through-composed, using ninth, eleventh and thirteenth chords, with chromatic melodies and frequent changes of metre and tonality, often modulating into remote keys. Chrétien's fame extended beyond France into England and the USA. Some of her songs were translated and published in England, and her wind quintet was reprinted in the USA.

WORKS
selective list

Dramatic: Ballet oriental, Paris, Théâtre National de l'Opéra; Le menuet de l'impératrice (comic opera, 1, Aylicson), 1889; La cinquantaine (comic opera, 1, Aylicson), Sermaize-les-Bains, 26 Feb 1911 (Paris, 1891)

Other vocal: Le calme (Dorchain), Bar, vn, pf; Chanson des pêcheurs de lune (Fortolis), 2 solo vv/chorus, pf; Fanatisme, 1v, vc, pf; Là-bas! (Marcel), 1v, pf, *c*1895; Point d'orgue (Marcel), 1v, pf, *c*1895; Pour ceux qui aiment (Magnien), 1v, vn, pf; Villanelle, 1v, fl ad lib; other songs, 1v, pf

Orch, inst ens: Arabesque, fl, ob, cl, hn, bn, pf (Paris, 1921); Allegro appassionato, vn, fl, cl, tpt, sax, ob/eng hn (also arr. with pf); Berceuse, vn, fl, cl, sax, ob/eng hn (also arr. with pf); Confidences, fl, cl, ob/eng hn (also arr. with pf); Danse rustique, pf, orch; Elégie, cl, eng hn (also arr. with pf); Escarpolette, orch/pf; Esquisse matinale, vc/vn, pf; Grand caprice, solo wind inst, pf; Idéal, vn, pf; Pastorale, fl, pf/fl; Polonaise, cl, pf/cl; Wind Qnt, fl, ob, cl, hn, bn; Romance (vn, ob/eng hn, pf)/fl; Scène rustique, ob, pf (Paris, 1921); Scherzettino, fl, ob/eng hn (also arr. with pf); Sérénade pathétique, fl, pf/fl; Sérénade sous bois, pf, fl, ob (Paris, 1922); Soir d'automne, vn/vc, pf/orch (also arr. orch); Source, pf, orch/pf

Solo inst: Ronde de nuit, vc; Sérénade, vn; Vers l'infini, vn; Pastels, pf 4 hands; Sur le lac, pf/harp; Tarantelle, pf 4 hands; other pf pieces

Principal publishers: Enoch, Grus, Durand, Leduc

BIBLIOGRAPHY
CohenE; *PazdirekH*; *WCBH*
A. Elson: *Woman's Work in Music* (Boston, 1903, 2/1931)

JUDY S. TSOU

Chudova, Tat'yana Alexeyevna (*b* Moscow, 16 June 1944). Russian composer. She studied at the Central Music School in Moscow, then at the Moscow Conservatory with Y. A. Shaporin (1963–6) and, at undergraduate and postgraduate level, with T. N. Khrennikov (1966–70); she has taught at both establishments since 1970. Chudova has participated in many folk expeditions and made a special study of folk culture, including folk singing skills. Her own music has been influenced by folk traditions, and she evolved a language where folk elements and techniques such as polytonality, pointillism and Sprechstimme are closely interwoven. The world of Russian fairy-tale and folklore pervades her symphonic suites and operas. In the 1970s the subject matter and style of her works changed, and she began to write bold and distinctive melodies, march- or toccata-like pieces, characterized by rapid changes of dynamics. Episodes from Russian history form the basis of her cantatas, and also of the symphonic trilogy *Sovetskoy molodyozhi* ('To Soviet Youth'), the third part of which was awarded the Lenin Komsomol Prize in 1984.

WORKS
selective list

Stage: Agitator (ballet, D. Plotkin), 1965; O myortvoy tsarevne i semi bogatïryakh [The Dead Princess and the Seven Heroes] (fairy-tale opera, Chudova, after A. S. Pushkin), 1966–7; Na derevnyu dedushke [To the Village, to Grandfather] (opera, V. Schuldzik and I. Maznina, after A. P. Chekhov: *Van'ka*), 1978

Orch: Iz russkikh skazok [From Russian Fairy-Tales], sym. suite, 1962; Pf Conc., 1969–70; 3 Suites, folk inst orch: no.1, 1980, no.2, 1981, no.3, 1982; Sovetskoy molodyozhi [To Soviet Youth], sym. trilogy: Timur i ego komanda [Timur and his Team] (after A. Gaydar), 1981–2, Kak zakalyalas' stal' [How the Steel was Tempered] (after N. Ostrovsky), 1983, Molodaya gvardiya [The Young Guard] (after A. Fadeyev), 1984; Sym. no.4, 1988

Choral: 4 choruses (folk texts), female vv, 1970; Bogatïri (cantata, I. Vekshegonova), 1971; Bagryanïy svet [The Crimson Light] (ballad, V. Rozhdestvensky), Bar, chorus, orch, 1973; Pro zverey, kotorïch net [Fabulous Beasts] (choral fairy-tales, E. Gulïga), unacc. chorus, 1975; Tramvay poezii [The Tram of Poetry] (Ye. Yevtushenko), unacc. chorus, 1975; Zodchiye [The Architects] (cantata, D. Kedrin), 1976

Vocal: 7 folk texts, female folksinger, 1969; Perepevki-pereplyasï [Songs and Dances] (L. Serostanova), Mez, pf, 1971, rev. 1974; O, thou Moon (V. Lebedeva), vocal qt, 1972

Inst: Sonata, solo vc, 1962; Sonata, solo trbn, 1967; 7 P'es v russkom stile [Pieces in Russian Style], pf, 1971; Vn Sonata no.1, 1974; Org Sonata, 1975; Khvala organu [In Praise of the Organ], org, 1981; Pieces, prepared bayan, 1981; Sonata, domra, pf, 1982; Vn Sonata no.2, 1987

BIBLIOGRAPHY

R. Petrushanskaya: 'Zhit': eto ochen' interesno' [Life is Very Interesting], *Sovetskiye kompozitorï: laureatï premii Leninskogo komsomola* [Soviet Composers: Laureates of the Lenin Komsomol Prize] (Moscow, 1989), 303–16

OLGA MANULKINA

Cianchettini, Veronica. Bohemian musician; *see* DUSSEK family, (1).

Ciani, Suzanne (*b* Edinburg, IN, 4 June 1946). American composer and keyboard player. Originally trained as a classical pianist, she then studied in California with electronic music pioneers Max Mathews, John Chowning and Donald Buchla. Her first important works were created with the Buchla Synthesizer. In the mid-1970s she moved to New York, where she worked with Philip Glass. Employing both acoustic and electronic instruments (Synclavier, Waveframe, IBM- and Macintosh-based software), she produced award-winning music for television, as well as film music and numerous albums. Her style combines popular and classical elements. She has continued to perform as a soloist and with chamber ensembles, playing the piano, the Midi piano and computer-driven synthesizers.

WORKS
selective list

Buchla synth: Voices of Packaged Souls, 1969; Dance Series: Perche? Perche, Stretch Dance, Baudelaire, Space, Glass Houses, 1971; Koddesh-Koddeshim, 1972; New York New York, 1974; Lixviation, 1974; New York II, 1975

Film scores: The Incredible Shrinking Woman, 1980; Mother Theresa, 1986

Albums: 7 Waves, 1982; Velocity of Love, 1986; Neverland, 1988; History of my Heart, 1989; Pianissimo, 1990; Hotel Luna, 1991

Also electronic music and arrs.

CHRISTINE AMMER

Cibbini-Kozeluch, Catherina [Catharina, Katharina] (*b* Vienna, 20 Feb 1785; *d* Zákupy, nr Česká Lípa, 12 Aug 1858). Austrian pianist and composer of Bohemian descent. She was the daughter of the renowned pianist, composer, conductor and teacher Leopold Kozeluch. After lessons with her father, she became a pupil of Muzio Clementi. In 1805 she made her début in Vienna as a concert pianist and soon joined the circle that included Beethoven, Ignaz Moscheles, J. V. Voříšek and, later, Chopin. In 1812 she married the court lawyer Anton Cibbini (1763–1836) and subsequently published her music in Vienna under the name Cibbini-Kozeluch. In 1820 Gustav Schilling referred to her in the *Allgemeine deutsche Musik-Zeitung* as 'among the most exquisite lady pianists of the capital Vienna'. For him, her playing was infused 'with impressive dexterity, delicacy, profound feeling and valuable knowledge of art'. Nevertheless, in 1825 she retired from public performance, because she was made chief lady-in-waiting to Empress Carolina Augusta (until 1831) and then to her successor, Empress Maria Anna Carolina Pia (until 1851), in Prague. She was also a teacher (her most accomplished pupil was Leopoldine Blahetka) and was on friendly terms with the Schumanns. On 10 October 1838 Robert Schumann wrote from Vienna: 'Our great hope is on Frau von Cibbini, she can make everything possible! Clara has confided everything to her in a wonderful letter'.

Her works for solo piano (including two *Divertissements brillants* op.3, Introduction and Variations in E♭ op.5, Introduction and Polonaise in A op.8, and six waltzes op.6) and *La rimembranza* op.10, for two pianos and cello (on themes by Rossini and others), show compositional skill and a taste for virtuosity. In spite of her long absence from public life, she played an important role as 'Exponentin der Reaktionäre Kräfte' in the Vienna uprising of 1848 (in which freedom of the press was demanded in opposition to Metternich). During this period her name appeared several times in the newspapers.

BIBLIOGRAPHY

PazdirekH; SchillingES; WurzbachL

L. Vojtíšková: 'Skladby žen z hudebních a hereckých rodin' [Compositions by Women from Musical and Theatrical Families], *Časopis národního musea* (1954), 1

— : 'Kateřina Koželuhová-Cibbini', *Zprávy Bertramky*, xii (1961), 29

A. Šerých: 'Po přeslici' [On the Distaff Side], *OM*, xx/2 (1988), 61–4, xvii

ROSARIO MARCIANO,
JORGE SANCHEZ-CHIONG,
ANNA ŠERÝCH

Ciobanu, Maya (*b* Bucharest, 5 May 1952). Romanian composer, pianist and educator. In Bucharest she studied at the George

Enescu High School for the Arts before attending the Conservatory (1971–5), where her teachers included Myriam Marbé and Dan Constantinescu (composition). She later won a scholarship to Darmstadt (1980, 1982) and an honourable mention at the 1982 GEDOK competition in Mannheim. Since 1981 she has taught piano and theory at the George Enescu High School. Drawn to poetry, dance and the use of metaphor, she favours the sonorities of chamber ensembles and pays great attention to detail, often writing within a modal framework. Ciobanu has written three cantatas for chorus and orchestra: *Ghicitori* ('Riddles', 1975), *Decembrie in Ardeal* ('December in Transylvania', 1983) and *Cele şase peceţi* ('The Six Seals', 1991). For orchestra alone she has written a symphonic movement (1975), a violin concerto (1980) and a symphony (1988). Her chamber music includes *Trei sculpturi* ('Three Sculptures', 1982), for string quartet, and various pieces for woodwind and for voices.

BIBLIOGRAPHY

V. Cosma: *Muzicieni din România*, i (Bucharest, 1989)

VIOREL COSMA

Claman, Dolores (Olga) (*b* Vancouver, 6 July 1927). Canadian composer and pianist. She studied in Vancouver and California before entering the Juilliard School, New York, where her teachers were Rosina Lhévinne and Edward Steuermann (piano) and Vittorio Giannini and Bernard Wagenaar (composition). Claman's early works include *Primitive Dance* (1945) for piano, three songs to texts by James Joyce (1948–50), *Prelude* (1950) for orchestra, the ballet *Le rêve fantasque* (1950) and the musical comedy *Timber!* (1952). She went to London in 1953, where she wrote music for television and songs for the theatre. She married the English writer Richard Morris and they lived in Toronto from 1958 until the mid-1970s, when they settled in London. They collaborated on writing jingles, for which they earned over 40 awards, and musicals such as *A Christmas Carol* (1963) and *In the Klondike* (1968). Among their film scores are *A Place to Stand* (Ontario Pavilion, Expo 67), *The Man who Wanted to Live Forever* (1970) and *Captain Apache* (1972). Claman's work for television includes music for documentaries and the theme song for 'Hockey Night in Canada'.

GAYNOR G. JONES

Claribel. *See* BARNARD, CHARLOTTE ALINGTON.

Clarke [Friskin], **Rebecca (Thacher)** (*b* Harrow, 27 Aug 1886; *d* New York, 13 Oct 1979). English composer and viola player of German-American descent. The most distinguished British woman composer of the generation between the late Victorians (Smyth, Lehmann, White) and the new independents (Maconchy, Lutyens), she was also pre-eminent as a viola player, numbering among the first six female full members of a professional London orchestra (Wood's New Queen's Hall Orchestra, 1912–14) and participating in professional chamber music with the greatest performers of her day. In both capacities she belongs with Frank Bridge and Eugene Goossens: all three were professional string players notable for performing and composing chamber music, and all three made a name for themselves in the USA after World War I, enjoying the patronage and friendship of Elizabeth Sprague Coolidge. Furthermore, they were all composition pupils of C. V. Stanford at the RCM and from a Brahmsian foundation developed urbanely post-impressionist idioms (influences including Debussy, Ravel, Skryabin and Bloch) which also owed something to Ralph Vaughan Williams and helped define the postwar British pastoral elegy with both its folk and radical undertones.

The three central works in Clarke's output, the Viola Sonata, Piano Trio and Rhapsody for cello and piano, best exemplify her range (as do some of the songs, in which a penchant for the macabre is striking). Motivic cells such as the [0, 3, 4] set of the Rhapsody are intensively worked with urgent harmonic rhetoric. Like Skryabin's, the dialectic can become monotonous, for while the chromaticism is post-tonal the textures and rhythms retain a good deal of late Romanticism. Sometimes Clarke fuses the exotic and primitive, and when her fanfare motif in the Piano Trio takes on the identity of the Last Post, or her *quasi pastorale* insert in the finale of the Viola Sonata evokes 'memories of England' that are then banished, as MacDonald describes it, her aggregated voice is impressive and thought-provoking.

Clarke's career seems a mixture of the circumscribed and independent. Her father was an American who came to England for Eastman Kodak, her mother a great-niece of the German historian Leopold von Ranke. Rebecca studied the violin at the RAM with Hans Wessely from 1902 but left when her harmony teacher, Percy Miles, proposed to her (he later bequeathed her a Stradivari which enabled her to institute the May Muklé Prize at the RAM). A second education as Stanford's first female composition student at the RCM from 1907 encountered no such hazards, and it was Stanford who suggested she change from violin to viola (she played a Grancino throughout her career and had private lessons with Lionel Tertis). But her father disapproved of her professional ambitions and she was without support on leaving the RCM in 1910. Work soon followed, and her chamber-music career was to include membership of three all-woman ensembles, the Norah Clench Quartet, the English Ensemble and a quartet with the d'Aranyi sisters and Guilhermina Suggia; she also toured a great deal – worldwide – particularly with the cellist May Muklé.

Clarke first visited the USA in 1916 and enjoyed success with *Morpheus* at Carnegie Hall in 1918. She won second prize in Mrs Coolidge's 1919 competition with the Viola Sonata; pseudonymous, like all the entries ('You should have seen the faces of the jury when it was revealed the composer was a woman!', Mrs Coolidge wrote), it initially tied for first place with Bloch's Viola Suite. The Piano Trio again came second in 1921 for Mrs Coolidge, who then commissioned the Rhapsody for her 1923 Pittsfield Festival. Clarke divided her time between the UK and the USA in the 1930s, and she herself said that an affair with a married man sapped her energy for composition at this period, when she wrote little. More works followed in the early 1940s, however, and the *Prelude, Allegro and Pastorale* was performed in Berkeley at the 1942 ISCM Festival.

She had to remain in the USA at the outbreak of World War II and married an old college friend, the pianist James Friskin, in 1944, having renewed contact with him after a chance meeting in New York, where they settled. Thenceforward she played and composed little but still pursued an active musical and social life. She also lived to enjoy the 'little renaissance' (as she put it) of her music that took place around and after her 90th birthday.

WORKS
works without parenthesized dates are unpubd
INSTRUMENTAL

Variations, c1907–8, ?lost; Vn Sonata, 1st movt, 1907–9; Vn Sonata, 1909; Danse bizarre, 2 vn, 1909, lost; Lullaby, va, pf, 1909; Morpheus, va, pf, 1917; [untitled movt], va, pf, 1918; Lullaby, vn, pf, 1918; 2 Pieces, va/vn, vc, 1918 (1930); Sonata, va/vc, pf, 1918–19 (1921); Chinese Puzzle, vn, pf, 1921 (1925); Epilogue, vc, pf, 1921; Pf Trio, 1921 (1928);

Rhapsody, vc, pf, 1923; Midsummer Moon, vn, pf, 1924 (1926); Str Qt, 1 movt, 1924; Adagio, str qt, 1926; Cortège, pf, 1930; [untitled movt], 2 vn, 1940; Combined Carols, str qt, str orch, 1941; Dumka, vn, va, pf, 1941; Passacaglia on an Old English Tune, va/vc, pf, 1941 (1943); Prelude, Allegro and Pastorale, va, cl, 1941

Arrs.

VOCAL

24 early songs (mostly German settings of R. Dehmel), 1903–11; 7 early partsongs, 1906–11
Songs, 1v, pf: 2 Songs (W. B. Yeats), 1912 (1920); Weep you no more, sad fountains, 1912; Infant Joy (W. Blake), 1913 (1924); Down by the salley gardens (Yeats), 1919 (1924); The Seal Man (J. Masefield), 1922 (1926); Cradle Song (Blake), 1924 (1929); June Twilight (Masefield), 1925 (1926); A Dream (Yeats), 1926 (1928); The Cherry-Blossom Wand (A. Wickham), 1927 (1929); Eight o'Clock (A. E. Housman), 1927 (1928); Greeting (E. Young) (1928); The Aspidistra (C. Flight), 1929 (1930); Tiger, tiger (Blake), 1933; The Donkey (G. K. Chesterton), 1942 (1984); God made a tree (K. Kendall), 1954
2 songs (J. Fletcher), 2vv, pf, 1912; Philomela (P. Sidney), SATB, 1914; A Psalm of David (Psalm lxiii), 1v, pf, 1920; Psalm xci, T, SATB, 1921; Come, O come, by life's delight (R. Clarke), 1926; Sleep (Fletcher), 2vv, pf, 1926; Ave Maria, SSA, 1937; Daybreak (J. Donne), 1v, str qt, 1940; Chorus (Shelley: *Hellas*), SSSAA, 1943

Arrs.

MSS in *US-NYp*, *Wc*

BIBLIOGRAPHY

J. Holbrooke: 'Women Composers', *Contemporary British Composers* (London, 1925), 293–304
E. Evans: 'Clarke, Rebecca', *Cobbett's Cyclopedic Survey of Chamber Music*, i, ed. W. W. Cobbett (London, 1929, 2/1963), 282–3
M. B. Stanfield: 'Rebecca Clarke: Violist and Composer', *The Strad*, lxxvii (1966), 297, 299
C. Johnson: *Rebecca Clarke: a Thematic Catalogue of her Works* (MS, 1977, *US-NYcu*)
—— : 'Introduction', *Rebecca Clarke: Trio for Piano, Violin and Cello* (New York, 1980)
E. Lerner: *A Modern European Quartet, c1900–c1960* (MS, 1981, rev. 1985, *US-NYp*)
M. Ponder: 'Rebecca Clarke', *British Music Society Journal*, v (1983), 82–8 [incl. list of works]
C. Johnson: record notes, *Rebecca Clarke: Music for Viola* (Northeastern Records NR 212, Boston, MA, 1985)
S. Banfield: ' "Too Much of Albion"? Mrs Coolidge and her British Connections', *American Music*, iv (1986), 59–88
C. MacDonald: 'Rebecca Clarke's Chamber Music (I)', *Tempo*, no.160 (1986), 15–26
A. M. Woodward: 'Introduction', *Rebecca Clarke: Sonata for Viola (or Cello) and Piano* (New York, 1986), pp.v–vi

STEPHEN BANFIELD

Clayton, Laura (*b* Lexington, 8 Dec 1943). American composer and pianist. She studied composition with Darius Milhaud at the Aspen Music School in Colorado, Charles

Wuorinen at the New England Conservatory in Boston, and Leslie Bassett, George Balch Wilson and Eugene Kurtz at the University of Michigan. She has received a Guggenheim Fellowship, NEA awards and two American Academy and Institute of Arts and Letters prizes. Her style has been described as rhythmically complex with a 'highly refined sense of mystery', inspired by images of nature. *Cree Songs for the Newborn*, based on creole poems, was chosen to represent the USA at the 1980 UNESCO International Rostrum of Composers in Paris.

WORKS
selective list

Orch: Sagarama, pf, orch, 1984; Terra lucida, 1988
Chamber: Mobile no.2, vc, pf, 1975; O Train Azul, gui, 1977; Cree Songs for the Newborn, S, chamber ens, 1978; Passaggio, pf, 1978; Herself the Tide, S, pf, 1981; Panels, chamber ens, 1983; Clara's Sea, women's vv, 1988; Joie, pf, 1990
Tape: Implosure, 2 dancers, slides, tape, 1977; Simichai-ya, a sax, echoplex, tape, 1987

CYNTHIA GREEN LIBBY

Clement, Sheree (*b* Baltimore, 8 Dec 1955). American composer. She trained at the Peabody Conservatory in Baltimore and has also worked with William Albright, George Balch Wilson and Leslie Bassett at the University of Michigan, but her most extensive study has been with Mario Davidovsky at Columbia University. She composes in an atonal idiom: her instrumental music is virtuoso, complex and 'crowded with colorful incident and event' (*Boston Globe*). Her tape pieces employ both analogue and digital sources. She has received a Guggenheim Fellowship and awards from the American Academy and Institute of Arts and Letters, as well as fellowships from Tanglewood and the MacDowell Colony.

WORKS
selective list

Orch: 5 Nocturnes, 1976; Music from a Summer Afternoon, 1978
Chamber: Belladonna Dreams, 1979; Str Qt, 1980; Concerto, 1982; Variations/Obsessions, 1985; preludes for piano
Tape: Thresholds, 1976; Second Threshold, 1977; Glinda Returns, 1979; One Breath, 1980

CYNTHIA GREEN LIBBY

Cléry [née Duverger; Duvergé], **Marie Elizabeth** (*b* ? Paris, 1761; *d* after 1795). French harpist and composer. The conjectural birthdate assumes she was the 15-year-old 'Mlle Duv★★' whose *air*, *Tout ce que je vois me rappelle*, was printed in the *Mercure de France* in 1776. As Mlle Duverger (or Duvergé) she sang and played the harp at the Concert Spirituel (1780–82), sometimes performing her own works. After her marriage (to Jean-Baptiste Cant-Hanet *dit* Cléry), she published three sonatas for harp accompanied by violin (op.1, 1785) as 'M^de Cléry, née Duvergé', with the title *musicienne des concerts de la Reine*. Her husband was later famous as the *valet de chambre* assigned to the imprisoned Louis XVI during the French Revolution (1792). Cléry (and perhaps also his wife) escaped in 1795 to Austria, where he entered the service of Louis XVI's daughter, Marie-Thérèse-Charlotte.

WORKS

Tout ce que je vois me rappelle, air, S, harp, b ['by Mlle Duv★★'], *Mercure de France* (June 1776), 62–7
3 sonates, harp/pf, vn acc., op.1 (Versailles, n.d.; Paris, 1785); edn (Fayetteville, AR, 1988)
Recueil d'airs arrangés pour la harpe avec accompagnement de flute et violon, op.2 (Versailles, 1785)
Le soldat patriote au champ de Mars (Paris, 1790)
Chanson patriotique (from vaudeville La piété filiale) (Paris, 1793)
5 romances . . . pour les illustres prisonniers du Temple, 1v, pf/harp acc., 1793–5 [no.3 for 2vv] (Paris, n.d.)
Potpourri, c, harp (Paris, n.d.)
Sonates, harp, vn acc., F-Pn

Lost works for harp, pubd Paris, n.d., listed in Whistling: Air de Bauer varié, 2 potpourris, Recueil d'airs variés

BIBLIOGRAPHY
C. F. Whistling: *Handbuch der musikalischen Literatur* (Leipzig, 1817)
F. Vernillat: 'La littérature de la harpe en France au XVIIIe siècle', *RMFC*, ix (1987), 162–76

BARBARA GARVEY JACKSON

Clingan, Judith Ann (*b* Sydney, 19 Jan 1945). Australian composer, conductor and teacher. She studied English and French at the Australian National University (BA 1966) and music with Larry Sitsky at the Canberra School of Music; later, she studied at the Kodály Institute in Hungary (Diploma of Music Education 1982). On her return to Canberra in 1983 she founded Gaudeamus, an institute for music teaching and performance for children, youth and adults. She has been particularly involved with composing and conducting vocal music – especially for children's voices – and her output includes much choral and church music. She has also written many stage works for children, most of them to her own texts, and incidental music for several plays.

WORKS
selective list

Stage (children's operas, libs by Clingan): Francis, 1986; Just Looking, 1988; Terra beata – Terra firma, 1991; Marco, 1991

Choral: Lux mundi, children's vv, children's orch, 1985; Modal Magic, SSA, 1986; Ngambra, multiple choirs, ens, 1988; The Birds' Noel, SATB, band, 1990; Kakadu, SAB, ens, 1990
Solo vocal: A Canberra Cycle, S, Bar, ens, 1991; Songs of Solitude, S, ens, 1991
Inst: Seven Deadly Sins, rec, perc, 1990

BIBLIOGRAPHY

Fuller-LeFanuRM

GRAHAM HAIR, GRETA MARY HAIR

Adrienne Clostre, 1986

Clostre, Adrienne (*b* Thomery, 9 Oct 1921). French composer. She studied at the Paris Conservatoire, where her teachers included Yves Nat for piano, Olivier Messiaen for analysis and aesthetics, and Darius Milhaud and Jean Rivier for composition. She was awarded the Prix de Rome for her cantata *La résurrection de Lazare* in 1949, since when she has dedicated herself exclusively to composition, winning the Grand Prix Musical de la Ville de Paris in 1955 and the Prix Florence Gould in 1976, as well as the Grand Prix de la Musique of the Société des Auteurs et Compositeurs Dramatiques in 1987.

Clostre has found her inspiration above all in extra-musical sources – visual and, more especially, literary – and composing for the theatre has naturally become her preferred medium. She has explored new forms and given renewed life to musical drama, with regard to both its presentation and its con-

tent, and her work is capable of being adapted to the most diverse theatrical environments. She has endeavoured to go beyond narrative to produce a kind of 'theatre of the soul', in which dramatic action is transcended in favour of a musical transfiguration of the inner, metaphysical quest of the protagonists. Believing that stage action only superficially communicates the social dimension, whereas music plumbs the depths of the human psyche, she has constructed most of her librettos from personal diaries and private letters. A technique essential to achieving the necessary sincerity of expression, and one already evident in *La résurrection de Lazare*, has been the gradual replacement of the normal vocal line by declamation and the spoken word; this development began to blossom in *Nietzsche* (1972–5) and found its culmination in *L'albatros* (1986–8).

Clostre's musical language, free from any system but with an underlying atonality, relies primarily on melody and rhythm; her formal structures of juxtaposed sequences favour a contrasting and ever-changing compositional style. Though her music is constantly evolving, there are nevertheless occasional moments of respite – in the form of chorales, where all the harmonic ideas are concentrated, as if to stop time momentarily. Clostre showed herself to be ahead of her time when in 1970 she introduced into her Oboe Concerto quarter-tones, multiphonics and multiple trills, instrumental techniques that were then barely known in France. Her latest works have tended towards an increasingly austere style.

WORKS
selective list

Stage: Le chant du cygne (chamber opera, 1, A. Clostre, after A. P. Chekhov), 1960; Julien l'apostat (drame lyrique, 8 scenes, Clostre, after H. Ibsen), 1970; Nietzsche (action musicale, 12 scenes, after F. Nietzsche), 1972–5; Cinq scènes de la vie italienne (Clostre), 1980; Le secret ([lecture musicale from the journal of] S. Kierkegaard), 1981; Romans, 1983; L'albatros (action dramatique, 9 scenes, Clostre, after C. P. Baudelaire), 1986–8; Annapurna (action musicale, 7 scenes, Clostre, after M. Herzog), 1988

Other dramatic and vocal: Tre fioretti di San Francesco d'Assisi, chamber cantata, 6vv, 10 insts, 1953; El tigre de oro y sombro, ([lecture musicale of 9 poems by] J. L. Borges), S, a fl, perc, celtic harp, 1979; Dans la nuit . . . le poète (dramatic cantata, F. Hölderlin), S, fl, vn, pf, tape, 1984; Froid comme le métal . . . brulant comme la passion (dramatic cantata, H. von Kleist), S, Mez, fl, vc, pf, tape, 1989; Peinture et liberté, radiophonic melodrama (J. Michelet and J. L. David), nar, inst ens, tape, 1989; Fantaisie à la manière de Callot (dramatic cantata,

E. T. A. Hoffmann), Mez, vn, 1990; L'écriture du Dieu, melodrama (Borges), nar, inst ens, 1991; Le Zaïre, sung melodrama (Borges), Bar, recorded music, tape, 1992

Orch: Sym., str, 1949, rev. 1962; Concert pour le souper du roi Louis II, 1957; Conc., ob, chamber orch, 1970; Conc., fl, vn, chamber orch, 1972

Inst: Permutations, tpt, ob, va, trbn, 1972; 6 dialogues, ob, 1972; Feux d'artifice pour le 111ème anniversaire de Bilbo, 8 variations, pf, 1976; Premier livre des rois, sonata, org, 1980; Brother Blue, celtic harp, perc, 1981; Variations italiennes, 4 interludes, pf, 1981; La reine de Saba, fresque musicale, org, perc, 1990; Sun, lecture de Virginia Woolf par le quatuor à cordes, str qt, 1991; Waves, lecture au piano de Virginia Woolf, pf, 1991

Principal publishers: Billaudot, Choudens, Editions Transatlantiques

FRANÇOISE ANDRIEUX

Coates, Dorothy Love (*b* Birmingham, AL, 30 Jan 1928). American gospel singer and composer. She was born into a musical family and by the age of ten was playing the piano for her church. As a teenager she sang with the Royal Travelers and a family group, the McGriff Singers. In 1945 she joined the Original Gospel Harmonettes, an all-female group in Birmingham, whose members were Vera Kilb, Mildred Miller Howard, Odessa Edwards, Willie Mae Newberry and the pianist Evelyn Starks. Their first recordings, *I'm sealed*, followed by *Get away Jordan* (1951), placed them in the front rank of gospel singers. The group made several successful recordings and appearances during the next seven years, performing predominantly works by Coates. Her compositional style is simple in its melody, harmony and rhythm; her lyrics make use of favourite church sayings and 'wandering couplets' taken from older hymns and spirituals (for example, *He may not come when you want him, but he's right on time*, 1953; *I've got Jesus and that's enough*, 1956). In her own performances she captures the emotion of the text by forcing her voice at the extremes of its range. Her songs have been recorded by such singers as Mahalia Jackson, Clara Ward and Johnny Cash. Coates has appeared at all the major gospel festivals and frequently at the Newport Jazz Festival.

BIBLIOGRAPHY

SouthernB

T. Heilbut: *The Gospel Sound: Good News and Bad Times* (New York, 1971)

I. V. Jackson: *Afro-American Religious Music: a Bibliography and Catalogue of Gospel Music* (Westport, CT, 1979)

HORACE CLARENCE BOYER

Coates, Gloria (*b* Wausau, WI, 10 Oct 1934). American composer. She obtained degrees from Columbia University (BA, theatre and ballet, 1963; BMus 1963) and from Louisiana State University (MMus 1965), and also studied with Jack Beeson, Otto Luening and Alexander Tcherepnin. A prolific composer, she began with works mainly for chamber forces, but after moving from New York to Munich in 1969 she wrote for large-scale ensembles as well. In 1972 she demonstrated her research into vocal multiphonics at the Darmstadt summer school. Her Symphony no.1 'Music on Open Strings', first performed in 1978 by the Polish Chamber Orchestra (conducted by Jerzy Maksymiuk) at the Warsaw Autumn Festival, brought her international acclaim; with this piece she later became the first woman composer to be performed in the Musica Viva series, Munich. Her compositions are notable for obtaining highly dramatic colouristic effects – sometimes employing microtones and scordatura – especially in string works (for example, the series of string quartets) and vocal works. She has received commissions from Henze for the Montepulciano Festival (*Lunar Loops II*, for two guitars and percussion) and from the Kronos Quartet.

WORKS
selective list

DRAMATIC

Fall of the House of Usher, 1962 (opera, G. Coates, after E. A. Poe), inc.

Ikarus, 1975 (ballet), Dreieich-Buchschlag, 16 May 1982

Machine Men (ballet), Dreieich-Buchschlag, 16 May 1982

Women's Movement (ballet), Erding, 1986

INSTRUMENTAL, VOCAL AND
MUSIQUE CONCRÈTE

Orch: Sym. no.1 'Music on Open Strings', str orch, 1973–4; Planets, 1974; Sinfonietta della notte, 1980 [based on Planets]; Sym. no.2 'Music in Abstract Lines' (Illuminatio in tenebris), 1987 [based on Sinfonietta della notte]; Sym. no.3 'Symphony Nocturne', str orch, 1976, rev. 1986; Sym. no.4 'Chiaroscuro', 1990 [based on Transitions, chamber orch, 1984–5]; Sym. no.5, 1985 [version of 3 Mystical Songs]; Sym. no.6 'Music in Microtones', 1986; Sym. no.7, 1990–91

Chamber: 5 str qts: no.1, 1966, rev. 1982, [no.2] Mobile for Str Qt, 1972 [rev. 1972 as Str Qt no.2], no.3, 1975–6, no.4, 1977, no.5, 1988–9; Trio, 3 fl, 1966; Lunar Loops, 2 gui, 1986; Lunar Loops II, 2 gui, perc, 1988; Light Splinters, fl, harp, va, 1988–9; Blue Monday, gui, perc, 1989; Light Splinters II, fl, harp, va, perc, 1990 [based on Light Splinters]; kbd works

Vocal orch: Fonte di Rimini (Sinfonia brevis) (Leonardo da Vinci), solo vv, chorus, orch, 1976–84;

Maria Rosa Coccia: portrait attributed to Antonio Cavallucci (1751–98)

3 Mystical Songs (A. Coates), SSAATTBBB, chamber orch, 1985; [7] Emily Dickinson Songs, 1v, chamber orch, 1989: 1 The sign in the scarlet prison, 2 Chanting to paradise, 3 There breathed a man, 4 One heart from breaking, 5 Thy dust to keep, 6 The place called morning, 7 To the Civil War dead; Rainbow across the night sky, vocalise, SSMezAA, vn, va, musical saw, perc, timp, 1991: 1 Canto I 'Bisema Tuwamoh', 2 Canto II 'Vah, Voh, Batami', 3 Canto III 'Tireje Famara'; Indian Sounds, American Indian vocalise, 1v, chamber orch, 1991–2: 1 Indian Rounds, 2 Indian Mounds, 3 Indian Grounds

Other vocal: [3] Ophelia Songs (W. Shakespeare), 1v, pf, 1964; [12] Transcendental Songs (E. Dickinson), 1v, pf, 1966–85: 1 They dropped like flakes, 2 I'm nobody, 3 I've seen a dying eye, 4 Wild night, wild nights, 5 I held a jewel in my fingers, 6 A word is dead, 7 Mine by the right, 8 Now I lay thee down to sleep, 9 If I can stop one heart from breaking, 10 Bind me, I still can sing, 11 Will there really be a morning, 12 In falling timbers buried; Go the great way (Dickinson), S, org/pf, 2 perc, 1985; Sperriges Morgen (Wir tönen allein) (Celan), S, tuba, vc, db, perc, 1989

Musique concrète: Ecology no.1, 1979; Ecology no.2 (G. Coates), 1v, insts, 2 tapes, 1980; Fiori and the

Princess, a rec, tape, 1987; Fiori, a rec, modified tape, 1987; Fiori and the Princess II, fl, tape, 1988; Fiori II, fl, perc, tape, 1988

CHRISTINE AMMER

Coccia, Maria Rosa (*b* Rome, 4 Jan 1759; *d* Rome, Nov 1833). Italian composer. As a child she achieved considerable fame. On 28 November 1774 she composed a canonic exercise in the presence of four examiners of the Roman Accademia di S Cecilia, who approved it as 'well executed in accordance with the rules of music'. This feat was celebrated in a publication the following year including the canon and her portrait. At about this time she was made a member of the Accademia Filarmonica of Bologna. A *Magnificat* dated 2 October 1774, for four voices and organ and including solo, duet and trio passages, and a *Dixit dominus* of 1775 for two four-part choirs and organ (both MSS in *GB-Cfm*) reveal considerable talent in a conservative idiom. In 1780 Michele Mallio published in Rome an *Elogio storico della* *signora Maria Rosa Coccia romana*, including letters written in praise of her by three of the most distinguished musical figures of the age, Pietro Metastasio, Padre Martini and Farinelli. Her early promise seems however not to have been fulfilled: all that is known of her adult life is a *Cantata per musica a 4 voci* dated 1783.

BIBLIOGRAPHY

FétisBS

ANTHONY BURTON

Coghill, Rhoda (Sinclair) (*b* Dublin, 14 Oct 1903). Irish composer and pianist. One of Ireland's finest pianists, she studied with Patricia Read in Dublin and with Artur Schnabel in Berlin, after gaining the MusB from Trinity College, Dublin. She followed a solo career in Ireland and was the official accompanist at Radio Eireann from 1939 for 30 years. Coghill's style is quite distinct, particularly in her introspective, atmospheric songs. Her rhapsody *Out of the cradle, endlessly rocking*, one of the most outstanding Irish works to be written before World War II, shows that she was influenced by Debussy, especially in her use of colour and whole-tone harmony. A gifted poet, she has published two collections of poems.

WORKS
selective list

Orch, vocal orch: Out of the cradle, endlessly rocking (W. Whitman), T, chorus, orch, 1923; Gaelic Fantasy, pf, orch
Songs: A Song of St Francis (A. N. Maugham), 1921; I love all beauteous things (R. Bridges), 1924; I will not let thee go (Bridges), 1924; Messages (F. Thompson), 1925; Among the heather (W. Allingham), 1926; 5 Songs (P. Colum), 1926; Meg Merrilees (J. Keats), 1927; Erster Schnee (O. Siepmann, trans. R. Coghill), 1931; 4 Songs ('A. E.', G. Russell), 1941
Pf: When Childher Plays (4 pieces for children), 1926; Gaelic Fantasy (on 3 Irish airs), 1939

Principal publishers: An Gúm, Pigott

SARAH M. BURN

Colaço Osorio-Swaab, Reine (*b* Amsterdam, 16 Jan 1881; *d* Amsterdam, 14 April 1971). Dutch composer. She began composing in her early forties and subsequently studied with Henk Badings. At first she wrote songs, then later produced instrumental works, choral works with biblical texts and several works for narrator and orchestra, all composed between 1930 and 1960, during which time her style developed from late Romantic to atonal. Her substantial list of chamber music includes a suite for woodwind quintet (1948), a flute quartet (1952)

and a string quartet (1955), while her larger-scale works include a dramatic overture (1953) and *Genezing van den Blinde*, for narrator and chamber orchestra (1955). Her music is published by Donemus.

BIBLIOGRAPHY

CohenE

HELEN METZELAAR

Colbran, Isabella [Isabel] **(Angela)** (*b* Madrid, 2 Feb 1785; *d* Castenaso, Bologna, 7 Oct 1845). Spanish soprano and composer. She had singing lessons with Francisco Pareja, finishing her studies with Gaetano Marinelli and the castrato Girolamo Crescentini. In 1801 she moved to Paris, where she was a pupil of Luigi Cherubini. After a warm reception at the court of Napoleon she went to Bologna, where she began her successful career in Italy. From 1811 until 1821 she was the prima donna of the Teatro S Carlo, Naples. Between 1815 and 1823 Rossini composed 18 operas for her voice, and they were married in 1822. She retired in 1829, and Rossini left her the same year; they were divorced in 1836, but she continued to live with Rossini's father until her death. She composed four collections of songs, dedicated to the Queen of Spain, Crescentini, the Empress of Russia and Prince Eugenio of Beaumarchais respectively.

BIBLIOGRAPHY

Choron-FayolleD; *DEUMM*; *FétisB*; *Grove1* (J. Marshall); *SchillingE*[†]; *SchmidlD*
G. Carpani: *Le rossiniane ossia Lettere musico-teatrali* (Padua, 1824)
Gaceta de Madrid (25 Feb 1857)
R. Osborne: *Rossini* (London, 1986, 2/1987)

MARIA ENCINA CORTIZO RODRIGUEZ

Cole, (Frances) Ulric (*b* New York, 9 Sept 1905; *d* Bridgeport, CT, 21 May 1992). American composer, teacher and editor. She studied with Homer Grunn in Los Angeles. In 1922 she toured the midwestern Chautauqua circuit as a pianist. She studied composition with Percy Goetschius (1922–3), Rubin Goldmark (1924–7, with fellowships from the Juilliard Graduate School) and Nadia Boulanger (1927); piano with George Boyle and Josef Lhévinne. Dissatisfied with teaching, she worked on the editorial staff of *Time* magazine from 1945 until 1952. Later she travelled widely, living for several years on Tahiti and Vanuatu.

Her music, which uses the pandiatonic harmonic vocabulary of its time, is marked by formal elegance and rhythmic forcefulness. The Piano Quintet and the Violin Sonata no.1 both won awards from the Society for the Publication of American Music. Her orchestral works have been performed by the symphony orchestras of Cincinnati, Rochester, Scranton and Sydney.

WORKS
selective list

Orch: Pf Conc., 1928; Divertimento, pf, str, 1931; 2 Sketches, str, 1938; Pf Conc., 1941; Nevada, 1947; Sunlight Channel, 1948

Chamber: Vn Sonatas, 1927, 1928; Suite, pf, vn, vc, 1930; Str Qts, 1932, 1934; Pf Qnt, 1936

Pf: Above the Clouds, 1924; Prelude and Fugue, 1924; Tunes & Sketches in Black & White, 1927; Purple Shadows, 1928; 3 Vignettes, 1936; 3 Metropolitones, 1940; Man-About Town, 2 pf, 1942

Principal publishers: John Church, J. Fischer, Galaxy, Theodore Presser, G. Schirmer, A. Weekes
MSS in American Music Center, Fleischer Library

BIBLIOGRAPHY

WAM
J. T. Howard: *Our Contemporary Composers: American Music in the Twentieth Century* (New York, 1941)
D. Ewen: *American Composers Today* (New York, 1949)
J. T. Howard: *Our American Music, Three Hundred Years of it* (New York, 3/1954)
W. Phemister: *One Hundred Years of American Piano Concertos* (Detroit, 1983)
CATHERINE PARSONS SMITH

Coleman, Ellen (*b* London, *c*1886; *d* London, 5 Feb 1973). English composer. She was privately educated and was composing sonatas at the age of 14; it was only in 1921 that she began to take composition lessons, studying with Lawrance Collingwood. She travelled widely and formed lifelong friendships with such notable musicians as Wilhelm Backhaus, Fyodor Shalyapin and harpsichordists Wanda Landowska and Marcelle de Lacour. She mounted three concerts of her works at the Salle Pleyel-Chopin in Paris, in 1937–8, each of which was extensively reviewed; at the second, on 31 March 1938, attended by André Gide, Landowska introduced the music and Lacour was among the performers.

Of Coleman's two operas, *The Walled Garden* in one act was twice broadcast by the BBC. She also wrote two masses, one of which (1928) was performed at Fribourg Cathedral; chamber music, for a variety of instruments, including a pair of ondes martenot; and over 300 songs. The work that brought her greatest acknowledgment was the Cello Sonata in A minor, issued on disc; it was published in London by Augener in 1937. Also published by Augener were *Swansong* (1935), a cycle of five songs to texts

by Robert Nichols, and several piano pieces. Her *Poems and Pictures* for piano were published by Arthur P. Schmidt in Boston. Although Coleman's musical language, frequently based on 'white-note' modality, and the emotional range of her utterance may be rather constricted, her works often reveal a lyrical charm and captivating directness. Her archive is housed at the University of Reading.

RHIAN SAMUEL

Avril Coleridge-Taylor

Coleridge-Taylor, Avril [Gwendolen] (*b* London, 8 March 1903). English composer and conductor. Daughter of the composer Samuel Coleridge-Taylor, she studied at the GSM and at Trinity College of Music, where she was taught composition by Gordon Jacob and Alec Rowley. Her earliest composition, the song *Goodbye Butterfly*, was published when she was 14. She made her début as a conductor at the Royal Albert Hall in 1933 and has been guest conductor with the LSO and the BBC SO. She founded and conducted several orchestras and ensembles, including the Coleridge-Taylor SO. Her compositions include large-scale orchestral works as well as songs, and keyboard and chamber music. In 1957 she wrote the Ceremonial March to celebrate Ghana's Independence. Coleridge-Taylor adopted the name Avril in place of Gwendolen, and has also published under the pseudonym Peter Riley.

WORKS
selective list

Orch: To April, 1933; Sussex Landscape, Pf Conc., op.27, f, 1936; Ceremonial March, 1957
Chamber: Idylle, op.21, fl, pf; Impromptu, op.33, a, fl, pf; Reverie, vc, pf; Fantasie, vn, pf, 1949; over 18 more pieces for solo kbd (pf, hpd, org)
Songs: over 35 written between 1917 and 1971, incl. Goodbye Butterfly (W. C. Berwick-Sayers) (London, 1917); Who knows? (P. L. Dunbar) (London, 1922); The Dreaming Water Lily (H. Heine), 1923; Regret (L. Granville), 1939; Love's Philosophy (P. B. Shelley); O'er all the hill-tops (H. W. Longfellow) (London, 1957); I can face it, Lord (E. Wilmot), 1971

BIBLIOGRAPHY

A. Coleridge-Taylor: *Samuel Coleridge-Taylor* (London, 1979)

SOPHIE FULLER

Colin-De Clerck, Jeanne (Albertine) (*b* Brussels, 9 Jan 1924). Belgian composer. At the Brussels Royal Conservatory of Music she obtained first prize for solfeggio (1942) and a mention for piano accompaniment, but as a composer she is self-taught. She was a professor of solfeggio at the Music Academy of Anderlecht from 1946 to 1977. Her works, which have an atonal basis, include *Matière habitée* op.9, for orchestra (1968), *Divertissement* op.13, for string orchestra (1970), and concertos for flute, op.17 (1972), and violin, op.22 (1974). Among her chamber works are a string quartet, op.8 (1968), a saxophone quartet, op.28 (1977), and *Petit concert à 7* op.31, for piano and six percussionists. She has also written pieces in collaboration with her husband, the composer Georges Colin.

MARIE CORNAZ

Collins, Laura Sedgwick (*b* Poughkeepsie, NY, *c*1859; *d* New York, 1927). American composer, actress and singer. She received early instruction from her mother and later studied with W. H. B. Matthews, H. W. Madeaus Beale, Oscar Coon and Carl Bergstein. She graduated from the Lyceum School of Acting in New York, and was apparently the first American woman to study with Dvořák; he praised her compositions as 'real American music – creative, not imitative'. She wrote the words for many of her songs, which were widely performed by the baritone David Bispham and others. She composed several patriotic songs for special groups, including the Daughters of the Revolution of the Empire State and the National Peace Federation Convention. Her other compositions include more 'than 200 melodies for children, German folksong arrangements, incidental music for several plays, an operetta, a cantata and chamber works. On the New York stage she presented a one-person show, *Sarah Tarbox, MA*, by Charles Barnard, in which she impersonated all 11 characters and performed her own songs; she also performed in Greek drama at Harvard College.

WORKS
selective list

Vocal: A Foolish Little Maiden (Boston, 1887); Graduates March, 1906; The Origin of the Rainbow (1908); My Easter Bonnet (New York, 1909); My Philosophy (New York, 1911); Sleepy Time (Boston, 1913); Making Love in the Choir (Mrs T. H. Whitney) (New York, 1914); Endymion, S, Bar, chamber ens; Ode to Beauty, solo vv and chorus
Incid. music: Pierrot (A. Thompson); Pygmalion and Galatea (W. S. Gilbert); The Lotus Pool (E. DeKay); Jonathon (T. Ewing jr).

BIBLIOGRAPHY

S. R. Crothers: 'Women Composers of America: Laura Sedgwick Collins', *MusAm*, x/4 (1909), 4–26; xi/22 (1910), 1–22

PAMELA FOX

Contini Anselmi, Lucia (*b* Vercelli, 15 Oct 1876; *d* ? after 1913). Italian pianist and composer. She studied at the Rome Conservatory with Giovanni Sgambati (piano) and Alessandro Parisotti (composition). As a concert pianist she performed in Italy and abroad. Her compositions include *Preludio, Gavotta* and *Minuetto* for string orchestra; a Piano Sonata in C minor; *Sibylla Cumaea* for piano (also arranged for two pianos and for orchestra); works for violin and piano and for cello and piano; and other piano works (some also arranged for orchestra). For her piano work *Ludentia* she was awarded a gold medal at the International Composers' Competition in Perugia in 1913.

BIBLIOGRAPHY

SchmidlD

A. de Angelis: *L'Italia musicale d'oggi: Dizionario dei musicisti* (Rome, 1918, 3/1928)
A. Bonaventura: 'Le donne italiane e la musica', *RMI*, xxxii (1925), 519–34

FRANCESCA PERRUCCIO SICA

Coolidge, Peggy Stuart. See STUART-COOLIDGE, PEGGY.

Corri, Ghita Auber. British musician of Italian descent; *see* DUSSEK family, (2).

Corri, Sophia. British musician of Italian descent; *see* DUSSEK family, (2).

Cory, Eleanor (*b* Englewood, NJ, 8 Sept 1943). American composer and teacher. Her teachers include Meyer Kupferman, Charles Wuorinen, Chou Wen-chung and Bülent Arel, and she holds the doctorate in composition from Columbia University. She has taught widely: at Yale University, the City University of New York, Manhattan School of Music, Sarah Lawrence College and the New School, New York. Cory composes principally for chamber ensembles and solo instruments; although she has occasionally employed serialism, her work is best described as atonal yet very lyrical and displays her acute ear for instrumental sonorities.

WORKS
selective list

Orch: Tapestry, 1982; Canyons, chamber orch, 1991
Chamber: Concertino, pf, 18 insts, 1970; Combinations, pf, 1970; Epithalamium, fl, 1973; Waking, S, cl, bn, tpt, t sax, pf, perc, vn, va, vc, db, 1974; Octagons, fl, cl, bn, pf, vib, gui, vn, vc, 1976; Designs, vn, vc, pf, 1979; Suite à la Brecque, pf, 1979; Str Qt, 1985, rev. 1988; Spectra, fl, cl, hn, tpt, pf, vn, vc, 1988; Fantasy, fl, gui, perc, 1991
Choral: Agnus Dei and Libera me, women's vv, 1964; Of Mere Being, SSATB, brass qnt, 1987

CHRISTINE AMMER

Coulthard, Jean (*b* Vancouver, 10 Feb 1908). Canadian composer. She wrote her first compositions under the direction of her mother, a pianist and teacher, and received her earliest musical training (theory and piano) in Canada. From 1928 to 1930 she studied in England, at the RCM, London, with Ralph Vaughan Williams, Kathleen Long and R. O. Morris, and she later took lessons with Arthur Benjamin in Vancouver (1939) and with Bernard Wagenaar (1945, 1949) and Gordon Jacob (1965–6) in New York. In the late 1930s and early 1940s she also received critiques of her work from Copland, Schoenberg, Milhaud and Bartók, and in 1955 from Nadia Boulanger. Her early works owe more to the French impressionists than to her English teachers. Urged by Arthur Benjamin in 1939 to move away from writing vocal and piano works, she composed during the next few years a series of scores for full orchestra, including *A Canadian Fantasy* (1939), *A Winter's Tale* (1940), *Excursion* (1940) and *Song to the Sea* (1942). After 1945 she began to develop a more personal style, which reached its full maturity during the 1950s and 60s, when she was also a teacher of composition at the University of British Columbia.

Coulthard's extensive output includes generally accessible works as well as more abstract pieces such as the *Octet* (1972). Her compositions combine traditional form with her own version of tonality coloured by polytonal and chromatic harmonies; in works written after her retirement from university teaching in 1973, she has incorporated more contemporary techniques such as microtones, *musique concrète* (birdsongs of Vancouver Island in *The Birds of Landsdowne*, 1972), tone clusters and aleatory devices (as in *The Pines of Emily Carr*, 1972). Coulthard was made an Officer of the Order of Canada and a Freeman of the City of Vancouver in 1978 and was named Composer of the Year by the Canadian Performing Rights Organization in 1984. She was awarded honorary doctorates by the University of British Columbia in 1988 and by Concordia University, Montreal, in 1991. Some of her works and her monologue 'Music is My Whole Life' are included in Radio Canada International's *Anthology of Canadian Music* (1982).

WORKS
selective list

Stage: Return of the Native (music-theatre, 4, J. Coulthard and E. Baxter, after T. Hardy), 1956–79; The Devil's Fanfare (chamber ballet), vn, pf, 3 dancers
Orch: A Canadian Fantasy, 1939; Excursion, 1940; A Winter's Tale, ballade, str orch, 1940; Song to the Sea, ov., 1942; A Prayer for Elizabeth, str orch, 1953; Rider on the Sands, 1953; Sym. no.1, 1953; Fantasy, vn, pf, chamber orch, 1961; Pf Conc., 1963; Sym. Ode, vc, orch, 1965; Endymion, sym. poem, 1966; Canada Mosaic, 1974; Kalamalka: Lake of Many Colours, 1974; Sym. no.3 'Lyric', bn, orch, 1975; Sym. Ode, va, chamber orch, 1976; Autumn Sym., str orch, 1984; Meditation and 3 Dances, va, str orch, 1988
Chamber and solo inst: Ob Sonata, 1947; Vc Sonata, 1947; Duo Sonata, vn, pf, 1952; Str Qt no.1 'In the Spring of the Year 1952', 1952; Threnody: Str Qt no.2, 1953, rev. 1969; Pf Qt 'Sketches from a Medieval Town', 1957; Vn sonatas, nos.2–3, 1965; Divertimento, ww qnt, pf, 1968; Lyric Trio, vn, vc, pf, 1968; Lyric Sonatina, bn, pf, 1970; Lyric Sonatina, fl, pf, 1971; The Birds of Landsdowne: a Fantasy, vn, vc, pf, tape of birdsongs, 1972; Octet, 2 str qt, 1972; Lyric Sonatina, cl, pf, 1976; Fanfare Sonata, tpt, pf, 1978; Sonata, vn, 1979; Fantasy Sonata, hn, pf, 1983; The Bird of Dawning Singeth All Night Long, fl, va, gui, 1983; Frescoes, vn, harp, 1985; Earth Music, vc, pf, 1986; Str Qt no.3, 1987; Duo Sonata, vn, vc, 1989
Pf: Sonata, 1947; Variations on B–A–C–H, 1951; Aegean Sketches, 1964; Daredevil, 1964; Requiem Piece [Threnody], 1968, arr. 2 pf, 1974; Sketches from the Western Woods, 1970; Sonata, 2 pf, 1978;

Image astrale, 1981; Sonata no.2, 1986; Image terrestre, 1990

Vocal: Spring Rhapsody (B. Carman, W. E. Marshall, L. MacKay, D. Campbell Scott), A, pf, 1958, also arr. orch; 6 Medieval Love Songs (anon. Lat., trans. H. Waddell), 1962; Songs from the Distaff Muse (Elizabeth I, K. Mansfield, E. Dickinson and others), S, A, vc, 1972; The Pines of Emily Carr, nar, A, str qt, pf, timp, 1972; 4 Prophetic Songs (E. Gourlay), A, fl, vc, pf, 1975; Song for Fine Weather of the Haida Indians, S, chamber orch, 1981; Christina Songs, high v, pf, 1983; Cycle of 5 Lyrics from the Chinese (trans. Waddell), S, fl, pf, glock, Chinese woodblock, 1984

Choral: Quebec May, 1948 (E. Birney), chorus, 2 pf, orch version, 1988; This Land, choral sym., S, A, T, B, SATB, speaking chorus, tape, orch, 1967; Hymn of Creation (after the Rig-Veda), 1975; Vancouver Lights: a Soliloquy (Birney), S, Bar, SATB, timp, perc, harp/str, 1980

Principal publishers: Berandol, Harmuse, Novello, OUP (Toronto), Waterloo

MSS in Canadian Music Centre, Toronto

BIBLIOGRAPHY

EMC 2 (J. Butler, B. N. S. Gooch)

G. Ridout. 'Two West-Coast Composers', Canadian Review of Music and Art, iii/Dec–Jan (1944–5)

V. W. Rowley: The Solo Piano Music of the Canadian Composer Jean Coulthard (diss., Boston U., 1973)

R. Kashak and B. Symaka: 'A Celebration of the Life and Work of Jean Coulthard', ILWC Journal (1994), Feb, 12–14

GAYNOR G. JONES

Couper [née Cooper], **Mildred** (b Buenos Aires, 10 Dec 1887; d Santa Barbara, CA, 9 Aug 1974). American composer and pianist. She studied in Karlsruhe, Paris and Rome; her teachers included Moritz Moszkowski, Alfred Cortot and Giovanni Sgambati. In 1915 she went to New York where she taught at the Mannes School until 1927. She composed several works for quarter-tone piano, starting with Xanadu, written for a 1930 production of Marco Millions in Santa Barbara. Dirge appeared in Cowell's New Music Edition in 1937; Rumba was performed at the Evenings on the Roof concerts in Los Angeles in 1951.

WORKS
selective list

Inst: Suite, pf, hpd, 1932; And on Earth Peace, ob, vn, va, vc, pf, c1933; Variations on The Irish Washerwoman, pf, c1935, arr. orch, 1945, also arr. 2 pf; The Nightingale, fl, ob, str qt, nar, 1951; The Days of Our Years, vn, ob, pf; Passacaglia Symbolizing the Unifying Principle of the United Nations, pf, also arr. sextet, also arr. orch; Pippa Passes, fl, str

Quarter-tone pf: Xanadu, incid. music for Marco Millions, 1930; Dirge (New York, 1937); Rumba, 1951

Pf music, songs, music for children

CATHERINE PARSONS SMITH

Cozzolani, Chiara Margarita (b Milan, 27 Nov 1602; d Milan, between 4 May 1676 and 20 April 1678). Italian singer and composer. In many ways, her life epitomizes the destiny of Milanese patrician women, most of whom became nuns in the early 17th century; some two-thirds of the 41 monasteries that housed them were renowned for music until the late 18th-century dissolutions. The youngest daughter of a wealthy merchant family, she entered the Benedictine monastery of S Radegonda. She began her novitiate in 1619 and professed final vows in 1620, taking 'Chiara' as her religious name. She is mentioned in documents from S Radegonda in connection with disputes over the regulation of music and may have served as the *maestra di cappella* of one of the house's two choirs.

Cozzolani's first publication (1640) and her secular cantatas are lost, along with the continuo part to the 1648 solo motets. But enough music remains to mark her as one of the leading composers of mid-century Milan. The duets and solos in the 1642 Concerti sacri, dedicated to Mathias de' Medici, are among the first Milanese examples of the Lombard style pioneered by Gasparo Casati (Isabella Leonarda's teacher) and as such testify to the porous ecclesiastical enclosure of Milanese female monasteries. These motets are characterized by highly affective texts, extended musical length by means of sequence, rapid declamation and irregularly spaced melismas, and by parallel 3rds. In contrast, the three- and four-voice pieces look back to earlier Milanese traditions; the Assumption Day dialogue Psallite superes, for instance, employs a tutti refrain.

The 1650 Vespers volume is an unusual combination of archaic (eight-voice psalm settings) and modern (two- to five-voice concerto) genres. Unlike other Milanese composers, Cozzolani mixed two-choir antiphony (in the tuttis and frequent refrains) with concertato solo and duet writing for the verses. These Vespers are among the largest-scale (and least traditional) settings of mid-century Milan, although their liberal use of repetition and sequence tempers their appeal. The concertos of the 1650 book, on the other hand, expand the characteristics of the 1642 collection in a somewhat more self-assured style (the awkward partwriting in the earlier book is largely absent); the duet O quam bonus es, for example, sets a double meditation (on the wounds of Christ and the milk of the Madonna) to balanced, well-crafted melodic periods in a multi-sectional form. A central genre in both prints is the dialogue, which even infiltrates the eight-voice psalm settings; Cozzolani's 1650 dialogue on Mary Magdalene at the tomb stands apart among Milanese treatments by its apportioning of long phrases to the Magdalene's lament, its closing section unified by an ostinato cadential figure, and its language taken from the Song of Songs.

After 1650 Cozzolani's musical production seems to have slackened off, partly because of her duties at S Radegonda (she was abbess in 1658–9 and 1672–3, and prioress in the 1660s), and the crusade against music and 'irregularities' launched by Archbishop Alfonso Litta in the mid-1660s.

WORKS

Primavera di fiori musicali, 1–4vv, bc, op.1 (Milan, 1640), lost; cited in Picinelli, Armellini and *Zur Feier des Wohlthätenfestes im Berlinischen Gymnasium zum grauen Kloster* (Berlin, 1856)

Concerti sacri, 2–4vv, bc, op.2 (Venice, 1642); O dulcis Jesu in 1649⁶; 1 ed. in Noske 1992, 2 ed. in Kendrick 1993

Scherzi di sacra melodia, 1v, bc, op.3 (bc lost) (Venice, 1648)

Salmi à otto . . . motetti et dialoghi, 2–8vv, bc, op.3 [*sic*], (Venice, 1650); 1 ed. in Noske 1992, 2 ed. in Kendrick 1993

1 aria, No, no no che mare, lost

BIBLIOGRAPHY

FétisB; *SchillingE*; *SchmidlD*

F. Picinelli: *Ateneo dei letterati milanesi* (Milan, 1670), 147

M. Armellini: *Biblioteca Benedictino-Casinensis* (Assisi, 1731–2)

F. Noske: 'Sul dialogo latino del seicento: Osservationi', *RIM*, xxiv (1989), 330–46

R. L. Kendrick: 'The Traditions of Milanese Convent Music and the Sacred Dialogues of Chiara Margarita Cozzolani', *The Crannied Wall: Women, Religion and the Arts in Early Modern Europe*, ed. C. Monson (Ann Arbor, 1992), 211–33

F. Noske: *Saints and Sinners: the Latin Musical Dialogue in the Seventeenth Century* (Oxford, 1992), 45–6, 110–11

R. L. Kendrick: *'Le Sirene Celesti': Generations, Gender and Genres in Seicento Milanese Nuns' Music* (diss., New York U., 1993), 479–702

ROBERT L. KENDRICK

Cramer, Anna M. (*b* Amsterdam, 15 July 1873; *d* Blaricum, 4 June 1968). Dutch composer. She studied the piano at the Amsterdam Conservatory and was living in Berlin in 1903. By 1910 four collections of her songs had been published. Some reviews were negative: critics were disturbed by the complex harmonies, the chromaticism, the surprising modulations and the expressive piano accompaniments. In her choice of poetry she revealed a highly developed sensitivity to literature. After her op.4 songs of 1910 she published nothing more. By 1934 she had returned to Amsterdam, where she remained as a recluse until she died, completely forgotten. She was only rediscovered as a composer some time after her death: research has unearthed 56 songs and three songs with orchestral accompaniment intended for an opera. Critics have been enthusiastic about these works, some of which resemble the songs of Richard Strauss and Hugo Wolf, while other pieces suggest Franz Schreker, and a few, surprisingly, Kurt Weill, because of their characteristic ironic tone.

HELEN METZELAAR

Craven, Elizabeth. *See* ANSPACH, ELIZABETH.

Crawford (Seeger), Ruth (Porter) (*b* East Liverpool, OH, 3 July 1901; *d* Chevy Chase, MD, 18 Nov 1953). American composer and folk music specialist. She had two important careers in a relatively short lifetime: as a composer, she was an outstanding figure among early American modernists in the 1920s and early 1930s; as a specialist in American traditional music, she transcribed, edited and arranged important anthologies in the 1940s and early 1950s.

Crawford received her earliest musical training while living in Jacksonville, Florida, between 1912 and 1921. Piano lessons with Madame Valborg Collett (a pupil of Agathe Grøndahl) from 1917 to 1920 led to further study at the American Conservatory of Music in Chicago with Heniot Levy (1921–3) and Louise Robyn (1921–4). She gained skill in composition from Adolph Weidig (*c*1923–1929). Equally formative were her piano studies from about 1925 to 1927 with the Canadian teacher Djane Lavoie Herz, a disciple of Skryabin. Through Madame Herz, Crawford came into contact with Henry Cowell and Dane Rudhyar. By 1926 Crawford was also acquainted with the leading Chicago poet Carl Sandburg, contributing folksong arrangements to his landmark anthology *The American Songbag* and absorbing his poetic and philosophical ideals.

Crawford's career flourished in the 1920s within the confines of the small modernist movement existing outside New York. In 1926 Cowell named Crawford for the board of his New Music Society and later published several of her works in the *New Music Quarterly*. In the mid-1920s Crawford became a board member of the Pro Musica Society and in 1928 a founder member of the Chicago chapter of the International Society for Contemporary Music (ISCM). Between 1924 and 1929 she composed almost two-thirds of her output, receiving several notable performances from new-music groups. The first professional performance of her music was given in New York in November 1925 by Gitta Gradova (another pupil of Lavoie Herz), who performed her second Piano Prelude. In 1927 her Violin Sonata was played at a League of Composers concert of music by six 'Young Americans' (including Aaron Copland and Marc Blitzstein); the following year it was performed at the inaugural concert of the Chicago chapter of the ISCM. Richard Buhlig included three piano preludes by Crawford in a recital on 6 May 1928 in the Copland–Sessions series in New York.

In autumn 1929, after spending the summer at the MacDowell Colony in New Hampshire, Crawford left Chicago for New York to study dissonant counterpoint with the composer and musicologist Charles Seeger. There she joined Cowell's circle of 'ultra-moderns', which included Seeger's close friend Carl Ruggles. Crawford became a protégée of Seeger and was influential in helping him to revise *Tradition and Experiment in New Music and a Manual on Dissonant Counterpoint* for publication. His ideas were crucial to the development of her second-style period (1930–33), a few short but fruitful years.

In 1930 Crawford was awarded a Guggenheim Fellowship in composition; she was the first woman to be named and one of only five in the next 15 years. She spent her year abroad mostly in Berlin (autumn 1930 to April 1931) and in Paris (June to early November 1931). 'In Berlin I studied with no-one', she later wrote (alluding to her lack of contact with Schoenberg). Yet she regarded her encounters with Bartók and Berg as high points of what was the most productive year of her life. Virgil Thomson later described the String Quartet '1931' as 'in every way a distinguished, a noble piece of work'. Crawford returned to New York in November 1931 and married Charles Seeger the following year. In the early 1930s her music was performed at the New School for Social Research, where both Seeger and Cowell were on the faculty. Her Three Songs for voice, oboe, percussion and strings represented the USA at the 1933 ISCM Festival in Amsterdam.

In 1936 the Seegers moved to Washington, DC: Charles was appointed to the music division of the Resettlement Agency (a federal New Deal organization), while Ruth worked closely with John and Alan Lomax at the Archive of American Folk Song at the Library of Congress, her interests having shifted from composition to the preservation and dissemination of American

Ruth Crawford

folk music. The Seegers became one of the most important 'families' in the folk music revival of the late 1930s and the 1940s. Her stepson Pete Seeger was the leading folk revival performer in the USA; her children Mike and Peggy also became professional musicians. Her only original composition during this period was *Rissolty Rossolty*, an 'American Fantasia for Orchestra' based on folk tunes, commissioned by CBS for its radio series American School of the Air.

With the publication of *Our Singing Country* (1941), Crawford became well known for her transcriptions. Later she developed music programmes utilizing folk music for progressive private schools in the Washington area. Compiled in 1941–6, the classic *American Folksongs for Children* (1948) won praise from both composers and music educators; it was followed by *Animal Folksongs for Children* (1950) and *American Folk*

Songs for Christmas (1953). The Suite for Wind Quintet (1952) marked a return to composition.

Crawford's original music falls into two style periods. Her Chicago compositions (1924–9) reveal her predilection for dissonance and for post-tonal harmonies influenced by Skryabin, as well as her fondness for irregular rhythms and metres. Unpublished diaries and poems suggest the influence of an eclectic legacy of philosophical and literary sources common to many American artists and writers of the early 20th century. Among these were theosophy and Eastern mysticism, and American literary transcendentalism, as well as the imaginative traditions of Walt Whitman and Sandburg, the latter supplying the texts for almost all of her vocal compositions.

However, Crawford's reputation as an innovative and experimental composer rests mainly on her New York compositions (1930–33), in which she concerned herself with dissonant counterpoint and indigenous American serial techniques. She was one of the earliest composers to extend serial controls to parameters other than pitch and to develop formal plans based on serial operations. As a folksong arranger, she was no less original and skilful. Her folksong transcriptions were praised as impeccable and her arrangements as faithful to both the sound and the spirit of the original field recordings that were so often their source. She summed up her credo as a desire to give people 'a taste for the thing itself'.

WORKS

CHAMBER

Vn Sonata, 1926; Chicago, 22 May 1926
Suite, 5 wind insts, pf, 1927, rev. 1929
Suite no.2, str, pf, 1929; New York, 9 March 1930; ed. J. Tick (Ann Arbor, 1993)
3 Songs (C. Sandburg), A, ob, perc, pf, opt. orch, 1930–32: Rat Riddles, 1930, New York, 21 April 1930; In Tall Grass, Berlin, 10 March 1932; Prayers of Steel, Amsterdam, 14 June 1933
4 Diaphonic Suites, 1930: no.1, 2 vc/bn, vc; no.2, 2 cl; no.3, fl; no.4, ob/va, vc
String Quartet '1931'; New York, 13 Nov 1933
Suite for Wind Quintet, 1952; Washington DC, 2 Dec 1952

OTHER WORKS

Vocal: Adventures of Tom Thumb (R. Crawford, after J. L. and W. C. Grimm), nar, pf, 1925; 5 Songs (Sandburg), Home Thoughts, White Moon, Joy, Loam, Sunsets, 1v, pf, 1929, ed. J. Tick (New York, 1990); 3 Chants, no.1, To an Unkind God, female chorus, no.2, To an Angel, S, SATB, no.3, S, A, female chorus, 1930; 2 Ricercari (H. T. Tsiang), no.1, Sacco, Vanzetti, no.2, Chinaman, Laundryman, 1v, pf, 1932
Orch: Music for Small Orch, fl, cl, bn, 4 vn, 2 vc, pf,

1926, ed. J. Tick (Ann Arbor, 1993); Rissolty Rossolty, 1939
Pf: Kaleidoscopic Changes on an Original Theme Ending with a Fugue, 1924; 5 Preludes, 1924–5, ed. R. Platt (Bryn Mawr, PA, 1993); 4 Preludes, 1927–8; Pf Study in Mixed Accents, 1930

Principal publishers: A–R Editions, Continuo Music Press, Merion Music, New Music, C. F. Peters
MSS in *US-Wc*

FOLKSONG ARRANGEMENTS AND TRANSCRIPTIONS

C. Sandburg: *American Songbag* (New York, 1927) [4 arrs.]
19 American folk tunes, pf, unpubd, 1936–8
J. A. Lomax and A. Lomax: *Our Singing Country* (New York, 1941)
G. Korson: *Coal Dust on the Fiddle* (Philadelphia, 1943)
with C. Seeger: *J. A. Lomax and A. Lomax: Folk Song U.S.A.* (New York, 1947)
American Folksongs for Children (Garden City, NY, 1948)
G. Korson: *Anthology of Pennsylvania Folklore* (New York, 1949)
Animal Folksongs for Children (Garden City, NY, 1950)
B. A. Botkin: *Treasury of Western Folklore* (New York, 1951)
American Folk Songs for Christmas (Garden City, NY, 1953)
Let's Build a Railroad (New York, 1954)
E. Garrido de Boggs: *Folklore Infantil do Santo Domingo* (Madrid, 1955) [transcr.]
with D. Emrich and C. Seeger: 1001 Folksongs, inc., unpubd [13 vols.]

BIBLIOGRAPHY

'Gitta Gradova to Play Compositions by Cowell, Rudhyar and Ruth Crawford', *MusAm*, xliii (28 Nov 1925)
P. Rosenfeld: *An Hour with American Music* (Philadelphia, 1929)
C. Seeger: 'Ruth Crawford', *American Composers on American Music*, ed. H. Cowell (Stanford, CA, 1933), 110–18
V. Thomson: 'Substantial Novelties', *New York Herald Tribune* (16 March 1949)
S. Thomson, ed.: *Four Symposia on Folklore* (Bloomington, IN, 1953), 191–4, 209, 243
S. R. Cowell: 'Ruth Crawford Seeger, 1901–1953', *JIFMC*, vii (1955), 55–6
G. Perle: 'Atonality and the Twelve-Tone System in the United States', *Score*, no.27 (1960), 51–61
E. Salzman: 'Distaff Disk: Ruth Crawford Seeger's Work Ahead of its Era', *New York Times* (16 April 1961)
C. Seeger: *Reminiscences of an American Musicologist* [Oral History Archives Transcript, U. of California, Los Angeles, 1972]
S. E. Gilbert: 'The Ultra-Modern Idiom: a Survey of New Music', *PNM*, xii/1–2 (1973–4), 282–314
E. Carter: 'Expressionism and American Music', *The Writings of Elliott Carter*, ed. E. Stone and K. Stone (Bloomington, IN, 1977), 230–42
B. Jepson: 'Ruth Crawford Seeger: a Study in Mixed Accents', *Feminist Art Journal* (1977), spr., 13–16, 50
R. Mead: *Henry Cowell's New Music 1925–1936: the Society, the Music Editions and the Recordings* (Ann Arbor, 1981)

D. Nicholls: 'Ruth Crawford Seeger: an Introduction', *MT*, cxxiv (1983), 421–5

M. Gaume: 'Ruth Crawford Seeger', *Women Making Music: the Western Art Tradition, 1150–1950*, ed. J. Bowers and J. Tick (Urbana and Chicago, 1986), 370–88

—— : *Ruth Crawford Seeger: Memoirs, Memories, Music* (Metuchen, NJ, 1986)

M. Nelson: 'In Pursuit of Charles Seeger's Heterophonic Ideal: Three Palindromic Works by Ruth Crawford', *MQ*, lxxii (1986), 458–75

E. Flemm: *The Preludes for Piano of Ruth Crawford Seeger* (diss., U. of Cincinnati, 1987)

M. Gaume: 'Ruth Crawford: a Promising Young Composer in New York, 1929–1930', *American Music*, v/1 (1987), 74–84

W. Mellers: *Music in a New Found Land* (New York, 2/1987)

R. W. White: 'Remembering Ruth Crawford Seeger: an Interview with Charles and Peggy Seeger', *American Music*, vi/4 (1988), 442–54

D. Nicholls: *American Experimental Music 1890–1940* (Cambridge, 1990)

J. Tick: 'Dissonant Counterpoint Revisited: the First Movement of Ruth Crawford Seeger's *String Quartet 1931*', *A Celebration of Words and Music: Essays in Honor of H. Wiley Hitchcock* (Ann Arbor, 1990), 405–22

—— : 'Ruth Crawford's "Spiritual Concept": the Sound-Ideals of an Early American Modernist, 1924–1930', *JAMS*, xliv (1991), 221–61

JUDITH TICK

D

Daiken, Melanie Ruth (*b* London, 27 July 1945). English composer and lecturer. She studied composition and the piano at the RAM, the University of Ghana, the Paris Conservatoire, where she was a pupil of Olivier Messiaen and Yvonne Loriod, and London University. She has taught composition at London University, Morley College and at the RAM, where she was appointed deputy head of composition and contemporary music studies in 1986. Daiken has written much vocal music, setting texts by authors as diverse as Paul Eluard, F. García Lorca, Charles Baudelaire, Rupert Brooke, Georg Trakl and Samuel Beckett. In 1971 her opera *Mayakovsky and the Sun* was commissioned by the Edinburgh Festival and performed by the Music Theatre Ensemble under Alexander Goehr. Several of her chamber works have been performed on BBC Radio 3, including the striking *Requiem* (1983) for solo piano.

WORKS
selective list

Opera: Eusebius (1, Daiken), Paris, Jan 1968; Mayakovsky and the Sun (V. Mayakovsky), Edinburgh, 1 Sept 1971; Playboy of the Western World (J. M. Synge), inc.
Orch and inst ens: Gems of Erin, wind/brass ens, pf, perc, db, 1980; Attica, orch, 1983; Der Gartner, 13 solo str, pf, 1988
Chamber and solo inst: Etudes pour Eusebius, pf, 1967; 3 Bagatelles, fl, 1968; Lorca pieces, pf, 1975; Va Sonata, 1978; Requiem, pf, 1983
Vocal: Les petits justes (P. Eluard), Mez, pf, 1967; Lorca songs (F. García Lorca), S, B, pf, 1974; Le Rancon (C. Baudelaire), SATB, str, perc, 1977; Songs of Attila Jozsef, Mez, va, pf, 1979; The Dead (R. Brooke and G. Trakl), SATB, brass ens, org, 1980

BIBLIOGRAPHY
Fuller-LeFanuRM

SOPHIE FULLER

Dalberg, Nancy (*b* Bødstrup, nr Slagelse, 6 July 1881; *d* Copenhagen, 28 Sept 1949). Danish composer. She was brought up in a wealthy middle-class home, and first wanted to become a pianist but had to give it up because of an arm disease. From 1909 she studied music theory and composition with Johan Svendsen, and from 1913 with Carl Nielsen whom she assisted in orchestrating and copying some of his compositions. In 1918 she gave a composition evening at which Carl Nielsen conducted three of her symphonic works, among them a three-movement symphony in C♯ minor; she later withdrew the first movement of this work and the *To orkesterstykker* remained. Besides instrumental music she wrote a large number of songs to texts by Selma Lagerlöf, Johannes Jørgensen and Martin Andersen Nexø.

WORKS
selective list

Orch: Scherzo, str orch, 1918; To orkesterstykker, op.9, 1918; Capriccio, 1918
Chamber: Str Qt, 1914; To fantasistykker, vn, pf, 1918; Scherzo grazioso, vn, pf, 1927; To violoncelstykker, vc, pf
Vocal: 3 Songs, 1914; To romancer og zigeunersang, 1922; 3 danske Duette, 1931; Svanerne og fire andre Sange, 1935

BIBLIOGRAPHY
G. Holmen: 'Hilda Sehested og Nancy Dalberg: to danske komponister', *Forum for kvindeforskning*, vi/1 (1986), 29–36

INGE BRULAND

Dale, Kathleen. *See* RICHARDS, KATHLEEN.

Dalebury, Jill. *See* FURZE, JESSIE.

Daniels, Mabel Wheeler (*b* Swampscott, MA, 27 Nov 1877; *d* Cambridge, MA, 10 March 1971). American composer. Both her grandfathers were church musicians and her parents were active in Boston's Handel and Haydn Society. She studied the piano from an early age and in 1888 wrote her first piece. While at Radcliffe College (BA 1900) she sang in the Glee Club, for which she wrote several operettas. She studied orchestration with George Chadwick at the New England Conservatory and in 1902 became the first woman in Ludwig Thuille's score-reading class at the Munich Conservatory. From 1911 to 1913 she directed the Radcliffe Glee

Mabel Daniels

Club and the Bradford Academy and from 1913 to 1918 she was head of music at Simmons College, Boston. From then on, with financial support from her family, she devoted herself to composition . After conducting *The Desolate City* at the MacDowell Colony, she returned there as a Fellow for 24 summers beginning in 1914.

Daniels's musical language encompasses nonfunctional triadic harmony with occasional diatonic dissonance; the melodic lines are sometimes angular, due partly to modal shifts and unpredictable triads. She preferred writing for voices, and indeed choral pieces are among her best-known works. She did not call herself a feminist or 'woman composer', yet she worked for women's suffrage and acknowledged discrimination against women musicians. A collection of her papers, scores and press cuttings is in the Schlesinger Library, Radcliffe College.

WORKS
selective list

Stage: A Copper Complication (operetta, R. L. Hooper), 3S, 3A, women's vv, orch, 1900; The Court of Hearts (operetta, Hooper), 2S, 2A, women's vv, pf, 1900; Alice in Wonderland Continued, 1902–4 (opera sketch), women's vv, Brookline, MA, 1904; The Legend of Marietta (operetta), women's vv, 1909; Digressions, op.41

no.2 (ballet), str, 1947; addl nos. for musical plays: The Show Girl (R. A. Barnet and D. K. Stevens), 1902; Baron Humbug (Barnet), 1903

Choral (with orch): The Desolate City, op.21 (W. S. Blunt), Bar, mixed vv, orch/pf, 1913; Peace in Liberty (Peace with a Sword), op.25 (A. F. Brown), mixed vv, orch/pf, 1917; Songs of Elfland, op.28 nos.1–2 (M. W. Daniels), S, women's vv, harp, fl, str/pf, 1924; The Holy Star, op.31 no.1 (N. B. Turner), mixed/women's vv, orch/pf, 1928; Exultate Deo: Song of Rejoicing, op.33 (Daniels, after *Psalms*), mixed vv, orch/org, pf, 1929; The Song of Jael, op.37 (E. A. Robinson), S, mixed vv, orch/pf, 1937; A Psalm of Praise, op.46, mixed vv, 3 tpt, perc, timp, str orch/org/pf, 1954

Other choral: Mavoureen, op.12 no.1 (Daniels), mixed vv, pf, 1906; In Springtime (R. Lincoln, A. F. Brown), choral cycle, women's vv, pf, 1910; The Voice of my Beloved, op.16 no.2, women's vv, pf, 2 vn, 1911; Veni creator spiritus, S, women's vv, pf, 1912; Secrets, op.22/1 (F. L. Knowles), men's vv, pf, 1913; The Ride (The Wild Ride) (L. I. Guiney), men's vv, pf, 1926; Dum Dianae vitrea, op.38/2 (12th century), women's vv, 1942; Carol of a Rose, women's vv, 1958; A Study in Grammar, men's vv; On the Road to Mandalay, women's vv

Orch: Deep Forest, op.34 no.1, ww qnt, tpt, perc, timp, str, 1931, arr. large orch, 1933; Pastoral Ode, op.40, fl, str, 1940

Inst: 3 Observations op.41, ob/fl, cl, bn, 1943; 4 Observations, 4 str, 1945; 2 Pieces, vn, pf, 1947; Vn sonata

Miscellaneous songs for voice and piano

Principal publishers: J. Fischer, H. W. Gray, E. C. Schirmer, A. P. Schmidt

BIBLIOGRAPHY

WAM

M. W. Daniels: *An American Girl in Munich: Impressions of a Music Student* (Boston, 1905) [excerpt in *Women in Music: an Anthology of Source Readings from the Middle Ages to the Present*, ed. C. Neuls-Bates (New York, 1982), 219–22]

J. T. Howard: *Our American Music* (New York, 3/1946)

C. Reis: *Composers in America: Biographical Sketches* (New York, 1947 [4th edn of *American Composers*])

R. Elie: 'The MacDowell Colony enters its 45th Year', *Boston Herald* (6 January 1951)

M. Goss: *Modern Music Makers* (New York, 1952), 61–9

P. S. Hurd: 'Composer joins Grace and Vigor: Modern but not Ultra', *Christian Science Monitor* (28 Dec 1955)

M. W. Daniels: 'Mabel Daniels Reads through her Score of Memories', *Christian Science Monitor* (22 April 1961)

C. Ammer: *Unsung: a History of Women in American Music* (Westport, CT, 1980), esp. 89–91

E. Kaledin: 'Daniels, Mabel Wheeler', *Notable American Women*, iv (Cambridge, MA, 1980), 177–9

E. R. Anderson: *Contemporary American Composers* (Boston, 2/1982)

J. MICHELE EDWARDS

Danzi, Franziska. *See* LEBRUN, FRANZISKA.

Danzi [née Marchand], **(Maria) Margarethe** (*b* Munich, 1768; *d* Munich, 11 June 1800). German soprano and composer. She was the daughter of the singer, actor and theatre director Theobald Marchand, who came from Strasbourg and whose troupe was active in Mainz, Frankfurt, Mannheim and Munich. From an early age she played children's roles in the theatre and performed as a pianist and singer. She and her younger brother Heinrich lived in Salzburg from 1781 to 1784 with Leopold Mozart, who taught her singing and the piano (she is often mentioned in his letters as 'Gretl'). He supported her first attempts at composition (sonatas for piano or for violin and piano) and tried to have them published, but without success. She made her singing début in Munich in 1787, in Vogler's *Castore e Polluce*, and became famous for her Mozart roles. In 1790 she married the composer Franz Danzi and toured with him in Germany, Austria and Italy; from 1796 she was a member of the Deutsches Theater in Munich. Two of her works were published by Falter in Munich: three sonatas for piano and violin op.1 (1801; no.1 ed. R. Münster in Varie musiche di Baviera, i, Giebing, 1967) and the *Marche de Marseillois varié* op.2 for piano (1802).

BIBLIOGRAPHY

GerberNL; *LipowskyBL*; *SchillingE*; *SchmidlD*†

AMZ, iv (1801), 124; xxviii (1826), 584

F. Walter: *Geschichte des Theaters und der Musik am kurpfälzischen Hofe* (Leipzig, 1898)

E. Reipschläger: *Schubaur, Danzi und Poissl als Opernkomponisten* (diss., U. of Rostock, 1911)

O. E. Deutsch, W. A. Bauer and J. H. Eibl, eds.: *Mozart: Briefe und Aufzeichnungen* (Kassel, 1962–75)

E. Anderson, ed.: *The Letters of Mozart and His Family* (London, 3/1985)

BRIGITTE HÖFT

Da Ponte, Vincenta (*fl* second half of the 18th century). Italian instrumentalist, singer and composer. She was a member of the *coro* (music school) of the Ospedale della Pietà in Venice during the tenure of the music director Bonaventura Furlanetto (1738–1817). Her patrician surname indicates that she was not a foundling, as were most of the wards of the Pietà, but an external, tuition-paying pupil or had been awarded a scholarship. (The music school had been founded in the late 17th century to train girls as musicians and was later reserved exclusively for daughters of the nobility.) Da Ponte is one of five composers so far identified among the members of the *coro* at the Pietà. Her known works are an unpublished set of four dances in a collection of *monferrine* (Piedmontese

dances), composed in about 1775. The manuscript is in the Conservatorio di Musica Benedetto Marcello, Venice (correr esposti, 72 no.30, 305–8).

BIBLIOGRAPHY

J. L. Baldauf-Berdes: *Women Musicians of Venice: Musical Foundations, 1525–1855* (Oxford, 1993)

JANE L. BERDES

D'Auenbrugg, Marianna. *See* AUENBRUGGER, MARIANNA VON.

Davidson, Tina (*b* Stockholm, 30 Dec 1952). American composer and pianist. She graduated in piano and composition from Bennington College, Vermont, where she studied with Henry Brant, Louis Calabro, Vivian Fine and Lionel Nowak. She has been composer-in-residence for the Orchestra Society of Philadelphia and director of the Philadelphia New Orchestral project, as well as president of the New Music Alliance, which sponsors New Music festivals internationally. Davidson has been awarded many prestigious commissions, state and national fellowships and Meet the Composer Awards. In 1988 her work *Transparent Victims* was selected by American Public Radio for the International Rostrum of Composers meeting at the UNESCO headquarters in Paris. In 1992 she received the Pew Fellowship.

Davidson has been influenced by the highly individual styles of Carl Ruggles, Henry Cowell, Ruth Crawford and Henry Brant as well as by the movement-styles of Merce Cunningham and Martha Graham. She gives equal attention to the intellectual and intuitive sides of the compositional process. Her works, several of which have been recorded, are usually in one movement and unfold in linear fashion, one event ending as the next begins, thus conveying a sense of seamless progress towards a goal.

WORKS
selective list

Orch: 2 Beasts from the Forest of Imaginary Beings, nar, orch, 1975; Dancers, 1980; Pf Conc., 1981; Blood Memory: a Long Quiet after the Call, vc, orch, 1985; In the Darkness I Find a Face (It is Mine), 1989; The Selkie Boy, nar, orch, 1991; Blessings (Sacred Space), a sax, orch, 1992; They Come Dancing, 1994

Chamber: Recollections of Darkness, str trio, 1975; Piece for Cello, pf, 1975; Snapshots, vc, pf, 1980; Wait for the End of Dreaming, 2 bar sax, db/bn, 1983; Dark Child Sings, 4 vc, 1988; Cassandra Sings, str qt, 1988; I Hear the Mermaid Singing, va, vc, pf, 1990; Bleached Thread, Sister Thread, str qt, 1991; Fire on the Mountain, vib, mar, pf, 1993

Vocal: 5 Songs (Native Indian), S, va, 1975; Witches'

Hammar (anon.), Mez, home-made perc, 1979; Unicorn/Tapestry (M. L. Polak), Mez, vc, tape, 1982; Black Riders and Other Lines (S. Crane), male v, pf, perc, 1985; Transparent Victims (no text), S, a sax, tape, 1987

Kbd: 7 Macabre Songs, 1979; Day of Rage, 1984; I am the Last Witness, pf 1 hand, 1984; Star Myths, 1987; The Dancing Sword, 2 pf, 1992

Mixed media: The Game of Silence (anon.), nar, mime, dance, 1976

BIBLIOGRAPHY

M. Wester: 'Between the Quiet and the Clamor: a Conversation with Tina Davidson', *American Women Composers News/Forum*, vii/5–6 (1987), 10

C. McCurdy: Applause and Curtain Calls for New Music Premieres in Philadelphia', *Chamber Music*, viii/2 (1991), 16–19

T. Davidson: 'Cassandra Sings', *Ms* (1992), Jan–Feb, 64

SAM DI BONAVENTURA

Davis, Miss [first name unknown] (*b* Dublin, *c*1726, *d* ?Dublin, after 1755). Harpsichord player, singer and composer. She was the daughter of Mr Davis (or Davies; *fl* 1735–48), a harpsichord player, and Mrs Davis (*fl* 1730–48), a singer. Mrs Davis promoted her daughter as a child prodigy, who first appeared on 5 February 1743, when she was said to be six years old. Her London début was at Hickford's Room on 10 May 1745, as 'a child of eight years of age, lately arrived from Ireland'. On 6 February 1748, at her annual benefit concert, besides playing the harpsichord she sang 'some fine Italian songs' composed by herself. This is her only claim to be listed as a composer. In November 1755 a notice in the *Dublin Journal* stated that 'Miss Davis having declined to play the Harpsichord in publick for some years past continues to teach Ladies.'

BRIAN BOYDELL

Davis, Alice Maude [Dotie]. *See* TEMPLE, HOPE.

De Blanck Martín, Olga (*b* Havana, 11 March 1916). Cuban music educationist and composer. She graduated in piano and music theory from the Hubert de Blanck Conservatory, Havana, took private lessons with Amadeo Roldán and Pedro San Juan, and also studied with Brazilian composer Burle Marx while living in New York (1935–8), and with Julián Carrillo and Jiménez Mabarak in Mexico (1943–4). She was appointed deputy director of the De Blanck Conservatory (founded by her father) in 1945 and director in 1955. Together with Gisela Hernández she developed a new system of music education and brought about profound changes in music teaching in Cuba; she also set up the educational and academic publishing firm Ediciones de Blanck, produced many musical editions, including works by contemporary Cuban composers, and helped establish the Museo de la Música in Havana. Her musical comedy *Vivimos hoy* was first performed in 1943 and her song *Mi guitarra guajira* won first prize in the Cuban National Song Competition in 1948. Many of her compositions are inspired by folk music and skilful use is made of Cuban rhythms and of traditional popular Cuban instruments, in particular the guitar, whose characteristic sound resonates throughout the whole of her output.

WORKS
selective list

Stage: Vivimos hoy (musical comedy, 3, M. J. Casanova), 1943; Hotel Tropical (musical comedy, 3, Casanova), 1944; Un cuento de Navidad (musical comedy, 3, Casanova), 1958; El cncuentro (ballct), 1962; Bohío (ballet), 1964; El mago de Oz (1), 1967; El caballito enano (musical tale, D. Alonso), 1967; Saltarín (musical tale, Alonso), 1967

Choral and sacred: Cantata guajira (E. Ballagas), solo v, mixed vv, orch, 1967; Misa cubana, mixed vv, org, 1987; Así dijo Santa Rosa Filipa, 1v, org, 1989

Inst: Pentasílabo, pf, güiro, quijada, tumbadora, 1972; Portocromía, pf, 1981

Also numerous songs (1v, pf), some with addl Cuban insts, 1935–1987; *c*110 children's songs; educational music, collab. G. Hernández; and arrs.

ALICIA VALDÉS CANTERO

Delaval, Mme (*fl* London, 1791–1802). French or English composer, harpist and pianist. She may have been a daughter of the French singer Henri Larrivée (either Adelaide or Agathe) and may have belonged to the Delaval family of Seaton Delaval, Northumberland. She studied the harp with J. B. Krumpholtz, who was in Paris from 1777 (*d* 1790). Her name appears on many London concert programmes of the 1790s, including those of the Salomon concerts at the Hanover Square Rooms. Her compositions for harp include three sonatas with violin ad lib, Prelude and Divertimento with two horns ad lib, a Grand Sonata with violin, tenor (instrument) and cello ad lib, and two sets of variations. She also wrote a cantata, *Les adieux de l'infortune Louis XVI à son peuple.*

BIBLIOGRAPHY

GerberNL; SainsburyD; SchillingE

R. Fiske: 'The Harp in Jane Austen's Day', *United Kingdom Harp Association Journal*, no.58 (1981), spr. 8–11

T. Milligan: 'Harp Concertos in London in the Late 18th Century', *American Harp Journal*, viii/1 (1981), 28

BONNIE SHALJEAN

Delfín, Carmelina (*b* Havana, *c*1900; *d* New York, after 1948). Cuban pianist and composer. She began her musical studies at the Peyrellade Conservatory, Havana, and was awarded several prizes for piano performance. In 1936 she moved to the USA, toured the country and Canada as a pianist during that and the following year, and in 1940 was engaged by NBC to write music for a regular weekly programme. Her *Himno de las Américas* won a national competition in 1942 and was recorded by the band of the US Marines. She was the soloist in an orchestral concert of Cuban music given in Carnegie Hall in 1943, and in 1946 and 1948 she gave piano recitals at Town Hall, New York, in which she included some of her own works. Although Delfín's music, which includes orchestral works, piano pieces and songs, is influenced by the 19th-century European Romantic tradition, compositions such as *Zapateo* for piano and the Piano Concertino clearly show that she was also influenced by the Hispanic and African legacies characteristic of Cuban culture.

BIBLIOGRAPHY

E. Martin: *Carmelina Delfín* (Havana, 1951) [programme of the Sociedad de Conciertos]

ALICIA VALDÉS CANTERO

Dell'Acqua, Eva (*b* Brussels, 25 Feb 1856; *d* Ixelles, 12 Feb 1930). Belgian singer and composer. She composed mainly vocal music, including about 15 operas and operettas, many of which were performed privately in Brussels and Paris during the 1880s. Five of her later works, however, were produced in Brussels and widely performed in Belgium. These include *La ruse de Pierrette* (1890), in which Dell'Acqua sang the title role. The one-act operetta *Pierrot Menteur* (1918) has modest vocal and theatrical demands: the mostly syllabic vocal writing for the two characters (the Bohemian lovers Pierrot and Musette) is in a series of single-movement arias and duets, often with characteristic dance rhythms. The only use of dissonance and syncopation for dramatic effect occurs in a brief orchestral passage ('Mélodrame') accompanying a comic supernatural episode. Dell'Acqua's coloratura song *Villanelle* is still a repertory showpiece.

WORKS
selective list

Operas and operettas: La ruse de Pierrette (1, F. van der Elst), Brussels, 1890; Bachelette (3, van der Elst), Brussels, Théâtre de la Galerie St Hubert, 1896; Tambour-Battant (3, van der Elst), Brussels, Théâtre de la Galerie St Hubert, 1900; Zizi (Lannoy and A. Lénéka), Brussels, Théâtre de la Galerie St Hubert; Pierrot Menteur (1, van der Elst) (1918); *c*9 other works

Other works: Au clair de la lune (pantomime), 1891; Chanson provençale, orch; Aveu romance, vn, pf; Sérénade, 2vv, pf; pieces for 1v, orch; songs, incl. Villanelle (J'ai vu passer l'hirondelle); pieces for pf solo

MARY ANN SMART

Della Pietà, Agata (*fl* Venice, *c*1800). Italian singer, teacher and composer. She was a foundling admitted in infancy to the Ospedale della Pietà in Venice. From early childhood she received a thorough musical education in the *coro* (music school) and became a soprano soloist, singing teacher and administrator in the school. She is identified as a soloist in manuscripts of motets commissioned from Giovanni Porta and Andrea Bernasconi, and is singled out for praise in the anonymous verse tribute to musicians of the *cori* at the Pietà dating from about 1740 (*I-Vmc* Codice Cicogna, 1178, *carte* 206–122, stanzas 18–20). Only two motet settings by her survive. The first, *Novo aprili*, in F major, is inscribed to 'Louisa Della Sga Agnatta' (*Vc* correr esposti, 94 no.545, 18); the second is of Psalm cxxxiv for compline, *Ecce nunc*, also in F (*Vc* correr esposti, 64 no.187, 42), for which only an instrumental bass part remains). She also produced a pedagogical text, *Regali per Gregoria*, for one of her pupils, Gregoria, an alto soloist between 1746 and 1777.

BIBLIOGRAPHY

K. Meyer-Baer: *Der chorische Gesang der Frauen* (Leipzig, 1917), 110
G. Rostirolla: 'L'organizzazione musicale nell'Ospedale veneziano della Pietà al tempo di Vivaldi', *NRMI*, xiii (1979), 168–95, esp. 192
J. L. Baldauf-Berdes: *Women Musicians of Venice: Musical Foundations, 1525–1855* (Oxford, 1993)

JANE L. BERDES

Della Pietà, Michielina [Michaelis, Michieletta] (*fl* Venice, *c*1701–44). Italian violinist, organist, teacher and composer. She was a foundling admitted in infancy to the Ospedale della Pietà in Venice. From early childhood she received a thorough education in the music school (*coro*), becoming a violinist in the orchestra and principal organist for the *coro*. She was a composer during the decades when it was directed by

Francesco Gasparini, Giovanni Porta, Nicola Porpora and Andrea Bernasconi and was licensed to teach in 1726. She composed a Litany for the Feast of the Nativity in 1740 and setting of the hymn *Pange lingua* for Corpus Christi in 1741 (*I-Vc* correr esposti, 54 no.127, 35–6).

BIBLIOGRAPHY
K. Meyer-Baer: *Der chorische Gesang der Frauen* (Leipzig, 1917), 109
P. Ryom: *Les manuscrits de Vivaldi* (Copenhagen, 1977), 34
J. Whittemore: *The Revision of Music Performed at the Venetian Conservatories in the Eighteenth Century* (diss., U. of Illinois, Champaign-Urbana, 1986), 140, 143
J. L. Baldauf-Berdes: *Women Musicians of Venice: Musical Foundations, 1525–1855* (Oxford, 1993)
JANE L. BERDES

Della Pietà, Santa [Sanza, Samaritana] (*fl c*1725–*c*1750; *d* after 1774). She was a foundling admitted in infancy to the Ospedale della Pietà in Venice. From early childhood she received a thorough musical education in the *coro* (music school), and was a contralto soloist, violinist, and composer during the tenures of Giovanni Porta, Nicola Porpora, and Andrea Bernasconi. She studied the violin under the maestra Anna Maria della Pietà, succeeded her as director of the orchestra in about 1740, and performed at least six of the violin concertos Vivaldi composed for Anna Maria. Her setting of the Vespers Psalm cxiii *Laudate pueri à 4* in D, survives (*I-Vc* correr esposti, 65 no.192, 13, 82).

BIBLIOGRAPHY
D. Arnold and E. Arnold: *The Oratorio in Venice* (London, 1986), 98, 108
G. Rostirolla: 'L'organizzazione musicale nell'Ospedale veneziano della Pietà al tempo di Vivaldi', *NRMI*, xiii (1979), 168–95, esp. 193
M. F. Tiepolo: *Vivaldi e l'ambiente musicale veneziano: mostra documentaria* (Venice, 1978), 82
M. A. Zorzi: 'Saggio di bibliografia sugli oratorii sacri eseguiti a Venezia', *Accademie e biblioteche d'Italia*, iv (Rome, 1930), 246; v (Rome, 1931), 90; vi (Rome, 1932), 261–2; vii (Rome, 1933)
J. L. Baldauf-Berdes: *Women Musicians of Venice: Musical Foundations, 1525–1855* (Oxford, 1993)
JANE L. BERDES

Dellaporta, Sophia (*b* Lixourion, Kefallinia; *fl* 2nd half of the 19th century). Greek composer. Her *Recueil musical* was published in Leipzig in August 1877 and consists of eight compositions bearing the names of various heroes of the 1821 Greek War of Independence. It won a prize at the Third Greek Composers' Competition, organized in Athens by the 1875 Olympic Exhibition.

According to Motsenigos, she was the sister of Spyridon Spathis (1852–1941), a composer at the Greek Orthodox Church in Paris; however, this has been disputed by Spathis's daughter, Hélène Spathis-Petersen.

BIBLIOGRAPHY
T. N. Synadinos: *Istoria tis neoellinikis moussikis, 1824–1919* [A History of Modern Greek Music, 1824–1919] (Athens, 1919), 214
S. G. Motsenigos: *Neoelliniki moussiki: symvoli is tin istoria tis* [Modern Greek Music: a Contribution to its History] (Athens, 1958), 255
GEORGE LEOTSAKOS

Delle Grazie, Gisella (*b* Trieste, 1 June 1868; *fl* 1894–5). Italian composer. She is known only for two operas: *Atala* (or *I Pellirossa*), performed on 14 April 1894 at the Teatro Balbo, Turin, and *La trecciaiuola di Firenze*, given in 1895 at the Teatro Filodrammatico in Trieste.

BIBLIOGRAPHY
A. de Angelis: *L'Italia musicale d'oggi: dizionario dei musicisti* (Rome, 1918, 3/1928)
A. Bonaventura: 'Le donne italiane e la musica', *RMI*, xxxii (1925), 519–34
MATTEO SANSONE

Demars, Hélène-Louise [Henriette-Louise] (*b* Paris, *c*1733; *d* after 1759). French composer, daughter of the Parisian organist and harpsichordist Jean Odo Demars. Her three *cantatilles à voix seule et simphonie* – *Hercule et Omphale* (dedicated to the Marquise de Villeroy), *Les avantages du buveur* (dedicated to the Marquis de La Salle; text by her cousin) and *L'horoscope* – were published in Paris about 1752. The title-page of *L'horoscope* reveals that Demars performed it for the dedicatee, Mlle de Soubise, as early as 21 November 1748; the text was printed (without the music) in the *Mercure de France* the following year. According to Fétis, she was 15 when they appeared.

Mlle Demars was a member of La Pouplinière's circle, the teacher of Stéphanie-Félicité du Crest de Saint-Aubin (later Mme de Genlis) and, from 1759, the wife of Jean-Baptiste Vernier, a violinist and music dealer specializing in foreign editions. As Mme Venieri (*sic*) she advertised herself as a harpsichord teacher in the 1759 *Tableau de Paris*. Later in the century a Thérèse Demars published works for harp or fortepiano – *Pot-pourri d'airs connus*, *Six nouvelles romances* and *Thème favori de Mysta tagoju uk raschennyil* – in Paris and Orléans (dates unknown).

BIBLIOGRAPHY
FétisB
M. Brenet: 'La librairie musical en France de 1653 à

1790 d'après les registres de privilèges', *SIMG*, viii (1906–7), 401–66, esp. 447

—— : 'Mme de Genlis, musicienne', *Revue internationale de musique*, ii/7 (1912), 4

G. Cucueil: *La Pouplinière et la musique de chambre au XVIIIe siècle* (Paris, 1913), 226

JULIE ANNE SADIE

Demessieux, Jeanne (*b* Montpellier, 14 Feb 1921; *d* Paris, 11 Nov 1968). French organist and composer. She became organist of the church of the Saint-Esprit, Paris, in 1933. A pupil of Magda Tagliaferro, Jean and Noël Gallon, and Marcel Dupré at the Paris Conservatoire, she won *premiers prix* in harmony (1937), piano (1938), fugue and counterpoint (1940). She continued her studies in organ playing, improvisation and composition with Dupré before giving her first public recital in Paris at the Salle Pleyel in 1946. She then travelled extensively as a recitalist, often visiting England where her first London recital (1947) ended with the improvisation of a four-movement organ symphony on themes submitted by four London music critics. In 1952 she became organ professor at the Liège Conservatory, and in 1962 organist of the Madeleine, Paris. The first woman invited to play in Westminster Cathedral and Westminster Abbey, she also took part in the inaugural ceremony at the Metropolitan Cathedral in Liverpool (1967).

Demessieux's published organ works are six *Etudes* (1946), *Sept méditations sur le Saint Esprit* (1947), *Triptyque* op.7 (1949), *Poème* for organ and orchestra op.9 (1949), *12 Chorale Preludes on Gregorian Themes* op.8 (1954), *Te Deum* op.11 (1965), Prelude and Fugue in C op.12 (1965) and *Répons pour le temps de Pâques* (1968: published posthumously). Her other works include *La chanson de Roland* for mezzo–soprano, choir and orchestra (unpublished) and Ballade for horn and piano op.10 (1958).

BIBLIOGRAPHY

P. Denis: 'Les organistes français d'aujourd'hui: Jeanne Demessieux', *L'orgue* (1955), no.75

J. Piccand: 'Quelques organistes français (3e serie)', *SMz*, cv (1965), 356–8

FELIX APRAHAMIAN

Dering [née Harvey], **Mary**, Lady (bap. 3 Sept 1629; *d* 1704). English composer. She was the daughter of Daniel Harvey, of Folkestone, Kent (brother of Sir William Harvey, discoverer of the circulation of the blood). She went to school at Hackney, where she began her friendship with Katherine Phillips ('the Matchless Orinda'). At the age of 19 she married Sir Edward Dering of Surrenden Dering, Kent (after some matrimonial 'escapades'; see Kerr), by whom she had ten children. She was a pupil of Henry Lawes, who included three of her songs in his *Select Ayres and Dialogues* (1655). In dedicating this book to her, he acknowledged that 'some which I esteem the best of these Ayres, were of your own Composition, after your Noble Husband was pleased to give the Words' (see MB, xxxiii, no.114). It is likely that she, along with Mrs Phillips and others, were among the 'brightest Dames' who attended concerts at Lawes's house during the Commonwealth.

BIBLIOGRAPHY

W. McC. Evans: *Henry Lawes: Musician and Friend of Poets* (New York, 1941), 202–8

J. M. Kerr: 'Mary Harvey – the Lady Dering', *ML*, xxv (1944), 23–33

IAN SPINK

Desportes, Yvonne (*b* Coburg, 18 July 1907; *d* Paris, 29 Dec 1993). French composer. She studied with Jean and Noël Gallon and Paul Dukas at the Paris Conservatoire, winning the Prix de Rome in 1932. In 1943 she returned to the Conservatoire to teach solfège, and in 1959 was appointed to teach counterpoint and fugue. A prolific composer and a well-known teacher, she is also the author of many theoretical and practical works for musical education purposes. Her style is vivid, bright, humorous and descriptive. Although she has composed in all genres, the greater part of her output is instrumental, much of it chamber music including wind and percussion instruments.

WORKS
selective list

Stage: Trifaldin (ballet), 1934; Le rossignol et l'orvet (scène lyrique), 1936; Les sept péchés capitaux (ballet), 1938; Maître Cornélius (opera, 3, M. Belvianes, after H. de Balzac), 1939–40; La farce du carabinier (opéra comique), 1943; La chanson de Mimi Pinson (opérette), 1952; Symphonie (ballet mécanique), 1961; Le forgeur de merveilles (opera, 3, Desportes, after F.-J. O'Brien), 1965, broadcast, French Radio, 30 June 1967

Orch: Variations symphoniques, pf, orch, 1942; Tpt Conc., 1948; Caprice champêtre, vn, orch, 1955; A bâtons rompus, conc., 2 perc, orch, 1957; 3 syms., 1958, 1964, 1969; Le tambourineur, conc., perc, orch, 1960; L'exploit de la coulisse, conc., trbn, orch, 1969; Variations sur le nom de Beethoven

Vocal: Le pardon, 1932; Requiem, solo vv, choir, orch, 1950; Ambiances, S, 2 perc, orch, 1963; Conc., 4 solo vv, orch, 1963; Discordances, 2 solo vv, choir, orch, 1966; Les importuns familiers, 4 solo vv, pf, 1967; Le bal des onomatopées, choir, fl/pf, 1976; works for unacc. choir, many mélodies, 1v, pf

Chamber: Aubade, fl, vn, va, vc, harp, 1946; Divertissement, 4 sax, pf, 1948; Vision cosmique, 3 perc, 1963; Idoles au rebut, pf, 1975; Plein air, 4 sax, 1975; Sérénade exotique, wind octet, 1975; Per sa pia, perc, sax, pf, 1978
Film scores, incid. music

Principal publishers: Billaudot, Eschig, Leduc
ALAIN LOUVIER,
FRANÇOISE ANDRIEUX

Dianda, Hilda (*b* Córdoba, Argentina, 13 April 1925). Argentine composer. She studied with Honorio Siccardi, Gian Francesco Malipiero and Hermann Scherchen. In 1958 she travelled to France on a French government scholarship and made contact with Pierre Schaeffer's Groupe de Recherches Musicales at the RTF in Paris. The following year she was one of a group of five composers (the others were John Cage, Henri Pousseur, André Boucourechliev and Dieter Schönbach) to whom the RAI in Milan first opened the doors of its Studio di Fonologia Musicale, enabling her to gain experience of electronic music. The *Dos estudios en oposición* for tape, which date from this time, mark her out as one of the first Argentine composers to use electronic techniques and resources. She received scholarships to attend the Darmstadt summer courses between 1960 and 1963, and in 1966 worked at the San Fernando Valley State College in Northridge, California, where *A 7* for cello and tape was written. Returning to Argentina in 1967, she was involved in an intensive schedule of teaching as a professor at the Universidad Nacional de Córdoba until 1971. After a period spent in Germany, she moved back to Argentina in 1976, composing . . . *después el silencio* for tape on her return.

There followed a seven-year break in her creative activity, after which she wrote the Requiem (1984). Dedicated 'to our dead' and based on the Latin mass for the dead (excluding the Dies irae, which, she felt, did not correspond to her intentions), the Requiem has vocal and instrumental textures of great variety and complexity, each movement being differently orchestrated, though always in accordance with the demands of the text. By contrast, the *Cántico* of 1988 inhabits a totally different world; based on St Francis of Assisi's *Cantico delle creature*, this chamber-style piece, 'stereophonically' conceived, achieves its effect through a spatial disposition of voices and instruments.

Dianda has participated in numerous international festivals of contemporary music and several of her works have been included in the study programmes of various European and North American Universities and other musical institutions as important examples of the contemporary composer's art. Among her many distinctions and awards are the Cultural Merit medal of the Italian government, Chevalier of the Ordre des Palmes Academiques of the French Republic, and official recognition of her work by the Fundación Alicia Moreau de Justo in Argentina. Dianda also devotes time to the educational and analytical aspects of contemporary music, writing in a number of publications and giving seminars, courses and lectures and published *La musica argentina de hoy* (Buenos Aires, 1966).

WORKS
selective list

Orch: Nucleos, str, 2 pf, vib, xyl, 8 perc, 1963; Resonancias 3, vc, orch, 1966; Ludus 1, 1969; Ludus 2, chamber orch, 1969; Impromptu, str, 1970; Canto, chamber orch, 1972; Va Conc., 1988; Mitos, perc, str, 1993
Vocal: Canciones (R. Alberti), S, gui, vib, 3 perc, 1962; Rituales, 1v + perc, pf + perc, 1962; Resonancias 5, 2 choruses, 1966–8; Requiem, B, chorus, orch, 1984; Cántico (Dianda, after St Francis of Assisi), chorus, chamber orch, 1985
Ens: Estructuras I–III, vc, pf, 1960; Qt III, str, 1963; Percusión 11, 11 perc, 1963; Resonancias 1, 5 hn, 1964; Divertimento a 6, 6 perc, 1969–70; Oda, 2 tpt, 3 trbn, 3 perc, 1974; Trío, cl, vc, pf, 1985; Cadencias, ww, perc, 1985; Cadencias 2, vn, pf, 1986; Paisaje (. . . sólo breves, fugaces colores . . .), 4 perc, 1992
Solo inst: Diedros, fl, 1962; Resonancias 2, pf, 1964; Ludus 3, org, 1969; Celebraciones, vc + perc, 1974; Rituales, mar, 1994
Tape: 2 estudios en oposición, 1959; A 7, vc, tape, 1966; . . . después el silencio . . ., 1976; Encantamientos, 1984

Principal publishers: EAC-Moeck, Ediciones Culturales Argentinas, Pan American Union, Ricordi Americana, Schott

BIBLIOGRAPHY
RiemannL 12
J. C. Paz: *Introducción a la música de nuestro tiempo* (Buenos Aires, 1955)
——: 'Una nueva etapa creadora en la música de la Argentina', *Revista musical mexicana* (1963), 62–8
'Portrait of Hilda Dianda', *Donaueschingen Festival 1969* [programme book]
R. Arizaga: *Enciclopedia de la música argentina* (Buenos Aires, 1971)

RAQUEL C. DE ARIAS

Dickson, Ellen (Elizabeth) [Dolores] (*b* Woolwich, 1819; *d* Lyndhurst, Hants., 4 July 1878). English composer. She was the daughter of General Sir Alexander Dickson, and lived most of her life at Lyndhurst in

Title-page of 'Good Night, Good Night, Beloved!' (London: Jefferys, 1854) by Ellen Dickson ('Dolores')

the New Forest. Her Latin pseudonym 'Dolores', which means sorrows or bodily pains, was, perhaps, a comment on her life as an invalid. She began to make her reputation in the late 1850s, composing drawing-room ballads in a style similar to that of Maria Lindsay, but with more originality, particularly in the figuration of her accompaniments, such as the elaborate use of grace notes in her setting (London, 1857) of Tennyson's *The Brook* and the irregular arpeggio patterns of *The Land of Long Ago* (London, 1873; words by Thomas Westwood).

BIBLIOGRAPHY

J. D. Brown and S. S. Stratton: *British Musical Biography* (Birmingham, 1897)
D. Hixon and D. Hennessee: *Women in Music: a Bio-Bibliography* (Metuchen, NJ, 1975)
D. Scott: *The Singing Bourgeois* (Milton Keynes, 1989)
                                        DEREK B. SCOTT

Diemer, Emma Lou (*b* Kansas City, MO, 24 Nov 1927). American composer, teacher and organist. A prodigy, she wrote several piano concertos by the age of 13 and took composition lessons with Gardner Read

during her high school years. She studied composition with Richard Donovan and Paul Hindemith at Yale University (BM 1949, MM 1950) and with Bernard Rogers and Howard Hanson at the Eastman School (PhD 1960). In addition she studied at the Conservatoire Royal de Musique in Brussels (1952–3), supported by a Fulbright Fellowship, and at the Berkshire Music Center with Ernst Toch and Roger Sessions (1954, 1955). Diemer was composer-in-residence in Arlington, Virginia (1959–61) and composer-consultant to Baltimore public schools (1964–5) before serving as professor of theory and composition at the University of Maryland (1965–70) and the University of California, Santa Barbara (1971–91). In 1990 she was appointed composer-in-residence with the Santa Barbara SO, and she has continued to work as a church organist in her home city.

Although Diemer is best known for her neo-classical and neo-romantic choral and keyboard works using free tonality, her compositions encompass many styles: *Declarations* (1973) uses strict 12-note technique and serialized rhythm as well as extended techniques for organ; her piano *Variations* (1987) combine a 12-chord series (following Schoenberg's principles) with a harmonic language reminiscent of Ravel. *Homage to Cowell, Cage, Crumb and Czerny* (1981), one of her most avant-garde works, employs note-clusters and techniques inside the piano. Diemer's interest in accessibility has led her to give particular attention to melody and formal unity. A search for greater timbral focus motivated both her initial involvement in electronic music during the early 1970s and her use of extended instrumental techniques (e.g. multiphonics, pitch-bending and flutter-tonguing, as in the Trio for flute, oboe, harpsichord and tape, 1973). Some works written in the 1990s feature slow-moving harmonic rhythm enlivened with melodic figuration (e.g. the concertos for piano and marimba) and might be viewed as an extension of techniques she used a decade earlier in *Encore* (for piano). She has written for both professional and amateur groups, aiming for accessibility in the music for school and church choirs through her use of simple vocal lines (often in unison or canon) with more challenging keyboard accompaniments.

WORKS
selective list

Orch: Sym. no.1, 1953; Pf Conc., 1953; Suite, 1954; Conc., hpd, chamber orch, 1958; Sym. no.2 (on

American Indian themes), 1959; Pavane, str orch, 1959; Youth Ov., 1959; Sym. no.3 'Antique', 1961; Festival Ov., 1961; Fl Conc., 1963; Fairfax Festival Ov., pf, orch, 1967; Concert Piece, org, orch, 1977; Tpt Conc., 1983; Vn Conc., 1983; Suite of Homages, 1985; Serenade, str orch, 1988; Mar Conc., 1991; Pf Conc., 1991

Chamber and inst: Suite, fl, pf, 1948; Vn Sonata, 1949; Pf Qt, 1954; Toccata, mar, 1955; Sonata, fl, pf/hpd, 1958; Ww Qnt, no.l, 1960; Déclamation, 2 hn, 4 tpt, bar hn, 2 trbn, tuba, timp, perc, 1960; Sextet, pf, ww qnt, 1962; Toccata, pic, 2 fl, a fl, b fl, 1968; Music, fl, ob, cl, bn, 1972; Movt, fl, ob, org, 1974; Movt, fl, ob, cl, pf, 1976; Solotrio, xyl + vib + mar, 1980; Echospace, gui, 1980; Summer of 82, vc, pf, 1982; Str Qt no.1, 1987; There's a certain slant of light, winter afternoons . . ., fl, gui, 1989; A Quiet, Lovely Piece, cl, pf, 1991; Sextet, fl, ob, cl, vn, vc, pf, 1992; Lovely Song, vn + va, pf, 1992

Kbd: Fantasie, org, 1958; Toccata, org, 1964; 7 Etudes, pf, 1965; Fantasy on 'O Sacred Head', org, 1967; Toccata and Fugue, org, 1969; Sound Pictures, pf, 1971; Declarations, org, 1973; Toccata, pf, 1979; Homage to Cowell, Cage, Crumb and Czerny, 2 pf, 1981; Encore, pf, 1981; Elegy, org duo, 1982; Variations: Homage to Ravel, Schoenberg and May Aufderheide, pf 4 hands, 1987; Space Suite, pf, 1988; 3 Pieces, pf, 1991; Toccata, hpd, 1992; 4 Biblical Settings, org, 1993; Fantasy, pf, 1993

Choral: St Chrysostom Cantata (Bible), S, A, T, B, chorus, org, 1956; 3 Madrigals (W. Shakespeare), mixed vv, pf/org, 1960; 4 Carols, SSA women's chorus, 1960; 3 Poems (O. Nash), TTB chorus, pf, 1960; Dance, dance my heart (H. Kabir), mixed vv, pf/org, opt. perc, 1967 [from A Service in Music and Poetry]; O to make the most jubilant song (W. Whitman, A. Tennyson), mixed vv, pf/org, 1970; Choruses on Freedom, mixed vv, pf, str, perc, 1975; 3 Poems (A. Meynell), mixed vv, ww qnt, mar, vib, 4 perc, pf, org, 1976; 3 Poems (O. Wilde), mixed vv, pf/org, 1984; Invocation (M. Sarton), mixed vv, orch/pf, 1985; The Sea, mixed vv, fl, cl, perc, pf, str, 1988; There is a morn unseen (E. Dickinson), S/T, mixed vv, orch/pf, 1991

Vocal: Songs of Reminiscence (D. D. Hendry), S, pf, 1958; 3 Mystic Songs (ancient Hindu), S, Bar, pf, 1963; The Four Seasons (E. Spenser), S/T, pf, 1969; 4 Poems (A. Meynell), S/T, 2 fl + pic, 2 perc, vib, xyl, harp, hpd, pf, str qt, 1976 [also version for S/T, pf]; I will sing of your steadfast love (Ps lxxxix), high v, org, 1986; Who can find a virtuous woman? (Bible, *Proverbs* xxxi), medium high v, pf, 1989; And I saw a new heaven and a new earth (Bible, *Revelation* xxi), medium high v, tpt, org/pf, 1991

Tape: Trio, fl, ob, hpd, tape, 1973; Patchworks, tape, 1978; Add One: no.1, elec pf, tape, 1981, no.2, tape, opt. synth, 1981, no.3, tape, opt. synth, 1982; A Day in the Country, cl, tape, 1984; Church Rock, org, tapc, 1986

Principal publishers: Boosey & Hawkes, Elkan-Vogel/T. Presser, C. Fisher, OUP, Seesaw

BIBLIOGRAPHY

CohenE; *KompA-Z*; *LePageWC*, i; *WAM*

J. L. Zaimont and K. Famera, eds.: *Contemporary Concert Music by Women* (Westport, CT, 1981), 38–9, passim

B. Grigsby: 'Women Composers of Electronic Music', *The Musical Woman: an International Perspective*, i: *1983*, ed. J. L. Zaimont and others (Westport, CT, 1984), 151–3, 191–3

C. C. Brown: *Emma Lou Diemer: Composer, Performer, Educator, Church Musician* (diss., Southern Baptist Theological Seminary, Louisville, 1985)

J. McCray: 'American Choral Music with Organ: the Music of Emma Lou Diemer', *American Organist*, xxi/11 (1987), 64–71

E. McDaniel: *The Choral Music of Emma Lou Diemer* (diss., Arizona State U., 1987)

E. L. Diemer: 'Women Composers as Professors of Composition', *The Musical Woman: an International Perspective*, iii: *1986–1990*, ed. J. L. Zaimont and others (Westport, CT, 1991), 714–38

T. Naus: *The Organ Works of Emma Lou Diemer* (diss., Michigan State U., 1991)

J. MICHELE EDWARDS

Dillon, Fannie Charles (*b* Denver, CO, 16 March 1881; *d* Altadena, CA, 21 Feb 1947). American composer, pianist and teacher. After graduating from Pomona College, Claremont, California, she moved to Berlin where she studied the piano with Leopold Godowsky (1900–06) and composition with Hugo Kaun and Heinrich Urban; she later studied composition with Rubin Goldmark in New York. Dillon made her début as a pianist in Los Angeles in 1908 and subsequently gave concerts on the West and East coasts of the USA. On 9 February 1918 she played her own works at a piano recital for the Beethoven Society of New York. She was a member of the music faculty at Pomona College (1910–13) and from 1918 until her retirement in 1941 taught in Los Angeles public schools. In 1921, 1923 and 1933 she was in residence at the MacDowell Colony.

The musical language of Dillon's early works (chiefly piano music) owes much to late 19th-century Romanticism, but by the time of her *Eight Descriptive Pieces* (1917) her style had become more pictorial: the pieces are freer in form and impressionist in character, with descriptive titles and texts. Dillon also wrote music for plays that were performed at the Woodland Theater she founded in Big Bear Lake, California.

WORKS
selective list

Orch: Celebration of Victory, 1918; The Cloud, 1918; The Alps, 1920; A Western Saga, pf conc., 1945, *US-Wc*; In a Mission Garden; A Letter from the Southland

Pf: 6 Preludes (Cincinnati, 1908); 8 Descriptive Pieces (Cincinnati, 1917); Heroic Etude (Cincinnati, 1917); Bird Stories in Music (New York, 1922); Songs of the Seven Hills (New York, 1927); From the Chinese (New York, 1944)

Solo inst: Woodland Flute Call, fl (Glen Rock, NJ, 1953); A Medieval Minstrelsy (suite), pipe org, Wc
Voice and pf: The Message of the Bells (Los Angeles, 1917); An April Day (New York, 1949); Saul (R. Browning), NYp
Incid. music for pf: Prince Su Ming (W. Fao), 1935, Wc; Nevertheless: Old Glory!, Wc; Tahquitz (G. Holme: *The Desert Play of Palm Springs*, rev. Whiting and D. Belasco), Wc; The Desert Calls

BIBLIOGRAPHY

'California's Brilliant Composer-Pianist, Fannie Dillon', *Musical Courier*, lxxiii/20 (1916), 45

CAROL NEULS-BATES

Di Lotti, Silvana (*b* Agliè Canavese, Turin, 29 Nov 1942). Italian composer. She studied in Turin with Amalia Pierangeli Mussato (piano) and Giorgio Ferrari (composition). After graduation she attended the International Sommer-Akademie in Salzburg, studying with Kurt Leimer, and took part in courses given by Goffredo Petrassi, Franco Evangelisti, Luis de Pablo, Luciano Berio and Pierre Boulez at the Accademia Chigiana, Siena. Her works have been performed at major contemporary music festivals, including Naples, and by prestigious groups in Italy and elsewhere. Her output includes *Conversari* for orchestra (1981) and *Serenata* for chamber orchestra (1982). Among her smaller-scale pieces are *Contrasti* for two clarinets (1981), *Duo in eco* for violin and guitar (1982), a piano trio (1986) and *A solo* for clarinet, violin, guitar, mandolin and percussion (1991). In addition to composing, she has taught harmony and counterpoint at the Turin Conservatory.

PAOLA DAMIANI

Dinescu, Violeta (*b* Bucharest, 13 July 1953). Romanian composer. She studied in Bucharest at the George Enescu school, and then at the Bucharest Conservatory (1973–8) with Myriam Marbé (composition) and in Germany (1972–82). In 1978 she taught harmony, theory and counterpoint at the Enescu school and then moved to Germany, lecturing in Heidelberg at the Hochschule für Kirchenmusik (1987–90), in Frankfurt (1989–91), at the Bayreuth International Youth Festival (1990) and from 1990 at the Hochschule für Kirchenmusik in Bayreuth. As a guest lecturer she has also visited many countries, including the USA and South Africa. A prolific composer, she has been awarded numerous international prizes.

Dinescu ranks among the most accomplished of Romanian women composers; her complex artistic personality is receptive to experiment and new concepts. Her compositional style has often been influenced by mathematical procedures and models; these ensure logical organization but, according to Dinescu herself, constitute only the 'starting-point of the musical architecture', determining a work's proportions. *Anna Perenna* (1978), named after the Roman goddess of spring and the mythological symbol of reincarnation, uses such principles and is typical of Dinescu's works between 1978, when she completed her studies, and her arrival in 1982 in Germany; in these pieces extreme, rigorous, predetermined structures form the background to improvisatory ideas, fantasies and sensuous sound-shapes. Whereas the number system also underpins the structure of the solo works *Echos* (1979–82) and the *Satya* cycle (1981), it is of no great importance in, for instance, her three music-theatre works, the Mörike ballet *Der Kreisel* (1985, Ulm), the Ionesco chamber opera *Hunger und Durst*, written for Freiburg (1986) and the chamber opera *Eréndira* after G. G. Marquez (1991, Stuttgart).

From 1972 to 1978 Dinescu worked on Romanian folk music; its figures have shaped numerous short motifs and thematic units in her works (for example, the suggestive, dreamy oboe melody at the beginning of *Hunger und Durst*), and its dialectic has influenced her parlando style and the frequent alternation of a free pulse with strict homorhythmic passages. In addition, two parlando/rubato techniques of folk music have strongly influenced her work: *doina* or *cântec lung* (which incorporates gradual transformations over long distances, somewhat analogous to minimalist music); and a pronounced heterophony, in which parallel voices emerge in unselfconscious 'floating islands' of autonomy. In folk music this produces a strikingly modern effect: the song of a Bulgarian farm woman, for example, begins to sound like avant-garde music. Such heterophonic 'islands' are clear features in two works from 1982, *Alternances* for brass quintet and *Dialogo* for flute and viola, and in the orchestral *Akrostichon* (1983) and the *Scherzo da fantasia III* for violin and cello (1985). Another marked characteristic of Dinescu's music is her use of relatively long solo passages in which individual voices alternate without interruption: a monologue art.

WORKS

selective list

Dramatic: Der Kreisel (ballet, after E. Mörike), Ulm, 26 May 1985; Hunger und Durst (chamber opera, after E. Ionesco: *Foame şi sete*), Freiburg, 1 Feb 1986; Der 35. Mai (children's opera, after E. Kästner), Dresden, 30 Nov 1986; Eréndira (chamber opera, after G. G. Marquez), Stuttgart, 1991

Orch: Anna Perenna, 1978; Memorii, str orch, 1980; Akrostichon, 1983; Map 67, chamber orch, 1987; Fresco, youth orch, 1989; Kybalion, str orch

Chamber, inst: Echos I, pf, 1979; Satya I–V, solo insts, 1981; Dialogo, fl, va, 1982; Aion, cl, bn, vc, 2 db, perc, 1982; Alternances, brass qnt, 1982; Echos II, pf + perc, 1982; Echos III, org, 1982; Auf der Suche nach Mozart, fl, bn, hn, sax, vn, harp, pf/cel, 1983; Terra Lonhdana, str qt, 1984; Melismen, 5 rec, 1985; Scherzo da fantasia III, vn, vc, 1985; Ostrov [Islet] I, 4 va, 1987; Ostrov II, 4 cl, 1988; Terra Lonhdana, fl, 2 vn, va, vc, pf, 1988; Kata, fl, pf, 1989; . . . wenn der Freude thränen fliessen . . ., vc, pf, 1990

Vocal: Bewitch me into a Silver Bird, chorus, orch, 1975; Euraculos, Mez, cl, 1980; Amont, 1v, hpd, 1984; Zebaoth, B, 2 org, 1986: Conc., 1v, orch, 1986; Quatrain, 1v, 1986; Mondnächte, 1v, sax, perc, 1986; Dona nobis pacem, 1v + perc, vc, 1987; Concertino, 1v, orch, 1988; Pfingstoratorium, 5 solo vv, chorus, chamber orch, 1993

Principal publisher: Ricordi

BIBLIOGRAPHY

CC (H. Maarten)

B. Schmalbrock: 'Violeta Dinescu – Personlichkeit, Werk, Analysen', *Komponistinnen unserer Zeit* (Essen, 1986)

B. Sonntag and R. Matthaei, eds.: *Annäherungen an sieben Komponistinnen*, ii (Kassel, 1987), 49–54

A. Olivier, ed.: *Komponistinnen: eine Bestandsaufnahme* (Düsseldorf, 1990)

VIOREL COSMA, GÁBOR HALÁSZ

Dlugoszewski, Lucia (*b* Detroit, 16 June 1934). American composer. After studying at the Detroit Conservatory and training in physics at Wayne State University, she moved to New York, where she studied the piano with Grete Sultan (1952–5), analysis with Felix Salzer (Mannes College, 1952–3) and between 1953 and 1965 composition with Edgard Varèse. She received a Guggenheim fellowship, grants from the NEA and the National Institute of Arts and Letters, and a Tompkins award for poetry. She has published articles on philosophical aesthetics and modern dance and a book of poetry, and has taught choreography.

During her early years in New York she was more closely associated with the poetic and artistic community than the musical one; supporters of her music included Robert Motherwell, John Ashbery and Ad Reinhardt. She was composer-in-residence for the Erick Hawkins Dance Company (1953–64), for which she wrote many scores. In her search for new sound qualities she invented the 'timbre piano', a conventional piano, of which the strings are struck, bowed and plucked with various implements; she also invented more than a hundred percussion instruments, which were made by the sculptor Ralph Dorazio (see illustration overleaf). Musicians began to take notice of her when Virgil Thomson described her music as 'of great delicacy, originality, and beauty of sound . . . of unusually high level in its intellectual and poetic aspects': the New York PO and the NEA commissioned her *Abyss and Caress* (1973–5), which was given its première by Pierre Boulez, and she has composed works for the Chamber Music Society of Lincoln Center, the Louisville Orchestra and the American Composers Orchestra. She was the first woman to win the Koussevitzky International Recording Award, in 1977, for *Fire Fragile Flight*.

Dlugoszewski's original approach to timbre was apparent from her earliest works, which were concerned with 'suchness' or Zen immediacy. *Balance Naked Flung* (1966) explored for the first time her non-linear 'leaping' structures of recklessness, and the architectonics of speed. She began to use 'otherness' or 'strangeness' as a compositional tool in the early 1980s – *Radical Otherness Concert* (1991) exemplifies this desire to make the listener hear as if for the first time – and later began to explore 'duende', the essence of 'look[ing] into the abyss and . . . surviv[ing]'. Her background as a poet is evident in her music as well as in its titles; her innovative and arresting compositions traverse timbral spectra in much the same way as poetry explores the richness of word meanings. She has written, 'Music must be intricate enough to slow up the murderous speed of our glibness [and] new enough to cheat the categories'. She has made recordings for Vox-Candide, Nonesuch, CRI and Folkways.

WORKS
selective list

DRAMATIC

Opera: Tiny Opera, 4 poets, moving v, dancers, pf, 1953; The Heidi Songs (J. Ashbery), 1972–

Dance scores: Openings of the (Eye), fl, timbre pf, perc, 1952–3; Here and Now with Watchers, 1954–7; Suchness Concert, 100 invented perc insts, 1958–60 [for 8 Clear Places]; Five Radiant Grounds, timbre pf, 1961 [for Early Floating]; Four Attention Spans, 1964 [for Cantilever, 1964]; Geography of Noon, 100 invented perc insts, 1964; To Everyone Out There, chamber orch, 1964; Balance Naked Flung, cl, tpt, b trbn, vn, perc, 1966 [for Lords of Persia]; Tight Rope, chamber orch, 1969; The Suchness of Nine Concerts, cl, vn, 2 perc, timbre pf, 1969–70 [for Black Lake, 1969–70]; Tender Theatre Flight Nageire, brass sextet, perc, 1971 [for Of Love], rev. 1978; Densities: Nova, Corona,

*Lucia Dlugoszewski playing
her wooden and glass ladder
harps, and skin tangent rattles;
these percussion instruments
were invented to achieve the
'suchness' (1960–61),
'quidditas' and 'otherness'
(1988–94) dimensions of music
which our standard instruments
cannot attain (Ralph Dorazio
constructed them as small pieces
of sculpture)*

Clear Core, brass qnt, 1972 [for Angels of the Inmost Heaven]; Avanti, 7 insts, 1983; Four Attention Spans, pf, orch or pf, 8 insts, perc, 1988 [for Cantilever 2]

Other theatrical: Moving Space Theater Piece for Everyday Sounds, 1949; Structure for the Poetry of Everyday Sounds (incid. music, A. Jarry: *Ubu roi*), 1952; Concert of Many Rooms and Moving Space (incid. music, E. Pound, after Sophocles: *Women of Trachis*), fl, cl, timbre pf, 4 rattles, 1960

Film scores: Visual Variations of Noguchi, everyday sounds, 1956; Guns of the Trees, 1961; A Zen in Ryoko-in, 1971

INSTRUMENTAL

Orch: Arithmetic Progression, 1954; Orchestral Radiant Ground, 1955; Beauty Music 2, perc, chamber orch, 1965; Beauty Music 3, timbre pf, chamber orch, 1965; Dazzle on a Knife's Edge, timbre pf, orch, 1966; Kireji: Spring and Tender Speed, chamber orch, 1972; Abyss and Caress, tpt, chamber orch, 1973–5; Strange Tenderness of Naked Leaping, str orch, 2 tpt, 2 fl/pic, 1977–; Amor Now Tilting Night, chamber orch, 1978–; Amor Elusive April Pierce, chamber orch, 1980; Startle Transparent Terrible Freedom, 1981–; Quidditas Sorrow Terrible Freedom, 1983–; Radical, Strange, Quidditas, Dew Tear, Duende, 1987–

Chamber (without perc) and solo inst: Sonata, fl, 1950; Transparencies, str qt, 1952; Flower Music for Left Ear in a Small Room, 8 insts, 1956; Rates of Speed in Space, ladder harp, chamber qnt, 1959; Flower Music, str qt, 1959; Skylark Cicada, vn, timbre pf, 1964; Vn music for Left Ear in a Small Room, vn, 1965; Naked Qnt, brass qnt, 1967; Hanging Bridge, str qt, 1968; Cicada Skylark Ten, 10 insts, 1969; Space Is a Diamond, tpt, 1970; Pure Flight, str qt, 1970; Sabi Music, vn, 1970; Fire Fragile Flight, 17 insts, 1974; Amor Elusive Empty August, ww qnt, 1979; Cicada Terrible Freedom, fl, str qt, b trbn, 1980–81; Wilderness, Elegant Tilt, 11 insts, 1981–; Duende Newfallen, b trbn, timbre pf, 1982–3; Quidditas, str qt, 1984; Radical Otherness Concert, fl, cl, tpt, trbn, vn, db, 1991; Radical Suchness Concert, fl, cl, tpt, trbn, vn, db, 1991; Radical Narrowness Concert, fl, cl, tpt, trbn, vn, db, 1992; Austere Suchness Concert . . . Outrageous Quod Libet Rims of Many Silences, 1993

Perc, other inst with perc: Naked Wabin, fl, cl, timbre pf, vn, db, perc, 1956; Delicate Accidents in Space, 5 rattles, 1959; Archaic Aggregates, timbre pf, perc, 1961; Beauty Music, cl, timbre pf, perc, 1965; Percussion Airplane Hetero, 100 invented perc insts, 1965; Percussion Flowers, 100 invented perc insts, 1965; Percussion Kitetails, 100 invented perc insts, 1965; Suchness with Radiant Ground, cl, perc, 1965; Kitetail Beauty Music, vn, timbre pf, perc, 1968; Naked Swift Music, vn, timbre pf, perc, 1968; Swift Diamond, timbre pf, tpt, perc, 1970; Velocity Shells, timbre pf, tpt, perc, 1970; Radical Quidditas for an Unborn Baby, 100 invented perc insts, 1991

Pf: Sonatas, no.1, 1949, nos.2–3, 1950; Melodic Sonata, 1950; Archaic Music, timbre pf, 1953–7; Music for Small Centers, 1958; Music for Left Ear, 1958; White Interval Music, timbre pf, 1961; Swift Music, 2 timbre pf, 1965; Naked Point Abyss, 1972–

OTHER WORKS

Vocal: Silent Paper, Spring and Summer Friends Songs, 1953–80; In Memory of my Feeling, T, chamber orch, 1972

Miscellaneous: Everyday Sounds for E. E. Cummings with Transparencies, 1952

Principal publisher: Margun

BIBLIOGRAPHY

CC (P. Collins); CohenE
V. Thomson: American Music Since 1910 (New York, 1971), 139
L. Dlugoszewski: 'What is Sound to Music?', Main Currents in Modern Thought, xxx/1 (1973), 3–11
C. Gagne: Soundpieces: Interviews with American Composers, ii (Metuchen, NJ, 1993), 55–83

J. HIGHWATER, SARA JOBIN

Dodd, Alison. See BRAHE, MAY HANNAH.

Dolby, Charlotte. See SAINTON-DOLBY, CHARLOTTE.

Dolores. See DICKSON, ELLEN.

Domange, Mélanie. See BONIS, MÉLANIE.

Donceanu, Felicia (b Bacău, 28 Jan 1931). Romanian composer. She studied at the Conservatory in Bucharest (1949–56) with Mihail Jora (composition), Paul Constantinescu (harmony) and Theodor Rogalski (orchestration). From 1956 to 1966 she worked as an editor at Editura Musicală in Bucharest. A member of the Romanian Composers' Union, she has won their

composition prize as well as an honourable mention at the GEDOK competition in Mannheim. She has written incidental music for many plays including works by Molière, Shakespeare and Thornton Wilder. A composer with a variety of artistic interests, including poetry and fine arts, she delights in mixing the timbres of old and modern instruments (e.g. viola da gamba, violin and clavichord) to produce light, sonorous works with a truly Romanian spirit.

WORKS
selective list

Orch: Meşterul Manole, sym. poem, 1956, rev. 1968; Ecouri Moldave [Moldavian Echoes], suite, str orch, 1985; Piatra Craiului, 3 sym. sketches, 1982

Chamber: Spinet Sonata, 1983; Eminesciana, Cl Sonata, 1985; Inscripţie pe un catarg [Inscription on a Mast], ballad, harp, 1989; Parlande–Rubato, harp, 1991

Solo vocal: Odinioară [Formerly], 1959 (Bucharest, 1965); Imagini [Images], 1965; Ponti Euxini Clepsydra, 1971 (Bucharest, 1974); Cîntînd cu lenă-chiţă Văcărescu [Singing with Lenăchita Văcărescu], 1984; The Music Lesson, 1992

Choral: Picolicomando, 1983; Clopoţelul cel isteţ [The Clever Bell], 1986; În căutarea lui Clopoţel [Searching Bell], 1989

Incid. and pf music

BIBLIOGRAPHY

V. Cosma: Muzicieni români: Lexicon (Bucharest, 1970)
C. Sârbu: 'Felicia Donceanu: Creaţia vocal-camerală', Muzica [Bucharest], i (1992), 59–82

VIOREL COSMA

Draganova, Dora (b Sofia, 29 Jan 1946). Bulgarian composer. A composition pupil of Veselin Stoyanov and Parashkev Chadjiev at the Sofia State Academy of Music, she graduated in 1972 and was immediately appointed lecturer in harmony at the Sofia State School of Music. In 1978 she began to work as an editor on Rodna pesen, the journal for choral music. Although much of her output is chamber music, she has written over 300 songs, three children's musicals and Car Koshnichar, a one-act comic opera to a libretto by Nikolaj Hajtov and Ivan Genov (1972). In her concern for contemporary issues she writes for a wide audience, often preferring children's themes; she has written a considerable amount of pop music. Some of her compositions have been published by Muzïka.

MAGDALENA MANOLOVA

Dring, Madeleine (Winefride Isabelle) (b Hornsey, London, 7 Sept 1923; d Streatham, London, 26 March 1977). English composer and actress. Born into a musical family, she

'The Kensington Gores', a Victorian variety duo, with Madeleine Dring (left), Margaret Rubel (right) and the pianist Alan Rowlands

won a violin scholarship on her tenth birthday to the junior department of the RCM, where the director, Angela Bull, channelled her theatrical talent into children's plays; Percy Buck was another early mentor at the RCM. Later, when she won a scholarship to study there as a senior student, her teachers were Herbert Howells, Ralph Vaughan Williams and Gordon Jacob for composition, W. H. Reed for violin (which she gave up after his death), Lillian Gaskell for piano and Topliss Green for singing. Dring also studied drama and mime and sustained a lifelong love of the theatre; she both wrote and composed for it (mostly incidental music and songs) and sang, played the piano and acted on the stage. She combined modesty with a lively sense of wit and mimicry, and for many years delighted RCM audiences with her compèring of the college 'At homes'. Her music for some of Laurier Lister's 'intimate revues' in the 1950s was complemented by her occasional appearances on stage at the Players' Theatre, and she also acted in television drama and ran a light entertainment group with her librettist D. F. Aitken and the dancer Felicity Andreae. In the 1970s she became interested in parapsychology and gave talks on it. She died suddenly of a brain haemorrhage.

Dring composed in a light style which accommodated her unpretentious and attractive chamber and instrumental works (several of the oboe pieces being written for her husband Roger Lord, a professional player), her teaching pieces and her many songs, and which gave her an affinity with Francis Poulenc, whom she admired. Like him she combined the frank enjoyment of vernacular idioms such as Latin American rhythms with a harmonic and melodic fastidiousness which, though firmly anchored to a love of the keyboard, was not easily won. Recently her work has been taken up and published in the USA, while the *Five Betjeman Songs*, classic encapsulations of the poet's observations of the British and their surroundings, serve as a prime memorial to her personality and his.

WORKS
printed works published in London

INSTRUMENTAL

Fantasy Sonata, pf, *c*1938, rev. (1948); 3 Fantastic Variations on Lilliburlero, 2 pf (1948); Jig, pf (1948); Prelude and Toccata, pf (1948); Tarantelle, 2 pf (1948); Festival Scherzo, pf, str orch, 1951 (1964); Sonata, 2 pf (1951); Jubilate, pf, 1953; March: for the New Year, pf (1954); Caribbean Dance (Tempo Tobago), 2 pf/1 pf (1959); Dance Suite, pf (1961): Italian Dance [also arr. 2 pf/ob, pf], West Indian Dance [also arr. 2 pf], American Dance, Waltz Finale; Polka (fl/ob, pf)/pf (1962); Colour Suite, pf (1963); Danza gaya, 2 pf/ob, pf (1965); 3 Dances, pf, 1968 (1981); Trio, fl, ob, pf, 1968 (1970); Prelude and Toccata, pf, 1976; Valse française, pf/2 pf (1980); 3 Pieces: WIB Waltz, Sarabande, Tango, fl, pf (1983); Waltz, ob, pf (1983); Suite, harmonica, pf [arr. P. Lord as Three Piece Suite, ob, pf (1984)]; Trio, ob, bn, hpd (1986); Moto perpetuo, pf; Spring Pastorale, pf; 12 Pieces in the Form of Studies, pf

Educational pieces for pf, tr rec etc, and contributions to Five by Ten, pf (1952), and Jack Brymer Series, cl, 1976

DRAMATIC

The Emperor and the Nightingale (incid. music, H. C. Andersen, adapted Dring), 1941; Tobias and the Angel (incid. music, J. Bridie), 1946;

Somebody's Murdered Uncle (incid. music, D. F. Aitken), BBC radio, 1947; Waiting for ITMA (ballet), BBC TV, 1947; The Wild Swans (children's play, A. Bull), 1950; The Fair Queen of Wu, (dance-drama, Aitken), BBC TV, 1951; The Marsh Kings's Daughter (children's play), 1952; Airs on a Shoe String (revue, L. Lister), 1953; Pay the Piper (revue, Lister), 1954; From Here and There (revue, Lister), 1955

Fresh Airs (revue, Lister), 1955; Child's Play (revue, S. Rafferty), 1958; The Buskers (incid. music, K. Jupp), 1959; Little Laura (cartoon series, V. H. Drummond), BBC TV, 1960; The Jackpot Question (incid. music, J. Bowen), Associated TV, 1961; Four to the Bar (revue, Lister), 1961; The Whisperers (incid. music, R. Nicolson and D. Webb), Associated TV, 1961; The Provok'd Wife (incid. music, J. Vanbrugh), 1963; The Lady and the Clerk (incid. music, J. Orde), Associated TV, 1964

I Can Walk Where I Like, Can't I? (incid. music), Associated TV, 1964; When the Wind Blows (incid. music, P. Nichols), Associated TV, 1965; Helen and Edward and Henry (incid. music), Associated TV, 1966; Variation on a Theme (incid. music, T. Rattigan), Associated TV, 1966; The Real Princess (ballet, Andersen), 2 pf, 1971; Cupboard Love (opera, 1, Aitken); The Lower Depths (M. Gorky); A Spring of Love (incid. music), Associated TV

SONGS WITH PIANO

3 Shakespeare Songs (1949); Thank you, Lord (L. Kyme) (1953); The Pigtail (A. von Chamisso), duet (1963); Dedications, 5 poems (R. Herrick), 1967; 5 Betjeman Songs, 1976 (1980); 4 Night Songs (M. Armstrong), 1976 (1985); Love and Time, cycle (Dryden, Sheffield, anon.)

c 35 songs, unpubd incl. Who killed the clock? (J. Ellison), 1942; Far, far in the east (Mélisande, trans. D. F. Aitken); My proper Bess (J. Skelton); Whenas I view your comely grace (anon.) [arr.]; Why so pale and wan (J. Suckling)

OTHER VOCAL

Bustopher Jones (T. S. Eliot), 5 male vv; The Lady Composer; The Sea-Gull of the Land-under-Waves, male vv; The Vocal Duettists

Principal publishers: Lengnick, Weinberger, Arcadia, Cambria

MSS/archive service: St James Music, the Old Meeting House, St James, Shaftesbury, Dorset

BIBLIOGRAPHY

M. Gough Matthews: 'Madeleine Dring', *RCM Magazine* lxxiii/2–3 (1977), 49 [obituary]

V. Twigg: *Madeleine Dring* (thesis, Trinity College, London, 1982) [copy at *GB-Lmic*]

H. Dawkes: record notes, *The Far Away Princess* (CBS E77050, 1982)

STEPHEN BANFIELD

Droste-Hülshoff, Annette von (*b* Hülshoff, nr Münster, Westphalia, 14 Jan 1797; *d* Meersburg, 24 May 1848). German poet and composer. She came from a musical family and studied the piano and singing, beginning to compose around 1820. Largely through the influence of her brother-in-law, Lassberg, she became interested in collecting old *Volkslieder* and contributed to the collections of Ludwig Uhland and August von Haxthausen. This interest culminated in her arrangement of the Lochamer Liederbuch for voice and piano (*c*1836). In addition, she composed many lieder to poetry by herself and others (e.g. Goethe, Brentano and Byron). Her literary talent was so highly respected that Robert Schumann, through Clara, requested an opera libretto from her in 1845. She began composing several operas of her own, but these were never completed. Compared to that of contemporary lieder, Droste-Hülshoff's style is simple, showing the influence of the *Volkslied*, and with the voice usually dominating the piano. A few lieder are recitative-like in texture (e.g. *Wer nie sein Brot*), while others contain occasional awkward melodic dissonances and harmonic cross-relations. Collections of her songs have been edited by Christoph Schlüter (*Lieder mit Klavier-Begleitung*, Münster, 1877) and by K. G. Fellerer (*Lieder und Gesänge*, Münster, 1954).

Although Droste-Hülshoff considered composition more important than writing poetry, she has been deemed more central to literature, recognized as a leading German Romantic poet. Perhaps (as Focher suggests) her approach to amalgamating poetry and music can best be viewed as Romantic individualism.

Annette von Droste-Hülshoff: portrait (1838) by Johannes Sprick

BIBLIOGRAPHY

J. Blaschke: 'Annette von Droste-Hülshoff und ihre Beziehungen zur Musik', *Neue Musikzeitung*, xxiii (1902), 77, 93, 105–06

E. Arens: 'Ein Byronisches Lied, von Annette von Droste komponiert', *Zeitung für Literatur, Kunst und Wissenschaft*, no.21 (1920)

J. Meier and E. Seeman: 'Volksliedaufzeichnungen der Dichterin Annette von Droste-Hülshoff', *Jb für Volkslied-Forschung*, i (1928), 79–118

K. G. Fellerer: 'Das Lochamer Liederbuch in der Bearbeitung der Annette von Droste-Hülshoff', *Mf*, v (1952), 200–05

—— : 'Annette von Droste-Hülshoff als Musikerin', *AMw*, x (1953), 41–59

M. J. Citron: 'Women and the Lied, 1775–1850', *Women Making Music: the Western Art Tradition, 1150–1950*, ed. J. Bowers and J. Tick (Urbana and Chicago, 1986), 224–48

A. Focher: 'Annette von Droste-Hülshoff: poetessa e musicista', *NRMI*, xx (1986), 564–78

A. Willison: *Women, Poetry and Song: Composer-Authors in German Romanticism* (diss., Indiana U., in preparation)

MARCIA J. CITRON

Duarte, Leonora (bap. Antwerp, 28 July 1610; *d* ?1678), South Netherlands amateur musician and composer. She belonged to a well-known Antwerp family of rich jewellers and diamond merchants, originally of Portuguese-Jewish (marran) origin. Her parents were Gaspar Duarte (bap. 11 Jan 1644; *d* 12 Nov 1653) and Catharina Rodrigues (*b* c1585; *d* 26 July 1644). Leonora had three sisters (Catharina, 1614–78, Francisca, 1619–78, and Isabella [Elisabeth], 1620–85) and two brothers (Diego [Jacques, Jacobus], 1612–91, and Gaspar 1616–85). (All the family baptisms, deaths and burials were recorded in Antwerp.) None of the children married, so that the Antwerp branch of the family died out in 1691.

The Duarte family residence at the Meir in Antwerp was a well-known centre for music and the visual arts. The correspondence of the elder Gaspar and his son Diego with the Dutch poet and amateur musician Constantijn Huygens shows that there were frequent contacts with the cultural élite of the Low Countries and England, including Huygens himself and his sons Constantijn and Christiaan, and William Cavendish and Margaret Lucas, Marquis and Marchioness of Newcastle. In 1644 Nicholas Lanier visited the family when he was in voluntary exile, and in 1653 Anne and Joseph de la Barre paid a visit when travelling from Paris to Stockholm.

Of the six Duarte children, Leonora, Francisca and Diego are mentioned most often in connection with family music-making. No details about their musical education are known, but for the family as a whole performing on the lute, viols and keyboard instruments was reported. Leonora and Diego are documented as composers. Leonora wrote a set of six abstract fantasies (one in two parts) for a consort of five viols; they are in late Jacobean style and called 'Symphonies' (in *GB-Och* Mus.ms.429). Her brother Diego composed vocal and instrumental works (all lost).

BIBLIOGRAPHY

M. Lucas: *CCXI Sociable Letters* (London, 1664)

W. J. A. Jonckbloet and J. P. N. Land, eds.: *Musique et musiciens au XVIIe siècle: correspondance et oeuvres musicales de Constantin Huygens* (Leiden, 1882)

Christiaan Huygens: Oeuvres complètes (The Hague, 1888–1905), vols. i–x [correspondence]

J. A. Worp, ed.: *De briefwisseling van Constantijn Huygens (1608–1687)* (The Hague, 1911–17)

E. R. Samuel: 'The Disposal of Diego Duarte's Stock of Painting 1692–1697', *Jaarboek van het Koninklijk Museum voor Schone Kunsten* (Antwerp, 1976), 305–24

RUDOLF A. RASCH

Duchambge [Du Chambge; née du Montet], **(Charlotte-Antoinette-)Pauline** (*b* Martinique, 1778; *d* Paris, 23 April 1858). French composer. The daughter of a noble family, she was taken to Paris, where she received a convent education and studied the piano with Jean-Baptiste Desormery. She left the convent in 1792 and married the Baron Duchambge four years later. In 1798, at the age of 20, she lost both her parents and the family fortune; to add to her misery, she was divorced soon afterwards. It was after these crises that Duchambge's musical education began in earnest. She studied with Jan Dussek, Luigi Cherubini and D.-F.-E. Auber, whom above all she greatly admired. Duchambge met the poet Marceline Desbordes-Valmore (1786–1859) in about 1815; their lifelong friendship is documented by a lengthy correspondence and a number of songs by Duchambge on Desbordes-Valmore's texts (including *L'adieu tout bas*, *La fiancée del marin*, *Je pense à lui*, *La jeune châtelaine*, *Rêve du mousse*, *La sincère* and *La valse et l'automne*). Through her Duchambge met the leading French poets of her day, including F. R. de Chateaubriand, Alphonse de Lamartine and Alfred de Vigny, who wrote texts specially for her *romances*. In addition to those of Desbordes-Valmore, Duchambge set the texts of other women writers such as Mme Amable Tastu (*Les cloches du couvent*) and Mme Emile de Girardin.

Pauline Duchambge: portrait by an unknown artist (possibly after Ingres)

Duchambge composed about 400 drawing-room style *romances*, most of which were published between 1816 and 1840. Her songs are straightforward, diatonic works, typically in strophic form without separate refrains. She also composed two sets of piano pieces (*Trois études et un caprice* and *Deux thèmes variés*).

BIBLIOGRAPHY
CohenE; *FétisB*; *RiemannL*; *MGG*
J. A. B. Boyer d'Agen: *M. Desbordes-Valmore: Lettres de Marceline Desbordes à Prosper Valmore* (Paris, 1924), ii, 267–325
P. Hédouin: 'Mme Pauline Duchambge', *Le ménestrel* (1858), June–July

JUDY S. TSOU

Du Coin, Mme **M.** *See* THYS, PAULINE-MARIE-ÉLISA.

Dufferin, Lady. *See* BLACKWOOD, HELEN.

Dusíkova, Kateřina Veronika Anna [Veronika Elisabeta]. Bohemian musician; *see* DUSSEK family, (1).

Dussek [Dusík, Dussik]. Family of musicians of Bohemian origin. The most famous member of the family was the pianist and composer Jan Ladislav Dussek (1760–1812). At least three of its members were women composers resident in London.

(1) Kateřina Veronika Anna Dusíkova [Veronika Rosalia Dussek; Veronika Elisabeta Dusíkova; Veronica Cianchettini] (*b* Čáslav, 8 March 1769; *d* London, 1833). Bohemian singer, pianist, harpist and composer, daughter of the organist and composer Jan Dussek. A pupil of her father, she went to London about 1795 to perform at the invitation of her brother Jan Ladislav Dussek. She married Francesco Cianchettini, a music dealer and publisher who in association with Sperati had the English rights for J. L. Dussek's works from 1807 to 1811. She was a successful teacher and performer. She composed two concertos and published some solo piano works, including three sonatas using 'favorite airs as adagios and rondos' (op.6), sets of variations and short pieces based on well-known tunes. Her son Pio Cianchettini was a pianist and composer.

(2) Sophia (Giustina) Dussek [née Corri] (*b* Edinburgh, 1 May 1775; *d* London, 1847). English singer, pianist, harpist and composer of Italian descent, wife of Jan Ladislav Dussek. She was taught the piano by her father, the composer, music publisher and teacher Domenico Corri, and performed in public at an early age. In 1788 the family moved from Edinburgh to London, where she studied singing with Luigi Marchesi, Giuseppe Viganoni and Giambattista Cimador. She made a successful début as a singer at the Salomon concerts in 1791 and thereafter sang regularly in the series, taking part in the first performance of Haydn's *The Storm* op.8a. In 1792 she married Dussek, with whom she performed, singing and playing the piano and harp. Their daughter, (3) Olivia, was also a pianist, harpist and composer. After Jan Ladislav's death in 1812 Sophia married the viola player John Alois Moralt; they lived in Paddington, where she established a music school. She published sonatas, rondos, variations and numerous arrangements for the piano or harp. The popular C minor harp sonata from op.2

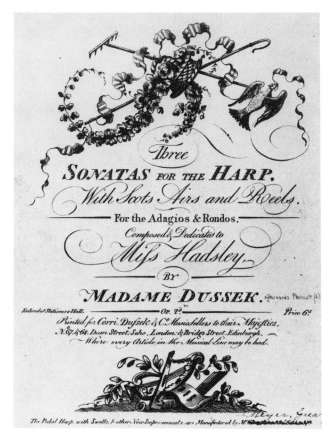

Title-page of Three Sonatas for Harp, op.2 (London and Edinburgh: Corri, Dussek & Co., ?1798) by Sophia Dussek

appears to have been incorrectly attributed to Jan Ladislav (see Dunn). The 1797 Pleyel edition lists only the composer's surname, probably deliberately, as the name of Sophia's famous husband would be expected to generate more sales. The piece was published in England between 1796 and 1801 by Corri-Dussek, and the title-page clearly states 'By Madame Dussek'. This firm was jointly owned by Sophia's father and husband and it is unlikely that they would have miscredited the sonata.

Sophia's great-niece, Ghita Auber Corri (1869/70–1937), composed songs and sang in the Carl Rosa Opera Company; she married the playwright Richard Neville Lynn in 1899.

WORKS
selective list

Kbd: Sonata, pf/hpd, vn/Ger. fl acc., op.1 (London, c1793); 3 Sonates, hpd/pf, vn acc., op.1 (Paris, n.d.); Sonata, pf (London, c1805)
Harp: 3 Sonatas, B♭, G, c, op.2 (London and Edinburgh, ?1798); 3 Sonatas, E♭, F, C (London and Edinburgh, c1795); 3 Favorite Airs with variations (London, ?1815); 4 Favorite Airs, bk 4 (London, n.d.); Variations on God Save the King (London, 1822); arrs., some with variations, of more than 30 airs, waltzes, rondos, some with fl/vn ad lib
Harp, pf: A Duett (London, ?1812); Introduction and Waltz (London, 1822); Duett . . . in which is Introduced a Favorite Air [Ah vous dirai-je], with variations and an introduction (London, 1823)

(3) Olivia Buckley [née Dussek] (*b* London, mid-1790s; *d* ? after 1845). English pianist, organist, harpist and composer. She was the daughter of Jan Ladislav Dussek and (2) Sophia Dussek. She composed a number of charming, if undemanding, pieces for harp, mainly settings of familiar folk melodies. Her London publishers advertised her music as by 'O. B. Dussek'. She is reported to have been organist of Kensington parish church, although her name does not appear in the registers.

BIBLIOGRAPHY

Choron-FayolleD (1); *GerberL* (2,3); *Grove1* (1[†], Mrs W. Carr; 2, W. H. Husk); *SainsburyD* (1,2,3); *SchillingE*[†] (2); *WaltherML* (2)
A. Obertello: 'Una famiglia di musicisti italiani in Inghilterra', *Nuova antologia* (1930), July, 244
H. A. Craw: 'Dussek, a Forgotten Composer', *American Harp Journal*, vi/4 (1978), 14–18

D. Dunn: 'Dussek vs Dussek', *United Kingdom Harpists Association Journal*, no.71 (1984), Feb, 11–14

HOWARD ALLEN CRAW,
BARBARA GARVEY JACKSON (2 work-list),
BONNIE SHALJEAN

Duval, Mlle [first name unknown] (*b* 1718; *d* Paris ? after 1775). French composer, dancer, singer and harpsichordist. In his contemporary manuscript, *Notices sur les oeuvres de théâtre*, the Marquis d'Argenson comments that Mlle Duval, 'une jeune fille de l'Opéra', was 18 in 1736 when she composed *Les Génies, ou Les caractères de l'Amour*. Fétis gives 1769 as her death date; Choron identifies her as a 'singer at the Paris Opera' and claims that she was 'still living in 1770'; the *Anecdotes dramatiques* for 1775 refer to her as a 'former actress at the Opera' and include a Mlle Duval as a supernumerary among the dancers.

Duval was best known as the composer of *Les Génies* (libretto by Fleury [de Lyon]), a *ballet-héroïque* in a prologue and four *entrées* (printed in Paris, date unknown). The title-page reveals that the Prince of Carignan was her 'Protecteur'. *Les Génies*, the second opera by a woman to have been performed at the Paris Opéra (the first was Jacquet de La Guerre's *Cephise et Procis* in 1694), was first heard on 18 October 1736. Although it was performed only nine times (the brothers Parfaict found the libretto 'détestable'), its music was roundly praised. Desfontaines, for one, found some pieces 'worthy of the harmony of J.-P. Rameau's *Les Indes galantes*'. The *Mercure de France* of November 1736 reported:

It is easy to be persuaded by this work that Mlle Duval is a young person with much talent. [The opera] is varied and extremely well developed [*travaillé*] in many regards. In general, the recitatives were applauded, the scenes well treated, some violin airs and choruses well composed and quite lively . . .

Most accounts refer to her as an 'actrice de l'Opéra', but 'Duval' is a very common French name. Was she the Mlle Duval who sang as a sailor (*matelote*) in the prologue to J. B. de Boismortier's pastoral *Daphnis et Chloé* (revival of 1752) and as a dryad in the prologue to J.-B. Lully's *Acis et Galatée* revived in the same year? Léris (2/1763) stated that she 'appeared on the stage of the Académie Royale de Musique for rather a long time and retired with a pension of 300 livres'. Was she the Mlle Duval described by Brenet as a 'young student of M. Royer' (the composer

J. N. P. Royer), director of the Concert Spirituel from 1748? If so, she sang a motet by J.-J. Mouret at the inaugural concert of the remodelled hall on 1 November that year. Duval was certainly an accomplished harpsichordist, judging from the *Mercure* review: 'To the astonishment and pleasure of the Public, this young person seated in the orchestra [Mlle Duval], accompanied her entire Opera from the Overture to the last Note'. One month earlier (October 1736) the *Mercure* printed a duo, *Du Dieu qui fait aimer*, by Mlle Duval (p.2307).

However, the *air Tout ce que je vois me rappelle* by 'Mlle Duv★★' (printed in the June 1776 *Mercure*) is not by Mlle Duval (as reported in *RISM* and *Grove6*), but probably by MARIE ELIZABETH CLÉRY. The treatise *Méthode agréable et utile pour apprende facilement à chanter juste*, attributed by Fétis and Choron to Mlle Duval is by Abbé Pierre Duval.

BIBLIOGRAPHY

Choron-FayolleD; FétisB; GerberL; SainsburyD

Recueil général des opéra (Paris, 1703–45)

Marquis d'Argenson [René Louis de Voyer de Paulmy]: *Notice sur les oeuvres de théâtre* (MS, 1725–56, *F-Pa*); ed. T. Besterman, *Studies on Voltaire and the Eighteenth Century*, nos.42–3 (1966)

P.-F. G. Desfontaines: *Observations sur les écrits modernes* (Paris, 1735–45), vi, 314–15

Mercure de France (Oct and Nov 1736)

C. Parfaict and F. Parfaict: *Histoire de l'Académie royale de musique* (MS, 1741, *F-Pn* nouv. acq. fr.6532)

[A. de Léris]: *Dictionnaire portatif des théâtres . . . de Paris* (Paris, 1754, 2/1763)

C. Parfaict and F. Parfaict: *Dictionnaire des théâtres de Paris* (Paris, 1756, 2/1767–70)

Anecdotes dramatiques, i (Paris, 1775)

J.-B. de La Borde: *Essai sur la musique ancienne et moderne* (Paris, 1780)

T. de Lajarte: *Bibliothèque musicale du théâtre de l'Opéra: catalogue historique, chronologique, anecdotique* (Paris, 1878)

M. Brenet [M. Bobillier]: *Les concerts en France sous l'ancien régime* (Paris, 1900)

M. Barthélemy: 'L'actualité musicale dans les publications périodiques de Pierre-François Guyot Desfontaines (1735–1746)', *RMFC*, x (1970), 107–16

S. Pitou: *The Paris Opera: an Encyclopedia of Operas, Ballets, Composers, and Performers*, ii: *1715–1815* (Westport, CT, 1983)

JAMES R. ANTHONY

Duverger [Duvergé]. See CLÉRY, MARIE ELIZABETH.

Dvorkin, Judith (*b* New York, *c*1927). American composer. Dvorkin studied music with Otto Luening at Barnard College, New York (BA) and with Luening and Elliott Carter at Columbia University (MA); she was also strongly influenced by Roger Sessions through his seminars at the

University of California at Berkeley. Her chamber operas (all to her own librettos) which include *Cyrano* (1964), *Humpty Dumpty and Alice* (1988) and *The Frog Prince* (1993), have been produced for schools and churches by several small companies. In addition to instrumental chamber music, such as the Suite for violin and clarinet (1957) and *Perspectives* for flute (1987), she has written a variety of small-scale vocal works. Her *Song Cycle* and *Four Women* (song cycle no.2, 1981) are both for mezzo-soprano and piano, while *The Children* (1956) is for bass, flute, oboe, piano and violin. Her choral works include *Maurice* (1955). Dvorkin's craft is marked by simplicity of harmonic means and effective text settings. Her music is available through the American Music Center.

BIBLIOGRAPHY

A. F. Block and C. Neuls-Bates: *Women in American Music: a Bibliography of Music and Literature* (Westport, CT, 1979)

CATHERINE PARSONS SMITH

Dziewulska, Maria (Amelia) (*b* Warsaw, 1 June 1909). Polish composer and teacher. After studying at the Warsaw Conservatory, where her teachers included Kazimierz Sikorski (1928–33), she taught at the State Higher School of Music in Kraków (1935–66), then at the corresponding school in Warsaw (1966–76), where she became a professor in 1967. She received the Prime Minister's Award in 1956 for her music for children and the Award of the Minister of Culture and Arts in 1965 and 1971. Dziewulska's rich educational experience is reflected in her works for young people, such as the *Eight Kurpian Songs* (1951) and *The Murmurs of Winnie the Pooh* (1961), both for children's voices. Her style is marked by a roundness of melodic phrase and sparse, polyphonic textures. She has often used Polish folk music and also made many arrangements of early music. Her principal publisher is PWM.

BARBARA ZWOLSKA-STĘSZEWSKA

E

Eckhardt-Gramatté, S(ophie)-C(armen)
[Fridman-Kochevskoy, Sonia de; Friedman
(-Gramatté), Sonia] (*b* Moscow, 25 Dec
1898/6 Jan 1899; *d* Stuttgart, 2 Dec 1974).
Canadian composer, pianist and violinist, of
Russian and French parentage. As an infant
she was placed with foster-parents in
England for four years before her mother, a
pupil of Nicholas Rubinstein, took her to
Paris in 1904 and began to teach her the
piano. She started to compose her first piano
pieces in Paris in 1905, and in 1910 her *Etude
de concert* was published there. From 1908
to 1913 she studied the piano and violin at
the Paris Conservatoire. A child prodigy, she
made her début at the age of 11, playing the
violin and piano in Paris, Geneva and Berlin.
She moved to Berlin in 1914 and studied the
violin with Bronisław Huberman; by 1919
she was performing concertos on both violin
and piano as well as becoming increasingly
drawn towards composition, particularly of
larger-scale works. She married the expressionist painter Walter Gramatté in 1920 and
from 1924 to 1926 lived in Spain, where
Pablo Casals was her mentor. In 1925 she
took part in a concert tour as duo pianist with
Edwin Fischer. After the death of her husband in 1929, she toured the USA, performing to critical acclaim her compositions for
piano and violin with Leopold Stokowski in
Philadelphia and Frederick Stock in Chicago.
She gave up her performing career in 1930 to
devote herself to composition.

In 1934 Gramatté married the art historian
Ferdinand Eckhardt, and from 1936 she
studied in Berlin with Max Trapp at the
Preussische Akademie. She moved to Vienna
in 1939 and in 1945 became a member of the
group that reopened the Austrian branch of
the ISCM. She left Vienna in 1954 for
Winnipeg, where she continued to work
relentlessly at her composition. In 1970 she
was awarded the honorary doctorate from
Brandon University, Manitoba, as well as
the title 'professor' by the Viennese minister
of education; in 1974 she was the first
Canadian composer to receive the Diplôme
d'honneur of the Canadian Conference of the
Arts. Her life was the subject of a two-hour
CBC documentary in 1974. Some of her
music and old performances are included in
Radio Canada International's *Anthology of
Canadian Music*. A project that she had
initiated to encourage young musicians to
study and play contemporary music was

S.-C. Eckhardt-Gramatté

only realized posthumously, in 1976, with the first annual Eckhardt-Gramatté competition for the performance of Canadian music.

As a composer Eckhardt-Gramatté was largely self-taught. She learned much from the virtuoso music she performed on both the piano and the violin, and her compositions from the 1920s in particular reflect this. By the late 1930s her unique contrapuntal idiom had reached full maturity, and in the following decade her style veered towards neo-classicism and bitonality with some use of jazz idioms. In 1950, with the Piano Sonata no.5, she began to adopt serialism, and by 1955 her use of metric manipulation showed similarities to that of Olivier Messiaen and Boris Blacher. She retained a lifelong admiration for the music of Bach – the ending of the 1955 Concerto for Orchestra reworks the prelude from his Partita in E – and, like Bartók, she also had a preference for the interval of the fourth as a structural device. Her music is dark, dense and dramatic, with relentless forward drive; although she admired the First Viennese School, her brand of counterpoint is individual and its dissonance owes much to the post-Romantics. Despite her use of modern techniques, she remained a Romantic in spirit. In addition to writing music, she developed a piano teaching method, the 'E-gré Piano Technique', whose basis is the use of rotary movement.

WORKS
selective list

Orch: Ziganka, ballet suite, 1920; Pf Conc. no.l, 1926, rev. 1931; Konzertstück, vc, chamber orch, 1928, rev. 1974; Grave funèbre, vn, chamber orch, 1931; Passacaglia und Fuge, 1937, rev. 1976; Molto sostenuto, str orch, 1938–52; Sym. in C [no.1], 1939–40; Capriccio concertante, 1941; Pf Conc. no.2, 1946; Concertino, str orch, 1947; Markantes Stück, 2 pf, orch, 1948; Tripel Konzert, tpt, cl, bn, orch, 1949; Bn Conc., 1950; Vn Conc., 1950; Conc., vn, concertante wind insts, orch, 1951; Concertino for Orch, 1954; Conc. for Orch, 1955; Sym.-Conc., pf, orch, 1967; Sym. no.2 'Manitoba', 1970; Sym.-Conc., tpt, chamber orch, 1974; arrs. of 3 Paganini Caprices, vn, orch

Chamber: Ein wenig Musik, pf trio, 1910; Suites, solo vn, nos.1–2, 1923, no.3 'Mallorca', 1924; 10 Caprices, solo vn, 1924–34; Berceuse, fl, pf, 1925; Conc., solo vn, 1925; Lagrima, va/vc, pf, 1926; Februar Suite, vn, pf, 1934; Presto I 'In the Old Style', fl, pf, 1934, rev. 1951 as Presto II; Str qts, no.1, 1938, no.2, 1943; Duos, nos.1–2, 2 vn, 1944; Ww Qt, fl, cl, basset hn/cl, b cl/bn, 1946; Triotino, str trio, 1947; Ruck-Ruck Sonate, cl, pf, 1947, rev. 1962; Nicolas Trio [Str Trio no.2], 1947; Duo concertante, fl, vn, 1956; Duo concertante, vc, pf, 1959; Ww Qnt, 1963; Str Qt no.3, 1964; Nonet, fl, ob, cl, bn, hn, vn, va, vc, db, 1966; Pf Trio,

1967; Suite no.4 'Pacifique', solo vn, 1968; Concertino, vc, pf, 1970; Fanfare, 8 brass insts, 1971

Pf: From my Childhood, i: 14 Alphabet Pieces, 1905–09, ii: Character Pieces, 1907–13; Etude de concert, 1910; Arabesque, 1923; Danse de nègre, 1923; Sonata no.1, 1924; Sonata no.2, 1924, rev. 1952; Sonatas, no.3, 1924, no.4, 1928; Sonata no.6 (3 Klavierstücke), 1928–51; Caprices, nos.2–5, 1932–7; Introduction and Variations on a Theme from My Childhood, 1936; Caprice no.6, 1948; Sonata no.5, 1950

Choral: 4 Christmas Songs (F. Eckhardt), SSATBB, fl, cl, bn, 2 tpt, 2 hn, pf, or vv and pf

Principal publishers: Eschig, Simrock, Universal, Vieu et Vieu

BIBLIOGRAPHY

EMC 2 (L. Watson, H. Kallmann, K. Winters)
J. Anderson: 'Winnipeg Composer Completes Four Centennial Commissions', *Canadian Composer*, no.25 (1968)
'Eckhardt-Gramatté', *Canadian Composer*, no.42 (1969)
'S.-C. Eckhardt-Gramatté: a Portrait', *Musicanada*, xxiii/Oct (1969), 8–9
'Manitoba Composers: a Collective Voice', *Canadian Composer*, no.52 (1970)
'S.-C. Eckhardt-Gramatté', *Canadian Music Educator*, xvii (1975)
M. E. Smith: *The Works for Violoncello by Sophie-Carmen Eckhardt-Gramatté* (thesis, U. of Western Ontario, 1978)
G. B. Carruthers: *The Career and Compositions of S.-C. Eckhardt-Gramatté* (thesis, Carleton U., Ottawa, 1981)
I. Harry: 'S.-C. Eckhardt-Gramatté's Life Story Adventures, Crises and Achievements', *Canadian Composer*, no.178 (1983)
F. Eckhardt: *Music from Within: a Biography of the Composer S.-C. Eckhardt-Gramatté*, ed. G. Bowler (Winnipeg, 1985) [vol.i of 23 vols. contains a catalogue of works]
The Eckhardts in Winnipeg: a Cultural Legacy, Winnipeg Art Gallery (Winnipeg, 1987) [exhibition catalogue]
GAYNOR G. JONES

Edwards [née Gerlich], **Clara** (*b* Mankato, MN, 18 March 1887; *d* New York, 17 Jan 1974). American composer, singer and pianist. She studied singing in Vienna and, returning to the USA in 1914, pursued an active career as a singer and pianist. A member of ASCAP from 1925, she wrote more than 50 songs that successfully blended the styles of art song and the sentimental parlour ballad; *With the Wind and the Rain in her Hair* (published in 1930, and a hit in 1940), *By the Bend of the River* and *When Jesus Walked on Galilee* were particularly popular. Some of her music was incorporated into the repertory of well-known artists: Ezio Pinza, for example, sang *Into the Night* on the 'Telephone Hour' radio programme several times. Edwards also wrote music for children's plays (e.g. *Alice in Wonderland*) and animated cartoons.

ROBERT FINN

Egeberg, Fredrikke (*b* Christiania [now Oslo], 23 Nov 1815; *d* Tønsberg, 6 May 1861). Norwegian composer. Although her education (in Christiania) was intermittent, she was the most distinguished Norwegian woman composer before Agathe Grøndahl; her compositions show formal and harmonic assurance allied to melodic imagination. She published more than 50 songs, many of which have survived in print to the present day. She also wrote many piano pieces.

WORKS
selective list;
all printed works published in Christiania

Songs (1v, pf): 4 Religious Songs (1849); 3 Norwegian Songs (1849); 4 Norwegian Songs (incl. Til min Gyldenlak) (1850); 2 Poems (H. Wergeland); 3 English Poems (1852); Lyksalig Pintse [Blissful Whitsun] (Swed. and Dan. poems) (1855); 3 Songs (1859); 3 Poems (B. Bjørnson) (1860); others

Pf: 6 Songs without Words, 1850; Arioso, Springdans (1850); many other pieces

BIBLIOGRAPHY

J. G. Conradi: *Musikens udvikling i Norge* [Musical Development in Norway] (Christiania, 1878)

K. Michelsen, ed.: *Cappelens musikkleksikon* (Oslo, 1978–80)

C. Dahm: *Kvinner komponerer: 9 portretter av norske kvinnelige komponister i tiden 1840–1930* [Women Composers: 9 Portraits of Norwegian Women Composers 1840–1930] (Oslo, 1987)

KARI MICHELSEN

Eggar, Katharine Emily (*b* London, 5 Jan 1874; *d* London, 15 Aug 1961). English composer and pianist. She studied the piano in Berlin, Brussels and in London, where she also studied composition at the RAM with Frederick Corder. She was one of the founder members of the Society of Women Musicians and spoke strongly at the inaugural meeting in 1911: 'The conventions of music must be challenged. Women are already challenging conventions in all kinds of ways. Everywhere we see them refusing to accept Artificialities for Realities . . . We believe in a great future for Women Composers . . .' In her composing she concentrated on chamber works, such as the Piano Quintet (?1907) and String Quartet (?1931), many of which, although well received in concert performances, remained unpublished. Among her songs are *Wolfram's Dirge* for voice with piano and cello accompaniment (1906), and *My Soul is an Enchanted Boat* for voice and string quartet.

SOPHIE FULLER

Eichner, Adelheid Maria (*b* ?Mannheim, before 1 Sept 1762; *d* Potsdam, 5 ?April 1787). German singer, pianist and composer. She was the daughter and only child of the bassoonist and composer Ernst Eichner and his wife Maria Magdalena Ritter. She grew up in Zweibrücken, where her father was employed in the Hofkapelle of Christian IV of Zweibrücken-Birkenfeld from autumn 1762 to spring 1773. According to Zelter, she was taught singing in Mannheim by an elderly Italian castrato.

At the end of 1773, she and her mother joined her father in Potsdam. He had travelled to Paris and London to give concerts and had begun his employment in the Hofkapelle of the prince of Prussia (later king Friedrich Wilhelm II) in August 1773. She was likewise employed at the Hofkapelle, as the only singer, appearing in public concerts in Berlin as the prince's 'Cammer Sängerin' from 1777 and, from 1781, at the Berlin Opera. Her contemporaries unanimously praised her voice, which was even throughout its range of three octaves, and her extraordinary vocal technique; only her acting was considered stiff and awkward. Of her piano playing the Freiburg *Musikalisches Taschenbuch* of 1784 remarked that she played 'with the same ease and skill [with which she sings] and particularly with regard to matters of taste in performance, her sensitive father's spirit seems to rest on her'.

As a composer, she wrote songs which demonstrate an instrumental rather than a vocal conception and which are unsuccessful as attempts to fuse words and melody. Her first collection, 12 *Lieder mit Melodien fürs Clavier*, was published in Potsdam in 1780; it includes one of the earliest settings of Goethe's *Jägers Nachtlied* ('Huntsman's Night Song'). Further individual songs were printed in musical almanachs until 1792. She also set poems by G. A. Bürger and J. D. Overbeck, as well as those of the Dutch General von Stamford, who from about 1775 until 1786 was tutor at the prince of Prussia's court, and, according to Zelter, was engaged to Eichner.

BIBLIOGRAPHY

Choron-FayolleD; *FétisB*; *GerberL*; *LipowskyBL*

J.-W. Schottländer, ed.: *Carl Friedrich Zelters Darstellungen seines Lebens* (Weimar, 1931)

MARIANNE REISSINGER

Eiríksdóttir, Karólína (*b* Reykjavík, 10 Jan 1951). Icelandic composer. She graduated as a piano teacher from the Reykjavík College of Music and continued her studies at the

University of Michigan, where she received master's degrees in musicology (1976) and composition (1978). Her principal teacher was William Albright. Most of her works are instrumental and include a few solo pieces, but mostly music for chamber ensembles or orchestra such as *Notes* (1978), *Nabulations* (1978), *Fragments* (1979), *Sonance* (1981), *Five Pieces* (1983), *Six Movements* for string quartet (1985), *Sinfonietta* (1985), *Climbing* (1991) and *Three Paragraphs* (1993). Although her earlier works are characterized by brevity, a certain terseness and scholarly objectivity, her lyrical side has gradually become more prominent, from the song-cycles *Some Days* (1982) and *Land Possessed by Poems* (1987) to the larger-scale chamber opera *Someone I have Seen* (1988) to a libretto by Marie Louise Ramnefalk.

BIBLIOGRAPHY

G. Bergendal: *New Music in Iceland* (Reykjavík, 1991)

THORKELL SIGURBJÖRNSSON

Ekizian, Michelle (*b* New York, 21 Nov 1956). American composer of Armenian descent. She studied composition with Nicolas Flagello at the Manhattan School of Music and with Chou Wen-chung at Columbia University. Among the awards she has received are a Guggenheim Fellowship (1986), an NEA Fellowship (1987), the Prix de Rome (1988) and a commission from the Meet the Composer/Reader's Digest Program (1992). Her works include the ongoing *The Exiled Heart Series* for orchestra (1982–), *Octoéchos* for double string quartet and soprano (1986), the chamber opera *David of Sassoun* (1992) and *Saber Dances* for orchestra (1992). Ekizian's music, often restive, displays a density of ideas and a concern for emotional contrast.

BIBLIOGRAPHY

R. Hershenson: 'Year in Rome Turns Composer's Requiem into a Celebration', *New York Times* [Westchester edn] (1 Oct 1989)

ŞAHAN ARZRUNI

Eksanishvili, Eleonora Grigor'yevna (*b* Tbilisi, 11 Feb 1919). Georgian composer, pianist and teacher. At the Tbilisi Conservatory she studied the piano with A. Tulashvili and then composition with A. Ryazanov and Andrey Balanchivadze, graduating in 1940 and 1945 respectively. Between 1947 and 1950 she was a postgraduate student at Moscow Conservatory, where her teachers were Alexander Goldenweizer for piano and G. Litinsky and V. Y. Shebalin

for composition. She was awarded the MMus degree in 1953 for her thesis on the piano transcriptions of M. A. Balakirev. From 1944 she was active as a pianist and she has taught in Tbilisi at the First Musical College, the Paliashvili Central Music School and, from 1953, at the conservatory, where she was appointed professor in 1973. As a result of Eksanishvili's initiative, the first Georgian experimental school-studio was set up in 1973; the teachers there have used the method she expounded in her textbook *Aisi* (published 1972) of developing creative abilities on the basis of Georgian folksong. Eksanishvili's piano music, consisting of original compositions and transcriptions of works by Georgian composers, and music for children are the most signifi parts of her output. Her writings incl rticles on Balakirev, Goldenweiser, th piano music of Georgian composers and the musical education of children. In 1967 the Supreme Soviet of Georgia conferred on her the rank of Honoured Artist.

WORKS
selective list

Stage: Progulka (Druz'ya lesa) [A Walk (Forest Friends)] (children's opera, 1, I. Sikharulidze), 1960; Lesnaya komediya [Forest Comedy] (children's opera, 2, V. Pshavela), 1972; other stage works for children

Orch: 2 pf concs., 1944, 1955; Vesna [Spring], children's suite, chamber orch, 1972

Chamber: Str Qt, 1944; Pf Qnt, 1945, rev. 1970; Str Qt, 1949; Vn Sonata, 1970

Pf: Detyam [For Children], 8 pieces, 1958; Sonata, 1973; 12 Georgian folksong arrs., 4 hands, 1974; Memorial: prelyudii, etyudï i elegiya [ded. to teachers and friends who fell in the war], 1980; other preludes and transcriptions

Vocal: Noch' [Night] (A. Abasheli), 1v, pf, 1940; Sumerki [Twilight] (H. Heine), 1v, pf, 1948; Tomborskiye nochi [Tomborsk Nights] (song cycle, I. Mosashvili), 1975; 2 romances (J. W. von Goethe), 1984; children's songs

BIBLIOGRAPHY

T. Yakovleva: 'Eleonora Grigor'yevna Yeksanishvili', *Oni pishut dlja detey* [They Write for Children], ed. T. Karïsheva (Moscow, 1988), 110–27

OLGA MANULKINA

Elcheva, Irina Mikhaylovna (*b* Leningrad [now St Petersburg], 28 Nov 1926). Russian composer and folksong collector. She was greatly influenced by her mother, the pianist, composer and music theorist, Nadezhda Bogolyubova. Elcheva studied with Sergey Volfenson at the Musorgsky College, Leningrad, during World War II; she then attended the Leningrad Conservatory, where she studied the piano with Alexander

compositions remained unpublished, including the cantatas *Henry of Navarre* and *Radiant Sister of the Dawn*, three overtures, a Fantasia in A minor for piano and orchestra, a cello sonata, a violin sonata and various string trios. Several critics thought that she treated the orchestra rather recklessly, but C. H. Parry once told her, 'You handle your brass as if you've been at it for 20 years.'

JOHN R. GARDNER

Elwyn-Edwards [née Roberts], **Dilys** (*b* Dolgellau, 19 Aug 1918). Welsh composer. After graduating with the BMus from University College, Cardiff, she studied composition with Herbert Howells at the RCM. She taught at various schools and later became a piano tutor at the Normal College and the University College of North Wales, both in Bangor. Elwyn-Edwards has devoted herself to small-scale vocal music: she has produced part-songs and anthems, including settings of Psalms xxiii, c and cxxi (1985), and a substantial quantity of songs and song cycles for voice and piano to both English and Welsh texts. These settings, which include the cycles *In Faëry* (1959), *Caneuon y Tri Aderyn* ('Songs of the Three Birds', 1962) and *Hwiangerddi* ('Lullabies', 1986), are well crafted, sensitive to the poetry and idiomatic, lying firmly within the British 20th-century art-song tradition.

BIBLIOGRAPHY

Fuller-LeFanuRM

D. Elwyn-Edwards and P. Kinney: 'Songwriter to Singer', *Welsh Music*, vi/4 (1980), 7–13

G. Lewis: 'Caneuon y Tri Aderyn', *Welsh Music*, viii/6 (1987), 26–9

A. J. HEWARD REES

Emingerová, Kateřina (*b* Prague, 13 July 1856; *d* Prague, 9 Sept 1934). Czech pianist, teacher, writer on music and composer, sister of the painter Helena Emingerová (1858–1943). She studied the piano with Josef Jiránek, Karel Slavkovský and Karl Heinrich Barth in Berlin (1882–3), then composition (privately) with Zdeněk Fibich and probably with Vítězslav Novák. She gave concerts and taught at the Prague Conservatory until 1928; she promoted and also published music, notably old Czech piano works. Her own compositions – piano pieces for two or four hands – were mainly dances, published by Klemm (Dresden, 1882) and Barvitius (Prague). Her *Polka melancholická* was published as a supplement to the magazine *Zlatá Praha* in 1901; earlier works include a violin sonata (1881), songs

Rosalind Frances Ellicott: lithograph from the 'Magazine of Music' (January 1888)

Kamensky (graduating in 1950) and composition with O. S. Chishko (graduating in 1958). In 1953 and 1956 she participated in folksong expeditions to the Pskov region, to northern Russia and to the lower reaches of the river Pechora. Since 1965 she has collected songs independently in the Ivanovo region; she published her edition of collected folksongs in 1968 and in the late 1970s recorded her own performances of some of these. Most of her original compositions reflect her two main concerns: impressions of war and Russian folk culture. She writes in a traditional style based on folktunes. Her output includes the opera *Spartak* (1962), a Symphony in memory of those who fell in the blockade of Leningrad (1965), solo songs and choral settings of her own texts and of folk texts.

OLGA MANULKINA

Ellicott, Rosalind Frances (*b* Cambridge, 14 Nov 1857; *d* London, 5 April 1924). English composer. She was a daughter of Charles John Ellicott, Bishop of Gloucester and Bristol. At 17 she embarked on two years' study at the RAM with Thomas Wingham, and continued for a further seven years. Many of her works were commissioned for the Gloucester Three Choirs Festival (the cantatas *Elysium*, 1889, and *The Birth of Song*, 1892). A number of important

(published by František Urbánek, 1882) and music for women's choir (Urbánek; 1900). *Starosvětské písničky* ('Songs from the Old Time') appeared in *Česká hudba* (xxxiv, 1930–31).

Even more important than her activities as a composer was her work as a lecturer and writer on music. She wrote on the history of music – on old Czech masters, Beethoven, Berlioz, Weber, Liszt and Smetana – as well as on musical pedagogy, the inheritance of musical gifts and the development of the musical ear. Her writings were published in the periodicals *Dalibor, Hudební revue, Hudba a škola, Ženský obzor, Český čtenář* and (from 1896) the Prague daily papers.

BIBLIOGRAPHY

ČSHS

E. Krásnohorská: 'Hlasatelka české hudby' [The Spokeswoman for Czech Music], *Ženské listy* [Women's Journal], liv/12 (1926), 154–7

K. Wíšková-Procházková: '40 let činnosti prof. K. Emingerové' [40 Years' Activity of Prof. K. Emingerová] *Česká hudba* [Czech Music], xxxiv/5–6 (1930), 25–6

Hudební zpravodaj [Musical Bulletin], iii (1934), no.9, p.12; vi (1937), no.7, p.14

Obituary, *Tempo* no.3 (1934), 95

V. Blažek: 'Kateřina Emingerová', *Sborník na pamět' 125 let konservatoře hudby v Praze* [125 Years of the Conservatory of Music in Prague, Memorial Volume] (Prague, 1936), 237–42

V. Helfert: 'Emingerová, Kateřina', *Pazdírkův hudební slovník naučný*, ii/1 (Brno, 1937)

L. Vojtíšková: 'Sté výroči narozeni Kateřiny Emingerové' [Emingerová's Hundredth Birthday], *HRo*, ix (1956), 635; repr. in *Časopis národního muzea* [Magazine of the National Museum], cxxv (1956), 162–8

MARKÉTA HALLOVÁ

Erding(-Swiridoff), Susanne (*b* Schwäbisch Hall, 16 Nov 1955). German composer. After a school trip to Manchester in 1972 she studied English language and literature at Stuttgart University. From 1974 to 1979 she studied school music at the Stuttgart Musikhochschule, where she was a composition pupil of Milko Kelemen. She also studied composition with Dieter Acker in Munich, Peter Maxwell Davies at Dartington, England, and Agosto Rattenbach in Buenos Aires, and undertook further studies in Oxford, Cambridge, New Haven and Montreal. She became a teacher at the Stuttgart Musikhochschule in 1979. In 1988 she married the writer Paul Swiridoff. Her many awards include a grant from the Villa Massimo, Rome, and prizes in the Città di Trieste, Weber (Dresden) and Turina

(Seville) competitions. In her music she synthesizes experimental techniques, using microtones and variable pitches, with a refined sense of expression and form.

WORKS
selective list

Stage: Yellan (ballet), 1981–2 [arr. of orch work]; Joy (chamber opera, R. Kift), 1983; Der Schneemann (opera, W. Jens), 1990; see also chamber work, Moment Musical

Orch: Yellan, 1981; Conc., vc, 2 orch groups, 1983; Modi giocosi I, II, youth chamber orch, 1985, 1990; Kassandra, 1986; Tierra Querida, vc, orch, 1986

Chamber and solo inst: Grotesques arabesques, vc, pf, 1980; Cadeau cosmique, pf, 1982; Suite, pf, 1982; Rotor, va qt, 1983; Moment musical, fl, gui, pantomime, 1983–4; Homage to the City of Dresden, org, 1985; Variations sérieuses, sax qt, 1985; Aragonesa, 12 vc, 1987; Delirio, tuba, 1987; Lieder, hn, paintings, 1988; Blumen und Blut, vc, 1988

Vocal: Spuren im Spiegellicht (H. Kromer), Bar/Mez, 1984, arr. Bar, chamber ens, 1985; Kein Ort, nirgends (W. Bauer), Mez, pf, 1988; Fröhliche Wehmut (S. Kierkegaard, P. Swiridoff), mixed chorus, 1990

BIBLIOGRAPHY

KompA-Z

DETLEF GOJOWY

Escot, (Olga) Pozzi (*b* Lima, 1 Oct 1933). American composer of French (Huguenot) and Moroccan (Jewish) descent. She was born in Peru, where her father was on diplomatic assignment, then moved to Europe but returned to Lima during World War II. There she studied mathematics at San Marcos University and received musical training at the Sas-Rosay Academy of Music (1949–53) before emigrating in 1953 to the USA (she took American citizenship in 1963). She attended the Juilliard School, New York (MS 1957) and the Hamburg Hochschule für Musik (1957–61). Her principal teachers were Andrés Sas, William Bergsma and Philipp Jarnach. She has lectured widely in Europe and taught at the New England Conservatory (1964–7, 1980–81) and Wheaton College, Norton, Massachusetts (from 1972), where she is director of the electronic music studio. She has held MacDowell Colony fellowships (1962–5) and won many other awards.

Escot's orchestral work *Sands* (1965), first performed by the New York PO in 1975, commanded considerable attention; Andrew Porter judged it 'an arresting composition, as direct as some of Xenakis' most formidably mathematical constructions' (*New Yorker*, 24 November 1975). Some have seen her exploratory inclinations as quintessentially American; at its first performance, at the

Nice international festival, Escot's Piano Concerto (1982) was placed by Jean-Etienne Marie 'in the path of Ives the discoverer . . . a reflection of Harry Partch's world view of the musical phenomenon' (*Musiques actuelles*, Nice, 16 February 1983).

Escot writes chiefly for chamber ensembles and solo instruments. Her rigorous precompositional mathematical planning, which is sometimes computer-assisted, yields a highly structured music that is clear, meticulous, striking in timbre and often dramatic. A discerning commentator on contemporary music, she has contributed to several theory journals and in 1985 co-founded and became editor of *Sonus: Journal of Investigation into Global Musical Possibilities*. With her husband, Robert Cogan, she has written two books on sonic design (1976, 1981), in which they propose analytic concepts and principles applicable to the understanding of music from diverse cultures and historical periods. In 1991 Escot became president of the International Society of Hildegard von Bingen Studies. It has been suggested that, 'Between Escot, 20th-century composer-writer-teacher, and the 12th-century scholar, Hildegard von Bingen, there is much similarity. Both brought to a brilliantly analytical perception of the universe an early training in mathematics [and] channeled an ebullient sensuous nature into that most orderly and disciplined of the arts, music' (Claire Rosenfield, *Radcliffe Quarterly*, centennial issue, 1978).

WORKS
selective list

Orch: Sands . . ., 5 sax, amp gui, 17 vn, 9 db, perc, 1965; Pf Conc., 1982
Inst: 3 Poems of Rilke, reciter, str qt, 1959; 3 Movts, vn, pf, 1959–60; Differences Group I, II, pf, 1960–61, 1963; Lamentus (Trilogy no.1) (Escot), S, 2 vn, 2 vc, pf, 3 perc, 1962; Cristhos (Trilogy no.2), a fl, dbn, 3 vn, perc, 1963; Visione (Trilogy no.3) (Escot, after A. Rimbaud, W. Kandinsky, G. Stein, G. Grass), S, spkr, fl/pic, a fl, a sax, db, perc, 1964; Neyrac lux, 2 gui, amp gui, 1978; Eure pax, vn, 1980; Our kindled valours bend (J. Donne), 1v, cl, pf, 1989; Jubilation, str qt, 1991; Mirabilis II, cl/sax/tpt, pf, perc, 1992; Sonatina no.4, pf, 1992
Tape: Interra, pf, tape, lights, film, 1968; Fergus Are, org, tape, 1975; Interra II, pf (left hand) tape, 1980 (Bryn Mawr, PA,1980); Pluies, a sax, tape, 1981; Mirabilis I, va, tape, 1990
Vocal: Ainu (Escot), 4 ens of 5 vv, 1970, arr. 1v, 1978; Missa triste (Escot), 3 female choruses, 3 opt. tr insts, 1981 (Bryn Mawr, PA, 1994); Bels dous amics, C, 1993
Many early works, 1942–58, withdrawn, incl. 3 str qts, 3 syms., 3 pf sonatinas, songs

Principal publisher: Publication Contract International

BIBLIOGRAPHY
LePageWC, ii
W. Thomson: 'Sonic Design by Robert Cogan and Pozzi Escot', *JMT*, xxiii (1979), 125–34
D. L. Sills: 'Three Sides of the Coin: an Appreciation', *ILWC Journal* (1993), Oct, 6–10
RICHARD S. JAMES/R

Escribano, María (*b* Madrid, 24 Jan 1954). Spanish pianist, composer and actress. After studying the piano and composition she undertook courses in the technique and analysis of contemporary music with Rodolfo Halffter, Mauricio Kagel and György Ligeti. In 1978 she was awarded a scholarship by the Juan March Foundation and moved to France, working as a pianist and composer with the Roy Hart theatre company for three years. She took part in a number of festivals (including Saintes, Montepulciano, Darmstadt, Galenia Göra and Alicante), performed with Brau Theatre, Teatro Vivo and Teatro de Cercanías and formed a duo with the German flautist Sputz Ronnenfeld. She returned to Spain in 1982 and founded the Taller de Música-Teatro AGADA workshop with the actor Manuel Aquinezer. Together they produced seven music-theatre entertainments for children and adults. In her music Escribano combines dramatic experimentation with a continuing investigation into the relationships between words, voice and sound.

WORKS
selective list

Music theatre: Cantos de Lorca (F. García Lorca), 3 actor-musicians, 1977; Lady Macbeth (W. Shakespeare), 2 actor-musicians, 1980; L'histoire d'un son (Lorca), 9 actor-singers, pf, 1981; La rosa amarga (R. Daumal), 2 actor-musicians, psaltery, 1983; Glo . . . Glo . . . Glorieta Viaje por Animalandia, 2 actor-musicians, synthesizer, perc inst, 1984
Chamber: Muñecas de Mimbre, 1975; Homenaje secreto, 1975; Flor de Azar, 1976; Jondo, 1989
Pf: Opening, 1980; Hombre pájaro, 1980; Ofrenda, 1988; Quejío, 1989

Principal publisher: RTVE Música
ALICIA CASARES-ALONSO

Ewart [née Donaldson], **Florence Maud** [Maude] [Alden, Sonia] (*b* London, 16 Nov 1864; *d* Melbourne, 8 Nov 1949). Australian composer. She studied at the Birmingham and Midland Institute and at the National Training School for Music in London (diploma 1882). She then studied the violin at the Hochschule für Musik in Leipzig, gaining sponsorship from Adolph Brodsky; she also worked for him as a tutor. She studied with Joseph Joachim in Berlin before returning to

Birmingham, where she gave violin recitals for musical societies. She conducted an orchestra until 1894, and during that period composed most of her first opera *Ekkehard*, several songs and two song cycles.

In 1898 she married the botanist Alfred James Ewart. In 1906 the family settled in Australia, where Alfred Ewart had been appointed first professor of botany at the University of Melbourne and government botanist. Gaining success with the *Ode to Australia* for the 1907 Exhibition of Women's Works, she was invited to compose for many musical and literary societies. By 1923 most of her works had been performed in Melbourne, and several songs in London. She travelled three times to England and elsewhere in Europe in unsuccessful efforts to have her large-scale works performed.

After an acrimonious divorce in 1927, Ewart again turned her attention to composition, having spent three years in Europe studying with Ottorino Respighi and Giacomo Settacciole. Between 1928 and 1933 she composed three operas, *The Courtship of Miles Standish*, *Mateo Falconé* and *Nala's Wooing*, and a string quartet in D minor. Only *Miles Standish* and the string quartet were performed at the time. Several songs were broadcast in radio recitals. Two operas were still incomplete at her death.

Her works are eclectic, with quotations from Wagner in *Ekkehard* and the symphonic poem, from Verdi, Bizet and Puccini in the symphonic poem, *Mateo Falconé*, *Nala's Wooing* and *Miles Standish*. A Greek ode provided references to Virgil's *Aeneid* in *Ekkehard*, Native American melodies in *Miles Standish*, Corsican folksongs in *Mateo Falconé*, and an Indian *rektah* in *Nala's Wooing*. There are correspondences in the string quartet with music by Respighi, but use is also made of modes and pentatonic scales. In the large-scale works and the songs a more refined and personal later style is developed. The songs, which include settings of Australian poetry, are characterized by finely-wrought textures and are representative of the genre in the 20th century.

Ewart combined her names in various ways when signing her works, and sometimes used the pseudonym Sonia Alden.

WORKS

STAGE
operas unless otherwise stated

Ekkehard (4, Ewart, after J. V. von Scheffel), *c*1910; excerpts, Melbourne, Queen's Hall, 23 Nov 1923
Audifax and Hadumoth (ballet, after von Scheffel), *c*1916, unperf.
The Courtship of Miles Standish (3, Ewart, after H. Longfellow), 1930; concert perf., Melbourne, New Conservatorium, May 1931
Mateo Falconé (2, Ewart, after P. Mérimée), 1933, unperf.
Nala's Wooing (after the Mahābhārata), 1933, unperf.
Pepita's Miracle (after A. Bridge), *c*1945, unperf.
A Game of Chess (after G. Giacosa), 1949, inc.

OTHER WORKS

Orch: Australian Pastoral Scenes, *c*1909; A Knight's Vigil in the Chapel, sym. poem, *c*1916
Chamber: Air with Violin and Viola, *c*1925; Fuga scherzosa, *c*1925; Fugue, str, *c*1925; Str Qt, d, 1930
Vocal: Ode to Australia (A. Rentoul), 1v, chorus, orch, 1907; Empire Pageant Opera (E. Derham), 1912; Abt Vogler (R. Browning), 1v, chorus, insts, *c*1920; My Country (D. Mackellar), 1v, chorus, orch, *c*1923; The days pass away (W. J. W. Turner), 1v, vn, str qt, str acc., 1925; Nocturne (V. Sackville West), 1v, orch, *c*1935; Song of the Crumleaf (E. P. Fox), 1v, brass, perc; *c*50 songs and duets, incl. 2 song cycles (H. Dan, E. Close)

BIBLIOGRAPHY
M. T. Radic: 'Ewart, Florence Maud', *Australian Dictionary of Biography, 1891–1939* (Melbourne, 1981)
F. Patton: 'Rediscovering our Musical Past: the Works of Mona McBurney and Florence Donaldson Ewart', *Sounds Australian: Journal of the Australian Music Centre*, xxi/aut. (1989), 10–12

FAYE E. PATTON

F

Faltis, Evelyn (*b* Trautenau, Bohemia, 20 Feb 1890; *d* Vienna, 19 May 1937). German composer of Bohemian origin. She was educated at the Assomption convent in Paris, then studied at the Vienna Music Academy, where her teachers included Robert Fuchs and Eusebius Mandyczewski; she also studied with Felix Draeseke and Eduard Reus at the Dresden Hochschule für Musik, where she won a prize for her *Phantastische Sinfonie* (op.2*a*), and with Sophie Menter in Munich. She was the first woman to coach solo singers at Bayreuth (1914) and became the soloists' répétiteur at the Nuremberg Stadttheater and Darmstadt Königliches Theater; from 1924 she worked for the Städtische Oper in Berlin. Her modest output of compositions includes the symphonic poem *Hamlet* (op.2*b*); a piano concerto (op.3); two string quartets (opp.13*a*, 15), a violin sonata (op.6) and other chamber works; choral works, including a Mass (op.13*b*); and about twenty songs (opp.7, 8, 10, 14, op. posth.). Many of her works were published by Ries & Erler.

BIBLIOGRAPHY

E. Köhrer, ed.: *Jb der Städtischen Oper Berlin* (Berlin, 1925–6), 63, 74

B. Brand and others, eds.: 'Faltis, Evelyn', *Komponistinnen in Berlin* (Berlin, 1987), 259–64

BIRGITTA MARIA SCHMID

Faria, Celeste Jaguaribe de Matos (*b* Rio de Janeiro, 5 April 1873; *d* Rio de Janeiro, 9 Sept 1938). Brazilian composer, singer and teacher. Her early music studies took place in Fortaleza, in north-east Brazil, where she lived until 1900. From there she went to Rio de Janeiro and in 1901 enrolled at the Instituto Nacional de Música, where her teachers included Alberto Nepomuceno (composition) and Francisco Braga (harmony, counterpoint and fugue). She was appointed singing monitor there in 1905, and professor of solfeggio in 1911. She also studied in Paris (1914) and Berlin (1928). Most of her compositions are vocal works and she wrote two solfeggio methods: *Curso superior de solfejo* and *Solfejos graduados* (both published in Rio de Janeiro in 1934).

WORKS
selective list

Cromo, 1v, pf; Meu coração, 1v, pf; A noite da boneca, 1v, pf; Num postal, 1v, pf; Trovas, 1v, pf; Mocidade e a roseirinha florida, 2vv; Perfume e luzes, 2vv; Seis cantos educativos e recreativos, 2vv

BIBLIOGRAPHY

Enciclopédia da música brasileira (São Paulo, 1977), i, 263

IRATI ANTONIO

Farrell, Eibhlis (*b* Rostrevor, Co. Down, 27 July 1953). Irish composer. She studied at Queen's University, Belfast (BMus), then with Raymond Warren at Bristol University, gaining the MMus in composition. She lectured at St Mary's College of Education, Belfast, before being appointed deputy principal and head of musicianship at the College of Music, Dublin Institute of Technology, in 1983. During 1988–90, she held a fellowship in composition at Rutgers University, New Jersey, studying with Charles Wuorinen (PhD 1991).

Texture and melody are of paramount importance in her strong, atonal works, which use flexible rhythms, polyrhythms and melodic cells. She prefers to write extended one-movement works, often in arch form, and acknowledges the influence of contemporary British and American composers. By the beginning of the 1990s, the forceful writing of the early 1980s had given way to lighter, sparser textures; many of her later compositions reflect her interest in early Baroque music.

WORKS
selective list

Orch and band: Interventions, str orch, 1975; Threnody, orch, 1979; Concerto grosso, 2 vn, vc, str orch, 1988; Sinfón, orch, 1990; Soundshock, concert band, 1993

Choral: Exultet (oratorio, liturgy and Boethius: *De consolatione philosophiae*), S, T, SATB, orch, 1990–91; Exaudi voces (anon.), S, A, T, B, SATB, 1991; A Garland for the President (anon.), S, SATB, 1991

Solo vocal: Now is a Moveable Feast (A. Hartigan), dramatic poem with music, S, vn, cl, gui, perc, 1979; Songs of Death (Hartigan), Mez, pf, 1980; Venus Turned (Hartigan), Bar, pf, 1987; The Lovesong of Isabella and Elias Cairel (Isabella, c12th century), S, ob, va, 1992; The Silken Bed (Nuala ni Dhomhonaill), Mez, vn, vc, hpd, 1993

Chamber and solo inst: Elegy, va, pf, 1977; Sonatina, cl, pf, 1977; Str Qt no.2, 1977; Quadralogue, cl, eng hn, bn, tpt, 1981; Play, org, 1985; Diversions, fl, vn, vc, hpd, 1986; Procession, fl, eng hn, vn, va, 1986; Dancing, org, 1988; Quintalogue, 2 tpt, hn, trbn, tuba, 1989; Time Drops, pf, 1989; Canson, vn, pf, 1991; Earthshine, harp, 1992

SARAH M. BURN

Farrenc [née Dumont], **(Jeanne-)Louise** (*b* Paris, 31 May 1804; *d* Paris, 15 Sept 1875). French composer, pianist, teacher and scholar. A descendant of a long line of royal artists (including several women painters) and a sister of the laureate sculptor Auguste Dumont, she displayed artistic and musical talent of a high order at a very early age. By mid-adolescence she had developed into a pianist of professional calibre and showed great promise as a composer; at 15 she began training in composition and orchestration with Antoine Reicha at the Paris Conservatoire. In 1821 she married Aristide Farrenc, a music publisher (formerly a flautist); her travels with him interrupted her studies for a time, but she resumed intensive work with Reicha a few years later.

Louise Farrenc's earliest compositions for piano were published by her husband's firm, between 1825 and 1839; most were issued also in London and on the Continent. Of special note are the *Air russe varié*, reviewed appreciatively in 1836 by Schumann in the *Neue Zeitschrift für Musik* ('so sure in outline, so logical in development . . . that one must fall under their [the variations'] charm, especially since a subtle aroma of romanticism hovers over them'), and the 30 Etudes in all the major and minor keys, extolled by the critic Maurice Bourges (*La revue et gazette musicale*, 1840), who prophesied that the collection would become a piano classic, 'not only to develop technique but also to mould taste'. The ensuing years substantiated Bourges' prediction: in 1845 the Conservatoire adopted the Etudes as required study for all piano classes, and the music was reissued in 1886.

Farrenc's orchestral compositions comprise two overtures (1834) and three symphonies (completed in the 1840s) – all unpublished, although each work had more than one Paris performance, and there were single performances in Copenhagen,

Louise Farrenc: wood engraving after the crayon portrait by J.-B. Laurens, from 'L'illustration' (13 January 1855)

Brussels and Geneva. Her most notable contribution is the corpus of chamber music, uniformly fine in craftsmanship and exceedingly tasteful and attractive, if a shade unadventurous. Two piano quintets (composed 1839 and 1840) established her reputation among critics and cognoscenti; both works were performed by the composer many times in the following years at musical soirées and matinées. In 1844 Farrenc completed two piano trios, also frequently performed and received with generous critical praise. Her compositions of 1848–58 include two violin sonatas, a cello sonata, two trios and two works for unusual combinations – a nonet for wind and strings, and a sextet for piano and wind. Despite the limited audience for instrumental music in opera-dominated Paris, the nonet catapulted its composer to near-celebrity, the more so because the young (but already legendary) violinist Joseph Joachim took part in the 1850 première. The Institut de France honoured Farrenc in 1861 and 1869 by awarding her the Chartier Prize for her contributions to chamber music.

In 1842 D.-F.-E. Auber, the director of the Conservatoire, appointed Farrenc professor of piano, a post she retained until her retirement on 1 January 1873. The only woman musician at the Conservatoire in the 19th century to hold a permanent chair of this rank and importance, she distinguished herself by the excellence of her teaching, demonstrated by the high proportion of her pupils who won competitions and went on to professional careers. Outstanding among them was the Farrencs' daughter Victorine Louise (1826–59), a rising star who, tragically, became ill in her twenties and died before she was 33.

Farrenc virtually abandoned composition after the death of her daughter. Instead, she became caught up in a project that had been occupying her husband for almost 20 years. Stimulated by the revelations of Fétis's *concerts historiques* (1832–5), Aristide Farrenc had become an ardent advocate of and researcher into early music. He dissolved his business enterprise in about 1840 and devoted his life to scholarship, concentrating on older music and treatises but also studying the musical thought of the recent past and of his contemporaries. What came from this research, ultimately, was *Le trésor des pianistes* (1861–74), a 23-volume anthology of harpsichord and piano music from a repertory encompassing 300 years. Inspired by her husband's enthusiasm, Louise Farrenc immersed herself in the task of compiling and editing the anthology, initially in collaboration with her husband and, after his death in 1865, as sole editor. She shared his ideal of reviving earlier keyboard music and helped to make it a reality through a number of *séances historiques*, in which she and her pupils performed selections from the 17th- and 18th-century repertory. From her own research and experimentation she had gained a remarkable comprehension of the essential problems of early music performance style, and her extended introduction to the first volume of *Le trésor*, 'Des signes d'agrément', was later issued as a separate manual entitled *Traité des abréviations* (1895).

Farrenc's role in music history carries significance beyond that ordinarily accorded to competent minor composers. Having worked in a society whose women musicians attained prominence mainly as performers, and in a cultural environment which valued only theatre and salon music, she merits recognition as a pioneering scholar and a forerunner of the French musical renaissance of the 1870s.

WORKS
printed works published in Paris
PIANO
Variations brillantes sur un thème d'Aristide Farrenc, op.2 (1825); Grandes variations sur . . . Le premier pas, op.4 (1825); Variations sur un air de la Cenerentola [Rossini], op.5 (?1829–30); Variations sur . . . O ma tendre musette, op.6 (1828); Air suisse varié, op.7 (1832); 3 rondos faciles, op.8 (1828); Rondo brillant sur un thème du Pirate [Bel-

Cover and first page of the programme for the soirée musicale (Salons de Madame Erard, 8 April 1861) at which Louise Farrenc's Piano Trio in D minor was performed, together with pieces from 'Le trésor des pianistes', the first volume of which appeared the same year

lini], op.9 (1833); Variations brillantes sur un thème du Colporteur [Onslow], op.10 (1828); Rondo brillant sur des thèmes d'Eurianthe [Weber], op.11 (1833)

Variations sur une galopade favorite, op.12 (1833); Rondo brillant sur une cavatine de Zelmire [Rossini], op.13 (1833); Les italiennes: 3 cavatines . . . variées [Bellini, Carafa], op.14 (1835); Les allemandes: 2 mélodies . . . variées, op.16 (?1835–6); Air russe varié, op.17 (?1835–6); La sylphide, rondo valse sur un motif de Masini, op.18 (c1836); Souvenir des Huguenots, fantaisie et variations, op.19 (c1837); Les jours heureux: 4 rondinos, op.21 (c1837)

Variations sur un thème du Comte Gallenberg, op.25 (c1838), also arr. pf, str qt/orch; 30 études, op.26 (c1839); Hymne russe varié, op.27 (c1839); Variations sur un thème allemand, op.28 (c1839); Variations sur un thème des Capuleti [Bellini], 4 hands, op.29 (c1839); 12 études brillantes, op.41 (1858); 20 études de moyenne difficulté, op.42 (1855); Mélodie, op.43 (1858); Scherzo, op.47 (1858); Valse brillante, op.48 (?1859–63); Nocturne, op.49 (?1859–63); 25 études faciles, op.50 (?1859–63); 2e valse brillante, op.51 (1864)

OTHER WORKS

Orch (all unpubd, F-Pn): Ov., op.23, 1834; Ov., op.24, 1834; Sym. no.1, c, op.32, 1841; Sym. no.2, D, op.35, 1845; Sym. no.3, g, op.36, 1847

Chamber: Variations concertantes sur un air suisse, pf, vn, op.20 (?1835–6); Qnt, a, vn, va, vc, db, pf, op.30 (1842); Qnt, E, vn, va, vc, db, pf, op.31 (?1844–51); Pf Trio, Eb, op.33 (?1850–55); Pf Trio, d, op.34 (?1850–55); Vn Sonata, c, op.37 (?1850–55); Nonet, Eb, op.38, 1849, Pn; Vn Sonata, A, op.39 (?1850–55); Sextet, c, fl, ob, cl, bn, hn, pf, op.40, 1851–2, also arr. str qt, db; Trio, Eb, cl/vn, vc, pf, op.44 (1861); Trio, e, fl/vn, vc, pf, op.45 (1862/R1979); Vc Sonata, Bb, op.46 (1861); Str Qt, Pn

Vocal: few works, most unpubd

EDITIONS

Le trésor des pianistes (Paris, 1861–74) [vols. i–viii with A. Farrenc]; introduction pubd separately as Traité des abréviations (Paris, 1895)

BIBLIOGRAPHY

FétisB; FétisBS; Grove1† (G. Chouquet); SainsburyD; SchmidlD

C. B. [C. Bannelier]: 'Nécrologie: Madame Louise Farrenc', Revue et gazette musicale, xlii (1875), 301

A. Marmontel: Les pianistes célèbres (Paris, 1878, 2/1887 [dated 1888])

G. Vattier: Une famille d'artistes: les Dumont (1660–1884) (Paris, 1890)

M. Brenet: 'Quatre femmes musiciennes', L'art, iv (1894), 183

B. Friedland: 'Louise Farrenc (1804–1875): Composer, Performer, Scholar', MQ, lx (1974), 257–74

—— : Louise Farrenc, 1804–1875: Composer, Performer, Scholar (Ann Arbor, 1980)

BEA FRIEDLAND

Feigin, Sarah (b Riga, 1 July 1928). Israeli composer of Latvian birth. She received her musical education at the Riga Music Academy and settled in Israel in 1972. That year she wrote a symphonic poem, Hakshev! ('Listen!'), for mezzo-soprano and orchestra, setting a text of E. Narusi. In 1973 she founded the first music conservatory for new immigrant teachers in Holon and was its director for approximately ten years.

Feigin developed an innovative system for teaching children in groups and has frequently conducted workshops at music education institutions throughout Israel. She has specialized in writing piano and organ works (especially for four or six hands) for use in her group teaching of children, and numbers among her progressive studies arrangements of Israeli and feast songs. Her music inclines towards traditional harmonies, inspired by the Russian nationalist school, and incorporates a great deal of folk material. While still in Riga, she composed five ballets on Russian epics: The Golden Tree and My Happy Days (both 1956), and three shorter works, Exercise (1968), Poem (1968) and The Storm (1969; after M. Gor'ky). She has also written a children's opera called The House of the Cat (1959, revised 1988) and various orchestral and instrumental pieces. Notable among these is her Violin Sonata (1968) with its beautiful, meditative slow movement. Original compositions and arrangements by Feigin have been performed regularly on Israeli radio. Her music is published principally by the Israel Music Institute.

WILLIAM Y. ELIAS

Fenger, Johanne Amalie (b Lynge, 5 Sept 1836; d Copenhagen, 11 Aug 1913). Danish composer. The daughter of a clergyman, she was herself deeply religious. Her family moved in the literary circle of the poet B. S. Ingemann, and this milieu was of great importance for her work as a composer. She composed as a child, but did not receive serious musical training until she was 18. She studied the piano and music theory with the composers Edvard Helsted and Christian Barnekow. She never married, but lived with her family, apart from a long period of illness (1885–96). She composed and published almost all of her music before 1885, including songs to texts by Danish and Swedish poets and a few occasional works for piano.

WORKS
selective list; all published in Copenhagen

Song collections: 6 Danske sange (1866); 6 sange (1869); 6 sange (B. S. Ingemann) (1871); Lyriske sange (1881); 5 sange (M. Rosing) (1882); Digte af Helene Nyblom (1884)

BIBLIOGRAPHY
H. K. Nielsen: *Mere end en Muse* (diss., Århus U., 1989)

INGE BRULAND

Fereyra, Beatriz (*b* Córdoba, Argentina, 21 June 1937). Argentine composer. Her early musical studies included piano lessons with Celia Bronstéin in Buenos Aires (1950–56). As a composer she was largely self-taught, although she spent a year in Paris in 1962–3, often meeting Nadia Boulanger, who advised and encouraged her, and then went on to study electronic and electroacoustic music with Edgardo Cantón at the RAI sound studio in Milan. She was a member of Pierre Schaeffer's Groupe de Recherches Musicales (1964–70), attended courses given by György Ligeti and Earle Brown at the 1967 Darmstadt summer school and was a collaborator on Bernard and François Baschets' *structures sonores*; she has also undertaken research in both music therapy and ethnomusicology. In 1969–70 she conducted seminars at the Paris Conservatoire in music and audio-visual techniques and in 1975 worked at Dartmouth College, Hanover, New Hampshire, on their digital computer system; she has otherwise lived in France and devoted herself entirely to composition. In her music Fereyra demonstrates an intuitive handling of sound materials – electronic, *concrète* or instrumental – and a freedom of approach to form. Her most representative works are *Siesta blanca, Petit poucet magazine* and *Mirage contemplatif*, all for tape.

WORKS
selective list

El-ac: Médisances, tape, 1968; L'Orvietan, tape, 1970; Siesta blanca, tape, 1972; Canto del loco, tape, 1974; Tierra quebrada, tape, vn, 1976; Echo, tape, 1978; Bruissements, tape, ob, 1982; Cercles de rondes, tape, 1982, version with pf as Jeux de rondes, 1984; Passacaille déboîtée pour un lutin, tape, lute/gui, 1984; Petit poucet magazine, tape, 1985; The UFO Forest, tape, 1985; L'autre . . . ou le chant des marécages, tape, 1987; Soufle d'un petit dieu distrait, tape, 1988; Mirage contemplatif, tape, 1992
Inst: Arabesque autour d'une corde raide, cl, 1988; Remolinos, fl, cl, pf, vn, va, vc, 1990
Filmscores: Documentary on J. L. Borges, 1969; Antartide (J. J. Flori), 1971; Mutations (Flori), 1972; Homo sapiens (F. Mariani), 1975; La baie St James (M. Lamour), 1980

MARIE NOËLLE MASSON

Ferrari, Carlotta (*b* Lodi, 27 Jan 1837; *d* Bologna, 23 Nov 1907). Italian composer and poet. She studied composition at the Milan Conservatory with Alberto Mazzucato. She lived mostly in Bologna, teaching the piano and singing. Her appreciable literary gifts are exemplified by her patriotic and dramatic poetry; she provided the librettos for her own operas and the texts of her songs. Benevolent critics referred to her as 'the Italian Sappho' (Dall'Ongaro) or 'a Bellini in skirts' (Sanelli) for her polished verses and the fluency of her melodies. Ferrari collected her poetic and prose works in four volumes, *Versi e prose* (Bologna, 1878–82), which testify to a wide range of interests (e.g. the poem *In morte di Felice Romani* and the four-act drama *Il vicario di Wakefield* from Goldsmith's novel). The third volume contains the librettos of her three operas. The style and format of Ferrari's musical works adhere to the conventions of the mid-19th century.

WORKS
OPERAS
all librettos by Ferrari

Ugo (dramma lirico, 4), Milan, Teatro di S Radegonda, 5 July 1857
Sofia (dramma lirico, 3), Lodi, Teatro Sociale, March 1866; rev. as Callista
Eleonora d'Arborea (dramma lirico, 4), Cagliari, Teatro Civico, March 1871

OTHER WORKS

Requiem Mass (Turin, 1868)
*c*40 other works, incl. Ave Maria; drawing-room songs; 12 Fronde Felsinee, pf; patriotic hymns

BIBLIOGRAPHY

FétisBS; SchmidlD
C. Ferrari: 'Memoria documentata sulle mie opere musicali', *Versi e prose* (Bologna, 1878), iii, 131–94
A. Bonaventura: 'Le donne italiane e la musica', *RMI*, xxxii (1925), 519–34
P. Adkins Chiti: *Donne in musica* (Rome, 1982)

MATTEO SANSONE

Ferrari [née Colombari de Montègre], **Gabrielle** [Gabriella] (*b* Paris, 14 Sept ?1851; *d* Paris, 4 July 1921). Italian-French composer and pianist. She first studied composition and the piano at the conservatories of Naples and Milan, where her teachers included Paolo Serrao; later, after her marriage to Francesco Ferrari (an Italian correspondent for *Le Figaro*), she studied in Paris with Théodore Dubois and Henri Ketten. Ferrari was encouraged as a composer by François Leborne and Charles Gounod. As a pianist she was renowned for her interpretations of Bach, Beethoven, Chopin, Liszt and contemporary Russian works. After Gounod's death, she studied at the Leipzig Conservatory. She returned to Paris, dedicating herself to composition from about 1895.

Ferrari's output includes orchestral pieces, solo piano works, many songs and five operas. *Sous le masque* (1874), *Le dernier amour* (*opéra comique* in one act, libretto by P. Berlier; 1895), *L'âme en peine* (1896) and the *tableau musical Le tartare* (libretto by H. Vacaresco; 1896) were all produced in Paris. Her final and greatest success was *Le Cobzar*, a *drame lyrique* (in one act to a libretto by Paul Milliet and Hélène Vacaresco) on a story of Romanian village life, first performed in Monte Carlo in 1909. It was well received by the public, but was the object of much debate and criticism by both pro- and anti-feminist writers when it was revived in a two-act version in Paris in 1912. Three other operas (*Le captif*, *Lorenzo Salvieri* and *Le corregidor*) were not completed.

BIBLIOGRAPHY

SchmidlD

MARGARET MONASTRA

Fine, Vivian (*b* Chicago, 28 Sept 1913). American composer and pianist. She became a scholarship piano student at the Chicago Musical College when only five years old. Later she studied the piano with Alexander Skryabin's pupil Djane Lavoie-Herz and harmony and composition with Ruth Crawford and Adolf Weidig. After moving to New York in 1931 she began to perform professionally. Later she studied the piano with Abby Whiteside and composition with Roger Sessions.

Fine's early compositions are in a stern, dissonant, mostly contrapuntal idiom which later turned markedly milder, almost diatonic (*The Race of Life* and Concertante for piano and orchestra). Soon, however, she returned to her dissonant style, although now less forbidding and with a wider expressive range, including a delightful sense of humour, as is evident in *A Guide to the Life Expectancy of a Rose*, an operatic setting of an article from the gardening page of a newspaper. Works such as *Paean* and *Missa brevis* employ free, multilineal textures.

For several years Fine was a composer and accompanist for modern dance groups led by Doris Humphrey, Charles Weidman and Hanya Holm. In addition to composing she has taught at New York University (1945–8), the Juilliard School (1948), and Bennington College, Vermont (1964–88). She was one of the founders of the ACA, serving as its vice-president from 1961 to 1965. She was also music director of the Rothschild Foundation (1953–60). Her honours include the Dollard Award (1966), a Ford Foundation grant (1970), an award from the American Academy and Institute of Arts and Letters (1979), a Guggenheim Fellowship (1980), and grants from the Martha Baird Rockefeller and Alice B. Ditson foundations (1981). Among her many commissioned works are the ballet *Alcestis* (Martha Graham), *Drama for Orchestra* (San Francisco SO), and the Piano Trio (Mirecourt Trio). Her recorded works include a suite from *Alcestis*, Concertante for piano and orchestra, *Missa brevis*, *Momenti*, *Paean*, Brass Quartet, and Sinfonia and Fugato, all on the CRI label.

WORKS

STAGE

for dance unless otherwise stated

The Race of Life (D. Humphrey), after drawings by J. Thurber, pf, perc, 1937; New York, 23 Jan 1938; arr. orch

Opus 51 (C. Weidman), pf, 1938; Bennington, VT, 6 Aug 1938

Tragic Exodus (H. Holm), 1v, pf, 1939; New York, 19 Feb 1939

They too are Exiles (Holm), pf 4 hands, vc, perc, 1939; New York, 7 Jan 1940

A Guide to the Life Expectancy of a Rose (fantasy, 1, Fine), S, T, fl, cl, vn, vc, harp, 1956; New York, 7 Feb 1956

Alcestis (M. Graham), orch, 1960; New York, 29 April 1960, cond. R. Irving

My Son, my Enemy (J. Limón), str qt, pf, perc, 1965; New London, CT, 15 Aug 1965, cond. Fine

The Women in the Garden (chamber opera, Fine), 5 solo vv, chamber ens, 1977; San Francisco, 12 Feb 1978

ORCHESTRAL

Elegiac Song (Piece for Muted Strings), str orch, 1937; The Race of Life [from the stage work], 1937; Dance Suite [4 dances from Opus 51 and The Race of Life], 1938; Concertante, pf, orch, 1944; Alcestis [suite from the stage work], 1960; Romantic Ode, vn, va, vc, str orch, 1976; 3 Sonnets (J. Keats), Bar, orch, 1976; Drama, 1982; Poetic Fires, pf, orch, 1984

CHAMBER

4 Pieces, 2 fl, 1930; Str Trio, 1930; Divertimento, ob, cl, bn, tpt, pf, perc, 1933, Lyric Piece, vc, pf, 1937; Prelude, str qt, 1937; Ob Sonatina, 1939, arr. vn, pf, arr. vc, pf; 3 Pieces, vn, pf, 1940; Capriccio, ob, str trio, 1946; Divertimento, vc, perc, 1951; Vn Sonata, 1952; Composition, str qt, 1954; Str Qt, 1957; Duo, fl, va, 1961; 3 Pieces, fl, bn, harp, 1961; Fantasy, vc, pf, 1962; Dreamscape, 3 fl, vc, pf, perc ens, 1964; Concertino, pf, perc ens, 1965; Chamber Conc., solo vc, ob, vn, va, vc, db, pf, 1966; Qnt, str trio, tpt, harp, 1967; Brass Qt (2 tpt, hn, b trbn)/(2 tpt, 2 trbn), 1978; Lieder, va, pf, 1979; Nightingales, motet, fl, ob, vn, 2 va, db, 1979; Music for fl, ob, vc, 1980; Pf Trio, 1980; Qnt, ob, cl, vn, vc, pf, 1984

SOLO INSTRUMENTAL

Solo, ob, 1929; 4 Polyphonic Pf Pieces, 1931–2; Music for Study, pf, 1938–41, 5 Preludes, pf, 1939–41; Suite, Eb, pf, 1940; Rhapsody on a Russian Folk Song, pf, 1944; Chaconne, pf, 1947; Solo no.2, ob,

1947; Sinfonia and Fugato, pf, 1952; Variations, pf, 1952; Variations, harp, 1953; Melos, db, 1964; The Song of Persephone, va, 1964; [4] Pf Pieces, 1966; The Flicker, fl/pf right hand, 1973; Momenti, pf, 1978; Double Variations, pf, 1982

VOCAL

Chorus: The Passionate Shepherd to his Love and her Reply (C. Marlowe, W. Raleigh), SAA, 1938; Psalm xiii, Bar, SSA, pf/org, 1953; Valedictions (J. Donne), S, T, mixed chorus, 10 insts, 1959; Morning (H. D. Thoreau), nar, mixed chorus, org, 1962; Epitaph (anon.), mixed chorus, orch, 1967; Paean (J. Keats), nar, women's chorus, brass ens, 1969; Sounds of the Nightingale (Keats, R. Barnefield and others), S, women's chorus, 9 insts, 1971; Meeting for Equal Rights 1866 (19th-century American), S, Bar, nar, mixed chorus, orch, 1976; Teishō (trad. Zen), small chorus/8 solo vv, str qt, 1976, parts arr. vn, pf; Oda a las ranas (P. Neruda), women's chorus, fl, ob, vc, perc, 1980

1v, insts: The Great Wall of China (F. Kafka), medium v, 2 vn, va, vc, 1947; The Confession (J. Racine), S, fl, vn, va, vc, pf, 1963; Missa brevis, 1 taped v, 4 vc, 1972; For a Bust of Erik Satie (G. Guy), S, Mez, nar, fl, bn, tpt, trbn, vc, db, 1979; Ode to Purcell, medium v, str qt, 1984

1v, pf: 4 Lyric Songs: The Riddle (E. Dickinson), 1933, A Flower Given to my Daughter (J. Joyce), 1935, Adios, bilbadito (anon.), 1939, Sonnet (Keats), 1939; Tragic Exodus, vocalise, 1939; 4 Elizabethan Songs: Daybreak (J. Donne), 1938, Spring's Welcome (J. Lyly), 1937, Dirge (W. Shakespeare), 1941, The Bargain (P. Sidney), 1938; Epigram and Epitaph (W. Jones, H. Wotton), 1941; Songs of our Time: Stabat mater (J. Wittlin), And what did she get, the soldier's wife? (B. Brecht), 1943; 2 Neruda Poems: La tortuga, Oda al piano, 1971; Canticles for Jerusalem, 1983

Principal publishers: Catamount Facsimile Editions, Margun

BIBLIOGRAPHY
CC (B. Weir); EwenD
W. T. Upton: 'Aspects of the Modern Art Song', MQ, xxiv (1938), 11–30
D. Humphrey: 'Music for an American Dance', ACAB, viii/1 (1958), 4–5
W. Riegger: 'The Music of Vivian Fine', ACAB, viii/1 (1958), 2–4
S. E. Gilbert: 'The Ultra-Modern Idiom: a Survey of New Music', PNM, xii/1–2 (1973–4), 310–14
N. Becker: 'Fine's Garden of Arias', East Bay Review [San Francisco] (9 Feb 1978)
R. Commanday: 'A Plotless "Garden" Gathering of Four Fantastic Personalities', San Francisco Chronicle (12 Feb 1978)
P. Hertelendy: 'Four Great Women – in Opera', Oakland Tribune (12 Feb 1978)
C. Ammer: 'Unsung': a History of Women in American Music (Westport, CT, 1980), 234–7
R. Commanday: 'Let the Music do the Talking', San Francisco Chronicle (31 March 1982)
KURT STONE

Finzi, Graciane (b Casablanca, 10 July 1945). French composer. Born into a musical family, she studied at the Paris Conserva-toire, obtaining premiers prix in harmony (1962), counterpoint (1964), fugue (1964) and composition (1969). She was artistic director of the music festival at La Défense (a suburb of Paris), 1975–1980, and in 1979 returned to the Conservatoire as a professor. Finzi has aimed to express emotion and life in her music. She combines a reliance on tradition – as is evident in her use of virtuoso writing and her sense of lyricism – with a contemporary musical language characterized, most notably, by juxtaposed rhythms, elements that evolve at different speeds and 'poles of attraction' between sounds. A fundamental aspect of her style is its formal dynamism, which is expressed as an ever-present, non-systematized chromaticism.

WORKS
selective list

Stage: Avis de recherche (J. P. Lemesle), 2 solo vv, spkr, 2 cl, 3 vc, 1981; Il était trois fois . . . (G. Levy), 6 solo vv, vn, va, vc, db, pf, tape, 1983–4; Pauvre assassin (opéra, 2, H. Christophe, after P. Kohout), 11 solo vv, actor, orch, 1987–91

Orch: Edifice, conc., vn, orch, 1972–3; Il était tant de fois, conc., vc, str orch, 1978–9; De la terre à la vie, conc., cl, str orch, 1979; Trames, 1980; Conc., 2 vn, orch, 1981; Soleil vert, 1983–4; Cadenza, bn, orch, 1987; Conc., fl, harp, orch, 1989; Sud, 1992

Chamber and solo inst: Profil sonore, hpd, 1970; Pf Trio, 1973; Songes, 2 pf, perc, db, 1973–4; Toujours plus, hpd, org, 1974; Paroxysme, cl, 1978; Free Qt no.1, str qt, pf, 1984; Non si muove una foglia, gui, 1986; Orchestra, 2 org/org 4 hands, 1986; Free Qt no.2, ob, eng hn, bn, hpd, 1988; Juxtapositions, 12 str, 1988–9; Phobie, vn, 1989; Ainsi la vie, va, 1990; Engrenage, ww qnt, 1992

Vocal: Univers de lumière (J. Audouze, M. Cassé), S, spkr, str qnt, cl, hpd, pf, bandoneon, gui, tape, 1990–1

Principal publishers: Billaudot, Durand

FRANÇOISE ANDRIEUX

Firsova, Elena [Yelena] **(Olegovna)** (b Leningrad [now St Petersburg], 21 March 1950). Russian composer. She began to compose at the age of 12 and, four years later, began attending music college in Moscow, where she quickly blossomed as the schoolgirl composer of ten pieces (including opp.1–3) that still figure in her list of works. Entering the Moscow Conservatory in 1970, she became a composition pupil of Alexander Pirumov for the next five years; she also studied analysis with Yury Kholopov. A further ten works (opp.4–13) date from these student years, including her first three orchestral works and her first chamber opera.

The 15 years after leaving the conservatory took her from op.14 to op.47 – not counting a number of smaller pieces without opus numbers. Her music was first performed abroad in 1979, and her first foreign commission (from the BBC) came in 1984. Within a few years, changes occurred internationally and personally, and not long after the travel barriers were removed, Firsova and her husband, the composer Dmitry Smirnov, left Moscow. Arriving in London in April 1991 with their two young children, both composers survived by writing music to commission (Firsova herself completing six works in 1991 alone) and by means of short-term residency invitations from Cambridge University and from Dartington College of Arts; in January 1993 they began a long-term attachment to the music department at the University of Keele.

Firsova's work may perhaps best be likened to that of the short-story writer; few of her pieces extend much beyond a quarter of an hour's duration and most are cast in a single unbroken span. As in the one-movement Piano Sonata (1986) she once thought to dedicate to Alban Berg, her harmonic language of the 1980s reveals its indebtedness to the early 20th-century Viennese composers; at the same time, loose-limbed rhythms and often unbarred metre owes much to the French influence of Olivier Messiaen and Pierre Boulez promoted by her friend and unofficial mentor Edison Denisov.

Like the partly private language of the poets she so admires and has so often set, her later musical secrets are contained by a more personalized library of characteristic gestures that may, but often do not, suggest narrative threads of a noticeably motivic kind. While the background pulse of her music is generally slow-moving, contrasts of speed and of mood are achieved less through metre or theme than through an increase or decrease in the amount of foreground activity that continues to animate the textures of the filigree style that she has made her own.

WORKS

STAGE

Pir vo vremya chumï [Feast in Plague Time], op.7 (chamber opera, Firsova, after A. Pushkin), 5 solo vv, chamber chorus, orch, 1972

Solovey i roza [The Nightingale and the Rose], op.46 (chamber opera, 1, after C. Rossetti and O. Wilde), 3 solo vv, SATB, inst ens, 1991; London, Almeida Theatre, 8 July 1994

ORCHESTRAL

5 p'yes [Pieces], op.6, 1971; Chamber Music, op.9, str orch, 1973; Vc Conc. no.1, op.10, 1973; Stansï [Stanzas], op.13, perc, harp, cel, str, 1975; Vn Conc. no.1, op.14, 1976; Postlyudiya [Postlude], op.18, harp, orch, 1977; Chamber Conc. no.1, op.19, fl, str, 1978 (Moscow, 1984); Chamber Conc. no.2 (Vc Conc. no.2), op.26, 1982; Vn

Elena Firsova

Conc. no.2, op.29, 1983; Chamber Conc. no.3, op.33, pf, orch, 1985; Osennyaya muzïka [Autumn Music], op.39, chamber orch, 1988; Nostal'giya, op.42, 1989; Cassandra, op.60, 1992

VOCAL
words by O. Mandel'shtam unless otherwise stated

Vocal-orch: Tristia, op.22, cantata, 1v, chamber orch, 1979; Kamen' [The Stone], op.28, cantata, 1v, orch, 1983

Choral: 3 stikhotvoreniya Mandel'shtama [3 Mandelstam Poems], op.3, chamber chorus, 1970; Kolokol [The Bell] (S. Yesenin), 1976, collab. Smirnov; Proritsaniye [Augury], op.38 (W. Blake), chorus, orch, 1988

Other: 3 romansa (B. Pasternak), 1v, pf, 1966–7, nos.2–3 (Moscow, 1986); Tvorchestvo [Creation] (song cycle, A. Akhmatova), high v, pf, 1967, nos.1 and 4 (Moscow, 1979); 3 romansa (V. Mayakovsky), 1v, pf, 1969; Osenniye pesni [Autumn Songs], op.12 (M. Tsvetayeva, Mandelstam, A. Blok, Pasternak), 1v, pf, 1974; Soneti Petrarki [Petrarch's Sonnets], op.17 (trans. Mandelstam), 1v, inst ens, 1976 (Moscow, 1983); Noch' [Night], op.20 (Pasternak), 1v, sax qt, 1978; 3 stikhotvoreniya Mandel'shtama, op.23, 1v, pf, 1980; Soneti Shekspira [Shakespeare's Sonnets], op.25, 1v, sax qt, 1981, arr. as op.25a, 1v, org, 1988; Zemnaya zhizn' [Earthly Life], op.31, cantata, S, chamber ens, 1984; Lesnïye progulki [Forest Walks], op.36, cantata, S, fl, cl, harp, str qt, 1987; Son [The Dream], op.39a (Pasternak), Mez, pf, 1988; Stigiyskaya pesnya [Stygian Song], op.43, S, ob, perc, pf, 1989; 7 Khokku [7 Haiku], op.47 (M. Basyo), S, lyre, 1991; Rakovina [Sea Shell], op.49, S, cl, va, vc, db (1991); Omut [Whirlpool], op.50, 1v, fl, perc, 1991; Silentium, op.51, 1v, str qt, 1991; Rasstoyaniye [Distance], op.53 (Tsvetayeva), 1v, cl, str qt, 1992; Taynïy put' [Secret Way], op.52, 1v, orch, 1992

INSTRUMENTAL

Chamber: Legenda, hn, pf, 1967 (Moscow, 1978); Scherzo, op.1, fl, ob, cl, bn, pf, 1967 (Moscow, 1975); 2 p'yesï [2 Pieces], vn, pf, 1968 (Moscow, 1977); Str Qt no.1 (5 Pieces), op.4, 1970 (Moscow, 1983); Sonata, op.5, vc, pf, 1971 (Moscow, 1979); Pf Trio, op.8, 1972; Str Qt no.2, op.11, 1974; Kaprichchio, op.15, fl, sax qt, 1976 (Moscow, 1979); Misterioso (Str Qt no.3), op.24, 1980 (Hamburg, 1982) [In memoriam Igor Stravinsky]; 3 Pieces, hn, pf, 1980; Spring Sonata, op.27, fl, pf, 1982 (Moscow, 1985); Taynstvo [Mysteria], op.30, org, perc, 1984; Muzïka dlya 12 [Music for 12], op.34, 1986; Chamber Conc. no.4, op.37, hn, ens, 1987; Amoroso (Str Qt no.4), op.40, 1989; Odyssey, op.44, fl, hn, perc, harp, vn, va, vc, 1990; Verdehr-Terzett, op.45, cl, vn, pf, 1990; Far Away, op.48, sax qt, 1991; Meditation in the Japanese Garden, op.54, fl, va, pf, 1992; You and I, op.55, vc, pf, 1992; Vigilia, op.57, vn, pf, 1992; Lagrimoso (Str Qt no.5), op.58, 1992; Otzvuki, op.59, fl, gui/harp, 1992; Phantom, op.61, 4 viols, 1993; Nochnïye demonï [The Night Demons], op.62, vc, pf, 1993; Crucifixion, op.63, vc, bayan/org, 1993

Solo inst: Invention à Two, pf, 1966 (Moscow, 1982); 2 polifonicheskiye p'yesï [2 Polyphonic Pieces], pf, 1966; Suite, op.2, va, 1967 (Moscow, 1979); Ofort, op.16, cl, 1976 (Moscow, 1978); 2 inventsii [2 Inventions], fl, 1977 (Moscow, 1980); 3 p'yesï, xyl, 1978 (Moscow, 1979); Elegiya, op.21, pf, 1979 (Moscow, 1980); Sfinks [Sphinx], harp, 1982; Fantasie, op.32, vn, 1985 (Hamburg, 1985); Sonata, op.35, pf, 1986; Monolog, op.41, bn, 1989; Starry Flute, op.56, fl, 1992; Hymn to Spring, op.64, pf, 1993; Monologue, op.65, sax, 1993

Also film scores (with Smirnov) and arrs., incl. vs of Denisov: L'écume des jours, prepared with Smirnov, 1980

Principal publishers: Boosey & Hawkes, Muzïka, Hans Sikorski, Sovetskiy Kompozitor

BIBLIOGRAPHY

CC (G. McBurney)

T. Baranova: 'Harmony and a Sense of Proportion', Music in the USSR (1990), July–Dec, 35–7

T. Porwoll: 'Die alternative Komponistengeneration in Moskau', Sowjetische Musik im licht der Perestroika (Laaber, 1990), 117–27

V. Yekimovsky: 'Lyogkich skladok burya' [A Storm of Light Folds], Melodia (1990), no.2, p.17

M. Miller: 'Firsova's Augury', Tempo, no.182 (1992), 25–6

V. Wern: 'At se verden i et sandskorn' [To See a World in a Grain of Sand], Dansk musiktidsskrift, lxvii/4 (1992–3), 134–7

B. Brand: Elena Firssowa, Klangportraits, Musikfrauen, vii (Berlin, 1993) [incl. articles by B.Brand, G. Eberle and D. Redepenning]

SUSAN BRADSHAW

Fisher, Helen (Wynfreda) (b Nelson, 4 Feb 1942). New Zealand composer and teacher. She graduated in English from the University of Canterbury (BA 1964) and taught for a number of years before taking the BMus first in music history (1982) and then in composition (1991) at Victoria University of Wellington. She has helped to develop the study of relationships between Polynesian and Western musical styles and has collaborated extensively with Maori performing artists. Her music is often expressively atonal or modal in style with frequent use of linear techniques and it displays her affinity with wind instruments. She has written many chamber and choral works but has specialized in music for dance and for performance in schools. Both Maori culture and the New Zealand environment are sources of inspiration for her.

WORKS

Te tangi a te matui (Maori karakia), fl + C, 1986; Ww Trio, fl, cl, bn, 1987; Ko wharepapa te maunga, 2 tpt, 4 hn, trbn, tuba, 1989; Pounamu (W. Whakatauki), SSAATB, fl/shakuhachi, 1989; Takiri mai te awatea (Fisher), SATB, poi, haka, patere, Maori insts, 1990; Nga taniwha, music for children's dance, vv, fl, cl, rec, pf, perc, rock band, 1991; Nga Tapuwae o Kupe, music for children's dance, chorus, fl, eng hn, cl, sax, koauau, gui, pf, perc, 1992; Wahine Toa, 'dance theatre', SATB, 2 fl, str qt, perc, pf, 1992, collab. G. Farr; Bone of Contention, 'dance theatre', Mez, cl/b cl, s/a sax, vn, vc, harp, mar, perc, bagpipes, 1993

BIBLIOGRAPHY

Fuller-LeFanuRM

A. Wells: 'Helen Fisher – Biculturalism: beyond 1900', Music in New Zealand (1991), aut., 28–31

'Wahine Toa – a Celebration of Maori Women', New Zealand Listener (12 Dec 1992) [reviews by A. Wells and Q. R. Hyland]

P. Katene: 'Wahine Toa – a Creative Partnership', Music in New Zealand (1992), sum., 12–14

J. M. THOMSON

Fleischer, Tsippi [Tsipporah] (b Haifa, 20 May 1946). Israeli composer. She graduated from the Music Teachers' College, Tel-Aviv, in 1967 and then took degrees in Middle Eastern subjects at Tel-Aviv University (BA 1970, 1973), and studied music at the Rubin Academy of Music (BMus 1969). She gained the MA in music education from New York University (1975) and later the PhD in musicology from Bar-Ilan University. She has taught theory at Tel-Aviv and Bar-Ilan universities and at the Hebrew Union College, Jerusalem. Her music combines Western and Eastern elements: her first stage work, A Girl Named Limonad (1977), is to a text by the Lebanese Christian poet Shawqi Abi-Shaqra and makes use of folk-inspired materials. Girl-Butterfly-Girl (1977), a song cycle for high voice and chamber ensemble, may be performed in either of two versions, for Western or oriental ensemble. Other works include Lamentations (1985) for soprano, women's chorus, two harps and percussion and *In the Mountains of Armenia* (for children's chorus), which represented Israel in the 1989 UNESCO International Rostrum for Composers in Paris.

BIBLIOGRAPHY

P. Roth: *Tsippi Fleischer: Music for Small Ensembles* (Hataklit DD 35362, 1986) [record notes]
E. Lauer: 'Vienna Modern Masters Recordings', *ILWC Journal* (1992), Oct, 21–3 [review of *Girl-Butterfly-Girl*]
G. Straughn: 'Profile: Tsippi Fleischer', *ILWC Journal* (1992), Oct, 17

Folville, Eugénie-Emilie Juliette (*b* Liège, 5 Jan 1870; *d* Castres or Dourgnes, 19 or 28 Oct 1946). Belgian pianist, violinist, teacher and composer. She began to study music with her father and later entered the violin class of Ovide Musin at the Liège Conservatory. She also studied the violin with Charles Malherbe and César Thomson, counterpoint and fugue (*premier prix* 1887) at the Conservatory, composition with Jean-Théodore Radoux and the piano with Delaborde in Paris. She embarked on a virtuoso career in both the violin and piano, beginning in 1879 and continuing to wide acclaim in Belgium, France, Holland, Germany and England. Folville is notable as a pioneer in the revival of the harpsichord, which she played in concerts, and its music of the 15th to the 18th centuries. She taught historical performing practice and the piano at the Liège Conservatory, the latter from 1897 to 1919.

Her many compositions exhibit a distinctive compositional craft, accomplished scoring, some chromaticism, and an elegance of style paralleling that of Massenet. Her only opera, *Atala* (1892), was well received when presented in Lille and Rouen in 1892 and 1893. Other significant works include the music for theatre *Jean de Chimay* (1905), the *Concertstück* and *Triptyque* for cello and orchestra, concertos for violin and for piano, the symphonic poem *Oceano Nox*, and three orchestral suites (*Scènes champêtres, Scènes d'hiver, Scènes de la mer*). Sacred works include *Chant de noël* for chorus and orchestra, *a cappella* motets and organ music. She also composed *mélodies*, cantatas, piano works and chamber music.

BIBLIOGRAPHY

SchmidlD

JAMES R. BRISCOE

Fontyn, Jacqueline (*b* Antwerp, 27 Dec 1930). Belgian composer. She was taught the

Jacqueline Fontyn

piano by Ignace Bolotine and Marcel Maas, and studied composition first with Marcel Quinet (1947–59), then in Paris (1954–5) with Max Deutsch, who introduced her to serial techniques. She furthered her studies in Vienna (1956) and at the Chapelle Musicale Reine Elisabeth, Belgium (1956–9). In 1961 she married the composer Camille Schmit, who encouraged and influenced her through the rigour of his work. She held appointments as professor of counterpoint at the conservatories in Antwerp (1963–70) and Brussels (1969–71), and taught composition at the latter (1971–90). In 1991 she began to devote herself entirely to her own composition. Among the awards she has received are the Prix de Rome (1959), the Oscar Espla Prize (Alicante, 1961), the Queen Elisabeth of Belgium prize (1964) and the Arthur Honegger prize (1987). Her Violin Concerto was commissioned for performance in 1976 at the Queen Elisabeth of Belgium International Competition.

Fontyn generally employed classical forms in those compositions written before 1956, of which the Piano Trio of that year, a form of tribute to her teacher Marcel Quinet, is one of the most representative works. *Capriccio* for piano was an exception: written in 1954, it was her first attempt at serialism. Thereafter, until 1969, she adopted free serialism and her style became profoundly atonal, as *Ballade* (1963) exemplifies; strict rhythm and the use of Klangfarben-melodien impart an indeterminate quality to her works of this period. In 1969, with *Filigrane*, she introduced a number of short but controlled sections in which she abandoned the bar-line in favour of free rhythm, and after 1979, with *Ephémères*, she moved away from serial technique, adopting a more modal language and combining rigorous writing with aleatory passages. Fontyn attaches great importance to matters of form, proportion and contrast; she has claimed that the orchestra is her preferred medium and more than half of her output is written for large ensembles.

WORKS
selective list

Stage: Piedigrotta (ballet, 5 scenes), women's vv, orch, 1958

Orch: Mouvements concertants, 2 pf, str, 1957; 6 ébauches, 1964; Evoluon, 1972; Per archi, 1973; Vn Conc., 1976; 4 sites, 1977; Halo, harp, 16 insts, or chamber orch, 1978; Créneaux, youth orch, 1983, rev. sym. band; In the Green Shade, 1988; Pf Conc. 'Rêverie et turbulence', 1989; Va Conc. 'A l'orée du songe', 1990; Vc Conc. 'Colinda', 1991; Aratoro, wind orch, 1992; On a Landscape by Turner, 1992

Chamber and solo inst: Capriccio, pf, 1954; Pf Trio, 1956; Ballade, pf, 1963; Musica a quattro, vn, cl/va, vc, pf, 1966; Nonetto, fl, ob, cl, bn, hn, vn, va, vc, db, 1969; Filigrane, fl, harp, 1969; Strophes, vn, pf, 1970; Spirales, 2 pf, 1971; 6 climats, vc, pf, 1972; Horizons, str qt, 1977; Zones, fl, cl, vc, perc, pf, 1979; Le gong, pf, 1980; Analecta, 2 vn, 1981; Either . . . or, str qnt/str qt, cl, 1984; Scurochiaro, fl, cl, bn, pf, vn, vc, db, 1989; Compagnon de la nuit, ob, pf, 1989; Polissonnerie, perc, pf, 1991; Cesare G., fl, vn, va, vc, harp, 1993, also version for fl, cl, vn, vc, pf

Vocal: Psalmus tertius, Bar, chorus, orch, 1959; Ephémères, Mez, 11 insts, 1979, orchd, 1979; Alba, S, cl, vc, harp/perc, pf, 1981; Pro et antiverb(e)s, S, vc, 1984; Cheminement, S, 9 insts, 1986; Rosa, rosae, S, C, cl, vn, harp, pf, 1986; Ku soko, S/Mez, pf, 1989; Rose des sables, Mez, spkr, women's vv, orch, 1990; Blake's Mirror, Mez/C, wind orch, 1993; 7 Galgenlieder (C. Morgenstern), S, ob, vc, pf, 1994

Principal publishers: Bote & Bock, Peer Southern, Perform Our Music, G. Schirmer

BIBLIOGRAPHY

CC (P. Heureux); CohenE; KompA-Z

P. Legrain, ed.: *Dictionnaire des Belges* (Brussels, 1981)

B. Sonntag and R. Matthei, eds.: *Annäherungen an sieben Komponistinnen*, iii (Kassel, 1987)

I. Coppens d'Eeckenbrugge: *Pour une approche de l'oeuvre de Jacqueline Fontyn* (thesis, Catholic U. of Louvain, 1987–8)

T. Beimel: 'Halo': *Erkundungen über ein Werk von Jacqueline Fontyn* (Düsseldorf, 1991)

B. Brand: *Jacqueline Fontyn, Klangportraits*, ii (Berlin, 1991)

CHRISTINE BALLMAN

Fowler, Jennifer (*b* Bunbury, 14 April 1939). British composer of Australian birth. She took degrees in music at the University of Western Australia (1960, 1967), then attended the University of Utrecht's Electronic Music Studio on a Dutch Government Scholarship (1968). From 1969 she lived in London, working as a freelance composer. Her music has been broadcast in many countries and performed at a number of international festivals. In 1975 she won a prize in the chamber music section of the GEDOK competition in Mannheim, and in 1971 she shared the Radcliffe Award of Great Britain. She received a BBC commission in 1989 for the vocal-chamber piece *And Ever Shall Be*, which was first performed in that year by Linda Hirst, mezzo-soprano, with Lontano. The work is a setting of four traditional texts united by their female stance; the title comments with resignation on women's lot.

Fowler is extremely resourceful in her concentrated exploration of sometimes quite simple ideas. *Chimes Fractured* (1971) is an amusing piece inspired by sounds heard on a visit to Liverpool Cathedral, with distinct strands in an oscillating equilibrium interacting and literally fracturing one another. In *Reeds, reflections . . .* (1990), instruments are set hauntingly in waves of motion that gradually distort as they mirror and echo.

Jennifer Fowler, 1983

WORKS
selective list

Orch: Look on this Oedipus, 1973; Chant with Garlands, 1974; Ring out the Changes, 1978

Chamber and solo inst: Ravelation, 2 vn, va, 2 vc, 1971; Chimes Fractured, 2 fl, 2 ob, 2 cl, 2 bn, org, bagpipes, perc, 1971; Piece for an Opera House, 2 pf//(pf, tape)/solo pf, 1973; Music for Piano: Ascending and Descending, pf, 1980; The Arrows of Saint Sebastian I, fl, ob, cl, bn, hn, tpt, trbn, tuba, pf, 2 vn, va, vc, 1981; The Arrows of Saint Sebastian II, b cl, vc, tape, 1981; Threaded Stars, harp, 1983; Lament, baroque ob, bass viol/vc, 1987; . . . between silence and the word, fl, ob, cl, bn, hn, 1987; Restless Dust, vc, pf, 1988, arr. va, vc, db, 1988; Reeds, reflections . . . ripples re-sound resound, ob, vn, va, vc, 1990

Vocal: Hours of the Day, 4 Mez, 2 ob, 2 cl, 1968; Veni Sancte Spiritus – Veni Creator, SATB chamber chorus/12 solo vv, 1971; Tell out, my Soul (Magnificat), S, vc, pf, 1980, rev. 1984; When David heard, chorus, pf, 1982; Letter from Haworth, Mez, cl, vc, pf, 1984; And Ever Shall Be, Mez, fl (pic), ob, cl, trbn, vn, va, vc, prc, 1989

Principal publisher: Universal (Australia)

BIBLIOGRAPHY
CC (J. Dawson); Fuller-LeFanuRM
K. Potter: 'Antipodean Connections', Classical Music, no.214 (8 January 1983), 19
J. Fowler: 'My Own Ears', New Music Articles, no.4 (1985), 3–6
——: 'An Emotional Geography of Australian Composition: Credo', Sounds Australian Journal, no.25 (1990), 6
——: 'Credo', Sounds Australian Journal, no.34 (1992), 28–9

TONI CALAM, THÉRÈSE RADIC

Fox, Erika (b Vienna, 3 Oct 1936). English composer and teacher. She came to England as a refugee at the age of three. She won a scholarship to the RCM, where she studied composition with Bernard Stevens; later she continued her studies with Jeremy Dale Roberts and Harrison Birtwistle. Her highly individual music is strongly influenced by the ancient Chassidic melodies that permeated her Orthodox Jewish childhood. She has written music for a wide variety of ensembles, from solo works, such as Nick's Lament (1984) for guitar, to powerful orchestral music, such as Osen Shomaat (1985). Her works have always been closely linked to music theatre and she has been increasingly involved with opera. The Dancer, Hotoke (1991), to a libretto by Ruth Fainlight, was commissioned by The Garden Venture, a scheme set up by the Royal Opera for the purpose of staging new, small-scale works.

WORKS
selective list

Stage: The Slaughterer (Fox, after I. B. Singer), 1975; The Bet (E. Feinstein), 1990; The Dancer, Hotoke (R. Fainlight), 1991

Orch: Cocytus, 1973; Osen Shomaat, 1985

Vocal: 8 Songs from Cavafy, Mez, fl, ob, bn, vn, pf, 1968; 9 Lessons from Isaiah, B, str qt, 1970; Jeder Engel ist schrecklich, S, Bar, cl, hn, trbn, str, 1976; Voices, 5 solo vv + perc, 1976; Frühling ist wiedergekommen, Mez, pf, 1988

Chamber and solo inst: In Memoriam Martin Luther King, vc, ob, 1969; Round, 14 solo str, 1972; Lamentations for Four, 2 vc, perc, 1973; Octet for Two, vc, pf, tape, 1977; Epitaph for Cathy, basset cl + perc, 1980; Paths where the Mourners Tread, fl, ob, harp, perc, str, 1980; Litany, str, 1981; Kaleidoscope, fl, harp, vib, vc, 1983; Quasi un cadenza, cl, hn, pf, 1983; Shir, ens, 1983; Nick's Lament, gui, 1984; On Visiting Stravinsky's Grave at San Michele, pf, 1988; Hungarian Rhapsody, fl, ob, cl, tpt, pf, 1989; The Moon of Moses, vc, 1992

BIBLIOGRAPHY
CC (N. Loseff); Fuller-LeFanuRM

SOPHIE FULLER

Frajt, Ludmila (b Belgrade, 31 Dec 1919). Serbian composer of Czech descent. She was a pupil of Miloje Milojević and Josep Slavenski at the Belgrade Music Academy; later she worked as music editor for the Avala film company and for Belgrade radio and television. A composer with a particular sensitivity towards timbral quality, she successfully assimilated elements of post-serial Klangmusik into her musical style, which is generally lyrical and intimate. Her vocal music, which is highly expressive and refined, is often inspired by folk music and rites, as exemplified by Pesme rastanka ('Songs of Departure', 1967) for mixed chorus and Zvona ('Bells', 1981) for mixed chorus with tape. For female chorus she has written Pesme noci ('Nocturnal Songs', 1970, with chamber orchestra) and Tužbalica ('Dirge', 1973). Her works for chamber orchestra include Eclogue (1975).

MELITA MILIN

Franchi, Dorothea Anne (b Auckland, 17 Feb 1920). New Zealand composer, pianist and harpist. Her early training in piano and singing was followed by a BMus from the University of Auckland in 1939. She became a music specialist in schools, then from 1948 studied the harp, composition and piano accompaniment at the RCM, London, where she won the Tertis Prize for her Rhapsody for viola and orchestra in 1950. In 1953 she became pianist and musical director for Poul Gnatt's newly formed New Zealand Ballet Company for whom she wrote Do-Wack-a-Do (1960), a piece evocative of the frenetic gaiety of the 1920s (she once commented that the syncopated rhythms of ragtime and jazz 'have stayed with me all my life'). From an early romanticism she has moved through more severe chromaticism towards atonality. She now describes herself as 'a neo-romantic'. It is as a spirited original that she has made her mark on New Zealand music.

WORKS
selective list

Stage: Do-Wack-a-Do, ballet, 1960; Twelfth Night, incid. music, 1965

Orch: Rhapsody, va, orch, 1950; Concertino, harp, harmonica, str, 1960; Suite of Dances, 1965 [arr. of Do-Wack-a-Do]

Choral: Magnificat, women's vv, org, 1947; The Oxen, chorus, 1949; Pilgrimage, chorus, 1950; Song to the Wind, Tr vv, 1953; The Young Patrick (E. O. E. Hill), chorus, orch, 1962

Solo vocal: 4 Pioneer Portraits, Mez, pf, 1949; Eventide, song cycle, T, str qt, harp, 1950; 3 Shakespeare Songs, Bar, pf, 1965; Mädchenliebe, song-cycle, S, harp, 1982; El Bailador, song-cycle, T, pf/orch, 1983; Advice to the Lovelorn, song-cycle, S, C, pf, 1990

Chamber and pf: Cross-Country, pf, 1947; Suite, fl/cl, hn, harp, 1947; Circus Suite, pf, 1950; Sonatina, pf, 1957

BIBLIOGRAPHY

O. Jensen: Interview, Radio New Zealand, 1969 [oral archive]

D. A. Franchi: 'A Personal Assessment: a Harpist Speaks', *IRMT Journal*, v (1983), 32–4

J. M. Thomson: Interview, Archive of New Zealand Music, *NZ-Wt*, 1984 [oral archive]

——: 'Franchi, Dorothea Anne', *Biographical Dictionary of New Zealand Composers* (Wellington, 1990)

J. M. THOMSON

François, M. See BAWR, SOPHIE DE.

Frank-Autheried, Hedy (*b* Vienna, 22 Jan 1902; *d* Vienna, 24 March 1979). Austrian composer. She studied at the Vienna Academy, but when she wanted to enter Richard Stöhr's composition class he refused to take her, arguing that it would be impossible to have one lady among his male students. Some years later, having married Ferdinand Frank, she was able to complete her composition studies with Camillo Horn, a pupil of Bruckner. Horn considered her one of his most gifted students. Her large output of 239 opuses includes 70 melodramas, choral works, piano sonatas and other piano pieces, works for violin and piano, lieder and chansons.

ROSARIO MARCIANO

Franks Williams, Joan (*b* New York, 1 April 1930). Israeli composer of American birth. She studied at the Eastman School, Rochester (BMus 1952), and at the Manhattan School, New York (MMus 1961), where her teachers included Wayne Barlow, Vittorio Giannini, Ralph Shapey, Stefan Wolpe and, for short courses, Vladimir Ussachevsky and Roman Haubenstock-Ramati. From 1962 to 1971 she directed the concert series 'New Dimensions in Music' in Seattle, and she also lectured there, at the New School of Music, on contemporary music. In 1971 she moved to Israel, where she continued her concert-giving activities at the Israel Broadcasting Authority and through her series 'New Dimensions in Music' and 'Israeli Composers Plus One'. In these she programmed specially written music sometimes involving audience participation, a technique that has influenced her own compositional style. Several of her works incorporate staging, acting and improvisation, such as her 'mini comic monodrama' *Shimshon Hagibor* ('Samson the Mighty'). Her 1975 piece *Frogs* includes a taped recording of the croaking of frogs in the pond of the Israel Philharmonic Orchestra courtyard. In 1989 she re-settled in Seattle, Washington, having made, during the previous 18 years, a strong impact on contemporary musical life in Israel.

WORKS
selective list

Inst: Composition, vn, pf, 1962; Str Qt, 1964; Concert Piece, vn, 1966; Haiku, fl, vc, perc, 1970; Rudolph Heinemann in Bonn, trbn, 1977; If Stones Send up their Witness, musique concrète, 1978, collab. P. Caryevschi; Sevens for Octet, fl, cl, brass, 2 vns, va, vc, 1979; Humpty Dumpty Sat on a Waltz, cl, trbn, vc, pf, 1980; Homage to Louise Nevelson, 2 pf, 1986–7; Fanfaria, 3 tpt, 1991; Hila-Ness, va da gamba, 1991

Vocal: From Patterson (W. C. Williams), S, tpt, vc, pf, 1968; Cassandra Monodrama, S, 5 insts, film, 1969; In Celebration (R. Jarvi), S, pf, tape, 1971; Frogs (Franks Williams), S, str, pf, tape, 1975; Shimshon Hagibor [Samson the Mighty] (mini comic monodrama, D. Avidan), S, nar, ens, tape, 1975; In the Fashion we've Invented for One Another, 1v, tape (Franks Williams and R. Ashley), 1978; Willie and Die Fledermaus, S, actor, 2 fl, pf, 1978; 2 Lea Goldberg Songs, S, va, pf, 1980–81; The Blue Eyed Lion, 1v, pf, 1982; For Henry Moore's Elephant Skull Etchings (S. Kauffman), Mez, vn, fl + b rec+ a fl, vc, 1982; Ceremonies, 1v, exotic insts (12 players), 1983; Song of Songs, Mez, fl, gui, 1983; Leah, Mez, fl, vn, vc, pf, 1986; Gulliver in Lilliput, children's choir, 1986–7; Frogs Revisited, 1v, fl, perc, pf (1992)

Principal publishers: ACA, Israel Music Institute

WILLIAM Y. ELIAS

Fraser, Shena (Eleanor) (*b* Stirling, 26 May 1910). Scottish composer, pianist and lecturer. She studied the violin and the piano at the RCM where she was a composition pupil of Herbert Howells. She has worked as a lecturer in adult education, as a pianist and accompanist and as an adjudicator. In 1982 she and the music education specialist Yvonne Enoch founded the music publishing company Fraser-Enoch Publications. Her output is predominantly vocal and reflects her interest in music for amateurs, particularly amateur choirs; several of her most significant works, such as *Carillon* (1957), *To Him Give Praise* (1959–60), *A Ring of Jewels* (1975) and *A Boy was Born* (1988), are for women's voices. Among her instrumental works are a Sonatina for flute (1989) and two *Sea Poems* for piano duo (1988), the latter adapted from her 1972 cantata *Full Fathom Five*. Her principal publishers are Associated Board, Banks, Boosey & Hawkes, Chappell, Curwen, Fraser-Enoch, Novello, OUP, Roberton, Thames Publishing and United Music Publishers. Some material is held at the British Music Information Centre in London.

BIBLIOGRAPHY

CohenE; *Fuller-LeFanuRM*

M. Barton: 'Pianists in Partnership (Raising the Standard of Teaching Music Available to Piano Teachers)', *Music Teacher*, lxviii (1989), 20–21 [interview]

MARIE FITZPATRICK

Freed, Dorothy Whitson (*b* Dunedin, 10 Feb 1919). New Zealand composer and librarian. She was part of the early group of students taught by Frederick Page and Douglas Lilburn at Victoria University College, Wellington (BMus, 1958). She also studied with Peter Racine Fricker and Elisabeth Lutyens in London during the early 1960s. She won the New Zealand Broadcasting Service/Australasian Performing Right Association (APRA) Award for a New Zealand song and the Philip Neill memorial prize in composition (both 1958), the APRA award for outstanding services to music (1980) and a Lilburn Trust grant for services to music librarianship and music in New Zealand (1991). She wrote many songs and instrumental music, some for radio and the theatre. Her music is traditional in style.

Composing as a profession was never an economic possibility for Freed, and she devoted herself to her career as a librarian. She has made an invaluable contribution to the dissemination of musical scores and information about music throughout New Zealand: she has published important books and articles on musical resources, and in 1982 she founded the New Zealand division of the International Association of Music Librarians, whose president she became.

WORKS
selective list

Orch and band: Suite, str, 1961; Variations on a Fanfare, orch, 1962; Aquarius, march, brass band, 1971

Chamber and inst: Ww Qnt, 1959; Diversion, 10 brass insts, 1967; 2 str qts, 1968, 1970; Nursery Tale, brass qnt, 1980; The Chinese Terracotta Soldiers, pf, 1982

Vocal: Suicide Deferred (Freed), farce, S, 2 pf, perc, vc, mime, 1965; Deserted Beach (R. Dallas), S, str, 1975; 20 solo songs

Also music for radio plays

BIBLIOGRAPHY

J. Body: 'A Discussion with Dorothy Freed', *Canzona*, ii/6 (1980), 25–30

O. Jensen: 'Dorothy Freed: an Appreciation', *Crescendo*, x (1985), 3

J. Palmer: 'Dorothy Freed: Pioneer of Music Librarianship in New Zealand', *Crescendo*, x (1985), 4–7

R. Wilson: Interview, Archive of New Zealand Music, *NZ-Wt*, 1989 [oral archive]

J. M. Thomson: 'Freed, Dorothy Whitson', *Biographical Dictionary of New Zealand Composers* (Wellington, 1990)

J. M. THOMSON

Freer, Eleanor Everest (*b* Philadelphia, 14 May 1864; *d* Chicago, 13 Dec 1942). American composer. Her father Cornelius Everest was an organist, her mother an accomplished singer. She began to play the piano at the age of five and during her childhood the family home was visited by various musicians including the operatic baritone David Bispham. In her teens Freer sang Josephine in *HMS Pinafore* and tried her hand at composition. She studied singing with Mathilde Marchesi in Paris (1883–6) and composition with Benjamin Godard. While in Europe she sang for Verdi and Liszt. On her return to the USA she taught the piano in Philadelphia and singing at the National Conservatory of Music, New York (1889–91), using the Marchesi method. She married in 1891 and, after an interim period devoted to family life, settled in Chicago where she spent much of her time promoting modern music. In 1921 she established the Opera in Our Language Foundation and the following year helped to set up the David Bispham Memorial Fund, the two merged as the American Opera Society of Chicago in 1924. According to her *Recollections* it was her work with the Foundation that prompted her to start writing operas, the first of which, *The Legend of the Piper*, was published in 1922 and performed three years later. She went on

Eleanor Everest Freer, c1927

to write another ten operas, one of which received a David Bispham Medal, and over 150 songs, including a cycle of 44 *Sonnets from the Portuguese* to texts by Elizabeth Barrett Browning. Freer's librettos are mostly set syllabically and in regular metres; the music, while tonal, is rich in seventh chords and decorative chromaticism.

WORKS

OPERAS

The Legend of the Piper, op.28 (1, Act 1 of J. P. Peabody: *The Piper*), 1922, vs (Boston, 1922); South Bend, IN, 24 Feb 1925

Massimilliano, the Court Jester, or The Love of a Caliban, op.30 (1, E. W. Peattie), 1925, vs (Chicago, 1925); Lincoln, NE, Temple, 19 Jan 1926

The Chilkoot Maiden, op.32 (1, Freer), 1926, vs (Milwaukee, 1926); Skagway, AL, 1927

A Christmas Tale, op.35 (1, B. H. Clark, after M. Bouchor), 1928, vs (Milwaukee, 1928); Houston, 27 Dec 1929

The Masque of Pandora, op.36 (1, Freer, after H. W. Longfellow), 1928, vs (Milwaukee, 1929)

Preciosa, or The Spanish Student, op.37 (Freer, after Longfellow), 1928, vs (Milwaukee, 1928)

Frithiof, op.40 (2, C. Shaw, after E. Tegner: *Frithiofs Saga*), 1929, vs (Milwaukee, 1929); Chicago, Illinois Women's Athletic Club, 11 April 1929

Joan of Arc, op.38 (1, Freer), 1929, vs (Milwaukee, 1929); Chicago, Junior Friends of Art, 3 Dec 1929

A Legend of Spain (1, Freer), 1931, vs (Milwaukee, 1931); Milwaukee, 19 June 1931

Little Women, op.42 (2, Freer, after L. M. Alcott),

1934, vs (Chicago, 1934); Chicago, Musician's Club of Women, 2 April 1934

The Brownings go to Italy, op.43 (1, G. A. Hawkins-Ambler), 1936, vs (Chicago, 1936); Chicago, Arts Club, 11 March 1938

SONGS

When is life's youth (A. Freer), op.4 no.3 (1905); An April Pastoral (E. R. McCormick), op.6 no.3 (1906); Apparitions (R. Browning), op.9 no.2 (1906); You (A. G. Foster), op.23 no.3 (Cincinnati, 1911); A Farewell (C. Kingsley), op.21 no.5 (Cincinnati, 1912); A Child's Quest (F. Shaw), op.27 no.2 (Chicago, 1915); Arachne (Freer), op.21 no.3 (n.p., 1927); A Dancing Girl (F. S. L. Osgood), op.40 no.6 (Chicago, 1935); [44] Sonnets from the Portuguese (E. B. Browning), op.22 (Chicago, 1939); Advent of Spring (A. Bard) (Chicago, 1941); Dream Caress (G. B. Lake), op.51 no.1 (Chicago, 1942)

BIBLIOGRAPHY

A. Farwell and W. D. Darby, eds.: *Music in America* (New York, 1915)

A. G. Foster: *Eleanor Freer, Patriot, and her Colleagues* (Chicago, 1927)

E. E. Hipsher: *American Opera and its Composers* (Philadelphia, 1927)

E. E. Freer: *Recollections and Reflections of an American Composer* (Chicago, 1929)

PHYLLIS BRUCE, THOMAS WARBURTON

Freixas (y Cruells), Narcisa (*b* Sabadell, Barcelona, 13 Dec 1859; *d* Barcelona, 20 Dec 1926). Spanish composer and teacher. She was a pupil of Juan B. Pujol, Felipe Pedrell and Enrique Granados. She founded a music school in Barcelona for children and young ladies, the Cultura Musical Popular (its choir performed in asylums, prisons, hospitals and working-men's clubs), and established children's theatre competitions and other choirs. After she gave a lecture in the Madrid Atheneum in 1917, the Ministry of Public Education put her in charge of a course for teachers, on the improvement of singing in schools, at the Biblioteca Nacional. This led to the setting up of a choir in Madrid. Freixas was also a sculptor and painter.

Most of Freixas's compositions were for children: settings of Catalan nationalist poets, inspired by traditional Catalan music. She published the collections *Cançons catalanes* (1900), *Cançons d'infants* (1905) and *Cançons amoroses* (1908). Two of her stage works for children were performed at the Teatre Principal in Barcelona: the one-act *Festa completa* (libretto by Federico Palma, given in October 1906) and the two-act *Rodamón* (libretto by R. Nogueras Oller; 8 November 1907). After her death a memorial album of about a hundred of her compositions was published, illustrated with drawings by her and other Catalan artists.

BIBLIOGRAPHY
LaborD

XOÁN M. CARREIRA

Fromm-Michaels, Ilse (*b* Hamburg, 30 Dec 1888; *d* Detmold, 22 Jan 1986). German pianist and composer. She studied in Berlin, first at the Hochschule für Musik (1902–5), then at the Sternsches Konservatorium (1905–8) with James Kwast (piano) and Hans Pfitzner (composition); from 1911 she studied at the Rheinische Musikschule in Cologne with Carl Friedberg (piano) and Fritz Steinbach (composition). As a pianist she promoted contemporary music from an early age and at 18 played Max Reger's Variations and Fugue on a Theme of Bach, one of the first to do so. As a soloist with orchestra she performed with Arthur Nikisch, Hermann Abendroth, Wilhelm Furtwängler and Arnold Schoenberg. From 1933, during the Third Reich, she had to curtail her concert-giving because her husband was Jewish according to Nazi laws. From 1946 to 1959 she taught the piano at the Hochschule für Musik in Hamburg, and was professor there from 1957. In 1961 she won first prize for her Symphony in C minor at the third international competition for women composers. Though she composed from youth onwards, her output was not large; being self-critical, she destroyed some of her works.

WORKS

Inst: 4 Puppen, op.4, pf, 1908, also arr. wind qnt; 8 Skizzen, op.5, pf, 1908; Pf Sonata, e, op.6, 1917; Walzerreigen, op.7, pf, 1917; Variations on an Original Theme, op.8, pf, 1918/19; Stimmungen eines Fauns, op.11, cl; Suite, e, op.15, vc, 1931; Passacaglia, f, op.16, pf, 1932, also arr. org; Sym., c, op.19, 1938; Musica larga, cl, str qt, 1944, also arr. cl, str orch; Waltzes, pf; 20 cadenzas for Mozart pf concs.; ? Vn Sonata, mentioned in Riemann
Vocal: 5 Lieder (Des Knaben Wunderhorn), op.9*a*, 1v, pf; 4 winzige Wunderhorn Lieder, op.9*b*, 1v, pf; Marien-Passion, chorus, 3 tpt, org, chamber orch, 1932/3; 3 Gesänge (R. M. Rilke), Bar, pf, 1948/9, arr. Bar, orch, 1955; 2 parodistische Lieder

Principal publishers: Ries & Erler, Sikorski

BIBLIOGRAPHY
RiemannL 11
F. Wohlfahrt: 'Ilse Fromm-Michaels', *Musica*, ii (1948), 337–8
B. Brand and others, eds.: 'Fromm-Michaels, Ilse', *Komponistinnen in Berlin* (Berlin, 1987), 341–6
K. Lessing: 'Ich kann die junge Dame wärmstens empfehlen', *5 Jahre internationales Festival Komponistinnen gestern–heute, Heidelberg, und 5th International Congress on Women in Music*, ed. R. Sperber and U. Feld (Heidelberg, 1989), 39–41

BIRGITTA MARIA SCHMID

Frykberg, Susan (*b* Hastings, New Zealand, 10 Oct 1954). New Zealand composer and teacher. Her studies began in 1973 at the University of Canterbury, where she subsequently became computer music research assistant. In 1978 she attended summer schools in Europe with John Cage and Iannis Xenakis. After experience as a computer programmer, composer, broadcaster and music journalist she held teaching positions at Simon Fraser University, Vancouver, and at the University of Auckland. She has published papers on computer music, produced radio programmes on new music and has written poetry. She sees music and theatre as one entity 'functioning to transform the people within the society' and 'real art [as] a transformative thing'. As a composer Frykberg has specialized in electro-acoustic music theatre. Several of her works (e.g. *The Garden, Woman and House*) deal with feminist issues. *Saxarba* examines aspects of women's spirituality, while *Caroline Herschel is Minding the Heavens* combines electronic techniques with acting and song to tell the story of the astronomer Sir William Herschel's sister. Frykberg has also written the script for the electronic music theatre piece *Machine Woman* by David McGee (1984).

WORKS
selective list
Fugitive, tape, 1980; Saxarba (Frykberg), elec music theatre, Ct, actress, 2 synth, tape, slides, signal-processing, 1982–5; Piano Study no.1, pf, tape, 1984; A Tarot Reading, tape, 1987; Caroline Herschel Is Minding the Heavens, el-ac music theatre, voices, synths, computers, 1988; The Garden, 1989 [music for multi-media work by D. Thorne]; Woman and House (Frykberg), el-ac music theatre, 1v, 2 actors, signal-processing, tape, diffusion, 1989–90; Mother Too, 1v, tape, signal-processing, 1991; Diaries, 1v, tape, signal processing multiple sound reproduction systems, 1993

BIBLIOGRAPHY
P. Dadson: 'Electro-Acoustic Music Theatre: Interview with Susan Frykberg', *Music in New Zealand* (1991), spr., 20–24

J. M. THOMSON

Fuchs, Lillian (*b* New York, 18 Nov 1903). American violist, composer and teacher, sister of the violinist and teacher Joseph Fuchs. She studied the violin with Louis Svecenski and Franz Kneisel, and composition with Percy Goetschius, at the New York Institute of Musical Art (now the Juilliard School), winning several awards on graduation. Her New York début in 1926 was as a violinist, but she began to make the viola her principal instrument soon afterwards, and was a member of the Perolé String Quartet from 1925 to the mid-1940s. She played a viola by Gaspare da Salò, handling it with ease, in spite of her small stature, and with flawless technique, obtaining a rich and expressive tone. Fuchs has taught at festivals in the USA and Canada and at many conservatories, including the Juilliard School, the Manhattan School of Music and the Mannes College of Music. She received the National Service Award of Chamber Music America in 1994.

Her own published works for solo viola include 12 *Caprices* (1950), *Sonata pastorale* (1956), 16 *Fantasy Etudes* (1961) and 15 *Characteristic Studies* (1965). She composed also a *Jota* and *Caprice fantastique* for violin and piano, and arranged Mozart's Violin Concerto in G (K216) for viola and provided it with cadenzas (1947).

BORIS SCHWARZ

Furgeri, Biancamaria (*b* Rovigo, 6 Oct 1935). Italian composer and organist. She was educated in Venice, Padua and Milan, studying the piano, the organ and composition; among her composition teachers were G. F. Ghedini and Bruno Bettinelli. In 1969 she was appointed to teach harmony and counterpoint at Bologna Conservatory. Among several important awards she has received are prizes from the GEDOK competition in Mannheim (1985), the Henryk Wieniawski competition in Poland and, for *Levia*, first prize at the first international competition of the Verein zur Förderung von Berufsmusikerinnen (1987) of Zurich. Furgeri's vast output includes orchestral works, chamber and choral music and collections of educational pieces. Her musical style, with its mainly atonal language and use of serial procedures, refers back to the music of the early 20th century, a period to which she feels closest. There are also in her works brief tonal and lyrical moments, always an indication of nostalgia for the recent musical past.

WORKS
selective list

Orch: Antifonie, pf, orch, 1975; Moods, 1983; Levia, str orch, 1987; Erzählung, vn, str orch, 1990
Vocal: Messa, 1v, chorus, org, 1973; Cantico, S, fl, harp, 1983
Inst: Org Sonata, 1964; Duplum, vn, pf, 1981; Il canto sognato, fl, 1989; Farben, fl, vn, pf, 1990; Immagini fluttuanti, fl, vn, va, harp, 1990

PAOLA DAMIANI

Furze, Jessie (Lilian) (*b* Wallington, Surrey, 4 Feb 1903; *d* Croydon, 5 Nov 1984). English composer and pianist. She studied at the RAM where she won the Cuthbert Nunn prize for composition. She married Willem L. F. Nijhof and lived for many years in the Netherlands. As a composer, Furze specialized in educational music. She wrote over 250 simple piano pieces including *The Truants* (1937), *All Alone: Two's Company* (1959), *Scenes from Holland* (1961) and *In Time of Spring* (1964), which have been used extensively by examining bodies such as the Associated Board and in music festivals. She also wrote many unison and two-part songs and made arrangements of traditional airs. She sometimes wrote under the pseudonyms Janet Bowditch and Jill Dalebury.

SOPHIE FULLER

G

Gabriel, Mary Ann Virginia (*b* Banstead, Surrey, 7 Feb 1825; *d* London, 7 Aug 1877). English composer and pianist. The daughter of Robert Gabriel, an Irish Colonel of the 7th Dragoon Guards, she was educated in Italy. She studied the piano with J. P. Pixis, Theodor Döhler and Sigismond Thalberg, and composition with Saverio Mercadante and Bernhard Molique. Many of her songs (she composed more than 300) and 30 piano works were popular and widely performed in the 1860s, and her cantata on Longfellow's poem *Evangeline* was highly acclaimed after its première at the Brighton Festival on 13 February 1873. She wrote about a dozen operettas, which were produced by the German Reed Company at the Gallery of Illustration, London, and on their provincial tours; *Widows Bewitched* had a long and successful run in 1867. In November 1874 she married George E. March, a Foreign Office official who wrote some of her librettos; she died three years later, after having been thrown from her carriage in Hyde Park.

WORKS

selective list; printed works published in London

Operettas: Widows Bewitched (H. Aidé), 1865; Who's the Heir (G. E. March), 1870; Grass Widows (March), 1873; Graziella (J. J. Lonsdale) (1875); The Love Tests (V. Amcotts); The Shepherd of Cournouailles (T. G. Lacy); *c*7 others

Cantatas: Evangeline (H. W. Longfellow) (1873); Dreamland (A. Matthison) (1875)

Songs: *c*300, incl. Forsaken (H. Aidé) (1855); At the Window (R. Browning) (1864); The Skipper and his Boy (Aidé) (1865); I will not ask to press that check (1865); White Dove (J. M. McNaughton) (1866); Deserter (1872); The Garden of Roses (W. Story); I really don't think I shall marry; Lost Dreams (C. G. Lelande) (1876); The Old Journal (H. Lockwood) (1876); O Willie Boy, come home

Pf: La gondola (1855); Long Ago (1861); Pavonia; Sunshine (1861); Valse élégante

BIBLIOGRAPHY

FétisB; *FétisBS*; *Grove1* (G. Grove)

J. D. Brown and S. S. Stratton: *British Musical Biography* (Birmingham, 1897)

PAMELA FOX, JOHN R. GARDNER

Gail [née **Garre**], **(Edmée) Sophie** (*b* Paris, 28 Aug 1775; *d* Paris, 24 July 1819).

French composer. Her first songs appeared from 1790 in the song magazines of Louis de La Chevardière and Antoine Bailleux. At the age of 18 she married the philologist Jean Baptiste Gail, but they separated some years later. She then studied singing with Bernardo Mengozzi, and made a successful tour of southern France and Spain. She studied musical theory with F.-J. Fétis and, later, with F.-L. Perne and Sigismund Neukomm. She wrote a number of songs and *romances*, and four one-act operas which were produced by the Opéra-Comique at the Théâtre Feydeau. The first and most successful of these, *Les deux jaloux* (1813), was followed by *Mlle de Launay à la Bastille* (1813), *Angéla, ou L'atelier de Jean Cousin* (with Adrien Boieldieu, 1814) and *La sérénade* (1818). The last contains accomplished music, but its libretto, adapted from a comedy by J.-F. Regnard, was considered scandalous, even 50 years later, by Félix Clément in his *Dictionnaire lyrique* (though he devoted much space to it). Gail sang in London in 1816, and in 1818 toured Germany and Austria with Angelica Catalani. She died prematurely of a chest ailment.

Sophie Gail enjoyed a high reputation both as singer and accompanist, and her songs, which cultivate a vein of plaintive, amorous sentiment fashionable in post-Revolutionary France, are original and carefully wrought. The most popular of them, *Celui qui sut toucher mon coeur*, was used as a theme for instrumental variations by five different composers. Her son, Jean François Gail (1795–1845), wrote songs and music criticism.

WORKS

selective list; all one-act opéras comiques, performed at Paris, Opéra-Comique (Théâtre Feydeau)

Les deux jaloux (C. R. Dufresny and J. B. C. Vial), 27 March 1813

Mademoiselle de Launay à la Bastille (C. de Lesser, R. Villiers and Mme Villiers), 16 Dec 1813

Angéla, ou L'atelier de Jean Cousin (C. Montcloux d'Epinay), *F-Pn*, collab. A. Boieldieu; 11 June 1814

La méprise (De Lesser), 20 Sept 1814

La sérénade (S. Gay, after J.-F. Regnard), 16 Sept 1818

BIBLIOGRAPHY
Choron-FayolleD; *SchillingE*; *SchmidlD*
Y. Gérard: 'Luigi Boccherini and Madame Sophie Gail', *The Consort*, xxiv (1967), 294–309
PHILIP ROBINSON

Galás, Diamanda [Dimitria Angeliki Elena] (*b* San Diego, 29 Aug 1955). American singer, composer and performance artist. Her early musical training was as a pianist; at the age of 14 she played Beethoven's Piano Concerto no.1 with the San Diego SO. She studied biochemistry, music and experimental performance at the University of California, San Diego (1974–9), and took singing lessons privately. After becoming known for her piano and vocal improvisations and as a jazz pianist, she began a career as a singer. Her musicianship and range of advanced vocal techniques interested composers: at Iannis Xenakis's request she sang the American première of his microtonal work *N'Shima* with Lukas Foss and the Brooklyn PO (1981); similarly she gave the first performance of Vinko Globokar's *Misère* (written especially for her) with the West German Radio Orchestra in Cologne (1980). She is perhaps best known for her extraordinary and theatrical performances of her own solo vocal works, given at a variety of places and events ranging from the Danceteria (a New York rock club) and the Moers Jazz Festival in Germany to the Donaueschingen Festival, the Paris Biennale and the Cathedral of St John the Divine in New York.

Galás's works, many of which use live electronics and pre-recorded tape, are improvised according to extreme, rigorously explored and widely divergent plans that the composer calls 'navigation[s] through specified mental states'. The inspiration for her works is a personal response to social and political circumstance. She uses words as a platform for her expression, but her emotional intensity and extremes of technique can blur the text's meaning. Galás's performances have stringent requirements for lighting and sound and at best create a shattering intensity. *Plague Mass* and *Vena cava*, are completed works that are still in a process of development; she has received Ford Foundation and Meet the Composer grants to continue work on them. She has also collaborated with several film makers and recording artists.

WORKS
Medea tarantula, solo v, 1977; Les yeux sans sang, solo v, elec, 1978; Tragouthia apo to aima exoun fonos [Song from the Blood of those Murdered], solo v, tape, 1981; Wild Women with Steak Knives, solo v, live elec, 1981–3; The Litanies of Satan (C. P. Baudelaire), solo v, live elec, tape, 1982; Panoptikon, solo v, live elec, tape, 1982; Solowork 1984, solo v, 1984; Masque of the Red Death, trilogy: The Divine Punishment, Saint of the Pit, You Must be Certain of the Devil, solo v, live elec, tape, 1984–8; Plague Mass, solo v, live elec, tape, perc, 1984–; Judgement Day, solo v, kbd, 1991; Vena cava, solo v, live elec, tape, 1991– ; Insekta, solo v, live elec, tape, 1993
Also arrs. of songs for solo v, kbd

BIBLIOGRAPHY
H. Charlton: 'Wild Women with Steak Knives', *Collusion*, no.1 (1981), 15
D. Galás: 'Intravenal Song', *PNM*, xx (1981–2), 59
L. Morra: 'Diamanda Galás: Rebellious Soprano', *East Village Eye* (March 1983) [interview]
R. Zvonar: 'Diamanda', *Diamanda Galás* (Metalanguage 119, 1984) [record notes]
S. Holden: 'Diamanda Galás, Avant-Garde Diva', *New York Times* (19 July 1985)
I. Burrell: 'Petal Power', *Melody Maker*, lxi (9 Aug 1986), 33 [interview]
C. V. P. Groome: 'Diamanda Galás: Masque of the Red Death', *Ear* [New York], xiii/2 (1988), 16–17 [interview]
K. Gann: 'Music: Searching for the Plague', *Village Voice* (15 Aug 1989)
R. Gehr: 'Mourning in America: Diamanda Galás', *Artforum*, xxvii/May (1989), 116–18
M. Sinker: 'The Demon Diva', *Melody Maker*, lxv (7 Jan 1989), 23 [interview]
ELLEN D. LERNER, GREGORY SANDOW

Galeotti, Margherita (*b* Mauern, Bavaria, 1867; *d* ? after 1912). Italian pianist and composer. She studied the piano with Giuseppe Buonamici and composition in Florence and graduated after completing her studies with Giuseppe Martucci in Bologna. She performed as a concert pianist in Italy, and in Linz, Monte Carlo, Paris and Zürich. Her compositions include a Piano Trio in D minor (Florence, 1912), a Violin Sonata, other pieces for violin and for cello, two piano suites and a few songs.

BIBLIOGRAPHY
SchmidlD
A. de Angelis: *L'Italia musicale d'oggi: Dizionario dei musicisti* (Rome, 1918, 3/1928)
FRANCESCA PERRUCCIO SICA

Gambarini, Elisabetta de (*b* London, 7 Sept 1731; *d* London, 9 Feb 1765). Soprano and composer of Italian descent. She was a daughter of Charles Gambarini, counsellor to the Landgrave of Hessen-Kassel. She sang in the first performance of Handel's *Occasional Oratorio* (14 February 1746) and the Covent Garden revival a year later. She created the Israelite Woman in *Judas Maccabaeus* at Covent Garden on 1 April 1747

Elisabetta de Gambarini: portrait by Nathanial Hone from her 'Lessons for the Harpsichord, Intermix'd with Italian and English Songs', op.2 (London, 1748)

and probably sang Asenath in *Joseph and his Brethren* the same year. Her name appears in the performing scores of *Samson* and *Messiah*, but it is not certain when she sang in these works. About 1748–50 she published three volumes of harpsichord pieces and songs in Italian and English, including a setting of 'Honour, riches, marriage-blessing' from *The Tempest*. Her op.2, dedicated to the Prince of Wales with an aristocratic subscription list, has a frontispiece portrait engraved by Nathaniel Hone in 1748; it gives the date of her birth as above, but this may understate her age. She had a benefit at the Great Room, Dean Street, on 15 April 1761, when an ode of her composition was performed together with a cantata by Francesco Geminiani; he may have been her teacher. In May 1764, as Mrs Chazal, she is said to have given a concert at which she appeared as organist and composer. According to Gerber's *Lexikon* she was also a painter.

WORKS

Six Sets of Lessons for the Harpsichord (London, 1748)

Lessons for the Harpsichord, Intermix'd with Italian and English Songs, op.2 (London, 1748)

XII English & Italian Songs, for a German Flute & Thorough Bass, op.3 (London, ?1750)

WINTON DEAN

García, Pauline. *See* VIARDOT, PAULINE.

Gardner, Kay ['C. W. Child', for 'Cosmos Wonder-Child'] (*b* Freeport, NY, 8 Feb 1941). American composer, flautist and conductor. In addition to formal study at the University of Michigan (1958–61) and SUNY at Stony Brook (MM 1974), she studied with Samuel Baron (flute) and Antonia Brico (conducting, 1977, 1978). A pioneer of women's music who declared her lesbianism in 1971, she has been an active composer-performer of women's music since 1973 and has appeared regularly at festivals of women's music. Her exploration of healing music has gained recognition through her presentations to medical schools and health workers, as well as her work to develop the use of music as a substitute for surgical anaesthesia. Her book *Sounding the Inner Landscape: Music as Medicine* (Stonington, ME, 1990) summarizes this work. Melody is the foundation for all her compositions, which often use modal scales and combine world music influences with contemporary techniques. She believes in specifically feminine modes of expression, for example cyclical form with central points of climax.

WORKS
selective list

Stage: Ladies Voices: a Short Opera (G. Stein), 6 solo vv, fl, ob, cl, va, vc, harp, 1981

Orch: Prayer to Aphrodite, a fl, str orch, 1974, arr. a fl, str ens, 1975; Rainforest, chamber orch, 1977; The Rising Sun [arr. of chamber work], chamber orch, 1985; Quiet Harbor, 1992

Chamber: Lunamuse, fl, gui, vc, perc, vocal drone (tape loop or audience), 1974–5; Atlantis Rising, fl + a fl + prepared pf, vn + va + wind chimes, vc + wind chimes, prepared pf, tape, 1978; 7 Modal Improvisation Studies, (tr inst, bass inst)/pf, 1978; A Rainbow Path (fls, ww, perc, harp, str ens)/pf, 1984; A River Sings, vc, 1986; Viriditas, fl + a fl +

b fl, ob + eng hn, bn + d bn, va, vc, perc, timp, harp, 1988; North Coast Nights, str qt, 1989
Vocal: 3 Mother Songs, Mez, gui, 1977; When we Made the Music, SSAA, pf/(eng hn, str qt), 1977; Sea Chantress, 1v, fl, hammered dulcimer, 1978; Anthem for an Aquarian Age, mixed chorus, 1988
Video and film scores

BIBLIOGRAPHY

Anderson 2; *LePageWC*, ii

G. Kimball: 'Female Composition: Interview with Kay Gardner', *Women's Culture: the Women's Renaissance of the 70s*, ed. G. Kimball (Metuchen, NJ, 1981), 163–76

J. L. Zaimont and K. Famera, eds.: *Contemporary Concert Music by Women* (Westport, CT, 1981), 46–7

M. Bourne: 'Women's Music Abloomin'', *Down Beat*, xlix/Sept (1982), 9

—— : 'Women's Fest More than Music', *Down Beat*, l/Sept (1983), 12

L. Koplewitz: 'Kay Gardner: Music and Healing', *Women Artists News*, viii/3 (1983), 17–19

B. Grigsby: 'Women Composers of Electronic Music', *The Musical Woman: an International Perspective*, i: *1983*, ed. J. L. Zaimont and others (Westport, CT, 1984), 175–7

C. Barrett: 'The Magic of Music', *Woman of Power*, no.19 (1990–91), 42–7 [interview]

S. Golden: 'Sounding the Inner Landscape', *Yoga Journal* (1992), May–June, 30–32, 34

J. MICHELE EDWARDS

Garelli della Morea, Vincenza, Countess **de Cardenas** [Della Morea, Centa] (*b* Valeggio, Pavia, 1859; *d* Rome, ? after 1924). Italian pianist and composer; she used the pseudonym Centa della Morea. She studied in Turin with Carlo Pedrotti and Giovanni Bolzoni, and later also with Giovanni Sgambati. She married the Count de Cardenas and lived in Milan, where she attended Countess Maffei's salon and played with Arrigo Boito, Franco Faccio and Gaetano Coronaro. In 1888 she moved to Rome where she met Gabriele D'Annunzio and Matilde Serao. Her drawing-room songs were performed at the meetings of the Fracassa, together with those by Paolo Tosti, Augusto Rotoli and Luigi Denza.

WORKS
Stage: Incantesimo (operetta, G. Drovetti), Padua, Teatro Garibaldi, 17 Nov 1915; Il viaggio dei Perrichon (operetta, 3, Drovetti, after E. Labiche), Turin, Teatro Alfieri, 20 July 1916; Le nozze di Leporello (commedia, 3, L. Almirante), Brescia, Teatro Sociale, 31 March 1924
Other works: 3 'pantomimes', orch: L'esultanza della stirpe, Idillio pastorale, La ballata d'Arlecchino; 1 str qt; pieces for pf; songs

BIBLIOGRAPHY

DEUMM, appx; *SchmidlD*

A. de Angelis: *L'Italia musicale d'oggi: Dizionario dei musicisti* (Rome, 1918, 3/1928)

A. Bonaventura: 'Le donne italiane e la musica', *RMI*, xxxii (1925), 519–34

U. Manferrari: *Dizionario universale delle opere melodrammatiche* (Florence, 1954–5)

P. Adkins Chiti: *Donne in musica* (Rome, 1982)

LAURA PISTOLESI

Garre, Sophie. *See* GAIL, SOPHIE.

Garsenda, Countess of Provence (*fl* early 13th century). Troubadour. She was the wife of Alphonse II of Provence, and the beloved of two other troubadours, Gui de Cavaillon and Elias de Barjols, Regent of Provence 1209–20. One of Garsenda's poems survives in two manuscripts, but without music.

BIBLIOGRAPHY

M. Bogin: *The Women Troubadours* (New York, 1976), 108–9, 170–73

MARIA V. COLDWELL

Kay Gardner

Gary-Schaffhauser, Marianne (*b* Vienna, 19 July 1903). Austrian composer. She studied the piano and singing at the Vienna Academy, as well as composition with Alfred Uhl; she also studied at Vienna University, gaining the PhD. For many years she was a professor of German and history, but retired early from this work and from 1948 was active as a composer. Many of her compositions had considerable success, including the *Oratorium von Leid und Heldentum der Ungenannten*, for soloists, choir and orchestra, which she has considered her most important work; it received its première in Vienna during the 1963–4 season. Gary-Schaffhauser's output includes 300 lieder, some with a single instrument (piano, harp or organ), others with violin and piano, string trio, string quartet or orchestra; she has also written chamber music and choral and orchestral works.

ROSARIO MARCIANO

Gazarossian, Koharik [Łazarosian, Goharik] (*b* Constantinople [now Istanbul], 21 Dec 1907; *d* Paris, 29 Oct 1967). Armenian composer and pianist. As a child she studied the piano with a Professor Hege, reportedly a pupil of Liszt. In 1926 she entered the Paris Conservatoire, where her teachers were Paul Dukas (composition) and Lazare Lévy (piano). She devised 24 programmes of piano music (by other composers), arranged according to tonality and named 'bien tempéré', which she performed on occasion in various musical capitals. Many of her compositions were inspired by Armenian liturgical chants and, in particular, the folksongs collected by Komitas. Her piano music is gracious, immediate and well-balanced, written with a sense of keyboard flair.

WORKS
selective list

Stage: Mi mor patmut'yun [The Story of a Mother] (ballet, after H. C. Andersen), 1960
Orch: Pf Conc. no.1, perf. 1960; Pf Conc. no.2, 1964
Vocal: Ařkayc črag [The Flickering Lantern] (after Varudan), 1v, orch; 3 chansons populaires arméniennes, 1v, pf, 1940; Prélude et fugue, 1v, str qt, 1951; 30 songs, choral works, folksong arrs.
Inst: Pf Suite, 1934; Les Arméniennes, pf, 1947; Sonatine, pf, 1956; 24 Etudes, pf, 1958; Mouvement perpétuel, vn, pf, 1961; 11 Préludes, pf, 1967

Principal publisher: Choudens

BIBLIOGRAPHY

Y. Hagopian: 'Goharik Łazarosiani mštadalar hišatakin hadagin' [To the Everlasting Memory of Koharik Gazarossian], *Haratch* [Paris] (1, 3 Nov 1972)

R. Haddejian: 'Hišelov Goharik Łazarosianĕ' [Remembering Koharik Gazarossian], *Marmara* [Istanbul] (21 Jan 1988)

ŞAHAN ARZRUNI

Geddes-Harvey [née Geddes], **(Anne Catherine) Roberta** (*b* Hamilton, Ont., 25 Dec 1849; *d* Guelph, Ont., 22 April 1930). Canadian composer. She studied with Arthur E. Fisher, Edward Fisher and Humfrey Anger before graduating from Trinity College, University of Toronto, with the BMus (1899). She was an organist in Hamilton and later organist and choirmaster at St George's Anglican Church, Guelph (1876–1926). She wrote a few instrumental pieces, anthems, hymns and over 20 songs, many of which were published between 1897 and 1919. Her major works are an opera *La terre bonne* (or *The Land of the Maple Leaf*), which was first performed at the Royal Opera House, Guelph, in 1903 (the music is now lost except for one song), and an oratorio *Salvator* (Boston, 1907).

GAYNOR G. JONES

Geertens, Gerda (*b* Wildervank, 11 Aug 1955). Dutch composer. After spending some years studying music and then philosophy, she took composition lessons with Klaas de Vries from 1981 to 1985, during which time she composed *Mexitli* (1982) for mixed voices and instrumental ensemble. Geertens's style lies within the atonal tradition; she often interweaves different musical effects in kaleidoscopic fashion, building up tension until it is released as a dramatic outburst. Her string trio *Slinger* was first performed at the Concertgebouw, Amsterdam, in January 1990 and repeated at Darmstadt the following summer. Among her other chamber works are *Trope* for cello (1987), *As en Seringen* for flute, oboe, clarinet, violin, viola, cello, piano, harp and percussion (1988), and *Contrast* for saxophone quartet (1990). Her principal publisher is Donemus.

HELEN METZELAAR

Gentile, Ada (*b* Avezzano, 26 July 1947). Italian composer and pianist. She attended the Conservatorio di S Cecilia, Rome, studying the piano before turning to composition as a pupil of Irma Ravinale (1974); she completed her composition studies at the Accademia di S Cecilia with Goffredo Petrassi (1975–6). She was later appointed to teach composition at the Conservatorio di S Cecilia; she was also artistic director of the Goffredo Petrassi Chamber Orchestra (1986–8) and has worked in the same capacity for the Nuovi Spazi Musicali festival in Rome (1978). She received an award in the Gaudeamus Composers' Competition (Amsterdam) in 1982 and an ISCM prize in 1986 (Budapest). Her works have been performed in Europe, North America and Australia.

In her music, Gentile generally explores the timbral possibilities and infinite combinations of conventional instruments and the human voice, often within a sound context favouring *piano* and *pianissimo* dynamics. Every sound parameter is broken down, investigated and reassembled in order to create a design from the myriad nuances and fascinating qualities of her chosen materials.

WORKS
selective list
Orch: Veränderungen, 1976; Criptografia, va, orch, 1985; Shading, gui, orch, 1988; Conc., fl, gui, orch, 1989
Inst: Bagamoyo, ens, 1981; Flash Back, fl, vc, 1984; Insight, 2 vn, va, 1984; Pour Pierre Yves, fl, 1987; Perilision, ens, 1989
Vocal: Canzon prima, female v, 3 cl, 1990; Paesaggi della mente, female v, str qt, 1991

PAOLA DAMIANI

Gerrish-Jones, Abbie (*b* Vallejo, CA, 10 Sept 1863; *d* Seattle, 5 Feb 1929). American composer, librettist and music critic. Her paternal grandfather was a bandmaster; her father, Samuel Howard Gerrish, a flautist; and her mother, Sarah Jones Rogers, a singer. Abbie Gerrish began serious music study at the age of seven, was composing for voice and piano at 12 and became a church organist at 14. Her first published works appeared when she was 18. Her teachers included Humphrey J. Stewart and Wallace Sabine. She married a naval officer, A. Widmore Jones.

Active chiefly as a composer of operas, Gerrish-Jones wrote eight (five to her own librettos): *Priscilla*, *Abon Hassan*, *The Milkmaid's Fair*, *The Snow Queen* (G. W. Hoffmann), *The Andalusians* (Percy Friars), *Two Roses*, *Sakura-San* (Hoffmann) and *Aztec Princess*. She also wrote five song cycles, 100 songs, piano works and teaching pieces. In 1906 she won a prize for her Prelude for piano in a competition sponsored by Josef Hofmann. She was a music critic for *Pacific Town Talk* and *Pacific Coast Musical Review*, and the West Coast representative for *Musical Courier*.

CAROL NEULS-BATES

Gertrude, Duchess of Lorraine. The wife of Thiebaut I, Duke of Lorraine, and probably a trouvère; *see* LORRAINE.

Gideon, Miriam (*b* Greeley, CO, 23 Oct 1906). American composer and teacher. She spent her formative years in Boston under the supervision of her uncle, Henry Gideon, an organist and choral director. After undergraduate work in music at Boston University (BA 1926), she received the MA in musicology at Columbia University (1946) and the DSM in composition at the Jewish Theological Seminary of America (1970). She also studied composition privately with Lazare Saminsky and Roger Sessions.

Gideon has served on the faculties of Brooklyn College (1944–54) and City College, CUNY (1947–55, 1971–6), where she was named professor emeritus. She became associate professor of music at the Jewish Theological Seminary in 1955 and a member of the faculty of the Manhattan School in 1967. She has received many awards (including one from the NEA), and among her honours is election in 1975 to the National Institute of Arts and Letters; she was only the second woman to have received this honour.

Gideon's works have been performed and recorded in the USA, Europe and the Far East. She does not use any precompositional system but allows each work to suggest its own language and design. Her idiom may be described as freely atonal, with wide dissonant leaps in the melodic lines and an intense harmonic underpinning. Although she has composed extensively in all categories, much of her later music has been for solo voice and instrumental ensemble. She is fascinated by setting the same poetic idea in more than one language and frequently uses both the original language and a translation in a single setting, finding the fitting musical idiom for each without interrupting the continuity of the entire work. There is a prevailing lyricism in her music, alternating with sharp dramatic contrasts; textures are 'characterized by lightness, the sudden exposure of individual notes, constantly shifting octave relationships [and] a technique that imposes economy and the exclusion of irrelevancies' (Perle). Several of her works have been recorded (chiefly by CRI and New World).

WORKS
all published unless otherwise stated
SONG CYCLES
Sonnets from Shakespeare, high/low v, tpt, str qt/str orch, 1950: Music to hear, Devouring time, Full

many a glorious morning, No longer mourn for me, No, time, thou shalt not boast

4 Epitaphs (R. Burns), high/low v, pf, 1952: Epitaph for a Wag in Mauchline, Epitaph on Wee Johnnie, Epitaph on the Author, Monody on a Lady Famed for her Caprice

Sonnets from 'Fatal Interview' (E. St V. Millay), high v, pf/(vn, va, vc), 1952: Gone in good sooth you are, Moon is my sister, Moon, that against the lintel of the west

Songs of Voyage, high/low v, pf, 1961: The Nightingale Unheard (Peabody), Farewell Tablet to Agathocles (Wilkinson)

The Condemned Playground, S, T, fl, bn, str qt, 1963: Pyrrha (Horace, J. Milton), Hiroshima (G. Spokes, S. Akiya), The Litanies of Satan (C. P. Baudelaire, Millay)

Questions on Nature (Adelard of Bath), medium v, ob, pf, tam-tam, glock, 1964: How the earth moves, Why the planets, Whence the winds arise, Whether the stars fall, Whether beasts have souls, Why we hear echoes, Why joy is the cause of weeping

Rhymes from the Hill (C. Morgenstern), medium v, cl, mar, vc, 1968: Bundeslied der Galgenbrueder, Galgenkindes Wiegenlied, Die korfsche Uhr, Palmstrom's Uhr, Der Seufzer

The Seasons of Time (ancient Jap. Tanka poetry), medium v, fl, pf + cel, vc, 1969, arr. medium v, pf: Now it is spring, The wild geese returning, Can it be that there is no moon, Gossip grows like trees, In the leafy treetops, A passing show'r, I have always known, To what shall I compare this world?, Yonder in the plum-tree

Nocturnes, medium v, fl, ob, vib, va, vc, 1976: To the Moon (P. Shelley), High Tide (J. S. Untermeyer), Witchery (F. D. Sherman)

Songs of Youth and Madness (F. Hölderlin, trans. M. Hamburger), high v, orch, 1977: To the Fates, To Diotima, Affirmation, The Walk

The Resounding Lyre, high v, fl, ob, bn, tpt, vn, va, vc, 1979 [previously titled Spiritual Airs]: Mutterbildniss (F. Ewen), Wähebuf und Nichtenvint (S. von Trimpberg), Halleluja (H. Heine)

Voices from Elysium (ancient Gk. poets, trans. J. A. Symonds, W. Barstone and R. Lattimore), high v, fl, cl, pf, vn, vc, 1979: The Swallow, Cicada, Prayer to Hermes, Epitaph for a Sailor, Of the Sensual World, Hesperos, Rest

Morning Star (Ayelet hashakhar), medium v, pf, 1980: The Nest (Ch. N. Bialik), The Cat is Angry (M. Stekelis), Morning Star (L. Goldberg), The See-Saw (Bialik)

Spirit above the Dust, medium v, fl, ob, bn, hn, str qt, 1980: Prologue (A. Bradstreet), Theory of Poetry (A. MacLeish), The Two Trees (MacLeish), The Linden Branch (MacLeish), Black Boy (N. Rosten), My Caliban Creature (Rosten), The Snow Fall (MacLeish)

A Woman of Valor (Eishet chayil) (Psalms, Proverbs), medium v, pf, 1981: Behold, an inheritance of the Lord, our children, A Woman of Valor, The Labor of thy Hands

Wing'd Hour, high v, pf/(fl, ob, vib, vn, vc), 1983: Prelude, Silent Noon (D. G. Rossetti), My heart is like a singing bird (C. Rossetti), Interlude, Autumn (W. de la Mare)

Creature to Creature (N. Cardozo), medium v, fl,

harp, 1985: The Fly, Spider, Snake, Firefly, Hoot-Owl, Interlude, L'envoi

Steeds of Darkness, high v, fl, ob, perc, pf, vc, 1986: Sovra un destrier dalle fumanti frogie (F. Pick), I hear the last shudder of your flesh (E. Mahon)

Poet to Poet, high v, pf, 1987: An Ode for Ben Jonson (R. Herrick), To Thomas Moore (G. Gordon, Byron), Ave atque vale (In Memory of Charles Baudelaire) (A. C. Swinburne)

The Shooting Starres Attend Thee, high v, fl, vn, vc, 1987: The shooting starres attend thee (Herrick), Give me more love, or more disdaine (T. Carew), Interlude, Know, Celia, since thou art so proud (Carew), Around my neck an amulet (S. Menashe)

Songs from the Greek, for Pipes and Strings (ancient Gk. poets), high v, ob, cl, bn, pf, 1989

CHORAL

Slow, Slow fresh fount (B. Jonson), SATB/TTBB, 1941; Sweet western wind (R. Herrick), SATB, 1943; How goodly are thy tents (Ps lxxxiv), SSA/SATB, org/pf, 1947; Adon olom (Heb. liturgy), S, A, T, SATB, ob, tpt, str orch, 1954, arr. SATB, pf/org; The Habitable Earth (Proverbs), cantata, S, A, T, B, SATB, ob, pf/org, 1965; Spiritual Madrigals (F. Ewen, S. von Trimpberg, H. Heine), TTB, bn, va, vc, 1965; Sacred Service for Sabbath Morning (Heb. liturgy), cantor, S, A, T, B, SATB, fl, ob, bn, tpt, org, va, vc, 1970; Shirat Miriam L'Shabbat (Heb. liturgy), cantor, SATB, org, 1974; Where wild carnations blow (C. Smart), solo vv, SATB, fl, ob, tpt, timp, 2 vn, va, vc, db, 1984

SONGS
1 voice and piano unless otherwise stated

Chanson (from P. Louÿs: Songs of Bilitis), 1929, unpubd; Das Mädchen im Kampf mit sich selbst (F. Hebbel), 1929, unpubd; Song from without the World (anon.), 1929, unpubd; Einsamkeit (N. Lenau), 1930; Les elfes (Leconte de Lisle), 1930, unpubd; Leise zieht durch mein Gemüt (H. Heine), 1930; La pluie au matin (from Louÿs: Songs of Bilitis), 1930, unpubd; Slumber Song (S. Sassoon), 1931, unpubd; Be still, the hanging gardens were a dream (T. Stickney), 1934, unpubd

Orion, 1934, unpubd; Abendlied (M. Claudius), 1937; Ach du, um die Blumen sich verliebt (J. Lenz), 1937; Lockung (J. Eichendorff), 1937; Vergiftet sind meine Lieder (Heine), 1937; At the Aquarium (M. Eastman), 1938, unpubd; Im Traum (Heine), 1938, unpubd; Sonnet (E. E. Cummings), 1938, unpubd; Southern Road (S. Brown), 1938, unpubd; She weeps over Rahoon (J. Joyce), 1939; The Too-Late Born (A. MacLeish), 1939; Gather ye rosebuds (R. Herrick), 1940, unpubd

The Hound of Heaven (F. Thompson), medium v, ob, vn, va, vc, 1945; Little Ivory Figures Pulled with String (A. Lowell), 1v, gui, 1950; Mixco (M. A. Asturias), 1957; To Music (Herrick), 1957; The Adorable Mouse (Gideon, after La Fontaine), 1v, fl, cl, bn, hn, timp, hpd, 1960, arr. nar, fl, cl, 2 hn, pf, timp, str; Bells (W. Jones), 1966; Böhmischer Krystall (H. Heilmann), medium v, fl, cl, pf, vn, vc, 1988

OTHER WORKS

Stage: Fortunato (opera, 3 scenes, Gideon, after S. Quintero and J. Quintero), Mez, T, 2 Bar, orch, 1958

Orch and vocal orch: Allegro and Andante, 1940, unpubd, withdrawn; Epigrams, suite, chamber orch, 1941, unpubd; Lyric Piece for Str Orch, 1941; Sonnets from Shakespeare, high/low v, tpt, str orch, 1950, arr. high/low v, tpt, str qt; Symphonia brevis (2 Movts for Orch), 1953; Songs of Youth and Madness (F. Hölderlin, trans. M. Hamburger), high v, orch, 1977

Chamber: Incantation on an Indian Theme, va, pf, 1939, unpubd; Lyric Piece, str qt, 1941, arr. str orch; Fl Sonata, 1943, unpubd; Str Qt, 1946; Divertimento, ww qt, 1948; Fantasy on a Javanese Motive, vc, pf, 1948; Va Sonata, 1948; Air, vn, pf, 1950; Vc Sonata, 1961; Suite, cl/bn, pf, 1972; Fantasy on Irish Folk Motives, ob, bn, vib, glock, tam-tam, va, 1975; Trio, cl, vc, pf, 1978; Eclogue, fl, pf, c1980

Pf: 2 Dances, 2 pf, 1934, unpubd; Sketches, 1934, unpubd; Sonatina 'Homage à ma jeunesse', 2 pf, 1935; 3-Cornered Pieces (Suite no.1), 1935, arr. fl, cl, pf, 1936; Sketches (Suite no.2), 1937–40; Canzona, 1945; Suite no.3, 1951; 6 Cuckoos in Quest of a Composer, suite, 1953; Walk, 1955; Biblical Masks, org, 1958, arr. vn, pf, 1960; Of Shadows Numberless, suite after J. Keats: *Ode to a Nightingale*, 1966; Sonata, 1977

Principal publishers: ACA, Mobart, Peters

BIBLIOGRAPHY

EwenD; *LePageWC*, ii; *WAM*

L. Saminsky: *Living Music of the Americas* (New York, 1949), 106

G. Perle: 'Miriam Gideon', *ACAB*, vii/4 (1958), 2–9

D. Stevens, ed.: *A History of Song* (New York, 1960), 452–3

A. Weisser: 'Miriam Gideon', *Dimensions in American Judaism* (New York, 1970)

—— : 'Miriam Gideon's New Service', *American Jewish Congress Bi-Weekly*, xxxix/9 (1972), 22

H. Hanani: 'Portrait of a Composer', *Music Journal*, xxxiv/4 (1976), 24–5

D. Rosenberg and R. Rosenberg, eds.: *The Music Makers* (New York, 1978), 62–9

B. A. Petersen: 'The Vocal Chamber Music of Miriam Gideon', *Musical Woman*, ii (1984–5), 222–55

LESTER TRIMBLE
(work-list with SARA JOBIN)

Gifford, Helen (Margaret) (*b* Melbourne, 5 Sept 1935). Australian composer. She studied at the University of Melbourne with Dorian Le Gallienne, who influenced her decision to become a full-time composer when she graduated (MusB) in 1958. In that year her second work, *Fantasy* for flute and piano, had its first performance, in The Netherlands, and was broadcast by Radio Hilversum II. In 1964 her *Phantasma* for string orchestra was chosen by the Australian jury for submission to the ISCM Festival, Copenhagen. She won the Dorian Le Gallienne Award for composition in 1965 and the commission under the award produced the string quartet (1965), first performed at the 1966 Adelaide Festival. In 1974 she held a senior composer's fellowship from the Australian Council for the

Arts and was composer-in-residence to the Australian Opera. She has since completed a number of commissioned works through grants from the Council. She was attached to the Melbourne Theatre Company as composer of incidental music from 1970 to 1982 and in 1980 was appointed to the Australia Council's Artists in the Schools programme. She has been involved with several arts organizations and was chairman of the Composers' Guild of Australia, 1976–8.

A sensitive and highly individual composer, Gifford was at first influenced by the music of the French impressionists. A year of travel in Europe in 1962 brought her into direct contact with contemporary idioms, and she has remained indebted to Witold Lutosławski and the Polish school in general. Her travels in India in 1967 and a visit to Indonesia in 1971 brought the increasing influence of Asian music into her work. Several of her scores for the Melbourne Theatre Company have been produced as the result of experimental workshops. Her intricately wrought scores reveal an assured but nonconformist style.

WORKS
selective list

Stage: Regarding Faustus (music-theatre, 1, Gifford, after C. Marlowe), 1983, Adelaide, 12 March 1988; Iphigenia in Exile (music-theatre, 1, R. Meredith, after Euripides), 1985, part perf. Melbourne, ABC FM Radio, 1 Oct 1990; Music for the Adonia (music-theatre), 1992; incid. music to Brecht, Congreve, Fry, Shaffer, Shakespeare, Stoppard, Tourneur

Orch: Phantasma, str, 1963; Chimaera, 1969; Imperium, 1969

Vocal: As Dew in Aprille, S, pf/harp/gui, 1955; The Wanderer, male spkr, fl, eng hn, va, perc, 1963; Red Autumn in Valvins, Mez, pf, 1964; The Glass Castle, S, chorus 5vv, 1968; Bird Calls from an Old Land, 5 S, female chorus, 5vv, perc, 1971

Chamber and solo inst: Fantasy, fl, pf, 1958; Pf Sonata, 1960; Catalysis, pf, 1964; Str Qt, 1965; Waltz, The Spell, Cantillation, pf, 1966; Fable, harp, 1967; Canzone, 9 wind, cel, 1968; Of Old Angkor, hn, mar, 1970; Company of Brass, 9 brass, 1972; Toccata attacco, pf, 1990

Principal publisher: Sounds Australian

BIBLIOGRAPHY

H. Gifford: autobiographical chapter in *The Half-Open Door*, ed. P. Grimshaw and L. Strahan (Sydney, 1982), 172–93

J. Murdoch: 'Regarding Faustus', *Arts National*, iii/2 (1985), 70–71

Lord Harewood: 'Festival Drama through Music', *Adelaide Festival Review*, xlviii/March (1988), 16–17

H. Gifford: 'Subliminal Co-ordinates – Drawing Threads', *New Music Articles*, vii (1989), 5–9 [autobiographical article]

THÉRÈSE RADIC

Ginés, Teodora (*b* Hispaniola, *c*1530; *d* ? after 1598). African–Cuban composer. After the middle of the 16th century she and her younger sister Micaela moved from Hispaniola to Santiago de Cuba, where they formed a quintet consisting of guitar-like instruments (which they played), recorders and a violin. In 1598 Micaela left for Havana, while Teodora elected to remain behind, claiming she was too old to make the trip. This event reportedly occasioned the tune she wrote known as *El son de la Má Teodora*.

If the versions that have come down to us are authentic, this work is stylistically similar to the Cuban *son*, an African–Cuban dance that originated in eastern Cuba. Like other early African–Latino music from Mexico, Spain and Portugal, it is notated in F major, performed in the traditional African call-and-response practice, and makes constant rhythmic shifts from two to three beats in a bar.

BIBLIOGRAPHY

R. E. Garrigo: *Historia documentada de la conspiración de los soles y rayos de Bolívar* (Havana, 1929)

E. Rodriguez Demorizi: *Música e baile en Santo Domingo* (Santo Domingo, 1971)

J. M. Coopersmith: *Música y músicos de la Republica Dominicana* (Santo Domingo, 1974)

G. Béhague: *Music in Latin America: an Introduction* (Englewood Cliffs, NJ, 1979)

D.-R. de Lerma: 'A Glimpse of Afro-Caribbean Music in the Early Seventeenth Century', *Black Music Research Newsletter*, iv/2 (1980), 2–3; repr. in *Black Music Research Journal*, x/1 (1990), 94–6

DOMINIQUE-RENÉ DE LERMA

Ruth Gipps rehearsing a concert at the Royal Festival Hall, London, in 1957

Gipps, Ruth (*b* Bexhill-on-Sea, 20 Feb 1921). English composer and conductor. Her musical education began at the age of four at the Bexhill School of Music, where her mother was principal; she gained the ARCM diploma in 1936. She entered the RCM in 1937 and there she studied composition with R. O. Morris, Gordon Jacob and Ralph Vaughan Williams, the piano with Arthur Alexander and Kendall Taylor and the oboe with Leon Goossens. She won five prizes and the Caird Travelling Scholarship, and later returned to the RCM as a professor. Her tone poem *Knight in Armour* was conducted by Sir Henry Wood at the last night of the Proms in 1942. In 1948 she was awarded the DMus at Durham University. She was then chorus master of the City of Birmingham Choir and lecturer for the Oxford extra-mural delegacy. Turning increasingly to conducting, she became musical director (in 1961) of the Chanticleer Orchestra, London, and of the London Repertoire Orchestra (1955–86).

In 1959 she toured the USA on an English-Speaking Union Ford Foundation Travel Award and in 1967 she was chairman of the Composers' Guild of Great Britain. Her early works showed some influence of Vaughan Williams, though with a degree of originality that has been developed in a brilliant and vigorous manner in her later music. She was created a MBE in 1981.

WORKS
selective list

Orch: Knight in Armour, op.8, chamber orch, 1940; Sym. no.1, f, op.22, 1942; Vn Conc., B♭, op.24, 1943; Sym. no.2, B, op.30, 1945; Pf Conc., op.34, 1948; Conc., op.49, vn, va, small orch, 1957; Sym. no.3, op.57, 1965; Hn Conc., op.58, 1968; Sym. no.4, op.61, 1972; Sym. no.5, op.63, 1980; Ambarvalia, chamber orch, op.70, 1988; Sinfonietta, op.73, 10 wind, tam-tam, 1989

Chamber: Vn Sonata, op.42, 1954; Cl Sonata, op.45, 1954; Str Qt, op.47, 1956; Theme and Variations, op.57, pf, 1965 [from Sym. no.3]; Wind Octet, 1983; Ob Sonata no.2, op.66, 1985; The St Francis Window, op.67, a fl, pf, 1986; The Riders of Rohan, op.69, trbn, pf, 1987; Threnody, op.74, eng hn, pf, 1990; The Pony Cart, op.75, fl, hn, pf, 1990; A Wealden Suite, op.76, E♭-cl, B♭-cl, A-cl, b cl, 1991; Pan and Apollo, op.78, 2 ob, eng hn, harp, 1992

Choral: The Cat, op.32, A, Bar, double chorus, orch, 1947; Goblin Market, op.40 (C. Rossetti), S, S, female chorus, str orch, 1953; An Easter Carol, op.52, 1958; Magnificat and Nunc dimittis, op.55, SSATB, org, 1959; Gloria in excelsis, op.62, unison vv, org, 1974

Principal publisher: Tickerage

BIBLIOGRAPHY

Fuller-LeFanuRM

D. C. F. Wright: 'Ruth Gipps', *British Music* [Journal of the British Music Society], xiii (1991), 3–13

C. Pluygers: 'Discrimination . . . the Career and Struggle for Recognition of Dr Ruth Gipps', *Winds* (1992), spr., 14–15

LEWIS FOREMAN, J. N. F. LAURIE-BECKETT

Giraud, Suzanne (*b* Metz, 31 July 1958). French composer. She was a student at the Strasbourg Conservatory and at the Paris Conservatoire (piano, viola, harmony, orchestration, conducting), after which she studied composition with Franco Donatoni, Brian Ferneyhough, Tristan Murail and Hugues Dufourt. She was resident at the Villa Medici, Rome, in 1986. Most of Giraud's works are written for chamber groups of varying size and configuration; her often unusual choice of instruments, as for example in *Episode en forme d'oubli* and *Le rouge des profondeurs*, enables her to create a noticeable interplay of subtle timbres, a feature reminiscent of, and maybe derived from, the work of Marius Constant. Although she uses strict combinatorial serialist techniques, the evocative titles of her compositions suggest that her work is informed by a natural aesthetic, one that is at once dreamlike and exultant.

WORKS
selective list

Orch: Terre essor, 1984

Chamber: Regards sur le jardin d'Eros, str qt, 1983; La dernière lumière, S, 8 insts, 1985; Ergo sum, 15 insts, 1985; L'offrande a Vénus, 8 insts, 1985; Voici la lune, S, fl, pf, 1986; Contrées d'une rêve, 15 insts, 1987; L'aube sur le désir, 2 fl, harp, str trio, 1988; Episode en forme d'oubli, cl, mar, db, 1989; Fantasia, 2 ob, bn, hpd, 1989; Le rouge des profondeurs, 6 insts, 1990; Crier vers l'horizon, bn, ens, 1991; Le rivage des transes, 2 pf, 2 perc, 1991; Str Trio, 1991

Solo perc: Tentative-univers, 1983; L'oeil et le jour, 1990

DANIEL KAWKA

Giteck, Janice (*b* New York, 27 June 1946). American composer and pianist. She studied at Mills College, California, with Darius Milhaud and Morton Subotnick (BA 1968, MA 1969), at the Paris Conservatoire with Olivier Messiaen (1969–70), and at the Aspen School, Colorado, with Milhaud and Charles Jones. She also studied electronic music with Lowell Cross and Anthony J. Gnazzo, Javanese gamelan with Daniel Schmidt and West African percussion with Obo Addy. She gained a second MA, in psychology, at Antioch University, Ohio (1986). Giteck held teaching positions at California State University, Hayward (1974) and the University of California, Berkeley (1974–6), before joining the faculty of the Cornish College of the Arts, Seattle (1979), as a teacher of both composition and women's studies. She was a founder and co-director of the Port Costa Players, a contemporary-music ensemble based in San Francisco (1972–9), and, in 1978–9, music director of KPFA Pacifica Radio, Berkeley. Her awards include grants from the California Arts Council (1978) and the NEA (1979, 1983), and she has received commissions from the San Francisco SO (*Tree*, 1981) and others, including a joint commission from new-music groups in Portland (Oregon), Syracuse and Atlanta (funded by the Meet the Composer/Reader's Digest Consortium Commissioning Program) for the 'performance piece' *The Screamer* (1993) on the theme of love and rage.

Giteck has long been concerned with music as ritual. From the early 1970s her works reflected her interest in the cultures of Native Americans. *A'agita*, an opera based on Pima and Papago mythologies, was performed by the Port Costa Players throughout the American West and in Europe. In the 1980s she began to pursue the relationship between music and healing, particularly in connection with AIDS. *Om Shanti* (1986), *Tapasya* (1987), *Home* (1989, revised 1992) and *Leningrad Spring* (1991) are part of a 'music and healing series', issued as recordings on CD as a benefit for the support of AIDS patients. The 1991 Merkin Hall, New York, performance of *Om Shanti* was described in a review (*Village Voice*, 30 April 1991) as 'the synthesis collage music has pointed to for thirty-five years'.

WORKS
selective list

Opera: A'agita (R. Giteck, after Pima and Papago texts), 3 singer-actors, dancer, 8 inst player-actors, 1976

Orch and inst: Trio, ob, vn, vc, 1964; Pf Qnt, 1965; Str Qt no.2, 1967; Trey, 3 Pieces, pf, 1968; Helixes, fl, trbn, vn, vc, gui, pf, perc, 1974; Breathing Songs from a Turning Sky, fl, cl, bn, vc, pf, perc, lights, 1980; When the Crones Stop Counting, 60 fl, 1980; Ah Ah Sh! Listen, gamelan, vcs, bns, drums, nar, dancer, 1981; Tree, chamber sym., orch, 1981; Loo-wit, va, orch, 1983; Tapasya, va, perc, 1987; Leningrad Spring, fl + pic + a fl, pf + mallets, perc, 1991

Choral: How to Invoke a Garden (cantata, J. Jones), SATB, 10 insts, 1969; Sun of the Center (cantata, R. Kelley), male v, fl, cl, vn, pf, 1970; Magic Words to Feel Better, SATB, 1974; Far North Beast Ghosts the Clearing (after Swampy Cree text, trans. H. Norman), chorus, 1978; Pictures of the Floating World, chorus, 10 insts, 1987; Home, chorus

400vv, 23 insts, 1989, rev. 1992 as Home (revisited), 6 male vv, gamelan pacifica, vc, synth; I am Singing (Giteck), women's chorus unacc., 1990; From Childhood (A. Rimbaud), men's chorus unacc., 1992

Vocal: Anew (L. Zukofsky), 1v, pf, 1969; L'ange Heurtebise (J. Cocteau), 1v, pf, 1971; Magic Words (Native American poems), T, S, pf, 1973; Messalina (A. Jarry), male v, vc, pf, 1973; Matinée d'ivresse, monody (A. Rimbaud), high v, 1976; 8 Sandbars on the Takano River (G. Snyder), 5 female vv, fl, bn, gui, 1976; Thunder like a White Bear Dancing (ritual based on the Ojibwa Mide Picture Songs), S, fl, pf, hand perc, slides, 1977; Callin' Home Coyote: a Burlesque (L. MacAdams), T, steel drums, db, 1978; Om Shanti (Shankaracharaya), S, sextet, 1986; The Screamer, performance piece, S, fl, cl, vn, vc, pf, perc, 1993

Elec: Traffic Acts, 4-track tape, 1969; Peter and the Wolves, trbn + actor, tape, 1978

Film scores: Hopi: Songs of the Fourth World, 1983; Hearts and Hands, 1987

BIBLIOGRAPHY
CC (B. Weir)

INGRAM D. MARSHALL,
CATHERINE PARSONS SMITH

Giuranna, Barbara [Barbàra, Elena Francesca Paola Maria Giuseppa] (b Palermo, 18 Nov 1899). Italian composer. She studied the piano in Palermo with G. A. Fano among others, then went to Naples, entering the conservatory in 1919 and studying composition with Antonio Savasta. After graduating in 1923 she completed her composition studies in Milan with G. F. Ghedini. The next year she married the composer and conductor Mario Giuranna, with whom she went to the USA. Two of her compositions, *Apina rapita dai nani della montagna* (1924) and *Marionette* (1925), had their first performances in Chicago in 1929 and were repeated at the Metropolitan. After returning to Italy, in 1933 Giuranna won a competition held by the Sindacato Musicisti Italiani, and in 1936 she was the first Italian woman composer represented at the Venice Biennale, with her Adagio and Allegro for nine instruments. During the fascist era she composed the heroic poem *X legio*, which won a prize in the Sindacato Musicisti competition, and *Patria*. She taught at the S Cecilia Conservatory in Rome from 1937 to 1976 and at the beginning of the 1950s was music consultant to RAI, for which she made transcriptions and realizations of operas by Giovanni Paisiello (*La molinara* and *Il re Teodoro in Venezia*) and Domenico Cimarosa (*Le astuzie femminili* and *I due baroni di Rocca Azzurra*). She won the international prize of the City of Trieste in 1967 for her second Concerto for Orchestra. In 1990 the International Leonard Bernstein

Academy organized a concert in Rome in her honour at which her mass *Sinite parvulos* was performed. Giuranna's works include three operas, all of which have been staged, and many orchestral and vocal works, as well as a solo viola piece for her son Bruno Giuranna. During her long career she has remained faithful to the Italian musical tradition in which she was trained – that of the previous generation; incursions into a non-tonal world are very rare. Some works, from the start of her career for example, show the influence of Debussy; others, such as her last work, the *Sinite parvulos* mass, testify to the inexhaustible vitality of her musical personality.

WORKS
selective list

Stage: Trappolo d'oro, ballet, 1929; Jamanto (opera lirica, 3), Bergamo, 1941; Mayerling (opera lirica, 3, A. Viviani), Naples, 1961; Hosanna (opera lirica, 1, C. Pinelli), Palermo, 1978

Orch: Notturno, 1923; Apina rapita dai nani della montagna, suite, small orch, 1924; Marionette, scherzo, 1925; X legio, poema eroico, 1936; Toccata, 1937: Patria, sym. poem, 1938; Conc. for Orch, 1942; Musica per Olivia, 1965; Conc. for Orch no.2, 1967

Chamber and solo inst: Adagio e allegro, vn, va, vc, db, hn, fl, ob, cl, bn, 1935; Sonatina, pf, 1935; Solo, va, 1980

Sacred: Messa 'Sinite parvulos', 1990

Many vocal works

Principal publisher: Ricordi

PAOLA DAMIANI

Glanville-Hicks, Peggy (b Melbourne, 29 Dec 1912; d Sydney, 25 June 1990). Australian composer. Her creative gifts appeared early, and she received her first training in composition from Fritz Hart at the Melbourne Conservatorium in 1927. In 1931 she won a scholarship to the RCM, where she studied until 1935 with Ralph Vaughan Williams (composition), Arthur Benjamin (piano), and Constant Lambert and Malcolm Sargent (conducting). The award of an Octavia Travelling Scholarship enabled her to further her studies with Egon Wellesz in Vienna and with Nadia Boulanger in Paris (1936–8). Other major awards have been a grant from the American Academy of Arts and Letters (1953–4), two Guggenheim fellowships (1956–8), a Fulbright Fellowship (1960), and a Rockefeller Grant (1961–3) for travel and research in the Middle and Far East.

In 1938 Glanville-Hicks married Stanley Bate and on occasion wrote as Peggy Bate until their divorce in 1949. She lived from 1942 to 1959 in the USA, where she was

Peggy Glanville-Hicks

naturalized in 1948. During this period many of her major works were composed, and she was engaged in notable activities for the propagation of new music and the encouragement of young composers. In 1943–4 she was a member of the League of Composers Committee, which gave concerts of modern music in New York's Central Park, and she collaborated with Carleton Sprague Smith in founding the International Music Fund, which operated through UNESCO to assist European artists in postwar re-establishment. She organized concerts of new music at the Museum of Modern Art and the Metropolitan Museum, assisted Yehudi Menuhin in presenting concerts of Indian music (1955) and, as a director of the New York Composers' Forum, helped to organize a series of seven concerts of new American music (1950–60). She also played an influential role as music critic of the *New York Herald Tribune* (1948–58) and through her contributions to various journals, her articles on American and Scandinavian music in *Grove's Dictionary* (5th edition), and her reports as Australian delegate to ISCM festivals. She acted as adviser on music to the Australian Ministry of Information in New York. In 1959 she went to live in Athens. Eight years later on a visit to New York, she underwent surgery for the removal of a

brain tumour; though she recovered fully, she composed little afterwards. In 1976 she returned to live in Sydney where she remained until her death.

Not only have many of her major works been recorded, but she was responsible for recordings made of works by her American colleagues, including George Antheil, Colin McPhee, Paul Bowles and Lou Harrison. The Artists' Company, which she established in 1958, was instrumental in reviving and producing new American operas, and her own works have been widely performed in Europe and America. Her Choral Suite was conducted by Adrian Boult at the 1938 ISCM Festival in London; the Concertino da camera was also first performed at an ISCM festival (1948, Amsterdam). Her early vocal music displays subtle wit and parody; for example *Thomsoniana* (1949) is set to words taken from Virgil Thomson's music reviews. Her championship of the percussion and harp repertories was reflected in works written in the 1950s.

The première of *Letters from Morocco*, given by Leopold Stokowski at the Museum of Modern Art in New York (1952), revealed her growing interest in musical exoticism, also explored in *Sinfonia da Pacifica*, which was first performed in Melbourne by Bernard Heinze (1953), and in her first major opera, *The Transposed Heads*. The latter was commissioned by the Louisville Orchestra and first performed in April 1954, with subsequent performances in New York (1958) and Sydney (1970); a recording of the opera (released in 1992) was made in the presence of the composer in 1984. Based on a novella by Thomas Mann, the music assimilates Hindu folk sources into a contemporary Western idiom; it is scored for three singers, two speaking roles, chorus, and chamber orchestra. *The Glittering Gate* (1959), her next opera, is a short curtain-raiser using electronics, which had its première in New York; it was also heard at the Adelaide Festival in 1972. Glanville-Hicks made a further study of oriental music after settling in Athens, where she made a comparative investigation into Aegean demotic music and Far Eastern folklorism. The influence of these is present in two of her later operas: *Nausicaa*, first performed at the Athens Festival in August 1961, and *Sappho*, commissioned by the Ford Foundation for the San Francisco Opera. Her stage works attempt to revive ancient Greek dramatic forms, musical modes, and meters, using modern theatrical means. But this creation of a style so divorced from the mainstream has resulted in her work receiving less attention than it merits.

WORKS
selective list
STAGE

Caedmon (3 scenes, P. Glanville-Hicks), 1933, ?unperf.

The Transposed Heads (6 scenes, Glanville-Hicks, after T. Mann: *Die vertauschten Köpfe*), *US-LOu*, vs (New York, 1953); Louisville, KY, Columbia Auditorium, 3 April 1954

The Glittering Gate (1, Glanville-Hicks, after Lord Dunsany), 1956, full score (New York, 1957); New York, 15 May 1959

Nausicaa (prol, 3, R. Graves and A. Reid, after Graves: *Homer's Daughter*), *AUS-Msl* (New York, n.d.); Athens, Herodus Atticus, 19 Aug 1961

Carlos among the Candles, 1962, unperf.

Sappho (3, L. Durrell, after his play), 1965, unperf.

OTHER WORKS

Inst: Concertino da camera, fl, cl, bn, pf, 1945; Sonata, harp, 1951; Sonata, pf, 5 perc, 1952; Sinfonia da Pacifica, 1953; Etruscan Conc., pf, chamber orch, 1956; Conc. romantico, va, orch, 1957

Vocal: Choral Suite (J. Fletcher), female chorus, ob, str orch, 1937; Last Poems (Housman), 5 songs, 1v, pf, 1945; Profiles from China (E. Tietjens), 5 songs, T, pf, chamber orch, 1945; Ballade (P. Bowles), 3 songs, 1v, pf, 1945; 13 Ways of Looking at a Blackbird (W. Stevens), S, pf, 1947; Thomsoniana (V. Thomson), S, T, fl, hn, str qt, pf, 1949; Letters from Morocco (Bowles), 6 songs, T, chamber orch, 1952

Film scores, incl. Tulsa, 1949, Tel, 1950, The African Story, 1956, A Scary Time, 1958

Principal publishers: Associated, Colfrank, Hargail, Peters, Schott, Weintraub

MSS in *AUS-Msl*

BIBLIOGRAPHY
EwenD

G. Antheil: 'Peggy Glanville-Hicks', *ACAB*, iv/1(1954), 2–9

Q. Eaton: *Opera Production: a Handbook* (Minneapolis, 1961–74)

P. Glanville-Hicks: 'At the Source', *ON*, xxvi/6 (1961–2), 8–13 [on *Nausicaa*]

R. Covell: *Australia's Music* (Melbourne, 1967), 168

D. Ewen, ed.: *Composers since 1900: a Biographical and Critical Guide* (New York, 1969), 233–5

A. D. McCredie: *Musical Composition in Australia* (Canberra, 1969), 14

—— : *Catalogue of 46 Australian Composers* (Canberra, 1969), 7

J. Murdoch: *Australia's Contemporary Composers* (Melbourne, 1972), 102–7

C. Northouse: *Twentieth-Century Opera in England and the U.S.* (Boston, 1976)

D. Hayes: *Peggy Glanville-Hicks: a Bio-Bibliography* (Westport, CT, 1990)

THÉRÈSE RADIC, ELIZABETH WOOD

Glatz [née Hunter], **Helen (Sinclair)** (*b* South Shields, Durham, 13 March 1908).

British composer and teacher. Taught by W. G. Whittaker in Newcastle, she won an open scholarship to the RCM in 1928, studying there with Ralph Vaughan Williams and Gordon Jacob. In 1933, on a travelling scholarship, she visited Florence, Vienna and then Budapest in the (vain) hope of studying with Zoltán Kodály. She married in Hungary in 1938. Returning to England in 1947, she taught at Dartington College of Arts (full-time from 1953 until her retirement), and resumed composing there in the 1950s. She has acknowledged the early influence of Vaughan Williams, Gustav Holst, Béla Bartók and Kodály, alongside a lifelong attraction to Hungarian folk music. Her extensive output includes three children's ballets (1954, 1956, 1958), *Dance Rhapsody* for harp and orchestra (1963–8) and a considerable amount of chamber music, including two string quartets (1932, 1936) and sonatas for viola (1929), flute (1971) and violin (1972). Among her choral compositions are a cantata and two psalm settings (1931, 1976). She has also written many works for woodwind, percussion and brass.

BIBLIOGRAPHY
Fuller-LeFanuRM

MARIE FITZPATRICK

Gonzaga, (Francisca Edwiges Neves) Chiquinha (*b* Rio de Janeiro, 17 Oct 1847; *d* Rio de Janeiro, 28 Feb 1935). Brazilian composer, pianist and conductor. She studied the piano in Rio de Janeiro with José de Sousa Lobo and the Portuguese pianist Arthur Napoleão dos Santos. However, her wealthy husband Jacinto Ribeiro do Amaral, whom she married in 1863, disapproved of her musical career and at the age of 20 she separated from him. She married again – her second husband was João Batista de Carvalho – and once more separated, in 1876; she found work as a piano teacher to help support her children. Her first success as a composer came with the publication in 1877 of the polka *Atraente*; two waltzes, a tango and another polka were also published in that year. She wrote music for several operettas; the first, *A corte na roça* (to a libretto by Francisco Sodré), first performed at the Teatro Príncipe Imperial on 17 January 1885, gained her the name 'the feminine Offenbach'. In 1885 she directed the theatre orchestra and the band of the military police – the first woman to conduct an orchestra in Brazil. She was an enthusiastic supporter of the Brazilian movements for the end of slavery (1888) and the proclamation of the Republic (1889).

Gonzaga composed 77 stage works (1885–1933) to subjects dealing mostly with local, everyday events, and she collaborated with the most famous Brazilian playwrights of the time. The popularity of these works is evidenced by the three-act operetta *Forrobodó* (1912), which received 1500 performances. Her tango *O Gaúcho*, written for the play *Zizinha maxixe* (1895) and based on the folk-dance *corta-jaca*, became one of her most famous pieces at the turn of the century. She travelled extensively between 1901 and 1910, performing in Spain, France, Italy, England and, especially, Portugal, where her operettas enjoyed unprecedented popularity. Her march *Ó abre-alas* (1899) became the prototype of the 'carnival march', a popular genre in the 1920s.

Over 300 of her works in dance and song forms were published, including waltzes, polkas, tangos, mazurkas, quadrilles, gavottes, habaneras, barcarolles, serenatas, *maxixes*, *lundus*, *fados*, *modinhas*, *marchas* and *choros* (the *Enciclopédia da música brasileira*, Diniz and Vasconcelos include complete lists).

BIBLIOGRAPHY

M. Lira: *Chiquinha Gonzaga: grande compositora brasileira* (Rio de Janeiro, 1939)

L. H. Corrêa de Azevedo: *150 anos de música no Brasil, 1800–1950* (Rio de Janeiro, 1956), 148–51

G. Béhague: *Popular Musical Currents in the Art Music of the Early Nationalistic Period in Brazil, circa 1870–1920* (diss., Tulane U., LA, 1966), 133–6

Enciclopédia da música brasileira (São Paulo, 1977), i, 322–7 [incl. list of works], 448; ii, 745

V. Mariz: *A canção brasileira* (Rio de Janeiro, 3/1977), 195–9

E. Diniz: *Chiquinha Gonzaga: uma história de vida* (Rio de Janeiro, 1984) [incl. list of works]

A. Vasconcelos: *Raízes da música brasileira* (Rio de Janeiro, 1991), 263–89 [incl. list of works]

CRISTINA MAGALDI

Goodeve [née Knowlys], **Florence Everilda** (*b* Heysham, Lancs., 1861; *d* London, Jan 1915). English composer. She married Louis Goodeve, a High Court advocate in Calcutta, where she spent some time; she was widowed in 1888. She published about 70 songs, some to her own words; *Ruth's Legacy* and *The Young Friar* became popular. Her only piece for piano (also her earliest composition), a *Glockenspiel Galop* (1875), was taken up by the principal military bands.

JOHN R. GARDNER

Gorne, Annette vande (*b* Charleroi, 6 Jan 1946). Belgian composer. After a conventional musical training at the conservatories in Mons and Brussels, and studies with Jean Absil, she discovered, together with F. Delalande and Pierre Henry, 'l'acousmatique' (music composed in the studio using tape or, later, digital sources, and relayed by an orchestra of loudspeakers); she went on to study electroacoustic composition at the Paris Conservatoire, where her teachers were Guy Reibel and Pierre Schaeffer. She was the founder of an information and research centre Musiques et Recherches and the studio Métamorphoses d'Orphée in Ohain (1982), which are designed to promote contemporary music, electroacoustics and 'l'acousmatique'. She has taught electroacoustic composition, first at the conservatory in Liège and then in Brussels. She has also published general articles on sonic research.

WORKS
selective list

ELECTROACOUSTIC

Lamento ou la délivrance du cercle, tape and orch of loudspeakers, 1980–82

Exil: chant II (Saint-Jean Perse), tape, large orch of loudspeakers, 1983

Tao: Métal, tape, 1983; Métal, tape, amplified zheng, 1984; Eau, tape, 1984; Eau, tape, amplified zheng, 1986; Feu, tape, 1986; Bois, tape, 1986; Terre, 8-track tape, 1991

Energie/Matière, tape, 1985

Faisceaux, tape, pf, 1985

Noces noires (W. Lambersy), 1986 [text recited by author]

Architecture/Nuit (Lambersy), 1989 [poems recited by A. Carré]

STAGE

Paysage/Vitesse (pour une nuit hexoise) (Ballet, choreog. O. Duboc), 1986

Action/Passion (ballet, choreog. P. Kuypers), 1987

Aglavaine et Selysette (incid. music, M. Maeterlinck), 1989

CHRISTINE BALLMAN

Gottsched [née Kulmus], **Luise Adelgunda Victoria** (*b* ?Danzig [now Gdańsk]; *d* Leipzig, 1762). German writer, translator, harpsichordist, lutenist and composer. Gottsched studied composition with J. L. Krebs, a pupil of J. S. Bach. In 1735 she married Johann Christoph Gottsched, a leading literary figure of the German Enlightenment who exerted a great influence on German opera and whose house was a centre of musical and intellectual activity. The Gottscheds were received at the court of Maria Theresa in Vienna in 1749.

BIBLIOGRAPHY
MGG ('Gottsched, Johann Christoph'; W. Serauky, H. Haase)

MARTHA FURMAN SCHLEIFER

Gow, Dorothy (*b* London, 1893; *d* London, 1 Nov 1982). English composer. In her thirties, Gow studied composition at the RCM with Ralph Vaughan Williams. She also studied with Egon Wellesz in Vienna. Her chamber music was regularly performed at the early Macnaghten-Lemare concerts in the 1930s and her Prelude and Fugue for orchestra (1931) was broadcast by the BBC. In spite of support from friends, such as Vaughan Williams and Elisabeth Lutyens, her extreme shyness and self-critical approach led to her few works being seldom performed in later years. Described by Lutyens as having 'an unconventional ear', Gow wrote chamber music of great beauty and individuality. Her best-known work is the String Quartet in One Movement (1947), published by OUP in 1957. Her manuscripts are held in the British Library (Add. 63000–63007) in London.

WORKS
selective list

Variations on a Diabelli Variation, pf; Kyrie, Gloria, Sanctus, Osanna, unacc. vv; Prelude and Fugue, orch, 1931; Fantasy Str Qt, 1932; Str Qt no.2, 1933; 3 Songs, T, str qt, 1933; Ob Qnt, 1936; Str Qt in One Movt, 1947; 2 Pieces, ob, ?1953; Theme and Variations, vn, 1955; Piece, vn, hn, 1971

BIBLIOGRAPHY
A. Macnaghten: 'Dorothy Gow', RCM Magazine, lxxix (1983), 61–2

SOPHIE FULLER

Graham, Janet (Christine) (*b* Consett, Co. Durham, 4 June 1948). English composer, teacher and music therapist. She studied composition with James Iliff at the RAM (1966–71) and privately with Elisabeth Lutyens (1972–4). During 1989-90 she trained as a music therapist. Her music, written mostly for small ensembles, achieves a distinctive balance of lyricism and angularity, particularly in the vocal works. Already evident in earlier pieces, such as *Atque in perpetuum* (1974), this quality is fully realized in *Until the Sunset Hour* (1985).

WORKS
selective list

Stage: The Journey of Everyman (music drama, 3, after morality play), 1977
Orch: The Sons of Cronos, 1982–3, arr. pf, 4 hands, 1987
Choral: The Call of the Tide, 1978; 2 Winter Songs, female vv, 1988
Other vocal: Cras Amet, S/T, pf, 1973; Atque in perpetuum, S, T, Bar, fl, 3 cl, vc, pf, 1974; Epitaphs, T, fl, 4 trbn, gui, chorus, 1975; This Great and Wide Sea, S, cl, pf, perc, 1980; Until the Sunset Hour, Mez, inst ens, 1985; Canta mihi aliquid, T, inst ens, 1986
Inst: Pf Sonata, 1972–3; Diversitas, 2 pf, 1974; Str Qt no.3, 1975; Persephone, pf, 1980; Evening Flights, fl, 1981; Str Qt no.4, 1982; Hecate, pf, 1983; Iris, pf, 1984; Pf Sonatina, 1985; 3 Pieces, org, 1986; 5 Pieces, vn, pf, 1987; 7 Songs from the North East, cl, vn, 1987; From Dusk to Dawn, fl, ob, pf, 1989; Earth Cry, ob, tpt, pf, 1990

Some material in *GB-Lmic*

BIBLIOGRAPHY
Fuller-LeFanuRM

MARIE FITZPATRICK

Grandval [née de Reiset], **Marie (Félicie Clémence),** Vicomtesse de [Blangy, Caroline; Reiset, Maria Felicita de; Reiset de Tesier, Maria; Valgrand, Clémence] (*b* St Rémy-des-Monts, Sarthe, 21 Jan 1830; *d* Paris, 15 Jan 1907). French composer. Born into a well-to-do family, Marie de Reiset started her musical studies at the age of six. Her earliest compositions were completed in her early teens under the tuition of Friedrich Flotow, a family friend; he left Paris, however, before her musical education was complete. After her marriage to the Vicomte de Grandval, she studied with Saint-Saëns for two years. In 1859 her one-act operetta *Le sou de Lise* was given its première at the Bouffes-Parisiens, Paris, and was published the same year under the pseudonym Caroline Blangy. Other works appeared under various pen names, including Clémence Valgrand, Maria Felicita de Reiset and Maria Reiset de Tesier.

In 1880 Grandval won the Concours Rossini for her oratorio *La fille de Jaïre*, which was first performed the following year at the Paris Conservatoire. In addition to the nine known dramatic works, Grandval left a manuscript of a grand opera in four acts. *Mazeppa*, a grand opera in five acts, was first performed on 24 April 1892. She also wrote three symphonies, two concertos, a concert overture (unpublished), music for a ballet, more than ten chamber works, and many piano pieces and vocal works. She continued to compose until her death.

Her friends were well-known composers and other musicians of the time, many of whom were dedicatees of her works: Gounod (*Sainte-Agnès*), Flotow (*Les fiancés de Rosa*), J. E. Pasdeloup (*Atala*), Victor Massé (*La pénitente*) and Saint-Saëns (*La forêt*). A copy of her *Messe* (in the Library of Congress, Washington, DC) is inscribed to her friend Bizet. Her stature as a respected

Cover of the 'Ballade suisse', arranged for voice and piano, from Marie Grandval's opera 'Piccolino' (1869), as sung by the soprano Gabrielle Krauss

composer is clear from the many favourable contemporary reviews of her works. Fétis remarked on the incontestable vigour with which she systematically tackled a range of musical genres, 'giving proof in each that if she was not a genius, she was at least genuinely talented'.

WORKS
selective list; printed works published in Paris

DRAMATIC

Le sou de Lise (opérette, 1) (1859); Paris, Théâtre des Bouffes-Parisiens, 1859

Les fiancés de Rosa (opéra comique, 1, A. Choler); Paris, Théâtre Lyrique, 1 May 1863

La comtesse Eva (opéra comique, 1, M. Carré); Baden-Baden, 7 Aug 1864

Donna Maria Infanta di Spagna (opera, 3, Leiser), 1865

La pénitente (opéra comique, 1, H. Meilhac and W. Busnach); Paris, Opéra-Comique (Salle Favart), 13 May 1868

Piccolino (opera, 3, A. de Lauzières, after V. Sardou), vs (1869); Paris, Théâtre Italien, 5 Jan 1869

La forêt (poème lyrique, 3 parties, Grandval); Paris, Salle de Ventadour, 30 March 1875

Atala (poème lyrique, L. Gallet), c1888

Mazeppa (opera, 5 acts and 6 tableaux, C. Grandmougin and G. Hartmann) (1899); Bordeaux, Grand Théâtre Municipal, 24 April 1892

VOCAL

Choral: Messe, chorus, orch, 1867; Stabat Mater, cantata, solo vv, chorus, orch, 1870 (1872); Sainte-Agnès (oratorio, Gallet), 1876 (1881); Villanelle (Passerat) S/T, chorus, fl (1877); La ronde des songes (scène fantastique, P. Collin), solo v, chorus, orch (1880); La fille de Jaïre (oratorio, Collin), 1881

Other vocal: Agnus dei, S/T, pf; Fleur de matin, (2vv/chorus, pf)/pf; Gratias, 2vv, pf/org; Heures, 4vv, pf; Jeanne d'Arc (C. Delavigne), C, pf/org (1862); Kyrie, S, A duo/women's chorus; Les lucioles, Mez, vn/pf/org; Noël (S. Prudhomme), 1v, pf, ob obbl (1901); O salutaris, S/(S, C); Pater noster, S, pf/org; Rose et Violette, 2 S; c50 songs, 1v, pf

OTHER WORKS

Orch: Amazones, lyric sym.; Callirhoe, ballet-symphonie; Concertino, vn, orch; Divertissement hongrois, c1890; Esquisses symphoniques, Paris, 8 March 1874; Gavotte, pf, orch (1885); Ob Conc., op.7 (n.d.), also arr. ob, pf; Ronde de nuit (1879), also arr. pf duet

Chamber and solo inst: Gavotte, vc, db, pf; Mazurka

du ballet, 2 pf; [4] Morceaux, eng hn/cl (?1900); Musette, vn; 2 nocturnes, pf, opp.5–6; Offertoire (vn, vc, harp, pf)/(lv, vc, pf/org); 2 pf trios, no.2 ed. L. Lydeen (Bryn Mawr, PA, 1994); 2 pièces, vn, pf (1882); 3 pièces, vc, pf (1882); 2 pièces, ob, vc, pf (1884); 2 pièces, cl, pf (1885); Prélude et variations, vn, pf (1882); Romance, vc, db, pf; Ronde de nuit, pf duet/orch (1883); Suite de morceaux, fl, pf (1877); Trio de salon, ob, bn, pf; Valse mélancolique, fl, harp; Vn Sonata, op.8; other works for solo pf

BIBLIOGRAPHY

CohenE; FétisB; FétisBS; PazdirekH; SchmidlD

F. Clément and P. Larousse: Dictionnaire lyrique (Paris, 1867–81, 2/1897, 3/1905 ed. A. Pougin as Dictionnaire des opéras)

H. Cohen: 'Cinquième concert', Chronique musicale, iii/18 (1874), 265–6 [on Esquisses symphoniques]

—— : 'Concerts Danbé', Chronique musicale, iv/20 (1874), 81–2 [on Stabat Mater]

—— : 'Théâtre Ventadour', Chronique musicale, viii/44 (1875), 83–4 [on La forêt]

'Concert spirituel de l'Odéon', Chronique musicale, xi/63 (1876), 125 [on Sainte-Agnès]

H. Buffenoir: La vicomtesse de Grandval (Paris, 1894)

JUDY S. TSOU

Grant, Micki [McCutcheon, Minnie Perkins] (b Chicago, 30 June 1941). African-American composer, singer and actress. She studied music in Chicago and at the University of Illinois. In 1962, her senior year, she left Illinois to sing in a Broadway musical, after which she performed as an actress and singer on and off Broadway, in regional theatre and in television dramas. As a composer of musicals she had her first major success with Don't Bother me, I Can't Cope (1972), produced on Broadway in collaboration with Vinette Carroll; the work, in which Grant also performed, received the Outer Circle Critics Best Musical award. She has composed for other musicals, including The Prodigal Sister (1974), Your Arm's too Short to Box with God (1976), The Ups and Downs of Theophilus Maitland (1977), Alice (1978), The Cradle will Rock (1978), It's so Nice to be Civilized (1979), Working (1980), and Croesus and the Witch and Hansel and Gretel (In the 1980s) (both 1984).

BIBLIOGRAPHY

SouthernB

O. Williams: American Black Women in the Arts and Sciences (Metuchen, NJ, 1973)

R. Abdul: Blacks in Classical Music (New York, 1977)

DORIS EVANS McGINTY

Grazianini, Caterina Benedicta (fl early 18th century). Italian composer, active in Vienna. Nothing is known about Grazianini's training or life. Her two surviving works are oratorios: S Gemignano vescovo e protettore di Modena (performed in 1705 and 1715; A-Wn 18.683) and S Teresa (date unknown; A-Wn 18.684). Both are in two parts, scored for four-part string orchestra and four soloists, and introduced by an Italian overture. The music exhibits the conventional early 18th-century spectrum of recitativo semplice, recitativo accompagnato, continuo and obbligato arias in ABA form, and ensembles. Grazianini seems to have been especially sensitive to the potential of using rhythm, syncopation and the relationship of an aria's vocal line to its orchestral accompaniment as means to delineate character. The madness of the young girl Flavia (and her interest in sexual adventures) in S Gemignano is portrayed by the use in her vocal line of syncopation and of motivic material that is not derived from orchestral motifs. Similar devices portray St Teresa's other-worldly sense of vocation. Possibly, these devices are also a means of constructing female character, for they are not applied to the music of the male characters: indeed, St Gemignano's saintliness and apparent wisdom are portrayed by the very regularity and tight motivic unity of his arias.

SUZANNE G. CUSICK

Grétry, Lucile [Angélique-Dorothée-Louise] (b Paris, 15 July 1772; d Paris, March 1790). French composer. She was the second daughter of the composer A.-E.-M. Grétry; like her two sisters, she was a youthful victim of tuberculosis. Lucile was named in the family after the heroine of Grétry's second Parisian opera (1769). Some details of her life emerge from her father's letter to the Journal de Paris of 29 July 1786, the day of the première of her Mariage d'Antonio. She had received early lessons from her father in counterpoint and declamation, and from Jean-François Tapray (b 1738) in harmony. J.-N. Bouilly's memoirs inform us of her unhappy marriage, as does Grétry's letter of 12 February 1790 (in Froidcourt).

Le mariage d'Antonio takes its point of departure from M.-J. Sedaine's libretto to Richard Coeur-de-lion (1784), in which the young Antonio had acted as Blondel's guide. Blondel now facilitates Antonio's betrothal. Lucile Grétry composed the vocal parts, the bass and a harp accompaniment, which her father scored for orchestra. The Correspondance littéraire praised its musical aptness, attractive melody, and freshness. The work was relatively successful, gaining 47 performances to February 1791. However,

Toinette et Louis, whose libretto was criticized, had only a single performance.

WORKS

Le mariage d'Antonio (comédie mêlée d'ariettes, 1, Mme de Beaunoir [A. L. B. Robineau]), full score (Paris, c1786); Paris, Comédie-Italienne, Salle Favart, 29 July 1786

Toinette et Louis (divertissement mêlée d'ariettes, 2, J. Patrat), Paris, Comédie-Italienne, Salle Favart, 22 March 1787

BIBLIOGRAPHY

Choron-FayolleD; *FétisB*; *GerberL*; *Grove1†* (G. Chouquet); *SainsburyD*; *SchillingE†*

A. D'Origny: *Annales du Théâtre Italien depuis son origine jusqu'à ce jour* (Paris, 1788), iii, 264–5, 299–300

A.-E.-M. Grétry: *Mémoires, ou Essais sur la musique* (Paris, 1789, enlarged 2/1797)

F. M. Grimm: *Correspondance littéraire, philosophique et critique* (Paris, 1813); complete edn, ed. M. Tourneux (Paris, 1877–82)

J.-N. Bouilly: *Mes récapitulations* (Paris, 1836–7)

M. Brenet: *Grétry, sa vie et ses oeuvres* (Paris, 1884), 190, 194–5

P. Long Des Clavières: *La jeunesse de Grétry et ses débuts à Paris* (Besançon, 1920)

G. de Froidcourt: *La correspondance générale de Grétry* (Brussels, 1962), 131–3, 151

D. Charlton: *Grétry and the Growth of Opéra-Comique* (Cambridge, 1986)

DAVID CHARLTON

Grever, María [La Portilla y Torres, María Joaquina de] (*b* León, Guanajuato, 16 Aug 1885; *d* New York, 15 Dec 1951). Mexican composer. The daughter of Francisco de la Portilla, a Spaniard, and Julia Torres Palomar, a Mexican, she was a child prodigy and was said to have composed a Christmas carol at the age of four. Taken to Spain in childhood, she travelled over Europe with her parents and later claimed to have received musical advice from Franz Lehár. On returning to Mexico she studied singing with her maternal aunt, Cuca Torres. In 1907 she married Leo Augusto Grever, an American oil company executive.

From 1916 she and her husband lived in New York. She appeared in four professional recitals there, in 1919, 1927 (a programme of her 'song dramas' at the Little Theatre, including the première of her one-act *The Gypsy*), 1928 (at the Pythian Temple, before the Mexican ambassador and involving six singers and a Japanese dancer) and 1939 (at the Guild Theatre, including the première of her miniature opera *El cantarito*; she was praised for 'her innate gift of spontaneous melody'). She is credited with 850 songs (see Moreno Rivas) of which at least 18 won enduring popularity in Mexico. She wrote her own opera librettos and most of her own romantic lyrics. Her first international popular song successes belonged to the 1920s. *Bésame* (*Kiss me*, 1921) was succeeded in 1928 by *Júrame* (*Promise me*), popularized by operatic tenor José Mojica. Her three greatest commercial triumphs were *Magic in the Moonlight* (*Te quiero dijiste*, 1929), sung by Jane Powell and by Ann Southern in the film *Nancy Goes to Rio* (1950); *What a Diff'rence a Day Made* (*Cuando vuelvo a tu lado*, 1934), revived in 1959 as a best-seller for Dinah Washington; and *Ti-Pi-Tin* (1938), introduced in the USA by Horace Heidt and his Brigadiers. On her death, Grever's remains were taken to Mexico City and her bust placed in the composers' gallery, Chapultepec Park. Her music is published by Peer, Edward B. Marks and Leo Feist.

BIBLIOGRAPHY

New York Times (15 Dec 1919, 14 Feb 1927, 27 Feb 1928, 6 March 1939)

Obituary, *New York Times* (16 Dec 1951)

Y. Moreno Rivas: *Historia de la música popular mexicana* (Mexico City, 1979), 174

Enciclopedia de México (Mexico City, 1987), vi, 3491

ROBERT STEVENSON

Grigsby [née Pinsky], **Beverly** (*b* Chicago, 11 Jan 1928). American composer and teacher. She studied ballet and frequently attended theatrical performances in Chicago before moving to Los Angeles in 1941. After three years of premedical study she changed to composition and became a pupil of Ernst Krenek, who introduced her to electronic music in 1958. She attended California State University, Northridge (BA 1961, MA 1963), and the University of Southern California (DMA 1986). She has also studied with Ingolf Dahl, Gerald Strang and Robert Linn. Grigsby's further studies included computer music at Stanford University and Carnegie Mellon University (Pittsburgh), where she was a fellow, and medieval music at Solesmes, France, and the RCM in London. In 1963 she returned to California State University, Northridge, where she founded the computer music studio and taught until she retired in 1992.

Grigsby's operas and dramatic cantatas have been produced in the USA, Europe and Brazil. Her music contains complex melodic and rhythmic elements, and she often uses a synthesizer to generate sonic layers horizontally interwoven with either acoustic or electronically altered sounds produced by live performers.

WORKS

selective list

Stage: Augustine the Saint (dramatic cantata), frags., 1975; Moses (opera), 1978, unperf; The Mask of Eleanor (opera), 1984; The Vision of Saint Joan, 1v, live/computer-generated orch, 1987

Vocal: Songs on Shakespeare Texts, S, 1949; Love Songs, T, gui, 1974

Orch: Conc., kbd, orch, 1993; Conc. for Orch, 1994

Chamber and solo inst: 2 Faces of Janus, str qt, 1963; 5 Studies on 2 Untransposed Hexachords, pf, 1971; Dithyrambos, vn, vc, 1975; 3 Movements, gui, 1982; Trio, vn, cl, pf, 1984; Wind Qnt, 1990

Computer (some with live performers): A Little Background Music, 1976; Shakti I, fl, tape, 1983; Occam's Razor, 1985; Shakti II, S, tape, 1985; Shakti III, cl + tabla, tape, 1989; Shakti IV, ob, tape

Also music for film, TV and video

CATHERINE PARSONS SMITH

Grimani, Maria Margherita (*fl* early 18th century). Italian composer, apparently active at Vienna. Nothing is known about Grimani's early training or her life; she may have lived intermittently in Vienna between 1713 and 1718, when her three extant oratorios were performed at the Vienna court theatre. (She was the last of several women composers for the Viennese court in the early 18th century believed by Wellesz to have been regular canonesses – certainly, they were not employed by the court as musicians.) She may have been related to Pietro Grimani, the Venetian ambassador extraordinary (later doge) who negotiated the alliance (against the Turks) between Venice and the Emperor Charles VI in 1713, the year in which the first oratorio, *Pallade e Marte*, was performed, on the emperor's name-day (4 November). That work and *La visitazione di Elisabetta* (performed immediately after *Pallade e Marte* and in 1718) celebrate Charles's martial success against 'infidels'. *La decollazione di S Giovanni Battista* was given in 1715. The librettists are unknown (Köchel's statement that the text of *La decollazione* was written by Domenico Fillipeschi rests on a confusion with A. M. Bononcini's oratorio of the same title, 1709).

Grimani's oratorios follow the pattern established by Alessandro Scarlatti: all begin with an Italian overture for four-part string orchestra. Most arias are da capo (a few are *AA'A*), accompanied by continuo, string orchestra, or, occasionally, obbligato instruments. In the extreme simplicity of their descriptive techniques and in their renunciation of dramatic effects the arias show 'an impressive command of the art of expression' (Schering). Unlike the works of J. J. Fux and Antonio Caldara, they use

virtually no counterpoint. Many arias exploit heroic and martial effects in both voice and accompaniment, even in a female context such as that of *La visitazione di Elisabetta*. In that work, the most varied of the three, the *Ave Maria* and *Magnificat* are both set as *recitativo semplice*; an accompanied recitative sung by Mary prophesies the birth of a new hero, son of an Austrian Emperor named Carlo. Mary's arias are distinctive in their short regular phrases and slow harmonic rhythm, adumbrating *galant* style as a means to characterize her humility.

WORKS

all oratorios

Pallade e Marte, S, S, ob, str orch, 4 Nov 1713; presentation score ded. from Bologna, 5 April 1713, *A-Wn* 17741

La visitazione di Elisabetta, S, A, A, B, str orch, 1713; full score, *Wn* 17668

La decollazione di S Giovanni Battista, 1715; 4 str pts, *Wn* 17667

BIBLIOGRAPHY

WurzbachL

L. von Köchel: *Johann Joseph Fux*, suppl. viii (Vienna, 1872)

A. von Weilen: *Zur Wiener Theatergeschichte* (Vienna, 1901)

A. Schering: *Geschichte des Oratoriums* (Leipzig, 1911)

E. Wellesz: 'Die Opern und Oratorien in Wien 1660–1708', *SMw*, vi (1919), 5–138

U. Manferrari: *Dizionario delle opere melodrammatiche* (Florence, 1955)

F. Hadamowsky: *Wien: Theater Geschichte von der Anfänge bis zum Ende des Ersten Weltkriegs* (Vienna, 1988)

SUZANNE G. CUSICK, RUDOLF KLEIN

Grøndahl [née Backer], **Agathe (Ursula)** (*b* Holmestrand, 1 Dec 1847; *d* Christiania [now Oslo], 4 June 1907). Norwegian composer and pianist. She first studied the piano in Christiania with Otto Winter-Hjelm and Halfdan Kjerulf, then in Berlin at Theodor Kullak's Music Academy (1865–7) and later (1871–2) with Hans von Bülow in Florence and Liszt in Weimar. She additionally studied theory and composition with L. M. Lindeman in Christiania. Influential in Norway as both performer and teacher, she also made concert tours in the other Scandinavian countries and in Germany and England. Her chief significance, however, was as a composer of songs (of which she wrote about 190) and piano pieces and a number of Norwegian folksong arrangements; her orchestral compositions are limited to two works, composed in Berlin, 1868–9, an 'Andante quasi allegretto' (lost) and a Scherzo in E major; only the MS of the Scherzo (for woodwind, horns and string orchestra) survives.

Agathe Grøndahl

The best of Grøndahl's songs, such as the cycles *Barnets vårdag* ('The Child's Spring Day') to poems of A. Jynge, and *Ahasverus*, to poems of B. S. Ingemann, belong to the standard Norwegian Romantic song repertory. Their strength lies in the shapely, singable melodies reflecting the moods of the texts. Although the piano generally plays a supporting role, only rarely functioning independently, the accompaniments are nonetheless carefully worked out and sometimes include elements of tone-painting. Most of Grøndahl's songs are in varied strophic form, but there are also simple strophic and through-composed examples.

Her piano works are for the most part descriptively titled lyric pieces in simple song forms or, less often, in larger fantasy-like forms. Among the best known are the *Serenade* (op.15 no.1), *Ballade* (op.36 no.5), *Sommervise* ('Summer Song'; op.45 no.3) and the fairy-tale suite *I blaafjellet* ('On the Blue Mountain'; op.44). The concert studies are among her finest works, and some of them make considerable technical demands on the performer. Although Grøndahl's career occurred in the heyday of late Romanticism, her style remained conservative and was principally modelled on the music of earlier composers, including Schubert and Mendelssohn. The folk-influenced Norwegian tradition, which left its stamp on

many of her contemporaries, seems not to have had much effect on her music; its principal qualities are melodic charm and an assured and balanced harmonic style.

WORKS

selective list;
published in Oslo unless otherwise stated

Songs: Sommerliv [Summer Life] (H. Hertz), 4 songs, op.7 (Stockholm, 1879); 4 Gesänge, op.10 (1879); 6 sange, op.16 (1884); 7 folkeviser og romanser, op.18 (1886); Serenade (E. von der Recke), op.21 (1888); Blomstervignetter (W. Bergsøe), 5 songs, op.23 (1888); Bryllupsmorgen [Wedding Song] (H. Gréville), op.28 (1890); 10 sange (V. Krag), op.29 (1892); [9] Norske folkeviser, op.34, arr. S (1894); Barnets vårdag [The Child's Spring Day] (A. Jynge), song cycle, S, pf, op.42 (1899); Sommer (Jynge), 8 songs, op.50 (1900); Ahasverus (B. Ingemann), 6 songs, op.56 (1902); 6 deutsche Liebeslieder aus der Jugend, op.60 (1903); Endnu et streif kun av sol [One More Glimpse of the Sun] (Somerset), op.70 (1907)

Pf character-pieces, incl. 3 morceaux, op.15 (Copenhagen, 1882); 4 skizzer, op.19 (1886); Suite, 5 movts, op.20 (1887); 6 idylles, op.24 (1888); 3 klaverstykker, op.25 (1890); [10] Fantasistykker, op.36 (1895); Serenade, F#, op.37 (Copenhagen, 1896); 3 ungarske studier, op.38 (1896); I blaafjellet [On the Blue Mountain], suite, 6 pieces, op.44 (1897); [5] Fantasistykker, op.45 (1897)

Pf studies incl. 6 consert-etuder, op.11 (1881); 3 études de concert, op.32 (Copenhagen, 1895); Etudes de concert, op.47 (1901), op.57 (1903), op.58 (1903)

Pf arrs.: [11] Norske folkeviser og folkedanse, op.30 (1891); [8] Folkeviser og folkdanse, op.33 (1894)

For fuller list see Sandvik

BIBLIOGRAPHY

I. Hoegsbro: *Biography of the Late Agathe Backer-Gröndahl* (New York, 1913)

W. P. Sommerfeldt: *Boktrykker Christopher Grøndahls efterkommore* (Oslo, 1916)

O. M. Sandvik: *Agathe og O. A. Grøndahl* (Oslo, 1948) [with catalogue of works]

K. M. Ganer: *Agathe Backer Grøndahls klaveretyder* (diss., U. of Oslo, 1968)

K. Michelsen, ed.: *Cappelens musikkleksikon* (Oslo, 1978–80)

G. Risa: *Agathe Backer Grøndahl som romansekomponist: en analyse av et utvalg romanser* (diss., U. of Oslo, 1980)

N. Grinde: *Norsk musikkhistorie* (Oslo, 3/1981; Eng. trans., 1991)

C. Dahm: *Kvinner komponerer: 9 portretter av norske kvinnelige komponister i tiden 1840–1930* (Oslo, 1987)

NILS GRINDE

Gubaydulina [Gubaidulina], **Sofiya Asgatovna** (*b* Chistopo'l, Tatarstan, 24 Oct 1931). Russian composer. She attended the Kazan' State Conservatory (1949–54), studying the piano with L. G. Lukomsky and G. M. Kogan and composition with A. S. Leman. She continued her composition studies with N. I. Peyko and V. Ya. Shebalin

Sofiya Asgatovna Gubaydulina in 1993, holding an Indian plucked drum, with (behind) sitar, tablā and bāyā, and (in front) a Japanese koto

at the Moscow Conservatory (1954–63). Since completing her education, she has worked primarily as a free-lance composer, although for a short time she was a member of staff at the Moscow Experimental Electronic Studio (1969–70).

Gubaydulina is regarded as one of the leading composers in Russia, with Al'fred Shnitke and Edison Denisov. Officially banned during the period of stagnation, she was an important representative of unofficial art. During this period, her works were familiar only to a narrow circle; in the 1980s, however, she achieved international recognition and later became known in her homeland as well. Between 1990 and 1992 festivals of her music took place in Russia, Japan, Italy and Germany.

In 1975 Gubaydulina founded the group Astreya with composers V. P. Artyomov and V. Ye. Suslin. Using a process of joint improvisation, the group aspired to achieve spiritual connection through sound, seeking absolute unity between an initial idea and its realisation. This experience coincided with Gubaydulina's own experiments with sound, an ongoing interest evident in the unusual performing techniques that are employed in her works, including 'shimmering' chords that involve glissandos of harmonics, *con le dita* variants such as tapping fingers on strings, and creating a 'breathing' effect on the bayan. She also assigns unusual roles to traditional instruments, for example featuring a double bass, a bass clarinet or a bassoon as soloist. She pays particular attention to percussion in her works, frequently utilizing exotic instruments.

According to Kholopova, Gubaydulina's output falls into discrete style periods. A preparatory period, during which she produced large-scale works, preceded the first main division, which began in 1965 with *Pyat' etyudov* ('Five Etudes'). From this time, the composer focussed on chamber works; the period is characterized by a radical expansion of sound expression and by the use of serial techniques, as in *Noch' v Memfise* ('Night in Memphis', (1968). During the second period, which started in 1978, Gubaydulina began to explore the potential of orchestral and vocal genres. She focussed more closely on rhythmic and temporal issues; in some works, structures are based on the Fibonacci series. The role of rests has also been investigated, culminating in the extraordinary conductor's solo in *Stimmen . . . Verstummen . . .* (1986; see illustration on p.202). In the score of *Alleluja* (1990), colour or coloured light is given a rhythmic function, the progression of which determines the structure of the work. During this latter period, the tension and anxiety of the late 1960s gave way to a more harmonious and stable mode of expression, evident in the works of her mature style.

Gubaydulina's music is marked by profound religious feeling. Every element of her compositions has symbolic meaning; entire works or movements are often associated with parts of the mass or are given titles derived from Biblical verse. Kholopova asserts that 'creation', 'spirituality', 'animation' and 'soul' are key concepts underlying the composer's work. Two parallel worlds frequently co-exist in her music, crossing at moments of climax; for example, contrasting sound images may alternate against a background of continuous crescendo until a break occurs and the instrumental drama begins. Moreover, the notion of 'binary oppositions' is manifest in titles such as 'Vivente – non vivente', 'Light and Dark', 'Pari e dispari'. By evoking such polarities, Gubaydulina creates her own religion, defining it as 're-ligio – the restoration of links, . . . the legato of life'. Her goal is the reconciliation of contradictory voices; this is articulated clearly in *Alleluja*, in which she unites plainsong, Russian Orthodox chant (*znamenniy rospev*), the 'Tuba mirum' (from the Requiem Mass) and Buddhist recitations. During the 1980s, the composer's idiom broadened to encompass additional polar extremes – microchromaticism versus archaic diatonicism, the avant garde versus reminiscences of the past – in

order to intensify internal contrasts even more vividly.

Gubaydulina's literary interests range from Hāfiz to T. S. Eliot. Her vocal chamber work *Perception* (1983) sprang from the correspondence, consisting of music and poetry, that she exchanged with the German writer Francisco Tanzer. She also receives inspiration from certain performers, whose gestures and intonations provide initial ideas for new pieces; for this reason, entire groups of compositions are connected with and dedicated to the percussionist M. I. Pekarsky, violinist Gidon Kremer, cellist V. K. Tonkha and bayan player F. R. Lips.

WORKS

Stage: Begushchaya po volnam [Flying on the Waves] (ballet, after A. Grin), 1963; Era vodoleya [Age of Aquarius], oratorio-opera-ballet, 1991

Orch: Sym., 1958; Pf Conc., 1959; Poema-skazka [Fairy-Tale Poem], 1971; Detto no.2, vc, inst ens, 1972; Conc., bn, low str, 1975; Conc., jazz band, orch, 1976 [after text by A. Fet]; Introitus, conc., pf, chamber orch, 1978; Te salutant, capriccio, 1978; Offertorium, conc., vn, orch, 1980, rev. 1982, rev. 1986; Sem' slov [Seven Last Words], vc, bayan, str, 1982; Stimmen . . . Verstummen . . ., sym., 12 movts, 1986; Pro et contra, 1989; The Unasked Answer, 3 orchs, 1989

Vocal orch: Fatseliya (vocal-sym. cycle, M. M. Prishvin), S, orch, 1956; Noch' v Memfise [Night in Memphis] (cantata, ancient Egyptian texts, trans. A. Akhmatova and V. Potapova), Mez, men's chorus, orch, 1968; Rubayyat (cantata, from Omar Khayyám, Hāfiz, Khakani), Bar, chamber orch, 1969; Stupeni [Stufen; Steps] (R. M. Rilke), speaking chorus, orch, 1972; Chas dushi [Hour of the Soul] (M. Tsvetayeva), Mez/C, wind ens, 1974, another version, Mez, perc, orch, 1976, rev. 1988; Laudatio pacis (oratorio, J. A. Comenius), S, A, T, B, spkr, 2 choruses, orch, 1975, collab. M. Kopelent and P.-H. Dittrich; Alleluja, boy's v, chorus, org, orch, 1990; Aus dem Stundenbuch (conc., R. M. Rilke), spkr, men's chorus, vc, orch, 1991

Other choral: Posvyashcheniye Marine Ivanovne Tsvetayevoy [Homage to Marina Tsvetayeva] (suite, Tsvetayeva), 1984; Likuyte pred Gospoda [Jauchzt der Gott; Rejoice before God], chorus, org, 1989

Vocal chamber: Rozï [Roses] (5 romances, G. Aygi), S, pf, 1972; Pesenki-schitalki [Counting Rhymes] (5 children's songs, J. Satunovsky), 1v, pf, 1973; Perception (from F. Tanzer and *Psalms*), S, Bar, 7 str, 1983; Posvyashcheniye T. S. Eliotu [Homage to T. S. Eliot], S, octet, 1987; Ein Walzerspass nach Johann Strauss, S, octet, 1987; 2 songs (Ger. folk poetry), Mez, fl, vc, hpd, 1988

Chamber and solo inst: Pf qnt, 1957; Intermezzo, 8 tpt, 16 harps, perc, 1961; Pf Sonata, 1965; 5 etyudov [études], harp, db, perc, 1965; Sonata, perc, 1966, rev. as Detto no.1, org, perc, 1978; Concordanza, chamber ens, 1971; Str Qt no.1, 1971; Muzïka dlya Klavesina i udarnïkh instrumentov iz kollektsii Marka Pekarskogo [Music for Hpd and Perc from Mark Pekarsky's Collection], 1972; Rumore e silen-

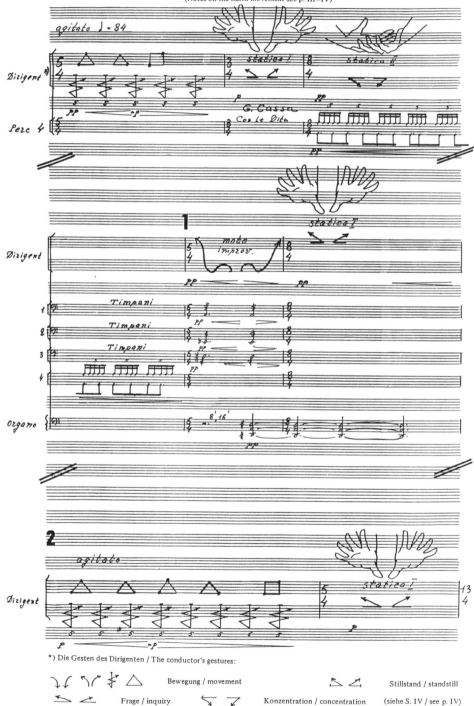

Page from Gubaydulina's 'Stimmen . . . Verstummen . . .' (1986) showing part of the solo for the conductor

zio, hpd/cel, perc, 1974; 10 etyudov (Preludii), vc, 1974; Quattro, 2 tpt, 2 trbn, 1974; Sonata, db, pf, 1975; Trio, 3 tpt, 1976; Svetloye i tyomnoye [Light and Darkness], org, 1976; Tochki, linii zigzagi [Dots, Lines and Zigzags], b cl, pf, 1976; Duo-Sonata, 2 bn, 1977; Misterioso, 7 perc, 1977; De profundis, bayan, 1978; Yubilyatsiya [Jubilation], 4 perc, 1979; In croce, vc, org, 1979; Sad radosti i pechali [Garten von Freuden und Traurigkeiten; Garden of Joy and Sadness], fl, harp, va, spkr (ad lib), 1980; Descensio, 3 trbn, 3 perc, harp, hpd/cel, cel/pf, 1981; Raduysya [Rejoice!], sonata, vn, vc, 1981; V nachale bïl ritm [In the Beginning there was Rhythm], 7 perc, 1984; Quasi hoquetus, bn, va, pf, 1984; Et ex-specto, sonata, bayan, 1985; Str Qt no.2, 1987; Str Qt no.3, 1987; Str Trio, 1989; Slïshish' li tï nas, Luidzhi, vot tanets, kotorïy stant-suyet dlya tebya obïknovennaya derevyannaya treshchotka [Do you Hear us, Luigi, This is the Dance that the Ordinary Wooden Rattle will Make for you], perc, 1991; Chyot i nechet [Pari e dispari; Even and Odd], 6 perc, hpd, 1991; Silenzio, bayan, vn, vc, 1991; pieces for pf, fl, hn, tpt, tuba, domra
Elec: Vivente – non vivente, synth, tape, 1970
Film scores: Vertikal', 1966, dir. S. Govorukhin; Maugli, 1971, after R. Kipling; Balagan [The Circus Tent], 1980, after F. García Lorca, dir. I. Garanina; Velikiy Samoyed, 1981, dir. A. Kordon; Kafedra [The University Chair], 1982; Chuchelo [The Scarecrow], dir. R. Bïkov; Koshka, Kotoraya gulyala sama po sebe [The Cat that Walked by himself], 1984, after Kipling, dir. Garanina

Principal publishers: Muzïka, Sovetskiy Kompozitor, Hans Sikorski

BIBLIOGRAPHY
V. Bobrovsky: 'Otkroyte vse okna!' [Open All the Windows], SovM (1962), no.2, pp.23–8
V. Kholopova: 'Obnovleniye palitrï' [New Colours on the Palette], SovM (1968), no.7, pp.28–30
—— : 'Dramaturgiya i muzïkal'nye formï v kantate S. Gubaydulinoy "Noch'" v Memfise"' [Dramaturgy and Musical Forms in Gubaydulina's 'Night in Memphis'], Muzïka i sovremennost', viii (1974), 109–30
M. Yakubov: Sofiya Gubaydulina (Moscow, 1981)
C. Bachmann: 'Konstruktiv vermittelte Gefühle', NZM, Jg.143 (1982), 43–5
L. E. Fay: 'Sofia Gubaidulina', Encore, iii/2 (1988), [1, 9–10]
V. Kholopova: 'Mir muzïki Sofii Gubaydolinoy' [The World of Gubaydulina's Music], Muzïkal'naya zizhn' (1988), no.14, pp.8–9
Yu. Makeyeva: 'I eto – shchast'ye' [And this is Happiness], SovM (1988), no.6, pp.22–7 [interview]
D. Kadantsev: 'Est muzïka nad nami . . .' [There is Music above us . . .], Ogonyok (1989), no.9, p.17 [interview]
M. Kurtz: 'Sofia Gubaidulina: an den Schwelle nach innen', Das Goetheanum, xl (1989)
G. Rozhdestvensky: Preambuly [Preambles] (Moscow, 1989)
V. Kholopova: 'Muzïka spasyot mir' [Music will Save the World], SovM (1990), no.9, pp.46–54
—— : 'Der sinfonische Kosmos Sofia Gubaidulina's', Sowjetische Musik im Licht Der Perestroika (Laaber, 1990)
—— : 'Zhertvoprinosheniye' [Offertorium], Muzïkal'naya zizhn' (1990), no.11, p.14
D. Redepenning: ' ". . . reingewaschen durch die Musik . . .", "Stunde der Seele" von Sofia Gubaidulina und Marina Zwetajewa', NZM, Jg.151 (1990), 17–22
V. Kholopova: 'Nikola Berdyayev i Sofiya Gubaydulina: v toi zhe chasti vselennoy' [Berdyayev and Gubaydulina: in the Same Part of the Universe], SovM (1991), no.10, pp.11–15
E. Restagno and V. Kholopova: Gubaidulina (Turin, 1991)
V. Kholopova: 'Atlantsky vzdokh dushi' [Atlas's Breath of a Soul], Muzïkal'naya zizhn' (1992), no.4, p.8
—— : Sofiya Gubaidulina: putevoditel' po proizvedeniyam [A Guide to Works] (Moscow, 1992)

OLGA MANULKINA

Gubitosi, Emilia (b Naples, 3 Feb 1887; d Naples, 17 Jan 1972). Italian pianist and composer. She studied at the Naples Conservatory with Beniamino Cesi, Simonetti and Nicola d'Arienzo, graduating in 1906. Her first work, the lyrical sketch Ave Maria, was performed in Naples in 1908, and two years later her one-act opera Nada Delvig was given in Pistoia; another theatre work Fatum was never staged. During her career she taught theory and solfeggio at the Naples Conservatory for over 40 years, was a noted pianist in Italy and abroad, and was responsible for the revival and performance of early Italian choral music, concerts of which she often conducted herself. In 1918 she and her husband the composer Franco Michele Napolitano (1887–1960) founded the Associazione Alessandro Scarlatti, out of which grew the first Neapolitan symphony orchestra. As well as works for the theatre, her orchestral output includes a Notturno and Cavalcata grottesca, and a Piano Concerto (1917) that shows the influence of the pianist and composer Giuseppe Martucci, who was director of the Naples Conservatory from 1902 and her husband's teacher; she also wrote vocal, chamber and instrumental works, including many pieces for solo piano. Like many other Italian musicians of her generation, she divided her interests between the 19th-century symphony orchestra and the rediscovery of the Baroque musical tradition and its sonorities. Gubitosi carried out her many musical activities with great commitment and was a much-respected figure in Italian music.

PAOLA DAMIANI

Guédon de Presles, Mlle (b early 18th century; d c1754). French composer, singer and actress. She may have been the daughter of Honoré-Claude Guédon de Presles. She spent most of her life in Paris, where she worked at the court theatre as a singer, actress and composer under the name 'Mlle Guédon'. Her song 'Sans une brillante fortune' was included in Ballard's *Meslanges de musique latine* (Paris, 1728); during the next four years further songs appeared, next to those of other women, in anthologies printed in The Hague (*Nouveau recueil de chansons choisies*, 1729) as well as Paris (*Meslanges*, 1728–32). Between 1742 and 1748 the *Mercure de France* published several of her *airs*; in 1742 alone her music appeared in six of twelve issues.

Mlle Guédon sang regularly in concerts at court, in the *chapelle* as well as in the *musique de chambre*, where Honoré-Claude had previously been employed; from 1748 she sang many secondary roles in operas at the Théâtre de la Reine in Paris, and her name appears in details of three opera performances in the dauphine's salon.

NICHOLAS ANDERSON, JULIE ANNE SADIE

Guerin, Mlle (*b* Amiens, *c*1739; *fl* 1755). French composer. At 16 she composed *Opera de Daphnis & d'Amalthée* which, according to a letter of 8 August 1755 published in the November *Mercure de France* (pp.214–15), was performed 'dans notre Concert' at Amiens. The writer particularly admired the chaconne for its precision and the beauty of its harmony; he held Mlle Guerin's precocious intellectual and musical accomplishments in highest esteem and offered special praise for the high standards of provincial music-making.

BIBLIOGRAPHY
GerberL; SainsburyD

JULIE ANNE SADIE

Guest [Miles], **Jane Mary** (*b* Bath, *c*1765; *d* after 1814). English pianist and composer. A child prodigy, she appeared in public at Bath before she was six. In London she was reported to have been one of J. C. Bach's last pupils and to have appeared publicly there from 1779. In 1783 and 1784 she played in the Professional Concerts and at Willis's Rooms. In 1783 or shortly after she published six sonatas (op.1) for keyboard with violin or flute accompaniment (the last sonata for piano alone). Their dedication to Queen Charlotte indicates that Guest had attracted the attention and encouragement of the court. The subscription list, headed by the queen, is an impressive register of London society, and the names of several prominent foreign musicians in London suggest that she

also held the respect of professionals. Much later (in 1806 or 1807) she was appointed music instructor to Princess Charlotte, daughter of the Prince of Wales (George IV). She remained on the royal rolls at least until 1814.

Guest's performance was compared by Parke to that of J. S. Schroeter, described as expressive and elegant, 'in so quiet a manner that [the] fingers were scarcely seen to move'. The published sonatas reinforce this comparison; like Schroeter's they stress singing-allegro style and are expressive in their melodic and harmonic chromaticism. The violin part is generally subordinate.

In the 1790s she often appeared under her married name in Rauzzini's concerts in Bath, where she was a prominent teacher. Sainsbury reported that some piano concertos, composed for her own performances at Bath during this period, were very attractive but remained unpublished. Apparently these works have not survived.

BIBLIOGRAPHY
EitnerQ; GerberL; GerberNL; SainsburyD
W. T. Parke: *Musical Memoirs (1784–1830)*, i (London, 1830), 89
C. F. Pohl: *Mozart und Haydn in London* (Vienna, 1867), i, 135; ii, 115, 173
C. L. H. Papendiek: *Court and Private Life in the Time of Queen Charlotte, Being the Journals of Mrs. Papendiek*, i (London, 1887), 152, 253
R. R. Kidd: *The Sonata for Keyboard with Violin Accompaniment in England (1750–1790)* (diss., Yale U., 1967), 443
Z. E. Pixley: *The Keyboard Concerto in London Society, 1760–1790* (diss., U. of Michigan, 1986), 247, 257, 668

RONALD R. KIDD

Guraieb, Rosa (*b* Matías Romero, Oaxaca, 20 May 1931). Mexican composer, of Lebanese origin. She was educated at the Mexico City Conservatory, before studying at Yale University (1954) and in Bayreuth. Her first composition teacher was José Pablo Moncayo; in 1970 she joined the Carlos Chávez Workshop and later studied with Mario Lavista and Daniel Catan. Among her principal works are two string quartets, a Trio for oboe, bassoon and piano, and a Piano Concerto.

BIBLIOGRAPHY
E. Pulido: 'Mexico's Women Musicians', in *The Musical Woman: an International Perspective*, ii: *1984–5*, ed. J. L. Zaimont and others (Westport, CT, 1987), 313–34.

Guran, Nazife (*b* Vienna, 5 Sept 1921). Turkish composer. As the daughter of a Turkish diplomat she spent a large part of her life abroad, studying music in Vienna and in Istanbul. In Berlin she studied composition with Paul Höffer and piano with Rudolf Schmidt. In 1959 she accompanied her husband to Eastern Anatolia where she set up a Philharmonic Society in Diyarbakir. In 1969 she spent some time in Germany, furthering her education, after which she returned to Turkey, settling in Istanbul. In addition to music for children's plays she has composed orchestral pieces, songs and choral works, some of which have been published in Turkey and elsewhere, and broadcast on radio and television. Her principal works are a Violin Sonata (1950), a Piano Sonata (the 'Sphinx', 1945) and Three Piano Pieces (1985).

FARUK YENER

Guy, Helen. *See* HARDELOT, GUY D'.

Gyring, Elizabeth (*b* Vienna, 1886; *d* New York, 1970). American composer of Austrian birth. She studied at the Vienna Academy of Music with Joseph Marx (harmony and counterpoint) and Ludwig Czaczkes (piano). She became a US citizen in 1944. Her music, which dates from the 1940s, is tonal, somewhat dissonant and well-constructed. She wrote one opera, *Night at Sea and Day in Court* (1954), and several other large-scale works, including the cantatas *The Reign of Violence is Over* (H. W. Longfellow) for chorus, string orchestra and piano (1943) and *The Secret of Liberty* (R. Davenport) for four solo voices, chorus and orchestra (1945). In addition to orchestral music she has composed many chamber pieces (mostly for wind instruments), solo works for piano and organ, and songs. Her manuscripts are at Washington State University and the American Music Center.

BIBLIOGRAPHY

CohenE; *WAM*

E. R. Anderson: *Contemporary American Composers* (Boston, 2/1982)

CATHERINE PARSONS SMITH

H

Haenel de Cronenthall, Louise (Augusta Marie Julia) (*b* Graz, 18 June 1839; *d* Paris, ? *c*1876). Austrian composer resident in France. At the age of 17 she went to Paris to study at the Conservatoire. She became a prolific composer in almost every genre, including dance forms, nocturnes, fugues and sonatas for piano; her output includes five symphonies, a string quartet and ten transcriptions of Chinese music. Some of the 22 piano sonatas were first given the title 'morceau de salon', others were arrangements from her symphonies. Of the 96 opus numbers, 29 were published between 1860 and 1880. Five are dedicated to her teachers at the Conservatoire – Auguste Franchomme, A.-J.-D. Tariot and Camille Stamaty – but most are dedicated to family members, a cross-section of the socio-political and military élite of Germany, Russia and the Netherlands. By 1870, apparently, 16 of her works had been performed, in orchestral arrangements, at the Théâtre du Champs-Elysées and in diverse concerts and casinos in France and Germany.

Many of her works have pastoral subjects, especially the early ones: the first sonata, 'Bonheur pastoral', includes a shepherd's song, a harvesters' song and a peasants' rondo; the first symphony, 'La cinquantaine villageoise', depicting a country wedding, also ends with a rondo. Except for the fugues, all her compositions have evocative titles. Sonata no.15, for example, first called 'Appassionata', later 'La pathétique' – in spite of the fact that its textures and form are more Schumannesque than Beethovenian – starts with a Fantasy-Adagio (rather than a sonata Allegro), subtitled 'Douleur', and continues with a scherzo movement, 'Espoir', and a finale, 'Allégresse'.

The Chinese transcriptions, dedicated to diplomats responsible for the Chinese pavilion at the Paris Exposition of 1867 and to a relative in the Dutch navy, are perhaps her most interesting works. The original music ranges from an ode from 860 BC and a Confucian air to an 18th-century tea song composed by an emperor, two dances, a pastoral and a Western-style drinking song. Several of them employ white-note pentatonic scales over series of parallel 5ths and have sinuous lines that presage Debussy's musical embroidery. These songs, for which she received an Exhibition medal, were performed each day during the Exhibition.

WORKS
*selective list; printed works published
in Paris unless otherwise stated*

Orch: 5 syms.: no.1 'La cinquantaine villageoise', no.2 'Salut au printemps', no.3 'La fantastique', no.4 'Apollonia', no.5 'Bonheur pastoral'

Pf: Bonheur pastoral (Morceau de salon no.1; Sonata no.1), op.3 (Naumburg and Paris, 1862); Regrets et souvenirs (Nocturne no.2), op.4 (Naumburg and Paris, 1860); Rosina (Varsovienne no.1), op.6 (1860); Josepha (Varsovienne no.2), op.11 (Naumburg, 1860); Le Burgergarten de Naumburg (Le jardin des bourgeois; Polka no.1), op.14 (1860); La gentillette (Polka no.3), op.24 (1861); Une partie de chasse (Morceau de salon no.9; Sonata no.9), op.28 (Naumburg and Paris, 1861); Frantziska (Valse no.4), op.29 (1860); Dorothea (Valse no.5), op.34 (1867); Jonquille, gavotte, op.38 (1878); Le val des roses (Valse no.6), op.39 (1860); Salut au printemps (Morceau de salon no.12; Sonata no.12), op.40 (1860); Filius dolorosus (Nocturne no.5), op.42 (Naumburg and Paris, 1861); Musettes gasconnes en forme de rondos, op.43 (Naumburg, 1862); Zufriedenheit (Satisfaction; Morceau de salon no.13; Sonata no.13), op.44 (Naumburg and Paris, 1862); La pathétique (Sonata no.15), op.48 (1870); La source, impromptu, op.60 (1869); Fleurs de mai, bagatelles, op.65 (1870); Les voix de la mer, andante, op.96 (1874); La vie en rose (Polka no.5), op.75 (1869); Antonia (Mazurka no.3) (1879); L'allarine, impromptu (1880)

Chinese transcrs. (arr. pf): La chanson du thé (18th-century, Emperor Ch'ien-lung), op.68 (1867); Le chalumeau de Niou-Va, op.69 (1867); La tasse d'or, op.73 (1867); La descente de l'hirondelle (1867); La grande tournante, danse chinoise (1867); La danse des plumes (1869)

BIBLIOGRAPHY
FétisBS; SchmidlD

JANN PASLER

Hagan, Helen Eugenia (*b* Portsmouth, NH, 10 Jan 1893; *d* New York, 6 March 1964). American composer, pianist and teacher. She attended the Yale University School of

*Title-page of 'La tasse d'or'
(Paris: Gérard & Cie, 1867)
by Louise Haenel de
Cronenthall*

Music (1906–12), studying composition with Horatio Parker. After graduation (BMus), she performed her Piano Concerto with the New Haven SO. A Yale fellowship enabled her to study with Vincent d'Indy and Blanche Selva at the Schola Cantorum in Paris. Having briefly pursued a performing career, she turned to education and became head of the music department at the George Peabody College for Teachers. Her one-movement concerto in C minor, one of the earliest extant works in the genre by an African-American woman composer, adheres to the Lisztian tradition, featuring a virtuoso solo part and fluid chromatic harmonies (the manuscript is held at Yale University; it was also arranged for two pianos). Hagan's other works included piano pieces and a violin sonata (before 1912), all lost.

BIBLIOGRAPHY
SouthernB
M. C. Hare: *Negro Musicians and their Music* (New York, 1936), 375
S. Dannett: *Profiles in Negro Womanhood*, v/1 (New York, 1966), 139
E. Southern: *The Music of Black Americans* (New York, 1971), 280
H. Walker-Hill: *Piano Music by Black Women Composers* (New York, 1992), 39

DAVID METZER

Hagen, Elizabeth Joanetta Catherine von [van] (*b* ?Amsterdam, 1750; *d* Suffolk Co., MA, 1809/10). Dutch-American keyboard player, teacher and composer. Nothing is known of her early years. She married Peter Albrecht van Hagen and in 1774 emigrated to the USA, settling first in Charleston, where their son Peter Albrecht von Hagen jr was born in about 1780. In 1789 they moved to New York, where they were active as performers, teachers and managers of a series called the 'Old City Concerts'. She performed piano sonatas and concertos in the series but published only a set of variations, *The Country Maid* ('L'amour est un enfant trompeur'). When they moved to Boston in

1796, they changed their name from 'van' to 'von' and established themselves as music dealers and publishers of patriotic and ballad opera songs. From 1799 she taught the piano, in Salem as well as in Boston, and succeeded her husband, on his death in 1803, as organist at King's Chapel.

BIBLIOGRAPHY

GroveAM ('Hagen, von'; B. Cantrell and others)
J. Tick: *American Women Composers before 1870* (Ann Arbor, 1983), 65–6

JULIE ANNE SADIE

Hajdú, Júlia (*b* Budapest, 8 Sept 1915; *d* Budapest, 23 Oct 1987). Hungarian composer and pianist. She was born into a well-established Jewish family in Budapest; they owned the city's 'English Park', a famous entertainment park, and her father was a well-known journalist. She graduated as a piano teacher from the Budapest Academy of Music, where she studied with Zoltán Kodály (folk music) and György Ránki (composition and instrumentation). For more than 40 years she was one of the most successful composers of light music in Budapest. Her song melodies perpetuated in an original manner the typical, operetta-like nostalgic atmosphere of the city. As a pianist she worked with leading Hungarian actors and singers, who generally congregated in the capital. Among her most famous partners were Lili Neményi, Mária Mezei, Hanna Honthy, the Latabár brothers and the opera singers Sándor (Alexander) Svéd and Mihály Székely. Her chansons and cabaret songs achieved remarkable popularity. She was one of the founders of Hungarian Television (1957) and until her death remained one of its most prolific producers of entertainment programmes. She received many awards in recognition of her artistic activities.

WORKS

Stage: 14 operettas, musicals etc., incl. Igaz mese [True Story] (musical comedy, 1, S. Darvas), Szolnok, Szígligeti Theatre, 28 April 1953; Füredi komédiások [The Comedians of Fured] (E. Kaszó and M. Tóth), Miskolc, National Theatre, 22 Dec 1959; Pest megér egy estet! [Pest is Worth an Evening] (T. Róna and I. Brand), Budapest, Margaret Island Open-Air Theatre, 15 July 1960; Doktorkisasszony [Miss Doctor] (I. Kertész and I. Bedő), 1960, Budapest, Vidám Theatre, 8 Feb 1962; Fedezzük fel Pestet [Let's Discover Pest!], 1961; Zénó és az asszonyok [Zeno and the Women] (musical, G. Rácz), 1970; Falusi esküvő [Village Wedding] (mini-musical, J. Kováts), 1970; Levendula [Lavender] (S. László, rev. K. Szász), Miskolc, National Theatre, 30 Dec 1974; incid. music, incl. Virágzó cseresznyefa [The Cherry Tree in Blossom] (melodrama, I. Simon), 1970; Act sans paroles (S. Becket), 1975

Orch: Keringő (Valse), pf, orch, 1964; Szilveszteri szvit [New Year's Eve Suite], 1964; Vidám nyitány [Happy Overture], 1964; Vidám percek [Happy Moments], 1964; Tánc-suite I–III, 1967; Téli örömök [Joyous Winter], 1967

Also *c*200 songs, chansons and cabaret songs; film scores and many musicals and reviews for TV and radio

RITA KAIZINGER

Halácsy, Irma von (*b* Vienna, 31 Dec 1880; *d* Vienna, 7 March 1953). Austrian violinist and composer. She was the daughter of Eugen Halácsy, a Hungarian botanist. She received piano lessons as a schoolgirl, then studied the violin with Jakob M. Grün and Siegmund Bachrich at the Vienna Conservatory. In spite of a sciatic illness she toured as a concert violinist until about 1912. She then gave up her performing career and devoted her time to teaching and composing. Her compositions include six operas: *Antinoos* (1909), *Abbé Mouret* (1921), *Der Puppenspieler* (1922), *Herz atout* (1923), *Schelmenerbschaft* (1943) and *Salambo* (1948); none has been performed complete. She also composed a Violin Concerto in E minor, op.1; a String Quartet in F, op.4; a Violin Sonata and a ballet. In 1986 many original manuscripts of her compositions were discovered (now in a private collection).

BIBLIOGRAPHY

C. M. Gruber: *Nicht nur Mozarts Rivalinnen: Leben und Schaffen der 22 österreichischen Opernkomponistinnen* (Munich, 1990)

EVA RIEGER

Hall, Pauline (Margrete) (*b* Hamar, 2 Aug 1890; *d* Oslo, 24 Jan 1969). Norwegian composer. She was the most notable Norwegian composer to follow Agathe Grøndahl. She studied composition with Catharinus Elling (1910–12) and in Paris and Dresden (1912–14). During the years 1934–42 and 1945–63 she was a respected music critic for the *Dagbladet* of Oslo. In this capacity and as president of Ny Musikk (1938–60), she played an important part in promoting new Norwegian music. In her early works, culminating with the *Verlaine-suite* for orchestra, she was influenced by Debussy; her later music is more neo-classical. According to Nils Grinde, 'Her French-inspired mode of expression contrasted strongly with the prevailing national tendencies in [Norwegian] musical life around 1930, and she experienced considerable resistance at the most productive time in her career. After 1945 [the] musical milieu became more receptive to international influence and Pauline Hall received full recognition.' She was made an honorary member of Ny Musikk in 1960, and from that year also received a state artist's pension. She is the author of *25 år Ny musikk* (Oslo, 1963).

WORKS
selective list

Stage: Markisen [The Marquise] (ballet), 1950; incid. music to plays by Aristophanes, M. Bulgakov, F. Dostoyevsky, T. S. Eliot, J. Giraudoux, K. Hansen, H. Ibsen, M. Maeterlinck, W. Shakespeare, T. Williams, among others, 1934–58

Orch: Poème élégiaque, 1920; Verlaine-suite, 1929; Circusbilleder [Circus Pictures], 1933

Chamber: Sonatina, str qt; Suite, fl, ob, cl, bn, hn, 1945

Choral: Smeden og Bageren [The Smith and the Baker], 1932; other choruses

Film and TV scores: Om kjærligheten synger de [They Sing about Love], 1946; Kranes konditori [Krane's Bakery], 1949; Den evige Eva [The Eternal Eve], 1953; Vintersolhverv [Winter Solstice], 1961; To mistenkelige personer [2 Suspicious People]; Skogen gir [The Forest Gives]

Also songs, pf pieces

BIBLIOGRAPHY

B. Wallner: *Vår tids musik i Norden* (Stockholm, 1968)

N. Grinde: *Norsk musikkhistorie* (Oslo, 1971)

A. L. Under: *Pauline Hall og hennes innsats i norsk musikkliv* [Pauline Hall and her Contribution to Norwegian Musical Life] (diss., U. of Oslo, 1977)

K. Michelsen, ed.: *Cappelens Musikkleksikon* (Oslo, 1978–80)

KARI MICHELSEN

Hannikainen, Ann-Elise (*b* Hanko, 14 Jan 1946). Finnish composer and pianist. One of a renowned family of musicians, she studied at the Sibelius Academy (1967–72) with Einar Englund (composition) and Tapani Valsta (piano). In 1972 she settled in Spain, where she studied composition with Ernesto Halffter. Her output consists exclusively of instrumental music, most of it for chamber ensembles. As a composer she is a representative of so-called moderate modernism and has been influenced by impressionism.

WORKS
selective list

Anerfalicas, theme and variations, orch, 1973; Pensamientos, pf, 1974; Toccata fantasia, pf, 1975; Pf Conc., 1976; Cosmos, orch, 1977; Sextet, wind insts, pf; Chachara, fl, pf, 1980; Trio, fl, va, pf; Duo, vn, pf, 1985

KIMMO KORHONEN

Hara, Kazuko (*b* Tokyo, 10 Feb 1935). Japanese composer and librettist. She graduated from Tokyo National University of Fine Arts and Music in 1957, where she studied composition with Tomojirō Ikenouchi. Subsequently, her teachers included Henri Dutilleux and Alexander Tcherepnin (composition), and Pierre Bernac and I. A. Corradetti (voice, 1962–3). She has taught at Osaka University (1968–85), Tokyo National University (1970–83) and Doshisha University (from 1986). Her earlier works were mostly atonal, sometimes dodecaphonic. Since 1981, she has devoted herself to opera, earning high praise, as well as many commissions and prizes. Her operatic style is often modal with a linear emphasis, employing transparent orchestration with colourful percussion embellishments. Her syllabic vocal writing places the focus on declamation, which ranges from Sprechstimme to lyricism.

WORKS
selective list

Opera: The Case Book of Sherlock Holmes: the Confession (J. Maeda, after A. Conan Doyle), 1981; On the Merry Night (Hara, after I. Kikumura), 1982–3; Chieko-Shō (Maeda), 1978, rev. 1984; Sute-hime (Hara, after S. Murō), 1985; Sonezaki-Shinjū (M. Chikamatsu), 1986; Beyond Brain Death (Hara, after S. Fujimura), 1987; The History of Yosakoi-bushi (Hara, after F. Tosa), 1988; Iwanaga-hime (B. Yoshida, after Chikamatsu), 1990; Petro Kibe (Hara, after G. Matsunaga), 1991; Nasu-no Yoichi (I. Narushima), 1991

Orch: Concertino, fl, hpd, str, 1966; Frammento, orch, 1969

Vocal: Yūgatō-Eika (Chūya Nakahara), S, T, fl, vn, va, vc, 1966; Shōmyō-Jion, S, Bar, cl, bn, hn, tpt, trbn, vn, vc, perc, 1972; Psyche: Ballade (Kimura), S, Bar, orch, 1979

Many other chamber pieces

J. MICHELE EDWARDS

Hardelot, Guy d' [Rhodes (née Guy), Helen M.] (*b* Chateau Hardelot, nr Boulogne, *c*1858; *d* London, 7 Jan 1936). French composer, pianist and singing teacher. She was the daughter of an English sea captain and the singer Helen Guy. At the age of 15 she was taken to Paris, where she studied at the Conservatoire under Renaud Maury, and success came in her early 20s with the song *Sans toi* (words by Victor Hugo). Gounod and Massenet were among those who encouraged her in composition, and those who introduced her songs included Nellie Melba, Victor Maurel and Pol Plançon, as well as Emma Calvé, with whom she went to the USA in 1896 as accompanist. After marrying an Englishman she settled in London, where she continued to produce sentimental songs, about 300 in all, notable for their easy melody and typical dramatic climax. They include *Three Green Bonnets* (H. L. Harris; 1901), *Because* (E. Teschemacher; 1902), *The Dawn* (Teschemacher; 1902), *I know a lovely garden*

Guy d'Hardelot

(Teschemacher; 1903) and the song cycle *Elle et lui* (F. E. Weatherly; 1895). She was also a singing teacher, her pupils including Miriam Licette.

ANDREW LAMB

Harraden [Glover], **R. Ethel** (*fl* late 19th century–early 20th century). English composer. She was the daughter of Samuel Harraden (1821–98), a musical instrument importer, and married Frank Glover. Herbert Harraden, who wrote the librettos for two of her operettas and the texts of many of her songs, may have been her brother. Her operettas *His Last Chance* and *The Taboo* were successfully produced in London and favourably received by the critics. Brown and Stratton erroneously credit her sister Beatrice (1864–1936) with the composition of *Ships that pass in the night* (1894), one of her most popular songs.

Harraden's slender talent is at its best in songs such as *Bridget's Reply* and *Peggy and Robin* (both to words by H. Harraden, published in 1882), which are in a bright English folk idiom, touched with tenderness; and Robert Schumann's influence rescues 'At Twilight' (no.2 of Six Characteristic Pieces for violin and piano). She failed, however, when attempting to express deeper emotions: her vocal waltzes are effusively saccharine, and the spoken dialogue of her theatre pieces is usually more interesting than the music.

WORKS
most published works printed in London

STAGE
All about a Bonnet (operetta, 1, H. Harraden), London, 1880s
His Last Chance (operetta, 1, Harraden), London, Gaiety Theatre, 1891 (1891)
The Taboo (operetta, 1, M. Carnes), London, Trafalgar Sq Theatre, 19 Jan 1895
Agatha's Doctor

INSTRUMENTAL
Pf: Une bonne histoire (1877); Sourire d'enfant (1878); 2 Romances, G, B♭ (1893); An Idyll, also for vn, pf (n.d.)
Vn, pf: Rêverie . . . sur le premier Prélude de S. Bach, vn/vc, pf (1885); 2 Melodies (1885); 2 gavottes, G (1887), F (1888); 6 Characteristic Pieces (1888); An Idyll, also for pf (n.d.); Légende (n.d.); Moto perpetuo (n.d.); 6 Pieces (n.d.)
Vc, pf: Rêverie (1885), also for vn, pf; Tristesse (Romance sans paroles) (1886)
Arrs. for pf trio: Andante (1893), from Gluck: Orfeo ed Euridice; Largo, from Handel: Serse (n.d.)

VOCAL
Choral: Over the sea our galleys went (R. Browning), perf. by the Browning Society, 28 Nov 1884; The Pearl, cantata, women's vv (n.d.); The Birth of Flora, women's vv (n.d.)
Duets: When the dew is on the grass (G. Harraden), canon (1889); There is gold upon the hills (G. Harraden), canon (1890); 6 others (n.d.)
Songs: 31 pubd 1877–94 (18 to words by H. Harraden); 13 others (n.d.)

BIBLIOGRAPHY
CohenE; *MEMM*; *PazdirekH*; *StiegerO*
J. D. Brown and S. S. Stratton: *British Musical Biography* (Birmingham, 1897)
J. Towers, ed.: *Dictionary-Catalogue of Operas and Operettas* (Morgantown, WV, 1910)

NIGEL BURTON

Harrison, Annie Fortescue [Hill, Lady Arthur] (*b* Crawleywood, Sussex, 1851; *d* Easthampton, Berks., 12 Feb 1944). English composer. Her famous song *In the Gloaming* (words by Meta Orred) was written in 1876 when she was considering a marriage proposal from the recently widowed Lord Arthur Hill. It was adopted as the regimental march of the 2nd Middlesex artillery, of which Lord Hill was the commanding officer. Her operetta *The Ferry Girl* was performed in London at the Gallery of Illustration, the Savoy Theatre and the Gaiety Theatre. Another operetta, *The Lost Husband*, was also produced in London, at the Opera Comique in April 1886 (vocal score, London, 1886).

JOHN R. GARDNER

Harrison, Pamela (*b* Orpington, 28 Nov 1915; *d* Firle, East Sussex, 28 Aug 1990).

English composer and pianist. She studied with Arthur Benjamin and Gordon Jacob at the RCM (1932–6), where the latter was an important influence. She made her Wigmore Hall début as pianist, and first made a mark as composer with her String Quartet (1944), which was performed at one of the wartime National Gallery Concerts, and the Six Poems of Baudelaire (1944–5). She was a schoolteacher during World War II and also studied Dalcroze eurhythmics, giving exhibitions with Emile Jaques-Dalcroze in Brighton. She died in a car accident.

A slow writer, she produced a small output characterized by gracefulness and clarity, no doubt reflecting her admiration for French music, and exhibiting traits common to her British exemplars, notably Arnold Bax, E. J. Moeran and John Ireland. Within these delimitations, however, she was not afraid of boldness of sound, false relations verging on bitonality being a part of her style that was perhaps suggestive of Ralph Vaughan Williams.

WORKS
most printed works published in London

Orch: A Suite for Timothy, str, 1948 (1953); An Evocation of the Weald, 1954; Concertante, pf, str, 1954; Brimstone Down, small orch, 1958

Vocal: The Lonely Landscape (E. Brontë), 1v, pf, 1944; 6 Poems of Baudelaire, T, str orch, 1944–5; 8 Poems of Walter de la Mare (A Present for Paul), 1v, pf, 1949 (1956); 5 Poems of Ernest Dowson, T, str orch, 1951–2; The Kindling of the Day, 1v, str qt, 1952; 2 Songs (De la Mare), 1v, pf (1954); The Dark Forest (E. Thomas), cycle, T, str, 1957; 8 Songs, 1v, rec, pf, 1959; Ladies' Choice, 1v, vn, harp, 1969; Songs (De la Mare), children's chorus, pf, 1969

Inst: Qnt, fl, ob, str trio, 1944; Str Qt, 1944; Str Trio, 1945; Ww Qt, 1948; Vc Sonata, 1947; Cl Sonata, 1954; Cl Qnt, 1956; Va Sonata, 1956; Idle Dan, vc, pf (1959); 2 Pieces, vc, pf (1959); Anderida, pf, 1960 (1963); 6 Eclogues of Portugal, pf, 1960; Badinage, fl, pf (1963); Chase a Shadow, ob, pf (1963); Faggot Dance, bn, pf (1963); Sonnet, vc, pf (1963); Lament, va, pf (1965); Epithalamium, org, 1967; Pf Trio, 1967; Qt, fl, vn, vc, pf, 1968; Qnt, fl, ob, vn, vc, pf, 1974; 6 Dances for Fanny Simmons, pf duet, 1976; 5 Pieces, fl, pf, 1976; Drifting Away, cl, pf, *c*1978; Septet, cl, bn, hn, vn, va, vc, db, 1980; Octetto Pastorale, 2 ob, 2 cl, 2 bn, 2 hn, 1981; Mariners Way, fl, pf, 1982; Lullaby, vc, pf; Rock Grove Suite, fl, vc, pf, 1989

Principal publishers: Chappell, OUP, Paterson
MSS in private collection; scores, some recordings and list of works in *GB-Lmic*

STEPHEN BANFIELD

Harrison [née Riley], **Susie** [Susan] **Frances** [King, Gilbert; Seranus] (*b* Toronto, 24 Feb 1859; *d* Toronto, 5 May 1935). Canadian composer and critic. She was an accomplished solo pianist and accompanist, and wrote several volumes of poetry and three novels as well as music criticism. She composed many songs and keyboard works, using the pseudonym Seranus for those published in England and the USA and for much of her music criticism; she also used the name Gilbert King for some of her English compositions. Harrison's three-act opera *Pipandor* (to a libretto by F. A. Dixon) incorporated French-Canadian folksongs, a subject on which she lectured. She arranged French-Canadian music for the piano, composed a string quartet on ancient Irish airs and three *Esquisses canadiennes* for piano, and wrote an *Address of Welcome to Lord Landsdowne* (Ottawa, 1883). As a music critic she wrote for a variety of publications; she was also editor of the Toronto (later Royal) Conservatory of Music's *Conservatory Monthly* (1912–13) and principal of the Rosedale branch of the conservatory. Her husband was the organist and conductor J. W. F. Harrison.

BIBLIOGRAPHY
EMC 2 (E. Keillor)
A. E. Wetherald: 'Some Canadian Literary Women – I: Seranus', *The Week* (1888), March

GAYNOR G. JONES

Hartmann [née Zinn], **Emma Sophie Amalie** [Palmer, Frederik] (*b* Copenhagen, 22 Aug 1807; *d* Copenhagen, 6 March 1851). Danish composer. She was the daughter of a wealthy merchant and musical amateur who held chamber music evenings in their home; on one of these occasions she met her future husband, J. P. E. Hartmann. They were married in 1829 and took up residence on the first floor of the Zinn home, where she bore ten children; she died in childbirth. She composed songs and in 1848 began publishing the first of several collections (22 songs in all) under the pseudonym Frederik Palmer, a name borrowed from Thomasine Gyllembourg's story *Extremerne*. In 1907 her youngest son published a collection of her dances for piano in facsimile to mark her centenary; other songs and piano pieces remain in manuscript. Hans Christian Andersen gave eloquent testimony of her in *Mit livs eventyr* (1855).

WORKS
selective list;
all printed works published in Copenhagen

Songs: Romancer (1848); Danske sange (1850); Danske sange (1851); Romancer og sange (1853); other songs, unpubd

Pf: Danse komponerede af Emma Hartmann født Zinn (1907); other pf pieces unpubd

BIBLIOGRAPHY
N. Schiørring: *Musikkens historie i Danmark*, ii (Copenhagen, 1978)
L. A. Jensen: *Emma Hartmann, kvinde og komponist i den borgerlige musikkultur* (thesis, U. of Copenhagen, 1988)

INGE BRULAND

Harvey, Mary. *See* DERING, MARY.

Hasnaş, Irina (*b* Bucharest, 15 July 1954). Romanian composer. She studied at the High School of Music (1961–73) and the Conservatory (1971–8) in Bucharest, where her teachers included Aurel Stroe for composition. In 1987 she became an editor at the Romania Broadcasting Station in Bucharest. Her output includes works for full orchestra, vocal and chamber music, and displays a particular concern for the creation of new musical timbres and combinations.

WORKS

Orch: Conc., 1978; Evocare [Evocation], sym. poem, 1980; Sym. no.1, 1991
Chamber and other inst: Melisme, pf, 1979; Polychromie I, str qnt, 3 ww, 3 brass insts, tape, 1982; Evolutio I–III, 1983–6; Monodie, bn, 1989; Games, vc, 1991
Vocal: Metamorphose, 8vv, wind insts, 1978; Vocile mioriței, 4 solo vv, chorus, 1980; România, choral fantasia, 1981

VIOREL COSMA

Haulteterre [Hauteterre, Hotteterre], **Elisabeth de** (*fl* 1737–68). French composer and violinist. She did not come from La Couture where the Hotteterre family of musicians originated, and there is no demonstrable connection between her and that family. In April 1737 the *Mercure de France* reported that 'Miss Hotteterre, young lady recently arrived from the provinces, has played [at the Concert Spirituel] several times on the violin various sonatas by Mr Leclair with all the intelligence, vivacity, and precision imaginable'. At the end of 1740 her *Premier livre de sonates* for violin and continuo appeared in Paris, dedicated to Jean-Marie Leclair (*l'aîné*). An 'investigation of bowstrokes for novices' included in this book suggests that she gave lessons on the violin. The publication of her 'second' *Concerto à cinq*, for four violins, organ and cello, was reported in the *Mercure* of January 1744. Because this work was announced as op.2, it seems unlikely that there was an earlier concerto, despite the label 'second'. The next known mention of her did not appear until 1768 (*Avant-courier*, 14 November, and *Mercure*, December), when the publication of a *Deuxième recueil d'airs choisis*, with accom-

paniments for the harp composed by 'Madame Lévesque, formerly mademoiselle de Haulteterre', was announced. These notices, and the title-pages of both this and a previously published *Recueil de chansons* with accompaniments for harp or harpsichord, probably indicate the correct spelling of her name. None of her violin compositions seems to have survived, and after the announcement of her second collection of *airs* nothing further about her is known.

BIBLIOGRAPHY
E. Thoinan: *Les Hotteterre et les Chédeville: célèbres joueurs et facteurs de flûtes, hautbois, bassons et musettes des XVIIe et XVIIIe siècles* (Paris, 1894)
M. Brenet: 'La librairie musicale en France de 1653 à 1790, d'après les registres de privilèges', *SIMG*, viii (1906–7), 441
N. Mauger: *Les Hotteterre: célèbres joueurs et facteurs de flûtes, hautbois, bassons et musettes des XVIIe & XVIIIe siècles: nouvelles recherches* (Paris, 1912)
L. de La Laurencie: *L'école française de violon de Lully à Viotti*, ii (Paris, 1923), 130–31
J. A. Sadie: '*Musiciennes* of the Ancien Régime', *Women Making Music: the Western Art Tradition, 1150–1950*, ed. J. Bowers and J. Tick (Urbana and Chicago, 1986), 191–223, esp. 207

JANE M. BOWERS

Havenstein, Birgit (*b* Berlin, 4 Jan 1954). German composer and flautist. She attended the Städtisches Konservatorium, Berlin, for her earliest musical training, after which she studied music education in Berlin, flute at the Berlin Hochschule der Künste, as well as in Zürich with André Jaunet, and composition (also at the Hochschule) with Witold Szalonek. The first performance of her *Szene für Orchester* was given by the Berlin PO in 1985 and the work was awarded a prize the same year at the Forum Junger Deutscher Komponisten für Orchestermusik. She also received prizes at the eighth international composition competition of the 1988 Sommerliche Musiktage Hitzacker for her *Graffiti* for flute, cello and harp. Her early works are predominantly for flute.

WORKS
selective list

Orch: Szene, 1984–5
Chamber and inst: Jeu, fl, 1982; 5 intermezzi, fl, 1983; 4 Gedichte (H. Budde), fl, Sprechstimme, 1984; Fragen, fl, spkr, 1984; Suite, fl, 1985; Niemals vergessen!, (collage, Budde), fl, spkr, 1985; Lament, str qt, 1985; 'alles Vergessene schreit im Traum um Hilfe': Graffiti, fl, vc, harp, 1987; Qarrtsiluni-Stille, fl, 1989; Im Jasmin, anagram, vc, 1989

BIBLIOGRAPHY
'Birgit Havenstein', *Komponistinnen in Berlin*, ed. B. Brand and others (Berlin, 1987), 315–18

BIRGITTA MARIA SCHMID

Hawaii, Queen of. *See* LILI'UOKALANI.

Sorrel Hays, 1988

Hay, Diana Pereira (*b* Sri Lanka, 20 Feb 1932). Danish composer. Her father was Australian, her mother of Irish descent, but she was educated at the Kongelige Danske Musikkonservatorium in Copenhagen. She studied the piano as her main subject, but also composition and orchestration with Vagn Holmboe. Her musical output is small yet original: it consists mainly of piano music, such as *Exercises in Metamorphosis I and II* (1966), *Sonata in Three Phases* (1978), Sonata no.2 (1979) and *I'm Still Alive* (1983), but also includes a further set of *Exercises in Metamorphosis* for string quartet (1967). Hay was a leading figure in the founding of the association Kvinder i Musik (Women in Music) in 1980, and by the 1990s had turned to the composition of computer music for educational purposes.

BIBLIOGRAPHY

I. Bruland: 'Fire danske kvindelige komponister fra det 20. århundrede' [4 Danish Women Composers from the 20th Century], *Kvinders former*, ed. I. Bruland, L. Busk-Jensen and T. Ørum (Copenhagen, 1986), 33–59

INGE BRULAND

Hay, Helen. *See* BLACKWOOD, HELEN.

Hays, Sorrel (Doris Ernestine) (*b* Memphis, 6 Aug 1941). American composer, pianist and mixed-media artist. She studied at the University of Tennessee, Chattanooga (BM 1963), the Munich Hochschule für Musik (piano and harpsichord diploma 1966), the University of Wisconsin (MM 1968) and the University of Iowa (composition and electronic music, 1969); her principal teachers included Harold Cadek, Paul Badura-Skoda, Hilde Somer and Richard Hervig. After winning first prize in the International Competition for Interpreters of New Music (Rotterdam) in 1971, she toured Europe and the USA numerous times as a performer and advocate of new music. In the 1970s and 80s she gave between 60 and 70 premières of other composers' music, including Henry Cowell's Piano Concerto (1978) and works by John Cage, Pauline Oliveros and Marga Richter.

Hays taught at Queens College, CUNY, in 1974–5, and served as artist-in-residence for the Georgia Council for the Arts, 1975–6. She was coordinator of the concert series Meet the Woman Composer, held at the New School for Social Research, New York, in 1976, and in 1980 she organized a conference on 20th-century string quartets composed by women; she has also been the producer of 'Expressions', a radio series about women composers and their music, sponsored by the International League of Women Composers, of which she was assistant chairman from 1979 to 1982. Hays has received many awards and commissions: from the NEA (1977, 1979, 1983), from Radio Cologne, Germany (1983–90), from Opera America and NEA for her opera *The Glass Woman* (1989, revised 1992), and from Meet the Composer, among others. From 1979 to 1989 she was a contributor to *Ear Magazine East*. She took the name Sorrel in place of Doris in 1985.

Hays's piano writing, in the tradition of Charles Ives and Henry Cowell, juxtaposes fiercely bombastic tone clusters with hymn-like passages of extreme serenity; finger stopping of the strings and microtonal experiments contribute to the great range of sonorities explored. The various chamber works entitled *Tunings* (1978–80), incorporating Appalachian fiddle riffs and a hymn tune, combine fine instrumental writing with rhythmic vitality and lyric beauty. The piano work *Sunday Nights* (1977) was the first of a number of pieces to evoke her Southern background, in which she grew increasingly interested in the mid-1970s, a time when she also began to expand her sound-palette. Her research into the musical aspects of Southern speech resulted in the tape music of *UNI* (1978) and *Southern Voices for Tape* (1980). These speech patterns also became the basis of her large orchestral work *Southern Voices for Orchestra* (1981, commissioned for the 50th anniversary of the Chattanooga Symphony), which translates spoken dialects into orchestral and vocal sound; the work was the subject of a television documentary in 1982. Her involvement in the feminist and peace movements in the mid-1970s became central to her work as a composer during the 1980s. *Exploitation* (1981), written for the first International Congress on Women in Music, commented wryly on the status of women as performers and composers at that conference and elsewhere. *Weaving* (1984) and *Disarming the World*, a political docudrama for radio, are products of her pacifism and her experience with the Seneca Women's Peace Encampment, as is her documentary film *CD: Civil Disobedience* (1988).

Hays has written many mixed-media compositions: the radio drama commissions from Radio Cologne in the 1980s enabled her to create substantial works in this genre, produced in studios in Cologne and New York. Her opera *The Glass Woman* (1989–93), a most ambitious work, concerns six renowned women collectors, including Bessie Smith and Peggy Guggenheim, commemorated by their own museums; another work dedicated to influential women, in this case Ethel Smyth and Ruth Crawford Seeger, is *90s: a Calendar Bracelet* (1990), a cycle of pieces for MIDI grand piano. *The Clearing Way* (1992), for contralto and orchestra, is based on Native American rituals for the passing of the spirit of the dead and cleansing of the departed's dwelling.

WORKS
selective list

OPERA
Love in Space (radio opera), 1986; Touch of Touch (video opera), 1989; The Glass Woman (S. Hays, S. Ordway, N. Rhodes), 1989–93; The Venus Project (radio opera, J. Smith); The Everybodydom (children's radio opera, Hays), 1994

CHAMBER, INSTRUMENTAL
Scheveningen Beach, fl qnt, 1972; Pieces from Last Year, 16 insts, 1976; SensEvents, 6 insts, tape, 1970–77 [several versions]; For A. B., cl, pf, 1977; Breathless, b fl, 1978; Characters, conc., hpd, str qt, 3 ww, 1978; Segment/Junctures, va, cl, pf, 1978; Tunings [nos.1–8]: [1] db, 1978, [2] fl, cl, bn, 1979, [3] solos for fl, cl, vn, S, 1979, [4] cl, pf, S, 1979, [5] str qt, 1980, [6] va, 1980, [7] 2 vn, 1980, [8] vn, vc, pf, S, 1981
UNI, dance suite (D. Hays), str qt, fl, chorus, tape, 1978; Winded, pic, 1978; Lullabye, fl, vn, pf, 1979; Tommy's Trumpet, 2 tpt, 1979; Fanfare Study, hn, tpt, trbn, 1980; Homing, vn, pf, 1981; Rocking, fl, vn, va, 1983; After Glass, 10 perc, 1984; Harmony, str, 1986; Bits, pf, DX7 synth, 1987; Juncture Dance III, 7 perc, 1988

PIANO
Chartres Red, 1972; If, pf, multiple tapes, 1972; Wildflowers, pf, synth, 1972–9; PAMP, pf, tape, bird whistles, 1973; Sunday Nights, 1977; Etude Base Basses, 1978; Past Present, 1978; Saturday Nights, pf, tape, 1980; Sunday Mornings, 1980; 90s: a Calendar Bracelet, MIDI grand pf, 1990

ELECTRONIC, MIXED-MEDIA
Hands and Lights, pf, lights, 1971; Duet for Pianist and Audience, 1971; Translations and Comments, pf, tape, 1971; Round Around, plastic sculptures, lights, tape, 1974; SensEvents for Lincoln Center Out of Doors Festival, 6 insts, dancers, sound sculpture, lights, tape, 1977; Certain: Change, pic, b fl, tape, 1978; Reading Richie's Paintings, synth, fl, slides, 1979; Southern Voices for Tape, tape, slides, S/nar, 1980
Exploitation, S/chanter, tape, 1981; The Gorilla and the Girl, tape, 1981; Only, pf, 2 tapes, slides, film, 1981; Water Music, S, tape, water pump, slides, opt. vn, opt. baby pool, 1981; Celebration of No, tape, film, opt. vn/S/pf trio, 1983 [several versions]; The Needy Sound, tape, 1983; M.O.M 'N P.O.P., 3 pf, tape, film, slides, mime, 1984; Something (to Do) Doing (G. Stein, Hays), 16 chanters, tape, 1984; Weaving (Interviews), opt. S, pf, film, slides, 1984
Flowing Quilt (M. Ries), video, soundtrack, 1987; CD: Civil Disobedience, documentary film with music and choreog., 1988; Echo US Continental, 1988; Whatchasay/Wie bitte? (radio play), 1988; Take a Back Country Road, DX7 kbd, Casio elec sax, ob, opt. v, 1989; The Hub: Megopolis Atlanta, 1989; Sound Shadows, kbds, ob, didjeridu, 1v, sax, perc, dance, video, 1990– ; Scaling, synth, didjeridu, 1991

VOCAL, VOCAL ORCHESTRAL
Star Music (Hays), chorus, tape, bells, 1974; For Women, 5 songs (A. Aldrich, B. Anderson, Hays, E. St V. Millay, A. Waldeman), S, pf, 1976; Set of Cheeky Tongues, S, pf, 1976; Hands Full, 2-pt chorus, drums, tape, 1977; Delta Dad (S. Ordway), 1v, pf, 1979; In-de-pen-dance, chanter, nylon str, 1979; Circling Around (B. Swan), 4 songs, Bar, fl, pf, 1981; Hush, 1v, reco-reco, sand block, 1981; Rest Song, SATB, opt. fl, 1981
Southern Voices for Orch, S, orch, 1981, excerpt Blues Fragments, arr. S, pf; Ex-, Rock-, In-, Re-, chant, tape, 1982; Rest Song, mixed chorus, 1982; Lullago, B, scat singer, 1982; Celebration of No, taped women's vv/(tape, vn, vc, prepared pf, slides, chanters), 1983; Hei-Ber-Ny-Pa-To-Sy-Bei-Mos, S, fl, perc, 1990; Searching Song, S, pf, 1990; The Clearing Way: a Chant for the 90s, C, orch, 1992; Dreaming the World, B, 4 perc, pf, 1993

Many film scores, 1971–5; works for children, incl. vocal, ens, tape, pf pieces

Principal publishers: A. Broude, Peer-Southern, C. F. Peters, Silver Burdett, Tallapoosa, Tetra

BIBLIOGRAPHY
CC (L. Goldberg)
H. Smith: 'She Creates Art Form with Sights, Sounds', *Atlanta Constitution* (10 Jan 1976)
M. Campbell: 'Doris Hays: Artist with a Vision', *Pittsburgh Post-Gazette* (10 Oct 1977)
P. Frank: 'Adoration of the Clash', *Fanfare*, iv/1 (1980), 263–5

E. Salzman: 'Classical Discs and Tapes: Special Merit', *Stereo Review*, xlv/3 (1980), 85 [review]
A. Kozinn: 'Women Composers Get Piccolo Forum', *News and Courier/Evening Post* [Charleston, SC] (30 May 1981)
S. Aeckerle: 'Thinking in Sound', *Troubadoura* [Munich] (12 June 1981)
A. Kozinn: 'Electronic Music on Discs Reflects a Maturing Genre', *New York Times* (5 June 1983)
A. Richter: *Frau und Musik* (diss., Hochschule für Musik, Lippe, 1985)
K. Gann: 'Opera Glasses', *Village Voice* (22 Aug 1989)

MYRNA S. NACHMAN,
CATHERINE PARSONS SMITH

Heckscher [née Massey]**, Celeste de Longpré** (*b* Philadelphia, 23 Feb 1860; *d* Philadelphia, 18 Feb 1928). American composer. She was born into an artistic family and began composing at the age of ten. Her early training in piano and composition, however, was obtained in spite of her parents' objections. In 1883 she married Austin Stevens Heckscher; they had two daughters and two sons. In the 1890s Heckscher studied composition with Henry Albert Lang and orchestration with Wasili Leps in Philadelphia; she is also reported to have studied in Europe. She composed two operas, *The Flight of Time* and *Rose of Destiny* (Philadelphia, 1918); an orchestral suite, *Dances of the Pyrenees*, which was also staged as a ballet (Philadelphia, 1916); chamber music, piano works and songs. In 1913 she gave a concert of her own compositions at the Aeolian Hall in New York. For many years she was president of the Philadelphia Operatic Society.

CAROL NEULS-BATES

Heiter, Amalie. *See* AMALIE.

Heller, Barbara (*b* Ludwigshafen am Rhein, 6 Nov 1936). German composer and pianist. From 1954 to 1957 she studied the piano with Helmut Vogel and composition with Hans Vogt at the Mannheim Hochschule für Musik, and went on to teach the piano there from 1958 to 1962. In 1962–3 she continued her studies at the Hochschule für Musik in Munich with Eric Ten Berg (piano) and Harald Genzmer (composition); she subsequently studied at the Accademia Chigiana, Siena, with A. F. Lavagnino (film music) and at Darmstadt summer schools. She was a founding member of the Internationaler Arbeitskreis Frau und Musik and from 1986 to 1992 was on the board of the Institut für Neue Musik und Musikerziehung in Darmstadt. Her output is centred on piano and chamber music; after

the mid-1980s, however, she began to work alongside women visual artists, and in her sound-installations she has experimented with tape and with sounds from the environment. As a performer and editor, Heller has dedicated herself principally to the music of forgotten women composers.

WORKS
selective list

Solo pf; 8 kurze Klavierstücke, 1962; Presto, 1966; Andantino, 1977; MMM – Meer Musik als Malerei, 1978, Pianomuziek voor Anje, 1980; Johannisbeeren – Currants, 1984; Tre lettere scarlattine, 1984; Furore – ein Traum, 1986; Intervaalles, 1987; Böhmisches Lied, 1989; Für Unica Zürn, 1992
Other inst: 3 Stücke, fl, pf, 1961; Meine Musica Domestica (J. Ringelnatz), S, pf, 1961; Kinderspiele, rec, pf, 1962; Früher oder später, cl, pf, 1981; Solovioline, vn, 1982; Solo, ob; 1984; Eins für zwei, vn, vc, 1985; Trauernde Sirenen, vn, pf, 1986; Drei mal dreiundzwanzig, rec qt, 1987; Lalai – ein Schlaflied zum Wachwerden?, vn, pf, 1989; Incantata I, kbd, 4 wine glasses, 1991; Auf der Suche nach dem Frühling, fl, 1993
Sound-installations, incl.: Schmerz, 1987; Hintergrund – Vordergrund, 1989; Traumreise, 1991; Klang-Zeichen, 1993
Film music

Principal publishers: Furore, Moeck, Schott

BIBLIOGRAPHY

R. von der Grün, ed.: 'Barbara Heller, Musik und Leben', *Venus Weltklang* (Berlin, 1983), 136–47
B. Heller: 'Musik ist geschlechtlos', *5th International Congress on Women in Music: Heidelberg 1989*, 280–82
B. Sonntag and R. Matthei, eds.: 'Am liebsten wär ich selbst Musik: Gespräch zwischen Barbara Heller und Klarenz Barlow', *Annäherungen an sieben Komponistinnen*, i (Kassel, n.d.), 7–16

ROSWITHA SPERBER

Henderson, Moya (*b* Quirindi, NSW, 2 Aug 1941). Australian composer. After leaving school she spent nine years as a nun at the Sacre-Coeur convent in Melbourne. In 1969 she received permission to study music at the University of Queensland, and subsequently left her Order. Later she studied music-theatre with Mauricio Kagel in Germany. The 50 or so compositions written since the late 1970s have been particularly concerned with cultural myths, including those of aboriginal people, women, and landscape and conservation. Characteristic works on such themes include *Sacred Site*, for organ and tape (1983), the piano concerto *Celebration 40 000* (1987) and *Meditations and Distractions on the Theme of the Singing Nun*, a radio music drama (1990). She rejects as misguided the description 'neo-romantic', which her music has sometimes attracted, but was prepared to describe her song cycle *Pellucid Days* (1989) as 'passionate, intense and lyrical'.

WORKS

selective list

Music-theatre: Clearing the Air, 4 wind insts, db, 1974; Mutti Kirche, 4 singer-actors, 1975; Secco, perc, 1976; Stubble, S, male v, 1976; Scene from Chloe, S, Mez, ens, 1984

Orch: The Dreaming, str orch, 1985; Celebration 40000, pf conc., 1987

Chamber and other inst: Alanbiq, perc, 1977, rev. 1985; Min-Min Light, cl, vn, va, vc, 1982; Sacred Site, org, tape, 1983; Cross-Hatching (Rarrk), pf, 1984; Who'd-a-thought-it, cl, va, pf, 1984; Kudikynah Cave, str qt, 1987; G'day Africa, cl, va, vc, pf, 1990; Waking up the Flies, pf trio, 1990

Vocal: 6 Urban Songs (P. White), Mez, orch, 1983; Confessions to my Dogs (M. Henderson), Bar, pf, 1986; Songs about Music (G. Harwood), mixed chorus, 1987; Pellucid Days (B. Beaver), S, Mez, hn, str orch, 1989; Wild Card (D. Hewett), S, vc, pf, 1991

Radio scores: Currawong: a Symphony of Bird Sounds, 1988; Meditations and Distractions on the Theme of the Singing Nun, music drama, 1990

BIBLIOGRAPHY

Fuller-LeFanuRM

GRAHAM HAIR, GRETA MARY HAIR

Henderson, Ruth Watson. *See* WATSON HENDERSON, RUTH.

Henneman, Ig (*b* Haarlem, 21 Dec 1945). Dutch composer. She studied the viola and violin at the conservatories of Amsterdam and Tilburg and began her career as an orchestral musician. Later (in the early 1990s), she studied composition with Robert Heppener. In 1978 she co-founded the all-female rock band F. C. Gerania; she has also played with Several Singers and a Horn and Nedly Elstak's Paradise Regained Orchestra. In 1985 she founded the Ig Henneman Quintet, for which she composes all written material. Since 1980 she has received numerous commissions as a composer for film scores and concert music, as well as jazz and improvised music. In 1983 she composed a score for the Russian silent film *Babï Ryazanskiye*, directed by Olga Preobrazhenskaya. Her output includes *Big Marble* for chamber orchestra (1986), *Le tigri de mare* for two alto saxophones and orchestra (1988), *Sottosuolo* for bass clarinet (1990) and *Si tira avanti* for accordion (1991). Her music is published by Donemus.

HELEN METZELAAR

Hensel, Fanny. *See* MENDELSSOHN, FANNY.

Hernández, Gonzalo Gisela (*b* Cardenas, 15 Sept 1912; *d* Havana, 23 Aug 1971). Cuban composer and teacher. She studied in Havana at the Bach Conservatory with Maria Muñoz de Quevedo (1929–35) and

at the Conservatorio Municipal with José Ardévol (1940–44), and then in the USA at the Peabody Conservatory (1944–7) with Gustav Strube and Theodore Chandler. From 1947 to 1953 she was conductor of the Choral de La Habana and until 1962 was also a teacher and administrator at the Hubert de Blanck Conservatory. She became particularly involved in music education, developing together with the composer Olga de Blanck Martín a new method of music teaching and writing educational material; she was also co-founder of Ediciones de Blanck, publishers of educational and academic music books. After the Cuban Revolution (1959) she taught at the Instituto Nacional de Cultura and became an adviser to several government and educational organizations and, in 1969, to Cuban Radio.

Hernández's early works, written between 1924 and 1940, consist mostly of small-scale and educational pieces, and include the *Pequeña suite* (1929) for piano. In the early 1940s she was a founder member of the Grupo de Renovación Musical (1942–8), which included Argeliers León, Harold Gramatges, Hilario González, Edgardo Martín and Serafín Pró and was led by Ardévol. She adopted a contemporary, neo-classical and impressionist language and continued to write mainly small-scale vocal, choral and chamber works, of increasing quality and individuality. In 1944 she was awarded the National Composition Prize of Cuba for her *Suite coral* (1942) to a text by F. García Lorca. During the final stage of her creative life, from 1947 until her death, a strengthening of the nationalist aesthetic is evident, a nationalism whose roots lay in the works of 19th-century composers Manuel Saumell Robredo and Ignacio Cervantes and which gained legitimacy between 1925 and 1940 with Amadeo Roldán and Alejandro García Caturlat. Hernández increasingly used melodic material from Afro-Cuban songs as well as the rhythmic content of forms such as the *son* and *guajira*; she also set the words of contemporary Cuban poets and wrote children's songs. A significant work from this period is the choral cycle *Tríptico* (1967) to verses by the poet Nicolás Guillén. The strongly nationalist aesthetic of the final years does not indicate a break with the past but rather the integration with and enrichment of previously established principles.

WORKS

selective list

Incid. music: Hamlet (W. Shakespeare), solo vv, women's vv, orch, 1948; El alcalde de zalamea (P.

Calderón de la Barca), solo v, women's vv, gui, 1949; Pedro de Urdemala (M. de Cervantes), solo v, vc, str orch, 1950; Juana de Lorena (M. Anderson), 1956; Blanca Nieves y los siete enanitos (D. Alonso), 1965

Choral: Canción (E. Ballagas), 4vv, 1942; Romance (R. Santos), 7vv, 1942; Suite coral (F. García Lorca), 4vv, 1942; Soneto coral (L. de Gongora), 5vv, 1943; 2 villancicos tradicionales: Noche buena, Tres reyes (M. Aguirre), 2/3vv, 1943–4; Aleluya (García Lorca), 3vv, 1944; 2 villancicos cubanos: Son de navidad, Palmas reales (C. Méndez), 4vv, 1948–9; Salmo Davidico, women's vv, str orch, 1954; Diálogo de octubre, 2 solo vv, women's vv, orch, 1965; Tríptico (N. Guillén), 4vv, 1967; Como allá (J. Martí), 4vv, 1967; La muchacha de Quang Nam, 1969

Chamber and orch: Pequeña suite, vn, vc, 1941; Vn Sonatina, 1945; Tríptico cubano, orch, 1954; Cubana no.3, guajira, 2 ob, 2 vn, va, vc, db, 1963

Pf: Pequeña suite, 1929; Sonata no.1, C, 1943; Sonatina Scarlatiana, 1944; Preludio cubano, 1953; Cubanas, 1957

Songs (1v, pf): Mi corazón lo trajo el mar (M. Aguirre), 1943; Romancillo (García Lorca), 1944; La palma (J. R. Jiménez), 1945; Tránsito (R. Tagore), 1945; Diálogo (D. M. Loynaz), 1955; Vispera (M. Brull), 1957; Miraba la noche el alma (A. Gaztel), 1964; Dones (C. Solis), 1964; Canto X (C. Vitier), 1966; Iba yo por un camino (Guillén), 1970; c50 children's songs

Also educational music (theoretical and practical, collab. O. de Blanck Martín) and arrs.

Principal publisher: Ediciones de Blanck
MSS in *CU-Hn*

BIBLIOGRAPHY

R. Martínez: *Gisela Hernández: biografía· y catálogo* (Havana, 1987)

A. Castro: *Acerca del estilo de creación en la obra de Gisela Hernández* (Havana, 1990)

ALICIA VALDÉS CANTERO

Hier, Ethel Glenn (*b* Cincinnati, 25 June 1889; *d* Winter Park, FL, 14 Jan 1971). American composer, teacher and pianist of Scottish origin. She received a diploma in piano from Cincinnati Conservatory in 1908 and immediately established what became a thriving piano studio. In 1911 she returned to the Conservatory for further piano study and took composition lessons with Edgar Kelley; in Germany during the summer of 1912 she studied composition with Hugo Kaun. In 1917 she moved to New York, opening teaching studios there and in New Jersey, and continued composition studies at the Institute of Musical Art, first with Percy Goetschius and later with Ernest Bloch. During subsequent summers she worked in Europe with Alban Berg, Egon Wellesz, and Gian Francesco Malipiero, and in 1923 she resumed piano study with Carl Friedberg.

Hier began publishing teaching pieces for piano in 1912. By 1918 her more ambitious works had won her the first of 14 fellowships at the MacDowell Colony. In 1925 her works were included in the Festival of American Women Composers in Washington, DC, and later that year, with Amy Beach, Mary Howe, Gena Branscombe and others, she founded the Society of American Women Composers. She organized the Composers Concerts in New York in 1948 and frequently gave lectures on modern music and other topics. *Asolo Bells* was played at the Festival of American Music at Eastman School of Music in 1939, and in 1945 by the Cincinnati SO; as part of Three Orchestral Pieces it won a Composers Press publication award in 1953. Hier's music combines elements of impressionism with popular and jazz styles (as in *Click o' the Latch* and *Badinage*). Her use of colouristic effects can be seen in *Asolo Bells*; in *A Day in the Peterborough Woods* and *The Song Sparrow* Hier drew on birdsong. Within an extended tonal scheme she often used parallel triads and tone clusters in a nonfunctional manner. Hier also wrote a play, *The Boyhood and Youth of Edward MacDowell* (1926). Her manuscripts are held at the American Music Center, the College Conservatory of Music at the University of Cincinnati, and the Delta Omicron Library, Cincinnati.

WORKS

Orch: 5 works, 1926–9, incl. Carolina Christmas; 3 Orch Pieces: Foreboding, Asolo Bells, Badinage (Study in Blues) (1954)

Chamber: 9 works, incl. 2 str qts, 3 qnts, suites

Pf: 34 works, incl. Theme and Variations, op.17 (1921); A Day in the Peterborough Woods, op.19 (1924)

Vocal: 20 songs, incl. Hail! Glorious Morn!, sacred song (1912); The Time to Woo (S. M. Peck) (1914); Dreamin' Town (P. L. Dunbar) (1919); La chanson du cordonnier (J. Bois), 1923; Click o' the Latch (N. B. Turner) (1938); The Hour (J. Rittenhouse) (1949); The Song Sparrow (N. Kreymborg) (1955)

Choral: 3 works, incl. The Mountain Preacher (J. Still) (1966)

Principal publishers: CFE, Composers Press, Willis

BIBLIOGRAPHY

'Contemporary American Musicians, no. 168: Ethel Glenn Hier', *MusAm*, xxxiv/2 (1921), 29

K. Pendle: *Ethel Glenn Hier* (MS, American Music Center)

ADRIENNE FRIED BLOCK

Hildegard of Bingen (*b* Bemersheim, nr Alzey, Rheinhessen, 1098; *d* Rupertsberg, nr Bingen, 17 Sept 1179). German abbess of Rupertsberg, mystic, writer and composer. She is known for her religious and diplomatic activities, and also for her literary works.

Miniature of Hildegard of Bingen with her amanuensis, from the 'Riesenkodex', 1180s

Clement V (1305–14) and John XXII (1316–34) it came to nothing. But her name is in the Roman Martyrology and her feast is 17 September.

Even in childhood she saw visions, which later intensified, and in 1141 with the aid of the monk Volmar she felt a divine command to record what she experienced. The result, *Scivias*, which contains 14 of the song texts of her *Symphonia armonie celestium revelationum*, took ten years to write and comprised 26 revelations. This was followed by the *Liber vite meritorum* (1158–63) and *Liber divinorum operum* (1163–70). The three works form a trilogy of apocalyptic, prophetic and symbolic visions. Her prophecies and miracles brought her fame. She was known as 'the Sybil of the Rhine' and was consulted by and held long correspondences with popes, emperors, kings, archbishops, abbots and abbesses, lower clergy and laymen, and was involved in politics and diplomacy. She later wrote lives of St Disibod (1170–72) and St Rupert (1172). Her two works on natural history and medicine, *Physica* and *Cause et cure*, both date from 1150–60. (A tropical deciduous tree, the *Hildegardia*, was named after her by Schott and Endlicher in the early 19th century.)

Hildegard's composition of lyrical poetry goes back to at least the 1140s. She collected it together in the early 1150s under the title *Symphonia armonie celestium revelationum*. As it survives (in two main sources, both in early German neumes: Dendermonde, Benedictine Abbey, MS 9, from the 1170s, and *D-Wll* 2, 'Riesenkodex', from the 1180s), it comprises 77 poems, all with music – though eight of these are placed together as two short successions of antiphons (six and two respectively), so that the total may sometimes be cited as 71. (Before the Dendermonde manuscript was discovered, with two unique items, the number was often given as 75 or 69; hence the confusion in the literature.) Of these, 43 (or 37) are called 'antiphons' in the sources, 18 'responds', seven 'sequences' and four 'hymns'; the remainder are a Kyrie, an alleluia and three miscellaneous items. Together they form a liturgical cycle, the majority bearing designations to feasts or classes of feast. Most feasts have a pair of items: antiphon-respond. Some, especially the locally revered saints, have more: thus St Rupert has three antiphons and a sequence, St Disibod two antiphons, two responds and sequence, St Ursula and her 11 000 virgins two responds, hymn and sequence. The remaining se-

The latter include recorded visions, medical and scientific treatises, hagiography and letters; also lyrical and dramatic poetry, which has survived with monophonic music.

Hildegard's parents, Hildebert and Mechtild, were members of the nobility. They promised her, as their tenth child, to the service of the Church. When she was eight they entrusted her for her novitiate to the recluse Jutta of Spanheim, sister of Count Meginhard, who with her followers occupied a cell of the Benedictine monastery of Disibodenberg. At 15 she took the veil. Jutta died in 1136, and Hildegard succeeded her as superior. Between 1147 and 1150 she founded a monastery on the Rupertsberg, in the Rhine valley near Bingen, and settled there with 18 sisters. In or around 1165 she founded a daughter house at Eibingen, on the opposite bank of the Rhine close to Rüdesheim. Shortly before this she was called 'abbess' in letters of protection drawn up by Frederick Barbarossa (16 April 1163). Between 1160 and 1170 she undertook four extended missions through Germany. After her death in 1179, Popes Gregory IX and Innocent IV (1227–41, 1243–54) ordered a process of information concerning her possible canonization. Although repeated by

quences are to the Holy Spirit, the BVM, St Eucharius and St Maximinus.

The poetry is laden with brilliant imagery and shares the apocalyptic language of the visionary writings. It has some affinity with the poetry of Notker Balbulus from the 9th century, and is akin in its richness and imaginative quality to that of Peter Abelard and Walter of Châtillon. The music is not drawn from plainchant and is in some respects highly individual. Hymns and sequences are the least elaborate, though rarely purely syllabic: responds are highly complex in style, with elaborate roulades; antiphons occupy a stylistic middle ground, often alternating syllabic and highly melismatic setting. The responds are supplied with verse and repetenda, and occasionally also *Gloria Patri* utilizing melodic material from the verse; the antiphons have 'EVOVAE' and the hymns 'Amen'. The sequences use poetic and melodic parallelism, but far from strictly.

The music of Hildegard is remarkable above all for its formulaic nature: it is made up of a comparatively small number of formulae, or melodic patterns, which recur many times under different melodic and modal conditions and are the common property of her poetic output. These formulae differ from the recurrent melodic elements ('timbres', to use Pierre Aubry's word) of Adam of St Victor's work. While the latter are fixed phrases which are assembled and reassembled in a patchwork quilt manner (akin to centonization), Hildegard's formulae are melodic 'frameworks' which occur in innumerable different guises.

Pfau (1988, 1990) has argued for a view of Hildegard's songs as 'text-music compounds'; that is, for text and music not as separate entities, but as intimately related, as parallel syntaxes mirroring one another, and at the same time functioning within an idiosyncratic system of modes.

Hildegard also wrote a morality play, *Ordo virtutum*, in dramatic verse. This contains 82 melodies, much more nearly syllabic in setting than the *Symphonia*. The earliest morality play by more than a century, it presents the battle for the soul, Anima, between the 16 Virtues and the Devil. Its language is highly mystical.

Dronke (1969–70) has proposed that the two manuscripts of the *Symphonia* represent the cycle in two states of development. Of these, the first (Dendermonde MS 9), completed by 1158, may have included the *Ordo virtutum* at the beginning as an integral part of the cycle. The second (*D-WIl* 2) excludes the

Ordo along with two other small items (*O frondens* and *Laus Trinitati*), and shows the cycle reshaped so that the items to the Holy Spirit precede those for the Virgin Mary and so that the items to St Ursula and her 11 000 virgins come under the heading of 'Virgins' rather than following 'Innocents'; it also has additional items, including all of those for the Trier saints, Matthew, Eucharius and Maximinus, the item for Boniface, and *O viridissima*, 'the most brilliant of Hildegard's compositions to the Virgin Mary'. The list below presents the second of these states, with the main material of *D-WIl* 2 and its supplementary material (mostly sequences and hymns) telescoped together, but with the two discarded items from the Dendermonde manuscript included.

Newman (1988, pp.8–12, 68–73) draws attention to a miscellany of homilies, letters, and other materials by Hildegard (in *D-WIl* 2; ed. Pitra, 1882), including the texts of 26 items of the *Symphonia*, these last lacking repetenda, doxologies, amens and liturgical cues. The 26 may, she speculates, be earlier, unpolished, pre-*Symphonia* versions, perhaps evidence that Hildegard did not initially plan a liturgical cycle, but only later collected her songs into a systematic order, her last songs

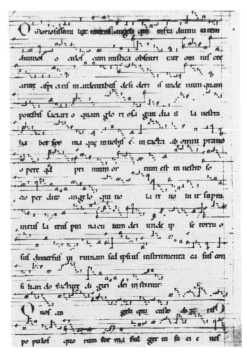

The antiphon 'O gloriosissimi' from Hildegard of Bingen's 'Symphonia armonie celestium revelationum', 1170s

being incorporated posthumously into the cycle. Newman tentatively suggests a division into early, middle and late compositions: the 14 pieces in *Scivias*, and all or part of the *Ordo virtutum*, by 1151; the 26 of the miscellany from the late 1150s; and the remaining pieces in Dendermonde and *D-Wll 2* after the 1150s.

WORKS

Editions:

Die Kompositionen der heiligen Hildegard, ed. J. Gmelch (Düsseldorf, 1913) [facs.]

Der heiligen Hildegard von Bingen Reigen der Tugenden: Ordo virtutum, ed. M. Böckeler and P. Barth (Berlin, 1927) [B]

Hildegard von Bingen: Lieder, ed. P. Barth, M.-I. Ritscher and J. Schmidt-Görg (Salzburg, 1969) [E]

Abbess Hildegard of Bingen (1098–1179): Sequences and Hymns, ed. C. Page (Newton Abbot, 1982) [P]

The 'Ordo virtutum' of Hildegard of Bingen, ed. A. E. Davidson (Kalamazoo, 1985) [V]

Manuscript sources:

Belgium, Dendermonde, Benedictine Abbey of St Peter and St Paul, MS 9, *Symphonia* [D]

D-Wll 2, ff.466r–478v, *Symphonia* [W]

D-Wll 2, ff.132v–133r, *Scivias* [S]

D-Wll 2, ff.404r–407v, 'Miscellany' [M]

Scivias and miscellany items are indicated after the title by S and M respectively, followed by the number, in parentheses: (S1), (M1)

Symphonia armonie celestium revelationum:

God, Father and Son
O vis eternitatis (M10) (ant), W 1; E 58
O magne pater (M6) (ant), W 2, D 1; E 1
O eterne Deus (ant), W 3, D 2; E 2
O virtus Sapientie (ant), W 4; E 59
O quam mirabilis (ant), W 5; E 60
O pastor animarum (M12) (ant), W 6; E 61
O cruor sanguinis (M11) (ant), W 7; E 77

Holy Spirit
Spiritus sanctus vivificans vita (ant), W 8, D 15; E 15
O ignis Spiritus Paraclitus (M16) (seq), W 59, D 19; E 19, P 4
O ignee Spiritus (M17) (hymn), W 60, D 18; E 18

Virgin Mary
O splendidissima gemma (S1) (ant), W 10, D 5; E 5
O tu illustrata (M21) (ant), W 11; E 62
Hodie aperuit nobis (M24) (ant), W12, D6; E 6
Quia ergo femina (M25) (ant), W 13, D 7; E 7
Cum processit factura (ant), W 14, D 8; E 8
Cum erubuerint infelices (ant), W 15, D 9; E 9
O frondens virga (M13) (ant), D 10; E 10
O quam magnum miraculum (M20) (ant), W 16, D 11; E 11
Ave Maria, O auctrix (M22) (ant), W 17, D 3; E 3
O clarissima mater (M23) (resp), W 18, D 4; E 4
O tu suavissima virga (S2) (resp), W 19, D 14; E 14
O quam pretiosa (M26) (resp), W 20; E 63
Alleluia, O virga mediatrix (M19), W 61; E 70
O virga ac diadema (M15), (seq), W 62, D 13; E 13, P 17
O viridissima virga (M18), W 63; E 71, P 10
Ave generosa (M14) (hymn), W 64, D 12; E 12, P 2

Trinity
Laus Trinitati (ant), D 17; E 17

Angels
O gloriosissimi lux vivens (S3) (ant), W 21, D 20; E 20
O vos angeli (S4) (ant), W 22, D 21; E 21

Patriarchs
O spectabiles viri (S5) (ant), W 23, D 22; E 22
O vos felices radices (S6) (resp), W 24, D 23; E 23

Apostles
O cohors militie floris (S7) (ant), W 25, D 24; E 24
O lucidissima apostolorum (S8) (resp), W 26, D 25; E 25
    St Matthew:
Matthias sanctus per electionem (hymn), W 65; E 72
    St John The Evangelist:
O speculum columbe (ant), W 27, D 26; E 26
O dulcis electe (resp), W 28, D 27; E 27

Martyrs
O victoriosissimi triumphatores (S9) (ant), W 29, D 31; E 31
Vos flores rosarum (S10) (resp), W 30, D 32; E 32

Confessors
O vos imitatores excelse (S12) (resp), W 31, D 33; E 33
O successores fortissimi (S11) (ant), W 32, D 34; E 34
    St Boniface:
O Bonifaci lux vivens (ant), W 66; E 73
    St Disibod [8 July; 619–700]:
O mirum admirandum (ant), W 33, D 28; E 28
O viriditas digiti Dei (resp), W 34, D 29; E 29
O presul vere civitatis (seq), W 67, D 30; E 30, P11
O felix anima (resp), W 35; E 64
O beata infantia (ant), W 36; E 65
    St Eucharius:
O Euchari, columba (resp), W 68; E 74
O Euchari, in leta via (seq), W 69; E 75, P 8
    St Maximinus:
Columba aspexit per cancellos (seq), W 70; E 76, P 1
    St Rupert:
O felix aparitio (M2) (ant), W 37, D 35; E 35
O beatissime Ruperte (M3) (ant), W 38, D 36; E 36
Quia felix pueritia (ant), W 39; E 66
O Jerusalem aurea civitas (M1) (seq), W 71, D 37; E 37

Virgins
O pulchre facies (S13) (ant), W 40, D 38; E 38
O nobilissima viriditas (S14) (resp), W 41, D 39; E 39
    [*St Ursula and her*] 11 000 *virgins*:
Favus distillans Ursula (resp), W 42, D 45; E 45
Spiritui Sancto honor sit (resp), W 43, D 43; E 43
O ecclesia oculi tui (seq), W 72, D 54; E 54
Cum vox sanguinis Ursule (hymn), W 73, D 55; E 55
    Symphony of Virgins:
O dulcissime amator (M4) W 74, D 40; E 40
    Symphony of Widows:
O pater omnium (M5) W 75, D 41; E 41
    Gospel:
O rubor sanguinis (ant), W 44, D 44; E 44
    Laudes at Matins:
Studium divinitas (ant), W 45, D 46; E 46
Unde quocumque venientes (ant), W 46, D 47; E 47
De patria etiam earum (ant), W 47, D 48; E 48
Deus enim in prima (ant), W 48, D 49; E 49
Aer enim volat (ant), W 49, D 50; E 50
Et ideo puelle iste (ant), W 50, D 51; E 51
    Gospel:
Deus enim rorem (ant), W 51, D 52; E 52
Sed diabolus (ant), W 52, D 53; E 53

Innocents
Rex noster promptus est (resp), W 53, D 42; E 42

Dedication of the Church
O virgo ecclesia pangendum est (M7) (ant), W 54, D 56; E 56
Nunc gaudeant materna viscera (M8) (ant), W 55, D 57; E 57
O orzchis ecclesia (M9) (ant), W 56; E 67
O coruscans lux stellarum (ant), W 57; E 68

Kyrie eleison, W 58; E 69

Ordo virtutum, morality play; B, V, E pp.165–205

BIBLIOGRAPHY

BIOGRAPHICAL STUDIES

[Gottfried of St Disibod and Dieter of Echternach]: *Vita Sanctae Hildegardis*, ed. J.-P. Migne in *PL*, cxcvii (1855), cols. 91–130; Eng. trans. by A. Silvas, in *Tjurunga: an Australasian Benedictine Review*, xxix (1985), 4–25; xxx (1986), 63–73; xxxi (1986); xxxii (1987), 46–59

J. P. Schmelzeis: *Das Leben und Wirken der Heiligen Hildegardis nebst einem Anhang hildegard'scher Lieder mit ihren Melodien* (Freiburg, 1879)

S. Flanagan: *Hildegard of Bingen, 1098–1179: a Visionary Life* (London, 1989)

EDITIONS AND TRANSLATIONS OF TEXTS

J.-P. Migne, ed.: *S. Hildegardis Abbatissae Opera Omnia*, Patrologiae cursus completus, i: Series latina, cxcvii (1855) [edns of 145 letters, *Scivias*, *Liber divinorum operum*, *Physica* and other works]

F. W. E. Roth: *Die Lieder und die unbekannte Sprache der heiligen Hildegardis*, Fontes rerum Nassoicarum, i/3 (Wiesbaden, 1880)

J.-B. Pitra: *Analecta sacra*, viii (Paris, 1882) [edns of *Liber vitae meritorum*, 145 letters, and other works; includes 26 items of the 'miscellany', pp.358–68]

A. Führkötter, ed.: *Hildegardis 'Scivias'* (Turnhout, 1978)

B. Newman, ed.: *Saint Hildegard of Bingen, Symphonia: a Critical Edition of the 'Symphonia armonie celestium revelationum'* (Ithaca, NY, 1988) [with Eng. trans., commentary and bibliography]

Hildegard of Bingen's 'Scivias', trans. B. Hozeski (Santa Fe, 1986) [abridged]

M. Fox, ed.: *Hildegard of Bingen's 'Book of Divine Works', with Letters and Songs*, trans. R. Cunningham (Santa Fe, 1987) [songs with music]

OTHER STUDIES

MGG (J. Schmidt-Görg)

L. Bronarski: *Die Lieder der heiligen Hildegard: ein Beitrag zur Geschichte der geistlichen Musik des Mittelalters*, Veröffentlichungen der Gregorianischen Akademie zu Freiburg, ix (Zürich, 1922) [analysis of melodies]

M. Böckeler: 'Aufbau und Grundgedanke des Ordo virtutum der heiligen Hildegard', *Benediktinische Monatsschrift*, v (1923), 300

—— : 'Beziehungen des "Ordo Virtutum" der heiligen Hildegard zu ihrem Hauptwerk "Scivias" ', *Benediktinische Monatsschrift*, vii (1925), 135

H. Liebeschütz: *Das allegorische Weltbild der heiligen Hildegard von Bingen* (Leipzig and Berlin, 1930)

B. Widmer: *Heilsordnung und Zeitgeschehen in der Mystik Hildegards von Bingen* (Basle, 1955)

J. Schmidt-Görg: 'Die Sequenzen der heiligen Hildegard', *Studien zur Musikgeschichte des Rheinlandes:*

Festschrift zum 80. Geburtstag von Ludwig Schiedermair (Cologne, 1956), 109

M. Schrader and A. Führkötter: *Die Echtheit des Schrifttums der heiligen Hildegard von Bingen: Quellenkritische Untersuchungen*, Beihefte zum Archiv für Kulturgeschichte, vi (Cologne and Graz, 1956)

J. Schmidt-Görg: 'Zur Musikanschauung in den Schriften der heiligen Hildegard', *Der Mensch und die Künste: Festschrift für Heinrich Lützeler* (Düsseldorf, 1962), 230

Hildegard von Bingen: Briefwechsel, trans. A. Führkötter (Salzburg, 1965)

J. Ritscher: 'Zur Musik der heiligen Hildegard', *Colloquium amicorum: Joseph Schmidt-Görg zum 70. Geburtstag* (Bonn, 1967), 309

P. Dronke: *The Medieval Lyric* (London, 1968), 75–6, 233ff

—— : 'The Composition of Hildegard of Bingen's "Symphonia" ', *Sacris Erudiri*, xix (1969–70), 381

—— : *Poetic Individuality in the Middle Ages: New Departures in Poetry 1000–1150* (Oxford, 1970), chap.5

B. L. Grant: 'Five Liturgical Songs by Hildegard von Bingen (1098–1179)', *Signs: Journal of Women in Culture and Society*, v/3 (1980), 557–67

P. Dronke: 'Problemata Hildegardiana', *Mittellateinisches Jb*, xvi (1981), 97

B. J. Newman: *'O feminea forma' : God and Woman in the Works of St Hildegard (1098–1179)* (diss., Yale U., 1981)

A. E. Davidson: 'The Music and Staging of Hildegard of Bingen's "Ordo Virtutum" ', *Atti del IV Colloquio della Société internationale pour l'étude du théâtre médiéval*, ed. M. Chiabò, F. Doglio and M. Maymone (Viterbo, 1984), 495–506

P. Dronke: *Women Writers in the Middle Ages* (Cambridge, 1984)

P. Escot: 'The Gothic Cathedral and Hidden Geometry of St Hildegard', *Sonus*, v/1 (1984), 14–31

B. Thornton: 'Hildegard von Bingen aus der Sicht des Interpreten', *Concerto*, ii/Jan (1984), 48–53

A. B. Yardley: ' "Ful weel she soong the service dyvyne": the Cloistered Musician in the Middle Ages', *Women Making Music*, ed. J. Bowers and J. Tick (Urbana and Chicago, 1986), 15–38

B. Newman: *Sister of Wisdom: St Hildegard's Theology of the Feminine* (Berkeley, 1987)

M. R. Pfau: 'Music and Text in Hildegard's Antiphons', *Saint Hildegard of Bingen, Symphonia: a Critical Edition of the 'Symphonia armonie celestium revelationum'*, ed. B. Newman (Ithaca, NY, 1988), 74–94

—— : *Hildegard von Bingen's 'Symphonia armonie celestium revelationum': an Analysis of Music Process, Modality, and Text-Music Relations* (diss., SUNY, Stony Brook, 1990)

Sonus, xi/1 (1990) [Hildegard issue, incl. articles by R. Cogan, P. Escot, S. Flanagan, K. Kraft and M. R. Pfau]

IAN D. BENT

Hill, Lady Arthur. *See* HARRISON, ANNIE FORTESCUE.

Hill [née Solomon], **Mirrie (Irma)** (*b* Sydney, 1 Dec 1892; *d* Sydney, 1 May 1986).

Australian composer. She was educated at the Sydney Conservatorium immediately after its opening in 1916, and shortly after graduating taught harmony and allied subjects there. In 1921 she married the composer Alfred Hill (*d* 1960). She composed a large body of orchestral, chamber and piano music, the last including much educational music, and songs. Many of the songs are to texts by Australian poets such as Hugh McCrae and Mary Gilmore. Her most ambitious works were the *Arnhem Land Symphony* (1954), based on aboriginal themes and rhythms, the five orchestral pieces *The Little Dream* (1930), and a string quartet written in her 88th year.

WORKS
selective list

Stage: Old Mr Sundown (children's operetta), 1935
Orch: Rhapsody, pf, orch, 1918; Cinderella Suite, 1925; The Little Dream, suite after J. Galsworthy, 1930; 3 Aboriginal Dances, pf, orch, 1950; Arnhem Land Sym., 1954; Avinu malkenu, vn, orch, 1971; Carnival Night, 1971
Other inst: All in a Day, 7 solos, pf, 1950; Blue Tongue Lizard, pf, 1952; Come Summer, cl, pf, 1969; Dancing Faun, fl, pf, 1969; Bonny Oh!, pf, 1973; Andante, ww, harp, str ens, 1975; Str Qt; Pf Trio, b; Improvisations, vn, pf
Vocal: Aboriginal Themes (M. Gilmore), Mez, Bar, ens, 1971; songs incl. And everyone will love me, Down in the sunlit glades, I heard a sound of singing, Let your song be delicate, My bird singing

BIBLIOGRAPHY

CohenE

GRAHAM HAIR, GRETA MARY HAIR

Hill-Handley, Delphine. *See* SCHAUROTH, DELPHINE.

Hodges, Faustina Hasse (*b* Malmesbury, 7 Aug 1822; *d* Philadelphia, 4 Feb 1895). English organist and composer. (She was named after the famous 18th-century opera singer Faustina Bordoni, who married the composer Johann Adolf Hasse.) The daughter of the organist Edward Hodges, who assumed the musical directorship of Trinity Church in New York in 1838, she followed his example and became a professional musician in New York and Philadelphia. Details of her career are sparse: she is listed as a 'professor' of organ, piano and singing at Emma Willard's Troy Seminary for Girls in 1852 and, in the late 1870s, she was the organist for two churches in Philadelphia. She began composing in the 1850s and her works include several keyboard pieces, a few sacred songs and about 25 drawing-room songs. She had a few signifi-

cant commercial successes, her most famous works being the songs *Dreams* (Boston, 1859) and *The Rose Bush* (1859) and a sacred duet *Suffer Little Children*. (Ebel claimed that she had sales of over 100 000 for *The Rose Bush*.) Hodges skilfully assimilated both Italian and German styles in her more cultivated songs, making them popular light recital pieces for opera singers such as Adelaide Phillipps in the 19th century and Alma Gluck in the early 1900s. She edited some of her father's works and published them in 1891 with her own hymn tunes.

WORKS
selective list
printed works published in New York

Pf: Reveries du Soir, 1862–3; Marigena: 3 Reveries by the Waterside, (*c*1860s)
Sacred songs: Cloister Memories of Sacred Song; Suffer Little Children, 2vv, 1860; The Holy Dead, 3vv (1861); Te Deum
Secular songs: Because I'm 25 (1850); Still o'er the Waters (1852); Dreams (1859); The Rose Bush (1859); L'amicizia, polka duet, women's vv, 1863; Farewell to North Maven, 1864; The Indignant Spinster (1867); Three Roses, 1874; As the hours pass on, 1882; Yearnings, 1893

BIBLIOGRAPHY

WCBH
F. H. Hodges: *Edward Hodges: Doctor in Music of Sydney Sussex College* (New York, 1896)
R. Hughes: 'Music in America – the Woman Composers', *Godey's Lady's Book*, cxxxii/Jan (1896), 30–40
J. Tick: *American Women Composers before 1870* (Ann Arbor, 1983)

JUDITH TICK

Hoenderdos, Margriet (*b* Santpoort, 6 May 1952). Dutch composer. After studying the piano at the Zwolle Conservatory, she entered the Sweelinck Conservatory in Amsterdam, where she studied composition with Ton de Leeuw and worked in the electronic studio. She graduated in 1985 and was awarded the Composition Prize that year. Hoenderdos is particularly concerned with exploring the relationships between time, tempo and timbre, as may be heard in her 1985 orchestral piece *Het nieuwe Verlaat*. Her compositions are characterized by a rigorous methodological approach rarely encountered in contemporary Dutch music. She concentrates mostly on orchestral pieces, such as *Hunker, Schor and Hasselaar* (1989) and *July '90* (1990), and chamber works such as *Blue Time* for two pianos (1981), *Borrowed Flesh* for organ (1987) and *De Lussen van Faverey* for wind quintet (1990). Her music is published by Donemus.

HELEN METZELAAR

Holland, Dulcie Sybil (*b* Sydney, 5 Jan 1913). Australian composer. Her composition teachers were Alfred Hill at the Sydney Conservatorium and Roy Agnew and John Ireland at the RCM in London. She became well known to several generations of young Australians as a piano examiner and broadcaster, and for her educational piano music and music for young choristers. Her large output includes many chamber works and music for about 40 documentary films.

WORKS
selective list

Elegy, fl, pf, 1954; Civic Ov., orch, 1957; Sym. for Pleasure, orch, 1974; Conc., pf, str orch; Conversation a 4, str qt; More Manly Tales, T, str qt; Sonata, a sax, pf

BIBLIOGRAPHY

CohenE [incl. fuller list of works]; *Fuller-LeFanuRM*

GRAHAM HAIR, GRETA MARY HAIR

Holmès [Holmes], Augusta (Mary Anne) (*b* Paris, 16 Dec 1847; *d* Paris, 28 Jan 1903). French composer of Irish parentage. She was the late and only daughter of an Irish officer who had settled in France and a mother of mixed Scottish and Irish origins; her parents were in close contact with many leading artistic personalities of the time. Alfred de Vigny was her godfather and may also have been her true father. Brought up in Versailles, she quickly showed an aptitude for music as well as poetry and painting. Because her mother discouraged her musical talents, it was not until after the latter's death that Augusta, then 11, had her first lessons with Henri Lambert, organist of Versailles Cathedral. Later she had instrumentation lessons from Hyacinthe Klosé, and in 1875 she joined the distinguished company of César Franck's pupils. By then, having heard *Das Rheingold* in 1869, she was already a devotee of Wagner's music, which is the dominant influence, with that of Franck, over her own. Much of it is conceived on an ample scale for large forces, based on strong classical or mythological subjects, and even in her songs the conception is often orchestral. She wrote an opera *Héro et Léandre* in 1875 (she wrote all her own librettos), followed by *Astarté* and *Lancelot du lac*. None of these was performed, and *La montagne noire*, played at the Paris Opéra in 1895, was not a success. She wrote a number of dramatic symphonies and symphonic poems including *Orlando furioso* (1877), *Lutèce* (1878), *Irlande* (1882), *Pologne* (1883) and *Andromède* (1901). She enjoyed some success with choral works, especially *Les Argonautes* (1881), vigorously dramatic and (as Saint-Saëns pointed out) too noisily orchestrated, *Ludus pro patria* (1888), and the *Ode triomphale*, composed for the centenary of the Revolution in 1889. Although her music has great breadth and virility – a quality observed by Jean de Villiers de l'Isle-Adam when she was only 16 – her harmony has none of Wagner's fluency and moves too much in static blocks. Ethel Smyth, who was by no means wholly sympathetic to her music, nevertheless declared that it contained 'jewels wrought by one who was evidently not among the giants, but for all that knew how to cut a gem'. Holmès's songs have indeed survived longer than anything else of her output.

The impact of Holmès's music was less striking than that of her personality, which dominated the musical and literary salons of her day to an extraordinary degree. She was a good linguist and mixed as easily with poets as with musicians. Saint-Saëns, whose offer of marriage she declined, said 'we were all in love with her', and there are many testimonies of her beauty and vivacity. Franck, Wagner, d'Indy, Villiers de l'Isle-Adam, and Mallarmé all admired her, and she was for a

Augusta Holmès

long time the mistress of Catulle Mendès, by whom she had three daughters. Her Irish ancestry revealed itself in her ebullient temperament and also in her passionate Irish patriotism. She converted to Roman Catholicism shortly before her death.

WORKS
all printed works published in Paris;
unpublished MSS in F-V unless otherwise stated

OPERAS
librettos by the composer

La montagne noir (4), Paris, Opéra, 8 Feb 1895, vs (1895)

Unperf.: Héro et Léandre (1), 1875; Astarté; Lancelot du lac

ORCHESTRAL
Symphonic: Hymne à Apollon, sym. poem (1872); Orlando furioso, sym. after Ariosto, 1877; Lutèce, dramatic sym., 1878 (1884); Les Argonautes, dramatic sym., solo vv, chorus, orch, vs (1881); Irlande, sym. poem, arr. pf (1882), full score (1885); Pologne, sym. poem, arr. pf (1883), full score, US-AA; Ludus pro patria (Puvis de Chavannes), sym. ode, chorus, orch, vs (1888); Au pays bleu, sym. suite (1892); Andromède, sym. poem (1901)

Other pubd works: Hymne à la paix, solo vv, chorus, orch (1889); Ode triomphale, solo vv, chorus, orch, vs (1889); Hymne à Vénus, 1v, orch (1894); Fleur de néflier, T, chorus, orch/pf (1902)

Unpubd: In exitu (Ps cxiii), chorus, orch, perf. 1873; Danse d'Almées, chorus, orch; La chanson de la caravane, chorus, orch; La vision de Ste Thérèse, S, orch; Retour, chorus, orch

OTHER WORKS
Vocal: Veni Creator, T, chorus, org (1887); La vision de la reine, scena, solo female vv, female chorus, pf, vc, harp (1895); 128 songs, incl. Les sept ivresses (1882), Les [5] sérénades (1883), [2] Rêves parisiens (1886–92), [4] Paysages d'amour (1889), [10] Contes de fées (1892), [6] Contes divins (1892), Les [4] heures (1900), 20 mélodies (1905), Les sept péchés capitaux, 63 songs pubd singly

Inst: Rêverie tzigane, pf (1887); 3 petites pièces, fl, pf (1897); Fantaisie, cl, pf (1900); Ce qu'on entend sur la montagne, pf (n.d.); Polonaise, pf

BIBLIOGRAPHY
FétisBS; SchmidlD

H. Imbert: *Nouveaux profils de musiciens* (Paris, 1892)

A. Jullien: *Musiciens d'aujourd'hui*, 2nd ser. (Paris, 1894)

P. Barillon-Bauché: *Augusta Holmès et la femme compositeur* (Paris, 1912)

R. P. Du Page: 'Une musicienne versaillaise: Augusta Holmès', *Revue de Versailles et de Seine-et-Oise* (1921)

E. Smyth: *A Final Burning of Boats* (London, 1928)

R. Berthelot: 'Trois anges sont venus ce soir . . . ou le roman d'Augusta Holmès', *Musica*, cv (1962), 20

R. Myers: 'Augusta Holmès: a Meteoric Career', *MQ*, liii (1967), 365–76

G. Gefen: *Augusta Holmès: l'outrancière* (Paris, 1987)

HUGH MACDONALD

Title-page, illustrated by Célestin Nanteuil, of the 'Chanson du chamelier' (Paris: Léon Grus, 1893) by Augusta Holmès

Imogen Holst rehearsing at the Snape Maltings, near Aldeburgh, 1977

Holmsen, Borghild (*b* Christiania [now Oslo], 22 Oct 1865; *d* Bergen, 6 Dec 1938). Norwegian composer and pianist. She was a pupil of Agathe Grøndahl and Otto Winter-Hjelm in Christiania and of Carl Reinecke in Leipzig and Albert Becker in Berlin. After her début in Christiania (1898) she gave many concerts in Scandinavia, England and the USA. She taught the piano at the Castberg Academy of Music in Bergen and worked as a music critic. Her compositions, mainly for small forces, show tonal originality; they were published between 1889 and 1911.

WORKS
all published in Christiania

Band: Festival March at Akershus Castle, military band, op.11 (1905); also for pf
Vn, pf: Romance, op.3 (1891); Sonata, D, op.10; Romance norvégienne, op.15 (1911)
Pf: Barcarolle and Scherzo, op.1 (1889); Capriccio (1898); 4 Sketches, op.12 (1902); Fjordbilleder [Pictures from the Fjord], op.17
Songs: Primula veris (1890); Wir liebten uns einst (1890); Spielmannslied (1893); Die junge Nonne (1893); Die Feder am Sturmhut (1900); Balvise, op.13 (1904); 3 Poems, op.14 (1908); other songs

BIBLIOGRAPHY
K. Michelsen, ed.: *Cappelens musikkleksikon* (Oslo, 1978–80)
C. Dahm: *Kvinner komponerer: 9 portretter av norske kvinnelige komponister i tiden 1840–1930* [Women Composers: 9 Portraits of Norwegian Women Composers 1840–1930] (Oslo, 1987)

KARI MICHELSEN

Holst, Imogen (Clare) (*b* Richmond, Surrey, 12 April 1907; *d* Aldeburgh, 9 March 1984). English writer on music, conductor, composer and administrator. She studied at the RCM, where she held a composition scholarship for tuition with George Dyson and Gordon Jacob. She won the Cobbett Prize in 1928 and the Octavia travelling scholarship in 1930. Though she is well known for folksong arrangements and music for amateurs, her serious compositions remained underestimated and largely unknown until the 1980s. Her earliest works were influenced by her father, Gustav Holst, but her own musical language developed great individuality during the 1940s: linear in construction, it is tonally ambiguous and often features the minor second. She wrote little during her appointment as amanuensis to Benjamin Britten between 1952 and 1964, but then regained her enthusiasm for composition. The latter period includes most of her finest music (e.g. the String Quintet of 1982), and she was busy with commissions at the time of her death in 1984.

WORKS
selective list

STAGE
Meddling in Magic (ballet, after J. W. von Goethe), comp. 1930
Love in a Mist or The Blue Haired Stranger (ballet), London, Rudolf Steiner Hall, 19 Jan 1935; music lost
Young Beichan (puppet opera, 7 scenes, B. de Zoete), 1945; Dartington, Devon, sum. 1946; withdrawn
Benedick and Beatrice (opera, 12 scenes), 1950; Dartington, 20 July 1951

OTHER WORKS
Orch: Suite, small orch, 1927; Suite, F, str orch, 1927; Persephone, ov., 1929; Conc. vn, str orch, 1935; Suite, str orch, 1943; Variations on 'Loth to Depart', str orch, 1963; Trianon Suite, 1965; Woodbridge Suite, 1969; Joyce's Divertimento, 1976; Deben Calendar, 1977
Chamber: Qnt, ob, str, 1928; Str Qt 'Phantasy', 1928; Sonata, vn, vc, 1930; Str Trio, 1944; 2 str qts, no.1, 1946, no.2, 1950; Str Trio, 1962; Fall of the Leaf, vc, 1963; Duo, va, pf, 1968; Str Qnt, 1982
Vocal: A Hymne to Christ (J. Donne), SATB, 1940; 4 Songs, S, pf, 1944; 5 Songs. SSSAA, 1944; Lavabo inter Innocentes, SSSAA. 1955; The Sun's Journey

(T. Dekker, J. Ford), cantata, SA, small orch, 1965; Hallo my Fancy (W. Cleland), Ct, T, SSBB, 1972; Homage to William Morris, B, db, 1984

Works for brass, wind band, rec, chorus with orch; many arrs. for chorus, orch and chamber groups

Principal publishers: Boosey & Hawkes, Cramer, Faber, Novello, OUP

BIBLIOGRAPHY

C. G. Tinker: 'Imogen Holst's Music, 1962–84, *Tempo*, no.166 (1988), 22–7

—— : *The Musical Output of Imogen Holst* (diss., U. of Lancaster, 1990)

—— : *Imogen Holst* (London, forthcoming)

CHRISTOPHER TINKER

Hölszky, Adriana (*b* Bucharest, 30 June 1953). Romanian composer of Austrian-German parentage. Her parents were scientists. She began to study the piano with Olga Rosca-Berdan at the Bucharest music school in 1959 and to compose in 1961. She studied composition with Ştefan Niculescu at the Bucharest Conservatory (1972–5) and in 1976, when the family moved to Germany, continued her studies with Milko Kelemen, Günter Louegk and Erhard Karkoschka (electronic music). She attended the summer academy at the Salzburg Mozarteum (1977, 1978), and the Accademia Chigiana, Siena (1980), with Franco Donatoni. She was the pianist of the Lipatti Trio, 1977–80, and taught at the Stuttgart Musikhochschule, 1980–89. Her awards include many prizes for composition: the Valentino Bucchi, Rome (1979); Gaudeamus (1981); Max Deutsch, Paris (1982); Stamitz, Mannheim (1985); German record critics' prize (1988–9); GEDOK, Mannheim (1985, 1989); the women composers' prize, Heidelberg (1990); and others. She has taught at the Darmstadt summer courses and been a member of international juries.

In her compositions Hölszky strives for originality, distancing herself, however, from the mainstream of the avant garde to an extent comparable to the gulf between Indian and Western thought: geometric forms, chemical processes and dramatic situations determine structural ideas, and the principles of mathematical ordering are set against 'chaotic' inspiration. In her opera *Bremer Freiheit* the main character, a murderess who kills with poison, can be seen as a female counterpart to Bartók's Bluebeard.

WORKS
selective list

Opera: Bremer Freiheit (Thomas Körner, after R. W. Fassbinder), 1987

Orch, ens: Constellation, orch, 1975–6; Space, 4 orch groups, 1979–80; Erewhon, 14 insts, 1984;

Klangwerfer, 12 str, 1984–5; New Erewhon, chamber ens, 1984–5, rev. 1990; Lichtflug, vn, fl, orch, 1990

Chamber and solo inst: Pf Sonata, 1975; Str Qt, 1975; Flux-re-Flux, a sax, 1981–3; Innere Welten I, str trio, 1981; Innere Welten II, str qt, 1981–2; Arkaden, 2 fl, str qt, 1982; Intarsien I, fl, vn, pf, 1982; Decorum, hpd, 1982–3; Intarsien II, fl, vn, hpd, pf, 1982–3; Intarsien III, fl, vn, 2 pf, 1982–3; Controversia, 2 fl, 2 ob, vn, 1983; Requisiten, 9 insts, 1985; . . . und wieder Dunkel I, timp, pf, 1985, rev. 1990; . . . und wieder Dunkel II, timp, org, 1986; Hörfenster für Franz Liszt, pf, 1986–7; Fragmente aus 'Bremer Freiheit', accordion, cymbal, timp, 1988; Hängebrücken, str qt 'an Schubert', 1989–90; Jagt die Wölfe zurück, 6 timp, 1989–90; Karawane 'Reflexion über den Wanderklang', 12 timp, 1989–90

Vocal: Monolog, female v, timp, 1977; . . . es kamen schwarze Vögel, 5 female vv, perc, 1978; Il était un homme rouge, 12 solo vv, 1978; Kommentar für Lauren, S, 8 wind insts, timp, 1978; Questions I, S, Bar, vn, vc, pf, 1980; Questions II, S, Bar, vn, vc, pic, gui, pf, 1981; Immer schweigender, 4 mixed choirs [each choir 8vv], 1986; Flöten des Lichts, 'Flächenspiel', female v, 5 wind insts, other insts ad lib, 1989–90; Message (E. Ionesco), Mez, Bar, spkr, sounds, elec, 1990; Gemälde eines Erschlagenen (J. M. R. Lenz), 72vv, 1993

Elec: OMION, tape, 1980

Principal publishers: Astoria, Breitkopf & Härtel

BIBLIOGRAPHY
KompA-Z

D. Gojowy: '7. Arbeitswoche junger Komponisten des Siegerlandorchesters in Hilchenbach mit Überraschungen', *Das Orchester*, ix (1981), 766

A. Hölszky: 'Wir haben unser Land und unsere Freiheit verloren', *Annäherungen an sieben Komponistinnen*, ii, ed. B. Sonntag and R. Matthei (Kassel, 1987)

M. Emigholz: 'Die Freiheit, mit Raum und Zeit zu spielen', *NZM*, Jg.150, no.9 (1989), 18–23

R. Sperber and U. Feld: *5 Jahre internationales Festival Komponistinnen gestern–heute und 5th International Congress on Women in Music* (Heidelberg, 1989)

G. R. Koch: 'Und es kamen schwarze Vögel: Laudatio auf die Komponistin Adriana Hölszky', *NZM*, Jg.151, no.12 (1990), 9–13

DETLEF GOJOWY

Holt, Patricia Blomfield. See BLOMFIELD HOLT, PATRICIA.

Hood, Helen Francis (*b* Chelsea, MA, 28 June 1863; *d* Brookline, MA, 22 Jan 1949). American pianist, composer and teacher. She studied in Boston with D. J. Lang (piano), J. C. D. Parker and J. K. Paine (harmony), and George Chadwick (composition); and in Berlin with Moritz Moszkowski and Scharwenka. She appeared as a pianist with many Boston organizations, had an extensive network of piano students for more than 40 years and composed steadily from an early age into the 1930s. She received a diploma and medal from the World's Columbian Exposition in Chicago, 1893, where her *Summer Song* was given a triple encore at its performance on 6 July. She is noted for her songs, which evolved from early sentimental ballads to an expansive and expressive idiom in the later works. Elson (2/1925), however, considered her piano trio to be her most important work.

WORKS
selective list

Stage: Die Bekehrte
Inst: Pf Trio; Suite de pièces, vn, pf, op.6; Str Qt; Romance, org, op.19; Novelette, A, pf
Vocal: Te Deum, Eb; The Robin, partsong; c100 songs, incl. Song Etchings, op.8 (Boston, 1893), A Disappointment, Message of the Rose, Skating, Sleighing, Summer Song and The River

MSS in US-Wc

BIBLIOGRAPHY
A. Elson: *Woman's Work in Music* (Boston, 1903, 2/1931), 207
L. C. Elson: *The History of American Music* (New York, 1904, 2/1925), 306
F. B. Lang: *Diaries* (MS, US-Bp)

PAMELA FOX

Hoover, Katherine (*b* Elkins, WV, 2 Dec 1937). American composer and flautist. She attended the Eastman School (BM 1959), Bryn Mawr, Yale Summer Session and the Manhattan School of Music (MM 1974). She has performed and taught in New York City while amassing a steady stream of commissions, residencies and awards. From 1978 to 1981 she organized the Women's Interart Center music festivals in New York. Although her output includes works for solo voice and chorus, her major works are instrumental. Extra-musical references include Barbara Tuchman's *A Distant Mirror* (in *Medieval Suite*) and Native American myths (in *Kokopeli* and *Canyon Echoes*). *Da pacem* takes its name from the 16th-century cantus firmus on which it is based.

WORKS
selective list

Orch: Nocturne, fl, str, perc, 1980; Summer Night, fl, hn, str, 1986 (1986); Cl Conc., 1987; Eleni: a Greek Tragedy, 1987; Double Conc., 2 vn, str, 1989; 2 Sketches, 1989; Night Skies, 1992
Chamber: Trio, 3 fl, 1974; Homage to Bartók, fl, ob, cl, hn, bn, 1975; Divertimento, fl, vn, va, vc, 1975; Sinfonia, 4 bn, 1976; Medieval Suite, fl, pf, 1979–80 (1986), orchd 1987; Serenade, cl, str qt, 1982, arr. cl, pf, also arr. as Aria, bn, pf, 1982; Qwindtet, fl, ob, cl, hn, 1987; Da pacem, pf qnt, 1988; Ob Sonata, 1991; Canyon Echos, fl, gui, 1991
Pf: Piano Book, 1977–82; Allegro e andante, pf, 1983
Choral: Lake Isle of Innisfree, SATB, pf, 1973; Songs of Joy, SATB, 2 tpt, 2 trbn, 1974; Songs of Celebration, SATB, kbd/brass qnt, 1983

Other vocal: To Many a Well, Mez/S, pf, 1977; Selima, or Ode on the Death of a Favourite Cat, Drowned in a Tub of Goldfishes, S, cl, pf, 1979; From the Testament of François Villon, B-Bar, bn, str qt, 1982

Principal publishers: Boelke-Bomart, Carl Fischer, Lawson Gould, Papagena, T. Presser

BIBLIOGRAPHY
WAM
J. L. Zaimont and K. Famera: *Contemporary Concert Music by Women* (Westport, CT, 1981)
A. Franco: 'A Study of Selected Piano Chamber Works by Twentieth Century American Woman Composers', (diss. U. of Columbia, 1985)
D. Jezic: *Women Composers: the Lost Tradition Found* (New York 1988)
A. Gray: *The Popular Guide to Classic Music* (Secaucus, NJ, 1993)

CATHERINE PARSONS SMITH

Hopekirk [Wilson], **Helen** (*b* Edinburgh, 20 May 1856; *d* Cambridge, MA, 19 Nov 1945). American pianist, composer and teacher of Scottish origin. Following early instruction in Edinburgh with G. Lichtenstein (piano) and A. C. Mackenzie (composition), she attended the Leipzig Conservatory from 1876 until 1878. There she studied with Carl Reinecke, Salomon Jadassohn (composition), Louis Maas (piano) and E. F. Richter (counterpoint), and formed lifelong friendships with fellow students Carl Muck and George Chadwick. Following successful débuts with the Leipzig Gewandhaus (28 Nov 1878) and at the Crystal Palace (15 March 1879), she toured England and Scotland. She married the music critic, painter and businessman William A. Wilson in 1882, and, with her husband as manager, made her American début on 7 December 1883 with the Boston SO. Following three highly successful years touring the USA, she felt the need for further development; in Vienna she studied the piano with Theodor Leschetizky and composition with Karel Navrátil. In 1892 they moved to Paris to enable further composition study with Richard Mandl. After her husband's severe injury in a traffic accident, Hopekirk accepted Chadwick's offer of a teaching post at the New England Conservatory in 1897. She became involved at every level of music-making in Boston, and promoted Edward MacDowell's piano works as well as introducing works by Fauré, Debussy and d'Indy. In 1901 she left the Conservatory to teach privately. She continued to perform, making her last appearance in April 1939 playing only her own compositions. Her music is characterized by Gaelic folk music and neo-classical tendencies. An ardent suffragette, she was widely acclaimed in her lifetime. Five of her scrapbooks are in the Library of Congress, Washington, DC.

WORKS
selective list

Orch: Concertstück, pf, orch, 1894; Pf Conc., 1900

Vocal: 100 songs, incl. 5 Songs (F. Macleod) (New York, 1903), 6 Songs (Macleod) (New York, 1907), 70 Scottish Songs (arrs.) (Boston, 1905), Requiescat (M. Arnold, 1886); sacred works

Other inst: Suite, pf (Boston, 1917); Serenata, pf (Boston, 1919); 2 vn sonatas, e, 1891, D, 1893

BIBLIOGRAPHY
A. G. Cameron: *Helen Hopekirk: a Critical and Biographical Sketch* (New York, 1885)
C. H. Hall and H. I. Tetlow: *Helen Hopekirk, 1856–1945* (Cambridge, MA, 1954) [incl. list of works]

PAMELA FOX

Hopkins, Sarah (*b* Lower Hutt, New Zealand, 13 Aug 1958). Australian composer and cellist of New Zealand origin. She emigrated to Australia with her family in 1964 and she studied at the Victorian College of the Arts (graduation 1979). As a composer-performer, she often uses the cello in combination with vocal sounds, handbells and 'whirly' instruments (plastic tubes of various lengths and diameters which play harmonic overtones when spiralled overhead). Her cello playing often employs extended techniques in combination with the vocalization of harmonic overtones. Her ensemble music essentially consists of an extension of this composer-performer persona, often involving aspects of music, poetry, theatre, dance, film, meditation, performance art, free and structured improvisation, and collective and community composition.

WORKS
w – whirly instrument(s)

Cello Timbre, amp vc, 1976, rev. 1978; Seasons II, amp vc, tape delay, 1978; Cellovoice, vc + v, 1982; Greeting Whirlies, 2 tuned w, 1983; Sunrise/Sunset, 6 tuned w, 1983; Deep Whirly Duo, 2 tuned deep w, 1984; Interweave, 6 tuned deep w, 1984; Aura Swirl, tuned handbells (14 players), 1986; Bougainvillea Bells, tuned w (15 players), handbells, cathedral bells, 1986; Cello Chi, vc + v, 1986; Eclipse, tuned w, handbells (14 players), 1986

Flight of the Wild Goose, vc, 1987; Ring, 2 tuned w, 1987; Circle Bell Mantra, 16 handbells, 1989; Heart Songs, ens incl. vv, w, wind chimes, handbells (17 players), 1989; Songs of the Wind, 1 deep w, 1989; Soul Song, 1989; Spiral Bells, 12 handbells, 1989; Transformation, 6 handbells, 1989; Celestial Song, ens incl. vv, w, wind chimes, 1990; Spirit of Gaia, vv, w, chime bars

BIBLIOGRAPHY
Fuller-LeFanuRM
J. Jenkins: 'Sarah Hopkins', *22 Contemporary Australian Composers* (Melbourne, 1988), 75–83

GRAHAM HAIR, GRETA MARY HAIR

Hori, Etsuko (*b* Kyoto, 22 Feb 1943). Japanese composer. She studied composition with Mareo Ishiketa at Tokyo National University of Fine Arts and Music (BA 1965, MA 1970). She was a lecturer (1967), then professor (1991) at the Tōhō Gakuen School of Music in Tokyo. Hori writes for Western as well as Japanese instruments but traditional Japanese influences can be heard in her choice of instrumentation (e.g. prominent flute parts; two harps in the Concerto for timpani and cello) and in her detailed dynamic indications and occasional extended techniques. Although she composes using regular metre, the constantly changing tempos of some pieces link them with the freer rhythm of traditional Japanese music (e.g. *Two Movements*).

WORKS
selective list

Orch: Hanka-shii (Meditazione di Maitreya), 1966; Vc and timp Conc., 1967; Va Conc., 1969

Chamber: 6 Classical Suites, ww qnt, harp, 1964; 2 Movts, fl + pic, fl + a fl, 1965

With trad. Japanese insts: Contrast, nōkan/shinobue, 3 shakuhachi, sangen chūzao, sangen futo-zao, biwa, 2 sō, jūshichigen, 2 perc, 1969; Duet for Nijugen-so and Flutes, fl + a fl, nijugen koto, 1969

Choral: Haru to Shura [Spring and Asura] (K. Miyazawa), men's vv, 1983

BIBLIOGRAPHY
A. Ueno: 'Hori Etsuko', *Saishin Ongaku Zenshuh* [Complete Works of the Latest Music], x, ed. Ongaku no Tomo Sha (Tokyo, 1980), 451–5

J. MICHELE EDWARDS

Horrocks, Amy Elsie (*b* Rio Grande do Sul, Brazil, 23 Feb 1867; *d* ? Brazil, ? after 1915). English composer, teacher and pianist. She entered the RAM in 1882, studying the piano with Adolph Schloesser and composition with F. W. Davenport. She won the Potter Exhibition in 1888 and the Sterndale Bennett Prize in 1889. She taught the piano in London and gave chamber concerts in the Prince's Hall in 1891. In 1895 she was made FRAM. She eventually returned to her birthplace, Brazil.

Horrocks's works suffer from a lack of musical substance, though her miniatures have a certain delicate charm. Her piano writing is usually derived from the style of Adolf Henselt and Anton Rubinstein; in larger works, however (such as the Cello Sonata and the Eight Variations op.11 for piano quartet), the texture is reminiscent of Brahms. She relied heavily on her rhythmic facility and was over-fond of canons. Her most successful piece is the experimental narrative *scena* with piano trio, *The Lady of Shalott*.

WORKS
printed works published in London

INSTRUMENTAL

Orch: Undine, legend, op.16, 1897, unpubd

Chamber: Pf Trio, B♭, 1887, unpubd; Cradle Song and Scherzo à la mazurka, vn, pf, op.12 (1893); 8 Variations on an Original Theme, pf qt, op.11 (1893); Irish Melody and Country Dance, vc, pf, op.17 (1894); Vc Sonata, G, op.7 (1896); Rigaudon, vn, pf (1900); 3 pièces faciles, vn, pf, op.34 (1900); Twilight, vc, pf (1901) [arr. from songs]

Pf: 2 Pieces, op.4 (1890): Berceuse, Waltz; 6 Pieces, op.14 (1893): Boat-Song, Minuet, Romance, Spinning-Song, Waltz, Mazurka; 2 Light Pieces (1915): A Tale of the Sea, Valse; Margory Gavotte (n.d.)

Incid. music for An Idyll of New Year's Eve, London, Chelsea, Jan 1890, unpubd

VOCAL

2 Fairy Songs (M. C. Gillington), S, women's chorus, str, harp, triangle, op.13 (1892); Love's Requiem (Gillington), 1v, pf, vc obbl (1894); The Night has a Thousand Eyes (F. W. Bourdillon), canon (1894); The Recompense (M. Byron), 1v, pf, vc obbl (1898); The Winds (Gillington), cantata, treble vv, op.22 (1898); The Lady of Shalott (A. Tennyson), nar, pf trio (1899); A Spanish Pastoral (M. Byron), 1v, pf, fl obbl (1899); Spring Morning, cantata; 2 Songs, with orch, op.3; The Wild Swan, cantata, op.9

Other songs, etc. (most pubd; *c*1890–1913): *c*100 songs, 1v, pf; 37 partsongs; 17 duets, mainly for female vv

BIBLIOGRAPHY

CohenE; *MEMM*; *PazdirekH*

J. D. Brown and S. S. Stratton: *British Musical Biography* (Birmingham, 1897)

S. Stern: *Women Composers: a Handbook* (Metuchen, NJ, 1978)

M. Stewart-Green: *Women Composers: a Checklist of Works for the Solo Voice* (Boston, 1980)

NIGEL BURTON

Hotteterre, Elisabeth de. *See* HAULTE-TERRE, ELISABETH DE.

Ho Wai-On (*b* Hong Kong, 26 May 1946). British composer born in Hong Kong. She studied Chinese and English literature at the Chinese University of Hong Kong and composition with James Iliff at the RAM (LRAM and ARCM 1969, professional certificate 1971). She studied electronic music at Stanford University, at a workshop directed by John Chowning, and at University College, Cardiff, where she gained the MMus (1984) in electronic and contemporary music. In the same year she was named ARAM. Many of her works involve performer interaction with computer or tape music. Since 1974 she has composed a number of staged multi-media works and music for three films. In 1988 she founded the group Inter-Artes and with it has created cross-cultural arts projects in Hong Kong and Britain.

WORKS
selective list

Stage: Metamorphosis (multi-media), 1979; Living Tradition (combined arts), London, 1989, rev. 1991; The Story so Far (music-theatre), 1990–91; Wiseman, Fool and Slave (music-theatre), 3 versions, 1990–93

Vocal: 4 Songs in Chinese, S, eng hn, 1974; Shadows' Farewell, S, str, 1975; Germination, S, S, T, T, fl, cl, vc, harp, perc, 1–3 Chin. insts, 1992

Inst: For You, fl, pf, 1977, rev. 1986; Intervals, str qt, 1977; Tai Chi, fl, gui, 1977; Spring River Flower Moon Night, fl, gui, harp, 1979, rev. 1987; Impression of an Opera, cl, 1982; Sapa, fl, vc, sitar, tablā, synth (hpd), 1989; Interwind, wind orch, 1990

Multi-media, combined arts: 3:10 AM, nar, va, gui, 1977; Impression of an Opera II, nar, mime, ob, cl, bn, hn, 1983; Acis and Galatea, 1987; Pygmalion and Galatea, mime, dance, pf, 1989

Computer, other elec: Dance Piece, 1975; Anxious Elements, 1978; Metamorphosis, 1979; 21-Part Composition, 1983

BIBLIOGRAPHY

Fuller-LeFanuRM

HARRISON RYKER

Howe, Mary (*b* Richmond, VA, 4 April 1882; *d* Washington, DC, 14 Sept 1964). American composer and pianist. Her early musical and piano training was under the private tutelage of Herminie Seron. In 1904 she briefly studied the piano with Richard Burmeister in Dresden; subsequently she became a pupil of Ernest Hutcheson and Harold Randolph at the Peabody Conservatory, and studied composition there with Gustav Strube. At the age of 40, married and the mother of three children, she took the diploma in composition at the Peabody (1922). In 1933, having already amassed a considerable output, she studied for a short period with Nadia Boulanger in Paris.

During her early mature years, Howe gave solo recitals and appeared as accompanist in the Washington area. Her first professional performances were as a duo-pianist with Anne Hull (1920–35). With her husband and others she helped found the National SO and served as a director. She was also a founder, with Elizabeth Sprague Coolidge and others, of the Chamber Music Society of Washington (from 1928, the Friends of Music in the Library of Congress); and with Amy Beach she helped organize the Society of American Women Composers in 1925. That year she undertook the first of many sojourns at the MacDowell Colony; she and her children, as the 'Four Howes', gave programmes of madrigals and early music on its behalf, 1935–40.

Although Howe did not begin to compose until about 1920, she was prolific and wrote over 20 large orchestral works as well as a substantial body of chamber, piano and vocal music. A traditionalist, she produced well-crafted pieces within a harmonic and formal language reminiscent of the late 19th century. She described her style of composition as one of 'spanning and bridging' – reaching from the past through the contemporary to develop her own language. Her music is thoroughly tonal and most notable for the assured way in which it exploits the rich expansiveness of the symphony orchestra. Many of her works are cast as tone poems, including three of her best-known pieces: *Castellana* is based on four Spanish folk tunes remembered from Howe's childhood; *Three Pieces after Emily Dickinson* (1941) is a string quartet inspired by the last lines of three of Dickinson's poems; and *Sand* is described by Howe as evoking the 'granular consistency and grittiness and . . . potential scattering quality' of sand on the shore. Also admired are her settings of J. W. von Goethe, R. M. Rilke, Elinor Wylie, Amy Lowell and others.

Mary Howe, ?early 1930s

WORKS
selective list

Catalogue: *Mary Howe: Works*, ed. C. Howe (MS, 1992)

CHORAL
published unless otherwise stated

Catalina, 1924; Chain Gang Song, 1925; Cavaliers, 1927, unpubd; Spring Pastoral, 1936; Laud for Christmas, 1936; Robin Hood's Heart, 1936, unpubd; Christmas Song, 1939; Song of Palms, 1939; Song of Ruth, 1939; Williamsburg Sunday, 1940; Prophecy, 1943; A Devotion, 1944; Great Land of Mine, 1953; Poem in Praise, 1955, unpubd; The Pavilion of the Lord, 1957, unpubd; Benedictus es Domine, 1960, unpubd; We Praise thee O God, 1962, unpubd

SONGS
published unless otherwise stated

Old English Lullaby, 1913; Somewhere in France, 1918; Cossack Cradle Song, 1922; Berceuse, 1925; Chanson souvenir, 1925; O mistress mine, 1925; Reach, 1925; Red Fields of France, 1925; The Prinkin' Leddie, 1925; Ma douleur, 1929; Ripe Apples, 1929; There has fallen a splendid tear, 1930; Der Einsame, 1931; Liebeslied, 1931; Mailied, 1931; Schlaflied, 1931; Abendlied, 1932, unpubd; Avalon, 1932; The Little Rose, 1932; The Rag Picker, 1932; The Lake Isle of Innisfree, 1933; Fair Annet's Song, 1934; Herbsttag, 1934
Little Elegy, 1934; Fragment, 1935; Now goes the light, 1935; Velvet Shoes, 1935; A Strange Story, 1936; Go down Death, 1936; Depart, 1938, unpubd; Soit, 1938; Viennese Waltz, 1938; Irish Lullaby, 1939, unpubd; You, 1939; Am Flusse, 1940; Die Gotter, 1940; Die Jahre, 1940; Heute geh' ich, 1940; Ich denke dein, 1940; Trocknet nicht, 1940, unpubd; Zweiful, 1940; General Store, 1941; Horses of Magic, 1941; Song at Dusk, 1941; The Bird's Nest, 1941

Traveling, 1941, unpubd; Were I to Die, 1941, unpubd; L'amant des roses, 1942; Mein Herz, 1942; Men, 1942; Nicht mit Engeln, 1942; Hymne, 1943; In Tauris, 1944; Look on this horizon, 1944, unpubd; To the Unknown Soldier, 1944; Lullaby for a Forester's Child, 1945; Rêve, 1945; O Proserpina, 1946; Spring come not too soon, 1947; The Christmas Story, 1948; The Bailey and the Bell, 1950; Horses, 1951; Einfaches Lied, 1955, unpubd; My lady comes, 1957; Three Hokku, 1958

OTHER WORKS

Orch: Poema, 1922; Stars, 1927 (New York, 1963); Sand, 1928 (New York, 1963); Castellana, 2 pf, orch, 1930; Dirge, 1931; Axiom, 1932; American Piece, 1933; Coulennes, 1936; Potomac River, 1940; Paean, 1941; Agreeable Overture, 1948; Rock, 1954 (New York, 1963); The Holy Baby of the Madonna, 1958
Chamber: Fugue, str qt, 1922; Sonata, D, vn, pf, 1922 (New York, 1962); Ballade fantasque, vc, pf, 1927; 3 Restaurant Pieces, vn, pf, 1927; Little Suite, str qt, 1928; Pf Qnt, 1928; Suite melancolique, vn, vc, pf, 1931; Patria, vc, pf, 1932; Quatuor, str qt, 1939; 3 Pieces after Emily Dickinson, str qt, 1941; Interlude between 2 Pieces, fl, pf, 1942; Wind Qnt, 1957
Pf (pubd unless otherwise stated): Andante douloureux, 1910; Nocturne, 1913 (New York, 1925); Prelude, 1920; Valse dansante, 2 pf, 1922, unpubd; Berceuse, 1924 (New York, 1925); Estudia brillante, 1925, unpubd; 3 Spanish Folk Tunes, 2 pf, 1925 (New York, 1926); Whimsy, 1931; Stars, 1934; Trifle, 1935, unpubd; Cards, ballet, 2 pf, 1936, unpubd; Le jongleur de Notre Dame, ballet, 2 pf, 1959, unpubd
Org: Elegy, 1939, pubd; For a Wedding, 1940
Also transcrs. of works by J. S. Bach

Principal publishers: Oliver Ditson, Edition Musicus, Carl Fischer, Galaxy, H. W. Gray, Mercury Music, OUP, C. F. Peters, E. C. Schirmer, G. Schirmer

BIBLIOGRAPHY

M. Howe: 'Paris to Me', *Peabody Bulletin* (1933), Dec

C. Reis: *Composers in America: Biographical Sketches* (New York, 3/1938 of *American Composers*, rev. and enlarged 4/1947)

K. Brooks: 'Washington Interest in Music has Centered around Inspiring Leadership of Mary Howe', *Washington Sunday Star* (2 May 1943)

M. Craig: 'Mary Howe, Composer, Honored for Works', *Musical Courier*, no.147 (1 Feb 1952), 22

E. Sharpe: 'Mary Howe, Independent Composer', *Washington Post* (26 Dec 1952)

F. D. Perkins: 'Music by Mary Howe', *New York Herald-Tribune* (25 Feb 1953)

W. Wallace: 'National Symphony', *Baltimore Sun* (1 Feb 1956)

M. Howe: *Jottings* (Washington, DC, 1959)

P. Hume: 'Mary Howe Honored on 80th Year with Concert of her Own Works', *Washington Post* (5 April 1962)

Z. Dressner: 'Mary Howe Remembered' *A[merican] W[omen] C[omposers] News*, ii/4 (1980)

R. C. Friedberg: *American Art Song and American Poetry*, ii: *Voices of Maturity* (Metuchen, NJ, 1984)

C. Shear: *The First Hundred Years of the Friday Morning Music Club of Washington DC* (Washington DC, 1987)

D. N. Allen: *The Works of Mary Howe: a Survey of Performance History and Critical Response* (diss., George Washington U., 1992)

S. C. McClain: *The Solo Vocal Repertoire of Mary Howe with Stylistic and Interpretive Analyses of Selected Works* (diss., Teachers College, Columbia U., 1992)

D. Indebaum: *Mary Howe: Composer, Pianist and Music Activist* (diss., New York U., 1993)

DOROTHY INDENBAUM, CAROL J. OJA

Howell, Dorothy (*b* Birmingham, 25 Feb 1898; *d* Malvern, 12 Jan 1982). English composer. She completed her general education early in order to study with John McEwen and Tobias Matthay at the RAM. She was a talented pianist as well as a composer, and much of her work is for the piano, most notably the concerto. She gained recognition in 1919 when her symphonic poem *Lamia* was given its première at the Promenade Concerts by Sir Henry Wood and was performed four more times that same season. Her style is essentially romantic, often drawing on nature and landscape for inspiration. The music is tonal, coloured by rich harmonies and chromaticism. The *Phantasy* for violin and piano won the Cobbett Prize in 1921. Her use of mainly small-scale genres in later works – for piano, voice or ensemble – was partly due to the restrictions of ill-health. From 1924 to 1970 she was professor of harmony and counterpoint at the RAM, and in 1971 was elected a member of the Royal Philharmonic Society. A catalogue of Howell's works (compiled by Celia Mike) is held at the British Library.

WORKS
selective list
printed works published in London

Stage: Christmas Eve, perf. 1922; Sanctity, perf. 1938

Orch: Lamia, sym. poem, 1918 (1921); Danse grotesque, 1919; 2 Dances, 1920; Humoresque, 1921; Koong Shee, 1921, rev. 1933; Minuet, str (1923); Pf Conc., 1923; 2 Pieces for Muted Strings, 1926; The Rock, 1928; Fanfare, ?1930; 3 Divertissements, ?1940; 1 sym., Concert Ov., Prelude, Valse caprice, all n.d.

Other inst: Pf Sonata, 1916; 5 Studies, pf (1919); Spindrift, pf (1920); Phantasy, vn, pf, 1921 (1925); The Moorings, vn, pf (1925); Vn Sonata, 1947 (1954); Pf Sonata, e, 1955; 1 str qt, other inst pieces, n.d.

Choral and other vocal works

Principal publishers: E. Arnold, L.J. Casy, Cramer

MSS held by the Dorothy Howell Trust, Bewdley, Worcs.

BIBLIOGRAPHY

E. Kuhe: 'A Girl Musician: Miss Dorothy Howell', *Lady's Pictorial* (4 Oct 1919)

D. Cox: *The Henry Wood Proms* (London, 1980)

C. Mike: 'Dorothy Howell', *British Music*, xiv (1992), 48–58

A. Jacobs: *Henry J. Wood: Maker of the Proms* (London, forthcoming)

CELIA MIKE

Hsiao, Shu-sien. *See* XIAO, SHUXIAN.

Huang, Zhun (*b* Huang Yan County, Zhe Jang Province, 25 June 1926). Chinese composer. She entered the Lu Xun Academy of Arts in Yanan as a drama student in 1938 but in the following year she began to study singing and composition with Xie Xinhai, Lü Ji and Zheng Lücheng. As a vocal performer and actress, she took part in many performances addressed to mass audiences. She composed her first film score in 1948. In 1949 she was appointed resident composer by the Beijing Film Studio and in 1951 became resident composer of the Shanghai Film Studio. Her film music is lyrical and expressive, often based on Chinese folk music materials. Many songs in her film music have become popular because of their mellow melodies. She is a member of the Board of the Chinese Musicians' Association.

WORKS
selective list

Film scores: Xin zhongguo de dansheng [The Birth of New China], 1949; Xin erlü yingxiong zhuan [New Hero and New Heroine], 1950; Xiao mao diaoyü [Little Cat Go Fishing], cartoon, 1952; Qiouweng yüxian ji [Old Man and Nymph], 1956; Lülan wuhao [No.5 in a Women's Basketball Team], 1957; Hongse niangzijün [Red Women Soldiers], 1960; Wutai jiemei [Sisters on Stage], 1964; Muma ren [Horsekeeper], 1982

Television scores: Cuotuo suiyüe [Difficult Years], 1982; Zhongguo guliang [Chinese Girls], 1985; Xihu mei [Beautiful West Lake], 1986; Lüyin [Green Shadow], 1989
Vocal: Meia, shenhuo [O how beautiful, the life], selected songs (1982)

YANDI YANG

Hugh-Jones, Elaine (*b* London, 14 June 1927). British composer, pianist and teacher. She studied the piano with Harold Craxton and Julian Isserlis, and composition with Lennox Berkeley. Alongside teaching (notably at Malvern Girls' College for which much of her choral music was written) she was a BBC accompanist for over 30 years. Almost all her works are vocal, ranging from solo and choral works to an operetta *The Dragon Fear* (1978). Of her song cycles, the seven Walter de la Mare Songs (1966–88) are the best known, blending French influence (in particular Fauré) with a sensitive English Romanticism inherited from Berkeley; her other cycles are *A Cornford Cycle* (1972–4), *Four American Songs* (1974–8) and *Six Songs of R. S. Thomas* (1991). Hugh-Jones's works are published by the Malvern Publishing Company, OUP and Thames; manuscripts and recordings are held at the British Music Information Centre in London.

BIBLIOGRAPHY
CohenE
J. Manning: *New Vocal Repertory: an Introduction* (London, 1986), 43–7 [on the De la Mare Songs]

MARIE FITZPATRICK

Hyde, Miriam Beatrice (*b* Adelaide, 15 Jan 1913). Australian composer and pianist. She studied at the Elder Conservatorium,

Adelaide (MusBac 1931), and in London at the RCM (1932–5). While in London she wrote two piano concertos, which she performed with the LPO and the LSO. Her style is lyrical and post-Romantic, and her principal works include many for the piano: a large sonata (*c*1940), a set of concert studies composed between 1934 and 1982, and numerous miniatures. There are also many songs and chamber works and several short orchestral pieces, including overtures commissioned for specific occasions. Hyde was made OBE in 1981. Her autobiography, *Complete Accord*, was published in Sydney in 1991.

WORKS
selective list
Ballet: Village Fair
Orch: Heroic Elegy, 1934; 2 pf concs., no.1, c♭, 1934, no.2, c♯, 1935; Adelaide Ov., 1957; The Symbolic Gate, sym. poem
Chamber: Cl Sonata, f, *c*1940; Va Sonata, b, *c*1940; Fantasy-Trio, b, op.10, vn/va, vc, pf; Fantasy-Qt, A, 2 vn, va, vc; Suite, a, op.24, fl, va, vc; Dryads' Dance, op.39, vn/fl; Str Qt, e, op.77; Canon and Rhapsody, op.88, cl, pf; Dancing Shadows, op.144 no.1, va; Seashell Fantasy, op.144 no.2, fl
Pf: Fantasy Sonata, c♯, op.14; 11 concert studies, 1934–82; Sonata, g, op.121, *c*1940; many other pieces
Vocal: Behold now, praise the Lord, op.9, anthem, mixed chorus, pf; Dreamland, op.15 (C. Rossetti), S, pf/orch, 1933; Motet, op.33 (Ps xcvi), unacc. chorus 5vv; The Wind in the Sedges, op.43a, 1v, orch, 1937; The Cedar Tree, op.58a, 1v, orch, 1944; The Illawarra Flame, op.97 (P. Francis), mixed chorus, 1955; Bridal Song, op.123 (V. Barton), S, fl, 1962; songs, 1v, pf

BIBLIOGRAPHY
CohenE

GRAHAM HAIR, GRETA MARY HAIR

I

Irman, Regina (*b* Winterthur, 22 March 1957). Swiss composer. She studied guitar at the Winterthur Conservatory, where she also began composing; this activity increased in importance after the completion of her studies, bringing her, in the mid-1980s, recognition in her native country, with radio and CD recordings and regular commissions from cultural institutions both local and national. She began to study percussion at the Winterthur Conservatory in 1989. An interest in the percussive possibilities of non-percussion instruments is also evident in her work, e.g. in the treatment of both voice and piano in the *Vatter-ländischer Liederbogen*. Here too is demonstrated her tendency towards a brittle form of humour uncharacteristic of her Swiss contemporaries.

WORKS
selective list

Vocal: 4 Galgenlieder (C. Morgenstern), Mez, pic + fl, gui, pf, perc, slides ad lib, 1981; In Darkness let me Dwell (after J. Dowland), Mez, ob, vn, va, vc, 1982; Ein vatter-ländischer Liederbogen (A. Wölfli), Mez/A, pf, 1985–6; Ein Trauermarsch (Wölfli), 3 perc, male spkr, 1987; Chopin in der Vertikalen (A. Akhmatova), spkr, timp, pf, tape, 1991; Requiem (Akhmatova), unacc. chorus, 1991–2

Inst: Hügel bei Céret, 2 va, db, 1983; Speculum, 4 cl, 2 perc, 1984; Zahlen, prepared pf, 1986; Klangspiel, prepared pf, 1986; Drive, quarter-tone gui, 1987; Schwarzes Glück, prepared pf, 1988–9; Passacaglia, cl, 1989–90; Schwarzes Glück 2, 4 perc, 1990

CHRIS WALTON

Isabella Leonarda [Leonardi, Anna Isabella] (*b* Novara, 6 Sept 1620; *d* Novara, 25 Feb 1704). Italian composer. Christened Anna Isabella Leonardi, she came from a prominent Novarese family; her father, Count Giannantonio Leonardi, was a Doctor of Law. In 1636 she entered the Collegio di S Orsola, an Ursuline convent, where she remained for the rest of her life. A document of 1658 identifies her as music instructor as well as 'mother and clerk' for her congregation. By 1676 she had attained the rank of

Portrait of Isabella Leonarda from a family tree belonging to the Leonardi family

mother superior and by 1693 *madre vicaria*; in her last years she served as 'counsellor'. She may have studied with Gasparo Casati (*maestro di cappella* at Novara Cathedral, 1635–41), who included two of her compositions in his *Terzo libro di sacri concenti* (*RISM* 1640³). Cotta called her 'la Musa novarese' and printed a sonnet by A. Saminiati Lucchese, comparing her musical talent to the military prowess of Emperor Leopold I.

Leonarda was a skilful, versatile composer whose approximately] 200 compositions include examples of nearly every sacred genre. In her concerted masses and psalm settings, sections for full chorus alternate with solo passages and instrumental ritornellos. Her sacred non-liturgical works frequently have intensely emotional Latin texts, some of which may have been written by Leonarda herself. Four-voice compositions in this genre are conservative: imitative writing is pervasive, and the organ provides the only instrumental accompaniment. Works for one to three voices are more modern, closely resembling chamber cantatas in form and melodic style. Many employ instrumental ritornellos and vocal refrains. In her numerous solo motets the sensuous lyricism of the arias balances the intense dramatic expression of the recitatives. Some arias are strophic, but most employ forms utilizing varied repetition, such as AA' and ABB'. The solo motets reveal the composer at her most expressive: word-painting abounds, and occasional Neapolitan 6ths, augmented 6ths and diminished 7ths enrich the harmonic vocabulary. The vocal writing shows occasional flashes of coloratura, particularly in concluding 'Alleluia' sections.

Leonarda's instrumental works (op.16, 1693) are apparently the earliest published sonatas by a woman. Her sonata for solo violin and continuo is one of her most advanced works harmonically, yet it is technically conservative. In five of the ensemble sonatas she varies the texture by giving solo passages to each of the string instruments.

WORKS

Editions:
Isabella Leonarda: Selected Compositions, ed. S. Carter, RRMBE, lix (1988)
Solo Motets from the Seventeenth Century, iv–v: *Novara I–II* (New York, 1987–8) [facs. edn with introduction by A. Schnoebelen] [S i, ii]

all with organ part;
published in Bologna unless otherwise stated
Motetti . . . libro primo, 3vv, op.2 (Milan, 1665), lost [cited in *FétisB*; possibly repr. from earlier edn]
[18] Sacri concenti, 1–4vv, 2 vn, op.3 (Milan, 1670)

Messa e [10] salmi, concertati, & a cappella con istromenti ad libitum, 4vv, 2 vn, op.4 (Milan, 1674)
[12] Motetti, 1v, 2 vn, op.6 (Venice, 1676)
[12] Mottetti . . . con le litanie della beata vergine, 1–4vv, 2 vn, op.7 (1677)
Vespro a cappella della beata vergine e [11] motetti concertati, 1–4vv, op.8 (1678)
[11] Motetti con le litanie della beata vergine, 4vv, op.10 (Milan, 1684)
[12] Motetti, 1v, op.11 (1684), S i
[14] Motetti, 1v, op.12 (Milan, 1686), S i
[12] Motetti, 1–3vv, 2 vn, op.13 (1687)
[10] Motetti, 1v, op.14 (1687), S ii
[11] Motetti, 1v, op.15 (1690), S ii
[12] Sonate, a 1–4, op.16 (1693)
[12] Motetti, 1v, op.17 (1695), S ii
[3] Messe concertate con stromenti, & [3] motetti, 1–4vv, 2 vn, vle/theorbo, op.18 (1696)
[10] Salmi concertati, 4vv, 2 vn, vle/theorbo, op.19 (1698)
[14] Motetti, 1v, 2 vn, 'bassetto', op.20 (1700)
2 sacred works, 1640³

BIBLIOGRAPHY

EitnerQ; *FétisB*; *GerberL*; *SchmidlD*
L. A. Cotta: *Museo novarese* (Milan, 1701), 269–70
V. Fedeli: 'Antichi musicisti novaresi', *Bollettino storico per la provincia di Novara*, xviii (1924), 308–12
L. Frati: 'Donne musiciste bolognesi', *RMI*, xxxvii (1930), 387–400
M. N. Schnoebelen [A. Schnoebelen]: *The Concerted Mass at San Petronio in Bologna, ca.1660–1700: a Documentary and Analytical Study* (diss., U. of Illinois, 1966), 362–4
S. Carter: *The Music of Isabella Leonarda (1620–1704)* (diss., Stanford U., 1982)
E. Dahnk Baroffio: 'La compositrice Isabella Leonarda', *Novarien*, xiii (1983), 75–92
J. Bowers: 'The Emergence of Women Composers in Italy, 1566–1700', *Women Making Music: the Western Art Tradition, 1150–1950*, ed. J. Bowers and J. Tick (Urbana and Chicago, 1986), 116–61
J. Briscoe, ed.: *Historical Anthology of Music by Women* (Bloomington and Indianapolis, 1987), 39–56

STEWART CARTER

Ivey, Jean Eichelberger (*b* Washington DC, 3 July 1923). American composer and pianist. She studied at Trinity College (BA 1944), the Peabody Conservatory (piano, MM 1946), the Eastman School (composition, MM 1956), and the University of Toronto (composition, DMus 1972). She is coordinator of the composition department at the Peabody Conservatory, Johns Hopkins University, Baltimore, where in 1967 she founded the Peabody Electronic Music Studio. As a pianist she has toured Europe, Mexico and the USA. From 1972 to 1975 and in 1979, she was a director of the League of Composers of the ISCM. She received grants from the NEA to compose *Sea-Change* (1979, première by the Baltimore SO, 1982) and a cello concerto (1983–5). Other awards include the Distinguished Achievement Citation of the National League of American

Pen Women and an Artists' Fellowship from the New York Foundation for the Arts (1992). She has written many articles on music and is herself the main subject of the television documentary (by WRC-TV) *A Woman is . . . a Composer.*

Ivey's early works were tonal and neo-classical, drawing particularly on the styles of Bartók and Ravel; in the 1960s she began to incorporate serial and electronic elements, which gave her music greater fluidity. She has been especially fond of writing for the voice in combination with the orchestra, instruments, piano or tape. Some of her works, including the monodrama *Testament of Eve* (1976), are to her own texts; in general she has preferred poems with a philosophical content, as in *Night Voyage* (1975), after Matthew Arnold's *Self-Dependence.*

WORKS
selective list

Stage: The Birthmark (opera, 1, Ivey, after N. Hawthorne), 1980–82; incid. music for 2 plays, 1963

Orch: Little Symphony, 1948; Passacaglia, chamber orch, 1954; Festive Symphony, 1955; Ov., small orch, 1955; Forms in Motion, sym., 1972; Sea-Change, large orch, tape, 1979; Conc., vc, 1983–5; Voyager, vc, orch, 1987; Short Sym., 1988

Inst: Theme and Variations, pf, 1952; Scherzo, wind septet, 1953; Sonata, pf, 1957; 6 Inventions, 2 vn, 1959; Str qt, 1960; Sonatina, cl, 1963; Ode, vn, pf, 1965, arr. orch, 1965; Aldebaran, va, tape, 1972; Skaniadaryo, pf, tape, 1973; Music, va, pf, 1974; Triton's Horn, t sax, pf, 1982; Ariel in Flight, vn, tape, 1983; Sonata da chiesa, harp, 1986; Suite, vc, pf, 1993; Flying Colors, brass fanfare, 1994; other works, incl. teaching pieces, pf

Vocal: Woman's Love (S. Teasdale), song cycle, Mez, pf, 1962; Tribute: Martin Luther King (spirituals), Bar, orch, 1969; Terminus (R. W. Emerson), Mez, tape, 1970; 3 Songs of Night (W. Whitman, Hovey and Callimachus), S, 5 insts, tape, 1971; Hera, Hung from the Sky (Kizer), Mez, 7 wind, 3 perc, pf, tape, 1973; Testament of Eve (Ivey), monodrama, Mez, orch, tape, 1976; Solstice (Ivey), S, fl/pic, perc, pf, 1977; Prospero (W. Shakespeare), scena, B, hn, perc, 4-track tape, 1978; Crossing Brooklyn Ferry (Whitman), Bar, pf, 1979; Notes toward Time (J. Jacobsen), 3 songs, Mez, fl/a fl, harp, 1984; Entreat me not to leave thee, SATB, 1985; My heart is like a singing bird (C. Rossetti), SSA, fl chorus, 1994; 5 other songs, 2 choruses, carols

Elec: Enter Three Witches, 4-track tape, 1964; Pinball [from film score], 1965; Continuous Form, 1967; Theater Piece, 1970; Cortège – for Charles Kent, 1979

2 film scores, 1963, 1965

Principal publishers: Boosey & Hawkes, C. Fischer, E. C. Schirmer

BIBLIOGRAPHY

LePageWC, i

B. E. Maris: *American Compositions for Piano and Tape-Recorded Sound* (diss., Peabody Conservatory, Johns Hopkins U., 1976) [incl. analysis of *Skaniadaryo*]

R. M. Muennich: *The Vocal Works of Jean Eichelberger Ivey* (diss., Michigan State U., 1983)

SAM DI BONAVENTURA

J

Jabor (Maia de Carvalho), Najla (*b* Rio de Janeiro, 25 Sept 1915). Brazilian composer. She graduated from the Escola Nacional de Música of the University of Brazil (now the University of Rio de Janeiro), where her teachers included Henrique Oswald (piano) and Francisco Braga (composition, fugue and orchestration). A member of the Ordem dos Músicos do Brasil, she participated in the movement to promote Brazilian composers. She was the first Brazilian woman to write a piano concerto (1953). Her compositions are mainly for piano, orchestra or chorus; the last include some occasional anthems. In 1952 she won first prize in the Courrier International competition (USA) with the piano piece *Jongo*; other solo piano pieces include two Nocturnes (1954, 1957) and *Estudo alvorada 1–3* (1970–76). Her orchestral works include *Prelúdio sinfônico* (1957), *Y Juca Pirama* (1957), *Américas* (1958), *Tango brasileiro* (1960) and *Batuquinho clássico* (1966); among her works for voice and piano are *Noturno com palavras* (1958) and a Suite of six pieces (1975). A catalogue of her works was published by the Ministério das Relações Exteriores (Brasília, 1977).

IRATI ANTONIO

Jacobs-Bond, Carrie. *See* BOND, CARRIE.

Jacquet de la Guerre, Elisabeth-Claude (bap. 17 March 1665; *d* Paris, 27 June 1729). French composer and harpsichordist, daughter of the organ builder Claude Jacquet. She was precociously talented as a musician and was first mentioned in 1677, in the July issue of the *Mercure galant*:

For four years a wonder has appeared here [i.e. in Paris]. She sings at sight the most difficult music. She accompanies herself, and others who wish to sing, at the harpsichord, which she plays in an inimitable manner. She composes pieces and plays them in all the keys asked of her. I have told you that for four years she has been appearing with these extraordinary qualities, and she still is only ten years old.

Elisabeth-Claude Jacquet de la Guerre: engraved medallion from 'Le Parnasse françois' (1732) by Evrard Titon du Tillet

In the December 1678 issue the same journal called her 'the marvel of our century'. She was singled out for special favour by Louis XIV, who placed her in the care of his mistress at that time, Mme de Montespan. The king always encouraged her career, giving audience to her performances and permitting her to dedicate her publications to him. Records show that by 1684 she had married the organist Marin de la Guerre. After the death of her only son and of her husband (in 1704) she remained in Paris and busied herself with a series of concerts that she gave at her home in the rue Regrattier in the parish of St Louis-en-l'Ile. Titon du Tillet wrote that 'all the great musicians and fine connoisseurs went eagerly to hear her . . . She had above all a talent for improvising and for playing fantasias extemporaneously'. She also performed at the Théâtre de la Foire, for which she composed a few songs and at least one comic scene. She retired from public performance in 1717 and moved to the rue de Prouvaires in the parish of St Eustache. Titon du Tillet reported that a *Te Deum* by her was sung to mark the recovery of Louis XV from smallpox in 1721, but it has not survived.

Shortly after her death a commemorative medal (reproduced in Titon du Tillet) was struck in her honour.

Her early works include a volume of harpsichord pieces (1687) and a ballet, *Les jeux à l'honneur de la victoire* (1685; this work has not been found). Her opera, *Cephale et Procris*, a tragedy in five acts with a prologue, was performed in Paris at the Académie Royale de Musique on 15 March 1694; it was revived with great success in 1989 by Jean-Claude Malgoire and Daniel Ogier in Saint-Etienne. A number of manuscripts from the 1690s survive, including solo and trio sonatas (some in Brossard's hand, others in a fine round hand presumably hers). More of her music was published after the turn of the century: another volume of harpsichord pieces, with a set of solo violin sonatas (both 1707), and two books of cantatas based on Old Testament stories (1708, 1711); three cantatas on the usual mythological and allegorical subjects were published later.

WORKS
STAGE
Les jeux à l'honneur de la victoire, ballet, 1685; lost, lib *F-Pn*

Cephale et Procris (prol, 5, Duché de Vancy), opera, 15 March 1694 (Paris, 1694)

VOCAL
Cantates françoises sur des sujets tiréz de l'écriture, livre I, 1v, bc, insts (Paris, 1708); 1 cantata, Le passage de la mer rouge, ed. D. Guthrie (Bryn Mawr, PA, 1994)

Cantates françoises, livre II, l, 2vv, bc, insts (Paris, 1711); 1 cantata, Jephté, ed. in Borroff

Cantates françoises, 1v, bc, insts (Paris, n.d.); also incl. Le raccomodement comique de Pierrot et de Nicole, 2vv, bc [perf. as part of Le ceinture de Vénus, Paris, Théâtre de la Foire, 1715]

La musette, ou Les bergers de Suresne (Paris, 1713); attrib. by Brossard

Te Deum, 1721, lost

Songs in Recueil d'airs sérieux et à boire, xxvii, xxx (Paris, 1721–4); Nouveau recueil de chansons choisies, iv (The Hague, 1729); Le théâtre de la Foire (Paris, 1721); Les amusemens de Monseigneur le Duc de Bretagne (Paris, 1712); all listed in Wallon

INSTRUMENTAL
Les pièces de clavessin . . . premier livre (Paris, 1687); ed. C. Bates, Le pupitre, lxvi (Paris, 1986)

Pieces de clavecin qui peuvent se joüer sur le viollon (Paris, 1707); ed. T. Dart and P. Brunold (Monaco, 1965); ed. C. Bates, Le pupitre, lxvi (Paris, 1986); sarabande, gigue, ed. in Borroff

Sonates pour le viollon et pour le clavecin (Paris, 1707)

2 sonatas, vn, va da gamba, bc (org), c1695, Pn

4 trio sonatas, 2 vn, vc, bc (org), c1695, Pn (score [?holograph] and parts)

BIBLIOGRAPHY
Choron-FayolleD; FétisB; GerberL; HawkinsH; SainsburyD; SchillingE; SchmidlD; WaltherML

E. Titon du Tillet: *Le Parnasse françois* (Paris, 1732)

M. Brenet: 'Quatre femmes musiciennes, I: Mademoiselle Jacquet de la Guerre', *L'art*, lix/Oct (1894), 108

R. Viollier: 'Les sonates pour violon et les sonates en trio d'Elisabeth Jacquet de La Guerre et de Jean-François d'Andrieu', *SMz*, xci (1951), 349–51

S. Wallon: 'Les testaments d'Elisabeth Jacquet de La Guerre', *RdM*, xl (1957), 206–14

E. Borroff: *An Introduction to Elisabeth-Claude Jacquet de La Guerre* (Brooklyn, NY, 1966)

C. Bates: *The Instrumental Music of Elizabeth-Claude Jacquet de la Guerre* (diss., Indiana U., 1978)

—— : 'Elizabeth Jacquet de la Guerre: a New Source of Seventeenth-Century French Harpsichord Music', *RMFC*, xxii (1984), 7–49

A. Rose: 'Elisabeth-Claude Jacquet de la Guerre and the Secular *cantate françoise*', *EMc*, xiii (1985), 529–41

J. A. Sadie: '*Musiciennes* of the Ancien Régime', *Women Making Music: the Western Art Tradition,*

Title-page of 'Les pièces de clavessin . . . premier livre' by Elisabeth-Claude Jacquet de la Guerre, privately printed for the composer (Paris, 1687)

1150–1950, ed. J. Bowers and J. Tick (Urbana and Chicago, 1986), 191–223

C. Cessac: *Elisabeth Jacquet de la Guerre (1665–1729): claveciniste et compositeur* (diss., U. of Paris, Sorbonne, 1993)

EDITH BORROFF

Jaëll [née Trautmann], **Marie** (*b* Steinseltz, nr Weissenburg, Alsace, 17 Aug 1846; *d* Paris, 4 Feb 1925). French pianist, teacher and composer. At the age of nine she appeared as a prodigy, giving concerts in Germany, Switzerland and France. At 16, having studied with Fridolin Hamma in Stuttgart, Ignaz Moscheles in Leipzig and Henri Herz in Paris, she won the *premier prix* in piano at the Conservatoire. In 1866 she married the Austrian piano virtuoso Alfred Jaëll and occasionally performed the piano duet repertory with him. Saint-Saëns dedicated his *Variations sur un thème de Beethoven* to them, and Chabrier his *Aubade* to Marie Jaëll. She studied composition with Saint-Saëns and Franck.

Marie Jaëll

She performed all of Liszt's solo piano music in Paris in 1891, all Beethoven's sonatas in 1893 (probably the first to do so in Paris) and the solo piano music of Robert Schumann in 1901. She must have become acquainted with Liszt in 1861 when both were giving concerts in Paris, for in November that year she added his transcription of the *William Tell* overture and other works to her standard repertory. Her husband died in 1881. Beginning in 1882 she participated regularly in the Liszt circle in Weimar. Appreciative of her opinions, he invited her to devise the final bars of the Third Mephisto Waltz and dedicated it to her. She assisted Liszt as secretary during the final three years of his life, and he composed variations (unpublished) on her most famous piece, the *Valses à quatres mains* (1877).

Her compositions include more than 80 pieces for the piano; concertos for cello and for violin (both unpublished), two piano concertos (one published, 1875), the symphonic poem *Ossiane* (1879), a string quartet in G minor and a cello sonata (both unpublished), and other chamber works, songs and choral music. They refer to Liszt in harmonic style and form but show a marked individuality when they dwell on a single emotional state or scene, such as in the piano series on Dante's *Divine Comedy* (*Pièces*, 1894) or the *Six esquisses romantiques*. Moreover, her later style reaches into impressionism and thus beyond the Romantic virtuoso.

She taught at the Paris Conservatoire for many years, almost completely leaving the concert platform for teaching and pedagogical writing after 1895. Her most pervasive legacy has been the emphasis on economy of movement, careful use of arm weight and hand posture, sitting low at the piano and practising slowly but not at extreme length. Originally aiming to explore the physiological basis of Liszt's technique, Jaëll went on to publish ten theoretical volumes, the main thrust of which was the formation of a perfected mental image of sound and its transference to the hand; her three-volume *Le toucher . . . basé sur la physiologie* (1895) and *La musique et la psycho-pédagogie* (1896) are representative. Albert Schweitzer was among her famous pupils, and Debussy knew of her method. It is still promoted by the Association Marie Jaëll in Paris.

WORKS

Orch: 2 pf concs., c (1875), d; Ossiane, sym. poem (1879); Harmonies d'Alsace, 1918; Vc Conc.

Choral: Pseaume, 4vv; Sur la tombe d'un enfant, chorus, orch

Other vocal (for 1v, pf, unless otherwise stated): 4 mélodies (Paris, 1889); La mer, 6 lieder (Paris, 1893); Les orientales, 6 lieder (Paris, 1893); Götterlieder, 1v, orch; La légende des ours, 6 lieder; Runéa, 1v, orch

Chamber: Romance, vn, pf (Paris, 1883); Str Qt, g; Vn Sonata; Vc Sonata

Pf solo: 2 méditations (Leipzig and Winterthur, 1871); Impromptu, 1872; 6 petits morceaux (Leipzig, 1872); Sonata, C (Milan, n.d.); 10 bagatelles (Paris, 1872); [6] Esquisses romantiques (Paris, 1884);

Sphinx, pubd in Album du Gaulois (Paris, 1885); [2] Prismes, pubd in *Le ménestrel* (1888); [6] Valses mignonnes (mélancoliques), pubd in *Le ménestrel* (1888); Promenade matériale (Paris, 1893); Les beaux jours, pubd in *Le ménestrel* (1894); Pièces [Ce qu'on entend dans l'Enfer, . . . dans le Purgatoire, . . . dans le Paradis], pubd in *Le ménestrel* (1894); Les jours pluvieux, pubd in *Le ménestrel* (1894); [10] Harmonies imitatives
Pf 4 hands: [10] Valses (1877); Les voix du printemps (Berlin, 1886)

BIBLIOGRAPHY
FétisBS; *MGG* (H. Klener); *SchmidlD*[†]
R. Delage: 'Trois figures de musiciens contemporains', *La musique en Alsace hier et aujourd'hui* (Paris, 1970), 287–306
M. Lang: *Collection M. Jaëll: pianiste, compositeur, auteur* (Strasbourg, 1980)
M.-H. Cautain: 'L'Association M. Jaëll', *Revue internationale de musique française*, vii/21 (1986), 83–6
JAMES R. BRISCOE

James, Dorothy (*b* Chicago, 1 Dec 1901; *d* St Petersburg, FL, 1 Dec 1982). American composer and teacher. She studied with Adolf Weidig, Howard Hanson, Louis Gruenberg, Healey Willan and Ernst Krenek. From 1927 to 1968 she taught at Eastern Michigan University, Ypsilanti, where she became professor in 1962; she was also music critic for the *Ypsilanti Press*. Her music is for the most part chromatic, well wrought and finely balanced; though based in 19th-century technique, it is not limited to traditional content. The clarity and fluidity of her choral writing create a quite individual luminous sound. James was an allied member of the MacDowell Colony Fellows. She published *Music of Living Michigan Women Composers* (1976).

WORKS
selective list
Opera: Paola and Francesca, 1933
Orch: 3 Sym. Fragments, 1931; Elegy for the Lately Dead, 1938; Suite, small orch, 1940
Choral: Tears (W. Whitman), SATB, orch, 1930; Christmas Night (E. Tatum), SATB, 1933; The Jumblies (E. Lear), SSAA, orch, 1935; The Little Jesus Came to Town (L. Reese), SATB, 1935; Mary's Lullaby (E. Coatsworth), SSAA, 1937; Paul Bunyan (Tatum), Bar, SSAA, orch, 1937; Niobe (J. H. Noyes), SSAA, chamber orch, 1941; The Night (H. Belloc), TTBB, pf, 1950; The Golden Years (A. Tennyson), SATB, orch, 1953; The Nativity Hymn (J. Milton), SSAA. 1957; Envoy (F. Thomson), SSAA, pf, 1958; Mutability (P. B. Shelley), SSAA, ens, 1967
Inst: 3 Pastorales, cl, str, cel, 1933; Autumnal, org, 1934; 2 Satirical Dances, pf, 1934; Recitative and Aria, va, 2 vn, 2 vc, 1944; Dedication, org, 1958; Dirge, pf, 1962; Impressionistic Study, pf, 1962; Tone Row Suite, pf, 1962; Two in One, pf, 1962; Morning Music, fl, pf, 1967; Motif, ob, org, 1970; Patterns, harp, 1977

Solo vocal: The White Moon (P. Verlaine), 1v, pf, 1924; Lacquer Prints (A. Lowell), 1v, pf, 1925; 4 Preludes from the Chinese, A/B, pf qnt, 1930: So sleeps the night (G. Goff), 1v, pf, 1930; Songs for Emily (E. Dickinson), 1v, pf, 1965; Sonnet after Michelangelo, Mez/Bar, hn, pf, 1967
Principal publishers: J. Fischer, Fitz Simmons
EDITH BORROFF

Janárčeková, Viera (*b* Svit, 23 Sept 1944). Czech composer. From 1956 to 1961 she studied the piano at the Bratislava Conservatory with Ilona Štěpánová-Kurzová. She then took part in Zuzana Růžičková's harpsichord masterclasses at the Prague Academy and Rudolf Firkušný's piano masterclasses in Lucerne. From 1972 she taught and performed in Germany, and from 1981 worked there as a freelance (self-taught) composer, painter and performer. Her radio plays *Asparagus contra Gaspara Stampa* and *Jede Nacht* have received awards, and her *Lieder auf der Flucht* for mezzo-soprano and chamber ensemble to poems by Ingeborg Bachmann, won first prize in the women composers' competition at Unna in 1987.

WORKS
selective list
Radio drama: Biomasse, 39 spkr, tpt, crotales, crumhorn, rec, tpt, tuba, clvd, pf, vib, synth, perc, str, 'noises', 1984
Inst: Holzkohle für das Feuerbecken einer Winternacht, 6 Haiku, spkr, fl, cl, pf, perc, 1983; Schlaflosigkeit, 3 movts, cl, ob, bn, 2 hn, pf, 1983; 3 str qts: no.1, 1983, no.2 'Vom Kahlschlag zur Lichtung', 1984–5, no.3 'Ernstfall', 1985–6; Heftige Landschaft mit dreizehn Bäumen, str orch, 1987; Pausenfabrik, cl, b cl, trbn, pf, perc, db, 1986–7; Str Qt no.4, 1989; Beschattungstheater, 4 vc, 1990; Phoenix, 8 vc, 1990; Verkalkung und Jungbrunnen, ob, eng hn, cl, b cl, 2 hn, bn, dbn, 1990; Pf Conc., 1990–91; Zusammenhang mit Sprung, org; [12] Abgestaubte Saiten, pf
Vocal: Ohr: 4 Gesänge (U. Holbein), T, fl, eng hn, pf, 1983–5; Bibeltextvertonungen, spkr, 11 str, synth, 1984; Sarastralien, T, B-Bar, orch, 1984–5; Melodramen (Holbein), 1987; Lieder auf der Flucht (I. Bachmann), Mez, 3 fl + pic + b fl, tpt, hn, trbn, harp, perc, 1987; Donna Laura (dramatic scene, C. Brückner), Mez, 15 insts, 1988–9; Zwischen on und off, 1v, fl, ob, cl, pf, 1989; Der Geheimnisvolle Nachen (F. Nietzsche), Mez, vc, 1989; 6 Siebenschläferinnen, 6 solo female vv, 1990; Der goldene Mantel, 2 lieder, 1v, gui

BIBLIOGRAPHY
KompA-Z
R. Sperber and U. Feld: *5 Jahre internationales Festival Komponistinnen gestern – heute und 5th International Congress on Women in Music* (Heidelberg, 1989), 199–204
DETLEF GOJOWY

Janotha, (Maria Cecylia) Natalia (*b* Warsaw, 8 June 1856; *d* The Hague, 9 June

1932). Polish pianist and composer. She studied with her father in Warsaw, later with Ernst Rudorff and Woldemar Bargiel in Berlin, and also with Brahms and Clara Schumann. She gave concerts throughout Europe and was regarded as one of the finest pianists of her time. In 1885 she was appointed court pianist in Berlin; she often performed at the Prussian and English courts. She lived for many years in London. Her compositions include the *Deutsche Kaisermarsch* (op.9) for piano and orchestra, an *Ave Maria* for soprano and organ (or choir), songs and about 400 piano works; the last include mazurkas, gavottes and other short pieces. Her music was published in Germany and in London. She greatly admired and was very much influenced by Chopin, whose Fugue in A minor she published in Leipzig in 1898. She also translated Polish books on Chopin into English and German.

BIBLIOGRAPHY

Grove1; (G. Grove); *MGG* (Z. Lissa); *PazdirekH* [incl. list of works]; *SchmidlD*

E. Altberg: *Polscy pianiści* (Warsaw, 1947)

ZOFIA CHECHLIŃSKA

Natalia Janotha

Jeske–Choińska–Mikorska, Ludmiła (*b* Małachów, nr Poznań, 1849; *d* Warsaw, 2 Nov 1898). Polish composer. She studied singing in Vienna with Mathilde Marchesi, and in Milan, Paris and Frankfurt. She also studied theory at the Paris Conservatoire and in Warsaw had lessons in composition with M. Zawirski, Gustaw Roguski and Zygmunt Noskowski, and in orchestration with Adam Münchheimer. She taught in Poznań from 1877, and later in Warsaw. She was a gifted composer, particularly of tuneful songs and comic operas. For her ballad *Rusałka* and operatic overtures she was awarded a special diploma at the World's Columbian Exposition in Chicago, 1893, and a medal at the 1894 exhibition at Amsterdam. She was married to the writer Teodor Choiński and wrote a novel, *Muzykanci*, which was published as a serial in the weekly *Rola* (1884). Some of her compositions were published by Gebethner in Warsaw.

WORKS

Stage: Zuch dziewczyna [The Brave Girl] (operetta), Warsaw, 1884; Markiz de Créqui (operetta), Warsaw, 1892

Orch: Rusałka, sym. poem, 1893; Na zamku [At the Castle], polonaise, pf, orch

Pf: Polka (Warsaw, n.d.); Ludmiła, polka (Warsaw, n.d.); Iskierka, polka; mazurkas: Zuch [The Brave One], Do upadłego [Until the Bitter End], Za mną kto żyje [Follow Me]; Mój luby [My Dearest], waltz

Songs: Do miłości [To Love]; Kołysanka 'Noc cudna, urocza' [Lullaby 'The Night is Beautiful and Bewitching'], in *Wędrowiec* (1900), no.11, also pubd separately (Warsaw, before 1907); Pożegnanie żołnierza [Soldier's Farewell]; Słowiczek [The Nightingale] (Warsaw, n.d.); Tyś moja [You're Mine]; Zalotna [The Flirt] (Warsaw, before 1907)

BIBLIOGRAPHY

PSB (W. Hordynski)

S. Sikorski: *Wielka encyklopedia powszechna ilustrowana* (Warsaw, 1890–1908)

K. Michałowski: *Opery polskie* (Kraków, 1954)

IRENA PONIATOWSKA

Jessye, Eva (*b* Coffeyville, KS, 20 Jan 1895; *d* Ann Arbor, 21 Feb 1992). American composer and conductor. She received her musical training at Western University, Kansas, and Langston University, Oklahoma, then taught for a while before settling in New York in the early 1920s. There she studied with Will Marion Cook and Percy Goetschius, and formed the Original Dixie Jubilee Singers (later the Eva Jessye Choir). She was choral director for the premières of Virgil Thomson's *Four Saints in Three Acts* (1934) and George Gershwin's *Porgy and Bess* (1935) and worked to promote interest in African–American musical forms, especially the spiritual. Her works include *The Life of Christ in Negro Spirituals* (1931), the folk oratorio *Paradise Lost and Regained* (1934) and *The Chronicle of Job* (1936).

BIBLIOGRAPHY

D. Cooper: *Eva Jessye, Afro-American Woman: her Contribution to American Music and Theater* (thesis, Hunter College, CUNY, 1979)

D. F. Black: *The Life and Work of Eva Jessye and her Contributions to American Music* (diss., U. of Michigan, 1986)

J. C. Smith, ed.: *Notable Black American Women* (Detroit, 1992)

MARK TUCKER

Non-staged el-ac: Ukolébavka [Lullaby], op.23a, 1978; Výhledy z balkonu [View from a Balcony], op.41, 1991; Včely a slunečnice [Bees and Sunflowers], op.44, fl, tape, 1992
Educational music for children

Principal publisher: Panton

BIBLIOGRAPHY

ČSS

ANNA ŠERÝCH

Jiráčková, Marta (*b* Kladno, 22 March 1932). Czech composer. She studied composition at the Prague Conservatory (1952–8) with Emil Hlobil and later (1962–4) with Alois Hába, whose teaching, together with her friendship with Sláva Vorlová, proved significant to her development as a composer. She undertook postgraduate study at the Janáček Academy of Music in Brno with Ctirad Kohoutek and particularly Alois Piňos (1976–8). For more than 30 years she has worked as a music editor for Czechoslovak Radio in Prague. This experience has not only profoundly enriched her musical knowledge but has also encouraged her to write electroacoustic music. Most of this music is for film and radio but it also includes a ballet, *Lod' bláznů* ('The Ship of Fools', 1991), which won a Czech Music Fund prize. Jiráčková enjoys writing for the human voice, which she treats as an instrument, but her output covers a wide range of genres and includes educational music.

WORKS
selective list

Stage: Lod' bláznů [The Ship of Fools], op.40 (ballet, after the painting by H. Bosch), el-ac, 1991; Pětkrát žena [5 Times a Woman], op.45 (ballet, female v, synth, 1992

Orch: Konfese Slávy Vorlové, op.8, S, tpt, orch, 1973; Nanda Devi (Sym. no.1), op.25, children's and women's vv, tower bells, orch, 1979; Ave Seikilos, op.31, str, perc, 1983; Motýlí efekt [The Butterfly Effect], op.32, vc, perc, str orch, 1984; Silbo (Sym. no.2), op.34, children's vv, large orch, 1987; Hodina skladby [A Lesson of Composition], op.35, org, perc, str orch, 1988

Vocal: Lokh Geet, op.2 (Indian folk poetry), female vv, 1972; Jen tak [Just So], op.3 (J. Prévert), S, fl, 1972; I, Charles Lounsbury, op.7, Bar, pf, 1973; Osm divů světa [8 Wonders of the World], op.18, chorus, harp, perc, 1976; De corde, op.29 (J. Tausinger), S, pf, tower bell, 1982; Svatý Václave [St Wenceslas], op.39 (S, va, pf)/(Mez, org), 1992

Chamber and solo inst: Čtyři preludia [4 Preludes], op.5, pf, 1973; Variace na ukradené téma [Variations on a Borrowed Theme], op.14, ens, 1975; Tři písně beze slov [3 Songs without Words], op.21, S, fl, cl, b cl, eng hn, 1977; Blankenburská fuga [The Blankenburg Fugue], op.33, str qt, 1985; Imago vitae, op.37, org, 1989; Dodekaria I, op.38, vn, pf, 1990; Dodekaria II, op.42, fl, cimb, 1992; Dodekaria tristis, op.43, basset-hn, pf, 1992

Jolas [Illouz], **Betsy** (*b* Paris, 5 Aug 1926). French composer. Her mother was the translator Maria Jolas, of Scottish origin, and her father was Eugène Jolas, a poet, journalist and founder of the magazine *Transition*. Betsy Jolas grew up, therefore, in an artistic milieu whose members included James Joyce, Ernest Hemingway, Henri Matisse, Edgard Varèse and Sylvia Beach. In 1940 her family left for New York, where she was educated at the Lycée Français and, from 1945, at Bennington College, where she studied music with Paul Boepple (theory), Carl Weinrich (organ) and Helen Schnabel (piano), taking the BA in 1946. During this time she sang in the Dessoff choir, and also accompanied on the piano or organ: this gave her constant exposure to Renaissance polyphony, which deeply marked her musical

Betsy Jolas

thought. Having returned to France, she resumed her musical studies from 1948 to 1955 with Simone Plé-Caussade (fugue), Olivier Messiaen (analysis) and Darius Milhaud (composition). She won first mention at a competition for young conductors at Besançon in 1953, and received the Copley Foundation Award (Chicago) in 1954 and the ORTF prize for French-speaking composers in 1961. Jolas did regular work for the ORTF between 1955 and 1970; she served as Messiaen's deputy in his composition class at the Paris Conservatoire, 1971–4, and was appointed a professor of composition and advanced analysis at the Conservatoire in 1975. She has also taught at various establishments in the USA, including Mills College, Yale University, the University of Southern California, Bennington College and Harvard University.

In her music, Jolas has shown a special predilection for the voice, or more generally for a vocal mode of writing, and she has been particularly concerned with relationships between word and music. These interests have been evident since the Reverdy song cycle *Plupart du temps* (1949). More than 20 years later, in her published lecture 'Voix et musique', Jolas quoted a letter from the poet – emphasizing the need for the composer to take great liberties with the text – which outlined her ideas about the relation between words and music. A further step was taken in the five Dupin poems (1959), written in a strict style close to serialism (Jolas has been influenced by serial procedures without completely subscribing to them). On the other hand, the cantata *Dans la chaleur vacante* (1963) is freely lyrical. *Mots* (1963) renewed Jolas's approach to vocal writing in a purified form: she began to write in a vocalistic style with a view to establishing equivalences between voices and instruments. The approach culminated in *Quatuor II* (1964), for coloratura soprano and string trio, in which the voice takes a role tantamount to that of the first violin in a string quartet.

J.D.E. (the significance of these initials remains undisclosed), an instrumental work of 1966, continued the search for a finely drawn style; the writing for harp is particularly noteworthy, and in the following year Jolas was motivated to write a solo piece, *Tranche* (for harp). *D'un opéra de voyage* (1967) for 22 instruments, one of her most engaging and frequently played works, may be seen as an extension of *Quatuor II*, but exploring in a contrary direction: instead of integrating the voice into an instrumental ensemble, this piece is a purely instrumental 'opera'. The instruments are treated as if they were vocalists, behaving 'like voices, singing, laughing, speaking or declaiming, murmuring or sighing', to achieve expressive intensity. There followed two concertante works for solo strings with homogeneous ensembles lacking strings: *Points d'aube* (1967, revised in 1969) for viola and 13 wind, and *Etats* (1969) for violin and six percussion. Both are concerned with confrontation rather than total opposition. *Points d'aube* is remarkable for its melody which, in a consistently atonal context, abounds in scalic patterns – almost invented modes – that are characteristic of Jolas's linear writing. In *Etats*, which balances violin and percussion, contemporary Western music and the musical traditions of the Far East, the percussion is used with refinement, its colouristic resources being drawn on more than its explosive power; the soloist clears the way in this sound world with great elegance thanks to a highly controlled treatment of textures and dynamics. In these works the violin relates to the ensemble like a voice to its instrumental support. Similarly, in *Motet II* (1965), the baritone oboe assumes a principal role, with a mixed choir of 36 voices and orchestra.

In *Quatre plages* (1968) Jolas turned to a standard formation, the string orchestra, finding unexpected possibilities in a body which might be thought exhausted of them. Still more telling is the structural conception, where the opposition between horizontal and vertical is dissolved and where timbres and variable tempos play a primary part. The choral *Sonate à 12* (1970) has particular beauty. Summarizing her experience since *Quatuor II*, Jolas essays a synthesis between different aspects and meanings of song. From vocal sound treated as a pure, almost abstract material to the voice in its essential role of verbal expression, Jolas creates a continuum, abolishing all dualism. The aesthetic and philosophical achievement, accomplished with lucidity and sensitivity, is deeply moving. *Lassus ricercare*, written in the same year, requires an instrumental ensemble dominated by two percussionists and two pianists. The notes are 'de-composed' from works by Lassus and then 're-composed' so as to point out the 'basic drives and . . . constants' in a kind of ' "aerial view" of his whole output', as Jolas wrote in the foreword to the score; 'as a composer', she has said, 'I feel myself indebted to the art of Orlande de Lassus in my preoccupation with the vocal dimension, with expressivity and the certainty that I must remain completely polyphonic'.

Jolas returned to concertante writing in *Musique d'hiver* (1971) for organ and orchestra, the solo part being closely integrated with the ensemble. This work, together with *Autour* (1972) for harpsichord and *Chanson d'approche* (1972) for piano, constitutes her gradual approach to a major keyboard piece. Also from 1971 are *Remember* (dedicated to the memory of the composer Jean-Pierre Guézec) and *Fusain*, linear works which testify to the development of a style which is, in the fullest sense, melodic.

But investigations in the realms of sonority have continued to provide one of the governing impulses of Jolas's invention. In *Musique de jour* (1976), for organ, the musical fabric is organized around timbral melodies and creates a self-amplifying texture, serving the work's meditative character. There are also works for unusual mixtures of sonorities and timbres, for example *D'un opéra de poupée en sept musiques* (composed in 1982 and given at IRCAM in 1984), where electric keyboards and guitar, ondes martenot and electroacoustical devices are combined with conventional wind instruments. Her works of the 1980s and 90s include, as well as a substantial quantity of chamber music, two stage works, following up her chamber opera of 1975 *Le pavillon au bord de la rivière*, which, for soprano and six choristers with three trombones, two flutes, english horn and percussion, and written to a 13th-century Chinese text, draws on elements of ancient Chinese popular theatre. *Le Cyclope* (1986), which treats of the confrontation between the civilized and the primitive, uses an orchestra of two saxophones, three trombones, electric and bass guitars and percussion, and makes use of jazz idioms. *Schliemann*, given in concert form at the opening of the Opéra Bastille in 1990, is scheduled for a stage première at Lyons in 1995.

Jolas's many awards and distinctions include a prize in 1973 from the American Academy of Arts, a Koussevitzky Foundation award and the French Grand Prix National de la Musique in 1974, the Grand Prix de la Ville de Paris in 1981 and the 1992 Prix International Maurice Ravel; she was elected a member of the Institute of the American Academy and Institute of Arts and Letters in 1983 and was named personality of the year by SACEM, Paris, in 1993. Several of her works, representing all stages of her career, have been recorded.

WORKS

STAGE

Le pavillon au bord de la rivière (chamber opera, 4, M. Raoul-Davis, after Kuan Han Chin), 1975; Avignon, 4 Aug 1975
Le Cyclope (opera, 1, after Euripides: *Cyclops*), 1986; Avignon, 27 July 1986
Schliemann (opera, 3, B. Bayen and B. Jolas, after Bayen), 1987; concert perf., Paris, Bastille, 4 April 1990

VOCAL AND CHORAL

With orch: 5 poèmes de Jacques Dupin, S, pf, orch, 1959; L'oeil égare dans les plis d'obéissance du vent (V. Hugo), radiophonic cantata, S, A, Bar, chorus, orch, 1961; Dans la chaleur vacante (A. du Bouchet), radiophonic cantata, solo vv, chorus, orch, 1963; Motet II (J. Dupin), chorus 36vv, chamber orch, 1965; Liring balade (E. Jolas), Bar, orch, 1980
With inst ens or pf: Plupart du temps (P. Reverdy), Mez, pf, 1949; Chansons pour Paule, S, pf, 1951; Everyone Sings, female double chorus, brass, 1955; Mots (B. Jolas), S, Mez, C, T, B, 8 insts, 1963; Plupart du temps II (P. Reverdy), T, t sax, vc, 1989
Unacc.: Arbres, 1954; Enfantillages, female chorus, 1954; Pantagruel, 1954; Et le reste à l'avenant, 1954; Orca, 1955; Diurnes, chorus 12–72vv, 1970; Sonate à 12, 12 solo vv, 1970; Voix premières, radiophonic work, 1974; Caprice à 1 voix, male or female v, 1975; Caprice à 2 voix, S, Ct/C, 1978; Perriault de la lune, chorus 12vv, 1993

ORCHESTRAL AND CHAMBER

9 or more insts: Figures, 9 insts, 1956–65; J. D. E, 14 insts, 1966; D'un opéra de voyage, 22 insts, 1967; Points d'aube, solo va, 13 wind insts, 1967, rev. 1969; 4 plages, str orch, 1968; Lassus ricercare, 10 insts, 1970; 3 rencontres, str trio, orch, 1970–72; Musique d'hiver, org, small orch, 1971; Well Met, 12 str, 1973; 11 Lieder, tpt, chamber orch, 1977; Tales of a Summer Sea, orch, 1977; Stances, pf, orch, 1978; D'un opéra de poupée en 7 musiques, 11 insts, 1982; 5 pièces pour Boulogne, small orch, 1982; Points d'or, sax, 15 insts, 1982; Préludes-Fanfares-Interludes-Sonneries, wind, perc, 1983; Frauenleben, 9 lieder, va conc., 1992
1–8 insts: Episode no.1, fl, 1964; Quatuor II, S, str trio, 1964; Tranche, harp, 1967; Etats, vn, 6 perc, 1969; Remember, eng hn/va, vc, 1971; Fusain, pic, b fl, 1971; How Now, 8 insts, 1973; Quatuor III, 9 études, str qt, 1973; Scion, vc, 1973; O Wall, wind qnt, 1976; Episode no.2 'Ohne Worte', fl, 1977; 4 duos, va, pf, 1979; Episode no.3, pf, 1982; 3 duos, tuba, pf, 1983; Episode no.4, t sax, 1983; Episode no.5, vc, 1983; 4 pièces en marge, vc, pf, 1983; Episode no.6, va, 1984; Episode no.7, el gui, 1984; Episode no.8, db, 1984; Trio, pf, vn, vc, 1988; Music for Joan, vib, pf, 1989; Quatuor IV 'Menus propos', str qt, 1989; E. A., petite suite variée, pf, vib, 1990; Episode no.9 'Forte magnum coloratum', cl, 1990; Trio 'Les heures', str trio, 1990; Etudes aperçues, vib, 5 cowbells, 1992; Musique pour Delphine, vn, vc, 1992; Musique pour Xavier, t sax, vn, 1992; Lettere amorosi, tpt, str qt, 1993; Quoth the Raven . . ., cl, pf, 1993

KEYBOARD

Pf: Chanson d'approche, 1972; B for Sonata, 1973; Mon ami, ariette variée, pf + v, 1974 [for female or child pianist-singer]; Pièce pour St Germain, 1981;

Calling E. C., 1982; Petite suite sérieuse pour concert de famille, 1983; Une journée de Gadad, 1983; Tango si, 1984; Signets: hommage à Maurice Ravel, 1987

Other kbd: Autour, hpd, 1972; Musique de jour, org, 1976; Auprès, hpd, 1980; 3 études campanaires, kbd carillon/pf, 1980; Etude la percues, vib, 1992

Also incid. and film music

Principal publishers: Billaudot, Editions Françaises de Musique, Heugel, Leduc, Ricordi, Salabert

BIBLIOGRAPHY

CC (V. Perlis); LePageWC, i

B. Jolas: 'Il fallait voter sériel même si . . .', Preuves, no.178 (1965), Dec, 40–42

M.-J. Chauvin: 'Entretien avec Betsy Jolas', Courrier musical France, xxvii (1969), 163–73

B. Jolas: 'Voix et musique', Bulletin de la Société française de philosophie, no.2 (1972), April–June

I. Krastewa: 'Betsy Jolas', SMz, cxiv (1974), 342–9

D. Henahan: 'Betsy Jolas Winning Recognition in the USA', New York Times (30 Aug 1976)

B. Massin: 'Betsy Jolas: Roland de Lassus me fascine', Panorama-musiques, no.41 (1981), May–June [interview]

'Voir la musique', L'âne, no.10 (1983), May–June [interview]

J.-P. Derrien, ed.: 20ème siècle: images de la musique française (Paris, 1985), 143–5 [interview]

ANDRÉ BOUCOURECHLIEV
(with DANIEL KAWKA, VIVIAN PERLIS)

K

Kainerstorfer, Clotilde (*fl* second half of 19th century). German composer. She probably lived in Swabia in Bavaria. Between 1874 and 1885, 11 sacred works by her were published by Böhm & Sohn of Augsburg. Opp.17, 39 and 60 are in German, for one to four voices and organ; opp.32, 36, 38, 40, 45, 49 and 51 are in Latin, for one to six voices and organ. Op.47 is a set of ten Christmas carols for voice and piano. All these works are *Gebrauchsmusik* of no great pretension.

ROBERT MÜNSTER

Kamaka'eha Paki, Lydia. *See* LILI'UOKALANI.

Kaminsky, Laura (*b* New York, 28 Sept 1956). She attended Oberlin College and the City College of New York (MA in composition 1980). She has received commissions from a number of organizations, including the New York State Council on the Arts and the 92nd Street Y Chorale, and has been awarded grants from Meet the Composer (1983–92) and a fellowship from the Tuch Foundation (1978–80). She is co-founder of the contemporary music ensemble Musicians' Accord (founded 1980) and from 1988 to 1992 was artistic director of Town Hall, New York. In 1992–3 she was a visiting lecturer at the National Academy of Music in Winneba, Ghana. Kaminsky's compositions consist mainly of intimate chamber works that are characterized by luminous textures and an understated sensuality.

WORKS
selective list

Orch: Untitled, 1992

Chamber, inst: Str Qt no.1, 1977; Enkomios, fl, pf, 1980; In memoriam Eleazer, tpt, 2 hn, trbn, 1980; Duo, fl, perc, 1982; Five for Three, fl, vc, pf, 1982; Remembering August, vn, va, vc, 1983; Still Life for the End of the Day, fl/a fl, ob, cl/b cl, vc, hp, 1984; A Dream Revisited, fl, perc, 1985; Juderla, vn, 1987; Just Here, Sitting Now, cl, pf, 1987; Proverbs of Hell, S, mar, pf, 1989; Whence It Comes, vc, perc, 1989; It Comes and It Goes, fl, gui, 1990; Triftmusik, pf, 1991; And Trouble Came: an African AIDS Diary, nar, va, vc, pf, 1993

Vocal: 13 Ways of Looking at a Blackbird, chorus, fl, 1977; 2 Songs of Emily Dickinson, S, fl, 1980; Para mi corazon, high v, fl, s sax/cl, vc, vib, pf, 1982; Sonnet Lines, Mez/S, fl, vib, pf, 1982; Sonnet Lines no.2, S, pf, 1982; Twilight Settings, S, str qt, perc, 1985, rev. 1988; There is a Season, chorus, cl, vc, perc, pf, 1986; Whitman Songs, Bar, pf, 1992

Dance scores: Steepletop Dances, dancer, ob, perc, 1984; Phaethon, dancer, perc, 1987

LISA B. ROBINSON

Kaprálová, Vítězslava (*b* Brno, 24 Jan 1915; *d* Montpellier, 16 June 1940). Czech composer. Encouraged by her father Václav Kaprál, she started to compose at the age of nine. At the Brno Conservatory (1930–35) she studied composition with Vilém Petrželka and conducting with Václav Chalabala; her graduation work was a piano concerto, which she conducted herself. For the next two years she participated in the

Vítězslava Kaprálová

245

masterclasses of Vítězslav Novák (composition) and Václav Talich (conducting) at the Prague Conservatory, after which a French government scholarship enabled her to move to Paris in 1937. There she studied conducting with Charles Münch and composition with Bohuslav Martinů. For Martinů she became more than a compatriot and talented pupil: they influenced each other when working on similar compositions (Martinů's *Madrigaly*, Kaprálová's *Koleda milostná*, 'Love Carol'), and their correspondence regarding Martinů's *Tre ricercari* and Kaprálová's *Partita* op.20 confirms their close cooperation.

The music Kaprálová wrote in Paris reveals a mature mastery of contemporary musical language as she mingles a concise polytonality with her own melancholy melodic expression. The outstanding works of this period are the Six Variations on the peal of St Etienne-du-Mont for piano, the *Deux ritournelles* for cello and piano, the Partita for piano and strings, the unfinished Concertino and the orchestral *Suita rustica* – the last perhaps her best work.

In 1938, to great acclaim, she conducted the BBC SO in her *Military Sinfonietta* at the ISCM Festival in London. At the end of that year she briefly visited her homeland, Moravia, but under the threat of war she returned to Paris in January 1939. There she married Jiří Mucha, son of the painter Alfons Mucha; she planned to join the theatre of the comic playwrights Jan Werich and Jiří Voskovec in New York, to replace Jaroslav Ježek, but she died of miliary tuberculosis during the evacuation of Paris. After World War II her ashes were sent home; much of her work and correspondence is preserved at the music department of the Moravian Museum in Brno.

WORKS
selective list

Orch: Military Sinfonietta, op.11; Suita rustica, op.19; Partita, op.20, pf, str orch; Concertino, vn, cl, orch, inc.

Chamber and solo inst: Dubnová preludia [April Prelude], op.l3, pf; 6 variace na zvonkovu hru kostela St Etienne du Mont v Paříži [6 Variations on the Peal of the Church of St Etienne–du–Mont in Paris], op.16, pf; Deux ritournelles, op.35, vc, pf; Burlesque, vn, pf; Groteskní passacaglia [Grotesque Passacaglia], pf

Vocal: Jablko s klína [The Apple from the Lap] (J. Seifert), op.10, 1v, pf; Navždy [Forever] (J. Čarek, Seifert), op.12, high v, pf; Sbohem a šáteček [Waving Farewell] (V. Nezval), op.14, S, orch/pf; Zpíváno do dálky [A Faraway Song], op.22, 1v, pf; Koleda milostná [Love Carol], 1v, pf

Principal publishers: Český hudebný fond, Hudební

matice Umělecké besedy, La sirène musicale, Supraphon
Some material in *CS-Bm*

BIBLIOGRAPHY

ČSHS (B. Štědroň)
J. Macek: *Vítězslava Kaprálová* (Prague, 1958)
J. Mucha: *Podivné lásky* [Ridiculous Loves] (Prague, 1988)

JIŘÍ MACEK, ANNA ŠERÝCH

Karamanuk, Sirvart (*b* Constantinople [now Istanbul], 1 Dec 1912). Armenian composer. She studied at the Istanbul Conservatory with Ferdi Statzer (piano) and later took masterclasses with Lazare Lévy and Jean Roger-Ducasse but was mainly self-taught as a composer. Her work includes the children's operetta *Valvan arvestagetnerě* ('Tomorrow's Artists', 1949), *Alt'amar* (symphonic poem, 1969), *Erg Petros Duryani* ('Song of Petros Duryan', choral cycle, 1972), piano compositions, about 90 songs, a collection of children's ditties and arrangements of liturgical chants. She possesses a facile melodic gift that is imbued with the spirit of traditional Armenian music. Often her work is vivid, opulent in colour and buoyant in texture.

BIBLIOGRAPHY

G. Muradian: 'Haskc'an, havatac'in u sirec'in' [They Understood it, Believed in it and Loved it], *Payk'ar* [Istanbul] (19 March 1970), 2
C'. Brutyan: 'Sp'yurk'ahay kin kompozitorner' [Armenian Women Composers of the Diaspora], *Žamanak* [Istanbul] (1 Oct 1990), 2
'Sp'yurk'ahay ergahanner: Sirvart Karamanuk' [Diasporan Composers: Sirvart Karamanuk], *Kanc* [Erevan] (21 Oct 1992), 3
R. Haddejian: 'Eražštaget-horinol tikin Sirvart Karamanukiani masin' [About the Musicologist and Composer Sirvart Karamanuk], *Marmara* [Istanbul] (28 Dec 1992), 3
L. Kasbarian: 'Music for the Bards', *Armenian International Magazine*, v/2 (1994), 46

ŞAHAN ARZRUNI

Karastoyanova, Elena (*b* Sofia, 1 Oct 1933). Bulgarian composer. She studied at the Sofia Academy of Music where her teachers included her father, Assen Karastoyanov (composition), Zdravko Manolov (polyphony) and Lili Atanasova (piano). After her graduation in 1958, she was appointed lecturer in harmony and music analysis at the Sofia State School of Music. She was director of the Institute for Music and Choreography (1979–82) and later of the Sofia State School of Choreography (1983–8). Her music couples the spirit of traditional Bulgarian folk music as revealed in the first half of this century with the more modern aesthetic of the 1950s. She is the author of studies of Bach polyphony and Bulgarian folk music.

WORKS
selective list

4 Pieces, pf, 1964; Vn Sonata, 1967; Symfonietta, str, 1969; Cantata, unacc. mixed vv, 1975; Dni [Days], unacc. mixed vv, 1975; Song cycle, unacc. vv, 1977; Allegro, tpt, pf, 1980; Summer, cycle of children's pieces, pf, 1982

Principal publishers: Muzïka, Nauka i Izkustvo

MAGDALENA MANOLOVA

Kasilag, Lucrecia Roces (*b* San Fernando, La Union, 31 Aug 1918). Filipina composer and writer. She studied at the Philippine Women's University (BA 1936, BMus 1949), at St Scholastica's College and at the Eastman School (MMus 1950); her principal teachers were Antonio Molina and Wayne Barlow. From 1953 to 1977 she was dean of the College of Music and Fine Arts of the Philippine Women's University, and from 1976 to 1986 president and artistic director of the Cultural Centre of the Philippines. She has held chairmanships of the League of Filipino Composers (1956–), the Asian Composers' League (1975–90) and the Federation for Asian Cultural Promotion (1981–6). Among many national and international honours, in 1989 she was named National Artist for Music of the Republic of the Philippines and in 1993 was elected an honorary member of the International Music Council. Kasilag's earliest works were solo songs dating from the late 1940s and early 50s. She went on to compose song cycles, chamber music and works for voice and orchestra, some of which demonstrate her interest in percussion and electronic music. Her contribution to Philippine music lies mainly in her introduction of contemporary Western techniques and in her combining of Western and oriental instrumental resources. A number of her theatrical works had their genesis in her association with the folkdance group Bayanihan.

WORKS
selective list

Orch, vocal orch: Divertissement, pf, orch, 1960; Legend of the Sarimanok, chamber orch, 1963; Handog sa Kababaihan [Apostrophe to Womanhood], S, orch, synth, 1974; Vn Conc., 1983; In the Beginning, Bar, mixed chorus, orch, 1988

Sacred: Missa brevis, female chorus, 1963; Filisiana, mixed chorus, Asian insts, 1965; De profundis, S, A, T, B, chorus, double chorus, orch, 1977; The Spiritual Canticle of St John of the Cross (eclogue-operatorio), solo vv, chorus, str, wind, perc, dancers, 1991

Dance scores: Dularawan: Golden Salakot, solo vv, chorus, insts; Sisa, orch, chant, synth, 1978; Tapestry, orch, 1983; Legende, orch, 1984

Chamber: Toccata, wind, perc, 1959; Larawan ng Kababaihan [Portrait of Womanhood], S, A, chorus, fl, hn, bn, str, timp, perc, 1980; Orientalia, pf, fl, ob, tpt, trbn, timp, perc, Philippine perc, 1981; Peking Interlude, kucheng, chamber ens, 1981; Munting principe [Small Prince], 1v, pf, synth, 1988

Kbd: Derivations I–V, prepared pf, 1961, 1963, 1966, 1969, 1982; Elegy on Mt Pinatubo, 1991

Elec: Trichotomy, 1v, insts, tape, 1967; Ekologie I, tape, perc, 1972; 5 Portraits, 2 amp pf, gongs, Kubing jew's harp, transistor radio, 1973

Principal publishers: Silliman Music Foundation (Dumagueta City); Southern Music (New York)

JOSÉ MACEDA/R

Kassia [Kasia, Eikasia, Ikasia; Kasiane, Kassiane] (*b* 810). Byzantine-Greek composer. She is identified in manuscripts by various forms of her name; in modern Greek literature she is referred to as Kasiane (or Kassiane). Kassia is the most important woman composer of medieval Byzantine chant. She also wrote liturgical and secular poems, as well as epigrams and moral sayings, and was considered the most beautiful and intelligent candidate in the selection of a bride for Emperor Theophilos. Kassia's musical compositions were written during the reigns of Theophilos (829–42) and his son Michael (842–67). She has been credited with writing 49 liturgical compositions, although the authenticity of 26 is disputed. She composed music to the texts of contemporary writers and may have set her own liturgical poems, as was the practice of early hymnographers.

Most of Kassia's music falls into the category of stichēron, a lengthy verse chanted in various parts of the morning and evening Offices. Her melodies closely reflect the rhythms of the text and exhibit a preference for the deuterus and tetrardus modes; she is also known to have used the medieval sequence form.

BIBLIOGRAPHY
D. Touliatos-Banker: 'Medieval Women Composers in Byzantium and the West', *Musica antiqua VI: acta scientifica: Bydgoszcz 1982*, 687–712 [incl. catalogue of Kassia's works]

—— : 'Women Composers of Medieval Byzantine Chant', *College Music Symposium*, xxiv/1 (1984), 62–80 [incl. catalogue of Kassia's works]

——: 'Kassia', *Historical Anthology of Music by Women*, ed. J. R. Briscoe (Bloomington, IN, 1987), 1–5

D. Touliatos: 'The Traditional Role of Greek Women in Music from Antiquity to the End of the Byzantine Empire', *Rediscovering the Muses: Women's Musical Traditions*, ed. K. Marshal (Boston, 1993), 111–23, 250–53

—— : 'Kassia', *Women Composers: an Historical Anthology*, i: *Early Middle Ages through the Renaissance*, ed. S. Glickman and M. Schleifer (in preparation) [incl. facs. and transcrs.]

DIANE TOULIATOS

Kats [Katz, Kats-Chernin], **Elena** (*b* Tashkent, 4 Nov 1957). Australian composer of Uzbek origin. She emigrated to Australia with her family in 1975. After graduating from the Sydney Conservatorium (1979) she studied with Helmut Lachenmann at the Hochschule für Musik in Hanover. Thereafter she produced numerous soundtracks for theatre performances in Bremen, Bochum and Vienna. She also composed orchestral, chamber and solo works. Although she has continued to live in Germany, she has maintained connections with Australia and Australian performing organizations. Her music often uses simple formulaic material which is treated in idiosyncratic textures.

WORKS
selective list

Music-theatre: Behind the Scenes, 1985; Choros, 1988; Hours, 1990

Orch: Pf Conc., pf, perc, double str orch, 1979; Bienie, 1980; Introduction to a Dance, 1983; Stairs, 1984; Vn Conc., 1990; Transfer, 1990

Other inst: Metro, 2 pf, 2 metronomes, 1976; Shestizvuchiya, pf, 1977; Veter, fl, cl, vc, 1977; Chu, trbn, perc, 1978; Chechyotka I, trbn, pf, 1979; Zeugspiel, vc, trbn, 1981; In Tension, fl, b cl, vn, vc, perc, 1982; Reductions, 2 pf, 1983; Duo I, vn, pf, 1984; Pre, fl, trbn, vc, perc, 2 pf, 1985; Solo January, accordion, 1985

Choral: Rasperry, mixed chorus, 1989

GRAHAM HAIR, GRETA MARY HAIR

Keal, Minna [Nerenstein, Mina] (*b* London, 22 March 1909). English composer. At the RAM she studied the piano with Thomas Knott and composition with William Alwyn; she received a bursary for composition in 1929. Domestic circumstances forced her to stop composing but in retirement she began again, taught by Justin Connolly (from 1975) and Oliver Knussen (from 1982). Her early pieces were influenced by Bruch and Debussy, but her later works, such as the string quartet (1976–8), show a new awareness of Bartók and Shostakovich. Her Symphony (1980–85), a powerful, stormy, dissonantly chromatic work, organized around Golden Sections and making free melodic use of 12-note technique, has attracted considerable attention and was given its first complete performance at a BBC Promenade Concert in 1989. Among her other later works are a wind quintet

(1978–80) and *Cantillation* for violin and orchestra (1985–8). Scores, recordings and other materials are held at the British Music Information Centre, London.

BIBLIOGRAPHY

CohenE; Fuller-LeFanuRM

K. Potter: 'Never too Late to Write', *Classical Music* (11 Feb 1984), 19

T. Sutcliffe: 'Minna's Music', *The Guardian* (13 Feb 1984) [interview]

F. Maddocks: 'Born Again Composer', *The Independent* (21 March 1988) [interview]

M. J. White: 'Veiled in Innocence', *The Independent* (6 Sept 1989)

MARIE FITZPATRICK

Kelly, Denise (*b* Belfast, 24 April 1954). Irish composer. In 1963 she moved to Dublin, where she studied the harp at the Royal Irish Academy of Music and graduated (BMus) from Trinity College. She also studied in London (GSM) with Robert Barclay Wilson (composition), Sidonie Goossens (harp) and Maria Korchinska (harp), and in Ireland with James Wilson (composition). Her ensembles often contain a harp, for example, *Journey of a Soul*, for voice and harp (a setting of five poems by James Joyce, 1977); *Dialogue to Unity*, for flute, harp and string quartet (1978); *Soundings*, for cello and harp (1984); *Hélas mon Dieu* (text by Claude le Jeune), for mezzo-soprano, flute and harp (1974); and *Idle Dreams* (translations of Chinese folk poems), for mezzo-soprano, flute and harp (1980). Her musical language is basically tonal, though in the 1970s she showed some interest in serialism. Her music has a definite Irish flavour (through Irish harp music), but she has also been particularly influenced by French music, including impressionism and the songs of Fauré and Duparc.

SARAH M. BURN

Kerkado, Mlle **Le Sénéchal de** (*b* c1786; *d* 1805 or later). French composer. In 1805 the archives of the Opéra-Comique in Paris recorded that she was then 19 years of age. Her one-act *comédie mêlée d'ariettes*, *La méprise volontaire ou La double leçon*, was first given on 24 June 1805 at the Opéra-Comique (not on 5 June as stated on the libretto issued in 1807, when the work was revived on 2 January that year); the libretto was by Alexandre Duval.

DAVID CHARLTON

Kern [née Seitz], **Frida** (*b* 9 March 1891; *d* Linz, 23 Dec 1988). Austrian composer. She spent her childhood and youth in Linz. In 1923 she entered the Vienna Music

Academy, where she studied composition with Franz Schmidt and conducting with Clemens Krauss and Robert Heger. By the time of her graduation in 1927 she was the only woman to have completed those subjects there. In 1942 the city of Linz awarded her its composition prize. For the next two years (1943–5) she was a lecturer in music theory at the University of Vienna, but thereafter dedicated herself exclusively to composing. In 1960 she received an honorary professorship from the Austrian president.

As a composer she described herself as neo-classical. Her output includes several large orchestral works and she composed prolifically for chamber ensembles (including five string quartets). She died in a car accident.

WORKS
selective list

Orch: Vn Conc., op.27, 1937; Vc Conc., op.28, 1937; Suite, op.33, 1939; Afrikanische Stimmungsbilder, op.34, small orch, 1934; Pf Conc., op.36, 1940; Variations, op.38, 1941; Passacaglia, op.45, 1943; Sym. no.1, op.46, 1943; Concertino, op.60, tpt, orch, 1951; Sym. March, op.73, 1956

Vocal: Auferstehungskantate, op.31, S, Bar, chorus, 1938; 3 Orchesterlieder, op.41, Bar, orch, 1942; Kinderchorlieder, op.52, 1952; 3 lieder cycles: op.65, A, pf, 1953, op.69, Mez, pf, 1954, op.83 (after Chin. texts), A, pf; Hymnus, op.78, A, str qt, 1959; Frau Musica, op.85, hymn, male chorus, brass

Chamber: Str Qt no.1, op.8, 1930; Vn Sonata, op.9, 1931; Vc Sonata, op.10, 1931; Pf Trio, op.15, 1933; Cl Qnt, op.19, 1933; Str Qt no.2, op.21, 1934; Ernste Musik, op.37, ww, brass, perc, 1940; Str Qt no.3, op.39, 1941; Str Trio, op.42, 1942; Str Qt no.4, op.48, 1948; Str Qnt, op.57, 1950; Rondino, op.58, pf, str qt, 1950; Fröhliche Impressionen, op.51, fl, vn, va, vc, harp, 1951; Ballade, op.59, harp, 1951; Variations, op.61, vn, harp, 1951; Serenade, op.62, fl, pf, 1952; Str Qt no.5, op.72, 1956; Etudes, op.80, mand, 1959

Pf: Russische Sonate, op.1, 1926; Scherzo, op.13, 2 pf, 1932; 3 Pieces, op.49, 2 pf, 1947; Elegy and Toccata, op.56, pf LH, 1949; Introduction and Toccata, op.66, 1953; Capriccio, op.70, 1955

BIBLIOGRAPHY
CohenE

ROSARIO MARCIANO

Khosrovidukht. *See* XOSROVIDUXT.

King, Gilbert. *See* HARRISON, SUSIE FRANCES.

Kinkel [Matthieux; née Mockel], **Johanna** (*b* Bonn, 8 July 1810; *d* London, 15 Nov 1858). German writer, composer and conductor. She was the daughter of Joseph Mockel (a teacher at the French lycée in Bonn) and Anna Maria Mockel. She studied the piano and composition with Franz Ries in Bonn and in 1829 took over the direction of the Musikalische Liebhabergesellschaft formed by his pupils and friends. Beginning in 1830 she composed lieder, duets and stage works for amateurs. She divided her time between conducting opera and writing poetry, political articles and art criticism. In 1831 she met Paul Matthieux (a book dealer) and was briefly married to him; they soon separated, but her divorce was not settled until 1839.

In 1836 she travelled to Berlin via Frankfurt, where she met Felix Mendelssohn, who became an admirer of her compositions. In Berlin she studied composition with Karl Böhmer and the piano with Wilhelm Taubert. Her friends included Fanny Mendelssohn and Bettina Brentano. Her stage works, full of humour and irony, were warmly received, and her lieder (many of them to her own texts) came to the attention of Robert Schumann.

In 1839 she returned to Bonn, where she composed, taught, took up again the direction of the Liebhabergesellschaft and wrote essays. There, in 1840, she met the theologian, amateur poet and future art-historian Gottfried Kinkel. They founded Der Maikäferbund (with Burkhard, Freiligrath and Simrock among many others) and in 1843 were married; four children were born during the first six years of their marriage. In 1848 Gottfried Kinkel gained prominence as a political leader and following a demonstration in 1849 was imprisoned. Johanna's political position at this time was no less critical, and she was forced to move to Cologne because of her activities as a newspaper publisher and writer. When Gottfried was freed the family made their way to London. Johanna stopped composing, became an advocate of women's rights and suffered a series of depressions which eventually drove her to commit suicide (by jumping out of a window).

WORKS

Stage: Die Assassinen (Liederspiel, G. Kinkel); Die Landpartie (operetta); Das Malzbier, oder Die Stadt-Bönnischen Gespenster (Lustspiel); Otto der Schütz (Liederspiel, 1, G. Kinkel); Themis und Savigny, oder Die Olympien in Berlin (vaudeville)

Choral, cantatas: Die Vogelkantate (J. Mockel), op.1; Hymnus in Coena Domini, chorus, orch, op.14; Chant du départ; Jubiläum des Grossvaters, 1849; Katzenkantate: Aus meiner Kindheit; other works

Other vocal: lieder collections, opp.6–8, 10, 16–19,

21; Schloss Boncourt (A. von Chamisso), op.9, 1v, pf; Duets, opp.11–12, female vv; Don Ramiro, Ballade, op.13, A/Bar, pf; Anleitung zum Singen, op.20, for children 3–6 years old; Tonleitern und Solfeggien, op.22, A, pf; arrs. of Gk. and Scottish folksongs; other pieces

BIBLIOGRAPHY

W. Hesse: *Gottfried und Johanna Kinkel* (Bonn, 1893)

E. Thalheimer: *Johanna Kinkel als Musikerin* (Bonn, 1922)

G. Kinkel: *Selbstbiographie* (Bonn, 1931)

S. Gustedt: *Johanna Kinkel: Leben und Werk* (Hamburg, 1981)

E. Weissweiler: *Komponistinnen aus 500 Jahren* (Frankfurt, 1981)

B. Schumacher: *Die Situation der Komponierende Frau im deutschen Biedermeier* (Frankfurt, 1983)

ROSARIO MARCIANO,
JORGE SANCHEZ-CHIONG

Kirkwood, Antoinette (*b* London, 26 Feb 1930). English composer. She studied the piano at the Royal Irish Academy of Music and composition in London with Dorothy Howell. In 1961 she married the writer Richard Phibbs. Accompanying her mother, the lieder singer Rome Lindsay, proved an enduring influence. Kirkwood's style has developed from her three orchestral Fantasias (each based on an Irish folksong), through her six Bartókian Intermezzos for piano (composed in 1959), to the technically demanding exploration of guitar idioms in *Soliloquy* (1990). Her output includes a symphony, music for two ballets, various instrumental pieces, including a cello sonata and *Rapsodie* for harp (both published in 1990), and many songs. Her music is published by Curlew and Andresier.

BIBLIOGRAPHY

Fuller-LeFanuRM

MARIE FITZPATRICK

Kistétényi, Melinda (*b* Budapest, 25 July 1926). Hungarian composer. She studied at the Budapest Academy of Music (1946–53), where her teachers included György Kósa (piano), Ferenc Szabó and János Viski (composition), and Sebetyén Pécsi (organ). She began her career as assistant choirmaster of the National Trade Unions Choir (1952–4) and the Home Office Choir (1954–6), and was later deputy choirmaster of the Central Choir of Hungarian State Railways (1958–63). From 1956 to 1989 she was professor of music theory at the Budapest Academy, and from 1959 gave organ recitals in Hungary and abroad. As a teacher she was among the most prominent Hungarian followers of Kodály's method and she wrote poetic texts to his *Epigrammák* (vocalises) and *Tricinia*.

She also translated many oratorio texts into Hungarian. Her compositions are basically tonal and technically accomplished, and combine gentle, refined lyricism with unusually dramatic expression.

WORKS

Stage: A halálratáncoltatott leány balladája [Ballad of the Girl Dancing to Death] (ballet, after Hung. folk ballad), 1958; Szerenád [Serenade] (ballet), 1958

Inst: 2 suites: ob, 1952, org, 1957; Org Conc., 1962; Járkály csak halálraítélt [You are just left to walk condemned to death] (after M. Radnóti), hn, org, harp, 1978; studies for vn, trbn

Vocal: Songs (E. Ady, S. Petőfi, R. M. Rilke, J. Vajda), 1954; Eng., Scottish, Welsh folksong settings, 1957; A vízrenéző [Looking on the Water], Bar, fl, gui, vc, 1972–3; Gondolatok [Ideas] (Petőfi), duets; songs and choruses to 20th-century Hungarian texts

RITA KAIZINGER

Klechniowska, Anna Maria (*b* Borówka, Ukraine, 15 April 1888; *d* Warsaw, 28 Aug 1973). Polish composer and teacher. She studied at the conservatories of Warsaw and Lemberg (now L'viv) in 1905 and then attended the Leipzig Conservatory (1906–8), where her teachers were Joseph Pembaur (piano) and Stephan Krehl (composition). Afterwards she studied the piano at the Kraków Music Institute with Klara Czop-Umlaufowa (until 1911) and at the Vienna Music Academy with R. Schmidt (graduating in 1917). From 1918 to 1939 she taught her own music courses for beginners in Warsaw, after which she studied composition with Nadia Boulanger in Paris. She was also a professor of piano at the Institute for Popular Music in Łódź. Though Klechniowska's educational music enjoys greater popularity than her other works, her output in most areas is quite extensive. Her orchestral music includes *Wawel*, a symphonic poem (1917), and *The Seasons* (1953), and among her several ballets are *Juria* (1939) and *Fantasma* (1964). Her elementary piano manual of 1916 is still used today for teaching beginners.

BARBARA ZWOLSKA-STĘSZEWSKA

Klinkova, Zhivka (*b* Samokov, 30 July 1924). Bulgarian composer, pianist and conductor. She graduated from the Sofia Academy of Music in 1951 where her teachers were Parashkev Hadjiev (composition) and Dimitar Nenov (piano). After working as a conductor and composer with the state-sponsored Philip Koutev Folksong and Dance Company (1951–60), she furthered her composition studies with

Rudolf Wagner-Régeny (1960–66) and then Boris Blacher in Berlin (1966–8). She is now a prolific freelance composer with an output that includes 11 ballets, four operas and a musical, most of which have been performed professionally in state theatres in Germany and the former Czechoslovakia. While Klinkova's emotional, quasi-Romantic idiom, which exhibits considerable melodic invention, draws on the characteristics of Bulgarian folk music, her themes are generally contemporary. In her ballet *Than saen* ('Vietnamese Poem'), for instance, she connects the magical world of fairies to that of the heroic, war-ridden Vietnamese, while the children's ballet *Quenny, the Little.Negro* examines the issue of racial oppression. The historical themes of both *Vassil Levski* and *Cyril and Methodius* contribute to the tradition of Bulgarian grand opera. The latter recounts one of the most significant episodes in Slav history – the appearance of Slavonic script – and tells of the fight of the eponymous brothers for recognition of the Slavonic liturgy. Klinkova employs the musical symbols of the Orthodox and Catholic churches – old Bulgarian and Gregorian chant – to help enact this struggle in music.

Barbara Kolb

WORKS
selective list

Stage: Petko Samohvalko [Boastful Petko], 1956 (children's opera, N. Trendafilova), Berlin, Theater der Freundschaft, 20 April 1960; Kaliakra, 1966 (ballet, S. Aladjov), Usti nad Labem, 30 March 1978; Than saen [Vietnamese Poem], 1972 (ballet, L. N. Kanh), Brno, Janáček Theatre, 17 Dec 1976; Quenny, the Little Negro, 1973 (children's ballet, Klinkova), Kiel, 30 Nov 1975; Isle of Dreams (musical, P. Panchev), Teplice, 11 Nov 1978; The Most Improbable (fairy-tale opera, Klinkova), 1980; Cyril and Methodius, 1981 (opera, V. Markovski and J. Gyermek), Bydgoszcz, 7 Feb 1986 [concert perf.]; Vassil Levski (opera, Klinkova), 1992

Orch: Sinfonietta no.1, 1960; Bulgarian Symphonic Suite no.1, 1963; Vn Conc., 1964; Ballad, 1972; Conc., 2 vn, timp, str, 1973; Sym. no.2, 1974; Cantata, chorus, orch, 1982; Conc., pf, str, 1992

Chamber, pf: Pf Sonata, 1950; Trio, bagpipes, 1955; Vn Sonata, 1963; Sonata, fl, va, 1969; Duo, 2 kavals, 1972; Trio, fl, ob, bn, 1974; 8 Preludes, 2 fl, 1975; 7 Frescoes, 2 fl, 1975; 10 Pieces, folk ens, 1978

Principal publisher: Muzika

MAGDALENA MANOLOVA

Kolb, Barbara (*b* Hartford, CT, 10 Feb 1939). American composer. She studied the clarinet, and composition with Arnold Franchetti, at Hartt College of Music (BM 1961, MM 1964); she also studied with Lukas Foss and Gunther Schuller at the Berkshire Music Center (1964, 1968). From 1960 to 1966 she was a clarinettist in the Hartford SO. She was the first American woman to receive the Prix de Rome (1969–71); among many other awards, enabling her to study in Vienna and Paris and at Mills College (electronic music), have been a Fulbright Scholarship, several MacDowell Colony fellowships, two Guggenheim fellowships, and the Kennedy Center Friedheim Award (1987, for *Millefoglie*). Major commissions include *Trobar Clus* and a work for chamber orchestra for the Fromm Foundation, *Soundings* for the Koussevitzky Foundation, *The Enchanted Loom* for the Atlanta SO and *All in Good Time* for the New York PO. She was composer-in-residence at the Marlboro Music Festival (1973), the American Academy in Rome (1975) and IRCAM (1983–4), and briefly held teaching positions in theory and composition at Brooklyn College, CUNY, Temple University and the Eastman School of Music. From 1979 to 1982 she served as artistic director of the contemporary music series Music New to New York at the 3rd Street Music School Settlement, and between 1982 and 1986 she developed a music theory course, sponsored by the Library of Congress, for the blind and physically disabled.

Kolb's music is highly eclectic, assimilating diverse styles and exploring different media; contemporary idioms, ranging from serialism to jazz, are uniquely synthesized. Many of her works also respond to a variety of extra-musical sources, including the visual arts (*Grisaille*) and poetry (*Appello* and *Spring River Flowers Moon Night*). *Appello* uses serial techniques, with a note row borrowed from Pierre Boulez's *Structures Ia*, but despite this kinship the two works produce highly contrasting effects: unlike Boulez's work, *Appello* features rich sonorities and repeated melodic and harmonic patterns. Jazz elements are incorporated most notably in *Chromatic Fantasy* and *Homage to Keith Jarrett and Gary Burton*. Besides fusing different styles, Kolb has combined electronic and acoustic media. In *Millefoglie* a computer-generated tape and a chamber orchestra blend diverse colours and interweave contrasting layers of sound. Many pieces in addition to *Millefoglie*, particularly the orchestral works *Grisaille*, *Soundings* and *The Enchanted Loom*, explore the superimposition of multiple harmonic and rhythmic layers. *Soundings*, her best-known work, is based on the technique of depth-measurement and cast in a tripartite, quasi-palindromic form. The first section 'descends' through successive layers to a climax and the last 'ascends' to the surface through different layers with rhythmic acceleration. In the central section the texture is dissipated, and motivic patterns from the opening are isolated and developed.

WORKS

Orch: Crosswinds, wind, perc, 1968; Trobar Clus, chamber orch, 1970; Soundings, chamber orch, tape, 1971–2, rev. 1975, 1978; Grisaille, 1978–9; Millefoglie, chamber orch, computer-generated tape, 1984–5; Yet that Things go Round, chamber orch, 1986–7, rev. 1988; The Enchanted Loom, 1988–9, rev. 1992; Voyants, pf, chamber orch, 1991; All in Good Time, 1994

Chamber and solo inst: Rebuttal, 2 cl, 1965; Figments, fl, pf, 1967, rev. 1969; Solitaire, pf, tape, 1971; Toccata, hpd, tape, 1971; Spring River Flowers Moon Night, 2 pf, perc, tape, 1974–5; Looking for Claudio, gui, tape, 1975; Appello, pf, 1976; Homage to Keith Jarrett and Gary Burton, fl, vib, 1976; Musique pour un vernissage, fl, gui, vn, va, withdrawn; 3 Lullabies, gui, 1980; Related Characters, pf, tpt/cl/sax/vn, 1980; Cantico, film score, tape, 1982; Cavatina, vn/va, 1983, rev. 1985; Time . . . and Again, ob, str qt, tape, 1985; Umbrian Colors, vn, gui, 1986; Extremes, fl, vc, 1989; Cloudspin, org, tape, 1991; Introduction and Allegro, gui, 1992 [replaces Molto Allegro, 1988]; Monticello Trio, vn, vc, pf, 1992

Vocal: [7] Chansons bas (S. Mallarmé), S, harp, perc,

1966; 3 Place Settings (I. Diamond, C., R. and B. Brown, R. Costa), nar, cl, perc, vn, db, 1968; [5] Songs before an Adieu (R. Pinsky, E. E. Cummings, H. Stern, V. Popa, G. Apollinaire), S, fl, gui, 1976–9; Chromatic Fantasy (Stern), amp nar, amp a fl, ob, sax, tpt, elec gui, vib, 1979; Poem, chorus, 1980; The Point that Divides the Wind (Franciscan and Gregorian chant), 3 solo male vv, org, perc, 1982; The Sundays of my Life, jazz song, 1982

Principal publishers: Boosey & Hawkes, C. Fischer, Peters

BIBLIOGRAPHY

CC (B. Weir); *LePageWC*, i

B. E. Maris: *American Compositions for Piano and Tape-Recorded Sound* (diss., Peabody Conservatory, Baltimore, 1976) [incl. discussion of *Solitaire*]

C. Gange and T. Caras: 'Barbara Kolb', *Soundpieces: Interviews with American Composers* (Metuchen, NJ, 1982), 269–79

D. P. Jezie: *Women Composers: the Lost Tradition Found* (New York, 1988), 193–200

DAVID METZER, LAWRENCE STARR

Konishi, Nagako (*b* Agematsu, Nagano, 16 Sept 1945). Japanese composer. She received an advanced degree from Tokyo National University of Fine Arts and Music (1971), where she studied with Tomojirō Ikenouchi, Makoto Moroi and Akio Yashiro. From 1976 to 1978 she continued composition studies with Andrew Imbrie as a graduate student at the University of California, Berkeley. She has been a leader in the Federation of Women Composers in Japan.

Nagako Konishi, 1993

Konishi's output includes works written for both Japanese and western instruments. In her 1982 piece for alto flute and harp, *Misty Poem*, longer lines often emerge from short motifs or even single inflected pitches.

WORKS
selective list

Inst: The Ring, 2 shakuhachi, futazao, 1974; Kalpa II, vn, va, vc, harp, 1977; 5 Romances, str qt, 1979; Transience I, vn, 1979; Transience II, va, pf, 1982; Misty Poem, a fl, harp, 1982; Elegy, fl, orch, 1983; Transience III, mar, 1985; Away the White, va, cl, pf, 1990

Vocal: S'radda, children's vv, org, 1975; Grave Post, SS, MezMez, AA, 1977; Moon Angel, S, fl, pf, 1979; The Spring, children's vv, 1982

J. MICHELE EDWARDS

Konshina, Yelena Sergeyevna (*b* Kirovgrad, Sverdlovsk [now Yekaterinburg] region, 9 Jan 1950). Russian composer. She has spent her working life teaching and writing in the ancient Russian town of Vladimir, far from the active musical centres of Moscow and St Petersburg. Her music, usually small in scale and quietist in aspiration, reflects the solitude in which she has chosen to live. Some time before the post-Gorbachev vogue for religious music, Konshina was already devoting much energy to *a cappella* choral works (many of which are called simply *Chorus*). These reflect a deep interest in the simplest traditions of the Orthodox church, as well as in the characteristic intonations of Russian folk music. Out of both these familiar traditions she has made a musical language of distinctive purity and restraint; her music is clearly an expression of her strong beliefs. Since the completion of her Piano Concerto in 1975, she has produced no other large-scale works. Her chamber compositions include a Cello Sonata (1973) and the highly refined Trio (1977) for oboe, bassoon and cello. Her more recent instrumental essays are mostly for solo piano and include the *Three Preludes* of 1985 (subtitled 'Morning Silences', 'Quietness and Stillness' and 'Evening Song').

GERARD McBURNEY

Koptagel, Yüksel (*b* Istanbul, 27 Oct 1931). Turkish composer. She began her musical studies in Istanbul with Cemal Reşit Rey and continued in Madrid with Joaquín Rodrigo. In Paris she studied the piano with Lazare Lévy and Alexandre Tansmann, and composition with Louis Jolivet. Later she graduated from the Schola Cantorum there, where she was awarded several medals. Her career as a solo pianist took her to several European countries. Her works include *Capriccio* for piano and orchestra, *Castilla romansa* for cello and piano, many songs, and several works for solo piano such as the 'Minorca' Sonata, the 'Fosil' Suite, *Tamzara* (a Turkish dance), *Toccata* (1959) and *Pastorale*. Her music is published by Max Eschig and Bote & Bock; several of her works have been recorded.

BIBLIOGRAPHY

Ş. Arzruni: 'Let's Talk Turkey: the Music of Yüksel Koptagel', *Keyboard Classics & Piano Stylist* (1993), May–June, 60–61

FARUK YENER

Korn [née Gerlach], **Clara Anna** (*b* Berlin, 30 Jan 1866; *d* New York, 14 July 1940). American pianist, composer and teacher of German birth. She went to the USA at the age of three, and later studied with William G. Vogt. After a brief career as a concert pianist she received a letter from Tchaikovsky, who had seen some of her compositions in manuscript while visiting New York. He urged her to devote her time to composing, and in late 1891 she won a scholarship to the National Conservatory in New York, where she studied with Dvořák, Horatio Parker and Bruno Klein. From 1893 until 1898 she taught theory at the conservatory. She was a founder of the National Federation of Music Clubs, the Women's Philharmonic Society and the Manuscript Society of New York. In 1899 she settled in Brooklyn, where she taught the piano privately.

Korn wrote for several music journals. She spoke out regarding the difficulty women faced in obtaining orchestral performances, and encouraged women composers not to isolate themselves or retreat to club work. Her articles include 'A Reply to Amy A. Fay' (*Musical Courier*, 24 June 1903, p.27), 'Women Composers and the Federation' (*Musical Courier*, 7 Aug 1907, p.26) and 'Women as Teachers' (*The Etude*, xvii, 1899, p.68). Her compositions are varied and numerous, including an opera, *Their Last War*, orchestral works, chamber music, piano works and songs. Few were published.

WORKS
selective list

Stage: Their Last War (opera, Korn) (Boston, 1932)

Orch: Sym., c; Morpheus, sym. poem; 2 suites: Ancient Dances, Rural Snapshots; Pf Conc.; Vn Conc.

Other inst: Suite, vn, vc, pf; Pf Sonata (Nautical), op.14 (East Orange, NJ, 1911); Gymnasium March, pf (Philadelphia, n.d.); Swinging (Philadelphia, n.d.); Overture solennelle (arr. of Tchaikovsky: 1812 Ov.), 2 pf (n.p. n.d.); pieces for vn, pf

Solo vocal: 9 Songs, S/T, pf (New York, 1903)

BIBLIOGRAPHY

S. R. Crothers: 'Woman Composers of America: Clara A. Korn', *MusAm*, x/4 (1909), 4–26

PAMELA FOX

Kozeluch, Catherina. *See* CIBBINI-KOZELUCH, CATHERINA.

Kralik von Mayerswalden [Kralik von Meyrswalden, Kralike, von Kralike], **Mathilde** (*b* Linz, 3 Dec 1857; *d* Vienna, 8 March 1944). Austrian composer and pianist. She studied the piano with Julius Epstein and counterpoint with Anton Bruckner in Vienna (1876–7), then entered the Vienna Conservatory, where she studied composition with Franz Krenn (1877–9). She was a member of the Austrian Composers' Union and the Vienna Bach Society, and president of the Vienna Women's Choral Society, for which she composed works. Many of her vocal works, which include operas, melodramas, and sacred and secular cantatas, are settings of texts by her brother, Richard Kralik.

WORKS
selective list

Operas: Blume und Weissblume; Der heilige Gral (R. Kralik), 1907

Melodramas: Amphortas; Jeanne d'Arc's Todesweg; Kaiser Karl der Grosse in Wien (Kralik), pf; Unter der Linde (Walther von der Vogelweide); Zwei Frauen

Sacred vocal: 4 masses, chorus, org, 1906; Der heilige Leopold (oratorio, Kralik), solo vv, chorus, orch; Der Kreuzweg (cantata, Kralik), solo vv, chorus, orch; Requiem, solo vv, chorus, orch; Weihnachtskantate (Kralik), solo vv, chorus, orch

Other vocal: Lieder aus R. Kralik's Buechlein der Unweisheit (Kralik), 1885; Maia (Kralik), 1895; Jugendlieder, 1899; Blumenlieder (I. Zoepf), 1912; Mutterlied, 1928; Auf Goethes Wegen, cantata; Prinz Eugen (Kralik); Der Rosenkranz, 1v, pf (n.d.); Weissblume (Kralik), mixed chorus

Orch: Heroische Ov., 1906

Chamber and solo inst: Vn Sonata, 1877; 5 pieces, pf, 1881; Nonett, str qt, 4 wind insts, pf, 1901; Pf Trio, F (n.d.); Str Qt; Rhapsody, pf; Variations, pf

Principal publisher: Gutman

BIBLIOGRAPHY

CohenE; *MEMM*; *SchmidlD*

A. Laurence: *Women of Notes* (New York, 1978)

M. Stewart-Green: *Women Composers: a Checklist of Works for the Solo Voice* (Boston, 1980)

MARTHA FURMAN SCHLEIFER

Krasteva, Neva (*b* Sofia, 2 Aug 1946). Bulgarian composer, musicologist and organist. She graduated from the Moscow Conservatory (1972), where her teachers included Jurii Holopov (theory) and Leonid Royzman (organ); she later studied with J. Rainberger in Prague and Zürich. In 1974 she was appointed lecturer in counterpoint at the Sofia State Academy of Music and, two years later, lecturer in organ. A founder of the first Bulgarian organ school, she is active as a performing artist. Krasteva writes mostly for chamber ensembles, often including an organ among the instruments. Her distinctive style is informed by her studies of Renaissance and Baroque music and her knowledge of Bulgarian folk and church music: in the cantata *Apokriff*, for example, fugues intermingle with fragments of Bulgarian sacred music. There are similar references in her *Sonata da chiesa*, which may be perceived as a dialogue between the flute and the organ symbolizing communication between two kinds of spiritual memory. In her *Five Songs from the Mountain of Pirin* for samodivi, she unites a spontaneous melismatic style of writing taken from folk music with jazz-like colouristic effects to recall the dramatic gestures of ancient rituals.

WORKS
selective list

Heterofoni miniaturi, org, 1974; Mitologichni pesni [Mythological Songs], S, folk vv, org, perc, 1976; Sonata da chiesa, fl, org, 1987; Starata ikona [The Old Icon], 1v, org, 1987; Varhat [The Pick], military madrigal, mixed vv, org, 1988; Apokriff, cantata, S, mixed vv, org, 1989; 5 Songs from the Mountain of Pirin, samodivi, 1989; Quantus tremor, small cantata, Mez, tpt, org, vc, 1989

MAGDALENA MANOLOVA

Krumpholtz [née Steckler or Stekler], **Anne-Marie** (*b* Metz, *c*1755; *d* London, 15 Nov 1813). French harpist and composer. Thought to be the daughter of the harp maker Christian Steckler of Metz, she studied the harp with Johann Baptist Krumpholtz, whom she married in 1783. She performed in Paris at the Concert Spirituel during the years 1779 to 1784. There is no record of her activities as a harpist between 1784 and 1788; two daughters may have been born during that time.

Anne-Marie Krumpholtz is said to have eloped to England with an unknown lover, and was certainly active there as a harpist in 1788. She continued to perform until 1803; her published harp works continued to appear until shortly before her death. She often took part in her own benefit concerts and at Salomon's concerts, together with Haydn, J. L. Dussek, Mme Mara, the young singer Sophia Corri (later Mme Dussek) and other great artists of the day. The reviewer of the *Oracle* (10 March 1792) wrote, 'Mme Krumpholtz is without doubt the first Player we have. There is an additional charm in manner; that too is her own'. She frequently performed J. L. Dussek's Concertante for harp and piano with him, which may be why he has been proposed as the unknown lover, although he did not go to London until 1789.

Like Mme Delaval and Sophia Dussek, she apparently composed in serious genres such as the sonata, but published mostly fashionable harp arrangements of well-known tunes and themes and variations – enormously popular types of music which found a ready market as domestic music for young women.

Anne-Marie Krumpholtz died of apoplexy. Her daughter, FANNY PITTAR, was also a composer. V. Krumpholtz, whose music for harp was published in London (*Quadrille*, *c*1820, and an arrangement of *Le rantz des vaches, or Un souvenir des vallées suisses*, *c*1825), may have been Fanny's younger sister.

WORKS
only printed works;
all published in London c1810

The Favorite Air of Pray Goody arranged for the Harp; The Favorite Air of Robin Adair arranged for the Harp; A Favorite Duet for the Harp and Pianoforte [Steibelt: Rondo] as arranged by Madame Krumpholtz; A Favorite Piemontois Air, with Variations by Dalvimare; Lison Dormoit with an Introduction and Variations arranged for the Harp

BIBLIOGRAPHY

Choron-FayolleD; FétisB; GerberNL; Grove1[†] (C. F. Pohl); *SainsburyD; SchillingE*

H. Tribout de Morembert: *Anne-Marie Steckler: une virtuose de la harpe au XVIIIe siècle* (Metz, 1962)

F. Vernillat: 'La littérature de la harpe en France au XVIIIe siècle', *RMFC*, ix (1969), 162–85, esp. 171

C. Pierre: *Histoire du Concert spirituel 1725–1790* (Paris, 1975)

U. Rempel: 'Fanny Krumpholtz and her Milieu', *American Harp Journal*, v/4 (1976), 11–15

—— : 'The Perils of Secondary Sources: an Annotated Bibliography of Encyclopedic and Dictionary Sources Relating to the Harpist Members of the Krumpholtz Family', *American Harp Journal*, vii/3 (1980), 25–30

R. Rensch: *Harps and Harpists* (Bloomington, IN, 1989)

BARBARA GARVEY JACKSON,
URSULA M. REMPEL

Krzanowska, Grażyna (*b* Legnica, 1 March 1952). Polish composer. She graduated with distinction from the composition class of Tadeusz Natanson at the State High School of Music in Wrocław (1976) and became a teacher at the music school in Bielsko-Biała. She has received the Young Composers award of the Polish Composers' Union (1978), and prizes at the Okanogan Music Festival in Canada (1983), the Poznań Spring Music Festival (1986), and in the Karol Szymanowski Competition (1988) and the GEDOK competition in Mannheim (1989). In her music Krzanowska draws freely on traditional techniques and classical forms, mixing aleatory features and note clusters with clear tonal references. Her use of chamber sonorities enables her, even in her orchestral music, to create moments of great intimacy and subtlety.

WORKS
selective list

Orch: Passacaglia, 1976; Pieśni bez słów [Songs without Words], chamber orch, 1978; Symfonia z uderzeniem w kotły [Paukenschlag Symphony], 1978; Mała symfonia chorałowa [The Little Choral Symphony], 1985; Zapomniana przestrzeń [Forgotten Space], 1985

Vocal: Melodies, cantata, solo vv, orch, 1975; Stabat mater, S, S, 2 mixed choirs, orch, 1975; Polanowe ognie [Bonfires], 2vv, chamber ens, 1979; Juhasko prośba [Shepherd's Request], S, org, 1983

Chamber: Concerto grosso, 15 str, 1976; Str Qt no.2, 1980: Silver Line, 15 str, 1991; Relief X, sax qt, 1991

Principal publisher: PWM

BARBARA ZWOLSKA-STĘSZEWSKA

Krzyżanowska, Halina (*b* Paris, 1860; *d* ? Rennes, 1937). Polish pianist and composer. She studied the piano at the Paris Conservatoire with Félix Le Couppey and at the age of 17 won the *prix d'honneur*. Then she studied counterpoint and composition with Andrès and Ernest Guiraud. She performed throughout Europe, though mainly in France and Poland, and in 1896 was made *officier* of the Académie de France. In 1900 she was appointed professor of piano at Rennes conservatory. Greatly influenced by Saint-Saëns, Krzyżanowska composed a symphony, a *Marche héroïque* for orchestra, a Fantasy for piano and orchestra, a string quartet and other chamber works, many solo piano works (including two sonatas, programmatic works and pieces in dance forms), settings of French and Polish poems, incidental music to S. Duchińska's play *Jasyr* ('Tatar Captivity'), a one-act opera *Magdusia* (to a libretto by H. Świejkowski, composed before 1894) and an oratorio. Her works, now forgotten, were published mainly in Paris and London. They were highly praised in their day by critics and audiences.

ZOFIA CHECHLIŃSKA

Kubisch, Christina (*b* Bremen, 31 Jan 1948). German composer and sound-installation artist. She studied at the Hochschule für Musik in Bremen and at the

Akademie der Bildenden Künste in Stuttgart (painting with K. H. Sonderborg) from 1967 to 1969, and at the Musikhochschulen in Hamburg, Graz and Zürich from 1969 to 1974, graduating in educational theory and flute. She then studied composition with Franco Donatoni at the Milan conservatory and electronic music with Angelo Paccagnini (1974–6), and gave concerts and created performances and videos (from 1975). From 1980 to 1981 she studied electrical engineering at the technical institute in Milan and since 1980 has created various types of indoor and outdoor sound installations. In 1987 she moved to Berlin. She was a guest lecturer at the Jan van Eyck Academie in Maastricht (1988–9) and became a sound-installation teacher at the Kunstakademie in Münster (1990). She won a research award from the cultural department of the Bund Deutscher Industrie (1988), received a Barkenhoff grant (1988–9) and won a further award from the Kunstfond in Bonn (1990).

WORKS
selective list

Sound installations: *c*75, including Listen to the Walls, Heidelberg, 1981; Der magnetische Garten, Vienna, 1983; On Air, Münster, 1984; Ocigam Trazom, Milan, 1985; Klangzelt, Amsterdam, 1986; Vogelbaum, Graz, 1987; Planetarium, Milan, 1988; Landscape, Banff, 1989; Landscape, Sydney, 1990; Iter magneticum, Kobe, Japan, 1991

Sound collages (with video, stage action, dance etc.): Liquid Movie, Milan, 1981; Fön, Bremen, 1985; Sie hütet es, Berlin, 1990

Other works: Language in Progress, 16vv, 1974; [7] Emergency Solos, fl, objects, 1975; Vibrations, str qt, elec vibrators, 1975; Two and Two, a fl, fl + ventilator, fl + steel drum, vc, vibrator, elec metronome, 1v + accordion, 1976–7 [video perf.]; Tempo liquido, acoustically strengthened plate glass, water filter, thimbles, tape, 1978 [video perf.]; Tam Tam, 2 people, 2 video cameras, 2 monitors, objects, insts, 1979–80; Konstante Variabile, 16-track tape, 1981; On Air – 6 Klanglandschaften, tape, 1984; Night Flights, tape, 1986–7; Vocrolls, tape, 1989

BIBLIOGRAPHY
M. Helmig, ed.: *Christina Kubisch* (1991)

BIRGITTA MARIA SCHMID

Kuliffay, Izabella (*b* Pest, 29 Dec 1863; *d* Budapest, 19 Jan 1945). Hungarian pianist and composer. She studied at the National Conservatory in Budapest (1877–9), then at the Budapest Academy of Music (1879–83) with Kornél Ábrányi and Gyula Erkel. In 1883 she became a music tutor at the Habsburg court at Alcsut; later, she was a professor at the conservatory. Between 1892 and 1895 she organized with Gyula Káldy (director of the conservatory) concert tours

of Hungarian music, which included some of her own compositions in traditional style. During that period she also taught herself to play the cimbalom and in 1894 published a tutor for the instrument (*Cimbalomiskola*, 'Cimbalom School') that soon became popular. She ran her own music school between 1901 and 1916, then taught at a girls' boarding school until she retired in 1932. She was vice-president of the Hungarian Women's Choral Union (from 1902) and president of the music department of the Hungarian Women's Art and Education Association (from 1904). Most of her compositions are solo songs.

BIBLIOGRAPHY
E. Fabricius: *Kuliffay Izabella zeneművésznő emlékezete* [In Remembrance of Izabella Kuliffay] (Budapest, 1947)

EVA KELEMEN

Kulmus, Luise Adelgunda Victoria. See GOTTSCHED, LUISE ADELGUNDA VICTORIA.

Kunkel, Renata (*b* Gdańsk, 1 Sept 1954). Polish composer. At the Warsaw Academy of Music she studied conducting with

Elisabeth Kuyper, conductor of the American Women's Symphony Orchestra, New York, 1924

Elisabeth Kuyper with her Berliner Tonkünstlerinnen-Orchester

Ryszard Dudek (diploma with distinction, 1979) and composition with Marian Borkowski, graduating in 1982, and was later appointed lecturer in composition there. Her works have been performed at concerts and festivals of contemporary music in several European countries, the USA, Mexico and Cuba, and have been broadcast in the USA and France as well as in Poland. She has won many prizes for symphonic, chamber and solo works at composers' competitions in Poland, including third prize for *Elegy* (for choir and orchestra) at the First Lutosławski International Composers' Competition (1990). At the GEDOK competition in Mannheim (1989) she received a special mention for . . . *Where Worlds are Naught* . . . . In her creative work, Kunkel strives for clarity of utterance and consistency in the development of her musical ideas, regardless of the complexity of the music.

WORKS
selective list

Orch: Shadows, 4 inst groups, 1981; Sym., 1983; Inner Landscapes, chamber orch, 1984; Music for Sirus B, ww ens, 1985; . . . Where Worlds are Naught . . ., str orch, 1987; The Stream, 1990

Chamber: Str Qt no.1, 1979; Penetrations, fl, perc, 1980; Str Qt no.2, 1986; In a Lit-up Streak of Sounds, fl, ob, cl, bn, 2 vn, va, vc, 1989; Str Qt no.3, 1991

Solo inst: Mimesis, vn, 1981; Phrases, pf, 1984; Eidos I, fl, 1986; Eidos II, cl, 1987; Anodos, vn, 1990

Vocal: Apógeios, vocal ens, orch, 1984; Idiochromie I, 2S, ens, 1985; Elegy (R. M. Rilke), mixed chorus, orch, 1988; . . . And Give us Silence to Drink (J. Lechoń), female vv/boys' chorus, 1990

BARBARA ZWOLSKA-STĘSZEWSKA

Kuyper, Elisabeth (*b* Amsterdam, 13 Sept 1877; *d* Viganello, Switzerland, 26 Feb 1953). Dutch composer and conductor. She studied with Daniël de Lange and Frans Coenen in Amsterdam (piano-teaching certificate 1895) and then with Max Bruch at the Berlin Hochschule für Musik, where from 1908 to 1920 she taught theory and composition – the first woman to do so there. She was also the first woman to win the Mendelssohn state prize for composition, in 1905. As a proponent of symphonic orchestral work for women, she founded four women's symphony orchestras – in Berlin (1910), The Hague (1922), London (1922–3) and New York (1924–5), all of them well received. The Hague orchestra was organized specifically to provide music for a conference of the International Women's Council in 1922, but the others, because of insufficient financial backing, were forced to disband. With the London Women's Symphony Orchestra Kuyper conducted the première of her *Das Lied von der Seele* for seven solo singers, orchestra and dance. Kuyper returned to Europe in 1925 and settled in Muzzano, Switzerland.

WORKS
selective list

Orch: Ballade, g, op.11, vc, orch, 1903 (Berlin, 1911); Serenade, d, op.8, 1905 (Leipzig, 1911); Vn Conc., b, op.10, 1908, pf score (Berlin, 1910); Sym., a, lost

Vocal orch: Festkantate (M. Bruch), solo vv, female chorus, nar, orch, 1912 (Leipzig, 1914); Hymne an die Arbeit, S/T, female/male chorus, orch, 1922 (Leipzig, 1936); Das Lied [von] der Seele, 7 solo vv, orch, dancers, 1923, unpubd

Chamber: Vn sonata, A, op.1, 1901 (Middelburg,

1902); Pf Trio, D, op.13, 1910 (Leipzig, 1913)

Pf: Serenata Ticinese, A, 1928 (Lugano, 1928); Dreams on the Hudson Waltz (Lugano, 1928)

Choral: Ewig jung ist nur die Sonne (C. F. Meyer), unacc. men's vv, 1941 (Leipzig and Zürich, 1941)

Solo vocal: 6 Lieder, op.17, 1v, pf, 1922 (Berlin, 1922); American Lovesong, S/T, pf (Muzzano and Lugano, 1944)

Principal publishers: Cranz, Eulenburg, Hug, Leuckart, A. A. Noske, N. Simrock

BIBLIOGRAPHY

SchmidlD

E. Kuyper: 'Mein Frauenorchester', *AMz*, xlvi (1919), 732–3

—— : 'Mein Lebensweg', *Führende Frauen Europas*, i (Munich, 1928), 214–27; repr. in E. Rieger, ed.: *Frau und Musik* (Frankfurt, 1980), 139–49

W. Jeths and P. Lelieveldt: 'Elisabeth Kuyper', *Zes vrouwelijke componisten*, ed. H. Metzelaar (Zutphen, 1991), 85–118

HELEN METZELAAR,
CAROL NEULS-BATES

L

La Barbara [née Lotz; Subotnick], **Joan** (*b* Philadelphia, 8 June 1947). American composer and vocal performer. She studied singing at Syracuse University with Helen Boatwright and composition at New York University (BS 1970), and received additional vocal training both from Phyllis Curtin at the Berkshire Music Center and from Marion Szekely Freschl at the Juilliard School. In 1973 she helped found the New Wilderness Preservation Band, a cooperative improvisational group that presented a two-year series of performances in New York with poets and writers; during the 1970s she was a vocalist with both Steve Reich's and Philip Glass's ensembles and performed in premières of works by John Cage, Alvin Lucier, Robert Ashley, Morton Subotnick (to whom she is married), Charles Dodge, Morton Feldman and others. La Barbara has toured extensively in the USA and in Europe, presenting concerts of her works and workshops in extended vocal techniques. In 1981 she was appointed to teach composition and singing at the California Institute of the Arts, Valencia. She has received grants from the New York State Council on the Arts (1975, 1978) and the NEA (1979, 1980); in 1979 she was a composer-in-residence in West Berlin under the sponsorship of the DAAD. She has received commissions from Joan Tower, Radio Bremen and RIAS Radio, Berlin, and the Los Angeles Olympic Arts Festival. Active as a writer and critic of new music, she became contributing editor of *High Fidelity/Musical America* in 1977. She has produced recordings of her own work, and worked as producer on recordings of music by Cage and Feldman.

La Barbara has been an influential figure in experimental music since the early 1970s, when she developed a repertory of extended vocal techniques, including multiphonics and circular breathing; some of these techniques, such as throat clicks and a high flutter, are recognized as her own 'signature' effects. Most of her compositions are designed for her specialized vocal skills. Early solo works like *Voice Piece: One-Note Internal Resonance Investigation* (1974) are rigorous explorations – for performer and listener alike – of vocal production. More often, however, she incorporates the vocal material into more elaborately textured ensemble and tape pieces.

WORKS

Dramatic: Layers (dance score), 1v, elec, acoustic and elec perc, tape, 1977; Anima (film score), 1v, vc, perc, elec kbd synths, gamelan, indigenous Diablo

Joan La Barbara, 1984

259

Canyon sounds, 1991; The Misfortune of the Immortals (interactive media opera), vv, dancers, video, interactive computer system, MIDI insts, 1993–

Large ens: Chandra, amp v/vv, 5 male vv, chamber orch, 1978, rev. 1983; The Solar Wind III, amp v, chamber orch, 1984

Vocal, inst ens: Thunder, amp v, 6 timp, elec, 1975; WARP–32375–1, 1v, perc, 1975; Ides of March I–VIII, amp v, insts, 1975–7; Chords and Gongs, amp v, cimb, gongs, 1976; Loisaida, amp v, kalimba [lamellaphone], cimb, steel drum, 1977; Silent Scroll, amp v, fl, cl/db, perc, gong, zoomoozophone, 1982; Vlissingen Harbor, amp v, fl + pic, cl, tpt, harp, pf + cel, vc, perc, 1982; The Solar Wind I, 1/2 solo vv, 8 insts, tape, perc, 1983; The Solar Wind, II, 16 amp solo vv, 2 perc, fl, elec kbd, 1983; A Rothko Study [no.1], 1v, chamber ens, 1985; Helga's Lied, 1v, chamber ens, 1986; A Rothko Study no.2, amp v, vc, computer (YCAMS), 1986; Urban Tropics, sound portrait, 1v, perc, indigenous Miami sounds, 1988; 'to hear the wind roar', (1v, perc, tape)/(vocal ens 8vv, perc)/(chorus, hand-held perc), 1991

Vocal, tape/other elec: Vocal Extensions, amp v, live elec, 1975; Cyclone, amp v, tape, light-panning activating device, 1976, rev. as sound installation, 16-track tape, 1979; An Exaltation of Larks, 1v, elec, 1976; Cathing, amp v, tape, 1977, rev. 1980; Twelvesong, amp v, tape, 1977; Klee Alee, amp v, tape, 1979; Shadowsong, amp v, tape, 1979; Erin, amp v, tape, 1980; October Music: Star Showers and Extraterrestrials, amp v, tape, 1980; Winds of the Canyon, amp v, tape, 1982; Berliner Träume (Berlin Dreaming), amp v, 16-track tape, 1983; After 'Obervogelsang', amp v, tape, 1984; Time(d) Trials and Unscheduled Events, 8 amp solo vv, tape, 1984; Loose Tongues, 8 amp solo vv, tape, 1985; Voice Windows, 1v, interactive video, 1986–7

Unacc. vocal: Hear what I feel, amp v, 1974; Performance Piece, amp v, 1974, rev. 1979; Voice Piece: One-Note Internal Resonance Investigation, amp v, 1974; Circular Song, amp v, 1975; Chords, amp v, 1976: Des accords pour Teeny, 1v, 1976; I have seen a rainbow, 1v (amp and acoustic), 1976–; Les oiseaux qui chantent dans ma tête, amp v, 1976; Space Testing, 1v, 1976; A Matter of Agreement, spoken and sung sounds, 1978–; California Chant, amp/acoustic v, 1979; Twelve for Five in Eight, 5 or more amp vv, 1979; Rothko, amp v, 16vv, 1986; Prologue to The Book of Knowing . . . (and) of Overthrowing, aria, 1v, 1987–8; Conversations, 1v, 1988

Other works: Hunters, video, 1975; Vermont II, video, 1975; Cyclone Con(s)t(r)ained, sound installation, 1978; Cyclone II, multi-media environment, audio, 1978–; Layers II, natural and elec sounds with quadraphonic panning, 1978–; Metamorphosis, spoken and sung sounds, elec, quadraphonic panning, 1978–; Windmill, amp sound environment, 1978; The Executioner's Bracelet, tape, 1979; Quatre petites bêtes, tape, 1979; Responsive Resonance with Feathers, pf, tape, 1979; She is always alone, video, 1979; As Lightning Comes, in Flashes, 2–6 amp vv, dancers, video, 1982; Autumn Signal, tape, 1982; 3 Space Trio/A Lament for the Wizard, video, 1982, collab. E. Emshwiller; L'albero della foglie azzurre (The Tree of Blue Leaves), ob, tape, 1989; In the Dreamtime, self-

portrait sound collage, 1990; Awakenings, chamber ens, 1991; Klangbild Köln, sound painting, voice perc, indigenous Cologne sounds, 1991

BIBLIOGRAPHY

T. Johnson: 'Research & Development', *Village Voice* (27 Jan 1975)

J. Rockwell: 'Joan La Barbara Sings Own Works', *New York Times* (19 Jan 1975)

W. Zimmermann: 'Joan La Barbara', *Desert Plants: Conversations with 23 American Musicians* (Vancouver, 1976), 149–62

P. Frank: 'New American Music on Records', *New York Arts Journal*, ii/1 (1977), 27

D. Sofer: 'Joan La Barbara: Voice is the Original Instrument', *Synapse*, i/6 (1977), 22

R. Palmer: 'Joan La Barbara Sings a "Collage"', *New York Times* (21 Feb 1978)

K. Jensen: 'Joan La Barbara', *Contact*, no.22 (1981), 21–3

J. Woodward: 'Joan La Barbara Pushes the Envelope', *Option* (1991), Jan–Feb

LINDA SANDERS, MICHELLE C. SWEET

Lachartre, Nicole (*b* Paris, 27 Feb 1934; *d* Versailles, 25 Nov 1991). French composer. She won first prizes for fugue and counterpoint at the Paris Conservatoire, where she studied composition with Darius Milhaud, Jean Rivier and André Jolivet. In 1974 she founded the Association pour la Collaboration des Interprètes et des Compositeurs to facilitate performances of her contemporaries' work. The music in Lachartre's own compositions, the majority of which were inspired by spiritual experiences, is expressly dominated by her creative imagination. To communicate this 'inner intensity' she does not hesitate to use traditional compositional methods, both vocal and instrumental, as well as electroacoustic techniques and mathematical devices. She also juxtaposes visual worlds with sound worlds, creating what she calls 'musivision'.

WORKS
selective list

Music-theatre and other stage: Couteau de clarté, 3vv, 6 insts, 2 actors, 1977; Joë Bousquet: Galant de neige, vn, vc, kbd, actor, 1980; Ogives désirs, 9 insts, 2 actors, 1982; Babylone malade, ou la nuit du thermomètre (mini-opéra comique, F. Meunier, other texts), vocal ens, 1981; Noce avec la folie (H. A. Müller), 6 insts, actor, 1983; Les grenouilles n'ont pas de dents (children's mini-opera, 1, J. Rosenmann), 5 male actors, vocal ens, mixed chorus, 4 tapes, 1984

Chamber: Va Sonata, 1964; Cl Qnt, 1965; Essai II, harp, hpd, gui, ẓarb, 1968; Résonance et paradoxe, ondes martenot, pf, perc, 1971; En sa mémoire l'hommesprit, 8 insts, 1975; Il y a mille et mille soleils, fl, harp, perc, 1975; Le jardin des tortues, 4 perc, 1984

Solo inst: Pf Sonata, 1965; Que le jour soit le jour et la nuit soit la nuit, pour toi, satellite de ton propre soleil, zheng, 1974; 10 présentations musicales du nom d'Hermann Sabbe, a fl, 1978; Requiem pour une compositrice, amp hpd, 1984

Inst with nar: Nidââ, B-nar, triple str qt, 1975; Papouil Tchatcharett, nar, 6 insts, 1982; Un dragon tombé à cheval (A. Wölfli), pianist-nar, 1985; Une robe tombé en poussière (B. Cendrars), harpsichordist-nar, 1986

Inst with tape: Ultimes, ondes martenot, tape, 1970; Hommage à Amiel, fl, tape, 1974; Le cri de cicogne peut même atteindre le ciel, pf, tape, 1978

Tape: Suicide cosmique, 1970; Mundus imaginabilis, 1970; Mundus sensibilis, 1972; Mundus intellectualis, 1973; Les champs de cinabre, 1977; Hommage à Ruysbroeck, 1979; Les coqs sont égorgés, 1984

Also pieces for 1v, insts

BIBLIOGRAPHY

N. Lachartre: 'Les musiques artificielles', Diagrammes du Monde, no.146 (1969), Apr, 1–96, esp. 5–84

FRANÇOISE ANDRIEUX

Lago. See NETZEL, LAURA CONSTANCE.

La Guerre, Elisabeth-Claude Jacquet de. See JACQUET DE LA GUERRE, ELISABETH-CLAUDE.

La Hye [née Rousseau], **Louise-Geneviève de** (b Charenton, 8 March 1810; d Paris, 17 Nov 1838). French pianist, organist and composer. She was a collateral descendant of Jean-Jacques Rousseau. A child prodigy, she studied first with her father, Charles-Louis Rousseau, then with Louis-Joseph Saint-Amans; when she was 11 she was admitted to the Paris Conservatoire. According to Fétis, she was invited in 1830 by the Conservatoire director, Luigi Cherubini, to teach harmony to a class of young women, and took the solo part in her fantasy for organ and orchestra in a Conservatoire performance on 10 April 1831. She married shortly thereafter and gave up her appointment to move to Cambrai, but returned to Paris at the end of 1834 and resumed teaching. In 1835 her dramatic choral work Le songe de la religieuse was performed at the Hôtel de Ville. She published a number of works (at least one under the pseudonym 'M. Léon Saint-Amans fils'), including a duo for horn and piano, a set of variations for piano and string quartet, and some settings of poems by her husband, but chronic ill-health prevented her from realizing many of her projects. She died at the age of 28 leaving two young children. Her Méthode d'orgue expressif and collection of Six mélodies italiennes (dedicated to the Princess Belgioioso) were published posthumously, while other works including masses and piano études remained in manuscript.

BIBLIOGRAPHY

FétisB; FétisBS; SchillingES; SchmidlD

Anon.: 'A List of Well-Known Women Composers', Etude, xxxvi (1918), 699–700

E. Barrell: 'Notable Musical Women', Etude, xlviii (1930), 121

JULIE ANNE SADIE

Lalauni, Lila (b Athens, 9 June 1918). Greek pianist and composer. Granddaughter of the composer Timotheos Xanthopoulos and a child prodigy, she entered the Vienna Music Academy in 1927, studying the piano until 1930, and then composition with Robert Konta, and graduating in 1934. She later took lessons privately with Marcel Dupré in Paris, where she settled. Lalauni became known primarily as a brilliant pianist; she made her début in Vienna as early as 1930. Four years later she performed Richard Strauss's Burleske, with the composer conducting. Although her international performing career overshadowed her achievements as a composer, some of her works, especially those for piano, were occasionally performed in Greece. Stylistically, her compositions, which include chamber music and songs as well as two piano concertos (1943, 1959) and a symphony ('Synthèses et catalyses', 1960–62), move between late Romanticism and neo-classicism and betray a profound lyrical gift tinged with emotional restraint. Indeed in terms of technique, let alone inspiration, she ranks among the best Greek composers of her generation.

GEORGE LEOTSAKOS

Lambertini, Marta (b San Isidro, Buenos Aires, 13 Nov 1937). Argentine composer. She studied with Luis Gianneo, Roberto Caamaño and Gerardo Gandini at the Universidad Católica Argentina (graduation 1972); she also studied electroacoustic composition at the Centro de Investigaciones de la Ciudad, Buenos Aires. She has received many prizes and takes part in national and international festivals and competitions, both as a composer and as a member of the jury.

Two subjects stand out in her music: the cosmos – reflected in compositions such as the string quartet Quasares (1971), the orchestral work Galileo descubre las cuatro lunas de Júpiter (1985) and Ultima filmación de los anillos de Saturno, for four clarinets (1991) – and musical humour, which is especially notable in the operas, Alice in Wonderland and ¡Oh, Eternidad . . .! ossia S. M. R. BACH. Both opera librettos are by Lambertini; they are based on works by other authors and employ a variety of languages. Many of her instrumental works are also inspired by literary texts, and sometimes by other composers' music. Later works show a developing interest in the principles of deconstructionism.

WORKS

Chamber operas: Alice in Wonderland (M. Lambertini, after L. Carroll), 1989; ¡Oh, Eternidad . . .! ossia S. M. R. BACH (Lambertini, after J. C. F. Hölderlin, E. A. Poe) [after J. S. Bach], 1990

Orch: Concertino-Serenata, fl, cl, str orch, perc, harp, pf, 1981; Misa de pájaros II, 1983; Galileo descubre las cuatro lunas de Júpiter, 1985

Other inst: Enroque a 7, fl, cl, str qt, pf, 1970; Quasares, str qt, 1971; Posters de una exposición, pf, 1972; Serenata, fl, cl, vc, pf, perc, 1973; Espacios interiores I, fl, pf, 1975–6; Espacios interiores II, cl, vc, pf, 1976; Gymel, fl, gui, 1977; Misa de pájaros I, fl, cl, vc, pf, perc, 1978; Vaghe stelle del'Orsa, str qt, 1978; Eridanus, fl, gui, 1979; Yggdrasil, el árbol, fl, cl, pf, 1979; Rigel, cl, pf, 1980; La espada de Orión, wind qnt, harp, pf, str qt, 1981; Anónimo italiano, 2 fl, gui, vn, va, vc, 1982; La Hydra, ob, pf, 1983; La question pataphysique, ens of insts held at Museo Azzarini,La Plata, 1983; 5 piezas transversales, pf, 1984; Los fuegos de San Telmo, pf trio, 1985; Antígona, va, 2 cl, mand, gui, pf, 1987; El Catedral sumergido, vc, pf, 1989; Como un jardín cerrado, bn, 1990; Una ofrenda musical, cl, bn, pf, 1990; Assorted Köchels (con Fantasía galopante), cl, bn, pf, 1991; Ultima filmación de los anillos de Saturno, 4 cl, 1991; Amanecer en el patio y apronte, 4 perc, 1992; Segundo jardín cerrado, cl, bn, 1992; Música para renacer en las aguas, ob, hn, str qt, pf, 1992

Vocal: Ad invocandum spiritum sanctum, chorus, 1969; Odas (F. Pessoa), chorus, orch, 1972; Proverbios (P. Eluard), chorus, orch, 1972; 3 poemas (O. Paz), Mez, pf, 1975; 3 canciones de cuna (M. Lambertini), children's chorus, 1975–6; 3 canti d'amore [after Dunstable, Gesualdo, Palestrina], S, fl, gui, 1981; O, Ewigkeit . . .! (M. Lambertini, after Hölderlin) [after J. S. Bach], Bar, str qt, pf, perc, 1985, rev., Bar, str orch, pf, perc, 1990; Lo stivale [It. folksongs],Bar, fl, cl, vn, vc, db, pf, perc, 1986; The Pool of Tears (Carroll), S, pf 6 hands, 1987; Tankas (J. L. Borges), Bar, pf, 1988; La nariz de Mozart (M. Lambertini) [after W. A. Mozart], Mez, fl, str qt, pf, 1991; Poemas del silencio (A. Lambertini), S, 2 fl, 1991; Escena de la Falsa Tortuga (M. Lambertini, after Carroll), S, Bar, fl, ob, cl, vn, va, vc, pf, perc, 1993

Tape: Estudio de materia, 1973

Principal publishers: EAC-Moeck, Ricordi Americana

BIBLIOGRAPHY

P. Ortiz: 'La citation dans la musique contemporaine argentine', Contrechamps, no.3 (1984), 136–7
R. Arias Usandivaras: 'Marta Lambertini, su obra', Temas y contracantos, (1986), May–June
G. Paraskevaidis: 'Acerca de las mujeres, que además de ser mujeres, componen', Pauta, v/17 (1986), 54–60
C. García Muñoz: 'Marta Lambertini: catálogo de su obra', Revista del Instituto de investigación musicológica Carlos Vega, viii (1987), 137–44

RAQUEL C. DE ARIAS

Lambiri, Eleni (b Athens, c1882–8; d Athens, 30 March 1960). Greek composer and conductor. The earliest modern Greek woman composer known to have had a full professional career, she was the daughter of the composer Georgios Lambiris and the niece of the well-known satirical poet Andreas Laskaratos. She studied theory and composition with Edoardo Sacerdote at the Athens Conservatory, graduating with a bronze medal. Shortly afterwards, in October 1908, she enrolled at the Leipzig Conservatory, where for four years she studied composition with Max Reger and conducting with Hans Schiedt. She returned to Athens, where her operetta To apokriatiko oneiro ('A Dream in Carnival') was successfully staged by the famed Papaïoannou company at the Panellinion theatre in June 1913. A second operetta, Isolma, to her own libretto, is said to have been successfully staged in Milan in 1915. Thereafter she worked in Milan as a conductor, but by 1925 she was back in Greece and settled in Patras. She was director of the Patras Conservatory until her retirement in 1953. She wrote a number of melodramas (music for performance against a spoken text) which were performed in Italy, a symphony, a string quartet, a piano sonata and songs (now in GR-Aleotsakos), and a Ballad for soprano and piano (1933, now lost). The music of her operas is lost, but a recording of extended excerpts from Isolma in the Sound Archives of Greek Radio and her extant songs betray a gift for flowing melody and, in comparison with some Greek composers at the turn of the century, a high degree of professionalism and sensibility in her approach to harmony.

BIBLIOGRAPHY

A. Theodoropoulou: 'Lambiri, Eleni', Megali elliniki engyklopaedia [The Great Hellenic Encyclopedia] (Athens, 1931)
I. Grékas: 'Lambiri, Eleni', Pangosmion lexikon ton ergon [The Universal Dictionary of Creative Works] (Athens, 1964)

GEORGE LEOTSAKOS

Lam Bun-ching (b Macau, 26 June 1954). Macau composer. She received the BA in music (1975) from the Chinese University of Hong Kong after an exchange year spent at the University of Redlands, California. She studied composition with Robert Erickson, Pauline Oliveros, Bernard Rands and Roger

Lam Bun-ching

Reynolds at the University of California, San Diego (PhD 1981), then taught at Cornish College of the Arts, Seattle (1981–6). She has been composer-in-residence for several organizations including the American Dance Festival, Durham, North Carolina (1986). Her music has been performed at concerts and festivals in Hong Kong, Japan, the USA and Europe, including the ISCM World Music Days (1988) and the UNESCO forum for contemporary compositions, Paris. She has received many awards including first prize at Aspen (1980), the Prix de Rome (1991) and the Lili Boulanger Award (1992). Her style makes colourful, sympathetic use of instruments and the voice; she achieves lyricism and transparency without discarding the avant-garde techniques acquired in California. Long attracted to Chinese poetry, painting and calligraphy, she has moved closer to these sources in her later compositions.

WORKS

Stage: E. O. 9066, dance, vocal qt, tape, 1989; The Child God (shadow-puppet opera, Ming Dynasty: *The Creation of the God*), New York, 1993

Orch: Lang Tao Sha, vn, orch, 1981; Yangguan Sandie, American gamelan, 1984; Impetus, conc. for Chin. orch, 1987; Saudades de Macau, 1987–9; Circle, 1992

Chamber and solo inst: 3 Tiny Bits, pf, 1977; Masks, fl, cl, hn, tpt, trbn, va, db, pf, 2 perc, 1978; Springwaters, pf, 2 fl, 3 cl, hn, tpt, trbn, 1980; Movement, str qt, 1980; Bittersweet Music I, pic, 1980; Bittersweet Music II, vn, 1981; After Spring, 2 pf, 1983; Lü, solo perc, 1983; 3 Easy Pieces, trbn, elec, 1985; 2 + 1 = 3, a fl, bn, pf, 1987; Böhmes Liebeslied, fl, pf, 1987; Social Accidents, fl, b cl, vn,

pf, accordion, perc, synth, 1988; Another Spring, a fl, vc, pf, 1988; Californian Duo, trbn, va, 1989; L'air du temps, str qt, 1989–90; Klang, solo perc, 1990; Last Spring, pf qnt, 1992

Vocal: Spring Yearning (Kuan Huan-ching), S, chamber orch/S, pf, 1976; 3 Yuan Dynasty Songs (Ma Chih-yuen), S, pf, 1978; 4 Beckett Songs (S. Beckett), S, vn, cl, perc, 1980; Autumn Sound (Li Ching-ch'ao), S, fl, 1983; 3 Dada Songs (H. Ball), S, fl, vc, pf, 1985; Clouds/Wolken (G. Kaldewey), nar, S, a fl, pf, 1986; Wolken II (Kaldewey), nar, double chorus, 10 insts, 1987; Wolken III (Kaldewey), nar, double chorus, pf, 1990; Walking Walking Keep Walking (Han Dynasty poems), T, Chin. insts, 1991

HARRISON RYKER

Landowska, Wanda (*b* Warsaw, 5 July 1879; *d* Lakeville, CT, 16 Aug 1959). Polish keyboard player and composer. She was a leading figure in the 20th-century revival of the harpsichord. After piano studies in Warsaw with Jan Kleczyński and Alexander Michałowski she went to Berlin in 1896; there she studied composition with Heinrich Urban, writing songs, piano pieces and works for orchestra. *Kolysanka* for piano and *Paysage triste* for string orchestra, on a poem of Paul Verlaine, were both performed in Warsaw, in 1899 and 1900 respectively. In 1900 Landowska married Henry Lew, an authority on Hebrew folklore, and settled in Paris. She continued to compose, playing her *Rhapsodie orientale* at a concert at Enoch's in Paris in 1901 (a version for english horn, harp and string quartet, dated June 1917, survives) and *Pologne*, variations for two pianos, with Alfredo Casella at the Fifth Concert Femina there in 1902. In 1903 or 1904, she entered the Musica International Competition with a piano piece, probably *Feux follets*, and a song; they won first and second prizes and Massenet pronounced, 'Elle a du talent, beaucoup de talent'.

She first played the harpsichord in public in 1903; in 1909 she published her book *Musique ancienne*, and in 1913 she began a harpsichord class at the Hochschule für Musik in Berlin, where she and her husband were detained as civil prisoners on parole during World War I. She gradually turned away from (though did not completely reject) original composition in favour of writing cadenzas for concertos by Mozart, Haydn, Handel and C. P. E. Bach (many of which have been published by Broude Bros., New York), and she made piano transcriptions of a *Chain of Ländler* by Schubert (1911), *Valses viennoises* by Lanner (1926) and

Mozart's dances K606 (1945). She also played and recorded, though never wrote down, two *Bourrées d'Auvergne* drawn from French folksongs, and arranged five Polish folksongs, collected in her youth, for harpsichord, wind and string instruments (Bryn Mawr, Pennsylvania, 1994).

Landowska's husband was killed in a car accident in 1919; in 1925 she settled in Leu-la-Forêt (north of Paris) and founded an Ecole de Musique Ancienne there. In 1940 the German occupation forced her to abandon her library of over 10000 volumes, her instruments and the manuscripts of her early compositions, though some piano pieces had been published. After her arrival in the USA she lived in Lakeville, Connecticut. Her *Liberation Fanfare*, composed in admiration of Charles de Gaulle, was orchestrated by Richard Franko Goldman and performed many times by the Goldman Band in the 1940s. For many years she toured widely, performing and teaching, and at the age of 70 she recorded the complete Bach '48'. She was decorated by both the French and the Polish governments.

BIBLIOGRAPHY

A. Schaeffner: 'Wanda Landowska et le retour aux "humanités" de la musique', *ReM*, viii/8 (1927), 254–78

B. Gavoty and R. Hauert: *Wanda Landowska* (Geneva, 1957)

D. Restout and R. Hawkins, eds.: *Landowska on Music* (New York, 1965)

DENISE RESTOUT, LIONEL SALTER

Lang, Josephine (Caroline) (*b* Munich, 14 March 1815; *d* Tübingen, 2 Dec 1880). German composer, singer, pianist and teacher. A prolific and accomplished composer of lieder, Lang inherited musical talent from both sides of the family, including her maternal grandmother, a famous coloratura; her mother's three sisters; and, especially, her mother, Regina Hitzelberger (1788–1827), a court singer who gave up much of her career upon marriage (1808). Her father, Theobald Lang (1783–1839), whose own father had been a horn virtuoso in Mannheim, was music director at the Munich court. Sickly and often homebound, Lang was first taught music by her mother. She made her début at 11, playing a set of variations by Henri Herz. Her earliest compositions date from 1828. In 1830 she met Felix Mendelssohn, her most important professional contact. Captivated by Lang's lieder and by her singing, Mendelssohn wrote a glowing report to his family (letter of 6 October 1831). He gave her daily lessons in theory and recommended that she study in Berlin, but Lang's father decided against it. In 1841, on her engagement to the Swabian poet and jurist Christian Reinhold Köstlin (1813–56), Mendelssohn urged that she remain active as a composer (letter to Köstlin, 15 December 1841). His enthusiasm was shared by his sister Fanny Hensel (letter of 13 July 1841).

During the 1830s Lang taught singing and the piano, sang in the Königliche Vokalkapelle (after 1835), and composed. About 1835 she became fascinated with the style and aesthetic of Robert Schumann, who praised her music in a review (1837) of *Das Traumbild* op.28 no.1 (see *Gesammelte Schriften*). Meanwhile, her compositions began to be published. She met Köstlin in 1840 and between July and August set 41 of his poems (a creative effusion comparable to the simultaneous 'Liederjahr' of Clara and Robert Schumann). After their marriage in 1842 they moved to Tübingen, and Lang gave priority to her role of wife and mother (they were to have six children). Although several collections were published in the 1840s, only a few pieces were written during her marriage. After Köstlin's death in 1856 Lang turned with renewed zeal to composition and with the help of friends, notably Ferdinand Hiller, she found publishers. In all, she published 46 opuses, almost all lieder (four are piano pieces). In 1882, two years after her death, Breitkopf & Härtel issued a retrospective collection of 40 lieder, many previously unpublished.

Lang wrote, 'my songs are my diary': the setting of texts allowed for a strong personal identification in the creative process. Of her approximately 150 songs, most deal with love or nature. Melodies are often daring and show the insight of a singer, while accompaniments usually function independently. Lang's style, although often likened to that of her contemporaries, is fresh and individual, and expands our notions of the genre.

The best list of her compositions is in Köstlin; 52 songs were reprinted in 1982 (see Tick).

BIBLIOGRAPHY

FétisB; *FétisBS*; *Grove1*[†]; *LipowskyBL*; *SchmidlD*

Reviews in *AMZ*, xliii (1841), col.1042; xlviii (1846), cols.36–7; l (1848), col.35

R. Schumann: *Gesammelte Schriften über Musik und Musiker*, ii (Leipzig, 1854)

F. Mendelssohn: *Briefe aus den Jahren 1830 bis 1847*, ed. J. Rietz (Leipzig, 1861–3)

F. Hiller: *Aus dem Tonleben unserer Zeit* (Leipzig, 1868–71), ii, 116–36

H. A. Köstlin: 'Josefine Lang', *Sammlung musikalischer*

Vorträge, iii, ed. P. Waldersee (Leipzig, 1881), 51–103 [incl. list of works]

E. Friedrichs: 'Josephine Lang', *Neue Musikzeitung*, xxvii/10 (1905), 220–22

H. H. Rosenwald: *Geschichte des deutschen Liedes zwischen Schubert und Schumann* (Berlin, 1930)

J. Tick: Introduction to *Josephine Lang: Selected Songs* (New York, 1982) [52 songs]

M. J. Citron: 'Women and the Lied, 1775–1850', *Women Making Music: the Western Art Tradition 1150–1950*, ed. J. Bowers and J. Tick (Urbana and Chicago, 1986), 224–48

—— : 'Introduction on Lang', *Historical Anthology of Music by Women*, ed. J. Briscoe (Bloomington, IN, 1987), 109–10

M. J. Citron, ed.: *Letters of Fanny Hensel to Felix Mendelssohn* (New York, 1987)

MARCIA J. CITRON

Lang, Margaret Ruthven (*b* Boston, 27 Nov 1867; *d* Boston, 30 May 1972). American composer. She studied the piano and composition with her father, Benjamin Johnson Lang, and wrote her first works at the age of 12. She studied the violin with Louis Schmidt in Boston, continuing with Franz Drechsler and Ludwig Abel in Munich (1886–7), where she also studied counterpoint and fugue with Victor Gluth. On her return to Boston she worked on orchestration with George Chadwick. Her father continued to act as her teacher and mentor: Lang submitted for publication only those works that pleased him and, as conductor of the Cecilia and Apollo Clubs, he was regularly able to include his daughter's works in his programmes.

Margaret Ruthven Lang: engraving from 'Century Magazine' (March 1898)

The first works by Lang to receive public performance were five songs included in a Boston recital by Myron W. Whitney on 14 December 1887, which received favourable reviews from local critics. Her song *Ojalá* was performed at a concert of representative American works given at the Trocadéro during the Paris Exposition of 1889; this established her reputation, and the same song was repeated at the inauguration of the Lincoln Concert Hall in Washington, DC, on 26 March 1890. The soprano Mrs Gerrit Smith gave the first of many all-Lang concerts in New York two years later. Many leading singers performed Lang's songs, including Ernestine Schumann-Heink, who favoured *An Irish Love Song* as an encore.

Lang was the first woman in the USA to have a work played by a major orchestra. On 7 April 1893 the Boston SO under Arthur Nikisch gave the première of her *Dramatic Overture* op.12. The same year her overture *Witichis* op.10 received three performances at the World's Columbian Exposition, Chi-

cago, conducted by Theodore Thomas and Max Bendix. Other orchestral works were given by leading orchestras, and the *Ballade* op.36 received its première on 14 March 1901 at the Women in Music Grand Concert given by the Baltimore SO. *Wind* op.53 was commissioned by Victor Harris for his St Cecilia Chorus of New York, and was regularly included in the group's programmes. Lang's last work appeared in 1919. She remained interested in new music, however, and continued to attend concerts of the Boston SO, which gave a concert in honour of her 100th birthday.

Unlike her contemporaries, Lang made use of a restrained harmonic vocabulary with judicious use of dissonance. A number of her works draw on Scottish and Irish folk elements (for example, the *Six Scotch Songs* and *An Irish Mother's Lullaby*). Others contain onomatopoeic effects and humour (*The Jumblies*). Many, such as *Day is Gone*, are strophic and brief; the *Nonsense Rhymes* are witty miniatures. Several works, including *Wind*, explore impressionist sonorities within a tonal frame. Manuscripts by Lang, together with printed music and correspondence, are in the Arthur P. Schmidt Collection at the Library of Congress; the Boston Public

Library has multiple family scrapbooks, as well as printed music.

WORKS

selective list: all printed works published in Boston

Choral: The Jumblies (E. Lear), B, male chorus 4vv, 2 pf, op.5 (1890); The Wild Huntsman, 1v, 4vv, orch, lost; Te Deum, 4vv, org, op.34 (1899); Praise the Lord, O my Soul, S, A, T, B, male chorus 4vv; The Lonely. Rose (cantata, P. B. Marston), S, female chorus 4vv, pf, op.43 (1906); Grant, we Beseech thee, Merciful Lord, 4vv, org, op.51 (1912); The Night of the Star (cantata, D. A. McCarthy), 4vv, orch, op.52 (1913); Wind (J. Galsworthy), female chorus 8vv, op. 53 (1913); In praesepio (R. L. Gales), 4vv, org ad lib, op.56 (1916); The Heavenly Noël (Gales), Mez, female chorus 4vv, orch, op.57 (1916); 8 others

Orch (all lost): Witichis, ov., op.10, perf. 1893; Dramatic Overture, op.12, perf. 1893; Sappho's Prayer to Aphrodite, Mez, orch, perf. 1895; Armida, S, orch, op.24, perf. 1896; Phoebus' Denunciation of the Furies at the Delphian Shrine, B, orch; Totila, ov., op.23; Ballade, d, op.36, perf. 1901; incid. music to E. Rostand: *The Princess Far Away*, perf. 1906

Chamber: Pf Qnt, 1879; Evening Chimes, vn, pf, op.29, perf. 1898; Str Qt

Pf: Petit roman, op.18 (1894); Rhapsody, op.21 (1895); Meditation, op.26 (1897); Springtime, op.30 (1899); Revery, op.31 (1899); A Spring Idyll, op.33 (1899); The Spirit of the Old House: Elegy, op.58 (1917); One Summer Day, [op.59] (1919); 3 Pieces for Young Players, [op.60] (1919)

Songs (for 1v, pf, unless otherwise stated): Ghosts (R. Munkittrick) (1889); Ojalá (G. Eliot) (1889); Lament (S. Galler), op.6 no.3 (1891); The Grief of Love (J. A. Symonds), op.19 no.2 (1894); 6 Scotch Songs, op.20; An Irish Love Song, op.22 (1895); An Irish Mother's Lullaby (M. E. Blake), with vn obbl, op.34 (1900); The Hills o' Skye (W. McLennan), op.37 no.3 (1901); Day is Gone (J. V. Cheney), op.40 no.2 (1904); Nonsense Rhymes and Pictures (E. Lear), op.42 (1905); More Nonsense Rhymes and Pictures (Lear), op.43 (1907); Spring, op.47 (1909); *c*140 others

Principal publisher: A. P. Schmidt

BIBLIOGRAPHY

WAM

T. F. Ryan: *Recollections of an Old Musician* (New York, 1899), 85–7

E. Syford: 'Margaret Ruthven Lang', *New England Magazine*, xlvi/March (1912), 22

Obituary, *Boston Globe* (31 May 1972)

C. Ammer: *Unsung: a History of Women in American Music* (Westport, CT, 1980), 86–8

J. Tick: *American Women Composers before 1870* (Ann Arbor, 1983), 228–30

G. Claghorn: *Women Composers and Hymnists: a Concise Biographical Dictionary* (Metuchen, NJ, 1984)

J. Tick: 'Passed Away is the Piano Girl: Changes in American Musical Life, 1870–1900', *Women Making Music: the Western Art Tradition, 1150–1950* (Urbana and Chicago, 1986), 325–48, esp. 338, 342–3

K. Pendle, ed.: *Women and Music: a History* (Indianapolis, IN, 1991), 160–61, 164–7

J. Cline: *Margaret Ruthven Lang: Her Life and Songs* (diss., Washington U., 1993)

ADRIENNE FRIED BLOCK

Lara, Ana (*b* Mexico City, 30 Nov 1959). Mexican composer. She began musical studies with Humberto Hernandez Medrano. In the early 1980s she studied composition at the Conservatorio Nacional de Música with Daniel Catán and Mario Lavista and subsequently at the Carlos Chávez National Centre for Musical Research, Documentation and Information (CENEDIM) with Federico Ibarra. She also studied the piano and singing. In 1986 the Polish government awarded her a fellowship to study at the Warsaw Academy of Music, with Witold Rudziński and Włodzimierz Kotoński. In 1994 she served as director of the ISCM World Music Days festival in Mexico City, and she is President of the Mexican Society for New Music. Although *Vitrales* ('Stained Glass', 1992), commissioned by the Trio Italiano Contemporaneo, was written for a low-pitched trio (viola, cello and double bass), it is hardly inhibited in tone colour: the composer creates a flow of sounds ranging from the lowest depths to the highest peaks. A subtle perversity is present, too, in *Icaro* for solo recorder, of which the composer has said, 'Icarus's myth is one of the most suggestive: the ascension towards the sun, with a feeling of being god and thus invulnerable, and at the end, the irremediable fall. . . . I wanted to have the theme of the fall repeated and alternated with other passages of virtuosity and . . . why not . . . a certain irony'.

BIBLIOGRAPHY

G. Béhague: *Sonidas de las Americas Festival*, New York, 30 Jan–6 Feb 1994, pp.26, 33 [American Composers' Orchestra programme booklet]

Larsen [Reece], Libby [Elizabeth] (Brown) (*b* Wilmington, DE, 24 Dec 1950). American composer. She studied at the University of Minnesota (BA 1971, MM 1975, PhD 1978) with Dominick Argento, Paul Fetler and Eric Stokes, and co-founded, with the composer Stephen Paulus, the Minnesota Composers Forum in Minneapolis, serving from 1973 as managing composer and later in an advisory role. From the 1983–4 season to 1987, she was a resident composer with the Minnesota Orchestra, which has given the premières of several of her works. In 1993 she organized and became artistic director of the Hot Notes Series (sponsored by the Schubert Club of St Paul), which focusses on the modern keyboard, notably on the interaction of performer and synthesized sound. This interaction has become a feature of Larsen's later works; the opera *Mrs Dalloway*, based

Libby Larsen (left) at Orchestra Hall, Minneapolis, working with the pianist Janina Fialkowska, who gave the première of Larsen's Piano Concerto 'Since Armstrong' with the Minnesota Orchestra, conducted by Kenneth Jean, 30 October 1991

on Virginia Woolf and produced in Cleveland in 1993, integrates electronic instruments with acoustic ensemble, enabling the characters to function in both real and fluid time. Her first exploration of technological sound was in the opera *Frankenstein, the Modern Prometheus* (1990).

Larsen is a prolific and widely performed composer in all genres. Her music, which includes seven operatic works and three symphonies, has increasingly been based on principles developed in popular music and cinema techniques. In *Mrs Dalloway* she explored the concept of cinematic timing, and her Marimba Concerto (1992) juxtaposes fluid and metric pulsation. Essentially a lyric composer of poetic imagination, she typically attaches to her works evocative titles suggesting extra-musical imagery, as in *Overture: Parachute Dancing* (1983), *Symphony: Water Music* (given its première in 1985 under Sir Neville Marriner) and the *Piano Concerto 'Since Armstrong'* (1990, written for Janina Fialkowska). The last work develops the conceit of conversation among the great jazz trumpeter Armstrong, Ravel, Schoenberg and other composers in order to examine the nature of the piano concerto at the end of the century. Convinced that concert format must undergo change, and determined to expand traditional boundaries, Larsen worked in conjunction with the choreographer Brenda Way to produce *Ghosts of an Old Ceremony* (1991), a dance–orchestral piece based on the experience of women pioneers of the American West. She has a continuing interest in composing biographical works that illuminate strong-minded women through music and words. These include the songs *ME (Brenda Ueland)*, *Songs from Letters* (Calamity Jane's letters to her daughter Janey) and *Black Birds, Red Hills* (on the

painter Georgia O'Keeffe), and *Mary Cassatt* for mezzo, trombone and orchestra. Larsen also probes contemporary issues: *Frankenstein, the Modern Prometheus*, a riveting stage work incorporating video devices, draws parallels between the ancient alchemists and 20th-century scientists. She is also at ease in small forms. Her ear for language, as well as her melodic impulse (within a freely dissonant framework), are reflected not only in her operas and in the oratorio *Coming Forth into Day*, but in the song cycle for soprano and chamber ensemble *Sonnets from the Portuguese*, written for Arleen Augér.

A much-commissioned composer who works swiftly to produce at least one large-scale work each year, Larsen is also in demand as a speaker and guest teacher. She is recognized as a crusader for musical causes, including music education, and as an advocate of American music and women composers. She has received numerous awards, including a composer fellowship from the NEA and, as a producer, a Grammy Award for *The Art of Arleen Augér* (1994), which includes Larsen's *Sonnets from the Portuguese*.

WORKS
selective list

Stage: The Silver Fox (children's opera, 1, J. Olive), St Paul, MN, 20 April 1979; Tumbledown Dick (opera, 2, V. Sutton, after H. Fielding), St Paul, 16 May 1980; Psyke and the Pskyskraper, chamber opera, S, T, B, pf, 1982; Clair de lune (romantic fantasy, 2, P. Hampl), Little Rock, AR, 22 Feb 1985; Frankenstein, the Modern Prometheus (music drama, 1, Larsen, after M. W. Shelley), St Paul, 25 May 1990; A Wrinkle in Time (opera, 1, W. Green), 1991–2; Mrs Dalloway (opera, 2, B. Grice, after V. Woolf), Cleveland, Lyric Theater, July 1993

Orch: Tom Twist, nar, mime, orch, 1975; Weaver's Song and Jig, str band, chamber orch, 1978; 3 Cartoons, 1980; Pinions, vn, chamber orch, 1981; Deep Summer Music, 1982; Ov. 'Parachute Dancing', 1983; Sym. 'Water Music', 1984;

Coriolis, 1986; What the Monster Saw, 1987; Conc. 'Cold Silent Snow', fl, harp, chamber orch, 1987; Collage: Boogie, 1988; Tpt Conc., 1988; Pf Conc. 'Since Armstrong', 1990; Tambourines. 1991; Ghosts of an Old Ceremony, dancers, orch, 1991; Sym. no.3 'Lyric', 1992; Mar Conc. 'After Hampton', 1992; The Atmosphere as a Fluid System, fl, str, perc, 1992

Inst: Black Roller, fl, ob, cl, bn, vn, va, vc, pf, 1975; Suite, pf, 1976; Argyle Sketches, gui, 1979; Bronze Veils, trbn, perc, 1979; Triage, harp, 1981; Aubade, fl, 1982; Sonata on Kalenda Maya, org, 1983; Alauda, str qt, 1986; Grand Rondo, concert band, 1988; Corker, cl, perc, 1989; Kathleen, as she was, ob, hpd, 1989; Trio, va, vc, pf, 1989; Sun Song, concert band, 1991; Quartet: Schoenberg, Schenker and Schillinger, str qt, 1991

Vocal: Saints without Tears (P. McGinley), S, fl, bn, 1976; Eurydice, S, str qnt, 1978; In a Winter Garden (Hampl), S, T, SATB, chamber orch, 1982; Clair de lune (P. Verlaine), TTBB, 1985; Coming Forth into Day (oratorio, J. Sadat and others), S, B, SATB, orch, 1985; Moon Door, 1v, tape, slides, 1985; Clair de lune in Blue, SATB, pf, 1986; Canticle of the Sun, women's vv, perc, synth, org, 1987; ME (Brenda Ueland), S, pf, 1987; The Settling Years, SATB, ww qnt, pf, 1988; 3 Summer Scenes, SATB, orch, 1988; Black Birds, Red Hills, S, pf, 1989; Songs from Letters (after Calamity Jane [M. J. Burke]), S, pf, 1989; Sonnets from the Portuguese, S, chamber orch, 1989; Everyone Sang (S. Sassoon), SATB, harp, 2 perc, 1991; Mary Cassatt, Mez, trbn, orch, 1994; various anthems

Principal publishers: OUP, E. C. Schirmer

BIBLIOGRAPHY

Anderson 2; CC (P. Collins); CohenE

L. Larsen: 'The Nature of Music', PanPipes of Sigma Alpha Iota, lxxvii/wint. (1984–5)

P. Lambert: 'Orchestrating a Life in Music', Wall Street Journal (8 Aug 1988)

N. Malitz: 'Song of the Monster', ON (1990), May

C. Green: 'Interview with Composer Libby Larsen', ILWC Journal (1992), June, 24–7

D. Boyer: 'Musical Style and Gesture in the Choral Music of Libby Larsen', Choral Journal, xxxiv/March (1993)

C. Fowler: 'Three Musical Creators: Aaron Copland, Duke Ellington, Libby Larsen', Music!: its Role and Importance in our Lives (New York, 1994), chap.18 [incl. CD and video]

MARY ANN FELDMAN

Last, Joan Mary (b Littlehampton, Sussex, 12 Jan 1908). English composer and piano teacher. She studied the piano with Mathilde Verne and made her début in London, at the Aeolian Hall, in 1926. A severe injury to her hand terminated her career as a concert pianist so, despite a lack of formal composition lessons, she started writing simple but appealing music for her piano pupils. Since 1935 she has published over 120 albums of piano pieces including The First Concert (1950), London Today (1967) and Alphabetically Yours (1978). Among her tutors and technical books are The Young

Pianist (1954), Interpretation in Piano Study (1960), Freedom in Piano Technique (1980) and Beginning in Style (1991). For 22 years she was a professor at the RAM and in 1988 was appointed OBE.

SOPHIE FULLER

Lauber, Anne (Marianne) (b Zürich, 28 July 1943). Canadian composer and conductor, of Swiss birth. She studied the piano and violin before attending the conservatory in Lausanne (1964–7), where her teachers included Andras Kovach and Jean Perrin; she also had private lessons with Darius Milhaud. After moving to Montreal in 1967, she studied composition with André Prévost from 1973 to 1977, and continued her studies at the Université de Montréal with Prévost and Serge Garant; she was awarded the MMus in 1982 and the DMus in composition in 1986. Although Lauber's techniques have changed and refined, she has never lost her individual lyrical imprint. Her early works show strong technical precision and what Milhaud called 'a charming sensitivity'. She turned to serial technique in 1978 with Cinq pièces pour orgue. The film score L'Affaire Coffin of 1979 uses tonality and atonality simultaneously for expressive purposes, as does the Valse concertante, for piano and orchestra, of 1981. Several of her compositions have achieved recognition, including Au-delà du mur du son (1983), commissioned jointly by the Quebec SO and the Toronto SO, a work intended for children but which has also become popular with adults in Canada and the USA. Arabesque was awarded a prize at the International Guitar Competition in Marl, Germany, in 1985, and the oratorio Jesus Christus received critical acclaim at its première in 1986. Her many commissions include works for the double bass player Gary Karr and pianist Janina Fialkowska, and among her awards are those from the Association des Musiciens Suisses, the Québec Ministère des Affaires Culturelles and the Canada Council. Lauber took up conducting in the 1980s, directing the first performance of Colin-Maillard and the recording of Au-delà du mur du son. She has taught at the Université du Québec at Montreal, the Université de Montréal, the Université du Québec at Trois-Rivières and Concordia University. She became president of the Canadian Music Centre in 1987.

WORKS
selective list

Orch: Divertimento, str, 1970; Conc., str, 1976; Poème pour une métamorphose, 1978; Fantaisie sur un thème inconnu, pf, timp, suspended cymbals, str, 1980; Osmose: pièce symphonique no.2, 1981; Valse concertante, pf, orch, 1981, rev. 1983; Colin-Maillard, 1982; Au-delà du mur du son (P. Tardif-Delorme), sym. tale, 2 nar, 5 mime artists, orch, 1983; Conc., str qt, orch, 1983; Vn Conc., 1985–6; Pf Conc., 1988; 3 Moods for Double Bass, conc., db, orch, 1988; Ouverture canadienne, 1989.

Chamber: 5 éléments, fl, s sax, bn, tuba, el/acoustic vn, 1972; Va Sonata no.1, 1975; Ww Qnt, 1977; Mollésiennes, fl, pf, 1978; Divertissement, fl, gui, 1979; Va Sonata [no.2], 1979; Mouvement, vn, pf, 1980; Mouvement, vc, pf, 1980; Mouvement, fl, pf, 1980; 7 mouvements, various insts, 1980; Arabesque, gui, 1983; Pf Qnt, 1983; Le songe, fl, nar, str qt, 1985; 3 intermezzi, db, pf, 1987; Pf Qt, 1989

Kbd: Pf Sonata, 1976; 5 pièces, org, 1978; Le Petit Prince, pf, 1979; Monologue, pf, 1980; Scherzo, pf, 1989

Vocal and choral: 3 poèmes de Monika (M. Merinat), Mez/Bar, pf, 1976; 4 mélodies (Saint-Denys-Garneau), T/S, pf, 1979; Contrastes (A. Lauber), 1v, pf, 1980; La joue de la poupée (Merinat), nar, 6vv, vc, 1982; Jesus Christus: à la mémoire d'un grand homme: le Fils de l'Homme, oratorio (B. Lacroix), S, A, T, Bar, B, SATB, timp, 2 perc, str, 1983–4; Requiem, 4 soloists, chorus, orch, 1988–9

Film scores: L'Affaire Coffin, pf, timp, perc, str, 1979; Marie Uguay, 1981

GAYNOR G. JONES

Lazarosian, Goharik. *See* GAZAROSSIAN, KOHARIK.

LeBaron, (Alice) Anne (*b* Baton Rouge, LA, 30 May 1953). American composer and harpist. She studied composition with Frederic Goossen at the University of Alabama (BA 1974) and with Daria Semegen and Bülent Arel at SUNY (MA 1978). After attending the 1980 summer course at Darmstadt she continued her composition studies with Mauricio Kagel and György Ligeti as a Fulbright Scholar (1980–81) and with Chou Wen-chung, Mario Davidovsky and Jack Beeson at Columbia University (DMA 1989). She has also studied the harp and, in Korea, the *kayvagum* (plucked zither). Whether writing for her own extended harp palette, for the unusually constituted LeBaron Quintet (trumpet, tuba, electric guitar, harp and percussion) or for conventional ensembles, LeBaron uses evocative, colourful timbres. In a desire to communicate with diverse audiences and to enliven musical languages in her opera *The E. & O. Line* (a reinterpretation of the Orpheus and Eurydice legend from Eurydice's point of view, written in collaboration with Thulani Davis), she mixed non-notational traditions of bebop and blues music with her own contemporary classical

style. She has often combined improvisation with highly structured elements, reflecting contemporary concepts of chaos (finding organized patterns within apparent randomness), as in her 1989 piece for chamber ensemble *Telluris theoria sacra*. LeBaron has received many awards, several NEA grants and, in 1991, a Guggenheim Fellowship. During 1994 she served as composer-in-residence in Washington, DC, under the auspices of New Residencies, sponsored by Meet the Composer.

WORKS
selective list; many works from early 1970s withdrawn

Opera: The E. & O. Line (elec blues opera, with T. Davis), 4 solo vv, 12 insts, 6-part mixed blues/gospel chorus, women's jazz/blues trio, 1991

Orch: Strange Attractors, 1987; Double Conc., 2 harps (one player), chamber orch, 1994

Chamber: Rite of the Black Sun (after A. Artaud), 4 perc playing c50 insts, 7 dancers (opt.), 1980; Noh Reflections, vn, va, vc, 1985; Telluris theoria sacra, fl + pic, cl + b cl, vn, va, vc, pf, perc, 1989; Bouquet of a Phantom Orchestra, tpt, tuba, el gui, harp, perc, 1990; North Coast Nights, str qt, 1991; Devil in the Belfry, vn, pf, 1993; Southern Ephemera, fl, vc, 2 Harry Partch insts (surrogate kithara, harmonic canon), 1993; In Celebration of Youth, str qt, 1994

Vocal: Concerto for Active Frogs (theatrical work), B-Bar, small mixed chorus, percussionist (playing insts of choice), 2nd player (vn/va/vc/ob/sax/cl), 3rd player (bn/trbn/tuba/db), tape, 1975; The Sea and the Honeycomb (A. Machado, trans. R. Bly), S/Mez, fl + pic, cl + b cl, pf, 2 perc, 1979; Lamentation/Invocation (E. Honig, after Orphic legend), Bar, cl, vc, harp, 1984; Dish, S, el vn, perc, el db, pf, 1990

Also electronic and film music; recorded improvisations

BIBLIOGRAPHY

CC (B.Weir)

A. LeBaron with D. Bouliane: 'Darmstadt 1980', *PNM*, xix (1980–81), 420–41

J. L. Zaimont and K. Famera, eds.: *Contemporary Concert Music by Women* (Westport, CT, 1981), 68–9, passim

J. R. Oestreich: 'Orchestra of Young Players in Five World Premieres', *New York Times* (21 Jan 1990) [on *Strange Attractors*]

J. M. Edwards: 'North America since 1920', *Women and Music: a History*, ed. K. Pendle (Bloomington, IN, 1991), 225

B. Shoemaker: 'Anne LeBaron's Career is on the Line', *Washington Post* (24 Oct 1993)

J. McLellan: 'Eurydice's New Blues', *Washington Post* (1 Nov 1993)

J. MICHELE EDWARDS

Le Beau, Luise Adolpha (*b* Rastatt, 25 April 1850; *d* Baden-Baden, 1927). German composer, pianist and critic. She wrote her first pieces at 15 and made her piano début three years later with the Baden court orchestra. She performed her own compositions for Hans von Bülow, gaining his lifelong encouragement, and was briefly a pupil of Clara Schumann. She studied mainly, however, with Joseph Rheinberger, for which purpose the family moved to Munich in 1874. This was her most fruitful period as a composer and pianist and resulted in many of her best works, composition prizes, many favourable reviews of performances of her works, and meetings with Brahms, Liszt and Hanslick during extensive concert tours. Le Beau's style, which changed little throughout her life, is characterized by strong, well-shaped themes and strict sonata structure, as well as some use of colourizing, nonfunctional chords and leitmotifs. Many development sections, however, consist of frequent repetitions of thematic material with little alteration. For this reason (as Hanslick noted) her choral works and smaller pieces with rigid strophic or dance structures are often more successful.

By the early 1880s Le Beau had begun to experience difficulties arranging performances of her works in Munich, because of an estrangement from the Rheinbergers (which she attributed to her successes) and her association with a faction of conservatives resistant to the increasing involvement of Wagner's adherents in local institutions. Her family moved to Wiesbaden (1885–90), then to Berlin (1890–93), seeking a milieu where Le Beau would be appreciated and her works performed, and finally to Baden-Baden (1893), where she played in chamber concerts and worked as a critic. A performance of her first opera, *Hadumoth*, in November 1894 was well received. Her memoirs, *Lebenserinnerungen einer Komponistin*, were published in Baden-Baden in 1910 and in 1925 a concert of her works was given there to celebrate her 75th birthday.

WORKS

MSS and printed works in D-Bim, Bsb, Mbs

Operas: Hadumoth op.40 ('Szenen' after J. V. von Scheffel: *Ekkehard*), 1888–91; Der verzauberte Kalif op.55 (fantasy opera, Le Beau and L. Hitz), 1901–3

Choral: 5 Pieces (Byron, L. Hensel, O. Roquette, J. Kinkel), mixed chorus unacc., op.9, *c*1875 (Reudnitz-Leipzig, 1879); 2 Ballads (S. C. Pape, L. Uhland), mixed chorus, pf, op.16, *c*1878 (Berlin, 1880); 4 Songs (J. V. von Scheffel, E. Geibel, W. Le Beau, W. Hauff), men's chorus, op.19, *c*1880 (Reudnitz-Leipzig, n.d.); Im Sängersaal, Bar/A, orch, op.22, before 1880; 2 Pieces, mixed chorus unacc., op.20, *c*1880 (Reudnitz-Leipzig, n.d.); Ruth, oratorio, solo vv, chorus, orch, op.27, 1881–2 (Leipzig, *c*1884); 2 Choruses, men's vv, op.36, 1886; Hegauer [dance and chorus from Hadumoth

op.40], 1896; Miriams Lied, 1v, women's/boys' chorus, op.51, 1899; 2 Choruses, women's vv, pf, op.60, incl. Der Wind, der wandernde Wind, *c*1904; Vater unser, mixed chorus, op.61; Sanctus, women's chorus 4vv, op.64

Other vocal (all with pf acc.): 5 Songs (L. Uhland, J. Mosen, M. Strachwitz, A. Hoffmann von Fallersleben, J. von Eichendorff), A, op.4, 1865–75 (Berlin, *c*1876); 4 Trios (A. Adolphi, T. Körner, K. Mayer, J. W. von Goethe), female vv, op.5, *c*1875 (Berlin, *c*1876); 2 Duets (F. Öser, K. Hoffmann von Nauborn), S, A, op.6, *c*1875 (Berlin, *c*1877); 5 Lieder (J. Sturm, W. von der Neun, R. Reineck, F. Loewe, Hoffmann von Fallersleben), S, op.7, *c*1875 (Berlin, *c*1876); 5 Lieder (G. von Dyherrn), Bar/Mez, op.11, *c*1876 (Berlin, 1879); 3 Lieder (Eichendorff, H. Beger, Hoffmann von Fallersleben), S, op.14, *c*1876 (Berlin, *c*1877); 3 Lieder (Öser, Sturm, M. Bernstein), medium v, op.18, *c*1880, pubd in *Deutsche Kunst- und Musikzeitung*, xiii/25 (1886); 2 Songs, low v, op.29, before 1885; 3 Lieder (A. Schmitt, E. Geibel, A. von Chamisso), high v, op.33 (Cologne, 1905); 3 Lieder (R. Gernss), Mez, op.39, *c*1884 (Berlin, 1905); 2 Ballads op.42, 1876; 3 Lieder (J. Kerner and other(s)), A, vn, pf, op.45, 1897 (Leipzig, 1905); 3 Duets, S, A, op.50, 1899; 8 Kinderlieder op.52, 1899; 2 Songs from Urania (C. A. Tiedge), op.56, 1903; 3 melodie per canto op.58, 1903

Orch: Concert Ov., large orch, op.23, *c*1880; Fantasy, pf, orch, op.25, *c*1882; Pf Conc. op.37, 1887; Sym., F, op.41, *c*1894; Hohenbaden, sym. poem, op.43, 1897

Chamber: Vn Sonata [no.1], op.10, *c*1875 (Berlin, n.d.); 5 leichte Stücke, vn, pf, op.13, *c*1876 (Leipzig, 1880); Pf Trio op.15, 1877 (Elberfeld, 1879); Sonata [no.1], D, op.17, *c*1878 (Leipzig, n.d.); 4 Pieces for Vc, E, op.24, 1881 (Leipzig, n.d.); Va Sonata, g, op.26, 1881 (Leipzig, n.d.); Pf Qt, f, op.28 (Leipzig, *c*1884); Romanze, harp, op.31, *c*1884; Str Qt op.34, *c*1884; Romanza, vn, pf, op.35, 1886 (Cologne, 1905); Canon, 2 vn, pf, op.38, 1887 (Heilbronn, 1905); Elegy, vn, pf, op.44, 1897 (Leipzig, 1905); Vn Sonata no.2, op.46, 1898; Str Qnt op.54, 1900; 5 Pieces, vn, pf, op.65

Pf: 3 Pieces op.1, 1874 and earlier (Bremen, *c*1876); Concert étude op.2, 1874 (Berlin, *c*1876); Theme and Variations, f, op.3, before 1874 (Berlin, *c*1876); Sonata, a, op.8, *c*1875 (Berlin, *c*1876); 8 Preludes, g, op.12, 1872 (Berlin, *c*1876); 6 Fugues (Studies), op.21, *c*1877 (Leipzig, n.d.); Improvisata for Left Hand, E♭, op.30, *c*1884 (Leipzig, *c*1884); Gavotte, f, op.32, *c*1884 (Leipzig, n.d.); Ballade, b, op.47, 1898; 3 danze antiche, a, op.48, 1898 (Milan, 1905); Deutscher Reigen op.49, 1899; Trauermarsch op.53, 1900; 3 Pieces op.57, 1903; Barcarole op.59, *c*1904; Im Walde op.62, n.d.; Abendklaenge op.63, n.d.

BIBLIOGRAPHY

SchmidlD

Kritiken über Kompositionen von L. A. Le Beau, 1876–1925 (4 scrapbooks, D-Bsb)

E. Rieger, ed.: *Frau und Musik* (Frankfurt, 1980), 45–59, 127–33, 229–30 [incl. excerpts from *Lebenserinnerungen* and Le Beau's articles, 'Über die musikalische Erziehung der weiblichen Jugend', *AMz*, v (1 Nov 1878), 365–6, and 'Über die Reform unserer Musik-Schulen', *AMz*, v (11 and 18 Oct 1978), 341–3 and 349–51 respectively]

Franziska Lebrun; portrait
(1780) by Thomas
Gainsborough

E. Weissweiler: *Komponistinnen aus 500 Jahren* (Frank-furt, 1981), 272–96
J. E. Olson: 'Luise Adolpha Le Beau' [trans. of excerpts from *Lebenserinnerungen*], *Women in Music: an Anthology of Source Materials from the Middle Ages to the Present*, ed. C. Neuls-Bates (New York, 1982), 167–74 [concerning *Hadumoth*]
—— : 'Luise Adolpha Le Beau: Composer in Late Nineteenth-Century Germany', *Women Making Music: the Western Art Tradition, 1150–1950*, ed. J. Bowers and J. Tick (Urbana and Chicago, 1986), 282–303
U. Keil: *Louise Adolpha Le Beau (1850–1927): und ihre Zeit und Werk* (diss., U. of Heidelberg, in preparation)

JUDITH E. OLSON

Lebrun [née Danzi], **Franziska** [Francesca] **(Dorothea)** (*b* Mannheim, 24 March 1756; *d* Berlin, 14 May 1791). German soprano and composer. She was the daughter of the cellist Innocenz Danzi and elder sister of the composer Franz Danzi (1763–1826). She made her début in 1772 at the Schwetzingen Hoftheater in Antonio Sacchini's *La contadina in corte* and sang in the Elector Carl Theodor's court opera at Mannheim, holding the title 'virtuosa da camera'. In 1777 she triumphed in the role of the countess in Ignaz Holzbauer's *Günther von Schwarzburg*, which was composed for her voice. She spent the next year in London and in 1778 married the Mannheim oboist and composer Ludwig August Lebrun (1752–90). On 3 August 1778 she sang the principal role in Antonio Salieri's *Europa riconosciuta* at the opening of La Scala, Milan. Early in 1779 she appeared with her husband at the Concert Spirituel in Paris, where she caused a stir by fitting Italian texts to the solo parts of *symphonies concertantes*. For the opera seasons of 1779–81 she was again engaged at the King's Theatre in London. Thomas Gainsborough painted her portrait in 1780. She published two sets of six sonatas for violin and piano (opp.1–2, 1780), which appeared in subsequent editions published in London, Paris, Amsterdam, Offenbach, Berlin and Mannheim. After the sudden death of her husband in December 1790 her health declined rapidly and she appeared in public only twice more.

BIBLIOGRAPHY
BurneyGN; *BurneyH*; *Choron-FayolleD*; *FétisBS*; *GerberNL*; *Grove1* (J. Marshall); *LipowskyBL* ('Brun'); *SchillingE*; *SchmidlD*
Musikalische Realzeitung, iii (1789), no.52, col.415; iv (1790), no.1, col.7, no.4, col.30, no.17, col.128
Musikalische Korrespondenz der teutschen Filarmonischen Gesellschaft (6 Jan 1791, 16 Feb 1791)

C. F. D. Schubart: *Ideen zu einer Ästhetik der Tonkunst* (Vienna, 1806)

F. Walter: *Geschichte des Theaters und der Musik am kurpfälzischen Hofe* (Leipzig, 1898)

H. Riemann: Introduction, DTB, xxviii, Jg.xvi (1915)

R. Fuhrmann: *Mannheimer Klavier-Kammermusik* (Marburg, 1963), 118–23, 185, 190

L. Finscher, ed.: *Die Mannheimer Hofkapelle im Zeitalter Carl Theodors* (Mannheim, 1992)

BRIGITTE HÖFT

Lebrun [Dülken], **Sophie** (*b* London, 20 July 1781; *d* Munich, 23 July 1863). German pianist and composer. She was the daughter of the Munich court oboist L. A. Lebrun and the court soprano Franziska Lebrun (née Danzi). Her teachers included the Munich court trumpeter Cajetan Knechtl (rudiments), Andreas Streicher (piano) and Franz Danzi (singing). Well known and respected from an early age as a pianist, she undertook concert tours to Switzerland, Italy and Paris. Weber, Spohr and Meyerbeer sought her acquaintance. Her compositions, mainly sonatas and concertos according to Lipowsky, were not published and are lost. She married the Munich court piano maker J. L. Dülken on 27 December 1799. Her daughters Louise (*b*1805) and Fanny (*b*1807) married the brothers Max and Anton Bohrer (both Munich court musicians) and her daughter Violande (*b*1810) became a concert singer.

BIBLIOGRAPHY

LipowskyBL

ROBERT MÜNSTER

Lecuona Casado, Ernestina (*b* Matanzas, 16 Jan 1882; *d* Havana, 3 Sept 1951). Cuban composer, pianist and teacher. Member of a remarkable musical family (including Ernesto Lecuona, her brother, and Leo Brouwer, her grandson), she studied at the Academia del Centro Asturiano in Havana and continued at the Municipal Conservatory (now the Amadeo Roldán School of Music) and then with Madame Calderón of the Paris Conservatoire. In 1932 she met the singer Esther Borja, her most faithful interpreter, with whom she toured Latin America, performing in theatres, on radio and on film. She also performed as a solo pianist in Cuba and abroad and gave concerts for two pianos with her brother, to whom she dedicated three pieces, *Danza negra* and the boleros *Mi vida es soñar* and *Anhelo besarte*. In 1937 she was a founder member of the Orquesta Feminina de Concierto. Her compositions are mostly small-scale, including canciones, hymns, waltzes and other Latin-

American dances. Like the traditional *trovadores* at the turn of the century, Leucona often wrote replies to the works of other composers: her *criolla ¿Me odias?* was a reply to *Te odio* by Felix B. Caignet; further works of this kind are the bolero *No lo dudes* (1932) and the bolero-canción *Ahora que eres mía* (1936). Some of her compositions have been recorded.

ALICIA VALDÉS CANTERO

Lee, Chan-Hae (*b* Seoul, 8 Oct 1945). Korean composer. She studied composition at Yonsei University, Seoul (BA), and at the Catholic University of America, Washington, DC (MM); she was later appointed lecturer at Yonsei University. Her works are typically contrapuntal and favour progressive structural developments over strict forms. In music that is simple and direct, Lee chooses subjects that reflect her Christianity and her interest in music education. One of her later works, *Glorification* (1991), for three percussionists, is her fifth piece based on John Bunyan's *Pilgrim's Progress*. It presents the pitch sequence D–E–B♭–G, gradually opening with central snare drums and moving outwards to low timpani and high tom-toms; halfway through, gongs, cymbals and bells take over as metal triumphs over wood and skin.

Lee's output includes *Hyesang* (1980) and *Chosaeng* (1981), both for two solo voices with chamber ensemble; two works for solo wind, *Galpiri* (clarinet; 1986) and *Three Fragments* (flute; 1989); *The Cross*, for mixed chorus (1988); and *Martyr*, for string orchestra (1990). Her music has been performed in Europe, the USA and Australasia.

KEITH HOWARD

Lee, Hope Anne Keng-Wai (*b* Taipei, 14 Jan 1953). Canadian composer and teacher of Chinese origin. She studied at the University of Toronto (BSc 1973; BMus 1978) and at McGill University (MMus 1981), having studied composition (including electronic composition) with Brian Cherney, Bengt Hambraeus, Jon Rea, Mariano Etkin and Alcides Lanza. In 1981 she won a German exchange scholarship to study composition for a year with Klaus Huber at the Staatliche Hochschule für Musik, Freiburg. She has worked as an accompanist, organist, choir director and piano teacher at the International Music Conservatory, Missisauga, and in Montreal. Her compositions include a number of orchestral, vocal and chamber pieces (including *Nabripamo*, 1982, for piano and

Nicola LeFanu

marimba, which won first prize in the Okanagan Music Composers' Festival) and a considerable amount of electronic music.

Lee, Young-ja (*b* Wŏnju, Kangwŏn province, 4 June 1936). Korean composer. The history of Western music in Korea goes back barely a century; women composers appeared more recently, and Lee is the most senior. She studied with La In-Yong at Ewha Women's University in Seoul (BA 1954, MA 1956); with Tony Aubin and Noël Gallon at the Paris Conservatoire (1958–61); with Marcel Quinet at the Brussels conservatory (1969–72); and at the Manhattan School of Music, New York (1969). She later gained a doctorate from the Sorbonne (1986–9). She was professor and director of the composition department at Ewha Women's University (1961–83), occasional lecturer at Seoul National University and other universities in Korea, and guest lecturer at the Sorbonne (1989). She is vice-president of the Korean National Committee of the International Music Council. In 1986 she was awarded the 8th Korean National Composer's Prize. In the West, her works have been performed in France, the Netherlands and Mexico.

Not surprisingly, Lee's works retain French influence. Her *Sonatine* for piano (1972) starts with a fluid Andantino that quickly develops oscillating bass ostinatos and blocks of descending chord clusters. Her

three-movement Piano Sonata (1985) begins with dissonant clusters coupled to rhythmic patterns imitating traditional percussion bands. The second movement describes *han*, Korean repression, using high block chords without vertical harmonic support. The finale emphasizes a regular oscillating bass, reminiscent of a country blacksmith. *Auto-portrait* for harp and piano (1990) couples the same features to glissandos and rapid melodic flurries that explore two non-complementary six-note scales. Other representative works include the Piano Concerto (1973) and *Mouvements concertanto* for violin and orchestra (1973). Lee is also the author of two books on counterpoint and a thesis on Olivier Messiaen's musical language.

WORKS

Orch: Suite, 1971; Movement symphoniques, 1972; Mouvements concertanto, vn, orch, 1973; Pf Conc., 1973; Festival Ov., 1975; Gae-chun, 1991
Chamber: Qnt, cl, vn, vc, db, pf, 1953; Trio, cl, bn, pf, 1955; Vc Sonata, 1956; Vn Sonata, 1956; Suite, vc, pf, 1967; Trio, ob, bn, pf, 1967; Ballade, cl, pf, 1970; Sonata 'Requiem', fl, 1983; Reflections, fl, cl, 1986; Music for Oboe and Piano, 1989; Auto-portrait, harp, pf, 1990; Qnt, fl, harp, str trio, 1992
Pf: 2 Preludes and Bagatelle, 1952; 2 Poems, 1958; Theme and Variations, 1961; Suite Romantic, 1967; Sonatine, 1972; Sonata, 1985; Reminiscence, 1988
Vocal: 5 Art Songs, 1955; 2 Art Songs, 1967; 3 Love Songs, S, harp, 1991

KEITH HOWARD

LeFanu, Nicola (Frances) (*b* Wickham Bishops, Essex, 28 April 1947). English composer and teacher, daughter of Elizabeth Maconchy. She studied at St Hilda's College, Oxford, where she was a pupil of Egon Wellesz, and at the RCM (1968–9). In 1973 she won the Mendelssohn Scholarship and a Harkness Award, which took her for a year to the USA (1973–4). By this time she was fulfilling many commissions and her first major orchestral work, *The Hidden Landscape*, had been performed at a Prom concert in London (1973).

She has held teaching appointments at St Paul's School for Girls (1975–7), at Morley College and at King's College, London (1977–94), where together with her husband David Lumsdaine she has developed a department of postgraduate composition. They have also worked together in Australia, and in 1979 were joint composers-in-residence at the NSW Conservatorium in Sydney. She was appointed Professor of Music at York University in 1994. LeFanu has been an active member of the SPNM and organizer of their composers' courses. She is a founder-member of the group Women in Music and her article 'Master Musicians: an Impregnable Taboo?' is a pioneering work in the study of the reception of British women composers. With Sophie Fuller, she organized the first 'Music and Gender' conference in Britain at King's College, London, in July 1991.

LeFanu is a practical composer with a solicitous regard for the particular character of instruments and voices. Many of her instrumental works can be regarded as explorations of the player–instrument relationship. In other works metaphors drawn from the natural world provide the controlling influence. *The Hidden Landscape* and *Columbia Falls* (inspired by Maine's 'blueberry barrens') can be described as sound landscapes in which the ear can find its own focus, moving at will from foreground to background. In *Deva* the cello descends from highest to lowest register, its sonority increasing 'like a stream . . . becoming river . . . becoming sea'.

Several of the theatre works bring together actors, dancers and singers as equal partners in the unfolding drama. While *Anti-World* deals in abstract terms with questions of freedom, control, influence and anti-influence, in *Dawnpath*, *The Old Woman of Beare* and *Blood Wedding* she has moved through myth to the musical representation of particular individuals and immediate human predicaments. It is perhaps in these later dramatic works that the 'exceptional gifts of heart and head' noted by the American critic Michael Steinberg find their fullest expression.

WORKS

STAGE

Anti-World (music-theatre piece, 1, N. Gorbanevskaya and A. Voznesensky), dancer; London, Cockpit Theatre, June 1972
The Last Laugh, (ballet) 1972; London, Young Vic Theatre, April 1973
Dawnpath (chamber opera, 1, LeFanu), S, Bar, dancer; London, Collegiate Theatre, 29 Sept 1977
The Old Woman of Beare (monodrama, 1, 9th/10th century Irish, adapted LeFanu), S, chamber ens; London, St John's, Smith Square, 3 Nov 1981
The Story of Mary O'Neill (radiophonic opera, 3, LeFanu and S. McInerney), S, 16 solo vv, 1986; BBC, 4 Jan 1989
The Green Children (children's opera, 2, K. Crossley-Holland), solo vv (adult and children's); King's Lynn, 18 July 1990
Blood Wedding (opera, 2, D. Levy, after F. García Lorca); London, Jacob Street Studios, 26 Oct 1992

INSTRUMENTAL

Orch: Preludio I, 1967; The Hidden Landscape, 1973; Columbia Falls, 1975; Preludio II, 1976; Farne, 1980; Variations, pf, orch, 1982
Chamber and solo inst: Soliloquy, ob, 1966;

Variations, ob qt, 1968; Chiaroscuro, pf, 1969; Abstracts and a Frame, vn, pf, 1971; Omega, org, 1972, rev. 1984; Collana, solo perc, ens, 1976; Deva, vc, ens, 1979; Trio I, fl + pic, vc, perc, 1980; Moon over Western Ridge Mootwingee, 4 sax, 1985; Invisible Places, cl qnt, 1986; Lament 1988, ob + eng hn, cl + b cl, va, vc, 1988; Str Qt, 1988; Lullaby, cl, pf, 1988; Nocturne, vc, pf, 1988; Concerto, a sax and str, 1989; Sundari and the Secret Message, fl + pic, vc, sitar, tabla, kbd, storyteller, 1993

VOCAL

Choral: Christ Calls Man Home (Eng. medieval), S, S, 3 SATB choruses, 1971; The Valleys Shall Sing (Psalms), SATB, ww ens, 1973; For We are the Stars (Native American), 16 solo vv, 1978; Verses from Psalm xc, S, 2 mixed choruses unacc., 1978; Like a Wave of the Sea (trad. Hindi, L. Carroll, Bible), mixed vv, early inst ens, 1981; Rory's Rounds (trad.), young vv, 1983; Stranded on my Heart (R. Tagore, J. Fuller, D. Sutton, Hindu texts), T, SATB, str orch, 1984
Solo vocal: Il cantico dei cantici II (Apocrypha), S, 1968; But Stars Remaining (C. Day Lewis), S, 1970; Rondeaux (Fr. medieval), T, hn, 1972; Paysage (G. Apollinaire), Bar, 1973; The Same Day Dawns (various sources), S, chamber ens, 1974; A Penny for a Song (Jap. and early Irish poems, W. de la Mare), S, pf, 1981; Trio II: Song for Peter (E. Dickinson, T. Hughes, A. Chekhov), S, cl, pf, 1983; I am Bread (B. Kennelly), S, pf, 1987; Wind among the Pines (S. Takahashi, trans. L. Stryk), S, orch, 1987

BIBLIOGRAPHY

CC   (R.   Matthew-Walker);   Fuller-LeFanuRM; LePageWC, iii
R. Cooke: 'Nicola LeFanu', MT, cxvi (1975), 961–3
V. O'Brien: 'Living British Women Composers: a Survey', The Musical Woman: an International Perspective, i: 1983, ed. J. L. Zaimont and others (Westport, CT, 1984), 209–34
N. LeFanu: 'Master Musicians: an Impregnable Taboo?', Contact, xxxi/aut. (1987), 4–9
A. Clements: 'Greening of the Opera', Financial Times (21 July 1990) [review of The Green Children]
G. Rickards: 'Nicola LeFanu's Blood Wedding', Tempo, no. 184 (1993), 60–61

HUGO COLE

Leginska [Liggins], Ethel (*b* Hull, 13 April 1886; *d* Los Angeles, 26 Feb 1970). English-American pianist and teacher, composer and conductor. While still a child she showed exceptional skill as a pianist, and with the patronage of a Hull shipping magnate and his wife, Arthur and Mary Smith Wilson, she undertook advanced training at the Hoch Conservatory in Frankfurt, with Theodor Leschetizky in Vienna for three years, and in Berlin. She adopted the name Leginska early in her professional career, and became widely known as the 'Paderewski of women pianists'.

She made her official début at 16 with the Queen's Hall Orchestra in London, then gave concert tours in Europe before going to the USA in 1913; there she gained the highest critical acclaim in the 1916–17 season. A great favourite with the public, she was noted for demanding programmes and innovations, such as playing an entire Chopin programme without an interval and wearing a tailored ('practical') dress rather than a glamorous one.

In 1914 Leginska began to compose and in 1918 studied with Ernest Bloch in New York. Her output was relatively small. Most of it was completed by the end of the 1920s and songs and piano music were published; other works include symphonic poems, a fantasy for piano and orchestra and two operas. Her music is progressive in its rhythmic intensity, its free approach to tonality, and its use of vocal declamation. It is to Leginska's credit that she was able to secure performances of the larger works in Europe and the USA.

Because of nervous crises, in 1926 Leginska retired as a concert pianist in favour of composition and conducting. After studying conducting with Eugene Goossens and Robert Hager in 1923, she established her pioneering role by directing major orchestras in Munich, Paris, London and Berlin in 1924.

Her American début took place on 9 January 1925 with the New York SO, and was followed by a triumphant performance at the Hollywood Bowl in August. She conducted the Boston PO, 1926–7, the Boston Woman's SO, 1926–30 (including extensive national tours in 1928 and 1929), and the Woman's SO of Chicago, 1927–9. In 1930–31 she conducted at leading European opera houses; other notable performances included Beethoven's Ninth Symphony in Havana (1933) and Dallas (1934).

The high point of her career, perhaps, was the première in 1935 of her one-act opera *Gale*, which was given by the Chicago City Opera under Leginska's direction. John Charles Thomas created the title role of this dark, atmospheric score depicting the Cornish seaside. After 1935 Leginska's novelty as a conductor faded. In 1940 she moved her studio to Los Angeles, where she taught the piano into the 1950s and in 1957 conducted a performance of her opera *The Rose and the Ring* (composed in 1932).

WORKS

Operas: The Rose and the Ring, 1932; Gale, 1935 [? = The Haunting (1, C. A. Dawson-Scott, H. D. Lowry), MS vs *US-NYp*]

Orch: Beyond the Fields we Know, 1921; Fantasy, pf, orch, *c*1922; 4 sujets barbares, 1923; 2 Short Poems, 1924

Chamber and solo inst: Str Qt, after 4 poems by R. Tagore; Triptych, 11 insts; The Gargoyles of Notre Dame, pf, *c*1920; Scherzo, after Tagore, pf, *c*1920; 3 Victorian Portraits, 1959

Songs: At Dawn, 1919; Bird Voices of Spring, 1919; The Frozen Heart, 1919; The Gallows' Tree, 1919; 6 Nursery Rhymes, 1928; In a Garden, 1928

BIBLIOGRAPHY

NAW (C. Neuls-Bates)

CAROL NEULS-BATES

Lehmann, Liza [Elizabeth] (**Nina Mary Frederica)** (*b* London, 11 July 1862; *d* Pinner, 19 Sept 1918). English soprano and composer. She was the daughter of Amelia Lehmann (widely known under the initials A. L. as a teacher, composer and arranger of songs) and Rudolf Lehmann, a German painter. She studied singing with Alberto Randegger and Jenny Lind in London, and composition with Raunkilde in Rome, Wilhelm Freudenberg in Wiesbaden and Hamish MacCunn in London. Realizing that despite her wide vocal range (*a* to *b″*) she lacked the stamina and power necessary for opera, she made her début as a recitalist at a Monday Popular Concert on 23 November 1885, and during the next nine years undertook many important engagements in

Ethel Leginska

England, receiving encouragement from Joseph Joachim and Clara Schumann. After a farewell concert at St James's Hall on 14 July 1894, she retired to marry Herbert Bedford, a painter and composer who after her death was to become a noted proponent of unaccompanied song. She had already published some songs, and in 1896 *In a Persian Garden* appeared, a cycle of selected quatrains from Edward FitzGerald's version of the *Rubāiyāt of Omar Khayyām*, for four soloists and piano; its exotic text and lyrical style appealed to contemporary taste, and it became popular. More song cycles and a number of musical comedies followed. In 1910 Lehmann undertook the first of two successful tours of the USA, accompanying her own songs in recitals. From 1911 to 1912 she was the first president of the Society of Women Musicians. She later became a professor of singing at the GSM and wrote *Practical Hints for Students of Singing*. Her memoirs make fascinating reading, giving a witty and humorous insight into musical society of the period in London and the USA, though they conclude with a great sense of loss at the death of one of her sons in training during World War I; she herself died shortly after completing them.

Lehmann and Maude Valérie White were England's foremost female composers of songs. Although both made solo settings of Tennyson's *In memoriam* (Lehmann's is on an extensive scale), they excelled in lighter material. Some of Lehmann's procedures, such as her penchant for four-voice cycles and for piano links between songs, seem fossilized as period taste while others remain fresh and have been undervalued. She wrote many children's songs, ranging from the pert triviality of 'There are fairies at the bottom of our garden' to the melodic and harmonic passion of 'Stars' from *The Daisy-Chain*. 'Ah, moon of my delight' from *In a Persian Garden* betokens a gift which would surely have flourished in the musical theatre had she been in a position to devote her career to it; as it was, her two comedy scores were received favourably, while in *Everyman*, a somewhat austere essay produced in a double bill with Debussy's *L'enfant prodigue*, she furthered the English morality genre.

Liza Lehmann

WORKS
selective list;
printed works published in vocal score in London
STAGE
Sergeant Brue (musical farce, 3, O. Hall [pseud. of J. Davis] and J. H. Wood), London, 14 June 1904 (1904); The Vicar of Wakefield (romantic light opera, 3, L. Housman, after O. Goldsmith), Manchester, 14 Nov 1906, London, 12 Dec 1906 (1907); Everyman (opera, 1), London, 28 Dec 1915 (1916); The Twin Sister (incid. music), unpubd

OTHER WORKS
Vocal with orch: Young Lochinvar (W. Scott), Bar, chorus, orch (1898); Once upon a Time, cantata (1903); The Golden Threshold (S. Naidu), S, A, T, Bar, chorus, orch (1906); Leaves from Ossian, cantata

Song sets and cycles: 8 German Songs (1888); 12 German Songs (1889); 9 English Songs (1895); In a Persian Garden (E. FitzGerald, after O. Khayyām), S, A, T, B, pf (1896); In memoriam (Tennyson) (1899); The Daisy-Chain (L. Alma Tadema, R. L. Stevenson and others), S, A, T, B, pf (1900); Cameos: 5 Greek Love-Songs (1901); 5 French Songs (G. Boutelleau, F. Plessis) (1901); More Daisies, S, A, T, B, pf (1902); Songs of Love and Spring (E. Geibel, A. P. Graves), A, Bar, pf (1903); The Life of a Rose (L. Lehmann) (1905); Bird Songs (A. S.) (1907); Nonsense Songs (from L. Carroll: *Alice in Wonderland*), S, A, T, B, pf (1908); 5 Little Love Songs (C. Fabbri) (1910); Prairie Pictures (Lehmann), S, A, T, B, pf (1911); Songs of a 'Flapper' (Lehmann) (1911); Cowboy Ballads (J. A. Lomax) (1912); The Well of Sorrow (H. Vacaresco: *The Bard of the Dimbovitza*) (1912); 5 Tenor Songs (1913); Hips and Haws (M. Radclyffe Hall) (1913); Songs of Good Luck (Superstitions) (H. Taylor) (1913); Parody Pie, S, A, T, B, pf (1914); Four Cautionary Tales and a Moral (H. Belloc), 2vv, pf (1919)

Other vocal works, incl. The Secrets of the Heart (H. Austin Dobson), S, A, pf (1895); Good-Night, Babette! (Austin Dobson), S, Bar, vn, vc, pf (1898); Endymion (scena, H. W. Longfellow), S, pf (1899); The Eternal Feminine (monologue, L. Eldée),

(1902); The Happy Prince (recitation, O. Wilde), (1908); 4 Shakespearean Part-Songs (1911); The High Tide (recitation, J. Ingelow), (1912) Chamber and inst works, incl. Romantic Suite, vn, pf; Cobweb Castles, pf

BIBLIOGRAPHY
GänzlBMT; *SchmidlD*
L. Lehmann: *The Life of Liza Lehmann, by Herself* (London, 1919)
G. Bush: 'Songs', *Music in Britain: the Romantic Age, 1800–1914*, ed. N. Temperley (London, 1981), 280–82
D. Hyde: *New-Found Voices: Women in Nineteenth-Century English Music* (Liskeard, 1984), 69–71
S. Banfield: *Sensibility and English Song: Critical Studies of the Early Twentieth Century* (Cambridge, 1985)
L. Foreman: 'British Opera Comes of Age: 1916–61', *British Opera in Retrospect* (n.p., 1986) [pubn of the British Music Society], 106–7
STEPHEN BANFIELD

Leite (Dias Batista), Clarisse (*b* São Paulo, 11 Jan 1917). Brazilian composer, pianist and teacher. She studied with Zilda Rizzo and José Kliass (piano), Teodoro Nogueira (composition), Orestes Farinello (orchestration) and João Sepe (harmony). In 1930 she graduated from the Conservatório Dramático e Musical, São Paulo, after having won a scholarship to study in France. As a pianist she toured Austria and Hungary and gave recital tours in Brazil playing Japanese music. She has taught at many music schools in São Paulo state. Most of her music is for piano, with or without other instruments; the solo music includes *Impressões de Vienna*, *Ciclo do jazz* and *Quilombo dos Palmares*. Of her two piano concertos (1972, 1975), the first was performed at the spring festival in Tokyo in 1977. She is a member of the International Academy of Music.

IRATI ANTONIO

Leite, Vânia Dantas (*b* Rio de Janeiro, 13 Aug 1945). Brazilian composer, pianist and conductor. She studied at the Escola Nacional de Música of the University of Brazil (now the University of Rio de Janeiro), where her teachers included Zilá de M. Brito (piano) and Frederico Egger (composition). Later she studied electronic music in London with Per Hartmann (1974) and in Paris, and completed her composition studies with Esther Scliar. Although she has performed as a concert pianist with several orchestras, she has dedicated most of her career to composing, conducting and teaching; she has held teaching posts at various schools, including the Conservatório Brasileiro de Música. In 1972 she won the first prize of the Ordem dos Músicos do

Brasil with the orchestral work *Abertura 1822*. Other orchestral pieces include the Symphony no.1 (1971), *Entre vidas* (1974) and, with chorus, *Réquiem para um poeta*. Her chamber music often involves electronics, for example *Vita vitae* for voice, flute, clarinet, viola, cello, tape and synthesizer (1975), and *Te quero verde*, 'electronic *merengue*' for computer tape, guitar and *berimbau* (musical bow) (1983).

IRATI ANTONIO

Leiviskä, Helvi (Lemmikki) (*b* Helsinki, 25 May 1902; *d* Helsinki, 12 Aug 1982). Finnish composer. She studied composition at the Helsinki Music Institute (now the Sibelius Academy) with Erkki Melartin (1919–27) and continued her studies in Vienna with Arthur Willner (1928–9). She worked as a librarian at the Sibelius Academy and as a music critic. Leiviskä's début took place in 1935 with a concert of her own compositions, most notably her Piano Concerto (1935). Her early works are Romantic, but after World War II she developed a highly contrapuntal style that in the last works moved towards free tonality; at the same time her music became more serious, sometimes even austere. Leiviskä's main compositions include three symphonies (1947, 1954 and 1971) and – perhaps her best-known work – the *Sinfonia brevis* (1962), a single movement piece with a concluding triple fugue. Her output also includes choral works, songs, chamber and piano music. The principal publisher of her music is the Finnish Broadcasting Corporation.

BIBLIOGRAPHY
E. Marvia, ed.: Suomalaisia säveltäjiä II [Finnish Composers II] (Porvoo, 1966)
M. Heiniö: 'Uusklassismin reseptio ja Suomen luova säveltaide 30-luvulta 50-luvun puoliväliin' [The Reception of Neo-Classicism and Finnish Music from the 1930s to the Mid-50s], *Musiikki*, iii–iv (1985), 171–260, esp. 205–07
KIMMO KORHONEN

Lejet, Edith (*b* Paris, 19 July 1941). French composer. She studied at the Paris Conservatoire, where she was a pupil of André Jolivet, and in 1968 won the Prix de Rome, after which she spent two years at the Casa de Velasquez. Her other awards include the Prix de la Vocation, the Prix Florence Gould (from the Académie des Beaux-Arts), the Prix Hervé Dugardin and the Grand Prix de la Musique de Chambre (from SACEM). Lejet's works are precisely structured and reflect her interest in extended instrumental

techniques, yet they also display her attachment to the French 'colourist' tradition. In
addition to writing music, she has taught
composition at the Paris Conservatoire.

WORKS
selective list

Orch: Monodrame, vn, orch, 1969; Ressac, 1985
Chamber: Musique, tpt, brass qnt, 1968; Musique,
trbn, pf, 1972; Musique pour René Char, fl, hn,
perc, harp, vn, va, vc, 1974; Sax Qt, 1974; 4 pièces
en duo, db, pf, 1975; Hauteurs-Lointains, 2 13-pièce
str ens, 1975; Méandres, b saxhorn, pf, 1976;
Espaces nocturnes, 2 fl, cl, b cl, perc, harp, db,
1976; Harmonie du soir, 12 str, 1977; 2 antiennes,
brass qnt, 1978; Fl Conc., ob, eng hn, cl, b cl, bn,
dbn, hn, tpt, trbn, harp, perc, 1980; Petits poèmes,
fl, va, harp, 1981; Aube marine, sax qt, 1982;
Améthyste, 12 str, 1990
Solo inst: 3 figures du zodiaque, gui, 1978–91;
Triptyque, org, 1979; Volubilis, vc, 1981; Couleurs
et contrastes, gui, 1983; La voix des voiles, gui,
1989; 3 eaux-fortes, pf, 1992
Vocal: Journal d'Anne Frank, girls' vv, fl, harp, hpd,
el gui, va, db, perc, 1970; L'homme qui avait perdu
sa voix, 5 vv, fl, cl, hn, tpt, perc, pf, va, db, 1984;
Les mille-pattes, musical tale, children's vv, variable inst ens, 1989; Les rois mages, oratorio, 6 solo
vv, mixed chorus, fl, cl, b sax, tpt, perc, gui, str
qnt, 1989; 7 chants sacres, chorus, org, 1990

MARIE NOËLLE MASSON

Leleu, Jeanne (*b* St Mihiel, 29 Dec 1898;
d Paris, 11 March 1979). French pianist and
composer. Her father was a bandmaster and
her mother a piano teacher. At the age of
nine she began studying at the Paris Conservatoire, where her teachers included
Marguerite Long, Alfred Cortot and
Charles-Marie Widor. In 1923, for her cantata *Béatrix*, she won the Prix de Rome; she
was later awarded two other prizes (Georges
Bizet and Monbinne) and was also honoured
by the Institut de France. She became a
professor of sight-reading at the Paris
Conservatoire in 1947, and was later
professor of harmony there. Stylistically
Leleu's compositions belong to no particular
school. Her clear, rhythmically alive and harmonically adventurous *Suite symphonique*
caused something of a sensation when it was
first heard in Rome. In 1937 she played her
own Piano Concerto with success at the
Concerts Lamoureux in Paris. *Transparences*
(1931), with its imaginative orchestral textures, was described by Florent Schmitt as 'a
marvel of freshness, finesse and feminine
grace', showing a high degree of invention,
sensibility, richness and technical assurance.
The ballets *Un jour d'été* and *Nautéos* have
been praised for their grace, wit and imagination; both have enjoyed considerable
success.

WORKS
selective list; printed works published in Paris

Stage: Le cyclope (incid. music, Euripides), 1928; Un
jour d'été (ballet), Paris, Opéra-Comique, 1940;
Nautéos (ballet), Monte Carlo, 1947
Orch: Esquisses italiennes, 1926 (1926); Suite sym-
phonique, wind, 1926 (1926); 2 danses, 1927;
Transparences, 1931 (1931); Pf Conc., 1935;
Femmes, suite, 1947; Virevoltes, suite, 1950
Other works: Pf Qt, 1922 (1926); pf pieces, songs

Principal publishers: Heugel, Leduc

DAVID COX

Lemon, Laura G(ertrude) (*b* Guelph,
Ont., 15 Oct 1866; *d* Redhill, Surrey, 18 Aug
1924). Canadian composer, resident in
England. She was born into a United Empire
Loyalist family. After growing up in Guelph
and Winnipeg, she decided in 1890 to study
at the RAM, London, and thereafter made
England her home. She attained recognition
as a song composer, especially for *My Ain
Folk: a Ballad of Home* (London, 1904), and
also the *Slumber Song* (London, 1895)
that Emma Albani performed for Queen
Victoria. Lemon often wrote the texts of her
songs, using the pseudonyms Austin
Fleming and Ian Macdonald. Boosey & Co.,
London, published several of her songs, and
the *Three Moravian Dances* for violin and
piano were published by Weekes & Co.
(London, 1910). Her works are held at the
National Library of Canada.

BIBLIOGRAPHY
EMC 2 (H. Kallmann)

GAYNOR G. JONES

León, Tania Justina (*b* Havana, Cuba, 14
May 1943). Cuban-American composer of
mixed descent (French, Spanish, African,
Chinese). She studied the piano from the age
of four, later graduated in music (BA 1963)
and in music education (MA 1964) from the
Peyrellade's Conservatorio de Música in
Havana, and began her career as a pianist.
After moving to the USA in 1967, she studied composition with Ursula Mamlok at
New York University (BS 1971, MS 1975)
and also began a long and productive association as pianist, conductor and composer
with Dance Theatre of Harlem. She has fulfilled numerous conducting engagements in
the USA, Europe and South Africa, and in
1992 became associate conductor of the
Brooklyn PO, whose Community Concert
Series she founded in 1977. In 1985 she was
appointed to teach and conduct at Brooklyn
College, and became adviser for new music
to the New York PO in 1993; she also served
as Artistic Director for Composers' Forum,

New York, from 1988 to 1991. During the late 1970s and early 80s, León's compositional style was influenced by such American idioms as gospel and jazz; beginning in the 1980s African and Cuban elements were incorporated alongside contemporary techniques. Her works are characterized by dense textures and colourful orchestration, with particular use of the intervals of the 2nd, minor 7th, and 9th. She has received commissions from the Cincinnati SO, the Women's Philharmonic, the American Composers Orchestra, the Da Capo Chamber Players and New Music Theatre (*Scourge of Hyacinths*, an opera for the 1994 Munich Biennale).

WORKS
selective list

Stage: The Beloved (ballet), fl, ob, cl, bn, pf, vc, db, 1972; Tones (ballet), pf, chamber ens, 1972, collab. A. Mitchell; Dougla (ballet), 2 fl, perc, 1974, collab. G. Holder; La ramera de la Cuena (musical, M. Pena), 1974; Maggie Magalita (R. Wilson), fl, cl, vc, 2 perc, pf, gui, 1980; Belé (ballet), pf, wind, str, perc, 1981; The Golden Windows (Wilson), fl + pic + a fl, ob + eng hn, tpt, perc, 1982; Scourge of Hyacinths (opera, 12 scenes, León, after W. Soyinka), Munich, 1 May 1994

Orch: Latin Lights, 1979; Conc. criollo, pf, 8 timp, orch, 1980; Pet's Suite, orch, 1980, also version for fl, pf; Batá, 1985; Kabiosile, pf, orch, 1988; Carabalí, 1991; Indigena, 1991

Chamber: Haiku, fl, bn, 5 perc, 1973; Pet's Suite, fl, pf, 1980; Ascend, 4 hn, 4 tpt, 3 trbn, tuba, 3 perc, 1983; Permutation 7, chamber ens, 1985; A la par, pf, perc, 1986; Parajota Delaté (From T to J), fl, cl, vn, vc, pf, 1988, rev. fl, ob, cl, bn, pf, 1990; Latin File, fl, cl, tpt, gui, pf, 1989; Arenas d'un tiempo, cl, vc, pf, 1992; Son sonora, fl, gui, 1992

Solo inst: Ensayos sobre una Toccata, pf, 1966; Preludes nos.1–2, pf, 1966; Sonata, vc, 1981; 4 Pieces, vc, 1983; Momentum, pf, 1984; Paisanos semos! (We's Hillbillies!), gui, 1984; Rituál, pf, 1987

Vocal: Namiac Poems, solo v, mixed chorus, orch, 1975; Spiritual Suite, nar, S, S, mixed chorus, ens, 1976; I Got Ovah, S, pf, perc, 1980; De-Orishas (Yoruban texts after B. Neals), S, S, Ct, T, T, B, 2 perc, 1982; Pueblo mulato: 3 Songs (N. Guillén), S, ob, gui, db, perc, pf, 1987; Heart of Ours: a Piece, men's chorus, fl, 4 tpt, 2 perc, 1988; Batéy, S, S, Ct, T, T, B, 2 perc, 1989, collab. M. Camilo; To and Fro, 1v, pf, 1990; Journey, 1v, fl, harp, 1990

Elec: Voices and Piccolo Flute, tape; Carmen and José (incid. music)

Principal publisher: Peer-Southern

BIBLIOGRAPHY

KompA–Z
A. Iadavaia-Cox: 'The Tug between Conducting and Composing', *Essence* (1976), Dec, 72, 120–22
P. J. Rabinowitz: 'Society for New Music: Women Composers', *HiFi/MusAm*, xxx/8 (1980), 28
D. A. Handy: *Black Women in American Bands and Orchestras* (Metuchen, NJ, 1981), 62–3
A. Porter: Review of 'New Music Consort', *New Yorker* (18 Feb 1985), 116
A. Lundy: 'Conversations with Three Symphonic Conductors', *BPiM*, xvi/2 (1988), 213–25, esp. 217–19
H. Mandel: 'Tania León: beyond Borders', *Ear Magazine* [New York] (1988–9), Dec–Jan, 12–13
J. M. Edwards: 'North America since 1920', *Women and Music: a History*, ed. K. Pendle (Bloomington, IN, 1991), 211–57, esp. 247, 250
M. Kinney: 'Composer's Forum: Tania León', *Composers' Forum Network News* [New York], x/1 (1992), 4–5

J. MICHELE EDWARDS

Leonarda, Isabella. *See* ISABELLA LEONARDA.

Leonardo, Luísa (*b* Rio de Janeiro, 22 Oct 1859; *d* Salvador, Bahia, 12 June 1926). Brazilian composer, pianist and actress. She studied the piano with Isidoro Bevilacqua and made her début at the age of eight playing the piano in a concert before Pedro II, Emperor of Brazil, at the Teatro Lírico Provisório. Dom Pedro was both her godfather and patron. Before leaving Brazil for Europe, she gave concerts with the Belgian flautist M. A. Reichert. In France she studied with A. F. Marmontel and Anton Rubinstein at the Paris Conservatoire (1873–9), where she was awarded a first prize in piano. She also studied harmony and composition with Albert Lavignac and performed her *Grande marcha triunfal* with the Pasdeloup Orchestra conducted by Lavignac at the Salle Herz on 9 May 1877. Upon her return to Rio de Janeiro in 1879, she gave a number of highly successful concerts, but left the following year to take up an appointment in Portugal as chamber music pianist at the court of Luís I. After two years she returned to Rio, and in 1885 abandoned her career as a pianist for that of a touring company actress. She nevertheless continued to compose, contributing incidental music to the theatre revues in which she took part. In 1901 she retired from the theatre and moved to Salvador, where she taught the piano and singing.

WORKS
selective list

Orch: Grande marcha triunfal, pf, orch, 1877; Pietosa, 1889; Marcha fúnebre, 1892; Hino a Carlos Gomes, 1903, orchd Sant 'Ana Gomes, 1903

Pf: Prière à la mémoire de Thalberg, 1869; Loin de la patrie, 1872; Dans la calme de la nuit, 1879; Appassionato, 1879; Un rêve du bal, 1879; Souvenir, 1879; Flor da noite, 1897; Teu sorriso, 1903; Poema do espaço (Suite de 6 morceaux caractéristiques), 1904; Plainte belge (Chopiniana), 1917

Vocal (all for 1v, pf): Solitude, 1873; Ma mère, 1873; 2 barcarolles, 1873; Innocence, 1873; Mes vers fuiraient vers vous (V. Hugo), 1877; Ave Maria, 1919

BIBLIOGRAPHY

S. Boccanera jr: *Autores e atores dramáticos* (Salvador [Bahia], 1923), 355–87

Enciclopédia da música brasileira (São Paulo, 1977), i, 411

IRATI ANTONIO

Lévesque, Elisabeth de. *See* HAULTE-TERRE, ELISABETH DE.

Levina, Zara Alexandrovna (*b* Simferopol', 23 Jan/5 Feb 1906; *d* Moscow, 27 June 1976). Russian composer and pianist. She studied the piano with D. Dronseyko-Mironovich at the Odessa Conservatory, graduating in 1923, and from 1925 to 1930 attended the Moscow Conservatory, where her teachers were R. M. Glier and N. Y. Myaskovsky for composition and F. Blumenfeld for piano. Levina participated in Procol, the production collective of conservatory students, and for a period up until 1931, as a devotee of the ideas of the Russian Association of Proletarian Musicians, she composed songs and marches, although these gave her little opportunity to express any real individuality. While studying in Moscow she also taught the piano at the Skryabin Music College, and afterwards she continued to teach at the worker's faculty attached to the conservatory (1930–2). She organized the Children's Music Committee of the Composers' Union of the USSR and was its chairwoman from 1943 to 1947, working with Dmitry Kabalevsky on children's education.

Although Levina wrote some large-scale compositions, she was first and foremost a master of the romance and of children's songs. Her finest love songs together with the reflective monologues on the poems of O. Shiraz, S. Kaputikyan and E. Moshkovskaya were written in the 1950s and 60s. Earlier, in the atmosphere of the 1930s, heroic and passionate monologues had been her natural choice, and a spirit of patriotism was present in her tragic monologues of the war years and in the severe and mournful romances on African poetry that she wrote during the 1960s. Light music extended the range of her output in the late 1940s, and children's music was always a central concern. Her melodies are simple, but their individuality is achieved through fine detail, delicate harmony, supple modulation and varied texture.

WORKS
selective list

Orch: 3 Sym.Waltzes, 1945; 2 pf concs., 1945, 1975
Choral: Burevestnik [Stormy Petrel] (after M.

Gorky), Bar, mixed chorus, pf, 1927 [extract from Put' Oktyabrya [October's Path], collab. Procol members]; Oda soldatu [Ode to a Soldier] (oratorio-triptych, A. Tvardovsky, L. Nekrasova), solo vv, mixed chorus, org, pf, orch, 1964; Choral songs, 1/2 vv, pf

Inst: Pf Sonata no.1, 1925; Vn Sonata no.1, 1925; Poem, va, pf, 1928; Poem, vc, pf, 1931; Vn Sonata no.2, 1952; Pf Sonata no.2, 1953; Yunosheskiy al'bom [Youth's Album], pf, 1972

Vocal: Vosstavshaya Vengriya [Hungary in Revolt], 4 monologues (A. Gidash), 1932; 4 romances (A. S. Pushkin), 1936; 5 romances (M. Yu. Lermontov), 1940; 5 romances (O. Shiraz), 1952; Songs and romances (O. Driz), 1959; Romances and monologues (African poets), 1960; Akvareli [Aquarelles], 10 miniatures (E. Moshkovskaya), 1964; 10 romances (S. Yesenin), 1975; other popular songs; arrs. of Russ., Belarus', American, Bulg., It., Nor. folksongs

Children's songs: Tsikl detskikh skazok [Children's Fairy-Tales] (K. Chukovsky and N. Konchalovskaya), 1944; Krugliÿ god [All Year Round] (S. Marshak), 1947; Masha (S. Kaputikyan), 1952; other songs (A. Barto, Marshak); songs for schools; songs and marches for young pioneers

BIBLIOGRAPHY

M. Nest'yeva: 'Poslushayte etu musïku!' [Listen to this Music], *SovM* (1962), no.12, pp.21–3

N. Mikhaylovskaya: *Zara Levina* (Moscow, 1969)

A. Pakhmutova: 'Absolyutnoe sluzheniye musïke' [An Absolute Devotion to Music], *SovM* (1986), no.5, pp.84–6

Z. Levina: 'Iz vospominaniy raznïkh let' [Memories of Different Years], *SovM* (1986), no.5, pp.87–90

OLGA MANULKINA

Liadova, Ludmila Alekseevna. *See* LYADOVA, LYUDMILA ALEXEYEVNA.

Licoshin, Ekaterina. *See* LIKOSHIN, EKATERINA.

Liddell, (Elizabeth) Claire (*b* Glasgow, 24 May, year undisclosed). Scottish composer and pianist. She studied at the Royal Scottish Academy of Music in Glasgow and, after winning a scholarship, at the RCM (1957–8), where her interest in composition developed and she began to publish her work. Her pianistic abilities, her knowledge of Robert Burns's poetry and a love of Scottish folksong come together in her many arrangements of Scottish songs. In *The Kindling Fire* (1974) Burns's chosen melodies are supported by skilful and sensitive accompaniments which reveal a Ravel-like fondness for parallel chord movement, with occasional jazzy inflections. Among her many original songs are several song cycles, including *Five Orkney Scenes* (1975) and *Orphead: a Spell for Rain* (1978), to texts by George Mackay Brown; *The Rhythm of Life* (1985) for female voice and piano, to words by Alice Meynell; and *Three Ballads* (1989), settings of J. C. Mathieson's translations of French poems. She has also written solo piano pieces and choral music. Her writings include *The Book of Keyboard Harmony* (London, 1979), *So you Want to Play by Ear?* (London, 1980) and articles in *The Music Teacher*. Her music is published mainly by Oecumuse/Barry Brunton and Roberton.

MARIE FITZPATRICK

Liebmann [née Riese], **Helene** (*b* Berlin, 1796; *d* after 1835). German composer and pianist. She was a child prodigy, performing to critical acclaim as a pianist before she was 13 and publishing compositions while still in her teens. Little is known of her personal life other than that she was from a well-to-do Berlin family, studied with Franz Lauska (one of Giacomo Meyerbeer's teachers), and was also a pupil of Ferdinand Ries. In the earliest reviews of her works, critics predicted a glowing career for her as a composer. Later reviews were cooler and her compositions were deemed to be merely pleasing. A few years after her marriage in about 1814, she settled in another city, possibly London, and evidently ceased all public musical activities. Her works reflect the influence of Mozart in style and form. The final movement of her Cello Sonata op.11 is based on the duet 'Là ci darem la mano' from *Don Giovanni*.

WORKS

★ MS lost

Chamber: ★2 Vn Sonatas, op.9 (Berlin, n.d.); Vc Sonata, op.11 (Leipzig and Berlin, n.d.), ed. N. Pyron (Fullerton, CA, 1982); ★Pf Trio, op.12 (Leipzig, n.d.); Pf Trio, op.13 (Leipzig, n.d.) [? reviewed in *AMZ*, xix (1817) as 'op.11']; ★Pf Qt (Leipzig, n.d.)

Kbd: 4 Pf Sonatas, opp.1–3 (Berlin, n.d.), op.15 (Leipzig, n.d.); ★Fantasie, op.16, pf (Leipzig, n.d.); ★6 Ländler, pf (Vienna, n.d.); Cendrillon Variations (Vienna, n.d.); other fantasies and variations, ? lost

Songs (1v, pf): Kennst du das Land (J. W. von Goethe), op.4 (Berlin, n.d.), ed. in Jackson; ★6 Lieder (Berlin, n.d.): Ach, aus diesen Thalen Gründen; Im Hain, am Bach; Ihr Weisen ohne Leidenschaft; Oede war des ersten Menschen Leben; Le matin dans une bruyère; Adieux bergère

BIBLIOGRAPHY

CohenE; FétisB

Reviews in *AMZ*, xiii (1811), 573–5 [opp.1, 2, 4]; xiv (1812), 614 [op.3]; xvi (1814), 292 [op.9]; xix (1817), 50–51 [op.12, ?13]

B. G. Jackson, ed.: 'Hélène Liebmann, née Riese', *Lieder by Women Composers of the Classic Era* (Fayetteville, AR, 1987), 1–2

NANCY B. REICH

Liebmann [née Lehmann], **Nanna Magdalene** (*b* Copenhagen, 27 Sept 1849; *d* Copenhagen, 11 May 1935). Danish composer. Her father was a doctor and an ardent amateur musician. Of the family's eight children Nanna was the only one who had a musical education, studying singing, the piano and music theory at the newly opened Kongelige Danske Musikkonservatorium (1869). Her teachers included the composers J. C. Gebauer, J. P. E. Hartmann and Niels Gade. She also studied in Paris, in 1880 and 1901. In 1874 she married the composer Axel Liebmann; he died two years later and Nanna Magdalene had to support herself and their child. Her compositions were written during the period 1869–1914, but she continued to work as a music teacher until 1929. Liebmann's musical style is firmly rooted in the Classical and Romantic traditions, but also contains elements of modality. Through a combination of majestic grace and powerful emotion, the expressive qualities in her works have been compared to those of Brahms. She joined the Danish composers' union, Dansk Komponistforening, at its founding in 1913, and had earlier helped develop a music teachers' union, Dansk Musikpaedagogisk Forening.

WORKS

printed works published in Copenhagen

Pf: Thème passionné et variations (1911); 7 pieces, 1910–12, unpubd

Songs: 7 sange (J. W. von Goethe, H. Heine, N. Lenau) (1885); Minnelieder (1903); 5 sange (T. Lange, L. Holstein) (1904); *c*16 other songs, 1869–1912, unpubd

BIBLIOGRAPHY

E. Dahlerup: *Nanna Liebmann – kvindelig komponist* (PAULA, 1987) [record notes]

INGE BRULAND

Likoshin [Licoshin, Likoshchina], **Ekaterina** (*fl c*1800–10, St Petersburg). Composer and pianist of Russian origin. She may have been employed in the service of Count Uvarov. She composed numerous short sets of keyboard pieces, at least two of which (a set of *Six polonaises et dix écossaises* and the unusually titled *Fragmens* [*sic*] *de mon passé temps contenant differentes* [*sic*] *danses*) were issued by the St Petersburg publisher F. A. Dittmar between 1800 and 1808 and later included in the 1810 catalogue of his successor, J. Paez. The polonaises of the former work, dedicated to Madame Dorothée Uvarov, are based on themes from Russian folksongs – a popular practice favoured by Likoshin's more prolific St Petersburg-based contemporary, Józef Kozłowski.

BIBLIOGRAPHY

N. J. Yandell: *Keyboard Music in Russia During the Late Eighteenth and Early Nineteenth Centuries* (diss., U. of Oxford, in progress)

NIGEL J. YANDELL

Lili'uokalani, Queen of Hawaii [Kamaka-'eha, Lili'u Loloku Walania; Kamaka'eha Paki, Lydia; Dominis, Lydia K.; Dominis, Lili'u K.] (*b* Honolulu, 2 Sept 1838; *d* Honolulu, 11 Nov 1917). Hawaiian composer. She played the piano, organ and various plucked string instruments, and was a choir director at Kawaiaha'o Church. When her brother King David Kalākaua designated her his heir apparent in 1877 he gave her the name Lili'uokalani. She reigned from 1891 to 1893, but was deposed by a group of American businessmen during an economic depression.

Lili'uokalani apparently began her musical training at the Chiefs' Children's School (1842–8). She was a skilled sight-reader and the first person of Hawaiian ancestry to become proficient in Western musical notation. Her published output began with the hymn-like *He mele lāhui Hawai'i* (1866), used until 1876 as the Hawaiian national anthem. Her *Nani nā pua* ('The Flower of Ko'olau') may be the first Hawaiian song to have been published on the American mainland (1869). She continued publishing in the USA, where her songs became popular (in 1898 she claimed to have written hundreds of songs, about a quarter of them printed). She was familiar with both Hawaiian and western European music and made an effort to synthesize the two. Many of her songs are of the *hīmeni*-type (secular texts with both melodic style and alternating verse-chorus form indebted to Anglo-American hymnody), and are sophisticated in harmony and appealing in melody. Her well-known and poignant song ('Farewell to thee') *Aloha 'oe* exemplifies these characteristics. Though it is a love song describing the parting of two lovers, it came to represent farewells in general and was used at Lili'uokalani's funeral. *Mōhailani* ('Offering to Heaven'), a three-act comic opera on a subject drawn from Hawaiian history (composed under the pseudonym Mme Aorena), was left incomplete. Lili'uokalani's diaries, letters, manuscript and printed music, and other documents are held in Honolulu, principally at the Hawaii State Archives, the 'Iolani Palace, the Bishop Museum and the Kamehameha Schools.

WORKS
selective list

Stage: Mōhailani (comic opera, 3), inc.

Songs: Nani nā pua (Ko'olau) [The Flower of Ko'olau], before 1862 (Boston, 1869); He mele lāhui Hawai'i (Hawaiian National Anthem), 1866 (Honolulu, 1867); 'Imi au iā 'oe e ke aloha [I have sought thee my beloved], 1866; Ahe lau makani [There is a breath], 1867, as Waltz Song no.3 (San Francisco, 1890s) [by 'The Three Graces of Hamohamo'], collab. Princess Likelike and ? L. Kapoli; Liko pua lehua [Tender Leaves of the Lehua Flower], 1867 [by 'The Three Graces of Hamohamo'], collab. Princess Likelike and ? L. Kapoli; Puīa ka nahele [The Fragrant Woods], 1868, as Waltz Song no.1 (San Francisco, ? 1892); E kala ku'u upu 'ana [Long years have I yearned for thee], 1873, as Mololani, in Book of Hawaiian Melodies (Honolulu, 1916); Aloha 'oe [Farewell to thee], 1877/8 (San Francisco, 1884); Ka makani līhau pua [Flower-misting Wind], 1877; A Chant (text after Hymn no.1134, Plymouth Collection), 1884 (San Francisco, ? 1892); Ka 'ōiwi nani [Beautiful One], 1886 (San Francisco, 1890s); The Queen's Jubilee, 1887 (San Francisco, ?1892); Ka wiliwiliwai [The Lawn Sprinkler], 1890; He aloha 'o ka haku [Beloved is the Lord] (Lili'uokalani's Prayer; The Queen's Prayer), 1895 (Honolulu and Washington DC, 1895); Ku'u pua i Paoakalani [My Flower at Paoakalani], 1895 (Honolulu, 1895); He inoa no Ka'iulani [A Name Song for Ka'iulani] (Lamalama i luna ka 'ōnohi lā); Maika 'i Waipi'o [Lovely Waipi'o], collab. Princess Likelike; *c*150 other songs, many in He buke mele Hawai'i (The Queen's Songbook) (compiled 1897)

Hawaiian solo chants and dance chants (*mele oli* and *mele hula*) and chant arrs.

BIBLIOGRAPHY

Lili'uokalani: *Hawaii's Story by Hawaii's Queen* (Boston, 1898)

Obituaries: *New York Times* (12 Nov 1917); *Pacific Commercial Advertiser* [Honolulu] (11–19 Nov 1917); *Star-Bulletin* [Honolulu] (12–17, 19 Nov 1917)

E. C. Smith: 'The Queen's Prayer', *Paradise of the Pacific*, lxvi/11 (1954), 10–11, 27

S. Elbert and N. Mahoe: *Nā mele o Hawai'i nei* [Songs of Hawaii] (Honolulu, 1970)

G. S. Kanahele, ed.: 'Aloha 'oe', 'Lili'uokalani', *Hawaiian Music and Musicians: an Illustrated History* (Honolulu, 1979), 11–13, 227–32

'Queen's Personal Songbook Found', *Ha 'ilono mele*, v/8 (1979), 1–3

'More Royal Songs Found: Three are Lili'uokalani's', *Ha 'ilono mele*, vi/2 (1980), 10

H. G. Allen: *The Betrayal of Liliuokalani* (Glendale, CA, 1982)

A. L. Korn and B. B. Peterson: 'Liliuokalani', *Notable Women of Hawaii*, ed. B. B. Peterson (Honolulu, 1984), 240–44

A. K. Stillman: 'Published Hawaiian Songbooks', *Notes*, xliv (1987–8), 221–39

A. K. Stillman: *Hawaiian Music: Published Songbooks (an Index)* (typescript, 1988)

D. Gillett and others, eds.: *The Queen's Songbook, by Her Majesty Queen Lili'uokalani* (Honolulu, forthcoming)

LESLEY A. WRIGHT
(work-list with D. GILLETT)

Lindsay, Maria [Mary] (*b* Wimbledon, 15 May 1827; *d* Betteshanger, Kent, 3 April 1898). English composer. Almost nothing is known of the personal life of 'Miss M. Lindsay', as she chose to be described. She married the Rev. John Worthington Bliss in 1858. In the early 1850s she became the first woman to achieve commercial success as a songwriter; the London publisher Robert Cocks obtained an exclusive contract. Her songs were tailored to the requirements of amateur music-making in the home, and often consist of strophic settings of admired contemporary poets: *Excelsior* of 1854 (H. W. Longfellow) and *Home they brought her warrior dead* of 1858 (Tennyson). She also composed sacred songs which took as their model the recitative and aria of contemporary English oratorio; *Absalom* (1868) was one of her most highly-regarded compositions in this vein.

BIBLIOGRAPHY
J. D. Brown and S. S. Stratton: *British Musical Biography* (Birmingham, 1897)
D. Scott: *The Singing Bourgeois* (Milton Keynes, 1989)
DEREK B. SCOTT

Linnet, Anne (*b* Århus, 30 July 1953). Danish composer and rock musician. She made her début as a rock singer and composer in 1971 with the jazz- and soul-inspired band Tears. In 1974 she formed an all-woman band, Shit og Chanel, which issued four recordings. She studied with Tage Nielsen and Per Nørgård at the conservatory in Århus (1976–85), graduating first in music education and then in composition, and was the first woman to complete the composition course at a Danish conservatory. In 1977 she made a solo recording, *Kvindesind*, in which she set poems by the Danish writer, Tove Ditlevsen. During the 1980s she wrote much theatre music and, with her bands, issued further recordings, including *Anne Linnet Band* (1981) and *Marquis de Sade* (1983). During this period, her score-notated works also received performances. Linnet does not consider that these two kinds of music exist in separate spheres, since both aim for a direct and intense personal expression and make equal use of her technical abilities.

WORKS
selective list

Inst: For symfoniorkester, orch, 1978; Quatuor brutale, str qt, 1978; Tivoli, perc, 1980; Spring Capricious, orch, 1985; Metal Blue Explo, 4 perc; Seul I, II, III, vn
Vocal: Sang til hjertet, 1v, harp, db, 1978; Hosiana, chorus, 1979

BIBLIOGRAPHY
D. Kjeldsen: *Anne Linnet og Marquis de Sade* (diss., U. of Copenhagen, 1992)

J. Levinsen: 'Det' så udansk', *Dansk musiktidsskrift*, lxvii (1992–3), 122–5
INGE BRULAND

Linwood, Mary (*b* Birmingham, 1755/6; *d* Leicester, 2 March 1845). English composer and artist in needlework. She ran an educational establishment for women in Leicester and published several pieces of vocal music. Her oratorio *David's First Victory* was performed in 1840 at the Queen's Concert Rooms, Hanover Square, conducted by Sir George Smart. She wrote at least two operas, *The Kellerin* and *The White Wreath*, which were never published. She is best known for her copies of famous paintings worked in embroidery that were exhibited in London from the late 1780s until her death in 1845; they were admired by Napoleon, the British royal family and Empress Catherine of Russia.

WORKS

The Kellerin (opera); The White Wreath (opera); David's First Victory (oratorio) (London, ?1840)
Songs (all pubd in London): Let us hence!, in *The Harmonicon*, vi/2 (1828), 101–5; Pretty Fairy, in *The Harmonicon*, vi/2 (1828), 45–9; The Sabbath Bridal, in *The Harmonicon*, x/2 (1832), 38–40; I ponder on those happy hours [from The Kellerin] (1853); Leave me to sorrow a while [from The White Wreath] (1853)

BIBLIOGRAPHY
N. Whitcomb: *Mary Linwood* (Leicester, 1951)
SOPHIE FULLER

Liu, Zhuang (*b* Shanghai, 24 Oct 1932). Chinese composer. She studied the piano with her father, and in 1950 entered the Shanghai Conservatory where she studied harmony, counterpoint, orchestration and composition with Ding Shande, Sang Tong and Den Erjin. After graduation in 1957, she took postgraduate courses with Guroff. She taught composition at Shanghai Conservatory (1958–60) and at the Central Conservatory of Music in Beijing, and in 1970 was appointed professional composer to the Central Philharmonic Society in Beijing. She is a member of the Chinese Musicians' Association and the Chinese Film Music Society and from 1989 to 1991 was Asian scholar-in-residence at Syracuse University on a Fulbright Fellowship. Liu's music is technically accomplished and characterized by clarity of structure and poetic expression. Many of her compositions have been performed and recorded both in China and abroad.

WORKS
selective list

Orch: Xiangei qing shao nian [To the Youth], pf conc., 1957; Vn Conc., 1963; Huang He [Yellow River], pf conc., 1971, collab. others; Meihua san nong [Plum Blossom Triptych], sym. picture, 1979; Guangling ballade, zhengs, orch, 1983; Impressions of Tash-gul-Kan, 1987

Chamber: Romance, vc, pf, 1955; Theme and Variations, pf, 1956; Chunjiang huayue yei [Moon Night by the Spring River], ww qnt, 1978; 3 Trios, fl, vc, harp, 1987

Vocal: Xiao niao [Little Bird], 1979; Yue zhi guxian [Hometown under the Moon], 1983; Song without words, 1987

Film scores: Xiaobin Zhang Ga [The Little Soldier Zheng Ga], 1963; Kunlun shanshang yike cao [A Leaf of Grass on the Mountain Kunlun], 1964; Miao miao, 1980; Bian cheng [The Border Town], 1985; Yueja er [A New Moon], 1986

Principal publisher: People's Music Publishing House, Beijing

YANDI YANG

Lockhart, Beatriz (*b* Montevideo, 17 Jan 1944). Uruguayan composer. She started her studies at the age of five with Emilia Conti de Alvarez (piano), and at 15 entered the Conservatorio Nacional de Música, being instructed by Carlos Estrada and Héctor Tosar. During 1969–70 she was an assistant at composition and electronic music courses given by Alberto Ginastera, Gerardo Gandini and Francisco Kroepfl at the Instituto Torcuato Di Tella, Buenos Aires. Her compositions include orchestral, chamber and piano works as well as electronic music; among them are Suite for chamber orchestra, Concerto grosso, *Ecos* for orchestra, *Tema y variaciones* for piano and *Ejercico I* for tape. From 1974 to 1988 she was in Venezuela, teaching in Caracas at the Conservatorio Nacional de Música Juan José Landaeta, the Escuela de Música José Lorenzo Llamozas and other institutions, and won several major composition awards from the Consejo Nacional de Cultura, the Consejo Municipal del Distrito Federal and Universidad Simón Bolívar. Two significant works are *Masia Mujú* (1987) for flute and orchestra, which has been given in Caracas and Montevideo, and *Visión de los vencidos* (1990) for voice and orchestra. She teaches at the University of Montevideo and is married to the composer Antonio Mastrogiovanni.

BIBLIOGRAPHY

S. Salgado: *Breve historia de la musicá culta en el Uruguay* (Montevideo, 1971, 2/1980)

SUSANA SALGADO

Lockwood, Annea [Anna] **(Ferguson)** (*b* Christchurch, New Zealand, 29 July 1939). New Zealand composer and instrument builder. After attending Canterbury University, New Zealand (BMus 1961), she studied the piano with E. Kendall Taylor and composition with Peter Racine Fricker at the RCM, London (diplomas 1963). She also studied composition at the Darmstadt summer courses (1961–2), with Gottfried Michael Koenig at the Staatliche Hochschule für Musik, Cologne, at the Bilthoven electronic music centre (1963–4), and in London at the Electronic Music Studios, Putney (1970). From 1969 to 1972 she studied psychoacoustics at the Southampton University Institute of Sound and Vibration Research. In 1973 Lockwood went to the USA and taught at Hunter College, CUNY; in 1982 she joined the faculty of Vassar College, where she has taught composition, theory and electronic music and served as Chair of the music department. She has given lectures on her works as well as performances in England, Scotland, New Zealand, Australia, France, West Germany and Sweden. Her honours include Arts Council awards (1970, 1972, 1973), Gulbenkian Foundation grants (1972, 1973), a Creative Artists Public Service grant (1977) and an NEA fellowship (1979–80).

Lockwood's early compositions, including the Violin Concerto (1962) and the chamber cantatas *A Abélard, Héloise* (1963) and *Aspekte einer Parabel* (1964), are atonal. Her work as an instrument builder began with *Glass Concert* for two performers and an environment of glass objects (which has come to be known by the same name) that serves as both scenery and instruments; the performers move about in it striking, rubbing, shaking, and even snapping the various pieces. Later Lockwood turned her attention increasingly to environmental installations and applications of taped sound. Her work in about 1970 included a variety of treatments of old, mainly upright, pianos under the collective title *Piano Transplants*. They were prepared, burnt, 'drowned' in a shallow lake, or installed in an outdoor 'piano garden'; the instruments were subjected in these ways to the activity of the four elements, and careful documentation on tape was made regularly of their rapid decay and transformation.

From 1970 Lockwood composed mainly electronic and performance pieces, including *Tiger Balm* (1970), *Malaman* (1974, for the Merce Cunningham Dance Company), *Spirit Catchers* (1974), *Conversations with the Ancestors* (1979) and *Delta Run* (1981; for the New Music America festival, Chicago,

1982). She also began to explore documentary forms, mixed media and environmental sound: in *The River Archive* (1973–) sounds of rivers such as the Ganges and Hudson are recorded, and in *World Rhythms* (1975) widely spaced strokes on a single gong resonate in response to natural sounds played back from ten tape tracks. These works demonstrate the holistic and meditation techniques Lockwood learnt from studying non-Western music and in her activities in avant-garde theatre and performance; they were performed during the 1980s at festivals and galleries and in concerts in the USA, Europe and Australasia. In 1987 Lockwood turned again to instrumental and vocal composition, producing works for various chamber ensembles.

WORKS

Inst: Vn Conc., 1962; Red Mesa, pf, 1989; Thousand Year Dreaming, ob, eng hn, cl, b cl, didjeridus, conchs, perc, projections, 1990

Vocal: Serenade no.1 (Sappho, Anacreon), S, fl, 1962; A Abélard, Héloïse (Heloise), chamber cantata, Mez, 10 insts, 1963; Aspekte einer Parabel (F. Kafka), Bar, 10 insts, 1964; Serenade no.2 (St John Perse), S, orch, tape, 1965; Humming, mixed chorus, 1972; Malaman, 1v/4 solo vv, 1974; Malolo (A. Lockwood), SSA, 1978; Saouah! (Lockwood), chorus, gongs, 1986; Night and Fog (Forché, O. Mandel'shtam), Bar, bar sax, pf, perc, 1987; Amazonia Dreaming, vocalist, snare drum, 1988; The Angle of Repose (R. M. Rilke, F. O. Matthiessen), Bar, a fl, shō [mouth organ], 1991

Elec and mixed media: Glass Concert, 2 performers, amp glass insts, 1966; Shone, mixed media, 1966; Sound Hat, Sound Umbrella, sound sculptures, 1969; Piano Transplants, sound sculptures, 1970; Tiger Balm, tape, 1970; Windhover, tape, 1972; Glide, wine glasses, 1973; Cloud Music, tape, 1973; Deep Dream Dive, db, elec, 1973; The River Archive: Play the Ganges backwards one more Time, Sam, mixed-media installation, 1973–4; Sound Map of the Hudson River, tape installation, 1982; Spirit Catchers, 4 amp vv, 1974; World Rhythms, 10-track tape, gong, 1975; Spirit Songs Unfolding, tape, slides, 1977; Woman Murder, tape, 1977; Conversations with the Ancestors, mixed-media installation, 1979; Delta Run, tape, slides, 1981; Secret Life, db, elec, tape, 1989

Principal publishers: Morrow, G. Schirmer, Source

BIBLIOGRAPHY

CC (B. Morton)

HUGH DAVIES, J. M. THOMSON, ELIZABETH WOOD

Loder, Kate (Fanny) (*b* Bath, 21 Aug 1825; *d* Headley, Surrey, 30 Aug 1904). English pianist and composer, cousin of the composer Edward Loder. Precociously musical, she possessed perfect pitch by the age of three. She studied the piano from the age of six with Miss Batterbury (who assisted her mother, the piano teacher Fanny Philpot) and at 12 transferred to Henry Field. A year later she entered the RAM, studying the piano with her aunt Lucy Anderson (pianist to the Queen) and composition with Charles Lucas, twice gaining the King's Scholarship. She took part in RAM concerts in March 1840, and played at Her Majesty's Theatre on 31 May 1844, when she performed Felix Mendelssohn's G minor concerto in the composer's presence, and at the Philharmonic Society on 15 March 1847, when she played Carl Maria von Weber's Concerto in E flat. Her own chamber music (including the String Quartet in G minor and the Violin Sonata in E major) was performed at the Society of British Musicians and reviewed in *The Musical World*.

In 1844 Loder was appointed a professor of harmony at the RAM. At the same time she became one of London's most sought-after piano teachers. On 16 December 1851 she married Henry Thompson, an eminent surgeon (he was knighted in 1867, created a baronet in 1899 and died on 18 April 1904). About 1871 Loder became gradually paralysed, but she remained a strong influence on English musicians. At her house on 7 July 1871 Brahms's *German Requiem* was first performed in England; she and Cipriani Potter played the accompaniments as a piano duet.

During her lifetime Loder achieved considerable success as a composer, especially of piano music. As a child she studied the works of Henri Herz, Sigismond Thalberg and J. L. Dussek (as well as Mozart and Beethoven) and their influence predominates in her piano writing. The 12 Studies of 1852 contain music of substance which systematically explores piano technique, but seldom ventures beyond the horizons of Carl Czerny: only in nos.11 and 12 can traces of Chopin's influence be discerned. Her early songs are formally experimental; one of the finest, *My faint spirit* (1854), compares favourably with Arthur Sullivan's setting of the same words: the first two verses are through-composed and at the start of the third and final stanza there is a telescoped reprise. However, individual touches became increasingly rare: a similar framework fails to lift the perfunctory vocabulary of *The Blind Boy* (1873), and the late organ voluntaries depend too heavily on Felix Mendelssohn and Louis Spohr.

WORKS
all printed works published in London

Stage: L'elisir d'amore (opera)

Orch and chamber: Ov., orch, 1844; Str Qt, g, 1846; Vn Sonata, E, 1847; Str Qt, e, 1848; Pf Trio

Pf: 12 Studies (1852); 3 Romances (1853); Pensée fugitive (1854); 3 Duettinos (1861); En avant galop (1863); 3 Duets (1869); Little Duets for the Pianoforte (1876); Mazurka (1899); Scherzo (1899); 2 sonatas

Org: 6 Easy Voluntaries, 2 bks [6 in each] (1889, 1891)

Songs: My faint spirit (P. B. Shelley) (1854); Sacred Sorrow (E. G. Winthrop) (1854); The Victim (1854); The Blind Boy (T. King) (1873); Where the stout nor-wester blows (M. A. Browne) (1880); Winter is past

Arrs.: Albinoni: Io morirei contento (?1880); composer unknown: Sta in tono mio core (?1880)

BIBLIOGRAPHY

CohenE; Grove5 (W. H. Husk); MEMM; PazdirekH; WCBH

Musical World, xix (1844), 145; xxi (1846), 553; xxii (1847), 658

W. W. Cazalet: The History of the Royal Academy of Music (London, 1854), 303–6

J. D. Champlin: Cyclopedia of Music and Musicians (New York, 1888–90)

J. D. Brown and S. S. Stratton: British Musical Biography (Birmingham, 1897)

M. B. Foster: The History of the Philharmonic Society of London (London, 1912)

S. Stern: Women Composers: a Handbook (Metuchen, NJ, 1978)

NIGEL BURTON, NICHOLAS TEMPERLEY

Lomax, Louisa Emily [Emma] (*b* Brighton, 22 June 1873; *d* Brighton, 29 Aug 1963). English composer and pianist. She studied at the Brighton School of Music and the RAM (Goring Thomas Scholar, 1907–10; Lucas Silver Medal, 1910; ARAM 1910), where she was later a professor of composition (1918–38). The innovative stage works for which she devised music, librettos and special effects led Frederick Corder to commend Lomax as a remarkable student, but her opera *The Marsh of Vervais* was never fully performed, and a toy theatre provided the main focus for her dramatic gift in later life. Among her other stage works are *The House of Shadows* (1905), *The Wolf* (1906) and *The Brownie and the Piano-Tuner* (1907), all set to her own texts. She wrote two cantatas for female voices, *The Stormbird* and *The Whirlpool*; her orchestral works include *Ida's Flowers* (1903), *Variations on a Quaint Theme* (1910) and the *Toy Overture, 1915*, a parody of Tchaikovsky's *1812*. She also composed solo and partsongs, recitations to music and piano pieces. She provided the libretto for Walton O'Donnell's comic opera *The Demon's Bride* (1909). Her works were published by Charles Avison.

BIBLIOGRAPHY

F. Corder: A History of the RAM from 1822 to 1922 (London, 1922)

RHIAN DAVIES

Kate Loder: lithograph (1851) by C. Baugniet

Lombardini Sirmen [Syrmen, Sijrmen, Seriman, Ceriman], **Maddalena Laura** (*b* Venice, 9 Dec 1745; *d* Venice, 18 May 1818). Italian composer, violinist and singer. She was the second child of Piero Lombardini and his second wife Gasparina Gambirasi. At the age of seven, she was musically advanced enough to attract the attention of the governors of the Mendicanti at an open audition to select young girls as apprentices to the *coro* (music school) of the *ospedale*. She was one of four chosen from 30 candidates to study one or two orchestral instruments, singing and solfeggio.

A letter to 'Signora Maddalena', dated 5 March 1760, from Giuseppe Tartini, shows that by the age of 14 she had been promoted to the rank of violin teacher. The governors sponsored her journeys to Padua for study with Tartini and others in 1760, 1761 and 1764. After two unsuccessful attempts to leave the Mendicanti, Lombardini was allowed to marry on 17 September 1767. Thereafter she was known as 'Laura Lombardini Sirmen di Ravenna'. She was independently wealthy, possessing about 3000 ducats, partly made up of a traditional dowry from the Mendicanti. Early in 1768 her husband, the violinist Lodovico Maria Gaspar Sirmen (1738–1812), was granted permission by the governors of the charitable consortium in Bergamo, Misericordia, to take his wife on a two-year tour. When they played in Turin, Quirino Gasparini, *maestro di cappella* of the cathedral, reported to Padre Martini: 'Maddalena Lombardini . . . won the hearts of all of Turin's music lovers with her playing. Last Saturday, I wrote to old Tartini in Padua about it. It will please him, I know, to hear how obvious it was to everyone here that this artist is one of his protégées'. In 1768 the couple appeared at the Concert Spirituel in Paris. The *Mercure de France* reported that her violin was 'the lyre of Orpheus in the hands of grace'. By March 1769 they had appeared five more times at the Concert Spirituel. The couple may have returned to Lodovico's native Ravenna, where their only child, Alessandra, was born in 1769. A second tour in 1770 took the Sirmens to London. Maddalena made her début as a soloist at the King's Theatre on 10 January 1771. She performed her own concertos in various London concert series 22 times during the first five months of 1771 alone, and later played concertos between the acts at the King's Theatre or at Covent Garden, and for concerts in series produced by J. C. Bach and C. F. Abel. She gave more

Maddalena Laura Lombardini Sirmen: engraving by Costa after 'F.C.'

than 200 performances in London up to 1773, including the singing of operatic roles at the King's Theatre and in Marylebone pleasure gardens.

By 1772 Lodovico had returned to Ravenna, while Maddalena remained in London, encountering some criticism despite the patronage of the royal family. Charles Burney spoke of 'her polished and expressive manner of playing' and found her style comparable to that of Pietro Nardini, also a pupil of Tartini. She appeared in 1774 in Turin and as a singer at the Opéra in Paris, and in 1776 in Parma. She was engaged in Naples in 1777 and later in Dresden. In spring 1783 she was appointed first woman singer at the Imperial Theatre in St Petersburg, with an annual salary of 8000 scudi; Lodovico joined her as leader of the orchestra but returned to Ravenna in 1784. She stayed on and performed in Moscow and St Petersburg before her final concerts, in Paris, in May 1785. In 1789 she was recalled to Venice from her post in Naples.

Lombardini Sirmen was highly regarded as a composer by her contemporaries. Leopold Mozart praised her Concerto no.1 in B♭ for violin in a letter to his wife and son (April 1778). (Leopold and his daughter Nannerl had taken part in a performance with the Mozarts' patron Count Johann Rudolf Czerny as soloist.) The Neapolitan composer Tommaso Giordani transcribed her concertos as both keyboard concertos and solo sonatas, the latter being printed in

London in three different editions during the 1770s and 1780s.

Sources for 35 instrumental compositions by Lombardini Sirmen have been located; this number exceeds the combined output of all other composers in the *cori*. Some of her works were issued in as many as seven editions. Music publishers' catalogues show that her music was available in Amsterdam, Berlin, Brussels, The Hague, Leipzig, London, Moscow, Paris, St Petersburg, Salzburg, Vienna and Turin, and in centres in Italy, Finland and Sweden.

The violin concertos represent the core of her known output and demonstrate all her stylistic characteristics: the ability to control large tonal plateaus, well-delineated cadenzas, frequent affective and purposeful chromaticism, use of multiple themes grouped by spatial design, exploitation of dynamics and tessitura, and instrumental articulation. Her harmonic vocabulary includes progressions from secondary dominants to 7th chords, augmented 6th and Neapolitan chords, and chordal transformations. In three-part solo textures, the principal violin is accompanied by the first and second violins in an obbligato setting (a technique learnt from Tartini). Her Paduan heritage is revealed in the consistency of three-movement, fast–slow–fast, sonata structure; homophonic rather than contrapuntal textures; long melodic lines, including three-octave leaps; technically demanding ornamentation; and expressivity.

WORKS

MSS in B-Lc; CS-BM; D-Bsb, WRz; I-AN, Bc, Gl, Mc, Nc, OS, Ria, TRa, Vc, Vnm; S-L, Skma

6 trios, 2 vn, vc obbl (Amsterdam, 1770); as op.1 (London, 1771)

6 quartetti (Paris, 1771); collab. L. Sirmen

6 concertos, vn, orch (Amsterdam, 1772–3), as op.3 (London, 1772–3); nos.1, 3, 5 ed. in RRMCE, xxxviii (1991); transcr. T. Giordani for kbd (London, 1773)

6 sonatas, 2 vn, op.4 (Amsterdam and London, 1773)

Sonata, A, vn, vc obbl (Vienna, 1776)

Str qt, F, frag. *GB-Cpl*

Trio, B♭, 2 vn, vc obbl, private collection

BIBLIOGRAPHY

Choron-FayolleD; *FétisB*; *GerberL*; *Grove1* (F. A. Marshall); *SainsburyD*; *SchillingE*; *SchmidlD*

M.-T. Bouquet: *Il Teatro di corte dalle origini al 1788*, Storia del Teatro regio di Torino, i (Turin, 1976), 334–5, 341

J. L. Berdes: *The Violin Concertos, Opp.2 and 3, by Maddalena Laura Lombardini Sirmen* (thesis, U. of Maryland, 1979)

L. Malusi: *L'arco degli strumenti musicali: storico tecnica costruttori valutazioni* (Padua, 1981)

C. White: 'First-Movement Form in the Violin Concerto from Vivaldi to Viotti', *Music East and West: Essays in Honor of Walter Kaufmann* (New York, 1981), 188–9

P. Fabbri: *Tre secoli di musica a Ravenna dalla controriforma alla caduta dell'antico regime* (Ravenna, 1983), 92–9

J. L. Berdes: Preface to M. L. Lombardini Sirmen: *Three Violin Concertos*, RRMCE, xxxviii (1991)

J. L. Baldauf-Berdes: *Women Musicians of Venice: Musical Foundations, 1525–1855* (Oxford, 1993)

JANE L. BERDES

Lomon, Ruth (Margaret) (*b* Montreal, 7 Nov 1930). American composer, pianist and teacher. She studied the piano, organ, theory and composition at the Quebec conservatory (performance diploma 1947), McGill University, Montreal (licentiate 1950), and the New England Conservatory (1951–4). She undertook further study with Frances Judd Cooke and Witold Lutosławski, and at the Darmstadt summer course (1963). From 1971 to 1983 she performed as part of the piano duo Lomon and Wenglin. She held Yaddo, MacDowell/Norlin and Helena Wurlitzer Foundation fellowships, and received a 'New Works' commission from the Massachusetts Council on the Arts and Humanities. Loman's inspiration comes not from conventional pitch organization but from techniques such as the pacing of speech patterns and from dramatic events, especially Native American ceremonials experienced in New Mexico.

WORKS

selective list

Stage: The Fisherman and his Soul (chamber opera, 1, O. Wilde), 1963; Many Moons (J. Thurber), fl, ob, tpt, perc, pf, vn, va, vc, synth, nar, mimes, 1990

Orch: Bn Conc., 1979; Spells, pf, chamber orch, 1985; Terra incognita, 1993

Chamber: Dialogue, vib, harps, 1964; Equinox, 2 tpt, 2 trbn, 1978; Vitruvian Scroll, str qt, 1981; Janus, str qt, 1984; Desiderata, ob, mar, opt. bow chime, 1984; Imprints, conc., pf, 4 perc, 1987; The Talisman, cl, cl/b cl, vn, va, vc, live elec, 1988; Butterfly Effect, str qt, 1989

Kbd: Toccata, pf, 1961; Soundings, pf, 4 hands, 1975; 5 Ceremonial Masks, pf, 1980; 7 Portals of Vision, org, 1982

Vocal: 5 Songs after Poems by William Blake, C, va, 1961; Dartington Quintet, S, fl, cl, vn, pf, 1964; Phase II (W. Whitman), S, vc, pf, 1972; Requiem (incl. verses by Lomon), S, SATB, fl, 2 cl, bn, 2 tpt, 2 trbn, 1977; Symbiosis (New Testament, Lomon), Mez, perc, pf, 1983; A Fantasy Journey into the Mind of a Machine, S, sax, 1985

Principal publisher: Arsis Press

BIBLIOGRAPHY

WAM

J. Zaimont and K. Famera: *Contemporary Concert Music by Women* (Westport, CT, 1981)

'Profile: Ruth Lomon: a Question of Individuality',

American Women Composers News/Forum (1985), Jan, 11

E. Cox-Cabrera: *Ethnic Influences in Contemporary Harp Music: Eastern and Amerindian Attributes in Selected Compositions by American Composers* (diss., California State U., Long Beach, 1989)

CATHERINE PARSONS SMITH

Lorraine, Duchess of (*fl* early 13th century). Trouvère. Two poems (R1640 and R1995) are attributed to the Duchess of Lorraine in one manuscript (*CH-BEsu* MS 389). One of these, *Un petit devant le jour*, is found in multiple sources, some with music. The duchess in question was probably Gertrude, heir to the counties of Metz and Dabo, wife of Thiebaut I, Duke of Lorraine.

BIBLIOGRAPHY

H. Spanke: G. *Raynauds Bibliographie des altfranzösischen Liedes* (Leiden, 1955) [R]

M. V. Coldwell: 'Jougleresses and Trobairitz: Secular Musicians in Medieval France', *Women Making Music: the Western Art Tradition, 1150–1950*, ed. J. Bowers and J. Tick (Urbana and Chicago, 1986), 39–61, esp. 50

MARIA V. COLDWELL

Loudová, Ivana (*b* Chlumec nad Cidlinou, 8 March 1941). Czech composer. She studied composition at the Prague Conservatory with Miloslav Kabeláč (1958–61) and at the Prague Academy of Musical Arts with Emil Hlobil (1961–6). From 1968 to 1972 she acted as an assistant in Kabeláč's composition class, and with the aid of a scholarship she undertook graduate work at the Centre Bourdan in Paris, where she studied with Olivier Messiaen and André Jolivet and worked with the Groupe de Recherches Musicales. She has an extensive command of contemporary compositional and instrumental techniques (especially in creating new sounds for wind and percussion) and writes in a wide variety of genres including large-scale works, experimental compositions, pieces for children and film and stage music. Many of her large-scale vocal works employ either Italian Renaissance or modern Czech poetry. Throughout her career Loudová has won awards, including a prize for *Rhapsody in Black* at the GEDOK competition in Mannheim (1967) and three prizes in the Guido d'Arezzo competition, for *Sonetto per voci bianche* (1978), *Italian Triptych* (1980) and *Occhi lucenti e belli* (1984). She has gained prizes for her choral compositions from the Jihlava and Jirkov competition and radio competitions in Moscow (1978) and Olomouc (1983).

WORKS
selective list

Dramatic: Rhapsody in Black (ballet), 1966

Orch, wind orch: Conc., chamber orch, 1961; Fantasie, 1961; 2 syms.: no.1, 1964, no.2, A, chorus, orch, 1965; Spleen, 1971; Hymnos, wind insts, perc, 1972; Chorale, 1973; Conc., org, perc, wind orch, 1974; Nocturne, va, str orch, 1975; Partita, D, fl, hpd, str orch, 1975; Magic Conc., xyl, mar, vib, wind orch, 1976; Luminous Voice, eng hn, wind orch, perc, 1986; Double Conc., vn, perc, str orch, 1989

Chamber and solo inst: Vn Sonata, 1961; Sonata, cl, pf, 1963; Str Qt, 1964; Per tromba, tpt, 1969; Solo for King David, harp, 1972; Air à Due Boemi, b cl, pf, 1972; Agamemnón, suite, perc, 1973; Romeo and Juliet, fl, vn, va, vc, harp/lute, 1974; Aulos, b cl, 1976; Str Qt, 1976; Mattinata, cl, trbn, vc, pf, 1978; Con umore, F, bn, 1978; Musica festiva, 3 tpt, 3 trbn, 1980; Posy for Emmanuel, jazz chamber orch, 1981; 2 Eclogues, fl, harp, 1982; 4 pezzi, cl, 1982; Hukvaldy Suite, str qt, 1984; Monumento, org, 1984; Tango Music, pf, 1984; Sleeping Landscape, brass insts, perc, 1985; Don Giovanni's Dream, wind octet, 1989; Str Qt, 1989; teaching pieces for vn, pf

Vocal: Stabat mater, male chorus, 1966; Kuroshio, dramatic frescoes, S, chorus, 1968; Gnomai, S, fl, harp, 1970; Sonetto per voci bianche, 1978; Italian Triptych, chorus, 1980; Looking Back, female chorus, 1981; Fortune, cantata, mixed chorus, children's chorus, 1983; Little Evening Music, ob, chorus, 1983; Occhi lucenti e belli, female chorus, 1984; Love!, female chorus, 1985; Life, stop for a while!, male chorus, 1987; children's choral cycles; see also Sym. no.2

Principal publishers: Panton, C. F. Peters (New York), G. Schirmer, Supraphon

MÍLAN KUNA, ANNA ŠERÝCH

Louie, Alexina (Diane) (*b* Vancouver, 30 July 1949). Canadian composer and pianist, of Chinese descent. Her first important piano teacher was Jean Lyons. She attended the University of British Columbia (BMus 1970), where she studied the piano with Barbara Custance and Frances Marr Adaskin and composition with Cortland Hultberg; she worked as a cocktail pianist to support herself during this time. Later, at the University of California at San Diego (MA 1973), she studied composition and sonic meditation with Pauline Oliveros and Robert Erickson. From 1971 to 1974 she participated in the ♀ ensemble in sonic meditation under Oliveros's direction. She subsequently taught the piano, theory and electronic music at Pasadena City College, 1974–80, and at Los Angeles City College, 1976–80. In California she listened to the music of China, Japan, Korea, India and Indonesia and studied the *ch'in* at UCLA. After returning to Canada in 1980 and taking up residence in Toronto, she devoted herself almost entirely to composition, although she also taught for York University, the Royal Conservatory of Music and the University of Western Ontario. She has fulfilled commissions from all the major Canadian orchestras and new music groups as well as from many prominent performers, and has written music for dance, film and television. In 1986 she was named Composer of the Year by the Canadian Music Council; she received a Juno award for best classical composition in 1988 for *Songs of Paradise*; and in 1990 she was the recipient of the first SOCAN concert music award. In 1994 she won the Jean A. Chalmers Award for Musical Composition (Chalmers Foundation, Ontario). Her *Music for a Thousand Autumns* was performed by the ISCM in 1988. She is the subject of the Rhombus Media and National Film Board film *The Eternal Earth* (1987) and a Canadian television programme *Beyond the Call* (1987). She is married to composer-conductor Alex Pauk.

Louie's music reveals an eclectic range of influences; whether these derive from her Chinese cultural background, her reading of literature or poetry, her exploration of the visual arts, her study of other musics or her concern for nature, hers is a truly unique voice. In her early works new techniques were combined with oriental influences, yet she did far more than create a fusion of east and west, even if some of the extreme contrasts evident in these works have been attributed to the 'contrasting principles of yin and yang'; dark as well as light colours, ranging from the lyrical to the percussive, co-exist within one work. It is her compositions for large orchestra that have enjoyed particular success, for in these her variegated instrumental colours and radiant, iridescent sound shine through most of all. Other works are more intense and introspective. Her humanitarian and environmental concerns have inspired several compositions, including *The Ringing Earth*, commissioned for the Expo '86 World Festival, and *Love Songs for a Small Planet* (1988), commissioned for the International Choral Festival of 1989. Many pieces suggest the music of the Indonesian gamelan with their gong-like sonorities, as in *The Eternal Earth* (1986) and in the *Music for Heaven and Earth* (1990) that was commissioned for the Toronto SO's Pacific Rim tour, but now the writing is more subtly evocative than in the earlier *Lotus* and *Lotus II* pieces (1977–8). Elsewhere, as in *O magnum mysterium: In memoriam Glenn Gould* (1982), Louie has used

Alexina Louie

musical quotation from Bach and Mahler. In *Molly* (1972) for four-channel tape, she has attempted to 'humanize' electronic music, whereas the opposite is the case in *O magnum mysterium* with its evocation of eastern-like sounds that sometimes create the effect of electronic music.

WORKS
selective list

Music-theatre: Journal (New York), 10 performers, 1980

Orch: O magnum mysterium: In Memoriam Glenn Gould, 44 str, 1982; Music for a Thousand Autumns, 1983, rev. 1985; Songs of Paradise, 1983; Pf Conc., 1984; Music for a Celebration, 1985; The Eternal Earth, 1986; The Ringing Earth, 1986; 3 Fanfares from the Ringing Earth, 1986, rev. 1987; Music for Heaven and Earth, 1990; Thunder Gate, vn, orch, 1991; Arc, solo v and orch, 1993; Gallery Fanfares, Arias and Interludes, 1993

Chamber: Lotus, 5 performers, tape, 1977; Lotus II, 10 performers, 1978; Incantation, cl, tape, 1980; Pearls, fl/a fl, ob, vc, pf, perc, 1980; Refuge, accordion, harp, vib, 1981; Sanctuary, 12 performers, 1982; Cadenzas, cl, perc, 1985, rev. 1987; Riffs, ob, cl, bn, 1985, rev. 1987; Demon Gate, 12 performers, 1987; Earth Cycles, accordion, tape, 1987; Music from Night's Edge, pf qnt, 1988; Winter Music, chamber conc., va, 11 performers, 1989; Bringing the Tiger down from the Mountain II, vc, pf, 1991; Ricochet, chamber conc., trbn, 6 performers, 1992

Solo inst: Dragon Bells, prepared pf, taped prepared pf, 1978; Afterimages, 2 pf, 1981; Music for Pf, 1982; Fantasia on a Theme by Bach, org, 1985; From the Eastern Gate, harp, 1985, rev. 1987; Star-

Filled Night, pf, 1987; Scenes from a Jade Terrace, pf, 1988, incl. Memories in an Ancient Garden, perf. separately; I Leap through the Sky with Stars, pf, 1991
Vocal: Songs of Enchantment, Mez, str qt, 1987; Love Songs for a Small Planet, S, chamber choir, harp, perc, 1989, rev. 1992 for chamber choir, harp, str, perc
El-ac: Molly (after J. Joyce: *Ulysses*), 4-channel tape, 1972
Also TV and film scores

BIBLIOGRAPHY
EMC 2 (E. Keillor)
M. Schulman: 'Exotic Sounds, Hypnotic Rhythm from Vancouver's Alexina Louie', *Canadian Composer*, no.150 (1980), 16–21
C. Goulet: 'Alexina Louie: Composition as a Soul-Searching Voyage into the Self', *Canadian Composer*, no.193 (1984), 20–23
R. Elliott: 'A Young Composer: Alexina Louie is Remarkably Successful', *Toronto Symphony Magazine*, xliv/March–April (1986)
R. Snider: 'New Music's Rising Star', *Maclean's*, xix/May (1986)
L. Lacey: 'A Young Composer's Remarkable Quest', *Toronto Globe and Mail* (21 March 1987)
J. K. Parker: *The Solo Piano Music of Alexina Louie: a Blend of East and West* (diss., Juilliard School, New York, 1989)
R. Flohil: 'Ms Louie Faces the Deadlines', *Canadian Composer*, i/sum. (1990)
GAYNOR G. JONES

Louis, Marie Emmanuelle. *See* BAYON, MARIE EMMANUELLE.

Lucas [née Anderson], **Mary** (*b* London, 24 May 1882; *d* London, 14 Jan 1952). English composer and pianist. She studied the piano at the Dresden Conservatory and in London. Although she retired temporarily after her marriage in 1903, she later studied composition with R. O. Morris, Herbert Howells and Maurice Jacobson. She became known when the Bournemouth Municipal Orchestra performed her Rhapsody (1928) and Fugue (1929). During the 1930s she published partsongs and had a minor reputation for chamber music and ballets (*Cupid and Death*, *Undine*, both 1936). She orchestrated the ballet *Sawdust* (1941) as the *Circus Suite* for the 1942 Promenade Concerts. Her Purcell variations for strings (1938) were performed by the New York Philharmonic Society at Saratoga Springs as well as by the Boyd Neel Orchestra in London, and the Flute Concertino (1940) by Gareth Morris in London in 1951.

WORKS
selective list

Stage: The Book of Thel (masque, W. Blake), 1935; Cupid and Death (ballet), 1936; Undine (ballet), 1936; Sawdust (ballet), pf, fl, str qnt, 1941, orchd as

Circus Suite, 1942; [4] Ballet Preludes, 1941, orchd 1945
Orch: Rhapsody, chamber orch, 1928; Fugue, str, 1929; Variations on a Theme of Purcell, str, 1938; Fl Concertino, 1940; Circus Suite [from ballet, Sawdust], 1942; ov.
Chamber: Str Qt no.2, 1933; Str Qt no.3, 1935; Lament and Rhapsody, cl, pf; Fugue, fl, ob, va; Sonata, cl, pf, 1938; Trio, cl, va, pf, 1939; Duo, cl, va, 1941; Rhapsody, fl, vc, pf, 1946
Choral works, partsongs, unison songs
LEWIS FOREMAN

Ludvig-Pečar, Nada (*b* Sarajevo, 12 May 1929). Croatian composer. She studied composition with Miroslav Špiler in Sarajevo and L. M. Škerjanc in Ljubljana. From 1969 she taught theory at the Sarajevo Music Academy. Her musical language is rooted in European music of the first decades of the 20th century. Ludvig-Pečar has contributed to almost all musical genres but most successfully to that of the solo song, as can be heard in her 1974 cycle *Sappho* for voice and piano. Notable among her chamber works are a violin suite (1965) and the String Quartet in D (1966). Her output for solo piano includes *Deset studija* (Ten Studies, 1965) and *Suita hexatonica* (1973).
MELITA MILIN

Luengo, Maria Teresa (*b* Quilmes, 25 Nov 1940). Argentine composer. She graduated in composition and musicology from the Catholic University of Argentina in 1969. Between 1973 and 1980 she experimented with a personal language influenced by north American music (as in *Cuatro soles*, 1973), which she later consolidated (in *Navegante*, 1983). Using consonant and dissonant 'regions', differentiated by particular groupings of small intervals, she builds modules of sounds and silence that have an archaic atmosphere and sonority, but without reference to Argentinian or Latin American folk music. Most of her works are for chamber groups, using various combinations of instruments. They have won many prizes. Luengo also teaches contemporary techniques and in 1990 instituted a course in electroacoustic composition at the Universidad Nacional in Quilmes.

WORKS
selective list

Chamber: 6 preludios, str qt, 1968, rev. 1970; Heptafón, fl, cl, str qt, pf, 1970; Ambitos, pf qnt, 1971; Duetto, vn, pf, 1972; 4 soles, fl, ob, vc, pf, perc, 1973; Del museo imaginario, pf qt, perc, 1975; El libro de los espejos, 2 fl, cl, vn, va, vc, pf, perc, 1976; 6 imágenes mágicas, fl, cl, vc, perc, 1978; Presencias, fl, vn, pf, 1980; Nao, wind qnt, 1983;

Navegante, pf, 6 perc, 1983; Ecos por Tupac, a fl, b cl, vc, 1984; Las aguas de la luz, 2 fl, b cl, vn, vc, 1989

Pf: Sonata, 1965; Mahlerianas, 1976; Saltos transparentes, 1990

Tape: Absolum, 1973

Film score: Taumanía, dir. P. Delfini

Principal publisher: EAC-Moeck

BIBLIOGRAPHY

D. Durañona y Vedia: 'Entrevista a Maria Teresa Luengo', *Realidad musical Argentina*, no.1 (1983), 11–12

A. M. Mondolo: 'Maria Teresa Luengo', *Revista del Instituto de investigación musicológica Carlos Vega*, ix (1988), 137–47

D. Grela: *Catálogo de obras musicales argentinas (1950–1992)* (Santa Fé, Argentina, 1993), 68

RAQUEL C. DE ARIAS

Luff, Enid (*b* Ebbw Vale, 21 Feb 1935). Welsh composer. She read modern languages at Cambridge (MA 1957), raised a family, then entered the Royal Northern College of Music to study the piano, 1964–5. In 1975 she was awarded a Welsh Arts Council Composers' Bursary after gaining the MMus from the University of Wales. She continued her studies with Elisabeth Lutyens, Anthony Payne and later Franco Donatoni (1977–8). In 1980 she co-founded, with Julia Usher, the self-publishing company Primavera. She has a particular interest in composing for dance and has written a considerable amount of piano music, including the sonata *Storm Tide* (1986), as well as chamber and vocal music.

WORKS
selective list

Chamber, inst: Tapestries, cl, va, vc, pf, 1971; Mixed Feelings, pf, 1973; 4 pieces, pf, 1973; Statements, pf, 1974; Mathematical Dream, harp, 1978, rev. 1983; Canto and Doubles, fl, 1979; Midsummer Night's Dream, 7 pieces, fl, pf, 1980; The Coastal Road, wind qnt, 1980; The Coming of the Rain, ob, 1981; Swiss Interiors, 2 fl, 1982; Belltower, pf, 1985; Dream Time for Bells, fl + pic + a fl, vib, harp, vc, 1985; Sky Whispering, pf, 1985; The Haunted Nightclub, pf, 1985; Today and Tomorrow, gui, 1986; Ships, pf, 1986; Sonata 'Storm Tide', pf, 1986; Come the Morning, fl, ob, cl, bn/hn, tpt, trbn, perc, 2 vn, va, vc, db, 1986; Sleep, Sleep, February, fl, ob, cl + b cl, pf, 1989; Peregrinus, org, 1991

Vocal: Lux in tenebris, S, pf, 1971; Spring Bereaved, song cycle, Bar, gui, 1971; 3 Jap. Songs, S, pf, 1973; The Bird, SATB, 1973; Counterpoints, S, pf, 1974; Thanksgiving at Morning Prayer, SATB, 1975; Nocturnes, S, pf, 1975; The Mad Maid in Summer, SATB, fl, hn, 1977; Weather and Mouth Music, S, db, 1977; 3 Shakespeare Sonnets, Mez, fl, pf, 1978; Vox ultima crucis, Bar, pf, 1979; Christmas Night, SATB, 1979; Marwnad Gwenhwyfar, S, pf, 1979; Swn dwr [The Sound of Water], Mez, fl, pf, 1981; Weary was the Walking, Christmas carol, 2 equal vv, 1982; Abendgebet, Bar, str orch, 1983; Sheila

Na Gig, S, pf, 1984; The Hands of God, SATB, 1987; Y lusern [The Lantern], SATB, 1988; Five God our Mother (Julian of Norwich), S, org, 1990

Theatrical: A Midsummer Night's Dream, incid. music, 1980; Since I am Coming, B, org, mime, 1988; Rags, solo mime, tape, 1990; Listen to the Roar of the Sun (G. Clarke), ob, mime/dancer, spkr, 1992

Orch: Star Trek, youth orch, 1977; Va Conc. 'Atlantic Crossing', 1991

BIBLIOGRAPHY

Fuller-LeFanuRM

TONI CALAM

Lund, Gudrun (*b* Copenhagen, 22 April 1930). Danish composer. She was educated in Copenhagen at the university, studying music, German and English, and at the Kongelige Danske Musikkonservatorium. She began to compose when she was 46; she then took lessons in composition and orchestration with Svend S. Schultz and Mogens Winkel Holm. In 1983–4 she studied in the USA at the Hartt College of Music. For a number of years she has been employed as a teacher at KDAS, a college of education in Copenhagen, but does not teach music. She is systematic and prolific, and has composed more than a hundred works. Her wide-ranging music embraces traditional tonal and rhythmic principles as well as more abstract and complex styles.

WORKS
selective list

Stage: Prinsessen på aerten [The Princess on the Pea], op.41 (musical fairytale, 2, Lund, after H. C. Andersen), 1980, Göteborg, Musikhögskolan, Feb 1992; Simple Johnny, op.128 (mini-opera, Lund, after Andersen), 8vv, 7 insts, 1991

Orch: A Festive Overture, op.15, 1977; Chamber Conc., op.18, ob, va, orch, 1977; Conc., op.26, a trbn, chamber orch, 1978; Consequences, op.32, 1979; Negotiations, op.76, wind band, 1983; Walking Along, op.86, cl, orch, 1984; Celebration, op.100, 1986

Chamber, inst: Str Qt no.1, op.8, 1976; Trio, op.10, fl, vn, va, 1976; Str Qt no.2, op.20, 1978; Serenata seriosa, op.42, str trio, 1980; 7 facetter [7 Facets], op.43, org, 1980; 5 Boys I Know, op.53, b trbn, 1981; Abstract, op.66, accordion, 1982; Str Qt no.4, op.70, 1983; Con anima, op.73, fl, vn, va, vc, 1983; Str Qt no.5, op.77, 1984; Diversions, op.88, fl, ob, cl, bn, hn, 2 vn, va, vc, db, 1985; Op og ned [Up and Down], op.93, mand ens, 1986; 5 Pieces for Grand Piano, op.109, 1988; 5 Girls I Know, op.114, tpt, trbn, 1988; Trio basso, op.119, va, vc, db, 1989; Spanish Lady, op.123, pf, 1990; Str Qt no.6, op.134, 1992; Suite, op.135, str, 1992

Vocal: 4 Songs, op.12 (J. A. Schade), SATB, 1977; Skisma, op.14 (T. Ditlevsen), S, orch, 1977; 3 sange om livet og døden [3 Songs about Life and Death], op.36 (G. Risbjerg Thomsen), S, trbn, org, 1979; Driving in the Fog, op.84, Mez, pf, 1984; A Woman's Nature?, op.98; S, wind qnt, hpd, 1986;

Summer, op.104, S/T, pf, tape, 1987; Jungle Music, op.117, S, vn, perc, tape, 1988; Snake, op.120 (D. H. Lawrence), T, mixed chorus, pf, 1989; Dejlige Danmark [Beautiful Denmark], op.133 (Lund), mixed chorus, 1992

Principal publisher: Samfundet

BIBLIOGRAPHY

CC; CohenE

L. Storm-Jørgensen: Kvindelige komponister: Gudrun Lund (diss., Copenhagen U., 1984)

I. Bruland: 'Fire danske kvindelige komponister fra det 20. århundrede' [Four Danish Women Composers from the 20th Century], Kvinders former, ed. I. Bruland, L. Busk-Jensen and T. Ødrum (Copenhagen, 1986)

INGE BRULAND

Lund, Signe (b Christiania [now Oslo], 15 April 1868; d Oslo, 6 April 1950). Norwegian composer. Her early studies were with Erika Nilsson, Per Winge and Iver Holter in Christiania; later she studied with Wilhelm Berger in Berlin and she undertook studies in Copenhagen and Paris. She worked as a teacher in both Norway and the USA; she lived in Chicago, 1902–20, and gave numerous concerts and lectures in the USA on Norwegian topics. In 1917 she was one of the founders of the Norwegian Association of Composers. She had swiftly gained recognition as a composer, through her piano pieces (of which the best-known are the Legende and Norske smaastubber) and her orchestral works. She was an accomplished craftswoman, and stylistically her music covers a range from simple folklike works to a dynamic, high Romantic manner.

WORKS
selective list

Orch: Berceuse, op.28, 1900; The Road to France, march, 1917; Andante, op.42, 1921; Armistice-Chimes, op.52, c1920; Pf Conc., op.63, 1931

Pf: 4 stykker, op.9, 1888; Petite valse coquette, op.10, 1888; Norske smaastubber, op.15, 1893 (London and Geneva, 1921); 4 morceaux [incl. Legende], op.16, 1896, Legende pubd (London, 1921); Impromptu, thema med variationer, op.18, 1896; Rondo, op.20, 1897; 6 lyriske smaastykker, op.25, 1898; 3 études poétiques, op.32, 1905; Ballade, c, op.37, 1910; Valse de concert, op.40, pf 4 hands, 1914; Fredsklokker 1918, 1918; Return of the Waltz, op.50, 1920; Naturstemninger, op.61, 1928

Other inst: Berceuse, op.28, vn, pf, 1900; Barcarolle et chanson, op.33, vn/fl, pf, 1906

Voice, pf: 5 songs, op.22, 1897; 3 songs, op.26, 1899; Chanson de Fortunio, op.31, 1911 (Chicago, 1911); The Dreamland Tree, op.35, 1911 (Chicago, 1911); Små blomsterviser, op.46, 1915; Til enhver, 1922

BIBLIOGRAPHY

S. Lund: Sol gjennem skyer (Oslo, 1944) [autobiography]

K. Michelsen, ed.: Cappelens musikkleksikon (Oslo, 1978–80)

B. Eika: Signe Lund: menneske og musiker (Oslo, 1983)

C. Dahm: Kvinner komponerer: 9 porteretter av norske kvinnelige komponister i tiden 1840–1930 (Oslo, 1987)

KARI MICHELSEN

Lutyens, (Agnes) Elisabeth (b London, 6 July 1906; d London, 14 April 1983). English composer. A daughter of the architect Sir Edwin Lutyens, she began serious music studies at the Ecole Normale, Paris, in 1922 and subsequently entered the RCM, where she studied composition with Harold Darke and the viola with Ernest Tomlinson. Her first important public performance was that of the ballet The Birthday of the Infanta in 1932. This score has been withdrawn, as have other works of the period performed at the Macnaghten-Lemare Concerts: indeed, Lutyens's stylistic evolution was a slow and arduous process worked out, she claimed, without knowledge of radical developments outside England. An important experience was her introduction to the Purcell string fantasias. Their independence of part-writing was to lead her to a personal brand of serialism in the Chamber Concerto no.1 (1939), one of the most innovatory British works of the period. The rigorously chromatic thematicism of this piece – and also the extremely attenuated textures – immediately marked Lutyens off from her English contemporaries. Her sense of isolation at this point seems to have been complete: she was driven to battle against the incomprehension of the English musical establishment, and she was not helped by her turbulent domestic life. In 1939 Lutyens left her first husband, the singer Ian Glennie, for Edward Clark, the influential BBC programme maker (1927–36) who had introduced most of the avant-garde composers of the time to British listeners. He was never to hold a steady job, however, and Lutyens was forced to compose for film and radio to support her four children. The situation lasted over twenty years and seriously hindered her artistic development. She was always to consider her commercial work artistically insignificant.

At the beginning of this period, which embraced World War II and after, she explored in many directions. The romantic expressionism and the bold dramatic outlines of the Three Symphonic Preludes, for example, contrast strongly with the unrhetorical First Chamber Concerto, while the neo-classical concertos for horn and bassoon are quite different again. Yet with each work Lutyens approached a little nearer the sensibility and style of her maturity. By the end of the war she was using with commanding ease a fully developed 12-note technique: *O saisons, o châteaux!* (1946) marked a new important stage in her development. Here the refined sensuousness and magical feeling of Arthur Rimbaud are embodied in a completely individual harmony. It only remained for her to evolve an equally original rhythmic style, and the seeds for this had already been sown in the Chamber Concerto no.1.

Three works mark her final steps to maturity. The *Concertante for Five Players* (1950) employs a new sparseness of texture with greater ease and freedom than in the Chamber Concerto, and it includes the first writing typical of her later work. This newly won ground was to some extent confirmed in the Sixth String Quartet (1952) where the rhythmic freedom and the independence of parts shows a considerable advance over the music of the previous decade. Lutyens's next work, the Motet on words of Ludwig Wittgenstein, at last took up the challenge of the First Chamber Concerto. Canonic and tightly organized in melodic flow, the Motet is based on a 12-note series itself formed from a three-note cell, so allowing quasi-Webernian symmetries.

Lutyens was now on the point of writing her finest music, yet her personal life was at a low ebb – as she related in her autobiography *A Goldfish Bowl* (London, 1972) – and the direction taken by her work had led to an almost total neglect. Her use of 12-note technique seems to have been considered almost morally reprehensible by some in England in the 1950s, but in the more sympathetic climate of the following decade Lutyens achieved a greater measure of recognition. Even so, works of her first full maturity, such as the chamber opera *Infidelio* (1954) and the very fine cantata *De amore* (1957), were not performed until 1973. These and other pieces of the period foreshadow lines of development that were to occupy her for some years. Music for Orchestra I (1955), however, is backward-looking in that its warm expressionism brings to fruition that vein that had run through other works back to the Three Symphonic Preludes. In *De amore* the emotional warmth is still present but now somewhat objectified. The process of refinement shortly yielded two of her finest works, *Six Tempi* (1957) with its impressively lean flow of events, and *Quincunx* (1959), whose balanced architecture presents a classically controlled passion and grandeur. A continuously evolving monody, scattered widely across the

orchestra, coalesces into, or is punctured by, harmonic incidents of varying density. This sombre and elegiac work marked a new level of achievement, a level maintained in Lutyens's later work.

The Wind Quintet (1960) aligned her new linguistic freedom with classical discourse, using in its first movement the palindromic form that became a preoccupation. The Symphonies (1961) for piano, wind and percussion, however, explored further aspects of Lutyens's imposing splendour, objective in its rhetoric and drama. Yet new ground was reached in *Catena* (1961) where atmospherically evocative and picturesque music illuminates a wide variety of texts. This was the first of several vocal anthologies, using various chamber ensembles, which constitute an important part of Lutyens's later music. Music for Orchestra II (1962), in which the strongest feelings are rigidly controlled, is one of her most uncompromisingly objective works but also one of her most deeply moving. A headlong Allegro, coloured by the searing sound of a large clarinet and saxophone section, subsides into a chorale which closes with a whisper – a swift cataclysm opposed by the colourful romantic drama of Music for Orchestra III (1963). The refinement of Lutyens's language at this time is epitomized in *The Valley of Hatsu-se* (1965). Here the extreme concentration of the Japanese poems is matched by lyrical traceries shorn of rhetoric and expansion.

At about this time there was a change of direction in Lutyens's work: a widening of vocabulary admitted more repetitive and simply patterned ideas; pictorial and atmospheric writing came to coexist with more abstract music, as in *Akapotik Rose* (1966). The less complex harmony, the simpler gestures and the block structuring of *And Suddenly it's Evening* (1966), for example, provide a strong contrast with the fluidly evolving lyricism of previous works. The full implications were realized in the magnificent choral and orchestral *Essence of our Happinesses* (1968) where airy textures and intercalated silences are crucial. Repetition and reduced eventfulness are carried to daring limits, giving a sense of timelessness and exactly conveying the metaphysical texts from Donne and Islam. Most of Lutyens's major works of the 1960s and early 1970s involved words, and from increasingly various sources. *Vision of Youth* (1970) finds a new context for triadic progressions and extended homophony in its valedictory settings of Joseph Conrad. *Islands* (1971), though perhaps too reliant on illustrative effect and on a loose succession of moods, presents a riot of colour and at times a wildness that is far from the emotional monotone of *Vision of Youth*. *The Tears of Night* (1971) combines Renaissance and modern vocal and instrumental resources in an intense nocturnal sadness, and *Counting your Steps* (1972) uses primitive poetry to create a starkly simple ritual with hypnotic repetition.

Before 1965 Lutyens had written two short chamber operas: *The Pit* (1947), concerning trapped miners, and *Infidelio* (1954), the story of a broken love affair traced back from the girl's suicide to the first meeting. Now, however, she began a series of three full-length works, of which the first staged was *Time Off? Not a Ghost of a Chance!* (1967–8). Described as a charade, it deals with ideas rather than events. Riddles, puns and free associations move from the nature of time to the workings of chance, from the ages of man to his spiritual existence; every facet of Lutyens's music is called upon, including parody. The first of the operas to be composed had been *The Numbered* (1965–7), one of Lutyens's finest achievements and the climax to the period of purity of language. The text, based on Elias Canetti's *Die Befristeten*, treats the problems of a society in which everyone knows his time of death but is sworn to keep his age secret; it drew some of Lutyens's most powerful music. Her third opera, *Isis and Osiris* (1969–70), is a ritual of the seasons and of life and death. Appropriately it uses her simpler, more hard-edged manner with repetitive figures and much block harmony.

In this phase of predominantly dramatic and vocal music Lutyens wrote few instrumental pieces, but in 1972 she embarked on the *Plenum* series, in which her scope and individuality, and her keen awareness of contemporary trends, enabled her to assimilate greater rhythmic flexibility in free notation. After 30 years of consistently excellent and often radical achievement Lutyens received some measure of official recognition with the award in 1969 of the City of London Midsummer Prize; in the same year she was made a CBE. It is unfortunate that during the last decade of her career a certain fading of the impulse that had energized her previous music took place. The rhythmic freedom led to a lack of structural focus. But she was still capable of arresting ideas and concentrated

Elisabeth Lutyens

thought, and it was touching that, crippled by arthritis, she was able to produce in her last year the marvellously fresh and pointed *Triolets*.

WORKS

A list of published works only. Most MSS, including many unpublished works, are held at *GB-Lbl*.

STAGE

The Pit, op.14 (dramatic scene, W. R. Rodgers), 1947; concert perf., London, Wigmore Hall, 18 May 1947; stage, Palermo, Teatro Massimo, 24 April 1949

Penelope (music drama for radio, Lutyens), 1950, unorchd

Infidelio, op.29 (opera, 7 scenes, T. E. Ranselm [Lutyens]), 1954; London, Sadler's Wells Theatre, 17 April 1973

The Numbered, op.63 (opera, prol, 2, M. Volonakis, after Canetti: *Die Befristeten*), 1965–7, unperf.

Time Off? Not a Ghost of a Chance!, op.68 (charade, 4 scenes and 3 interruptions, Lutyens), 1967–8; London, Sadler's Wells Theatre, 1 March 1972

Isis and Osiris, op.74 (lyric drama, Lutyens, after Plutarch), 1969–70; London, Morley College, 26 Nov 1976

The Linnet from the Leaf, op.89 (music-theatre work, Lutyens), 1972; BBC, 11 Nov 1979

The Waiting Game, op.91 (opera, 3 scenes, Lutyens), 1973, unperf.

One and the Same, op.97 (scena, Lutyens), 1973–4; York, 21 June 1976

The Goldfish Bowl, op.102 (ballad opera, Lutyens), 1975, unperf.

Like a Window, op.109 (opera, after letters of V. Van Gogh), 1976; BBC, 24 Nov 1977

VOCAL

Choral: Motet 'Excerpta Tractatus logico-philosophici', op.27 (L. Wittgenstein), chorus, 1953; De amore, op.39 (cantata, G. Chaucer), S, T, chorus, orch, 1957; Encomion, op.54 (*Apocrypha*), chorus, brass, perc, 1963; Motet 'The Country of the Stars' (H. Boethius, trans. Chaucer), chorus, 1963; Magnificat, Nunc dimittis, male chorus, 1965, rev. SATB, 1970; Motet 'The Hymn of Man', op.61 (A. C. Swinburne), male chorus, 1965, rev. SATB, 1970; The Essence of our Happinesses, op.69 (Abü-Yasïd trans. R. C. Zaehner, J. Donne, A. Rimbaud), T, chorus, orch, 1968; The Tyme doth Flete, op.70 (Petrarch and Ovid, trans. T. Wyatt), chorus, ad lib prelude and postlude for 2 tpt, 2 trbn, 1968; Verses of Love (B. Jonson), chorus, 1970; Voice of Quiet Waters, op.84, chorus, orch, 1972; Counting your Steps, op.85 (African trad.), chorus, 4 fl, 4 perc, 1972; It is the Hour, op.111a (Byron), SSTB, 1976; The Roots of the World, op.136, vv, vc, 1979

Solo v(v) with orch or inst ens: O saisons, o châteaux!, op.13 (cantata, A. Rimbaud), S, mand, gui, harp, str orch, 1946; Nativity (W. R. Rodgers), S, str orch/org, 1951; 3 songs and incid. music for Group Theatre 'Homage to Dylan Thomas', S, (fl, va)/accordion/pf, 1953; Quincunx, op.44 (after T. Browne), S, Bar, orch, 1959–60; Catena, op.47, cantata, S, T, 21 insts, 1961; The Valley of Hatsu-Se, op.62 (Jap.), S, fl, cl, vc, pf, 1965; Akapotik Rose, op.64 (E. Paolozzi), S, fl + pic + a fl, cl + b cl, cl + t sax, vn, va, vc, pf, 1966; And Suddenly it's Evening, op.66 (S. Quasimodo, trans. J. Bevan), T, inst ens, 1966; A Phoenix, op.71 (Ovid, trans. A. Goulding), S, cl, vn, pf, 1968, arr. as op.71a, S, pf, 1968; Anerca, op.77 (Eskimo trad.), spkr/actress, 10 gui + perc, 1970; Vision of Youth, op.79 (J. Conrad), S, 3 cl + b cl, pf + cel, perc, 1970; Islands, op.80 (Sophocles trans. M. Volonakis, P. B. Shelley, R. L. Stevenson, F. Rabelais trans. T. Urquhart and P. A. Motteux), S, T, nar, 8 insts, 1971; Requiescat [in memory of Stravinsky], (S, str trio)/(Mez, 2 cl + b cl), 1971; The Tears of Night, op.82 (14th century), 6 S, Ct, 3 inst ens, 1971; Dirge for the Proud World, op.83 (T. Merton), S, Ct, hpd, vc, 1971; Chimes and Cantos, op.86 (R. Herrick), Bar, 2 tpt, 2 trbn, perc, 4 vn, 2 db, 1972; Laudi, op.96 (Lutyens), S, 3 cl, pf, perc, 1973; Concert Aria, op.112, female v, orch, 1976; Cascando, op.117 (S. Beckett), C, vn, str orch, 1977; Chorale Prelude and Paraphrase, op.123 (J. Keats), T, str qnt, 3 perc, pf, 1977; Elegy of the Flowers, op. 127 (C. Cavafy, trans. R. Devlen), T, 3 inst ens, 1978; Echoi, op.129, Mez, orch, 1979; Cantata, op.130 (U. Vaughan Williams), S, inst ens, 1979; Cantata, op.134 (C. Baudelaire), S, C, B, inst ens, 1979; Echoes, op.138 (H. Sudo), C, a fl, eng hn, str qt, 1979; Concert Aria: Dialogo, op.142 (Quasimodo), S, inst ens, 1980; Mine Eyes, my Bread, my Spade, op.143 (T. Tanner), Bar, str qt, 1980; Fleur du silence, op.150 (R. de Gourment), T, inst ens, 1980

Solo v(v) with 1 inst or unacc.: The Virgin's Cradle Hymn (S. T. Coleridge), 1v, pf, 1939; 2 Songs (W. H. Auden), S/Bar, pf, 1942; 9 Songs (S. Smith), Mez, pf, 1948–53; In the Temple of a Bird's Wing, op.37 (T. Tanner), Bar, pf, 1956, rev. 1965; The Egocentric (index I, *Oxford Book of English Verse*), T/Bar, pf, 1968; The Supplicant [from Isis and Osiris, op.74], B/Bar, pf, 1969–70; In the Direction of the Beginning, op.76 (D. Thomas), B, pf, 1970; Lament of Isis on the Death of Osiris [from Isis and Osiris, op.74], S, 1970; Oda a la tormenta, op.78 (P. Neruda), Mez, pf, 1970; Dialogo, op.88 (S. Quasimodo), T, lute, 1972;

Roads, op.95 (Lutyens), 2 S, Ct, T, Bar, B, 1973; The Hidden Power (P. B. Shelley), 2 equal vv, 1974; Of the Snow (F. Martens), 3 equal vv, 1974; Sloth – One of the 7 Deadly Sins (Lutyens), 2 Ct, T, 2 Bar, B, 1974; 2 Songs (D. H. Lawrence), 1v, 1974; Nocturnes and Interludes, op.111 (R. Burns, R. Kipling, A. Tennyson, R. Graves, C. Marlowe, Lutyens, J. Milton, H. Newbolt, G. Peele), S, pf, 1976; Variations: Winter Series – Spring Sowing, op.115 (U. Vaughan Williams), S, pf, 1977; By all These, op.120 (R. Jeffries), S, gui, 1977; She Tells her Love while Half Asleep, op.131 (Graves), S, 1979; That Sun, op.137 (G. Flaubert, trans. J. Cohen), C, pf, 1979; The Singing Birds, op.151 (W. B. Yeats, Lutyens, after M. Silverthorne, after Plato), actress/spkr, va, 1980

ORCHESTRAL

3 Pieces, op.7, 1939; Chamber Conc. no. 1, op.8/1, ob, cl, bn, hn, tpt, trbn, str trio, 1939; Chamber Conc. no.2, op.8/2, cl, t sax, pf, str orch, 1940–41; 3 Sym. Preludes, 1942; Chamber Conc. no.3, op.8/3, bn, str orch, 1945; Chamber Conc. no.4, op.8/4, hn, chamber orch, 1946–7; Chamber Conc. no 5, op.8/5, str qt, chamber orch, 1946; Va Conc., op.15, 1947; Music for Orch I, op.31, 1955; Chorale (Hommage à Stravinsky), op.36, 1956; Symphonies for Solo Piano, Wind, Harps and Percussion, op.46, 1961; Music for Orch II, op.48, 1962; Music for Orch III, op.56, 1963–4; Music for Pf and Orch, op.59, 1964; Novenaria, op.67/1, 1967; The Winter of the World, op.98, vc, 2 inst ens, 1974; Eos, op.101, small orch, 1974–5; Rondel, op.108, 1976; 6 Bagatelles, op.113, chamber orch, 1976; Nox, op.118, pf, 2 chamber orchs, 1977; Tides, op.124, 1978; Wild Decembers, op.149, chamber orch, 1980; Music for Orch IV: Gone Like a Sea-Covered Stone, op.152, chamber orch, 1981

INSTRUMENTAL

3 or more insts: Str Qt no.2, op.5/5, 1938; Str Trio, op.5/6, 1939; Str Qt no.3, op. 18, 1949; Concertante for 5 Players, op.22, fl + pic, cl + b cl, vn + va, vc, pf, 1950; Str Qt no.6, op.25/3, 1952; Nocturnes, op.30, vn, vc, gui, 1955; Capriccii, op.33, 2 harp, perc, 1955; 6 Tempi, op.42, fl, ob, cl, bn, tpt, hn, pf, vn, va, vc, 1957; Wind Qnt, op.45, 1960; Str Qnt, op.51, 1963; Wind Trio, op.52, 1963; Fantasie-Trio, op.55, fl, cl, pf, 1963; Str Trio, op.57, 1964; Scena, op.58, vn, vc, perc, 1964; Music for Wind, op.60, double wind qnt, 1964; The Fall of the Leafe, ob, str qt, 1966; Music for 3, op.65, fl + pic + a fl, ob, pf, 1966; Horai, op.67/4, vn, hn, pf, 1968; Driving out the Death, op.81, ob, str trio, 1971; Rape of the Moone, op.90, wind octet, 1973; Plenum II, op.92, ob, 13 inst, 1973; Plenum III, op.93, str qt, 1973; Kareniana, op.99, solo va, fl + a fl, ob, cl + b cl, tpt, trbn, hn, harp, pf + cel, 2 perc, 1974; Fanfare for a Festival, 3 tpt, 3 trbn, 1975; Go, Said the Bird, op.105, el gui, str qt, 1975; Mare et minutiae, op.107, str qt, 1976; Fantasia, op.114, a sax, 3 inst ens, 1977; O Absalom, op.122, ob + eng hn, vn, va, vc, 1977; Doubles, op.125, str qt, 1978; Trio, op.135, cl, vc, pf, 1979; Str Qt, op.139, 1979; Rapprochement, op.144, solo hn, solo harp, fl + a fl, ob, cl + b cl, perc, cel, pf, vn, va, vc, 1980; Str Qt: Diurnal, op. 146, 1980; Six, op. 147, cl + b cl + Eb-cl, Bb- tpt + D-tpt + flugel hn, perc, pf, vn, db, 1980; Branches of the Night and of the Day, op.153, (hn, vn, 2 va,

vc)/(hn, 2 vn, va, vc), 1981; Str Qt no.12, op.155, 1981; Str Qt no.13, op.158, 1982; Triolets op.160a, cl, vc, mand, op.160b, vc, harp, mar, 1982
1 or 2 insts: The Check Book (12 Pieces for Children), pf, 1937–8; Sonata, op.5/4, va, 1938; 5 Intermezzi, pf, 1941; 9 Bagatelles, vc, pf, 1942; Suite gauloise, vn, pf, 1944 [also arr. wind octet; movt 1 arr. chamber orch]; 5 Little Pieces, cl, pf, 1945; Aptote, vn, 1948; 3 Improvisations, pf, 1948; Ninepins, 2 vn, 1948; Prelude and Capriccio, op.20, vc, 1949; Valediction [in memory of Dylan Thomas], op.28, cl, pf, 1953–4; Sinfonia, op.32, org, 1955; 3 Duos, op.34: (1) hn, pf, (2) vc, pf, (3) vn, pf, 1956–7; Variations, op.38, fl, 1957; Piano e forte, op.43, pf, 1958; 5 Bagatelles, op.49, pf, 1962; Présages, op.53, ob, 1963; Helix, op.67/2, pf 4 hands, 1967; Scroll for Li-Ho, op.67/3, vn, pf, 1967; Epithalamion, op.67/5, org, S ad lib (E. Spenser), 1968; Temenos, op.72, org, 1969; The Dying of the Sun, op.73, gui, 1969; 3 pièces brèves [from Isis and Osiris, op.74], chamber org, 1969; The Tides of Time, op.75, db, pf, 1969; Plenum I, op.87, pf, 1972; Tre, op.94, cl, 1973; Plenum IV, op.100, org 4 hands, 1974; This Green Tide, op.103, basset-hn, pf, 1975; Pietà, op.104, hpd, 1975; The Ring of Bone, op.106, pf, opt. spkr(s), 1975; Constants, op.110, vc, pf, 1976; 5 Impromptus, op.116, pf, 1977; Madrigal, op.119, ob, vn, 1977; Romanza, op.121, gui, 1977; 7 Preludes, op.126, pf, 1978; Footfalls, op.128, fl, pf, opt. spkr(s), 1978; The Great Seas, op.132, pf, 1979; Prelude, op.133, vn, 1979; Morning Sea, op.140, ob + ob d'amore, pf, 1979; Bagatelles (3 bks), op.141, pf, 1979; Déroulement, op.145, ob, gui, 1980; Soli, op.148, cl + b cl, db, 1980; La natura dell'aqua, op.154, pf, 1981; The Living Night, op.156, perc, 1981; Echo of the Wind, op.157, va, 1981; Encore-Maybe, op.159, pf, 1982; Solo Fanfare (Jubilate), va, 1982

Arr.: Purcell: Air-Dance-Ground, va, pf, 1946
Many film, theatre and radio scores, light music

Principal publishers: Augener, Chester/Belwin Mills, Lengnick, Novello, Olivan/Universal, Schott, de Wolfe, Yorke

BIBLIOGRAPHY
R. M. Schafer: 'Elisabeth Lutyens', British Composers in Interview (London, 1963), 103–11
N. O'Loughlin: 'Elisabeth Lutyens's "Novenaria"', Tempo, no.88 (1969), 55–6
A. Payne: 'Elisabeth Lutyens's "Essence of our Happinesses"', Tempo, no.95 (1970–71), 33–4
S. Bradshaw: 'The Music of Elisabeth Lutyens', MT, cxii (1971), 653–6
L. East: 'Time Off? . . . with Lis Lutyens', Music and Musicians, xx/6 (1971–2), 18, 20
R. R. Bennett: 'Time Off? Not a Ghost of a Chance!', Opera, xxiii (1972), 102–5
S. Walsh: '"Time Off" and "The Scene Machine"', MT, cxiii (1972), 137–9 [interview]
R. Saxton: 'Composer Portraits: Elisabeth Lutyens', New Music 88, ed. M. Finnissy, M. Hayes and R. Wright (Oxford, 1988), 9–21
M. Harries and S. Harries: A Pilgrim Soul: the Life and Work of Elisabeth Lutyens (London, 1989)
S. J. Tenant-Flowers: A Study of Style and Techniques in the Music of Elisabeth Lutyens (diss., U. of Durham, 1991)

ANTHONY PAYNE
(work-list, bibliography with TONI CALAM)

Lyadova, Lyudmila Alexeyevna

(b Sverdlovsk [now Yekaterinburg], 29 March 1925). Russian composer. She studied at the Sverdlovsk Conservatory from 1943 to 1948: piano with B. Marants and composition with V. Trambitsky. Together with N. Panteleyeva she formed a vocal duet, which performed with great success in the late 1940s and won the 1946 All-Union Variety Artists Competition. As an integral part of her work, Lyadova also gave many concert tours of the USSR, performing her own songs (as pianist and singer).

Optimism and buoyancy of mood are the constant, fundamental features of Lyadova's style, as revealed in the majority of her songs, which range from folklike comic songs, sometimes in the character of chastushki (humorous and topical two- or four-line folk verses), to more lyrical songs. She has not sought to be an innovator: her lively melodies and energetic rhythms mostly conform to what was official Soviet pop-music style. She has written music in response to important events, such as the struggle for peace or even Komsomol construction projects, but her main topics concern sport or love. A festive mood also prevails in her orchestral works. Of her stage works, the first operetta Pod chyornoy maskoy ('Behind a Black Mask', 1960) was the most successful, remaining in the repertory for 20 years.

WORKS
selective list

Stage: Pod chyornoy maskoy [Behind a Black Mask] (operetta, Y. Lelgant), 1960; Skaska pro Yeryomu, Danilu i nechistuyu silu [A Fairy-Tale about Erioma, Danila and the Evil One] (musical, I. Petrova), 1977; Shakhtyorskiye nevestï [Miners' Brides] (operetta, Petrova), 1984; Dva tsveta vremeni [Two Colours of the Time] (opera, E. Kushakov and A. Snitsarenko), 1986

Orch: Kolkhoznaya pol'ka [Collective-Farm Polka], folk insts, orch, 1950; Ural'skaya rhapsodiya, folk insts, orch, 1951; Russkiy suvenir, light orch, 1961; Pf Conc., 1965; Intermezzo, pf, orch, 1978; Rhapsodies, pf, orch, 1980, 1981

Choral: Velikaya bitva [The Great Battle] (V. Petrov), 1967; Komsomolu: pionerskiy nash salyut! [Our Young Pioneers Salute the Komsomol!] (G. Chodosov), 1970; Tyumen'-Surgut (Petrov), 1972

c500 songs, incl. Chudo-pesenka [A Song-Wonder] (L. Davidovich and V. Dragunsky), Starïy marsh [Old March] (M. Vladimov), Zhenshchina [A Woman] (V. Lazarev), Pesnya o dome [Song about Home] (L. Zaval'nyuk)

BIBLIOGRAPHY
Yu. Milyutin: 'Pesni Lyudmilï Lyadovoy' [Songs by Lyudmila Lyadova], SovM (1954), no.12, pp.29–32
E. Dobrïnina: 'Lyudmila Lyadova', Muzïkal'naya zhizn' (1976), no.15, pp.18–19
G. Golub: Lyudmila Lyadova (Moscow, 1990)

OLGA MANULKINA

M

Macfarren [née Bennett], **Emma Maria** [Brissac, Jules] (*b* London, 19 June 1824; *d* London, 9 Nov 1895). English composer. She married John Macfarren (brother of the composer George Macfarren) in 1846. They spent three years in the USA and between 1862 and 1873 she was constantly on tour with her 'Mornings at the Piano' lecture recitals. Under her pseudonym Jules Brissac she published many original, brilliant piano pieces and fantasias (mainly on operas by Auber, Bellini, Donizetti, Flotow, Meyerbeer, Rossini, Verdi and Weber); she also published songs and a few piano pieces under her real name.

JOHN R. GARDNER

McIntosh [née Lowes], **Diana** (*b* Calgary, 4 March 1937). Canadian composer and pianist. She studied in Calgary with Gladys Egbert, at the Banff School of Fine Arts and the Toronto Royal Conservatory with Boris Roubakine, in Winnipeg with Alma Brock-Smith and Leonard Isaacs, in Toronto with Michael Colgrass and in the USA with Adele Marcus. As a pianist she has performed in North America and Europe. She made Winnipeg her home in 1959 and has served as composer-in-residence at the University of Manitoba. She has continued to be a major force in the performance of Canadian new music and has given the premières of many major works. In 1977, together with composer Ann Southam, she founded the Winnipeg-based Music Inter Alia, of which she is artistic director; the organization presents and commissions new works and in 1981–2 began to hold annual competitions.

McIntosh is regarded as a 'free spirit', an eclectic composer who has not confined herself to one school or style. Her works range from the light and cheery – *scherzando*-like pieces – to the expansive and evocative – works that sometimes reflect the Canadian landscape and its art. Her *Paraphrase no.1*, *Paraphrase no.2* and *Sound Assemblings* were inspired by paintings by Lawren Harris, Marcel Barbeau and Bertram Booker re-spectively. The multi-media works include slide projections, mime and narration; in these and in some of her keyboard works, the pianist may be required to play percussion instruments and narrate. A recording, *The Original McIntosh*, featuring performances of her music dating from 1978 to 1983, her video *Serious Fun with McIntosh* (1989) and her one-woman show 'Solitary Climb' (1990–91) have helped illuminate this multi-faceted musical personality.

WORKS
selective list

Music-theatre and multi-media, incl. el-ac: Music at the Centre (narration from W. Wordsworth: *Tintern Abbey*), cl, pf + perc + nar, tape, slide projections, 1981; Kiviuq (puppet theatre piece), taped music, 1982; A Different Point of View, tape, synchronized slide projections, 1983; Roles Renverses (theatre piece), Mez, pf, 1986; Sampling the Communication Parameters in the Ambience of Structural Phrasing and Dynamics in Contemporary Music (theatre piece), spkr, pf, 1986

Orch: Kiviuq: an Inuit Legend, nar, orch, 1985; Toward Mountains, 1985; Margins of Reality, str orch, 1989

Chamber: Luminaries, fl, pf, 1978; Sonograph, sopranino/s/a rec, ob, bn, 1980; Gulliver, b + t + s + sopranino rec, pf + perc, 1981; Aiby-Aicy-Aidyai, amplified mouth perc, toy pf, 1983; Tea for Two at Whipsnade Zoo, a rec, tape, 1983; Four or Five for Four or Five, rec/fl, ob, bn/vc, hpd, perc, 1984; Gut Reaction, va, tape, 1986; Patterns and Digressions, ww qnt, 1987; Playback, vn, vc, pf, 1987; Dance for Daedalus, a sax, pf, 1989

Kbd (solo and ens): Paraphrases, nos.1–2, pf, 1978; Extensions, pf, tape, 1981; Gradatim ad summum: Summit by Steps, pf duet, 1982; Sound Assemblings, pf, tape, 1983; Go Between, 3 pf + perc, tape, 1985; Channels, pf, 1986; All in Good Time, pf, taped v, mouth sounds, 1987; Music for Wire and Wood, pf + perc, 1987

Vocal: Colours (text based on Eng., Fr., Ger., It., Sp. words for colours), SATB, fl, opt. lighting, 1979; Eliptosonics, spkr, pf, 1979; . . . and eight thirty in Newfoundland, with perc and digital delay, 1985; Doubletalk, amplified v, tape, 1985; Tongues of Angels (*1 Corinthians*), Mez + perc, pf + perc, 1986; Shadowed Voices, vocalist + perc + pf, with digital delay, 1988

GAYNOR G. JONES

Macirone, Clara Angela (*b* London, 20 Jan 1821; *d* London, 19 Aug 1895). English

298

Clara Angela Macirone: portrait (c1870) by her sister Emily

pianist and composer. She was the daughter of Italian musicians; her father was a singer and her mother a pianist. This seems to have influenced her own career, since she studied singing and the piano at the RAM and composed little else but vocal and piano music. She first built a reputation as a pianist, then as a teacher, developing a system of music teaching which won the support of George Macfarren. Most of her compositions are partsongs, and these achieved wide recognition through performances by massed choirs at the Crystal Palace and at Exeter Hall (her *Sir Knight* was the first music heard by Queen Victoria over the telephone in 1878). Most of her songs are for mixed voices or treble voices, but her setting of Byron's *Fare thee well, and if for ever* (London, 1885) shows that she was equally at home writing a five-part song for men's voices. Her piano compositions are modest in scale, representative works being *Summer Serenade* (London, 1870) and a *Rondino* in G (London, 1889).

BIBLIOGRAPHY

CohenE; *MEMM*

J. D. Brown and S. S. Stratton: *British Musical Biography* (Birmingham, 1897)

S. Stern: *Women Composers: a Handbook* (Metuchen, NJ, 1978)

DEREK B. SCOTT

Mackenna (Subercaseaux), Carmela
(*b* Santiago, 31 July 1879; *d* Santiago, 30 Jan

1962). Chilean composer and pianist. She began her music studies in Chile under Bindo Paoli, continuing them in 1926 with Konrad Ansorge and Hans Mersmann in Berlin. Most of her works were composed, published and first performed in Europe, but in 1934 her Piano Concerto (1933) was performed in both Chile and Berlin. In 1936 her Mass for unaccompanied voices won second prize in the International Religious Music Competition in Frankfurt. Her style reflects the interests of her time, in particular expressionism and neo-classicism. In addition to her two *Kleine Orchesterstücke* (1935) she wrote many chamber works including two string quartets (1940, 1942) and *Visiones chilenas* for string quartet with percussion. Among her works for solo voice are settings of texts by Pablo Neruda and Paul Verlaine.

BIBLIOGRAPHY

V. Salas Viu: *La creación musical en Chile 1900–1951* (Santiago, 1951), 27–8

R. Bustos: 'Carmela Mackenna Subercaseaux', *Revista musical chilena*, xxxvii/159 (1983), 50–75

RAQUEL BUSTOS VALDERRAMA

McLean [née Taylor], **Priscilla (Anne)**
(*b* Fitchburg, MA, 27 May 1942). American composer and performer of electroacoustic music. She graduated from the State College at Fitchburg (BEd 1963) and the University of Massachusetts, Lowell (BME 1965). At

Indiana University, Bloomington (MM 1969) she was greatly influenced by the music of Iannis Xenakis, who was teaching there. She has taught at Indiana University, Kokomo (1971–3), St Mary's College, Notre Dame (1973–6), and the University of Hawaii (visiting professor, 1985). From 1976 to 1980 she produced the American Society of Composers 'Radiofest' series. In 1974 she and her husband, Barton McLean, began to perform together as the McLean Mix, and in 1983 to present concerts of their own music full-time. She sings and plays the piano, synthesizer, percussion and Native American wooden flutes, as well as newly created instruments.

McLean's works cover a wide range, from abstract orchestral and chamber music to visceral, dramatic electroacoustic music. Since 1978 most of her music has focussed on the concept of the wilderness and has incorporated sounds from animals and nature along with synthesized music according to an 'imago–abstract' concept. Her compositions, unquestionably dramatic, are neither busy nor fussy and are unencumbered by complex electronics. The sonic tension and large-scale coherence of her music and its unique sound-world have been widely admired.

WORKS
selective list

Orch and band: Holiday for Youth, concert band, 1964–5; Variations and Mozaics on a Theme of Stravinsky, orch, 1967–9, rev. 1975; A Magic Dwells, orch, tape, 1982–4; Voices of the Wild [Movt 1: (Printemps) Rites], live elec soloist, orch, 1986–8 [movt 2 by B. McLean]

Chamber: Interplanes, 2 pf, 1970; Spectra I, perc ens, synth, 1971; Spectra II, perc ens, prepared pf, 1972; Ah-Syn!, autoharp, synth, 1974, rev. 1976; Beneath the Horizon I, 4 tubas, tape [whale sounds], 1977–8; Beneath the Horizon II, china, tape [whale sounds], 1978, rev. as Beneath the Horizon III, 1979; Elan! A Dance to all Rising Things from the Earth, fl, vn, vc, perc, pf, 1982–4; Where the Wild Geese Go, cl, stereo tape, 1993–4

Multi-media: Inner Universe, 8 tone poems, amp pf, tape, slide projections, 1979–82; Beneath the Horizon, quadrophonic/stereo tape, slide projections, 1982; Dance of Shiva, stereo computer music, slide projections, 1989–90; Rainforest, 'audience-interactive multi-media installation', 2 synth, 2 microphones, tape, digital processors, slide projections, 1989–90, collab. B. McLean; Rain Forest Images II, stereo tape, videotape, 1993, collab. B. McLean

Tape: Night Images, 2-track, 1973; Dance of Dawn, 4-track, 1974; Invisible Chariots, 4-track, 1975–7; Rain Forest Images, 2-track, 1992, collab. B. McLean

Vocal: Men and Angels Share, chorus, pf, 1959; 4 Songs in Season: Chant of Autumn, Lullaby of Winter, Song to the Spring, Summer Soliloquy, chorus, pf, 1963, rev. 1967; 3 Songs (R. M. Rilke),

S, vn, 1965, rev. 1975; There Must be a Time, chorus, fl, pf, 1970; Messages, 4 solo vv, double chorus, chamber ens, elec, 1972–4; Fantasies for Adults and Other Children (E. E. Cummings), S, amp pf, 1978–80; Invocation, S, chorus, audience singing, created perc and ww, tape, 1984–5; O Beautiful Suburbia!, S + autoharp, audience singing, bongo drums + bicycle wheel, tape, 1984–6; On Wings of Song, S, bicycle wheel, tape, 1985; Wilderness, S, fl, cl, 2 sax, bn, accordion, 2 perc, pf, 1985–8; In Celebration (of the Historic Alaskan Wilderness Act and of All Consciousness of Our Bond with Nature), chorus, perc, tape, 1987–8; Wilderness, S, flexatone, tape, 1989–90; 6 (Sage) Songs about Life (and Thyme . . .), S, pf, 1990; also works for children's chorus, pf

Principal publishers: Bourne, Elkan-Vogel, Greenwood, MLC Publications, Silver-Burdett

BIBLIOGRAPHY

LePageWC, iii
P. McLean and B. McLean: 'The McLean Mix: Philosophics and Soliloquies', *Asterisk: a Journal of New Music*, no.2 (1976), 5–7
P. McLean: 'Fire and Ice: a Query', *PNM*, xvi/1 (1977), 205–11
D. Ernst: 'The Electronic Music of Barton and Priscilla McLean', *Polyphony*, iv/3 (1978), 40–42
P. McLean: 'Thoughts as a (Woman) Composer', *PNM*, xx/1 (1982), 308–10
P. McLean and B. McLean: 'The McLean Mix: the Inner Tension of the Surrealistic', *AWC News*, iii/3 (1982), 8–13
J. Aiken: 'Barton and Priscilla McLean', *The Art of Electronic Music*, ed. T. Darter (New York, 1984), 231–5

BARBARA A. PETERSEN,
LESLEY A. WRIGHT

McLeod, Jenny [Jennifer] **Helen** (*b* Wellington, 12 Nov 1941). New Zealand composer. From a musical family, in her youth she accompanied local singers, violinists and choirs in Levin, where she also made Maori friends and was introduced to their poetry and legends. Following an American Field Service scholarship at 16 to the Midwest, she took part in her first Cambridge (New Zealand) Summer School of Music. She began writing small pieces when she became a student of Douglas Lilburn and David Farquhar at Victoria University, Wellington (BMus 1964). Olivier Messiaen's *Quatuor pour la fin du temps* moved her profoundly and on being awarded an Arts Council bursary she joined the composer's classes at the Paris Conservatoire. She later studied with Karlheinz Stockhausen, Henri Pousseur, Luciano Berio and Earle Brown and in 1965 attended Pierre Boulez's conducting course in Basle. Appointed lecturer in music at Victoria University in 1967, she was professor there from 1971 to 1976.

McLeod's first works, *Cambridge Suite*

(1962) and the *Little Symphony* (1963), were written for students at Cambridge. In Paris she wrote *Piano Piece 1965* using the 12-note method and *For Seven* (1967), embodying contemporary European avant-garde techniques. Her ambitious music-theatre piece for children, *Earth and Sky* (1968), draws on a variety of indigenous and contemporary idioms in its bringing to life of the Maori creation myth; it also enabled McLeod to use her immense organizational abilities, galvanizing into action the small town of Masterton. *Under the Sun* (1971), written partly in rock style for children and amateurs in Palmerston North, contemplated the breaking down of the universe, but did not match *Earth and Sky* in quality. On resigning the professorship in 1976 McLeod devoted herself for a time to the artistic activities of the Divine Light Mission in America. After her return to New Zealand she became a full-time professional composer writing highly successful film and television scores. She has been influenced by the 'tone clock' harmonic theories of Peter Schat and has translated two of his books into English. Her own book on the chromatic system is a 'sort of codification and composer's handbook'. McLeod's later style varies from simple to complex depending on her intended audience: 'Some may find my music an odd mixture, but at least it is my own. I find I cannot separate the quality of people's art from their quality as human beings'.

WORKS

Music theatre (for children and amateurs): Earth and Sky, 1968; Under the Sun, 1971
Orch: Cambridge Suite, chamber orch, 1962; Little Symphony, chamber orch, 1963; The Emperor and the Nightingale, after H. C. Andersen, nar, chamber orch, 1985; 3 Celebrations, 1986
Vocal: Childhood, 10 songs, chorus, 1981; Through the World, song cycle (W. Blake), Mez, pf, 1982; Dirge for Doomsday, chorus, 1984
Chamber: Str Trio, 1963–4; For Seven, fl, cl, vn, va, vc, mar/vib, pf, 1966; Music for Four, 2 pf, 2 perc, 1985; Suite: Jazz Sketches, chamber ens, 1986
Pf: Piano Piece 1965, 1965; Rock Sonatas nos.1, 2, 1987; Tone Clock Pieces, 1988

BIBLIOGRAPHY

Fuller-LeFanuRM
J. McLeod: 'He Mana Toa', *Landfall*, xxi (1967), 189–91
F. Page: 'Reports: New Zealand', *MT*, cx (1969), 64
— : 'New Zealand Composers', *MT*, cxi (1970), 992
H. McNaughton: 'Earth and Sky', *Landfall*, xxv (1971), 176–81
D. Simmonds: 'London Music', *MO*, xcv (1971–2), 232
J. McCracken: 'Composer in Transit', *Landfall*, xxvi (1972), 335–44
J. McLeod: 'Jenny McLeod: New Directions for 1975', *Composers Association of New Zealand Newsletter* (1975), Oct, 4–7
D. Freed: 'Jenny McLeod: Composer', *Music News*, nos.14–15 (1985), 3–4, 14
E. Kerr: 'Jenny McLeod Talks to *Music in New Zealand*', *Music in New Zealand* (1988), spr., 7–13, 40
J. M. Thomson: *Biographical Dictionary of New Zealand Composers* (Wellington, 1990), 97–101

J. M. THOMSON

Elizabeth Maconchy

Maconchy, Elizabeth (*b* Broxbourne, Herts., 19 March 1907). English composer of Irish descent. The only musician in her family, she began to compose when she was six. She received her musical education at the RCM (1923–9), studying composition with Charles Wood and Vaughan Williams. Throughout her student years, she was strongly encouraged to pursue a compositional career by her teachers, by the college director and by a circle of peers, who included her life-long friends, Grace Williams, Dorothy Gow and Ina Boyle. During this period, she became acquainted with Bartók's music, an important influence on the development of her own style.

In 1929 Maconchy won an Octavia Travelling Scholarship which took her to Prague, where she had lessons with K. B. Jirák; her music first came to public attention when her Piano Concertino was performed there by Ervín Schulhoff in spring 1930. She returned to London, and the following August – just a week after she married William LeFanu – her suite, *The Land*, was given at a Promenade Concert to great acclaim. The Proms triumph launched Maconchy into the professional world; in November 1930 three of her songs were published, and she became known for her chamber works, which received frequent hearings in public concerts, including the Macnaghten-Lemare Concerts, in BBC broadcasts and at ISCM festivals. Her career changed course in 1932 when she contracted tuberculosis and was forced to move from London. She never again returned there to live, but continued to compose steadily. By 1936 her works had been played in Eastern Europe, Paris, Germany, the USA and Australia, as well as in Britain.

During the war, Maconchy and her family were evacuated to Shropshire. By this time she had one daughter, and she gave birth to her second – the composer Nicola LeFanu – in 1947. After the war, she re-established herself in the musical world as a composer of individuality and resource. She won the Edwin Evans Prize with String Quartet no.5 (composed 1948) and took the London County Council prize for Coronation Year with the overture *Proud Thames* (1952). She became the first woman chairman of the Composers' Guild of Great Britain in 1959 and was for many years associated with the SPNM, of which she became president in 1976. She was made a CBE in 1977 and a DBE in 1987. She has written many pieces to commission for professional and amateur organizations and for schools, her later output including a large proportion of operas, theatre works, choral pieces and song cycles.

Maconchy's particular musical individuality emerges most distinctly in her chamber pieces, and most of all in the 13 string quartets, written between 1933 and 1984, which she has described as 'my best and most deeply-felt works'. She conceives the dialogue within the quartet as 'impassioned argument' rigorously carried through, every note being essential to the whole structure. The music is largely linear, involving counterpoint of rhythms as well as of melody. Motifs, like Bartók's, tend to be short and compact, often turning back chromatically on themselves. Many movements are driven by strong motor rhythms, while developments concern themselves with a few basic themes and their transformations. From the Second Quartet onwards thematic connections may be established between movements. A quartet may be based on a single idea (as in no.2) or on a group of ideas (as in no.3). No.5 is dominated by an opening canon, no.6 by a passacaglia, in no.8 a single chord provides all melodic and harmonic material, and no.10 is unified by a viola motif linked to a short repeated-chord phrase.

In later years she enjoyed close associations with various performers whose intelligent virtuosity helped to inspire and shape commissioned pieces. In the chamber works of the 1970s and 80s she exploited in Haydn-like fashion the characteristics and foibles of particular voices or instruments. *Ariadne* (1970–71) is remarkable for the freedom and expressive quality of its wide-ranging vocal line and for its intricate, multi-linear, orchestration. In *Epyllion* (1974–5) the character of the solo cello is explored in melodic coloratura of a fantastic, semi-improvisatory, kind.

Maconchy was stimulated rather than inhibited by the inevitable limitations involved in writing for children or amateurs. *The Birds* (1967–8) has something of the gusto and good humour of Vaughan Williams's more popular works for amateurs; *Samson and the Gates of Gaza* (1963–4) and *The King of the Golden River* (1975) are strongly dramatic, yet never overstep the limits of what is practicable for children.

Her belief that music is worth nothing if it does not spring from passionate emotion is reflected strongly in the works of her maturity. Her three chamber operas are properly and vividly theatrical. The cantata *Heloise and Abelard* (1976–8), which is also operatic in mood and form, is a work of Italianate passion and intensity. At the other end of the emotional scale, the song cycle *My Dark Heart* (1981) deals in intimate, half-articulated thoughts and desires. By this time, she had moved a long way from the businesslike, no-nonsense mood of the early quartets, gaining expressive freedom, but without denying or outdistancing her earlier self.

WORKS
selective list
STAGE
operas unless otherwise stated

Great Agrippa (ballet), 1935; concert perf., London, 4 Feb 1935

Puck Fair (ballet), 2 pf, 1939–40; Dublin, Gaiety Theatre, 1940; orchd I. Boyle

The Sofa (1, U. Vaughan Williams), 1956–7; London, Sadler's Wells Theatre, 13 Dec 1959

The Three Strangers (1, Maconchy, after T. Hardy), 1957–8, orchd 1967; Bishop's Stortford College, 5 June 1968
The Departure (1, A. Ridler), 1960–61; London, Sadler's Wells Theatre, 16 Dec 1962
The Birds (1, Maconchy, after Aristophanes), 1968; Bishop's Stortford College, 5 June 1968 (London, 1974)
The Jesse Tree (church opera, 1, Ridler), 1969; Dorchester Abbey, 7 Oct 1970
Johnny and the Mohawks (children's opera, 1, Maconchy), 1969; London, Francis Holland School, March 1970 (London, 1970)
The King of the Golden River (children's opera, 1, Maconchy, after J. Ruskin), 1975; Oxford, University Church of St Mary, 29 Oct 1975

VOCAL

Choral: 2 Motets: A Hymn to Christ, A Hymn to God the Father (J. Donne), double chorus, 1931; The Voice of the City, female vv, 1943; 6 Yeats Settings, S, SSA, cl, 2 hn, harp, 1951; Christmas Morning, S, female vv, pf/inst ens, 1961; The Armado, SATB, pf, 1962; Samson and the Gates of Gaza [rev. of solo vocal work] (N. V. Lindsay), SATB, orch, 1963–4, arr. brass band, 1973; Nocturnal (W. Barnes, E. Thomas, P. B. Shelley), SATB, 1965; Propheta mendax, 3vv, 1965; 2 carols: I sing of a maiden, 4vv, This Day, 3vv, 1966; And death shall have no dominion (D. Thomas), SATB, brass ens, 1968–9; Prayer before Birth (L. MacNeice), SSAA, 1971; Fly-by-nights (anon.), children's vv, harp, 1973; The Isles of Greece (Byron), SATB, orch, 1973; Siren's Song (W. Browne), SSATB, 1974; 2 Epitaphs (F. Quarles, anon.), SSA, 1975; Pied Beauty, Heaven Haven (G. M. Hopkins), (Tr/S)ATB, brass, 1975; Heloise and Abelard (dramatic cantata, Maconchy), S, T, Bar, chorus, orch, 1976–8; The Leaden Echo and the Golden Echo (Hopkins), SATB, a fl, va, harp, 1978; 4 Miniatures (E. Farjeon), SATB, 1978; Creatures (I. Seraillier), SATB, 1979; O time turn back (W. Shakespeare, W. Raleigh, H. Vaughan, W. Blake, R. Herrick), SATB, wind qnt, vc, 1984; There is no rose (anon.), SATB, 1984; The Bellman's Carol (anon.), SATB, 1985; Still falls the rain (E. Sitwell), S, double SATB, 1985; Ode on St Stephen's Day, SSA, 1989
Solo: The Woodspurge (D. G. Rossetti), S, pf, 1930; How Samson bore away the Gates of Gaza (scena, N. V. Lindsay), T/S, pf, 1937, rev. as Samson and the Gates of Gaza [see choral section]; The Garland (song cycle, Anacreon, trans. W. LeFanu), S, pf, 1938; Sonnet Sequence (K. Gee), S, str orch, 1946–7; A Winter's Tale (Gee), S, str qt, 1949; A Hymn to God the Father (J. Donne), T, pf, 1959; 3 songs (G. M. Hopkins), S/T, chamber orch: The Starlight Night, 1964, Peace, 1964, May Magnificat, 1970; 4 Shakespeare Songs, S/T, pf, 1965; Hymn to Christ, The Sun Rising (Donne), T, pf, 1965–6; Ariadne (C. Day Lewis), S, chamber orch, 1970–71; Faustus (scena, C. Marlowe), T, pf, 1971; 3 Songs (P. B. Shelley, Byron, T. Campbell), T, harp, 1974; Sun, Moon and Stars (song cycle, T. Traherne), S, pf, 1977; My Dark Heart (Petrarch, trans. J. M. Synge), S, fl + a fl, ob, eng hn, vn, va, vc, 1981; L'horloge (C. Baudelaire), S, cl, pf, 1982; 3 songs: 2 Songs in Memory of W. B. Yeats (W. H. Auden), It's no go (L. MacNeice), S, pf, 1985; Butterflies (J. Rae), Mez, harp, 1986

ORCHESTRAL

Concertino, pf, chamber orch, 1928, rev. 1929–30; Sym., 1928–9, withdrawn; The Land, suite, 1929; Dialogue, pf, orch, 1940–41; Theme and Variations, str orch, 1942–3; Puck Fair [suite from the ballet], 1943; Concertino, cl, str orch, 1945; Sym., 1945–8, withdrawn; Concertino, pf, str orch, 1949; Concertino, bn, str orch, 1950–51; Nocturne, 1950–51; Proud Thames (Coronation Ov.), 1952; Sym., double str orch, 1953; Double Conc., ob, bn, str orch, 1955–6; Serenata concertante, vn, orch, 1962; Variazioni concertante, ob, cl, bn, hn, str orch, 1964–5; An Essex Ov., 1966; Music for Ww and Brass, timp, 1966; 3 Cloudscapes, 1968; Genesis, 1972–3, withdrawn; Epyllion, vc, str orch, 1974–5; Sinfonietta, 1976; Romanza, va, inst ens, 1979; Little Sym., 1980; Music for Str, 1981–2; Concertino, cl, small orch, 1984; Life Story, str orch, 1985

CHAMBER AND INSTRUMENTAL

Str qts: no.1, 1932–3; no.2, 1936; no.3, 1938; no.4, 1939–43; no.5, 1948; no.6, 1950; no.7, 1954–6; no.8, 1966; no.9, 1968–9; no.10, 1971–2; no.11, 1976–7; no.12, 1979; Quartetto corto, 1983
Other works for 3–9 insts: Qnt, ob, str, 1932; Reflections, ob, cl, va, harp, 1960; Qnt, cl, str, 1963; Sonatina, str qt, 1963; Qt, ob, vn, va, vc, 1972; Piccola musica, str trio, 1980; Trittico, 2 ob, bn, hpd, 1980; Qnt, fl, ob, cl, bn, hn, 1981; Tribute [for Iris Lemare's 80th birthday], vn solo, 2 fl, 2 ob, 2 cl, 2 bn, 1983
Works for 1–2 insts: Prelude, Interlude and Fugue, 2 vn, 1934; 5 Pieces, va, 1937; Sonata, va, pf, 1937–8; A Country Town, 9 pieces, pf, 1939; Sonata, vn, pf, 1943; Divertimento, vc, pf, 1944; Duo: Theme and Variations, vn, vc, 1951; 4 pieces, db, 1954; Variations on a Theme from Vaughan Williams's 'Job', vc, 1957; 4 pieces, pf, 1962: Conversation, Moonlight Night, Mill Race, The Yaffle; Notebook, hpd, 1965; Sonatina, hpd, 1965; 6 Pieces, vn, 1966; Preludio, Fugato and Finale, pf, 4 hands, 1967; Conversations, cl, va, 1967–8; Music for Db and Pf, 1970; 3 Preludes, vn, pf, 1970; 3 Bagatelles, ob, hpd, 1972; Touchstone, ob, chamber org, 1975; Morning, Noon and Night, harp, 1976; Contemplation, vc, pf, 1978; Colloquy, fl, pf, 1979; Fantasia, cl, pf, 1980; 5 Sketches, va, 1983; Excursion, bn, 1984; Narration, vc, 1984

Principal publishers: Boosey & Hawkes, Chappell, Chester, Faber, Lengnick, OUP
MSS in St Hilda's College, Oxford; some material in GB-Lmic

BIBLIOGRAPHY

Fuller-LeFanuRM (N. LeFanu)
A. Macnaghten: 'Elizabeth Maconchy', MT, xcvi (1955), 298–302
E. Maconchy: 'A Composer Speaks', Composer, no.42 (1971–2), 25–9
Elizabeth Maconchy, Arts Council videotape dir. M. Williams (London, 1985)
N. LeFanu: 'Elizabeth Maconchy', Composer, no.83 (1987), 113–14

HUGO COLE, JENNIFER R. DOCTOR

McTee, Cindy (b Tacoma, WA, 20 Feb 1953). American composer. She studied with

David Robbins at the Pacific Lutheran University, Tacoma (BM 1975), and with Jacob Druckman, Krzysztof Penderecki and Bruce McCombie at Yale University (MM 1978), and gained the PhD in 1981 under the direction of Richard Hervig at the University of Iowa; she also studied with Penderecki, Marek Stachowski and Krystyna Moszumańska-Nazar at the Kraków Conservatory. She taught at the Pacific Lutheran University, 1981–4, then at North Texas State University, Denton, where she became associate professor of music. She has received a Goddard Liebeson Fellowship from the American Academy and Institute of Arts and Letters, a Senior Fulbright Scholar Lecturing award in electronic music at the Kraków music academy and other awards, and commissions from the Barlow Endowment for Music Composition, the American Guild of Organists and other organizations.

McTee composes for both acoustic and electronic media, and her works have been performed in Asia and Europe as well as the USA.

WORKS
selective list

Orch: Unisonance, 1978; On Wings of Infinite Night, 1985; Circuits, 1990 [also arr. wind ens]

Chamber: 3 Miniatures, cl, 1973; Organism, org, 1975; Str Qt no.1, 1976; Wind Qnt no.1, 1981; Octonal Escalade, 20 tpt, 1985; Circle Music, I–IV, 1988: I, va, pf, II, fl, pf, III, bn, pf, IV, hn, pf; Circuits, wind ens, 1990; The Twittering Machine, chamber ens/chamber orch, 1993; California Counterpoint, wind ens, 1993 [arr. of The Twittering Machine]; Capriccio per Krzysztof Penderecki, vn, 1993; Stepping Out, fl, clapping hands, 1993

Vocal: King Lear Fragments, Bar, b fl, perc, 1980; Frau Musica, Mez, chorus, orch, 1983; Songs of Spring and the Moon, S, 8 insts, 1983; Psalm cxlii (Threnody), medium v, org, 1984

Elec: Metal Music, computer-generated tape, 1989; 8 études, 4 insts, tape, 1991; Circle Music V, trbn, tape, 1992; Etudes, a sax, tape, 1992; 'M' Music, computer-generated tape, 1992

Principal publisher: MMB Music

ELIZABETH HINKLE-TURNER

Maddison [née Tindal], **(Katherine Mary) Adela** (*b* 15 Dec 1866; *d* Ealing, 12 June 1929). Irish composer. A friend and pupil of Fauré, Maddison moved to Paris from London in the late 1890s. There she gave concerts of her works and musical parties, moving in circles which included Debussy, Delius and the Polignacs. She spent several years in Germany and her opera *Der Talisman* was performed to enthusiastic reviews at the Leipzig Stadttheater in 1910. She returned to England during World War I and became involved with Rutland Boughton's Glastonbury Festivals. Much of her music has not survived; her songs display a lyrical individuality and power.

WORKS
printed works published in London

Operas: Der Talisman (after L. Fulda), Leipzig, Stadttheater, 1910; The Children of Lir, 1920; Ippolita in the Hills (M. Hewlett), 1920s

Inst: Brer Rabbit Polka, pf (1882); Diana Waltz, pf (1888); Irische Ballade, orch, 1909; Pf Qnt (1925)

Songs: For a Day and a Night (A. C. Swinburne) (1888); 2 mélodies (Sully Prudhomme [R. F. A. Prudhomme], F. E. J. Coppée) (1893); 12 songs, opp.9–10 (E. W. Wheeler, Swinburne, D. G. Rossetti, A. Tennyson, P. B. Shelley, H. Heine) (1895); 3 mélodies (E. Harancourt) (1915); National Hymn for India (K. N. Das Gupta) (1917); If you would have it so (R. Tagore) (1919); Tears (Wang Sen-ju) (1924); other songs

SOPHIE FULLER

Mageau, Mary (Jane) (*b* Milwaukee, 4 Sept 1934). Australian composer of American origin. She studied at DePaul University, Chicago, and the University of Michigan (MMus); her principal teachers were Leon Stein, Leslie Bassett and Ross Lee Finney. She taught in Minnesota and Wisconsin before going to Australia in 1974; she married the architect Kenneth White and became a permanent resident in Australia. She has been particularly prominent in lobbying for opportunities for women composers. Her major work is the Triple Concerto (1990), composed for the Queensland SO, but she has also composed chamber, keyboard, choral and educational works.

WORKS
selective list

Stage: Mighty Skity, or The Rabbit who Knew too Much (children's opera, R. Woodhouse), 1985; Australis 1788 (music drama, J. Bradhurst), 1987

Orch: Variegations, 1968; Montage, 1970; Conc. grosso, fl, vc, hpd, timp, perc, str orch, 1982; Conc., hpd, str orch, 1988; Dance Suite, vc, str orch, 1989; Triple Conc., vn, vc, pf, orch, 1990

Choral: Mass for Our Lady of Victory, unison chorus, org, 1967; A Chime of Windbells, chorus, fl, perc, 1971; Lacrimae, chorus, perc, 1972; Community Mass, chorus, congregation, org, 1978; The Line Always There, female chorus, fl, perc, pf 4 hands, 1981; Serenade, str qt, 1986

Chamber and solo inst: Cycles and Series, pf, 1970; Fantasy Music, vn, pf, 1972; Forensis, fl, ob, cl, bn, 2 perc, 1973; Forecasts, pf, 1974; Australia's Animals, 6 solos, pf, 1976; Contrasts, vc, 1976; Ragtime, pf, 1977; Cityscapes, pf, 1978; Dialogues, cl, vc, pf, 1979; Pacific Ports, pf 4 hands, 1979; Statement and Variations, va, 1979; March, pf 4 hands, 1980; Sonata concertante, fl, vc, hpd, 1980; Cantilena, fl, perc, 1981; Winter's Shadow, hpd,

Alma Maria Mahler

chimes, 1983; Soliloquy, pf, 1984; Concert Pieces, pf trio, 1985

Elec: I Never Saw Another Butterfly, 5 songs, S, cl, va, pf, 2-track tape, 1972; Arches, cl, vn, pf, tape; Interaction, cl, tape

GRAHAM HAIR, GRETA MARY HAIR

Mahler(-Werfel) [née Schindler], **Alma Maria** (*b* Vienna, 31 Aug 1879; *d* New York, 11 Dec 1964). Austrian composer. A daughter of the Viennese landscape-painter Emil Schindler, she was educated privately under the supervision of her mother (whose remarriage to the painter Carl Moll, after Schindler's death in 1892, Alma bitterly resented). After studying music with Joseph Labor, Alma took composition lessons with Alexander Zemlinsky. Thoughts of marriage to Zemlinsky were dropped in 1901 after she met Gustav Mahler, then aged 41 and recently appointed Director of the Vienna Hofoper. She married him in 1902, agreeing to abandon her compositional aspirations. Their complex and often unhappy marriage lasted until his death in 1911; of their two daughters only Anna Mahler, the sculptor, survived. In 1910 marital crisis had played its part in persuading Gustav to select and have published five of Alma's songs. Other song collections appeared in 1915 and 1924, in which year she published her influential edi-

tion of his letters and the facsimile manuscript of his uncompleted Tenth Symphony. By that time, following an intense relationship with the painter Oskar Kokoschka, she had married and then divorced the architect Walter Gropius (their daughter, Manon, died in 1935). In 1929 she married her third husband, the poet and novelist Franz Werfel, with whom she subsequently fled Nazi Austria, via France, for America, arriving there in 1940. In California Alma became an influential, if contentious, hostess to the emigré community that included Thomas Mann, Bruno Walter and Arnold Schoenberg. She maintained a similar lifestyle in New York after Werfel's death in 1945 (she declined to attend his funeral, saying 'I never go'). She died in 1964 and was buried beside her daughter Manon in Grinzing, near Vienna.

Few have so effectively made themselves a legend in their own lifetime. Of Alma's two widely read autobiographical works, the first dealt specifically with her life with Gustav Mahler. The frankness and, by period standards, indiscretion of that book, published in 1940 (but written earlier), was matched by that of her later autobiography (first published in 1959 in an abridged English edition as *And the Bridge is Love*). These confirmed her rumoured attraction to 'great men' and her tendency to discard them in a manner conventionally permitted only to men in their dealings with women. The problem was compounded not only by her insistence upon the style of a Nietzsche-inspired New Woman of the 1890s but also by her sympathy with Mussolini and certain German fascists (not Hitler) whose anti-semitism she affected to share, to the distress of Werfel (a Jew).

Her songs, in a *fin-de-siècle* style that owes something to Hugo Wolf and Zemlinsky, are striking for their often bold chromatic harmony, whose lyrical effect is occasionally comparable with that of the earliest songs of Schoenberg. The five songs published in 1924, to texts by Novalis, Bierbaum, Dehmel and Werfel ('Der Erkennende'), are characterized by declamatory passages and an expansive, hymnic manner. Of 11 surviving songs attributable originally to the period about 1900–01, nine were published (by Universal) as Fünf Lieder (1910) and Vier Lieder (1915). Her last published song-collection, containing the Werfel setting composed in 1915, was Fünf Gesänge (published by Weinberger in 1924). No other works are known to survive.

WRITINGS

ed.: *Gustav Mahler Briefe 1879–1911* (Vienna, 1924)
ed.: *Gustav Mahler: Erinnerungen und Briefe* (Amsterdam, 1940; Eng. trans. as *Gustav Mahler: Memories and Letters*, 1946, 3/1975, ed. D. Mitchell and K. Martner)
And the Bridge is Love (London and New York, 1959) [with E. B. Ashton]
Mein Leben (Frankfurt, 1960)

BIBLIOGRAPHY

W. Storey Smith: 'The Songs of Alma Mahler', *Chord and Discord*, ii (1950), 74–8
B. Colerus: 'Alma Mahler', *Die schöne Wienerin*, ed. G. Sebestyen (Munich, 1971), 168–82
P. Mahony: 'Alma Mahler-Werfel', *Composer*, xlv (1972), 13–17
W. Sorrell: 'Alma Mahler-Werfel: Body and Mind', *Three Women, Lives of Sex and Genius* (London and New York, 1975), 3–69
R. Schollum: 'Die Lieder von Alma Maria Schindler-Mahler', *ÖMz*, xxxiv (1979), 544–51
G. Perle: 'Mein geliebtes Almschi . . . ', *ÖMz*, xxxv (1980), 2–15
S. Filler: 'A Composer's Wife as Composer: the Songs of Alma Mahler', *Journal of Musicological Research*, iv (1983), 427–42
K. Monson: *Alma Mahler: Muse to Genius – from Fin-de-Siècle Vienna to Hollywood's Heyday* (Boston, 1983)
B. Wessling: *Alma: Gefährtin von Gustav Mahler, Oskar Kokoschka, Walter Gropius, Franz Werfel* (Düsseldorf, 1983)
F. Xenakis: 'Alma Schindler, 1880–1964', *Zut, on a encore oublié Madame Freud* (Paris, 1985), 191–276
S. Filler: 'Alma Mahler: "Der Erkennende" ', *Historical Anthology of Music by Women*, ed. James R. Briscoe (Bloomington, IN, 1987), 245–7
F. Giroud: *Alma Mahler, ou l'art d'être aimée* (Paris, 1988)
S. Filler: *Gustav and Alma Mahler: a Guide to Research* (New York and London, 1989)
S. Keegan: *The Bride of the Wind: the Life and Times of Alma Mahler-Werfel* (London, 1991)

PETER FRANKLIN

Maier [Maier-Schiatti, Maier-Schiati], **Katerina** (*fl* St Petersburg, *c*1800). Composer and pianist of Italian parentage. Daughter of Luigi Schiatti, a prominent violinist who arrived in Russia in 1760 and was employed in the main court orchestra, she lived in St Petersburg for most of her composing life. The earliest reference to her as a composer appears in 1795 in a St Petersburg journal (*Magazin obshchepoleznykh znaniy i izobretiniy s prisovokupleniyem modnago zhurnala, raskrashenniïkh risunkov, i muzïkal'nïkh not*; 'Magazine of Generally Useful Knowledge and Inventions, Supplemented by a Fashion Journal with Coloured Pictures and Musical Scores') which advertises the publication of a set of three keyboard sonatas. The publisher J. D. Gerstenberg issued some ten further keyboard works by her over the following three-year period, principally fantasias and

Maria Malibran: lithograph

sets of variations based on popular songs of the day. In 1803, as part of a series of weekly concerts organized by A. G. Teplov, she performed as soloist in a keyboard concerto (now lost) of her own composition, after which date no further references to her as either composer or pianist are known.

BIBLIOGRAPHY

R.-A. Mooser: *Annales de la musique et des musiciens en Russie au XVIIIme siècle* (Geneva, 1948–51)
N. J. Yandell: *Keyboard Music in Russia During the Late Eighteenth and Early Nineteenth Centuries* (diss., U. of Oxford, forthcoming)

NIGEL J. YANDELL

Malibran [née Garcia], **Maria(-Felicia)** (*b* Paris, 24 March 1808; *d* Manchester, 23 Sept 1836). Spanish mezzo-soprano and composer, the elder daughter of the tenor Manuel Garcia and sister of Pauline Viardot. Her first stage appearance was in 1814 at Naples in Ferdinando Paer's *Agnese*. She studied with her father, whose harshness towards her was notorious, and made her London début at the King's Theatre on 11 June 1825 in Rossini's *Il barbiere di Siviglia*. The same work opened the Garcia family's season at the Park Theatre, New York, on 29 November 1825. Maria's marriage to Eugène Malibran, contracted as a means of escape from her father, was a failure, and in 1827 she returned to Europe alone. She made her Paris début at the Théâtre Italien in *Semiramide* on 8 April 1828, reappeared at the King's Theatre in 1829 in *Otello*, and then sang alternately in Paris and London until 1832, when she went to Italy. She first sang the title role of Bellini's *Norma* at Naples in February 1834, repeating it for her début at La Scala on 15 May. On 29 March 1836 she married the violinist Charles de Bériot. She died only months later following a riding accident when she was pregnant. On 17 March 1837 the cantata *In morte di María Malibrán* was performed at La Scala, Milan; the libretto was by A. Piazza and the music by Pietro Coppola, Donizetti, Mercadante, Pacini and Nicola Vaccai.

Malibran liked to include in her private recitals songs in which she would accompany herself on the guitar or at the piano. She would very often perform her own compositions, which were widely published in French, English and Italian editions and earned her the name of the 'Sévigné de la romance'. Her *romances*, nocturnes, *ariettes*, ballads and Tyrolean songs were published individually and embellished with lithographs. Her posthumous album *Dernières pensées musicales* (which contains ten *romances* and two Italian songs) was published in Paris (1836) and London (1837).

BIBLIOGRAPHY

FétisB; *FétisBS*; *Grove1* (J. Marshall); *SchillingE*; *SchmidlD*

R. Parkinson: *A Sermon Preached . . . the day after the funeral of the late Mme Malibran . . . in the Collegiate Church of Manchester* (Manchester, 1836)

J. Thompson: *Memoirs of the Public and Private Life of the Celebrated Maria Malibran* (London, 1836)

H. Berlioz: Article on *Dernières pensées musicales*, *Revue et gazette musicale* (2 July 1837)

Part of the chansonnette 'Rataplan' (Paris: E. Troupenas, c1832) by Maria Malibran with a lithograph by Mlle Formenlin after F. Grenier

A. de Musset: 'Concert de Mademoiselle Garcia', *Revue des deux mondes* (1 Nov 1839)
—— : 'Stances à la Malibran', *Poésies nouvelles* (Paris, 1852)
M. Sterling-Mackinlay: *Garcia the Centenarian and his Times* (Edinburgh, 1908)
L. Héritte-Viardot: *Memories and Adventures*, trans. E. S. Buchheim (London, 1913; Fr. orig., Paris, 1922, as L. Héritte de la Tour: *Mémoires de Louise Héritte-Viardot: . . . notes . . . sur Garcia, Pauline Viardot, La Malibran, Louise Héritte-Viardot, et leur entourage*)
A. Flamant: *L'enchanteresse errante: La Malibran* (Paris, 1937)
G. Lauri-Volpi: *Voci parallele* (Milan, 1955)
T. Marix-Spire, ed.: *Lettres inédites de George Sand et de Pauline Viardot 1839–49* (Paris, 1959)
C. de Reparaz: *María Malibrán* (Madrid, 1976)
A. FitzLyon: *Maria Malibran: Diva of the Romantic Age* (London, 1987)

XOÁN M. CARREIRA, ELIZABETH FORBES

Mallá, Florentina (*b* Čakovice, 14 July 1891; *d* Prague, 7 June 1973). Czech composer and pianist. She studied the piano at the Prague Conservatory with Josef Jiránek, graduating in 1913. After some years as a solo pianist and piano teacher, she studied composition with the expressionist composer Vítězslav Novák and became receptive to the new ideas of the time about expanded tonality and atonality. Her output, though small, is notable for its spontaneity and strict musical logic. She gave up composing under the Communist regime. Her music reviews in Czech journals confirm her up-to-date orientation. Mallá was the accompanist for Emmy Destinn's last recitals in Prague in 1929.

WORKS
selective list

Pět písní s průvodem klavíru pro vyšší hlas [5 Songs for High Voice and Piano] (Prague, 1918); Meistersinger, pf, 1925; Sonatina, pf, 1930; Preludium, pf, 1944, rev. 1945, 1948; over 50 songs on Cz. and Ger. symbolist texts; educational pf music

BIBLIOGRAPHY
ČSHS
K. Emingerová: 'Pět písní F. Mallé' [5 Songs by Mallá], *Ženský svět*, xxii (1918), 3–4
—— : 'Žena v hudbě' [Woman in Music], *Ženský svět*, xxvii (1923), 19–20
R. Rosenkrancová: 'F. Mallá', *Umělec*, ii (1946), 46
A. Šerých: 'Po přeslici' [On the Distaff Side], *Opus musicum*, xx/2 (1988), 61–4, p.xvii
—— : 'Ema Destinnová, Florentině Mallé', *Opus musicum*, xx/10 (1988), pp.i–v

ANNA ŠERÝCH

Malmlöf-Forssling, Carin (*b* Gävle, 6 March 1916). Swedish composer. She studied counterpoint (1938–40) and composition (1941–3) at the Kungliga Musikaliska Akademien in Stockholm, graduating as a music teacher in 1942. In 1957 she studied composition with Nadia Boulanger in Paris. From 1952 she worked in Falun and was elected to the Society of Swedish Composers in 1970 – for many years she was its only woman member. Her music has a strongly personal, expressive touch. Her song settings, brief and intense, are thoroughly sensitive to their texts; for this reason in particular she is often called 'the master of the miniature', but even her large-scale works are notable for their idiomatic instrumental sonorities.

WORKS
selective list

Orch: Revival, str orch, 1976; Flowings, 1985
Choral: Biblia Dalecarlica, reciter, S, T, B, mixed chorus, cl, 1971; Ecce jubile, T, male vv, tape, 1975; 3 bevingade ord [Familiar Quotations] (Lat. text), mixed chorus, 1984
Other vocal: Litania, 3 songs, 1v, pf, 1974; 6 sånger om ljus och mörker [Songs about Light and Dark], S, pf, 1975; 3 upplevelser [Experiences], S, fl, 1976; Vollmond (3 Haiku), 1979; 3 latinska sentenser [Latin Maxims], S, fl, hn, pf, 1986; Aum, S, 1987; Shanti, S, orch, 1990
Chamber and solo inst: Sonata svickel, fl, 1964; Lalendo, vc, 1970; Viewpoints, pf, 1979; Orizzonte, hn, 1981; Silverkvartetten (Str Qt no.1), 1988

EVA ÖHRSTRÖM

Malumbres, Maria Dolores (*b* Alfaro, 11 April 1931). Spanish composer. She was first taught music by her father, a violinist, and afterwards became a pupil of Fernando Remacha for composition and piano and Paquita Velerda for piano. She later studied contemporary techniques with Carmelo Bernaola, whose ideas have influenced her works written after 1982. The greater part of her output consists of chamber works, among which are pieces for two pianos and percussion, solo instruments and piano, including *Diálogos* for guitar and piano, a wind quintet *Pax Domine*, a string trio and quartet, and *Collage* for flute, clarinet, cello and piano. She has also written keyboard works, including five pieces for piano *Homenaje a Remacha*, and *Tríptico* for harpsichord.

TERESA CASCUDO

Mamlok, Ursula (*b* Berlin, 1 Feb 1928). American composer and teacher of German birth. She studied the piano and composition as a child in Berlin; when her family moved to Ecuador for a year she continued her studies there. After emigrating to the USA in 1941, she finished her schooling in New York, where she continued to live. She became an American citizen in 1945. At the Mannes College (1942–6) she was a pupil of George Szell and at the Manhattan School of Music (BM 1957, MM 1958) she studied with Vittorio Giannini; she also studied privately with Stefan Wolpe, Roger Sessions, Edward Steuermann and Ralph Shapey. She has taught at New York University (1967–76), Kingsborough Community College (1972–5) and the Manhattan School (from 1974). Her awards include two NEA grants (1974, 1981), a BMI Commendation of Excellence (1987), the Walter Hinrichsen Award (1989), prizes for recordings and commissions from organizations including the Koussevitzky Foundation and the San Francisco SO. *When Summer Sang* was chosen to represent the USA at the 1984 International Rostrum of Composers. *Die Laterne*, for soprano and chamber ensemble, is her contribution to the 'Pierrot Project' of the Schoenberg Institute at the University of Southern California.

Mamlok has always shown an affinity for chamber music and piano works, and has written many teaching pieces in these media. As a young composer she was greatly influenced by Schoenberg and his circle. The difficult and uncompromising String Quartet (1962) in particular invites comparison with the works of Elliott Carter. Elegantly crafted, her music has considerable nuance and delicacy as well as dramatic intensity. In her own words, she has consolidated 'old and new techniques which best serve to express the work at hand'. Examining the interplay of sonorities and silence, she writes eloquent music, more often gentle and reflective than harsh or aggressive. A 1987 retrospective concert at Merkin Hall, New York, drew attention to her works written between 1956 and 1986. Among her most frequently performed scores are *Panta rhei*, the Violin Sonata (1989), Five Intermezzi, *Girasol* and *Der Andreas Garten*, the last with texts by her husband, Gerard Mamlok. In addition, her thoughtful, deftly constructed, challenging pieces for students are important additions to the genre.

WORKS
printed works published in New York
unless otherwise stated

Orch: Conc., str, 1950; Grasshoppers (6 Humoresques) [arr. of pf piece], 1957; Divertimento, youth orch, 1958; Ob Conc., 1976 [arr. of chamber work, 1974]; Concertino, ww qnt, perc, str orch, 1985 (1989); Constellations, 1993

Vocal: 5 Songs from Stray Birds, song cycle, S, fl + pic + a fl, vc, 1963 (1990); Haiku Settings, S, fl, 1967; Mosaics, S, C, T, B, chorus, 1969; Der Andreas Garten (G. Mamlok), Mez, fl + pic + a fl, harp, 1987 (1989); Die Laterne, S, fl, cl, vn, vc, pf, 1989 (1993); songs

Chamber and solo inst: Grasshoppers (6 Humoresques), pf, 1956 (Bryn Mawr, PA, 1993), orchd 1957; Ww Qnt, 1956; Lament, 4 vc, 1957, rev. 1988; Sonatina, 2 cl, 1957; 8 Easy Duets, 2 cl, 1958; Variations, fl, 1961; Composition, vc, 1962; Designs, vn, pf, 1962; Str Qt, 1962; Concert Piece for 4, fl, ob, va, perc, 1964; Music, va, harp, 1965; Sculpture I, pf, 1965; Capriccios, ob, pf, 1968 (1975); Polyphony, cl, 1968; Sintra, a fl, vc, 1969; Variations and Interludes, perc qt, 1971 (1978); Polyphony II, eng hn, 1972; Conc., ob, perc, 2 pf, 1974, orchd 1976; Sextet, fl + pic, cl, b cl, vn, db, pf, 1977 (1978); Festive Sounds, ww qnt, 1978 (1978); When Summer Sang, fl, cl, vn, vc, pf, 1980 (1987); Panta rhei (Time in Flux), vn, vc, pf, 1981 (1982); Str Qnt, 1981; Fantasie Variations, vc, 1983; From my Garden, vn/va, 1983 (1987); Alariana, rec/fl, cl, bn, vn, vc, 1985; 3 Bagatelles, pf/hpd, 1987 (1991); 5 Bagatelles, cl, vn, vc, 1988 (1991); Music for Stony Brook, fl + a fl, vn, vc (1989); Rhapsody, cl, va, pf, 1989 (1992); Vn Sonata, 1989 (1992); Girasol (Sunflowers), fl, cl, vn, va, vc, pf, 1990 (1992); 5 Intermezzi, gui, 1991 (1992); other works for solo inst or small ens; teaching and recital pieces for pf, pf duo

Elec: Sonar Trajectory, tape, 1966

Principal publishers: ACA, C. F. Peters

BIBLIOGRAPHY
KompA-Z; *LePageWC*, iii
D. L. Sills: 'Three Sides of a Coin: an Appreciation', *ILWC Journal* (1993), Oct, 6–10
BARBARA A. PETERSEN

Mana Zucca [Zuckermann, Augusta; Zuckermann, Gussie] (*b* New York, 25 Dec 1885; *d* Miami, 8 March 1981). American composer and pianist. She changed her name to Mana Zucca in her teens and became a protégée of the pianist and teacher Alexander Lambert; according to her unpublished memoirs she performed with major orchestras in New York before the age of ten (although this and other claims in her memoirs have not been verified). In 1902 she played an arrangement of Liszt's 14th Hungarian Rhapsody with Frank Damrosch as part of his concert series for young people at Carnegie Hall. About 1907 she went to Europe, where she met several prominent musicians and gave successful concert tours with the Spanish violinist Juan Manon. Her lively descriptions of Teresa Carreño, Ferruccio Busoni, Leopold Godowsky and the composition teacher Max Vogrich were published in American music magazines. She also performed as a singer, notably in Franz Lehár's *Der Graf von Luxemburg* in London (1919). After her marriage in 1921, and especially after 1941, Mana Zucca's musical activities were concentrated in her home town of Miami.

On her return to the USA in 1915, she began to publish her compositions. Her privately issued catalogue of published works lists approximately 390 titles (all undated), though she claimed to have published around 1100 works and to have written 1000 more. Included in the catalogue are the operas *Hypatia* and *Queue of Ki-Lu* (both *c*1920), the Piano Concerto op.49 (1919) and Violin Concerto op.224 (1955), 172 songs, three choral works, more than 20 chamber works and numerous educational pieces. She was a gifted melodist. Many of her songs performed by leading singers in the 1920s and 30s: Johanna Gadski favoured the *Kinder-Lieder*; Amelita Galli-Curci often sang *Le petit papillon*; and the most famous, *I Love Life* (1923), was performed by Lawrence Tibbett, John Charles Thomas and Nelson Eddy. *Honey Lamb*, *There's Joy in my Heart*, *Time and Time Again* and *The Big Brown Bear* were also well known. Many of her songs with Yiddish texts, among them *Rachem* (1919) and *Nichevo* (1921), were dramatic set-pieces. Mana Zucca's more serious ambitions as a composer met limited yet noteworthy recognition: the Cincinnati SO performed *Novelette* and *Fugato humoresque* in 1917; the New York PO also played the latter piece in 1917; Mana Zucca herself gave the first performance of her Piano Concerto on 20 August 1919 with the Los Angeles SO; and in 1955 the American SO gave the première of the Violin Concerto. Her manuscripts and papers are at the University of Miami; her principal publishers are Boston Music, Congress Music and G. Schirmer.

BIBLIOGRAPHY

'Mana Zucca, Humorist', *Musical Courier*, lxxv/3 (1917), 42

H. Brower: 'American Women Pianists: their Views and Achievements', *MusAm*, xxviii/26 (1918), 18–19

M. Stanley: 'Mana Zucca Tells why Rachem was Written', *MusAm*, xxxi/4 (1919), 19

J. T. Howard: *Our American Music* (New York, 1931, 4/1965)

JUDITH TICK

Manning, Kathleen Lockhart (*b* Hollywood, CA, 24 Oct 1890; *d* Los Angeles, 20 March 1951). American composer and singer. She studied composition in Paris with Moritz Moszkowski in 1908 and then toured France and England between 1909 and 1914, spending the 1911–12 season as a singer with the Hammerstein Opera Company in London. She performed briefly in the USA in 1926 and joined ASCAP in 1932. As a composer, Manning specialized in vocal compositions, for which she usually wrote her own texts, and was influenced by the orientalisms used by impressionist composers. This is most apparent in *Nang-Ping* and *Pagoda Bells* (from *Chinese Impressions*). Several of her song cycles evoke the cities and countries of their titles and one of these, *In the Luxembourg Gardens* (from the *Sketches of Paris*), was so popular that she arranged it for women's choir.

WORKS

SONGS

unless otherwise stated, words by Manning and printed works published in New York

The Water Lily: Louis XV Love Song (New York and London, 1923); Japanese Ghost Songs: In the Bamboo, The Maid of Mystery (1924); Sketches of Paris, song cycle (1925); 2 Sketches of Childhood: The Truant, Mother's Cookie Jar (1926); Autumn Leaves (1929); Chinese Impressions: 1 Pagoda Bells, 2 Incense, 3 Chinoise, 4 Nang-Ping, 5 Hop-Li, the Rickshaw Man (1931), no.5 arr. women's chorus 4vv (1933); 5 Fragments: Streets, Image, Miss Wing-fu, Silhouette, Voyage (1931); Nostalgia (1931); Shoes (1931); Vignettes, 25 songs (1933); Sketches of New York, 1936; 4 Songs of Bilitis, high v, pf (1944)

OTHER WORKS

Stage: Operetta in Mozartian Style; Mr Wu (L. J. Milu), 1925–6; For the Soul of Rafael

Pf: Playtime, 1924; Sundown Tales, 1924; 3 Dance Impressions; In the Summer

Also 4 sym. poems, 1 pf conc., 1 str qt

Principal publishers: Boosey & Hawkes, Composers' Music Corporation, C. Fischer, G. Schirmer

BARBARA L. TISCHLER

Manziarly, Marcelle de (*b* Kharkiv, 1/13 Oct 1899; *d* Ojai, CA, 12 May 1989). French composer. A pupil of Nadia Boulanger in Paris, she later followed courses in conducting with Felix Weingartner in Basle (1930–31) and piano with Isabelle Vengerova in New York (1943). Her career was divided between France and the USA: she appeared as a pianist and conductor in America, and taught privately in Paris and New York. She gave the first performance of her Piano Concerto, with the Concertgebouw under Casella, at the 1933 ISCM Festival; but the earliest of her works to achieve wider fame was the *Sonate pour Notre-Dame de Paris*, an orchestral piece sparked off by the liberation of the French capital in 1944. The music is in D major, but the harmony encompasses modal melodic lines. Further extensions to tonality followed: the Sonata for two pianos (1946) is, in its central section, tetratonal; *Musique pour orchestre* (1950) employs an 11-note scale based on C; *Trilogue* (1957) includes atonal serial features; and *Incidences*

(1964) is based on magic squares that govern aspects of melody, harmony and rhythm.

WORKS
selective list

Stage: La femme en flèche, chamber opera, 1954
Orch: Pf Conc., 1932; Sonate pour Notre-Dame de Paris, 1944–5; Musique pour orchestre, small orch, 1950; Incidences, pf, orch, 1964
Chamber: Str Qt, 1943; Trio, fl, vc, pf, 1952; Trilogue, a fl, va da gamba, hpd, 1957; Dialogue, vc, pf, 1970; Périple, ob, pf, 1972
Vocal: 3 fables de La Fontaine, 1935; Choeurs pour enfants, 1938; Poèmes en trio (L. de Vilmorein), 3 female vv, pf, 1940; Duos, 2 S/T, pf, 1952; Duos, S, cl, 1953; 3 chants, S, pf, 1954; 2 odes de Grégoire de Narek, C, pf, 1955; 3 sonnets de Pétrarque, Bar, pf, 1958; Le cygne et le cuisinier, 4 solo vv, pf, 1959
Pf: Mouvement, 1935; Arabesque, 1937; Toccata, 1939; Bagatelle, 1940; Sonata, 2 pf, 1946; 6 études, 1949; Stances, 1967

Principal publishers: Associated, Durand, Heugel, Salabert

Marbé, Myriam Lucia (*b* Bucharest, 9 April 1931). Romanian composer. She studied composition with Mihail Jora and Leon Klepper and instrumentation with Theodor Rogalski at the Bucharest Conservatory (1944–54). She remained in Bucharest, becoming music editor at the Cinema Studio (1953–4) and professor of composition at the conservatory (1954–88), and attended the Darmstadt summer schools in 1968, 1969 and 1972. She is a member of the Romanian Composers' Union. She has taught courses in composition in several other countries, including Germany and the Netherlands. Her many awards include prizes at the GEDOK competition in Mannheim (1961, 1966, 1970), six first prizes from the Composers' Union of Romania (1970–82), the Bernier prize of the Académie des Beaux-Arts, Paris (1972), the Romanian Academy prize (1977) and the Heidelberg Künstlerinnen prize (1987).

In her early works Marbé adopted the latest avant-garde techniques, while still maintaining some freedom of expression. Acknowledging the limitations of conventional musical language, she attempted in works such as *Ritual pentru setea pămintului* ('Ritual for the Thirst of the Earth'; 1968) to replace musical sounds with words; later, however, she not only accepted these limitations but took veritable pleasure in them, as for example in the concertos for viola (1977) and for harpsichord (1978) and in *Les oiseaux artificiels* (1979). She has also shown a concern for certain fundamental aspects of music: with temporal issues, in *Le temps inévitable* (1968–71) and *Timpul regăsit* ('Time Rediscovered'; 1982), and specifically with remembrance, in *Jocus secundus* (1969). Some

works draw in a variety of sources: her Requiem, *Fra Angelico – Chagal – Voronet* (1990), combines texts from the Latin Mass for the Dead, the Byzantine Hymn of the Resurrection, a fragment of the *Kaddish* (the Hebrew prayer for the dead), old Romanian folklore rituals for the initiation of the dead, and the Greek word 'ania', which expresses the sorrow of the soul. Other works, such as *Trommelbass* (1985), *Sonata per due* (1985) and *E–Y–Thé* (1990), present the theme of human dignity in the face of a totalitarian system. In the 1990s Marbé has moved towards a simpler, more purified style, as for example in *Passages in the Wind* (1994).

Marbé's writings on music include articles in the Romanian periodical *Muzica* and an essay on the role of women in Romanian folklore (in *5. Jahre Internationales Festival Komponistinnen gestern–heute und 5th International Congress on Women in Music*, ed. R. Sperber and U. Feld, Heidelberg, 1989, pp.75ff).

WORKS
selective list

Vocal: Colind (T. Arghezi), 1v, pf, 1950; Madrigale din lirica japoneza (Jap. haiku), women's vv, 1964; Clime [Atmospheres] (I. Negoitescu), Mez, women's vv, children's vv, chamber orch, 1966; Ritual pentru setea pămintului [Ritual for the Thirst of the Earth] (Rom. folk texts), 7/14 solo vv, chorus, perc, prepared pf ad lib, 1968; Jocus secundus, cl, vn, va, vc, pf, perc, tape ad lib, small chorus, 1969; Vocabulaire I – chanson, S, cl, pf, prepared bells, 1974; Les oiseaux artificiels (after W. Shakespeare), cl, vn, va, vc, hpd + cel, spkr, 1979; Timpul regăsit [Time Rediscovered], S/T, ens, 1982; An die Musik (R. M. Rilke), A, fl, org, 1983; An die Sonne (Delphic hymn, Roumanian folk text), Mez, wind qnt, 1986; Sym. no.1 'Ur Ariadne' (Lat. poets, J. G. Herder, F. Nietzsche and others), Mez, sax, orch, 1988; Farbe und Klang (H. Heine, C. Morgenstern and others), song cycle, Mez, fl, hpd/gui/pf, 1989–90; Fra Angelico – Chagall – Voronet (Requiem), Mez, chorus, orch, 1990; Der Schätzer (P. Aristide), spkr, T, trbn, perc, qt, 1990; Stabat mater, 12vv, ens, 1991; Passages in the Wind (J. G. Brown), T, rec, vc, hpd, 1994
Orch: Musica festiva, divertimento, str, brass, perc, 1961; Le temps inévitable, pf, orch, 1971; Evocări, str, perc, 1976; Va Conc., 1977; Trium, 1978; Conc., va da gamba/vc, 1982; Sax Conc., 1986
Chamber, inst: Pf Sonata, 1956; Cl Sonata, 1961; Incantatio, cl, 1964; Sonata, 2 va, 1965; Le temps inévitable, pf, tape, 1968–71; Cyclus, fl, gui, other insts ad lib, 1974; Eine kleine Sonnenmusik, serenata, ens, 1974; La parabole du grenier I, pf/hpd/cel, 1975–6, rev. 1979; La parabole du grenier II, hpd, ens, 1977; Conc., hpd, 8 insts, 1978; Les musiques compatibles (Str Qt no.1), 1981; Sonata per due, fl, va, 1985; Trommelbass, str trio, drum, 1985; Str Qt no.2, 1985, reorchd str, 1986; Des-cantec, wind qnt, 1986; The World is a Stage . . ., cl, trbn, vn, db, perc, 1987; After Nau, vc, org, 1987; Lui Nau (Str Qt no.3), 1988; Kontakte, cl, vn, va, db, 1989; Diapente, 5 vc, 1990; E – Y – Thé, cl, 4 vc, 1990

Principal publishers: Breitkopf & Härkel, Editura Muzicală (Bucharest)

BIBLIOGRAPHY

CohenE; KompAZ

V. Cosma: 'Marbé, Myriam', Muzicieni români (Bucharest, 1970), 289–90

L. Danceanu: 'Portrait Myriam Marbé', Muzica, xxx/7 (1983), 41; Ger. trans. in H. Henck, G. Gronemeyer and D. Richards, eds., Ansätze zur Musik der Gegenwart, iv (Bergisch-Gladbach, 1984), 68

D. Gojowy: 'Myriam Marbé', Annäherungen an sieben Komponistinnen, ed. B. Sonntag and R. Matthei, ii (Kassel, 1987), 41–7

——: 'Zwischen Absolutem und Alltäglichen: Myriam Marbé im Gespräch', 5-Jahre Internationales Festival Komponistinnen gestern–heute und 5th International Congress on Women in Music, ed. R. Sperber and U. Feld (Heidelberg, 1989), 91ff

G. Gronemeyer: 'Myriam Lucia Marbé', Klangporträt, v, Musikfrauen e. V. Berlin (Berlin, 1990)

T. Beimel: Vom Ritual zur Abstraktion (Unna and Wuppertal, 1994)

THOMAS BEIMEL, VIOREL COSMA

Marcelli, Anaïs. See PERRIÈRE-PILTE, ANAÏS.

Marcello, Rosanna Scalfi (fl 1723–42). Italian singer and composer. A singer of Venetian arie di battello (simple strophic songs sung in gondolas), Rosanna Scalfi was taken, according to legend, as a singing pupil by the nobleman Benedetto Marcello in about 1723. It is said that he was enchanted with her voice, which he heard from his window overlooking the Grand Canal.

On 20 May 1728 the two were secretly wed in a religious ceremony performed by the patriarch of Venice, but because no civil ceremony was ever conducted, the marriage was considered null by the state. This caused Rosanna, who was named the primary beneficiary of Benedetto's estate when he died in 1739, to live her later years in destitution. On 1 February 1742, she filed suit against Benedetto's brother Alessandro for financial support. That same year, she appeared as Arbace in Paganelli's Artaserse at S Salvatore during the Ascension season.

She composed a set of 12 cantatas for alto and basso continuo (I-Rsc, preserved in A MS 3819; indexed in Selfridge-Field). Some of the texts are also credited to her. They are far simpler than Benedetto Marcello's numerous cantatas but show a basic mastery of compositional technique. Some of his dramatic cantatas with marked shifts of register appear to have been written for her. She is also known to have participated in private performances of Marcello's psalm settings.

BIBLIOGRAPHY

Choron-FayolleD†; FétisB; SchillingE†; SchmidlD

E. Selfridge-Field: The Music of Benedetto and Alessandro Marcello: a Thematic Catalogue with Commentary on the Composers, Repertory and Sources (Oxford, 1990)

ELEANOR SELFRIDGE-FIELD

Marchand, Margarethe. See DANZI, MARGARETHE.

Marez Oyens, Tera de (b Velsen, 5 Aug 1932). Dutch composer. She graduated from the Amsterdam Conservatory in 1953, where she studied the piano with Jan Odé. She then studied composition with Hans Henkemans and, later, electronic composition with Gottfried Koenig. She has performed as a concert pianist, led music improvisation groups for children and for adults and conducted amateur and professional choirs and orchestras. She has also produced music programmes for the radio and lectured internationally on music education, group improvisation and the role of women in music. Until 1988 she taught composition at the conservatory in Zwolle. She is a prolific composer with an output of over 200 works, including orchestral, chamber and electronic pieces, church and choral music, and children's operas. Many of her compositions were commissioned by the Dutch Ministry of Culture and various broadcasting networks.

WORKS
selective list

Orch and vocal-orch: Der chinesische Spiegel, T, orch, 1962; The Odyssey of Mr Good-Evil (oratorio, M. S. Arnoni), 4 solo vv, 2 nar, 2 mixed choruses, orch, 1981; Litany of the Victims of War, 1985; Sinfonia Testimonial, 1987; Symmetrical Memories, vc, orch, 1989; Confrontations, pf, orch, 1990

Chamber and solo inst: Deducties, ob, hpd, 1964; Conc., hn, tape, 1980; Ballerina on a Cliff, 1980; Str Qt Contrafactus, 1981; Octopus, b cl, perc, 1982; Charon's Gift, pf, tape, 1982; Möbius by Ear, va, pf, 1983; Valalan, gui, 1985; Parallels, perc, 1986; Gilgamesh Quartet, 4 trbn, 1988

Unacc. choral: Canto di parole, 1971; Bist du Bist II, 1973; From Death to Birth, 1974; Black, 1981; Abschied, 1983

Other vocal: Vignettes, S, fl, perc, pf, 1986; Thoughts of a Haunted Traveller, S, sax qt, 1990

For amateurs: Snapshots, orch, 1979; Free for All, 5 insts, 1986; Music for a Small Planet, 1v, 8 insts, perc, 1988

Principal publishers: Annie Bank, Broekmans & Van Poppel, Donemus, Harmonia

BIBLIOGRAPHY

T. de Marez Oyens: ' "Wenn ich Musik höre, dann ist es, als ob ich die Klänge einatme" ', Annäherungen an sieben Komponistinnen, ed. B. Sonntag and R. Matthei, v (Kassel, 1989), 53–60

Maria Antonia Walpurgis (right) with her brother Maximilian III Joseph of Bavaria (playing the viol) and his wife Maria Anna: group portrait (1758) by J. N. Grooth

E. Overweel: 'Tera de Marez Oyens', *Zes vrouwelijke componisten*, ed. H. Metzelaar (Zutphen, 1991), 199–232

HELEN METZELAAR, ROGIER STARREVELD

Margot, Dame, and **Maroie,** Dame (*fl* 13th century). Trouvères from Arras. They wrote a *jeu-parti* (debate song) which is preserved with music in two manuscripts (*F-AS* MS 657, f.141*v* and *I-Rvat* Reg. MS 1490, f.140*r*). The two different melodies preserved for the piece are unrelated.

BIBLIOGRAPHY

A. Långfors: *Recueil général des jeux-partis français* (Paris, 1926), no.144 [text edn]
M. V. Coldwell: 'Jougleresses and Trobairitz: Secular Musicians in Medieval France', *Women Making Music: the Western Art Tradition, 1150–1950*, ed. J. Bowers and J. Tick (Urbana and Chicago, 1986), 39–61, esp.50–51, 53, 54 [music edn]

MARIA V. COLDWELL

Maria Antonia Walpurgis, Electress of Saxony (*b* Munich, 18 July 1724; *d* Dresden, 23 April 1780). German princess, amateur musician and writer. The eldest daughter of the Elector Karl Albert of Bavaria (later Emperor Karl VII) and of Archduchess Maria Amalia of Austria, she received her first musical training in Munich from Giovanni Ferrandini and Giovanni Porta. After her marriage in 1747 to Friedrich Christian, later Elector of Saxony, she continued her studies in Dresden with Nicola Porpora and J. A. Hasse. She was also a painter and wrote poetry in French and Italian. From 1747 she was a member of the Arcadian Academy in Rome, and published her works as 'ETPA' (Ermelinda Talea Pastorella Arcada). With the Seven Years War and the death of the elector (1763) the cultural life at the Dresden court declined. Her lively exchange of letters with Frederick the Great of Prussia from 1763 to 1779 bears witness to her increasing sense of personal and artistic isolation; the musical ideals she had grown up with as a pupil and devotee of Hasse and a correspondent of Pietro Metastasio lost their validity, and new music, in particular the new Neapolitan operatic style, found no favour with her.

Maria Antonia Walpurgis is of interest principally as a patron (for example of the painter Raphael Mengs, the composers Hasse, Porpora and J. G. Naumann and the singers Regina Mingotti and Gertrud Mara, the latter making her début in Maria Antonia's *Talestri* in 1767), but she herself was an active participant in the arts. She frequently performed at court as a singer or keyboard player; Burney warmly praised her singing. She took leading roles in court performances of her own operas – *Il trionfo della fedeltà* (summer 1754, Dresden) and *Talestri, regina delle amazoni* (6 February 1760, Nymphenburg) – both to her own texts. They were published by Breitkopf, performed in other European capitals and translated into several languages. Their texts are clearly modelled on Metastasio (who made alterations to *Trionfo*), and their music on Hasse, who may have had a hand in the composition of *Trionfo*. The published score of *Trionfo* included her self-portrait, engraved by Giuseppe Canale, on the title page. Many other compositions in manuscript in Dresden bear her name, but cannot be authenticated; in many cases her name merely indicates ownership. Among the compositions attributed to her are arias, a pastorale, intermezzos, meditations and motets. She wrote the texts of Hasse's oratorio *La conversione di Sant'Agostino* and several cantatas, and her poems were set to music by Hasse, Naumann, G. B. Ferrandini and Gennaro Manna, among others. Antonio Eximeno's *Dell'origine e delle regole della musica* (Rome, 1774) was dedicated to her and included her portrait. A manuscript thematic catalogue of her library (compiled *c*1750–90) is in the Bayerische Staatsbibliothek, Munich.

BIBLIOGRAPHY

BurneyGN; *Choron-FayolleD*; *EitnerQ*; *FétisB*; *GerberL*; *LipowskyBL*; *SchillingE*; *SchmidlD*

J.-D.-E. Preuss, ed.: *Correspondance de Frédéric avec l'Electrice Marie-Antonie de Saxe*, Oeuvres de Frédéric le Grand, xxiv (Berlin, 1854)

J. Petzholdt: 'Biographisch-litterarische Mittheilungen über Maria Antonia Walpurgis von Sachsen', *Neuer Anzeiger für Bibliographie und Bibliothekwissenschaft* (1856), 336, 367 [incl. list of her works and those dedicated to her]

C. von Weber: *Maria Antonia Walpurgis, Churfürstin zu Sachsen* (Dresden, 1857) [incl. list of works, writings and paintings]

F. M. Rudhart: *Geschichte der Oper am Hofe zu München* (Freising, 1865)

M. Fürstenau: 'Maria Antonia Walpurgis, Kurfürstin von Sachsen: eine biographische Skizze', *MMg*, xi (1879), 167–81

W. Lippert, ed.: *Kaiserin Maria Theresia und Kurfürstin Maria Antonia von Sachsen: Briefwechsel 1747–1772* (Leipzig, 1908)

H. Drewes: *Maria Antonia Walpurgis als Komponistin* (Leipzig, 1934) [incl. list of MSS in Dresden]

A. Yorke-Long: *Music at Court: Four Eighteenth Century Studies* (London, 1954), 73–93

M. N. Massaro: 'Il ballo pantomimo al Teatro Nuovo di Padova (1751–1830)', *AcM*, lvii (1985), 215–75, esp. 245

GERHARD ALLROGGEN

María (Teresa) Barbara (de Bragança), Queen of Spain, 1746–58 (*b* Lisbon, 4 Dec 1711; *d* Madrid, 27 Aug 1758). Portuguese composer. The daughter of João V of Portugal and Maria Ana of Austria, she studied the harpsichord with Domenico Scarlatti, who had been brought to Lisbon from Rome

in 1719 or 1720. On 11 January 1729 she married the future Fernando VI of Spain, taking Scarlatti with her to Seville and four years later to Madrid. Padre Martini, when dedicating the first volume of his *Storia della musica* (1757) to her, claimed that she had learnt from Scarlatti 'the most intimate knowledge of music and its profoundest artifices'. According to Soriano Fuertes she composed an orchestrally accompanied *Salve regina*, which was performed by members of the Spanish royal chapel at the Salesian monastery she founded in Madrid in 1750 (see Vieira). Her musical legacy, itemized in an appendix to her will (in the Biblioteca del Palacio Real, Madrid), included 12 keyboard instruments distributed among royal residences at Aranjuez, Buen Retiro, and El Escorial. At her death Manuel de Figueiredo eulogized her playing as sufficient to cause 'ecstasy' in those who heard her.

BIBLIOGRAPHY

E. Vieira: *Diccionário biográphico de músicos portuguezes*, ii (Lisbon, 1900), 63

R. Kirkpatrick: *Domenico Scarlatti* (Princeton, 1953, 3/1968)

—— : 'Who Wrote the Scarlatti Sonatas? a Study in Reverse Scholarship', *Notes*, xxix (1972–3), 426–31 [on María Barbara's musical accomplishments]

ROBERT STEVENSON

Maria Cattarina. *See* CALEGARI, CORNELIA.

Maria de Ventadorn (*fl* late 12th century). The daughter of Raimon II, Viscount of Turenne, and wife of Ebles V, Viscount of Ventadorn, she was a patron of many troubadours. She exchanged a *tenso* (debate song), with Gui d'Ussel. This one poem is the only extant example of her work, and no music survives.

BIBLIOGRAPHY

M. Bogin: *The Women Troubadours* (New York, 1976)

MARIA V. COLDWELL

Mariani Campolieti, Virginia (*b* Genoa, 4 Dec 1869; *d* Milan, 1941). Italian composer and pianist. She studied the piano with Mario Vitali and composition with Carlo Pedrotti in Pesaro. She won the Bodoi Prize for her cantata *Apoteosi di Rossini* (for soloists, chorus and orchestra). Her three-act melodrama *Dal sogno alla vita* (libretto by Fulvio Fulgonio) was peformed at Vercelli in February 1898. She also composed chamber music and drawing-room songs.

BIBLIOGRAPHY

SchmidlD

A. de Angelis: *L'Italia musicale d'oggi: Dizionario dei musicisti* (Rome, 1918, 3/1928)

A. Bonaventura: 'Le donne italiane e la musica', *RMI*, xxxii (1925), 519–34

U. Manferrari: *Dizionario universale delle opere melodrammatiche* (Florence, 1954–5)

P. Adkins Chiti: *Donne in musica* (Rome, 1982)

LAURA PISTOLESI

Marić, Ljubica (*b* Kragujevac, 18 March 1909). Serbian composer. She studied composition with Josip Slavenski at the Stanković Music School, Belgrade, and with Josef Suk at the Prague Conservatory, where she also attended Alois Hába's classes in quarter-tone music and the conducting classes of Method Doležil and Nikolai Malko. She later returned to Belgrade as a professor at the Stanković School and as a teacher of theory at the Academy of Music, and in 1963 was elected a member of the Serbian Academy of Sciences and Arts. Marić's early compositions boldly explored atonality, athematicism and quarter-tone music and were well-received at festivals in Amsterdam and Strasbourg (1933). Her affinity with Serbian medieval culture, which she expressed in a personal and contemporary manner, enriched her mature style of the 1950s. The novel combination of old and new is best exemplified in her much-acclaimed cantata *Pesme prostora* ('Songs of Space', 1956), based on texts taken from Bogumil tombstones. Many of her orchestral and chamber works were inspired by the melodic principles of the *oktōēchos*, the ancient cycle of Orthodox liturgical music that acted on her as a kind of 'ancestral memory' and provided a tonal basis for her music.

WORKS
selective list

Oktōēchos cycle: Muzika oktoiha, nos.1–3, orch, 1958–62; Vizantijski koncert [Byzantine Conc.], pf, orch, 1959; Prag sna [The Threshold of Dreams], cantata, 2 vv, reciter, chamber orch, 1961; Ostinato super thema octoicha, harp, pf, str orch, 1963; Simfonija octoiha, orch, 1964

Other orch and inst: Str Qt, 1931; Wind Qnt, 1932; Muzika za orkestre, orch, 1933; Pf Suite, 1937 [1/4 tone]; Trio, cl, trbn, db, 1937 [1/4 tone]; Brankovo kolo [Branko's Dance], pf, 1947; Skice [Sketches], pf, 1947; Vn Sonata, 1948; Passacaglia, orch, 1958; Čarobnica (Virgil), S, pf, 1964; Monodija oktoiha [Monody of the Octōēchos], vc, 1984; other chamber and pf pieces

Other vocal and choral: Stihovi iz gorskog venca [Verses from the Alpine Region], Bar, orch, 1947; Pesme prostora [Songs of Space], cantata, chorus, orch, 1956; Slovo svetlosti [Word of Light] (medieval Serbian poetry), 6 nar, choir, orch, 1965; Iz tmine pojanje [Chant from Darkness], 1v, pf, 1984; other songs and choral pieces, incl. Tri narodne korovi [3 Folk Choruses]

Principal publishers: Prosveta, Srpska Akademija Nauka i Umetnosti, Udruženje Kompozitora Srbije

BIBLIOGRAPHY

P. Stefanović: 'Stvaralački podvig Ljubice Marić', *Knijizevne novine*, xxi (1956)

—— : 'O jednom velikom delu savremene muzike', *Delo*, vii (1958)

J. Milojkovic-Djuric: 'Das Byzantinische Konzert für Klavier und Orchester von Ljubica Marić', *MZ*, xv (1979), 102–08

M. Bergamo: *Elementi ekspresionističke orijentacije u srpskoj muzici od 1945 godine* [Elements of Expressionist Orientation in Serbian Music to 1945] (Belgrade, 1980)

M. Veselinović: *Stavaralačka prisutnost evropske avangarde u nas* [The Creative Presence of the European Avant-Garde in Serbia] (diss., U. of Belgrade, 1981)

M. Blagojević: 'Najnovije delo Ljubice Marić: recitativna kantata "Iz tmine pojanje" (1984)', *Zvuk*, iii (1984), 30–33

STANA DURIĆ-KLAJN, MELITA MILIN

Maroie, Dame. *See* MARGOT AND MAROIE.

Maroie de Dregnau de Lille (*fl* 13th century). Trouvère. She was the author and composer of a chanson, *Mout m'abelist quant je voi revenir*, preserved with music in one source (*F-Pn* f.f. 844, f.181). Only one seven-line strophe of text is extant. The musical form displays the initial repetition typical of trouvère songs: ABABCDE.

BIBLIOGRAPHY

M. V. Coldwell: 'Jougleresses and Trobairitz: Secular Musicians in Medieval France', *Women Making Music: the Western Art Tradition, 1150–1950*, ed. J. Bowers and J. Tick (Urbana and Chicago, 1986), 39–61, esp. 50–52 [incl. facs. of music, p.51]

MARIA V. COLDWELL

Marshall [née Thomas], **Florence Ashton** [Marshall, Mrs Julian] (*b* Rome, 30 March 1843; *d* ? after 1911). English composer, conductor and writer. She studied with William Sterndale Bennett, John Goss and G. A. Macfarren at the RAM and was made an Associate of the Philharmonic Society. Her writings include a biography of Handel (London, 1885), contributions to the first edition of Grove's *Dictionary of Music and Musicians* and articles in periodicals.

Marshall's music consistently achieves a level of accomplished excellence. Though non-sentimental Mendelssohnian traits are apparent, chromatic shadings and original melodic contours define a personal idiom of freshness and beauty. The timeless quality of *Sweet and Low* and the depiction of 'a soldier's sepulchre' (in *Hohenlinden*) both testify to her strength of intellect, while the dominant chord which concludes *Ask me no more* perfectly expresses the poem's ambiguity. Whatever the medium, her writing is always idiomatic, and the 'la-la' refrains of the Choral Dances form *Prince Sprite* momentarily suggest the world of Delius.

WORKS
all printed works published in London

STAGE
The Masked Shepherd (operetta, E. Simpson-Baikie); 1 partsong (1879)
Prince Sprite (fairy operetta, B. Thomas), London, 1897; Choral Dances (1897), str pts. (1900)

ORCHESTRAL
Nocturne, cl, orch; other works, lost

VOCAL
Choral: Hohenlinden (T. Campbell), SSAA, pf (1892); School March, unison/2-pt chorus (1903)
Partsongs: Behold the sun in gold descending (from The Masked Shepherd), 4vv (1879); Rest hath come (L. Leigh) dirge, 4vv (1884); To sea! the calm is o'er (T. L. Beddoes), 5vv (1884)
Songs (for 1v, pf): Il poeta moriente (1867); Solitude (A. Cowley) (1867); A little while (D. G. Rossetti) (1870); The Withered Primrose (F. Marshall) (1870); Mutability (P. B. Shelley) (1874); I arise from dreams of thee (Shelley) (1877); A New Year's Burden (Rossetti) (1877); Sweet and Low (A. Tennyson) (1877); Ask me no more (Tennyson) (1880); A Lullaby (L. A. Tadema) (1898)
Pedagogical: 70 Solfeggi for Class-Singing (1885); Interval Exercises for Singing Classes . . . [and] a Few Two-Part Time Exercises (1893)
Cantata

EDITIONS AND ARRANGEMENTS
Spohr: Violin School, trans. (1878); 5 Minutes' Exercises, choral 2vv (1889); ballet music from Mozart: Idomeneo, str orch (1908); Ov. from Cimarosa: Il matrimonio segreto, str orch (1911)

BIBLIOGRAPHY
CohenE; MEMM; StiegerO
J. D. Brown and S. S. Stratton: *British Musical Biography* (Birmingham, 1897)
J. Towers, ed.: *Dictionary-Catalogue of Operas and Operettas* (Morgantown, WV, 1910)
D. L. Hixon and D. Hennessee: *Women in Music: a Bio-Bibliography* (Metuchen, NJ, 1975)
                                    NIGEL BURTON

Martin, Roberta (*b* Helena, AR, 12 Feb 1907; *d* Chicago, 18 Jan 1969). American gospel singer, pianist and composer. She began piano lessons at an early age with the intention of becoming a concert pianist. After her family moved to Chicago when she was a teenager, she sang in Thomas A. Dorsey's newly formed gospel choir at the Ebenezer Baptist Church and shortly afterwards became its pianist. With the composer

Theodore R. Frye, an associate of Dorsey, she organized in 1933 the Martin-Frye Quartet; its original members were Willie Webb, Narsalus McKissick, Eugene Smith and Robert Anderson, and Martin was the accompanist. By 1935 the group had become known as the Roberta Martin Singers. Although they occasionally performed routine jubilee or 'shout' songs, their style was generally refined and controlled. Martin's style of accompaniment was characterized by middle-register chords punctuated rhythmically in the bass.

Martin wrote her first gospel song, *Try Jesus, he satisfies*, in 1943. The most popular of her approximately 100 works are *God is still on the throne* (1959), *Let it be* (1962), and *Just Jesus and me* (1966). Her songs are characterized by a sophisticated use of melody in the verse section and exotic harmonies in the chorus. She published her music through her own company, the Roberta Martin Studio of Music, which was established in Chicago in 1939. She was honoured in a series of lectures and recitals at the Smithsonian Institution in February 1981.

BIBLIOGRAPHY
SouthernB
H. C. Boyer: *The Gospel Song: a Historical and Analytical Study* (thesis, Eastman School of Music, 1964)
T. Heilbut: *The Gospel Sound: Good News and Bad Times* (New York, 1971)
I. V. Jackson: *Afro-American Gospel Music and its Social Setting with Special Attention to Roberta Martin* (diss., Wesleyan U., 1974)
—— : *Afro-American Religious Music: a Bibliography and Catalogue of Gospel Music* (Westport, CT, 1979)
                    HORACE CLARENCE BOYER

Martínez, Marianne [Anna Katharina] **von** (*b* Vienna, 4 May 1744; *d* Vienna, 13 Dec 1812). Austrian composer of Spanish descent. She was the daughter of a Neapolitan who had come to Vienna as 'gentiluomo' to the papal nuncio. She spent her childhood under the educational guidance of Pietro Metastasio, a friend of the family who lived in the same house; she was taught singing, the piano and composition by Nicola Porpora and Haydn, who were also living there, by Giuseppe Bonno and possibly by J. A. Hasse. As a child she had attracted attention at court with her beautiful voice and her keyboard playing, and in 1761 a mass by her was performed in the court church.

She acknowledged in 1773, when she became an honorary member of the Bologna Accademia Filarmonica, that as a composer she took as her principal models Hasse, Nicolò Jommelli and Baldassare Galuppi. Not only did she possess a thorough understanding of imitation and fugue, but she also knew how to set words in the Baroque manner. Her predilection for coloratura passages, leaps over wide intervals and trills indicate that she herself must have been an excellent singer. In 1772 Charles Burney praised her singing for all the typical virtues of the Italian school as well as for 'touching expression'.

Marianne von Martínez: portrait (n.d.) by Anton von Maron

Burney's remark that her vocal works were 'neither common, nor unnaturally new' applies to her instrumental works as well. A typical composer of the early Classical period in Vienna, she wrote in the Italian style. As a harpsichordist she was influenced by C. P. E. Bach. Sometimes she created a composition of several movements from a single idea (e.g. the Harpsichord Concerto in G, 1772). Her frequent development of motifs, decoration techniques and rapid runs show that she was concerned to impress her public with virtuosity, suiting the taste of the Viennese salons.

After Metastasio's death in 1782, the Martínez family, as heirs of his large estate (Marianne was bequeathed 20 000 florins, Metastasio's harpsichord and his music library), were able to maintain a large household. Many notable personalities, including Haydn and Mozart, attended her musical soirées there; Michael Kelly heard her play-

ing one of Mozart's four-hand sonatas with the composer and described her as still 'possessing the gaiety and vivacity of a girl'. In the 1790s she started a singing school in her house, which produced several outstanding singers.

WORKS

★ – *autograph score*

Oratorios: Isacco, figura del Redentore (P. Metastasio), Vienna, 1782, *A-Wgm*★; Santa Elena al Calvario, *Wgm*★

Other sacred vocal: 4 masses, *Wgm*; 6 motets, inst acc., *Wgm*; Dixit Dominus (Ps cix), 5vv, orch, 1774, *D-Bsb*★; Et vitam venturi, 4vv, *I-Bc*★; In exitu Israel (Ps cxiii), 4vv, orch, *Fc*; Kyrie, 4vv, orch, *Bc*★; 3 Litanie della BVM, *A-Wgm*; Miserere (Ps l), soloists, chorus, orch, 1769, *Wgm*★, *I-Bc*; Miserere, 4vv, bc, *D-Bsb*★; Psalm cxii, 4vv, orch, *I-Fc*; Quemadmodum desiderat cervus (Ps xli), soloists, chorus, orch, 1770, *D-Bsb*★; Regina coeli, *A-Wgm*★; 2 other psalms, 4vv, orch, 1769, 1770, *D-Bsb*

Secular vocal: La tempestà (Metastasio), cantata, S, orch, 1778, *A-Wn*★; Amor timido, cantata, S, orch, 1779, *Wgm*★; Il nido degli amori, cantata, 1783, *Wgm*★; Orgoglioso fiumicello, cantata, S, orch, *Wst*; Perchè, compagna amata, cantata, S, 2 vn, bc, *I-Bc*★; 24 arias, S, bc, 1767, *Nc*; 2 other arias, S, orch, 1769, *D-Dlb*; Deh dammi un altro core, 1v, bc, *Bsb*; Dell'amore i bei momenti, 1v, bc, *I-Mc*; Tu vittime non vuoi, 1v, orch, *D-Bsb*

Inst: Ov. (Sinfonie), C, 1770, *A-Wgm*★; 2 kbd concs., G, 1772, *Wgm*★, A, *Wgm*★, pts *Wgm*; 2 pf sonatas, in Raccolta musicale, op.4 (?1763), op.5 (1765)

BIBLIOGRAPHY

BurneyGN; Choron-FayolleD; FétisB; GerberL; Grove1 (C. F. Pohl); *SainsburyD; SchillingE; SchmidlD*

C. Burney: *Memoirs of the Life and Writings of the Abate Metastasio* (London, 1796), iii, 279–80

M. Kelly: *Reminiscences* (London, 2/1826), i, 249

A. Schmid: 'Zwei musikalische Berühmtheiten Wien's aus dem Schönen Geschlecht in der zweiten Hälfte des verflossenen Jahrhunderts', *Wiener allgemeine Musikzeitung*, vi (1846), 513, 517

C. Pichler: *Denkwürdigkeiten aus meinem Leben*, ed. E. K. Blümml, i (Munich, 1914), 191, 296, 343, 515

A. Costa: *Pagine metastasiane* (Milan, 1923), 140ff

K. L. Fremar: *The Life and Selected Works of Marianna Martines (1744–1812)* (diss., U. of Kansas, 1983)

R. Stevenson: 'Marianna Martines = Martínez (1744–1812): Pupil of Haydn and Friend of Mozart', *Inter-American Music Review*, xi (1990–91), 25–44

HELENE WESSELY

Martinez(-Mijares), Odaline de la (Caridad) ['Chachi'] (*b* Matanzas, Cuba, 31 Oct 1949). American conductor and composer of Cuban birth. She moved to the USA in 1961 and became an American citizen in 1971; since 1972 she has lived in London. After attending Tulane University (BFA 1972), she gained a scholarship to the RAM, London, where she studied composition with Paul Patterson (1972–6); at the University of Surrey (MM 1977; PhD 1980) she studied composition with Reginald Smith Brindle. She has been the recipient of Watson (1975–6), Danforth (1975–80) and Guggenheim (1980–81) fellowships. She is best known in Europe as the conductor of Lontano, a professional, London-based chamber ensemble that she helped found in 1976 to perform and record contemporary music. In 1982 she founded the Contemporary Chamber Orchestra (later the London Chamber Symphony), of which she is principal conductor. She organized an all-women orchestra for the first Chard Festival of Women in Music in May 1990; this was officially re-formed as the European Women's Orchestra, still with Martinez as director, for the London Women in Music festival later the same year. In 1991 she co-founded a recording company to specialize in contemporary, Latin American and women's music.

Martinez's own works are eclectic, influenced by George Crumb, by electronic music, and by her Latin American heritage. Much of her music possesses a simple and direct minimalist quality. The opera *Sister Aimée* (1978–83), based on the life of the American evangelist Aimée Semple McPherson, makes use of a host of styles and techniques, including gospel music and aleatory procedures. She is the author of an 'everywoman's guide' to women composers and performers entitled *Mendelssohn's Sister* (in preparation).

WORKS

Stage: Sister Aimée (opera, 2, J. Whiting), 1978–83, New Orleans, Newcomb College Theatre, 12 April 1984
Inst: Little Piece, fl, 1975; Phasing, chamber orch, 1975; Eos, org, 1976; A Moment's Madness, fl, pf, 1977; Improvisations, vn, 1977; Colour Studies, pf, 1978; A Mind of its Own, eng hn, 1981; Litanies, 2 fl, harp, str trio, 1981; Asonancias, vn, 1982; Suite, eng hn, vc, 1982; Str Qt, 1984–5
Vocal: 5 Imagist Songs (D. H. Lawrence, W. C. Williams, R. Aldington, H. D.), S, cl, pf, 1974; After Sylvia (S. Plath), S, pf, 1976; Absalom (2 Samuel, xviii, 33), Ct, T, T, Bar, B, 1977; Psalmos, chorus, brass qnt, timp, org, 1977; 2 American Madrigals (E. Dickinson), unacc. chorus, 1979; Canciones (F. García Lorca), S, perc, pf, 1983; Cantos de amor, S, pf, str trio, 1985; 5 Russ. songs, S, chamber orch, 1986
Elec: Hallucination, tape, 1975; Visions and Dreams, tape, 1977–8; Lamento, S, A, T, B (all amp), unacc. chorus, tape, 1978; 3 Studies, perc, elec (all amp), 1980

Some material in AMC, GB-Lmic

BIBLIOGRAPHY

Fuller-LeFanuRM (T. Calam)
O. Maxwell: 'Odaline de la Martinez', *Music and Musicians* (1983), Oct, 10

Odaline de la Martinez

H. Cole: 'First Lady of the Proms', *Guardian* (17 Aug 1984)
A. Burn: 'Odaline de la Martinez', *MT*, cxxvi (1985), 401–4
K. Brookes: 'Women's Room', *Classical Music* (11 Jan 1992), 11
H. Finch: 'Are Women So Different?', *The Times* (4 Feb 1992)
A. Stewart: 'Restoring the Balance', *Gramophone*, lxx/Sept (1992), 23
N. Kimberley: 'It's Still an Unsuitable Job for a Woman', *Independent on Sunday* (11 April 1994)

TONI CALAM, STEPHEN MONTAGUE

Martins, Maria de Lourdes (Clara da Silva) (*b* Lisbon, 26 May 1926). Portuguese composer and teacher. She studied the piano and composition at the Conservatório Nacional in Lisbon, then was awarded a Gulbenkian Foundation scholarship and studied with Harald Genzmer and Karlheinz Stockhausen in Germany. In 1960, having received a diploma from the Orff Institut at the Mozarteum in Salzburg, she was appointed director of the Orff-Schulwerk courses promoted by the Gulbenkian Foundation in Lisbon. She taught music education and composition at the Lisbon conservatory (1971–8) and was director of the Portuguese branch of the ISME (1972–6). The works between the Piano Sonatina no.1 (1947) and the Sonatina for wind quintet (1959) reveal the influence of Stravinsky and Bartók, but with *O Encoberto* (1965) she made a sharp turn towards more modern preoccupations, incorporating timbral experimentation, polystylism, development of the percussion and aleatory techniques into her music. She has also gained inspiration from Portuguese poetry and popular music, as is most clearly evident in her works for band and for choir. Martins's compositional achievements have been recognized not only by the Gulbenkian Foundation (1965, 1971) but also by the granting of the Carlos de Seixas award of the SNI (1959) and Juventide Musical Portuguesa (1960).

WORKS
selective list
Dramatic: Silêncio, onde estás tu?, op.15 (radio opera, D. Moreno), 1958; As três máscaras (opera), Lisbon, Teatro de S Carlos, 1984
Orch: Pezzo grotesco, op.19, 1959
Band: Rondó, op.34, 1978; Rapsódia do Natal, op.35, 1978; Suite de danças tradicionais portuguesas, 1978
Choral: Cantata de Natal, op.8, S, A, female vv, fl, rec, vn, pf, 1951; Tia Anica do Loulé, op.18, unacc., 1959; O Encoberto, op.25 (F. Pessoa), S, A, Bar, spkr, chorus, orch, 1965; O litoral, op.29 (A. Negreiros), 3 choruses SATB, perc, 1971; 20 canções, 1981
Chamber: Vn Sonata, op.4, 1948; Sonatina, op.5, ob, pf, 1949; Dança, op.7, 2 pf, 1950; Cromos, op.16, vn, pf, 1958; Esqueletos, fl, bn, vn, pf, 1962; Divertimento, op.26, wind qnt, 1967; Convergências, op.27, ens, 1970; Painéis, ens, 1982; Str Qt no.2, 1989
Songs: 4 poemas (Pessoa), A, fl, cl, pf, 1985; Soneto, Bar, gui; Soneto, S, pf
Also pieces for pf; educational music, incl. vocal works with Orff insts

Principal publishers: EMI Valentim de Carvalho, Schott

JOSÉ CARLOS PICOTO/DULÇE BRITO

Massarenghi [Mazarenghi], **Paola** (*b* Parma, 5 Aug 1565; *fl* 1585). Italian composer. Her parents were probably well-to-do bourgeois, perhaps civil servants, as they were able to obtain the aid of Duke Ranuccio Farnese in the education of her younger brother, Giovanni Battista (*b* 3 April 1569), also a composer. One madrigal by Massarenghi is known, *Quando spiega l'insegn'al sommo padre*, published in the *Primo libro de' madrigali a cinque voci* of Arcangelo Gherardini (Ferrara, 1585). It is listed in the table of contents as 'Quando spiega, di Madonna Paola Massarenghi da Parma'. Gherardini's dedication (dated 25 May 1585) is to Alfonso Fontanelli, a Ferrarese nobleman-composer originally from Reggio, and mentions other composers – Salvatore Essenga, Orazio Vecchi and Arcangelo da Reggio – but not Massarenghi, whose contribution may have been supplied by someone other than Gherardini.

BIBLIOGRAPHY
SchmidlD; VogelB
N. Pelicelli: 'Musicisti in Parma nei secoli XV–XVI', *NA*, ix (1932), 126
J. Bowers: 'Women Composers in Italy, 1566–1700', *Women Making Music: the Western Art Tradition, 1150–1950*, ed. J. Bowers and J. Tick (Urbana and Chicago, 1986), 116–67, esp. 117, 132, 155 n.77, 162

THOMAS W. BRIDGES

Masson, Elizabeth (*b* Scotland, 1806; *d* London, 9 Jan 1865). British composer, contralto and teacher. She was taught singing by Mrs Henry Smart senior, and by Giuditta Pasta in Italy. She made her début at John Ella's second subscription concert in the Argyll Rooms, London, on 11 March 1831, and sang afterwards at the Ancient Concerts and the Philharmonic Society. During about 12 years with these societies she revived music by Purcell, Handel, Pergolesi, Gluck and Mozart. She helped to found the Royal Society of Female Musicians in 1839 and remained its honorary treasurer until her death. She sang in oratorios of Handel: the title part in *Solomon*, at the Sacred Harmonic Society (22 November 1839), and Storgè in the revival of *Jephtha* (7 April 1841). Later, she devoted herself to teaching and composition.

Masson's Scottish origins are seen to advantage in her compositions. The *Original Jacobite Songs* (1839) were deservedly popular in their day; their authentic folk melodies are set to highly apposite accompaniments, written with a sparseness that is unusual for the period. In her settings of Byron she responded to his irregular metres with rhythmic flexibility, breaking up the music's phrase patterns with considerable subtlety. Her songs in the Italian vein demonstrate an intimate knowledge of contemporary opera, and her vocal experience is reflected in their beautifully shaped melodic contours. Her sense of quasi-symphonic development results in some remarkable experiments with binary form in songs such as *Mary, adieu* (1837) and *The lark now leaves his wat'ry nest* (1840).

WORKS
all printed works published in London
Songs (1v, pf): Ah! love was never yet without the pang (Byron) (1837); Mary, adieu (Byron) (1837); An Italian Sunset (Byron) (?1840); The lark now leaves his wat'ry nest (W. Davenant) (1840); 12 Songs (E. Bulwer-Lytton, Byron, J. H. Caunter, Mrs Jameson, Masson, P. Metastasio, R. M. Milnes and others) (1843); Wishes (B. Cornwall) (1845), also in Vocal Sketches (1848); O thou art the lad of my heart (Smyth) (1846); [10] Vocal Sketches (Byron, W. Scott and others) (1848); Is my lover on the sea? (Cornwall) (1852); Come off to the moors

(Masson) (1853); The Parting Song (F. Hemans) (1853); Scotland (J. Sheerer) (1857); Welcome, welcome (Masson) (1857); A Woman's Question (A. Procter) (1863); J'aime un artilleur; ?2 other songs
Duets: Hope's Requiem ('a lady of rank') (1851); All yesterday I was spinning (Byron) (1859); A Doubting Heart (Procter) (1859)
Pedagogical: Vocal Exercises (1855)
Song arrs.: [5] Original Jacobite Songs (1839); 12 Songs for the Classical Vocalist, 2 ser. (1845, 1860); 13 others pubd separately (1840–c1880)
Edns incl. 6 songs by C. Krebs (1847); 4 Songs by L. Weyrauch (1849); Pezzi scelti di bel canto (1851)

BIBLIOGRAPHY
MEMM; PazdirekH; SchmidlD; WCBH
J. D. Brown and S. S. Stratton: British Musical Biography (Birmingham, 1897)
G. Claghorn: Women Composers and Hymnists: a Concise Biographical Dictionary (Metuchen, NJ, 1984)
ALEXIS CHITTY/NIGEL BURTON

Massumoto [Masumoto], **Kikuko** (*b* Tokyo, 2 Feb 1937). Japanese composer and ethnomusicologist. Her musical study began with piano lessons from her mother. In 1963 she graduated from Tōhō Gakuen School of Music, having studied with composers from various stylistic backgrounds: Minao Shibata and Yoshirō Irino (serialism) and Sadao Bekku and Akio Yashiro (French school). She went on to study ethnomusicology at the Tokyo National University of Fine Arts and Music with Fumio Koizumi and Shigeo Kishibe, and pursued private study of gagaku with Masataro Togi and Sukehiro Shiba. In 1982 she was appointed an assistant professor at Tōhō Gakuen University.

Influences of gagaku, noh and shōmyō (Buddhist chanting) stemming from Massumoto's work in ethnomusicology gradually became apparent in her compositions; these include microtones, proportional and free rhythm and, in *Ranjoh*, a meditative atmosphere. In general her works favour linear writing and gradual unfolding of themes rather than thematic contrasts. Her vocal music employs the range of utterance between singing and speaking, drawing on narration styles from noh (*sashi*) and bunraku (*jiai*) in, for example, *Three Songs from Medieval Japan*. In ensemble works combining Japanese and European instruments she uses related instruments (e.g. three reeds in *Kawa*). Her writings include *Gagaku: dentō ongaku e no atarashii aprōchi* ('A Theoretical Analysis of Japanese Court Music', Tokyo, 1968).

WORKS
selective list

Chamber and solo inst: Chiisa-na-kaze (A Short Piece), 2 kotos, 2 shakuhachis, 1972; 12 Tableaux, 2

pf (6 hands), 1972; Kaiko [Encounter], 2 rec, 2 shakuhachis, 1974; Chaos, kotos, gagaku ens, perc, str ens, 1975; Roei (Ancient Court Song in the Heian Era), va d'amore, 1976; Ranjoh, fl, 1983; Kawa (An Image of the Great River), ob, shō, hichiriki, Ō-tsuzumi/woodblock, 1984
Vocal: 3 Songs from Medieval Japan, S, pf, perc, 1980; Asaji-ga-yado [The House amid the Thickets] (chamber opera, Massumoto, after kabuki lib by F. Enchi from A. Ueda: U-getsu-monogatari), 1984–6

Principal publisher: Japanese Federation of Composers

BIBLIOGRAPHY
'Frauengipfel: deutsche und japanische Komponistinnen', Stuttgarter Zeitung (7 Oct 1991)
T. Hoffman: 'The Sounds of Music: Japan's Modern Composers and Performers', Japan Society Newsletter (1985), March, 2–6, esp.4
T. Kakinuma: 'Japan', Ear Magazine, xv/10 (1991), 18
K. Massumoto: '. . . nehme ich beim komponieren eine natürliche, oder dem Verlauf der Sache angepasste Haltung ein', Komponistinnen in Japan und Deutschland: eine Dokumentation, ed. R. Matthei (Kassel, 1991), 25–31
Discussion [K. Massumoto, N. Funayama, E. Rieger, A. Hölszky, H. Miyake, R. Matthei], ibid., 45–56
J. MICHELE EDWARDS

Matthieux, Johanna. *See* KINKEL, JOHANNA.

Matuszczak, Bernadetta (*b* Toruń, 10 March 1937). Polish composer. She was a pupil of Z. Sitowski (theory) and J. Kurpisz-Stefan (piano) at the State Higher School of Music in Poznań, graduating in 1958. She then studied composition with Tadeusz Szeligowski and Kazimierz Sikorski in Warsaw (MA 1964) and completed her education under Nadia Boulanger in Paris (1968). A freelance composer, she has worked frequently with Polish music theatres, enabling her to pursue an avid interest in composing operas and oratorios. The distinctive feature of her compositional style is strong expressivity realized using frugal means. Her works have received prizes in Poland and at international competitions, and have been performed at numerous European music festivals; the choral work *Septem tubae* was performed at the ISCM Weltmusikfest in Hamburg (1969) and her opera *Julia i Romeo* was first given at the Internationale Maifestspiele in Wiesbaden (1972).

WORKS
selective list

Stage: Julia i Romeo (chamber opera, 5 scenes, after W. Shakespeare), 1967 (Kraków, 1979); Humanae voces (opera-oratorio), S, reciting vv, chorus, orch, 1971; Mysterium Heloizy (opera, 7 scenes), solo vv, chorus, orch, actors, dancers, mimers, 1974; Pamiętnik wariata [A Madman's Diary] (opera-monodrama, M. Gogol), Bar, chamber ens, actor, 1976; Apocalypsis (opera-oratorio), S, Bar, reciting vv, chorus, orch, 1977; Prometeo (opera da camera, after Eschilo), solo vv, chorus, orch, 1982; W noch na Rynku Starego Miasta [A Night in the Old Market Square] (pantomime, after I. L. Perec), solo vv, chorus, orch, 1986; Dzikie łabędzie [The Wild Swans] (ballet fairy-tale, after H. C. Andersen), elec, 1990

Orch: Kontrasty, 1970; 12 Preludes, str, 1982; Momenti musicali, fl, str, 1983; Miniatury baletowe, orch, 1985

Choral: Septem tubae (Revolution), chorus, org, orch, 1966; Elegia o chłopcu polskim [Elegy for a Polish Boy] (K. K. Baczyński), S, spkr, 2 female choruses, orch, 1974; Fraszki [Epigrams] (J. Kochanowski), chorus, 1982; Wiersze dziecięce [Poems for Children] (K. Iłłakowicz), chorus, 1982

Other vocal: Dramat kameralny [A Chamber Drama] (T. S. Eliot: The Hollow Men), Bar, taped Bar, spkr, b cl, vc, db, perc, 1965; 7 Songs (R. M. Rilke), Bar, orch, 1971; Salmi per uno gruppo di cinque (Psalms), Bar, spkr, perc, harp, db, 1972; Tryptyk Norwida [Norwid's Triptych], Bar, b cl, vc, 1983; Pejzaże [Landscapes], Mez, pf, 1984; Pieśni żałobne [Funeral Song], S, org, 1991; Libera me, Bar, tape, 1991

Inst: Musica da camera, pic, 3 fl, 4 tpt, 5 tom toms, 1967; Aforyzmy [Aphorism], fl, 1975; Ossessioni concertanti, perc, 1980; Quartetto in 12 parti, str qt, 1980; Aforyzmy, pf, 1984; Dźwiękowe zabawki: 24 bajki [Sound Toys: 24 Fairy-Tales], pf, 1984

Principal publisher: PWM

BARBARA ZWOLSKA-STĘSZEWSKA

Mayer, Emilie (b Friedland, Mecklenburg, 14 May 1821; d Berlin, 10 April 1883). German composer and sculptor. The daughter of an apothecary, she received piano lessons and soon began to compose short piano pieces. After her schooling she moved to Stettin (now Szczecin), then the capital of Pomerania, and took lessons with the ballad composer Carl Loewe. During this period she composed songs, chamber music, overtures and symphonies. In 1847 she moved to Berlin, where she studied fugue and counterpoint with the theorist and composer Adolf Bernhard Marx and orchestration with the military musician Wilhelm Wieprecht. She organized private performances of her music at home and in other houses. Her sinfonia in B minor (1852), one of her most successful compositions, was given at least eight public performances by Karl Liebig. She went with her brothers to Vienna, where she was received by the Archduchess Sophie, and travelled between Berlin, Stettin and Pasewalk, spending considerable money and energy on having her music printed and performed. Later, her financial affairs seem to have deteriorated. Her music was performed in Brussels, Lyons, Budapest, Dessau, Halle, Leipzig and Munich, and was much acclaimed during her lifetime. In 1885 she was appointed an honorary member of the Munich Philharmonic Society. She was the most prolific German woman composer of the Romantic period, yet most of her music (which is in the Berlin Staatsbibliothek) has remained unperformed since her death. Besides composing, she worked as a sculptor, and some of her works were retained in royal collections.

WORKS
selective list

Stage: Die Fischerin (Spl, after J. W. von Goethe), c1842

Sinfonias (unpubd unless otherwise stated): no.1, c; no.2, e; no.3 'Sinfonia militaire', C; no.4, E; no.5, f; no.6, b, 1852, arr. pf 4 hands, pubd Berlin

Other orch: Ov., d; Ov., c, inc.; Ov., d; Conc., pf, orch, d; Faust Ov., op.46, 1880, pubd Stettin, arr. pf 4 hands, pubd Stettin

VOCAL

Choral: 5 Gesänge: Immortelle, An sie, Lied, Schwäbisches Bauernlied, Warum bist du so ferne, op.6, men's vv, 1848, pubd Neustrelitz; Ps cxviii, solo vv, chorus, orch, before 1861; Erlkönig, vv, pf, 1870; 23 Lieder, men's vv

1v, pf: Erlkönig (J. W. von Goethe), 1842; 2 Gesänge: Abendglocken (N. Vogl), Das Schlüsselloch (Nathusius); 3 Lieder: Du bist wie eine Blume (H. Heine), O lass mich dein gedenken (Kletke), Wenn der Abendstern die Rosen (H. von Chezy), op.7, S/T, pf, 1849, pubd Neustrelitz

CHAMBER
works published in Berlin unless otherwise stated

9 vn sonatas, incl.: a, op.10; F, op.17 (from Vc Sonata, F), 1863; a, op.18, 1864; e, op.19, 1867; A, op.21, 1867; d, op.29, 1869

13 vc sonatas, incl.: d. op.38, 1873; C, op.40, 1874; D, op.47, 1883

11 pf trios, incl.: e, op.12, 1861; D, op.13, 1861; bb, op.15; b, op.16, 1861; F, unpubd

7 str qts, incl.: g, op.14, 1864

3 str qnts, 2 pf qts

PIANO

Tanz der Horen, op.26, Melodie, pubd Berlin; Aus der Jugendzeit, op.27, Walzer, pubd Berlin; Allemande fantastique, op.29, pubd Stettin; Tonwellen-Walzer, op.30, pubd Stettin; Ungaraise, op.31, pubd Stettin; Valse, op.32, pubd Stettin; Mazurka, op.33, pubd Stettin; Drei Humoresken, op.41, pubd Berlin; Impromptu, op.44, pubd Berlin; La Modesta (Salonstück), op.45, pubd Berlin; 6 Klavierstücke für die Kinderwelt, op.48a, pubd Bremen; 3 sonatas (all unpubd): no.1, D, no.2, d, no.3, d

Principal publishers: Bote & Bock, Challier, Prütz & Mauri

MSS in D-Bsb

BIBLIOGRAPHY

C. von Ledebur: Tonkünstlerlexikon Berlins von den Anfängen bis auf die Gegenwart (Berlin, 1861)
M. Sichardt: 'Auf den Spuren einer vergessenen Komponistin: Emilie Mayer', Komponistinnen in Berlin, ed. B. Brand and others (Berlin, 1987), 150–78 [incl. complete list of works]

EVA RIEGER

Mazur, Marilyn (*b* New York, 18 Jan 1955). Danish composer and jazz musician. She moved to Denmark at the age of six, and first studied the piano and later the drums and percussion at the conservatory in Copenhagen. In 1970 she began to work as a dancer with the Creative Dance Theatre, but from about 1973 concentrated on composition. She was the organizer of several female groups, Zirenes, Primi Band and Feminist Improvising Group, and worked too with mixed groups, Six Winds and Mazur Markussen Quartet. After playing in a recording of Mikkelborg's *Aura* with Miles Davis (1985), she worked with bands led by Davis, Gil Evans and Wayne Shorter, among others; in 1990 she formed the international group Future Song. In form as well as sound and timbre Mazur's music is strongly experimental, and her band provides a distinguished vehicle for her ideas. Her works appear on several recordings, including *Six Winds* and *Primi* (both 1982), *MM 4* (1984), *Ocean Fables* (1986) and *Future Song* (1991).

BIBLIOGRAPHY
C. Irgens-Møller: 'Marilyn Mazur: sirene og magiker', *Dansk musiktidsskrift*, lxii (1987–8), 4–16
E. Wiedemann: 'Tre jazz-kvinder', *Dansk musiktidsskrift*, lxiii (1992–3), 126–31

INGE BRULAND

Mekeel, Joyce (*b* New Haven, CT, 6 July 1931). American composer and teacher. Educated principally in Paris and at Yale University, she also studied privately with Nadia Boulanger, Gustav Leonhardt, Ralph Kirkpatrick and Earl Kim. She has taught at the New England Conservatory, and at Boston University (from 1970). Her works treat conventional voices and instruments in unusual ways, such as requiring instrumentalists to walk, whisper or sing, or singers to shriek, declaim or gesticulate. Even her non-theatrical compositions tend to be highly dramatic. They often employ multilingual texts and seem less concerned with the direct setting of the words than with evoking their mood and atmosphere.

WORKS
selective list; dates are of first performance

Stage: Chains, 7 chains, 5 dancers, 1969; Feast, tape, dancers, 1970; Soundings (music-theatre event), 1972, collab. P. Earls and L. Davidson; Kisses and Kazoos (music-theatre), 1977, collab. Earls and Davidson
Orch: Vigil, large orch, 1978; Obscurities of Order, reader, orch, 1990
Chamber and vocal: Dark Rime, S, pf, 1966; Corridors of Dream, Mez, a fl, b cl, va, vc, harp, 1972; Planh, vn, 1975; Alarums and Excursions, actress/Mez, fl, cl, vn, va, vc, perc, pf, 1978; Sigil, actor, actress/Mez, cl, eng hn, 2 hn, 2 tuba, str qnt,

harp, 1981; Tessera, s sax, eng hn, dbn, tpt, hn, str qnt, hpd, 1982; Voices, cl, vn, pf, 1985; Journeys of Remembrance, actress/Mez, S, Bar, fl, cl, eng hn, vn, va, vc, perc, 1986; Pantoum, vn, pf, 1991; choral works

CHRISTINE AMMER

Mel-Bonis. *See* BONIS, MÉLANIE.

Mendelssohn (–Bartholdy) [Hensel], **Fanny (Cäcilie)** (*b* Hamburg, 14 Nov 1805; *d* Berlin, 14 May 1847). German composer, pianist and conductor, sister of the composer Felix Mendelssohn. She was the eldest of four children born into a post-Enlightenment, cultured Jewish family. Of her illustrious ancestors, her great-aunts Fanny Arnstein and Sarah Levy provided important role models, especially in their participation in salon life. Her paternal grandfather, Moses Mendelssohn, was the pivotal figure in effecting a rapprochement between Judaism and German secular culture. In Fanny Mendelssohn's generation this movement resulted in the conversion of the immediate family to Lutheranism. Despite baptism, however, Fanny retained the cultural values of liberal Judaism.

An important element in the family circle was her special relationship with her younger brother Felix (1809–47). In close contact their entire life, they stimulated and challenged each other musically and intellectually. Fanny played a major role in shaping some of Felix's compositions, notably his oratorio *St Paul* (completed in 1837), and advised him on musical matters. Felix, likewise, encouraged her compositional activities, but he discouraged publication. Although his attitudes echoed his father's views and reflected the prevailing cultural values, they may have been motivated by jealousy, fear of competition, protectiveness, or paternalism. In any case, these negative aspects exacerbated Fanny's own feelings of ambivalence towards composition.

From 1809 Fanny Mendelssohn lived in Berlin. She received her earliest musical instruction from her mother, Lea, who taught her the piano (she is reputed to have noted her daughter's 'Bach fingers' at birth). She then studied the piano with Ludwig Berger, and in 1816 with Marie Bigot in Paris. A few years later she embarked on theory and composition with C. F. Zelter, a conservative musician and early champion of J. S. Bach. Her first composition dates from December 1819, a lied in honour of her father's birthday. In 1820 she enrolled at the newly opened Berlin Singakademie. During

Fanny Mendelssohn: drawing (1829) by her husband Wilhelm Hensel

the next few years Mendelssohn produced many lieder and piano pieces; such works were to be the mainstay of her output of about 500 compositions. On 3 October 1829 she married the Prussian court painter Wilhelm Hensel. Their only child, Sebastian, was born the following year (recent evidence shows that there was at least one stillbirth).

Beginning in the early 1830s, Mendelssohn became the central figure in a flourishing salon, for which she created most of her compositions and where she performed on the piano and conducted. Her tastes favoured composers who were then unfashionable, including Mozart and Handel, and especially Bach. Her only known public appearance was in February 1838, performing her brother's First Piano Concerto at a charity benefit. Two trips to Italy, in 1839–40 and 1845, were among the high points of her life. Her last composition, the lied *Bergeslust*, was written on 13 May 1847, a day before her sudden death from a stroke.

While lieder and piano pieces dominate her output, she composed a few large-scale dramatic works in the early 1830s, perhaps to test her role as *saloniste*. Of note among the relatively small number of instrumental chamber works is the Piano Trio op.11 (composed 1846), and the unpublished String Quartet. Only a very small amount of her music was published – 11 opuses and about 16 single pieces without opus number. This fact, combined with the previously restricted access to her manuscripts (many still in private hands), has impeded a thorough evaluation of her style. Nonetheless, the available music suggests certain traits we may assume to be typical: lyricism, as in the published piano pieces; neo-Bachian procedures, as in the Prelude in E minor and in the *Oratorium nach den Bildern der Bibel* (composed 1831); and, above all, attention to craftsmanship and respect for traditional syntax and procedures. It further suggests that her music has been unduly neglected.

Fanny Mendelssohn's letters and diaries reveal a witty, perceptive and intelligent woman, fully conversant with intellectual life. Her strong self-image in this regard contrasts with her shaky confidence in her creativity (not uncommon in women composers).

Yet despite her doubts, she created and maintained in her salon a flourishing showcase for her many musical talents. Any full-scale evaluation will have to take into account the importance of the salon for Mendelssohn as for countless other female composers, writers and artists.

WORKS

Editions:

Ausgewählte Klavierwerke, ed. F. Kistner-Hensel (Munich, 1986) [K]

Weltliche a cappella Chöre von 1846, ed. E. M. Blankenburg (Kassel, 1988) [B]

Ausgewählte Lieder, ed. A. Assenbaum (Düsseldorf, 1991) [A]

Ausgewählte Lieder, ed. A. Maurer (Wiesbaden, 1993) [M]

Six Pieces from 1824–1827, ed. J. Radell (Bryn Mawr, PA, 1994) [R]

printed works published in Berlin unless otherwise stated

SONGS

for 1v and piano unless otherwise stated

Lieder: at least 250 works, incl.: Sehnsucht nach Italien, 1822, A; An Suleika, *c*1825, M; Harfners Lied, 1825, M; Mignon, 1826, A; Ave Maria, in *The Harmonicon*, x (London, 1832), 54–5; In die Ferne, 1833, A; Über allen Gipfeln ist Ruh, 1835, M; Suleika, 1836, M; Ach, die Augen sind es wieder, 1837, M; Fichtenbaum und Palme, 1838, M; Die Schiffende (1837); Schloss Liebeneck (Cologne, 1839); Sehnsucht, 1839, A; Anklänge nos.1–3, 1841,

Autograph manuscript of 'Der Maiabend' by Fanny Mendelssohn, with a vignette by Wilhelm Hensel

A, M; Auf dem See, 1841, A; Traurige Wege, 1841, A, M; Dämmerung senkte sich, 1843, M; Im Herbst, 1844, M; Liebe in der Fremde, 1844, A; Ich kann wohl manchmal singen, c1946, M; 6 Lieder, op.1 (1846/R1985); Nacht ist wie ein stilles Meer, c1846, M; Bergeslust, 1847; 6 Lieder, op.7 (1848), no.1 (Nachtwanderer) ed. in J. Thym: *100 Years of Eichendorff Songs* (Madison, WI, 1983); 6 Lieder, op.9 (Leipzig, 1850); 5 Lieder, op.10 (Leipzig, 1850); Wandrers Nachtlied, M

Lieder pubd under Felix Mendelssohn's name: Das Heimweh (F. Robert), c1824, Italien (F. Grillparzer), 1825, Suleika und Hatem (J. W. von Goethe), 2vv, pf, 1825 [op.8 nos.2, 3, 12, pubd 1827]; Sehnsucht (J. G. Droysen), before 1830, Verlust (H. Heine), before 1830, Die Nonne (L. Uhland), 1822 [op.9 nos.7, 10, 12, pubd 1830]

OTHER VOCAL

Choral: c28 works, incl.: Nachtreigen, double chorus, 1829; Hiob, cantata, S, A, T, B, SATB, orch, 1831, ed. C. Misch (Kassel, 1992); Lobgesang, cantata, S, A, SATB, orch, c1831, ed. C. Misch (Kassel, 1992); Oratorium nach den Bildern der Bibel, S, A, T, B, chorus, orch, 1831; Zum Fest der heiligen Cäcilia, mixed chorus, pf, 1833; Einleitung zu lebenden Bilder, nar, chorus, pf, 1841; Gartenlieder: 6 Gesänge, op.3, SATB, 1846, (1847), B; Lockung, 1846, B; O Herbst, 1846, B; Schon kehren die Vögel, 1846, B

12 vocal trios, 1825–41

INSTRUMENTAL

Orch: Ov., C, c1830

Chamber: Adagio, E, vn, pf, 1823, ed. R. Marciano (Kassel, 1989); Pf Qt, Ab, 1823, ed. R. Eggebrecht-Kupsa (Kassel, 1990); Capriccio, Ab, vc, pf, 1829; Die frühen Gräber, va, 2 vc, db, 1829; Fantasia, g, vc, pf, c1830, C. Lambour (Wiesbaden, 1994); St Qt, Eb, 1834, ed, G. Marx (Wiesbaden, 1988); Pf Trio, op.11, 1846 (Leipzig, 1850/R1980)

Pf: at least 125 works incl.: Übungsstück, 1822, K; Übungsstück, 1823, K; Allegro, c, 1824, R; Sonata, c, 1824, ed. L. G. Serbescu and B. Heller (Kassel, 1991), ed. J. Radell (Bryn Mawr, PA, 1992); Andante con moto, c, 1825, R; Capriccio, F#, 1825, R; Allegro ma non troppo, f, c1826, R; Andante con espressione, c, 1826, R; Fugata, Eb, 1827, R; Prelude, e, 1827, ed. R. Marciano (Kassel, 1989); Notturno, 1838, K; Abschied von Rom, c1840, K; Das Jahr: 12 Characterstücke, 1841, ed, L. G. Serbescu and B. Heller (Kassel, 1989); Sonata, g, 1843, ed. L. G. Serbescu and B. Heller (Kassel, 1991), ed. J. Radell (Bryn Mawr, PA, 1992); Allegretto, c1846, K; Allegro molto, 1846, K; Allegro vivace, 1846, K; Andante cantabile, 1846, K; 4 Lieder, op.2 (1846/R1983); O Traum der Jugend, o goldener Stern, 1846, K; 6 mélodies, op.4 (1847/R1982); 6 mélodies, op.5 (1847/R1982); 4 Lieder, op.6 (1847/R1983); 2 Bagatellen für die Schüler des Schindelmeisser'schen Musik-Instituts (1848); Pastorella (1848/R1983); 4 Lieder, op.8 (Leipzig, 1850/R1989); Sonatensatz, E, ed. L. G. Serbescu and G. Heller (Kassel, 1991); 3 Stücke, pf 4 hands, ed. B. Gabler (Kassel, 1990)

Org: Präludium, F, 1829, ed. B. Harbach (Pullman, WA, 1993); Präludium, G, c1829–33

Most MSS are in D-Bsb (Mendelssohn-Archiv) and private collections; some are in D-Dük, GB-Ob, S-Smf and US-Wc

BIBLIOGRAPHY

FétisB; Grove1 (G. Grove); *SchmidlD*[†]

S. Hensel: *Die Familie Mendelssohn 1729–1847, nach Briefen und Tagebüchern* (Berlin, 1879; Eng. trans., 1882)

R. Elvers, ed.: *Fanny Hensel, geb. Mendelssohn Bartholdy: Dokumente ihres Lebens: Ausstellung zum 125. Todestage im Mendelssohn-Archiv*, Staatsbibliothek Preussischer Kulturbesitz, Ausstellungen, ii (Berlin, 1972)

R. Elvers: 'Verzeichnis der Musik-Autographen von Fanny Hensel in dem Mendelssohn-Arkiv zu Berlin', *Mendelssohn-Studien*, i (1972), 169–74

—— : 'Weitere Quellen zu den Werken von Fanny Hensel', *Mendelssohn-Studien*, ii (1975), 215–20

C. L. Quin: *Fanny Mendelssohn Hensel: Her Contributions to Nineteenth-Century Musical Life* (diss., U. of Kentucky, 1981)

V. R. Sirota: *The Life and Works of Fanny Mendelssohn Hensel* (diss. Boston U., 1981)

M. J. Citron: 'The Lieder of Fanny Mendelssohn Hensel', *MQ*, lxix (1983), 570–93

E. Weissweiler, ed.: *Fanny Mendelssohn: italienisches Tagebuch* (Frankfurt, 2/1983)

M. J. Citron: 'Felix Mendelssohn's Influence on Fanny Mendelssohn Hensel as a Professional Composer', *CMc*, nos.37–8 (1984), 9–17

E. Weissweiler, ed.: *Fanny Mendelssohn: ein Portrait in Briefen* (Frankfurt, 1985)

M. J. Citron, ed.: *The Letters of Fanny Hensel to Felix Mendelssohn* (New York, 1987)

P. Benjamin: 'A Diary-Album for Fanny Mendelssohn Bartholdy', *Mendelssohn-Studien*, vii (1990), 178–217

N. Reich: 'The Power of Class: Fanny Hensel', *Mendelssohn and his World*, ed. R. L. Todd (Princeton, 1991), 86–99

F. Tillard: *Fanny Mendelssohn* (Paris, 1992)

MARCIA J. CITRON

Ménétou, Françoise-Charlotte de Senneterre, Mlle de

(*b* Paris, 1680; *fl* 1691). French harpsichordist and composer. At the age of nine she played for the Dauphine Marie Anne Christine Victoire of Bavaria and Louis XIV who, according to the Marquis de Dangeau (18 August 1689), found her playing 'délicieuse'; a 118-page manuscript dated 1689 contains pieces by her as well as by J.-H. D'Anglebert, Michel Lambert, N.-A. Lebègue and J.-B. Lully (*US-BE* MS 777). Two years later, she published her own *recueil d'airs* (1691). She was the daughter of the Duc de La Ferté and a pupil of François Couperin (whose second book of harpsichord pieces includes one entitled *La Ménétou*).

BIBLIOGRAPHY

C. Masson: 'Journal du Marquis de Dangeau, 1684–1720: extrait concernant la vie à la cour', *RMFC*, ii (1961–2), 193–221, esp. 203

A. Curtis: 'Musique classique française à Berkeley: pièces inédites de Louis Couperin, Lebègue, De La Barre, etc', *RdM*, lvi (1970), 123–64

B. L. Gustafson: *The Sources of Seventeenth-Century French Harpsichord Music: Thematic Catalog and Commentary* (diss., U. of Michigan, 1977)

JULIE ANNE SADIE

Menter, Sophie (*b* Munich, 29 July 1846; *d* Stockdorf, nr Munich, 23 Feb 1918). German pianist and composer. The daughter of the cellist Josef Menter and the singer Wilhelmine Menter [née Diepold], she was taught the piano by Siegmund Lebert and, later, by Friedrich Niest. At 15 she played Weber's *Konzertstück* for piano and orchestra with F. P. Lachner conducting. Her first concert performances took her to Stuttgart, Frankfurt and Switzerland. In 1867 she was acclaimed for her interpretation of Liszt's piano music at the Leipzig Gewandhaus. In Berlin she became acquainted with the famous pianist Carl Tausig and occasionally joined the circle of pianists studying with Liszt, who described her as 'my only legitimate piano daughter'; Anton Rubinstein called her 'the sole ruler of all piano keys and hearts'. From 1872 until 1886 she was married to the cellist David Popper. In 1883 she became piano professor at the St Petersburg Conservatory but left in 1886 to continue her concert tours. She first appeared in England in 1881 and in 1883 was awarded honorary membership of the Philharmonic Society. She was regarded as one of the greatest piano virtuosos of her time. She composed various pieces for piano, mostly in a brilliant style, yet spoke of herself as having a 'miserable talent for composing'.

WORKS
all for piano

Tarantelle, op.4; Romance, op.5; Mazurka, op.6; Petit valse, op.7; Sextenstudie, op.8; Etude, A♭, op.9; Consolation, op.10; Ungarische Zigeunerweisen, arr. pf, orchd Tchaikovsky

BIBLIOGRAPHY
SchmidlD
La Mara (M. Lipsius): *Musikalische Studienköpfe* (Leipzig, 1868, enlarged 2/1875–82), v: *Die Frauen im Tonleben der Gegenwart*

EVA RIEGER

Messager, Dotie. See TEMPLE, HOPE.

Metallidi, Zhanneta Lazarevna (*b* Leningrad [now St Petersburg], 1 June 1934). Russian composer and teacher. She studied composition with Galina Ustvol'skaya at the music college attached to the Leningrad Conservatory (1952–5) and with Orest Alexandrovich Yevlakhov at the conservatory itself (1955–60). She worked at the Leningrad Drama Institute as an accompanist and a composer of incidental music (1959–63). From 1960 she taught composition, solfeggio and theory at a children's music school in Leningrad, which provided her with opportunities to compose for specific performing ensembles, enabling her to test her ideas. She has created a diverse repertory of children's music, which has been in continuous use in Russian schools. She was greatly influenced by Ustvol'skaya: both composers aspire to clarity of conception and exactness of realization. Metallidi attaches particular importance to melody, especially in music for children. Joviality reigns, and witty jokes and nonsense words occur often.

WORKS
selective list

Stage: Strana (Valyay, forsi!) [The Country (Swagger: Go Ahead!)] (musical, Yu. Kruznov), 1989; Tarakanishche [The Cockroach] (opera, K. Chukovsky), 1992

Orch: Sym., 1962, rev. 1993; Concertino, fl, chamber orch, 1965; Concertino, fl, vn, pf, str orch, 1981; Zolotoy klyuchik [The Little Golden Key], suite, 1981–2; Conc.-Fantasia, fl, pf, str orch, 1982; Conc., tpt, fl, str orch, perc, 1984; Lukomor'ye [Curved Seashore], suite, 1987; Sinfonietta, 1993

Chamber, inst: Wind Qnt, 1972; Str Qt, 1974; Pf cycles: Vospominaniya o Severe [Reminiscence of the North], 1975, Zolotoye kol'tso Rossii [The Golden Ring of Russia], 1988; Ermitazhnïye zarisovki [Hermitage Sketches], 1992; numerous children's pieces for various insts

Song cycles: Romances (V. Mayakovsky), 1963; (M. Tsvetayeva), 1966; (P. Eluard), 1973; Zimniye solov'i [Winter Nightingales] (Pol. poets, trans. B. Zakhoder and Yu. Vronsky), 1978; other cycles and songs for children

Choral: Smeyantsï [Merry Fellows], (cantata, G. Sagpir), children's chorus, perc, pf, 1981; Mir glazami detey [The World through Children's Eyes], children's chorus, orch, 1988; unacc. choral songs

Also educational music

BIBLIOGRAPHY
S. Tikhaya, ed.: 'Rasskazïvayet Zh. L. Metallidi' [Metallidi Speaks], *Chto uslïshal kompozitor* [What the Composer has Heard], no.3 (Leningrad, 1987), 53–65

OLGA MANULKINA

Meyer [née Tuxen], **(Katharina) Elisabeth** (*b* Svendborg, 19 July 1859; *d* Copenhagen, 4 July 1927). Danish composer. Her parents' home was the centre of musical life in Svendborg; her mother gave singing lessons and her sister, Marie English, became a famous singer. Meyer was taught by her mother and probably by the composers Jørgen Malling and L. H. G. Birkedal-Barfod. She married and had four children, but, being well off, found time and energy for composing. She wrote about 60 songs,

Teresa Milanollo: lithograph by M. Alophe

almost exclusively on Danish texts, and a cantata (now lost).

WORKS
printed works published in Copenhagen
Inst: Berceuse, vn, pf (1900); Naar Duggen falder, pf (1913)
Vocal: 5 sange (1892); Blandede digte (1893); Madonnafest (1893); 3 sange (1893); 4 sange, (1895); Tove (1895); c35 other songs, unpubd; cantata, soloists, female chorus, 2 pf, lost

BIBLIOGRAPHY
H. K. Nielsen: *Mere end en Muse* (diss., Århus U., 1989)

INGE BRULAND

Mezari, Maddalena. *See* CASULANA, MADDALENA.

Michielina [Michaelis, Michieletta]. *See* DELLA PIETÀ, MICHIELINA.

Milanollo, (Domenica Maria) Teresa (*b* Savigliano, nr Turin, 28 Aug 1827; *d* Paris, 25 Oct 1904). Italian violinist and composer. She studied solfège with her father and the violin with Giovanni Ferrero, Mauro Caldera and Giovanni Morra. She made her début on 17 April 1836 in Mondovi before moving with her family to France; there she met the violinist Charles Philippe Lafont,

who took her on tour to the Netherlands. In December 1836 she gave a benefit concert in Brussels, which marked the beginning of a lifelong concern for the poor.

Early in 1837 the Milanollo family went to England, where Teresa performed with Johann Strauss and became the protégée and pupil of Francis Mori. In 1838 she toured Wales with the harpist N. C. Bochsa. She then returned with her family to France, and in 1842 she and her sister Maria (1832–48), also a violinist, began a series of European concert tours which rivalled those of Nicolò Paganini in artistic and financial success. For a time they settled in Brussels, where Teresa studied composition with Hubert-Ferdinand Kufferath. During their second tour to England (1845) they appeared at the Philharmonic concerts. In Lyons they surpassed the earlier successes of Sigismond Thalberg, H. W. Ernst and even Liszt; after her sister's death, Teresa established the Concerts des Pauvres there. From 1852 she toured France, Switzerland, Germany and Austria, and on the day of her last public concert (16 April 1857) she married Théodore Parmentier, a military engineer and an amateur musician of some repute, who wrote for the *Revue et gazette musicale*.

Milanollo's compositions include opera transcriptions for two violins and orchestra, numerous pieces for solo violin, including a *Fantaisie élégiaque* (written in 1853 in memory of her sister), and an Ave Maria for male chorus.

BIBLIOGRAPHY
FétisB; *FétisBS*; *Grove1* (P. David); *SchmidlD*
A. Pougin: 'Les soeurs Milanollo', *RIM*, xxiii (1916), 345–89
A. Moser: *Geschichte des Violinspiels* (Berlin, 1923, rev., enlarged 2/1966–7)
E. van der Straeten: *The History of the Violin* (London, 1933), ii, 32ff

ALBERT MELL

Miles, Jane Mary. *See* GUEST, JANE MARY.

Milstein, Silvina [née Mendzylewski] (*b* Buenos Aires, 12 Feb 1956). Argentine composer, resident in Britain. Her early musical training took place at the Collegium Musicum in Buenos Aires; subsequent study at the University of La Plata was curtailed by her emigration to Britain after the Argentine military coup in 1976. In 1979 she entered Glasgow University, where her composition teachers were Judith Weir and Lyell Cresswell, and after graduation in 1983 she went to Cambridge University to study composition and to research into the music of Arnold Schoenberg with Alexander Goehr. In that year she wrote the serial composition *Sombras*, which became co-winner of the Ralph Vaughan Williams Trust/SPNM Orchestral Award in 1985. At Cambridge she held fellowships at Jesus College and King's College and wrote the book *Arnold Schoenberg: Notes, Sets, Forms* (Cambridge, 1992). A composing hiatus of four years ended with the String Quartet (1989), which abandons serial writing in favour of a melodically motivated mode of composition. Later works in her modest output have proved more referential: the *Piano Phantasy* (1992) takes Mozart's Fantasia K475 as its model, while *Music of the City* (1993) for orchestra draws on the vernacular music of Buenos Aires. In 1989 Milstein became a lecturer in music at King's College, London.

BIBLIOGRAPHY
Fuller-LeFanuRM

RHIAN SAMUEL

Miyake, Haruna [Shibata, Haruna] (*b* Tokyo, 20 Sept 1942). Japanese pianist and composer. She studied in Tokyo and then at the Juilliard School of Music, New York, with Vincent Persichetti. As a pianist she made her début with the Tokyo SO at the age of 14 playing Mozart and continues to perform standard repertory as well as experimental works. A frequent collaborator with the pianist-composer Yuji Takahashi, she has also collaborated in improvisatory work with a range of artists (Christian Marclay, Sergei Kuryokhin, Richard Teitelbaum, Wayne Shorter and Frederic Rzewski).

Miyake has sought to create music comparable to the avant-garde novels of Masuji Ibuse and Hyakken Uchida: art which differs from European forms but which Westerners would not perceive as Asian. Her compositional influences range from childhood experiences with Japanese traditional instruments and attendance at *bunraku* puppet theatre to Charles Ives's writings about music. From 1977 to 1985 she presented a concert series that mixed Japanese *enka* (a nostalgic style of pop music) with European avant-garde idioms. In a desire to link her music with the concreteness of daily life and its chaotic nature, she composed a series of pieces called *Why Not, My Baby?* (for soprano, piano and trumpet) reflecting her experiences as a mother and blending avant-garde style, Baroque music and *enka*. Some

works combine tone clusters and glissandos within traditional Western forms.

WORKS
selective list

Poem for Str Orch: Shiyoku, 1964; Pf Conc., 1966; Music for Pic, Fl and Gui, 1967; Fantasy for 'Milky Way Railroad', 2 fl, 2 ob, 2 tpt, gui, 1970; Why Not, My Baby?, S, pf, tpt, n.d.; Why Not, My Baby? II: Sutego Elegy, pf, 1974; Phantom of a Flower (T. Hara), S, tpt, pf, 1977; Poem Harmonica, harmonica, pf/2 pf/pf, pf + synth/accordion, 1980; Es war einmal ein Igel, 2 pf, 1983; Requiem, orch, 1984, also pf version Bird Shadows (The Shadow of a Bird), 1984; 43° North: a Tango, Type II, pf, pf + synth, 1986; Psalm on the Anti-World, 2 pf, 1987; Toward the East, snare drum + yunluo [small Chin. gongs], pf, 1987; Air Music, pf + synth, synth, str bass, 1989; Playtime (P. Celan), pf + synth, large wind orch [players recite text], 1989; Inner Paradise VI (13th-century love songs from *Shin-Kokin Waka-shu*, shamisen + v, v, tape, 1991; The Time of Melancholy, double conc., pf + synth, perc, orch, 1991

BIBLIOGRAPHY
R. Joseph: 'New Faces: Haruna Miyake', *Ear Magazine*, xv/8 (1990–91), 66
Discussion [H. Miyake, K. Massumoto, N. Funayama, E. Rieger, A. Hölszky, R. Matthei], *Komponistinnen in Japan und Deutschland: eine Dokumentation*, ed. R. Matthei (Kassel, 1991), 45–56
T. Kakinuma: 'Japan', *Ear Magazine*, xv/10 (1991), 18
H. Miyake: '. . . in den siebziger Jahren konnte ich mit der Zeit fühlen und eins mit ihr sein', *Komponistinnen in Japan und Deutschland: eine Dokumentation*, ed. R. Matthei (Kassel, 1991), 41–4
J. MICHELE EDWARDS

Moberg, Ida Georgina (*b* Helsinki, 13 Feb 1859; *d* Helsinki, 2 Aug 1947). Finnish composer and conductor. After taking piano and singing lessons, she studied counterpoint with Richard Faltin and composition with Sibelius at the Helsinki Orchestral School. In 1893–4 she was at the St Petersburg Conservatory and from 1901 to 1905 at the Dresden Conservatory, where she was a pupil of Felix Draeseke. She completed her training at the Dalcroze Institute in Berlin (1911–12) and then returned to Helsinki. From 1914 she taught at the Helsinki Music Institute and conducted choirs, which sometimes performed her music. In 1906 Moberg conducted her symphony, an Overture in A minor, *Lantlig dans* ('Country Dance') for orchestra, and *Vaknen* ('Awaken') for male chorus and orchestra, and in 1908 her *Tyrannens natt* ('The Night of the Tyrant'), also for male chorus and orchestra. Intermittently, and as late as 1945–6, she worked on an opera about Buddha, *Asiens Ijus* ('The Light of Asia'), based on a poem by Viktor Rydberg; although it was never completed, fragments were performed.

BIBLIOGRAPHY

G. von Klosse: 'Ida Moberg: ensimmäinen soomalai-
nen naissäveltäja [The First Finnish Woman
Composer], *Musiikki*, no.7 (1948)
T. Karila, ed.: *Composers of Finland* (Porvoo, 2/1965)

FABIAN DAHLSTRÖM

Mockel, Johanna. See KINKEL, JOHANNA.

Moe, Benna (*b* Copenhagen, 14 Jan 1897; *d*
Copenhagen, 30 May 1983). Danish composer and organist. In 1915 she took a degree
in organ playing at the Kongelige Danske
Musikkonservatorium in Copenhagen. She
gave concerts throughout her life, enjoying
particular success in Sweden, where, in the
1940s, she made long stays in Stockholm and
in Mora, working partly as town composer
and music teacher. From 1948 to 1950 she
was cinema organist at the Palladium,
Copenhagen, but in later years she concentrated more on church concerts (though she
never held a church post). Moe composed a
large amount of music, serious as well as
light. Her ballet *Hybris*, which she did not
orchestrate, was performed in Copenhagen
in 1930.

WORKS
selective list

Stage: Hybris, ballet, 1929; Copenhagen, Kongelige
Teater, 1930
Chamber and solo inst: Berceuse, vn, pf, 1914; 3
instruktive etuder, pf, op.6 (1918), op.9 (1923);
Gondolier's Serenade, op.11, pf (1927); Alpine
Suite, op.l2, org, 1927; Danse espagnole, vn, pf,
1928; Festival Polonaise, pf 4 hands, 1928;
Intermezzo, vn, pf, 1931; Str Qt, f, 1934;
Meditation, vn, pf, 1969; Koncert suite, org (1971);
Cantilena, org (1972); Une petite suite ancienne,
org (1972); Praeludie, org, 1977; Legend, org, 1980
Vocal: More than 200 solo songs, mostly from the
period 1925–45, of which 20 are children's songs;
occasional cantatas, incl. Kantate vid Mora, 1945
Many marches, waltzes, tangos and foxtrots, orches-
trated by others

BIBLIOGRAPHY

I. Bruland: 'Benna Moe, overgangskvinde og profes-
sionel musiker', *KIM-NYT*, vii/21 (1990), 9–16

INGE BRULAND

Monk, Meredith (*b* Lima, Peru, 20 Nov
1943). American composer and singer. She
was born in Peru while her mother – a pop
and show singer known professionally as
Audrey Marsh – was on tour; she grew up in
New York and Connecticut, and in 1964
graduated from Sarah Lawrence College (BA
in performing arts). From the beginning of
her career Monk's interests have included
solo singing, film making (she made her first
film in 1966), choreography and directing;

her first theatre piece, *Juice*, was given its
première at the Guggenheim Museum, New
York, in 1969. During the 1970s she became
one of the most popular members of the
'downtown' avant garde and, subsequently,
a highly regarded creator of music-theatre.

Monk views the human voice as the aboriginal instrument. Her compositions depend
on extended vocal techniques – including
(with conventionally sung notes over a four-
octave range) a variety of insistent, wistful,
fey or humorous cries (always wordless); at
times Monk sounds as if she might be singing ethnic music from a culture she invented
herself. Her solo pieces, some with repetitive
piano accompaniments derived both from
minimalism and from popular music, are
built from simple, often modal melodies and
melodic cells, repeated with constant small
variations and alternated with other material
to form additive structures reminiscent of
birdsong. In the late 1970s the composer
shifted her focus from essentially solo voice
to ensemble singing and in 1978 founded the
Meredith Monk Vocal Ensemble, a chamber
group that performs with her in the USA and
in Europe. Her ensemble pieces, such as
Dolmen Music (1979), are somewhat tenta-
tive: the added voices are muted, at least
compared with Monk's solo singing, and the
variety they introduce is accommodated at
the expense of continuity. Nevertheless these
pieces enjoy tremendous popularity. Monk's
most highly developed works are powerfully
affecting theatre pieces such as *Quarry* (1976),
in which music, film, dance, acting and
scraps of text are combined to create the
assured flow produced in conventional opera
by music alone. However, *The Games*
(1983), a view of reconstruction after a
nuclear holocaust, relies more heavily on its
unusually dissonant and varied score.

Monk has received several awards and
commissions for her music-theatre pieces,
including two Obie awards (1972, for *Vessel*,
and 1976, for *Quarry*) and first prize in the
music-theatre category at the 1975 Venice
Biennale (for *Education of the Girlchild*). She
conceived, wrote and directed her first
feature-length film, *Book of Days*, in 1988,
the music for which is a re-working and re-
scoring of an earlier work. Her 1991 opera
Atlas was commissioned by the Houston
Grand Opera (see illustration, p. 330).

WORKS
SOLO VOCAL

16 Millimeter Earrings, 1v, gui, 1966; Candy Bullets
and Moon, 1v, el org, el db, perc, 1967, collab. D.
Preston; Blueprint: Overload/Blueprint 2, 1v, tape,

Scene from Meredith Monk's opera 'Atlas' commissioned by Houston Grand Opera (1991): Alexandra Daniels (Meredith Monk) speaks with the Ancient Man (Wilbur Pauley) in 'Forest Questions' from part 2 ('Night Travel')

live elec, 1967; A Raw Recital, 1v, el org, 1970; Our Lady of the Late, 1v, wine glass, 1972–3, arr. 1v, wine glass, perc, 1974; Songs from the Hill, 1976–7; View no.2, 1v, synth, 1982; Double Fiesta, 1v, 2 pf, 1986; I don't Know, 1v, pf, 1986; Scared Song, 1v, synth, pf, 1986; String, 1v, 1986; Cat Song, 1v, 1988; Fayum Music, 1v, hammered dulcimer, double ocarina, 1988; Light Songs, 1v, 1988; Processional, 1v, pf, 1988

VOCAL ENSEMBLE

Tablet, 4 solo vv, 2 s rec, pf 4 hands, 1977; Dolmen Music, 6 solo vv, vc, perc, 1979; Tokyo Cha-cha, 6 solo vv, 2 el org, 1983; 2 Men Walking, 3 solo vv, el org, 1983; Panda Chant I, 4 vv, 1984; Panda Chant II, 8 vv, 1984; Graduation Song, 16 vv, 1984; Book of Days, 5 solo vv, chorus, synth, pf, 1985, arr. 7 solo vv, synth, also rev. for film version; Do You Be, 10 vv, 2 pf, synth, vn, bagpipes, 1987; Duet Behavior, 2 vv, 1987; 3 Heavens and Hells, 4 vv, 1992

THEATRE PIECES

Juice, theatre cantata, 85 solo vv, 85 jew's harps, 2 vn, 1969; Needle-Brain Lloyd and the Systems Kid, 150 solo vv, el org, fl, gui, 1970; Plainsong for Bill's Bojo (incid. music, W. Dunas), el org, 1971; Vessel (opera epic), 75 solo vv, el org, accordion, 2 dulcimers, 1971; Paris, 2 solo vv, pf, 1972; Education of the Girlchild (opera), 6 solo vv, el org, pf, 1972–3; Chacon, 25 vv, pf, perc, 1974; Quarry (opera), 38 solo vv, 2 harmoniums, 2 s rec, tape, 1976; Venice/Milan, 15 solo vv, pf 4 hands, 1976; The Plateau Series, 5 solo vv, tape, 1977

Recent Ruins, 12 vv, vc, 1979; Specimen Days (opera), 14 solo vv, 2 pf, 2 el org, 1981; View no.1, 1v, pf, synth, 1981, collab. Ping Chong; The Games, 16 solo vv, synth, el kbds, bagpipes, Flemish bagpipes, Chin. hn, Rauschpfeife, 1983, collab. Ping Chong; Turtle Dreams (cabaret), 4 solo vv, 2 el org, 1983; The Ringing Place, 9 vv, 1987; Facing North, 2 vv, tape, 1990, collab. R. Een; Atlas (opera), 18 vv, 2 kbd, cl, b cl, sheng, bamboo sax, 2 vn, va, 2 vc, hn, perc, 1991

OTHER WORKS

View no.1, video score, 1v, pf, synth, 1981, collab. Ping Chong; Engine Steps, tape collage, 1983; Window in 7s, pf, 1986; Parlour Games, 2 pf, 1988; Raven, pf, 1988; Phantom Waltz, 2 pf, 1990; Book of Days, film score [from vocal ensemble work], 10 vv, vc, shawm, synth, hammered dulcimer, bagpipe, hurdy-gurdy, 1988, dir. Monk

BIBLIOGRAPHY

M. Monk and F. Quadri: 'Il tempo e gli ambienti di Meredith Monk: con il testo parlato di Quarry', *Edizioni de La Biennale di Venezia 1976*

L. K. Telberg: 'Meredith Monk – Renaissance Woman', *Music Journal*, xxxvii/6 (1979), 6

H. Budweg: 'Meredith Monk: ein Portrait', *NZM*, Jg.141 (1980), 543–4

M. Monk: 'Notes on the Voice', *Terpsichore in Sneakers*, ed. S. Banes (Boston, 1980), 166–7

K. Bernard: 'Some Observations on Meredith Monk's *Specimen Days*', *Theater* [Yale School of Drama], xiii/2 (1982), 88–90

R. Oehlschlägel: 'Dances for the Voice: Meredith

Monk – Tänzerin, Performerin, Musikerin',
Neuland Ansätze zur Musik der Gegenwart, iv (1983–
4), 234–38
G. Sandow: 'Invisible Theater: the Music of Meredith
Monk', *The Musical Woman: an International
Perspective*, i: *1983*, ed. J. L. Zaimont and others
(Westport, CT, 1984), 147–50
R. Baker: 'Living Spaces: 20 Years of Theatre with
Meredith Monk', *Theatre Crafts*, xix/March (1985),
32–7
S. Foster: 'The Signifying Body: Reaction and
Resistance in Postmodern Dance', *Theatre Journal*,
xxxvii/1 (1985), 45–64
J. K. Forte: *Women in Performance Art: Feminism and
Postmodernism* (diss., U. of Washington, 1986)
C. Ryan: 'Meet the Composer: Meredith Monk', *Ear*
xii/8 (1987), 16–19 [interview]
D. Sterritt: 'Summen, Keuchen, Wispern, Singen:
Performance Künstlerin Meredith Monk', *NZM*,
Jg.148, no.6 (1987), 19–21
S. Mayer: 'Meredith Monk', *Jazz Podium*, xxxvii/Dec
(1988), 35
E. Strickland: 'Voices/Visions: an Interview with
Meredith Monk', *Fanfare*, xi/3 (1988), 354–65
R. Sandla: 'Dream weaver', *ON*, lv (1990–91), 8–11
B. Marranca: 'Meredith Monk's Atlas of Sound: New
Opera and the American Performance Tradition',
Performing Arts Journal, xiv/Jan (1992), 16–29
ELLEN D. LERNER, GREGORY SANDOW

Montgeroult, Hélène de Nervo de
[Countess de Charnay] (*b* Lyons, 2 March
1764; *d* Florence, 20 May 1836). French
virtuoso fortepianist and composer. She was
trained as a fortepianist by N.-J. Hüllmandel
and then J. L. Dussek (in 1786). She was
briefly married to the Marquis de Montgeroult, who served in the French army in
Italy before perishing while a prisoner of the
Austrians en route home in 1793. As a
vulnerable widow of aristocratic stock, Mme
de Montgeroult seems to have entered into a
temporary marriage of convenience in order
to evade persecution during the Reign of
Terror.

Though appointed *professeur de première
classe* at the newly established Paris
Conservatoire in 1795, her name disappeared
from the list after the second year. However,
through her pupils (who included L.-B.
Pradère, A. P. F. Boëly and I. A. Ladurner),
her two collections of *Trois sonates pour le
forte-piano* and a *Cours complet pour l'enseignement du forte-piano* (the second part contains
70 etudes), which all appear to have been
published during 1795–6, she continued to
exert an important influence on early French
piano pedagogy.

BIBLIOGRAPHY
Choron-FayolleD 2; FétisB; SainsburyD
M. Brenet: 'Quatre femmes musiciennes', *L'art*, lix
(1894), 142–7
JULIE ANNE SADIE

Moore, Dorothy Rudd (*b* New Castle, DE,
4 June 1940). American composer and poet.
She studied composition with Mark Fax
at Howard University, Washington, DC
(BM 1963), with Nadia Boulanger at the
American Conservatory at Fontainebleau
(summer 1963), and with Chou Wen-chung
in New York (1965). She taught theory and
piano at the Harlem School of the Arts
(1965–6) and music history and appreciation
at New York University (1969) and Bronx
Community College, CUNY (1971). She
has also published poetry, some of which she
has set, and has worked as a singer in New
York. In 1968 she helped to found the
Society of Black Composers. Her works
are predominantly contrapuntal, sometimes
with block harmonies, clusters, and chords
built in 2nds and 4ths. Her husband Kermit
Moore, a cellist, is among those who have
given premières of her works.

WORKS
selective list
Stage: Frederick Douglas (opera, 3, Moore), 1979–85
Orch: Reflections, sym. wind, 1962; Sym. no.1, 1963;
  Transcension ('I have been to the mountaintop'),
  chamber orch, 1986
Chamber and solo inst: Adagio, va, vc, 1965; Baroque
  Suite, vc, 1965; 3 Pieces, vn, pf, 1967; Modes, str
  qt, 1968; Moods, va, vc, 1969; Pf Trio, 1970; Dirge
  and Deliverance, vc, pf, 1971; Dream and
  Variations (Theme and Variations), pf, 1974; Night
  Fantasy, cl, pf, 1978; A Little Whimsy, pf, 1982
Vocal: Songs (*Rubáiyát of Omar Khayyám*), cycle of 12
  songs, S, ob, 1962; From the Dark Tower (J. W.
  Johnson, A. Bontemps, H. C. Johnson, G. D.
  Johnson, W. Cuney, L. Hughes, C. Cullen), cycle
  of 8 songs, Mez, vc, pf, 1970, nos.1, 3, 6, and 8 arr.
  Mez, chamber ens, 1972; The Weary Blues
  (Hughes), Bar, vc, pf, 1972, arr. Bar, chamber
  orch, 1979; Sonnets on Love, Rosebuds, and Death
  (A. D. Nelson, C. S. Delaney, G. B. Bennett,
  Hughes, Bontemps, Cullen, H. Johnson), cycle of 8
  songs, S, vn, pf, 1976; In Celebration (Hughes),
  Bar, SATB, pf, 1977; Flowers of Darkness, T, pf,
  1989

Principal publishers: ACA, Belwin–Mills
MSS in Howard University, Washington, DC

BIBLIOGRAPHY
SouthernB
A. Tischler: *Fifteen Black American Composers: a
  Bibliography of their Works* (Detroit, 1981)
A. Horne: *String Music of Black Composers: a
  Bibliography* (New York, 1991)
H. Walker-Hill: *Piano Music by Black Women
  Composers* (New York, 1992)
D. C. Hine, ed.: *Black Women in America: an Historical
  Encyclopedia* (Brooklyn, NY, 1993)
DORIS EVANS McGINTY

Moore, Mary (Louise) Carr (*b* Memphis,
6 Aug 1873; *d* Inglewood, CA, 9 Jan 1957).

American composer and teacher. She studied in San Francisco with J. H. Pratt (composition) and H. B. Pasmore (singing). By 1889 she had begun teaching and composing (a song from that year was later published) and in 1894 she sang the leading role in the première of her first operetta *The Oracle*. The following year she abandoned her singing career; for the rest of her life she taught and composed in Lemoore, California (from 1895), Seattle (1901), San Francisco (1915) and Los Angeles (1926). In Los Angeles she taught at the Olga Steeb Piano School (1926–43) and was concurrently professor of theory and composition at Chapman College, Orange, California (1928–47) which awarded her the honorary DMus in 1936. Moore was a tireless promoter of American music; she organized an American Music Center in Seattle (1909) and worked for Federal Music Project performances by local composers in Los Angeles (1936–42).

The American music movement of the 'progressive' era greatly inspired Moore as a composer. Her early study of late 19th-century European compositional models was tempered by her location on the West Coast, where the boundaries between élite and vernacular styles in music tended to blur. Moore was at her best in opera, frequently challenging the limitations of the genteel culture to which she remained bound by inclination and family obligations. Her largest work,

Mary Carr Moore

Narcissa (1909–11), has a legitimate claim to be the first major 'American' opera, but it went unrecognized and was misunderstood. Its three productions (1912, Seattle; 1925, San Francisco; 1945, Los Angeles; all with the composer conducting) failed to draw serious attention. Based on the 1847 massacre of missionaries Narcissa and Marcus Whitman in the Oregon Territory, neither the opera's theme nor its setting fit the already established stereotype of the colonial East Coast as the proper setting for 'American' opera. Its main character, Narcissa Prentiss Whitman, is presented, like her husband, as missionary, patriot, pioneer and teacher, but with the added, exalted role of mother. The absence of romantic interest led even those critics who were moved by the work's dramatic power and who admired its music to wonder whether it was really an opera at all. *Narcissa* was belatedly awarded a David Bispham Memorial Medal in 1930.

Moore altered her musical language substantially after *Narcissa*. *David Rizzio* (completed in 1928), whose action takes place during the brief reign of Mary, Queen of Scots, makes much use of the whole tone scale. In *Legende provençale*, a tale of love, faith and sorcery set in the 15th century, the harmonic vocabulary is expanded still further. Vocal scores of *Narcissa* (1912) and *David Rizzio* (1937) were published in Moore's lifetime. Mixed groups of amateurs and professionals, assembled through her own efforts, performed her operas, although she considered *Narcissa*, *David Rizzio*, *Los Rubios* and especially the delicate and demanding *Legende provençale* too difficult for amateur singers. All except *The Leper* and *Legende provençale*, which were never produced, had at least limited revivals. In addition to the operas, her chamber works and many of her songs deserve revival; her published works include 65 songs, 15 choral works and piano pieces.

WORKS

OPERAS

★ – *autograph*

The Oracle (operetta, 2, Moore), San Francisco, Golden Gate Hall, 19 March 1894; rev. (3), Seattle, 10 Jan 1902, vs *US-LAu*★

Narcissa, or The Cost of Empire (grand opera, 4, S. P. Carr), 1909–11; Seattle, Moore Theatre, 22 April 1912, conductor's score (pts) *LAu*, vs (New York, 1912)

The Leper (1, D. Burrows), 1912, unperf., vs *LAu*★

Memories (vaudeville sketch, 1, C. E. Banks), Seattle, Orpheum Theatre, 31 Oct 1914, vs *LAu*★

Harmony (operetta, 1, various students), San Francisco, Mission High School, 25 May 1917, vs (pts) *LAu*★

Mary Carr Moore's opera 'Narcissa, or The Cost of Empire' (1909–11): scene from Act 1 of the original Seattle production (1912), from 'Musical America' (11 May 1912)

The Flaming Arrow, or The Shaft of Ku'pish-ta-ya (operetta, 1, Carr), 1919–20; San Francisco, Pacific Music Society, 27 March 1922, vs *LAu*

David Rizzio (2, E. M. Browne), 1927–8; Los Angeles, Shrine Auditorium, 26 May 1932, *LAu★*, vs (San Bruno, CA, 1937)

Legende provençale (3, E. Flaig), 1929–35, unperf., vs *LAu*

Los rubios (3, N. Marquis), Los Angeles, Greek Theatre, 10 Sept 1931, *LAu*, vs *Wc*

Flutes of Jade Happiness (operetta, 3, L. S. Moore), 1932–3; Los Angeles, Los Angeles High School, 2 March 1934, vs (pts) *LAu★*

OTHER WORKS

Orch: Ka-mi-a-kin, 1930; Pf Conc., 1933–4; Kidnap, 1937–8

Chamber and solo inst: 2 pf trios, 1895, 1906; Saul (R. Browning), pf trio, nar, 1916, arr. pf, str qt, pts *LAu*, arr. orch, nar, 1930; Vn Sonata, c1918–19; Str Qt, g, 1926; Str Qt, f, 1930; Str Trio, g, 1936; Pf Trio, 1941; Brief Furlough, qnt, 1942; 57 pf pieces; 20 other pieces for various insts and pf

Vocal: Beyond These Hills (G. Moyle), cycle, S, A, T, B, pf, 1923–4; 250 songs, 1889–1952; 57 choral pieces

Principal publishers: C. Fischer, G. Schirmer, Webster, Witmark

MSS in *US-LAu*

BIBLIOGRAPHY

M. C. Moore: 'Writing and Producing an Opera', *Pacific Coast Musician*, iv/7 (1915), 51

F. H. Martens: *A Thousand and One Nights of Opera* (New York, 1926)

E. E. Hipsher: *American Opera and its Composers* (Philadelphia, c1927, 2/1934)

'Mary Carr Moore – American Composer', *Christian Science Monitor* (16 April 1929), 11

M. Couche: 'Mary Carr Moore: American Composer', *Music of the West*, ix/6 (1954), 13, 18

H. E. Johnson: *Operas on American Subjects* (New York, 1964)

C. P. Smith: Introduction in M. C. Moore: *David Rizzio*, Women Composers Series, xii (New York, 1981) [repr. of 1937 edn]

—— : Liner Notes, *The Songs of Mary Carr Moore* (Cambria 1022, 1985)

C. P. Smith and C. S. Richardson: *Mary Carr Moore, American Composer* (Ann Arbor, 1987)

B. Rogers: *The Works for Piano Solo and Piano with Other Instruments of Mary Carr Moore (1873–1957)*, (diss., U. of Cincinnati, 1992)

CYNTHIA S. RICHARDSON,
CATHERINE PARSONS SMITH

Moore, Undine Smith (*b* Jarratt, VA, 25 Aug 1905; *d* Petersburg, VA, 6 Feb 1989). American composer and educator. She studied the piano and organ with Alice M. Grass at Fisk University, Nashville (BA, BMus), and continued her education at the Juilliard School, the Manhattan School, Columbia University Teachers College and the Eastman School. After teaching in schools in Goldsboro, North Carolina, she taught at Virginia State College, Petersburg, from 1927 to her retirement in 1972; there she co-founded and co-directed the Black Music Center (1969–72). She also lectured extensively and was a visiting professor at several colleges, including Virginia Union University in Richmond.

Moore's earlier vocal compositions were built on diatonic harmonies with melodic emphasis and ethnic identification, while her instrumental works and later vocal compositions included dissonant polyphony and occasional passages of atonality.

WORKS
selective list; for a fuller list see
Baker, Belt and Hudson

Inst: Scherzo, pf, 1930; Valse Caprice, pf, 1930; Fugue, str trio, 1952; Reflections, pf, org, 1952; Romance, 2 pf, 1952; Romantic Young Clown, pf, 1952; Introduction, March and Allegro, cl, pf, 1958; 3 Pieces, fl, pf, 1958; Afro-American Suite, 2 fl, vc, pf, 1969; Variations on 'Nettleton', org, 1976; Soweto, pf trio, 1987

Choral: Sir Olaf and the Erl King's Daughter, cantata, SSA, pf, 1925; Into my Heart's Treasury, 1950; Thou has made us for thyself, 1952; Teach me to hear mermaids singing, SSA, 1953; Mother to Son, 1955; When Susanna Jones wears red, c1958; Let us make man in our image, 1960; O spirit who dost prefer before all temples, chorus, pf/org, 1966; Lord, we give thanks to thee, 1971; Tambourines to Glory, 1973; Glory to God, cantata, nar, TTBB, fl, org/pf, 1974; A Time for Remembering, chorus, pf, 1976; Scenes from the Life of a Martyr, oratorio, nar, chorus, orch, 1982; many arrs. of spirituals

1v, pf: Heart, have you heard the news?, 1926; Uphill, 1926; Set Down!, 1951; Love, let the wind cry how I adore thee, 1961; To be Baptized, 1973; Watch and Pray, 1973; I want to die while you love me, 1975; I am in doubt, 1975; Lyric for True Love, 1975

BIBLIOGRAPHY
CohenE; SouthernB

H. Roach: *Black American Music: Past and Present* (Boston, 1973)

D. N. Baker, L. M. Belt and H. C. Hudson, eds.: *The Black Composer Speaks* (Metuchen, NJ, 1978) [incl. list of works]

S. Stern: *Women Composers: a Handbook* (Metuchen, NJ, 1978)

R. D. Jones: *The Choral Works of Undine Smith Moore: a Study of her Life and Work* (diss., New York U., 1980)

A. Horne: *String Music of Black Composers: a Bibliography* (New York, 1991)

—— : *Keyboard Music of Black Composers: a Bibliography* (Westport, CT, 1992)

DORIS EVANS McGINTY

Moorman, (Madeline) Charlotte (*b* Little Rock, AR, 18 Nov 1933; *d* New York, 8 Nov 1991). American cellist and performance artist. She studied at Centenary College, Shreveport, Louisiana (BM 1955), and the University of Texas at Austin (1956–7), where she was a cello pupil of Horace Britt. In 1957–8 she began studying with Leonard Rose at the Juilliard School. She played in the Boccherini Players (1958–63) and the American SO (until 1967). Influenced by Yoko Ono, a close friend, in 1963 she founded the annual New York Avant Garde Festival, and in 1964 collaborated for the first time with the composer and video and performance artist Nam June Paik. They interpreted and collaborated on a large number of works diverse in aim, from the *Cello Sonata no.1 for Adults Only* (1965), in which music is associated with sex and violence, to *Global Grove* (1973). Some of these works use non-traditional instruments, as in *TV Cello* (1971), while others juxtapose the human and the technological (*TV Bra for Living Sculpture*, 1969). Moorman's cello performance in Paik's *Opéra sextronique* in February 1967 resulted in her conviction for indecent exposure, an event commemorated by their *The People of the State of New York against Charlotte Moorman* (1977). In such works as Yoko Ono's *Cut Piece* Moorman performed showing her mastectomy scars; on other occasions she played her cello under water, in a gondola or wrapped only in cellophane.

BIBLIOGRAPHY
C. Barnes: 'Don't Move! The Case of the Topless Cellist', *Financial Times* (17 May 1967); repr. in *Music and Musicians*, xv/12 (1967), 25

C. Moore: 'Miss Moorman's Music', *Village Voice* (16 Feb 1967)

'When Festival is 10, is it Avant-Garde?', *New York Times* (10 Dec 1973)

C. Tomkins: 'Video Visionary', *New Yorker* (5 May 1975)

N. J. Paik and C. Moorman: 'Videa, Vidiot, Videology', *New Artists Video: a Critical Anthology*, ed. G. Battcock (New York, 1978), 121–37

J. G. Hanhardt, ed.: *Nam June Paik* (New York, 1982)

'From Jail to Jungle, 1967–1977: the Work of Charlotte Moorman and Nam June Paik', *The Art of Performance: a Critical Anthology*, ed. G. Battcock and R. Nickas (New York, 1984), 278–88

J. Johnston: 'Remembering Charlotte Moorman', *Village Voice* (10 Dec 1991)

SEVERINE NEFF

Moralt, Sophie. English musician of Italian descent; *see* DUSSEK family, (2).

Moratori Scanabecchi, Angiola Teresa (*b* Bologna, 1662; *d* 19 April 1708, bur. Bologna). Italian composer and painter. The daughter of the Bolognese physician Roberto

Moratori, who arranged for her to be trained in singing, instrumental performance and painting, Moratori composed at least four oratorios. *Il martirio di S Colomba* (1689), *Li giochi di Sansone* (1694) and *L'Esterre* (1695), all to librettos by Giacomo Antonio Bergamori, were for performance on major feast days at the Oratorio of S Filippo Neri; *Cristo morto* (1696), also set to a text by Bergamori, was performed on Good Friday at the oratory of the Arciconfraternità di S Maria della Morte.

Although Moratori's scores do not survive, it is clear from the librettos (*I-Bc*, Lo.O.1252 and Lo.O.1224) that she would have had to compose recitatives, duets and arias in strophic and *ABA* form. Each libretto highlights the contribution of feminine heroism to Catholic tradition: the virgin martyr St Colomba is supported in her endurance by her mother Teodosia; both Esther and Samson are likened in their strength of purpose to the Virgin (to whom the works are dedicated by the composer); and the Virgin and Mary Magdalene are the principal characters of *Cristo morto*, representing in their responses to Christ's death fortitude and humility respectively.

Moratori married Tommaso Scanabecchi Monetta. Her paintings, admired by contemporaries for their architectural conception and intelligence, can be seen in various churches in Bologna (S Stefano, S Giovanni in Monte and Madonna di Galliera) and Ferrara (S Domenico). She is buried in Madonna di Galliera in Bologna, beneath her own painting of St Thomas.

BIBLIOGRAPHY

M. Oretti: *Notizie di professori del dissegno cioè pittori scultori ed architetti Bolognesi*, ix (MS, *I-Bca*)

A. Machiavelli: *Delle donne bolognese illustri* (MS, *I-Bca*)

SUZANNE G. CUSICK

Moretto, Nelly (*b* Rosario, Argentina, 20 Sept 1925; *d* Buenos Aries, 24 Nov 1978). Argentine composer and pianist. She studied at the Conservatorio Nacional de Música in Buenos Aires and at the University of Illinois. On her return to Argentina she studied contemporary techniques with Juan Carlos Paz and composed her first works, beginning with chamber and symphonic music. From the mid-1960s, while working at the electronic institute of the University of Buenos Aires, she began to add electroacoustic techniques to traditional ones. She was a member of the Agrupación Nueva Música from 1951 until her death (vice-president from 1970) and participated in its educational work.

WORKS

Orch: Hipocicloides no.2, chamber orch, 1954; Composition no.11, 1970

Chamber: 7 Inventions, pf, 1948: Hipocicloides no.1, 1953; Music for 2 Pianos, 1955; Duo, cl, tpt, 1956; Trio, ob, vn, vc, 1957; Composition no.7, fl, va, b cl, gui, 1958; Composition no.8, 3 ens (perc; 2 fl, cl, pic cl, b cl; harp, vib, gui, vn, va), 1962; Composition no.12 'Marcha fúnebre para un violinista', str qt

Tape: Composition no.9*b*, 1966; Ella es Marcia, ballet music, collage

Mixed-media: Composition no.9*a* (G. Moretto), 2 ens (prepared pf, 2 trbn, 2 cl, perc; fl, pic cl, tpt, harp, perc), dance, tape, lights, 1965; Coribattenti, str qt, tape, 1967; Composition no.13 'In memoriam Juan Carlos Paz', tpt, tape, 1972; Composition no.14 'Bah! le dije al tiempo', 1v, tpt, pf, tape, 1974–5

Principal publisher: Ediciones Culturales Argentinas

BIBLIOGRAPHY

J. C. Paz: *Introducción a la música de nuestro tiempo* (Buenos Aires, 1955)

—— :'Una nueva etapa creadora en la música de la Argentina', *Revista musical mexicana* (1963), 62–8

R. Arizaga: *Enciclopedia de la música argentina* (Buenos Aires, 1971)

RAQUEL C. DE ARIAS

Mori, Junko (*b* Niigata-ken, 13 Feb 1948). Japanese composer and teacher. She attended the Tokyo National University of Fine Arts and Music, studying music (BA 1971), composition (MM 1975) and musicology and solfeggio (MM 1978); her composition teachers

Junko Mori, 1990

included Tomojirō Ikenouchi, Akio Yashiro and Teizō Matsumura. In 1979 she became a lecturer at the same university as well as at Aichi Gakuin University. She is a founding member of the Federation of Women Composers in Japan.

Mori's compositions are regularly performed and broadcast in Japan and the USA. Characteristics of French impressionism evident in her songs and piano works reveal the influences of her composition teachers. Her lyrical, melodic writing displays linear clarity, and the texture frequently involves a melodic foreground with accompaniment. Although she often uses triadic harmonies, her harmonic vocabulary extends beyond referential tonality. Several works, including *Autumn Mist* and *Imagery*, have been recorded.

WORKS
selective list

Stage: Songs of the Sea Shell (Y. Kusaka), 2S, A, T, B, pf, 1980, rev. version (Kusaka and S. Nakamura), 4S, A, 3T, 2Bar, 2B, pf, 1988; Shogamura wa Osawagi [Turmoil at Shoga Village] (R. Usagi), 2S, 2 Mez, T, Bar, pf, 1987; Abarajō no Kyōfu [The Terror of the Dilapidated Castle] (Usagi), 4S, 2 Mez, A, 2T, 2Bar, 2B, pf, xyl, 1990
Choral: Ajisai no Hana [Hydrangea], women's chorus, 1982; Kudamono no Uta [Song of Fruits], children's/women's chorus, pf, 1984; Fujisan no Uta [Songs of Mt Fuji], children's/women's chorus, pf, 1989
Other vocal: Kawabe [Riverside], Bar, pf, 1982; Tsuyukusa no Hana [5 Songs of Flowers], S, pf, 1983; A Birthday (C. Rossetti), Mez/S, pf, 1986; The Book of Songs, S, pf, 1986; Rengesō [Chinese Milk Vetch], S, pf, 1991
Chamber and solo inst: Str Qt no.3, 1975; Spring Dawn, vn/va, gui, 1983; Twilight, gui, 1983; Autumn Mist, fl/shakuhachi, gui, 1984; Sleep at Sea, b cl, pf, 1986; Imagery, pf, 1987; Jūninnin no kodomo [12 Children], pf, 1988; Song in the Songless, gui, 1991

Principal publisher: Ongaku no Tomo Sha

J. MICHELE EDWARDS

Morley, Angela (*b* Leeds, 10 March 1924). English composer and conductor, resident in the USA. After working as an orchestral woodwind player, she studied composition with Mátyás Seiber (1947–50) and Hugh Wood, and conducting with Walter Goehr. Between 1974 and 1989 she was a frequent conductor of the BBC Radio Orchestra. As a composer she has worked mainly in film music and is perhaps best known for her music for *Watership Down* (1977); her involvement with films also includes conducting (*The Slipper and the Rose*) and making adaptations, arrangements and orchestrations

(*The Little Prince*). She has also composed music for popular American television series, including *Dallas*, *Dynasty* and *Cagney and Lacey*, and has written many arrangements for the Boston Pops Orchestra. Her concert music includes *Tehuantapec* for chorus and orchestra (1965) and *Romance* for cello and orchestra (1976). Her principal publishers are April Music, Carlin Music, Chappell and Warner Bros Music.

BIBLIOGRAPHY
C. Palmer: 'Angela Morley in Conversation'; 'Bringing the Slipper and the Rose to Life', *Crescendo*, xv (1976), 10–12 [interviews]
K. Gronau: 'How to Score', *Songwriter*, iv (1979), 16–19 [interview]
'You Ought to be in Pictures', The Songwriters Resources and Services Workshop Series (New York, 1979) [tape recorded discussion]
L. Shropshire: 'Where are the Woman Composers?', *Cue Sheet*, vi/2 (1989), 53–62 [biography]

MARIE FITZPATRICK

Mosusova, Nadežda (*b* Subotica, 4 Aug 1928). Serbian composer and musicologist. She studied composition with Predrag Milošević at the Belgrade Academy of Music (1948–53) and in 1970 she gained the PhD in musicology at Ljubljana University. She was appointed assistant at the Musicological Institute in Belgrade in 1959, where she holds the post of Higher Scientific Adviser. Most of her compositions are chamber works; they are often rhapsodic in form, with a marked linearity displaying Mosusova's refined, often polytonal thinking. Her output includes the *Fantasy* for clarinet and piano quartet (1968) and *Pièce romantique* for piano trio (1972). Among her larger-scale works are the *Introduction and Largo* for string orchestra (1969) and *Hommage à Scriabine* for strings (1982).

MELITA MILIN

Moszumańska-Nazar, Krystyna (*b* Lwów, 5 Sept 1924). Polish composer. She studied composition with Stanisław Wiechowicz and the piano with Jan Hoffman at the Kraków Conservatory (later renamed the Academy of Music), with which she has maintained her association: in 1982 she was appointed to teach composition there and in 1987 became rector. Several of her works have won prizes and honourable mentions at competitions in Buenos Aires (in 1962 for *Music for Strings*), Mannheim (at the GEDOK competition in 1962 for *Hexaèdre* and in 1966 for *Exodus*), Kraków (for *Variazioni concertanti* at the

Ann Mounsey: lithograph by I. W. Slater after Joshua Slater for 'The Musical Keepsake' (1834)

Malawski competition, 1966) and Warsaw (for *Polish Madonnas* at the Szymanowski competition, 1974). She has also received three awards from the Polish Ministry of Culture and Arts and the award of the Polish Composers' Union. Moszumańska-Nazar's works represent distinguished achievements in timbral exploration; they played an important role in the 1960s, when Polish composers were showing a particular interest in orchestral and vocal colour. She has composed a number of works for and including percussion in which the technical problems of performance are perfectly reconciled with the demands of her artistic ideas.

WORKS
selective list

Orch (incl. vocal-orch): Hexaèdre, 1962; Exodus, orch, tape, 1964; Variazioni concertanti, fl, chamber orch, 1966; Intonations, 2 choirs, orch, 1968; Pour orchestre, 1969; Madonny polskie [Polish Madonnas], mixed choir, orch, 1974; Rhapsody I, 1976; Rhapsody II, 1980; Sinfonietta, str chamber orch, 1983; Pieśń nad pieśniami [The Song of Songs], S, spkr, speaking chorus, inst ens, 1984; Conc. for Orch, 1986; Essay, 1988; Fresco, 1989; Fresco II, 1991

Chamber: Muzyka na smyczki [Music for Str], vns, vas, vcs, 1962; Interpretations, fl, tape, perc, 1967; Bel canto, S, cel, perc, 1972; Str Qt, 1974; Variants, pf, perc, 1979; Str Qt no.2, 1980; Music for Five, 5 perc groups, 1989

Solo inst: 3 Concert Studies, perc, 1969; Constellations, pf, 1972; Bagatelle, pf, 1973; From End to End Percussion, 1976; Canzona, vn, 1985; Fantasy, mar, 1987

Principal publisher: PWM

BIBLIOGRAPHY
H. Schiller: '"Muzyka na smyczki" Krystyny Moszumańskiej-Nazarowej', *Ruch muzyczny* (1963), no.22, p.13 [on Music for Strings]
K. Moszumańska-Nazar: 'Composer's Workshop: Krystyna Moszumańska-Nazar', *Polish Music*, ix/2 (1974), 10–13
E. Mizerska-Golonek: '"Madonny polskie" Krystyny Moszumańskiej-Nazar: wybrane zagadnienia z zakresu faktury wokalnej' [K. Moszumańska-Nazar's *Polish Madonna*: Selected Problems in the Field of Vocal Composition], *Zeszyt naukowy* [Akademia Muzyczna Kraków], no.7 (1984), 60–91
—— : '"Pieśń nad pieśniami" Krystyny Moszumańskiej-Nazar' [K. Moszumańska-Nazar's *Song of Songs*], *Krakowska szkoła kompozytorska, 1888–1988*, ed. T. Malecka (Kraków, 1992), 109–47
BARBARA ZWOLSKA-STĘSZEWSKA

Mounsey, Ann (Sheppard) (*b* London, 17 April 1811; *d* London, 24 June 1891). English composer, organist and teacher. At the age of six she became the pupil of Johann Bernhard Logier. In 1820 she attracted the interest of Louis Spohr, who published her harmonization of a melody in his autobiographical account of a visit to Logier's academy. She later studied with Samuel Wesley and Thomas Attwood. In 1828 she was appointed organist at Clapton and four years later became an associate of the Philharmonic Society. Her earliest known work was the ballad *Mary meet me there* (1832). In 1843 she gave the first of six series of Classical Concerts, at Crosby Hall, London. She became a friend of Felix Mendelssohn and on 8 January 1845 gave the première of his anthem *Hear my Prayer* for voice and organ, which he especially composed for her Classical Concerts. In 1853 she married William Bartholomew, a scientist, writer and violinist chiefly known as the adapter of librettos for Mendelssohn's works. In the same year she composed the oratorio *The Nativity* op.29, which was performed on 17 January 1855 under the direction of John Hullah at St Martin's Hall. Mounsey was well known in London as a teacher and organist; she published a sacred cantata, *Supplication and Thanksgiving* (1864), more than a hundred songs, 40 partsongs, several hymns, and a large number of works for piano and for organ. Among her lieder, her settings of Goethe's *Erlkönig* op.12 (translated by W. Bartholomew), and *Kennst du das*

Title-page of the ballad 'The Bridesmaid' (London: Johanning, c1835) by Ann Mounsey

Land (translated by W. Ball) compare favourably with those of her German contemporaries.

Her sister, Elizabeth Mounsey (*b* London, 8 Oct 1819; *d* London, 3 Oct 1905), was also an organist and composer. They collaborated in the publication of the collection of psalm and hymn tunes and chants *Sacred Harmony* (London, ?1860) and *Hymns of Prayer and Praise* (London, 1868). Elizabeth also composed works for the organ, the piano and the guitar.

BIBLIOGRAPHY

Grove1 (G. Grove)

J. D. Brown and S. S. Stratton: *British Musical Biography* (Birmingham, 1897)

JANE A. BERNSTEIN

Moyseowicz, Gabriela (*b* Lwów, 4 May 1944). Polish composer. By the age of 13 she had composed her first concerto, for two pianos, which was performed at the Kraków Conservatory. She studied at the music high school in Kraków (1958–62), then spent a year at the Conservatory there; she continued her studies in Katowice (1963–7), where she gained a Master's degree in theory, composition and conducting. During the next seven years she received grants from the Ministry for Art and Culture and commissions, and taught at the high school in Gliwice. However she found herself increasingly ostracized on account of her compositional style, which was still in the Romantic, tonal tradition of Chopin, and she left the composers' union in 1970. In 1974 she moved to Berlin to work as a music teacher and church musician.

WORKS
selective list

Orch: Pf Conc. no.1, 1960–61; Conc. rapsod, vn, orch, 1964; Pf Conc. no.2, 1965–6; Capriccio, str orch, 1968; Rapsod, va, orch, 1968; Pf Conc. no.3, 1971; Memento mori, 2 pf, tpt, trbn, vn, va da gamba, vc, 1988

Vocal: Media vita, male spkr, S, 2 vn, vc, 1961–2; Dies irae, chorus, 2 fl, 2 ob, 2 bn, 2 tpt, str, 1963; Riconoscimento (after C. K. Norwid), C, B, 2 fl, 2 ob, 2 bn, 2 hn, str qnt, 1968; Cantata solemnis (I. Iszkowska), Bar, women's chorus, orch, 1969; Stabat mater, oratorio, Mez, T, chorus, inst ens, 1972–3; 2 Sprechlieder (P. Verlaine), spkr, pf, 1989; Memento mori II (M. Luther), chorus 4vv, 2 pf, tpt, trbn, vn, va da gamba, vc, 1990

Chamber: Musique en trois styles, pf trio, 1969; Vc Sonata no.1, 1977; 2 canzonen, va da gamba, 1980; Vc Sonata no.2, 1985–6; Vn Sonata no.2, 1987

Pf: Conc., 2 pf, 1957; Sonata no.1, 1960; Variations, 1961; sonatas, no.2, 1962, no.3, 1963, no.4, 1964; Passacaglia und Fuga, 1967; Sonatas, no.5, 1974, no.6 'Noumenon', 1976, no.7, 1978, no.8 'Concatenatio', 1981; 3 rhapsodies, no.1, 1983–4, no.2, 1984–5, no.3 'Empyreum', 1989

Principal publisher: Ries & Erler

BIBLIOGRAPHY

KompA-Z

G. Moyseowicz: *Egzemplifikacja własnej estetyki na podstawie II Koncertu Fortepianowego* [An Explanation of my Aesthetic as Illustrated in my Second Piano Concerto] (Katowice, 1967)

E. Weissweiler: *Komponistinnen aus 500 Jahren* (Frankfurt, 1981)

M. Gutierrez-Denhoff: 'Inspiration als Quelle des Komponierens', *Neuland*, iv (1984), 107–10

B. Brand: ' "Wer sein Klavier nicht tritt" ', *Neue berlinische Musikzeitung*, iii (1988), 8–12

DETLEF GOJOWY

Mozart, Maria Anna (Walburga Ignatia) [Nannerl] (*b* Salzburg, 30–31 July 1751; *d* Salzburg, 29 Oct 1829). Austrian pianist and composer. She studied with her father, the composer and violinist Leopold Mozart, and showed a precocious talent at the keyboard. With her even more gifted younger brother, Wolfgang Amadeus Mozart (1756–91), she toured extensively in western Europe and the Vienna region; she was noted as an exceptionally brilliant and precise keyboard player, and a skilled improviser, but was outshone by her brother in improvisation and composition. She was too old to be exhibited as a child prodigy when, in 1769, Wolfgang and their father went to Italy, and thereafter stayed at home in the Salzburg region except for brief journeys to Munich. In 1784 she married Johann Baptist von Berchtold zu Sonnenburg (1736–1801) and had three children, of whom only the eldest, a son, survived childhood; later she was active as a teacher. Maria Anna was a capable composer, but her gifts remained undeveloped in the social climate of the time; when in 1770 she sent her brother a song, he wrote from Italy that he had forgotten how well she could compose. It is not known what else she wrote and none of her compositions survives.

BIBLIOGRAPHY

W. Hummel: *Nannerl: Wolfgang Amadeus Mozarts Schwester* (Vienna, 1952)

N. Medici di Marignano and R. Hughes: *A Mozart Pilgrimage: Being the Travel Diaries of Vincent and Mary Novello in the Year 1829* (London, 1955)

E. Rieger: 'Maria Anna Mozart (1751–1829)', *Schwestern berühmter Männer*, ed. L. F. Pusch (Frankfurt, 1985), 123–54

E. Schwerin: 'Maria Anna ("Nannerl") Mozart: a Profile of Mozart's Sister', *Friends of Mozart Newsletter*, no.19 (1985), 1–4

E. Rieger: *Nannerl Mozart: Leben eine Künstlerin im 18. Jahrhundert* (Frankfurt, 1991)

STANLEY SADIE

Geraldine Mucha

Mucha [née Thomsen; Muchová-Thomsenová], **Geraldine** (*b* London, 5 July 1917). Scottish composer, of Orcadian descent. She studied first with her father, a professor of singing at the RAM. In 1936 she won a scholarship to the RAM, where her teachers included William Alwyn, Benjamin Dale and Alan Bush. During the war she married the Czech writer Jiří Mucha (son of Alphonse Mucha, pioneer of *art nouveau*); they moved to Prague in 1945, and their son was born in 1948. She immersed herself in Czech music, which she had first heard in London at a concert of works by Janáček, Martinů and his highly gifted pupil Vitězslava Kaprálová (Jiří Mucha's first wife, who had conducted the concert; she died in 1940).

The infectious dance rhythms of Czech music played a formative role in Mucha's development. Her work, although espoused by leading Czech composers and performers, was little heard outside that country until the Glasgow world première by Jill Gomez of *En los pinares de Júcar*, a setting of a poem by Luis de Góngora for soprano, oboe d'amore and string ensemble. This was the first of several works specially written for Gomez and performed by her. The spontaneous quality of lyricism in Mucha's music and her fondness for syncopated dance rhythms (often in quintuple time) are exemplified in *Epitaph*, a hauntingly beautiful work for string quintet and oboe dedicated to Jiří Mucha, who died in 1991. Her works have been broadcast by Czech Radio and the BBC and some of them recorded by Supraphon.

WORKS
selective list

Stage: Nausicaa (ballet, after Homer), 1940s; Macbeth (ballet, after W. Shakespeare), 1965

Orch: Fantasy, vc, orch, 1946; Ov., 1951; Pictures from the Šumava, 1952; Pf Conc., 1960; Carmina Orcadiana, 2 vn, str orch, arr. 2 ob, hpd, 1960; Ov. to a Ballet, 1961; The Tempest, ov., 1964

Chamber and solo inst: Str Qt, 1941; Parting and Teasing, pf, 1942; Va Sonatina, 1945; Vn Sonata no.1, 1947; Children's Pieces, pf, 1953; 16 Variations on a Scottish Folksong, pf, 1957; Sea Scenes, vn, pf, 1958; Nonet, 1959; Vn Sonata no.2, 1961; Sonnets from Shakespeare, spkr, fl, hp, 1961; Str Qt, 1962; Song of Songs, spkr, fl, hp, 1963; Str Qt, 1963; Wind Qnt, 1964; Intermezzo, eng hn, str; Str Qt, 1988; Music for Pf and Harp, 1990; Epitaph, ob, str qnt, 1991

Vocal: Collection of Czech and Slovak Songs, Bar, pf, 1943; Folk Lullabies, 1952; 2 Women's Choruses (anon. 16th-century poet), 1956–8; Incantation from Byron's Manfred, Bar, orch, 1960; En los pinares de Júcar (Luis de Góngora), S, ob d'amore, str, also pf version, 1975; 3 Jersey Folksongs, S, Bar, pf, 1975; 3 Winter Songs (W. de la Mare), S, Bar, pf, 1975; John Webster Songs, S, orch, also

versions for ob d'amore, hpd, and for pf, 1975–88;
5 canciones de Antonio Machado, S, 7 solo insts,
1980s; Sonnets of Hawthornden (W. Drummond),
S, ob, str qnt, 1990

MARGOT LEIGH MILNER
(with PATRICK CARNEGY)

Müller-Hermann, Johanna (*b* Vienna, 15
Jan 1878; *d* Vienna, 19 April 1941). Austrian
composer. She studied with Guido Adler and
Alexander Zemlinsky and later with J. B.
Foerster, whom she succeeded as professor
of composition at the Neues Konservatorium
in Vienna. Although her works adhere to
traditional form and tonality, they reveal
considerable harmonic richness and resourceful instrumentation.

WORKS
selective list

Orch: Heroische Ov., op.21; Sym. Fantasy (after H.
Ibsen: *Brand*), op.25; Sym., d, op.28
Choral orch: 2 Frauenchöre, op.10, 3vv, incl. Von
Tod und Gedenken; Der sterbende Schwan, op.16;
Deutscher Schwur, op.22; Sym., d, op.27 (R.
Huch), solo vv, chorus, orch, vs (? Vienna, 1919);
Ode, op.29; In memoriam, op.30 (oratorio, J.
Schlaf, after W. Whitman), 4 solo vv, chorus, orch,
org, vs (Vienna and Leipzig, 1930)
Chamber: Vn Sonata, op.5; Str Qt, Eb, op.6 (?Vienna,
*c*1910); Str Qnt, op.7; Pf Sonata, op.8; Vc Sonata,
op.17; Pf Qnt, g, op.31; pieces for pf, opp.3, 12, 19
Other vocal: 2 duets, op.15; Songs, op.26, 1v, orch;
songs, 1v, pf; unacc. choral works

KARL GEIRINGER/ROSARIO MARCIANO

Munktell, Helena (Mathilda) (*b* Grycksbo,
Dalarna, 24 Nov 1852; *d* Stockholm, 10 Sept
1919). Swedish composer. She was born into
a wealthy and cultured family. Her father was
a talented amateur musician and a successful
industrialist. Her mother was well educated
and arranged lively salons in Stockholm.
Munktell was taught the piano by Carl Fexer
and composition by Ludvig Norman, Johan
Lindegren and Joseph Dente. She studied in
Paris, 1877–9, and, until about 1910, spent
every winter there. Composition, which she
studied with Benjamin Godard (1885–92),
gradually became her main interest. About
1890 she met Vincent d'Indy, with whom
she continued her studies (*c*1892–1910). She
became a member of the Kungliga Musikaliska Akademien of Sweden in 1915.

Munktell made a name for herself as a
composer in Stockholm in 1885. Her début
programme included some of her own songs
(*Sof, sof* and *Ater i Sorrento*), which showed
an individual style (with some French influence) and were well received. During the
1890s she was especially productive, composing songs and choral works. Her ballad
for baritone and orchestra Isjungfrun (*Vision*

polaire), composed in 1889, was performed in
Paris at the Salle Pleyel and her comic opera
In Firenze was given in Stockholm in 1889
and 1891. One of her best works is the Violin
Sonata op.21 (1905). Munktell's music
exhibits bold harmony and has a typical
Nordic tone; some of the songs and the
violin sonata are among the finest works by
Swedish women composers.

WORKS
selective list

Stage: In Firenze (opéra comique, 1), Stockholm, 1889
Orch: Suite symphonique; 3 sym. poems: Bränningar
(Sur les brisants), op.19; Dalsvit (Suite dalécar-
lienne), op.22, perf. 1910; Valborgsmässoeld, op.24
Vocal: Isjungfrun (Vision polaire), ballad, Bar, orch,
op.20, 1889; Majnattsröster, S, orch, op.25; 2 cantatas; *c*20 choruses, mixed vv, women's vv, male vv;
10 mélodies, 1v, pf (Paris, 1900)
1–2 inst: Vn Sonata, Eb, op.21 (Paris, 1905);
Humoresque, pf

BIBLIOGRAPHY

K. Lindén: *H. M.s musikaliska verksamhet o produktion*
(MS, 1968, Uppsala)
A. Edling: *Franskt i svensk musik 1880–1920* (Uppsala,
1982)
E. Öhrström: *Borgerliga kvinnors musicerande i 1800-
talets Sverige* [Middle-Class Women Playing Music
in 19th-Century Sweden] (Göteborg, 1987)

EVA ÖHRSTRÖM

Musgrave, Thea (*b* Barnton, Midlothian, 27
May 1928). Scottish composer. She studied
for three years at the University of Edinburgh
and privately with Hans Gál before going to
Paris to work with Nadia Boulanger (1950–
54). Meanwhile her music began to arouse
interest in Scotland. In 1953 she fulfilled her
first commission (from the Scottish Festival at
Braemar) with the *Suite o' Bairnsangs*, and in
the following year the BBC commissioned a
major vocal work, the *Cantata for a Summer's
Day*. During this period she also composed
two medium-length stage works, the ballet *A
Tale for Thieves* and the chamber opera *The
Abbot of Drimock*.

These scores, predominantly diatonic in
style, show a predilection for ancient, dialect
or in other ways picturesque texts. After her
return from Paris, however, Musgrave's style
underwent a gradual change towards chromaticism and her forms became more abstract.
From this period date her first important instrumental works: the Piano Sonata, the
String Quartet, *Obliques* for orchestra and, a
little later, *Colloquy* for violin and piano, and
the Trio for flute, oboe and piano. By 1960,
the year of the Trio, Musgrave was using a
fairly orthodox serial technique (there is
already a free but distinct serialism deployed
in the *Triptych* for tenor and orchestra, a short

Thea Musgrave

Chaucer setting, first performed at a Prom in 1960). In 1959 she had taken up an extramural lectureship for London University at Teddington. Her position was representative of the *via media* of British music: a tempering of strict orthodoxy with an instinctive moderation which also disposed her against experiment with any more *outré* forms of the avant garde. The tone of her music was serious but not solemn, its personality somewhat retiring.

The 1960s brought an enlargement, at first slow, later rapid. The main catalyst for this change was the opera *The Decision*, to which Musgrave devoted most of her energies in 1964–5 (it was staged in 1967). This was her biggest undertaking to date and, for all the prevailing sombreness appropriate to the subject of a mining accident and the conflicting moral dilemmas in which it places those involved, its music shows a marked enrichment of both expressive and technical means as compared with the two main works that preceded it: *The Phoenix and the Turtle*, a well-wrought but elusive (as well as allusive) setting of the Shakespeare poem, commissioned for the 1962 Proms; and the Sinfonia of 1963, a serial work of no great individuality. *The Decision* forced an extroversion that the earlier works had generally lacked, and the benefit is apparent in most of Musgrave's subsequent work. *Nocturnes and Arias* (1966) stands slightly apart in being based on actual material from the opera. The first technical departures

came in the Second and Third Chamber Concertos (both 1966). Here for the first time Musgrave wrote asynchronous music (music where each part is fully notated but need not be exactly coordinated with the others). In the Second Concerto there are also Ivesian borrowings from popular music. But, whereas in Charles Ives such quotations often have an impressionistic function, Musgrave uses the tunes as *dramatis personae*, giving the music the character of a charade or harlequinade (there is a parallel with the role of *commedia dell'arte* characters in the Venetian classical theatre). In later works, this dramatic function is taken over by solo instrumentalists performing simple gestures and sometimes moving physically around the orchestra or around the hall (an idea much in vogue during the late 1960s and early 70s). Her use of this device is striking, and fully integrated into the form of the work. The concertos for clarinet (1967), horn (1971) and viola (1973), as well as the earlier Concerto for Orchestra, amplify latent subversive oppositional traits: accompanying groups admit division and the soloist leads its supporters in an independent direction.

Since *The Decision* Musgrave has composed mainly to commission. In 1967 she wrote the Concerto for Orchestra for the Feeney Trust, and in the same year the Royal Philharmonic Society commissioned the Clarinet Concerto (not performed until 1969). *Night Music*, the concerto-like *Memento vitae* and the Viola Concerto (first performed by her husband, Peter Mark) were all composed for the BBC. In 1969 Scottish Theatre Ballet produced the full-length ballet *Beauty and the Beast* at Sadler's Wells Theatre, London. There are also works for solo instrumental or chamber forces, including some (the Impromptu for flute and oboe, and the Music for Horn and Piano) which develop in an étude-like manner the concerto techniques already mentioned. *Soliloquy* (1969) for guitar and *From One to Another* (1970) for viola use the solo instrument in conjunction with a pre-recorded tape – a further extension of what Musgrave calls the 'dramatic-abstract' procedures of her works of the period. Finally, the chamber opera *The Voice of Ariadne*, commissioned by the Royal Opera House for the 1974 Aldeburgh Festival, renders these procedures concrete and may be seen as the natural culmination of the theatrical tendencies in Musgrave's concert works since *The Decision*. In *The Voice of Ariadne* the asynchronous techniques of the concertos are carried over with good effect into the vocal ensembles, where they become a natural extension of what has always been an essentially declamatory type of music.

Musgrave has also won international renown as a conductor of opera and concert music. In the early 1970s she moved to the USA with her husband. In 1976 she became the first woman to conduct her own composition with the Philadelphia Orchestra (Concerto for Orchestra); the next year she made her New York conducting début in *The Voice of Ariadne* with the New York City Opera (30 September 1977), which also produced *Mary, Queen of Scots* in 1981. She has conducted her own compositions in performances by numerous other British and American ensembles, including the English Opera Group, the Scottish and the San Francisco Spring opera companies, the Scottish Ballet, the BBC, London, San Diego and San Francisco symphony orchestras, the Scottish National Orchestra, the English, Los Angeles and St Paul chamber orchestras, and the RPO.

Musgrave's output covers a wide range, from full-length stage works to simple *a cappella* choral motets, music for brass band and a set of teacher–pupil piano duets, *Excursions*. However, since 1966 her music has been predominantly instrumental, and if these works leave a stronger impression than their predecessors it is above all because they are more brilliant and direct. The instrumental works of the late 1950s and early 1960s, while tending towards serial procedure, are technically conservative or, where more ambitious, inclined to mannerism (for instance, rising semiquaver figuration and augmented octave pedals recur repeatedly). In the later works serialism is subsumed in a confident, individual atonal style, drawing new rhythmic and structural energy from the bolder, less inhibited instrumental writing. Witold Lutosławski's 'controlled aleatoricism' is used freely and with definite harmonic and textural purpose. In contrast, the solo lines regain something of Musgrave's early lyricism, recapturing spontaneity without loss of sinew. On these and other grounds, *Night Music* (1969), the Horn Concerto (1971) and the Viola Concerto (1973), in particular, must count among the most striking achievements in British music of the time.

This is not to discount Musgrave's earlier works, which are seldom less than effective. The vocal works before *The Decision* are eclectic in style, but with a tendency to florid and rhapsodic word-setting which remains characteristic and seems to refer forward to the bravura instrumental writing of the concertos. The early *Cantata for a Summer's Day* (1954) is an unusually felicitous example of melodrama. Of the mature works, the ballad *Sir Patrick Spens* (written for Peter Pears and Julian Bream; 1961) and the declamatory *Song for Christmas* (1958) for high voice and piano cover familiar ground with distinction. The earlier stage works, up to *Beauty and the Beast*, impress rather as important steps in Musgrave's development than as completely fulfilled achievements. *The Voice of Ariadne*, coming after a series of works in which the composer perfected a naturally gestural style, may be considered a first fertile exploitation of the theatre.

Musgrave continued to move towards stage and dramatic works. *Mary, Queen of Scots*, commissioned by Scottish Opera and first performed at the 1977 Edinburgh Festival with the composer conducting, demonstrates her ability to distil the dramatic essence and thus focus upon the core of an idea; it treats of a relatively short period of Mary's life. Similarly, *A Christmas Carol* (1979) reduces a large body of material from Dickens's popular work in order to obtain a coherent nucleus which yet retains the spirit of the original. Its inclusion of well-known carols marked an expansion of her earlier interest in the borrowing techniques, which were further exploited in *Harriet, the Woman Called Moses* (1984), where the dramatic impetus is enhanced by the incorporation of spirituals; it was commissioned jointly by the Royal Opera House, Covent Garden, and the Virginia Opera Association. Her next opera, *Simon Bolívar* (1992), was commissioned jointly by the Los Angeles Music Center Opera and Scottish Opera.

Musgrave has consistently demonstrated her capacity for an intensely personal revitalization, which recognizes and incorporates contemporary musical developments while clearly retaining a personal, stylistic integrity. The dramatic element in her work is very strong, and while earlier works now seem restrained, their clarity and spirit clearly foreshadow the poised technical control which has facilitated the development of her innately dramatic handling of music.

WORKS

STAGE

A Tale for Thieves (ballet, 1, after G. Chaucer: *The Pardoner's Tale*), 1953

The Abbott of Drimock (comic opera, 1, M. Lindsay), 1955; London, Morley College, 15 March 1962

Marko the Miser (children's opera, 1, Musgrave and F. Samson, after A. N. Afanas'yev), 1962; Farnham, Surrey, 1963

The Decision (opera, 3, Lindsay), 1964–5; London, Sadler's Wells Theatre, 30 Nov 1967 (London, 1967)

Beauty and the Beast (ballet, 2, C. Graham), 1968–9; London, Sadler's Wells Theatre, 1969

The Voice of Ariadne (chamber opera, 3, A. Elguera, after H. James: *The Last of the Valerii*), 1973, vs (Borough Green, 1977); Snape, Maltings, 11 June 1974

Orfeo (ballet, fl, str ens/str orch/tape, dancer, 1975; BBC TV, 17 March 1977

Mary Queen of Scots (opera, 3, Musgrave, after Elguera: *Moray*), 1977, vs (Borough Green, 1978); Edinburgh, King's Theatre, 6 Sept 1977

A Christmas Carol (opera, 2, Musgrave, after C. Dickens), 1979, full score (Borough Green, 1981); Norfolk, VA, 7 Dec 1979

An Occurrence at Owl Creek Bridge (radio opera, Musgrave, after A. Bierce), 1981; BBC, 14 Sept 1982; stage, Bracknell, Wilde Theatre, 23 June 1988

Harriet, the Woman Called Moses (opera, 2, Musgrave), 1984, rev. 1985; Norfolk, VA, 1 March 1985; rev. as The Story of Harriet Tubman, 1990, orchd J. Grant

Simon Bolívar (opera, 2, Musgrave), 1992

ORCHESTRAL

A Tale for Thieves, suite [from ballet], 1953; Divertimento, str orch, 1957; Obliques, 1958 (London, 1961); Scottish Dance Suite, 1959; Theme and Interludes, amateur orch, 1960 (London, 1962); Perspectives, ov., 1961; Sinfonia, 1963; Festival Ov., 1965; Variations, brass band, 1966; Nocturnes and Arias, 1966; Conc. for Orch, 1967 (London, 1968); Cl Conc., 1967 (London, 1969); Night Music, chamber orch, 1969 (London, 1972); Memento vitae (Conc. in Homage to Beethoven), 1970 (London, 1975)

Hn Conc., 1971 (London, 1974); Va Conc., 1973 (Borough Green, 1975); Orfeo II [arr. of chamber version], fl, 15 str/str orch, 1975 (Borough Green, 1976); From One to Another [arr. of chamber version], va, 15 str, 1980; Peripeteia, 1981 (Borough Green, c1983); Moving into Aquarius, 1984, collab. R. R. Bennett [in honour of Sir Michael Tippett]; The Seasons, 1988; Rainbow, 1990 (London, 1991); Song of the Enchanter, 1990

CHORAL

4 Madrigals (T. Wyatt), SATB, 1953 (London, 1958); Cantata for a Summer's Day (D. Hume, M. Lindsay), S, A, T, B, spkr, chorus (opt.), (fl, cl, str qt, db)/(fl, cl, str orch), 1954; Song of the Burn [from Cantata for a Summer's Day] (Lindsay), SATB, 1954 (London, 1964); Make ye Merry for Him that is Come (15th century), children's chorus, female chorus, org ad lib, 1961 (London, 1963); The Phoenix and the Turtle (W. Shakespeare), small chorus, orch, 1962

2 Christmas Carols in Traditional Style (N. Nicholson), SA, TB ad lib, str, 1963 (London, 1968); The Five Ages of Man (Hesiod, trans. R. Lattimore), chorus, orch, 1963 (London, 1965); John Cook (anon.), SATB, 1963 (London, 1963); Memento creatoris (J. Donne), SATB, org ad lib, 1967 (London, 1967); Rorate coeli (W. Dunbar),

SATB, 1974, rev. 1976 (Borough Green, 1977); O caro mé sonno (Michelangelo), SATB, 1978 (Borough Green, 1978)

The Last Twilight (D. H. Lawrence), SATB, brass, perc, 1980 (Borough Green, 1991); The Lord's Prayer, SATB, org, 1983 (Borough Green, c1984); Black Tambourine (H. Crane), SA (with perc insts), pf, 1985; For the Time Being: Advent (W. H. Auden), SATB, nar, 1986 (London, 1991); Echoes Through Time, dramatic choral work, SA, spoken chorus, orch, 3 dancers (opt.), 1988; Midnight (J. Keats: *To Sleep*), SATB, 1992

VOCAL

2 Songs (E. Pound), Bar, pf, 1951; Suite o' Bairnsangs (M. Lindsay), 1v, pf, 1953 (London, 1962); 5 Love Songs (medieval Eng.), S, gui, 1955 (London, 1970); 4 Portraits (J. Davies), Bar, cl, pf, 1956; A Song for Christmas (attrib. W. Dunbar), S/T, pf, 1958; Triptych (G. Chaucer), T, orch, 1959 (London, 1960); Sir Patrick Spens (trad.), T, gui, 1961 (London, 1976); Primavera, S, fl, 1971 (London, 1976); Monologues of Mary Queen of Scots [from opera], S, orch, 1986

CHAMBER, SOLO INSTRUMENTAL

Pf sonatas, no.1, withdrawn, no.2, 1956; Str Qt, 1958 (London, 1959); Colloquy, vn, pf, 1960 (London, 1961); Monologue, pf, 1960 (London, 1970); Trio, fl, ob, pf, 1960 (London, 1964); Serenade, fl, cl, harp, va, vc, 1961 (London, 1962); Chamber Conc. no.1, ob, cl, bn, hn, tpt, trbn, str trio, 1962 (London, 1977); Excursions, pf 4 hands, 1965 (London, 1966); Sonata for Three, fl, vn, gui, 1966 (Borough Green, 1979); Chamber Conc. no.2, pic + fl + a fl, cl + b cl, vn + va, vc, pf, 1966 (London, 1967)

Chamber Conc. no.3, cl, bn, hn, str qt, db, 1966 (London 1968); Impromptu no.1, fl, ob, 1967 (London, 1968); Music, hn, pf, 1967 (London, 1969); Soliloquy, gui, tape, 1969; Elegy, va, vc, 1970 (London, 1971); From One to Another, va, tape, 1970, rev. as orch version, 1980 (London, c1987); Impromptu no.2, fl, ob, cl, 1970 (London, 1974); Space Play, wind qnt, vn, va, vc, db, 1974 (Borough Green, 1975); Orfeo I, fl, tape, 1975, rev. as orch version

Fanfare, brass qnt, 1982; Pierrot, cl, vn, pf, 1985 (London, c1990); The Golden Echo I, hn, tape, 1986 (London, c1987), rev. as The Golden Echo II, solo hn, 16 hn, 1986; Narcissus, fl (with digital delay), 1987 (London, c1988), arr. cl (with digital delay), 1988 (London, c1989); Niobe, ob, tape, 1987; Piccolo Play, pic, pf, 1989 (London, c1989); Fanfare for a New Hall, 2 tpt, 1990; Wind Qnt, 1992

Principal publishers: Chester, Novello

BIBLIOGRAPHY

CC (J. Weir); *Fuller-LeFanuRM* (J. Hamer); *GroveO* (H. Cole); *LePageWC*, i

S. Bradshaw: 'Thea Musgrave', *MT*, civ (1963), 866–8

M. Lindsay: 'The Disaster and *The Decision*', *Opera*, xviii (1967), 974–6

T. Musgrave: '*The Decision*', *MT*, cviii (1967), 988–91

A. Payne: 'Thea Musgrave's Clarinet Concerto', *Tempo*, no.88 (1969), 50–53

N. Kay: 'Thea Musgrave', *Music and Musicians*, xviii/4 (1969–70), 34–6, 40

T. Musgrave: 'A New Viola Concerto', *MT*, cxiv (1973), 790–91

S. Walsh: 'Musgrave's "The Voice of Ariadne" ', *MT*, cxv (1974), 465–7

L. East: 'The Problem of Communication – Two Solutions: Thea Musgrave and Gordon Crosse', *British Music Now*, ed. L. Foreman (London, 1975), 19ff

T. Musgrave: 'Mary Queen of Scots', *MT*, cxvii (1977), 625–7

R. Milnes: 'Dickens into Opera', *MT*, cxxii (1981), 818–20

H. Cole: 'The Song at the Heart of Scrooge', *Guardian* (11 Dec 1981)

D. L. Hixon: *Thea Musgrave: a Bio-Bibliography* (Westport, CT, 1984)

H. Kupferberg: 'Thea Musgrave', *HiFi/MusAm*, xxxv/3 (1985), 4–5, 21

P. J. Smith: 'Thea Musgrave's New Success', *Opera*, xxxvi (1985), 492–3

C. Roma: 'The Choral Music of Thea Musgrave', *American Choral Review*, xxxi/1 (1989), 5–31

R. Dick: 'Instrumental Solo and Ensemble Music', *Notes*, xlvi (1989–90), 236–7

R. H. Kornick: *Recent American Opera: a Production Guide* (New York, 1991), 202–12

STEPHEN WALSH (with TONI CALAM)

N

Nascinbeni, Maria Francesca (*b* Ancona, 1658; *fl* 1674). Italian composer. She was a 'discepola' of Scipione Lazzarini, an Augustinian monk in Ancona, who included her motet *Sitientes venite* (for two sopranos, bass and organ) and those of two other students in his *Motetti a due e tre voci* (*RISM* 1674[1]). In Ancona in December 1674 she published a complete volume of her own music, *Canzoni e madrigali morali e spirituali a una, due e tre voci e organo* (one ed. in Jackson), dedicated to Olimpia Aldobrandini Pamphili (mother of Pope Innocent X and Cardinal Benedetto Pamphili, the librettist and lavish patron of music). In the dedication she describes herself as 16 years of age. Although her name is spelt with an 'm' (Nascimbeni) in all modern reference works, it appears in the form 'Signora Maria Francesca Nascinbeni' in the two publications that are the only sources of information about her.

BIBLIOGRAPHY
SchmidlD
B. G. Jackson, ed.: Preface to *Two Sacred Works for Three Treble Voices* [incl. *Non tema nò di morte*, from *Canzoni e madrigali*] (Fayetteville, AR, 1990)

BARBARA GARVEY JACKSON

Needham [née Montgomery], **Alicia Adélaïde** (*b* Old Castle, Co. Meath, 1872; *d* London, 24 Dec 1945). Irish composer. She studied first at Victoria College, Londonderry, and then at the RAM with Ebenezer Prout and F. W. Davenport (1889–96). She married the physician Joseph Needham in 1892, was a Red Cross Searcher for the wounded and missing during World War I, and was widowed in 1920. She published a few piano pieces and over 600 songs, winning prizes at the Irish Music Festival (Feis Ceoil) for six consecutive years. The songs are simple and appealing and were popular in their day. Many are settings of traditional Irish melodies with Irish texts; the piano accompaniments often reflect Needham's academic training. In 1902 she won the prize for the best coronation song with *The Seventh English Edward*. In 1918 she was awarded a civil list pension 'in consideration of her work as a composer, and of her straitened circumstances'.

WORKS
selective list; all published in London

Pf: 4 Pf Sketches, op.30 (1898); Scherzo (1899)
Song cycles (all for S, A, T, B, pf): A Bunch of Shamrocks (1904); A Bunch of Heather (1910); A Branch of Arbutus (1913)
Over 600 songs, incl.: Who Carries the Gun? (A. C. Doyle) (1897); O'Shanaghan Dhu (J. J. Bourke) (1898); The Despairing Lover [Gradh gan Dóchas] (O'Curnane) (1899); The Seventh English Edward (H. Begbie) (1902); It was a lover and his lass (W. Shakespeare) (1907); 4 Songs for Women Suffragists (1908)

SOPHIE FULLER, JOHN R. GARDNER

Nelson, Sheila Mary (*b* Manchester, 5 March 1936). English string teacher and composer. After study at the RCM, she played the violin in several London orchestras during the 1960s and early 70s, and taught. In 1976 she studied in the USA with Paul Rolland, whose methods influenced her teaching and encouraged her to continue composing graded music suitable for string groups of all sizes (*Right from the Start* and *Tetratunes* for beginners) and ultimately imaginatively crafted works for different combinations of instruments (including *Two in One*, *Together from the Start*, *Quartet Club* and *Tunes for my String Orchestra*). Both her music and her pedagogical work, *Beginners Please* (London, 1987, 2/1993), which appeared after a television series about her work with children of ethnic minorities in the East End of London, are published by Boosey & Hawkes. She has written two monographs, *The Violin Family* (London, 1964) and *The Violin and Viola* (London, 1972).

JULIE ANNE SADIE

Nerantzi, Susanna (*b* ? Zakinthos; *fl* ?1830–40). Greek composer and pianist. The earliest known modern Greek woman composer, she was a composition and piano pupil of Nicolaos Mantzaros in Corfu. Her fantasias

Les souvenirs (op.26) and *Fantasia sulla romanza 'Il lago di Como'* (op.27), and *Regret pour la patrie* (op.28), were published in 1839 by Francesco Lucca in Milan.

BIBLIOGRAPHY

S. G. Motsenigos: *Neoelliniki moussiki: symvoli is tin istoria tis* [Modern Greek Music: a Contribution to its History] (Athens, 1958), 247

GEORGE LEOTSAKOS

Nešić, Vojna (*b* Sarajevo, 6 Oct 1947). Serbian composer. She studied composition with Enrico Josif at the Belgrade Academy of Music and later with Komadina in Sarajevo. In 1977 she was appointed to teach at the music school in Kragujevac. She has composed for a variety of forces, including solo flute (*Sonnets*, 1985) and brass band (*Impressions*, 1989), and employs a broad range in *Deca sa glasovima cvrčaka* ('Children with Voices of Crickets', 1986), scored for soprano, children's choir and mixed choir, speaker, flute, trumpet, percussion and strings. Her music is strongly polyphonic and freely atonal. In some works she has experimented with 12-note serialism and aleatory techniques.

MELITA MILIN

Netzel [née Pistolekors], **Laura Constance** [Lago] (*b* Rantasalmi, Finland, 1 March 1839; *d* Stockholm, 10 Feb 1927). Swedish composer and pianist. She studied the piano and singing in Stockholm during the 1860s and composition with Charles-Marie Widor in Paris during the 1880s. She made her début as a pianist at the age of 17 and performed in Stockholm for about 40 years. In 1866 she married Professor W. Netzel. She began composing during the 1880s in order to raise money for hospitals for homeless women and children. During the 1890s and 1900s she regularly organized 'cheap concerts for workers' in Stockholm which were much praised. Under the pseudonym Lago she composed about 70 works (including five for choir, three piano trios, 11 works for violin and piano, eight for piano and one for organ, and about 40 songs). They are in a late Romantic, chromatic style inspired by Wagner. Her manuscripts are in the library of the Kungliga Musikaliska Akademien, Stockholm.

BIBLIOGRAPHY

E. Öhrström: *Borgerliga kvinnors musicerande i 1800-talets Sverige* [Middle-Class Women Playing Music in 19th-Century Sweden] (Göteborg, 1987)

EVA ÖHRSTRÖM

Newlin, Dika (*b* Portland, OR, 22 Nov 1923). American musicologist and composer. She was educated at Michigan State University (BA 1939), UCLA (MA 1941) and Columbia University, receiving that institution's first PhD in musicology (1945). At the same time she studied composition with Arthur Farwell, Arnold Schoenberg and Roger Sessions. She taught at various American universities and in 1978 was appointed to the faculty of Virginia Commonwealth University in Richmond. Newlin's research has centred on Austrian composers of the late 19th century and the 20th century, including Bruckner, Mahler and Schoenberg. She has edited and translated some of the major writings by and about Schoenberg, and is the author of *Schoenberg Remembered: Diaries and Recollections, 1938–1976* (New York, 1980). Her interests include electronic and computer music, mixed-media works and experimental music-theatre, and she is active in all these areas as a composer, teacher and performer. She has written three operas (*Feathertop*, in one act, 1942; *The Scarlet Letter*, three acts, 1945; and *Smile Right to the Bone*), songs, piano and chamber works (Piano Quintet, 1941; Violin Sonata, 1942; Piano Trio, *c*1951), a piano concerto, and a symphony for chorus and orchestra (*The Eumenides*, 1941).

BIBLIOGRAPHY

K. Wolff: 'Dika Newlin', *ACAB*, x/4 (1962), 1

T. Albrecht, ed.: *Dika Newlin, Friend and Mentor: a Birthday Anthology* (Denton, TX, 1973)

——: *Dika Caecilia: Essays for Dika Newlin, November 22, 1988* (Kansas City, MO, 1988)

PAULA MORGAN

Niewiarowska-Brzozowska, Julia (*b* Warsaw, 1827; *d* Warsaw, Dec 1891). Polish pianist and composer. She studied music with August Freyer in Warsaw. In 1845 and 1848 she performed in Berlin and Warsaw. After marrying the writer Aleksander Niewiarowski, she led an important artistic salon in Warsaw. For this salon she composed piano music (mainly pieces in dance forms and fantasies, apart from the serenade *Sylfida*) and songs – *Dwa śpiewy* ('Two Songs'), *Przypomnienie* ('Reminder'), *Śpeiwak w obcej stronie* ('A Singer in a Foreign Country'), *Szatan* ('The Devil') and *Chant d'amour*. Several pieces were published in the 1850s.

ZOFIA CHECHLIŃSKA

Nikolayeva, Tat'yana (Petrovna) (*b* Bezhitza, 4 May 1924; *d* San Francisco, 22

Nov 1993). Russian pianist, composer and teacher. She studied the piano with Alexander Goldenweiser at the Moscow Central School of Music, then graduated from his class at the conservatory in 1947; it was through his teaching that she developed her considerable skills as a player of contrapuntal works. She also studied composition in Yevgeny Golubev's class, graduating in 1950; as her degree exercise she presented a cantata, Pesn' o schast'ye ('Song about Happiness'), and a piano concerto. Even before she was a student she had made her début as a pianist (in 1945) and begun her intensive performing career in the USSR and abroad. In 1950 she won the Leipzig International Competition for the best Bach performance. Nikolayeva began teaching at the Moscow Conservatory in 1959 and became a professor in 1965; she was made Honoured Artist of the RSFSR in 1955.

Nikolayeva was a strikingly individual artist, who possessed a profound, strong temperament and a virtuoso technique; her passionate emotional impulsiveness was balanced by clarity of purpose. Her works include symphonies, two piano concertos and a violin concerto, various compositions for piano – including sonatas, Variatsii pamyati N. Myaskovskogo ('Variations in Memory of N. Myaskovsky'), Polifonicheskaya triada ('The Polyphonic Triad') and 24 concert studies – a piano quintet and other instrumental chamber music, songs and the song cycle Islandiya ('Iceland').

BIBLIOGRAPHY

G. Tsïpin: 'Tat'yana Nikolayeva', Portreti sovetskikh pianistov [Portraits of Soviet Pianists] (Moscow, 1982), 111–20; (2/1990), 141–52

'Tat'yana Nikolayeva: beseda s Ye. Petrushanskoy' [Nikolayeva: in Conversation with Petrushanskaya], Muzïkal'naya zhizn', no.21–2 (1993), 6–7

I. M. YAMPOL'SKY

Nogueira, Ilza (b Salvador, Bahia, 12 Dec 1948). Brazilian composer and teacher. She graduated in literature (1971) and music (1972) from the Federal University, Bahia, where she studied the piano with Fritz Klose and composition with the Swiss-Brazilian composer Ernst Widmer. In 1972 she received a German government fellowship to study with Mauricio Kagel at the Rheinische Hochschule für Musik, Cologne. She was appointed to teach music at the Federal University of Paraíba in 1977. From 1982 to 1985 she pursued doctoral work in composition at the State University of New York at Buffalo under the supervision of Lejaren

Hiller and in 1990 was a post-doctoral fellow at Yale University. As a researcher, she has focussed on the work of her teacher Widmer. Her earlier compositions (1969–78) are characterized by the use of extra-musical and electroacoustic materials; later works (after 1982) reflect her contact with serialism and set theory.

WORKS
selective list

El-ac: Metástase, choir, tape, 1971; Idiossincrasia, stage work [with dance and audience participation], S, chorus, 7 vn, ronda, perc, tape, synth, 1972; Triloquia, vn, hn, bn, pf, perc, tape with pic, tpt, vc, 1977; Cromossons, 3 orchs pre-recorded, 1977; Transforms, sax qt, tape, 1985

Inst and vocal: Kaleidoscope, brass ens, 1984; Urtext, S, Bar, ww, str qt, perc, 1985; In memoriam Morton Feldman, S, perc, 1988; Ode aos Jamais Iluminados, str qt, pf, 2 reciters, 1993

CRISTINA MAGALDI

Nordenstrom, Gladys Mercedes (b Pokegama Township, MN, 23 May 1924). American composer. She studied music and philosophy at Hamline University, St Paul, Minnesota, and at the University of Minnesota. In 1950 she married the composer Ernst Krenek (1900–91). Her El Greco Phantasy for string orchestra (1965) was commissioned by the Gesellschaft für Neue Musik in Mannheim; some of her works have been published by Bärenreiter. She writes in expressionist style. Her output includes Antitheses for chorus and orchestra (1946), a piano concerto (1947), the orchestral Elegy for Robert F. Kennedy (1968), Orchestra Work no.3 (1975), Zeit, XXIV for solo soprano (text by R. Pandula; 1975), Parabola of Light for women's chorus and piano (to her own text; 1980), chamber music and electronic works. In 1993 she was working on the chamber opera The Neighbors (text by Krenek).

BIBLIOGRAPHY

B. Grigsby: 'Women Composers of Electronic Music in the United States', The Musical Woman: an International Perspective, i: 1983, ed. J. L. Zaimont and others (Westport, CT, 1984), 193

SARA JOBIN

Norton [née Sheridan], **Caroline Elizabeth Sarah** (b Huddersfield, 22 March 1808; d London, 15 June 1877). English poet and composer. She was a granddaughter of Richard Brinsley Sheridan, the statesman and dramatist, and Elizabeth Sheridan (née Linley), a celebrated English soprano; her elder sister was HELEN BLACKWOOD, Lady Dufferin, with whom she collaborated on an early publication entitled *A Set of Ten Songs and Two Duets . . . by Two Sisters* (London, 1833). In the 1840s, when most women composers chose to remain anonymous, she allowed the publication of her songs to reveal her identity, thus setting an example for other women to emulate. Her song *Juanita* (London, 1853) was the first drawing-room ballad by a woman composer to achieve substantial sales. Her stormy relationship with her husband, George Norton (*d* 1875), prompted her to write pamphlets and agitate on behalf of married women's rights. Her poetry was admired, and one of her poems, *The Arab's Farewell to his Favourite Steed*, became a favourite drawing-room ballad in a setting by John Blockley (*c*1865). Shortly before her death she married Sir William Stirling-Maxwell.

BIBLIOGRAPHY
A. Acland: *Caroline Norton* (New York, 1948)
D. Scott: *The Singing Bourgeois* (Milton Keynes, 1989)
DEREK B. SCOTT

Nova (Sondag), Jacqueline (*b* Ghent, 6 Jan 1935; *d* Bogotá, 13 June 1975). Colombian composer of Belgian origin. She studied with Fabio González-Zuleta, Olav Roots and Blas Emilio Atehortúa at the Bogotá Conservatory, graduating in composition. She is considered one of the finest Colombian composers of the 20th century and a progressive exponent of trends that dominated contemporary music in the 1960s, including aleatory and electronic techniques. One of the first Latin American women to obtain international acclaim for her compositions, she won a first prize in Caracas in 1966 for the chamber work *Doce móviles* (subsequently published by Pan American Union). Her *Metamorfosis III* (1966) was given its première by the Colombia SO, conducted by Roots. In 1967 she was awarded a scholarship for two years' study at the Instituto Torcuato Di Tella, Buenos Aires. Several works were first performed in Buenos Aires, including *Asimetrias* (1967), conducted by Armando Krieger, the electronic work *Oposición-fusión* (1968), and *Cantos de la creación del mundo* (1972; performed by Nueva Música), which was later

performed in France (1973). The oratorio *Hiroshima* (1972) was commissioned by Colcultura.

WORKS
selective list

Vocal, vocal with elec: Uerhayas: Invocation to the Gods (text in Tunebo [Am. Indian] dialect), S, male chorus, 1967; 14–35, orch, elec transformed vv, 1969; Pitecanthropus, vv, orch, elec, 1971; Hiroshima (oratorio, D. Castellanos), vv, orch, elec, 1972; Omaggio a Catullus, nar, vv, harmonium, perc, chamber orch, elec, 1972
Other elec: Música para audiovisual sobre Machu-Pichu, 1968; Oposición-fusión, 1968; Resonancias I, pf, elec, 1969; Cantos de la creación del mundo (Tunebo text), elec transformed v, 1972
Orch and inst: Secuencias, pf, 1963; Doce móviles, chamber ens, 1965; Metamorfosis III, orch, 1966; Asimetrias, fl, timp, tam-tam, 1967
Other works: Espacios, audiovisual experience, 1970; Camilo (film score, dir. F. Norden), 1974 [on Camilo Torres]

SUSANA FRIEDMANN

Nugent [Jerome], Maude (*b* Brooklyn, NY, 12 Jan 1873 or 1874; *d* New York, 3 June 1958). American singer and composer. She began her career in vaudeville, achieving tremendous success in 1896 with her song *Sweet Rosie O'Grady*, which became the archetypal waltz ballad of the 1890s. Over the next few years Nugent's songs included *Mamie Reilly* (1897), *I can't forget you, honey* (1899) and *Somebody wants you* (1909), but none were more than minor successes. Nugent introduced many of her songs herself; for most she wrote both words and music, but the lyrics were occasionally supplied by her husband, William Jerome. At the age of 28 she retired from the stage to raise a family, although she made a brief return seven years later. After several decades in relative obscurity Nugent began appearing in 'Gay Nineties' shows in the 1940s and, with her nostalgic appeal and lively presence, she enjoyed a brief vogue as a television personality in the 1950s.

BIBLIOGRAPHY
D. Gilbert: 'Maude Nugent launched Sweet Rosie O'Grady, own song, at Tony Pastor's', *New York World Telegram* (17 April 1934)
Obituary, *New York Times* (4 June 1958)
WILLIAM BROOKS (with PAMELA FOX)

O

Obrovská, Jana (*b* Prague, 13 Sept 1930; *d* Prague, 4 April 1987). Czech composer. Born into an artistic family, she had a short but significant musical career. She studied the piano with Berta Kabeláčová, music theory with Jaroslav Řídký and composition with Emil Hlobil at the Prague Conservatory (1949–55), where her graduation composition, an acclaimed Piano Concerto, revealed her talent for concertante forms. She worked as an editor for the Supraphon music publishing house in Prague. She was married to the guitar player Milan Zelenka. Her guitar pieces show a delicate stylization: *Passacaglia-Toccata* won the prize at the international guitar competition in Paris in 1972, and *Hommage à Béla Bartók* was the compulsory piece for the 1975 competition.

WORKS
selective list

Orch: 2 pf concs., 1955, 1960; Scherzino, wind, 1962; Concerto meditativo, gui, str, 1971; Pf Conc. 'Da Tasca', 1973; Conc., 2 gui, orch, 1977; Smutek sluší viole [Melancholy Suits the Viola], va, orch, 1978; Suita, str, 1979; Concertino, vn, va, db, str, 1981; Quasi concerto, vn, str, 1982

Chamber and solo inst: Podzimní preludia [Autumn Preludes], vn, pf, 1956; Wind Qnt, 1968; Hommage à Béla Bartók, gui, 1970; Passacaglia-Toccata, gui, 1972; Suoni, b cl, pf, 1974; Str Qt, 1976; Fanfárová suita [Fanfare Suite], 13 brass insts, 1976; Tryptych, gui, accordion, 1982

Vocal: 5 songs (folk texts), 1955; Canzoni in stilo antiquo, A, gui, 1969

Principal publishers: Max Eschig, Panton, Supraphon

BIBLIOGRAPHY
CohenE; CŠHS; ČSS

ANNA ŠERÝCH

Odăgescu, Irina (*b* Bucharest, 23 May 1937). Romanian composer. After completing her studies at the Bucharest Conservatory (1957–63), where she studied composition with Alfred Mendelsohn and Tiberiu Olah, she remained in that city, becoming a professor at the conservatory in 1967. In 1962 and 1976 she participated in the Darmstadt summer school, where resident teachers included Iannis Xenakis, Karlheinz Stockhausen, György Ligeti, Mauricio Kagel and Helmut Lachenmann, and later won national prizes for composition in Romania and international prizes in Ibagué, Colombia (1981) and at the Viotti Competition, Vercelli, Italy (1982). She has published musicological and didactic (vocal) studies. In the majority of her works, often devoted to Romanian themes, Odăgescu seems to be concerned to synthesize traditional and contemporary elements and to amalgamate modal and serial languages.

WORKS
selective list; printed works published in Bucharest

Choral: Tinerețe [Youth], op.7 (cantata, M. Duțescu), mixed vv, orch, 1963; Cîntec în memoria eroilor [Song to the Memory of the Heroes], op.10 (N. Constantinescu), mixed vv, 1965; Imn țării mele [Hymn to my Country], op.17 (M. Negulescu), mixed vv, 1971 (1972); Cîntec de drumeție [Song of Travel], op.20 (T. Bratu), children's choir 2vv, pf, 1972; Imn tineretii [Hymn to Youth], op.21 (D. M. Ioan), mixed vv, pf, 1972 (1973); Zi de lumină [Day of Light], op.26 (cantata, Negulescu), mixed vv, orch, 1976; Mîndria muncii [Work's Pride], op.28 (Constantinescu), 2vv, pf, 1976; Și-am pornit in drumeție [And I Started on a Journey], op.29 (Constantinescu), children's choir 2vv, pf, 1977 (1981); Numele patriei [Homeland's Name], op.36 (V. Nicolescu), mixed vv/male vv, 1979 (1981); Ție țară [To you, Country], op.37 (Constantinescu), women's vv, pf, 1980 (1981); Rădăcini străbune [Ancient Roots], op.52 (I. Crînguleanu), mixed vv, perc, 1983; Chemarea pămîntului [The Appeal of the Earth], op.55a (cantata, Crînguleanu), mixed vv, reciters, perc, 1984, rev. as oratorio, with orch, op.55b, 1985

Orch: Noapte de August [Night of August], op.8, sym. movt, 1964; Passacaglia, op.11, 1966; Piscuri [Peaks], op.15, sym. poem, 1970 (1973); Improvizații dramatice, op.22, 1972; Momente, op.25, concertino, str, 1974; Bătălia cu facle [The Battle with Torches], op.31, choreographic poem after painting by T. Aman, 1977 (1980); Cîntec înalt [High Song], op.50, choreographic poem, 1983; Cetatea de pămînt [The Earth Fortress], op.54 (P. Ghelmez), sym. poem, B-Bar, orch, 1985

Chamber: 3 Preludes, op.1, pf, 1960–61; Passacaglia, op.3, org, 1962; Sonata monopartita, op.5, pf, 1963; Str Qt, op.6, 1963; Vn Sonata, op.13, 1967 (1971); Scherzo-Toccata, op.14, pf, 1968; Melos I, op.44, S, cl, vc, perc, 1981; Melos II, op.45, fl, pf, 1982; Sonata, op.48, va, 1982; Music, op.51, 2 pf, perc, 1983

BIBLIOGRAPHY

D. Buciu: ' "Piscuri" de Irina Odăgescu', *Muzica*, xxii/8 (1972), 8–10

G. Constantinescu: 'Simfonicul Filarmonicii' [The Philharmonic's Symphony Concert], *Informaţia Bucureştiului* (27 Dec 1972) [on op.22]

D. Buciu: ' "Bătălia cu facle" de Irina Odăgescu' [Odăgescu's *Battle with Torches*], *Muzica*, xxix/3 (1979), 16–17

M. Popescu: *Repertoriul general al creaţiei muzicale româneşti* (Bucharest, 1979–81)

D. Popovici: ' "Bătălia cu facle" ' [*The Battle with Torches*], *Săptămîna culturală a Capitalei* (23 March 1980)

A. Hoffman: 'Cîntece pentru tineret' [Songs for Youth], *România liberă* (2 Dec 1981)

E. Zăvoianu: 'Balada de argint' [The Silver Ballad], *Săptămîna culturală a Capitalei* (20 Nov 1981)

I. Bănăţeanu: 'Discul' [The Disc], *Săptămîna culturală a Capitalei* (1 Jan 1982)

I. Dumitrescu: 'Cronică', *Săptămîna culturală a Capitalei* (26 Feb 1982)

G. Sbârcea: 'Un muzician complex', *România liberă* (25 Feb 1982)

VIOREL COSMA

Oh, Sook-Ja (*b* Seoul, 26 May 1941). Korean composer. She studied first at Kyung Hee University (BA 1971, MA 1973); in 1975–6 she studied electronic music at the Peabody Conservatory, Baltimore, and in 1979 took part in the conductors' summer course at the Salzburg Mozarteum. She taught at Kyung Hee University from 1973 to 1989. Her compositional inspiration typically comes from Korean traditions. For example, the orchestral work *Doet-Boe-Ki*, first performed in Sydney in 1981, is constructed from blocks of sound inspired by old mask dances; in the same way that masks express joy, agony, fury or courage, Oh's music conjures up the spectrum of human experience. *Mu-ak* for piano and percussion, first performed in Rome in 1982, explores the world of shamanism. The solo violin work *Nyoum II* imitates Korean scales and ornaments. Oh's works have been widely performed in Korea, Japan, Thailand, Taiwan and Australia. Like her compositions, her writings, published in Korea, focus on Korean musical traditions and shamanism.

WORKS
selective list

Stage: Won-Sul-Lang [Wŏnsullang; The Son of a Knight], opera, 1990

Orch: A Stone, 1972; The Heaven and the Earth, 1974; Asteroid B612, 1975; Vn Conc., 1977; Doet-Boe-Ki [Toetpaegi; Mask Dancer], pf, orch, 1981; Mysterious Dawn, 1984

Inst: Premagnet, fl qt, 1973; Mu-Ak [Muak; Shaman Music], pf, perc, 1976; Nyoum I–IV [Yŏŭm I–IV; Thought]: I, vc, perc, 1981, II, vn, 1983, III, cl, 1985, IV, fl, vn, va, vc, pf, 1986; Monologue, ob, dancer, 1992

Vocal: Art Songs, 1977; Waterdrop, 7 solo vv, harp, cel, perc, 1977; A Word of St Mary, chorus, 1979; A Prayer for Peace, chorus, 1980; An Orphan, male v, str qt, 1988

KEITH HOWARD

O'Leary [née Strong]**, Jane** (*b* Hartford, CT, 13 Oct 1946). American composer, resident in Ireland. She took the BA in music at Vassar College (1968) and the PhD at Princeton University (1978), where she studied composition with Milton Babbitt. In 1972 she moved to Ireland. She has received international awards, notably at the GEDOK competition in Mannheim (1985), for her String Quartet, and a Vienna Modern Masters recording award for *Islands of Discovery* (1992). In 1981 she was elected to Aosdána, which honours those who have contributed significantly to the creative arts in Ireland. Her appointments include Chairman of the Contemporary Music Centre, Dublin, from 1989, and membership of the Executive Board of the International League of Women Composers, 1986–94. In addition, she founded (1976), directs and performs in Concorde, an ensemble devoted to the performance of 20th-century music, and became director of the National Concert Hall, Dublin, in 1986.

O'Leary's early works explore aspects of serialism, focussing especially on structural elements that arise from pre-determined pitch patterns. Since 1983 she has adopted a freer approach to composition, which is evident in longer melodic lines, a particular attention to beauty of sound, and fluid textures.

WORKS
selective list

Orch: From the Flatirons, chamber conc., fl, ob, cl, str orch, 1985; Summer Stillness, 1986–9; The Petals Fall, chamber orch, 1987; Sky of Revelation, str orch, 1989; Islands of Discovery, 1991

Vocal: Filled Wine Cup (B. Kennelly, after Irish trad.), SATB, 1982; Is it Summer? (M. Cannon), S, fl, 1988; To Listen and to Trust, SSAA (Cannon, Kennelly), 1990

Pf: Pf Piece, 1974; Pf Piece II, 1980; Reflections: A Set of Five Images, 1985–6; Cartoline da Sicilia, 1987; Forgotten Worlds, 1987; When the Bells have Stopped Ringing, 1989; From the Crest of a Green Wave, 1993

Other inst: Sinfonia for Three, fl, vn, pf, 1980; Str Qt, 1983; Variations, fl, pf, 1984; Two for One, rec, 1986; A Silver Thread, vn, perc, 1988; Memories Grown Dim, tr rec, hpd, 1988; A Woman's Beauty (W. B. Yeats), fl, perc, dancer, spkr, 1991; Pf Trio, 1992; 4 Pieces, gui, 1993; Silenzio della terra, fl, perc, 1993; Duo, vn, vc, 1994

Principal publisher: Contemporary Music Centre (Dublin)

BIBLIOGRAPHY

Fuller-LeFanuRM

SARAH M. BURN

Olive, Vivienne (*b* London, 31 May 1950). English composer and harpsichordist, resident in Germany. She studied the organ with James Stevens and the harpsichord with Valda Aveling at Trinity College of Music, London (1966–8), taking the diploma in music theory. After completing an undergraduate degree (University of York, 1971), she studied composition with Bernard Rands in York, Franco Donatoni in Milan and Roman Haubenstock-Ramati in Vienna. She took the doctorate at the University of York in 1975 and continued studying at the Hochschule in Freiburg with Klaus Huber (composition) and Stanislav Heller (harpsichord). In 1973 she was appointed lecturer in music theory at the Fachakademie für Musik in Nuremberg.

Olive combines serial techniques with tonal elements in her compositions, but aims to communicate on a musical rather than an intellectual level. Rands and Huber have had a lasting influence on her work, which also shows an affinity with Lutyens, Musgrave and Zechlin.

WORKS
selective list

Orch: Tomba di Bruno: Hommage à Bruno Maderna, fl, orch, 1975
Ens, vocal: C (V. Woolf), 30vv, 5 perc, 1972; Lusciniae lacrimae: Klagelied für die Opfer von Seveso, 8 insts, 1979; Stabat mater, (Mez, org)/(8 female vv), 1980; A Thing which Fades: Klagelieder für die Opfer von Hiroshima, S, fl, gui, perc, 1987

BIBLIOGRAPHY

B. Sonntag and R. Matthei: 'Vivienne Olive', *Annäherungen an sieben Komponistinnen*, ii (Kassel, 1987), 55–64

ROSWITHA SPERBER

Oliveira, Jocy de (*b* Curitiba, Paraná, 11 April 1936). Brazilian composer and pianist. She studied the piano with José Kliass in São Paulo (1946–53) and Marguerite Long in Paris (1953–60). In 1963 she and her husband, the conductor Eleazar de Carvalho, moved to St Louis, Missouri, where she studied composition with Robert Wykes at Washington University (MA 1968). She played Stravinsky's *Capriccio* with the St Louis SO under the composer's direction; she subsequently played with the Boston SO and the French radio orchestra. Since then Luciano Berio, Iannis Xenakis, Lejaren Hiller and the Brazilian composer Cláudio Santoro have dedicated pieces to her. She later taught

for a year at the University of South Florida at Tampa and then at the New School for Social Research, New York (1977).

Oliveira has promoted new music in Brazil, coordinating concerts and pioneering the use of mixed and electronic media in works such as her play, *Apague meu Spotlight*, staged in São Paulo with music by Berio in 1961, the series *Estória* (1967–80), *Dimensões* for four amplified or electronic keyboard instruments (1976) and *Wave Song* (1977). She has written about her life and work in *Days and Routes through Maps and Scores* (Rio de Janeiro, 1984).

WORKS
selective list

Ens: Estória II, 1v, perc, tape, 1967; Polinterações I and II, happenings, 1970; Dimensões para 4 teclados, amp pf, amp hpd, el org, el pf, 1976; Wave Song, pf, tape, 1977; Estória IV, vv, el vn, perc, gui, db, 1978, rev. 1980; Música no espaço, multimedia, 1982; Fata Morgana, magic opera

Principal publisher: Source Music of the Avant Garde

BIBLIOGRAPHY

Enciclopédia da música brasileira (São Paulo, 2/1977), 569
V. Mariz: *Historia da música no Brasil* (Rio de Janeiro, 2/1986), 335–6

IRATI ANTONIO

Olivero, Betty (*b* Tel-Aviv, 16 May 1954). Israeli composer. From 1972 to 1978 she studied at the Rubin Academy of Music at Tel-Aviv University with Ilona Vincze-Kraus for piano and Yizhak Sadai and Leon Schidlowsky for composition. In 1982 she went to the USA for further study at Yale University, where her composition teachers were Jacob Druckman and Gilbert Amy. She was also awarded a Leonard Bernstein Scholarship to Tanglewood where she studied with Luciano Berio, who had a considerable influence on her career. In her music Olivero takes the rich variety of music to be found in the world's various Jewish communities and blends it with contemporary composition techniques. Although these folkloric elements are her source of inspiration, she does not quote them directly but subjects them to a process of metamorphosis while incorporating them in her music, thus preserving both their flavour and their spiritual and dramatic content. Her orchestration is massive, with occasional aquarelle-like treatment, while her musical textures, reflecting in some measure the influence of her teacher Schidlowsky, reveal a wide range of simultaneous rhythmic complexities using very small note values.

WORKS
selective list

Inst: Tehilim [Psalm], 12 vc, 4 db, 1980; Pan, 5 fl, 1984, rev. 1988; Batnun, db, chamber orch, 1985; Duo, vn, pf, 1987; Cubi, vc, db, 1987; Presenze, 10 players, 1987; Ketarim [Crowns], vn, orch, 1989; Adagio, orch, 1990

Vocal: Cantes amargos, Mez, chamber orch, 1981, rev. 1984; Maqamat, 5 folksongs, female v, 9 insts, 1988; Behind the Fence, scene for Mez, 4 puppet players, 7 insts, 1990

Principal publisher: Ricordi (Milan)

WILLIAM Y. ELIAS

Oliveros, Pauline (*b* Houston, 30 May 1932). American composer. As a child she studied the piano, violin, accordion and horn. She attended the University of Houston (1949–52), where she studied composition with Paul Koepke and the accordion with William Palmer, and San Francisco State College (BA 1957); she also had private composition lessons with Robert Erickson (1954–60). She was a co-director (1961–5), with Ramon Sender and Morton Subotnick, of the San Francisco Tape Music Center, and director (1966–7) when it became the Mills Tape Music Center. From 1967 to 1981 she taught at the University of California at San Diego. She has held appointments as composer-in-residence at a number of universities and conservatories as well as at the Walker Art Center, the Cleveland Museum of Art and the Cabrillo (California) Festival. Her many honours have included the Beethovenpreis der Stadt Bonn (1977, for *Bonn Feier*) and an NEA commission (*Portrait of Quintet of the Americas*, 1988). She is founder-director of Deep Listening Publications (1984) and the Pauline Oliveros Foundation (1988). In 1988 she began to work with Stuart Dempster and Panaiotis; a variety of composing and performing projects have resulted from the collaboration.

Oliveros's compositions range from music for acoustic instruments to mixed-media pieces incorporating both electronically produced and live sounds, film, texts, theatrical events and dance, and her works frequently involve audience participation. She uses sonic meditations, characterized by drone effects and the prolongation of sounds, to foster a sense of communion between performers in works involving improvisation. Her own performances often combine these ideas with an exploration of the relationship between sounds and the acoustic properties of the environments in which they are produced. She has written *Pauline's Proverbs* (New York, 1976) and articles for period-icals; her collected writings were published as *Software for People: Collected Writings 1963–80* (New York, 1981).

WORKS
selective list

DRAMATIC

Seven Passages, dancer, mobile, 2-channel tape, 1963; Apple Box Conc., performers, amp apple boxes, 1964; George Washington Slept Here Too (theatre piece), 4 performers, 1965; Pieces of Eight (theatre piece), wind octet, tape, 1965; Seven Sets of Mnemonics (mixed media), 1965; Theater Piece for Trbn Player, garden hoses, tape, 1966; Double Basses at 20 Paces, 2 db, tape, slides, cond. + referee, 2 performers, 1968

Evidence for Competing Bimolecular and Thermonuclear Mechanisms in the Hydrochlorination of Cyclohexene, performers, sonic events, audience, 1968; Valentine for SAG, 4 card players, amp sound, 1968; The Dying Alchemist Preview, nar, vn, tpt, pic, perc, slides, 1969; Please don't shoot the piano player, he's doing the best he can (theatre piece), 1969; Sonic Meditations, vv, insts, performers, 1971–2

Postcard Theater (multi-media event), 1972; What to Do, performers, sonic and mixed media, 1972; Crow Two (ceremonial opera), 1974; Theatre of Substitution, 1975; Bonn Feier (theatre piece), 1977; Theatre of Substitutions: Blind/Dumb/Director, 1977; The Yellow River Map (theatre piece), 50 or more performers, 1977; Traveling Companions (theatre piece), dancers, perc ens, 1980: Nzinga, the Queen King (theatre piece), 1993

INSTRUMENTAL

Trio, cl, hn, bn, 1955; Variations for Sextet, fl, cl, tpt, hn, vc, pf, 1960; Trio, fl, pf, p. turner, 1961; Trio, tpt, accordion, db, 1961; Outline, fl, perc, db, 1963; Duo, accordion, bandoneon, opt. mynah bird, 1964; Engineer's Delight, pic, 7 cond., 1967; Circuitry, 5 perc, lights, 1968; Night Jar, va d'amore, 1968; To Valerie Solanas and Marilyn Monroe in Recognition of their Desperation, orch/ chamber ens, 1970

1000 Acres, str qt, 1972; Horse Sings from Cloud, harmonium, accordion, bandoneon, concertina, 1975; Double X, meditation, pairs of like insts with overlapping compasses, 1979; Gone with the Wind, assorted ens, 1980; Tashi gomang, orch, 1981; Monkey, chamber ens, 1981; Mother's Day, 2 concertinas, 1981; . . . Jam, accordion, ens, 1982; Rattlesnake Mountain, accordion, 1982

The Wanderer, accordions, 1982; Gathering Together, pf 8 hands, 1983; The Seventh Mansion: from the Interior Castle, amp accordion, effects, 1983; The Wheel of Time, str qt, 1983; Earth Ears, accordion, vib, vn, 1984; Letting Go, accordion ens/solo, 1984; Spiral Mandala, 4 cl, 8 crystal glasses, b drum, finger cymbals, 1984; Three/Peace, vn, vc, pf, 1984

Waking the Heart, accordion solo/ens, 1984; Wings of a Dove, 2 pf, double wind qnt, 1984; Lion's Eye, gamelan orch/synclavier, 1985; Tasting the Blaze, perc, elec, trbn, vc, cl, 4 accordions, gagaku orch, 1985; Portrait of Qnt of the Americas, fl, ob + eng hn, cl + b cl, 1988; Portraits for Brass Qnt, 1989; All Fours for the Drum Bum, drum set, 1990; Grand Improvisation, b accordion, ob, db, synth, 1990; What If, accordion, 1991

VOCAL

3 Songs, S, pf, 1957; Sound Patterns, chorus, 1961; The C(s) for Once, vv, fls, tpts, tape delay, 1966; O HA AH, chorus, cond., 2 perc, 1968; AOK, chorus, accordion, vns, conds., 8 country fiddles, tape, 1969; SY*YdY = 1, 4 readers (4 solo vv), 4 vc, 4 bn, amp heartbeat, shakuhachi, 1969; Meditations on the Points of a Compass, 12 solo vv, chorus, perc, 1970; Music for Tai Chi, vv, accordion, str, wind, perc, 1970; Horse Sings from a Cloud (Rose Mountain), 1v, accordion, 1977

King Kong Sings Along, chorus, 1977; The Wheel of Life, vv, 1978; Carol Plantamura, 1v, 20 insts, 1979; Angels and Demons, chorus, ens, 1980; The Wandering: a Love Song, 1v, digital delay, 1983; Aga, 1v, concertina, whistle conch, tpt, electronics, digital delay, 1984; Drama of the 5 Families, nar, soloist, chorus, 1984; Oh Sister whose Name is Goddess, 1v, digital delay, 1984; Open Circuits om mani padme hum for 1984 Summer Olympics

Song for the Ancestors, 1v, shell tpt, didjeridu, 1984; Talking Bottles and Bones, 1v, effects, digital delay, 1984; The Chicken who Learned how to Fly, vv, nar, synth, 1985; Legend, amp accordion, chorus, perc, 1985; The New Sound Meditation, vv, 1989; Deep Listening Pieces, 1v, ens, 1990; In Memory of the Future, 1v, 1991; Reflections on the Persian Gulf, accordion, 1v, 1991; Uncensored Sound, accordion, trbn, 1v, kbd, 1991; Midnight Operas, chorus, 1992

ELECTRONIC

Time Perspectives, tape, 1961; Before the Music Ends, tape, dancer, 1965; Bye Bye Butterfly, oscillators, amplifiers, tape, 1965; 5000 Miles, tape, elec, 1965; Mnemonics III, IV and V, tape, elec, 1965; Rock Symphony, tape, 1965; Winter Light, tape, mobile, figure, 1965; Big Mother is Watching you, tape, 1966

The Day I Disconnected the Erase Head and Forgot to Reconnect it, tape, elec, 1966; I, II, III, IV and V of IV, tape, 1966; Participle Dangling in Honor of Gertrude Stein, tape, mobile, work crew, 1966; Music for Lysistrata, tape, elec, 1968; Live Elec Piece for Merce Cunningham's Dance, 1969; Bog Road with Bird Call Patch, tape, 1970; Listening for Life, 1991

Principal publishers: Deep Listening, Smith

BIBLIOGRAPHY

CC (D. Revill)

M. Subotnick: 'Pauline Oliveros: Trio', PNM, ii/1 (1963), 77–82

E. Kefalas: 'Pauline Oliveros', HiFi/MusAm, xxv/6 (1975), 24

W. Zimmermann: 'Pauline Oliveros', Desert Plants: Conversations with 23 American Musicians (Vancouver, BC, 1976)

H. Von Gunden: The Music of Pauline Oliveros (Metuchen, NJ, 1983)

M. Roth: The Amazing Decade: Women and Performance Art in America (Los Angeles, 1983) [on Bonn Feier]

G. Gronemeyer: 'Hast du jemals den Klang eines schmelzenden Eisbergs gehört? Porträt von Pauline Oliveros', Neuland, iv (1983–4), 277–86

M. E. Young: The Life and Music of Pauline Oliveros (diss., U. of Minnesota, 1984)

H. Von Gunden: 'The Music of Pauline Oliveros: a Model for Feminist Criticism', ILWC Journal (1992), June, 6–8

P. Pannke: 'Deep Listening: Pauline Oliveros und ihre Stratagien des Hörens', NZM, Jg. 153, no.3 (1992), 28–30

LISA B. ROBINSON, RICHARD SWIFT

Oosterzee, Cornélie van (*b* Batavia [now Jakarta], 16 Aug 1863; *d* Berlin, 12 Aug 1943). Dutch composer. After studying music theory in The Hague with Willem Nicolaï, she went to Berlin to study composition with Rudolf Radecke and instrumentation with Heinrich Urban. Although she remained in Berlin for the rest of her life, she maintained contact with the Netherlands as a music correspondent for a Dutch newspaper, *Algemeen Handelsblad*, and by conducting Dutch orchestras. She was one of the first Dutch women to write orchestral works; these include the overture *Jolanthe*, *IJsbrand*, *Königs-Idyllen* (based on Tennyson's *Idylls of the King*) and a symphony in F minor. She also composed an Italian *verismo* music drama, *Das Gelöbnis*. In 1898 she composed a cantata for women's choir, soloists and orchestra for the opening ceremony of the National Exhibition on Women's Work in The Hague. Van Oosterzee was made a Knight of the Order of Oranje-Nassau in 1897 and a corresponding member of the Maatschappij tot Bevordering der Toonkunst (Association for the Promotion of Music) in 1901. Much of her work was apparently lost in Berlin during World War II.

HELEN METZELAAR

Oram, Daphne (Blake) (*b* Devizes, Wilts., 31 Dec 1925). English composer. She was educated at Sherborne School for Girls. She worked at the BBC from 1943 to 1959, at first as a music balancer for classical music programmes. A pioneer in integrating music and technology, she was one of the initiators of the BBC Radiophonic Workshop in 1958 and established her own studio in 1959. Her experiments in converting graphic information into sound – from 1944, with the aid of Gulbenkian grants in 1962 and 1965 – led to the development of her Oramics system, a photo-electric digital and analogue composition machine, which gives the composer control of subtle nuances in all parameters: amplitude, envelope shaping, rhythm, timbre control, microtonal pitch and vibrato (the last hand drawn, not 'mechanically' cyclic). In the 1990s she began to convert the system to RISC computer technology, suitable for composers to use at home. A number of her works have been composed using the system, including *Broceleande* for Oramics tape (1970), and *Sardonica* for piano and Oramics tape (1972, written in collaboration with Ivor Walsworth). She has written music for films, including *The Innocents* (1961); for television and radio; for exhibitions, including *Pulse Persephone* (1965); for the theatre, including the ballet *Xallaraparallax* (1972); and for concert performance.

BIBLIOGRAPHY

Fuller-LeFanuRM; *GroveI* ('Oramics'; H. Davies)

D. Oram: *An Individual Note of Music: Sound and Electronics* (London and New York, 1972)

A. Douglas: *Electronic Music Production* (London, 1973), 92; (2/1982), 102

P. Manning: *Electronic and Computer Music* (Oxford, 1985), 152

SOPHIE FULLER

Ørbeck, Anne-Marie (*b* Oslo, 1 April 1911). Norwegian composer and pianist. She studied the piano in Oslo and Berlin (début 1933, Oslo), and composition with Mark Lothar and Paul Höffer in Berlin, Nadia Boulanger in Paris and Hanns Jelinek in Vienna. Cecilie Dahm has said (*Cappelens musikkleksikon*) that Ørbeck's songs are characterized by 'a marked lyrical thread and a natural freshness which derives its effect from an independent and thoroughly prepared accompaniment'. Her music is tonal, and the early works show a strong Romantic influence. According to Dahm, this is most marked in the Symphony, her largest work, completed in 1944 (recorded in 1989).

WORKS
selective list

Orch: Concertino, pf, orch, 1938; Sym., 1944; Miniatursuite, 1945; Pastorale and Allegro, fl, str orch, 1959

Pf: Capriccio, Humoreske, Melodi, Stemning [Mood], all 1931; Runemarsjen [The Runa March], 1941; Sonatina, 1967; Valse piccante, 1971; cadenzas for Mozart concs. K365/316a, 415/387b, 467, 482, and Haydn conc., D, H XVIII:2; arr. of R. Strauss: Der Rosenkavalier, 1938

Vn, pf: Norsk springar [Norwegian Dance], 1928; Romanse, 1928; Melodi, 1931

Vocal (for 1v, pf): c40 romanser and other works, incl.: Snefald [Snowfall], 1927; Ein Jüngling liebt ein Mädchen, 1929; Barn [Children], 1939; 3 songs (Swed. texts), 1951; So rodde dei fjordan [And across the fjord they rowed], 1954, arr. 1v, orch, 1962; Vill-Guri [Wild Guri], 1955, arr. 1v, orch, 1962; En hustavle [Proverbs], 1957; Sne [Snow], 1959; Staresong [Song of the Starling], 1964

BIBLIOGRAPHY

K. Michelsen, ed.: *Cappelens musikkleksikon* (Oslo, 1978–80)

KARI MICHELSEN

Daphne Oram composing, using the photo-electric prototype instrument which she built (1962–5) for her 'Oramics' graphic sound system

Ore, Cecilie (*b* Oslo, 19 July 1954). Norwegian composer. She graduated as a pianist and teacher at the Oslo Musikkhøgskole, then studied composition at the Sweelinck Conservatory in Amsterdam with Ton de Leeuw and electroacoustic music at the Institute of Sonology at Utrecht. Ore's main compositional tool is the computer. Bjørn Billing has described her music as 'a matter of time'; in it the concept of time is 'like a prism mirroring different nuances, different aspects of temporal relations; non-linear movements, simultaneous processes, polycentricity'. Her aim is to avoid traditional 'melodic-rhythmical temporal and spatial processes', using instead 'sonorous-rhythmical structures'. Her works have been performed at the ISCM and other international festivals. In 1988 at the International Rostrum for Electroacoustic Music in Stockholm she was awarded the first prize for young composers and second prize for her composition *Etapper*; in the same year her orchestral work *Porphyre* (1986) was named Work of the Year in Norway.

WORKS
selective list

Vocal: Carnathus, S, unacc. chorus, 1982; Calliope, S, 1984; Ex oculis, T, T, Bar, B, 1985; Cantus aquatoris, S, A, T, B, 1987

Inst: Helices, wind qnt, 1984; Janus, vc, 1985; Porphyre, orch, 1986; Contracanthus, db, 1987; Praesens subitus, amp str qt, 1989; Erat erit est, amp chamber ens, 1991; Futurum exactum, amp str ens, 1992; Lex temporis, amp str qt, 1992

Elec: Im-mobile IV, video, 1984; Kald verden, film score, 1986; Etapper, 1988; Prologos, theatre music, 1990; see also inst works

BIBLIOGRAPHY

CC (B. Billing)

B. Billing: 'A Matter of Time', Cecilie Ore (Oslo, 1992) [Norwegian Music Information Centre and Norsk Musikforlag brochure]

KARI MICHELSEN

Orger [Reinagle], **Caroline** (b London, 1818; d Tiverton, Devon, 11 March 1892). English pianist, composer and writer. She was the daughter of Mary Ann Orger (1788–1849), an actress and dramatic author. She began her recital career in 1840 and performed her Piano Concerto at the Hanover Square Rooms on 3 May 1843. In 1844 she played her Piano Trio there at a concert given with Charlotte Sainton-Dolby. Other chamber works by her were performed at the Society of British Musicians in 1844, 1846 (Cello Sonata) and 1847. In 1846 she married the organist and composer A. R. Reinagle.

Orger's music is the product of an original, cultured mind. Her songs, especially the Browning settings (1868), are characterized by unremitting psychological power: the intensely Victorian imagery of the texts serves only to affirm the music's emotional grandeur. Even when not setting words, she seems to have worked to an inner programme: this is particularly true of the Piano Sonata, one of the most significant English keyboard works of the 19th century. Its stylistic base is Schubert, on whose idiom it continually enlarges, reaching a point (in the finale) where technical demands far exceed those of the 'London piano school' (Muzio Clementi, J. B. Cramer and others, most of whose music can be played without arm weight). The only defect is occasional prolixity, but this may be a consequence of the work's massive structure.

WORKS

all printed works published in London

Orch: Pf Conc.

Chamber: Pf Qt; Pf Trio; Vc Sonata, G; chamber work, Eb, insts unknown, perf. London, 1847

Pf: Tarantella (1846); Sonata, A, op.6 (1855); Volunteer Rifle March (1860)

Songs: The Pilgrims (A. Procter) (1862); A Dead Past (Procter) (1863); A Shadow (Procter) (1864); Would it were I had been false, not you! (R. Browning) (1864); 3 Songs (Browning) (1868): In a year, I would that you were all to me, This is a spray the bird clung to; 2 Songs (A. Tennyson and C. Rossetti) (1880)

Pedagogical: A Few Words on Piano Playing (1855)

BIBLIOGRAPHY

CohenE; MEMM; WCBH

J. D. Brown and S. S. Stratton: British Music Biography (Birmingham, 1897)

O. Thompson, ed.: The International Cyclopedia of Music and Musicians (London, 4/1942)

J. Bowers and J. Tick, eds.: Women Making Music: the Western Art Tradition, 1150–1950 (Urbana and Chicago, 1986), 306–7

NIGEL BURTON

Orsina, Lucrezia. See VIZZANA, LUCREZIA ORSINA.

Oury [née de Belleville], **Anna Caroline** (b Landshut, 24 June 1808; d Munich, 22 July 1880). German pianist and composer, of French descent. The daughter of a French nobleman who was director of the Munich Opera, she spent her childhood in Augsburg, where she studied with the cathedral organist. From 1816 to 1820 she studied with Carl Czerny in Vienna, where she was introduced to Beethoven and heard him improvise on the piano. In 1820 she returned to Munich, performing there with great success; she spent the next year in Paris and then resumed her studies in Vienna with Johann Andreas Streicher. She subsequently toured to Warsaw and Berlin. In July 1831 she made her London début in a concert at Her Majesty's Theatre with Nicolò Paganini and in October married the English violinist Antonio James Oury. Between 1831 and 1839, they toured in Russia, Germany, Austria, Holland, France and Belgium, before settling in England. In 1846 and 1847 they visited Italy; afterwards, until her retirement in 1866, she devoted herself primarily to composition, producing some 180 drawing-room pieces – mainly dances and fantasies for piano.

BIBLIOGRAPHY

Grove1 (J. A. Fuller-Maitland); SchillingES

J. A. FULLER MAITLAND/ANDREW LAMB

Owen [Llwyn-Owen], **Morfydd** (b Treforest, 1 Oct 1891; d Oystermouth, 7 Sept 1918). Welsh composer, mezzo-soprano and pianist. She was educated at University College, Cardiff (BMus 1912), and at the RAM with Frederick Corder (Lucas Silver Medal 1913; ARAM 1918). World War I frustrated her ambition to study folk music in St Petersburg in 1915, and she developed instead her collaboration with Ruth Lewis, the pioneering Welsh ethnomusicologist. Many of her 150 compositions – orchestral works, choral, chamber and piano music, and a wealth of exquisite vocal miniatures –

bear the imprint of folksong. Her mercurial yet emotionally intense personality, which intrigued a wide circle from David Lloyd George to D. H. Lawrence, also shines through. Her output and engagements dwindled after her sudden marriage in 1917 to the Freudian psychoanalyst Ernest Jones, with whom she had a chequered relationship. Her early death was the result of a failed appendicectomy. A memorial edition of her songs, orchestral and piano music (four volumes) was published in London about 1923.

WORKS

Orch: Romance, str, 1911; Nocturne, 1913; Prelude, 1913; Morfa Rhuddlan, 1914; Death Music: The Passing of Branwen, str, Funeral March to Branwen, 1916

Vocal: Fierce raged the tempest (S. Thring), SATB, pf, 1911; The Refugee (F. von Schiller), SATB, pf, 1911; Sea Drift (W. Whitman), Mez, orch, 1911; Sweet and Low (A. Tennyson), SATB, 1911; Ave Maria, Mez, SSATB, str, 1912; A Cycle of Sea Songs (C. Rossetti, W. Watson, C. Mackay, T. Campbell), Mez, orch, 1912; Love's Music (P. Bourke Marston), S, orch, 1912; Mad Song (W. Blake), SATB, 1912; My luve's like a red, red rose (R. Burns), SATB, 1912; My Sorrow (E. Crawshay-Williams), S, orch, 1912; Y Fwyalchen (Welsh folksong), SSA, 1912; Jubilate Deo, SSATB, brass insts, org, 1913; Toward the Unknown Region (Whitman), Mez/T, orch, 1913; Choric Song (Tennyson), S, str, cel, 1914; An Old Man's Darling (Normandy folksong), Mez, orch, 1914; My luve's like a red, red rose (Burns), S, T, pf, 1914; Pro Patria (Elidir Sais), cantata, S, Bar, SATB, orch, 1915; Trugarha wrthyf, O Dduw [Have mercy, O Lord], unison vv, org, 1915; 2 Songs: In Cradle Land, The Fairies' Wedding (Eos Gwalia), S, orch, 1916; 2 Songs: An Irish Lullabye (anon.), Pitter Patter (D. Ainslie), S, orch, 1917; 18 hymns, SATB, 1909–16; 75 songs, 1v, pf, 1910–18; transcrs. and arrs. of Welsh, Eng. and Russ. folksongs, 1v, pf, 1913–16

Chamber: Romance, vn, pf, 1911; Pf Trio, 1912; Pf Trio, Lenavanmo, 1915

Pf: Sonata, 1910; Impromptu, 1910; Etude, 1911; Fantaisie, 1911; Mélodie, 1911; Minuet and Trio, 1911; Chromatic Fugue, 1911; Rhapsody, 1911; Causerie gracieuse de riens, 1911; Story Fantaisie, ?1911; Fantaisie appassionata, 1912; Berceuse, 1912; Prelude and Fugue in the Ancient Style, 1914; Preludes: Beti Bwt, Citi Cariadus, Glantaf, Little Eric, Nant-y-Ffrith, Talyllyn, Waiting for Eirlys, 1914–15; Minuet and Trio, ?1915 [arr. of Beti Bwt]

Principal publishers: Anglo-French Music Co./OUP, Boosey, Hughes & Son, Welsh Music Information Centre (Cardiff)

MSS in GB-CDu, AB

BIBLIOGRAPHY

E. Crawshay-Williams: 'Morfydd Owen', Wales, iv (1958), 50–56

'The Tragedy of Morfydd', Y Ddinas (1959), March, 17–18

K. I. Jones: 'The Enigma of Morfydd Owen', Welsh Music, v/1 (1975–6), 8–21

R. Davies: Never So Pure a Sight: Morfydd Owen (1891–1918): a Life in Pictures (Llandysul, 1994)

—— : The Life and Music of Morfydd Owen (1891–1918) (diss., U. of Wales, Bangor, in preparation)

RHIAN DAVIES

Ozaita, María Luisa (b Baracaldo, 20 April 1939). Spanish composer and harpsichordist. She studied with J. C. Gómez Zubeldia (piano), Fernando Remacha (composition) and Kenneth Gilbert (harpsichord), and was awarded scholarships to attend courses at Santiago de Compostela, Granada, Darmstadt, and the Copenhagen Kongelige Danske Musikkonservatorium, where her teachers were K. J. Isaksen (harpsichord) and Leif Thybo (composition). She has pursued a career as a composer, performer, teacher and researcher and has given many lectures on women composers. In 1988 she was the founding president of Mujeres en la Música and in 1991, together with the cellist Rosario Ramos, founded the association's Orquestra de Cámara Femenina. She also took part in Radio Nacional de España's 'La otra música' and has contributed to several periodicals. Her music combines a wide variety of contemporary styles with elements of classical counterpoint, and some pieces are clearly impressionistic.

WORKS
selective list

Stage: La fuente del Halcón (ballet), 1961 [arr. of chamber work, 1961]; Balada de Atta Troll (music-theatre, A. Casona), 1963; Pelleas y Melisenda (ballet-cantata, P. Neruda), 1974

Chamber and orch: La fuente del Halcón, va, harmonium, perc, 1961; Vn Sonata, 1968; Canción, str orch, 1970; Urte berri eta ametza 'n Dantza, film score, wind qnt, 1971; In memóriam, 2 vc, fl, ob, cl, bn, 1975; Esto nos pasa por no tener director, wind qnt, 1981; ¡Oh!, vn, cl, vc, 1982; Tríptico encadenado, vn, vc, pf, 1987; Pieza en trio, vn, cl, vc, 1987

Solo inst: 3 pequeñas piezas, fl, 1968; Para órgano no.1, org, 1971; Irurak Bat, pf, 1973; Módulos canónicos, hpd, 1981; A modo de improvisación, hpd, 1982; Preludio, danza con 3 variaciones y fantasía, gui, 1982; Tema con 10 variaciones, pf, 1983; Recordando, org, 1987; Fantasía, vc, 1988

Vocal: Aforismos (S. Kierkegaard), 1v, triangle, 1974; Irrintzi, 1976; Aleluyas, S, fl, 1982; La balada de Atta Troll, S, fl, pf, 1982 [new version]; Homenaje a Goya, S, gui, 1983; 3 canciones españolas (F. García Lorca), 1v, pf, 1983; other songs

BIBLIOGRAPHY

KompA-Z

J. A. Arana Martija: Música vasca (Bilbao, 1987)

Catálogo de obras de la Asociación de Compositores Sinfónicos Españoles (Madrid, 1987)

E. Kay, ed.: The World Who's Who of Women 1990–1991 (Cambridge, 1990)

ALICIA CASARES-ALONSO

P

Pade, Else Marie (*b* Århus, 2 Dec 1924).
Danish composer. After participating in the
resistance during World War II, she trained as
a pianist at the Kongelige Danske Musikkonservatorium in Copenhagen. Later she
had lessons in 12-note technique with
Jan Maegaard. Primarily inspired by Pierre
Schaeffer's *A la recherche d'une musique concrète*
(1952) and taking advantage of the facilities at
Danish Radio, where she was employed from
1952, she became the first Danish composer to
write electronic music, beginning sound experiments in 1954. In the late 1970s she participated in a research project at the National
Hospital in Copenhagen, where *musique concrète* was used to stimulate the imagination of
mentally handicapped children. Her output
includes ballets and other theatre works, and
music for films. Her children's opera *Far, mor
og børn* ('Father, Mother and Children', 1974)
won second prize in a competition organized
by Scandinavian opera companies.

WORKS
selective list

Dramatic: Far, mor og børn [Father, Mother and
Children] (children's opera), 1974; see also elec
works
Inst: Conc., tpt, orch, 1954; Parametre, str orch, 1962;
Historien om skabelsen [The Story about Creation],
toy insts, 1969; Efterklange [Echoes], perc, 1984;
see also elec works
Vocal: Tullerulle Tappenstreg, children's songs, 1951;
4 Anon. Songs, A, cl, 1955; Volo spa hoc est,
female chorus, 1956
Elec, el-ac: En dag på Dyrehavsbakken [A Day at
Dyrehavsbakken] (television film score), 1954–5; 6
eventyr [6 Fairy-Tales] (incid. music for radio),
1955–6; Symphonie magnétophonique, 1958–9;
Glasperlespil [Glass Bead Game], 1960; Afsnit I–III
[Sections I–III], vn, 11 perc insts, elec, 1960;
Vikingerne (film score), 1961; Faust, suite, 1962;
Symphonie heroica, 1962; Graesstrået [The Blade of
Grass] (television ballet), vn, prepared pf, elec,
1964; Immortella (ballet pantomime), 7 perc insts,
elec, 1969–70; Maria, 1972; Teresa af Avila (incid.
music, church play), 1980

BIBLIOGRAPHY

S. Christiansen: 'Portraet af Else Marie Pade', *DEMS
Bulletin*, no.3 (1979) [interview]
I. Bruland: 'Fire danske kvindelige komponister fra
det 20. århundrede' [4 Danish Women Composers
of the 20th Century], *Kvinders former*, ed. I.
Bruland, L. Busk-Jensen and T. Ødrum (Copenhagen, 1986), 33–59, esp. 34–9

INGE BRULAND

Pagh-Paan, Younghi (*b* Cheongju, 1945).
South Korean composer, resident in
Germany. She studied music theory and
composition at the National University in
Seoul (1965–72) before moving to Germany
on a DAAD grant (1974). She continued her
studies with Klaus Huber and Brian
Ferneyhough at the Hochschule in Freiburg.
She has received many honours, including
the jury prize at the fifth International
Composers' Seminar in Boswil, Switzerland
(1978), the music prize of Korea and first
prize at the UNESCO International Rostrum
of Composers, Paris (both 1979), and a
scholarship from the Heinrich Strobel
Foundation (1980–81).

Pagh-Paan attained international recognition following the premières at Donaueschingen festivals of her orchestral works
SORI (1980) and *NIM* (1987), and her works
have been heard frequently at contemporary
music festivals across Europe. She was guest
professor at the Musikhochschule in Graz
and in Karlsruhe, and became professor of
composition at the Hochschule für Kunste,
Bremen, in February 1994. Although her
early works were principally instrumental,
her later compositions reveal a growing
interest in vocal writing. In her music she
combines avant-garde techniques with the
traditions and aesthetics of her east Asian
origins.

WORKS
selective list

Orch: SORI, 1980; NIM, 1986–7; Hong (Ständig wie-
derkehrend), 1992–3
Inst: Dreisam-Nore, fl, 1975; Man-Nam I, cl, vn, va,
vc, 1977; Man-Nam II, a fl, vn, vc, db, 1977–86;
Madi, 12 insts, 1981, rev. 1983; Pyon-Kyong, pf,
perc, 1982; Aa-Ga, vc, 1984; No-Ul, va, vc, db,
1984–5; Ta-Ryong II, 16 insts, 1987–8; Bi-Dan-Sil
(Seidener Faden), ob, 8 insts, 1993; Trio, cl, va, pf,
1994
Vocal: Nun, 5 women's vv (all with perc insts), 18
insts, 1978–9; Flammenzeichen (H. Scholl, S. Scholl

357

and extracts from a World War II resistance pamphlet: *Weissen Rose*), Mez (with perc insts), 1983; Hin-Nun, 6 women's vv (all with perc insts), 1985; Hwang-To [Gelbe Erde] (Kim Chi-Ha), solo vv, chorus, 9 insts, 1989; Ma-Am, woman's voice, 1990; Ma-Um, Mez, 12 insts, 1990

Principal publisher: Ricordi

DETLEF GOJOWY, ROSWITHA SPERBER

Pakhmutova, Alexandra Nikolayevna (*b* Volgograd, 9 Nov 1929). Russian composer. She studied composition with V. Y. Shebalin at the Moscow Conservatory, as an undergraduate (until 1953) and at postgraduate level (1953–6). She made an immediate impact on the world of Soviet song, securing a reputation among popular songwriters through her individual voice and unfailing ability to respond acutely to contemporary events, whether it be the heroism of Gagarin or the tragedy of Chernobyl. Her treatment of important social themes carries a personal stamp, and even the 'official' songs she was obliged to write – Pakhmutova's heyday occurred during the 'period of stagnation' under Brezhnev – are individual and of high quality. Her songs are also inseparably linked with the Komsomol movement of the 1960s; their performance was a high point of congresses, and the songs became popular because the composer succeeded in emphasizing the best aspects of the movement – its spirit rather than its formal ideology. Pakhmutova was secretary to the Board of the USSR Composers' Union and enjoyed not only official Soviet recognition, rare for a composer, but also international renown. She was the first composer to be awarded the Komsomol prize, was twice a state prizewinner and was decorated with the Order of Lenin and the Order of the Red Banner of Labour.

Pakhmutova is a true romantic who is fully aware of the dramatic possibilities of the song genre and who possesses an unerring sense of how to express the essence of each song. Her characters are drawn from all aspects of life – from astronauts to ice-hockey players – and she skilfully combines within her simple diatonic melodies soulfulness, passion and every shade of emotion, while always maintaining dignity of expression. Although she has set existing poetry to music, in most cases it is the musical idea that precedes the writing of the words, collaboration with the poet beginning once the latter has responded to the theme and established the verse structure; this is particularly true of her work with

N. Dobronravov. In her early songs Pakhmutova combined different styles, often boldly juxtaposed: art song, folksong, Soviet songs, guitar songs, military music and Western pop music. Later her range of contrasting styles extended, to include operatic arioso, love songs, disco and rock music. The songs have not dated, and the composer is continually in search of new materials and inspiration.

WORKS
selective list

Stage: Ozaryonnost' [Illumination] (ballet, 1, N. Dobronravov), 1973

Orch: Russkaya syuita, 1952; Tpt Conc., 1955; Tyuringiya (Poema na nemetskiye narodnïye temï) [Thuringia (Poem on German Folk Themes)], 1957; Yunost' [Youth], festive ov., 1957; Vesyalïye devchata [Jolly Girls], ov., variety light orch, 1964; Dinamo-marsh [Dynamo March], variety light orch, 1965; Lyubov' moya, sport [Sport, my Love], ov., variety light orch, 1974; Pieces, 1982; Pieces for circus perf., 1983

Choral: Vasily Tyorkin (cantata, A. Tvardovsky), 1953; Lenin v serdtse u nas [Lenin in our Heart] (cantata, S. Grebennikov and Dobronravov), spkr, children's chorus, orch, 1957; Prekrasnaya, kak molodost', strana [The Country Beautiful as a Youth] (cantata, V. Lebedev-Kumach, S. Orlov, N. Dorizo and Dobronravov), spkr, 1v, children's chorus, mixed chorus, orch, 1977; Oda na zazhzheniye olimpiyskogo ognya [Ode on the Lighting of the Olympic Fire], wordless mixed chorus, orch, 1980

Song cycles: Tayozhnïye zvyozdï [Stars of the Taiga] (Grebennikov and Dobronravov), 1963; Obnimaya nebo [Embracing the Sky] (Grebennikov and Dobronravov), 1966; Sozvezdiye Gagarina [Constellation of Gagarin] (Dobronravov), 1971

Over 300 songs, incl. Pesnya o trevozhnoy molodosti [A Song about Troubled Youth] (Yu. Drunina and L. Oshanin), Starïy klyon [Old Maple] (M. Matusovsky), Geologi [Geologists], Trus ne igrayet v khokkey [A Coward doesn't Play Hockey] (Grebennikov and Dobronravov), Orlyata uchatsya letat' [Young Eagles Learn to Fly], Ne rasstanus' s komsomolom [I will not Leave the Komsomol], I vnov' prodolzhayetsya boy [And the Battle Still Goes on], Nadezhda [Hope], Kak molodï mï bïli [How Young we were], Do svidan'ya, Moskva [Goodbye, Moscow], Komanda molodosti nashey [The Team of Our Youth], Ya ne mogu inache [I Cannot Otherwise], Dobraya skazka [A Good Tale] (Dobronravov)

Also film music

BIBLIOGRAPHY

E. Dobrynina: 'Aleksandra Pakhmutova', *Muzïkal'naya zhizn'* (1961), no.5, p.11

—— : 'Kompozitor i ego pesni' [The Composer and his Songs], *Muzïkal'naya zhizn'* (1965), no.5, p.4; also pubd in E. Dobrynina: *Lyubitel'yam muzïki posvyashchayetsya* [Dedicated to Music Lovers] (Moscow, 1980), 104–10

V. Zak: *Pesni Aleksandrï Pakhmutovoy* [The Songs of Pakhmutova], *SovM* (1965), no.3, pp.6–11

E. Dobrïnina: *Aleksandra Pakhmutova* (Moscow, 1973)

D. B. Kabalevsky: 'Glavnïy komsomol'skïy kompositor' [The Principal Komsomol Composer], *SovM* (1975), no.9, pp.16–18

L. Genina: 'Rodnikovaya pravda pesni' [The Pure Truth of a Song], *SovM* (1980), no.1, pp.32–6

R. Petrushanskaya: 'Trubadur komsomol'skogo plemeni' [The Troubadour of the Komsomol Generation], *Sovetskiye kompoẓitori: laureatï premii Leninskogo komsomola* [Soviet Composers: Laureates of the Lenin Komsomol Prize] (Moscow, 1989), 7–28

OLGA MANULKINA

Palmer, Frederik. Pseudonym of HARTMANN, EMMA SOPHIE AMALIA.

Papavoine [Pellecier], Mme [first name unknown] (*b* c1735; *fl* 1755–61). French composer. By 1755, she was married to the violinist Papavoine (*d* 1793), the composer of symphonies and comic operas, by whom she had two children, Angélique (*b* Paris, 1759) and a son (? Jean-Noël; *d* Paris, 1796). The *Mercure de France* of January 1755 contains a 'Catalogue des oeuvres de M. et Mme Papavoine', ascribing six *cantatilles* to her as Mlle Pellecier (*Les arrets d'amour, La tourterelle, Les charmes de la voix, La fête de l'amour, Issé* and *Le joli rien*) and two as Mme Papavoine (*Le triomphe des plaisirs* and *Le Cabriolet*, which contains a tempest movement). That issue (January 1755) also includes a short, 12-bar unaccompanied *air* by her, and the following year a modest little chanson appeared in the July issue; lastly, a texted *pastorale* melody was offered in May 1761. At least one more *cantatille*, *La France sauvée ou Le triomphe de la vertù*, has been attributed to her.

BIBLIOGRAPHY

SchmidlD†

JULIE ANNE SADIE

Paradis [Paradies], **Maria Theresia von** (*b* Vienna, ? 15 May 1759; *d* Vienna, 1 Feb 1824). Austrian composer and pianist. She was the child of the Imperial Secretary and Court Councillor to Empress Maria Theresa, after whom she was named (the empress was not however her godmother, as was formerly believed; the date of birth is also in question). She developed normally until 9 December 1762, when she became blind, perhaps because of a nervous ocular disorder. In spite of treatment, from Dr Anton Mesmer among others, her affliction proved to be permanent. Nevertheless, she showed such remarkable musical talent that the empress granted her a stipend for a broad musical and general education. Her teachers

included Leopold Kozeluch (piano), Vincenzo Righini and Antonio Salieri (singing and composition) and Karl Frieberth and G. J. Vogler (theory and composition). By 1775 she was performing as a pianist and singer in Viennese concert rooms and salons; she is said to have played at least 60 sonatas and concertos from memory. Composers who wrote for her include Salieri (an organ concerto, 1773), Mozart (a piano concerto, probably K456) and Haydn (a piano concerto, H XVIII:4).

On 18 August 1783, Paradis, her friend and librettist Johann Riedinger (who invented a composition board for her) and her mother left Vienna on a concert tour that lasted almost three years. On 27 August she visited Mozart, his father, his wife and his sister in Salzburg (when presumably the concerto was commissioned); she played in Frankfurt and other German cities, then in Switzerland and France, reaching Paris in March 1784 and playing at the Concert Spirituel there on 1 April. She played at least 14 times in Paris. She also assisted Valentin Haüy, 'father and apostle of the blind', in establishing the first school for the blind, which he opened in Paris in 1785. She arrived on 3 November in London, where Charles Burney championed her and wrote several articles about her. She played Handel fugues to George III and later accompanied the Prince of Wales, a cellist. She left England in March 1784, resuming her concert tour in Brussels, Amsterdam, Hamburg (where she met C. P. E. Bach), Berlin and Prague, returning to Vienna in February 1786. Plans to tour in Russia and Italy did not materialize, but she returned to Prague in 1797 for the production of her opera *Rinaldo und Alcina*.

During her journey Paradis began composing solo piano music as well as pieces for voice and keyboard. The earliest music attributed to her was a set of four sonatas of about 1777, but these are probably the work of Pietro Domenico Paradies, with whom she is often confused (the Toccata in A sometimes ascribed to her is from a sonata by him). Many of her authentic works of this period are lost. Her earliest extant major work is the collection *Zwölf Lieder auf ihrer Reise in Musik gesetzt*, composed 1784–6. By 1789, she was devoting more time to composition than performance; between then and 1797 she wrote at least five operas and three cantatas. After the failure of *Rinaldo und Alcina*, she increasingly devoted her energy to teaching; in 1808 she founded her own

Title-page of the 'Zwölf Lieder' (Leipzig: Breitkopf, 1786) by Maria Theresia von Paradis

music school where she taught the piano, singing and theory, primarily to young girls. A Sunday concert series at the school featured the work of her outstanding students. She continued to teach up to the time of her death.

Paradis was not a prolific composer. Her works total about 30, and of them all the piano sonatas as well as some lost Italian canzonets are of dubious authenticity. The famous *Sicilienne* is spurious, probably the work (after a Weber violin sonata op.10 no.1) of its purported discoverer, Samuel Dushkin. Her authentic compositions combine the lyrical features of the Viennese and Italian styles with the more dramatic nature of the Berlin School. Her tours as a pianist and her work on behalf of the blind and young women musicians earned her a distinctive place in musical history.

WORKS

STAGE

Ariadne und Bacchus (melodrama, 1, J. Riedinger), Laxenburg, Schlosstheater, 20 June 1791, lost

Der Schulkandidat (ländliches Singspiel, 3, ?Riedinger), Vienna, Marinellitheater, 5 Dec 1792; *A-LIm* (Act 3 and pt of Act 2 lost); ov. ed. H. Matsushita (Fayetteville, AR, 1992)

Rinaldo und Alcina [Die Insel der Verführung] (Zauberoper, 3, L. von Baczko), Prague, Estates Theatre, 30 June 1797, lost

Grosse militärische Oper (F. von Niederstradon), ?1805, lost

Zwei ländliche Opern, lost

OTHER WORKS

Cantatas: Trauerkantate auf den Tod Leopolds II (Riedinger), 1792, lost, lib *Wgm*; Deutsches Monument Ludwigs des Unglücklichen (Riedinger), vs (Vienna, 1793); Kantate auf Wiedergenesung meines Vaters, lost

Other vocal: Lied auf die Blindheit des Frl. M. Th. v. Paradis (Ich war ein kleines Würmchen) (G. K. Pfeffel), in *Wiener Musenalmanach* (1785); 12 Lieder auf ihrer Reise in Musik gesetzt (Leipzig, 1786), 2 ed. in DTÖ, liv, Jg.xxvii/2 (1920), ed. H. Matsushita (Fayetteville, AR, 1987); Lenore (G. A. Bürger), ballade (Vienna, 1790), ed. H. Matsushita (Fayetteville, AR, 1989); Auf die Damen, welche statt Gold, nun Leinwand für die verwundeten Krieger zupfen (?Bürger) (Vienna, 1794); Da eben seinen Lauf (Mlle Jerusalem), rev. as aria (Vienna, 1813); Auf Brüder, auf, geniesst des Lebens Wonne (Riedinger), chorus (Vienna, 1813), lost; other lieder, lost

Inst: 2 pf concs., g, C, lost; 12 pf sonatas, opp.1–2 (Paris, 1792), probably by D. Paradies, lost; Pf Trio (Vienna, 1800), lost; Fantasie, G, pf (Vienna, 1807); Fantasie, C, 1811; Variations, kbd, lost; An meine entfernten Lieben, pf, lost

BIBLIOGRAPHY

Choron-FayolleD; *FétisB*; *GerberL*; *Grove1* (C. F. Pohl); *SainsburyD*; *SchillingE*; *SchmidlD*

C. Burney: 'An Account of Mademoiselle Theresa Paradis of Vienna', *London Magazine*, iv (1785), 30

J. Riedinger: 'Notenschrift für Blinde', *AMZ*, xii (1810), 905–10

G. J. Dlabacž: *Allgemeines historisches Künstler-Lexikon* (Prague, 1815)

L. Frankl: *Biographie der M. Th. Paradis* (Linz, 1876)

H. Ullrich: 'Maria Theresia Paradis and Mozart', *ML*, xxvii (1946), 224–33

O. Brües: *Mozart und das Frl. von Paradis* (Tübingen, 1952)

E. Komorzynski: 'Mozart und Maria Theresia Paradis', *MJb 1952*, 110–16

H. Ullrich: 'Maria Theresia Paradis' grosse Kunstreise', *ÖMz*, xv (1960), 470–80; xvii (1962), 11–26; xviii (1963), 475–83; xix (1964), 430–35; xx

(1965), 589–97 [see also *BMw*, vi (1964), 129ff; *Sächsische Heimatblätter 1964*, 393ff]

—— : 'Maria Theresia Paradis (1759–1824) als Musikpädagogin', *Musikerziehung*, xiv (1960–61), 9–13

—— : 'Das Stammbuch der Maria Theresia Paradis', *Jb des Bonner Heimat- und Geschichtsvereins*, xv (1961), 340–84

—— : 'Die Bildnisse der blinden Musikerin Maria Theresia Paradis', *Musikerziehung*, xv (1961–2), 69–72

—— : 'Maria Theresia Paradis in London', *ML*, xliii (1962), 16–24

—— : 'Maria Theresia Paradis und Dr. Franz Anton Mesmer', *Jb des Vereines für Geschichte des Stadt Wien*, xvii–xviii (1962), 149–88

—— : 'Die erste öffentliche Musikschule der Maria Theresia Paradis in Wien (1808–1824)', *Musikerziehung*, xvi (1962–3), 187–91; xvii (1963–4), 56–61

—— : 'Drei wiederaufgefundene Werke von Maria Theresia Paradis', *ÖMz*, xvii (1962), 458–71 [see also xxi (1966), 400]

—— : 'Maria Theresia Paradis: Werkverzeichnis', *BMw*, v (1963), 117–54 [see also viii (1966), 256–8]

E. Badura-Skoda: 'Zur Entstehung des Klavierkonzertes in B-Dur K V 456', *MJb 1964*, 193–7

H. Ullrich: 'Maria Theresia Paradis' zweite Reise nach Prag 1797: die Uraufführung von "Rinaldo und Alcina"', *Mf*, xix (1966), 152–63

H. Matsushita: *The Musical Career and Composition of Marie Theresia von Paradis 1759–1824* (Ann Arbor, 1990)

HIDEMI MATSUSHITA

Paraskevaidis, Graciela (*b* Buenos Aires, 1940). Argentinian composer, resident in Uruguay. She studied the piano and composition at the Conservatorio Nacional de Música and the Instituto Torcuato Di Tella in Buenos Aires, and at the Institut für Neue Musik in Freiburg. Since 1975 she has taught composition in Montevideo, Uruguay, and at the Latin American Courses for Contemporary Music, of which she is also a member of the board. She was a guest of the DAAD-Künstlerprogramm in West Berlin during 1984. Her compositions include *Huaqui* (1975) and *A entera rivisación del público en general* (1981), both for tape, *Magma I* for nine brass (1967), *Magma VII* for 14 winds (1984) and *Un lado, otra lado* for piano (1984).

BIBLIOGRAPHY

G. Paraskevaidis: 'An Introduction to 12-Tone Music and Serialism in Latin America', *Interface*, xiii (1984), 133–47

Paredes, Hilda (*b* Puebla, Mexico, 22 Sept 1959). Mexican composer. She began her musical studies in Mexico City, then moved in 1979 to London, where she studied the flute and composition at the GSM. She also participated in masterclasses with Peter Maxwell Davies and Harrison Birtwistle at Dartington Summer School. She returned to Mexico and became a university professor. Paredes has written dance, choral and orchestral music, as well as chamber music for various ensembles. In 1989, Covent Garden invited her to take part in the first Garden Venture project on new opera at Dartington; as a result she wrote her first chamber opera, *La séptima semilla*. *Ikal* (Mayan for 'human spirit, breath') for solo recorder includes three main sections separated by distinctive transitions in which sounds of the voice and the recorder are blended. Recorders with different tunings are used to define different harmonic regions while historic temperaments are used as a reference to the past.

BIBLIOGRAPHY

G. Béhague: *Sonidas de las Americas Festival*, New York, 30 Jan–6 Feb 1994, p.25 [American Composers' Orchestra; programme booklet]

Park [née Reynolds], **Maria Hester** (*b* 29 Sept 1760; *d* Hampstead, 7 June 1813). English composer and teacher. She played the harpsichord and piano in public concerts before her marriage to the antiquarian and man of letters Thomas Park (1759–1834), and taught music to members of the nobility, including the Duchess of Devonshire and her daughters. Although she suffered from ill-health for many years, her family life was a happy one; her husband wrote several touching poems to her. Her surviving music, spanning a quarter of a century, is that of a very competent, professional composer. Her sonatas are varied and spirited, while the concerto for keyboard and strings reveals an individual voice, particularly in the final rondo.

Earlier reference works confuse her with the singer and composer Maria F. Parke, to the extent of calling the singer Maria Hester Parke; the British Library *Catalogue of Printed Music* clearly distinguishes the two. Her keyboard sonatas opp.1 and 2 were published under her maiden name.

WORKS
published in London

op.

1 Sonatas, hpd/pf, vn acc. (1785), ded. Countess of Uxbridge

2 3 Sonatas, hpd/pf (*c*1790)

3 A Set of Glees with the Dirge in Cymbeline (?1790)

4 2 Sonatas, pf/hpd (1790)

6 Concerto, pf/hpd, str (?1795)

7 Sonata, pf (?1796)

13   2 Sonatas, pf, vn acc. (?1801)
—   Waltz, pf (?1800)
—   Divertimento, pf, vn acc. (?1811)

Possibly lost, advertised in op.13: 6 Divertimentos, harp, pf, op.8; 6 Duets, harp, pf, op.9; Sonata with the Berlin Favourite; Sonata with Prince Adolphus Fancy

BIBLIOGRAPHY
A. Seward: *Letters* (Edinburgh, 1811)
Gentleman's Magazine, lxxxiii (1813), 596
T. Park: *Morning Thoughts and Midnight Musings* (London, 1818)
'Thomas Park, Esq.', *Annual Biography*, xx (1835), 257–63

OLIVE BALDWIN, THELMA WILSON

Parke, Dorothy (*b* Londonderry, 29 July 1904; *d* Portrush, Co. Antrim, 15 Feb 1990). Northern Ireland composer. She was a piano pupil of Ambrose Coviello and a composition pupil of Paul Corder at the RAM in London, after which she returned to Northern Ireland and settled in Belfast. She married Douglas Brown, a musician and teacher, and became established as a highly-regarded piano teacher in Belfast. She was a prolific writer for children, composing many songs and piano pieces· that were used in music competitions. Her compositional style is generally in the tradition of C. V. Stanford and the simpler pieces of Ralph Vaughan Williams and Herbert Howells – very approachable but of a rather naive simplicity and with ingenuous harmonies. Nevertheless, her music is distinctive and effective; many of her choral and vocal settings in particular achieve poignancy and considerable expressiveness. She occasionally used a more advanced idiom, as in her choral settings of texts by James Stephens. A collection of her music has been acquired by the National Library in Dublin.

WORKS
selective list
Inst: Vn Sonata, A, 1929; A Short Fantasia on Christmas Carols, pf duet, 1946, arr. orch, 1972; The Faery Fiddler, 2 pf, 1947, arr. str orch, 1949; 2 Interlinked Irish Airs, 2 pf, 1947; Improvisation on 'The· Snowy-Breasted Pearl', pf, orch, 1955; chamber and pf works for children
Choral: Wind from the West (E. Younger), SA, pf, 1938; A Snowy Field (J. Stephens), SATB, 1950; As it was Windy Weather (Stephens), SATB, 1962; A Cradle Song (P. Colum), SSA, pf, 1963
Songs (1v, pf): Kilkeel (R. Rowley), 1933; Moon Magic (J. Irvine), 1938; The Road to Ballydare (Irvine), 1939; The House and the Road (J. Peabody), 1947; Sing Heigh-Ho (C. Kingsley), 1952; A Honeycombe (Stephens), 6 songs, 1957; The Cupboard (W. de la Mare), 1962; The Ferryman (C. Rossetti), 1962; The Falling of the Leaves (W. B. Yeats), 1963; Somewhere (De la Mare), 1980; Wee Hughie (E. Shane), 1980; many songs for children

Principal publishers: Ashdown, Boosey & Hawkes, Lengnick

SARAH M. BURN

Parke, Maria F. (*b* London, 1772/3; *d* London, 31 July 1822). English soprano, composer and pianist. The eldest daughter of the oboist John Parke, she was taught by her father and made her first appearance as both singer and pianist at his benefit concert in April 1782, when she was nine. She sang among the trebles in the Handel Commemoration concerts in 1784, played a piano concerto in a Drury Lane oratorio interval in 1785 and performed in J. P. Salomon's concerts the next year. From 1790 she was a leading soprano soloist in concerts and oratorios in London and the provinces. Her uncle W. T. Parke remembered her singing in *Messiah* 'with great taste and judgement'. She both sang and played at her benefit in May 1794, and Haydn directed the concert from the piano. He later wrote to her father: 'I tack me the liberty to Send for the Mistris Park a little Sonat'. She retired on her marriage to John Beardmore in 1815.

She has been confused with the composer Maria Hester Park, but her published compositions are all attributed to 'Miss Parke' and often signed 'MFP' on the title-page. The British Library *Catalogue of Printed Music* clearly differentiates the two composers.

WORKS
published in London
Inst: 3 Grand Sonatas, pf, op.1 (1799); 2 Grand Sonatas, pf, vn acc. ad lib, op.2 (?1800); Divertimento and Military Rondo, pf (?1807)
Vocal: I have often been told (1787); God of Slaughter, duet (?1806); What is beauty, duet (?1810)

BIBLIOGRAPHY
BDA; *SainsburyD*
W. T. Parke: *Musical Memoirs* (London, 1830)
H. C. R. Landon: *Haydn in England 1791–1795* (London, 1976)

OLIVE BALDWIN, THELMA WILSON

Parker, Alice (*b* Boston, 16 Dec 1925). American composer, arranger and choral conductor. After studying at Smith College (BA 1947) and the Juilliard School (MS 1949), she worked as principal arranger for the Robert Shaw Chorale (1948–67), producing more than 400 published arrangements of folksongs, hymns and carols. From 1965 she devoted herself increasingly to composing her own music, as well as to conducting and teaching. Her works are primarily vocal, many of them sacred; they are tonal and adhere to traditional forms, reflecting her close association with American hymnody and folksong.

WORKS
selective list

OPERAS

The Martyrs' Mirror (2), Lansdale, PA, 10 Oct 1971
The Family Reunion (1), Norman, OK, 8 Dec 1975
Singers Glen (prol, 2), Lancaster, PA, 1 April 1978
The Ponder Heart (2), Jackson, MS, 10 Sept 1982

OTHER VOCAL

Choral, orch: 7 Carols, 1975; Journeys: Pilgrims and Strangers, 1975; Gaudete: 6 Latin Christmas Hymns, 1976; Commentaries, SSA, SSAA, orch, 1978; Songs from the Dragon Quilt, nar, SATB, orch, 1984; Earth, Sky, Spirit, children's vv (SSA), orch, 1986; The World's One Song, 1990

Cantatas: A Sermon from the Mountain (M. L. King), nar, SATB, str, ad lib jazz insts, 1969; The Feast of Ingathering, SATB, organ, 1972; Melodious Accord, SSATB, brass qt, harp, 1974; In Praise of Singing, SATB, str qnt, 1981; Sacred Symphonies, SATB, fl, vn, vc, org, 1983; Elinor Wylie: Incantations, SSA, cl, pf, 1984; Kentucky Psalms, SATB, str qnt, 1984; The Babe of Bethlehem, SSAA, handbells/pf, 1986; A Gift from the Sea, 5 groups: (children's SSA), (orch), (pf), (banjo, db), (fl, harp, db), 1989; Angels and Challengers, SATB, ob, 2 cl, bn, pf, 1990

Other choral: Psalms of Praise, TB, perc, 1964; Street Corner Spirituals, SATB, tpt, drum, gui, 1964; 5 American Folk Songs, SATB, 1968; Away, Melancholy, SSA/SSAA, tambourine, 1971; Carols to Play and Sing, SATB, perc, org, 1971; 6 Hymns to Dr Watts, (SATB)/(Bar, ww qt), 1975; There and Back Again, SATB, ww qt, 1977; Play–Party Songs, SATB, pf, 1982; 3 folksongs, SAB, pf, 1983; SongStream, SATB, pf 4 hands, 1983; Millay Madrigals, SATB, 1985; Stars and Stones, SATB, ob, bn, pf, 1987; Dem Bells, chorus, handbells, 1988; Women on the Plains, SSA, pf, 1988; American Dances, SA, pf, 1989; Anniversary Hymns, SATB, 1989; Roll Round with the Year, TTBB, gui/pf, 1989; Sacred Madrigals, SSATB, 1989; Three Seas, SSAA, fl, bn, harp, 1989; Water Songs, unison/SA, pf, 1989; Wren Songs, SATB, 1991

Song cycles: Astrometaphysical: 4 Songs to Robert Frost, S, pf, 1968; A Gnasherie (O. Nash), Mez, pf, 1971; Songs for Eve (A. MacLeish), vocal qt, str qt, 1975; Echoes from the Hills (E. Dickinson), S, fl, cl, hn, str, 1979; Of Irlaunde, Bar, fl, pf, 1979; Mountain Hymns, S, pf, 1982

CHRISTINE AMMER

Parkhurst, Susan McFarland [Parkhurst, Mrs E. A.] (*b* Leicester, MA, 5 June 1836; *d* Brooklyn, NY, 4 May 1918). American composer. She composed popular songs and parlour piano solos during the 1860s. A skilful writer, she gained most recognition for songs on such topical themes as temperance and abolition. *Father's a Drunkard and Mother is Dead* (1866), which she and her daughter ('Little Effie') performed at concerts and temperance meetings in New York, became a standard of the period. Other successful songs include *New Emancipation Song, There are Voices, Spirit Voices* and *Weep no more for Lilly* (all 1864).

Horace Waters, the New York publisher associated mainly with Stephen Foster, promoted Parkhurst's work, printing a *Select Catalogue of Mrs. E. A. Parkhurst's Compositions* in 1864. She contributed tunes to Waters's collections of 'Sunday school' hymns: *The Athenaeum* (1863), *The Golden Harp* (1863) and *Zion's Refreshing Showers* (1867). In the early 1860s Parkhurst worked at Waters's music store, where she encountered Foster. She published 'Personal Recollections of the Last Days of Stephen Foster' in the September 1916 issue of the magazine *The Etude*, describing herself as a 'lady who in her youth was known as a successful composer, and who, when a young girl, took a friendly interest in Stephen Foster'.

Writing in the standard 'song and chorus' format of the period, Parkhurst infused popular song formulae with a more ambitious musical language. Her harmonic vocabulary was more expansive and richer than that found in most average songs of the period, and the piano postludes she often used to round off her songs were more imaginative. Original prints of about 60 songs are held in the Music Division of the New York Public Library; instrumental works are at the American Antiquarian Society, Worcester, Massachusetts.

BIBLIOGRAPHY

E. M. Smith, ed.: *Women in Sacred Song: a Library of Hymns, Religious Poems and Sacred Music by Women* (Boston, 1885)
M. R. Turner: *The Parlour Song Book* (London, 1972)
R. Crawford, ed.: *Civil War Songs* (New York, 1977)
J. Tick: *American Women Composers before 1870* (Ann Arbor, 1983)

JUDITH TICK

Patterson, Annie (Wilson) (*b* Lurgan, 27 Oct 1868; *d* Cork, 16 Jan 1934). Irish folksong collector and arranger, composer, organist and writer on music. She studied at the Royal Irish Academy of Music (organ, with Robert Stewart) and the Royal University of Ireland (now the National University), where she obtained the BMus in 1887 and DMus in 1889. In 1897 she organized the first Feis Ceoil festival of Irish music. In 1924 she was appointed to a lectureship in Irish music at University College, Cork (Carl Hardebeck had earlier resigned from a chair in that subject, which had then been discontinued). Her writings include *The Music of Ireland* (London, 1926). She edited musical 'agony columns' in various periodicals, signing herself 'Dr Annie', and gave lecture recitals throughout Britain and on the radio. She spent the last years of her life in Cork as an organist. Her dedication to Irish folk music is reflected in her many arrangements, and in a number of compositions which are no longer performed. She is reported to have written some large-scale works including two operas, *The High-King's Daughter* and *Oisín*. No record has been found of any public performance of these operas, and they were not published.

WORKS
selective list

Operas: The High-King's Daughter; Oisín
Other works: 6 Original Gaelic Songs (T. O. Russell and others) (London, 1896), rev. 1912 [in Gaelic and Eng.]; The Bells of Shandon, SATB (London, 1914); Shandon Bells, tone poem, pf (London, *c*1932); choral marching songs; many arrs. of Irish airs

BRIAN BOYDELL

Payne, Maggi (*b* Temple, TX, 23 Dec 1945). American composer, flautist and video artist. She studied the flute and composition at Northwestern University (BM 1968) and, after a brief period at Yale University, at the University of Illinois (MM in flute, 1970), where her composition teachers were Salvatore Martirano and Ben Johnston and where she began to compose electronic music. After studying at Mills College (MFA 1972) she remained there, working as a recording engineer until 1981 with Robert Ashley and other composers, including Alvin Lucier, Gordon Mumma, David Behrman and Christian Wolff. In 1982–3 she taught sound design at the San Francisco Sound Institute and in 1988–9 was artist-in-residence at the Exploratorium in San Francisco. She began to give courses in recording engineering and electronic music at Mills College in 1980, and in 1992 became co-director of the college's Center for Contemporary Music. She has received grants from the NEA and the Mellon Foundation among other honours.

Payne composes mostly electronic music using synthesized material and extensive multi-tracking. Spatial location of sound, acute attention to gradual alterations of timbre and rhythm, and visual elements – usually abstract imagery produced on video-tape, film or 35 mm slides – are vital concerns in her work. In several of her compositions (*Airwaves (realities)*, *Resonant Places*, *Subterranean Network*) she has used these techniques to evoke states of mind associated with the features of geographical locations. Since the mid-1980s she has collaborated with the video artist Ed Tannenbaum on a number of projects.

WORKS

Elec: Hum, fl, tape, 1973; Orion (film), 1973; VDO (film), 1973; Scirocco, fl, tape, 1983; White Night, tape, 1984; Subterranean Network, 1986; Phase Transitions, 1989; Resonant Places, 1992; Aeolian Confluence, tape, 1993
Mixed media (for tape, slides, unless otherwise stated):Allusions, dancers, lighting, video, tape, 1974; Farewell, 1975; Transparencies, 1976; Spheres, 1977; Spirals, 1977; Lunar Earthrise, 1978; Lunar Dusk, 1979; Blue Metallics, tape, film/slides, 1980; Rising, dancers, 1980; Circular Motions, tape, video, 1981; Ling, tape, video, slides, 1981; Crystal, tape, video, slides, 1982; Io, tape, video, 1982; Solar Wind, tape, video, slides, 1983; Airwaves (realities), tape, video, 1987
Dance/Video: Music for Carolyn Brown's House Party, 1974; Music for Carolyn Brown's Synergy II, 1974; Flights of Fancy, tape, 1985; Shimmer, tape, 1985; Back to Forth, tape, 1986; Ahh Ahh, tape, 1987; Heavy Water, tape, 1991
Other works: Ametropia, fl, 1970; A Winter's Tale (incid. music, W. Shakespeare), 1975; Song of Flights (G. Snyder), S, pf, 1988; Desertscapes (M. Payne), 2 choruses, 1991

LISA B. ROBINSON, STEPHEN RUPPENTHAL

Pejačević [Pejacsevich], **Dora** (*b* Budapest, 10 Sept 1885; *d* Munich, 5 March 1923). Croatian composer. The daughter of the Croatian *ban* (civil governor) Count Teodor Pejačević and the Hungarian Baroness Lilla Vay de Vaya – a talented musician and actress, and patron of the arts – she studied at the Croatian Music Institute in Zagreb, then briefly in Dresden with Percy Sherwood and in Munich with Walter Courvoisier. For the most part, however, she was self-taught and developed her musical talents through contact with other artists and intellectuals, such as Karl Kraus. At her ancestral home at Našice (near Osijek) she usually devoted herself to her work, but she also travelled extensively to cultural centres, including Budapest, Munich, Prague and Vienna, and to the Janovice estate in Bohemia, the home of her friend Sidonie Nádherný von Borutin. After her marriage to Ottomar von Lumbe in 1921 she lived mainly in Munich.

Her works were performed most frequently outside Croatia: part of her Symphony (op.41, composed 1916–18) was given in Vienna (25 January 1918), conducted by Oskar Nedbal; it was later performed in Dresden (10 February 1920), conducted by Edwin Lindner. Her late-Romantic idiom, enriched with impressionist harmonies and lush orchestral colours, evolved continually as she strove to break free from drawing-room mannerisms and conventions. She introduced the orchestral song, a characteristic *fin-de-siècle* form into Croatian music, but among her vocal works her greatest achievement was in the *Drei Gesänge* op.53, for voice and piano, to texts by Friedrich Nietzsche. Her late piano miniatures (the two nocturnes op.50, *Humoreske und Caprice* op.54) juxtapose bizarre or grotesque elements and lyrical and meditative passages. The Piano Quintet op.40, String Quartet op.58, the Symphony and the Piano Concerto display both an accomplished technique and a striving towards integration of motivic and thematic material. In the *Phantasie concertante* op.48 for piano and orchestra and in the Piano Sonata in Ab, op.57, she followed the Lisztian concept of the single movement sonata-fantasy.

In Croatia Pejačević's work was hand in hand with the modernist movement in literature and the Secession in the visual arts: without breaking new ground, but with nuance, she helped bring a new range of expression into the traditional musical language. She and others of her generation opened up new vistas for Croatian composers and established new standards of professionalism. Almost all of her 57 known compositions survive as a single collection, in the Croatian Music Institute in Zagreb.

WORKS
selective list

Orch: Pf Conc., g, op.33, 1913; Sym., f♯, op.41, 1916–18; Phantasie concertante, d, op.48, pf, orch, 1919; Ov., d, op.49, 1919
Vocal: 7 Lieder, op.23 (W. Wickenburg-Almásy), 1v, pf, 1907; Verwandlung, op.37*b* (K. Kraus), 1v, orch, 1915; Liebeslied, op.39 (R. M. Rilke), 1v, orch, 1915; Mädchengestalten, op.42 (Rilke), 1v, pf, 1916; 2 Schmetterlingslieder, op.52 (K. Henckell), 1v, orch, 1920; 3 Gesänge, op.53 (F. Nietzsche), 1v, pf, 1920
Chamber: Pf trio, D, op.15, 1902; Pf Qt, d, op.25, 1908; Vn Sonata, D, op.26, 1909; Pf Trio, C, op.29, 1910; Str Qt, F, op.31, 1911 [lost]; Elégie, op.34, vn, pf, 1913; Vc Sonata, e, op.35, 1913; Pf Qnt, op.40, 1915–18; Slawische Sonate, bb, op.43, vn, pf, 1917; Méditation, op.51, vn, pf, 1919; Str Qt, C, op.58, 1922
Pf: 6 Phantasiestücke, op.17, 1903; Blumeleben, op.19, 1904–5; 4 Klavierstücke, op.32*a*, 1912; Sonata: bb, op.36, 1914; 2 nocturnes, op.50, 1919, 1920; Humoreske und Caprice, op.54, 1920; Sonata, Ab, op.57, 1921

BIBLIOGRAPHY
K. Kos: *Dora Pejačević: Leben und Werk* (Zagreb, 1987)
Z. Veber, ed.: *Dora Pejačević, 1885–1923* (Zagreb, 1987) [colloquium, *Našice 1985*; Croatian text, Eng. summaries]

KORALJKA KOS

Pelegrí i Marimón, Maria Teresa (*b* Barcelona, 4 March 1907). Spanish composer. She studied the piano with Gilbert Camins and Carles Pellicer, but it was more than 20 years after her marriage before she began to write music seriously. She studied composition with José Soler, and 20th-century music with Carles Guinovart; her desire for a wider knowledge of modern trends led to a particular interest in the Second Viennese School, from which her own compositional methods derive (with some deviation from strict orthodoxy). She is a member of the Asociació de Catalana Compositors, and her work has become more widely known in Catalonia through the series Muestras de Música Catalana Contemporanea.

WORKS
selective list

Stage: Herodes und Mariamne (opera, 2, F. Hebbel), 1979–83
Orch: Variaciones, 1975; 4 ideas en cien compases, 1976; 3 piezas, 1976; Poema trágico, 1978; Herodes und Mariamne, sym. frags., 1979; Passacaglia, tape, 1985; Tríptico, 1985; Movimiento sinfónico, 1986; 7 piezas, small orch, 1986; Sinfonieta, 1986
Chamber: Música, pf, db, perc, 1977; Trio, cl, vn, pf, 1977; 2 piezas, solo va, cl, ob, bn, harp, cel, 1978; Cuarteto para música XXI, str qt, 1979; Indivisus, fl, cl, 2 tpt, vn, vc, db, pf, perc, 1980; Wind und Percussion, 1981; Str Qt no.2, 1984; Str Qt no.3, 1984; Música per a sis, 1989
Solo inst: Praeludium und tiento, org, 1975; Pieza, cl, 1977; Tríptico celeste, org, 1977; Memento, org, 1978; Praeludium, mar, 1978; 2 impromptus, pf, 1978; Suite, pf, 1986; other pf pieces
Vocal: 4 chansons sentimentales (P. Verlaine, G. Apollinaire, J. Supervielle, C. P. Baudelaire), S, pf, 1975; Infant Joy – Spring (W. Blake), mixed chorus, 1976; Pater noster, Bar, org, 1976; Requiem, SATB, fl, vc, org, 1976

BIBLIOGRAPHY
68 compositors catalans (Barcelona, 1989) [pubn of the Associació Catalana de Compositors]

ALICIA CASARES-ALONSO

Pellecier, Mlle. *See* PAPAVOINE.

Pentland, Barbara (Lally) (*b* Winnipeg, 2 Jan 1912). Canadian composer. She began composing at the age of nine, shortly after her first piano lessons, persisting in her pursuit of music despite poor health and parental opposition. Winnipeg provided a flourishing, if limited, musical environment in the

1920s, and it was the piano sonata writing of Beethoven that Pentland emulated during this period. While attending a private boarding school in Montreal (1927–9) she studied the piano and theory with an English organist, Frederick H. Blair, who encouraged her to continue music studies. She proceeded to Paris in 1929 and became a composition pupil of Cécile Gauthiez. Gauthiez's teaching was in the Franckian tradition, and the characteristic thick textures and chromatic harmonies remained in Pentland's music until the late 1930s, as is evident in the Five Piano Preludes (1938), the Rhapsody for piano (1939) and the Piano Quartet (1939).

After returning to Winnipeg in 1930, Pentland continued her studies with Gauthiez by correspondence for 18 months. During the next six years she composed a great deal, winning several local competitions; at the same time she studied the piano and organ and frequently performed her piano music in public. She then won a fellowship in composition to the Juilliard School, where she studied with Frederick Jacobi (1936–8) and Bernard Wagenaar (1938–9). Exposure to new music in New York had a decisive effect: she was particularly impressed by the work of Paul Hindemith, which provided a model for her increasing interest in counterpoint. She returned again to Winnipeg in 1939 and was appointed to the music advisory committee and an examiner in theory at the University of Manitoba. In the summers of 1941 and 1942 she studied at Tanglewood with Aaron Copland, whose influence, which encouraged her to a more lucid style, is shown most strikingly in the similarity between her Piano Variations (1942) and Copland's own (1930). Also contributing to the leaner textures of her music was a neoclassical tendency, a primary feature from the early 1940s to the late 1950s.

Persuaded that her works would have more chance of performance in a larger centre, Pentland moved to Toronto in 1942, and in the following year she was appointed to teach theory and composition at the conservatory. During the 1940s she gained a reputation as a headstrong member of the avant garde. Her developing contrapuntal leanings are seen in the Sonata Fantasy (1947), in which the opening few bars present the material for the entire work. This direction was stimulated by her first significant exposure to serial music, in the summers of 1947 and 1948 at the MacDowell Colony, where Dika Newlin introduced her to many of Arnold Schoenberg's compositions; the

Barbara Pentland

Wind Octet (1948) was her first consciously serial work. In 1949 she joined the music department of the University of British Columbia, Vancouver, where she taught until 1963, when she resigned to give her attention to composition.

The main influence on Pentland's mature style was the music of Anton Webern, which impressed her during a European visit in 1955. She attended the Darmstadt summer courses and the ISCM Festival, and in the following year returned to hear her Second Quartet played at the ISCM Festival in Stockholm. The Symphony for Ten Parts (1957), in its compactness and clarity, displays Webern's influence: three tightly-knit movements are built from melodic and rhythmic shapes established in the short introduction. A new interest in timbre, also Webernian, is expressed in such instrumental combinations as that of xylophone with double bass, as well as in the alternation of dry, percussive sections with passages of greater lyricism.

Pentland's later works are economical, the textures swept clean of the scales and arpeggios of her music of the 1940s. 12-note serialism, used freely, is a means of control. A distinctive feature is the touch of humour in the syncopated rhythms, light melodies or brisk staccatos. Retrograde is also a frequently-encountered technique: a work or section often concludes with a reversal of the initial serial statement, sometimes providing material for a coda or recapitulation.

In the late 1960s Pentland began to use aleatory techniques and quarter-tones. There are short aleatory passages in the *Trio con alea* (1966), the Third String Quartet (1969), *News* (1970) and *Mutations* (1972), permitting the performer freedom in rhythmically varying, repeating and articulating given pitches; the last aleatory section in a work may function as a cadenza. The use of quarter-tones is principally decorative and confined to string parts, though there are some in the vocal line of *News*. Also during this period Pentland wrote numerous short piano pieces for children, strictly miniatures of her mature style.

WORKS
selective list

Stage: Beauty and the Beast (ballet-pantomime), 2 pf, 1940; The Lake (chamber opera, 1, D. Livesay), SATB, small orch, 1952

Orch and vocal orch: Lament, 1939; Arioso and Rondo, 1941; Holiday Suite, 1941; Conc., vn, small orch, 1942, arr. vn, pf, 1945; Colony Music, pf, str, 1945; Sym. no.1, 1945–8; Variations on a Boccherini Tune, 1948; Conc., org, str, 1949; Sym. no.2, 1950; Ave atque vale, 1951; Ricercar, str, 1955; Conc., pf, str orch, 1956; Sym. for 10 Parts (Sym. no.3), 1957; Sym. no.4, 1959; Strata, 1964; Cinescene, chamber orch, 1968; News, Mez, orch, tape, 1970; Variations concertantes, pf, orch, 1970, also arr. 2 pf; Five Plus (Simple Pieces for Str), 1971; Res musica, str orch, 1975

Vocal: Ballad of Trees and the Master (S. Lanier), chorus, 1937; Dirge for a Violet (D. C. Scott), chorus, 1939; Song Cycle (A. Marriott), 1v, pf, 1942–5; At Early Dawn (Hsiang Hao), T, fl, pf, 1945; Epigrams and Epitaphs, rounds, chorus 2–4vv, 1952; Salutation of the Dawn (Sanskrit), SATB, 1954; What is Man? (Apocrypha, *Ecclesiasticus* xviii), SATB, 1954; 3 Sung Songs (Chin., trans. C. M. Candlin), SATB, 1964, also arr. medium v, pf, 1964; Sung Songs nos.4–5 (J'Sin Ch'I-Chi, trans. Candlin), 1v, pf, 1964; Disasters of the Sun (D. Livesay), Mez, inst ens, tape, 1976; Ice Age (Livesay), S, pf, 1986

Chamber: Pf Qt, 1939; Sonata, vc, pf, 1943; Str Qt no.1, 1945; Vista, vn, pf, 1945; Sonata, vn, pf, 1946; Wind Octet, 1948; Weekend Ov. for Resort Combo, cl, tpt, pf, perc, 1949; Sonata, vn, 1950; Str Qt no.2, 1953; Duo, va, pf, 1960; Canzona, fl, ob, hpd, 1961; Trio, vn, vc, pf, 1963; Variations, va, 1965; Trio con alea, str trio, 1966; Septet, hn, tpt, trbn, org, vn, va, vc, 1967; Str Qt no.3, 1969; Reflections, accordion, 1971; Interplay, accordion, str qt, 1972; Mutations, vc, pf, 1972; Occasions, brass qnt, 1974; Phases, cl, cl, trbn, vn, vc, harp, 2 perc, 1978; Trance, fl, pf/harp, 1978; Variable Winds, solo ww (4 versions), 1979; Elegy, hn, pf, 1980; Str Qt no.4, 1980; Commenta, harp, 1981; Tellus, fl, vc, pf, perc, cel, 1981–2; Qnt, pf, str, 1983; Tides, vn, mar, harp, 1984; Str Qt no.5, 1985; Intrada and Canzona, rec qt, 1988

Pf: 5 Preludes, 1938; Rhapsody, 1939; Studies in Line, 1941; Variations, 1942; Sonata, 1945; Sonata Fantasy, 1947; Dirge, 1948; 2 Sonatinas, 1951; Sonata, 2 pf, 1953; Interlude, 1955; 3 Duets after

Pictures by Paul Klee, pf 4 hands, 1958; Toccata, 1958; Fantasy, 1962; Echoes no.1 and no.2, 1964; Maze, Casse-Tete (Labyrinthe, Puzzle), 1964; Puppet Show, pf 4 hands, 1964; Shadows (Ombres), 1964; 3 Pairs, 1964; Hands Across the C, 1965; Space Studies, 1966; Suite Borealis, 1966; Music of Now, bks 1–3, 1969–70; Vita brevis, 1973; Ephemera, 1974–8; Tenebrae, 1976; Vincula, 1983; Horizons, 1985; Canticum, Burlesca, Finale, 1987

Also incid. music for radio plays and film scores, incl. The Living Gallery, 1947

BIBLIOGRAPHY

EMC 2 (K. Winters and J. Beckwith)
M. Wilson: 'The Lake, One-Act Chamber Opera', *Canadian Forum* (1954), April
R. Turner: 'Barbara Pentland', *Canadian Music Journal*, ii/4 (1958), 15–26
'Barbara Pentland in Dual Role', *CBC Times* (27 July–2 Aug 1963)
P. Huse: 'Barbara Pentland', *Music Scene*, no.242 (1968), 9
'Barbara Pentland: a Portrait', *Musicanada* (1969), July–Aug, 8–9
R. MacMillan: 'Vancouver Composer at 70 Concentrates on Chamber Works', *Music Scene*, no.327 (1982), 6ff
J. Adames: 'The Art of Composition: an Interview with Barbara Pentland', *Performing Arts in Canada*, xx (1983), fall
S. Eastman and T. J. McGee: *Barbara Pentland* (Toronto, 1983)
P. Margles: 'The Arduous Journey of Barbara Pentland', *Music*, vi (1983), July–Aug
T. J. McGee: 'Barbara Pentland in the 1950s: String Quartet No.2 and Symphony for Ten Parts', *Studies in Music from the U. of Western Ontario*, ix (1984), 133–52
G. Dixon: 'The String Quartets of Barbara Pentland', *Canadian University Music Review*, xi/2 (1991), 94–121
L. Hartig: *Violet Archer: a Bio-Bibliography* (Westport, CT, 1991)

SHEILA EASTMAN LOOSLEY
(work-list, bibliography
with GAYNOR G. JONES)

Pereyra-Lizaso, Nydia (*b* Rocha, 12 May 1916). Uruguayan composer. She began her musical studies at the Conservatorio Teresiano in Rocha with Dolores Bell and Carmen Barrera; later she moved to Montevideo for advanced studies with Wilhelm Kolischer (piano), Tomás Mujica (counterpoint and fugue) and Enrique Casal-Chapí (composition). Her *Cuatro miniaturas* for violin and viola won a chamber music award at the GEDOK competition in Mannheim in 1966 (with Ernst Krenek, Werner Egk and Nadia Boulanger as the jurors); she also won several times (1959, 1964, 1966, 1967, 1978) the Casa de Teatro stage music award with incidental music for plays performed by the Comedia Nacional de Montevideo. Besides a large output of compositions, mainly of chamber and vocal music, she has written pedagogical works for children. She taught for many years at the Kolischer conservatory and at the Instituto de Enseñanza Musical.

BIBLIOGRAPHY
Uruguayos contemporáneos, iii (Montevideo, 1965)
S. Salgado: Breve historia de la música culta en el Uruguay (Montevideo, 1971, 2/1980)

SUSANA SALGADO

Perrière-Pilte, Anaïs, Countess of [Marcelli, Anaïs] (b Paris, 1836; d Paris, Dec 1878). French amateur poet and composer. Her wealth enabled her to have her works performed at her salon and, to accommodate her theatre pieces, she had a large 'salle de spectacle' constructed in her town house where works such as her three-act opéra comique Les vacances de l'Amour (August 1867) and La Dryade (April 1870) were mounted. Three operettas – Le sorcier (1866), Jaloux de soi (1873) and Le talon d'Achille (1875) – were performed in public, though none was well received.

BIBLIOGRAPHY
FétisBS; StiegerO

JULIE ANNE SADIE

Perry, Julia (Amanda) (b Lexington, KY, 25 March 1924; d Akron, OH, 24 April 1979). American composer. She studied at Westminster Choir College, Princeton (MMus 1948), the Juilliard School and in Europe, her principal teachers being Henry Switten, Nadia Boulanger and Luigi Dallapiccola for composition, and Emanuel Balaban and Alceo Galliera for conducting. Her honours included two Guggenheim fellowships, an award from the National Institute of Arts and Letters, and the Boulanger Grand Prix. She was active as a lecturer in Europe and the USA and also as a college teacher. Her music reflects wide cultural interests; its style is neo-classical, with richly dissonant harmonies, contrapuntal textures and an intense lyricism. In her late works (e.g. Soul Symphony, 1972) she used black folk idioms.

WORKS

Stage: The Bottle (opera, 1, Perry, after E. A. Poe: The Cask of Amontillado), 1953; The Cask of Amontillado (opera, 1, Perry and V. Card, after Poe), New York, 1954; The Selfish Giant (opera-ballet, 3, after O. Wilde) (1964); Three Warnings (opera)
Orch: Short Piece, 1952; Study, 1952; Pastoral, fl, str, 1959; Requiem, 1959; 12 syms., 1959–72; Contre-temps, 1963; Pf Conc., 1964; Vn Conc., 1964; Pf Conc., 1965; Episodes; Homage to Vivaldi; Module, 1975; works for band

Vocal: Chicago (cantata, after C. Sandburg), Bar, nar, chorus, orch, 1948; Ruth (after Bible), cantata, chorus, org, 1950; Stabat mater (trans. Perry), A, str orch/qt, 1951; Quinary Quixotic Songs, B-Bar, 5 insts, 1976; Frammenti dalle lettere de S Caterina, S, chorus, small orch; Missa brevis; 7 Contrasts, Bar, chamber ens; many songs, arrs. of spirituals, sacred choral pieces
Chamber and inst: Homunculus C. F., harp, 10 perc, 1960; Ww Trio; Str Qt; pf pieces

Principal publishers: Fischer, Galaxy, Peer-Southern, Southern

BIBLIOGRAPHY
SouthernB
E. Southern: The Music of Black Americans: a History (New York, 1971, 2/1983)
M. Green: Black Women Composers: a Genesis (Boston, 1983)

EILEEN SOUTHERN

Pessiak-Schmerling, Anna (b Vienna, 1834; d Vienna, 14 March 1896). Austrian composer and teacher. She studied with Marchesi and taught singing for many years at the Vienna Conservatory. She composed piano pieces, masses, other large sacred works, choral works, vocal studies and songs. Her masses were frequently performed in Vienna.

BIBLIOGRAPHY
CohenE; MEMM
A. Elson: Woman's Work in Music (Boston, 1903, 2/1931)
A. Laurence: Women of Notes (New York, 1978)

MARTHA FURMAN SCHLEIFER

Petkova, Rosica (b Plovdiv, 18 Feb 1947). Bulgarian composer. She studied composition with Emil Hlobil at the Prague Academy of Music (1966–7) and later with Alexander Raichev at the Sofia State Academy of Music. She worked for 12 years as an editor for the music journal Muzikalna Estrada (1979–91). Her works, often in a popular, laconic style, show an understanding of Bulgarian folk music. Her large-scale works include a Cantata for bass, chorus and orchestra (1976) and a Concertino for clarinet and orchestra (1981), while her chamber works include a Scherzo (1974) and Sonata (1976), both for flute and piano. Her output of solo vocal and choral works reflects her special love for children's songs.

MAGDALENA MANOLOVA

Petra-Basacopol, Carmen (b Sibiu, 5 Sept 1926). Romanian composer and teacher. She was educated in Bucharest, studying at the conservatory (1949–56) with Leon Klepper and Mihail Jora (composition), and, simultaneously for a time, attended the Faculty of

Philosophy (1945–9). She attended the Darmstadt summer school (1968), and later took the doctorate in musicology at the Sorbonne in Paris (1976). She has taught musical form at the Bucharest Conservatory, 1962–86, and again from 1993) and is a member of the Composers' Union in Romania. Consistent with the Romanian tradition of composition, she incorporates folk music in her work; she specializes in ballet and chamber music, as well as in writing for the harp.

WORKS
selective list

Stage: Fata și masca [The Girl and the Mask], op.32 (ballet, 1, N. Coman), 1969; Miorița [The Ewe], op.47 (ballet), 1980; Cuore, op.52 (opera, 2, after E. d'Amicis), 1983; Ciuleandra, op.54 (ballet, 2, after L. Rebreanu), 1986; Apostol Bologa, op.58 (opera, prol, 2, epilogue, after Rebreanu), 1989

Orch: Sym. no.1, op.6, 1955; Pf Conc., 1961; Sym. Triptych, op.19, 1962; 2 vn concs, 1963, 1965; Vc Conc., op.50, 1982

Vocal orch: Crengile [The Branches], op.26, orch, 1966; Moartea căprioarei [The Death of the Deer], op.27, Bar, orch, 1966

Chamber, vocal: Sonata, op.17, fl, harp, 1961 (Bucharest, 1963); Octet, op.30, ww qnt, harp, db, xyl, 1969; File de acatist [Leaves of Prayer for the Dead], op.68, 1v, fl, 1993; Spiritual Songs, op.70, low v, pf, 1994

BIBLIOGRAPHY
V. Cosma: *Muzicieni români* (Bucharest, 1970)

VIOREL COSMA

Petrová, Elena (*b* Modrý Kameň, 9 Nov 1929). Czech composer. She studied the piano with Karel Hoffmeister, musicology at Charles University, Prague, and composition under Jan Kapr at the Janáček Academy of Music, Brno. She has spent her whole career teaching music theory at Charles University. Her main creative interest is in vocal and dramatic music, for which she writes her own texts and scenarios. Her opera *Kdyby se slunce nevrátilo* ('Suppose the Sun did not Return') demonstrates her concise approach to musical utterance and a tendency towards modality in her harmonic language. Petrová's works have won several prizes, in her own country and abroad (Philadelphia, 1968; Denver, 1975; Mannheim, 1976).

WORKS
selective list

Opera: Kdyby se slunce nevrátilo [Suppose the Sun did not Return] (Petrová, after F. C. Ramuz), 1982–3

Ballets: Slavík a růže [The Nightingale and the Rose] (after O. Wilde), 1969; Podivuhodná raketa [The Remarkable Rocket] (after Wilde), 1970; Slunečnice [Sunflower] (after Ovid), Plzeň, Tyl Theatre, 1976

Orch: Sym., 1968; Slavnostní předehra [Festive Overture], 1975; Sym., 1976; Smuteční hudba [Mourning Music], 1981; Passacaglia, 1982; Slavnostní hudba [Festive Music], 1982; Sym., 1990

Vocal: Písně o čase [Songs about Time], Bar, pf, 1958; Madrigaly, chamber chorus, 1966; Noci [To the Night], cantata, T, chorus, orch, 1969; Pět slovenských písní [5 Slovak Songs], men's vv, 1969; Tanbakzan, melodrama, spkr, chamber orch, 1981; Nářek královny Ningal [Mourners of Queen Ningal], S, chamber chorus, 1992; Sluneční sonáta [Sunny Sonata], S, pf, 1992

Inst: Pf Sonata, 1960; Eclogues, b cl, 1965; 2 str qts, 1965, 1968; Inspirace [Inspirations], pf 4 hands, 1973; Pantomime, va d'amore, 1974; Impromptus, pf, 1979, 1989; Str Qt, 1991; Pf Sonata, 1992; Capricci, b cl, perc, 1993

Principal publishers: ČHF (Czech Music Fund), Panton

BIBLIOGRAPHY
CohenE; ČSHS; ČSS

A. Šerých: 'Konfese Eleny Petrové' [Confession of Elena Petrová], *Opus musicum*, xviii/8 (1986), 239–41

ANNA ŠERÝCH

Petrova, Mara (*b* Sliven, 15 May 1921). Bulgarian composer. One of the earliest Bulgarian woman composers to be well documented, she graduated in 1945 from the Sofia Academy of Music, where her teachers were Veselin Stoyanov (composition), Pancho Vladigerov (piano) and Marin Goleminov (orchestral conducting). Her talent revealed itself at an early age through her children's songs, instrumental pieces and a short operetta. She has been an editor, a teacher at the Institute for Music and Choreography in Sofia (1972–83) and a critic. Her large output, embracing many genres, includes over 260 children's songs, as well as orchestral and chamber works. Her music, based on Bulgarian classical and folk traditions, exhibits clear formal structures and rich melodic invention; it has been performed and recorded not only in Bulgaria but also in Poland, Germany, the former Czechoslovakia, Switzerland and the former USSR.

WORKS
selective list

Orch: Mladezhka suita [Youth Suite], 1953; Mojata rodina [My Homeland], ov., 1965; Junosheska suita [Youth Suite], str orch, timp, 1970; Sym. 'April 1876', 1981

Vocal: Blue-Eyed, song, 1v, orch, 1947; Lullaby, song, 1v, orch, 1953; Triptych, 1v, orch, 1972

Chamber and solo inst: Pf Variations, 1945; Small Sonata, pf, 1946; Prelude, pf, 1948; Bulgarian Dance, 1951; Dance, 3 bn, 1957; Prelude, 3 bn, 1960; Scherzo, fl, pf, 1964; Sofijska suita [Sofia Suite], 1969; Skici [Sketches], fl, ob, bn, 1977

Children's songs

Principal publishers: Muzika, Nauka i Izkustvo

BIBLIOGRAPHY

S. Lazarov: 'Mara Petrova', *Balgarska muzika* (1972), no.5, p.15

N. Kaufman: 'Za muzikata na Mara Petrova', *Balgarska muzika* (1981), no.5, p.30

MAGDALENA MANOLOVA

Philarmonica, Mrs. Pseudonym. A set of 12 trio sonatas for two violins was published under the pseudonym 'Mrs Philarmonica' by Richard Meares in London about 1715: six *Sonate* with obbligato cello parts and six *Divertimenti da camera*. While showing the influence of Arcangelo Corelli, they are written in an individual and often witty style.

MARGARET CHRISTIE

Phillips, Liz [Elizabeth] (*b* Jersey City, NJ, 13 June 1951). American composer and artist. She graduated from Bennington College in 1973 with a degree in art and music. In her early career as an artist she created sculptures using light. Later she incorporated sound as a logical extension of her work: 'What I wanted to do . . . was to change three dimensional space over time, and sound was the best way to do this', Phillips stated in an interview (Close). She has earned considerable recognition for her sound sculptures, created for indoor and outdoor installation. They contain electronic circuitry that responds to elements of the environment in which they are positioned – in some cases the presence and movement of people (as in *Sunspots*) and in others a changing landscape (as in *Windspun* and *Come About*). From a visual standpoint *Windspun* is typical of many of Phillips's sculptures in that the 'sensor' (in this case a windmill) serves both an artistic and a practical purpose. Information about the speed and direction of the wind and the presence of nearby people is gathered by the sensor and then transformed into sound by means of a synthesizer, using the hollow shaft of the windmill as a resonator. Phillips's sculptures have been exhibited throughout Europe and the USA.

WORKS

Sound sculptures: T. V. Dinner, 1971; Electric Spaghetti, 1972; Sound Structure, 1972; Sumtime, 1973, collab. Y. Wada and A. Knowles; Broken/Unbroken Terracotta, 1975; Cityflow, 1977; Metrosonic Province, 1978; Sunspots, 1979; Windspun for Minneapolis, 1980; Come About, 1981; Windspun, 1981; Multiple Perspectives, 1982; Sound Syzygy, 1982; Sonar Eclipse, 1983, collab. M. Cunningham

BIBLIOGRAPHY

R. Cohen: 'Sound Articulates Space', *Synapse* (1977), Jan–Feb, 14–15

J. La Barbara: 'New Music', *HiFi/MusAm*, xxix/5 (1979), 12–13, 40

C. Drewes: 'A Sculptor with Sound', *San Francisco Examiner* (21 June 1981)

D. Ahlstrom: 'Liz Phillips: Sunspots', *Computer Music Journal*, vi/3 (1982), 5–6

R. Close: 'Composer's Works Lend New Meaning to Movement', *St Paul Pioneer Press* (13 Dec 1982)

CHARLES PASSY

Philp, Elizabeth (*b* Falmouth, 1827; *d* London, 26 Nov 1885). English singer and composer. She was the elder daughter of James Philp, a geographer. Her early education was in Bristol and Paris; in 1867 she studied with Ferdinand Hiller in Cologne. She also studied singing in London with Manuel Garcia and Marchesi, and gave annual concerts, usually in aid of a philanthropic project. She wrote well over 100 songs (most of them published in London) and some duets and partsongs. Her style was summed up by the *Musical World* (11 May 1872): 'It is because Miss Philp always writes with true expressiveness and simplicity that her songs have wide patronage. But why, we ask, does Miss Philp select so many subjects from the graveyard and surrounding parts?'.

JOHN R. GARDNER

Picconi, Maria Antonietta (*b* Rome, 23 Sept 1869; *d* Rome, 1926). Italian pianist and composer. She studied at the S Cecilia conservatory in Rome, where her teachers included Giovanni Sgambati (piano) and Eugenio Terziani (composition). From 1886 to 1896 she was active as a concert pianist in Rome, then concentrated on teaching the piano and singing. She composed many drawing-room songs.

BIBLIOGRAPHY

SchmidlD

A. de Angelis: *L'Italia musicale d'oggi: Dizionario dei musicisti* (Rome, 1918, 3/1928)

FRANCESCA PERRUCCIO SICA

Pinel, Julie (*fl* Paris, ?1710–1737). French composer. A member of the Pinel dynasty of court lutenists whose immediate family had served the house of Soubise from the 1680s, she may have been the 'Mlle. Pinet [*sic*] la fille' who published an *air* in Ballard's 1710 *recueil*. In December 1736 she acquired an eight-year *privilège*, enabling her to publish vocal and instrumental chamber music. Before the year was out Pinel published a book of *airs* and in 1737 a *Nouveau recueil* *d'airs sérieux et à boire à une et deux voix, de Brunettes à 2 dessus, scène pastorale, et cantatille avec accompagnement*, dedicated to the Prince of Soubise; concertante flute parts contribute to trio textures in a delicately ornamented *air sérieux* and *cantatille*, both entitled 'Le Printemps'.

BIBLIOGRAPHY

M. Brenet: 'La librairie musicale en France de 1653 à 1790 d'après les registres de privilèges', *SIMG*, viii (1906–7), 401–66, esp. 437

J. A. Sadie: '*Musiciennes* of the Ancien Régime', *Women Making Music: the Western Art Tradition, 1150–1950*, ed. J. Bowers and J. Tick (Urbana and Chicago, 1986), 191–223

JULIE ANNE SADIE

Pistono, Piera (*b* Bangkok, 15 July 1938). Italian composer. She went to Rome for her musical studies, graduating in piano, choral music and choral conducting; her composition teachers included Barbara Giuranna, Irma Ravinale and Vieri Tosatti. She remained in Rome as a member of the teaching staff at the Conservatorio di S Cecilia, to which she was appointed in 1979. As a composer Pistono does not belong to any particular school or trend; indeed, eclecticism is a hallmark of her style. Her output consists mostly of solo instrumental and chamber works, but she has also written vocal works to texts by the Japanese poet Matsuo Bashō and by the Italian poet Guido Gozzano, from whom she is descended.

WORKS
selective list

Vocal: I miei pensieri (6 songs, Matsuo Bashō), S, 1980; Ignorabimus (G. Gozzano), chorus, orch, 1992; Parametri delle parti, S, fl, cl, tape, 1992; Haikai (Matsuo Bashō), mixed chorus, 1994
Chamber: Divertimento, wind qnt, pf, 1988; Oasi, sax qt, 1988; Dal fondo . . . la luce, sax qt, 1990; Tokamak, fl, ob, cl, vn, va, vc, pf, 1991
Solo inst: 8 Stücke, pf, 1988; Alle soglie dell'irreale, cl, 1990; Ricordando Sandro, vn, 1990

PAOLA DAMIANI

Pittar [née Krumpholtz], **Fanny** (*b* ?London, *c*1785; *d* ? after 1815). English harpist and composer, daughter of ANNE-MARIE KRUMPHOLTZ. She married a diamond merchant, Isaac Pittar, some time before March 1814, with a marriage settlement from the Earl of Hardwicke (Rempel suggests that he may have been her father). In about 1812 she published a march 'for a Regiment of Bengal Sepoys, adapted for either a Military Band or Piano Forte', and in about 1815 *A Military Divertimento* (for harp or piano) and an air and variations for harp, *Dedans mon petit réduit* (dedicated to the

memory of her mother). Her manuscript book (1811, in the British Library) contains 20 short pieces (allemandes, waltzes, themes and variations, marches, rondos and allegrettos for harp and/or piano), which show a wide range of compositional skills.

BIBLIOGRAPHY

U. Rempel: 'Fanny Krumpholtz and her Milieu', *American Harp Journal*, v/4 (1976), 11–15

—— : *A Critical Edition of British Library Additional Manuscript 49288: Fanny Krumpholtz's Manuscript Book of her own Compositions for the Harp, 1811* (thesis, U. of California, Santa Barbara, 1979)

—— : 'The Perils of Secondary Sources: an Annotated Bibliography of Encyclopedic and Dictionary Sources Relating to the Harpist Members of the Krumpholtz Family', *American Harp Journal*, vii/3 (1980), 25–30

BARBARA GARVEY JACKSON,
URSULA M. REMPEL

Pizer, Elizabeth [Faw] **Hayden** (*b* Watertown, NY, 1 Sept 1954). American composer. After completing her formal education at the Boston Conservatory of Music, she moved to the West Coast, working as an opera répétiteur at San Jose State University. She began her work in radio broadcast production at the studios in Berkeley and then worked in San Mateo. She has received several awards for her vocal and choral music, including First Prize in the Delius Composition Contest, 1982, for *Madrigals Anon* for unaccompanied chorus, and several first prizes in National League of Pen Women composition contests, for works including *Five Haiku II*, String Quartet and *Nightsongs*. She has also written a large number of jazz-inspired works and several for electronic tape, including *Arlington* and *Embryonic Climactus* (both 1989). Her music has been widely performed, in Europe and Australia as well as in the USA. In 1974, with her husband Charles Pizer, she formed an archival library for music not commercially available, and in 1988 developed the International Women's Music Sound Archive, a collection of classical music by women composers. She chaired the International League of Women Composers, 1982–3. She maintains her archives at Three Mile Bay, New York.

WORKS
selective list

Orch: Under and Overture, op.37, orch without str, 1979; Elegy in Amber: In Memoriam Leonard Bernstein, str orch, 1993
Band: Fanfare Ov., 1977–9
Vocal: Alleluia, op.25, 2S, chorus, 1976; Kyrie, op.39, chorus, 1976; Look down, fair moon (W. Whitman), 1v, pf, 1976; Slow, slow, fresh fount (B. Jonson), fl, chorus, 1977; Holy Eucharist Rite

II, op.46, 1v, chorus, pf/org, 1978; When to the sessions of sweet silent thought (W. Shakespeare), op.47, 1978; 5 Haiku, op.48, S, chamber ens, 1978; 5 Haiku II, op.50, Mez, pf, 1979; Madrigals Anon, op.51, chorus, 1979; Kyrie eleison, chorus, 1983

Chamber: Nocturne, op.28, ob, va, vc, cel, harp, 1976; Quilisoly, op.38, fl/vn, pf, 1976; Elegy, op.43, str orch/str qt/(fl, eng hn, hn, bn) 1977 [formerly known as Interfuguelude]; Piece of Eight, op.42, 2 ob, 2 cl, 2 hn, 2 bn, 1977; Str Qt, 1981; Nightsongs, vc, pf

Pf: Sonata no.2, op.10, 1974; 2 Brief Pieces, op.12–13, 1975; Expressions intimes, op.14–18, 1975; Jimnobody no.1, op.22, 1976; Jimnobody no.2, op.24, 1976; A mon père, pour mon père, op.40, 1977; Lyric Fancies, 1983

Elec: In the Land of Nod, synth, tape, 1979; Sunken Flutes, synth, tape, 1979; Arlington, tape, 1989; Embryonic Climactus, tape, 1989; Aquasphere, tape, 1990; The Infinite Sea, tape/(nar, tape), 1990; Momentum: a Glimpse of the Sea, tape, 1990

BIBLIOGRAPHY

G. Straughn: Composer Profile: 'Elizabeth Faw Hayden Pizer', *ILWC Journal* (1994), Feb, 33

Poldowski [Wieniawska, Irena Regina] (*b* Brussels, 16 May 1880; *d* London, 28 Jan 1932). Polish composer. She was a daughter of the Polish violinist Henryk Wieniawski and Isabella Hampton, a niece of the pianist and composer George A. Osborne. She studied at the Brussels Conservatory with F. A. Gevaert (composition) and Stork (piano), in London with Percy Pitt and Michael Hambourg, and in Paris with André Gédalge. Later she studied with Vincent d'Indy at the Schola Cantorum in Paris. She married Sir Aubrey Dean Paul and lived in London. Her compositions are mainly for small forces and include about 30 songs, to texts by Paul Verlaine, William Blake, Jean Dominique, Jean Moréas, Albert Samain, Anatole Le Braz and Adolphe Retté. The best and most interesting are the 16 songs on texts by Verlaine (1915–20), in a style close to that of contemporary French composers.

Except for two songs published under the name Wieniawska in 1900, all of her music was published in London by Chester, under the pseudonym Poldowski. Her orchestral *Nocturnes* had its first performance at the Queen's Hall Promenade Concerts in 1912.

WORKS
printed works published in London

Stage: Laughter, operetta

Orch: Pat Malone's Wake, pf, orch; Nocturnes, sym. sketch; Tenements, sym. sketch

Other inst: Berceuse de l'enfant mourant, vn, pf (1923); Caledonian Market, suite, pf (1923); Tango, vn, pf (1923); Pastorale, cl, pf (1927); The Hall of Machinery – Wembley, pf (1928); Sonatina, pf (1928); Study, pf (1928); L'heure exquise, pf; Suite miniature de chansons à danser, wind ens; Vn Sonata, d

Vocal: Soir, 1v, pf, ob d'amore (1920); Narcisse, 1v, str qt (1927); *c*30 songs

BIBLIOGRAPHY

M. F. Brand: *Poldowski (Lady Dean Paul): her Life and her Song Settings of French and English Poetry* (diss., U. of Oregon, 1979)

ZOFIA CHECHLIŃSKA

Polin, Claire (*b* Philadelphia, 1 Jan 1926). American composer, musicologist and flautist. She studied composition with Vincent Persichetti at the Philadelphia Conservatory (MMus 1950, DMus 1955), with Peter Mennin at the Juilliard School of Music, and with Roger Sessions and Lukas Foss at Tanglewood. She also studied the flute with William Kincaid, with whom she collaborated on five tutors for the instrument. From 1958 until her retirement in 1991 she taught at Rutgers University. Her works have been widely performed, and she has received many honours and awards. Besides showing the influence of her flute playing, her compositions reflect her scholarly concerns (especially early Welsh music and folklore, the music of biblical and medieval times, and Native American and Russian folk music) and her interest in birdsong. She also explores instrumental sonorities in a dissonant contrapuntal style. Her publications include *Music of the Ancient Near East* (New York, 1954) and an edition of the Ap Huw Manuscript (Musicological Studies, xxxiv, Henryville, PA, 1982).

WORKS
selective list

Orch: Scenes from Gilgamesh, fl, str (1972); Journey of Owain Madoc, brass qnt, perc orch (1973); Mythos, conc., harp, str (1983)

Chamber: Cader Idris, brass qnt (1972); O, Aderyn Pur, fl, sax, tape (1973); Death of Procris, fl, tuba (1974); Ma'alot, va, perc qt (1981); Kuequenaku-Cambriola, pf, perc (1982); Walum olum, pf, cl, va (1984); Freltic Sonata, vn, pf (1985)

Solo inst: Summer Settings, harp (1967); Margoa, fl (1972); Eligmos archaios, harp (1974); Georgics, fl (1986); Shirildang, pf (1991)

Vocal: Infinito, a sax, S, nar, dancer, SATB (1972); Paraselen, S, fl, pf (1982); Mystic Rondo, song cycle, T, vn, pf (1987–8)

Principal publisher: Seesaw Music

CHRISTINE AMMER

Poole, Chris (*b* New York, 23 June 1952). Danish composer, flautist and saxophonist of American birth. She was the first woman to complete the applied music programme at Berklee College of Music in Boston (1974). In 1975 she moved to Denmark, taking

Danish citizenship in 1986. In addition to establishing herself as a performer, she grew rapidly as a composer during the 1980s and early 90s, her musical activities marked by her feminism. She has composed music for the ballet and for the theatre, collaborating with the Norwegian actress Juni Dahr in *Joan of Arc* (1988) and *The Lady from the Sea* (1993); she and Dahr performed these works in Pakistan, India, Venezuela, Colombia, Russia and the USA, as well as in Europe. In her music Poole explores a broad spectrum of traditional and untraditional flute sounds in a synthesis of jazz, minimalist, folk and New Age styles.

WORKS
selective list

Dramatic: Joan of Arc, theatre, 1988; Ibsen Women, theatre, 1990; Liv Lage, slide projections, 1991; Rodder (Trio no.1), modern dance theatre, 1991; Troll, film, 1991; Spejl, modern dance theatre for children, 1992; The Lady from the Sea, theatre, 1993

Chamber: Swim!, 1v, fl, digital dclay, 1986; Bamboo Boogie, bamboo fl, synth, 1988; Memories of Thailand, 3 bamboo fl, 1988; Regnbuen Synger, 4 solo vv, fl, 1990; Sangen til Hildegard von Bingen, 1v, a fl, 1990

Solo fl: Breath/Attack, 1985; Langeland Ladies, 1985; En hilsen til gudinderne, 1986; A Woman Unfolding, 1986; Mavedans for Ishtar, 1988; Missing You Mazdier-a, 1988; Til minde om Maren Urtegaard, 1988; Silly Spheres, 1990; Hilsen til Godtved Salen, 1991; Nr.40, 1992

Fl, elec: Krystal Lys, 1987; Legen i en jàpansk have, 1988

INGE BRULAND

Poston, Elizabeth (*b* Highfield, Herts., 24 Oct 1905; *d* Highfield, 18 March 1987). English composer, writer and pianist. She received her musical education at the RAM and on the Continent, and also studied the piano with Harold Samuel and the organ with Stanley Marchant. Later in her career she received support from Ralph Vaughan Williams. She emerged as a composer in 1925, when seven of her songs were published (her popular early setting of *Sweet Suffolk Owl* was one of these). Her first work to be broadcast, from the BBC at Savoy Hill, was an RAM prize-winning violin sonata. In 1928 she published five songs in a more personal style. From 1930 to 1939 most of her time was spent abroad where, among other studies, she collected folksong. On returning to England she joined the BBC's music staff, and her war service was thus a period of intensive broadcasting which included the direction of music in the European Service. She resigned in 1945, but after a period in the

USA and Canada returned to the BBC in 1947 to broadcast and advise for a year at the inception of the Third Programme. She was elected president of the Society of Women Musicians (1955–61).

Poston distinguished herself in a wide field of musical activities. In collaboration with David Jones, Terence Tiller, Dylan Thomas, C. S. Lewis and others, she produced many important scores for radio productions. Outstanding among her film scores is that for *Howards End* (1970; she lived in the house which was the subject of E. M. Forster's novel). Her extended choral works include *An English Kalendar* (1969) for female voices and harp and *An English Day Book* (1971) for mixed voices and piano, both commissoned by the Farnham Festival. A *Concertino da camera* (1950) for recorder, oboe d'amore, viola da gamba and harpsichord and a Trio (1958) for flute, clarinet (or viola) and harp (or piano) are her most significant chamber works.

Although her output was modest, Poston evolved a personal style which derived from the neo-classical tradition and laid great emphasis on clean craftsmanship and melodic fluency. She won particular respect as the editor of folksong, carol and hymn collections. Her association with Peter Warlock made her a unique authority on the subject of the man and his music.

WORKS
selective list

Choral: The Nativity, S, Mez, C, T, B, chorus, str, 1951; Antiphon and Psalm: Laudate Dominum, chorus, org, 1955; Song of Wisdom, 1956; 2 Carols in Memory of Peter Warlock, 1956; Happy are thy Men, 1958; Sing unto the Lord, 1959; An English Kalendar, female vv, harp, 1969; An English Day Book, chorus, pf, 1971

Vocal: Aubade (The lark now leaves his wat'ry nest) (W. Davenant), 1925; Brown is my love, 1925; A Little Candle to St Anthony (S. Russell), 1925; Salve Jesus, little lad, 1925; Sweet Suffolk Owl (T. Vautor), 1925; The Bellman's Song (T. Ravenscroft), 1925; The Lake Isle of Innisfree (W. B. Yeats), 1926; Maid Quiet (Yeats), 1926; Balulalow, 2 solo vv, 1928; 5 Songs, 1928; She is all so slight (R. Aldington), 1942; The Stockdoves (A. Young), 1945; 6 Canzoni (6 Italian Folksongs), 1950; Sheepfolds (M. Madeleva), 1958; Jesus Christ, the Apple Tree, 1967

Inst: Concertino da camera, rec, ob d'amore, va da gamba, hpd, 1950; Trio, fl, cl/va, harp/pf, 1958; Lullaby and Festa, pf, 1960; Sonatina, vc, pf, 1972

Other works: Comus (incid. music for radio, J. Milton), 1946; In Parenthesis (incid. music for radio, D. Jones), 1946; Paradise Lost (incid. music for radio, Milton), 1947; Twelfth Night (incid. music for radio, W. Shakespeare), 1947; A Room with a View (film score, E. M. Forster); Howard's End (film score, Forster), 1970

Principal publishers: Boosey & Hawkes, Chester, Novello, OUP

BIBLIOGRAPHY

J. Littlejohn: 'Senior British Composers, II: Elizabeth Poston', *Composer*, no.56 (1975–6), 15–18; no.57 (1976), 27–32

SOPHIE FULLER, MICHAEL HURD

Pownall, Mary Ann (*b* London, Feb 1751; *d* Charleston, SC, 11 Aug 1796). English actress, singer and composer. She made her performing début at Drury Lane in 1770 under the name Mrs James Wrighton, and was praised by the critics for her role as Lucy Lockit in John Gay's *The Beggar's Opera*. In 1792 she went to the USA with Mr Pownall, her second husband, and became a member of the Old American Company; in the next few years she appeared in concerts in Charleston, Philadelphia, New York and Boston. Her repertory ranged from popular songs to opera, oratorio and dramatic readings. Her songs *Jenny of the Glen*, *Lavinia* and *The Straw Bonnet* (all included in *Six Songs for the Harpsichord*, written in collaboration with James Hewitt, New York, 1794), and *Kisses sued for* (New York, 1795), were among the first by a woman to be published in the USA. Her vocal writing is characterized by strong leaps in the melody and a variety of rhythmic patterns; her harmonic language, however, is straightforward.

BIBLIOGRAPHY

O. G. T. Sonneck: *A Bibliography of Early Secular American Music* (Washington, DC, 1905, rev. and enlarged by W. T. Upton, 2/1945)

—— : *Early Concert-Life in America (1731–1800)* (Leipzig, 1907)

J. Tick: *American Women Composers before 1870* (Ann Arbor, 1983)

LORETTA GOLDBERG

Prescott, Oliveria Louisa (*b* London, 3 Sept 1843; *d* London, 9 Sept 1919). English composer. She studied at the RAM in the mid-1870s with Lindsay Sloper and George Macfarren, and acted as Macfarren's amanuensis when he became blind. She published about 20 substantial partsongs, songs and anthems, and a Concert Finale for piano duet (London, 1878). But her 'Alkestis' Symphony, a Piano Concerto in A minor and an Orchestral Suite ('In Woodland') remained unpublished, as did a large amount of chamber music. Her three-act musical comedy *Carrigraphuga, the Castle of the Fairies* (words by S. Phillips) was published in 1914.

JOHN R. GARDNER

Price [née Smith], **Florence Bea(trice)** (*b* Little Rock, AR, 9 April 1887; *d* Chicago,

3 June 1953). American composer. She was the first African-American woman to win widespread recognition as a symphonic composer, rising to prominence (with William Grant Still and William Dawson) in the 1930s. After early training with her mother she studied composition at the New England Conservatory in Boston with Wallace Goodrich and Frederick Converse (1903–6) and privately with George Whitefield Chadwick. She gained an Artist's Diploma (organ) and a piano teacher's diploma. She returned to the South to teach at the Cotton Plant – Arkadelphia Academy (1906–7) and Shorter College (1907–10) in Little Rock, then headed the music department of Clark College in Atlanta until 1912, when she returned to Little Rock to marry. In 1927, presumably to escape the increasing racial oppression in the South, the Price family moved to Chicago. There Florence Price began a period of compositional creativity and study at the American Conservatory and with Carl Busch, Wesley LaViolette and Arthur Olaf Anderson at the Chicago Musical College. In the 1920s she began to win awards for her compositions, and in 1932 she achieved national recognition when she won first prize in the Wanamaker competition for her Symphony in E minor. With the symphony's première in 1933 by the Chicago SO under Frederick Stock, Price became the first African-American woman to have an orchestral work performed by a major American orchestra. Her music was taken up by other orchestras, and she won further recognition after Marian Anderson's performance of her arrangement of the spiritual *My soul's been anchored in de Lord* and *Songs to the Dark Virgin*. The latter, a setting of a text by Langston Hughes, is one of her most powerful art songs and was hailed by the *Chicago Daily News* as 'one of the greatest immediate successes ever won by an American song'. She remained active as a composer and teacher until her death.

Price played the theatre organ for silent films, wrote popular music for commercial purposes and orchestrated arrangements for soloists and choirs who performed with the WGN Radio orchestra in Chicago. She is best known for her songs: her art songs and arrangements of spirituals were sung by many of the most renowned singers of the day including, besides Marian Anderson, Blanche Thebom, Etta Moten and Leontyne Price. Although her music was widely performed, her output, comprising over 300 compositions, remains unpublished, apart from a handful of songs and piano pieces. In her large-scale works Price's musical language is often conservative, in keeping with the romantic nationalist style of the 1920s–40s, but it also reflects the influence of her cultural heritage and the ideals of the 'Harlem renaissance' of the 1920s–30s. She incorporated spirituals and characteristic dance music within classical forms and at times deviated from traditional structures in deference to influences which are implicitly African-American, for example call-and-response techniques and Juba dance rhythms. To her art songs and piano music she brought a thorough knowledge of instrumental and vocal writing, colourful harmonies and exotic modulations.

WORKS
selective list

Orch: Sym. no.1, e, 1931–2; Ethiopia's Shadow in America, 1932; Mississippi River, sym., 1934; Pf Conc., d, perf. 1934; Sym. no.2, g; Sym. no.3, c, 1940, US-NH; Sym. [no.4]; Vn Conc. no.2, D, 1952; Chicago Suite; Colonial Dance, sym.; Dances in the Canebrakes [arr. of pf piece]; 2 concert ovs. [based on spirituals]; Rhapsody, pf, orch; Songs of the Oak, tone poem; Suite of Negro Dances

Choral: The Moon Bridge (anon.), SSA, 1930; The Wind and the Sea (P. L. Dunbar), SSAATTBB, pf, str qt, 1934; Witch of the Meadow (M. R. Gamble), SSA (1947); Nature's Magic (Gamble), SSA (1953); Song for Snow (E. Coatsworth), SATB (1957); Sea Gulls, female chorus, by 1951; Abraham Lincoln walks at midnight (V. Lindsay), mixed vv, orch, org; After the 1st and 6th Commandments, SATB; Communion Service, F, SATB, org; Nod (W. de la Mare), TTBB; other works for female/mixed vv, pf

Solo vocal (all with pf): Dreamin' Town (Dunbar), 1934; Songs to the Dark Virgin (L. Hughes) (1941); Night (L. C. Wallace) (1946); Out of the South blew a Wind (F. C. Woods) (1946); An April Day (J. F. Cotter) (1949); Dawn's Awakening (J. J. Burke); The Envious Wren (A. Carey and P. Carey); Fantasy in Purple (Hughes); Forever (Dunbar); Love-in-a-Mist (Gamble); Nightfall (Dunbar); Resignation (Price), also arr. chorus; Song of the Open Road; Sympathy (I know why the caged bird sings) (Dunbar); To my Little Son (J. J. Davis); Travel's End (M. F. Hoisington); c75 other works

Chamber: Moods, fl, cl, pf, 1953; Negro Folksongs in Counterpoint, str qt; 2 pf qnts; other works for str qt; pieces for vn, pf

Pf: At the Cotton Gin (1928); Fantasie negre, 1929; Sonata, e (1932); 3 Little Negro Dances, 1933, arr. band, 1939, arr. 2 pf (1949); Bayou Dance, 1938; Dance of the Cotton Blossoms, 1938; Dances in the Canebrakes (1953); c10 other works, c70 teaching pieces

Org: Impromptu, 1941; Adoration (1951); Evening Song, 1951; In Quiet Mood, 1951; Passacaglia and Fugue; Retrospection (An Elf on a Moonbeam); Sonata no.1; Suite no.1; Variations on a Folksong

Arrs. of spirituals: My soul's been anchored in de Lord, 1v, pf (1937), also arr. chorus; Nobody knows the trouble I see, pf (1938); Were you there when they crucified my Lord?, pf (1942); I am bound for the kingdom, 1v, pf (1948); I'm workin' on my building, 1v, pf (1948); Heav'n Bound Soldier (1949); I couldn't hear nobody pray, SSAATTBB; Save me, Lord, save me, 1v, pf: Trouble done come my way, 1v, pf

Principal publishers: Fischer, Gamble-Hinged, Handy, McKinley, Presser

MSS of 40 songs in US-PHu; other MSS in private collections; papers and duplicate MSS in University of Arkansas, Fayetteville

BIBLIOGRAPHY

NAW (B. G. Jackson); *SouthernB*
E. Southern: *The Music of Black Americans: a History* (New York, 1971, 2/1983)
H. E. Roach: *Black American Music Past and Present* (Boston, 1973)
M. D. Green: *A Study of the Lives and Works of Five Black Women Composers in America* (diss., U. of Oklahoma, 1975)
R. Abdul: *Blacks in Classical Music: a Personal History* (New York, 1977)
B. G. Jackson: 'Florence Price, Composer', *BPiM*, v (1977), 30–43
O. Williams: *American Black Women in the Arts and Social Sciences* (Metuchen, NJ, 2/1978)
C. Ammer: *Unsung: a History of Women in American Music* (Westport, CT, 1980)
M. D. Green: 'Florence Price', *Black Women Composers: a Genesis* (Boston, 1983), 31–46
R. L. Brown: *Selected Orchestral Music of Florence B. Price in the Context of her Life and Work* (diss., Yale U., 1987)
—— 'Florence B. Price and Margaret Bonds: the Chicago Years', *Black Music Research Bulletin*, xii/2 (1990), 11
—— 'William Grant Still, Florence Price, and William Dawson: Echoes of the Harlem Renaissance', *Black Music in the Harlem Renaissance*, ed. S. A. Floyd jr (Westport, CT, 1990), 71–86
—— 'The Woman's Symphony Orchestra of Chicago and Florence Price's Piano Concerto in One Movement', *American Music*, xi/2 (1993), 185–205

RAE LINDA BROWN, MYRNA S. NACHMAN
(work-list with BARBARA GARVEY JACKSON)

Prieto, María Teresa (*b* Oviedo, 1896; *d* Mexico, 24 Jan 1982). Spanish composer. Born into a musical family, she first studied in Oviedo, where she was a piano and composition pupil of Saturnino del Fresno, who had a strong interest in traditional Asturian music; she was profoundly influenced by the music of Bach, and was to become particularly noted for her contrapuntal style and rational temperament. She continued her studies at the Conservatorio Real, Madrid, with Benito García de la Parra, whose advocacy of the use of modes also influenced her decisively. In addition, Asturian regionalism, which dominated the intellectual climate of her home town, remained an inspiration throughout her life. At the outbreak of the Spanish Civil War in 1936, Prieto went to

Mexico to live with her brother Carlos, an important financier, patron and friend of Igor Stravinsky, Darius Milhaud and many Mexican composers. There she formed contacts with other Spanish musicians in exile, such as Adolfo Salazar, Rodolfo Halffter, Jesús Bal y Gay and Rosita García Ascot. Her last teacher was the nationalist Manuel Ponce, with whom she studied from 1937 to 1939.

Prieto's early compositions, which are nationalist in character and inspiration, include small-scale pieces such as *Añada* (1937) for piano and *Seis melodias* (1940) for voice and piano, as well as grander works (from 1942), notably the Romantic *Impresión sinfónica* for piano and orchestra, the three-movement *Sinfonía asturiana* (1942) and the symphonic poem *Chichen Itza* (1944), a musical vision of Mayan culture that shows considerable mastery of orchestral writing. In the later 1940s she worked with Milhaud at Mills College, California, and her musical style began to change: although melody was still important, her particular use of modulating harmony and harsh dissonances, as for example in *Odas celestes* (1947) for voice and piano, gave a more expressionist character to her work. During the 1950s she was attracted by the quartet genre; the *Cuarteto modal* won the Samuel Ros prize in Madrid in 1958. There was a further change of style after 1956 when, prompted by her work with Halffter, she adopted 12-note technique; the main serial compositions of this period are her *Doce variaciones seriales* (1961) for piano and the *Tema variado y fuga (dodecafónico)* (1968) for orchestra, although such works as the *Suite sinfónica* (1967) show that she also continued to write in her earlier style.

WORKS
selective list

Orch, vocal-orch: Impresión sinfónica, pf, orch, 1942; Sinfonía asturiana, 1942; Chichen Itza, sym. poem, 1944; Sinfonía breve, 1945; Variaciones y fuga, 1947; Adagio y fuga, vc, orch, 1948, also arr. vc, pf; Oración de quietud, sym. poem, 1v, orch, 1949; Sinfonía de la danza prima, 1955; Sinfonía cantabile, 1956; 12 miniaturas, vn, orch, 1957; 6 canciones modales (J. Inés and others), 1v, orch, 1964; Ave Maria, 1v, orch, 1966, also for chorus, org/pf; Suite sinfónica, ballet suite, 1967; Cuadro de la naturaleza, 1967; Tema variado y fuga (dodecafónico), 1968; Sonata modal: Pt.1, Palabras divinas, 1v, orch, 1972, Pt.2, Doble fuga, D, orch, Pt.3, Aleluya (Bible, *Song of Songs*), 1v, orch, 1974

Songs: 6 melodias (R. de Alcázar and others), 1v, pf, 1940; Odas celestes (V. Aleixandre and others), 1v, pf, 1947; Córdoba, lejana y sola (F. García Lorca), 1v, pf, 1970; Camino (García Lorca), 1v, pf, 1971; 4 canciones (Prieto and others), 1v, pf, 1971

Chamber and solo inst: Str Qt, G, 1951; Fuga, b♭, str

qt, 1952; Fuga postdodecafónica, str qt, 1953; Str Qt, f, 1954; Cuarteto modal, str qt, 1958; 24 variaciones: 12 seriales y 12 tonales, pf, 1961; Fuga para aliento, str qt, 1969

BIBLIOGRAPHY

E. Casares Rodico: 'La compositora Maria Teresa Prieto: del postromanticismo al estructuralismo dodecafónico', *Boletín del Instituto de Estudios Asturianos*, no.95 (1978)

EMILIO CASARES RODICIO

Priuli [Prioli], **Marieta Morosina** (*fl* 1665). Italian composer. She was a noblewoman, a member of the distinguished Venetian Morosina family. She dedicated a volume of *Balletti e correnti* (Venice, 1665) for three string instruments and harpsichord continuo to the Habsburg Dowager Empress Eleonora. It contains five sets of pieces paired by key, though not by theme, and eight independent *correnti*. They are conservative in style.

ELEANOR SELFRIDGE-FIELD

Procaccini, Teresa (*b* Cerignola, Foggia, 23 March 1934). Italian composer. She began to compose when very young, and studied the piano at the Foggia Conservatory, graduating in 1952. Later, under the guidance of Fernando Germani, she graduated also in organ and composition, having studied with Achille Lango, Enzo Masetti and Virgilio Mortari. She undertook advanced studies at the Conservatorio di Musica S Cecilia in Rome (film music) and at the Accademia Musicale Chigiana in Siena (composition). She has won various prizes, including the Viotti competition (1956), the Casella prize (1970) and the International String Quartet Competition, San Francisco (1981). She taught the organ and composition at the Foggia Conservatory and became director there (1972–3), and in 1979 became a lecturer in composition at the Conservatorio di S Cecilia in Rome. Procaccini's large output covers all genres and includes many chamber and orchestral works. Her style is firmly rooted in the preceding musical generation and she remains faithful to Classical formal values, but her creative facility and spontaneity of expression make her a versatile composer and her works immediately accessible. Much of her music relates to the world of childhood, and many works are intended for young performers.

WORKS
selective list

Stage: La vendetta di Luzbel (opera, Proccacini, after F. Lopé de Vega), 1970, rev. 1974; Piazza della musica no.1, op.54 (ballet, after S. Massaron), 1972, rev. 1978; La prima notte, op.55 (comic opera, 1, Massaron), 1973; Questione di fiducia, op.56 (comic opera, 1, Massaron), 1973; Medea, op.84 (ballet), 1981

Orch: Sonata in tricromia, op.11, pf, orch, 1957; Org Conc., op.12, 1957; Un cavallino avventuroso, op.23, fairy-tale, chamber orch, 1960; 3 danze, op.24, tpt, str orch, 1961; Sensazioni sonore, op.41, 4 pieces, 1969; Musica per archi, op.50, str orch, 1971; Harp Conc., op.78, 1980; Intersecazioni, str orch, 1989

Chamber: Pf Trio, op.5, 1956; 9 preludi, op.29, pf, 1966; 3 pezzi, op.30, bn, pf, 1966; Dialogo, op.34, va, pf, 1968; Clown Music, op.37, 4 pieces, wind qnt, 1968; Str Qt, op.43, 1969; Duo, op.85, vn, va, 1982; Meeting, 4 sax, 1988; Qnt, ob, cl, bn, hn, pf, 1992

Vocal: Il giudizio di Salomone, op.15, cantata, soloists, chorus, orch, 1958; La peste di Atene, op.17 (cantata, after Lucretius), chorus, orch, 1958; In memoriam, op.96 (cantata, C. de Flumeri), spkr, chorus, orch, 1984; La pioggia nel pineto, fl, pf, women's chorus, reciter, 1988; Ave Maria, chorus, orch, 1990

BIBLIOGRAPHY

CohenE
J. L. Zaimont and others, eds.: *The Musical Woman: an International Perspective*, i: *1983* (Westport, CT, 1984)

PAOLA DAMIANI

Pstrokońska-Nawratil, Grażyna (Hanna) (*b* Wrocław, 16 July 1947). Polish composer. She studied composition at the State High School (later Academy) of Music in Wrocław with Stefan Poradowski and Tadeusz Natanson, graduating in 1971. She completed her studies in France with Olivier Messiaen and Pierre Boulez, participated in seminars in Aix-en-Provence on the music of Iannis Xenakis and worked at the experimental music studios in Paris and Marseilles. In 1971 she began to teach at the Wrocław Academy of Music, later becoming professor (1993) and head of the theory and composition department. Among the many prizes she has won in international competitions is honourable mention for *Ostinato* at the 1975 GEDOK competition in Mannheim and third prize for *Icarus* at the UNESCO International Rostrum of Composers in Paris in 1987. Her works have received frequent festival and broadcast performances. She has written several articles on contemporary music, music therapy and theory. Pstrokońska-Nawratil favours musical forms grounded in tradition while eschewing classical stylization; her rich and varied resources are always subordinated to her main goal, expression. She has developed her own formal methods, which she calls 'structure shifting'.

WORKS
selective list

Orch: Conc. grosso, cl, hn, pf, perc, str, 1971; Reanimacja [Reanimation] (Fresco I), 1972; Epitaphios (Fresco II), 1975; Ikar [Icarus] (Fresco III), 1979; Incrustation, vn, orch, 1979; Conc. alla campana: Tadeusz Baird in memoriam (Fresco IV), pf, orch, 1984; Płomienie: Ryszard Bukowski in memoriam [Flames], str, hpd, 1988; Le soleil: Conc. for perc and orch after Monet, Seurat, Van Gogh, 1991

Vocal: Po słońca czerwone [For the Red Suns], vv, 5 insts, 1972; Abecadło [Alphabet Book], mixed chorus, inst ens, 1973; Ymnodia, vocalise, 3vv, tape, perc, 1977; Pieśni niespokojne [Unquiet Songs] (T. Różewicz), Bar, orch, 1985; Pejaż z pluszczem [Landscape with a Dipper], vocalise, S, 2 vn, 1986; Eternel (Fresco V), S, 2 choruses, orch, 1989

Chamber: Nocturne, vc, prepared pf, 1973; Ostinato, perc ens, 1975; Canon for Motoric Group, 4 perc, pf, 1976; Studio, vn, large tam-tam, 1976; Arabesque, str qt, 1980; Bis & Joke, perc, pf, 1985; Str Qt no.2: Andrzej Krzanowski in memoriam, 1991

Other works: La vetrata, pf, 1979; W. królestwie jesiennych liści [In a Kingdom of Autumn Leaves] (ballet for children, 2), 1987; Triangle, 6 perc, 1991

Principal publisher: PWM

BARBARA ZWOLSKA-STĘSZEWSKA

Ptaszyńska, Marta (*b* Warsaw, 29 July 1943). Polish composer and percussionist. After graduating from the music academies of Warsaw and Poznań she received a French government grant to study with Nadia Boulanger (1969–70). In 1972 she settled in the USA when a grant from the Kosciuszko Foundation enabled her to study at the Cleveland Institute of Music (1972–4) with Cloyd Duff, Richard Weiner and Donald Erb. During her time there she gave many lectures on Polish music and made concert appearances throughout the USA with a wide repertory that included her own works. She taught intermittently at Bennington College, Vermont (1974–7), and in 1977 was appointed composer-in-residence at the University of California at Berkeley and Santa Barbara, a position she has continued to occupy. From 1981 to 1984 she served on the board of directors of the Percussive Arts Society, and in 1984–5 she taught at Indiana University. In 1974 the Cleveland Orchestra gave the première of her *Spectri sonori*. *Siderals* and *Classical Variations* won prizes in Percussive Arts Society competitions in 1974 and 1976, and in 1986 *La novella d'inverno* was placed second at the UNESCO International Rostrum of Composers in Paris. The Marimba Concerto received honourable mention at the International Composers' Competition in New York in 1987. As well

Loïsa Puget: lithograph by M. Alophe

as composing Ptaszyńska remains active as a recitalist and holds performance clinics. Her music, which ranges widely from pointillism to cantabile writing, is colourful and often delicate, with a keen sense of architecture and occasional use of aleatory procedures. Percussion instruments feature prominently in her works, and she often specifies a precise spatial arrangement of performers.

WORKS
selective list

Stage: Oskar z Alwy [Oscar from Alva] (opera, 6 scenes, Z. Kopalko, after Byron), S, Mez, T, Bar, B, chorus, orch, 1971; Soirée snobe chez la princesse (music-theatre), 2 kbd, tape, mimes, light projection, 1979

Orch: Improvisations, 1968; Phantasy in Black and White, 1973; Spectri sonori, 1973; Crystallites, 1974; Perc Conc., 1974; Conductus: a Ceremonial for Winds, ww, 1982; La novella d'inverno, str, 1984; Mar Conc., 1985; Sax Conc., 1988; Ode to Praise all Famous Women, 1992

Chamber: 4 Preludes, vib, pf, 1965; Scherzo, xyl, pf, 1967; Passacaglia and Fugue, org, perc, 1968; Jeu-parti, harp, vib, 1970; Madrigals (Canticum sonarum), wind qt, str qt, tpt, trbn, gong, 1971; Sonospheres III, fl, cl, trbn, vc, pf, perc, 1973; Siderals, 2 perc qnts, light projection, 1974; Mobile, perc, 1975; Classical Variations, timp, str qt, 1976; Dream Lands, Magic Spaces, vn, pf, perc (6 players), 1978; Kwiaty Księżyca [Moon Flowers], vc, pf, 1986; Ajikan: Unfolding Light, fl, perc, 1990; Poetic Impressions, ww qnt, pf, 1991

Solo inst: Model przestrzenny [Space Model], perc, 1971–5; Arabesque, harp, 1972; Stress, tape, perc, 1972; 2 Poems, tuba, 1973–5; Touracou, hpd, 1974; Quodlibet, db, tape, 1976; 6 Bagatelles, harp, 1979;

Graffito, mar, 1988; Hommage à I. J. Paderewski, pf, 1992

Vocal: Epigrams (Gk. poems), chorus, fl, harp, pf, perc, 1977; Sonety do Orfeusza [Sonnets to Orpheus] (R. M. Rilke), 1v, chamber orch, 1981; Listy polskie [Polish Letters] (cantata, Pol. poems), S, Mez, Bar, chorus, chamber orch, 1988; Pieśni rozpaczy i samotności [Songs of Despair and Loneliness] (Rilke, P. Verlaine, W. Shakespeare, F. García Lorca, L. Staff), Mez, pf, 1989

Principal publishers: Marks, Presser, PWM

BIBLIOGRAPHY

T. Marek: 'Composer's Workshop: Marta Ptaszyńska's *Siderals*', *Polish Music* (1975). no.2, pp.20–23

B. Murray: 'The Influence of Polish Music on American Culture', *Polish Music* (1976), no.1, p.6; no.2, pp.10–18

D. Szwarcman: 'The Colorful World of Marta Ptaszyńska', *Polish Music* (1988), no.2–3, pp.25ff

MICHAEL MECKNA,
BARBARA ZWOLSKA-STĘSZEWSKA

Puget, Loïsa [Louise-Françoise] (*b* Paris, 11 Feb 1810; *d* Pau, 27 Nov 1889). French composer and singer. She was taught music by her mother, a singer. She composed more than 300 *romances*, which were extraordinarily popular, due in part to her frequent performances of them in Parisian salons.

Title-page, illustrated by Célestin Nanteuil, of 'Le Rhin Allemand' (Mainz: Schott, c1842) by Loïsa Puget

Their popularity reached well beyond Paris, however. They appeared in bilingual (French and German) editions, English editions and in piano arrangements; illustrated volumes, entitled *Album* or *Collection des romances*, were published in Paris between 1830 and 1845. Most of her texts were written by the actor Gustave Lemoine, who became her husband in 1842. Lemoine's texts treat a wide variety of subjects typical of the 19th-century spirit, from the innocence of *Demain, je serai dame* or the flagrant sentimentality of *Le ciel sur terre* and *Appelle-moi ta mère*, to the sensational treatment of suicide in *Morte d'amour!*, inspired by an actual event.

Encouraged by the success of her *romances*, and because of her interest in the theatre, Puget studied with Adolphe Adam and composed two one-act operettas. On 1 October 1836 the première of her *Le mauvais oeil* (text by Eugène Scribe and Gustave Lemoine) was given by the Opéra-Comique, with Laure Cinti-Damoreau and Louis-Antoine-Eléonore Ponchard. Her second operetta, *La veilleuse, ou Les nuits de milady* (also to a text by Lemoine) was performed at the Théâtre du Gymnase, Paris, on 27 September 1869, with Irma Marié, Pradeau and Vois. Puget's output also includes a few solo piano works and *Mystère de Paris*, a set of quadrilles for four hands.

BIBLIOGRAPHY

CohenE; *FétisB*; *FétisBS*; *Grove1* (G. Chouquet); *PazdirekH*; *SchmidlD*

P. Scudo: 'Esquisse d'une histoire de la romance', *Critique et littérature musicales*, i (Paris, 1850, enlarged 3/1856)

F. Clément and P. Larousse: *Dictionnaire lyrique* (Paris, 1867–81, 2/1897, 3/1905 ed. A. Pougin as *Dictionnaire des opéras*)

JUDY S. TSOU

Q

Qü, Xixian (*b* Shanghai, 23 Sept 1919). Chinese composer. From 1940 to 1948 she studied the piano and composition at the Shanghai Academy, where her teachers included Tan Xiaolin, a former pupil of Paul Hindemith and one of the ·founders of modern Chinese music. After graduating she taught at the Beipin (now Beijing) Arts School. In 1949 she began to compose professionally, working with the Central Song and Dance Ensemble (later the Central National Music Ensemble) and the Central Philharmonic Society. She was elected vice-chairman of the Chinese Musicians' Association in 1985. A large proportion of Qü's compositions are vocal. She is particularly interested in choral writing, and her keen exploration of different voice combinations has resulted in some highly individual effects. Her many choral arrangements of folksongs have won praise in China.

WORKS
selective list

Vocal: Hongjun genjüdi dahechang [Cantata of the Red Army Base], solo vv, chorus, orch, 1954; Mu ge [Pastoral Song], chorus, 1954; 2 albums of solo songs (1985); Ba wode naiminger jiao [Call me by my Pet Name], chorus, pf; Wusuli chuange [Boatmen's Song], chorus, pf

Film scores: Qinchun zhi ge [Song of Youth], 1959; Hognqi pu [Music of the Red Flag], 1960; Luotuo Xiangzi [Xiangzi the Camel], 1981

YANDI YANG

Quinault, Marie-Anne-Catherine (*b* Strasbourg, 26 Aug 1695; *d* Paris, 1791). French singer and composer. She was the daughter of the actor Jean Quinault (1656–1728) and the sister of Jean-Baptiste Maurice Quinault. Mlle Quinault (known as 'l'aînée') made her début at the Paris Opéra in 1709 in Lully's *Bellérophon* and remained there until 1713; she acted and sang at the Comédie Française, 1714–22. According to Fétis, she composed several motets for the royal chapel at Versailles, one of which won for her the decoration of the order of St Michel, never before given to a woman.

BIBLIOGRAPHY
FétisB

JAMES R. ANTHONY

Quinciani, Lucia (*b c*1566; *fl c*1611). Italian composer. She was a pupil of Marc'Antonio Negri and may have worked in Verona or Venice. She is known by a single composition, a setting of 'Udite lagrimosi spirti d'Averno, udite', from G. B. Guarini's *Il pastor fido* (Act 3 scene vi), included in the second book of Marc'Antonio Negri's *Affetti amorosi* (Venice, 1611), identified in the table as 'della Sig.ra Lucia Quinciani, sua Discepola'. The book consists mainly of monodies and duets, with a concluding cantata on a text by G. B. Marino. Quinciani's piece is the earliest published monody by a woman. Nothing further is known about her. She appears not to be related to the composer Lucrezio Quintiani.

BIBLIOGRAPHY
SartoriB; SchmidlD
J. Bowers: 'Women Composers in Italy, 1566–1700', *Women Making Music: the Western Art Tradition, 1150–1950*, ed. J. Bowers and J. Tick (Urbana and Chicago, 1986), 116–67, esp. 118, 163

THOMAS W. BRIDGES

R

Radermacher, Erika (*b* Eschweiler, 16 April 1936). Swiss pianist, singer and composer of German birth. She studied the piano in Cologne and Vienna, won major prizes in Germany and Austria, and has performed throughout Europe. After marrying the Swiss composer Urs Peter Schneider she moved to Switzerland, where she was appointed to teach at the Berne Conservatory. She is a member of the Berne contemporary music group Ensemble Neue Horizonte. As a singer one of her principal interests is experimental improvisation. She began to compose in the 1970s and many works have been recorded by Swiss radio. Her compositions include the opera *Das Tanzlegendchen* (1990), a Concerto grosso for strings (1987–8), *Der Tod des Empedokles* for two pianos with ensemble or orchestra ad lib (1992) and a considerable number of chamber works.

WORKS
selective list

Stage: Das Tanzlegendchen, op.26 (opera, after G. Keller), 1990
Orch: Concerto grosso, op.22, str, 1987–8; Der Tod des Empedokles, op.31, 2 pf, opt. ens/orch, 1992
Vocal: 7 Rosen später, op.5 (P. Célan), S, ens, 1981; 21 Eisgesänge, op.23, 1v, pf, 1988
Inst: Alle Uhren, selbst die trägsten, op.4, 11 fantasies after E. T. A. Hoffmann, 2 pf, 1981–3; Chi order X, op.7, variations, vn, pf, 1983; Pf Trio, op.12, 1985; Str Qt, op.13, 1970, rev. 1984–5; Ein apoka-lyptisches Fragment, op.17, ritual after K. von Günderode, fl, 2 gongs, 1987; 7 Verehrungen der Glühwürmer und der Selbstzufriedenheit, op.20, pf, 1987; 11 Lobgesänge auf das Erwachen der Blüten und der Frösche, op.24, fl, pf, antique cymbals, 1989; 15 Ahnungen der Vergänglichkeit allen Lebens und der Vogelscheuche, op.25, hn, pf, 1989; 5 Glücksrufe, op.28, 3 trbn, 4 gongs, 1990

CHRIS WALTON

Radigue, Eliane (*b* Paris, 24 Jan 1932). French composer. She studied in Paris with Pierre Schaeffer at the Studio d'Essai (1957–8) and with Pierre Henry at the Apsone-Cabasse Studio (1967–8). In 1970 she was artist-in-residence at New York University's School of Arts, and she has subsequently worked in the electronic music studios at the University of Iowa and the California Institute of the Arts (1973), as well as making regular visits to the USA to give concerts of her works. Radigue became a disciple of Tibetan Buddhism in 1975, and after four years of study began a large-scale cycle of works based on the life of the Tibetan master Milarepa. Her electronic works include *Ohmt* (1968), *Adnos* (1974), *Jetsun Mila* (1986), *Kyema* (1988) and *Kailasha* (1991).

JEAN-NOËL VON DER WEID

Raffaelli, Francesca. *See* CACCINI, FRANCESCA.

Rainier, Priaulx (*b* Howick, Natal, 3 Feb 1903; *d* Besse-en-Chandesse, France, 10 Oct 1986). South African-English composer of English-Huguenot origin. After early childhood in Zululand, she entered the South African College of Music, Cape Town, as a violin student (1913); in 1920 her playing won her the Cape University Scholarship to the RAM. She then settled permanently in London, earning her living as a violinist and teacher until 1935, when an anonymous grant enabled her to concentrate on composition. In 1937 she studied with Nadia Boulanger for three months, and she was a professor of composition at the RAM (1943–61). In 1952 she won the John Clementi Collard Fellowship. After her retirement in 1961 she received many commissions, some funded by the Arts Council of Great Britain (*Vision and Prayer*; the *Concertante* for two winds and orchestra) and others by the BBC (Cello Concerto; *Ploërmel*); *Aequora lunae* was written for the Cheltenham Festival and *Due canti e finale* for Yehudi Menuhin. In June 1982 she received the honorary DMus from the University of Cape Town. She had a long association with the Worshipful Company of Musicians, becoming a Freeman (1955) and their first Lady Liveryman (1983); after her death they established a Priaulx Rainier Fund for young composers at the RAM and the University of Cape Town.

Rainier developed a fastidious language drawing little from other 20th-century styles. Rather, the most important influences were the language and music of the Zulus, and the natural sounds of their country; beyond this, the visual insights of Barbara Hepworth and Ben Nicholson, with both of whom she had contact, greatly extended the range of her music. She came to the attention of a wider public after the success of the String Quartet, a work whose originality is particularly clear in the scherzo and in the finale. Crystalline textures and short ostinato rhythms assist in the building of fast movements independent of Bartók and Stravinsky and of more conventional styles. Although Rainier never consciously used African musical techniques, these movements obviously reflect her origins, and at the same time introduce a characteristic distancing, both literally – as if sounds were being heard across the open air – and metaphorically, the product of classically disciplined musical thinking. Subsequent works of the 1940s emphasize rhythmic novelty, chief among them the Clarinet Suite and the *Barbaric Dance Suite*, where, despite its title, the dominant impression is of delicacy rather than savagery.

At this time Rainier's harmony was triadic and even diatonic; chromaticism was the consequence of melodic inflection and bitonality. Her melodic writing was typified by concise motivic phrases. The promise of functional harmony and extended melodic line was amply realized in *Requiem*, a work of beauty and passion, whose simple yet expressive neo-tonal harmony and incantatory solo part mark the culmination of a period in her output. During the 1960s her music became more compressed, owing in part to a fondness for clusters and an associated emphasis on melodic semitones and minor 9ths, in part to a continuing use of short, pulsating rhythmic figures, but more particularly to the gestures themselves. These retain Rainier's meticulously polished sounds, but are isolated, often abruptly contrasted, and highly concentrated, suggesting an energy activated only briefly. Continuity is achieved more through patterns of timbre and texture than through consistent impulse. A more relaxed expression is evident in the works of the 1970s, although the uncompromisingly objective sounds remain distinctive.

Except for *Quanta* and *Due canti e finale*, which were bequeathed to the British

Priaulx Rainier, 1981

Library, her manuscripts are housed at the University of Cape Town; a collection of her papers is held at the RAM.

WORKS

Orch: Sinfonia da camera, str, 1947; Phalaphala, dance conc., 1960; Vc Conc., 1963–4; Aequora lunae, 1966–7; Ploërmel, wind insts, perc, 1972–3; Due canti e finale, vn, orch, 1977; Concertante, ob, cl, orch, 1980–81; Celebration, vn, orch, 1984

Chamber and solo inst: Str Qt, 1939; Suite, cl, pf, 1943; Sonata, va, pf, 1946; Barbaric Dance Suite, pf, 1949; 5 Pieces, kbd, 1955; 6 Pieces, 5 wind insts, 1957; Pastoral Triptych, ob, 1958–9; Trio-Suite, pf trio, 1960; Quanta, ob, str trio, 1961–2; Suite, vc/va, 1963–5; Str Trio, 1965–6; Quinque, hpd, 1971; Organ Gloriana, org, 1972; Primordial Canticles, org, 1974; Grand Duo, vc, pf, 1982

Vocal: 3 Greek Epigrams (Anyte of Tegea, trans. R. Aldington), S, pf, 1937; Dance of the Rain (E. Marais, trans. U. Krige), T/S, gui, 1947; Ubunzima [Misfortune], T/S, gui, 1948; Cycle for Declamation (J. Donne), T/S unacc., 1953; Requiem (D. Gascoigne), T, SATB unacc., 1955–6; The Bee Oracles (E. Sitwell), T/Bar, fl, ob, vn, vc, hpd, 1969; Vision and Prayer (D. Thomas), T, pf, 1973; Prayers from the Ark, T, harp, 1974–5

Principal publisher: Schott

BIBLIOGRAPHY

W. Glock: 'The Music of Priaulx Rainier', *The Listener*, xxxviii (1947), 872

J. Amis: 'Priaulx Rainier', *MT*, xcvi (1955), 354–7

F. Routh: *Contemporary British Music* (London, 1972), 346ff

T. Baxter: 'Priaulx Rainier: a Study of her Musical Style', *Composer*, no.60 (1977), 19–26

H. H. van der Spuy: 'Priaulx Rainier', *Musicus*, vii/1 (1979), 7–14

Obituaries: 'Miss Priaulx Rainier: Notable Composer and Teacher', *The Times* (13 Oct 1986); J. Amis, *Independent* (15 Oct 1986); *Gramophone*, lxiv (1986–7), 810; *MT*, cxxvii (1986), 705; *Das Orchester*, xxxiv (1986), 1945

J. Opie: *Come and Listen to the Stars Singing: Priaulx Rainier, a Pictorial Biography* (Penzance, 1988)

H. H. van der Spuy: *The Compositions of Priaulx Rainier: an Annotated Catalogue* (diss., U. of Stellenbosch, 1988)

—— : 'Priaulx Rainier: 1903–86', *Musicus*, xxi/i (1993), 47

IAN KEMP, HUBERT VAN DER SPUY

Rampazzi, Teresa (*b* Vicenza, 31 Oct 1914). Italian composer and pianist. She graduated in piano and composition from the Conservatorio di Musica G. Verdi, Milan, where her teachers included Arrigo Pedrollo. Later, in Verona, she became acquainted with Camillo Togni, Franco Donatoni (both of whom dedicated compositions to her), Sylvano Bussotti and, most importantly, Bruno Maderna, whom she had met a few years earlier in Venice and with whom she became very close friends. It was Maderna who introduced her to the Darmstadt summer courses, which she continued to attend until 1959. As a pianist Rampazzi committed herself to the dissemination of contemporary music, giving many first performances both as a soloist and as a member of the Bartók Trio (which included the clarinettist Elio Peruzzi and the violinist Edda Pitton). After moving to Padua she concentrated on electroacoustic experimentation, and in 1965 she and Enio Chioggio founded the group Nuove Proposte Sonore, one of the main research projects of the period; Alvise Vindolin also collaborated with them. In 1967 she was invited to realize several works at the experimental studio of Radio Warsaw. The next year she set up a pilot course in electronic music at the Conservatorio C. Pollini, Padua, and in 1972 was appointed lecturer in the subject there. Her international reputation increased: she was invited to the Sonology Institute of the University of Utrecht (1974) and to Stockholm (1976), and twice won second prizes for electronic music at the international festival at Bourges (for *Whit the Light Pen*, 1976, and *Atmen noch*, 1980). When the activities of Nuove Proposte Sonore ceased in 1972, Rampazzi and her pupils at the Padua Conservatory began a collaboration with the University of Padua which in 1979 became the university's Centro di Sonologia Computazionale, one of the most important computer music research centres in Italy.

WORKS
selective list

Masse, 1968; Glassrequiem, 1973; Breath, 1974; Whit the Light Pen, 1976; Fluxus, 1979; Atmen noch, 1980; Geometrie in moto, 1982; Requiem per Ananda, 1982; Quasi un haiku, 1987; Polifonie di novembre, 1989

PAOLA DAMIANI

Ran, Shulamit (*b* Tel-Aviv, 21 Oct 1949). Israeli composer and pianist. She studied composition with Alexander Uriah Boskovich and Paul Ben Haim and the piano with Miriam Boskovich and Emma Gorochov. In 1962, already an accomplished composer, she was awarded scholarships for study in the USA by the America-Israel Cultural Foundation and Mannes College, from which she graduated in 1967. While at Mannes she studied the piano with Nadia Reisenberg and composition with Norman Dello Joio; subsequently she studied the piano with Dorothy Taubman and, in 1976, composition with Ralph Shapey. As a pianist, she performed her *Capriccio* with the New York PO under Leonard Bernstein in 1963 and gave tours of the USA and Europe between 1968 and 1973; in July 1971 she gave the première of her *Concert Piece* with the Israel PO under Zubin Mehta. After a year as artist-in-residence at St Mary's University, Halifax, Nova Scotia (1972–3), she joined the faculty of the University of Chicago where in 1978 she became associate professor (later professor) of composition. In 1987 she was a visiting professor at Princeton University and in 1990 was appointed composer-in-residence with the Chicago SO. She has received Guggenheim fellowships (1977, 1990), a grant from the Illinois Arts Council for the completion of *Excursions* (1980), and commissions from the Fromm Foundation (*Ensembles for Seventeen*), the NEA (Piano Concerto), the radio station WFMT, Chicago (*Apprehensions*, *Fanfare*), the Da Capo Chamber Players (*Private Game*) and individual performers. *Ensembles for Seventeen* was performed at the Berkshire Music Festival in 1975, and *Hyperbolae* was selected as the required piece for the Second Annual Artur Rubinstein International Piano Competition (Israel, 1977). Her String Quartet no.2 'Vistas' (1989) was commissioned for the Taneyev String Quartet of Leningrad; her symphony (1989–90), commissioned by the Philadelphia Orchestra, won the Pulitzer Prize in 1991.

Ran's early works were influenced by the somewhat conservative 'Mediterranean' style of her teachers Paul Ben Haim and Alexander

Boscovich. Later, however, she turned to more avant-garde styles, making use of tonal nuclei and creating a driving rhythmic energy, while retaining clarity of form. Her output also includes electronic music, which she studied in the Netherlands in 1969.

WORKS
selective list

Orch: Capriccio, pf, orch, 1963; Sym. Poem, pf, orch, 1967; 10 Children's Scenes, 1970 [arr. of early pf work]; Concert Piece, pf, orch, 1971; Pf Conc., 1977; Conc., 1986; Sym., 1989–90

Inst: Qt, fl, cl, vc, pf, 1967; 3 Fantasy Pieces, vc, pf, 1972; Double Vision, ww qnt, brass qnt, pf, 1976; For an Actor: Monologue for Cl, 1978; Fantasy Variations, vc, 1979; Private Game, cl, vc, 1979; Excursions, vn, vc, pf, 1980; A Prayer, cl, b cl, bn, hn, timp, 1981; Str Qt no.1, 1984; Concerto da camera I, ww qnt, 1985; Concerto da camera II, cl, str qt, pf, 1987; East Wind, fl, 1988; Str Qt no.2 'Vistas', 1989

Kbd: Structures, pf, 1968; Sonata brevis, hpd, 1975; Hyperbolae, pf, 1976; Sonata Waltzer, pf, 1981–2; Verticals, pf, 1982

Vocal: Harzvi Israel Eulogie, Mez, fl, harp, str qt, 1968, arr. Mez, chamber orch; 7 Japanese Love Poems, Mez, pf, 1968; O the Chimneys (N. Sachs), Mez, ens, tape, 1969; Ensembles for 17 (W. Shakespeare: Othello), S, 16 insts, 1974–5; Apprehensions (S. Plath), 1v, cl, pf, 1979; Adonai malach (Ps xciii), cantor, pic, ob, cl, hn, 1985; Amichai Songs, Mez, ob/eng hn, va da gamba, hpd, 1985

Other: The Laughing Man (television programme), 1967; Fanfare, 2 taped S, 1981; a few early works, some withdrawn

Principal publishers: C. Fischer, Israel Music Institute, Presser

BIBLIOGRAPHY

K. Monson: 'As a Composer, Shulamit's no also-Ran', *Panorama – Chicago Daily News* (5–6 April 1975)
'Career Alternatives in Music: Some Advice from Outstanding Women Musicians', *The Instrumentalist*, xxxi/5 (1976), 34
'In Response (questionnaire to women composers)', *PNM*, xx/1–2 (1982–3), 311
WILLIAM Y. ELIAS, MARGARETH OWENS

Raschenau, Maria Anna de (*fl* early 18th century). Composer, active in Vienna. Nothing is known about her training or life. Egon Wellesz believed that she and her contemporaries Caterina Benedicta Grazianini, Maria Grimani and Camilla de Rossi were regular canonesses (certainly, they were not employed as singers or musicians by the court). Raschenau is known only through her oratorio *Le sacre visioni di Santa Teresa*, on a text by M. A. Signorini, which was performed on 20 March 1703. The score, formerly in the Österreichische Nationalbibliothek, was no longer listed in that library's catalogue by 1991 and is assumed to be lost.

BIBLIOGRAPHY

SchmidlDS
E. Wellesz: 'Die Opern und Oratorien in Wien 1660–1708', *SMw*, vi (1919), 5–138, esp. 89
SUZANNE G. CUSICK

Raum [Hodges], **Elizabeth** (*b* Berlin, NH, 13 Jan 1945). American, later Canadian, composer and oboist. She was educated in Boston and graduated as an oboist from the Eastman School of Music (BMus 1966). She had an active career as an oboist, in Boston, in Halifax, Nova Scotia, from 1968 as principal oboist in the Atlantic SO, and from 1975 in Regina, Saskatchewan, where she eventually became principal oboist in the Regina SO. She was one of the founding members there of the Contemporary Directions Ensemble. Before embarking on operas, Raum wrote the poetry for Thomas Schudel's *Winterpiece* and won a top place in a Saskatchewan writers' short story contest; she has written the librettos for all her operas. She completed her first opera (her first major work) in 1979. In 1983 she took the MMus in composition at the University of Regina. It was *The Garden of Alice* (1984), a Kafkaesque *Alice in Wonderland*, that established her as an opera composer.

Raum's conservative musical style makes her music accessible, and frequently more popular with audiences than with critics. Her instrumental pieces are eclectic and range from pieces for full orchestra to chamber, keyboard, vocal, electroacoustic and band works; in her operas she writes idiomatically for chamber ensemble. *Eos: the Dream of Nicholas Flood Davin* explores the struggles that faced the Canadian politician who committed suicide in 1901 and brought culture to western Canada.

WORKS
selective list

Stage: The Final Bid (opera, 1, Raum), Regina, Open Stage Theatre, 27 Feb 1981; The Garden of Alice (opera, 2, Raum, after L. Carroll: *Alice in Wonderland*), Regina, Globe Theatre, 19 Jan 1985, condensed version, Regina, Norman MacKenzie Art Gallery, 4 March 1984; Thunder in a Concave Vacuum (multi-media, with tape, musicians, actors, lighting, audience participation, Regina, Globe Theatre, 10 May 1986; Mulligan's Toy Shop (musical for children); Eos: the Dream of Nicholas Flood Davin (opera, 3, Raum), Regina, Norman MacKenzie Art Gallery, 26 Jan 1991

Orch: Evolution: a Theme with Variations, str, 1985; The Adventures of Ian the Oboe, 1985; Fantasy, double orch, 1988

GAYNOR G. JONES

Ravinale, Irma (*b* Naples, 1 Oct 1937). Italian composer and teacher. She graduated from the Conservatorio di Musica S Cecilia in Rome, where she studied composition with Goffredo Petrassi, as well as the piano, choral music, choral conducting and band instrumentation, and at the same time engaged in literary research. She has received many awards for her compositions, which embrace many musical genres and have received performances by leading musicians both in Italy and abroad. Particularly noteworthy is her one-act opera *Il ritratto di Dorian Gray* (after Oscar Wilde; 1970), which was given a concert première by RAI in Turin (1975). Ravinale has always been closely involved with teaching and in 1966 was appointed to the chair of composition at the Conservatorio di S Cecilia in Rome; her composition courses there proved a training ground for many well-known Italian musicians. In 1982 she was appointed director of the Conservatorio di Musica S Pietro a Majella in Naples, but in 1989 she returned to Rome as director of the conservatory.

WORKS
selective list

Opera: Il ritratto di Dorian Gray (1, after O. Wilde), 1970, concert perf., Turin, RAI, 1975

Orch: Conc., ob, hn, timp, str, 1967; Conc., str, 1968; Sinfonia concertante, gui, orch, 1972; Elegia del silenzio, chamber orch, 1988

Inst: Sequentia, gui, str qt, 1975; Per Ada, cl, 1984; Sombras, gui, 1982

Vocal: Spleen, Bar, orch, 1976; La ballata del vassallo, female vv, 1989

PAOLA DAMIANI

Ravissa, Mme [first name unknown] (*fl* late 18th century). Italian singer, keyboard player, teacher and composer. Originally from Turin, but in Paris at least from 1778 until 1783, Madame Ravissa quickly made her talents known by singing airs by Pasquale Anfossi and Antonio Sacchini at the Concert Spirituel (25 March 1778), publishing a collection of *Six sonates pour le clavecin ou le forte piano* (op.1, 1778), and finally advertising herself in the *Almanach Musical* variously as a teacher of composition, harp, harpsichord, *chant italien* and *goût italien*. The 1778 issue (iv, 77) describes the compositional style of her sonatas as sparkling – noting in particular that 'ces transitions hardies' were more daring than French composers would permit themselves – and praises her honesty and character, not omitting to remark upon the popularity and availability of the lessons she gave at her home in the rue St André-des-Arts.

JULIE ANNE SADIE

Recli, Giulia (*b* Milan, 4 Dec 1890; *d* Milan, 19 Dec 1970). Italian composer. She studied the humanities, singing and the piano, and composition with Ildebrando Pizzetti and Victor de Sabata. She received several important awards, including the 'Arti' prize of Trieste, and many public honours. She was the first Italian woman composer to enter the symphonic repertory and to attract the attention of such institutions as the Teatro alla Scala, Milan, and the Metropolitan Opera, New York. She was also a music critic and vice-secretary of the Sindacato Musicisti Italiani. Among her large output, covering many genres, the lyric opera *Cento ducati e Belluccia* (after Giulio Cesare Croce) and the ballet *Piume d'oro* are particularly noteworthy, as are many of her songs (of which there are more than 200). The songs are often grouped into cycles and include Spanish, Greek and Persian themes.

WORKS
selective list

Stage: Cento ducati e Belluccia (azione fiabesca, after G. C. Croce); Eliduc; Piume d'oro (ballet); Villidiana (leggenda)

Orch: Alba dell'anima, sym. poem, 1914; L'isola dei pastori, 1953

Choral orch: Alisa e Dafni, poemetto pastorale, 1913; Cantate Domino, 1927

Other vocal: Invocazione, chorus, pf, 1936; Perla via del Calvario, S chorus, pf, 1936; 2 masses, Requiem, *c*200 songs

Chamber: Str Qt, 1913–14; Leggenda, vn, pf; Pf Trio; Vn Sonata

PAOLA DAMIANI

Rehnqvist, Karin (*b* Stockholm, 21 Aug 1957). Swedish composer. After graduating as a teacher in 1980 from the Kungliga Musikhögskolan, Stockholm, she spent a further four years studying composition with, among others, Gunnar Bucht and Brian Ferneyhough. In 1976 she became conductor of the amateur choir Stans Kör and was elected a member of the Society of Swedish Composers in 1985. Her work for string orchestra, *Stråk*, drew considerable critical attention after its first performance (in Reykjavík) in 1982, as did *Davids nimm*, for three women's voices, in 1984. She is particularly noted for her thorough knowledge of the voice, and also for her use of folk material, often boldly transformed, as in *Davids nimm*, *Puksånger-lockrop* and the violin concerto *Skrin*.

WORKS
selective list

Orch: Stråk, str, 1982; Kast, str, 1986; Vn Conc. 'Skrin', 1990 [with S. Ahlbäck]

Chamber: Lod, t rec, archlute, vc, 1986; Time of Taromir, 11 str, fl/vn, cl/va, 1987
Elec: Musik från vårt klimat [Music from our Climate], 1982
Pf: Dans [Dance], 1984
Vocal: Davids nimm, 3 female vv, 1984; Tilt. Drama, mixed chorus unacc., 1985; Sång ur Sagan om Fatumeh [Song from the Saga of Fatumeh], male chorus 12vv, 1988; Här är jag. Var är du? [Here I am. Where are you?], girls' vv, 1989; Puksånger-lockrop, 2 female vv, perc, 1989; Triumf att finnas till [The Triumph of Being], girls' vv, 1990

EVA ÖHRSTRÖM

Reichardt [née Benda], **(Bernhardine) Juliane** (*b* Berlin, 14 May 1752; *d* Berlin, 9 May 1783). German singer, pianist and composer. A member of an illustrious musical family, she was the daughter of Franz Benda and his wife Franziska Louise, the sister of Maria Carolina Wolf, and the mother of Louise Reichardt. She had a reputation as an unusually expressive singer and even before her marriage to J. F. Reichardt in 1777 was a published composer. Two piano sonatas and about 30 songs appeared during her lifetime in almanacs, in a collection of *Oden und Lieder* (1779–81) by her husband and in her *Lieder und Klaviersonaten* (Hamburg, 1782).

BIBLIOGRAPHY
Choron-FayolleD; *GerberL*; *SchillingE*†
A. Krille: *Beiträge zur Geschichte der Musikerziehung und Musikausübung der deutschen Frau (von 1750 bis 1820)* (Berlin, 1938), 174–5
F. Lorenz: *Die Musikerfamilie Benda: Franz Benda und seine Nachkommen* (Berlin, 1967), 101ff

NANCY B. REICH

Reichardt, Louise (*b* Berlin, 11 April 1779; *d* Hamburg, 17 Nov 1826). German composer and singing teacher. The daughter of J. F. Reichardt and his first wife, Juliane (née Benda), Louise Reichardt was educated by her father. She knew many of the philosophers and poets of the German Romantic era, and such literary figures as the Grimm brothers, Ludwig Tieck, Novalis (F. L. von Hardenberg), Joseph von Eichendorff, Clemens Brentano and Ludwig von Arnim frequented her home in Giebichenstein (near Halle) and admired her song settings. In 1809 she settled in Hamburg, where she supported herself as a singing teacher and composer. She also organized and directed a women's chorus which became the nucleus of the Hamburg Singverein (1819). Reichardt was known for her untiring efforts in the production of Handel oratorios; she translated the texts and prepared the choruses for performances conducted by her male colleagues. She composed more than 90 songs and

choruses, both sacred and secular, which were popular throughout the 19th century and appear in many anthologies; a number have achieved the status of folksongs. Reichardt's songs have unusually graceful and lyrical vocal lines with inappositely simple piano accompaniments. Among her best – and best known – songs are *Hoffnung* ('Wenn die Rosen blühen', F. G. Wetzel), *Unruhiger Schlaf* (Arnim), and *Nach Sevilla*, *Für die Laute* and *Der Spinnerin Nachtlied*, all to texts by Brentano.

WORKS
printed works published in Hamburg unless otherwise stated

Editions:
L. Reichardt: Ausgewählte Lieder, ed. G. Rheinhardt (Munich, 1922)
L. Reichardt: Songs, ed. N. B. Reich (New York, 1981)
Songs: 12 deutsche Lieder (Zerbst, 1800), collab. J. F. Reichardt; 12 deutsche und italiänische romantische Gesänge (Berlin, 1806); 6 Canzoni (P. Metastasio) (1811); 12 Gesänge (1811); 12 Gesänge (1819); 12 Gesänge, gui acc. (Breslau, before 1819); 6 Lieder (Novalis [F. L. von Hardenberg]) (1819); Christliche, liebliche Lieder (*c*1820), arr. 2–4vv unacc. (1827; Leipzig, 2/1836); Choral-Buch, 1822, *D-Hs*; 7 romantische Gesänge (L. Tieck) (*c*1822); 6 geistliche Lieder unserer besten Dichter, arr. 4 female vv, pf (1823); 6 deutsche Lieder (*c*1826); Choralbuch (Basle, *c*1827); Des Schäfers Klage (J. W. von Goethe) (n.d.); 6 deutsche Gesänge (n.d.)
Arr. of J. F. Reichardt: Weihnachts-Cantilene (M. Claudius), vs (Hamburg, 1827)

BIBLIOGRAPHY
GerberNL; *SchillingE*†
M. G. W. Brandt: *Leben der Luise Reichardt* (Karlsruhe, 1858, 2/1865)
H. Weber: 'Luise Reichardt', *Neujahrsgeschenk von der Allgemeinen Musik-Gesellschaft in Zürich*, lxviii (1880), 3–20
A. Krille: *Beiträge zur Geschichte der Musikerziehung und Musikausübung der deutschen Frau (von 1750 bis 1820)* (Berlin, 1938), 123ff
F. Lorenz: *Die Musikerfamilie Benda: Franz Benda und seine Nachkommen* (Berlin, 1967), 123ff
N. B. Reich: 'Louise Reichardt', *Ars musica, musica scientia: Festschrift Heinrich Hüschen* (Cologne, 1980), 369–77
—— : Introduction, *L. Reichardt: Songs* (New York, 1981)

NANCY B. REICH

Reid, Sally [Sarah] **Johnston** (*b* East Liverpool, OH, 30 Jan 1948). American composer and oboist. She studied music education and the oboe at Abilene Christian University, Texas (BME 1969), and music theory and composition at Hardin-Simmons University, Texas (MM 1971). She gained the PhD (1980) from the University of Texas at Austin, where she studied composition with Karl Korte and the oboe with Richard

Blair. She became professor of theory and composition at Abilene Christian University and director of the electronic music studios, and has been a guest performer with the Abilene PO. She is editor of the *ILWC Journal*.

Reid composes for both acoustic and electronic forces, often combining them. Her works have been performed throughout the USA and Europe.

WORKS
selective list

Dramatic: Healing (chamber opera, 8 scenes, C. Willerton), 1986

Inst: Wasatch Symphony, wind band, 1970; Escape Wheel for Five, 3 cl, db, pf, 1976; 3 miniatures: eng hn, tape, 1984, rev. 1987, vn, tape, 1984, a sax, tape, 1985; Suite for the Ears of a Child, pf, 1985; A Rainbow Shines There, rhapsody, orch, digital sounds, 1991: A Carousel Fantasy, brass qnt, synth, 1993

Vocal: 5 Haiku, Mez, pf, 1973, rev. 1986; Note the Silence, 1v, brass qnt, pf, perc, 1975; Tear on a Child's Cheek (J. Shieman), 5 haiku, Mez, pf, 1987; I cry out in the night (Ps lxxxviii), chorus, tape, 1988; Songs from Alaska, Mez, cl, 1993–

Tape: Gyro-Space, 1979; Celebration in Sound and Space, 1981; Ballet of the 13 Clocks, 1982; 10 Miniatures, 1983

Principal publisher: American Music Center

BIBLIOGRAPHY

B. Grigsby: 'Women Composers of Electronic Music in the United States', *The Musical Woman: an International Perspective*, i: *1983*, ed. J. L. Zaimont and others (Westport, CT, 1984), 151–96

E. Hinkle-Turner: 'Recent Electro-Acoustic Music by Women: a Survey', *ILWC Journal* (1992), Oct, 8–14

S. Mabry: 'New Directions: Miniatures', *NATS Journal* (1993), May–June, 29

ELIZABETH HINKLE-TURNER

Reinagle, Caroline. See ORGER, CAROLINE.

Reiset, Maria Felicita de. See GRANDVAL, MARIE.

Reiset de Tesier, Maria. See GRANDVAL, MARIE.

Reisserová [née Kühnlová], **Julie** (*b* Prague, 9 Oct 1888; *d* Prague, 25 Feb 1938). Czech composer. She studied composition in Prague with J. B. Foerster (1919–21), in Berne with Ernst Hohlfeld, and in Paris with Albert Roussel (1924–9) and with Nadia Boulanger at the Ecole Normale. Her works, which blend neo-romanticism and impressionism, were frequently given during her lifetime by eminent performers. As the wife of a Czech diplomat and musicologist, she played some part in spreading a knowledge of modern Czech music outside her own country.

WORKS
selective list

Březen [March] (song cycle, Reisserová, E. Mörike, Chin. poets), 1923–5, version for S, orch, 1931; Suita, orch, 1928–31; Esquisses, pf, 1928–32; Pastorale maritimo, orch, 1933; Předjaří [Early Spring], coloratura S, orch, 1936; Slavnostní den [Festive Day], women's vv, 1936

BIBLIOGRAPHY

ČSHS

J. Vacková: *Julie Reisserová: osobnost a dílo* [Personality and Works] (Prague, 1948)

ANNA ŠERÝCH

Renard, Claire (*b* Neuilly-sur-Seine, 10 Dec 1944). French composer and educationist. She studied law in Paris (1963–6) and, later, music at the Paris Conservatoire (1971–3) and computer music at IRCAM (1983). She concentrated at first on research into contemporary music teaching (Institut National de l'Audiovisuel, 1973–7; Centre Européen pour la Recherche Musicale de Metz, 1978–81; IRCAM, 1983) and is the author of several works in this field, notably *Le geste musical* (Paris, 1982). As a composer, she allots pride of place to the voice, which is treated as an instrument. Her electroacoustic music is mainly for the theatre, dance or film, yet in handling her chosen sound sources – instrumental, vocal, *concrète* – she avoids purely electronic colours. She has worked increasingly on the role of time, memory and silence in music. Renard was awarded prizes by the Villa Medici and the Fondation Beaumarchais in 1990.

WORKS
selective list

Dramatic: Le brouillon du muet, tape, 1984; Dom Perlimplin et l'amour de Bélise en son jardin (F. García Lorca), tape, 1984; Chansons d'Ophélie (incid. music, W. Shakespeare: Hamlet), 1989; Dove esita l'immagine del mondo, 1v, perc, 1992

Vocal and inst: Musique à mots, musique à gestes, concert-spectacle, 1979; Le bonhomme-son, concert-spectacle, 1981; Qui pit bulle, children's vv, objects, 1985; Chips, children's vv, objects, 1986; La vallée close, 3 choruses, 6 perc, 1986; Toekoetschak, children's vv, db, 1987; La danse de l'air, chorus, wind insts, 1988; Pour Octave, concert-spectacle, 1v, fl, harp, db, perc, 1988; Un éclat de son rire, haute-contre, fl, db, 1989; Le 11 mai, 3 choruses (women's vv/children's vv), fl, vn, 7 cl, 5 a sax, 5 tpt, 5 gui, 5 pf, tuba, accordion, 3 perc, 1993; Brèves d'été (scenography A. Mecarelli), lute, harp, va de gamba, tape, lights, 1994

Other elec: Incertitude, 1973; Sable, perc, tape, 1985

Film scores: Arménie 1900 (dir. J. Kébadian), 1981; Pixel planète (dir. A. Longuet), 1985; La sirène et le ballon (dir. B. Germain), 1988

PIERRE SABY

Rennes, Catharina van (*b* Utrecht, 2 Aug 1858; *d* Amsterdam, 23 Nov 1940). Dutch music educator and composer. In contrast to many women composers van Rennes enjoyed a good deal of fame during her lifetime, both for her pedagogical activities and for her songs. After studying theory, singing and composition with Richard Hol and completing her vocal studies with Johan Messchaert, she began her career as a soloist, appearing in operas and oratorios. In 1887 she founded her own music school in Utrecht, teaching singing, music theory and Dalcroze rhythmical gymnastics. For more than 40 years she inspired a love of music in generations of young people. For the coronation of Queen Wilhelmina in 1898 she conducted her *Oranje-Nassau-Cantate* op.33, with a choir of 1800 children and orchestra. She composed more than a hundred children's songs, which, together with the songs written by Hendrika van Tussenbroek (1854–1943), were highly regarded for their freshness and appeal to children's imagination. She also composed vocal duets, trios and quartets with accompaniment for her own women's chorus.

BIBLIOGRAPHY
N. van der Elst: 'Catharina van Rennes', *Zes vrouwelijke componisten*, ed. H. Metzelaar (Zutphen, 1991), 63–84

HELEN METZELAAR

Respighi [née Olivieri-Sangiacomo], **Elsa** (*b* Rome, 24 March 1894). Italian composer and singer. She began studying the piano and solfeggio privately before enrolling at the Istituto Nazionale di Musica, Rome, in 1905. She attended the Liceo (later Conservatorio) di S Cecilia in 1911, studying the piano with Giovanni Sgambati, harmony and counterpoint with Remigio Renzi and composition with Ottorino Respighi, whom she married in 1919.

Her first published songs appeared in 1916 and were followed by others in 1918, 1919 and 1921 (issued by Ricordi). During her marriage, she gave precedence to her husband's career; they worked closely together, performing on tour in North and South America as well as in Europe, and she collaborated with him on the ballet version of *Gli uccelli* (1927) and the transcription of the Bach Passacaglia (1930–31).

After his death in 1936 she returned to composition, finishing the score of his nearly completed opera *Lucrezia* ('un atto in tre momenti'), with assistance from Ennio Porrino; it was performed at La Scala on 24 February 1937. The following year she and Claudio Guastalla (her husband's librettist) prepared a ballet version of the *Antiche arie e danze*. Guastalla wrote revealingly of their division of labour in his notebooks: 'I wrote the scenario as a guide for the choreographer, but it was Elsa who made the more important and enterprising contribution. Boldly and skilfully she cut, arranged and integrated Respighi's music'. The first of her articles on her husband's music, which appeared in 1938, culminated in a biography (*Ottorino Respighi: dati biografici ordinati*, Milan, 1954; Eng. trans., 1962); she later collaborated on *Il teatro di Respighi* (1978) with Leonardo Bragaglia. In 1969 she founded the Fondo Respighi in Venice to improve music teaching in Italy and she continued to a great age in the devoted promotion of her husband's music.

Respighi did in fact compose her most significant music as a widow: her work on *Lucrezia* stimulated her to compose *Il pianto della Madonna* (1938, text by Angelo Poliziano), a sacred drama, then *Alcesti* (1941), a one-act opera to a text by Guastalla. During World War II she composed *Tre canti corali* (Poliziano) for *a cappella* choir (1944) and, in 1945, a cantata for soprano and chamber ensemble, *Caterina da Siena* (Guastalla), and a three-act opera, *Samurai* (Guastalla). Other works include *Fior di neve* (a fairy opera in three acts), the *Serenata di maschere* (a symphonic poem), several orchestral suites and the *Intermezzo romantico* for viola, flute and harp.

PAOLA DAMIANI, JULIE ANNE SADIE

Reverdy, Michèle (*b* Alexandria, Egypt, 12 Dec 1943). French composer and musicologist. She studied at the Paris Conservatoire with Claude Ballif (analysis), Olivier Messiaen (composition) and Alain Weber (counterpoint), gaining first prize in counterpoint and in analysis and the composition prize. She also holds a degree in literature from the Sorbonne. Reverdy was resident at the Casa de Velasquez, Madrid, 1979–81, teaches analysis at the Paris Conservatoire and is a prolific composer who has received numerous commissions. Her many vocal works include four operas; *Un signe dans l'espace* (1990) was commissioned for Péniche Opéra (première March 1991). Hallmarks of her style include slow transformation of sound material, as in *Météores* and *Les jeux de Protée*, and the use of repetition, as in *Le cercle du vent*. Her sophisticated technique is always at the service of the emotional content of the music, whose substance is inspired by visual art and literature. Reverdy's writings include two books on the music of Olivier Messiaen: *L'oeuvre pour piano d'Olivier Messiaen* (Paris, 1978) and *L'oeuvre pour orchestre d'Olivier Messiaen* (Paris, 1988).

WORKS
selective list

Stage: Le chateau (opera, 10 tableaux, after F. Kafka), 1980–86; Mimodrame (ballet), 3 dancers, 2 trbn, 8 perc, 1981; La nuit qui suivit notre dernier dîner (opéra de poche, J.-C. Buchard), 1984, Saint-Brieuc, 30 May 1985; Vincent (7 paroles de la vie et de la mort de Vincent Van Gogh) (opera, M. S. Gille), 1984–9, Alessandria, 18 Sept 1990; Un signe dans l'espace (mimodrame, after I. Calvino: *Cosmicomics*), 1990, Paris, Aulnay-sous-Bois, L'espace Jacques Prévert, 18 March 1991
Orch, large ens: Météores, 17 insts, 1978; Scenic Railway, 16 insts, 1983; Le cercle du vent, orch, 1988
Other inst: Kaleidoscope, fl, hpd, 1975; Tétramorphie, va, perc, 1976; Figure, pf, 1976; Number One, gui, 1977; Les jeux de Protée, fl + a fl, va, harp, 1984; Messe pour les blancs-manteaux, org, 1990; L'intranquillité, str qt, 1991; En terre inconnue, pf trio, 1992
Choral: 3 fantaisies de Gaspard de la Nuit, chorus/ens 12vv, 1987; Propos félins (A. Reverdy), children's chorus, str orch, 1988; Messe pour la paix, coloratura S, Mez, Bar, large chorus, small chorus 16vv, congregation, org, 1991
Other vocal: Through the Looking Glass (L. Carroll), 7 scènettes, female v, cl, va, 2 trbn, pf, 1979; 7 enluminures (S. Poliakoff), S, cl, b cl, pf, perc, 1987

Principal publisher: Salabert

DANIEL KAWKA

Reynolds, Maria Hester. *See* PARK, MARIA HESTER.

Ricci, Cesarina (*b* Cingoli, nr Ancona, *c*1573; *fl* 1597). Italian composer. The book *Il primo libro de madrigali a cinque voci, con un dialogo a otto novamente composti & dati in luce*, 'di Madonna Cesarina Ricci de Tingoli' (Venice, 1597), contains 20 madrigals for which the cantus and quintus have not survived. The dedication to 'Monsignore il Cardinale San Giorgio' (Cinzio Passeri Aldobrandini, 1551–1610), is dated Monte Colombo (Colombano in Vogel), 10 February 1597. The texts include one by Ongaro, two by Tasso (one set in two parts), and one, the concluding *Dialogo*, by Guarini. Two of the madrigals are by the otherwise unknown Alberto Ghirlinzoni.

BIBLIOGRAPHY
SchmidlD; VogelB

THOMAS W. BRIDGES

Richards [Dale], **Kathleen** (*b* London, 29 June 1895; *d* Woking, 3 March 1984). English musicologist, composer and pianist. Her music studies were pursued privately with York Bowen and Fanny Davies for piano and with Benjamin Dale (whom she later married) for composition. Active as a pianist in the early part of her career, she broadcast frequently during the period 1927–31. From 1926 to 1928 she studied Swedish language and literature at University College, London, and she subsequently published translations from that and other languages (e.g. Hans Redlich's *Claudio Monteverdi* and Reimar Riefling's *Piano Pedalling*). She taught theoretical subjects at the Matthay School (1925–31) and taught and lectured for the Workers' Educational Association (1945–50, 1957). She served on the council of the Society of Women Musicians (1920–25, 1946–9) and acted as Ethel Smyth's musical executor in 1944. Under the name Kathleen Dale she published a biography of Brahms (London, 1970), personal reminiscences of, and critical articles on, Ethel Smyth (in *Music and Letters*, 1944, 1949) and two essays in *Ethel Smyth*, edited by C. St John (London, 1959).

WORKS
selective list

Chamber: Pastoral, vn, pf, 1920; 6 Duets, 2 vn, 1934; Wayfaring, vn, pf, 1939; 2 Divertimenti, 2 vn, 1940
Pf: Dance in Spring, 1919; Versailles, miniature suite, 1920; Greek Myths (Echo, Ganymede, Lethe), 1921; Minuet, Gavotte and Gigue, 1922; Frozen Landscape, 1948; Music, 5 pieces, 1951
Vocal: The God of love my shepherd is (J. Herbert), 1934; How long, O Lord, wilt thou forget (Ps xiii), 1934; The Horn (W. de la Mare), 1947; The Window (De la Mare), 1947; The Flight (De la Mare), 1949; Winter (De la Mare), 1949

FRANK DAWES/LEWIS FOREMAN

Richter, Marga (*b* Reedsburg, nr Madison, WI, 21 Oct 1926). American composer. At the Juilliard School she studied the piano with Rosalyn Tureck and composition with William Bergsma and Vincent Persichetti (BS, MS 1951). As an undergraduate she had three compositions performed at a Composer's Forum series in New York. Her Sonata for piano (1954), written for and recorded by Menahem Pressler, is one of four works commissioned by MGM Records; two commissions by the Harkness Ballet resulted in scores for *Abyss* (1964) and *Bird of Yearning* (1967–8). Inspired by two Georgia O'Keeffe paintings, her piano concerto (1968–74) makes effective use of an Indian raga; it is the first of a series of works,

Marga Richter

entitled *Landscapes of the Mind*, that share thematic material and were composed between 1968 and 1979. Her compositions have been performed by major orchestras and she has received grants, awards and commissions from the NEA, the Martha Baird Rockefeller Fund, the National Federation of Music Clubs and Meet the Composer. In her compositions she uses multi-textural structures in a modern idiom, creating works that are easily accessible and which have been enthusiastically received. Evidence of the continued expansion and enrichment of her musical expression is to be found in such works as *Out of Shadows and Solitude* (1985) and *Qhanri*, subtitled 'Tibetan Variations' (1988).

WORKS
selective list

Ballet scores: Abyss, 1964; Bird of Yearning, 1967–8
Orch: Lament, str, 1956; Aria and Toccata, va, str/pf, 1957; Landscapes of the Mind I, pf conc., 1968–74; Blackberry Vines and Winter Fruit, 1976; Spectral Chimes/Enshrouded Hills, 3 qnts, orch, 1980; Düsseldorf Conc., fl, va, harp, perc, str, 1981; Out of Shadows and Solitude, 1985; Quantum Quirks of a Quick Quaint Quark, 1991; '. . . beside the still waters', conc., pf, vn, vc, orch, 1992
Chamber and solo inst: Pf Sonata, 1954; Melodrama, 2 pf, 1958; Str Qt no.2, 1958; 8 Pieces, pf, 1961; Darkening of the Light, va, 1962, arr. vc, 1976; Soundings, hpd, 1965; Landscapes of the Mind II, vn, pf, 1971; Requiem, pf, 1978; Landscapes of the Mind III, pf, vn, vc, 1979; Sonora, 2 cl, pf, 1981; Seacliff Variations, pf, vn, va, vc, 1984; Obsessions,

trbn, 1986; Qhanri (Tibetan Variations), vc, pf, 1988
Vocal: Transmutation (Chin., trans. H. Hart), 1v, pf, 1948; 2 Chinese Songs, 1v, pf, 1953; Lament for Art O'Leary (E. O'Leary), S, pf, 1984; 7 Lieder (F. Tanzer), 1v, pf, 1985; Into my Heart, SATB/pf 4 hands/chamber ens, 1988

Principal publishers: Belwin-Mills, Broude, C. Fisher, G. Schirmer

BIBLIOGRAPHY

LePageWC, i
L. Van Gelder: 'For a Composer, a Week of Special Note', *New York Times* (9 April 1978)
C. Ammer: *Unsung: a History of Women in American Music* (Westport, CT, 1980)
D. P. Jezic: *Women Composers: the Lost Tradition Found* (New York, 1988)

JUDITH ROSEN

Riego, Teresa Clotilde del (*b* London, 7 April 1876; *d* London, 23 Jan 1968). English composer of English-Spanish parentage. Educated at the West Central College of Music, she was best known as a songwriter, although she also composed piano, chamber and orchestral works. She published more than 300 songs and ballads, many of which were sung by the great singers of her time, including Emma Albani, Nellie Melba, Gervase Elwes, Clara Butt and Maggie Teyte, and which became extremely popular. *O Dry Those Tears*, for example, sold 23000 copies within six weeks of its publication in 1901. Her best-known song,

Teresa Clotilde del Riego

Nadezhda Nikolayevna
Rimskaya-Korsakova:
photograph, early 1870s

Homing, has been published, recorded and broadcast in many different arrangements.

SOPHIE FULLER

Riley, Peter. *See* COLERIDGE-TAYLOR, AVRIL.

Rimskaya-Korsakova [née Purgold], **Nadezhda Nikolayevna** (*b* St Petersburg, 19/31 Oct 1848; *d* Petrograd, 24 May 1919). Russian pianist and composer. She studied with Anton Gerke (piano) and Nikolay Zaremba (theory) at the St Petersburg Conservatory (but did not graduate), and later with Nikolay Rimsky-Korsakov (composition and orchestration). During the 1860s and 70s, she was pianist for the music-making at the home of Alexander Dargomïzhsky (who taught her to reduce orchestral scores), then at the soirées sponsored by Balakirev and the *kuchka* ('The Five'): Musorgsky dubbed her 'our darling orchestra'. Her transcriptions include works (for piano four hands) by Dargomïzhsky, Rimsky-Korsakov, Tchaikovsky, Borodin

and Glazunov, and vocal scores of Rimsky-Korsakov's operas *Pskovityanka* ('The Maid of Pskov') and *Boyarïnya Vera Sheloga* ('The Noblewoman Vera Sheloga'). Autographs survive of her own symphonic tableau, *Zakoldovannoye mesto* ('The Bewitched Place'), after Nikolay Gogol, dedicated to Musorgsky, and a Scherzo in Bb for piano. After her marriage to Rimsky-Korsakov in 1872, her activity as a composer came gradually to naught, in part because of unfavourable comparison with her husband's works, but doubtless also because of family responsibilities (she bore seven children). She published recollections of Dargomïzhsky (*Russkaya molva*, 2 February 1913) and wrote a memoir of Musorgsky, and edited her husband's autobiography. Rimsky-Korsakov, Cui, Tchaikovsky, Borodin, Musorgsky and Glazunov dedicated works to her.

BIBLIOGRAPHY

ME (I. M. Yampol'sky)

N. A. Rimsky-Korsakov: *Letopis' moyey muzïkal'noy zhizni* [Chronicle of my Musical Life] (St Petersburg, 1909); Eng. trans., as *My Musical Life*, ed. C. van Vechten (New York, 1942) [incl. Eng. trans. of Rimskaya-Korsakova's introduction to the 1st edn]

A. N. Rimsky-Korsakov: *M. P. Musorgsky: pis'ma i dokumentï* [Letters and Documents] (Moscow and Leningrad, 1932), 158–61 [incl. biographical sketch of Rimskaya-Korsakova and her rough-draft memoir of Musorgsky]

G. B. Bernandt and I. M. Yampol'sky: *Kto pisal o muzïke* [Writers on Music] (Moscow, 1971–89)

MALCOLM HAMRICK BROWN

Rimskaya-Korsakova, Yuliya Lazarevna. *See* VEYSBERG, YULIYA LAZAREVNA.

Riseman, Shoshana [Shosh] (*b* Cyprus, 10 April 1948). Israeli composer, teacher and stage director. She was born while her parents were in Cyprus en route to Israel. First taught music at the Tel-Aviv Conservatory and Telma Yalin Music High School, she graduated in 1970 from the Tel-Aviv Academy of Music, where her main study was the piano (she was a pupil of Madeleine Aufhauser); she also completed a degree in philosophy. During her period of compulsory military service, from 1970 to 1972, she was responsible for classical music at Galei-Zahal, the radio station of the Israeli Defence Forces, and wrote on music for *Bahmane*, the IDF's weekly magazine. From 1973 to 1974 she studied composition with Hans Heimler in Guildford, England.

After Riseman's return to Israel, her song cycle *Eize yom yafe* ('What a Beautiful Day') for male voice and chamber ensemble was recorded; a further cycle, *Nine Haiku Songs*, received its première at the Israel Festival in 1984. During the mid-1970s she composed music for educational television programmes, one of which was the operetta *The Brave Soldier Zweig*; she also wrote the musical *Hakol po* ('Everything is Here') for the Tel-Aviv Drama School, and music for two other productions, *The Persian* by the Jerusalem Khan Theatre and *Under Milk Wood* by the Beer Sheva Theatre. In 1976 she furthered her studies in composition with Ralph Shapey in Chicago.

By the end of 1990 Riseman had composed the music for about 50 plays, for all the major theatres in Israel, including *The Rubber Merchants* (Hannoch Levin) for the Cameri Theatre in 1977 (also performed at the Edinburgh Festival in 1983) and *Hamlet* for the Matam Theatre (also given at Munich). She also composed ballet music. In 1987 she

began to combine writing theatre music with stage direction and lighting design. Riseman also teaches voice training and singing for the stage at the Theatre School in Tel-Aviv and at Tel-Aviv University.

WILLIAM Y. ELIAS

Rivé-King [née Rivé], **Julie** (*b* Cincinnati, 31 Oct 1854; *d* Indianapolis, IN, 24 July 1937). American pianist and composer. From 1870 to 1872 she studied in New York with S. B. Mills and briefly with William Mason, and in 1873 went to Europe to work with Carl Reinecke in Leipzig and Franz Liszt in Weimar. After her return to the USA in 1874 she began a performing career managed by Frank H. King and in 1877 they married. Her career was more successful than that of many male American pianists during the last quarter of the 19th century. Devoted to educating the musical public, Rivé-King played throughout the USA and Canada and made at least two transcontinental tours, including one with Theodore Thomas and his orchestra. Piano companies including Steinway, Chickering, Decker Brothers and Weber sponsored numerous tours. She performed many of her own compositions and in 1887 the New York critic James Huneker declared

Julie Rivé-King

her 'the best composer among the fair sex' in the USA. She also taught at the Bush Conservatory in Chicago (1908–37).

Because most concert pianists of the late 19th century also composed, King persuaded her to publish his own works under her name to enhance her reputation. During her lifetime six companies published compositions by King but bearing Rivé-King's name. In addition the couple allowed their major publisher, Charles Kunkel of St Louis, Missouri, to publish Kunkel's transcriptions under her name. Rivé-King helped her husband with 'the passage work' on the most popular piece, *Bubbling Spring*, which continued to appear in original and simplified editions until 1950. Piano-roll companies recorded at least 14 of the works attributed to Rivé-King during the early 20th century.

WORKS

all for piano; published in St Louis unless otherwise stated

Gems of Scotland (1878); Hand in Hand (1878); On Blooming Meadows (1878); Pensées dansantes (1878); Bubbling Spring (1879); Impromptu (New York, 1879); Impromptu Mazurka (Boston, 1879); March of the Goblins (1879); Mazurka des grâces (1879); Polonaise héroïque (1879); Popular Sketches (1879); Coeur de lion March (Chicago and New York, 1880); La scintilla (Cincinnati, 1907)

BIBLIOGRAPHY

J. C. Fillmore: 'Piano Teachers and Concert Pianists', *Dwight's Journal of Music*, xxxvii (1877), 84–5

J. Huneker: 'American Piano Composers', *The Etude*, v (1887), 93

W. S. B. Mathews: 'Madame Julia Rivé-King', *Music*, xiii (1897), 223–5

V. E. B.: 'Madame Julie Rivé-King', *The Musician*, xvi (1911), 160

M. L. Petteys: *Julie Rivé-King, American Pianist* (diss., U. of Missouri-Kansas City, 1987)

M. LESLIE PETTEYS

Rodrigo, Maria (*b* Madrid, 1888; *d* Puerto Rico, 1967). Spanish composer and teacher. She was a pupil of José Tragó (piano) and Emilio Serrano (composition) at the Conservatorio Real Madrid; and after working in popular musical theatre she continued her studies in Munich. From 1933 until 1939 she taught choral and instrumental groups at the Madrid Conservatory. She then lived in exile in Puerto Rico; no works were composed during that time. Immediately after her period of study in Munich her musical style in non-theatrical works, such as the symphonic poem *Alma española* and the song cycle *Tres ayes*, changed from German academicism to a national style similar to the neoclassicism of the Republican school of composers.

WORKS

Stage: Becqueriana (opera, 1, J. Alvárez Quintero and S. Alvárez Quintero), Madrid, Teatro de la Zarzuela, 9 April 1915; Diana cazadora (sainete, 1, J. Alvárez Quintero and S. Alvárez Quintero), Madrid, Teatro Apolo, 19 Nov 1915; La romería del rocío (zarzuela, 2, S. Valverde), Barcelona, Teatro reina Victoria, 1921; Canción de amor (zarzuela); La flor de la vida (opera)

Orch: 1 sym.; Alma española, sym. poem; Rimas infantiles, suite; Gánciara, ov.

Other inst: Qnt, pf, wind insts; 1 str qt; Pf Sonata 'La copla intrusa'; 1 piece for vn, pf

Vocal: Caprichos de Goya, chorus, orch; Tres ayes, song cycle; other songs

BIBLIOGRAPHY

LaborD

XOÁN M. CARREIRA

Rodriguez, Marcela (*b* Mexico City, 18 April 1951). Mexican composer and guitarist. She has participated in several composition seminars, including those at Brown University in Providence, Rhode Island and the Hochschule in Freiburg; among her composition teachers have been Maria Antonieta Lozano and Leo Brouwer. Her most significant works include *Religiosos incendios* for symphony orchestra, *La fábula de las regiones* for string orchestra, and the opera *La Sunamita* (1991). She also has written a considerable amount of chamber music and music for theatre. The Concerto for Recorders and Orchestra (1993) is in four movements, each requiring a different recorder: sopranino, tenor, bass and, in the last movement, two soprano recorders played simultaneously.

BIBLIOGRAPHY

G. Béhague: *Sonidas de las Americas Festival*, New York, 30 Jan–6 Feb 1994 [American Composers' Orchestra; programme booklet]

Roe, Betty (*b* London, 30 July 1930). English composer. She studied the piano, the cello and singing at the RAM, London, and, briefly, composition with Lennox Berkeley. In 1952 she began a teaching career and later was appointed director of music at St Helen's Church, Kensington. She has also taught at the London Academy of Music and Dramatic Art (1968–78). Her works, primarily small-scale, include songs, church and choral music, and music for children; she has also written five operas, including *Gaslight* (1983), *Canterbury Morning* (1986) and *A Flight of Pilgrims* (1993). Her works are published by Thames Publishing.

Rogers [née Barnett], **Clara Kathleen** (*b* Cheltenham, 14 Jan 1844; *d* Boston, MA, 8

March 1931). American singer, composer and teacher of English origin. The granddaughter of the cellist Robert Lindley and daughter of the composer John Barnett, she received musical instruction from her parents before entering the Leipzig Conservatory at the age of 12. She studied the piano with Ignaz Moscheles and Louis Plaidy, harmony with Paperitz and E. F. Richter, and singing with Hermann Goetz. After further piano study (with Hans von Bülow) and singing lessons, she made her début in 1863 in Italy as Isabelle in Meyerbeer's *Robert le diable*, using the stage name Clara Doria. After triumphs in Genoa, Naples and Florence, she returned to London in 1866 and continued her concert career. In 1871 she went to the USA with the Parepa-Rosa troupe, and the following year toured with the Maretzek company. She settled in Boston (1873) and concentrated on composition and teaching after her marriage in 1878 to the Boston lawyer Henry M. Rogers. In 1902 she was appointed Professor of Voice at the New England Conservatory. Her published writings were extensive and significant: several books on singing – including *The Philosophy of Singing* (London, 1893), *My Voice and I, or the Relation of the Singer to the Song* (Chicago, 1910) and *Your Voice and You . . . a Practical Application of Psychology to Singing* (Boston, 1925) – convey her novel approaches as singer and teacher, and her autobiography, *Memories of a Musical Career* (Boston, 1919), reveals acute observations on musical life. Her early chamber works show solid craftsmanship and her songs display a steady development towards an expressive chromatic language, often tinged with humour. Her manuscripts and correspondence are in the Library of Congress, Washington, DC.

WORKS
selective list

Vocal: c100 songs, incl. 2 cycles (R. Browning), op.27 (Boston, 1893), op.32 (Boston, 1900); Aubade, with vn obbl (1883)

Inst: Str Qt (1866); Rhapsody, pf (Boston, 1880); Scherzo, pf, op.15 (Boston, 1883); Vn Sonata, op.25 (Boston, 1893); Romanza, pf, op.31 (1895); Vc Sonata

BIBLIOGRAPHY

SchmidlD
R. Hughes: 'Women Composers', *Century Magazine*, lv/5 (1898), 768–79, esp. 777
W. Upton: *Art Song in America* (Boston, 1930), 109

PAMELA FOX

Roma, Caro [Northey, Carrie] (*b* East Oakland, CA, 10 Sept 1869; *d* East Oakland,

23 Sept 1937). American soprano and composer. She performed in public as a small child, and while still a teenager directed an opera company that toured Canada. After graduating from the New England Conservatory in 1890, she appeared frequently with the Castle Square Opera Company in Boston and sang for eight seasons at the Tivoli Opera House in San Francisco. She toured regularly in the USA, Canada and Europe and in 1906 sang with the Turner Grand Opera in London. She also sang in vaudeville. In 1919 she moved to Miami, where she joined the faculty of the Florida Conservatory of Music and Art and directed the choir at a large Presbyterian church. She published more than 1000 songs, among which are sea songs, sacred songs and the song cycles *The Swan* and *The Wandering One*. She also wrote an opera *God of the Sea* (unpublished).

BIBLIOGRAPHY

'Born in God's Country – California', *MusAm*, ix/10 (1909), 2
'Caro Roma Charms the South', *Musical Courier*, lxxix (11 Dec 1919), 8
I. Witmark and I. Goldberg: *The Story of the House of Witmark: from Ragtime to Swingtime* (New York, 1939)

SALLY MERRILL

Romero, Elena (*b* Madrid, 7 Nov 1923). Spanish composer, pianist and conductor. After studying with José Balsa, she began her concert career at the age of 12. In Barcelona she studied the piano with Frank Marshall and composition with Ricardo Lamote de Grignon; later, in Madrid, she studied composition with Joaquin Turina, Julio Gómez and Lopez Varela, and conducting with Ataúlfo Argenta. She also attended courses in Freiburg, Breslau (Wrocław) and Heidelberg, studying Baroque keyboard music in particular, and in Paris where her tutor was Salvador Bacarisse. She toured in Spain and abroad as a pianist, and is probably the first Spanish woman to have conducted large symphony orchestras (including the Orquesta Sinfónica de RTVE and the Orquesta Ciutat de Barcelona). Among awards for her compositions are the Premio Pedrell for the ballet *Títeres* and a BBC prize for *Ensayo para orquesta sobre dos canciones sudafricanas*. In the context of her generation in Spain, her work is distinguished by its modernity. This takes on different guises: a nationalism inherited from Manuel de Falla and Turina in *Títeres* and *Canto a Turina*, atonal expressionism in *Preludio, fugueta y rondó* and Debussyan impressionism in many of the piano works.

WORKS

Stage: Títeres (ballet), 1950; Marcela (chamber opera, Milán), 1957

Orch: Pequeña suite 'Penibética', 1949, also arr. pf qnt; Aristeo, 1952: Canto a Turina, 1952, also arr. str orch/pf/lute orch; Balada de Castilla, pf, orch, 1953; Ensayo para orquesta sobre dos canciones sudafricanas, 1956, also arr. wind orch; Sinfonietta concertante, fl, vn, vc, orch, 1958; Sym. 'del recuerdo', c, 1973; 2 movimientos, str orch, 1985

Choral: Canción antigua, 4vv, 1952; Ave María, 4vv, 1956; Romance del caballero (anon. 17th-, 18th-century texts), female vv, pf, 1966; Mingo Revulgo (anon. 15th-century text), 7vv, 1968; Agachaté mi niño, mixed vv, 1984; other works

Chamber: En el Castillo de Torremolinos, pf trio, 1948; Canzonetta, vn, pf, 1949; Pequeña suite, 1949 [arr. of orch work]; Fantasía española, pf trio, 1952; Canción de cuna, vn, pf, 1953; Danza rústica, vn, pf, 1953; Vn Sonata, g, 1953; Adagio y rondó, va, pf, 1958; Preludio, fugueta y rondó, ob, cl, va, vc, 1963; Habanera, vn, pf, 1979; Divertimento, pf trio, 1983; 2 movimientos, str qt, 1984; Str Qt, g, 1988; 2 tiempos atonales, vn, harp, 1988

Solo inst (pf unless otherwise stated): Sonata, D, 1947; Canto a Turina, 1950 [arr. of orch work]; Danza del clown, 1950; De noche en el Albaicín, 1955; 2 movimientos temáticos, gui/harp, 1957; Tres de junio, nocturne, gui, 1960; 3 piezas breves, 1970; Fantasia temática, 1979; 3 movimientos, org, 1980; Idilio, 1985; Sugerencias, 1991; other pieces

Other vocal (1v, pf, unless otherwise stated): Antiprimavera, 1948; Madrugada (J. R. Jiménez), 1948; Cantiga (G. Vicente), 1952; El cantar (M. Machado), 1953; Fulla per fulla, 4 solo vv, 1982; El angel de los números (R. Alberti), 1983; other songs

BIBLIOGRAPHY

J. Piñeiro García: Músicos españoles de todos los tiempos: diccionario biográfico (Madrid, 1984)

Catálogo de obras de la Asociación de compositores sinfónicos españoles [ACSE] (Madrid, 1987)
                                    ALICIA CASARES-ALONSO

Rosas-Fernandes, Maria Helena (b Brazópolis, Minas Gerais, 8 July 1933). Brazilian composer, conductor and pianist. She graduated from the Conservatório Brasileiro de Música, Rio de Janeiro, where she studied the piano with Liddy Mignone and João de Souza Lima. In 1977 she pursued further studies, in composition and conducting, at the Escola Superior de Musica Santa Marcelina, São Paulo, where her teachers were Osvaldo Lacerda and José de Almeida Prado. She has also studied music education and in 1992 held a teaching appointment at Campinas University, São Paulo. Her output consists mainly of chamber works, including Território e Ocas (1979) for string quartet and percussion, and In memoriam (1980) for oboe, clarinet and strings; piano music, of which the prize-winning Ciclos (second prize in a Brazilian composers' competition in 1979) has entered the repertory of many Brazilian pianists; and, most importantly, vocal and choral music, which often incorporates Native American material, including Marawawa (1978) for choir and chamber ensemble, Dawawa Tsawidi (1979) for soprano and percussion and Daprava (1980) for mixed chorus.

BIBLIOGRAPHY

V. Mariz: História da música no Brazil (Rio de Janeiro, 2/1983), 337–8
                                    CRISTINA MAGALDI

Rosselli-Nissim, Mary (b Florence, 9 June 1864; d Viareggio, 26 Sept 1937). Italian composer, painter and sculptor. She began her musical studies with her mother Janet Nathan Rosselli and continued with Giuseppe Menichetti. In the 1890s she became well known as a composer of drawing-room songs. In 1896 she received an honourable mention at the Vienna Steiner Contest for her one-act opera Nephta (composed in 1891). Her second opera, Max (two acts; libretto by Enrico Golisciani), written in collaboration with Menichetti, was performed in Florence in 1898. In the following years she devoted herself to painting, sculpture and industrial design and was awarded the first prize at the 1911 Turin International Exhibition. She nevertheless continued to compose operas: Fiamme (three acts; libretto by Giovacchino Forzano) was completed in 1915 and Andrea del Sarto (three acts; Antonio Lega, after Alfred de Musset) was performed in Bari in 1931.

BIBLIOGRAPHY

SchmidlD

A. de Angelis: L'Italia musicale d'oggi: Dizionario dei musicisti (Rome, 1918, 3/1928)

A. Bonaventura: 'Le donne italiane e la musica', RMI, xxxii (1925), 519–34

U. Manferrari: Dizionario universale delle opere melodrammatiche (Florence, 1954–5)

P. Adkins Chiti: Donne in musica (Rome, 1982)
                                    LAURA PISTOLESI

Rossi, Camilla de (b ? Rome; fl Vienna, 1707–10). Italian composer. Nothing is known of her life except that 'Romana' appears on the title pages of her manuscripts, indicating Roman origin. She wrote four oratorios for solo voices and orchestra, which were performed in the Vienna court chapel between 1707 and 1710. A cantata also survives. Her first known work, Santa Beatrice d'Este, was commissioned by Emperor Joseph I. The second oratorio, Il sacrifizio di Abramo (1708), uses chalumeaux, only a year after their first orchestral use in Vienna. According to the title page of the manuscript, Rossi wrote the text as well as the music for *Il figliuol prodigo* (1709).

WORKS

Oratorios, for solo vv, orch (MSS incl. some orch pts in *A-Wm*; arias ed. B. G. Jackson in *Arias from Oratorios by Women Composers of the Eighteenth Century*, Fayetteville, AR, 1987–90): Santa Beatrice d'Este (B. Pamphili), 1707, ed. B. G. Jackson (Fayetteville, 1986); Il sacrifizio di Abramo (F. Dario), 1708, ed. B. G. Jackson (Fayetteville, 1984); Il figliuol prodigo (Rossi), 1709; Sant'Alessio, 1710
Frà Dori, e Fileno, cantata, S, A, str orch, *D-Dlb*

BIBLIOGRAPHY

B. G. Jackson: 'Oratorios by Command of the Emperor: the Music of Camilla de Rossi', *CMc*, no. 42 (1986), 7–19

BARBARA GARVEY JACKSON

Rotaru [Nemţeanu-Rotaru], **Doina Marilena** (*b* Bucharest, 14 Sept 1951). Romanian composer. She studied at the Bucharest Conservatory (1970–75), where her teachers included Tiberiu Olah (composition), attended the Darmstadt summer courses in 1984, 1990 and 1992 and participated in the Gaudeamus composition workshop in Amsterdam in 1990. She has been awarded prizes by the Romanian Academy and by the Composers' Union, of which she is a member, and her music has been played at international festivals in Europe, the USA and Australia. In 1986 she published, with Liviu Comes, a treatise on counterpoint and in 1991 became professor of harmony at the Bucharest Conservatory. In 1994 she was awarded first prize at the GEDOK competition in Mannheim. From Romanian folk music Rotaru has borrowed heterophony, modal harmony and the principle of continuous variation to create music which blends a strong lyricism with clear formal structure. Rhythmically, she often implies a sense of rubato or even improvisation in her works, sometimes by means of proportional notation. She is particularly concerned with timbre, making frequent use of less familiar instruments to create original sonorities. *Troiţe* (the title signifies a small traditional funeral monument consisting of three intertwined crosses) was composed after the Romanian revolution of 1989. Each of its three movements illustrates an emotional condition experienced in the face of death, the last portraying the revival of hope through Christian belief. The musical discourse relies on a slow and steady variation of several folklike themes.

WORKS
selective list

Orch: Cl Conc., 1984; Sym. no.1, 1985; Conc., fl, str, perc, 1986; Vc Conc., 1987; Sym. no.2, 1988; Fl Conc. no.2, 1991
Chamber: Str Qt no.1, 1974; Vc Sonata, 1978; Chrisalide, fl, vn, pf, 1979; Noaptea sânzienelor [The Golden-Haired Fairy's Night], cl, tape, 1980; Str Qt no.2, 1981; Cumpăna luminilor [Balance of Light], cl, vn, va, vc, pf, 1982; Str Qt no.3, 1982; Ww Qnt, 1983; Joc de oglinzi [Mirror Play], 4 fl, 1984; Quatro-tempi, vc, perc, 1984; Aux portes du rêve, fl, perc, 1985; Ceasuri [Clocks], (cl, bn, vn, vc, gui, pf, perc)/(cl, pf, perc), 1987; Măşti [Masks], cl, vc, 1989; Troiţe, cl, pf + synth, perc, 1990; Runa, fl, ob + ob d'amore, gui, cel, hpd, 1991
Solo inst: Răscrucea macilor [The Crossroad of the Poppies], pf, 1980; Legend, fl, 1982; Metamorphosis, b cl, 1987; Spyralis, hp, 1989; Dor, a fl, 1989

Principal publisher: Editura Muzicală (Bucharest)

VIOREL COSMA

Rubin, Anna (*b* Akron, OH, 5 Sept 1946). American composer. She studied sociology at Pomona College in Claremont, California (BA 1968) and music at the California Institute of the Arts (BFA 1975, MFA 1981). Her teachers included Pauline Oliveros, Mel Powell, Leonard Stein and Morton Subotnick; she also studied with Ton de Leeuw in the Netherlands. She has received fellowships and held residencies in the USA and elsewhere (Brahmshaus, Baden-Baden), and has received commissions from the New York State Council on the Arts and for radio. Her work for soprano and ten instruments, *Die Nacht: Lament for Malcolm X*, won an award from the Gaudeamus Foundation in 1983. Rubin's compositions are lyrical, dramatic and heterophonic in style, and her electroacoustic pieces are often inspired by vocal models. Both her instrumental and her electronic works have been performed throughout North and South America, Mexico and Europe. She also teaches in New York.

WORKS
selective list

Sappho, women's chorus, chamber ens, 1979, rev. 1989; Die Nacht: Lament for Malcolm X, S, 10 insts, 1983; The Light and so much Else, 4 t trbn, 1986; Chiaroscuro, cl/ob, perc, 1987; Viola a tre, 3 va, 1989; Mr Moses, Mr Moses, sound collage for radio, 1989; Carousel Suite, tape, 1990; Remembering, S, pf, tape, 1990; Dreaming he Spoke, tape, 1991; Freedom, Sweet and Bitter, orch, tape, 1991; Treasures, cl, live elec, tape, 1991; Breezes, wind qnt, 1992; Ice Song, Mez, perc, 1993; Lullabies for Eli, Bar, fl, vc, pf, perc, tape, 1994

BIBLIOGRAPHY

B. Grigsby: 'Women Composers of Electronic Music in the United States', *The Musical Woman: an*

International Perspective, i: *1983*, ed. J. L. Zaimont and others (Westport, CT, 1984), 151–96

E. Hinkle-Turner: 'Recent Electro-Acoustic Music by Women: a Survey', *ILWC Journal* (1992), Oct, 8–14

ELIZABETH HINKLE-TURNER

Ruiz Lastres, Magaly (*b* Santa Clara, 2 Oct 1941). Cuban composer. In 1959 she won a scholarship to the Guillermo Tomás Conservatory, Havana, to study the piano with César Pérez. She continued her education at the Instituto Superior de Arte, specializing in composition with Roberto Valera and taking a degree in music in 1981. From her first years as a student she taught music and she has maintained an intensive teaching schedule as a member of the Facultad de Enseñanza Artistica del Instituto Superior Pedagógico Enrique José Varona in Havana. Her creative work has been closely linked to that of the composers José Ardévol, Félix Guerrero Díaz, Alfredo Díez-Nieto, Dolores Torres and Harold Gramatges. The greater part of her output consists of very short pieces for small groups, especially duos, in which the timbre of the piano dominates. She often employs the themes, sonorities and rhythms of Cuban popular music forms such as the *son* and the *danzón*, transformed into a contemporary language by means of bitonality, polytonality and randomism. She has won prizes in various Cuban composition competitions.

WORKS
selective list

Orch: Ob Conc., 1979; 3 ambientes sonoros, 1981; Variaciones en habaneras, ob, orch, 1983

Choral (unacc. mixed vv): Altura y pelos, 1976; Canciones para 2 pueblos: Pueblo entre lomas, La Habana, 1990

Songs: A Conrado Benítez, T, pf, 1978; 2 canciones para niños: Abuelita, Trota que trota mi caballito, 1v, pf, 1984; Tríptico a mi madre: Te recuerdo en canto, Mi mariposa, Esa cabeza blanca, Mez, pf, 1985

Inst: Obra aleatoria, 2 cl, perc, 1975; Pf Trio, 1976; Juego con metales, 6 pieces, various insts, pf, 1977; Vc Sonata, 1977; Str Qt, 1978; 3 piezas cubanas para niños, vn, pf, 1978; Pequeña pieza, trbn, pf, 1979; Str Qt, 1980; Pieza no.2, trbn, pf, 1983; Pieza, vn, pf, 1986; Canción para un amigo, sax, pf, 1988; Pieza no.3, trbn, pf, 1988; Fantasia, vn, pf, 1994

Pf: 3 preludios, 1978; 3 estudios cubanos, 1980; Estudios cubanos nos.4–14, 1988; [26] Pequeñas piezas cubanas, 1988; Piezas, 4 hands, 1990–94

ALICIA VALDÉS CANTERO

Runcie, Constance Faunt Le Roy (*b* Indianapolis, IN, 15 Jan 1836; *d* Winnetka, IL, 17 May 1911). American composer, pianist and writer. Runcie's maternal grandfather was Robert Owen, and she grew up in New Harmony, Indiana. Her father, Robert Henry Faunt Le Roy, was an amateur flautist and composer; her mother, Jane Owen, was a pianist and harpist. In 1852, following her father's death, Runcie went to Germany with her family for six years. Her initial plans were to study the piano and harp, but she turned to composition. In 1861 she married James Runcie, an Episcopalian minister in New Harmony, and after 1871 they lived in St Joseph, Missouri; they had two daughters and two sons.

It appears that Runcie was the first American woman to compose in large forms. She is credited with a symphony, a piano concerto, a violin concerto, an opera (*The Prince of Asturia*), chamber music and 50 songs, many to her own texts. Annie Louise Cary and William Mason praised her songs, of which the most widely sung were *I've wandered far away*, *Invocation to Love*, *Das Vöglein singt* and *Take my Soul, O Lord*. William Mason once remarked to Runcie that he had thought her music was 'that of a man. It is both virile and dramatic'.

According to tradition no musical composition submitted by Runcie for publication was rejected. She also wrote poetry, two novels (unpublished) and a biography of Felix Mendelssohn. She is credited with being the founder of one of the first women's clubs in the USA, the Minerva Society in New Harmony, in 1859. In 1897 an accident deprived her of her hearing, and she curtailed her activities thereafter.

CAROL NEULS-BATES

Rusca, Claudia (*b* Milan, 1593; *d* Milan, 6 Oct 1676). Italian composer. She was a nun at the Umiliate monastery of S Caterina in Brera, where she was a soprano, organist and music teacher. According to the house's necrology, she had learnt music, including composition, at home before professing final vows at S Caterina. A letter from Sister Angela Flaminia Confaloniera to Archbishop Federigo Borromeo (in *I-Ma*) describes her *Sacri concerti à 1–5 con salmi e canzoni francesi* (published in Milan, probably by Rolla, in 1630) as having originated at S Caterina and as being particularly suited to the needs of other female monastic institutions. The only known copy of this print was destroyed in the fire at the Biblioteca Ambrosiana in 1943; it probably exhibited the simplicity and directness of other Milanese concerto books of Federigo's tenure.

BIBLIOGRAPHY

*Biografia delle monache umiliate di S. Caterina di Brera,
anno 1684* (MS, *I-Ma*)

Letters between nuns at S Caterina and Federigo
Borromeo (MS, *I-Ma*)

U. Saba: *Federico Borromeo ed i mistici del suo tempo*
(Florence, 1933), 91

R. L. Kendrick: *'Le sirene celesti': Generations, Gender
and Genres in Seicento Milanese Nuns' Music* (diss.,
New York U., 1993), 323

ROBERT L. KENDRICK

Ruta, Gilda (*b* Naples, 13 Oct 1856; *d* New
York, ?1932). Italian pianist, composer and
singer. Her mother, Emilia Sutton, was an
English singer; her father, Michele Ruta, was
a composer and co-director of the Naples
Conservatory. She studied with her father,
then with Liszt in Rome and became one of
the most distinguished pianists of the
19th-century Neapolitan school. Francesco
Florimo mentions her as a singer (as Isolina
in Melchiorre Delfico's opera *Il parafulmine*)
in 1876. After an early début in Naples, she
embarked on a period of intense activity as a
concert pianist, eventually performing in
New York. She settled there in 1896 and
devoted herself to teaching the piano and
composing. Her works include a Piano
Concerto, *Bolero* and *Andante rondò* for piano
and strings, a Violin Sonata, pieces for solo
piano and songs. Some instrumental compositions show the influence of Classical style;
in others the melodic vein is reminiscent of
Chopin (in the *Allegro appassionato* for piano;
Milan, 1884) and in keeping with the trend
followed by pianists of the Neapolitan
school. The simpler style of the late 19th-
century Italian *romanza* and *canzone* is apparent in songs such as *Alle stelle*, *Canzone mari-
naresca* and *Voglio guarire*. Ruta was awarded
a gold medal at the 1890 international exhibition of Florence for her vocal and orchestral works. Some of her piano pieces were
published by Lucca and Ricordi and were
favourably reviewed by Filippo Filippi,
music critic of *La perseveranza* in Milan.

BIBLIOGRAPHY

DEUMM; *FétisB*; *FlorimoN*; *SchmidlD*

'Gilda Ruta', *Gazzetta musicale di Milano*, xxxix
(1884), 249

'Bibliografia musicale', ibid, 354–5

A. de Angelis: *L'Italia musicale d'oggi: Dizionario dei
musicisti* (Rome, 1918, 3/1928)

A. Bonaventura: 'Le donne italiane e la musica', *RMI*,
xxxii (1925), 519–34

P. Adkins Chiti: *Donne in musica* (Rome, 1982)

V. Vitale: *Il pianoforte a Napoli nell'Ottocento* (Naples,
1983)

FRANCESCA PERRUCCIO SICA

S

Saariaho, Kaija (*b* Helsinki, 14 Oct 1952). Finnish composer. After completing her composition studies with Paavo Heininen at the Sibelius Academy, Helsinki, in 1981, she went to Freiburg to study at the Musikhochschule with Brian Ferneyhough and Klaus Huber (1981–2), receiving her diploma in 1983. In 1982 she attended a computer music course at IRCAM in Paris, then settled in Paris. She spent the 1988–9 season at San Diego, California.

Interested in enlarging the potential of traditional instruments, Saariaho has used electronic technology in almost all of her works. Very often she also makes use of extra-musical stimuli, such as texts, visual impulses or natural phenomena. Harmony and timbre, primary features in all of her music, form the basis of works up to *Verblendungen* (1982–4, for orchestra and tape). *Jardin secret II* (1984–6), for harpsichord and tape, introduces a strong rhythmic aspect. *Lichtbogen* (1985–6), for nine instruments and live electronics, shows her interest in the use of the computer in the precompositional phase of creating a work. With the computer, she analyses individual instrumental sounds, which provide material to structure the whole piece. This technique was taken even further in *Io* (1986–7), for ensemble, tape and live electronics, commissioned by IRCAM for the 10th anniversary of the Pompidou Centre in Paris.

Nymphea (Jardin secret III) (1987) for string quartet and live electronics (written for the Kronos Quartet), employs models from nature for abstract musical composition; here, symmetrical shapes are in constant evolution. The same kind of impulse engendered the orchestral diptych *Du cristal* (1989–90) and *. . . à la fumée* (1990), two pieces for large symphony orchestra, the second with alto flute and cello soloists (commissioned by the Los Angeles PO, the Helsinki Festival and Finnish Radio). Saariaho's interest in other art forms is most clearly manifest in the ballet *Maa* ('Earth', 1991), performed by the Finnish National Ballet (choreographed by Carolyn Carlson). In *Amers* (1992), for cello, ensemble and electronics, and the work closely related to it, *Près* (1992), for cello and electronics (both realized at IRCAM), she continued her research in sound synthesis.

Of Scandinavian contemporary composers, she is among those who have received most recognition. Her awards include the Kranichsteiner Musikpreis, Darmstadt (1986); the Prix Italia for *Stilleben* (1988, commissioned by Finnish Radio) and the Ars Electronica prize, Linz (1989). Most of her later works have been recorded for the Finlandia, Ondine or Bis labels.

WORKS
Theatre: 3 Interludes and other music (for J. Groot: *Skotten in Helsingfors*), tape, 1983; Kollisionen, perc, tape, 1984; Collisions, tape, 1986; Csokolom, elec, 1985; Piipää, 2vv, tape, live elec, 1987; Maa [Earth] (ballet, 7 pts., choreog. C. Carlson), chamber ens, live elec, 1991 [pts. 2, 3, 6, 7: see also chamber and inst works]

Orch: Verblendungen, orch, tape, 1982–4; Du cristal,

Kaija Saariaho

399

orch, 1989–90; . . . à la fumée, a fl, vc, orch, live elec, 1990; Graal Theatre, vn, orch, 1994

Chamber and inst: Canvas, fl, 1978; Im Traume, vc, pf, 1980; Yellows, hn, perc, 1980; Laconisme de l'aile, fl, 1982; Jardin secret II, hpd, tape, 1984–6; Lichtbogen, fl, 2 vn, va, vc, db, harp, pf, perc, live elec, 1985–6; Io, chamber ens, tape, live elec, 1986–7; Nymphea (Jardin secret III), str qt, live elec, 1987; Petals, vc, 1988; Oi kuu [For the Moon], b cl, vc, 1990; Aer, fl, vn, va, vc, harp, hpd/other kbd, perc, live elec, 1991 [pt 7 of Maa]; . . . de la terre, vn, live elec, 1991 [pt 3 of Maa]; Fall, harp, opt. elec, 1991 [pt 6 of Maa]; Gates, fl, vc, hpd, opt. live elec, 1991 [pt 2 of Maa]; Amers, vc, ens, elec, 1992; NoaNoa, fl, elec, 1992; Près, vc, 1992; Trois rivières, 4 perc, elec, 1993; Nocturne, vn, 1994

Vocal: Bruden [The Bride] (E. Södergran), song cycle, S, 2 fl, perc, 1977; Jing (Li Ch-ing Chao), S, vc, 1979 [Finnish text]; Nej och inte [No and Not] (G. Björling), 3 songs, 4 female vv/choir, 1979; Suomenkielinen sekakuorokappale [Finnish Piece], mixed choir, 1979; Preludi-Tunnustus-Postludi [Prelude–Confession–Postlude] (M. Waltari), S, prepared grand pf, 1980; Study for Life, female v, dancer, tape, light, 1980; 3 Preludes (Bible), S, org, 1980 [Finnish text]; . . . sah den Vögeln, S, fl, ob, vc, prepared pf, live elec, text collage, 1981; Du gick, flög [You Went, Fled] (Björling), S, pf, 1982; Adjö (S. von Schoultz), S, fl, gui, 1985 [rev. version of Ju lägre solen, 1982, withdrawn]; From the Grammar of Dreams (S. Plath), 2S, 1988; Grammaire des rêves, S, A, 2 fl, va, vc, harp, text collage, 1988; Nuits, adieux (H. de Balzac, J. Roubaud), 4vv, live elec, 1991

Other works: Study II for Life, tape, 1981; Vers le blanc, tape, 1982; Jardin secret I, tape, 1984–5; Suuri illusioni [The Big Illusion] (film score), 1985; Stilleben, tape, 1987–8; La dame à la licorne, sound installation, tape, 1993

Principal publishers: Chester, Hansen

BIBLIOGRAPHY

CC (B. Morton); Fuller-LeFanuRM

R. Nieminen: 'Kaija Saariahos Besuche im Wunderland', Neuland, iv (1983–4), 89–93

S. McAdams and K. Saariaho: 'Qualities and Functions of Musical Timbre', International Computer Music Conference: Vancouver 1985, 367–74

R. Nieminen: 'A Portrait of Kaija Saariaho', Nordic Sounds (1986), June

S. Winterfeldt, ed.: Kaija Saariaho (Berlin, 1991)

J. Anderson: 'Seductive Solitary: Kaija Saariaho' MT, cxxxiii (1992), 616–19

A. Ford: Composer to Composer: Conversations about Contemporary Music (London, 1993)

R. Nieminen, ed.: Kaija Saariaho (Paris, 1994)

RISTO NIEMINEN

Sabinin, Martha von [Sabinina, Marfa Stepanovna] (b Copenhagen, 30 May 1831; d Crimea, 14 Dec 1892). Russian pianist and composer. The daughter of the Eastern Orthodox priest to the Grand Duchess of Weimar, Sabinin was court pianist and teacher at the Noble Girls' Institute in Weimar (1854–60). Tsar Alexander II, nephew of the Grand Duchess, then appointed his aunt's protégée court music teacher to his children. She was a pupil of the Schumanns (1850–51), Peter Cornelius (1853–5) and Liszt (1853–60), who praised her 'musically well-tempered freedom and flow'. She wrote the text as well as the music for her choral work Franziskus-Lied and Liszt later set her text for male voices (soloists, chorus and instrumental ensemble) as An den heiligen Franziskus von Paula. She excelled in Classical and ensemble performance, and as the accompanist of such gifted singers as Johanna Wagner (niece of Richard Wagner). New artistic influences inspired her pieces for salon and court; songs to contemporary German Romantic lyrics led to the composition of music for the new genre melodrama and impressionistic piano solos. A nurse from 1868 with the Tsarina's Sisters of the Annunciation, she served heroically in the field (manning ambulances and establishing hospitals) during the Russo-Turkish war (1876–8) and was subsequently made Abbess of the Crimean mother house.

WORKS

VOCAL

op.

— Franziskus-Lied (M. von Sabinin), chorus, pf, harp, perf. Weimar, 22 Oct 1857

1 Acht Lieder, 1851–5 (Leipzig, n.d.)
2 Sechs Gesänge, 1851–5 (Weimar, 1881)
3 Sechs Gedichte, 1851–5 (Weimar, 1881)

DRAMATIC

4 Rolf's Fahne (Ballade), 1860–67 (Leipzig, n.d.)
— Vorspiel zur 'Loreley' (melodrama), c1860

PIANO

5 Musikalische Bilder (11 Salonstücke), 1860–67 (Leipzig, n.d.)
— Vesennya Vody [Spring Waters], 1861–8 (Moscow, n.d.)

BIBLIOGRAPHY

La Mara [M. Lipsius], ed.: Franz Liszts Briefe (Leipzig, 1893–1902), esp. i, 171; vi, 48; vii, 134; viii, 328

Franz von Milde: Ein ideales Künstlerpaar, Rosa und Feodor von Milde (Leipzig, 1918), i, 55–6, 66

N. Szolncev: 'Liszt Ferenc Tizenhat Levele Orosz Tanítványához, Marfa Szabinyinához', Magyar zene, xiv (1973), 281–98

P. Pocknell: 'Author! Author! Liszt's Prayer An den heiligen Franziskus von Paula', Journal of the American Liszt Society, no.30 (1991), 28–43

PAULINE POCKNELL

Sahakduxt (fl early 8th century). Armenian hymnographer, poet and pedagogue. Sister of the music theorist Step'annos Siwnec'i, she was an ascetic who lived in a cave in the Garni valley (near Erevan) and produced ecclesiastical poems and liturgical chants. Srp'uhi Mariam ('Saint Mary'), consisting of nine stanzas in acrostic formation, is her only verse to have survived. Reportedly, many of her *šarakaner* (hymns) were devoted to the Mother of God (akin to the *theotokion* in the music of the Byzantine rite) and helped to shape the development of the genre during subsequent centuries. Seated behind a curtain, as the mores of the period required, Sahakduxt taught sacred melodies to clerical students and lay music lovers.

BIBLIOGRAPHY

S. Örbelyan: *Patmut'yun nahangin Sisakan* [History of the Province of Sis] (Tbilisi, 1910), 139

Archbishop Covakan Norayr [Połarian]: *Sahakduxt Siwnec'i ev Srp'uhi Mariam* [Sahakduxt of Siunik and Saint Mary], *Hask* (Antilias, 1951), 366–7

M. Örmanian: *Azgapatum* [National History], i (Beirut, 2/1959), 867–8

D. Der Hovhanessian and M. Margossian, trans. and eds.: *Anthology of Armenian Poetry* (New York, 1978), 45–6

G. A. Hakobyan: *Šarakanneri žanrě hay mijnadaryan grakannt'yan mej* [The Genre of the *šarakan* in Medieval Armenian Literature] (Erevan, 1980), 159–72

ŞAHAN ARZRUNI

Saint-Marcoux, Micheline Coulombe (*b* Notre-Dame-de-la-Doré, Quebec, 9 Aug 1938; *d* Montreal, 2 Feb 1985). Canadian composer. She studied with Claude Champagne at the Ecole Vincent-d'Indy, Montreal (1956–8), and later with Gilles Tremblay and Clermont Pépin at the Montreal conservatory (CMM), winning a *premier prix* for *Modulaire* in 1967. She worked with Tony Aubin in Nice in summer 1965 and from 1968 to 1970 lived in Paris, where she worked with Pierre Schaeffer and members of the Groupe de Recherches Musicales, which commissioned her *Arksalalartôq* (1971). With five others, she co-founded in 1969 the Paris-based Groupe International de Musique Electro-Acoustique, which gave concerts until 1973 in Europe, Canada and South America. On her return to Quebec in 1971, she taught at the CMM and was a co-founder of the Ensemble Polycousmie. She has received commissions from the Montreal SO, the CBC, the Société de Musique Contemporaine du Québec (SMCQ) and others. Her mature works show a rejection of her earlier serialism in favour of ensemble and orchestral pieces with atmospheric effects and titles evocative of a unique sound world, in which intervallic modules are constantly manipulated.

WORKS
selective list

Dramatic: Comment Wang-fô fut sauvé (incid. music for marionettes), 1983; Transit (opera, F. Théoret), 1984

Orch: Modulaire, 1967; Hétéromorphie, 1970; Luminance, 1978

Other inst: Variations sur un thème personnel, pf, 1963; Evocations doranes, ww qt, 1964; Fl Sonata, 1964; Kaleidoscope, pf LH, 1964; Str Qt, 1966; Equation I, 2 gui, 1967; Séquences, 2 ondes martenot, perc, 1968, rev. 1973; Assemblages, pf, 1969; Episodie II, 3 perc, 1972; Génésis, wind qnt, 1975; Intégration I, vc, 1980; Intégration II, vn, 1980; Mandala I, 1980; Mandala II, pf, 1980; Composition I, hn, 1981; Horizon I, fl, 1981; Horizon II, ob, 1981; L'Etre et son double, 2 fl, *c*1981; Etreinte, 4 ondes martenot, 1983; see also elec works

Vocal: Chanson d'automne (P. Verlaine), S/T, pf, 1963, rev. 1966 [orig. for S/T, fl, vn, pf]; Wing tra la, chorus, chamber ens, 1964; Makazoti (N. Audet, G. Marsolais), SATB, chamber ens, 1971; Alchera (N. Brossard), Mez, chamber ens, 1973; Ishuma (Inuit texts, P. Chamberland), S/Mez, trbn, vn, db, 3 perc, ondes martenot, synth, Hammond org, 1974; Moments, S, fl, va, vc, 1977; Jesod I, II, S, pf, 1981; Moments, 1981

Elec: Bernavir (N. Audet), 1970; Trakadie, perc, tape, 1970; Artsalalartôq, tape, 1971; Contrastances, tape, 1971; Moustières, tape, 1971; Zones, tape, 1972; Tel qu'en Lemieux, film score, tape, 1973; Miroirs, hpd, tape, 1975; Regards, chamber ens, tape, 1978; Constellations I, tape, 1981; see also 'other instrumental' and vocal works

GAYNOR G. JONES

Sainton-Dolby [née Dolby], **Charlotte (Helen)** (*b* London, 17 May 1821; *d* London, 18 Feb 1885). English contralto, teacher and composer. From 1832 she studied at the RAM, where she gained the King's Scholarship (1837). Her first performance as a soloist was at the Philharmonic Society on 14 April 1842. Felix Mendelssohn was impressed by her singing; he obtained an engagement for her at the Leipzig Gewandhaus Concerts (1845–6), dedicated his Six Songs op.57 to her and wrote the contralto part in *Elijah* with her in mind. In 1860 she married the French violinist Prosper Sainton. During the 1860s she was in demand in Britain, especially in oratorio. She retired from public performance in 1870 and set up a vocal academy in 1872. Shortly after her death the RAM founded a scholarship in her memory.

Sainton-Dolby's works were popular in her day, but now seem insipid, her songs relying too heavily on the duller aspects of Mendelssohn's style. Even her best work, *The Legend of St Dorothea*, is marred by a lack of dramatic credibility. She is best remembered as the writer of the excellent *Tutor for English Singers*, and as the leading contralto of her generation.

WORKS
all printed works published in London

Choral: The Legend of St Dorothea (J. C. H.), cantata, 1876, vs (1876); The Story of the Faithful Soul

(A. Procter), cantata, 1879, vs (1880); The Glove on the Snow (H. Hodgson), female vv (1883); Our Happy Home (J. Roscoe), trio/chorus (1883); Florimel (J. A. Blaikie), cantata, female vv, 1885, vs (1885); Thalassa, cantata

Other vocal: *c*65 songs (1856–85); The Angel's Home, duet; folksong arrs.; arr. of Handel: Cangio d'aspetto (Admeto) (1884)

Pedagogical: Tutor for English Singers (?1872)

BIBLIOGRAPHY

CohenE; *DNB* ('Sainton, Prosper'; R. H. Legge); *FétisBS*; *Grove1*, 5 (W. Barclay Squire); *MEMM*; *PazdirekH*; *WCBH*

Obituary, *MT*, xxvi (1885), 145–6

J. D. Champlin: *Cyclopedia of Music and Musicians* (New York, 1888–90)

J. D. Brown and S. S. Stratton: *British Musical Biography* (Birmingham, 1897)

O. Thompson, ed.: *The International Cyclopedia of Music and Musicians* (London, 4/1942)

NIGEL BURTON

Saint-Simon, Mme de. *See* BAWR, SOPHIE DE.

Salter, Mary Elizabeth Turner (*b* Peoria, IL, 15 March 1856; *d* Orangeburg, NY, 12 Sept 1938). American soprano, teacher and composer. Instructed in music from an early age by her parents, she then studied singing with Alfred Arthur and Gustav Schilling in Iowa, and with John O'Neill, Lillian Norton and Erminia Rudersdorff in Boston. From 1874 to 1893 she sang in Boston and New York churches and in many choral society concerts conducted by B. J. Lang and Theodore Thomas. She taught singing at Wellesley College from 1879 until 1881, when she married the organist and composer Sumner Salter. After her marriage, she continued to teach and began to compose while rearing a family of five children, producing more than 200 songs (many set to her own texts) and numerous choral works. Her song *The Cry of Rachel* was widely performed by Madame Schumann-Heink. Influential in promoting her work, her husband often corrected works for publication, as evidenced in her manuscripts. Despite her lack of formal training in harmony and composition, her songs are lyrical and especially strong in word-setting and interpretation. Her manuscripts and correspondence are in the Library of Congress, Washington, DC.

WORKS
selective list

Songs: *c*200, including The Cry of Rachel (New York, 1905); Lyrics from Sappho, op.18 (New York, 1909); 3 cycles: Love's Epitome (New York, 1905), Night in Naishapur (New York, 1906), From Old Japan, op.23 (Chicago, 1911)

Other vocal: Ballad of the Nautilus, partsong; As

Pants the Heart, anthem; Christmas Song, sacred song, 1936; musical illustrations for J. S. Gates: *One Day in Betty's Life* (Indianapolis, IN, 1913) [children's book]

BIBLIOGRAPHY

H. G. Kinscella: 'How Mary Turner Salter Composes her Songs', *MusAm*, xxix/18 (1919), 29

D. A. Clippinger: 'The Songs of Mary Turner Salter', *Musical West*, vi/4 (1929), 22

[S. Salter]: *In Memoriam Mary Turner Salter* (privately pubd, n.p., 1939)

PAMELA FOX

Samter, Alice (*b* Berlin, 11 June 1908). German composer. She studied the piano, choral music and conducting in Berlin and, after an interruption in her training because of World War II, graduated in music education in 1946 from the Berlin Hochschule für Musik, where her teacher was Heinrich Martens. From 1946 to 1970 she was active as an art and music teacher in various Berlin high schools, and she has been a member of the council of the Verband Deutscher Musikerzieher und Konzertierender Künstler in Berlin. She received a state service award in 1988. Her first compositions date from early childhood, but works written before 1945 were destroyed in the war. Samter's style is not based on any particular models, although she has an affinity with the music of Stravinsky, and her music is strongly aphoristic. Most of her works are commissioned, and take into account the practicalities of performance. Her large output consists mainly of chamber music, songs and educational music.

WORKS
selective list

Incid. music: Die Schule der Frauen (J. Cocteau), spkr, vn, vc, pf, 1967; Die Nachtwache (N. Sachs), solo vv, chorus, spkr, inst ens, 1967; Proteus (P. Claudel), inst ens, 1967

Vocal: 4 Lieder (C. Morgenstern), 1954; 3 Lieder (R. M. Rilke), 1954; Erfindungen (Morgenstern), 5 choruses, 3vv, rec, pf, 1966; 3 Lieder (S. George), 1968; Ode an Singer (P. van Ostaijen), S, spkr, pf, 1969; 3 Lieder (C. Reinig), 1971; Hellbrunn-Zyklus (R. Magnus), S, fl, ob, bn, 1971; 5 Lieder (A. Gustas), 1973; 8 Oboenlieder, 1v, ob, 1978; Stimme des Heiligen Landes (Sachs), 1v, trbn, org, 1986; Freiheit-Gleichheit-Brüderlichkeit, cantata, A, chorus, fl, cl, bn, tpt, vc, db, perc, 1988

Chamber: Permutation, vc, pf, 1970; Mobile, ob, pf, 1971; Rivalités, fl, cl, vc, pf, 1974; Essay, vn, cymbal, 1977; Pf Trio, 1979; Gemini, pf 4 hands, 1979; Dedikation, cl, hn, pf, 1981; Zueignung, fl, trbn, pf, 1983; Imaginationen, fl, cl, tpt, vc, perc, pf, 1985; Duettino, cl, org, 1986; 4 Ungleiche, fl, vc, perc, pf, 1990

Solo inst: 3 Phasen, pf, 1968; Match, pf, 1970; Prisma, org, 1972; Monolog, vn, 1973; Monolog, fl, 1973; Eskapaden, pf, 1974; Monolog, vc, 1975; Mosaik, db, 1978; Monolog, b cl, 1984; Monolog, cl, 1985;

Monolog, trbn, 1986; Oboe d'amore allein, 1987; Für ein Fagott, 1989

Educational music, incl. an opera, masques and puppet plays

BIBLIOGRAPHY

R. Matthei and B. Sonntag, eds.: 'Alice Samter', *Annäherungen an sieben Komponistinnen*, i (Kassel, 1986), 27–34

'Alice Samter', *Komponistinnen in Berlin*, ed. B. Brand and others (Berlin, 1987), 359–69

ROSWITHA SPERBER

Samuel, Rhian (*b* Aberdare, 3 Feb 1944). British composer. She studied with Andrew Byrne at the University of Reading (BA 1966, BMus 1967) and in the USA with Robert Wykes and Paul Pisk at Washington University, St Louis (MA 1970; PhD 1978, with a dissertation *Tonality, Modality and Musica Ficta in the Renaissance Chanson*). From 1977 to 1983 she taught at the St Louis Conservatory of Music. She returned to Britain in 1983 and to the University of Reading as lecturer in 1984, becoming head of the music department in 1993 and Reader the next year.

Her acknowledged output dates from 1978, when she won the first of a number of awards including the 1983 ASCAP/Nissim Composers Award for *La belle dame sans merci*. *Before Dawn* was given at the first concert of the New Music Orchestral Project in New York (director Jorge Mester) in 1989. Among commissioned works are the *Elegy-Symphony* (St Louis SO), *Clytemnestra* (BBC National Orchestra of Wales) and *The Cool Heart* (Ensemble Bartók, Santiago, Chile).

Samuel's understanding of vocal genres betokens her Welsh background as well as American influences; they come together in her direct, sympathetic settings of women's poetry (e.g. of Emily Dickinson in *Lovesongs and Observations*, and of May Sarton). Her instrumental writing, on the other hand, already mature in the *Elegy-Symphony*, is fully equal to the techniques of abstract modernism, though 12-note procedures are residual, with recent works more tonally forthright.

Her writings encompass articles on Harrison Birtwistle's *Gawain*, women composers, feminist musicology and new music.

WORKS
selective list

Dramatic: Pasquinade (incid. music, D. Nokes), 2 fl, ob, cl, bn, a sax, hn, tpt, trbn, pf, str, 1984

Orch: Elegy-Sym, 1981; Encounters (Pf Conc.), 1991

Orch with v: Intimations of Immortality (W. Wordsworth), T, small orch, 1978; Before Dawn (M. Sarton), Mez/Bar, orch, 1988; The White Amaryllis (Sarton), medium v, orch/pf, 1988–91

[incl. Before Dawn]; Clytemnestra (after Aeschylus), coloratura S, orch, 1994

Choral orch: La belle dame sans merci (J. Keats), 1982, rev. 1987; A Song for the Divine Miss C (A. D. Hope and others), S, T, chorus, orch, 1986

Chamber: Winter Cantata, fl, ob, cl, bn, tpt, hn, vn, vc, db, perc, 1980; Rondo pizzicato, youth str qt, 1982 (London, 1986); Encounter, bn, vn, va, vc, 1983; Midwinter Spring, wind qnt, 1984, rev. 1989; Shadow Dance, fl, ob, pf, 1984, rev. 1985; Caprice I, fl, pf, 1986; Caprice II, fl/pic, ob, cl, bn, hn, tpt, trbn, mar, str, 1986; Ariel, fl, pf, 1988; Variations, 4 trbn, 1988; To Become the Song, solo inst, pf, 1990

Solo inst: Mosaics, pf, 1988; Traquair Music, ob, 1989; Fel Blodeuyn (Like a Flower), org, 1992

Vocal chamber: The Hare in the Moon (Ryokan), (S, mar, vib, db)/(S, pf), 1978, rev. 1979; Rondeau (H. Daigaku), Mez/Bar, fl, cl, va, vc, vib, 1979; Songs of Earth and Air (L. Lee, W. H. Davies, J. Silkin, K. Leslie), Mez/Bar, pf, 1983 (recorded 1985); In the Hall of Mirrors (J. Merrill), Mez/Bar, pf, 1984; The Witch's Manuscript (C. Rumens), Mez, brass qnt, 1985; 3 Songs with Guitar (E. A. Poe, W. Soyinka, J. Haines), 1v, gui, 1985 (London, 1987); Of Swans, Snails and Geese (M. Sarton), 4 amp vv, 3 el gui, 1990; The Cool Heart (E. Bishop) (1v, cl, vn, vc, pf)/(1v, pf, tape), 1992

Other choral (unacc. unless otherwise stated): Changes (Priest Saigyo), chorus, vib, 1973, rev. 1978; Jacobean Lyrics (G. Herbert, B. Jonson, F. Beaumont, J. Fletcher), 1979; So Long Ago (J. Pudney), 1979; Opposites (W. Shakespeare, T. Campion), 1980, rev. 1992; Lovesongs and Observations (E. Dickinson), 1989

BIBLIOGRAPHY

Fuller-LeFanuRM

J. Wierzbicki: 'SLSO to Play New Work by Conservatory Composer', *St Louis Globe-Democrat* (26–7 Sept 1981)

S. Mabry: 'New Directions: New British Song', *NATS Journal* (1989), Sept–Oct, 25

A. Kozinn: 'New Works, Writers, and Orchestra', *New York Times* (27 Feb 1989)

A. Maack: 'La música no se explica con palabras', *El Sur* [Concepción, Chile] (17 May 1992)

STEPHEN BANFIELD

Santa [Sanza, Samaritana]. *See* DELLA PIETÀ, SANTA.

Santos Ocampo, Amada (Galvez) (*b* Manila, 23 June 1925). Filipina composer. She studied at St Paul College, Manila (music teacher's diploma), the Centro Escolar University Conservatory (BMus), DePauw University, Indiana (MMus) and the University of Indiana at Bloomington. Among her composition teachers were Antonio Molina, Antonino Buenaventura and Lucio San Pedro in the Philippines, and Roy Harris, Donald White, Bernhard Heiden and Juan Orrego Salas in the USA. In addition, she had advanced piano lessons with Glen Sherman and Sidney Fosters, and toured the Philippines and the USA as a composer-pianist. She taught at Centro

Escolar University (1955–8, 1964–7) and Stella Maris College (1965–7) before returning to the USA to take up a post as pianist and assistant professor at the Pennsylvania State University. She retired in 1992.

Santos Ocampo's varied compositional style ranges from neo-classical to atonal, using contemporary harmonic and contrapuntal idioms.

WORKS
selective list

Stage: Masquerade (musical), 1976
Orch: Tone Poem, 1956; Pf Conc., 1957; Variations, 1960; 2 syms., 1964
Chamber: Sonata, cl, pf, 1960; Quintet, ww, 1961; Str Qt, 1961; Concert Piece, 2 pf, 1962; Sonata, vn, pf, 1965; Five Songs, Mez, orch, 1966; Orchesis, vn, pf, 1978
Vocal: Gloom Casts the Candle, Bar, pf, 1966; The Beggar, Bar, pf, 1967; Universal Peace, Mez, pf, 1974; Sumikat ka ina [Shine on the Motherland], Mez, pf, 1985
Choral pieces, pf music, music for dance and gymnastics

LUCRECIA R. KASILAG

Sanz, Rocío (*b* San José, Costa Rica, 28 Jan 1933; *d* Mexico City, 14 April 1993). Costa Rican composer. She began her studies at the Conservatorio Nacional de Música and continued, working on piano and composition studies, in Los Angeles and at the Conservatorio Nacional de México and the Moscow State Tchaikovsky Conservatory. From 1953 she was based in Mexico City, where almost all her works were written; there she studied with the composers Jiménez Mabarak, Rodolfo Halffter and Blas Galindo Dimas. She taught at the Academia de Danza Mexicana, the Escuela de Arte Dramático of the Instituto Nacional de Bellas Artes and the Centro Universitario de Teatro and was Special Projects Coordinator for the Ballet Folklórico de México. Her output includes stories and songs for children, chamber music, orchestral works, music for numerous short documentaries and theatrical productions and for the film *La Sunamita*, the ballet *El forastero* and for the Griselda Alvarez success, *Letania erótica para la paz*. Her *Cantata de la Independencia de Centroamérica* won her first prize in the competition on the 150th anniversary, in 1971, of Costa Rican independence; it had its première in 1984. In 1976 she received first prize in the choral music competition of the Teatro Nacional of Costa Rica for her *Sucedió en Belén*, five villancicos to texts by Sister Juana de la Cruz. In her later years she devoted herself almost exclusively to the important and highly successful radio programme *El rincón de niños* ('Children's Corner'), broadcast from 1972 by Radio UNAN, in which she made known the music of many composers. A prize named after her, for children's music and songs, was created by the Grupo Signo de México in 1981. Notable among her works are *Hilos*, a suite for string orchestra, and *Canciones de la muerte* for soprano, both of which were given at the 1993 congress of women composers in Mexico. Sanz was a member of the Liga de Compositores de Música de Conciertos and the Sindicato de Músicos y Compositores de México.

BIBLIOGRAPHY
B. Flores Zeller: *La música en Costa Rica* (San José, 1978)
—— : *La música en Costa Rica contemporánea* (San José, 1979)
G. Moreno and C. Valverde: 'Rocío inolvidable', *Ancora*, xxi/19, *La nación* (1993), May
JORGE LUIS ACEVEDO VARGAS

Sappho (*b* Lesbos, 7th century BC). Greek lyric poet. Perhaps the most famous woman poet of the Western world, Sappho lived in Lesbos in the 7th and 6th centuries BC. As with other early Greek lyric, most of her output of monody and choral poetry is lost,

Sappho and Alcaeus; detail from an Attic red-figure krater, BC c460

but papyrus finds have added to poems and fragments preserved by other writers. These, mostly of sensuous, erotic beauty, were subject to both admiration and moral reproof, and it became common to call her 'the tenth Muse'. She would accompany herself on the long-stringed barbiton – there is a famous vase (see illustration) showing her with her contemporary, Alcaeus – and she mentions also the small harp called *pēktis*. Late authorities declare her the inventor of the plectrum, and the Mixolydian mode of Greek music, of a highly emotional character. The beguiling Sapphic stanza of much of her verse has been imitated in later poetry, especially Latin and German. Her emotional relationship with the many girls her monodies address has aroused controversy whether the modern sense of 'Lesbian' can justly be applied to her, but names of husband and daughter have been handed down. Plutarch's description (*Moralia*, 762f) 'her words are mingled with fire, and in her songs she draws up from her heart a violent heat' anticipates Byron's famous epithet 'burning Sappho' (*Don Juan*, Canto iii, first verse of the 'hymn' following stanza 86).

WRITINGS

In *Poetarum Lesbiorum fragmenta*, ed. E. Lobel and D. L. Page (Oxford, 1955)
In *Greek Lyric Poetry*, ed. D. A. Campbell (Cambridge, Mass., and London, 1982) [with trans.]

BIBLIOGRAPHY

Choron-FayolleD; *FétisB*; *GerberL*; *SchillingE*; *WaltherML*
D. L. Page: *Sappho and Alcaeus* (Oxford, 1955)
C. M. Bowra: *Greek Lyric Poetry from Alcman to Simonides* (Oxford, 1961)
R. Jenkyns: *Three Classical Poets: Sappho, Catullus and Juvenal* (London, 1982)
A. P. Burnett: *Three Archaic Poets: Archilochus, Alcaeus, Sappho* (London, 1983)
                                                                E. KERR BORTHWICK

Sato, Kimi (*b* Sendai, 5 March 1949). Japanese composer. In 1971 she graduated in composition and piano from the Tōhō Gakuen School of Music, Tokyo, where she studied composition with Yoshirō Irino. She attended the Darmstadt summer course in 1972 and in December began composition studies with Olivier Messiaen at the Paris Conservatoire, graduating in 1978. In 1981, after nearly ten years in France, Sato returned to Japan. On the recommendation of Messiaen she was awarded the Prix de Rome (1984); she was the first foreign recipient of the prize. Her works rely heavily on timbre and dynamics for shape and motion, and are characterized by rich, colourful orchestration, ranging from slow-moving timbral blocks to shimmering, virtuoso passagework.

WORKS

Orch: Espace, 1974; Ailleurs . . ., 1984 [rev. of chamber work]; Genso-Teien [The Imaginary Garden], 1987
Vocal: Perspectif du brouillard, mixed chorus, 1986
Other inst: Le cadre blanc, fl, 1972; Beyond Space, Sound, pf, 1976; Le bleu du ciel, 12 str, 1977; Sol dièse, 27 performers, 1977; Journal d'été, 15 performers, 1978; Ailleurs . . ., 14 performers, 1979; Bleu et bleu, 2 pf, 1982; Sphere, Crystal, Moon, shō [mouth organ], 1987; Du côté de la maison d'Ingre, vn, pf, 1989

BIBLIOGRAPHY

T. Hoffman: 'The Sounds of Music – Japan's Modern Composers and Performers', *Japan Society Newsletter* (1985), March, 2–6, esp. 4, 6
                                                          J. MICHELE EDWARDS

Savage, Jane (*fl c*1780–90). English composer, daughter of William Savage, a Gentleman-in-Ordinary in the Chapel Royal. She was a virtuoso keyboard player and an accomplished composer of keyboard music and songs. Her music is in the typically untaxing *galant* style of the late 18th century, and was quite popular in its time.

WORKS
all published in London

op.
2 Six Easy Lessons, hpd/pf (1783)
3 Six Rondos, hpd/pf (*c*1790)
4 Strephan and Flavia, cantata, 1v, kbd (*c*1790)
5 Hall the Woodman, a Favourite Song, 1v, kbd (*c*1790)
6 A Favorite Duett, pf/hpd (1789)
7 Two Duetts for Voices, 2vv, bc (*c*1790)
8 God Save the King, adapted as a Double Lesson, hpd/pf (*c*1790)

BIBLIOGRAPHY

R. J. S. Stevens: *Life of Mr William Savage* (MS, *GB-Ge*); repr. in H. G. Farmer: 'A Forgotten Composer of Anthems', *ML*, xvii (1936), 188–99 [*Life*, p.190]
—— : Diaries and Memoirs (MSS, *GB-Cp*); ed. M. Argent as *Recollections of R. J. S. Stevens: an Organist in Georgian London* (London, 1992)
                                                          CHARLES CUDWORTH

Scalfi, Rosanna. *See* MARCELLO, ROSANNA SCALFI.

Scarborough, (Frances) Ethel (*b* Crouch End, London, 10 Jan 1880; *d* Graffham, Sussex, 9 Dec 1956). English composer, pianist and politician. She studied harmony with Philipp Scharwenka in Berlin, and at the RAM (1900–03). Her large output of compositions includes orchestral and choral works, piano concertos (she played one while on tour in 1905 and another was performed with the Bournemouth Municipal Orchestra in 1908) and a symphony (1909). She also wrote piano music and song cycles; the latter were broadcast by her in the 1930s. She conducted her *Scherzo* at Brighton (1914) and it was subsequently given by Dan Godfrey at Bournemouth (1915). There she also conducted her overture *Aspiration* (1909), an orchestral fantasy, *Promise* (given twice in 1923) and the suite *Moods* (1925). The last was revived by David John with the Dorset Philharmonic in 1988.

After 1925 she devoted more time to Labour politics, taking part in the Jarrow March, and competing unsuccessfully with Aneurin Bevan for adoption as parliamentary candidate at Ebbw Vale (she composed songs for the miners). She also wrote songs for BBC Children's Hour. Her manuscripts are held in a private collection.

LEWIS FOREMAN

Schapira, Claire (*b* Paris, 7 Nov 1946). French composer. She studied the theatre and then music (harpsichord and composition) and graduated in electroacoustics from the Schola Cantorum; she was resident at the Villa Medici from 1976 to 1978. Her output is small yet finely crafted. Formal rigour and an ever-present 'directionality' impart to her music a strong sense of dramatic tension, as in *Acheminement* (1980) and *Chant cousu* (1983), which are of a truly theatrical nature. Her style is further characterized by a pervasive use of polyrhythms (*Rumeur*, 1986) and dense sound textures resulting from the superposition of lines (*La chaine*, 1981 and *A choeur perdu*, 1986).

WORKS
selective list

Orch: Regards, 1977; Conc., harp, 40 str, 1985
Chamber and inst: Cendres, vn, fl, hpd, 1981; La chaîne, 12 str, 1981; Trame, 2 amp harps, tape, 1984; Sans craindre le vertige et le vent, str trio, harp, 1986
Vocal: In pace, S, chorus, orch, 1978; Immobiles, S, 14 insts, 1978; Acheminement, S, S, fl, hpd, pf, dbn, perc, 1980; Interjections, S, double perc, 1982; Contes, S, 1983; Ténèbres (De profundis), 12 soloists, chorus, orch, 1983; Chant cousu, S, chamber orch, 1983; Rumeur, S, insts, 1986; A choeur perdu, 6 mixed vv, 1986; Mémorial, Mez, ens, 1989

DANIEL KAWKA

Schauroth [Hill-Handley], **Delphine (Adolphine) von** (*b* Magdeburg, 1814; *d* ?Charlottenburg, 1887). Bavarian pianist and composer. She is said to have been a piano pupil of Frédéric Kalkbrenner (presumably in Paris), whose music she performed in London in July 1823. She was only 16 when she came to the attention of Felix Mendelssohn during his stay in Munich en route to Italy in June 1830. In his letters of 11 and 26 June he wrote to his sister Fanny of flirtation and duet-playing, and later inscribed a dedication to Delphine Schauroth in the margins of the manuscript of his *Venetianische Gondellied*, dated 16 October, which became no.6 of his first collection of *Songs without Words*. They met again on his return in October 1831, according to his letter of 6 October; it was to Schauroth that he dedicated his op.25 Piano Concerto in G minor, which he performed for the first time in Munich on 17 October. However, nothing came of their relationship and by 1835 she had been briefly married to the Englishman Hill-Handley.

Fanny Mendelssohn and her husband, Wilhelm Hensel, visited her in Munich en route to Italy in 1839; the two women got on well and Fanny described her to Felix in a letter of 23 September as 'a charming person and an extraordinary talent' and praised her performance of his concerto, adding that 'what I especially like about her playing is her inspired improvisations, a rare talent in women'. Schauroth permitted Hensel to sketch her, and, according to Fanny, was 'delighted with the result'. Her lasting affection for Felix Mendelssohn is evident from the 1870 birthday recital she gave in his honour, at which she performed works of her own and by Chopin.

Robert Schumann wrote paternalistically about her Caprice ('charming in spite of its little weak points', *NZM*, v, 1836, p.132) and a Piano Sonata in A minor ('amiable, thoughtless, – not wholly so; – self-sacrificing, and even somewhat learned', *NZM*, ii, 1835, p.125), questioning consecutive 5ths, false relations and other marks of inexperience in composing, but pardoning them all for the thoroughly musical nature which her pieces displayed. However, he later warmly reviewed her 1839 Munich performance of Beethoven's 'Emperor' Concerto. Her affection for Felix Mendelssohn is alluded to in the fifth and sixth of her *Sechs Lieder ohne Worte* (Leipzig and Weimar, 1870), entitled 'Venezia' and 'Am Arno'. In 1881 she was living at Charlottenburg.

BIBLIOGRAPHY
Grove1 (G. Grove); *SchillingE*
F. R. Ritter, trans. and ed.: *Music and Musicians: Essays and Criticisms of Robert Schumann* (London, 4/1880)

Title-page of 'Sechs Lieder ohne Worte', op.18 (Leipzig and Weimar: R. Seitz, 1870) by Delphine von Schauroth

O. Ebel: *Women Composers: a Biographical Handbook of Women's Work in Music* (Brooklyn, NY, 1902; Fr. trans., 1910 as *Les femmes compositeurs de musique*)

M. J. Citron, trans. and ed.: *The Letters of Fanny Hensel to Felix Mendelssohn* (New York, 1987)

GEORGE GROVE/JULIE ANNE SADIE

Scherchen(-Hsiao), Tona (*b* Neuchâtel, 12 March 1938). French composer of Eurasian origin. She was trained in traditional Chinese music in China by her mother, the composer Xiao Shuxian (Hsiao Shu-sien), and in Western music by her father, the conductor Hermann Scherchen. She later studied with Hans Werner Henze (Salzburg Mozarteum, 1961–3), Olivier Messiaen (Paris Conservatoire, 1963–5) and György Ligeti (in Vienna). An overt oriental influence can be detected in her original approach to sound and to form, which she ties to the internal development of rhythm and tempo. In 1979 she received a Koussevitsky award in recognition of the whole of her output.

WORKS
selective list

Dramatic: Tzan-Shen (ballet) [from Shen, 1968], 1971

Orch: Tzang, chamber orch, 1966; Kouang, 1968; Tao, va, orch, 1971; Vague-Tao, 1975; 'S . . .', 1975; L'invitation au voyage, chamber orch, 1977; Oeil de chat, 1977; L'illégitime, orch, tape, 1986

Other inst: In, Sin, 2 pieces, fl, 1965; Hsun, ob, tpt, trbn, 2 vc, perc, 1968; Shen, 6 perc, 1968; Tzoue, (cl, vc, hpd)/(fl, db, hpd), 1970; Yun-yu, 2 vn/2 va, vib, 1972; Bien, cl + b cl, hn, tpt, trbn, 2 vn, va, vc, db, 2 perc, pf, 1973; Lien, va, 1973; Tjao-houen, fl, ob, trbn, va, vc, 3 perc, pf, 1973; Yi, mar (2 players), 1973; Ziguidor, wind qnt, 1977; Escargots volants, cl, 1979; Once upon a Time, harp, 1979; Lo, trbn, 12 str, 1979; Tzing, hn, 2 tpt, 2 trbn, 1979; Radar, pf, 1980; Tarots, hpd, 3 cl, tpt, trbn, vn, db, 1982

Vocal: Wai, Mez, str qt, perc, 1967; Tzi, chorus, 1970; La larme de crocodile, 1v, 1977

Elec and mixed-media: Eclats obscurs, tape, 1982; Cancer, solstice '83, 1v, sounds, lights, tape, 1983; Un cadre univers ouvert, 'jeu publique sur table magnétique', 1985; Between, architectural spectacle, son et lumière, trbn, tape, 1986; Spaceflight, tape, 1987; Fou-fou, tape, 1987; Fuite?, 1v, cl + b cl, perc, tape, 1987; see also orchestral works

Principal publishers: Boosey & Hawkes, Universal

BIBLIOGRAPHY
CC (C. Paquelet)

MARIE NOËLLE MASSON

Schjelderup, Mon [Maria Gustava] (*b* Halden, 16 June 1870; *d* Oslo, 21 Nov 1934).

Norwegian composer and pianist. She was a pupil of Agathe Grøndahl and Gustav Lange in Christiania (now Oslo), Woldemar Bargiel in Berlin and Jules Massenet in Paris. She gave concerts in Norway and abroad, and taught at the Christiania conservatory from 1899 to 1906; she then retired because of ill health. Schjelderup is known especially for her 40 songs, but she also wrote orchestral and chamber works. Her music contains frequent allusions to Norwegian folktunes.

WORKS
printed works published in Christiania unless otherwise stated

Orch: Prelude to H. Ibsen: *The Wild Duck*, 1894; Festival March to B. Bjørnson, op.30 (1902)
Vn, pf: Berceuse, op.1 (1893); Ballade, op.2 (1906); 2 Romances, op.6 (1902); Sonata, op.12 (Paris, 1896)
Songs: 40 romances, incl. 3 songs (V. Krag) (1895); 2 Vestlandsviser (1899); 2 Songs, op.10 (1900); 2 Songs (Caspari), op.31 (1901); Barnerim [Children's Rhymes] (1902); Et Savn, op.33 (1902); To Crown Prince Olav, op.52 (1905)
Pf: 2 Pieces, op.13 (1898); Bjerken i brudeslør [Birch in Bridal Veil] (1898); 4 Bagatelles (1903); Serenade, op.55 (1906)

BIBLIOGRAPHY
SchmidlD
K. Michelsen, ed.: *Cappelens musikkleksikon* (Oslo, 1978–80)
C. Dahm: *Kvinner komponerer: 9 portretter av norske kvinnelige komponister i tiden 1840–1930* [Women Composers: 9 Portraits of Norwegian Women Composers 1840–1930] (Oslo, 1987)
                                        KARI MICHELSEN

Schonthal, Ruth (*b* Hamburg, 27 June 1924). American composer and pianist of German origin. She studied at the Sternsches Konservatorium, Berlin, from the age of five until her parents emigrated to Sweden in 1934, then at the Kungliga Musikaliska Akademien in Stockholm (1937–40). In early 1941, the family travelled east across the USSR to Mexico City, where Schonthal studied composition with Rodolfo Halffter and Manuel Ponce, and the piano with Pablo Castellanos. Then, on Hindemith's recommendation, she studied composition at Yale University (AB 1950). In Mexico City she gave an acclaimed performance of her own piano concerto; she also played the piano in bars in both Mexico and the USA (sometimes using the name 'Carmelita') to support herself and her family, and from 1954 held many part-time teaching positions and taught privately in New York. Schonthal is a prolific composer and her works are widely performed and recorded. She draws on a variety of styles, most of which reflect her European background, and achieves an expressiveness that suggests the unusual range of her experience.

WORKS
selective list

Operas: The Courtship of Camilla (1, A. A. Milne), 1979–80; Princess Maleen (2, J. L. Grimm and W. C. Grimm, Schonthal, W. Wood), 1988
Orch: Conc. romantico, pf, orch, 1942; Pf Conc. no.2, 1977; The Beautiful Days of Aranjuez, harp, str orch, 1981, rev. 1983; Evening Music (Night Fantasy with Ocean Waves), 1992; Soundtracks for a Dark Street, orch, el gui, 1993
Chamber and solo inst: Str Qt no.1, 1962; Vn Sonata, 1962, arr. cl, pf, 1975; Sonata concertante (vc, pf)/(cl, pf)/(va, pf), 1973; 4 Epiphanies, va, 1975; Fantasia in a Nostalgic Mood, gui, 1978; Music for Horn and Piano, 1978, arr. hn, chamber orch, 1979; Love Letters, cl, vc, 1979; Letters to Cunegonde, cl, vc, 1979, rev. as Sonata, vc, pf, 1989; Str Qt no.2 'in the Viennese manner', 1983; A Bird's Song about . . ., fl, pf, 1991; A Bird over Jerusalem, fl, pf, tape, 1992; Abendruhe mit süssem Traum, vc, pf, vib, 1993; Improvisation in 3 Interconnected Sections, vn, 1993; Variations on a Jewish Liturgical Theme, el gui, 1993
Vocal: 6 Early Songs (R. M. Rilke), S, 1939–42; 9 Lyric-Dramatic Songs (W. B. Yeats), Mez, chamber orch/pf, 1960; Hommage à García Lorca (F. García Lorca), S, fl, va, vc, harp, 1962, rev. 1992; Totengesänge (Schonthal), S, 1963; By the Roadside (W. Whitman), S, pf, 1975; Songs of Love and Sorrow (various authors), S, pf, 1977; The Young Dead Soldiers (A. MacLeish), SATB, 10 insts, 1986; Six Times Solitude (Milne), S, pf, 1987, rev. 1990; Collages (from *Des Knaben Wunderhorn*), S, fl, 2 cl, 2 perc, vc, pf, synth, 1990; Ingrid's Lieder (Olbricht), Mez, pf, 1993; Trompeten Gesänge (Schonthal), medium v, tpt, vn, vc, pf, small drum, 1993
Pf: Sonatina, a, 1939; Sonata, E♭, 1947; Sonata, b, 1950; Fiestas y danzas, 1961; Nachklänge, pf with added timbres, 1967–74; Sonata brève, 1973; Variations in Search of a Theme, 1974; Gestures, 1978; Fragments from a Woman's Diary, 1982; Canticles of Hieronymus, 1987; Self-Portrait of the Artist as an Older Woman, 1991
Other kbd: Temptation of St Anthony, org, 1989

Principal publishers: Cornucopia, Fine Arts Music, Carl Fischer, OUP

BIBLIOGRAPHY
LePageWC, iii
J. Zaimont and K. Famera: *Contemporary Concert Music by Women* (Westport, CT, 1981)
D. Jezic: *Women Composers: the Lost Tradition Found* (New York, 1988)
C. Bisda: *The Piano Works of Ruth Schonthal* (diss., Manhattan School of Music, New York, 1991)
M. Helmig: *Ruth Schonthal: ein kompositorischer Werdegang im Exil* (diss., Freie U., Berlin, 1993)
S. Epstein and D. Hayes: 'Composer Interview: Ruth Schonthal', *ILWC Journal* (1994), Feb, 5–8
                          CATHERINE PARSONS SMITH

Schorr [née Weller], **Eva** (*b* Crailsheim, Württemberg, 28 Sept 1927). German com-

Corona Schröter (as Iphigenia) and Goethe (as Orestes) in the first performance of his 'Iphigenie auf Tauris', Weimar, 6 April 1779: painting by Georg Melchior Kraus

poser and painter. She started learning music and art from her father at the age of five and began composing when she was eight. At 15 and 16 she won prizes for composition and organ. From 1947 to 1952 she studied at the Staatliche Hochschule für Musik in Stuttgart with J. N. David (composition) and A. A. Nowakowski (organ); she took the Staatsexamen in church music (1950) and composition (1951). In 1952 she took part in the Darmstadt summer course with Olivier Messiaen; she has won awards in the GEDOK competitions in Mannheim and is a member of the Freie Akademie der Künste there, and won the gold medal at the 4th International Competition in Buenos Aires. She settled in Stuttgart in 1954.

Her output includes orchestral and chamber music, and works for piano and organ. The opera *Die Katze des Königs*, in six 'Bilder', is for 'children and adults' and includes a children's chorus and a ballet. Her compositional technique, like her painting, bears the stamp of her predilection for architecture. It is strictly serial and characterized by the juxtaposition of linear colouring supported by contrapuntal structures. The differing aspects of tradition, the present and the future are apparent in all her works. Schorr's graphic art works have been shown in many individual and group exhibitions.

WORKS
selective list

Opera: Die Katze des Königs (6 Bilder, B. Frank), 1989
Orch: Kammersinfonie, 1953; 2 vn concs., 1964, 'Septuarchie', 1975; Sinfomobil, 1979; Mixed Suite, 1984
Chamber and solo inst: Wind Qnt, 1971; Fantasie, Choral und Fuge, eng hn, org, 1977; Vc Sonata, 1977; . . . und predigte den Vögeln . . ., harp, 1980; Nonet 'Rondo d'Austria', wind qnt, vn, va, vc, db, 1986; 3 Canzonen, 2 vc, org, 1989; Zeiträume (Variations on Two Themes), wind qnt, pf, 1990
Kbd: 8 Preludes and Fugues, pf, 1949; Deutsche Messe, org, 1952; 4 rhythmische Etüden, pf, 1961; 2 Fugues, 2 hpd, 1990
Vocal: Wände, S, str qt, 1974; Terra magica (cantata, after J. Poethen: *Ach Erde du alte*), Mez, fl, cl, vc, 1986

BIBLIOGRAPHY
R. Matthei and B. Sonntag, eds.: 'Eva Schorr', *Annäherungen an sieben Komponistinnen*, i (Kassel, 1987), 35–41

ROSWITHA SPERBER

Schröter, Corona Elisabeth Wilhelmine (*b* Guben, 14 Jan 1751; *d* Ilmenau, 23 Aug 1802). German singer, actress and composer.

She was the daughter of the oboist Johann Friedrich Schröter, who gave her her earliest instruction in music. She studied various instruments, including keyboard and guitar, but was most successful as a singer. When the family moved to Leipzig (about 1763) she continued her studies with J. A. Hiller (whose wife was probably her godmother) and from 1765 she appeared in Hiller's Grand Concerts. She became the darling of Leipzig musical audiences, although she shared the limelight with Gertrud Schmeling (later Mme Mara) until 1771. Schröter's voice lacked the strength and italianate agility of her rival but the purity of sound and her delivery gave her the advantage in the eyes of many admirers. From 1771 J. F. Schröter took his talented family on extended tours in Germany, the Netherlands and England. After they returned from London in about 1774 Schröter became ever more prominent in Leipzig musical circles but also gained acclaim as an actress in amateur theatricals. She was the dedicatee of the 1775 Chronologie des deutschen Theaters (H. Schmid and J. G. Dyck), an acknowledgment of her growing reputation as an actress. In 1776 Goethe, who had earlier seen and admired her, met her again and arranged her appointment as chamber musician to the Duchess Anna Amalia at Weimar, where she first performed on 23 November that year. While there she also created many of the leading roles of Goethe's early dramas, often playing opposite Goethe in the amateur court theatre. She not only created the title role in his Singspiel Die Fischerin (1782) but also composed music for it, including Der Erlkönig, which opened the play. This first setting of Goethe's famous ballad is simple, folklike and strophic, and (unlike Franz Schubert's later setting) does not attempt to dramatize the poem's inherent dialogue. (In his eulogy Auf Miedings Tod, 1782, for the deceased theatre director, Goethe immortalized Schröter's contribution to the Weimar stage and implicitly acknowledged her impact on his own development in drama.)

Some biographers place Corona Schröter in the Leipzig concert series again in 1782–4, but the 'Mlle Schröter' in question could have been her younger sister Marie. When the court theatre was replaced by a professional company in 1783, Schröter sang in more informal salons and taught singing, as well as acting. (She also devoted herself to poetry, drawing and painting, for which she had a respectable talent.) She had withdrawn from the court altogether by about 1788.

During these years she formed a warm friendship with Friedrich von Schiller, some of whose poems she set. About 1801 she went to Ilmenau with her lifelong companion Wilhelmine Probst in the hope of alleviating a respiratory disease, but she died in the following year. Ten of her letters, 1774–1802, survive (in D-WRgs).

Schröter composed and published two collections of lieder, the first (including Der Erlkönig) in 1786, the second in 1794. The first reflects the strophic simplicity of the folksong revival, but is nevertheless regarded as more effective than the second, which contains more artistically elaborate works, including French and Italian songs. Several other vocal works, among them her settings of Schiller, are lost.

WORKS

Lieder: 25 Lieder in Musik gesetzt, 1v, pf (Weimar, 1786), ed. L. Schmidt (Leipzig, 1907) [facs. edn.]; [16] Gesänge, 1v, pf (Weimar, 1794)

Other vocal: music for Die Fischerin (J. W. von Goethe), 1782, inc., D-WRdn, WRtl; further music for stage works, incl. Der Taucher and Die Würde der Frauen (F. von Schiller), lost; anthology of 360 It. arias and duets, cited in GerberNL, lost; further single works in contemporary anthologies

BIBLIOGRAPHY

ADB (H. M. Schletterer); Choron-FayolleD; EitnerQ; FétisB; GerberL; GerberNL; SainsburyD; SchillingE; SchmidlD

R. Keil: Vor Hundert Jahren, ii: Corona Schröter: eine Lebenskizze mit Beiträgen zur Geschichte der Genie-Periode (Leipzig, 1875)

H. Düntzer: Charlotte von Stein und Corona Schröter: eine Vertheidigung (Stuttgart, 1876)

A. Dörffel: Geschichte der Gewandhausconcerte zu Leipzig (Leipzig, 1884)

H. Burkhardt: 'Das Grabmal der Corona Schroeter in Ilmenau', 5 Volkslieder, ed. M. Friedlaender (Ilmenau, 1902)

P. Pasig: Goethe und Ilmenau mit einer Beigabe: Goethe und Corona Schroeter (Ilmenau, 1902)

H. Stümcke: Corona Schroeter (Bielefeld, 1904 , 2/1926)

L. Schmidt: 'Nachwort', 25 Lieder (Leipzig, 1907) [facs. of Corona Schröter's songs]

H. Holle: Goethes Lyrik in Weisen deutscher Tonsetzer bis zur Gegenwart (Munich, 1914)

E. Herrmann: Das Weimarer Lied in der zweiten Hälfte des 18. Jahrhunderts (diss., U. of Leipzig, 1925), 251ff

M. J. Citron: 'Corona Schröter: Singer, Composer, Actress', ML, lxi (1980), 15–27

C. Neuls-Bates: Women in Music (New York, 1982), 87–8

M. J. Citron: 'Women and the Lied, 1775–1850', Women Making Music: the Western Art Tradition, 1150–1950, ed. J. Bowers and J. Tick (Urbana and Chicago, 1986), 224–48

A. J. Randall: 'The Mysterious Disappearance of Corona Schröter's Autobiography', Journal of Musicological Research, xiv (1994), 1–15

RONALD R. KIDD

Clara Schumann, 1846

Schultz, Ella Georgiyevna. *See* ADA-YEVSKAYA, ELLA GEORGIYEVNA.

Schumann [née Wieck], **Clara (Josephine)** (*b* Leipzig, 13 Sept 1819; *d* Frankfurt, 20 May 1896). German pianist and composer. The daughter of Marianne and Friedrich Wieck, Clara was destined by her father for the concert stage from birth. Her mother (née Tromlitz), the daughter and granddaughter of professional musicians, performed in the Leipzig Gewandhaus as a singer and solo pianist and in later years taught the piano in Berlin. Friedrich Wieck established a music business, selling and hiring out music and pianos, and repairing pianos; he also taught the piano and singing (he devised his own piano method and published singing exercises). The divorce of Clara's parents in 1824 left her in the custody of her father at the age of five. She learnt the piano with him and under his management played in the Gewandhaus at nine, made her formal solo début there at 11, performed in Paris at 12, and dazzled audiences in Vienna at 18. She was appointed *k.k. Kammervirtuosin* to the

Austrian court and an honorary member of the Gesellschaft der Musikfreunde. She pursued a successful career as a concert pianist for more than 60 years.

Following a legendary legal battle with her father, she married the composer Robert Schumann in 1840. Schumann, who had been Friedrich Wieck's student and with whom she had been acquainted since childhood, was relatively unknown as a composer, while she was already a pianist with an international reputation. The Schumanns settled first in Leipzig and subsequently lived in Dresden and Düsseldorf. Between 1841 and 1854, Clara Schumann had eight children, but continued to give concerts, to compose and to teach. Her husband, whose growing mental illness had been a cause for concern for many years, attempted suicide in 1854, was hospitalized in Bonn-Endenich and died there in July 1856.

After her husband's death, Clara Schumann moved to Berlin and resumed her work as a touring *virtuosa*, travelling throughout Europe and the British Isles. She was popular in England and made 19 concert tours there. In 1878 she became principal teacher of piano at the Hoch Conservatory and settled in Frankfurt, but did not relinquish her performing career. She made her last public appearance as a pianist in that city in 1891.

Clara Schumann's life was one of triumph and tragedy. One child died in infancy, and three adult children predeceased her. Her one surviving son was in a mental hospital for more than 40 years and died three years after she did. She supported her children and grandchildren by her earnings. For many years she was her own concert manager and was sought out by students from all over the world. At the same time, she took responsibility for the complete edition of Robert Schumann's works, prepared the instructive edition of his piano music and arranged other works for piano. Her close friends included Felix Mendelssohn, Pauline Viardot, Joseph Joachim and Johannes Brahms. The last was her closest friend from 1854 until her death at the age of 76. She helped advance Brahms's career by performing his works when he was young and unknown, and although they lived in widely separated cities their correspondence testifies to the close musical and personal bonds between them.

Clara Schumann was considered the peer of such keyboard giants as Franz Liszt, Sigismond Thalberg and Anton Rubinstein, and dubbed Europe's 'Queen of the piano'. Her playing was characterized by masterful technique, beautiful tone and poetic spirit; her attention to the composer's text, in an age of improvisation on the score, was almost unique. Although she performed virtuoso works by such composers as Pixis, Frédéric Kalkbrenner and Liszt, her programming was always considered 'serious'. She introduced J. S. Bach, Domenico Scarlatti, Beethoven and Schubert to audiences accustomed to showy variations on popular and operatic melodies. She often performed the works of Felix Mendelssohn and Fryderyk Chopin and, since Robert Schumann was the only composer of piano music among his contemporaries who did not perform in public, she took on this task

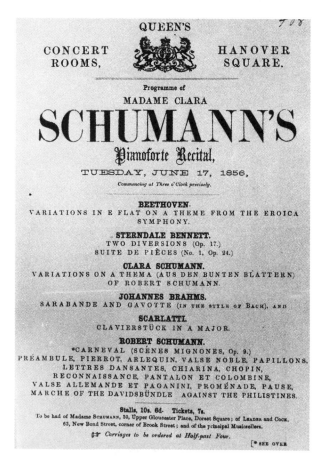

Programme of Clara Schumann's recital at the Hanover Square Rooms, London, 17 June 1856, the month before Robert died

Title-page of 'Soirées musicales' (Leipzig: Hofmeister, 1838), a collection of Clara Schumann's piano music

for him, from childhood introducing and continuing to play his works. Because of her reputation and long career as a pianist, she had a great influence on concert life in the 19th century: the piano recital became an event in which attention was focussed on the composer rather than the virtuoso performer.

Although Robert Schumann strongly supported her efforts at composition and contacted publishers for her, his work took priority over hers, and for many years her composing and practising were relegated to hours when her husband would not be disturbed. Despite her obvious gifts, she exhibited considerable ambivalence towards her own creative work, and she ceased composing after Robert's death (apart from a March written for a friend's anniversary in 1879).

The composer-pianist was an accepted phenomenon in the early 19th century, so the young Clara Wieck wrote primarily for her own concerts. Her father provided her with the best teachers in composition, singing, the violin, instrumentation, counterpoint and fugue. Beginning with her four Polonaises op.1 (1831), almost all her works were published and favourably reviewed. In the use of bold harmonies, rhythmic freedom and the genres she chose, her compositions reflect the advanced tendencies of their day and resemble the works of young composers of the new Romantic school such as Robert Schumann, Felix Mendelssohn and Chopin. (Robert Schumann paid homage to her in the many quotations from her works that appear in his own.) Outstanding among the works before her marriage are the piano pieces opp.5 and 6 – imaginative, poetically conceived character pieces – and the Piano Concerto op.7 (dedicated to Louis Spohr), a dramatic work, testifying to her own virtuosity and independent musical thinking; the three movements are continuous and the work has a unity unusual for its time.

In 1840, she turned, as Robert Schumann had, to songs; three (*Am Strande*, *Volkslied* and *Ich stand in dunkeln Träumen*) were presented to her husband on their first Christmas together. These were followed by four songs, three of which (op.12) were incorporated in a joint collection (Robert Schumann's op.37). Two later groups of songs (opp.13 and 23) are not as well known but deserve recognition. The songs are not distinguished for their lyric qualities but exhibit great feeling, power and sensitivity to the text.

Her Piano Trio op.17 is probably her greatest achievement. Written at a time of great stress (1846), it has an autumnal, melancholy quality but demonstrates the mastery of sonata form and polyphonic techniques, which she and Robert had studied together.

She arranged works by Brahms and William Sterndale Bennett for piano. Her piano arrangements of Robert Schumann's works that were published include the vocal score of the opera *Genoveva* (1850), Studies for the Pedal-Piano from opp.56 and 58 (1896), a four-hand arrangement of his Piano Quintet op.44 (1845), and transcriptions of a number of songs (1873).

WORKS

Editions:

Clara Schumann: Romantische Klaviermusik, ed. F. Goebels, i (Heidelberg, 1967); ii (Heidelberg, 1976) [G i, ii]

Clara Wieck Schumann: Selected Piano Music (New York, 1979 [repr. of Leipzig and Vienna edn, 1836–46]) [S]

Clara Wieck-Schumann: Ausgewählte Klavierwerke, ed. J. Klassen (Munich, 1987) [K]

Clara Schumann: Sämtliche Lieder, ed. J. Draheim and B. Höft, i (Wiesbaden, 1990); ii (Wiesbaden, 1992) [D i, ii]

Clara Schumann: Seven Songs, ed. K. Norderval (Bryn Mawr, PA, 1993) [N]

Printed works published in Leipzig unless otherwise stated; MSS are in D-Bsb, Dlb and Zsch

op.

ORCHESTRAL AND CHAMBER

7   Piano Concerto, a, orch/qnt acc., 1833–5 (1837), ed. J. Klassen (Wiesbaden, 1990)

17   Piano Trio, g, 1846 (1847); (Munich, 1972)

—   Piano Concerto, f, 1847, sketch *D-Zsch*; completed and orchd J. De Beenhouwer and G. Nauhaus (Wiesbaden, 1994)

22   Drei Romanzen, vn, pf, Db, g, Bb, 1853 (1855); (Wiesbaden, 1983)

PIANO

1   Quatre Polonaises, Eb, C, D, C, 1829–30 (1831), ed. B. Hierholzer (Berlin, 1987)

—   Etude, Ab, early 1830s, *Bsb*

2   Caprices en forme de valse, 1831–2 (Paris and Leipzig, 1832)

3   Romance variée, C, 1831–3 (1833), G ii

4   Valses romantiques, 1835 (1835)

5   Quatre pièces caractéristiques, 1833–6 (1836), S, K, G ii [no.3]: 1. Impromptu, Le sabbat; 2. Caprice à la boléro; 3. Romance; 4. Scène fantastique, Ballet des revenants; no.1 as Hexentanz (Vienna, 1838), nos. 1–4 with op.6 as Soirées

musicales (1838)

6   Soirées musicales, 1834–6 (1836), S, K [4 pieces]: Toccatina, Ballade, Nocturne, Polonaise, 2 Mazurkas; reissued with op.5 (1838)

8   Variations de concert sur la cavatine du Pirate de Bellini, 1837 (Vienna, 1837), S

9   Souvenir de Vienne, Impromptu, G, 1838 (Vienna, 1838)

10   Scherzo, d, 1838 (1838), S, K

11   Trois romances, eb, g, Ab, 1838–9 (Vienna, 1840), G ii, S, K; no.2 also pubd as Andante und Allegro, *NZM*, vi (1839), suppl.3

14   Deuxième scherzo, c, after 1841 (1845), G ii

15   Quatre pièces fugitives, F, a, D, G, 1840–44 (1845), G ii; ed. J. Draheim (Wiesbaden, 1994)

—   Sonata, g, 1841–2: Allegro, Scherzo, Adagio, Rondo [orig. titled Sonatine; Scherzo identical with op.15 no.4]; ed. G. Nauhaus (Wiesbaden, 1991)

—   Impromptu, E, ?1844, in Album du Gaulois (Paris, 1885)

16   Drei Präludien und Fugen, g, Bb, d, 1845 (1845), G i, S

—   Three fugues, Eb, E, g, 1845, *Zsch*

—   Praeludium und Fuge, f#, 1845, *Dlb*, fugue inc.

—   Präludium, f, 1845, *Bsb*

20   Variationen . . . über ein Thema von Robert Schumann, f#, 1853 (1854), G i, K

21   Drei Romanzen, a, F, g, 1853–5 (1855), K, G i [no.1], G ii [no.3]; ed. J. Draheim, *Johannes Brahms und seine Freunde* (Wiesbaden, 1983)

—   Romance, a, 1853, in Girl's Own Paper (London, 1891), K

—   Romanze, b, 1856, G ii

—   March, 1879, *Zsch*, first public perf., Frankfurt, Oct 1888; arr. 4 hands, *Zsch*; orchd J. O. Grimm, 1888, *Zsch*

—   Präludien und Vorspiele, improvisations written out 1895, *Bsb*, *Zsch*

VOCAL

—   Der Abendstern, early 1830s, *Zsch*, D ii

—   Walzer (J. Lyser), ?1833 (1834), D ii

12   Three songs (F. Rückert), 1841 (1841), D i: Er ist gekommen, Liebst du um Schönheit, Warum willst du and're fragen [pubd as nos. 2, 4, 11 of 12 Gedichte aus Friedrich Rückert's 'Liebesfrühling' für Gesang und Pianoforte von Robert und Clara Schumann; other nos. = R. Schumann, op.37]

—   Am Strande (R. Burns, trans. Gerhard), 1840, *NZM*, viii (1841), suppl.2; D ii

—   Volkslied (H. Heine), 1840, *Zsch*, D ii, N

—   Die gute Nacht (Rückert), 1841, *Zsch*, D ii, N

13   Sechs Lieder, 1840–43 (1844), D i: Ich stand in dunklen Träumen (Heine) [also in D ii as Ihr Bildnis], Sie liebten sich beide (Heine) [also in D ii], Liebeszauber (E. Geibel), Der Mond kommt still gegangen (Geibel), Ich hab' in deinem Auge (Rückert), Die stille Lotosblume (Geibel)

—   Loreley (Heine), 1843, *Zsch*, D ii, N

—   O weh des Scheidens (Rückert), 1843, *Zsch*, D ii, N

—   O Thou my Star (F. Serre), 1846 (London, 1848) [= trans. of Mein Stern, *Zsch*, D ii, N]

—   Beim Abschied (Serre), 1846, *Zsch*, D ii, N

—   Drei gemischte Chöre (Geibel), SATB, 1848: Abendfeyer in Venedig, Vorwärts, Gondoliera; ed. G. Nauhaus (Wiesbaden, 1989)

23 Sechs Lieder aus Jucunde (H. Rollett), 1853 (1856), D i: Was weinst du Blümlein, An einem lichten Morgen, Geheimes Flüstern, Auf einem grünen Hügel, Das ist ein Tag, O Lust, O Lust
— Das Veilchen (J. W. von Goethe), 1853, *Bsb*, D ii, N

Doubtful: Der Wanderer in der Sägemühle, D ii

CADENZAS

— 2 for Beethoven: Pf Conc., G, op.58, 1846 (1870)
— 1 for Beethoven: Pf Conc., c, op.37, 1868 (1870)
— 2 for Mozart: Pf Conc., d, K466, n.d. (1891)

JUVENILIA
*all lost; cited in C. Schumann's diary,
programmes and Albumblätter*

Orch: Scherzo, 1830–31; Ov., ?1833; orch version of op.4
Songs: Der Traum, 1831 (C. A. Tiedge); Alte Heimath, 1831 (J. Kerner); Der Wanderer, 1831 (Kerner); others listed as Lied/Lieder on programmes from 1830 on
Pf: Waltz, 1828; Variationen über ein Originalthema, 1830; Variationen über ein Tyrolerlied, 1830; Phantasie-Variationen über ein Wieck Romanze, 1830–31; An Alexis, 1832; Rondo, b, 1833; other works mentioned, incl. Capriccio, chorales, variations, scherzos, impromptus, n.d.

BIBLIOGRAPHY

ADB (C. Krebs); *FétisB*; *Grove1* (G. Grove); *MGG* (I. Fellinger); *SchillingE*
F. Wieck: *Clavier und Gesang: Didaktisches und Polemisches* (Leipzig, 1853); Eng. trans. as *Piano and Singing: Didactical and Polemical for Professionals and Amateurs* (Aberdeen, 1875), as *Piano and Song: How to Teach, How to Learn, and How to Form a Judgment of Musical Performances* (Boston, 1875)
A. von Meichsner: *Friedrich Wieck und seine beiden Töchter, Clara Schumann, geb. Wieck, und Marie Wieck* (Leipzig, 1875)
V. Joss: *Friedrich Wieck und sein Verhältnis zu Robert Schumann* (Dresden, 1900; enlarged 2/1902 as *Der Musikpädagoge Friedrich Wieck und seine Familie: mit besonderer Berücksichtigung seines Schwiegersohnes Robert Schumann*)
B. Litzmann: *Clara Schumann: ein Künstlerleben nach Tagebüchern und Briefen*, i (Leipzig, 1902, 8/1925), ii (1905, 7/1925), iii (1908, 6/1923); Eng. trans., abridged (1913 and 1979)
R. Hohenemser: 'Clara Wieck-Schumann als Komponistin', *Die Musik*, v/4 (1905–6), 113ff, 166ff
Johannes Joachim and A. Moser, eds.: *Briefe von und an Joseph Joachim* (Berlin, 1911–13; Eng. trans., abridged, 1914)
F. May: *The Girlhood of Clara Schumann: Clara Wieck and her Time* (London, 1912)
M. Wieck: *Aus dem Kreise Wieck-Schumann* (Dresden, 2/1914)
F. Schumann: 'Brahms and Clara Schumann', *MQ*, ii (1916), 507–15, Eng. trans. of 'Erinnerungen an Johannes Brahms', *NZM*, lxxxii (1915), 225–8, 233–6, 241–3
——: 'Erinnerungen an Clara Schumann', *NZM*, lxxxiv (1917), 69–72, 77–80, 85–8, 93–6, 101–4; Eng. trans., abridged, as *Reminiscences of Clara Schumann as Found in the Diary of her Grandson Ferdinand Schumann of Dresden*, ed. J. Dickinson (Rochester, NY, 1949)

M. Kreisig: 'Einige Briefe Clara Schumanns', *Neue Musik-Zeitung*, xl (1920), 35–6
F. Davies: 'On Schumann – and Reading between the Lines', *ML*, vi (1925), 214–23
E. Schumann: *Erinnerungen* (Stuttgart, 1925); Eng. trans. as *The Memoirs of Eugenie Schumann* (London, 1927) and *The Schumanns and Johannes Brahms: the Memoirs of Eugenie Schumann* (New York, 1927)
B. Litzmann, ed.: *Clara Schumann–Johannes Brahms Briefe aus den Jahren 1853–1896* (Leipzig, 1927; Eng. trans., abridged, 1927)
E. Schumann: *Robert Schumann: ein Lebensbild meines Vaters* (Leipzig, 1931)
M. Fromm: 'Some Reminiscences of my Music Studies with Clara Schumann', *MT*, lxxiii (1932), 615–6
J. Burk: *Clara Schumann: a Romantic Biography* (New York, 1940)
A. de Lara: 'Clara Schumann's Teaching', *ML*, xxvi (1945), 143–4
K. Walch-Schumann, ed.: *Friedrich Wieck: Briefe aus den Jahren 1830–1838* (Cologne, 1968)
K. Stephenson: *Clara Schumann: 1819–1896* (Godesberg [Bonn], 1969)
Robert Schumann: Tagebücher, i: *(1827–1838)*, ed. G. Eismann (Leipzig, 1971, 2/1987); ii: *(1836–1854)*, ed. G. Nauhaus (Leipzig, 1987) [excerpts trans. P. Ostwald; see Nauhaus 1994]; iii: *Haushaltbücher (1837–1856)*, ed. G. Nauhaus (Leipzig, 1982)
P. Susskind: *Clara Schumann as Pianist and Composer: a Study of her Life and Works* (diss., U. of California, 1977)
S. C. Fang: *Clara Schumann as Teacher* (diss., U. of Illinois, 1978)
S. Kross, ed.: *Briefe und Notizen Robert und Clara Schumanns* (Bonn, 1978, 2/1982)
W. Boetticher, ed.: *Briefe und Gedichte aus dem Album Robert und Clara Schumann* (Leipzig, 1979)
P. Ostwald: 'Florestan, Eusebius, Clara, and Schumann's Right Hand', *19th Century Music*, iv (1980–81), 17–31
P. S. Pettler: 'Clara Schumann's Recitals, 1832–50', *19th Century Music*, iv (1980–81), 70–76
J. Chissell: *Clara Schumann: a Dedicated Spirit* (London, 1983)
N. B. Reich and A. Burton: 'Clara Schumann: Old Sources, New Readings', *MQ*, lxx (1984), 332–54
E. Weissweiler, ed.: *Clara und Robert Schumann Briefwechsel: kritische Gesamtausgabe 1832–1838*, i (Basle, 1984), ii (Basle, 1987)
N. B. Reich: *Clara Schumann: the Artist and the Woman* (Ithaca, NY, 1985)
——: 'Clara Schumann', *Women Making Music: the Western Art Tradition, 1150–1950*, ed. J. Bowers and J. Tick (Urbana and Chicago, 1986), 249–81
A. Burton: 'Robert Schumann and Clara Wieck – a Creative Partnership', *ML*, lx (1988), 211–28
N. B. Reich: 'Clara Schumann's *Romance*: Discovered in an 1891 London Weekly', *Keyboard Classics* (1989), Sept–Oct, 18ff
A. Burton: 'A Psychoanalyst's View of Clara Schumann', *Psychoanalytic Explorations in Music* (Madison, CT, 1990), 97–113
J. Klassen: *Clara Wieck-Schumann: die Virtuosin als Komponistin* (Kassel, 1990)
N. B. Reich: 'Clara Schumann and Johannes Brahms', *Brahms and his World* (Princeton, 1990), 37–47
G. Nauhaus, ed.: *The Marriage Diaries of Robert and Clara Schumann*, trans. P. Ostwald (London, 1994)

N. B. Reich: 'The Correspondence between Clara Wieck Schumann and Felix and Paul Mendelssohn', *Schumann and his World* (Princeton, 1994)

NANCY B. REICH

Schuyler, Philippa Duke (*b* New York, 2 Aug 1931; *d* Da Nang, Vietnam, 9 May 1967). American pianist, composer and writer. She began piano studies at the age of three and gave her first formal recital when she was six, having already begun to compose. By the time she was 11 she had won honours several years in succession in a competition sponsored by the New York Philharmonic Young People's Society. She made her first major New York appearance on 13 July 1946, playing Saint-Saëns's Concerto in G minor with the New York PO at Lewisohn Stadium, and her Town Hall recital début on 12 May 1953. Her later life was spent in concert tours of Europe, South America, the Far East and Africa. Among her teachers were Josef Hoffman, Dean Dixon, Antonia Brico, Arnetta Jones, Paul Wittgenstein and Otto Cesana. Although the majority of her compositions are juvenilia for piano, her best-known works are the orchestral *Manhattan Nocturne* (1943), *Sleepy Hollow Sketches* (1945–6), *Rhapsody of Youth* (1948) and *Nile Fantasy* (1965); her later works show the influence of Béla Bartók and of African music. Five books related to her travels were published between 1960 and 1962. She died in a helicopter accident while helping in the evacuation of schoolchildren in Vietnam, where she had been working as a journalist for the *Manchester* (New Hampshire) *Union-Leader*. Subsequently a Philippa Duke Schuyler Memorial Foundation was established in New York. Her manuscripts are in the Schomberg Center for Research and Black Culture (New York).

BIBLIOGRAPHY

CohenE; SouthernB

Obituary, *New York Times* (10 May 1967)

J. Schuyler: *Philippa the Beautiful American: the Travelled History of a Troubadour* (New York, 1969)

O. Williams: *American Black Women in the Arts and Social Sciences: a Bibliographic Survey* (Metuchen, NJ, 1973, 2/1978), 82–7

K. Talalay: 'Philippa Duke Schuyler, Pianist/ Composer/Writer', *BPiM*, x/1 (1982), 43–68 [incl. list of works]

DOMINIQUE-RENÉ DE LERMA

Scliar (Cabral), Esther (*b* Porto Alegre, 28 Sept 1926; *d* Rio de Janeiro, March 1978). Brazilian composer, pianist and teacher. She first studied the piano and harmony in Porto Alegre and undertook further studies, in composition, in Rio de Janeiro with H. J. Koellreutter, Cláudio Santoro and Edino Krieger from 1948 to 1952, with a period spent in Italy in 1948 as a conducting pupil of Hermann Scherchen. In 1952, in Porto Alegre, she formed the chorus of the Associação Juvenil Musical, with which she toured Europe the following year. In 1956 she settled in Rio de Janeiro and taught musical analysis and form at the Instituto Villa-Lobos and at the Pró-Arte music school (1962–75). She composed mainly chamber and vocal works, and among the awards she received were first prize for her Piano Sonata in the 1961 Brazilian National Radio competition and a prize at Brasília in 1966 for her music for the film *A Derrota*; she also wrote two theoretical works, *Elementos de teoria musical* (São Paulo, 2/1985–7) and *Fraseologia musical* (Porto Alegre, 1982).

WORKS

selective list

Orch: O auto da barca do inferno, prelude, 1962

Chamber and solo inst: Pf Sonata, 1961; Sonata, fl, pf, 1962; Str Qt, 1963; Imbricata, fl, ob, pf, 1976; Estudo no.1, gui, 1976

Choral and vocal: Desenho leve, chorus, 1962; Canto menor com final heróico, chorus, 1964; A busca da identidade entre o homem e o rio, chorus, 1971; Entre o ser e as coisas, 1v, pf, 1973; Toada de gabinete, chorus, 1976

BIBLIOGRAPHY

J. M. Neves: *Música contemporânea brasileira* (São Paulo, 1977), 104, 141

V. Mariz: *História da música no Brazil* (Rio de Janeiro, 2/1983), 281

IRATI ANTONIO

Scott [née Spottiswoode], **Alicia Ann** [Lady John Scott] (*b* Spottiswoode, 1810; *d* Spottiswoode, 12 March 1900). Scottish author and composer. She married the Hon. John Montagu-Douglas-Scott, son of the Duke of Buccleuch. As a composer, she remained anonymous until 1854, when a collection of six songs was published bearing her name. She composed drawing-room ballads to harp accompaniment, but they were published in piano arrangements by others. Her best-known song, *Annie Laurie*, appeared in 1838, arranged by Finlay Dun in the third volume of *The Vocal Melodies of Scotland*; it was an 'improved' and expanded version of two stanzas found in Allan Cunningham's *Songs of Scotland* (1825). Her work marks an important stage in the involvement of women songwriters with Scottish song, since her melodies were original, unlike those of Carolina Nairne and others. Most of her songs adopt a sentimentalized Lallans dialect, but not all; among the latter is *Think on me*, which acquired popularity after its posthumous publication (1910, in *Thirty Songs*, ed. Ross).

BIBLIOGRAPHY

D. Ross, ed.: *Thirty Songs by Lady John Scott* (Edinburgh, 1910) [incl. discussion of the music]
D. Scott: *The Singing Bourgeois* (Milton Keynes, 1989)

DEREK B. SCOTT

Sehested, Hilda (*b* Fyn [Fünen], 27 April 1858; *d* Copenhagen, 15 April 1936). Danish composer. Her father owned an estate, Broholm, where she was born, one of 14 children. She studied the piano with C. E. F. Hornemann and later with Louise Aglaé Massart, during a stay in Paris. The composer Orla Rosenhoff (the teacher of Carl Nielsen) also taught her. In 1901 she graduated from the Kongelige Danske Musikkonservatorium as an organist, but never applied for an appointment, concentrating on composing for the rest of her life. She was an active member of the committees of two concert societies, Dansk Koncertforening and Kammermusikforeningen (1911). She never married; during her last years she lived with the violinist Ebba Høyrup, and counted among her closest friends the musicologist Hortense Panum and the pianist Anna Bendix. As an anti-feminist, she had refused to take part in the musical events during the Kvindernes Udstilling (Women's Exhibition) in Copenhagen in 1895, but in 1916 she accepted the offer of writing and conducting a cantata for Dansk Kvindesamfund (a Danish women's organization). In 1914 her opera, *Agnete og Havmanden*, was accepted at the Kongelige Teater in Copenhagen, though never performed.

WORKS

Opera: Agnete og Havmanden (S. Michaëlis), 1913
Orch: Suite, cornet, str, 1906; 2 Miniatures, 1914; Suite, 1915 [version of Suite, cornet, pf, 1905]; Nocturne, hn, vc, orch, 1919; Course des athlètes du nord, trbn, orch, 1925
Chamber: 4 Fantasistykker, vn, pf, 1904; Intermezzi, vn, vc, pf, 1904; Suite, cornet, pf, 1905; Fantasistykker, vc, pf, 1908; Intermezzo pastorale, cl, pf, 1910; Str Qt, G, 1911 [part lost, 2 movts survive]; Fynske Billeder, cl, vc, pf, 1920; Morceau pathétique, trbn, pf, 1923; Pièce de concert, trbn, pf, 1924; 4 Fantasistykker, fl, pf, 1927
Choral: 3 Sange, SATB, 1917; Cantata, S, SSAA, pf, str, 1916; 3 Sange, male chorus, 1922; Fuglekor, T, SATB, pf, 1910
Songs: 8 Gedichte (H. von Gilm), 1v, pf, 1894; 6 Sange, 1v, pf, 1907; Foraarsvers og Sommersange, 1v, pf, 1908; 2 songs, 1v, cl, vc, pf, 1910; 3 Sange,

1v, pf, 1912; 4 Sange, 1v, pf, 1914; Dansk Lyrik, 1v, pf, 1915; Moderen synger, 1v, pf, 1920
Pf: Fantasistykker, 1892; Sonata, 1904; 3 Klaverstykker, 1907; Sommerminder, 1920

BIBLIOGRAPHY

G. Holmen: 'Hilda Sehested og Nancy Dalberg – to danske komponister', *Forum for kvindeforskning*, vi/1 (1986)
G. Holmen, M. Magnussen and O. Kongsted: 'Komponisten Hilda Sehested', *Meddelelser fra Musikhistorisk Museum og Carl Claudius' Samling*, iii (1986), 17–42 [incl. list of works]
D. V. Hansen and T. B. Sørensen: *Hilda Sehested: en dansk komponists liv og musik* (diss., Copenhagen U., 1993)

INGE BRULAND

Sekacz, Ilona (*b* Blackpool, 6 April 1948). English composer. She studied at Birmingham University, initially reading music then changing to drama and theatre arts. She worked for three years as resident composer for the Unicorn Theatre for Children (London) writing *musique concrète* scores and then worked for the Shared Experience theatre company. She wrote the music for the 1982 Royal Shakespeare Company productions of *King Lear* and Edward Bond's *Lear* and has since worked extensively for the company on a freelance basis, providing music for many plays by Shakespeare and others. As well as her music for the theatre, she has produced much work for television including the music for the series *Boys from the Blackstuff* (1982) and *Maigret* (1992). Sekacz is firmly committed to composing what she describes as 'useful' music and meeting the differing demands and challenges of each new production. In 1989 her opera *A Small Green Space* for amateur and professional performers, with a libretto by Fay Weldon, was taken on tour throughout England by the Baylis Programme at the ENO. Her instrumental works, which include a Serenade for double bass and orchestra, a violin sonata (both 1988) and a brass quintet (1990), and her several choral pieces, including Processional Hymn (1986) as well as other hymns and anthems, were mainly composed in aid of conservation and wildlife causes.

BIBLIOGRAPHY

Fuller-LeFanuRM

SOPHIE FULLER

Semegen, Daria (*b* Bamberg, 27 June 1946). American composer of German origin. She emigrated to the USA in 1951· and took American citizenship in 1957. She studied composition with Phillip Bezanson, on a

Chautauqua scholarship, before entering the Eastman School (BM 1968), where she was a pupil of Burrill Phillips and Samuel Adler. As a Fulbright scholar (1969) she studied in Poland with Witold Lutosławski and Włodzimierz Kotoński, afterwards winning a fellowship to Yale University (MM 1971), where she studied with Bülent Arel and Alexander Goehr. She also studied with Vladimir Ussachevsky at Columbia University (DMA 1973) and was his assistant at the Columbia-Princeton Electronic Music Center, where she taught from 1971 to 1975. In 1974 she joined the music faculty of SUNY, Stony Brook, and later became director of its electronic music studio, which she had helped to design.

Semegen's music focusses on the aural perception of colour and shapes. Her compositions are purely instrumental in nature even when she uses the voice. She does not write 12-note music but often uses note rows like traditional scales. Both her musical works and her writings (the latter published in *Music Journal* and elsewhere) reflect her belief that electronic music has evolved naturally from traditional instrumental styles. She favours such 'primitive' electronic composing techniques as physically cutting and splicing tape; exposition of themes and contrapuntal development provide a Classical structure for her music, whatever the genre. Her droll sense of humour is evident in both her writings and her music (e.g. *Jeux des quatres*). She has also written the lyrics for a set of songs with music by Alice Shields.

Semegen has won many honours and awards including six NEA grants, two BMI awards, two MacDowell Colony fellowships, a National Academy of Recording Arts and Sciences award and several Meet the Composer grants. In 1987 she was the first woman to be awarded the McKim Commission from the Library of Congress (*Music for Violin and Piano*).

WORKS
selective list

Orch: Fantasia, 1963; Triptych, 1966

Chamber and inst: 2 str qts, 1963, 1964; Composition, str qt, 1965; Six Plus, tape, fl, vn, vc, hn, harp, cond., 1965; Suite, fl, vn, 1965; 3 Pieces, pf, 1966; 5 Early Pieces, pf, 1967; Quattro, fl, pf, 1967; 3 Pieces, cl, pf, 1968; Study for 16 Str, 1968; Jeux des quatres, cl, trbn, vc, pf, 1970; Music for Vn Solo, 1973; Music for Cl Solo, 1980; Music for Contrabass Solo, 1981; Music for Va and Tape, 1982; Music for Vn and Pf, 1988; Rhapsody for Midi Grand Pf, 1990

Vocal: Silent, Silent Night (W. Blake), T, pf, 1965; Lieder auf der Flucht (I. Bachmann), S, ens, 1967; Poem: For (R. Sward), SATB, 1967; Psalm xliii,

SATB, 1967; Prayer of Hannah (Bible, *1 Samuel*), S, pf, 1968; Poème 1er: Dans la nuit (H. Michaux), Bar, chamber orch, 1969

Elec: Out of Into, film score, 1971; Study on a Trill, 1971, collab. B. Arel; Elec Composition no.1, 1972; Spectra Studies, 1974–6; Arc: Music for Dancers, 1977; Elec Composition no.2, 1979; Epicycles: Music for Dancers, 1982; Arabesque, 1992

BIBLIOGRAPHY

D. Semegen: 'Once More with Feeling', *Heresies*, iii/2 (1980), 32–3

—— : 'The Composer between Man and Music', *Interface*, ix/3–4 (1980), 235–6

J. I. Lochhead and G. Fisher: 'The Performer as Theorist: Preparing a Performance of Daria Semegen's *Three Pieces for Clarinet and Piano (1968)*', *In Theory Only*, vi/7 (1982), 23–39 [incl. complete score]

J. I. Lochhead: 'Temporal Structure in Recent Music', *Journal of Musicological Research*, vi/1–2 (1986), 49–93

D. Semegen: 'Electronic Music: Art beyond Technology', *On the Wires of our Nerves: the Art of Electroacoustic Music*, ed. R. J. Heifetz (Lewisburg, PA, 1989), 32–6

A. E. Hinkle-Turner: *Daria Semegen: her Life, Work and Music* (diss., U. of Illinois, 1991)

—— : 'The Electronic Music of Daria Semegen', *ILWC Journal* (1991), Dec, 1–5

E. Lerner: *The Music of Selected American Women Composers: a Stylistic Analysis* (diss., U. of Massachusetts, 1976 [incl. analysis of *Jeux des quatres*]

C. Grantier: 'Daria Semegen', *The Triangle* [Mu Phi Epsilon], no.4 (1978)

ELLEN D. LERNER, DAVID WRIGHT

Senfter, Johanna (*b* Oppenheim, 27 Nov 1879; *d* Oppenheim, 11 Aug 1961). German composer, pianist and violinist. At the age of 14 she entered Dr Hoch's conservatory in Frankfurt, where she studied with Iwan Knorr (composition), Carl Friedberg (piano) and Adolf Rebner (violin). She studied in Leipzig with Max Reger and won the Arthur Nikisch prize for composition there in 1910. Senfter's large output includes nine symphonies, and concertos for piano, violin, viola and cello. She composed in a late-Romantic style and the formal design of the symphonies reveals the influence of Bruckner. Composition dates for most of her works have not been established.

WORKS
selective list

Syms.: no.1, F, op.22; no.2, d, op.27; no.3, A, op.43; no.4, B, op.50; no.5, e, op.67; no.6, Eb, op.74; no.7, f, op.84; no.8, Eb, op.107; no.9 [details unknown]

Concs. Vn: e, op.1, d, op.35, B, op.71; Pf, g, op.90; Fl, ob, hn, str orch, op.98; Vc, b, op.105

Str qts: d, op.4; f#, op.28; f, op.46; B, op.64; c, op.115

Other chamber: Pf Qt, d, op.112; Cl Qnt, op.119

Vocal: 2 choruses, op.16, female vv, orch; Weihnachtskantilene (Claudius), op.31, soloists, mixed chorus, orch; Maria vor dem Kreuz, op.51, 4 solo vv, str qt; 6 Orchesterlieder, op.82, A, orch; Chor der Toten, op.114, chorus, orch; 6 Lieder, op.131, S, orch

BIRGITTA MARIA SCHMID

Sepúlveda (Maira), María Luisa (*b* Chillán, 14 Aug 1896; *d* Santiago, 5 April 1958). Chilean composer, pianist and teacher. She was the first woman composer to graduate in Chile, and the only one whose works are included within the nationalist movement. She was a pioneer in the compilation, study and research of Chilean folk music. Her compositions, which show a variety of influences – Romantic, impressionist and neo-classical as well as national folklore – range from teaching pieces for piano and choral works for children to chamber music and orchestral works, the last including *Estudio sinfónico* (1932), *Greca* (1932), *Canción de las corhuillas* (1940) and *Trutruka* (1940).

BIBLIOGRAPHY
V. Salas Viu: *La creación musical en Chile (1900–1951)* (Santiago, 1951), 423–6
R. Bustos: 'María Luisa Sepúlveda Maira', *Revista musical chilena*, xxxv/153–5 (1981), 117–40

RAQUEL BUSTOS VALDERRAMA

Seranus. *See* HARRISON, SUSIE FRANCES.

Serena, Amalie. *See* AMALIE.

Sergeyeva, Tat'yana Pavlovna (*b* Kalinin [now Tver'], 28 Nov 1951). Russian composer, pianist and organist. At the Moscow Conservatory she studied the piano with L. Roshchina, organ and harpsichord with Natal'ya Gureyeva (1970–75) and composition, at undergraduate and postgraduate levels, with Alexander Nikolayev (1977–81). Her career as a pianist and organist began in 1974 and she also worked at the conservatory from 1975 to 1988. She was twice laureate of the All-Union Young Composers' competitions, in 1977 and 1979, and was a winner of the 1987 prize of the Composers' Union of Russia.

Sergeyeva's music dwells in a world of antiquity and classicism, and the texts of her vocal works are drawn from 18th-century Russian poetry or older stylized forms. Yet, despite the frequent use of Classical forms and genres, her work is very much part of a living tradition rather than of a lost age of perfection. She employs both direct and disguised quotation, mostly of well-known 'popular classics', and her own themes are concise; close attention to detail results in a noticeable clarity of texture. Lightness and

joy – rare qualities in modern music – are hallmarks of her work.

WORKS
Orch: Pf Conc. no.1, 1979; Db Conc., 1980; Pf Conc. no.2, with solo tpt, 1985; Trbn Conc., 1986; Sym., with solo org, 1987; Fantaziya na temï starinnïkh russkikh val'sov [Fantasia on Themes of Old Russian Waltzes], pf, orch, 1988; Conc., vn, kbd insts, 1989
Inst: Dionis, septet, ob, pf, str, 1980; Sextet, brass, ww, pf, 1980; Sonata, trbn, pf, 1982; Dafne, trio, va/vc, sax, org, 1983; Sonata, vc, pf, 1986; Sonata, vc, org, 1988; Antichnïye pesni [Ancient Songs], trbn, org, 1990–91; Variations [on a theme by T. Tolstaya], vn, org, a sax, tpt, 2 trbn, 1991; Serenade, vc, org, 1992
Vocal: Afrodita i Del'fin [Aphrodite and Dolphin] (songs, E. Krukova), 1v, pf, 1980; Arias (N. Yelagin, V. Trediakovsky), Mez, ens, 1981; Aria (I. Pisarev), 1v, org, 1984; Aria (A. Sumarokov), 1v, org, 1985; O prikhode vesnï [On the Arrival of Spring] (Pentady), Mez, pf, 1990–91

BIBLIOGRAPHY
I. Stepanova: 'Avangard bez avangarda' [Avant Garde without Avant Garde], *SovM* (1990), no.11, pp.17–21
I. Romashchuk: 'Tvorcheski razvivaya traditsii' [Developing Traditions Creatively], *Muzïke Rossii*, ix, ed. A. Grigor'yeva (Moscow, 1991), 194–204

OLGA MANULKINA

Serova [née Bergman], **Valentina Semyonovna** (*b* Moscow, 1846; *d* Moscow, 24 June 1924). Russian composer and writer on music. She was the wife of the composer Alexander Serov and mother of the painter Valentin Serov. In 1862 she entered the St Petersburg Conservatory with a scholarship to study the piano with Anton Rubinstein. Serov, hearing her skilful improvisation, exclaimed, 'Too bad you're not a boy!' Valentina rejoined, 'And why can't a girl be a composer?' She left the conservatory and studied privately with Serov, whom she married in 1863. Together they published *Muzïka i teatr* (1867–8), which included her earliest writings on music. In January 1871, Serov's opera *Vrazh'ya sila* ('The Power of the Fiend') was in production when the composer died, leaving Act 5 incomplete. Serova, aided by Nikolay Solov'yov, finished it in time for the première at the Mariinsky Theatre, St Petersburg, on 19 April/1 May 1871. The intense emotional experience revived her interest in composition and resulted in four original operas. Her first opera, *Uriel Acosta* (1885), was the only one to be performed at the Bol'shoy in Moscow; *Marie d'Orval* (composed during the 1880s) is set in the French Revolution; *Il'ya Muromets* (given by the Mamontov Private Opera in Moscow in 1899) is based

Valentina Serova (right), with her son Valentin and his nanny, 1872

on a Russian heroic tale; the last, *Vstrepenulis'* ('They Roused Themselves Up'), relates to the political unrest of 1904–5. Serova also wrote music criticism in the leading Russian musical, literary and educational journals between 1865 and 1915 and vigorously promoted music education among the people.

WORKS

Uriel Acosta (opera, 5, Serova and P. Blaramberg, after C. von Gutschow's novel), Moscow, Bol'shoy Theatre, 15/27 April 1885, vs (Moscow, 1892)

Marie d'Orval (opera, 5, Serova), 1880s, lost

Il'ya Muromets (opera, 4, Serova), Moscow, Solodovnikov Theatre, 22 Feb/6 March 1899, lib (Moscow, 1899)

Vstrepenulis' [They Roused Themselves Up], 1904–5 (opera, 5, Serova), lost

Miscellaneous works for pf, incl. Muzïkal'nïye vin'yetki [Musical Vignettes]; Suite, orch, arr. from Serov's unfinished opera Kuznets Vakula [Vakula the Smith]; completion (with N. Solov'yov) of Serov: Vrazh'ya sila [The Power of the Fiend]: Act 5, ov., Pyotr's aria

BIBLIOGRAPHY

ME (Yu. V. Keldïsh)

V. Serova: *Serovï, Aleksandr Nikolayevich i Valentin Aleksandrovich: vospominaniya* [Reminiscences of A. N. and V. A. Serov] (St Petersburg, 1914)

N. Yefimova-Simonovich: 'Pamyati muzïkanta-obshchestvennika V. S. Serovoy' [In Memory of the Musician and Public Figure V. S. Serova], *SovM* (1947), no.4, pp.56–60

G. N. Khubov, ed.: *A. N. Serov: izbrannïye stat'i* [Selected Essays] (Moscow, 1950, and Leningrad, 1957), i: 29 n.1, 75, 598 (commentary to p.75)

G. B. Bernandt: 'Uriel Acosta', 'Il'ya Muromets', *Slovar' oper* [A Dictionary of Operas] (Moscow, 1962)

N. Zelov: 'Podvig muzïkanta' [The Heroic Deed of the Musician], *SovM* (1966), no.11, pp.50–53

M. Kopshitser: *Valentin Serov* (Moscow, 1967), 7–8

V. Kolomiytsov: 'Pamyati V. S. Serovoy' [In Memory of Serova], *Stat'i i pis'ma* [Essays and Letters] (Leningrad, 1971),156–7

G. B. Bernandt and I. M. Yampol'sky: 'Serova (urozh. Bergman)', *Kto pisal o muzïke* [Writers on Music] (Moscow, 1974–89)

MALCOLM HAMRICK BROWN

Sessa, Claudia (*b* *c*1570; *d* Milan, between 1613 and 1619). Italian composer. She was a nun at the Lateran Canoness house of S Maria Annunciata in Milan; her singing abilities were praised by Puteanus (*Modulata Pallas*, 1599) and Borsieri's encomium (1619) remarks on her outstanding musical talents and model life as a nun. Her two sacred songs, *Vattene pur, lasciva orechia humana* and *Occhi io vissi di voi* (for soprano and basso continuo; in *Canoro pianto di Maria Vergine*, RISM 1613[3]), belong to the north Italian monodic tradition; *Vattene pur* employs shifting modal centres to underline the surprise conceits of Angelo Grillo's poem.

BIBLIOGRAPHY
SchmidlD
E. Puteanus: *Modulata Pallas* (Milan, 1599; rev. as *Musathena*, Hanover, 1602), chap.5, p.29
G. Borsieri: *Supplimento* to P. Morigia: *La nobiltà di Milano* (Milan, 1619), 51–4
J. Bowers: 'The Emergence of Women Composers in Italy, 1566–1700', *Women Making Music: the Western Art Tradition, 1150–1950*, ed. J. Bowers and J. Tick (Urbana and Chicago, 1986), 116–61, esp. 126–7
R. L. Kendrick: *'Le Sirene Celesti': Generations, Gender and Genres in Seicento Milanese Nuns' Music* (diss., New York U., 1993), 270, 430

ROBERT L. KENDRICK

Setti (de Castro Lima), Kilza (*b* São Paulo, 26 Jan 1932). Brazilian ethnomusicologist, composer and pianist. She graduated as a pianist in 1953 from the Conservatório Dramático e Musical, São Paulo, where she also studied composition with Camargo Guarnieri. She undertook private studies in ethnomusicology and anthropology, and in 1970 a Gulbenkian Foundation grant enabled her to continue her ethnomusicological research in Portugal, with the cooperation of Michel Giacometti and Fernando Lopes-Graça. She subsequently obtained the doctorate in social anthropology from São Paulo University with a dissertation (published in 1985) on the music and culture of the Brazilian Caiçara fishermen; she has also conducted research into the music of the Mbyá-Guarani Indians of Brazil. She taught folklore and ethnomusicology at the Santa Marcellina music faculty, Perdizes, 1975–7, and postgraduate courses in musical anthropology at São Paulo University in 1985 and ethnomusicology at Bahia University, Salvador, in 1991. As a researcher, she has given conferences and published articles in Brazil and abroad. She is a member of the International Council for Traditional Music and of the Sociedade Brasileira de Musicologia. Setti's compositional output reflects a preference for choral music, songs and chamber works. She has developed a free and individual musical style, and a few of her works are based on popular folk melodies. She has won several composition prizes, among them the Rádio MEC awards in 1961 and 1962; her *Canoa em dois tempos* for chorus was commended by the musical institute of the Fundação Nacional de Arte in 1982. A catalogue of her works was published in Brasília in 1976.

WORKS
selective list
Inst: Folgança, suite, chamber orch; Suite, fl, cl, str; 2 momentos, fl, 1972, fl, pf, 1975; Conversainvento, bn, pf, 1991
Pf: Toada, 1952; 8 variações, 1958; Série, 1960; 2 peças, 1972; Multisarabanda, 1987
Choral: 2 corais mistos (Obialá korô, Iemanjá otô), unacc. choir, 1958; Balada do rei das sereias (cantata, M. Bandeira), unacc. choir, 1959; Lenda do Céu (cantata, M. de Andrade), choir, perc, 1962; Canoa em dois tempos, c1982; Missa caiçara, 1990
Vocal: A estrela (Bandeira), 1v, pf, 1961; 3 lembranças do folclore infantil (S. Romero), 1v, pf, 1961; Cantorias paulistas, 1v, pf, 1962; Trova de muito amor (H. Hilst), 1v, pf; Ore ru ñamandu ete tenondeguá, 1v, fl, pf, perc, 1993

BIBLIOGRAPHY
J. M. Neves: *Música contemporânea brasileira* (São Paulo, 1977), 143–4

IRATI ANTONIO

Sfakianaki, Marielli (*b* Athens, 12 Jan 1945). Greek composer, singer and writer. The daughter of the composer and pianist Kostas Sfakianakis, she studied singing at the Athens Conservatory (1963–71) and then composition with Yannis Papaioannou (1971–84). She has devoted herself almost exclusively to the composition of vocal and especially choral music, drawing on her long experience as a member of the Hellenic Radio chorus since its inception in 1978. Her flowing, melodious musical style tends towards neo-classicism, and the formal balance and occasional harmonic boldness evident in her works reflect the shape and character of the poetic texts, several of which she has written herself. Most of her works have been performed at the Moussikos Avgoustos Festival in Iraklion, Crete. Her works include two operas (both to her own texts), *The Pagic Muper* (performed at Iraklion, 1988) and *Minos* (1988–93); *Eyeopelayitika traghoudia* ('Six Aegean Folksongs') for mixed chorus (1986); and a cycle of 12 songs to a text by Nikos Demou, *To vivlio ton gaton* ('The Book of Cats'), for baritone, female chorus, string quintet and percussion (1986–7). She is also the author of a novel and a satirical work.

GEORGE LEOTSAKOS

Shatin [Shatin Allen], **Judith** (*b* Boston, 21 Nov 1949). American composer. She studied at Douglas College (AB 1971), the Juilliard School (MM 1974) and Princeton University (PhD 1979). Her teachers included Milton Babbitt, Otto Luening, Jacob Druckman and Gunther Schuller. She has won four NEA composer fellowships and has received many commissions, among them one from the Bay Area Women's Philharmonic (*Piping the Earth*). In 1979 she joined the faculty of the University of Virginia, where she became director of the Virginia Center for Computer Music, and from 1989 served as president of American Women Composers, Inc. Shatin has written for both electronic and acoustic media, combining the two in several works.

WORKS
selective list

Opera: Job (opera–oratorio), 1978–9; Follies and Fancies (chamber opera, after Molière: *Les précieuses ridicules*), 1981–2

Orch: Arche, va, orch, 1978; Aura, 1981; The Passion of St Cecilia, pf, orch, 1983–4; Ruah, fl, chamber orch, 1985; Piping the Earth, 1990; Stringing the Bow, 1991

Other inst: When the Moon of Wildflowers is Full, fl, vc, 1972; Quatrain, vn, va, cl, b cl, 1975; Constellations, str qt, 1979; Lost Angels, tpt, bn, pf, 1979; Study in Black, fl, perc, 1981; Sphinx, pf, 1982; Icarus, vn, pf, 1983; L'étude du coeur, va, 1983, rev. 1987; Werther, fl, cl, vn, vc, pf, 1983; Widdershins, pf, 1983; Ignoto Numine, vn, vc, pf, 1986; Monument in Brass, brass qnt, 1986; View from Mt Nebo, vn, vc, pf, 1986; Doxa, va, pf, 1989; Gabriel's Wing, fl, pf, 1989; Round 3, trbn, 1989; Secret Ground, fl, cl, vn, vc, 1990; 1492, pf, perc, 1992

Vocal: Ruth, S, 1971; Wedding Song, S, eng hn, 1974; Akhmatova Songs, Mez, fl, cl, vn, vc, pf, 1982; Carreno, Mez/pf, 1987; Marvelous Pursuits, 4vv, pf, 1987; We Bring you Peace, chorus, 1990; Hark my Love, chorus, pf, 1991; see also elec works

Elec: Music for Emergence, 1988; Hearing Things, amp vn, MIDI kbd, computer, elec insts, 1989; Three Summers' Heat, Mez, tape, 1989; Spinnerets, S, actress, kbd, tape, 1990; Tenebrae super faciem abyssi, 1990; Kairos, fl, computers, 1991

Principal publishers: ACA, Arsis, Peters

BIBLIOGRAPHY

J. L. Zaimont and K. Famera, eds.: *Contemporary Concert Music by Women* (Westport, CT, 1981), 2

J. M. Keller: 'Teresa Carreña Returns to the Stage', *Piano Quarterly*, xxxviii/Fall (1990), 18–27, esp. 24

DAVID METZER

Sheppard, Ann. *See* MOUNSEY, ANN.

Sheridan, Caroline Elizabeth Sarah. *See* NORTON, CAROLINE ELIZABETH SARAH.

Sheridan, Helen. *See* BLACKWOOD, HELEN.

Shiomi, Mieko [Chieko] (*b* Okayama, 13 Dec 1938). Japanese composer, performing artist and pianist. She wrote her first composition at the age of 11 and later studied composition with Minao Shibata, Yoshio Hasegawa and Koji Taku at the National University of Fine Arts and Music, Tokyo; she graduated in musicology in 1961. Shiomi has worked exclusively as a freelance composer-performer since 1961, when she, Takehisa Kosugi and Shūkō Mizuno organized Group-Ongaku, an experimental ensemble focussing on improvisation, tape music and 'events'. In 1963 Nam June Paik introduced her to the group Fluxus, whose members created events and collective documents representing the major directions of concept music; with the encouragement of the founder, George Maciunas, she went to New York to participate with Fluxus in 1964–5. Most of her works before 1976 are events and 'inter-media' art (for example the event piece *Direction Music*, 1965, in which ten performers pull strings attached to a pianist's fingers, or the series of international mail events, 1965–75, which were published as *Spatial Poem*). She resumed notated composition, but still produced mainly intermedia and theatrical works for voices. In *If we were a Pentagonal Memory Device*, a humorous theatrical work, each singer focusses on a single vowel sound; pseudo-madrigal sections and occasional block chords using extended triads contrast with polyphony concentrated on vocal timbres and the sounds of individual words. Another theatrical work, *A Trick of Time*, uses extensive quotation and plays with the perception of time through independent and fluctuating tempos. In 1990 Shiomi began collaborating with a computer musician on pieces for a 'media opera' and in 1991 began to cultivate 'an art form uniting female and male elements that would survive in the future' (Shiomi quoted by Kakinuma).

WORKS
selective list

Wind music, 1964, rev. 1991; Direction Music, event piece, pf, 10 performers, 1965; Compound View no.2, 1967; Amplified Dream nos.1–2, 2 pf, elec, tapes, slides, performers, 1969; Intermezzo, 1974; As it were Floating Granules nos.1–6, perf. by audience, 1975; Phantom, monodrama, S, 1978; Polarization, 2 pf; Bird Dictionary, S, pf, tape, 1978; Do you Hear the Theorem by Pythagoras?, 1979

If we were a Pentagonal Memory Device, theatre piece, S, S, T, T, B, 1979; In the Afternoon or the Structure of the Dream, 1v, pf, 1979, rev., with computer obbl, 1991; And a Nightingale has Flown, 1980; The Sun Sets over the Prairie, 1980; Spring, S, S, Ct, T, Bar, 1981; Have you Seen Milpass?, 1983; A Trick of Time [pt 1], pf, nar, vc, metronome, endless box [folded paper], 1984; Maboroshi no Uta, 1986

Compound View no.3, 1987; A Poem by Globules, synth/sampler, performer-nar, 1988; A Trick of Time, pt.2, 2 pf, nar, vc, 1988; Direction Music for a Pianist, pf, 1990; Requiem for George Maciunas, tape, 1990; An Episode by Glass Marbles, 1991; A Celestial Tune by 108 Glass Marbles, 1992

Visual poetry and objects, 1963–91, incl: Endless Box, 1963; Spatial Poem nos.1–9, mail events, 1965–75; Flying Poem no.2, 1989; Balance Poem nos.1–24, visual poetry, 1991; Fluxus Balance, mail event, 1991

BIBLIOGRAPHY

K. Akiyama: 'Japan', Dictionary of Contemporary Music, ed. J. Vinton (New York, 1971)

D. H. Cope: New Directions in Music (Dubuque, IA, 1971, 5/1989)

B. Dittrich: 'Anschauungsunterricht auf höchstem Niveau', Reutlinger General-Anzeiger (21 Feb 1981)

B. H.: 'Dadaistische Köstlichkeiten', Südwest Presse–Schwäbisches Tagblatt (21 Feb 1981)

T. Hoffman: 'The Sounds of Music – Japan's Modern Composers and Performers', Japan Society Newsletter (1985), March, 2–6, esp. 4

J. Hendricks: Fluxus Codex (New York, 1988), esp. 475–84

C. Phillpot and J. Hendricks: Fluxus: Selections from the Gilbert and Lila Silverman Collection (New York, 1988) [pubn of the Museum of Modern Art], 58–9

T. Kakinuma: 'Japan', Ear Magazine, xv/10 (1991), 18

N. J. Paik: '2 × Mini Giants', Artforum, xxix/7 (1991), 90–91

J. MICHELE EDWARDS

Shlonsky, Verdina (b Kremenshug, Ukraine, 19 Jan 1905; d Tel-Aviv, 20 Feb 1990). Israeli composer and pianist. While studying at the Berlin Hochschule für Musik she took piano lessons with Egon Petri and Artur Schnabel and later studied composition with Nadia Boulanger, Edgard Varèse and Max Deutsch in Paris (1930–32). After arriving in Israel (then Palestine) in 1929 she worked as a concert pianist and theatre composer, and later taught at the Tel-Aviv Academy of Music for many years. In 1931 her Poème hébraïque won first prize in a French government competition for women composers, and in 1948 her String Quartet won the Bartók Prize. She composed many piano works, including pedagogical and educational pieces, and a substantial number of art songs to texts by French, German and Israeli poets. Noteworthy are the songs to texts by her brother, the Israeli poet Abraham Shlonsky.

Shlonsky's style developed over the years from traditional with modal elements to Romantic, then to the 12-note system which prevailed in most of her later works. Her achievement, especially in areas where she excelled – piano works and art songs, may have been unjustly overshadowed by her brother's reputation as a poet and his status as a 'national treasure'.

WORKS
selective list

Inst: Sym., 1935; Jeremiah, sym. poem, 1936; Pf Conc., 1942; Str Qt, 1948; 5 Sketches, pf, 1949; 2 sonatas, vn, pf, 1951; Divertimento, wind qnt, 1952; Reflexion symphonique, orch, 1966; Vn Conc., 1967; Pf Conc. no.2, 1968; Concertino, pf, orch, 1970; Silhouettes, vn/cl, perc, 1977; Euphony, chamber orch, 1980

Vocal (1v, pf, unless otherwise stated): Poème hébraïque, 1931; Images (Temunot) (A. Shlonsky), 6 songs, 1933; 8 Songs (R. Eliaz, S. Melzer, S. Shabazi, S. Shalom, A. Shlonsky), 1936–44; 5 Songs (G. Apollinaire), 1939; 4 Songs (A. Shlonsky), 1947; Gedi [Kid] (A. Shlonsky), Mez, pf, 1954; Glühende Rätsel [Glowing Riddles] (N. Sachs), 1v, chamber orch, 1967; Oreah·[Guest] (A. Shlonsky), 1984

Principal publishers: Israeli Music Publications, Israel Music Institute

WILLIAM Y. ELIAS, ZVI KEREN

Sianovine, Caterina. See SINYAVINA, EKATERINA ALEXEYEVNA.

Siegling, Marie [Mary] **Regina** (b Charleston, SC, 1824; d London, 1919). American amateur singer, pianist, harpist and composer. She was the eldest daughter of John Siegling, an emigrant from Erfurt and the founder, in 1819, of the Siegling Music House of Charleston. Her father encouraged her musical talents by taking her on his business trips to New York and Havana, where she sang with Ole Bull, and she studied composition in Erfurt with her paternal grandmother, Regina von Schröder Siegling. Her piano pieces La capricieuse, La gracieuse, Souvenir de Charleston and Souvenir de la Saxe were published in the mid-1840s by George Willig jr of Baltimore. In 1850 she married Edward Schuman-LeClercq of Dresden and remained in Europe, looking after their five children.

BIBLIOGRAPHY

M. R. Schuman-LeClercq: Memoirs of a Dowager (typescript, 1908, South Caroliniana Library, Columbia, SC)

E. O. S. Horlbeck: Sketch of my Father's Life as Related to his Children, Collected . . . by his Youngest Daughter Eliza Ottelia (MS, 1912, South Caroliniana Library, Columbia, SC)

J. J. Hindman: Concert Life in Ante Bellum Charleston (diss., U. of N. Carolina, 1971)

J. Tick: American Women Composers before 1870 (Ann Arbor, 1983), 139

CAROLINE CEPIN BENSER

Signorini [Signorini-Malaspina], **Francesca**. See CACCINI, FRANCESCA.

Sikora, Elżbieta (*b* Lwów, 20 Oct 1943). Polish composer. She graduated in sound engineering from the State Higher School of Music in Warsaw (MA 1968) and completed her studies in electroacoustic music with Pierre Schaeffer and François Bayle at the Groupe de Recherches Musicales in Paris (1968–70). She returned to the Warsaw music school and studied composition with Tadeusz Baird and Zbigniew Rudziński (MA 1977). During that period she founded with the composers Krzysztof Knittel and Wojciech Michniewski the group KEW, which gave performances in Poland, Sweden, Austria and Germany. Scholarships from the French government and from the Kościuszko Foundation for work with John Chowning at the Computer Center for Research in Music and Acoustics in Stanford enriched Sikora's international outlook. In 1981 she moved to France, where she took part in computer music courses at IRCAM and studied with Betsy Jolas. In 1989 she became professor of electronic music at the conservatory in Angoulême. She collaborates with French radio as a composer and promoter of new music; her works have been performed in most European countries and in the USA. Awards include the GEDOK (Mannheim) first prize in 1982 for *Guernica* and second prize for the chamber opera *Ariadne* at the 1978 Weber Competition in Dresden.

WORKS
selective list

Dramatic: Ariadne, chamber opera, 1977; Derrière son double, radio opera, 1v, inst ens, elec, 1983; L'arrache-coeur, radio opera, 1984–6; La clef de verre, ballet, 1986
Orch: Cercles, 1975: Sym. no.1, 1984; Rappel II, orch, SYTER system, 1988
Vocal: Pieśni rozweselające serce [Heart Brightening Songs], S, 5 insts, 1973; Guernica – Hommage à Pablo Picasso, unacc. chorus, 1975–9; . . . according to Pascal, reciter, tpt, harp, hpd, vc, 1976; Stworzenie swiata [The Creation of the World], 2 vocal ens, chamber orch, 1976; Salve regina, chorus, org, 1981; Lorelay, S, inst ens, 1987; Chant de Salomon, S, chamber ens, 1991; see also elec works
Chamber: Str Qt, 1975; Podróż pierwswa [Journey no.1], tuba, 1977 [version of elec work, 1974]; Interludes, fl, harp, 1980; Piaski [Sands], fl, perc, 1980; Str Qt no.2, 1980; Podróz trzecia [Journey no.3], fl, 1981; Eine kleine Tagmusik, 7 insts, 1983; Solo, vn, 1980; see also elec works
Elec (for tape unless otherwise stated): First Name, 1970; Widok z okna [The View from the Window], 1971; Uncertainty of Summer, 1973; Podróż pierwswa [Journey no.1], db, 2 tape recorders, 1974; Podróż druga [Journey no.2], 1976; Nocą twarzą ku niebu [In the Night Face to Heaven], 1978; Rapsodia na śmierć republiki [Rhapsody for

the Death of the Republic], 1979; Głowa Orfeusza I [The Head of Orpheus I], 1981; Janek Wiśniewski – Grudzien – Polska [Janek Wiśniewski, December, Poland], 1981–2; Głowa Orfeusza II [The Head of Orpheus II], fl, tape, 1982; Pięć pór roku [5 Years' Seasons, vc, tape, 1989; A peine le temps que dure une vision, reciter, tape, 1989 [2nd version of work for S, chamber ens, n.d.]; Géométries variables, 1991; On the Line, S, tape, 1992; see also dramatic and orch works

BARBARA ZWOLSKA-STĘSZEWSKA

Silva, Adelaide Pereira da (*b* Rio Claro, São Paulo, 5 July 1928). Brazilian pianist and composer. She studied the piano first with Nair de Souza and Hans Bruch and later with Dinorá de Carvalho, harmony and counterpoint with Oswaldo Lacerda and composition with Camargo Guarnieri. Although most of her career has been dedicated to performing and teaching, she has also been active in developing research into Brazilian folk music, at the Museu do Folclore in São Paulo. Her compositions, which are mainly instrumental and choral, include, for piano, two suites (1965) and a sonatina (1975), and, for chorus, *Ele nasceu lá na Loanda* (1964), *Reza de umbanda* (1971), *Coros infantis brasileiros* (1977) and *Canto da terra* (1980). Some pieces have been published by Ricordi Brasileira (São Paulo), and a catalogue of her works was produced by the Ministério das Relações Exteriores, Brasília, in 1977.

IRATI ANTONIO

Silver, Sheila (*b* Seattle, 3 Oct 1946). American composer and painter. She studied composition in Paris and Stuttgart with Erhard Karkoschka and György Ligeti, and at Brandeis University with Arthur Berger, Harold Shapero and Seymour Shifrin. She has received numerous awards, prizes and residencies including the Prix de Paris, Prix de Rome, a Koussevitsky Fellowship and a Composer Award from the American Academy and Institute of Arts and Letters and the ISCM. One critic has described her output as comprising 'impressive transcultural works in which elements of, say, Buddhist chanting are worked into Western-style textures'. Other sources for her melodically rich music include classical Greek, Roman and Indian mythology, American jazz and Jewish chant. Her allegorical opera, *The Thief of Love*, for which she also wrote the libretto, is based on a 17th-century Bengali tale.

WORKS

Opera: The Thief of Love (S. Silver), 1986
Orch and chamber orch: Galixidi, 1976; Shirat Sarah,

1985–7; Dance of Wild Angels, 1990; 3 Preludes, 1992

Chamber: Str Qt, 1975; Canto (E. Pound), Bar, ens, 1979; Vc Sonata, 1988; 6 Preludes, after C. Baudelaire, pf, 1990; To the Spirit Unconquered, vn, vc, pf, 1992

Vocal: Chariessa (cycle of 6 songs, Sappho), S, pf, 1978, arr. S, orch, 1980; Ek Ong Kar, SATB chorus, 1981

CYNTHIA GREEN LIBBY

Simons, Julie. See CANDEILLE, JULIE.

Simons, Netty (b New York, 26 Oct 1913; d New York, 1 April 1994). American composer. Originally trained as a pianist, she later studied at New York University with Percy Grainger and privately (1938–41) with Stefan Wolpe; she regarded Wolpe as her most influential teacher. Her early compositions are characterized by extreme economy of means and imaginative interplay of tone colour. By 1960 she had become more experimental, often including aleatory elements; later she frequently used graphic notation (*Buckeye has Wings, Design Groups I and II, Silver Thaw*). Many of her compositions may be performed as theatre pieces, employing dancers and actors as well as (or instead of) musicians. Her musical materials have been donated to New York Public Library, Lincoln Center.

WORKS
selective list

Stage: The Bell Witch of Tennessee (1, J. Simons) (1956); Buckeye has Wings (theatre piece), any number of players (1971); Too Late, the Bridge is Closed (theatre piece), any number of players (1972); see also 'Other inst'

Orch: Piece for Orchestra (1949); Lamentations I (1961); Lamentations II (1965); Variables, 5 insts/ multiples of 5 up to full orch (1967); Illuminations in Space, va, orch (1972); Pied Piper of Hamelin (R. Browning), nar, fl, pf, str orch (1972); Big Sur (1981)

Other inst: Piano Work, pf (1952); Night Sounds, pf (1953); Qnt, 4 wind, db (1953); Sonata, 2 vn (1954); Circle of Attitudes, dance suite, vn, opt. dancer (1960); Facets II, fl/pic, cl, db (1961); Time Groups I (Gate of the 100 Sorrows), dance suite, pf, opt. dancer (1963); Windfall, pf (1965); Design Groups I, 1–3 perc (1966); Design Groups II, duo, 1 tr, 1 b (1968); Silver Thaw, 1–8 players (1969); 5 Illuminations, pf (1970)

Vocal: Set of Poems for Children (C. Rossetti, C. Sandburg, J. Stephens, R. L. Stevenson), nar, inst octet (1949); 3 Songs (H. Morley), Mez, pf (1950); Puddintame (limericks), nar, any number of players (1972); Songs for Wendy (W. Blake, J. Keats, Rossetti), 1v, va (1975); Songs for Jenny, 1v, db, amp pf (1974–5); see also orch

Principal publisher: Presser

CHRISTINE AMMER

Sinyavina [Sianovine, Sinavina, Sinavin], **Yekaterina Alexeyevna** (d St Petersburg, 1784). Russian composer and keyboard player. The daughter of Admiral Alexey Naumovich Sinyavin, she was the dedicatee of a keyboard concerto by Giovanni Paisiello, probably first performed at the court of Catherine II in 1781 with Sinyavina as soloist. She was active at the court as a composer of instrumental music from the late 1770s. According to the concerto's title-page she was a maid of honour to the Empress (*Concerto . . . alla Signora de Sianovine, dame di onore de S. M. I. l'Imperatrice di tutte le Russie*). In 1781 she married S. R. Vorontsov (later Russian Ambassador in London) and died three years later, having composed numerous short instrumental and keyboard pieces for private court occasions; the only extant examples survive in manuscript form (keyboard dances in *RU-SPsc*). The lost *Sonate per cembalo accomp. di un violino* are among the earliest-known examples of keyboard sonatas by a composer of Russian origin, predating the *Sonate di cembalo* by the Ukrainian Dmitri Bortnyansky.

BIBLIOGRAPHY

N. J. Yandell: *Keyboard Music in Russia during the Late Eighteenth and Early Nineteenth Centuries* (diss., U. of Oxford, in preparation)

NIGEL J. YANDELL

Sirmen, Maddalena Laura Lombardini. See LOMBARDINI SIRMEN, MADDALENA LAURA.

Skouen, Synne (b Oslo, 8 Aug 1950). Norwegian composer and writer. She studied at the Vienna Academy of Music, where her composition teachers included Alfred Uhl and Dieter Kaufmann (electronic music), then at the Oslo School of Music (1973–6) with Finn Mortensen. During the period 1977–86 she was editor of the newly-established periodical for contemporary music *Ballade*, and for some years was also a music critic for *Arbeiderbladet* in Oslo; in the 1980s she began to work full-time as a composer. Her works are mostly based on dramatic concepts and are written in a mainly atonal language with tonal passages interspersed. In 1983 the radio production of Cecilie Løveid's play *Måkespisere* ('The Gull Eaters'), for which Skouen wrote incidental music, won the Prix Italia; the full-length ballet *Volven* was commissioned in 1987 by the Norwegian State Opera. In 1993 she became head of music for channel two of the Norwegian broadcasting corporation, NRK.

WORKS
selective list

Dramatic: Måkespisere [The Gull Eaters] (incid. music, C. Løveid), 1981; Volven (ballet, choreog. K. Alveberg), 1987–8; Froskeprinsen [The Frog Prince] (television fable), S, T, elec, 1988–9

Vocal: Rug [Rye] (Løveid, S. Obstfelder), female v, vc, grand pf, 1982–4; 3 haner galer [3 Cocks Crowing], S, S, A, A, orch, 1985; Rosa, S, grand pf, tape, 1984

Inst: Tombeau to Minnona, orch, 1976; Hils Domitila! [Greet Domitila!], pf, 1980: P.s.: pianissimo, pf, 1980; Canto delle balene, orch, tape, 1988

Principal publisher: Norsk Musikforlag

KARI MICHELSEN

Sloman, Jane [Torry, Sloman] (*b* Ipswich, 15 Dec 1824; *d* after 1850). English composer, also active as a concert pianist and singer. As a child prodigy, she studied with Louise Dulcken (pianist to Queen Victoria), made early appearances at court and played privately with Nicolò Paganini and Sigismond Thalberg. She was one of the first female virtuoso pianists in the USA when she arrived in 1839. She gave piano lessons to a few students before she made her American début at Niblo's Gardens in New York on 16 July 1841; this was part of a concert tour that included performances in Philadelphia and Boston. Her first concerts were accompanied by a biographical sketch which established her as a child prodigy who was entirely self-taught in composition, yet also modest and of the 'good character' appropriate for a Victorian professional woman. The date of her death is unknown; her last concert took place in 1850. Her compositions were published under the name Sloman Torry after 1862, and appeared in the USA until 1902. She edited a vocal collection, *The Melodist*, which included her piano accompaniments to popular tunes and eight original choral melodies and settings. The tune of her most popular vocal work, *Roll on, Silver Moon*, was incorporated into Stephen Foster's *Social Orchestra*; Charles Grobe wrote a transcription of it, Nathan Barker arranged it for chorus and Mark Twain mentioned the song in his catalogue of music popular in a Southern parlour (*Life on the Mississippi*, 1883). Sloman wrote many of her own texts, frequently depicting some aspect of courtship through the voice of a female narrator. Her musical writing ranges from the simple hymns in the *Melodist* to a more chromatic style characteristic of the mid-19th century.

WORKS
VOCAL

Forget thee?, 1v, pf (Boston, 1843); The Maiden's Farewell (Boston, 1843); Roll on, Silver Moon, S,

mixed chorus, pf (New York, 1848) [? orig. for 1v, pf]; I'll make him speak out (New York, 1852); Take back the ring (New York, 1860); The Butterfly, pubd as La farfalletta, trans. E. C. Sebastiani (New York, 1861); So far away (New York, 1869); Queen of the Night (Del Ciel Regina), 1v, pf (Boston, 1873); Margery Drew; Titania (n.p., 1902)

The Melodist: Containing selected gems . . . arranged expressly for the use of female seminaries, 1–4 female vv, pf (New York, 1871): 48 arrs. of melodies by Bellini, Donizetti, Charles Horn, Jenny Lind, Felix Mendelssohn, Mozart and others; and 21 hymns, 8 by Sloman (Ailse, Cardross, Dismission Hymn, Holmes, Mutter, Parsons, Prosser, The Academy Hymn)

PIANO

Boz Quadrilles, as played . . . at the complementary ball to Charles Dickens, Esq., Park Theatre, New York (Boston, 1842): Pickwick, Oliver Twist, Nicholas Nickleby, Barnaby Rudge, Master Humphrey's Clock
Ericsson's Schottische (New York, 1853)

BIBLIOGRAPHY
CohenE; WAM
A Biographical Sketch of Jane Sloman the Celebrated Pianiste (Boston, 1841)
C. Ammer: Unsung: a History of Women in American Music (Westport, CT, 1980), 44, 75
J. Tick: American Women Composers before 1870 (Ann Arbor, 1983), esp. 188–91
K. Pendle, ed.: Women and Music: a History (Indianapolis, IN, 1991)

NAOMI ANDRÉ

Smiley, Pril (*b* Mohonk Lake, NY, 19 March 1943). American composer, teacher and percussionist. She studied with Henry Brant, Louis Calabro, Vivian Fine and Vladimir Ussachevsky. In 1963 she became associated with the Columbia-Princeton Electronic Music Center (now the Electronic Music Center of Columbia University) and in 1985 was appointed its associate director. She also taught electronic music and was composer-in-residence at other American universities. Particularly known for her film and theatre compositions, Smiley was electronic music consultant for the Lincoln Center Repertory Theater from 1968 to 1974 and created scores for nine major productions there. She has also occasionally worked as a freelance percussionist.

WORKS
selective list; all electronic
DRAMATIC

Elephant steps (occult opera), Tanglewood, MA, 1968; Operation Sidewinder, New York, Vivian Beaumont Theater, 1970; Dr Faust . . ., Cleveland, OH, Playhouse, 1972; Creation of the World and Other Business, New York, 1972, rev. 1981 as Up from Paradise; The Crazy Locomotive, New York, Chelsea Theater, 1976

Incid. music for W. Shakespeare: Macbeth, 1966,

1973; Richard III, 1967; King Lear, 1968; Twelfth Night, 1972; A Midsummer Night's Dream, 1980
Also scores for films, TV, dance

OTHER WORKS

Eclipse, 4-track tape, 1967; Kolyosa, 2-track tape, 1970; Forty-three, 2-track tape, 1983

CHRISTINE AMMER

Smith [Meadows White], **Alice Mary** (*b* London, 19 May 1839; *d* London, 4 Dec 1884). English composer. The daughter of Richard Smith, a lace merchant, she was a pupil of William Sterndale Bennett and G. A. Macfarren and at 21 attracted attention when her First Piano Quartet was performed at a trial of new compositions by the London Musical Society; the Society subsequently performed her First String Quartet, Symphony and other orchestral works. On 2 January 1867 she married Frederick Meadows White, QC (afterwards Recorder of Canterbury and a judge for the County of Middlesex, but not Director of the RAM as is sometimes stated); in November of that year she was elected Female Professional Associate of the Philharmonic Society, and in 1884 Hon RAM.

A prolific composer of both large- and small-scale works, Smith was accounted 'of considerable distinction in her day' (*MEMM*). Her Clarinet Concerto was performed at the Norwich Festival in 1872 and her ode *The Passions* at the Hereford Festival in 1882. Her obituary in *The Athenaeum* noted that

Her music is marked by elegance and grace rather than by any great individuality . . . that she was not deficient in power and energy is proved by portions of the *Ode to the North-East Wind* and *The Passions*. Her forms were always clear and her ideas free from eccentricity; her sympathies were evidently with the classic rather than with the romantic school.

Time has endorsed the negative aspects of this judgment, principally because of Smith's pallid and anachronistic harmonic idiom. She is seen to advantage only in a few pretty miniatures such as *Love's Summer-Land* and the deservedly popular duet *Maying*, of which she sold the copyright in 1883 for £663.

WORKS

all printed works published in London

VOCAL

Operetta: Rüdesheim, or Gisela, solo vv/chorus, 1865
Secular choral: The Masque of Pandora (H. W. Longfellow), cantata, 1865, ov. perf. London, 1878, 2 Intermezzi perf. London, 1879; Ode to the North-East Wind (C. Kingsley), chorus, orch, 1880 (1880); The Passions (W. Collins), ode, soloists, chorus, orch, 1882 (1882); Song of the Little Baltung (AD 395) (Kingsley), choral ballad, male vv, orch, 1883 (1883); The Red King (Kingsley), choral ballad, male vv, orch, vs (1885), str pts (1886); The Valley of Remorse (Miss Bevington), cantata
Sacred choral (SATB, org, unless otherwise stated): Who so hath this world's goods (1864); 4 anthems: By the waters of Babylon, with solo vv, Come unto him, Out of the deep, The Soul's Longing
Partsongs (SATB, unless otherwise stated): The Dream (E. Waller) (1867); Lovers' Melancholy (J. Ford) (1870); Queen of Love (F. J. Palgrave) (1870); Rock them, rock them (T. Decker) (1870); Blow, bugle blow (A. Tennyson); Farewell, fair day (R. Burns), TTBB; Pack clouds away!; Peace, O peace, ATTB; The Question; Venus' Looking Glass, 5vv
Duets (with pf acc.): The Night-Bird (C. Kingsley) (1869); Maying (Kingsley) (1870); Love's Summer-Land (F. E. Weatherly) (1873); When the dimpled water slippeth (J. Ingelow) (1876); Cupid's Curse (G. Peele) (1881); Peace to this dwelling
Songs (1v, pf): Sing on, sweet thrush (R. Burns), canzonet (1857); Weep no more! (J. Fletcher), canzonet (1858); Love and Fear (E. Sandars) (1859); The Last Footfall, in *Chambers' Journal* (1862); West wind, O west wind (Sandars) (1866); L'ange et l'enfant (1869); The First Snow-Fall (J. R. Lowell) (1869); None will be nigh to hear (J. Ingelow) (1869); Binding Sheaves (Ingelow) (1874); O let the solid ground (A. Tennyson) (1876); The Last Goodbye (E. Oxenford) (1882); The Brook; The Dream of Home; Fair daffodils, we weep to see; Fairest Fair (Ingelow); Flow down, cold rivulet (A Farewell; Tennyson); From flow'r to flow'r; I wept as I lay dreaming; If I thought thou could'st have died (C. Wolfe); If thou wilt remember; Mary (Burns); The Mother's Lament (Burns); O forbear to bid me slight her (A. Hill); O sleep, of sleeps thou sweetest; O where art thou dreaming?; Please, Sherry, my dear; Silent night yields no repose; Spring; There's not a joy (Byron)

INSTRUMENTAL

Orch: Sym., c, perf. 1863; Endymion (after J. Keats), ov., 1864; Introduction and Allegro, pf, orch, 1865; Lalla Rookh (after T. Moore), ov., 1865; Endymion, ov., 1869; Cl Conc., 1872; Jason, or The Argonauts and the Sirens, ov., 1879; 2 syms., a, G; Vivien, ov.; untitled movt, b
Chamber: Pf Qt no.1, B♭, 1861; Str Qt no.1, D, 1862; Pf Qt no.3, D, 1864; Pf Qt no.4, g, 1867; Melody and Scherzo, vc, pf (1869); Cl Sonata, A, 1870, slow movt also arr. cl, orch; Str Qt no.2, a, 1870; Pf Trio, G, 1872; Pf Qt [?no.2], E; Str Qt 'Jubal Cain'
Pf: Fugue, f, 2vv, 1961; Fugue, F, 3vv, 1861; Fugue, 2vv, 1861; Vale of Tempe, rondo (1862); Impromptu (1869); 6 Short Pieces (1873); The Fleur de Lys Quadrille, 5 pieces; Fugue, G, 3vv

BIBLIOGRAPHY

Baker6; *DNB* (J. C. Hadden); *Grove1* ('White, Meadows'); *MEMM*; *PazdirekH*; *RiemannL 12*; *SchmidlD*
Obituaries: *The Times* (8 Dec 1884); *The Athenaeum* (13 Dec 1884); *Musical World*, lxii (13 Dec 1884), 779; *MT*, xxvi (1885), 24 [incl. list of major works]
J. D. Champlin: *Cyclopedia of Music and Musicians* (New York, 1888–90)
J. D. Brown and S. S. Stratton: *British Musical Biography* (Birmingham, 1897)

W. W. Cobbett, ed.: *Cyclopedic Survey of Chamber Music* (London, 2/1963)

E. Blom, ed.: *Everyman's Dictionary of Music* (London, 5/1971)

NIGEL BURTON

Smith [Vielehr], **Julia (Frances)** (*b* Denton, TX, 25 Jan 1911; *d* New York, 27 April 1989). American composer, pianist, and writer on music. She graduated from North Texas State University (1930) and studied piano and then composition on a fellowship at the Juilliard Graduate School (1932–9), where she gained a diploma. At New York University she completed the MA (1933) and the PhD (1952). She was the pianist for the Orchestrette Classique of New York, a women's orchestra (1932–9), and gave concerts in Latin America, Europe, and the USA, playing much American music, especially that of Aaron Copland. She taught at Hartt College (1941–6), where she founded the department of music education.

All Smith's operas and orchestral works have been performed, some frequently. Her music, which has an appealing directness, is tonal, often dissonant, and incorporates elements of jazz, folk, and 20th-century French harmony. The String Quartet, her best chamber work, uses irregular metres and driving rhythms; and the operas *Cynthia Parker* and *Cockcrow* employ folk music within a generally conservative tonal idiom. A recipient of several commissions and awards, among them two Ford Foundation recording grants and three Meet the Composer grants, Smith was also active in music organizations, especially the National Federation of Music Clubs, for which she chaired the Decade of Women Committee (1970–79). Among her publications are *Aaron Copland: his Work and Contribution to American Music* (New York, 1955), and a *Directory of American Women Composers* (Indianapolis, IN, 1970), of which she was the editor.

WORKS
selective list

Operas: Cynthia Parker (3, J. Fortune), 1938, rev. 1977; The Stranger of Manzano (1, J. W. Rogers) (1943); The Gooseherd and the Goblin (1, J. F. Royle) (1946); Cockcrow (1, C. D. Mackay), 1953; The Shepherdess and the Chimneysweep (1, Mackay), 1963; Daisy (2, B. Harding), 1973

Orch: Episodic Suite, 1936; Pf Conc., 1938, rev. 1971, arr. 2 pf, 1971; Folkways Sym., 1948; 3 suites incl. American Dance Suite, 1963 [rev. of withdrawn work]; other works for band

Chamber and solo inst: Pf Sonatine, 1943–4; 2 Pieces, va, pf, 1944; Sonatine, fl, bn, 1945; Pf Trio:

Cornwall, 1955; Str Qt, 1964; Suite, wind octet, 1980; 5 Pieces, db, 1988; other works incl. pf pieces

Vocal: 3 Love Songs (K. Flaster), 1v, pf, 1955; Our Heritage (A. M. Sampley), SSAATTBB, orch, 1958; Remember the Alamo (W. J. Marsh, G. Y. Wright), collab. C. Vashaw, sym. band/full band, opt. nar, chorus (1965); Prairie Kaleidoscope (O. M. Ratcliffe), song cycle, S, str qt, 1982; other songs

Principal publisher: Mowbray

BIBLIOGRAPHY

LePageWC, ii; *GroveO*

C. Ammer: *Unsung: a History of Women in American Music* (Westport, CT, 1980)

J. L. Zaimont and K. Famera, eds.: *Contemporary Concert Music by Women* (Westport, CT, 1981)

R. H. Kornick: *Recent American Opera: a Production Guide* (New York, 1991), 286–8

ADRIENNE FRIED BLOCK

Smith, Linda Catlin (*b* White Plains, NY, 27 April 1957). Canadian composer of American birth. She was brought up in Manhattan and received her early musical education from her mother, who was a piano teacher. Between the ages of 12 and 18 she studied the piano with John Verbalis; from the age of 15 to 18 she was a composition pupil of Allen Shawn in New York. Later, at SUNY, Stony Brook, 1975–7, she studied the piano with Nurit Tilles and Gilbert Kalish. At the University of Victoria she studied music theory and Japanese music with Jo Kondo, piano with Kathleen Solose and harpsichord with Erich Schwandt, and composition with Martin Bartlett, John Celona, Rudolf Komorous and Michael Longton (BMus 1979, MMus 1981). She later attended lectures given by Morton Feldman, 1986–7. As well as winning prizes for her compositions in several Canadian contests, she received a Canada Council grant in 1988 to attend the Darmstadt summer school and a Canada Council commission in the same year for *Versailles*. She co-produced a series of contemporary music concerts at the Mercer Union Gallery in Toronto, 1982–5, and was artistic director of Arraymusic, a Toronto-based contemporary music ensemble, 1988–93.

The transparency, clarity and orchestration of Baroque music, as well as the timbre and invention of impressionism have proved influential in the forging of Smith's style; her pointillistic use of instruments, economy of means and subdued dynamics seem indebted to the later Webern. But, although she applies a serial-inspired pitch logic, her music is neither serial nor yet minimalist; she is concerned, rather, with ambiguity. Later compositions tend towards the abstract and use a layering technique: in *Diagonal Forms* (1991) she superimposes one colour on another; and in *Morandi* (1991) the painter Giorgio Morandi's water-colours of bottles and jars, each in a different, muted colour, are reflected in the pastel shades of iridescent sonorities. *Infinity* (1987) is dedicated to Morton Feldman, while the one-page piece *Music for John Cage* (1991), written for Toronto's *Impulse Magazine*, uses the notes C–A–G–E and those a semitone sharper. Her works have been performed throughout Canada and in the USA, England, France, Sweden and Switzerland.

WORKS

selective list

Orch: Link, 1980

Chamber: Periphery, fl, sax, tpt, vn, vc, db, pf, vib, mar, chimes, 1978; Clay, str qt, 1979; Flowers of Emptiness, acoustic or el str trio, 1986; Machinery, b rec, vn, db, harp, perc, melodica, t banjo, 1987; Versailles, baroque fl, baroque vn, va da gamba, hpd, 1988; Diagonal Forms, cl, tpt, db, pf, vib, mar/glockenspiel, 1991; Morandi, 2 pf, 2 vib, 1991; The Disposition of the Forms in Space (fl, va, vib)/ (baroque fl, baroque va, vib), 1992; Topology, rec, tuba, pf, vib, accordion, 1993

Solo inst: Silhouette, cornet, 1981; Invisible Cities, vib, 1982; Gravity, hpd, 1988; Zart, pf, 1989; Music for John Cage, pf, 1990; 9 Memos, b cl, 1990; The View from Here, pf, 1992; Consolation, pf, 1993

Vocal: Grey Broken, S, baroque fl, hpd, 1982; Infinity: for Morton, S, cl, pf, 1987; Gold Sandals (after Sappho), S, S, Mez, pf, 1989

GAYNOR G. JONES

Smyth, Dame **Ethel (Mary)** (*b* London, 23 April 1858; *d* Woking, 9 May 1944). English composer and writer. She was one of the most original figures of British music history, attaining international recognition as an opera composer at a time when women were still considered amateur musicians.

Her early education, with private tutors followed by boarding school, was typical of the upbringing of an upper middle-class Victorian lady. Demonstrating a talent for music, she began formal training at the age of 17 with Alexander Ewing. In 1877, with the grudging consent of her parents, she entered the Leipzig Conservatory as a composition student and took classes with Carl Reinecke, Salomon Jadassohn and Louis Maas. After one year, dissatisfied with the low standards there, she left and took private lessons with the Austrian composer Heinrich Herzogenberg. Through him she gained entrance into the musical circle of Brahms and Clara Schumann. She also met Grieg, Dvořák, and Tchaikovsky, all students at the

Ethel Smyth

conservatory. Her apprentice works include a string quintet, a sonata for violin and piano, a sonata for cello and piano and two sets of German lieder. Written in a Brahmsian vein, they demonstrate her command of contrapuntal and harmonic techniques. In 1878 she submitted her lieder to Breitkopf & Härtel for publication. The publisher told her that 'no woman composer had ever succeeded, barring Frau Schumann and Fräulein Mendelssohn, whose songs had been published together with those of their husband and brother respectively . . . that a certain Frau Lang had written some really very good songs but they had no sale'. In spite of this, he was willing to print her songs; Smyth, however, discouraged by the failure of women composers, did not ask for a fee.

After her lessons with Herzogenberg, she continued to study orchestration on her own. On 26 April 1890 she made her orchestral début with a four-movement Serenade, conducted by August Manns at Crystal Palace; Manns gave the première of her overture to *Antony and Cleopatra* six months later. The critics heralded her as a 'promising young composer'. In summer 1891 she completed one of her most important works, the Mass in D. Donald Tovey described the work as a *locus classicus* in choral orchestration, com-

Title-page of 'The March of the Women', dedicated to The Women's Social and Political Union and published by The Woman's Press (London, 1911)

paring it with the power and grandeur of Beethoven's *Missa solemnis*. When the German conductor Hermann Levi saw the work, he commented on her dramatic abilities, and insisted that she write an opera. From that time, she devoted herself to the composition of musico–dramatic works. Her first opera, *Fantasio*, set to a libretto by Henry Brewster after Alfred de Musset's comedy, was given its première at the Hoftheater in Weimar in 1898. It was not well received by the critics, who praised only its rich orchestration. Three years later, Felix Mottl conducted a second, more successful performance by the court opera in Karlsruhe. Her second opera, *Der Wald*, was first performed by the royal opera in Berlin on 21 April 1902; three months later it was produced at Covent Garden and the next year, on 11 March, it made history as the first opera by a woman to be performed at the Metropolitan Opera House in New York. Much of the libretto, with its forest setting and theme of salvation through death, is indicative of German symbolism and, in particular, Wagnerism. Both operas were originally set to German texts. Smyth, like

other English composers before World War I, was forced to write her operas in German in order to gain first performances on the Continent, since London musical life at that time was not propitious to English opera.

In 1904 Smyth completed her third opera, *The Wreckers*, considered by many to be her masterpiece. She again collaborated with her friend Henry Brewster on the libretto. At that time rumour had it that André Messager of the Opéra Comique would be the new director of Covent Garden. In the hope of securing a première in London, Smyth decided to write the opera in French as *Les naufrageurs*. Ironically, *The Wreckers* was never presented in its original French version. In 1906 it received its first two productions, in Leipzig and Prague, as *Strandrecht* (translated by H. Decker and J. Bernhoff). Smyth then translated the opera into English and on 28 May 1908 Arthur Nikisch conducted the LSO in a concert version of the first two acts. The first English stage production, on 22 June 1909, was conducted at His Majesty's Theatre by Thomas Beecham, who included it in his début season at Covent Garden a year later. Beecham called *The Wreckers* 'one of the three or four English operas of real musical merit and vitality'. Unlike her earlier works, *The Wreckers* betrays Smyth's British origins in its evocation of the sea and characterization of an isolated sea town. The subject as well as certain musical devices, in particular the unaccompanied chorale sung by the townspeople in Act 1, bring to mind Britten's later opera *Peter Grimes*. Smyth's music, however, with its use of ballad form, its colourful orchestration, leitmotifs and dense contrapuntal writing, recalls the Wagnerian style.

In 1910 Smyth was awarded the honorary DMus by the University of Durham. (She was created DBE in 1922 and received the honorary DMus at Oxford University in 1926.) This same year she halted her musical career to take an active role in the women's suffrage movement. She became a close friend of Emmeline Pankhurst, the charismatic leader of the Women's Social and Political Union, taking care of her during the final Cat

and Mouse Act phase of the fight. In 1912 she served two months in Holloway Prison for smashing the window of a cabinet minister. Her greatest contribution to the cause, however, was the *March of the Women* (1911), which, as the anthem of the WSPU membership, was sung at meetings, in the streets and even in prison.

In 1913 she composed her fourth and most popular opera, *The Boatswain's Mate*. Set to an English text by W. W. Jacobs, this two-act comedy comes closest to the composer's native tradition in that the first act is written in the English ballad opera style with spoken dialogue and folksong quotations. At this time, Smyth realized that she was gradually going deaf. Despite this hardship, she composed two more operas, the 'dance-dream' *Fête galante* (1922), based on a short story by Maurice Baring, and the comedy *Entente cordiale* (1925). Her other major works were a Concerto for violin, horn and orchestra (1927) and *The Prison* (1930), a symphony for

Cover for the programme of the concert at Queen's Hall, London (30 April 1921) at which Ethel Smyth conducted the love duet from her opera 'The Wreckers'

soprano, bass-baritone and orchestra, based on a metaphysical poem by Henry Brewster.

When World War I put an end to performances of her works on the Continent, she embarked upon a second career as a writer. She wrote ten books, mostly of an autobiographical nature, which not only remain an invaluable source on her own life but also offer brilliant portrayals of many notable contemporaries. Among her friends were several leading British writers of her day, most notably Vernon Lee, Edith Somerville, Vita Sackville-West, and Virginia Woolf, to whom Smyth dedicated her seventh book, *As Time Went On*. Smyth also wrote many essays championing equal rights for women musicians. Her strong feelings about discrimination against women in music led her to campaign in newspaper articles and books to secure places for women in orchestras.

Smyth was an eclectic in that she absorbed, adopted, and experimented with music from a wide range of sources; her youthful works follow the Mendelssohn-Brahms style, while the Mass in D and *The Wreckers* reflect the dynamism and turbulence of Beethoven and Wagner. The Four Songs (1908) and *Three Moods of the Sea* (1913) have an affinity with early 20th-century French style, and her later opera, *Fête galante*, captures the neo-classical idiom. Yet her music remains strikingly original in its bold energy, skilful counterpoint, novel harmonic progressions and unusual orchestrations. Smyth was a first-rate composer, who ranks easily with such contemporaries as Hubert Parry, C. V. Stanford and Arthur Sullivan. As a feminist, writer and composer, she stands alone as an important pioneer whose fight for recognition helped change the attitudes of her time.

WORKS

STAGE

Fantasio (phantastische Komödie, 2, H. Brewster and Smyth, after A. de Musset), 1892–4; Weimar, Hoftheater, 24 May 1898, *GB-Lbl★*, vs (Leipzig, 1899)

Der Wald (Musik-Drama, 1, Brewster and Smyth), 1899–1901; Berlin, Königliches Schauspielhaus, 9 April 1902; as The Forest, London, Covent Garden, 18 July 1902, *Lbl★*; (London, 1902)

Les naufrageurs [The Wreckers] (lyrical drama, 3, Brewster and Smyth), 1902–4; trans. H. Decker and J. Bernhoff as Strandrecht, Leipzig, Neuestheater, 11 Nov 1906; trans. A. Strettell and Smyth, London, His Majesty's Theatre, 22 June 1909; *Lbl★*, vs (Leipzig, 1906)

The Boatswain's Mate [Der gute Freund] (comedy, 1, Smyth, after W. W. Jacobs), 1913–14; London, Shaftesbury Theatre, 28 Jan 1916, *Lbl★*, vs (Vienna, 1915)

Fête galante (dance-dream, 1, E. Shanks and Smyth, after M. Baring), Birmingham, Repertory Theatre, 4 June 1923, *Lue*, vs (Vienna, 1923); arr. as ballet (Vienna, 1933)

Entente cordiale (postwar comedy, 1, Smyth), London, RCM, 22 July 1925; Bristol, Royal Theatre, 20 Oct 1926, *Lfm*, vs (London, 1925)

VOCAL

[5] Lieder und Balladen (J. Eichendorff, E. Mörike, folksong), 1v, pf, op.3, c1886; [5] Lieder (G. Buchner, E. von Wildenbruch, Eichendorff, K. Groth, P. Heyse), 1v, pf, op.4, c1886; The Song of Love (Solomon's Song), soloists, chorus, orch, op.8, 1888, unpubd; Mass, D, S, A, T, B, chorus, orch, 1891, rev. 1925; 4 Songs (H. de Régnier, Anacreon), 1v, ens, 1908; Songs of Sunrise (Smyth, C. Hamilton), SATB, 1911; Hey nonny no, SATB, orch, 1911; Sleepless Dreams (D. G. Rossetti), chorus, orch, 1912

3 Moods of the Sea (A. Symons), 1v, orch, 1913; 3 Songs (M. Baring, E. Carnie, anon.), 1v, orch, 1913; Dreamings (P. Mcgill), SATB, 1920; Soul's Joy, SATB, 1923; A Spring Canticle (Der Wald) (Smyth), chorus, orch, 1926; The Prison (H. Brewster), S, B, chorus, orch, 1930; We watched her breathing through the night (T. Hood), unacc. chorus, unpubd; 5 partsongs on German church tunes, unpubd; songs to French and German texts, 1v, pf, unpubd

ORCHESTRAL

Serenade, D, 1890, unpubd; Antony and Cleopatra, ov., 1890, unpubd; March of the Women, 1911; Conc., vn, hn, orch, 1927; On the Cliffs of Cornwall [from The Wreckers], 1928; 2 Interlinked French Melodies [from Entente cordiale], 1929

Frags.: sym., D, small orch (1 movt); Tragi-komische Ouvertüre (sketch)

CHAMBER AND INSTRUMENTAL

2 pf sonatas, C, 1877, c♯, 1877, unpubd; Variations on an Original Theme, pf, 1878, unpubd; Prelude and Fugue, f♯, pf, 1880, unpubd; Str Qt, d, 1880, unpubd; Str Qnt, E, op.1, 1884; Sonata, vc, pf, op.5, 1887; Sonata, vn, pf, op.7, 1887; Str Qt, e, 1902–12; 5 Short Chorale Preludes, org, 1913; 2 Trios, vn, ob, pf, 1927; Prelude on a Traditional Irish Melody, org, 1939

Frags. and other unpubd works, n.d.: Str Qnt (1 movt: Largo and Andante, b); 5 str qts, a♯ 'no.1' (1 movt), E♭, E♭ (Andante only), C, c; Pf Trio, d; Str Trio, D; Pf Sonata, D (2 movts); Suite in dance forms, pf; Fugue, b, org; Fugue, C, pf; canons, pf; chorale preludes, org

Principal publishers: Curwen/Faber, Novello, Universal

Other MSS in *GB-Lbl*, *DRu*

WRITINGS

Impressions that Remained (London, 1919)
Streaks of Life (London, 1921, 2/1924)
A Three-Legged Tour in Greece (London, 1927)
A Final Burning of Boats (London, 1928)
Female Pipings in Eden (London, 1933)
As Time Went on (London, 1935)
Beecham and Pharaoh (London, 1935)
Inordinate (?) Affection (London, 1936)
What Happened Next (London, 1940)

BIBLIOGRAPHY

W. McNaught: 'Dame Ethel Smyth', *MT*, lxxxv (1944), 207

K. Dale: 'Dame Ethel Smyth', *ML*, xxv (1944), 191

—— : 'Ethel Smyth's Prentice Work', *ML*, xxx (1949), 329

E. W. White: *The Rise of English Opera* (London, 1951), 129–35

T. Beecham: 'Dame Ethel Smyth (1858–1944)', *MT*, xcix (1958), 363

C. St John: *Ethel Smyth* (London, 1959) [incl. list of works]

F. Howes: *The English Musical Renaissance* (London, 1966), 65–7

E. W. White: *A History of English Opera* (London, 1983), 354–64

L. Collis: *Impetuous Heart: the Story of Ethel Smyth* (London, 1984)

D. Hyde: 'Ethel Smyth (1858–1944): a Reappraisal', *New-Found Voices: Women in Nineteenth-Century English Music* (Liskeard, 1984), 138–65

J. A. Bernstein: ' "Shout, shout up with your song!": Dame Ethel Smyth and the Changing Role of British Women Composers', *Women Making Music: the Western Art Tradition 1150–1950*, ed. J. Bowers and J. Tick (Urbana and Chicago, 1986), 304–24

R. Crichton, ed.: *The Memoirs of Ethel Smyth* (Harmondsworth, 1987) [incl. excerpts from her writings and a list of works]

E. Wood: 'Gender and Genre, in Ethel Smyth's Operas', *The Musical Woman: an International Perspective*, ii: *1984–5*, ed. J. L. Zaimont and others (Westport, CT, 1987), 493–507

K. A. Abromeit: 'Ethel Smyth, *The Wreckers* and Sir Thomas Beecham', *MQ*, lxxiii (1989), 196–211

E. A. Copley: *A Survey of the Choral Works of Dame Ethel Smyth with an Analysis of the Mass in D* (diss., U. of Cincinnati, 1990)

J. Nichols: *Women Music Makers: an Introduction to Women Composers* (New York, 1992)

C. S. Ripley: 'The Chorale Preludes of Ethel Smyth', *American Organist*, xxvii/7 (1993), 56

R. Crichton: 'Salvaging the "Wreckers"', *Opera*, xlv (1994), 783–6

JANE A. BERNSTEIN

Snížková(-Škrhová), Jitka (*b* Prague, 14 Sept 1924; *d* Prague, 11 May 1989). Czech composer and musicologist. Her father, a professor at Charles University, Prague, supervised her education and musical studies. After private music lessons, she attended the Prague Conservatory, 1945–8, studying the piano with Jan Heřman and composition with Alois Hába, and Charles University, where she graduated in musicology, aesthetics and literature. Her career encompassed composing, teaching theory at the Prague Conservatory, and research, notably in medieval music and Czech Renaissance polyphony. Within her vast output, vocal, especially choral, works predominate; her oratorios and cantatas in particular reveal the influence of medieval music. She also produced educational music and many chamber works, several to commission.

WORKS
selective list

Orch: Symfonietta balatta, chamber orch, 1957; Interludia fantastica, fl, tambourine, str, 1958; Vzpomínky na Evropu [Remembrance of Europe], chamber orch, 1983; Ludus paragensis propter Michaelem Haydn, 1987

Inst: Str Qt, 1949–51; Str Qt no.2 'Starodávný' [Old-Fashioned], 1955; Str Qt no.3, 1956; Start, pf 4 hands, 1958; Trio, fl, ob, bc, 1962; 'Choral' Str Qt, 1967; Medieval Reminiscences, org, 1969; Epithalamia, fl, 1970; Alfa solaris, b cl, pf, 1976–80; Fantasticon, 2 pf, 1981; Sonata pastoricia, vn, pf, 1981; Die Glocke der Hoffnung, hn, trbn, pf, 1985; Lesní znělky [Forest Tune], 3 trbn, 1989

Solo vocal: Ave Maria, 1v, vn, org, 1950; Gitanjali (R. Tagore), S, 1969; Jarní pozdravení [Spring Greeting] (melodrama, J. Kutina), 1v, fl, pf, 1971; Píseň písní [Song of Songs], 1v, fl, vc, pf, 1975; Stopy světců [Traces of Saints] (Snížková), S/A, 1982–4; Eminy písně [Song of Emmy Destinn] (E. Destinn), 1v, va, pf, 1989

Choral: Píseň [Song], S, women's vv, cl, str qnt, 1949; Cantata, 1969 [on J. A. Comenius]; Kruh domova [The Home Circle] (Snížková), S, spkr, men's vv, 1972; In honorem Sancti Adalberti, oratorio, B, men's vv, children's chorus, org, 1972; Agnes regis filia, chorus, 1979; Kdo vzpomene Giovanni Punto [Who Remembers Giovanni Punta] (B. Pospíšil), 4 hn, chorus, 1986; Dopis Karla Čapka [Čapek's Letter], chorus, 1989

Principal publishers: Panton, Supraphon

BIBLIOGRAPHY

CohenE; *ČSHS*; *ČSS*

A. Šerých: 'Konfese Jitky Snížkové [Confession of Jitka Snížková], *OM*, xvi (1984), 315–18

ANNA ŠERÝCH

Sodré, Joanídia (Núñez) (*b* Porto Alegre, Rio Grande do Sul, 22 Dec 1903; *d* Rio de Janeiro, 7 Sept 1975). Brazilian composer. She studied the piano from an early age with Alberto Nepomuceno and later went to the Instituto Nacional de Música in Rio de Janeiro, where her teachers included João Nunes for piano and Francisco Braga for composition. She was appointed professor of harmony and form at the Instituto in 1925. For her opera *Casa forte* she was awarded a trip to Germany in 1927; she stayed three years, studying composition with Paul Juon and conducting with Ignatz Waghalter in Berlin. After her return to Brazil she founded and conducted the Coral Feminino (1930), the Orquestra Sinfônica Infantil (1939) and the Orquestra da Juventude (1939). She was director of the Escola Nacional de Música of the University of Brazil, 1946–67. Her compositions include, for stage, *A cheia do Paraíba* (1927) and, for chorus and orchestra, *Girassol* and *Incêndio em Roma*. She also wrote works on music theory.

IRATI ANTONIO

Sommer, Silvia (*b* Vienna, 9 April 1944). Austrian pianist and composer. Born into a family of musicians, she played the piano from the age of three and began to compose at 11. She studied the piano with Joseph Dichler and composition with Alfred Uhl at the Vienna Music Academy. Since 1968 her music has been performed in Austria, in many other European countries and in North and South America. She received the City of Vienna composition prize in 1970 and the Lower Austria prize in 1982. During the 1980s she began to compose light music (including *Autumn Melody* and *Sarah's Song*, both 1984; *Laura's Dream*, 1987; and *Flowers in the Rain*, 1988).

WORKS
selective list

Orch: 5 israelische Tänze, str orch: Kyriat Shmona; No Sunshine Today, str orch; Onic 123, vc, str orch, fl ad lib

Other inst: Artardecer, fl, gui; Canción para desear una buenas noches, 2 gui; Dance on the Roof, vn, pf; Sonatine, fl, pf; Der Traum eines jungen Elefanten, der im Zirkus auftreten wollte, vc; Trio, fl, gui, db; La vida de cada canto, pf; Yarma, ob

Songs: 3 Lieder (B. Mosa): Blumen-Samen, Urrt, Der Säufer, Mez, fl, pf; Der Riese vor der Stadt (W. Petzwinkler), S, pf

BIBLIOGRAPHY
KompA–Z

ROSARIO MARCIANO

Sonntag, Brunhilde (*b* Kassel, 27 Sept 1936). German composer. During her school years she played the organ and took lessons in harmony, and after training as a teacher she studied music in Frankfurt with Kurt Hessenberg. From 1963 she studied composition in Vienna with Otto Siegl and Gottfried von Einem, whose teaching was very much in the tradition of the Second Viennese School. Sonntag went on to study musicology in Marburg, where she obtained the doctorate with a dissertation on collage techniques in 20th-century music. From 1968 to 1975 she taught at the University of Giessen, then held a senior academic post at the Pädagogische Hochschule in Münster; in 1981 she was appointed professor of applied music theory at the Gesamthochschule in Duisburg. Sonntag's compositions, written in a subtle, chamber-music style, extend the tradition of the Second Viennese School; they may even be considered as belonging to a kind of 'Third Viennese School'. Sonntag is co-editor, with Renate Matthei, of the series of studies of women composers *Annäherungen an sieben Komponistinnen*, published by Furore, Kassel (1986–). She has also published articles on issues in 20th-century music.

WORKS
selective list

Orch: Verwandlungen, 1983; O Tod, wie bitter bist du, 1991

Chamber: EKG, Collage, spkr, str qt, org, 5 timp, tàpe, 1981; 2 str qts, no.1, 1984, no.2 'Animus', 1988; Akrostichon, gui, 1987; Dialog, 2 gui, 1989, also arr. hpd, 1989; Str Qt no.3 'Es ist ein Schnitter, Leisst der Tod', 1993

Kbd: Klavierstück, pf, 1959; [4] Klavierstücke für H., pf, 1978, 1981, 1982, 1984; Kum, kum, Geselle min, org, 1982; Spiegelungen (with text), pf, 1987; Farbenkugel, org, 1988

Vocal: Auf einem Baum ein Kuckuck sass, cantata, chorus, 3 fl, 1958; Wenn die Tale blühn, cantata, chorus, 1958; Ovid-Metamorphosen, men's choir 4vv; Hallelujah (Variations on 'When the Saints'), S, cl, pf, 1981; Der tragische Tausendfüssler (after F. Hohler), spkr, pf, 1981; Von guten Mächten (D. Bonhoeffer), 4 vv, 1982; Aber ich sage euch: liebet eure Feinde (M. Luther King and others), spkr, chorus, 1983; 5 Lieder (R. Ausländer, P. Celan), S, pf, 1983; 3 Lieder (U. Hahn), S, pf, 1988

Principal publisher: Furore

BIBLIOGRAPHY
KompA–Z

B. Sonntag: 'Komponieren, eine der schönsten Formen menschlicher Selbstverwirklichung', *Annäherungen an sieben Komponistinnen*, i, ed. B. Matthei and B. Sonntag (Kassel, 1986)

DETLEF GOJOWY

Sønstevold [née Lundén], **Maj** (*b* Sollefteå, Sweden, 9 Sept 1917). Norwegian composer of Swedish parentage. She studied the piano with Sven Brandel and Gottfried Bohn in Stockholm, and jazz piano, theory and composition with Billy Mayerl in London. She settled in Norway in 1945, working there as a composer and teacher. In 1966 she received a diploma in composition from the Vienna Music Academy, where her teachers were Hanns Jelinek and Karl Schiske. In 1971 she became a lecturer at Oslo University, teaching a variety of subjects including jazz and instrumentation; in the same year she joined the music department of the Norwegian broadcasting corporation (NRK), teaching programme engineers and technicians. In 1974 she and her husband, Gunnar Sønstevold, formed a music institute at Rakkestad near Oslo.

Her music exhibits a versatile range of styles: several orchestral suites, for example *Sørlandssommer* and *Den gamle majors forunderlige drømme* ('The Old Major's Wonderful Dream'), are simply for entertainment, in traditional style, whereas works written in Vienna in the mid-1960s employ 12-note techniques, rigorously as in *Ni Haiku* ('Nine

Haiku'), or more freely, as in *Vårvon* ('Spring Yearning'). She has written more than 50 scores for films, plays and television and radio drama, some in partnership with her husband. She has also produced two jazz manuals (1947, 1977), which include examples of her own compositions.

WORKS
selective list

Orch: Sørlandssommer, suite, 1956; Den gamle majors forunderlige drømme [The Old Major's Wonderful Dream], suite, 1970; Festival ov., 1983

Vocal: Vårvon [Spring Yearning] (P. Sivle), ballad, T, 2 choirs male vv, orch, 1965; 9 Haiku, op.5, C, fl, harp, 1966; Stillhet [Silence], 8 solo vv, fl, cl, vn, vc, pf, perc, 1978; Itacha, Bar, vn, vc, harp, pf, 1983

Solo inst (pf unless otherwise stated): Suite, op.1, 1962; Theme and Variations, op. 2, 1963; Sonata, op.3, 1964; 11 polytonale blues, 1978; 4 gjøglere [4 Jugglers], bn, 1983; Per aspera ad astra (Reflections on South America), 1983; The Merry Herbal Gardener, 1992

Other works: more than 50 scores for films, plays and TV and radio drama, some collab. G. Sønstevold

CECILIE DAHM

Sophie [Sophia] **Elisabeth,** Duchess of Brunswick-Lüneburg (*b* Güstrow, 20 Aug 1613; *d* Lüchow, 12 July 1676). German composer and poet. She received an all-round musical training at the court of her father, Duke Johann Albrecht of Mecklenburg-Güstrow, where the orchestra was noted at the time for its employment of outstanding English instrumentalists, among them William Brade. In 1628 she was obliged to flee from the Thirty Years War, and for some years she lived at the Kassel court, a lively centre of music. In July 1635 she married Duke August the Younger of Brunswick-Lüneburg, the learned founder of the Wolfenbüttel library. The court orchestra, established for their Brunswick residence in 1638, twice required reorganization, in 1644 after the move to the ancestral castle at Wolfenbüttel and again in 1665; on each occasion she was responsible for it. Heinrich Schütz, who was connected with the court for almost 30 years and was a frequent guest at Brunswick and Wolfenbüttel, was her musical adviser. Friedrich Chrysander described the correspondence between them. Sophie Elisabeth was responsible for Schütz's initial engagement as *absentes* Kapellmeister in 1655, and he taught her composition. In 1644, referring to 'newly despatched arias' (probably for the *Theatralische neue Vorstellung von der Maria Magdalena*, on which they collaborated), he commended her noticeable improvement 'after a little guid-

ance from me'. In 1661 he called her a 'uniquely accomplished princess, particularly in the worshipful calling of music'.

Sophie Elizabeth's compositions, the earliest of which date from her youth at Güstrow, have for the most part survived anonymously. Most are sacred songs, a genre that continued to occupy her during her widowhood at Lüchow, where she lived from 1666. The melodies of the two printed collections (1651 and 1667) are aria-like in idiom and more suited to private than to congregational worship. Sophie Elisabeth also contributed to numerous secular celebrations and theatrical performances, although the extent of her creative contributions to these events is not known. Allegorical celebratory plays, ballets and masquerades were performed annually, most of them in honour of Duke August's birthday and with the participation of the ducal family. Sophie Elisabeth played an essential part in establishing this tradition (G. P. Harsdörffer and S. T. Staden's *Seelewig* was given in 1654) and apparently composed the music for most of the productions up to 1656; only a little of it has survived. In *FriedensSieg* the spoken voice, solo and choral singing, instrumental music and dance are combined within an operetta-like action, while *Freudensdarstellung* is conceived in the manner of a scenic festival cantata.

WORKS

Edition: *Sophie Elisabeth, Herzogin zu Braunschweig und Lüneburg: Dichtungen*, i: *Spiele*, ed. H.-G. Roloff (Frankfurt, 1980)

FESTSPIELE

Neuerfundenes FreudenSpiel genandt FriedensSieg (J. G. Schottelius), solo vv, chorus, insts, Brunswick, 1642 (Wolfenbüttel, 1648, 2/1649); music exx. repr. in Schneider

Die Gebuhrt unsers Heylandes (Schottelius), 1645, music lost; facs. in M. Burkhard, *Justus Georg Schottel, Fruchtbringender Lustgarte* [1647] (Munich, 1967), 92

Glückwünschende Freudensdarstellung Dem . . . Herrn Augusten Hertzogen zu Brunschwig und Lüneburg, 4vv, chorus 4vv, 4 str, bc (Lüneburg, 1652, 2/1655); facs., incl. score, in Bircher and Bürger, 114–29; two sections in *MGG*, xiv, pls.43–4; text in Roloff, 9

librettos by Sophie Elisabeth

Der Natur Banquet, 1654; Roloff, 27
Der Minervae Banquet, 1655; Roloff, 43
Ballet der Zeit, 1655; Roloff, 67
Glückwünschende Waarsagung und Ankunft der Königin Nicaulae, 1656; Roloff, 85

OTHER VOCAL

21 chansons, 1v, bc, *D-W* (autograph; begun Güstrow, 1633) [arrs. of airs de cour]
3 sacred concertos, 1 song, 1v, bc/1 inst, *W* (autograph MS, dated 1642–53)

6 sinfonies, 2 vn, bc, 45 songs and 1 sacred concerto, 1v, bc, *W* (autograph, dated 1647–55); 1 ed. in Brauer, ii, 63; 1 facs. in Schottelius, 46f

Vinetum evangelicum, Evangelischer Weinberg (J. von Glasenapp) (83 hymn melodies), 1v, bc (Wolfenbüttel, 1651)

Glückwünschende Gedancken über den Geburts-Tag des . . . Herren Augusten Herzogen zu Braunschwieg und Lüneburg, aria, 1v, 3 insts (Wolfenbüttel, 1653); facs., incl. score, in Bircher and Bürger, 106–9

ChristFürstliches Davids-Harpfen-Spiel (Duke Anton Ulrich) (60 hymn melodies), 1v, bc (Nuremberg, 1667, 2/1670 with 63 melodies); 5 ed. in von Winterfeld, 39 ed. in Zahn; facs. in B. L. Spahr, *Classics in Germanic Literatures and Philosophy* (New York and London, 1969)

BIBLIOGRAPHY

Choron-FayolleD; *EitnerQ*; *GerberL*

B. Daetrius: *Königes Davids Hertzens-Lust und Liebe zum steten Lobe Gottes* (Wolfenbüttel, 1677) [funeral oration for Sophie Elisabeth]

C. von Winterfeld: *Der evangelische Kirchengesang*, ii (Leipzig, 1845, repr. 1966), 446f, 484ff, appx nos.175ff

F. Chrysander: 'Geschichte der Braunschweig-Wolfenbüttelschen Capelle und Oper', *Jb für musikalische Wissenschaft*, i (Leipzig, 1863), 159ff

J. Zahn: *Die Melodien der deutschen evangelischen Kirchenlieder* (Gütersloh, 1889–93)

S. Kümmerle: *Encyklopädie der evangelischen Kirchenmusik*, iii (Gütersloh, 1894)

F. Saffe: 'Wolfenbüttel in der Musikgeschichte', *Die Lessingstadt Wolfenbüttel und ihre Dichter* (Wolfenbüttel, 1929), 50, 56

H. J. Moser: *Heinrich Schütz: sein Leben und Werk* (Kassel, 1936, 2/1954; Eng. trans., 1959)

M. Schneider: 'Ein Braunschweiger Freudenspiel aus dem Jahre 1648', *Musik und Bild: Festschrift Max Seiffert* (Kassel, 1938), 87

H. Sievers: 'Aus den Anfängen zum Nationaltheater', *250 Jahre Braunschweigisches Staatstheater 1690–1940* (Brunswick, 1941), 26ff

W. Schmieder and G. Hartwieg: *Kataloge der Herzog August Bibliothek Wolfenbüttel*, xii: *Musik: alte Drucke bis etwa 1750* (Frankfurt, 1967)

E. Thiel and G. Rohr: *Kataloge der Herzog August Bibliothek Wolfenbüttel*, xiv: *Libretti, Verzeichnis der bis 1800 erschienenen Textbücher* (Frankfurt, 1970)

Justus Georg Schottelius 1612–1676: ein Teutscher Gelehrter am Wolfenbütteler Hof. Ausstellung der Herzog August Bibliothek Wolfenbüttel vom 23.10.1976 bis 2.1.1977, Ausstellungskataloge der Herzog August Bibliothek, xviii (Brunswick, 1976)

J. Leighton: 'Die Wolfenbütteler Aufführung von Harsdörffers und Stadens Seelewig im Jahre 1654', *Wolfenbütteler Beiträge*, iii (Frankfurt, 1978), 115ff

M. Bircher and T. Bürger, eds.: *Alles mit Bedacht: Barockes Fürstenlob auf Herzog August (1579–1666) in Wort, Bild und Musik* (Wolfenbüttel, 1979)

Sammler Fürst Gelehrter: Herzog August zu Braunschweig und Lüneburg 1579–1666: Niedersächsische Landesausstellung in Wolfenbüttel 26.5. bis 31.10.1979, Ausstellungskataloge der Herzog August Bibliothek, xxvii (Brunswick, 1979)

J. L. Brauer: *Instruments in Sacred Vocal Music at Braunschweig-Wolfenbüttel: a Study of Changing Tastes in the Seventeenth Century* (diss., CUNY, 1983), 168ff

S. Smart: *Doppelte Freude der Musen: Court Festivities in Brunswick-Wolfenbüttel 1642–1700* (Wiesbaden, 1989)

G. Busch: 'Herzogin Sophie Elisabeth und die Musik der Lieder in den Singspielen Herzog Anton Ulrichs zu Braunschweig und Lüneburg', *Chloe*, xii (1992), 127ff

K. W. Geck: *Sophie Elisabeth Herzogin zu Braunschweig und Lüneburg (1613–1667) als Musikerin* (Saarbrücken, 1992)

HORST WALTER

Sophie Friederike Wilhelmina. *See* WILHELMINA.

Sousa, Berta Alves de (*b* Liège, 8 April 1906). Portuguese composer, teacher and critic. She studied at the Oporto Conservatory. Between 1927 and 1929 she worked in Paris with Wilhelm Backhaus, Theodore Szanto and Georges Migot. She was also a pupil of the pianist José Vianna da Motta in Lisbon and the conductor Clemens Krauss in Berlin. Later, she attended courses given by Alfred Cortot (piano) and Edgar Willems (music education). She received the 1941 Moreira de Sá prize in composition. In 1939 she became a critic for the Oporto newspaper *Primeiro de Janeiro*, and from 1946 she taught at the Oporto Conservatory. After an initial tonal period, Sousa's music reflects a closer affinity with the impressionist movement, but also employs polytonal techniques. Some of her works are based on Correia de Oliveira's system of 'sound symmetry' (expounded – in Portuguese and English – in his *Simetria sonora*, Oporto, 1969).

WORKS
selective list

Stage (all before 1955): Bailado oriental (ballet); Ker Keb (ballet); incid. music to *João Landim*

Orch: O jovem rei, suite after O. Wilde: *The Happy Prince*, 1934; Dança exótica, 1935; Vasco da Gama, sym. poem, 1936; Pavana, 1948; Bolero, 1951; Tremor de terra, 1952; A rivedere i stelle, 1966; Scherzo-marcha, 1969

Vocal orch: O virgens que passais ao sol poente (A. Nobre), 1941; A noite (M. Angelo), 1946; Canção Marinha (Teixeira de Pascoais), 1958

Sacred: Salve regina, female vv, 1932; Ave Maria, female vv, 1946; Pai nosso, male vv, 1946; Eia mater fons amoris, female vv, 1950; Stabat mater, before 1955

Other choral works, 14 songs, chamber and piano music

GABRIELA CRUZ

Southam, Ann (*b* Winnipeg, 4 Feb 1937). Canadian composer. She studied composition with Samuel Dolin at the Royal Conservatory of Music, Toronto, and electronic music at the University of Toronto (1960–63) with Gustav Ciamaga. She taught electronic music at the Royal Conservatory from 1966 and from 1968 was composer-in-residence with the New Dance Group of Canada (later known as the Toronto Dance Theatre). In 1977 she co-founded Music Inter Alia with the pianist Diana McIntosh, which aimed to present and to commission new works and to hold an annual composition competition in Winnipeg. She was the first president of the Association of Canadian Women Composers (1980–88). As a composer, Southam is best known for her electroacoustic works written for dance, although she has also composed for the piano and for string instruments. The lyricism of her early atonal works continues in her later music.

WORKS
selective list

Orch: Waves, str orch, 1976
Chamber: Networks, 1978; Qnt, 1986; Alternate Currents, 1987
Pf: Altitude Lake, 1963; Rivers: 1st and 2nd sets, 1979; Cool Blue, RedHot, 1980; Four in Hand, pf 4 hands, 1981; Glass Houses no.5, 1981; Rivers: 3rd set, 1981; Soundings for a New Pf, 1986; Spatial View of Pond, 1986; In a Measure of Time, 1988
El-ac: Against Sleep, 1969; Encounter, 1969; Boat, River, Moon, 1972; Walls and Passageways, 1974; Arrival of All Time, 1975; The Reprieve, 1975; Seastill, 1979; Emerging Ground, 1983; Rewind, 1984; Music for Slow Dancing, 1985; Goblin Market, 1986; Fluke Sound, 1989

GAYNOR G. JONES

Spiegel, Laurie (*b* Chicago, 20 Sept 1945). American composer. She studied social sciences at Shimer College in Mt Carroll, Illinois (BA 1967), and composition with Jacob Druckman at the Juilliard School, New York (1969–72), and Brooklyn College, CUNY (MA 1975), where she also took courses in American music with H. Wiley Hitchcock and Richard Crawford. She also studied philosophy at Oxford University and the lute and guitar with Oscar Ghiglia and John Duarte. Between 1973 and 1979 and again in 1984 she worked on computer music at the Bell Telephone Laboratories, with Emmanuel Ghent, Max Mathews and Kenneth Knowlton, and she taught composition and electronic and computer music at the Aspen Music Festival, 1971–3, at Bucks County Community College (Pennsylvania), 1981–5, and at the Cooper Union for the Advancement of Science and Art in New York, 1980–81. She was artist-in-residence at the WNET Experimental Television Laboratory, 1976, and founded the New York University computer music studio, teaching there in 1982–3. During the 1970s she worked as a composer and music editor for film and television and created computer-generated visual art and animation software. She has been the recipient of many grants and awards, notably from Meet the Composer (1975–7, 1979–80) and the New York Foundation for the Arts (1991–2).

Spiegel has written instrumental pieces but is best known as a composer of electronic and computer music. Her mature works, which are somewhat Romantic in style, are characterized by emotional intensity and often reflect an interest in folk music. Such pieces as *Voyages* (1978), for sound and videotape, and *A Living Painting* (1979), for videotape alone, employ abstract visual images that move and develop in time, creating in silence the effect of music. Her *Realization of Kepler's Harmony of the Planets* was used as the first item in the 'Sounds of Earth' recording on the Voyager spacecrafts of 1977. Spiegel has been deeply involved in the development of the computer as a compositional tool and musical instrument. She has served as a consultant to firms involved in computer technology and helped design the AlphaSyntauri synthesizer (for use with the Apple II microcomputer), the McLeyvier synthesizer and her widely used computer programme, Music Mouse – An Intelligent Instrument; she has also worked on interactive process composition and logic-based instruments. With Beth Anderson she was co-editor, 1977–8, of *Ear*. She has written many articles on music and computers, software design, analogies between music and the visual arts, and kindred topics.

WORKS

Elec and computer: A Tombeau, 1971; Before Completion, 1971; Harmonic Spheres, 1971; Mines, 1971; Orchestras, 1971; Sojourn, 1971; Rāga, 1972; Return to Zero, 1972; Sediment, 1972; 2 Fanfares, 1973; Introit, 1973; Purification, 1973; Sunsets, 1973; Appalachian Grove, 1974; A Meditation, 1974; The Orient Express, 1974; Patchwork, 1974, rev. 1976; Pentachrome, 1974; The Unquestioned Answer, 1974, arr. harp, 1981; Water Music, 1974; Clockworks, 1975; Drums, 1975; The Expanding Universe, 1975; Old Wave, 1975; A Folk Study, 1976; Music for a Garden of Electronic Delights, 1976; Voyages, 1976, rev. with videotape, 1978; Conc., digital synth, 1977; Evolutions, with videotape, 1977; Realization of Kepler's Harmony of the Planets, 1977; 5 Short Visits to Different Worlds, 1977; An Acceleration, 1978; A Living Painting, silent visual study, videotape, 1979; Voices Within, 1979; A Canon, 1980; Modes, 1980; 2 Nocturnes, 1980; Phantoms, 1980; A Quadruple Canon, 1980; A Harmonic Algorithm, 1981, rev. 1990; A Cosmos, 1982; Progression, 1982; Harmonic Rhythm, 1983; Idea

Pieces, 1983; Immersion, 1983; 3 Modal Pieces, 1983; Over Time, 1984; All Star Video, 1985 [for videotape by N. J. Paik]; Cavis Muris, 1986; Music Mouse Demonstration Music, 1986; Passage, 1987; Finding Voice, 1988, 3 Sonic Spaces, 1989, 2 Archetypes: Hall of Mirrors, The Hollows, 1990; Hurricane's Eye, 1990; 2 Intellectual Interludes (Data and Process): Viroid, A Harmonic Algorithm, 1990; Riding the Storm, 1990; Sound Zones, 1990

Film and video scores: Cathode Ray Theater, 1974; Studies for Philharmonia, 1974; War Mime, 1974; War Walls, 1974; Zierrot the Fool, 1974; Emma, 1975; Just a Day in the Life, 1975; Raster's Muse, 1975; Das Ring, 1975; Narcissicon, 1976; Guadalcanal Requiem, 1977; Zierrot in Outta Space, 1978; The Avenue of the Just, 1979; The Phantom Wolf, 1980; Precious Metal Variations, 1983; Point, 1984; Dissipative Fantasies, 1986; Dryads, 1988; Continuous Transformations, 1990; Stacked Julia Set, 1990; many other commercial, television, film and video scores

Inst: A Deploration, fl, vib, 1970; An Earlier Time, gui, 1972; A Canon, chamber ens, computer/tape, 1980; A History of Music in 1 Movt, pf, 1980, elec version, 1980; Phantoms, chamber ens, tape, 1980; Hearing Things, chamber orch, 1983; A Stream, mand, 1984; Song without Words, gui, mand, 1986; After the Mountains, pf, 1990; 3 Movts, hpd, 1990; Returning East, 1990; other works for inst ens; solo gui and pf pieces

Dance scores: Music for Dance, 1975; Waves, 1975; East River, 1976; Escalante, 1977; Nomads, 1981; Over Time, 1984; Gravity's Joke, 1985; Rain Pieces, 1985; Signals, 1986

Incid. music: The Library of Babel (P. Ahrens), 1972; White Devil (J. Webster), 1972; The Clinic (R. Goldman), 1973; The House of Bernarda Alba, 1973; The Devils, 1974

BIBLIOGRAPHY

L. Spiegel: 'Comments on Common Complaints: Notes on Feminists in Music', *Ear Magazine East* (1981), April–May [Women in Music issue]; excerpt repr. in *Ear*, xv/5 (1990)

—— : 'In Response', *PNM*, xx/1–2 (1981–2) [320–22; on gender and composition]

'Laurie Spiegel: Computers and Music', *On Key* (1984), Jan–Feb, 121–3 [interview]

'Laurie Spiegel: Computer Music Pioneer', *Mix*, x/2 (1986), 60–67

P. Lehrman: 'Laurie Spiegel: Esthetic Engineer', *Keyboard* (1986), Nov, 18–19

L. Spiegel: 'An Open Letter on Women in Computer Music', *ICMA Array*, xi/3 (1991)

'Laurie Spiegel: Technofolk', *Ear*, xvi (1991), April, 16–18 [interview]

C. Gagne: *Soundpieces 2: Interviews with American Composers* (Metuchen, NJ, 1993), 295–332 [incl. list of works, discography and bibliography]

NEIL B. ROLNICK/R

Stair, Patty (*b* Cleveland, 12 Nov 1869; *d* Cleveland, 26 April 1926). American teacher, organist and composer. She attended the Cleveland School of Music from 1882 and joined its faculty in 1889; three years later she started teaching at the University School, where she was organist and offered instruction in piano and organ. She continued to teach at both institutions until her death and also gave private lessons in piano, composition and theory. She was organist at five Cleveland churches and in 1914 became a Fellow of the American Guild of Organists. From 1916 she conducted choruses of the Cleveland Women's Club. An active composer, Stair wrote a variety of works, including *Woodland Scene* for an orchestra of toy instruments, pieces for violin and piano, several solo songs, partsongs and over 20 anthems. Many of her manuscripts are preserved in the Library of Congress, Washington, DC.

WILLIAM OSBORNE

Steckler, Anne–Marie. *See* KRUMPHOLTZ, ANNE-MARIE.

Stefanović, Ivana (*b* Belgrade, 14 Sept 1948). Serbian composer. She studied composition with Enrico Josif at the Belgrade Academy of Music and in 1976 began an association with Radio Belgrade, working as an editor, founding the Sound Workshop in 1985 and becoming head of music production on the First Programme in 1990. Her works show an extraordinary variety of compositional techniques, ranging from the manipulation of different sound sources – electronic, *concrète*, environmental as well as traditional instrumental – to the application of mathematical proportions. Almost all her works are designed for varied and unconventional ensembles, and most of the compositions that include the voice reveal her use of diverse verbal elements.

WORKS
selective list

Hommage à François Villon, early insts, vv, 1978; Fragment mogueg reda [Fragment of a Possible Order], 2 pf, hpd, org, cel, accordion, 1979; Kuda sa pticom na dlanu [Where to with the Bird on the Palm of the Hand], perc, tape, 1980; Tumačenje sna [Interpretation of a Dream], fl, 2 spkrs, tape, 1984; Lingua/Phonia/Patria, experimental radiophonic work, 1988–9; Psalam [Psalm], Mez, mixed vv, 1990; Isidora, ballet, tape, 1992; Lacrimosa, tape, 1993

MELITA MILIN

Steinberg, Carolyn (*b* San Antonio, TX, 17 May 1956). American composer. She was educated at North Texas State University, Denton (BM 1978), and the Manhattan School of Music (MM 1980), then undertook private study with Cathy Berberian (1980–81), at the Accademia Chigiana, Siena

(1981–2), and at the Staatliche Hochschule für Musik, Freiburg (1983). She later studied at the Juilliard School (1987–9), taking the DMA. Her composition teachers have included Ludmila Ulehla, Franco Donatoni, Bernard Rands and Brian Ferneyhough, to whom she was married, 1984–9. She has taught at various institutions in New York City since 1987. Her move to Europe in 1980 triggered in her an intense interest in the rigorous control of musical parameters; she ventures even further in *Rauhreif/Frost* (1987, first performed in Darmstadt, 1988), where groups of instruments rotate according to an autonomous design. According to Rulon, after the chamber opera *Cors de chasse* (1990, New York) the composer allowed acoustic phenomena to achieve for her a complexity she had previously sought through technical invention.

BIBLIOGRAPHY
CC (C. B. Rulon)

Steiner, Emma Roberto (*b* ?Baltimore, 1850; *d* New York, 27 Feb 1928). American composer and conductor. Her paternal ancestors were military officers; her mother was an excellent amateur pianist. Mainly self-taught, Steiner composed from the age of seven, despite a lack of encouragement from her parents. In the early 1870s she went to Chicago to make music her career, initially as a singer in the chorus of an opera company, then – after attracting the interest of Edward Everett Rice – as a conductor in a company under Rice's direction. Over the next 30 years Steiner is said to have conducted 6000 performances of more than 50 operas and operettas, including 700 performances of *The Mikado*. She and Caroline B. Nichols were the earliest women conductors in the USA to have had a full career. Heinrich Conried, whose company she conducted before he became manager of the Metropolitan Opera in 1903, is said to have wanted to hire her for the Met, but dared not because she was a woman.

Steiner composed throughout her lifetime, chiefly light operas, overtures, songs and piano music. She also prepared orchestrations. Theodore Thomas selected four of her works for performance at the World's Columbian Exposition in Chicago, 1893. On at least five occasions she conducted concerts of her own works in New York: in 1894 in Chickering Hall, in 1918 at the Morosco Theater, in 1920 and 1925 at the Metro-

politan Opera House and in 1921 at the Museum of Natural History. The 1925 concert included excerpts from her three-act light opera *The Burra Pundit* (1907, libretto by Katherine Stagg and 'Joe-Ker') and an orchestral transcription from it (1914); the overture to the two-act comic opera *Fleurette* (1877, libretto by B. W. Doremus and Edgar Smith); excerpts from the two-act *opéra bouffe The Man from Paris* (1900, libretto by M. I. Macdonald and J. W. Castle); and an orchestral work, *The Flag – Forever may it Wave* (1918, dedicated to Steiner's grandfather, Colonel Stephen Steiner), commemorating the American victory at North Point and incorporating melodies of 1814. The 1921 concert included the songs *Beautiful Eyes*, *Tecolote* (a Mexican 'idyl') and *I Envy the Rose* (composed at the age of 12), and excerpts from *The Burra Pundit* and *The Man from Paris*.

Steiner published her works with Margaret MacDonald. In response to failing eyesight, she emigrated to Alaska after 1900 and worked as a tin miner for ten years.

CAROL NEULS-BATES

Steiner, Gitta (Hana) (*b* Prague, 17 April 1932; *d* New York, 1 Jan 1990). American composer, pianist, teacher and poet. She studied composition at the Juilliard School (MusB 1967, MS 1969) with Vincent Persichetti, Gunther Schuller, and Elliott Carter, and gained several awards. She was co-founder of the Composers Group for International Performance (1968) and taught at Brooklyn Conservatory (1962–6 and 1983–4). Her works for percussion are particularly well known (many are published by Seesaw).

WORKS
selective list

Orch: Suite, 1958; Vn Conc., 1963; Pf Conc., 1967
Chamber: Suite, fl, cl, bn, 1958; Str Trio, 1964; Wind Qnt, 2 tpt, hn, trbn, tuba, 1964; Refractions, vn, 1967; Str Qt, 1968; Perc Qt, 1968; Trio, 2 perc, pf, 1969; Duo, vc, perc, 1971; Dialogue, 2 perc, 1975; 3 Pieces, perc, 1978; Duo, trbn, perc, 1981; Sonatine, vib, mar, 1983; 5 Pieces, trbn, pf, 1984; Str Qt, 1984; Pf Trio, 1985; Sonata, vib, 1985; Bagatelles, vib, 1990
Pf: 3 Pieces, 1963; 2 sonatas, 1963, 1964; Fantasy Piece, 1966; Music for Piano, 1985
Vocal: 3 Songs, medium v, 1960; Interlúdes, medium v, vib, 1968; 4 Songs, medium v, vib, 1970; Settings, chorus, 1970; 5 Poems, mixed chorus, 1970; Trio, 1v, pf, perc, 1971; 2 Songs, 1v, pf, 1971; [2] Concert Pieces for Seven, high v, fl, 2 perc, pf, vc, cond., 1971; Pages From a Summer Journal,

medium v, pf, 1971; 4 Choruses, 1972; New Poems, 1v, vib, 1974; Dream Dialogues, 1v, perc, 1974

Principal publishers: Belwin Mills, Seesaw

CATHERINE PARSONS SMITH

Stirling, Elizabeth (*b* Greenwich, 26 Feb 1819; *d* London, 25 March 1895). English organist and composer. She studied the organ and piano with W. B. Wilson and Edward Holmes, and harmony with J. A. Hamilton and G. A. Macfarren. In November 1839, she was elected organist of All Saint's, Poplar, a post she retained until September 1858, when she gained a similar one at St Andrew's Undershaft, by competition. This she resigned in 1880. In 1856 she submitted an exercise (Psalm cxxx, for five voices and orchestra) for the Oxford BMus; though accepted, it was not performed, since at that time women were not eligible for degrees. She published some original pedal fugues and slow movements, other pieces for the organ and organ arrangements from the works of Handel, Bach and Mozart, songs and duets, and many partsongs for four voices, of which a favourite was *All among the Barley*. In 1863 she married the organist F. A. Bridge. Her opera *Bleakmoor for Copseleigh* (unpublished) was in the repertory of their chamber opera company.

GEORGE GROVE/JOHN R. GARDNER

Stirling-Maxwell, Caroline Elizabeth Sarah. *See* NORTON, CAROLINE ELIZABETH SARAH.

Stocker [née Prince], **Stella** (*b* Jacksonville, IL, 3 April 1858; *d* 1925). American composer and specialist in American Indian culture. Stocker began her study of music at the Jacksonville Conservatory. After graduating from the University of Michigan, she attended Wellesley College and then the Sorbonne. She studied singing with Giovanni Sbriglia in Paris, the piano with Xaver Scharwenka in Berlin, and composition with Bruno Klein in New York. Native American music was of special interest to her, and she became a member of the Ojibwa people. She lectured on Native American music and legends both in the USA and abroad, and she incorporated melodies from this repertory in her works, for example, in the choruses for her play *Sieur du Lhut* and in a pantomime, *The Marvels of Manabush*. Stocker also wrote four operettas – *Beulah, Queen of Hearts, Ganymede*

and *Raoul* – as well as piano works and songs.

CAROL NEULS-BATES

Strickland [Anderson], **Lily (Theresa)** (*b* Anderson, SC, 28 Jan 1887; *d* Hendersonville, NC, 6 June 1958). American composer. Her musical talents were noticed at an early age and she started to compose while in her teens. She attended Converse College from 1901 to 1904, and in 1905 was offered a scholarship by Frank Damrosch to study at the Institute of Musical Art in New York; her teachers at the Institute were Albert Mildenberg, William Henry Humiston, Daniel Gregory Mason, and Percy Goetschius. She also studied privately with Alfred John Goodrich. In 1920 she accompanied her husband, J. Courtney Anderson, on a business trip to India; they lived there until early 1929, during which time Strickland became fascinated with non-Western music and wrote a number of articles comparing Indian with European idioms. From 1930 to 1948 the Andersons lived in Woodstock and Great Neck, New York, finally retiring to Hendersonville.

Some of Strickland's early pieces, such as *Honey Chile* (1922), *Pickaninny Sleep Song* (1911) and *Heah dem Bells* (1926), were influenced by the black music she used to hear on her grandparents' estate. After 1910 she was drawn to Native American music and incorporated some of its melodies in such pieces as *Two Shawnee Indian Dances* (1919) and the operetta *Laughing Star of Zuni* (1946). Her sojourn in India influenced many of her works composed after 1930, notably *The Cosmic Dance of Siva* (1933) and *Oriental and Character Dances*. Strickland composed approximately 400 pieces; in addition to many songs and piano pieces she wrote several operettas, including *Jewel of the Desert* (1933), a sacred cantata *St John the Beloved* (1930), orchestral suites, and other works. They are cast in a conservative harmonic idiom; many are salon pieces influenced by the works of Charles Cadman and Arthur Farwell.

BIBLIOGRAPHY

A. W. Howe: *Lily Strickland: her Contribution to American Music in the Early Twentieth Century* (diss., Catholic U. of America, 1968)

JOHN GRAZIANO

Strozzi, Barbara [Valle, Barbara] (*b* Venice, 1619; *d* ?Venice, after 1664). Italian composer and singer, adopted (possibly illegitimate) daughter of Giulio Strozzi, some-

Female Musician with a Viola da Gamba: portrait (c1637) by Bernardo Strozzi, probably of Barbara Strozzi

times referred to by him as Barbara Valle; by 1650 she was his sole heir. Her mother was Isabella Garzoni, called 'la Greghetta', Strozzi's longtime servant. She was a pupil of Francesco Cavalli and the dedicatee of two volumes of solo songs by Nicolò Fontei, the *Bizzarrie poetiche* of 1635 and 1636, for which Giulio Strozzi wrote most of the texts, and which Barbara sang at his home in the presence of various Venetian *letterati*. Her performances were institutionalized in 1637 when Giulio founded the Accademia degli Unisoni, a musical offshoot of a more important literary academy, the Accademia degli Incogniti. As indicated by published minutes of the Unisoni (*Le veglie de' Signori Unisoni*, 1638), she sang at the meetings and suggested the subjects on which the members exercised their debating skills.

Strozzi's career as a professional composer began in 1644 with the first of her eight publications, a volume of madrigals for two to five voices on texts by Giulio Strozzi, which she dedicated to Vittoria della Rovere, Grand Duchess of Tuscany. All but one of her subsequent surviving publications – op.4 is missing – appeared after Giulio's death in

1652. Dedicated to a variety of important patrons, including Ferdinand II of Austria and Eleanora of Mantua (op.2, 1651), Anne of Austria, Archduchess of Innsbruck (op.5, 1655), Nicolo Sagredo, Doge of Venice (op.7, 1659) and Sophia, Duchess of Brunswick and Lüneburg (op.8, 1664), they suggest that she may have been forced to rely on her abilities as a composer for her livelihood after her father's death. She disappears from history after her op.8.

Apart from the madrigals of op.1 and the solo motets of op.5, nearly all of Strozzi's surviving works are ariettas, arias and cantatas for solo voice (mainly soprano) and continuo. A few works call for strings as well. Although the generic categories are not fixed, and terminology is only loosely applied in the publications themselves, the simplest pieces are the ariettas, which are essentially short arias in strophic form (such as most of the pieces in op.6). The most complex are the cantatas (such as those in opp.7 and 8). These are lengthy, varied works containing several sections and a mixture of vocal styles: recitative, arioso and aria, responding to textual distinctions between open narration and formal lyricism. The arias are generally shorter than the cantatas, often strophic, and frequently enclosed by a refrain at beginning and end.

The texts, many of them apparently written to order and about half of them anonymous, are in the Marinist vein: precious love poetry filled with various conceits, ironic and lachrymose by turns. The known poets include, besides Giulio Strozzi, several figures associated with the world of opera in Venice around the middle of the 17th century: Pietro Paolo Bissari, Aurelio Aureli, Pietro Dolfino, Marc'Antonio Corraro, Nicola Beregani and Francesco Piccoli. Although she wrote no operas, the best of her works (most notably the *lamento* 'Sul Rodano severo', opp.2 and 3) convey dramatic action in which the progress of a protagonist – partly described by a narrator – towards a resolution of his predicament unfolds in a carefully calculated series of musico–dramatic events. In cantatas as well as arias, her primary formal procedure is contrast, usually combined with some kind of refrain idea. Strozzi's style, with its easy shifts between unmeasured and measured passages and between duple and triple metre, and her occasional use of the *stile concitato*, all in response to a faithful aherence to the form and meaning of the texts, reflects her training in the *seconda prattica* tradition, as exemplified in the music of her teacher, Cavalli. But her melismatic expansions are longer and repetitions of text more frequent than his, and her style altogether more pointedly lyrical, more dependent on sheer vocal sound. It is emphatically singer's music, and very grateful to the lyrical soprano voice, neither excessively virtuoso nor especially demanding as far as range or tessitura is concerned. The similarity in vocal style among her works, the scoring for soprano and continuo, and the frequent puns on her name in the texts suggest that she sang most of her music herself, at academic meetings and similar social occasions.

The *Female Musician with Viola da Gamba* painted in Venice by the Genoese Bernardo Strozzi, probably around 1637 (now in the Gemäldegalerie, Dresden), may be her portrait (see illustration).

WORKS
all printed works published in Venice

Editions:
Ariette di Francesca Caccini e Barbara Strozzi, ed. A. Bonaventura (Rome, 1930)
The Italian Cantata in the Seventeenth Century, v, ed. E. Rosand (New York, 1986) [facs. edn] [ICSC]

Il primo libro de madrigali, 2–5vv, bc (1644); 2 madrigals ed. C. Raney, *Nine Centuries of Music by Women* (New York, 1978)
Cantate, ariette e duetti, 1–2vv, bc, op.2 (1651); facs. edn, 21 cantatas and ariettas, ICSC; 2 ariettas ed. K. Jeppesen, *La flora*, ii (Copenhagen, 1949); 1 arietta ed. V. Ricci, *Antiche gemme italiane* (Milan, 1949/R1975); 1 arietta ed. F. Vatielli, *Antiche cantate d'amore* (Bologna, n.d.)
Cantate e ariette, 1–3vv, bc, op.3 (1654); 5 cantatas and ariettas, ICSC
Sacri musicali affetti, libro I, op.5 (1655); facs. edn, ed. E. Rosand (New York, 1988)
Ariette a voce sola, op.6 (1657) [incl. 1 for 2vv]; 2 ariettas repr. in F. Tonalli, ed., *Arie a voce sola di diversi auttori* (1656); 17 ariettas, ICSC
Diporti di Euterpe, overo Cantate e ariette a voce sola, op.7 (1659); facs. edn, *Archivum musicum: la cantata barocca*, iii (Florence, 1980); 8 ariettas and cantatas, ICSC; 1 cantata, Lagrime mie, pr. in Racek, 251ff, and ed. C. MacClintock, *The Solo Song 1580–1730: a Norton Music Anthology* (New York, 1973), 81ff
Arie a voce sola, op.8 (1664); facs. edn, Antiquae Musicae Italicae Studiosi (Bologna, 1970); 5 arias (*I-Bc* BB.422), ICSC
Quis dabit mihi, motet, 3vv, in B. Marcesso, *Sacra corona, motetti a due e tre voci di diversi eccelentissimi autori moderni* (1656)

BIBLIOGRAPHY
ChoronFayolleD; FétisB; GerberL; HawkinsH; SainsburyD; SchillingE; SchmidlD
Veglie de' Signori Unisoni (Venice, 1638)
Satire, e altra raccolte per l'Accademia de gli Unisoni in casa di Giulio Strozzi (*I-Vnm* Cl.X, Cod.CXV [7193])
G. F. Loredano: *Bizzarrie academiche* (Venice, 1638), 182ff
E. A. Cicogna: *Delle iscrizioni veneziane* (Venice, 1824–53), v, 278–9, 663
A. Bonaventura: 'Un'arietta di Barbara Strozzi', *Nuova musica*, x (1905), 61
E. Schmitz: *Geschicte der weltlichen Solokantate* (Leipzig, 1914, 2/1955), 81–2
A. Bonaventura: 'Le donne italiane e la musica', *RMI*, xxxii (1925), 522
M. Maylander: *Storie delle accademie d'Italia*, v (Bologna, 1930), 396–7
J. Racek: *Stilprobleme der italienischen Monodie* (Prague, 1965)
L. Bianconi and T. Walker: 'Dalla "Finta pazza" alla "Veremonda": storie di Febiarmonici', *RIM*, x (1975), 379–425, esp. 410ff
E. Rosand: 'Barbara Strozzi, *virtuosissima cantatrice*: the Composer's Voice', *JAMS*, xxxi (1978), 241–81
E. Rosand and D. Rosand: 'Barbara di Santa Sofia and Il Prete Genovese: on the Identity of a Portrait by Bernardo Strozzi', *Art Bulletin*, lxiii (1981), 249–58
E. Rosand: 'The Voice of Barbara Strozzi', in *Women Making Music: the Western Art Tradition, 1150–1950*, ed. J. Bowers and J. Tick (Urbana and Chicago, 1986), 168–90
—— : 'Cantatas by Barbara Strozzi', in *The Italian Cantata in the Seventeenth Century*, v (New York, 1986) [Introduction]
R. K. Wong: *Barbara Strozzi's 'Arie', op.8 (1664): an Edition and Commentary* (thesis, Stanford U., 1992)
ELLEN ROSAND

Stuart-Coolidge [Coolidge; Stuart], **Peggy** (*b* Swampscott, MA, 19 July 1913; *d* Cushing,

Peggy Stuart-Coolidge

ME, 7 May 1981). Privately educated, she studied the piano with Heinrich Gebhard and composition with Raymond Robinson and Quincy Porter. Coolidge's orchestral works were performed by the Boston Pops from the late 1930s; commissions included *American Mosaic* for the American Wind Symphony and *The Blue Planet* for the World Wildlife Fund. Her works were performed in Europe from 1963 and, on Aram Khachaturian's invitation, a concert of her music was presented by the USSR Union of Composers in Moscow in 1970. Coolidge was the first American to be honoured thus, and at the same time she was awarded the medal of the Soviet Union of Workers in Art. Coolidge's music is skilfully orchestrated and accessible, with a distinctive style reminiscent of George Gershwin and Aaron Copland.

Her manuscripts and personal papers are held by Joseph R. Coolidge and will eventually be lodged at the Schlesinger Library on the History of Women in America, Radcliffe College, Cambridge, Massachusetts.

WORKS

Ballet: Cracked Ice, 1937; An Evening in New Orleans, *c*1966

Orch: Rhapsody, harp, orch, 1965; Spirituals in Sunshine and Shadow, 1969; New England Autumn, suite, chamber orch, 1971; Pioneer Dances, 1980; The Blue Planet (J. R. Coolidge), nar, orch; Dublin Town [arr. of incid. music for Red Roses for Me]; The Island; Look to the Wind, 1v, orch [orchd G. Ghal]; O'er Silent Snow (J. R.

Coolidge); Out of the Dark; Night Froth; Smoke Drift; Twilight City

Band: American Mosaic, 1978; Pioneer Dances

Incid. music: Voices (R. Lortz), 1972; Red Roses for Me (S. O'Casey)

Film score: The Silken Affair, late 1950s

Chamber music, pf pieces, songs, music for children's stories: The Angel's Christmas (R. Lortz), Salisbury Seagull (J. R. Coolidge)

CATHERINE PARSONS SMITH

Stubenberg, Maria Anna, Countess (*b* Graz, 9 Aug 1821; *d* Graz, 1 Dec 1912). Austrian pianist and composer. A member of the ancient Stubenberg family of Graz, she was brought up in Pesth (Budapest). Her early interest in music was nurtured by her family and she soon became known as a gifted improviser. She composed numerous virtuoso piano pieces of national character (polkas, mazurkas and *csárdás*) and a few songs. She was married three times: on 15 February 1840 to Johann Remekhazy von Gurahoucz (*d* 1843); on 22 February 1848 to Count Friedrich Zichy von Zichy und Vasonykeö (who died three months later) and on 28 February 1872 to Count Otto Buttlar, Freiherr von Brandenfels.

BIBLIOGRAPHY

PazdirekH; *WurzbachL*

ROSARIO MARCIANO

Suh, Kyungsun (*b* Seoul, 8 Nov 1942). Korean composer. She studied at Seoul National University, presenting a concert of her first works in 1966 shortly after graduation, and later continued her studies at Amherst College, Massachusetts. In 1981 she joined a music-theatre project with Mauricio Kagel in Cologne. She lectures at Hanyang University and in 1993 was elected president of the Korean Society of Women Composers. Her works have been performed in Seoul, Rome (1981), Wellington (1984), Taipei (1985), Sendai (1986) and Los Angeles. She favours small ensembles: *An Illusion* (1977) for three flutes and percussion and *Phenomenon I* (1982) for two pianos are representative works. Monody coupled to elaborate serial techniques features in the Concerto for nine string instruments and the solo violin piece *Pentastisch* (1987). The former comprises a seven-section arch and the latter five short sections; both gradually open up distinct pitch areas contrasting, for example, blocks of low *col legno* and pizzicato notes against high legato melodies. Her writings include studies of the music of C. P. E. Bach and of Allen Forte's atonal theory.

WORKS
selective list

Inst: 3 Movements, cl, vc, 1973; For Clarinet and Violoncello, 1975; Prelude, str, 1975; An Illusion, 3 fl, harp, perc, 1977; Poem, fl, 1979; A Movement for Flute and Harp, 1980; Poem, pf, 1981; Phenomenon I, 2 pf, 1982; Poem, vc, pf, 1982; Concerto, 9 str, 1983; Lamentation, pf, perc, 1983: Poem, str ens, 1983; Pentastisch, vn, 1987; Music for 16 String Players, 1989; At the Soo-kook, hn, pf, perc, 1991

Vocal: For a Child, 1v, fl, cl, perc, 1975; 2 Images, 1v, vn, pf, 1975; 3 Songs for Autumn, 1v, 1987; A Song: the Winter Sea, 1v, 1991

Principal publisher: Soomoondang

KEITH HOWARD

Sullivan, Marion Dix (*fl* 1840–50). American composer. Although little is known about her life, Marion Dix came from New England and married J. W. Sullivan of Boston in 1825. She was the first American woman composer to produce a commercial hit song, *The Blue Juniata* (1844). It was published in several collections and set as piano variations by Charles Grobe and Gould, and was mentioned in Mark Twain's autobiography. Her music is in the parlour-song tradition of memorable melodies supported by diatonic harmonies, with simple chordal accompaniments. She wrote the texts as well as the melodies for most of her songs. However, some of her publications include collaborations with other composers; for example, *Bible Songs* (1856) was published with piano accompaniments by Benjamin Johnson Lang.

WORKS
for 1v, piano, unless otherwise stated;
printed works published in Boston unless otherwise stated

The Blue Juniata (Sullivan), 1v, gui (1844), arr. pf by E. L. White; Jessie Cook (1844); Marion Day (1844); Oh! Boatman, row me o'er the stream, duet (1844), arr. pf by White; The Field of Monterey (1846); Gypsy, perf. Madison Female College, 27 July 1853, lost; Mary Lindsay (1848); O'er our way when first we parted (n.d.; 1840s); The Bridal, pubd in Godey's Lady's Book, xl/March (1850); We cross the prairie as of old (J. G. Whittier: Song of the Kansas emigrants) (1854); When the bright waves are dashing (n.p., 1858); The Evening Bugle

Collections: [48] Juniata Ballads (Sullivan), 1v unacc. (1855); [24] Bible Songs (1856), pf accs. by B. J. Lang

BIBLIOGRAPHY

CohenE; WAM

J. Tick: *American Women Composers before 1870* (Ann Arbor, 1983)

K. Pendle, ed.: *Women and Music: a History* (Indianapolis, IN, 1991)

NAOMI ANDRÉ

Sutherland, Margaret (Ada) (*b* Adelaide, 20 Nov 1897; *d* Melbourne, 12 Aug 1984).

Margaret Sutherland, awarded an honorary doctorate of music by the University of Melbourne in 1969

Australian composer and pianist. Her father was a writer and amateur pianist, and other relatives included musicians, artists, scientists and academics. Her musical education included studies with Edward Goll (piano) and Fritz Hart (composition) at the Marshall Hall (now Melba) Conservatorium and later at the Melbourne University Conservatorium. At the age of 19 she was invited by the director of the New South Wales State Conservatorium of Music, Henri Verbrugghen, to appear as soloist with the NSW State Orchestra in public concerts under his direction. She gave recitals and taught theory and piano during World War I and up to 1923, and wrote a number of short teaching pieces for the piano. She left Australia in 1923 for further study in composition, orchestration and conducting in London and Vienna. In London she was for a time a pupil of Arnold Bax; during this period she produced her first published works, including the Violin Sonata, which received especially warm praise from Bax. She returned to Melbourne in 1925.

The period between 1925 and 1935 was fallow, but during the next 35 years she was active as a composer, performer (principally of chamber music) and teacher, contributing greatly to the musical and cultural development of Australia. She was also a vigorous champion of the music of Australian composers. For many years, her own works gained comparatively little recognition. During the 1960s, however, the rapid growth of performances, recordings, publication and commissioning of Australian compositions made some reparation. Her considerable services to Australian music received official recognition in 1969 when she was awarded an honorary DMus from the University of Melbourne, and again in 1970 when she was made an OBE. Failing eyesight precluded further composition in the final decade or so of her life.

Sutherland has become recognized as one of the first 20th-century Australian composers to write in an idiom comparable with that of her generation in Europe. Her music was influenced by that of her teacher, Bax, and by the English pastoral idiom; the richer, more sensuous elements of this style are most noticeable in some early songs, keyboard and chamber music. Unlike many Australian composers of the first half of the 20th century, however, she soon integrated these influences in a personal idiom, absorbing a wide range of stylistic sources, contemporary continental as well as English. The influence of Bartók and Hindemith is particularly evident, and also the neo-classicism found in Ravel, Milhaud or Poulenc.

Her music at times betrays romantic warmth and often displays considerable strength of utterance and rhythmic vitality, although restraint, conciseness of expression and a strong taste for contrapuntal development must be considered basic qualities. This last element is especially prominent in many of her chamber works and is aptly reflected in the title of one of the best of these, *Discussion* (1954) for string quartet. Her chamber music also shows a typically 20th-century interest in varied, often unusual instrumental combinations. Romantic elements are perhaps most marked in orchestral works such as the Violin Concerto (1954) and the tone poem *Haunted Hills* (1954; a musical evocation of the Dandenong Ranges near Melbourne and one of her few works with programmatic intentions). One of the finest and most characteristic of her larger works is the Concerto grosso (1955), in which two fast movements, characterized by an effective use of dissonant counterpoint as well as by rhythmic drive and rhetorical strength, enclose a lyrical slow movement of brooding melancholy. Lyrical qualities are also to be found in her many songs; the settings of poems by Judith Wright contain some fine examples. Her single opera, *The Young Kabbarli*, a one-act chamber opera, was given its première at the Festival of Contemporary Opera and Music in Hobart in 1965.

WORKS
selective list

STAGE AND ORCHESTRAL

Opera: The Young Kabbarli (1, M. Casey), Hobart, July 1965

Ballets: Dithyramb, pf, 1937, orchd ?1941; The Selfish Giant

Incid. music: A Midsummer Night's Dream

Orch: Pavan, 1938; Prelude and Jig, str, 1939; Suite on a Theme of Purcell, 1939; Pf Concertino, 1940; Conc., str, 1945; Rondel, 1945; Adagio, 2 vn, orch, 1946; Threesome, 1947; Ballad Ov., 1948; 4 Sym. Concepts (Studies), 1949; Bush Ballad, ?1950; Haunted Hills, 1950; Open Air Piece, 1953; Vn Conc., 1954; Conc. grosso, 1955; Outdoor Ov., 1958; 3 Temperaments, 1958; Movt, 1959; Concertante, ob, str, perc, 1961; Fantasy, vn, orch, 1962

VOCAL

Choral: The Passing, SATB, orch, ?1939; A Company of Carols, SATB, pf, 1966; miscellaneous short pieces

Solo vocal: Songs for Children (Martyr), 1v, pf, ?1929; 3 Songs (F. Thompson), 1v, vn, pf, 1930; 5 Songs (J. Shaw Neilson), 1v, pf, 1936; The Gentle Water Bird (Shaw Neilson), 1v, vn/ob, pf; The Orange Tree (Shaw Neilson), 1v, cl, pf, ?1938; 4 Blake Songs, 1v, pf, ?1950; The World and the Child (J. Wright), Mez, pf/str qt, 1960; Sequence of Verses into Music (Casey), speaker, fl, bn, va, 1964; 6 Australian Songs (Wright), 1v, pf, 1967; other settings, folksong arrs.

CHAMBER AND INSTRUMENTAL

For 3–4 insts: Trio, cl, va, pf, 1934; House Qt, cl/vn, va, hn/vc, pf, 1936; Str Qt no.1, ?1939; Adagio and Allegro giocoso, 2 vn, pf, ?1945; Trio, ob, 2 vn, 1951; Discussion (Str Qt no.2), 1954; Qt, eng hn, str, 1955; Divertimento, str trio, 1958; Little Suite, wind trio, ?1960; Str Qt no.3, 1967; Qt, cl, str, 1967

For 2 insts: Sonata, vn, pf, 1925; Fantasy Sonatina, sax, pf, ?1935; Rhapsody, vn, pf, 1938; Sonata, vc/sax, pf, 1942; Ballad and Nocturne, vn, pf, 1944; Sonata, cl/va, pf, 1947; Contrasts, 2 vn, 1953; 6 Bagatelles, vn, va, 1956; Sonatina, ob/vn, pf, ?1957; Fantasy, vn, pf, ?1960

For kbd: Burlesque, 2 pf, ?1927; 2 Chorale Preludes on Bach's Chorales, pf (1935); 2 suites, pf (1937); Miniature Ballet Suite, pf (1937); Miniature Sonata, pf, ?1939; 6 Profiles, pf, ?1946; Pf Sonatina (1956); Pavan, 2 pf (1957); Canonical Piece, 2 pf (1957); Pf Sonata (1966); Extension, pf, 1967; Chiaroscuro I–II, pf, 1968; Voices I–II, pf, 1968; 3 Pieces, hpd

Educational: str pieces (1967), pf pieces

Principal publisher: Albert (Sydney)

BIBLIOGRAPHY

LePageWC, iii

I. Moresby: *Australia Makes Music* (London, 1948), 127

J. Garretty: *Three Australian Composers* (diss., U. of Melbourne, 1963), 49–102

R. Covell: *Australia's Music: Themes of a New Society* (Melbourne, 1967), 152–4, 261

A. McCredie: *A Catalogue of 46 Australian Composers and Selected Works* (Canberra, 1969), 18

— : *Musical Composition in Australia* (Canberra, 1969)

F. Callaway and D. Tunley, eds.: *Australian Composers in the Twentieth Century* (London, 1979)

H. Coles: 'Margaret Sutherland: Australian Composer', *Lip* [Melbourne] (1978–9), 111–13

I. Morgan: *An Analysis of Margaret Sutherland's Sonata for Clarinet and Piano (1947)* (diss., U. of Melbourne, 1986)

DAVID SYMONS

Svanidze, Natela Damianovna (*b* Ahalzih, 4 Sept 1926). Georgian composer. She studied at the Tbilisi Conservatory with Andrey Balanchivadze, graduating in 1951, and at the Moscow Conservatory with Yury Fortunatov, Revol Bunin and Nicolay Peyko. In 1956 she became a member of the Georgian Drama Institute, where she was later appointed professor. Before 1962 Svanidze's music was rooted in the traditions of the Georgian Romantic school, but as a result of experimenting with polytonality, assimilating contemporary techniques and studying Georgian folk part-singing, she began to use the principles of west Georgian folk polyphony as the constructive basis of her style. Individual, contrasting parts are created by means of a variety of techniques – serial, colourist and aleatory – to which are added original counterpoint, electronic sounds and collages of authentic folk music. The composer has sought to cultivate a style that is expressionist, grotesque and yet concise.

WORKS
selective list

Stage: Gaul-Gavkhe (opera, 3, N. Svanidze, after T. Maglaperidze), 1987, unperf.

Orch: Simfonicheskiye tantsï [Symphonic Dances], 1949; Samgori, sym. poem, 1951; Kvarkvare, sym. poem, 1963; Sym. no.1, pf, perc, str, 1967; Burleska, pf, ww, brass, perc, 1968; Sym. no.2, sym.-ballet, 1983

Vocal: Pirosmani (chamber oratorio, T. Tabidze, P. Antokol'sky and B. Pasternak), vocal sextet, spkr, 1v, inst ens, 1969; Gruzinskiye plachi [Georgian Lamentations] (oratorio, J. Charkviani), 2 mixed choruses, female sextet, 1v, fl, vn, 2 vc, bells, organ, tape, 1974; Skazaniye ob odnoy devushke [The Legend about a Girl] (I. Noneshvili), 1v, pf, 1974

Chamber and pf: Improvisation, vn, pf, 1956; Skazka [Fairy-Tale], pf, 1960; Krugovorot [Rotation], pf, 1972

OLGA MANULKINA

Swados, Elizabeth [Liz] (*b* Buffalo, NY, 5 Feb 1951). American composer. She attended Bennington College in Vermont (BA 1972), where she studied composition with Henry Brant. She became associated with the La Mama Experimental Theater Company, based in New York, in 1970. For the Romanian director Andrei Serban she composed scores to accompany several of his adaptations of Greek tragedies; she also acted as music director of the International Theater Group, led by Peter Brooks. In 1978 her innovative musical *Runaways* was given its première in New York. Later she collaborated with Garry B. Trudeau, creator of the *Doonesbury* comic strip, on a musical based on the strip and on a revue about Ronald Reagan (*Rap Master Ronnie*).

In her music for theatre of the 1970s Swados drew on a number of non-Western influences. *Runaways* established her as a force in American musical theatre; like her other so-called collage musicals, it treats a common theme in songs and sketches without relying on a plot. She uses a wide range of popular music from pop and punk to salsa in her revues and other shows.

WORKS
selective list

Stage (dates are of first perf., in New York unless otherwise stated): Nightclub Cantata (revue, Swados), 9 Jan 1977; Runaways (musical, Swados), 9 March 1978; Alice in Concert (after L. Carroll), 27 Dec 1978; The Incredible Feeling Show (musical), Feb 1979; Dispatches (musical, after M. Herr), 6 April 1979; Haggadah (cantata, after E. Wiesel), 31 March 1980; Under Fire (musical, Swados), 6 Aug 1980; Lullabye and Goodnight (musical, Swados), Feb 1982; A Summer Fable (musical), Boston, June 1983; Doonesbury (musical, G. Trudeau), 10 Nov 1983; Jerusalem (oratorio, after Y. Amichai), May 1984; Rap Master Ronnie (revue, Trudeau), Oct 1984; The Three Travels of Aladdin (musical)

Incid. music (all plays dir. A. Serban): Medea (Euripides), 1972; Electra (Sophocles), 1973; The Trojan Women (Euripides), 1974; The Good Woman of Setzuan (B. Brecht), 1975; Agamemnon (Aeschylus), 1977; The Cherry Orchard (A. Chekhov), 1977

Film scores: Four Friends; Too Far to Go

Other works: Sylvia Plath Song Cycle; New York Gypsy Suite, orch, 1980; Truth and Variations; Symphonic Ov.; other ens works

BIBLIOGRAPHY

CBY 1979

M. Gussow: 'Eiizabeth Swados, a Runaway Talent', *New York Times Magazine* (5 March 1978), 19–57

C. Bentsen: 'Swados in Wonderland', *New York* (29 Dec 1980), 38–42

CHARLES PASSY

Swain, Freda (*b* Portsmouth, 31 Oct 1902; *d* Chinnor, 29 Jan 1985). English composer and pianist. One of the last composition pupils of C. V. Stanford at the RCM, she also studied the piano with Dora Matthay (1913–17) and with Arthur Alexander, whom she married in 1921. She was appointed professor at the RCM in 1924, the year from which her first mature compositions may be said to date. Of the works written in her student days, only the *Mauresque* for violin and piano and some song settings of Chinese poems have survived. She first came to prominence with *The Harp of Aengus* for violin and orchestra (based on a poem by W. B. Yeats), played by Achille Rivarde at Queen's Hall in January 1925. In 1936 she founded the British Music Movement for the promotion of new music and after World War II she set up the NEMO Concerts, which again promoted her contemporaries' music as well as her own. The intention of both was not to isolate British music from the work of foreign composers, but to prove that it could hold its own with the music of any other school.

At the beginning of the war Arthur Alexander was marooned in South Africa. Swain wrote a piano concerto for him; it was scored on very thin paper and sent by airmail in a number of instalments. Alexander performed it at Cape Town and elsewhere and it became known as the 'Airmail Concerto'. Despite its success abroad, however, and protests by the composer and her supporters, the concerto was never accepted for broadcast by the BBC. In 1940 Swain joined her husband and they toured the country widely, giving recitals for two pianos. They repeated the tour in Australia, returned to South Africa, and thence home to England in May 1943.

Swain's affinities are with the English school immediately preceding her generation, John Ireland especially. Although the range of her music is limited, the music is vital, individual and presented with technical assurance. While her later music introduces a more dissonant harmony, her earlier instrumental works and especially one or two songs, such as the folklike *The Lark on Portsdown Hill* and sympathetic settings of Housman, show her at her best.

WORKS
selective list

Operas: Second Chance (1, Swain and M. Rodd), concert perf., London, Royal Festival Hall, Recital Room, 1959; The Spell (3), inc.

Orch: The Harp of Aengus, after W. B. Yeats, vn, orch, 1924; Pastoral Fantasy, chamber orch, 1936–7; 'Airmail' Conc., pf, orch, 1939; Perihelion, vn, str orch; Lumina naturi, cl, hn, str orch, 1948; Concertino, pf, str orch; The Lion of England, coronation march, 1953

Chamber and solo inst: Mauresque, vn, pf, 1920; Str Qt no.1 'Norfolk', 1924; 2 vn sonatas, 'The River', 1925, b, 1925; Sonata, vn, 1933; Satyr's Dance, sax, pf, 1935; Summer Rhapsody, va/cl, pf, 1936; Suite, sax, 1937; Pf Qt 'The Sea', 1938; The Willow Tree,

cl, pf, 1946; Vn Sonata, g, 1947; Str Qt no.2, g, 1949; pf pieces

Choral works, songs, educational music

BIBLIOGRAPHY
E. Blom: 'The Younger English Composers, 8: Freda Swain', *MMR*, lix (1929), 257–8

D. Francke: Obituary, *The Times* (4 Feb 1985)
ERIC BLOM/LEWIS FOREMAN

Swepstone, Edith (*fl* 1885–1930). English composer and teacher. Little about her is known. She studied at the GSM and was lecturing on music at the City of London School in 1895. Of the works by various women composers performed by Sir Dan Godfrey with the Bournemouth Municipal Orchestra during the first quarter of the 20th century, the largest number by any one composer were by her, but the music has not been located. Between 1899 and 1933, 14 orchestral works by her were given a total of 24 performances. There is only record of two having been performed elsewhere: a movement from the Symphony in G minor, first heard at Leyton in March 1887, and *Les ténèbres* at Queen's Hall in February 1897.

WORKS
selective list

ORCHESTRAL
dates are of performances at Bournemouth

Daramona, sym. poem, 1899; The Ice Maiden, suite, 1900; Sym., g, 1902; A Vision, sym. poem, 1903; Les ténèbres, elegiac ov., 1903; Paola and Francesca, prelude, 1904; Mors Janua Vitae, funeral march, 1906; The Wind in the Pines, sym. poem, 1909; The Horn of Roland, ov., 1910; Moonrise on the Mountains, sym. poem, 1912; Woods in April, sym. poem, 1914; The Roll of Honour, march, 1916; Morte d'Arthur, sym. poem, 1920; The Four Ships, suite, 1927

OTHER WORKS

Pf Qnt, f; Str Qt, g; The Ice Queen, cantata, female vv; Idylls of the Morn, cantata, female vv; songs, other inst works

LEWIS FOREMAN

Swift, Kay (*b* New York, 19 April 1897; *d* Southington, CT, 28 Jan 1993). American composer, lyricist, author and pianist. Born into a musical family (her father was the music critic Samuel Swift), she began music lessons at the age of seven. She studied the piano with Bertha Tapper and composition with A. E. Johnstone at the Institute of Musical Art (now the Juilliard School), then continued with Charles Loeffler (composition) and Heinrich Gebhard (piano) at the New England Conservatory. She also studied counterpoint and orchestration with Percy Goetschius. On graduation she became a pianist, accompanying singers and instrumentalists, and a member of a trio which toured the northeastern USA.

Swift has two claims to a place in American musical history: first, in the 1920s, among the massed ranks of Tin Pan Alleymen, she (along with the lyricist Dorothy Fields and a few others) was a rare female songwriter; second, as an intimate friend and a fellow composer, she was among George Gershwin's closest musical confidants apart from his brother Ira. Swift had classical credentials; Gershwin was best known as a song-plugger who had graduated to musical comedy. At one stage, she was writing a fugue a week; he was writing a song a day. She assisted his translation to the concert hall; he led her to Broadway and popular music.

Her first hit song was 'Can't we be friends?', interpolated into *The Little Show* in 1929. On paper, it looks busy and cluttered, but it swings with a breeziness that belies its musical surprises. The words were by 'Paul James' (her husband, the banker James Paul Warburg), who also collaborated on her next success, *Fine and Dandy* (1930), an enduring song combining a strong lyric thrust with an irresistible rhythmic device of a recurring syncopated fourth beat.

Swift was an early champion of *Porgy and Bess*. When Gershwin died, she and Ira Gershwin preserved and numbered his unused jottings and, over the years, began turning the best into new songs, for example in the score for the film *The Shocking Miss Pilgrim* (1946). Although Swift declined co-composing credit and insisted that every note was Gershwin's, in some cases she was taking two- or four-bar phrases and organizing them into song form. Like Ira Gershwin, she seemed content to neglect her own career to serve what she saw as Gershwin's genius.

Her second marriage, to a cowboy, prompted a quirky memoir, *Who Could Ask for Anything More?* (1943), and an Irene Dunne film *Never a Dull Moment* (1950), which she scored. Swift continued to compose for the theatre, writing her own lyrics for the musical *Paris '90* (1952). A number of her works were commissioned for special occasions, including *One Little Girl* (1960, composed for the 50th anniversary of the Campfire Girls), *Century 21* (1962, for the Century 21 Exposition, Seattle), and *Dr Rush Pays a House Call* (1976, for the American Medical Association). Her song cycle *Reaching for the Brass Ring* is a continuing work, new songs being added to celebrate the birth of grandchildren and great-grandchildren.

WORKS

Stage: 9:15 Revue (musical, P. James [J. P. Warburg]), New York, 11 Feb 1930; Fine and Dandy (musical, James), New York, 23 Sept 1930; Alma mater (ballet), New York, 1935, rev. 1974; Paris '90 (musical, Swift), New York, 4 March 1952

Vocal and orch: Reaching for the Brass Ring, song cycle, S, orch, 1953–; One Little Girl (D. Frankel), solo vv, chorus, orch, 1960; Century 21, suite, 1962; All about Elsie (J. Oliansky), S, S, Bar, chorus, orch, 1964; Man have Pity on Man (U. Vaughan Williams), 1v, orch, 1972; Dr. Rush Pays a House Call, 1976

Songs: Can't we be friends?, 1929; Can this be love?, 1930; Fine and Dandy, 1930; Up among the chimney pots, 1930

Chamber and pf: Theme and Variations, vc, pf, 1960; Off-beat Waltz Plus Four, pf, 1974

Film score: Never a Dull Moment, 1950

EDWARD JABLONSKI, MARK STEYN

Szajna-Lewandowska, Jadwiga (*b* Brody, Ukraine, 22 Feb 1912; *d* Wrocław, 14 March 1994). Polish composer. She began her musical education at the conservatory in L'wów and after World War II studied composition at the Wrocław State Higher School of Music, first with Tadeusz Szeligowski and then with Stefan Poradowski, graduating in 1956. She taught the piano, theory and composition for a time, but her main activity became composition, especially for the musical stage (ballets and musicals for children); she also composed incidental music for more than 50 plays. Her ability to characterize while using an accessible contemporary musical language ensured the popularity of her stage works among young people. Several of her works received prizes, including *Gramy w zielone* ('We Play "Green"'; All-Polish Composers' Competition, 1970) and a ballet suite (GEDOK competition, Mannheim, 1970); she also received national awards for her works for children, in 1974, and for *Błekitny kot* ('The Blue Cat'), in 1983.

WORKS
selective list

Stage: Pinocchio (ballet, 3 scenes, Collodi [C. Lorenzini]), 1956; Harfista [The Harpist] (mimodrama, E. A. Poe: *The Harpist or the Exchanged Hands*), 1962; Porwanie w Tiutiurlistanie [Kidnapping in Tiutiurlistan] (ballet, 3, W. Żukrowski), 1966; Thais (ballet, 3, Z. Kosidowski), 1970; Księżniczka w ośłej skórze [A Princess in an Ass's Hide] (musical, 3, C. Perrault), 1974; Błekitny kot [The Blue Cat] (musical fairy-tale, 3), 1976; Zaczarowany krawiec [The Magic Tailor] (musical, 7 scenes), 1977; Czerwony Kapturek [Little Red Riding Hood] (ballet, 2 scenes, J. L. Grimm and W. C. Grimm), 1984

Orch: Concertino, fl, str orch, 1956; Pf Conc. [for pupils], 1979

Vocal: A Regiment, cantata, mixed chorus, orch, 1960; Song Cycle (T. Zasadny), S, chamber orch, 1961; 3 Jocular Songs (L. J. Kern), chorus, str, perc, 1962; O El Mole rachmim, reciter, chorus, orch, 1964; Wierszyki Pana Leara [Little Poems of Mr Lear], reciter, chamber orch, 1968; Gramy w zielone [We Play 'Green'] (M. Jasnorzewska-Pawlikowska), S, str qt, c1970; Poems (J. Iwaszkiewicz), reciter, pf, 1977

Chamber and pf: Sonatina, ob, pf, 1954; Sonatina giocosa, pf, 1959; Funérailles, 2 pf, 1970, arr. pf, str orch, perc, 1974; 10 Studies, 2 pf, 1975; 5 Pieces, pf qnt, 1978; 6 Pieces, pf, str qt, 1978; 4 tańce w dawnym stylu [4 Dances in the Old Style], fl, ob, 2 cl, bn, perc, 1979; 6 Triollets, 2 fl, pf, 1980

Principal publisher: PWM

BARBARA ZWOLSKA-STĘSZEWSKA

Szőnyi, Erzsébet [Elisabeth] (b Budapest, 25 April 1924). Hungarian composer, conductor and educationist. She began composing at the age of 13. In 1942 she entered the Budapest Academy of Music, where she graduated with diplomas in music teaching (1945), composition, conducting and the piano (1947); she deputized there for Zoltán Kodály in 1945–6, teaching his folk music classes. She received a French government scholarship to pursue graduate studies with Tony Aubin (composition) and Olivier Messiaen (musical aesthetics) at the Paris Conservatoire (1947–8); she also studied piano accompaniment with Nadia Boulanger. During that time she was awarded the Conservatoire composition prize for her orchestral Divertimento no.1. On 5 June 1948 the première of her Parlando és giusto was broadcast by French Radio (RTF) with Aubin conducting.

Between 1948 and 1981 Szőnyi taught at the Budapest Academy, becoming head of the teacher-training department in 1960. During that time she published her pioneering work A zenei írás-olvasás módszertana ('Methods of Musical Reading and Writing', Budapest, 1953–65). She also wrote on Kodály's teaching methods (Budapest, 1973), and it was largely owing to her efforts that Kodály's educational theories became world renowned. In addition to pedagogical works, Szőnyi's vocal compositions are among her most significant contributions. She was awarded the Erkel Prize in 1959 and is considered one of Hungary's most important musical personalities.

WORKS
selective list
STAGE

Dalma (opera, 3, after M. Jókai), 1953; studio perf., Budapest, Dec 1953

Makrancos királylány [The Stubborn Princess] (children's opera, 2, E. Kováts); Budapest, 10 June 1955

Firenzei tragédia [The Florentine Tragedy] (opera, 1, after O. Wilde), 1957; Meiningen, 8 March 1960

Képzelt beteg [The Hypochondriac] (musical comedy, 3, after Molière), 1961; Budapest, 18 Oct 1961

Az aranyszárnyu méhecske [The Little Bee with Golden Wing] (children's opera, 1, É. Orbán), 1974; Philadelphia, 24 May 1979

Adáshiba [Break in Transmission] (opera, 1, after K. Szakonyi), 1980; Szeged, Nemzeti Theatre, 7 May 1982

OTHER WORKS

Vocal: József Attila kantáta, chorus, orch, 1968; Radnóti kantáta, chorus, orch, 1974; oratorios, other choral works, vocal chamber music

Orch: Parlando és giusto, 1947; 2 divertimentos, no.1, 1948, no.2, 1951; Org Conc., Trio concertino, vn, vc, pf, str orch, 1958; Musica festiva, 1964; Allegro, 1969; Prelude and Fugue, 1969; Három ötlet négy tételben [3 Ideas in 4 Movts], pf, orch, 1980

Works for wind band, solo insts, youth orch

Principal publisher: Editio Musica Budapest

KATALIN SZERZŐ

Szymanowska [née Wolowska], **Maria Aghate** (b Warsaw, 14 Dec 1789; d St Petersburg, 25 July 1831). Polish pianist and composer. Her parents were born middle-class Jews, then were baptized Christians. She early displayed a precocious musical talent and studied with Antoni Lisowski (1798–1800) and Tomasz Gremm (1800–04). Later mentors included József Elsner, Franciszek Lessel, the composer John Field (whom she met in Moscow) and Luigi Cherubini (whom she met in Paris). In 1810, she made her performing début in Warsaw and Paris, and married the wealthy landowner Josef Szymanowski. They had three children before their marriage was dissolved because of his reluctance to allow her to pursue a professional musical career. After leaving her husband, she travelled widely, playing in several European countries. In 1822 she was appointed court pianist to the Tsar of Russia in St Petersburg. She toured until 1828 in Germany, France, Italy, England, Poland, Austria, Belgium, Holland and Russia, commanding high ticket prices and playing to large audiences. Her sostenuto cantabile style of playing, based on her desire to emulate the famous singers of the day, was considered an innovation on the fortepiano. Critics differed, as some noted her brilliant technique, others criticized her use of rubato, and yet others applauded her musical understanding; all were agreed on her personal beauty and intellect. She composed more than a hundred pieces, many of them short,

Maria Aghate Szymanowska: portrait by Alexander Kokular

virtuoso piano works, based on folk melodies and dances and imbued with the ideals of revolutionary patriotism. Most were published in Leipzig by Breitkopf & Härtel during the 19th century, some of them after her death.

Johann Nepomuk Hummel and Field dedicated piano pieces to her. Goethe is said to have fallen madly in love with her (she was the inspiration for his poem *Aussöhnung*). Cherubini dedicated his Fantasia in C major to her. Robert Schumann described her études as 'written by the "feminine Field", . . . in character and invention . . . present-[ing] the most remarkable qualities, for a woman composer, that we have met with'. Other critics described her as a musician who defined Romanticism in her compositions and in her playing. Her salon in St Petersburg became the centre of cultural life, patriotic conspiracy and a place where Polish émigrés could find assistance. Her musical autograph album is filled with short pieces of music by those who visited her salon, including Robert and Clara Schumann, Chopin, Liszt, Beethoven, Field, Rossini, Meyerbeer and Franz Xaver Mozart.

WORKS

Edition:

Maria Szymanowska: Music for Piano, ed. S. Glickman (Bryn Mawr, PA, 1990) [G]

CHAMBER

Divertimento, vn, pf (Leipzig, 1820); Sérénade, vc, pf (Leipzig, 1820); Fanfara dwugłosowa [Fanfare Duet], 2 hn, 2 tpt, *PL-Kj*; Thème varié, pf, fl/vn, lost

PIANO

18 Danses de différent genre (Leipzig, 1819), Mazurek, C, ed. I. Poniatowska (Bryn Mawr, PA, 1993); Caprice sur la romance de Joconde (Leipzig, 1820); Grande valse, pf 4 hands (Leipzig, 1820); 20 exercices et préludes (Leipzig, 1820); 6 Marches (Leipzig, 1820); 6 Minuets (Leipzig, 1820); Polonaise sur l'air national du feu Prince Joseph Poniatowsky (Leipzig, 1820); Romance de Monsieur le Prince Alexandre Galitzin (Leipzig, 1820)

Fantasie (Leipzig, 1820); 4 valses, pf 3 hands (Warsaw, 1822), ed. in G; Cotillon ou valse figurée (Paris, 1824); Danse polonaise (Paris, 1824); Nocturne, A♭, 'Le murmure' (Paris, 1825); 24 Mazurkas (Leipzig, 1826), ed. I. Poniatowska (Bryn Mawr, PA, 1993); Nocturne, B♭ (St Petersburg, 1852); Nocturne, f (Leipzig, n.d.); 5 études, C, d, E, E♭, F, nos.1, 2 and 5 ed. in G; Menuet, E, ed. in G; Preludium, B, *Kj*; Serenada; Temat wariacji [Theme for Variations], *Kj*; Valse, d, *Kj*

VOCAL

[5] śpiewów historycznych [Historical Songs] (J. U. Niemcewicz): 1 Jadwiga, królowa Polski [Jadwiga, Queen of Poland], 2 Jan Albrycht, 3 Duma o Kniaziu Michale Glińskim [The Muses of Prince Michal Glinski], 4 Kazimierz Wielki [Kazimierz the Great], 5 Stefan Czarniecki, nos.1, 2, 3 (Warsaw, 1816); Le départ (M. de Cervantes) (Leipzig, 1820); Nie będę łez ronić [I will not shed tears] (A. Gorecki) (n.p., 1822); Śpiewka no powrót wojsk polskich [Song of Welcome to the Returning Polish Army] (L. A. Dmuszewski) (Warsaw, 1822) 3 settings from Konrad Wallenrod (A. Mickiewicz) (Kiev and Odessa, 1828); Świtezianka (Mickiewicz) (Moscow, 1828); other songs incl. Alpuhara (W. Skarbek), Ballade (Saint-Onge), Peine et plaisir (W. Shakespeare), Pieśń z wieży [Song from the Tower] (Skarbek), Romance à Josephine, Romance à la nuit (F. de Berni), Se spiegar potessi oh Dio, Wilia (Skarbek), W tych przedsionkach szezęście gości [In These Vestibules Happiness Resides] (Skarbek)

BIBLIOGRAPHY

FétisB; *Grove1* (G. Grove); *SchillingE*; *SchmidlD*

J. Mirscy and M. Mirscy, eds.: *Maria Szymanowska, 1789–1831: Album* (Kraków, 1953) [incl. facsimiles and portrait]

I. Betzo: *Tsaritsa zvukov: Zhizn' i tvorchestvo Marii Szhimanovskoy* [Tsarina of Tones: the Life and Works of Maria Szymanowska] (Moscow, 1956, 2/1989; Pol. trans., Krakow, 1987, as *Maria Szymanowska*)

M. Iwancjko: *Maria Szymanowska* (Kraków, 1959)

J. Davies: 'Maria Szymanowska', *The Consort*, no.23 (1966), 167–74

J. M. Meggett: *Keyboard Music by Women Composers: a Catalog and Bibliography* (Westport, CT, 1981)

N. B. Reich: *Clara Schumann: the Artist and the Woman* (Ithaca, NY, 1985)

S. Glickman, ed.: Introduction to *Maria Szymanowska: Music for Piano* (Bryn Mawr, PA, 1990)

I. Poniatowska, ed.: Introduction to *M. A. Szymanowska: 25 Mazurkas* (Bryn Mawr, PA, 1993)

SYLVIA GLICKMAN

T

Tailleferre, Germaine (Marcelle) (*b* Parc–St-Maur, nr Paris, 19 April 1892; *d* Paris, 7 Nov 1983). French composer. Despite her father's opposition and her equal skills in art she entered the Paris Conservatoire in 1904, her formative studies being undertaken with Eva Sautereau-Meyer. As a pianist prodigy with an amazing memory she won numerous prizes, and in 1913 she met Georges Auric, Arthur Honegger and Darius Milhaud in Georges Caussade's counterpoint class. In 1917 Erik Satie was so impressed with her two-piano piece *Jeux de plein air* that he christened her his 'musical daughter', and it was he who first brought her to prominence as one of his group of Nouveaux Jeunes. She then went on to become the only female member of Les Six when it was formed in 1920. Her career was also assisted by the Princesse Edmond de Polignac, who liked her ballet *Le marchand d'oiseaux* (1923) enough to commission a Piano Concerto (1923–4), which proved similarly successful and demonstrated her natural affinities with the 18th-century *clavecinistes*. Tailleferre's talents fitted in perfectly with the prevailing spirit of Stravinskian neo-classicism, though she was also influenced by Gabriel Fauré and Maurice Ravel, remaining in close contact with the latter throughout the 1920s.

Unfortunately, Tailleferre never regained the acclaim she had enjoyed through her early associations with Les Six. Two unhappy marriages (to the caricaturist Ralph Barton in 1926 and to the lawyer Jean Lageat in 1931) proved a considerable drain on her creative energies, and her continual financial problems led her to compose mostly to commission, resulting in many uneven and quickly written works. Also, her natural modesty and unjustified sense of artistic insecurity prevented her from promoting herself properly, and she regarded herself primarily as an artisan who wrote optimistic, accessible music as 'a release' from the difficulties of her private life. However, her concertos of the 1930s enjoyed a measure of success, as did her impassioned *Cantate de Narcisse* (1938,

words by Paul Valéry), and she was much in demand as a skilful composer of film music. After a fallow period in the USA (1942–6) she produced the superb Second Violin Sonata (1947–8) and turned her attention towards opera – her lighthearted approach being epitomized in the four short comic pastiches written with Denise Centore in 1955 ('Du style galant au style méchant'). She also gave successful concert tours with the baritone Bernard Lefort, for whom she wrote the *Concerto des vaines paroles* (1954), and in 1957 she flirted briefly with serial techniques in her Clarinet Sonata. Although she continued to compose prolifically and teach until the end of her life, she resorted increasingly to self-borrowing and familiar formulae (like the *perpetuum mobile*), and the circularity of her career can be seen in the stylistic ease with which she was able to complete her 1916–17 Piano Trio in 1978. Meeting the conductor Désiré Dondeyne in

Germaine Tailleferre

1969 led to a new interest in composing for wind band and she also remained devoted to children and their music, a link which helps explain the spontaneity, freshness and charm that characterize her best compositions.

WORKS

selective list

unless otherwise stated, printed works published in Paris

OPERAS

opéras bouffes unless otherwise stated

Zoulaina (opéra comique, 3, C.-H. Hirsch), 1930–31, unperf.

Le marin du Bolivar (1, H. Jeanson), Paris Exhibition, 1937

Dolorès (opérette), Paris, Opéra-Comique, 1950

Il était un petit navire (satire lyrique, 3 tableaux, Jeanson), Paris, Opéra-Comique, 9 March 1951

Parfums (comédie musicale, 3, G. Hirsch and J. Bouchor), Monte Carlo, Opéra, 11 April 1951

La fille d'opéra (1, D. Centore), RTF, 28 Dec 1955

Le bel ambitieux (1, Centore), RTF, 28 Dec 1955

Monsieur Petitpois achète un château (1, Centore), RTF, 28 Dec 1955

La pauvre Eugénie (1, Centore), RTF, 28 Dec 1955

Mémoires d'une bergère (1, P. Jullian), RTF, 22 Dec 1959

Le maître (chamber opera, 1, E. Ionesco), RTF, 12 July 1960

La petite sirène (opéra, 3, P. Soupault, after H. C. Andersen), RTF, 27 Dec 1960

BALLETS

Les mariés de la Tour Eiffel [Valse des dépêches and Quadrille only] (1, J. Cocteau), Paris, Théâtre des Champs-Elysées, 18 June 1921, collab. Les Six

Le marchand d'oiseaux (1, H. Perdriat), Paris, Champs-Elysées, 25 May 1923

Paris-Magie (1, L. Deharme), Paris, Opéra-Comique, 13 May 1949

Parisiana (1, Laudes), Copenhagen Opera, 1953

INCIDENTAL MUSIC

for theatre and radio

Mon cousin de Cayenne (comedy, 3, J. Blanchon), Paris, 1925; Sous le rempart d'Athènes (play, P. Claudel), Paris, Elysée Palace, 24 Oct 1927; Madame Quinze (play, J. Serment), Paris, 1935; Le cantate de Narcisse (mélodrame, 7 scenes, P. Valéry), 1938, Marseilles, RTF, 1942; Conférence des animaux (M. Oswald), Paris, RTF, 1952; La bohème éternelle (A. Antoine), Paris, RTF, 1952; Ici la voix (G. Hugnet), Paris, RTF, 25 Aug 1954; Adalbert (D. Centore), Paris, RTF, 1 Jan 1958; Au paradis avec les ânes (F. Jammes), Paris, RTF, 18 Feb 1962; Le Cid (P. Corneille), Paris, 1978

FILM AND TELEVISION SCORES

Terre d'amour et de liberté (documentary, M. Cloche), 1936; Provincia (documentary, Cloche), 1937; Sur les routes d'acier (documentary, B. Peskine), 1937; Symphonie graphique (Cloche), 1937; Ces dames aux chapeaux verts (Cloche), 1938; Le Jura ou Terre d'effort et de liberté (documentary, Cloche), 1938; Le petit chose [*sic*] (Cloche), 1938; [La] Bretagne (documentary, J. Epstein), 1941

Les deux timides (Y. Allégret), 1942; Les confidences d'un micro (M. Courmes), 1946; Torrents (S. de Poligny), 1946, collab. G. Auric; Coincidences (S. Debecque), 1947; Les souliers, 1948, collab.

Devred; Cher vieux Paris! (M. de Gastyne), 1950; Ce siècle à 50 ans (documentary, N. Védrès), 1950; Caroline au pays natal (Gastyne), 1951; Le roi de la création (Gastyne), 1952

Caroline au palace [*sic*] (Gastyne), 1952; Caroline du Sud (Gastyne), 1952; Caroline fait du cinéma (Gastyne), 1953; Gavarni et son temps (Gastyne), 1953; Adler – L'aigle des rues (J. Funke), 1954; L'homme, notre ami (Gastyne), 1956; Le travail fait par le patron (G. Roze), 1956; Les plus beaux jours (Gastyne), 1957; Robinson (Gastyne), 1957; Les requins sur nos plages (documentary, G. Bollore), 1959

La rentrée des Foin (G. Jarlot), ?1960; Les grandes personnes (J. Valère), 1961; Sans merveille (TV film, M. Mitrani), 1963; Evariste Galois ou L'éloge des mathématiques (TV film, A. Astruc), 1964; Anatole (TV film, J. Valère), 1966; Impressions: soleil levant (documentary, A. Daumant), 1970

ORCHESTRAL AND WIND BAND

Morceau symphonique (later Ballade), pf, orch, 1920; Ballade, pf, orch, 1920–22 (1923); Pf Conc. no.1, 1923–4 (1924); Concertino, harp, orch, 1926–7 (1928); Pavane, nocturne, final, 1928; Ouverture [orig. for Zoulaina], 1930, rev. 1932 (1934); Conc., 2 pf, 1v, orch, 1933–4; Vn Conc., 1936; 3 études, pf, orch, 1940, inc.; Suite, 1949; Divertissement dans le style de Louis XV, 1950 [from incid. music to Madame Quinze, 1935]

Pf Conc. [no.2], 1951; Sarabande pour 'La guirlande de Campra', chamber orch, 1952 (1954); Conc., fl, pf, orch, 1952–3; Conc. des vaines paroles (J. Tardieu), Bar, pf, orch, 1954 [adaptation of Conc., 1933–4]; Conc., S, orch, 1957 [transcr. of Sonata, harp]; Petite suite, 1957 (1958); Partita, fl, cl, ob, str, 1962, also arr. wind band by D. Dondeyne, 1969; Concertino, fl, orch, 1962; Partita, 2 pf, perc, 1964 [uses material from operas La petite sirène and Le maître]

Etonnement, amertume, jacasseries, angoisse (4 miniature pieces), 1969; Sinfonietta, tpt, timp, str, 1974–5; March militare, wind band, arr. Dondeyne, 1976; Suite-divertimento, wind band, 1977 [Wormerveer, 1986], orchd Dondeyne; Conc. de la fidélité, wordless coloratura S, orch, 1981 [reworking of Conc., 1957, orch rev. Dondeyne]

CHORAL AND SONGS

Berceuse du petit éléphant, 1v, chorus, hns, 1925; Ban'da, wordless chorus, orch, 1925; Nocturno, Fox (2 songs), 2 Bar, small ens, 1928, rev. 1958 (1958); Vocalise-étude pour voix élevées, 1v, pf, 1929 (1929); 6 chansons françaises (15th-, 17th-, 18th-century texts), 1v, pf/orch, 1929 (1930); La chasse à l'enfant (J. Prévert), 1v, pf, 1934

Ave Maria, chorus, 1942; Paris sentimental (cycle of 6 songs, M. Lacloche), 1v, pf, 1949; Chansons du folklore de France (9 songs), 1v, pf/small ens, 1952–5, collab. D. Centore; C'est facile à dire (A. Burgaud), 1v, pf, 1955; Une rouillé à l'arsenic (cycle, Centore), 1v, pf, 1955; Déjeuner sur l'herbe (C. Marny), 1v, pf, 1955

La rue Chagrin (Centore), 1v, pf, 1955 (1956); Pancarte pour une porte d'entrée (cycle of 11 songs, R. Pinget), 1v, pf, 1961; L'adieu du cavalier (G. Apollinaire), 1v, pf, 1963; [12 pieces] (J. Tardieu), children's vv, pf, 1982–3, only 3 completed

CHAMBER AND SOLO INSTRUMENTAL
for piano music, see below

Morceau de lecture, harp, 1910; Fantaisie sur un thème donné de Georges Caussade, str qt, pf, 1912; Berceuse, vn, pf, 1913 (1924); Pf Trio, 1916–17, completed version/rev., 1978 (1980); Sonatine, str, 1917, finale added to make Str Qt, 1919 (1921); Image (orig. Pastorale), fl, cl, cel, pf, str qt, 1918 (London, 1921); Vn Sonata no.1, 1920–21 (1923); Pastorale, fl, pf, 1942 (Philadelphia, 1946)

Vn Sonata no.2, 1947–8 (1951) [rev. of Vn Conc., 1936]; Sonata, harp, 1957 (1957); Sonata, cl, 1957 (1958); Galliarde, tpt, pf, 1972 (1973); Choral, tpt, pf, 1972 (1973); Rondo, ob, pf, 1972 (1973); Forlane, fl, pf, 1972 (1973); Sonatine, vn, pf, 1973 (1974); Arabesque, cl, pf, 1973 (1973) [uses material from opera La petite sirène]; Sonate, cl, ob, bn, pf, 1974; Vn Sonata no.3, 1974; Chant et pastourelle, wind qnt, 1979

PIANO

Premières prouesses (6 pieces), pf 4 hands, 1910 (1911); Impromptu, 1912 (1912); Romance, 1913 (1913), rev. 1924 (1924); Jeux de plein air, 2 pieces, 2 pf, 1917 (1919), arr. orch, 1924; Pastorale, 1919 (1920), also arr. small orch; Fandango, 1920; Très vite, 1920; Hommage à Debussy, 1920; 2 valses, 2 pf, 1928 (1928); Sicilienne, 1928 (1928); Pastorale, Ab, 1928 (1929); Pastorale, C, 1929 (1930); Fleurs de France, 8 easy pieces, pf 4 hands, 1930 (1962), orchd as Fleurs de France, suite à danser

Berceuse, 1936; Au Pavillon d'Alsace, 1937 (1937) [last of 8 Illustrations musicales commissioned for Paris Exhibition, entitled A l'exposition]; Charlie valse, 1954; 2 pièces: Larghetto, Valse lente, 1954 (1963); Sonate, 2 pf, 1974; Sonatine, pf 4 hands, 1974–5; Escarpolète, singeries, rondeau, ?1975–6; Suite burlesque, 6 easy pieces, pf 4 hands, 1979 (1980)

See also children's pieces in La forêt enchantée (1952); Scènes de cirque (1953); Pages choisies d'hier et d'aujourd'hui (1955); Printemps musical (1958); Jardin d'enfants, ii (1962); Premier recital (1971); Musique des jours heureux (1981)

Edns, incl. 6 vols. of 18th-century Fr. and It. arias in Les maîtres du chant: répertoire de musique vocale ancienne, ed. H. Prunières (Paris, 1924–7)

Principal publishers: Billaudot, Chester, Durand, Heugel, Lemoine

WRITINGS

'Quelques mots de l'une des "Six"', *L'intransigeant* (3 June 1923), section 'La vie du théâtre', 4
'From the South of France', *Modern Music* (1942), Nov-Dec, 13–16
Mémoires à l'emporte-pièce (Paris, 1974); repr., ed. F. Robert, in *Revue internationale de musique française*, no.19 (1986), 6–82
'Musique pour Claudel', *Sang neuf*, no.43 (1980), 10–11

BIBLIOGRAPHY

Roland-Manuel: 'Esquisse pour un portrait de Germaine Tailleferre', *Revue Pleyel*, xxxviii/Nov (1926), 54–5
J. Bruyr: 'Entretien avec Germaine Tailleferre', *Guide du Concert* (1930), Oct, 7–9
O. Pannetier: 'Avec Germaine Tailleferre', *Candide* (19 Nov 1931)

J. Bruyr: 'Germaine Tailleferre', *L'écran des musiciens*, 2nd ser. (Paris, 1933), 91–8
C. Chaplin: *My Autobiography* (New York, 1954)
S. Trickey: *Les Six* (thesis, North Texas State College, 1955)
J. Bruyr: 'Germaine Tailleferre', *Musica*, xxxvi/March (1957), 29–33
R. Bobbitt: *The Harmonic Idiom in the Works of 'Les Six'* (diss., Boston U., 1963)
C. Chamfray: 'Germaine Tailleferre', *Courrier musical de France*, no.9/Jan–March (1965), fiche biographique
F. Robert: 'Cinquante ans après . . . A propos du Groupe des Six', *Journal musical français*, nos.193–4 (1970), 29ff
C. Chamfray: 'Hommage à Germaine Tailleferre', *Courrier musical de France*, no.39 (1972), 119
M. de Cossart: *The Food of Love: Princesse Edmond de Polignac (1865–1943) and her Salon* (London, 1978)
R. Lyon: 'Visite à Germaine Tailleferre', *Courrier musical de France*, no.61 (1978), 3–4
G. Auric: *Quand j'étais là . . .* (Paris, 1979)
M. Hacquard: 'Germaine Tailleferre: mon temps c'est le présent', *Nouvelles rive-gauche*, lxxvi–lxxvii (1982)
A. Lacombe: *Des compositeurs pour l'image* (Paris, 1982)
L. Mitgang: *'La Princesse des Six': a Life of Germaine Tailleferre* (thesis, Oberlin College, OH, 1982)
—— : 'One of "Les Six" is Still at Work', *International Herald Tribune* (8 June 1982)
E. Hurard-Viltard: *Le Groupe des Six, ou Le matin d'un jour de fête* (Paris, 1987)
L. Mitgang: 'Germaine Tailleferre', *The Musical Woman: an International Perspective*, ii: *1984–5*, ed. J. L. Zaimont and others (Westport, CT, 1987), 177–221
R. Orledge: 'A Chronological Catalogue of the Compositions of Germaine Tailleferre (1892–1983)', *Muziek & Wetenschap*, ii/2 (1992), 129–52
C. Potter: 'Germaine Tailleferre (1892–1983): a Centenary Appraisal', ibid., 109–28
J. Roy: 'Un souvenir de Germaine Tailleferre', *Diapason* (1992), Oct, 50–51
R. Shapiro: *Germaine Tailleferre: a Bio-Bibliography* (Westport, CT, 1994)

ROBERT ORLEDGE

Talma, Louise (*b* Arcachon, France, 31 Oct 1906). American composer. She studied theory and composition from 1922 to 1930 at the Institute of Musical Art, New York. During the summers of 1926 to 1939 she attended the Fontainebleau School of Music, France, studying the piano with Isidore Philipp, and harmony, counterpoint, fugue, composition and organ with Nadia Boulanger; she became the first American member of the faculty there in 1936. She received the BMus from New York University in 1931 and the MA from Columbia in 1933, and taught at Hunter College, CUNY, from 1928 to 1979. She became a Fellow of the MacDowell Colony in New Hampshire in 1943. Among the many honours she has received are two Guggenheim fellowships – she was the first woman to be awarded two – in 1946 and

1947; a Senior Fulbright Research Grant, 1955–6, to compose *The Alcestiad*; and the Sibelius Medal for Composition from the Harriet Cohen International Awards, London, in 1963 – she was the first woman recipient of this prize. Talma was also the first American woman to have an opera (*The Alcestiad*) performed in a major European opera house (1962, Frankfurt) and the first woman composer elected to the National Institute of Arts and Letters (1974). Much of her piano music and several other chamber and orchestral works have been recorded. She has also written two textbooks: *Harmony for the College Student* (1966) and *Functional Harmony* (with J. Harrison and R. Levin, 1970).

Louise Talma

Talma's early works are tonal and neo-classical. Stylistically, the influence of her strong background in counterpoint and her study of Igor Stravinsky with Boulanger is evident, though in fact her whole output is marked by clarity of line, gesture and pro-portion. The Piano Sonata no.1 (1943) and the exuberant Toccata for Orchestra (1944), both superbly tailored to their respective instrumentations, incorporate elements of jazz and Americana. Exemplifying the range of her style during this early period is the rhythmic vitality of the *Alleluia in Form of Toccata* for solo piano (1945) and, by con-trast, the impressionistic languor of *Terre de France* (1943–5). In 1952, after hearing Irving Fine's String Quartet, Talma began to ex-periment with serialism; she developed a

mature style that incorporates 12-note tech-nique into a freely tonal context. Important works from this later period include the String Quartet (1954), *The Alcestiad* (1955–8), whose première received a 20-minute ovation, *Dialogues* for piano and orchestra (1963–4) and the triptych *The Tolling Bell* (1967–9). She has not adhered to strict set technique, but has adapted it by arranging subsets in tonally related patterns, such as in the Violin Sonata (1962), or by distributing row elements among voices, as in the cantata *All the Days of my Life* (1965). In the song cycle *Diadem* (1978–9), made up of clever character sketches of seven gems, shimmer-ing clarinet trills illustrating the 'Aqua-marine' give way to the bold angularity of 'Diamond'. The circular structure of this work and its septuple division of form may also be found in *Full Circle* for orchestra (1985), whose last section (the seventh of seven) is a modified reversal of the first. The linear simplicity of *Seven Episodes* for flute, viola and piano (1987) highlights Talma's talent for shaping a phrase; based on a row whose first and last notes form a perfect 5th, this work exemplifies the dodecaphonic writing grounded in tonal relationship that is a characteristic of her late style.

WORKS

STAGE

The Alcestiad (opera, 3, T. Wilder), 1955–8, Frankfurt, 1 March 1962

CHORAL

In principio erat verbum (St John), mixed chorus, org, 1939; The Divine Flame (oratorio, Bible, liturgy), Mez, Bar, mixed chorus, org, 1946–8; The Leaden Echo and the Golden Echo (G. M. Hopkins), S, double mixed chorus, pf, 1950–51; Let's Touch the Sky (E. E. Cummings), mixed chorus, fl, ob, cl, 1952; La corona (7 sonnets, J. Donne), unacc. mixed chorus, 1954–5; A Time to Remember (Bible, J. F. Kennedy, A. M. Schlesinger jr), mixed chorus, orch, 1966–7

Voices of Peace (Bible, Hopkins, liturgy, St Francis), mixed chorus, str, 1973; Celebration, women's chorus, small orch, 1976–7; Psalm lxxxiv, unacc. mixed chorus, 1978; Mass for the Sundays of the Year,1984; Mass in English, unacc. mixed chorus, 1984; A Wreath of Blessings, unacc. mixed chorus, 1985; Give Thanks and Praise (Bible, W. Cowper), antiphonal double chorus, pf, 1989; In Praise of a Virtuous Woman (Bible), women's vv, pf, 1990; Psalm cxv, unacc. mixed chorus, 1992

OTHER VOCAL

One need not be a chamber to be haunted (E. Dickinson), S, pf, 1941; Carmina Mariana (liturgy), 2S, pf, 1943, also arr. women's chorus, org, and women's chorus, small orch; Terre de France (song cycle, C. Peguy, J. du Bellay, C. d'Orléans, P. de Ronsard), S, pf, 1943–5; Leap before you look (W. H. Auden), Letter to St Peter (E. Dean), S, pf,

1945; Pied beauty, spring and fall (Hopkins), S, pf, 1946; 2 Sonnets (Hopkins), Bar, pf, 1946–50; Birthday Song (E. Spenser), T, fl, va, 1960
All the Days of my Life (cantata, Bible), T, cl, vc, pf, perc, 1963–5; The Tolling Bell (W. Shakespeare, C. Marlowe, Donne), Bar, orch, 1967–9; Rain Song (J. Garrigue), S/T, pf, 1973; Have you Heard? Do you Know? (divertimento in 7 scenes, Talma), S, Mez, T, inst ens, 1974–80; Diadem (song cycle, Confucius, medieval), T, pf/(vn, vc, fl, cl, pf), 1978–9; Variations on 13 Ways of Looking at a Blackbird (W. Stevens), S/T, fl/ob/vn, pf, 1979; Wishing Well, S, fl, 1986; Infanta Marina (Stevens), S, pf, 1988

ORCHESTRAL
Toccata, 1944; Dialogues, pf, orch, 1963–4; Full circle, chamber orch, 1985

CHAMBER
Song and Dance, vn, pf, 1951; Str Qt, 1954; Vn Sonata, 1962; 3 Duologues, cl, pf, 1967–8; Summer Sounds, cl, 2 vn, va, vc, 1969–73; Lament, vc, pf, 1980; The Ambient Air, fl, vn, vc, pf, 1980–83; Studies in Spacing, cl, pf, 1982; Fanfare for Hunter College, 2 tpt, 3 trbn, 1983; 7 Episodes, fl, va, pf, 1986–7; Conversations, fl, pf, 1987

KEYBOARD
Four-Handed Fun, pf 4 hands/2 pf, 1939; Pf Sonata no.1, 1943; Pf Sonata no.2, 1944–55; Soundshots, 20 short pieces, pf, 1944–74; Alleluia in Form of Toccata, pf, 1945; Wedding Piece, org, 1946; Pastoral Prelude, pf, 1949; Bagatelle, pf, 1950; 6 Etudes, pf, 1953–4; 3 Bagatelles, pf, 1955; Passacaglia and Fugue, pf, 1955–62; Textures, pf, 1977; Kaleidoscopic Variations, pf, 1984; Ave atque vale, pf, 1989

Principal publisher: C. Fischer

BIBLIOGRAPHY
LePageWC, i
M. Goss: 'Louise Talma', Modern Music Makers (New York, 1952), 382–91
R. Berges: 'The German Scene: "Alcestiad" in Frankfurt: Hamburg and Munich Seasons', Musical Courier, clxiv/4 (1962), 33–4
P. Moor: 'Louise Talma's "The Alcestiad" in Première at Frankfurt Opera', New York Times (2 March 1962), 25
'The Singing Greeks', Time, lxxix (23 March 1962), 54
V. Thomson: American Music since 1910 (New York, 1971)
E. Barkin: 'Louise Talma: "The Tolling Bell" ', PNM, x/2 (1972), 142–52
R. Ericson: 'Celebrating Louise Talma', New York Times (4 Feb 1977)
C. Ammer: Unsung: a History of Women in Music (Westport, CT, 1980)
D. Ewen: Composers since 1900: a Biographical and Critical Guide (New York, 1981)
S. C. Teicher: The Solo Works for Piano of Louise Talma (diss., Peabody Institute, Johns Hopkins U., 1983)
—— : Louise Talma: Essentials of her Style as Seen through the Piano Works', The Musical Woman: an International Perspective, i: 1983, ed. J. L. Zaimont and others (Westport, CT, 1984), 128–46
ARTHUR COHN,
DOROTHY REGINA HOLCOMB,
SARA JOBIN

Tanco Cordovez de Herrera, Teresa (b 1859; d Bogotá, 1946). Colombian composer and pianist. A member of one of the most prominent Colombian families, Tanco went to Europe at the age of 15 and studied with A. F. Marmontel at the Paris Conservatoire. Her performance at the Salle Pleyel in 1883 in the presence of Camille Saint-Saëns drew favourable comment from the Parisian press. After her return to Colombia her salon became an important forum for novelists, poets and politicians. She is renowned for her zarzuela Simila similibus (musically a rather insignificant work), first performed in 1883. Her other compositions are virtually unknown; they include the a cappella motets Bone pastor, Ecce panis, Jesus dulcis, O salutaris (all SAT) and Tantum ergo (SATB), orchestral and piano works, and songs. Some of the choral works were written for the women's choir of the church of San Ignacio.

SUSANA FRIEDMANN

Tann, Hilary (b Ferndale, Mid Glam., 2 Nov 1947). Welsh composer resident in the USA. She studied with Alun Hoddinott at University College, Cardiff (BMus 1968), then with Jonathan Harvey at Southampton University (research into Roberto Gerhard's music) and from 1972 at Princeton University with J. K. Randall (PhD 1981). She took up a teaching appointment at Union College, Schenectady, New York, in 1980. After co-editing, in 1989, a volume (xxvii/2) of Perspectives of New Music about Japanese music, she visited Japan a year later, teaching at Kansai University and pursuing her studies of the shakuhachi (bamboo flute) and noh performing traditions. She serves on the executive board of the International League of Women Composers and was the editor of its journal from 1982 to 1988. Her music, whose stimulus often derives from environmental phenomena, is spare in texture, meticulous in its sensitivity to timbre, and frequently rich in growth patterns; though generally marked by a strong lyrical impulse, there are also moments of vehement expression.

WORKS
selective list

Orch: As Ferns, str (vn, va, vc), 1979; The Open Field, 1989; Adirondack Light, nar, chamber orch, 1992
Ens: Duo, ob, va, 1981; Winter Sun, Summer Rain, fl, cl, va, vc, cel, 1986; Llef, fl, vc, 1988; Of Erthe and Aire, fl + pic, cl + b cl, frame drums, 1990; Water's Edge, pf duet, 1993
Solo inst: Aftermath, pf, 1973; A Sad Pavan Forbidding Mourning, gui, 1982; Doppelgänger,

pf, 1984; Windhover, fl/s sax, 1985; Look Little Low Heavens, C-tpt, 1993

Vocal: Sound Dawn, men's chorus, pf, 1983; Arachne, solo S, 1987

Tape: Templum, computer synthesized tape, 1976

Principal publisher: OUP

A. J. HEWARD REES

Tate, Phyllis (Margaret Duncan) (*b* Gerrards Cross, 6 April 1911: *d* London, 29 May 1987). English composer. Her earliest attempts at composition, dating from her teenage years, were foxtrots for her ukulele. From 1928 to 1932 she studied composition (with Harry Farjeon), the piano, conducting and timpani at the RAM. Her early works, including an operetta (*The Policeman's Serenade*), songs, a string quartet, a violin sonata, a cello concerto and a symphony, were variously performed at the RAM, at the Macnaghten-Lemare Concerts, by the Bournemouth Municipal Orchestra and at concerts organized by Hubert Foss of OUP. She also wrote and arranged commercial light music, often using the pseudonyms Max Morelle or Janos. In 1935 she married the music publisher Alan Frank. She lived and worked in London and was at various times involved with the Hampstead Music Club, the Barnet Choral Society, the PRS Member's Fund (from 1976 to 1981 she was the first woman to serve on the management committee) and the Composers' Guild.

Tate destroyed almost all her pre-war music. The first work she acknowledged was the Saxophone Concerto of 1944, which had been commissioned by the BBC. In 1947 she came to public attention when her Sonata for clarinet and cello was performed at a London Contemporary Music Centre concert and her *Nocturne for Four Voices* (composed 1945) was broadcast on the Third Programme. She was often attracted by the sounds and textures of unusual combinations of instruments: the voices in *Nocturne*, a setting of a poem by Sidney Keyes, are accompanied by string quartet, double bass, celesta and bass clarinet; later works included a setting of Tennyson's *The Lady of Shalott* (1956) for tenor, viola, two pianos, celesta and nine percussion instruments, and a *Sonatina pastorale* for harmonica and harpsichord (1974). She was particularly drawn to vocal music and wrote vocal chamber music, several large-scale choral works, such as *A Secular Requiem* (1967) and *St Martha and the Dragon* (1976), as well as her acclaimed opera, a musical thriller, *The Lodger* (1960). In later life she wrote much music for young people, includ-

ing several operettas. Exploring a wide variety of formal structures and harmonic languages, Tate's elegant and expressive music is always clear and accessible.

WORKS
selective list

Operas: The Lodger, 1960 (D. Franklin, after B. Lowdnes), workshop perf., London, 14 July 1960, rev. version, April 1965; Dark Pilgrimage (TV opera, Franklin), 1963; The What d'ye Call it, 1966 (V. C. Clinton-Baddeley, after J. Gay), Cheltenham, 1966

Choral: Choral Scene from The Bacchae (Euripides), double chorus, 1953; Witches and Spells, choral suite, 1959; 7 Lincolnshire Folksongs, chorus, insts, 1966; A Secular Requiem (attrib. W. Shakespeare), chorus, insts, 1967; Christmas Ale, 1v, chorus, orch, 1967; To Words by Joseph Beaumont, SSA, pf, 1970; Serenade to Christmas, Mez, chorus, orch, 1972; St Martha and the Dragon (C. Causely), nar, S, T, chorus, children's chorus, chamber orch, 1976; All the World's a Stage (Shakespeare), chorus, orch, 1977; Compassion (U. Vaughan Williams), chorus, org/orch, 1978

Vocal: Nocturne for 4 Voices (chamber cantata, S. Keyes), Mez, T, Bar, B, str qt, db, b cl, cel, 1945; Songs of Sundry Natures, Bar, fl, cl, bn, hn, harp, 1947; The Lady of Shalott (Tennyson), T, va, 2 pf, cel, perc, 1956; A Victorian Garland (M. Arnold), S, C, hn, pf, 1965; Gravestones [for Cleo Laine], 1966; Apparitions, T, harmonica, str qt, pf, 1968; 3 Gaelic Ballads, S, pf, 1968; Coastal Ballads, Bar, insts, 1969; Creature Great and Small, Mez, gui, db, perc, 1973; 2 Ballads (Causely), Mez, gui, 1974; Songs of Sundrie Kindes, T, lute, 1976; Scenes from Kipling, Bar, pf, 1976; Scenes from Tyneside, Mez, cl, pf, 1978; The Ballad of Reading Gaol (O. Wilde), Bar, org, vc, 1980

Orch and band: Conc., a sax, str, 1944; Illustrations, brass band, 1969; Songs without Words, 1976; Panorama, str, 1977

Chamber: Sonata, cl, vc, 1947; Str Qt, F, 1952, rev. as Movements for Str Qt, 1982; Triptych, vn, pf, 1954; Air and Variations, vn, cl, pf, 1958; The Rainbow and the Cuckoo, ob, str trio, 1974; Sonatina pastorale, harmonica, hpd, 1974; A Seasonal Sequence, va, pf, 1977; Prelude, Aria, Interlude, cl, pf, 1981

Solo inst: Pf Sonatina no.2, 1959; Variegations, va, 1970; Explorations around a Troubadour Song, pf, 1973; Lyric Suite, pf 4 hands, 1973–4; 3 Pieces, cl, 1979

Also educational music

BIBLIOGRAPHY

CohenE
M. Carner: 'The Music of Phyllis Tate', *ML*, xxxv (1954), 128–33
H. Searle: 'Phyllis Tate', *MT*, xcvi (1955), 244–7
M. Carner: 'Phyllis Tate', *MT*, cv (1964), 20–21
N. Kay: 'Phyllis Tate', *MT*, cxvi (1975), 429–30

SOPHIE FULLER

Tăutu, Cornelia (*b* Odorhei, 10 March 1938). Romanian composer. She graduated from the Bucharest Conservatory (1967) and completed her studies at Long Island

University, New York (1971–2). On her return to Bucharest, she became a researcher at the Institute of Folklore and then an editor at the musical publishing house there. She is well known for her film music and has written a considerable amount of 'serious' music, which often obliquely invokes the sounds and materials of folk music, and is original and dramatic, with minimalist tendencies. In the first section of *Stampe* ('Engravings', 1984), for example, the piano supports the orchestra like a slow metronome, mercilessly obsessive; it again marks time in the fifth and final section, but delicately. The First Symphony (1987) is full of suppressed grief, its third (and last) movement serving as a requiem for the fallen. In the Piano Sonata (1973), the motivic workings are traditionally developmental, while in the *Five Inventions* for piano and orchestra (1988), the percussive, geometric motifs of the piano engage in an intense dialogue with the woodwind to produce unusual and exciting timbres.

WORKS
selective list

Orch: Concertino, str orch, 1967; Mişçare simfonică [Symphonic Movement], 1967; Contrapunct [Counterpoint], str orch, 1968; Segmente [Segments], 1969; Zaruri [Dice], 1971; Stampe [Engravings], 1984; Sym. no.1 '1907', 1987; Five Inventions, pf, orch, 1988; Pf Conc., 1989

Chamber and solo inst: 2 str qts: no.1, 1965, no.2, 1972; Trio, fl, pf, harp, 1965; Inventions, pf, 1971; Pf Sonata, 1973

Incid. music: Prometeu [Prometheus] (Aeschylus), 1972; Medea (Seneca), 1974

Film scores: Coasa [The Scythe], dir. C. Vaeni, 1983; Trenul de Aur [The Golden Train], dir. B. Poreba, 1985; Moromeţii [Moromete Family Story], dir. S. Gulea, 1986; The Enigma, 1988; Forgotten by God, 1991

BIBLIOGRAPHY

CohenE
Z. Dumitrescu-Buşulenga: record notes, *Cornelia Tăutu* (RGM [Romanian Women Composers]/ Electrecord ST-ECE 03735, 1988)
VIOREL COSMA, RHIAN SAMUEL

Tegnér [née Sandström], **Alice** (*b* Stockholm, 12 March 1864; *d* Stockholm, 26 May 1943). Swedish composer and teacher. She trained as a teacher and at the same time studied music, especially composition. She was the originator of the Swedish repertory of children's songs: her first songbook, *Sjung med oss, Mamma!*, was published in 1892 and eight further collections appeared during the next 32 years. Most of the songs, as for example *Bä, bä vita lamm* ('Baa baa, Black Sheep'), *Mors lille Olle* ('Mother's Little

Olle'), and *Ekorrn satt i granen* ('The Squirrel Sat in the Fir-Tree'), are well known throughout Sweden, and *Betlehems stjärna* has become one of the most famous Swedish Christmas songs. Several of the song anthologies edited by her, including *Unga röster* ('Young Voices'; 1904), *Sjung svenska folk* (1905) and *Nu ska vi sjunga* ('Now we will Sing'; 1943), have also been widely disseminated throughout the country. Her own cantatas and piano music are no longer performed.

EVA ÖHRSTRÖM

Telfer [Lindsey], **Nancy (Ellen)** (*b* Brampton, Ont., 8 May 1950). Canadian composer and choral conductor. She studied the piano from the age of six and played the french horn in school and at the University of Western Ontario, where she took the BA in 1971. From 1972 to 1976 she was a schoolteacher but in 1977 she returned to specialize in composition at the University of Western Ontario, where her teachers were Jack Behrens, Alan Heard, Peter Paul Koprowski and Gerhard Wuensch in composition, Kenneth Bray in arranging and Deral Johnson in choral conducting. She gained the BMus in 1979, after which she became a full-time composer.

Telfer has received numerous commissions and has produced a huge and diversified output. She is best known as a composer of secular choral works, which illustrate her knowledge of choral technique and her sensitivity to the varied texts she has set. Her interest in the outdoors is often reflected in the titles of her works, many of which have been inspired by specific natural settings. Although she is regarded as a traditionalist in matters of form, she is an individualist in her sensitive manipulation of it, often interpolating modal harmonies and open 5ths to enhance the text, expressive setting of which is paramount in her works. Significant performances include *The Journey* at the World Council of Churches in 1983, *Sing Praises* at the 12th Biennial Conference of the Lutheran Churches in America in 1984 and *Birdflight* at the Festival of Music from Around the World in 1986.

WORKS
selective list

Stage: A Time for Sharing, children's chorus, fl, perc, pf, 1987

Orch and band: Dance no.1, str orch, 1982; Dance no.2, str orch, 1982; Release the Captives, sym. band, 1985; 2 Canadian Folksongs, orch, opt. solo v/unison choir, 1988; other band works

Choral: Songs of Love and Loneliness, SATB, 1979; Winter Flowers (E. Brester), C, chorus, orch, 1980; Bushed (Birney), SATB, pf, 1981; From Quiet Winter Skies (G. Nodwell), nar, SATB, fl, ob, org, 1981; High Flight (Magee), SSA, 1982; Hodie, SATB, 1982; The Journey, oratorio, 3 female vv, SATB, str orch, 1982; The Spell of Time Long Past, SATB, pf, 1982; Missa brevis, SSA, 1983; This Holy Time (T. Merton, H. Thurman), SATB, rec sextet/ww sextet, kbd, 1983; Hope's Lantern, SATB, brass insts, org, 1984; Lullaby of the Iroquois (Johnson), SSA, 1984; Sing Praises, SATB, 1984; 99 Names of God, SATB, 1985; Requiem, SATB, 1985 [Lat. and Eng. text]; Canadian Kaleidoscope, SATB/SA/unison, pf, 1986; Magnificat, SSA, 1986; Of Things Eternal, SSA, pf, 1986; Noell, SATB, fl, harp, 1987; 2 Canadian Folksongs, solo v/unison choir, orch, 1988; c100 other works

Other vocal: The Ballad of Princess Caraboo, Mez, pf, 1982; Jesus, my Love, my Joy, S, pf, 1983; A Child's Christmas in Wales (D. Thomas), nar, orch, 1984; Christlove, 1984; Portraits, S, pf, 1984; Trio, S, fl, pf, 1986; The Sea's Strong Voice (E. J. Pratt), Mez, orch, 1989

Chamber and solo inst: Inner Space, brass qnt, 1981; Meditations of Lent, org, 1983; Put on your Dancing Shoes, kbd, 1984; Birdflight, 2 pic, 4/6 fl, a fl, b fl, 1985; Bird's-Eye View, ob, pf, 1985; The Crystal Forest, 2 pic, 6 fl, 1985; Voluntaries, org, 1985; Dinosaurus, hn, 4 tpt, 4 trbn, tuba, perc, 1989

GAYNOR G. JONES

Hope Temple

Temple, Hope [Davis, Alice Maude; Davis, Dotie] (*b* Dublin, 27 Dec 1859; *d* Folkestone, 10 May 1938). Irish composer and pianist. Hope Temple was the pseudonym under which all her compositions were published. She originally trained as a pianist, but had to abandon that career because of sporting accidents. At 13 she was sent to London to finish her general education, and while there also studied the piano, harmony and counterpoint. She then moved to Paris to take further lessons with André Wormser, and later studied with André Messager, becoming his second wife in 1895. Her beauty and charm were remarked upon both by William Boosey and by Isidore de Lara, who first met her in Paris between 1892 and 1894; she seems also to have known Frederick Delius at this time. During Messager's employment at the Opéra–Comique (1898–1904) she became something of a society hostess, forsaking her own compositional activity. Her compositions (around 50) are all songs, with the exception of the operetta *The Wooden Spoon*, a one-act piece consisting of only six numbers and an overture, which was performed in London during 1892 and 1893. Messager claimed that she also had a hand in the composition of his *Mirette*, produced at the Savoy Theatre in July 1894, but her name does not appear on the published vocal score. One of her biographers noted, as testimony to her facility in song composition, that her melody *Love and Friendship* was written in half an hour, and that another work was composed in a hansom cab. Given the formulaic nature of most of her pieces, these statements have a ring of truth. The majority of her works are sentimental ballads. Temple's fondness for 4/4 time, and a predominantly syllabic word-setting, gives them a heavy, earthbound tread, and her habit of beginning a melody on an anacrusis quickly palls. Most of her texts are of mediocre quality, but she also set Longfellow, Tennyson (*The Poet's Song*) and Byron (*She Walks in Beauty*), and seems to have enjoyed considerable popular success in her own day.

BIBLIOGRAPHY

WCBH

A. T. C. Pratt: *People of the Period* (London, 1897)

W. Boosey: *Fifty Years of Music* (London, 1931)

I. de Lara: *Many Tales of Many Cities* (London, 1938)

Who was Who, iii: *1929–1940* (London, 1947)

J. Wagstaff: *André Messager: a Bio-Bibliography* (Westport, CT, and London, 1991)

JOHN WAGSTAFF

Terzian, Alicia (*b* Córdoba, 1 July 1934). Argentine composer, musicologist and conductor of Armenian descent. She studied composition with Alberto Ginastera at the

Conservatorio Nacional de Música, Buenos Aires, where she graduated in 1958 and won the Gold Medal in 1959. She also studied Armenian sacred music in Italy, with Father Leoncio Dayan at the S Lazzaro monastery near Venice, and pursued private studies in conducting with Mariano Drago. She has won many honours in Argentina and France and from Catholicos Vazken I of Armenia, and has received commissions not only in Argentina but also from Lisbon, London, Zagreb, Grenoble and Salzburg. In 1978, she founded Encountros Internacionales de Música Contemporánea to introduce international audiences to Latin American, and specifically Argentine, avant-garde music; under her direction, the group has participated in over 150 festivals. Her posts include the directorship of the Society for the Promotion of New Music in the Three Americas, as well as executive secretary of the Latin American and Caribbean divisions of the International Music Council of UNESCO. She has been professor of composition at the Conservatorio Nacional and has lectured widely on contemporary music.

Terzian's works possess both a bold imaginative drive and a solid inner logic, and often exploit tone colour as an element of musical form. In the Violin Concerto (1955), Terzian employs microtones; scored for large orchestra, the concerto is virtuoso yet lyrical, and the brilliant technical display of the solo instrument is supported by a classical design. Its elegiac slow movement is based on an Armenian folksong. Cuaderno de imágenes (1964) features stationary and shifting tone-clusters, its unconventional organ registrations creating striking effects; it incorporates a tiento by a 17th-century organist of Lima Cathedral. Carmen criaturalis (1969–71) reveals an elemental grandeur, its horn soliloquy formed within a framework of amorphous and grotesque sonorities, while Voces (1979) dramatically exploits the relationship of verbal sounds and musical tones. Many of her large-scale compositions, as well as the piano pieces, have been recorded.

WORKS
selective list

Stage: Hacia la luz (ballet), 1965 [arr. of orch work, Movimientos contrastantes]; Génesis (ballet), with tape, 1972; Achtamar [Aŀt'amar] (ballet), 1979; Bestiela (theatre music, C. de Marigny), 1981; El Dr Brecht en el Teatro Colón (theatre music, A. Castillo), 1981; El otro Judas (theatre music, Castillo), 1981; El enano (theatre music, L. Lagerkvist), 1984

Orch: Vn Conc., 1955; El gris de la noche, str orch,

cymbals, 1960–70; Movimientos contrastantes, 1964; Proagon, vn, str orch, 1969–70; Carmen criaturalis, hn, str orch, vib, cymbals, 1969–71; Narek, 1v, chamber orch, tape, 1979; Voces, 1v, chamber orch, tape,1979; Y cuya luz es como la profunda oscuridad, chamber orch, M. A. Vidal's paintings, 1982; Y la luz se oira, chamber orch, 1982; Amores, 1v, inst ens, 1984–7; Off the Edge, 1v, orch, 1993

Other inst: Danza criolla, pf, 1954; Toccata, pf, 1954; 3 piezas, str qt, 1955; Juegos para Diana, pf, 1956–65; Cuaderno de imágenes, org, 1964; Atmósferas, 2 pf, 1969; Shantiniketan, fl, 1970

Vocal (1v, pf, unless otherwise stated): Libro de poemas de Lorca, 1954–6; 3 canciones (Byron), 1954; Tristeza (Byron), 1956; 3 madrigales, SSA, 1958; Canciones para niños (F. García Lorca), 1960; Padre nuestro y Ave Maria, SATB, 1966; Embryo, 1v, va, 1969

Multi-media, el-ac: Atmósferas, tape, 1970; Musidanzavisión, tape, slides, lasers, sculptures, paintings, improvised dance, 1970; Sinfonía visual en 2 movimientos, tape, slides, 1972; Sinfonía apocalíptica, tape, 1978–80; Canto a mí misma, str orch, digital delay, digital transposition in real time, sonorous system in hall, 1986; Buesnos Aires me vas a matar, pf, actors, tape, 1990; Canto a mí misma, str orch, tam-tam, sound transformation, 1993

Principal publishers: Barry, Ricordi Americana, Salabert

BIBLIOGRAPHY
E. Alemann: 'Alicia Terzian: Multi-Talented Musician', *Ararat* (1984), aut., 35–7
Ş. Arzruni: 'Alicia Terzian's *Juegos para Diana*', *Keyboard Classics*, xii/3 (1992), 42–3

ŞAHAN ARZRUNI

Teyber [Tayber], **Eleonora**. *See* ASACHI, ELENA.

Thisse-Derouette, Rose (*b* Liège, 20 July 1902; *d* Liège, 16 Sept 1989). Belgian composer and folklorist. Born into a family of musicians and singers, she studied at the Liège Conservatory, where the composer Sylvain Dupuis was among her teachers, and won several prizes, including those for piano, chamber music, harmony and fugue; she later became a professor of solfège at the conservatory. She was awarded second prize in the Prix de Rome contest in 1929. Her output is dominated by vocal music, whether for the stage, solo voice or choir, in a style that is influenced by Walloon popular folk music; some pieces are in Walloon dialect and describe the people of her region. As a folklorist, she transcribed the music of many dances and songs and wrote several books and articles about her country's folk traditions.

WORKS
selective list

Stage: Coûr d'amoûr (A. Ledoux), 1928; Gloire à la Meuse!; Po l'vî Maîsse (L. Lagauche); L'étoile qui danse (féerie, 8 scenes, M. Shérac); Andrian et Jusémina (féerie, M. de Ghelderode); Le berger des loups (J. Chot); Amaury (féerie, 3, F. Bodson); Un jour d'été (poème musical, F. Roland); Lès Bwèh'lîs (3, Lagauche); On djoûr ol Fagne (H. Bragard); Li Sotê (C. Bicheroux)

Choral: Poètes du clocher, male chorus, 1930 [for the centenary of Belgium]; Errant éternel, 1933; Les lys, 1933; Le petit faune, 1933; Refrains de chasse, 1933

Songs: 3 chants plaisants de Ronsard; 3 mélodies, low/mixed vv, pf; Campanule; Paysages wallons, lieder (A. Lovegnée)

BIBLIOGRAPHY

A. Guller: 'Les musiques légères', La musique en Wallonie et à Bruxelles, ed. R. Wangermée and P. Mercier, ii (Brussels, 1982), 283–96

MARIE CORNAZ

Thome, Diane (b Pearl River, NY, 25 Jan 1942). American composer, teacher and pianist. She studied at the Eastman School (BM in composition and performer's certificate, 1963); the University of Pennsylvania (MA in theory and composition, 1965); and at Princeton (MFA in composition, 1970), where she was the first woman to receive the PhD in music (for her dissertation Toward Structural Characterization of the Timbral Domain, 1973). Her teachers included Dorothy Taubman, for piano, and Robert Strassburg, Roy Harris, Darius Milhaud, Alexander Boscovich and Milton Babbitt, for composition. In 1963–4 she was pianist for the Israel Dance Theatre, Tel-Aviv. Thome has taught at Princeton and SUNY, Binghamton, and in 1977 was appointed to the University of Washington. In her music, which has frequently been written to commission and which is widely performed, she explores the boundaries between live performance and computer-synthesized sounds. Polyvalence (1972), for computer and ensemble, was among the earliest computer-synthesized compositions by a woman.

WORKS
selective list

Mixed media: Night Passage (environmental theatre piece), 1973, collab. B. Tromler and J. Vassallo; Angels (virtual reality artwork, N. Stenger), 1992

Orch and vocal orch: 3 Sonnets (Sri Aurobindo), S, chamber orch, 1984; The Golden Messengers, orch, 1985; Lucent Flowers, S, chamber orch, 1988; Indra's net, orch, 1989

Tape and computer: Polyvalence, computer, 6 players, 1972; January Variations, computer-synthesized tape, 1973; Anais, vc, pf, tape, 1976; Sunflower Space, fl, pf, tape, 1978; Levadi, S, tape, 1986; Ringing, Stillness, Pearl Light, pf, tape, 1988; The Ruins of the Heart, S, orch, tape, 1990; Into her Embrace: Musings on Savitri, tape, 1991; The Palaces of Memory, chamber orch, tape, 1993

Also chamber and vocal music

BIBLIOGRAPHY

B. Becker: 'Diane Thome: Electronic Music Composition', Northwest Originals: Washington Women and their Art, ed. E. Nichols (Portland, OR, 1990)

CATHERINE PARSONS SMITH

Thys [Sébault], **Pauline-Marie-Elisa** (b Paris, c1836; d 1909). French librettist and composer. The daughter of the opéra comique composer Alphonse Thys, she first became known as a composer of salon music (chansonnettes and romances) before trying her hand at larger-scale works. Then, over a period of 40 years (1857–1907), she wrote and composed at least 16 theatre pieces – dramas (without music), operettas, opéras comiques and operas – many of which were staged at Paris theatres (including the Bouffes-Parisiens, the Théâtre Impérial du Cirque, the Théâtre Lyrique, the Théâtre du Vaudeville and the Théâtre de l'Athénée) while others received concert performances. Her operetta Nedgeya (libretto by P. Nemo) was given in Naples in December 1880 and her two-act serious opera Le mariage de Tabarin, ou La congiura di Chevreuse (1876) a year later in Florence. She used the pseudonym 'Mme M. Du Coin' and wrote at least one novel, Les bonnes bêtes (Paris, 1885).

BIBLIOGRAPHY

FétisB; FétisBS; StiegerO

JULIE ANNE SADIE

Tibors (fl mid-12th century). Troubadour. She was the sister and guardian of the troubadour Raimbaut d'Orange and the wife of the troubadour Bertrand des Baux. Only one poem, without music, is extant, but she is one of only eight women given an official vida.

BIBLIOGRAPHY

M. Bogin: The Women Troubadours (New York, 1976), 80–81, 162–3

MARIA V. COLDWELL

Ticharich, Zdenka (b Vukovar, 26 Sept 1900; d Budapest, 15 Feb 1979). Hungarian pianist and composer. After studying the piano at the National Conservatory (from 1904) with István Tompa and then in Vienna (1916–17) with Emil Sauer, at the age of 17 she embarked on an international performing career with concerts in Berlin, Rome, Vienna and Scandinavia. From the early 1920s she lived in Berlin, studying the piano with Ferruccio Busoni and composition with Franz Schreker, for whom she worked for two years as an assistant professor at the

Berlin Hochschule für Musik. For the next 20 years she toured extensively in Europe and beyond. She often included her own compositions in the programme and in 1926 (Paris), 1935, 1938 and 1943 (Budapest), gave concerts exclusively of her own music. She ceased performing after World War II and from 1947 until her retirement was professor of piano at the Budapest Academy of Music. She won several awards for her achievements.

As well as being an exceptionally talented pianist, Ticharich was a composer of much individuality. The success of her compositions, however, owed much to her own performance of them. Her exoticism inspired a great number of painters and sculptors, including József Rippl-Rónai, Käthe Kollwitz and Matthew Smith. Published works include an *Ave Maria* setting and *Stimmungsbilder* for piano (both 1911), a series of settings of Deszö Kosztolányi poems (1938) and *Old Hungarian Dances* for piano (1944). Some unpublished manuscripts, including orchestral works (*Symphonietta*, an overture, *Praeludium quasi Fantasia et Fugue*), two string quartets, piano music (including a sonata) and songs (among them settings of Guillaume Apollinaire), are in the Hungarian National Library, Budapest.

BIBLIOGRAPHY

G. Thurzó: 'A Zdenka', *Film, Szinház, Muzsika* (1972), April
J. Breuer: 'Ticharich Zdenka', *Muzsika*, xviii/9 (1975), 26–7
I. Raics: 'Ticharich Zdenka távozására', *Muzsika*, xxii/4 (1979), 26–7 [obituary]

EVA KELEMEN

Tindal, Adela. See MADDISON, ADELA.

Tolkowsky, Denise (*b* Brighton, 11 Aug 1918; *d* Antwerp, 9 March 1991). Belgian composer. She studied at the Antwerp Conservatory, where her composition teacher was Flor Alpaerts, and gave piano concerts in Belgium and elsewhere; she also occasionally worked as a journalist. After the death of her husband, the Belgian pianist Alex de Vries, in 1964, she founded the Fonds Alex de Vries, an association to help young musicians begin their careers. In 1979 she became director of the Flemish section of Live Music Now – Belgium. Her early compositions show impressionist influences, but the later ones are more expressionist in style. The most prominent of her works are *Hulde aan Béla Bartók* for flute, violin, piano and percussion, broadcast in New York in 1957,

and the three-movement Piano Concerto, first performed in 1958 with her husband as soloist.

WORKS
selective list

Ballets: Van 't Kwezelke, 1939, choreog. V. Belowa; Le jeu du coeur, choreog. R. Avermaete; Van aarde en mensen, choreog. Belowa; La sulamite
Orch and chamber: Adagio, str; Hulde aan Béla Bartok, fl, vn, pf, perc, 1950; Conc., fl, str; Pf Conc., 1958
Pf: Sonatine; Rythmic; 2 études; 6 préludes; 5 chants hébraïques; North-American Impressions, 2 pf; Variaties op een russisch thema, 1961
Vocal: Het kamp (M. Coole), 1v, chamber orch, 1939; songs

BIBLIOGRAPHY

AMe
R. Wangermée: *La musique belge contemporaine* (Brussels, 1959)

MARIE CORNAZ

Torry, Sloman. See SLOMAN, JANE.

Tower, Joan (*b* New Rochelle, NY, 6 Sept 1938). American composer and pianist. She spent her childhood in South America and returned to the USA in 1955, studying at Bennington College, Vermont (1958–61), and at Columbia University (MA 1967, DMA 1978), where Otto Luening and Chou Wen-chung were among her teachers. In 1969 she founded and became the pianist for the Da Capo Chamber Players, an ensemble specializing in the performance of contemporary music; the group won a Naumburg

Joan Tower

award in 1973. Tower has received many awards, including three NEA composer fellowships (1974, 1975, 1980) and a Guggenheim fellowship (1977), and commissions from the Koussevitzky Foundation (for *Music for Cello and Orchestra*), the Naumburg Foundation (1985), several major American orchestras and the Carnegie Hall Centennial commission (1992–3). She became assistant professor at Bard College, Annandale-on-Hudson, New York, in 1972 and was composer-in-residence with the St Louis SO from 1985 to 1987. Her *Silver Ladders* was awarded a prize in the Kennedy Center Friedheim Awards in 1988, and a Grawemeyer prize in 1990. She returned to Bard College in 1988 and was appointed to the Asher Edelman endowed chair there. Her works are widely performed in the USA and Europe, and a number of them have been recorded.

Tower's music is vividly evocative and strongly rhythmic; balances of gesture, register, tempo, rhythm, texture, timbre and dynamics are among her main concerns. She acknowledges the influences of Beethoven and Stravinsky, to whom, respectively, she paid homage with her Piano Concerto (1985) and *Petroushskates* (1980). Works written before 1974 rely heavily on serial techniques and complex 'mapping' procedures. *Hexachords* (1972) is a representative work of this period, its harmony based on a 6–note unordered chromatic series. *Breakfast Rhythms I and II* (1974–5) are transitional works, the second of which moves away from serialism towards simpler, Debussyan textures and sonorities. Later works are more lyrical and many are inspired by images: *Platinum Spirals* (1976) is a musical representation of the malleable properties of platinum; *Wings* (1981) was inspired by the wingspan and flight of a falcon; and the contrasting textures of *Silver Ladders* (1986) mirror the variegated properties of silver while rising 4ths and ascending symmetrical scales evoke the image of ladders. In *Sequoia* (1981), her first major orchestral work and one of her most frequently performed compositions, Tower uses carefully controlled registral, timbral and harmonic balances – a musical parallel to the precarious equilibrium suggested by the Sequoia tree's majestic height in contrast to the smallness of its pine needles.

In the early 1980s Tower began to concentrate increasingly on the temporal aspects of music; in this respect Olivier Messiaen's *Quatuor pour la fin du temps* was a seminal

influence. During her tenure at St Louis she continued to write mainly large orchestral works, including several concertos that exhibit her gifts for virtuoso solo writing and vibrant orchestration. The Clarinet Concerto (1988), with its subtle manipulations of tempo and metre, gradual transformations of melodic material within the context of rapid ostinato patterns, and extensive use of long pedal points, trills and cadenzas, is typical of the works which during this period mostly take the form of long single movements that avoid large-scale repetition. In many of these works the added force of an expanded percussion section intensifies the energy and exuberant rhythmic drive characteristic of Tower's music.

WORKS

Orch: Amazon II, 1979; Sequoia, 1981; Amazon III, chamber orch, 1982; Music for Vc and Orch, 1984; Island Rhythms, 1985; Pf Conc. (Homage to Beethoven), 1985; Silver Ladders, 1986; Cl Conc., 1988; Fl Conc., 1989; Island Prelude, ob, str orch/wind qnt, 1989; Conc. for Orch, 1991; Vn Conc., 1992; For the Uncommon Woman, 1993; Stepping Stones: a Ballet, 1993

Chamber: Perc Qt, 1963, rev. 1969; Brimset, fl, perc, 1965; Movements for Fl and Pf, 1968; Prelude for 5 Players, fl, ob/vn, cl, bn/vc, pf, 1970; Breakfast Rhythms I–II, cl, 5 insts, 1974–5; Black Topaz, pf, 6 insts, 1976; Amazon I, fl, cl, va, vc, pf, 1977; Petroushskates, fl, cl, vn, vc, pf, 1980; Noon Dance, fl, cl, vn, vc, pf, perc, 1982; Fantasy . . . Harbour Lights, cl, pf, 1983; Snow Dreams, fl, gui, 1983; Fanfare for the Uncommon Woman, brass, timp, perc, 1987; Second Fanfare for the Uncommon Woman, brass, timp, perc, 1989; Third Fanfare for the Uncommon Woman, double brass qnt, 1991

Solo inst: 6 Variations, vc, 1971; Hexachords, fl, 1972; Platinum Spirals, vn, 1976; Red Garnet Waltz, pf, 1977; Wings, cl/a sax, 1981; Clocks, gui,1985

Principal publishers: ACA, Associated, Peters, G. Schirmer

BIBLIOGRAPHY

CC (R. Johnson)

G. Levin: 'Current Chronicle', *MQ*, lx (1974), 625–32

C. Amner: *Unsung: a History of Women in American Music* (Westport, CT, 1980)

L. Valdes: 'Women Composers can be in Harmony without Making Music Together', *Baltimore Sun* (30 May 1981)

V. O'Brien: 'Joan Tower: Musician of the Month', *HiFi/MusAm*, xxxii/9 (1982), 6–7

L. Koplewitz: 'Joan Tower: Building Bridges for New Music', *Symphony Magazine*, xxxiv/3 (1983), 36

B. Jepson: 'For an Uncommon Woman, Fanfare Comes Full Circle', *New York Times* (2 Jan 1994)

MYRNA S. NACHMAN, LISA B. ROBINSON

Trautmann, Marie. *See* JAËLL, MARIE.

Trimble, Joan (*b* Enniskillen, 18 June 1915). Irish composer. She was awarded piano, violin and composition scholarships while studying at the Royal Irish Academy of Music, Dublin (1930–36), and also graduated from Trinity College, Dublin (BA 1936, MusB 1937), after which she studied at the RCM, London, with Ralph Vaughan Williams and Herbert Howells for composition and Arthur Benjamin for piano. In 1940 her Phantasy Trio won the RCM Cobbett Prize and she was also awarded the RCM Sullivan Prize for composition. With her sister Valerie she formed a two-piano duo, which was to have a long and distinguished performing history, and she wrote many original works for the medium, including the Sonatina (1940). BBC commissions included *Érin Go Bragh*, a march-rhapsody for brass band (1943), *Ulster Airs* (arrangements, 1939–40) for the BBC Northern Ireland Orchestra (Ulster Airs Scheme), and the television opera *Blind Raftery* (1957). Her setting for voice and orchestra *How dear to me the hour when daylight dies* won the Radio Éireann Centenary Prize in 1953. She has lived permanently in Ireland since 1977, and her *Three Diversions for Wind Quintet* was commissioned by the Arts Council of Northern Ireland for her 75th birthday in 1990. An Irish idiom, particularly with regard to certain rhythmic and rhapsodic qualities, informs her distinctive style, but her compositions also convey something of the colour and clarity of French music.

WORKS

Operatic and film: The Voice of Ulster (film incid. music), 1948; Blind Raftery (TV opera, C. Cliffe, after D. Byrne), 1957

Orch and band: Ulster Airs, arrs., 1939–40; In Glenade, 1942; Érin Go Bragh, march-rhapsody, brass band, 1943; Suite, str, 1953

Vocal: My Grief on the Sea (D. Hyde), 1v, pf, 1937; Green Rain (M. Webb), 1v, pf, 1938; The County Mayo (4 songs, J. Stephens), Bar, 2 pf, 1949; How dear to me the hour when daylight dies (T. Moore), 1v, orch, 1953; 2 songs: The Milkmaid (T. Nobbes), The Lamb (W. Blake), 2vv, pf, 1953

Chamber: Phantasy Trio, vn, vc, pf, 1940; The Pool among the Rushes, cl, pf, 1940; Rosa breatnach, vn, pf, 1940; Air for 2 Irish Harps, 1969; 3 Diversions for Wind Qnt, 1990

2 pf: Buttermilk Point, 1938; The Humours of Carrick, The Bard of Lisgoole, 1938; Sonatina, 1940; The Green Bough, 1941; Pastorale, 1943; Puck Fair, 1951; arrs. of Irish airs

BIBLIOGRAPHY

Fuller-LeFanuRM

SARAH M. BURN

Trissina, Alba (*fl* 1622). Italian composer. She was a nun at the monastery of Araceli in Vicenza and a pupil of Leone Leoni there. The four motets included in Leoni's *Sacri fiori: quarto libro de motetti a 1–4* (Venice, 1622) are her only known compositions; all involve an alto voice. *Vulnerasti cor meum*, a solo piece, has well-balanced phrases and modest melismas in a style typical of the Veneto in the 1620s.

ROBERT L. KENDRICK

Troup, (Emily) Josephine (*d* 1912). English composer. Little is known of her life: Brown and Stratton refer to her simply as a 'composer of [the] present time', while Wier (*MEMM*) vouches for the date of her death. The former also imply that, during her lifetime, her songs were her best-known compositions, especially *Spring Showers*, *On a Faded Violet* and *Portuguese Love Song*. Troup's music is of excellent quality, and its style hints strongly at a thorough German (or Germanic) training: there is little of Felix Mendelssohn about it, but it displays the influence of C. M. von Weber (in particular) and lesser masters such as Adolf Henselt and Anton Rubinstein. Yet the basic idiom is unquestionably English, and the *Kleines Wiegenlied* (1909) for violin and piano demonstrates an engaging use of uncloying secondary 7ths that is all her own. Of her solo and choral songs, the finest are for children: she possessed a unique ability to conceive bright, airy music with the freshness of a childlike imagination. Today she is deservedly remembered for her setting of H. W. Longfellow's Christmas hymn, *I heard the bells on Christmas Day*.

WORKS
selective list; all printed works published in London

INSTRUMENTAL

Kleines Wiegenlied, vn, pf (1909); 2 Sketches, vn, pf; pieces for pf

VOCAL

Songs (1v, pf): Cradle Song (W. C. Bennett) (1878); Vivien's Song (A. Tennyson) (1878); When love doth pace (W. A. Gibbs) (1883); On a Faded Violet (P. B. Shelley) (1884); Portuguese Love Song (J. de Vasconcellos) (1884); Spring Showers (R. Buchanan) (1884); [4] Nonsense Songs (E. Lear) (1885–9); Unless (E. B. Browning) (1887); An Apparition (song cycle, S. Phillips) (1899); I bring a garland for your head (E. Gosse) (1901); The Singers (H. W. Longfellow) (1914)

Duets: Constancy, C, T, pf (1889); Give (A. Procter), C, T, pf (1889); When o'er the hill (R. Burns), Mez, T, pf (1889)

Partsongs: 2vv: Everyday Songs for Boys and Girls, 3 vols. (c1892); 3vv: 6 Part-Songs for Female Voices (1887–8): Hark! hark! the lark (W. Shakespeare), It was a lover and his lass (Shakespeare), The rose is

Weeping (P. J. Bailey), Song by the River (M. Collins), Sweet Chloe, 1 song lost

Sacred: I cannot find thee! (E. Scudder), 1v, pf (1878); Oh may I join the choir invisible, SATB; I heard the bells on Christmas Day (Longfellow), hymn

BIBLIOGRAPHY

MEMM; *WCBH*

J. D. Brown and S. S. Stratton: *British Music Biography* (Birmingham, 1897)

A. Laurence: *Women of Notes: 1000 Women Composers Born before 1900* (New York, 1978)

NIGEL BURTON

Tucker, Tui St George (*b* Fullerton, CA, 25 Nov 1924). American composer and recorder player. She was named after the *tui* bird of her mother's native New Zealand. She attended Occidental College, Los Angeles, from 1941 to 1944 and in 1946 moved to New York, where she became known as a recorder virtuoso and a composer, describing herself as 'underground'. Much of the inspiration for her compositions has come from her yearly summer retreats to the mountains of North Carolina (where she settled permanently in 1985). A strong melodic bias, ranging from plainsong-like expanses and baroque angularities to expressionist convolutions, characterizes much of her music, in which a pervasive sense of tonality, folk elements, musical quotations and startling, often humorous juxtapositions of disparate elements can also be found. Tucker's music for recorder reflects her highly developed capacities as a performer, making use of extended ranges, quarter-tones, unusual trills, nature sounds and multiphonics. Some of these devices, especially quarter-tones, are also used in other works, for example *Little Pieces for Quarter Tone Piano* (1972) and *Indian Summer* (1983). In later microtonal compositions such as *Vigil 1* (1985) and *Vigil 2* (1989), for microtonal organ, she has continued to focus on key-orientated explorations of intervals above and beyond the outlined major triad of the overtone series (past harmonics 4:5:6). *Ave verum* (1992), an evening-length piano work, is written for a conventionally tuned instrument. Several of her works have been recorded.

WORKS

Orch and chamber: Rosa mystica, any insts, 1941–; Vn Sonata, 1958; 2 str qts, no.1, 1958, no.2, n.d.; Sym., 1961; other chamber works incl.: Serenade, 2 va; Vn Partita; Lift up your heads, ww trio; Sing Cuckoo, 2 brass sextets, perc, audience

Rec: Sonata no.1 'The Bullfinch', 1960; Romanza, 1962; Sonata no.2 'The Hypertonic', 1967; There are Different Kinds of Writing I, b rec, nar, 1970; Amoroso, variations, 1972; Quartertone Rec Duets,

1973; There are Different Kinds of Writing II, 2 rec, nar, 1980; Quartertone Lullaby, I, rec trio, 1981, II, rec trio, 1982, III 'Midnight Microtone', rec trio/other ww, 1983; The Canary Concertino, small rec/wooden pic, 1988; The Mocking Bird, 2 rec, 1990; Amoroso 2, 1990; other works incl.: Rec Sonata; Happy Birthday, Dear Krzysztof, rec, str, hpd; Ralph and Edward, rondo, rec, hpd; The Syrinx, sonata, 2 rec/other ww

Solo kbd: 2 pf sonatas, no.1, n.d., no.2 'The Peyote', 1956; O Head Full of Blood and Wounds, org, 1958; Tantum ergo, pf, 1970; Little Pieces for Quarter Tone Pf, 1972; My Melancholy Baby, fantasy, quarter-tone pf, 1984; Sarabande, microtonal hpd, 1985; Vigil 1, microtonal org, 1985; Vigil 2, microtonal org, 1989; Ave verum, pf, 1992; other pf works incl.: Notes from the Blue Mountains, Pine Mountain, tòccata; other org works

Choral: Requiem, chorus, orch, 1966; De profundis, 1973; Summer Alleluia, chorus, orch, 1980; 2 motets: Adoramus te, 1986, Venite exultemus, 1991; All Colors of Light, carol, 1991; other works incl.: Drum-Taps (cantata, W. Whitman), Bar, men's chorus, cl trio, pf, vc; 5 Zen Songs, Mass in Popular Style, Missa brevis, Shma Yisrael, 3 hymns, 6 arrs. of spirituals

Other vocal: Indian Summer, 2 Bar, inst ens, 1983; 2 songs (V. Lachmann), 1984; other songs, incl. several sets

Principal publisher: Anfor Music

DOUGLAS LEEDY, JOHNNY REINHARD

Tyrrell, Agnes (*b* Brno, 20 Sept 1846; *d* Brno, 18 April 1883). Czech-Austrian composer and pianist. She was the daughter of Henry Tyrrell, an English language-teacher who had established himself among the German-speaking community in Brno. She studied the piano at the Vienna Conservatory (1862) and composition with Otto Ritzler, the director of the Brno Musikverein. Her frail health prevented an active career as a pianist, though she gave some concerts; instead she devoted herself to composition, encouraged by Count Haugwitz of Námĕst, whom she visited in 1867, and Liszt, who in 1874 praised her piano studies, suggesting some alternative fingerings. These and other piano pieces were published in Vienna; she also wrote songs (some to English texts), choruses, an opera and some orchestral music. Her most adventurous compositions are her choruses, though her piano pieces show Liszt's influence, which is rare in 19th-century Moravia.

WORKS
all MSS in CS-Bm,
including letters and other documents

Stage: Bertran de Born (opera, 2, F. Keim, after L. Uhland), unperf.

Orch: Sym., C, 1875; 2 ovs., 1 mazurka

Other inst: Str Qt; 12 grosse Studien, pf, op.48 (Vienna, c1874); 2 pf sonatas; many miscellaneous pieces, pf

Vocal: Die Könige in Israel, oratorio, unfinished; 20 choruses; 70 songs

BIBLIOGRAPHY

C. F. d'Elvert: *Geschichte der Musik in Mähren und Oesterr.-Schlesien* (Brno, 1873), 185–6

J. Fukač: 'Zur Frage der neuromantischen Stilmerkmale in der Musikentwicklung Mährens', *Sborník prací filosofické fakulty brněnské university*, H5 (Brno, 1971), 63 [list of works, 87ff]

—— : 'Agnes Tyrrellová: zapomenutý zjev moravské romantiky' [Agnes Tyrrell: a Forgotten Figure of the Moravian Romantic Period], *OM*, iii (1971), 269

JOHN TYRRELL

U

Uccelli [née Pazzini], **Carolina** (*b* Florence, 1810; *d* ?Paris, 1885). Italian composer. She made her début in Florence on 21 June 1830 with the successful performance at the Teatro della Pergola of *Saul*, a sacred opera, in two acts, of which she wrote both libretto and music. Her two-act *melodramma Anna di Resburgo* (libretto by Gaetano Rossi) was performed in Naples two years later. The overture of her opera *Eufemio da Messina* was performed in Milan in 1833. Uccelli's only other known work is a cantata for chorus and orchestra, *Sulla morte di Maria Malibran*. She was widowed in 1843 and moved to Paris with her daughter Giulia, a singer. They performed together on concert tours in Belgium, the Netherlands and Switzerland.

BIBLIOGRAPHY
FétisB; *FétisBS*; *SchmidlD*

A. Bonaventura: 'Le donne italiane e la musica', *RMI*, xxxii (1925), 519–34

U. Manferrari: *Dizionario universale delle opere melodrammatiche* (Florence, 1954–5)
MATTEO SANSONE

Ulehla, Ludmila (*b* Flushing, NY, 20 May 1923). American composer, pianist and teacher, of Czech descent. She began writing music at the age of five and later studied at the Manhattan School of Music (BMus 1946, MMus 1947), where her composition teacher was Vittorio Giannini. She became a professor at the Manhattan School in 1947 and was chairperson of the Composition Department there from 1970 to 1989. Additionally she taught at the Hoff-Barthelson Music School, Scarsdale, New York (1968–91), and acted as chairperson of the American Society of University Composers (1972–3) and programme chairperson for the National Association for American Composers and Conductors (1967–74). She has received awards and grants from ASCAP and Meet the Composer.

Although Ulehla's musical language is contemporary, the legacy of the classical canon as well as Slav influences have clearly contributed to its evolution. Her works are tonal, but are not organized by key; emphasis is given to the function of phrases rather than bar-lines, and the balance of contrast and unity helps to articulate formal structures.

WORKS
selective list

Stage: Sybil of the Revolution (chamber opera, 2, S. Schefflein), S, Mez, T, T, B–Bar, fl/pic, ob, cl, bn, 2 hn, perc, pf, str qnt, 1993

Orch and band: Glory and Death, 1942; Pf Conc., 1947; Vc Conc., 1948; Music for Minstrels, 1969; Michelangelo: a Tone Portrait, ww, brass, perc, 1970, orchd 1971; Temple at Abydos, solo trbn, harp, ww, str, 1981; Sym. in Search of Sources, 1990

Chamber: Str Qt, e, 1953; Vn Sonata no.1, 1955; Aria, Fugue and Toccata, str qt, 1968; Trio, vn, hn, pf, 1969; Divertimento, fl, pf, 1972; Duo, hn, vc, 1972; Five Around, 2 tpt, hn, trbn, b trbn/tuba, 1972; In memoriam, vn, vc, pf, 1972; American Scenes, fl, ob/cl, bn, 1976; The China Closet, mar qt, 1984; Lebewohl Variations, fl, ob, bn, hpd, 1986; Vn Sonata no.2, 1988; Remembrances, I, II, vn, pf, 1989; 6 Silhouettes, gui, str qt, 1991; Bn Sonata, 1992

Pf: Sonata no.1, 1951; Sonata no.2, 1956; Variations on a Theme by Bach, 1970; Diversions Four/Two, pf 4 hands, 1971; Harlequinade, 1971; Five over Twelve: Preludes, 1976; Inspirations from Nature, 1985; Diversion Two/Scherzo, pf 4 hands, 1990; children's pieces

Choral and solo vocal: 3 Sonnets from Shakespeare, S/T, chamber orch, 1948, version for 1v, pf, 1960; Gargoyles (G. Corso), S, bn, pf, 1970; Piovean di foco dilatate faldo (Dante), SATB qt/madrigal ens, solo vc, 1973; Time is a Cunning Thief (J. T. Shotwell), S/T, pf, 1973; Fountains, Castles and Gardens (P. Viereck), S, cl, hpd/pf, 1977; The Great God Pan (E. B. Browning), SATB, solo fl, 1979

Principal publisher: General Music Publishing Co.

BIBLIOGRAPHY
D. Amram: *Vibrations* (New York, 1968), 221–2

Who's Who of American Women (Chicago, 8/1972)
SAM DI BONAVENTURA

Urner, Catherine Murphy (*b* Mitchell, IN, 23 March 1891; *d* San Diego, 30 April 1942). American composer and singer. At the University of California, Berkeley, she won the first George Ladd Prix de Paris, enabling her in 1920 to go to Paris to study composition with Charles Koechlin, who considered her remarkably gifted. From 1921 to 1924 she was director of vocal music at Mills College, Oakland, California. She was active as a composer and singer in the USA, France and Italy, and first performances of her music were given in Paris by the Société Musicale Indépendante and at the Salle Pleyel. A talented singer, she specialized in Native American tribal melodies, which she used in many of her compositions to create a stark, poetic effect. Through her teaching Urner transmitted the classical French heritage of Charles Koechlin; she translated several of his treatises and arranged for him to give lectures in California. Koechlin regarded her as influential upon his own modal–contrapuntal style. She collaborated with him on various works and he orchestrated her *Esquisses normandes* (1929), the first performance of which was given by the Bay Area Women's Philharmonic in Berkeley in 1990. In 1937 Urner married the Californian composer and organist Charles Shatto.

WORKS
selective list

Choral and orch: Esquisses normandes, suite, 1929, rev. and orchd C. Koechlin, 1945; Rhapsody of Aimairgin of the Golden Knee, chorus, orch, 1936; 3 Movements, chamber orch, 1938; Fl Conc., 1940; c30 other works

Songs (all for S, pf): 4 mélodies (Paris, 1928): Ici-bas (S. Prudhomme), La lune se lève (J. Madeleine), Le papillon (A. M. L. de Lamartine), Colloque sentimental (P. Verlaine); 6 Songs (Paris, 1928): Sonnet (M. Meagher), Song (I. R. McCleod), Come away, death (W. Shakespeare), Music I heard with you (C. Aitken), Dusk at Sea (T. Jones), The Lake Isle of Innisfree (W. B. Yeats); c90 others

Chamber and solo inst: Petite suite, fl, vn, va, vc, 1930; Jubilee Suite, fl, pf, 1931; Barcarolle, org, 1932; Vn Sonata, C, 1942; 2 Traditional American Indian Songs, org; Pf Suite for Children; The Mystic Trumpeter, tpt; other pieces, pf

Also transcrs., arrs.

MSS in *US-BE*

BIBLIOGRAPHY

E. K. Kirk: 'A Parisian in America: the Lectures and Legacies of Charles Koechlin', *CMc*, xxv (1978), 50–68

C. Shatto and D. Zea: *The Musical Works of Catherine Urner* (MS, 1983, Eugene F. Miller Foundation, Carpenteria, CA)

D. Zea: 'Composer Profile: Catherine Urner', *ILWC Journal* (1994), Feb, 20

ELISE K. KIRK

Urreta [Urrueta] **(Arroyo), Alicia** (*b* Veracruz, 12 Oct 1933; *d* Mexico City, 20 Dec 1987). Mexican composer and pianist. She began six years of piano study with Joaquín Amparán in Mexico City in 1948. In 1952 she entered the Conservatorio Nacional de Música, studying harmony with Rodolfo Halffter, and other subjects with Hernández Moncada, León Mariscal and Sandor Roth. After graduation she continued studying the piano privately with Alfred Brendel and Alicia de Larrocha, and she studied acoustics and electronic music at the Schola Cantorum in Paris. From 1957, while titular pianist of the Orquesta Sinfónica Nacional and instructor in acoustics at the Instituto Politécnico Nacional, she was the chosen performer in the Mexico City premières of all works including piano by Stockhausen, Cage, Gilbert Amy, Manuel Enríquez and Halffter. Meanwhile she composed many works showing her mastery of the avant-garde techniques emanating from Darmstadt. These works favour aleatory procedures with a Boulez-like notion of control: specific markings indicate the exact durations of particular passages and precise dynamic contours; pedalling too is indicated. In the 1970s she co-founded the Festival Hispano-Mexicano do Música Contemporánea, founded the Camerata de México and made recordings (for Voz Viva de México and Creaciones Cisne). Her many awards include prizes for the music for the film *El ídolo de los orígenes* (1967) and for incidental dramatic music, and a citation for her own mixed-media creation, *Pequeña historia de la música* (1980). Her incidental music for plays kept her name constantly before the Mexico City public. In 1981 the Orquesta Sinfónica Nacional gave the first performance of her concerto for amplified piano and orchestra, *Arcana*, in which she herself was the soloist; the première of her *Esferas poéticas* was given in 1983 by the same orchestra. Manuel Enriquez, Halffter, Mario Lavista and Héctor Quintanar are among those to have dedicated works to her.

WORKS
selective list

Stage: Romance de Doña Balada (chamber opera, Urreta), 1972; Canto (Homage to Falla), 1v, actor, dancers; Tributo (ballet); Ven a conocernos [for marionettes]

Orch: Arcana, conc., amp pf, orch, perf. 1981; Esferas poéticas, perf. 1983; Estudio sonoro para una escultura; Hasta aquí la memoria, S, pf, perc, gui, str orch; Homenaje a Castro, str orch; Rallenti; Teogonía mixteca

Elec: De natura mortis o La verdadera historia de Caperucita Roja [The True Story of Little Red Riding Hood], vv, insts, tape, 1972

Other: El ídolo de los orígines, film score; Pequeña historia de la música, mixed media work

BIBLIOGRAPHY

E. Pulido: 'Con Alicia Urreta', *Heterofonía*, iv/22 (1972), 23

—— : 'La mujer mexicana en la música Alicia Urreta', *Heterofonía*, iv/24 (1972), 24

50 años de música: Palacio de Bellas Artes (Mexico City, 1986), 513, 527 [pubn of the Instituto Nacional de Bellas Artes]

E. Pulido: 'Mexico's Women Musicians', *The Musical Woman: an International Perspective*, ii: *1984–5*, ed. J. L. Zaimont and others (Westport, CT, 1987), 327–8

ROBERT STEVENSON

Urteaga, Irma (*b* San Nicolás, Argentina, 7 March 1929). Argentine composer and pianist. She studied in Buenos Aires at the National Conservatory and at the Instituto del Teatro Colón, where she studied choral and orchestral conducting. She later taught at both institutions. Between 1974 and 1978 she was director of the opera studio and house répétiteur at the Teatro Colón; she did similar work for Ecuador Opera during the 1986–8 seasons. Urteaga's compositions, mainly vocal works, have won several prizes. Her style is essentially neo-romantic but she occasionally uses avant-garde techniques. This combination is particularly apparent in *La maldolida* (1987), a humorous and affectionate operatic parody.

WORKS

Dramatic: La maldolida (chamber opera, A. Dimant), 1987

Orch and vocal orch: Ambitos, orch, 1970; Paolo e Francesca (Dante), S, T, chamber orch, 1971; El mundo del ser (E. Frías), Mez, orch, 1989–90

Choral: L'Inferno (Dante), chorus, orch, 1971; Expectación (C. Costa Lima), S, chorus, 1977; Motivos de pecera (A. L. Frega, C. A. Merlino), children's chorus, fl, pf, 1989; Luz de mundos (I. Gruss), chorus, 1990; Los alumbramientos (N. Candegabe), children's chorus, chamber orch, 1992

Other vocal (for 1v, pf unless otherwise stated): 2 canciones (J. F. Giacobbe, C. Nalé Roxlo), 1967; Existenciales (A. Storni), 1974; Sueños de Yerma (F. García Lorca), Mez, fl, cl, vn, vc, pf, 1986; Celebérrimas andanzas del ingenioso fidalgo Don Eduardo Cogorno (Dimant), 1989; Himno a San Rafael (E. Frías), 1992; Cánticos para soñar (Frías, O. Sussel-Marie), 1993; Enigma de la palabra (A. Requeni), 1993

Chamber and pf: 2 Preludes, pf, 1967; Variations and Toccata, pf, 1968; Pf Sonata, 1969; Str Qt, 1969; Designios, fl, cl, va, pf, 1976; Turbulencias, vn, pf, 1979; Escalónicas, pf, 1992; A través, db, pf, 1993

Principal publishers: Cosentino IRCA, EAC-Moeck

BIBLIOGRAPHY

L. Kurucz: *Vademecum de la música argentina* (Buenos Aires, 1983), 24

P. Adkins Chiti: *Donne in musica* (Rome, 1982)

B. Luccheli: *Guía de la música argentina* (Buenos Aires, 1985)

RAQUEL C. DE ARIAS

Usher, Julia (*b* Oxford, 21 July 1945). English composer. A pianist and flautist, she studied composition at Cambridge University with Richard Orton and subsequently at York University with Robert Sherlaw Johnson. She later trained as a music therapist (1985–6). In 1980 she and the composer Enid Luff jointly set up the music publishing company Primavera.

Usher's solo instrumental pieces are dramatic, technically demanding and well-structured monodies. She has also written chamber works and a number of multi-media compositions. The powerful and arresting *A Grain of Sand in Lambeth* (1986) graphically demonstrates the melodic and rhythmic flexibility of her musical language. Some of her piano works, including *Pentimento* (1979) and *Marak* (1989), have been recorded.

WORKS
selective list

Theatre and multi-media: A Dance for the Son-Rising (Dance Mass), chorus, viols, harp, brass band, str orch, actors, dancers, 1976; Handbook (music-theatre), actor/reciter, nar, b cl, sax, tpt, va, slide projections, 1984; A Grain of Sand in Lambeth, chorus, orch, sound sculptures by D. Shiel, 1986; The Orford Merman, actor/singer, fl, ob, cl, hn, vc, pf, dancer, 1987–90; Unfinished Business, tpt, perc, live elec, dancer, sound sculptures, 1990–91; Hope's Perpetual Breath (Lu Hsun), T, fl, cl, vc, harp, perc, dancer, 1992–3

Orch: De revolutionibus, 1975; The Bridge, 1980

Vocal: Season's End (R. Frost), chorus, org, perc, 1967; Ordnance Survey, T, fl, cl, va, vc, 1978; Rites of Transition (Usher), S, A, T, B, 1978; Sacred Physic (madrigal, after W. Shakespeare), S, rec/crumhorn, vc + va da gamba, hpd, 1979; Wellsprings (Usher and J. le Carré), T, wind octet, 1991

Chamber and solo inst: Byzantine Mosaics, fl, 1968; Encounter, cl qnt, 1973; Asolando, fl, 1975; Pentimento, pf, 1979; A Reed in the Wind, ob, 1980; Subsequent Darkness, cl, pf, 1981; Aquarelles, fl + pic + a fl, 1983; L'isole della Laguna, rec, pf, 1983–4; The Old Man of the Sea, hn, pf, 1988–9; Marak, pf, 1989; Mental Maps and Perceived Distance, ob, cl, tpt, pf, 1990; Sacred Conversations, fl, ob, cl, tpt, pf, 1993–4

Principal publisher: Primavera
Some material in *GB-Lmic*

BIBLIOGRAPHY

CohenE; *Fuller-LeFanuRM* (J. Usher)

J. Usher: 'The Composer Minds the Shop', *Composer*, no.81 (1984), 17–18

J. M. East: 'About Turning Point', *Composer*, no.88 (1986), 1–6 [on *Handbook*]

H. Mosby: 'Sound Sculptures', *Composer*, no.89 (1986), 12–14 [on *A Grain of Sand in Lambeth*]

MARIE FITZPATRICK

Ustvol'skaya, Galina Ivanovna (*b* Petrograd [now St Petersburg], 17 June 1919). Russian composer. She studied at the college attached to the Leningrad Conservatory (1937–9) and then with Shostakovich at the conservatory itself (1939–50); her education was interrupted by a period of service in a military hospital during World War II. In 1947 she was appointed to teach composition at the college attached to the conservatory and taught there until 1975. Shostakovich so admired her music that he incorporated some of her ideas into his works; for example, the second theme of the Finale of her Trio for clarinet, violin and piano (1949) appears in Shostakovich's Fifth String Quartet op.92 and in the Suite op.145 (no.9, 'Immortality').

Galina Ustvol'skaya

Ustvol'skaya's First Piano Sonata may be regarded as the starting point in her compositional evolution. Although her early pieces reflect the influence of Shostakovich and neo-classicism, the strong, ascetic style of her mature works stands apart from mainstream contemporary techniques. The profound, emotional world of her music is polarized between the opposing forces of silence and tense protest. Abrupt changes in mood are effected through extreme shifts in texture and dynamics: meditative moments, with broad textures and dynamics as low as *ppppp*, are contrasted with raging sections of dense textures and *fffff* dynamic markings. At

times, bar-lines are dispensed with and lines move independently of each other, invoking, in appearance at least, different types of psalmodic chant – Gregorian plainsong, Russian Orthodox chant (*znamennïy rospev*) or the mourning ritual of the folk tradition. At other times, Ustvol'skaya introduces bars with single beats, the presence of a strong beat without its antithesis giving the music hypnotic power. Another characteristic technique involves chains of single notes, or clusters, of equal duration moving along the diatonic scale.

In her mature works, Ustvol'skaya has concentrated on composing for instruments. Although several of her symphonies include voice, the vocal part either is conceived as an instrumental line, albeit the principal one, or is used to recite a proclamation or prayer (e.g. the speaker's role in symphonies no.2–4). Avoiding the traditional orchestra, she composes for unusual combinations of soloists. Nevertheless, the composer maintains that the works are not chamber music and are unconnected with the early music renaissance. Ustvol'skaya has been a resident of St Petersburg for her entire life, and her music is linked with the artistic tradition of F. M. Dostoyevsky and Andrey Bely.

WORKS
selective list

Syms.: no.1, 2 descant vv, orch, 1955; no.2 'Istinnaya, vechnaya blagost'!' [True and Eternal Bliss], boy spkr, orch, 1979; no.3 'Iisuse, Messiya, spasi nas!', [Jesus, Messiah, Save us!], boy spkr, orch, 1983; no.4 'Molitva' [Prayer], C, tpt, tam-tam, pf, 1985–7; no.5 'Amen', male spkr, ob, tpt, tuba, perc, vn, 1989–90

Other orch: Conc., pf, timp, str orch, 1946

Chamber: Trio, cl, vn, pf, 1949; Octet, 2 ob, timp, 4 vn, pf, 1949–50; Vn sonata, 1952; Bol'shoy duet [Grand Duet], vc, pf, 1959; Duet, vn, pf, 1964; Composition no.1 'Dona nobis pacem', pic, tuba, pf, 1970–71; Composition no.2 'Dies irae', 8 db, perc, pf, 1972–3; Composition no.3 'Benedictus, qui venit', 4 fl, 4 bn, pf, 1974–5

Pf: Sonatas no.1, 1947, no.2, 1949, no.3, 1952; 12 Preludes, 1953; Sonatas no.4, 1957, no.5, 1986, no.6, 1988

Principal publishers: Muzïka, Hans Sikorski, Sovetskïy Kompozitor

BIBLIOGRAPHY

A. Sokhor: 'Dorogami iskaniy' [By the Roads of Quest], *SovM* (1959), no.1, pp.50–55; also in A. Sokhor: *Stat'i o sovetskoy muzike* [Essays on Soviet Music] (Leningrad, 1974), 164–70

K. Yuzhak: 'Iz nablyudeniy nad stilem G. Ustvol'skoy' [Observing Ustvol'skaya's Style], *Stileviye tendentsii v sovetskoy muzïke 1960–1970gg* (Leningrad, 1979), 83–103

B. Kats: 'Sem' vzglyadov na odno sochineniye'

[Seven Looks at One Work], *SovM* (1980), no.2, pp.9–17
A. Andreyev: 'Zametki o stile Galinï Ustvol'skoy' [Notes on Ustvol'skaya's Style], *Music of Russia*, iv (Moscow, 1982), 240–60
A. Sanin: 'Galina Ustvol'skaya: slovo skazano' [Ustvol'skaya: the Word is Said], *SovM* (1990), no.10, pp.10–15
V. Suslin: article in *Galina Ustvolskaya* (Hamburg, 1990) [Sikorski catalogue]
B. Tishchenko: 'V vechnom poiske istinï' [In the Eternal Search for Truth], *Muzïka v SSSR* (1990), no.4, pp.22–3

LUDMILA KOVNATSKAYA

Uyttenhove, Yolande (*b* Leuze, 25 July 1925). Belgian composer and pianist. She studied at the Brussels Conservatory, gained in addition the licentiate diploma of the RAM, London, and received several international awards, both for piano, in the Barcelona competition, and for composition, in the Lutèce (France) and Viotti (Italy) competitions. Uyttenhove's works belong within a post-Fauré or medieval-inspired tradition, but her non-serial musical language, which she describes as 'intemporel', is enhanced through the use of resolutely modern harmonies.

WORKS
selective list

Orch: Vn Conc., op. 102, 1982
Chamber and solo inst: Pf Sonatina, op.16, 1962; Fl Sonata, op.17, 1962; Trio, op.23, tpt, 4 timp, pf, 1964; Dîner à Cajarc, op.30, pf, 1967; Triptyque, op.37, fl, 1967; Etude, op.54, snare drum, pf; Stèle pour Aliénor d'Aquitaine, op.58, gui qt, 1975; Tpt Sonatina, op.78, 1977; Cendrillon, op.93, pf 4 hands, 1980; Sonata, op.94, fl, hpd, 1980; Vn Sonata, op.95, 1980; Sonata, op.119, a sax, pf, 1985; Berdikir, op.128, vc, pf, 1987; Va Sonata, op.146, 1989
Vocal and choral: Cancole, op.25 (A. Lepage), C, pf, 1967; Retour, op.26 (Lepage), S, pf, 1967; Ps cxx, op.43, medium v, chorus 2vv, 1970; Elévation, op.75 (C. Baudelaire), SATB, 1976; Mes souvenirs de Tours, op.76 (H. de Balzac), women's chorus 2vv, 1976

Principal publishers: CeBeDeM, Maurer (Brussels), Vevey

BIBLIOGRAPHY
CohenE
P. Legrain: *Dictionnaire des Belges* (Brussels, 1981)

CHRISTINE BALLMAN

V

Valentine, Ann (bap. Leicester, 15 March 1762; *d* Leicester, 13 Oct 1842). English organist, music-seller and composer of keyboard music. She was a member of a prominent Leicester family of musicians; her father, John Valentine, composed music for amateur orchestras. She lived in Belgrave Gate. In 1785 she performed music by Handel at a subscription concert, perhaps at St Margaret's Church, where she served as organist until as late as 1834. In 1798 Ann Valentine published *Monny Music* for keyboard, along with ten sonatas (op.1) for piano or harpsichord, with violin or flute accompaniment, and, in 1803, further pieces.

BIBLIOGRAPHY
M. Medforth: 'The Valentines of Leicester: a Reappraisal of an 18th-Century Musical Family', *MT*, cxxxii (1981), 812–18

JULIE ANNE SADIE

Valette, Pierre. *See* VIEU, JANE.

Valgrand, Clémence. *See* GRANDVAL, MARIE.

Valle, Barbara. *See* STROZZI, BARBARA.

Van Appledorn, Mary Jeanne (*b* Holland, MI, 2 Oct 1927). American composer. She attended the Eastman School of Music (BM 1948, MM 1950, PhD 1966), where she studied composition with Bernard Rogers and Alan Hovhaness. Her doctoral thesis was a study of Debussy's *Pelléas et Mélisande*. She has been recognized for her compositional achievements through many prizes, including awards from ASCAP (1980–88) and the Texas Composers Guild (1987), and through commissions from the Women Band Directors National Association and the National Intercollegiate Bands. In 1967 she was appointed to teach at Texas Tech University.

Van Appledorn's works are intense and introspective. She often incorporates jazz elements and striking timbral effects into tightly controlled formal structures. Her compositions have received frequent performances in the USA and have also been presented in Europe, Russia and Japan. Several of her works, including the Concerto for Trumpet and Band and *Set of Five*, have been recorded.

WORKS
selective list

Orch and band: Conc., tpt, band, 1960; Passacaglia and Chorale, orch, 1973; Cacophony, wind ens, perc, toys, 1980; Lux: Legend of Sankta Lucia, harp, handbells, perc ens, sym. band, 1981; Terrestrial Music, vn, pf, str orch, 1992

Choral: 2 Shakespeare Songs, chorus, pf, 1953; Darest thou now, O soul, female chorus, org, 1975; West Texas Suite, chorus, perc ens, sym. band, 1975; Rising Night after Night, nar, 3 vv, chorus, orch, 1978

Other vocal: Communiqué, 1v, pf, 1960; Danza impresión de España, 8vv, dancers, 1979; Azaleas, Bar, fl, pf, 1980; Freedom of Youth, spkr, synth, 1986

Chamber and solo inst: Contrasts, pf, 1947; Cellano Rhapsody, vc, pf, 1948; Set of Five, pf, 1953; Patterns, brass qnt, 1956; Sonnet, org, 1959; Matrices, sax, pf, 1979; Liquid Gold, sax, pf, 1982; A Liszt Fantasie, pf, 1984; 4 Duos, va, vc, 1986; Sonic Mutation, harp, 1986; Ayre, str, 1989; Windsongs, brass qnt, 1991; Incantations, tpt, pf, 1992

Carillon: Suite, 1976; A Celestial Clockwork, 1983; Skybells, 1991

Dance: Set of Seven [from Set of Five and Contrasts], pf, 1988

Principal publishers: Arsis, Dorn, Carl Fischer

LISA B. ROBINSON

Van den Boorn-Coclet, Henriette. *See* BOORN-COCLET, HENRIETTE VAN DEN.

Van de Vate [née Hayes], **Nancy** (*b* Plainfield, NJ, 30 Dec 1930). American composer. She studied the piano, viola and composition before taking the doctorate in composition at Florida State University (1968). During the 1960s and 70s she taught at various American educational institutions, including Memphis State University and Hawaii Loa College. She founded the International League of Women Composers in

1975. In 1985 she became a resident of Vienna.

During the 1960s Van de Vate composed mainly chamber music and songs, but has since turned to larger works for orchestra and chorus. Her musical style has been influenced by extended visits to Indonesia and Hawaii. After moving to Europe, she worked closely with Polish composers, including Penderecki and Lutosławski, and this influence is reflected in her music. Her large-scale works feature clusters, aleatory passages, lyric solos and background ostinatos within a carefully devised formal structure.

WORKS
selective list

Orch: Pf Conc., 1968; Dark Nebulae, 1981; Journeys, 1984, rev. 1984; Distant Worlds, vn, orch, 1985; Vn Conc., 1986; Chernobyl, 1987; Pura Besakih, 1987; Kracow Conc., perc, orch, 1988; Va Conc., 1990
Choral: An American Essay, 1972; Cantata, female chorus, 1979; Katyn, chorus, orch, 1989
Songs and other vocal: 4 Somber Songs, 1970, orchd 1991; To the East and to the West, 1972; Letter to a Friend's Loneliness, S, str qt, 1976; A Night in the Royal Ontario Museum, 1983; Songs for the Four Parts of the Night, 1983; Cocaine Lil, S, 4 actors, 1986
Chamber: Va sonata, 1964; Str Qt no.1, 1969; 3 Sound Pieces, brass, perc, 1973; Brass Qnt, 1974, rev. 1979; Qnt, fl, cl, vn, vc, pf, 1975; Music, va, perc, pf, 1976; Trio, vn, vc, pf, 1983; Teufelstanz, perc ens, 1988
Kbd: 9 Preludes, pf, 1978; Pf Sonata no.1, 1978; Hpd Sonata, 1982; Pf Sonata no.2, 1983; Contrasts, 2 pf, 3 performers, 1984; 12 Pieces on One to Twelve Notes, pf, 1986

CHRISTINE AMMER

Vázquez, Alida (*b* Mexico City, *c*1931). American composer of Mexican birth. She attended the Conservatorio Nacional de Música, 1941–7, studying the piano with Esperanza Cruz de Vasconcelos and theory with Julián Carrillo. In the next year she moved to New York City where the Diller-Quaile Music School gave her a scholarship; she also studied with Mario Davidovsky at City College. In 1959 she enrolled in the Columbia University School of Journalism, but from 1960 worked as a music therapist and from 1976 taught in the Bank Street College of Education. Her compositions include numerous solo and chamber works, song cycles (*Acuarelas de México*, 1970), electronic music for dance and electro-acoustic works (*Electronic Moods and Piano Sounds*, 1977). Her works are notable for their rhythmic energy. For example, in the *Pieza para clarinete y piano* (1971), in two movements, after an opening clarinet solo which presents several contiguous expo-

sitions of a 12-note row, the instruments continue in a duo in constantly changing metre; and the second movement, Giocoso energico, is in 3/8 time with dance rhythms irregularly placed. While *Música para siete instrumentos* (wind quintet with trumpet and viola, 1974), a work in two parts with the viola and bassoon fulfilling *obbligato* roles, generally more mournful (it was written in memory of the composer's sister), the exploration of rhythmic motifs leads eventually to a greater vitality, signifying hope and reconciliation. Vázquez's principal publisher is See-Saw Music (New York).

BIBLIOGRAPHY
WAM
E. Pulido: 'Fichero de compositores mexicanos jóvenes', *Heterofonía*, xi/3 (1978), 27, 48
—— : 'Mexico's Women Musicians', *The Musical Woman: an International Perspective*, ii: *1984–5*, ed. J. L. Zaimont and others (Westport, CT, 1987), 313–34
G. Béhague: *Sonidas de las Americas Festival*, New York, 30 Jan–6 Feb 1994, pp.29–30 [American Composers' Orchestra programme booklet]

ROBERT STEVENSON

Veisberg, Yuliya Lazarevna. *See* VEYSBERG, YULIYA LAZAREVNA.

Velázquez, Consuelo (*b* Ciudad Guzmán, Jalisco, 19 Aug 1920). Mexican composer. On graduating with the title *profesora de piano* from the Escuela Nacional de Música, Mexico City, with the intention of becoming a concert artist, she was hired by the Mexico City radio station XEQ. She there formed her own ensemble and broadcast her own songs. *Bésame mucho* (1941), with her own words, published in Mexico City when she was 21 and reissued in New York in 1943, became a best seller in the USA for Jimmy Dorsey and his orchestra in 1944; it was a great hit with North American servicemen fighting in Asia and Europe during World War II. Recorded three times by the Beatles in 1962, this song (now a New Year's Eve favourite) lifted her into an international stardom eclipsed by no other woman in Mexican history. Her next great success, *Qué seas feliz* (1956), won the Desfile de éxitos ('Parade of Bestsellers') and within three months was recorded by 21 artists including Nat King Cole, Ray Coniff, Percy Faith and Mantovani. By 1989 she had copyrighted 47 songs. Although she studied the piano with Ramón Serratos (a pupil of Lhévinne), Velázquez was self-taught as a composer. Because of her classical training, however, her harmonizations generally far exceed in richness those of American ballad composers. She has received many prizes and honours. Her principal publishers are Promotora Hispano Americana de Música (Mexico City) and Peer (New York).

BIBLIOGRAPHY

E. Pulido: 'Mexico's Women Musicians', *The Musical Woman: an International Perspective*, ii: *1984–5*, ed. J. L. Zaimont and others (Westport, CT, 1987), 313–34

Enciclopedia de México (1988), 7986

Y. Moreno Rivas: *Historia de la música popular mexicana* (Mexico City, 1989), 179

ROBERT STEVENSON

Velkiers, Esther Elizabeth (*b* Geneva, *c*1640; *d* after 1685). Swiss composer. She was blind from before the age of one, the result of an accident. Her father taught her to read with a wooden alphabet; she mastered Latin, French and German as well as mathematics, philosophy and theology. She also took up music, in Hawkins's words, 'as a relief to her severer studies', singing, playing the harpsichord and composing. However, according to Hawkins, none of her music survives.

BIBLIOGRAPHY

Choron-FayolleD; *GerberL*; *HawkinsH*

JULIE ANNE SADIE

Vellère [Weiler], **Lucie** (*b* Brussels, 23 Dec 1896; *d* Brussels, 12 Oct 1966). Belgian composer. She studied the piano from the age of six and then the violin, and was later a composition pupil of Joseph Jongen. A pharmacist by profession, she pursued her musical career outside the official establishment. She received several awards, including first prize in the Comité National de Propagande de la Musique Belge competition (1935), the Brabant prize (1957), and first prize in the National Council of Women of the USA competition (1957) for her unaccompanied choral work *Air de Syrinx* (text by Paul Claudel). She has written mostly vocal, instrumental and chamber works. Her musical style belongs to no particular school, although the influence of impressionism is evident; the language is often modal with fairly free use of atonal passages.

WORKS
selective list

Orch: Nuits, suite, str orch, 1946; Petite sym., str orch, 1956; Fantaisie en 3 mouvements, vn, orch, 1958; La route ascendante, chamber orch, 1962; Epitaphe pour un ami, va, str orch, 1964

Chamber: Chanson nocturne, vn, pf, 1920; Pf Trio, 1947; Str Qt no.3, 1951; Vn Sonata, 1952; Bagatelles, str trio, 1960; Prélude, ob, cl, hn, bn,

1961; Sonata, vn, va, 1961; Str Qt no.4, 1962; Qt, 4 cl, 1963; Qt, fl, ob, cl, bn, 1964

Pf: Deux danses, 1930; Promenade au bord du lac, 1949; Préludes pour la jeunesse, 1950; 2 sonatinas, 1960, 1965

Songs: Harmonie lunaire (P. Fort), S/T, pf, 1917; La ronde (Fort), 1917; Toi et moi (P. Géraldy), S/T, pf, 1921; O blanche fleur des airs (C. Van Lerberghe), S/T, pf/double str qt, 1934; Croquis (M. Carême), S/T, pf, 1948; Les cloches (G. Apollinaire), S/T, pf, 1949; Egarement (F. Ardel), S/T, pf, 1952; Les chants de l'ombre (M. Maurel), Mez, pf/str trio, 1964

Also choral music, incl. Air de Syrinx (P. Claudel), unacc. women's vv, 1957; and music for children, incl. Puck compositeur (conte musical, O. Robert), spkrs, ww qt, pf, 1964

Principal publishers: CeBeDeM, Eschig, J. Maurer

BIBLIOGRAPHY

CohenE; *KompA–Z*

CHRISTINE BALLMAN

Vercoe, Elizabeth (*b* Washington DC, 23 April 1941). American composer and writer. She was educated at Wellesley College (BA 1962), the University of Michigan (MM 1963) and Boston University (DMA 1978), where she studied composition with Gardner Read. She was a fellow at the Charles Ives Center (1984, 1992) and at the Cité Internationale des Arts in Paris (1983–5) and has received grants from the Artists Foundation and the National Endowment for the Arts. She was director of the Women's Music Festival/85 in Boston and was a member of the boards of the International League of Women Composers (1980–87) and the Artists Foundation (1985–90). Her writings include articles and reviews about music by women composers.

Read has described Vercoe as 'a composer with a fine technical command and keen sensitivity to sound materials'. These qualities have enabled her to produce highly contrasting works, ranging from the powerful, disturbing *Herstory* series to the spare and suggestive *Changes* for orchestra. Several of her works, including *Herstory II*, *Herstory III* and the satirical yet elegant *Irreveries from Sappho*, have been recorded.

WORKS
selective list

Orch: Rhapsody, vn, orch, 1977; Despite our Differences no.2, pf, chamber orch, 1988; Changes: a Little Music for Mozart, 1991

Vocal: Herstory I (texts by American women poets), S, vib, pf, 1975; Herstory II: 13 Japanese Lyrics, S, perc, pf, 1979; Irreveries from Sappho, S/SSA trio, pf, 1981; Herstory III: Jehanne de Lorraine, monodrama, Mez, pf, 1986; A Dangerous Man: a Monodrama on John Brown, Bar, pf, 1990

Inst: Fantasy, pf, 1975; Persona, pf, 1980; Sonaria, vc,

1980; Fanfare, 3 tpt, timp, 1981; Suite française, vn, 1983; Despite our Differences no.1, vn, vc, pf, 1984; A la fin-tout seul, mand, opt. pf, 1985

BIBLIOGRAPHY

S. Mabry: record notes, *Herstory III: Jehanne de Lorraine* (Owl Recording, CD 35, 1991)

SHARON MABRY

Verne, Mary. *See* WURM, MARY J. A.

Vernier [Venieri], Mme. *See* DEMARS, HÉLÈNE-LOUISE.

Veysberg [Weissberg, Veisberg, Rimskaya-Korsakova], **Yuliya Lazarevna** (*b* Orenburg, 25 Dec/6 Jan 1880; *d* Leningrad [now St Petersburg], 1 or 4 March 1942). Russian composer. She became a pupil at the St Petersburg Conservatory in 1903, studying piano with Rimsky-Korsakov and instrumentation with Alexander Glazunov. She was dismissed in 1905 for participating in a strike and continued her studies with Engelbert Humperdinck and Max Reger in Germany, 1907–12. She returned to St Petersburg to take her examinations and receive her degree (1912). She later worked on the editorial board of the periodical *Muzïkal'nïy sovremennik* (1915–17) and as choral director at the Young Workers' Conservatory (1921–3). Her nine-volume translation of the musical writings of Romain Rolland was published as *Sobraniye muzïkal'no-istoricheskikh sochineniy* (Moscow, 1938). She was married to Rimsky-Korsakov's son, Andrey Nikolayevich.

In her compositions, Veysberg focussed on vocal genres, writing primarily operas, vocal-orchestral and vocal-chamber works. Her musical style, as exemplified in the song cycle *Rautendelein*, a setting of Gerhart Hauptmann's *Die versunkene Glocke*, is characterized by its highly chromatic harmonic language. Although rhythms are simple and phrasing occurs in regular two-bar units, tension is achieved through tritone skips in the melody and through sinuous, chromatic shifts in the harmonic accompaniment. A substantial part of Veysberg's oeuvre is devoted to works for children, including two 'opera-games', *Zaykin dom* ('A Little Rabbit's House') and *Gusi-lebedi* ('Geese-Swans'), cycles of 'song-riddles' and pieces written for children's choirs. These works feature simple rhythms, regular phrasings and unadventurous diatonic harmonies.

WORKS
selective list
OPERAS

Rusalochka [The Little Mermaid] (S. Parnok, after H. C. Andersen), 1923
Gyul'nara (Veysberg and Parnok), 1935, excerpts pubd
Gusi-lebedi [Geese-Swans] (children's opera, Veysberg and S. Marshak), 1937 (Moscow, 1938); Moscow, 1937
Myortvaya tsarevna [The Dead Princess] (radio opera, after A. S. Pushkin), 1937; broadcast, 1938
Zaykin dom [A Little Rabbit's House] (children's opera, W. Weltmann), 1937 (Moscow, 1938); Moscow, 1937

OTHER WORKS

Orch: Skazochka [Tale], 1928; Noch'yu [At Night], sym. picture, after F. I. Tyutchev, 1929; Ballade, 1930; Fantasia; Dramatic Scherzo; Sym., g
Vocal orch: Rautendelein (G. Hauptmann: *Die versunkene Glocke*), S, orch, 1912, vs (Leipzig, 1912); Poyot pechal'nïy golos [A Sad Voice Sings] (F. Sologub), 1v, orch, 1924; Dvenadtsat' [The Twelve] (A. A. Blok), chorus, orch, 1928; 5 detskiye pesni [Children's Songs] (V. P. Katayev), 1v, orch, 1929
Chamber: Lunnaya skazka [The Story of the Moon] (P. Dehmel), 1v, fl, str qt, 1929; 4 Pieces, 2 vn, pf, 1937; Garafitsa (Moldavian folksong), 1v, vc, harp/pf, 1938
Many songs for 1v, pf; duets with pf; solo and choral children's songs; folksong arrs.

Principal publishers: Iskusstvo, Kapella, Muzgiz

DETLEF GOJOWY

Viardot [née García], **(Michelle Ferdinande) Pauline** (*b* Paris, 18 July 1821; *d* Paris, 18 May 1910). French mezzo-soprano, composer and singing teacher, of Spanish origin. The younger daughter of Manuel García (1775–1832), she was his studio accompanist at the time of his death (when she was 11). She acquired additional vocal training from her mother, Joaquina Sitches García. She studied composition with Antoine Reicha and the piano with Meysenberg and Franz Liszt. On 13 December 1837 she made her début as a singer in Brussels, and her Paris début the following year. Like her sister, Maria Malibran, she made her stage début at 17, as Desdemona in Rossini's *Otello* in London (9 May 1839) and Paris (8 October 1839). Her musical and dramatic gifts were immediately acclaimed.

In 1840 she married Louis Viardot, a distinguished French writer 21 years her senior. Their house became a centre for writers, musicians and artists, their circle one of the most distinguished in Paris. In 1843 she visited Russia for the first time, singing both Italian and Russian music (Mikhail Glinka and Alexander Dargomïzhsky), performing

Salon at the Paris home of Pauline Viardot: wood engraving by H. Valentin from 'L'illustration', xxi (1853)

the latter in Russian, the first foreigner to do so. She became one of the principal channels through which Russian music reached the West. Viardot also helped to launch the careers of Gounod, Massenet and Fauré. The second act of Wagner's *Tristan und Isolde* was first heard in Paris in a private performance at her home (February 1860), with Viardot singing Isolde. Robert Schumann's op.24, Saint-Saëns's *Samson et Dalila* and Fauré's opp.4 and 7 are dedicated to her.

In 1849 she appeared at the Paris Opéra as Fidès in Meyerbeer's *Le prophète*, a role written specifically for her. Her success was immense, provoking Berlioz to write that 'Madame Viardot is one of the greatest artists . . . in the past and present history of music'. The summit of her singing career was in 1859 when Berlioz, at the suggestion of Léon Carvalho (director of the Théâtre Italien in Paris), prepared an edition of the French version of Gluck's *Orfeo ed Euridice* in which she sang Orpheus. All who witnessed those performances (some 150 in three years) agreed that in them she reached tragic heights rarely seen on the stage (see illustration on p.476).

Charles Dickens, seeing her Orpheus in 1862, called it 'a most extraordinary performance – pathetic in the highest degree, and full of quite sublime acting'. In 1863 she retired with her family to Baden-Baden, but moved to London in 1870 (after giving the first performances of Brahms's Alto Rhapsody in Jena), because of the Franco-Prussian War. In 1871 the family returned to Paris, where Viardot composed and taught.

Pauline Viardot's compositions are dominated by vocal music. Her early attempts at composition included transcriptions of Chopin Mazurkas (first performed in 1848, with Chopin at the piano) and of the string quartet attributed to Haydn as op.3 no.5 (published in 1845). Her published songs (about 100) link the *romance* and the *mélodie*, being distinguished from the *romance* by the use of complex accompaniments (reflecting her near-virtuoso piano skills) and in the vocal lines, which often contain fioritura and coloratura reminiscent of Italian bel canto opera. The dramatic style and use of pre-symbolist poetry prevent her songs from attaining the qualities of the *mélodie*.

She composed four operettas (three with librettos by Ivan Turgenev), which were performed by her students at her weekly salons. One, *Le dernier sorcier*, was performed in Weimar (1869, conducted by Brahms), Karlsruhe and Riga. Her opera *Cendrillon* (1904) was successfully revived in Newport, Rhode Island, in 1971, and given several performances in Great Britain in 1972 and 1981.

She arranged and compiled song collections; and, with George Sand, collected and transcribed French folksongs (*chansons populaires*). The character of the heroine in Sand's novel *Consuelo* was inspired by Viardot. Viardot was the friend and inspiration of many other writers, among them Alfred de Musset and Ivan Turgenev, who spent much of his life in the Viardot household. Viardot's own writings include the method *Ecole classique de chant* (Paris, 1861). Her singing pupils included Désirée Artôt, Aglaja Orgeni, Marianne Brandt and Antoinette Sterling.

She bore four children. Her eldest daughter, Louise (Pauline Marie) Héritte (*b* Paris, 14 Dec 1841; *d* Heidelberg, 17 Jan 1918) was a contralto, teacher and composer. She taught singing in St Petersburg, Frankfurt, Berlin and Heidelberg. Her comic opera *Lindoro* was performed at Weimar in 1879 and a cantata, *Das Bacchusfest*, in Stockholm in 1880. She published many songs and a string quartet; her *Memories and Adventures* appeared in London in 1913. Viardot's second daughter, Claudie (1852–1914), a painter, married the master printer Georges Chamerot. Her third daughter, Marianne (*b* 1854), was engaged to Fauré but married the French pianist and composer V. A. Duvernoy. Viardot's son Paul (Louis Joachim) (*b* Courtavenel, 20 July 1857; *d* Algiers, 11 Dec 1941) was a violinist, conductor and composer.

WORKS

Stage (operettas unless otherwise stated): Trop de femmes (I. Turgenev), 1867; L'ogre (Turgenev), 1868; Le dernier sorcier (Der letzte Zauberer) (Turgenev), Weimar, 1869; Le conte de fées, 1879; Cendrillon (opéra comique), 1904

Choral: Choeur bohémien, soloists, SSA; Choeur des elfes, soloists, SSA; Choeur de fileuses (from L'ogre); La Jeune République (P. Dupont), 1v, chorus (Paris, ?1848)

Other vocal: Duo, 2 solo vv, pf; *c*100 songs incl. 5 Gedichte (St Petersburg, 1874); 4 Lieder (Berlin, 1880); [5] Poésies toscanes (L. Pomey) (Paris, 1881), 6 mélodies (Paris, 1884), [6] Airs italiens du XVIIIe siècle (trans. Pomey) (Paris, 1886), 6 chansons du XVe siècle (Paris, 1886), [3] Album russe; Canti popolari toscani; vocal arrs. of inst works by Brahms, Haydn, Schubert; other arrs.

Inst: 2 airs de ballet, pf; Défilé bohémien, pf 4 hands, also as song; Gavotte et sérénade, pf (Paris, 1885); Introduction et polonaise, pf 4 hands (Paris, 1874); Marche militaire, 2 fl + pic, 2 ob, 2 brass choirs; Mazourke, pf; 6 morceaux, vn, pf (Berlin, 1868); Second album russe, pf; Sonatine, vn, pf (Paris, 1874); Suite arménienne, pf 4 hands

BIBLIOGRAPHY

G. Sand: 'Le Théâtre-Italien et Mlle Pauline Garcia', *Revue des deux mondes*, xxi (1840), 580–90

F. Liszt: 'Pauline Viardot-Garcia', *NZM*, i (1859), 49–54

H. Berlioz: *A travers chants* (Paris, 1862; Eng. trans., 1913–18)

L. Torrigi-Heiroth: *Mme Pauline Viardot-Garcia: sa biographie, ses compositions, son enseignement* (Geneva, 1901)

A. Sol: 'Mme Pauline Viardot', *RHCM*, v (1905), 322

'Turgenieff and the Woman he Loved', *Current Literature and Art*, xlix (1910), 213–15

L. Héritte-Viardot: *Memories and Adventures*, trans. E. S. Buchheim (London, 1913; Fr. orig., Paris, 1922, as L. Héritte de la Tour: *Mémoires de Louise Héritte-*

Pauline Viardot as Orpheus in Gluck's 'Orfeo ed Euridice' (in the version by Berlioz), Paris, c1860

Title-page of six 'Mélodies' (Paris:
G. Miran, 1884) by Pauline Viardot

Viardot: . . . notes . . . sur Garcia, Pauline Viardot, La
    Malibran, Louise Héritte-Viardot, et leur entourage)
T. Baker, trans.: 'Pauline Viardot Garcia to Julius
    Rietz – Letters of Friendship', *MQ*, i (1915), 350–80,
    526–59; ii (1916), 32–60
W. Rieck: 'Pauline Viardot – her Life and Career',
    Musical Courier (21 July 1921), 6–7, 18
T. Marix-Spire: 'Vicissitudes d'un opéra comique *La
    Mare au Diable* de George Sand et Pauline Viardot',
    Romanic Review, xxxv (1944), 125–46
— : 'Gounod and his First Interpreter, Pauline
    Viardot', *MQ*, xxxi (1945), 193–211, 299–317
F. Noske: *La mélodie française de Berlioz à Duparc*
    (Amsterdam, 1954; Eng. trans., rev., 1970)
T. Marix-Spire, ed.: *Lettres inédites de George Sand et de
    Pauline Viardot, 1839–1849* (Paris, 1959)
J. A. FitzLyon: *The Price of Genius: a Biography of
    Pauline Viardot* (London, 1964)
A. Rozanov: *Polina Viardo-Garsia* (Leningrad, 1969,
    2/1982)
A. FitzLyon: 'Pauline Viardot: a 150th Anniversary
    Tribute', *Opera*, vii (1971), 582–8
A. Zviguilsky, ed.: *Ivan Tourguénev: nouvelle corres-
    pondance inédite* (Paris, 1971) [8 letters from Viardot]
H. Granjard and A. Zviguilsky, eds.: *Lettres inédites de
    Tourguénev à Pauline Viardot et sa famille* (Lausanne,
    1972) [12 letters from Viardot]
P. Waddington: 'Pauline Viardot-Garcia as Berlioz's
    Counselor and Physician', *MQ*, lix (1973), 382–98
— : 'Dickens, Pauline Viardot, Turgenev: a Study in
    Mutual Admiration', *New Zealand Slavonic Journal*,
    i (1974), 55–73
*Cahiers Ivan Tourgueniev Pauline Viardot Maria
    Malibran* [pubn of Association des Amis D'Ivan
    Tourgueniev, Pauline Viardot et Maria Malibran]
    (Paris, 1977–)

G. Marek and M. Gordon-Smith: 'Pauline Viardot
    and Frédéric Chopin', *About the House*, v/7 (1978),
    28–31
B. Meister: *Nineteenth Century French Song* (Bloom-
    ington, IN, and London, 1980)
P. Waddington: 'Henry Chorley, Pauline Viardot and
    Turgenev: a Musical and Literary Friendship', *MQ*,
    lxvii (1981), 165–92
P. J. Viardot: 'Les jeudis de Pauline Viardot', *Revue
    internationale de musique française*, viii (1982), 87–104
P. Waddington: 'Turgenev and Pauline Viardot: an
    Unofficial Marriage', *Canadian Slavonic Papers*, xxvi
    (1984), 42–64
S. H. Stewart: *The Vocal Compositions of Pauline
    Viardot-Garcia* (thesis, Yale U., 1985)
G. Dulong: *Pauline Viardot: tragédienne lyrique* (Paris,
    2/1987)
Y. Sieffert-Rigaud: 'Pauline Viardot: femme et
    artiste', *Romantisme*, xvii/57 (1987), 17–32
A. F. Cofer: *Pauline Viardot-Garcia: the Influence of the
    Performer on Nineteenth Century Opera* (diss., U. of
    Cincinnati, 1988)
J. Rose: 'Chopin's Collaborator', *Keyboard Classics*,
    viii/6 (1988), 7–8
A. Tubeuf: 'Réparation à Mme Viardot', *L'avant-scène
    opéra*, no.108 (1988), 116 [*Don Pasquale* issue]
P. Citron, ed.: *Hector Berlioz: Correspondance générale*,
    v (Paris, 1989); vi (Paris, forthcoming)
N. G. Zekulin: *The Story of an Operetta: Le dernier
    sorcier by Pauline Viardot and Ivan Turgenev* (Munich,
    1989)
N. Barry: *Pauline Viardot: l'Egérie de George Sand et de
    Tourgueniev* (Paris, 1990)
D. Fischer-Dieskau: *Wenn Musik der Liebe Nahrung ist*
    (Stuttgart, 1990)

J. Ard: *The Songs of Pauline Viardot* (diss., Juilliard School, 1993)

JAMÉE ARD, APRIL FITZLYON

Viðar, Jórunn (*b* Reykjavík, 7 Dec 1918). Icelandic pianist and composer. She was a pupil of Árni Kristjánsson at the Reykjavík College of Music, from which she graduated in 1936. For the next two years she was a piano student at the Berlin Hochschule für Musik, and later studied composition with Vittorio Giannini at the Juilliard School, New York (1943–5). She completed her education with further piano studies in Vienna (1959–60). As a composer, she is best known for her songs. The modal language and metrical schemes of Icelandic folksong have been an important influence on her style, as is evident in the *Five Meditations on Icelandic Themes* for piano (1965), in the ballet scores, *Fire* (1950) and *Ólafur liljurós* ('Olafur "Lily-rose" ', 1952), and in the piano concerto, *Slátta* ('Hay-making', 1977).

WORKS
selective list

Stage: Fire, ballet, 1950; Ólafur liljurós [Olafur 'Lily-rose'], ballet, 1952
Orch: Slátta [Hay-Making], pf conc., 1977
Vocal: Olafsrímur Graenländings [The Ballad of Olafur the Greenlander], chorus, str, 1950; Icelandic Folk Songs, 1v, pf, 1972 (Reykjavík, 1974); 15 songs (texts by Icelandic poets), 1v, pf, 8 pubd (Reykjavík, 1977)
Chamber and pf: Variations on an Icelandic Song, vc, pf, 1962; 5 Meditations on Icelandic Themes, pf, 1965; Suite, vn, pf, 1974
Also incid. music for plays and films

Principal publisher: Iceland Music Information Centre

BIBLIOGRAPHY

A. M. Burt: *Iceland's Twentieth-Century Composers and a Listing of their Works* (Annandale, VA, 1977)
G. Bergendal: *New Music in Iceland* (Reykjavík, 1991)

AMANDA M. BURT,
THORKELL SIGURBJÖRNSSON

Vieu, Jane [Jeanne Elisabeth Marie; Valette, Pierre] (*b* 1871; *d* Paris, 8 April 1955). French composer. Little is known about Vieu's life. She composed about 100 works – orchestral, operatic, chamber, piano and vocal – some of which were published under the pseudonym Pierre Valette. Her musical idiom is decidedly 19th-century in its formal and harmonic character, despite the fact that she lived well into the 20th century. Her operetta *Arlette* received its première in Brussels, at the Théâtre Royal des Galeries St Hubert, on 28 October 1904.

From 1907 onwards, Vieu's compositions were published by Maurice Vieu, presumably her husband, with whom she later formed a publishing house (Maurice Vieu and Jane Vieu) in Paris. She wrote a solfège manual, *Dix leçons de solfège manuscrites à changement clès* (Paris, 1913), designed for use at the Paris Conservatoire and dedicated to the director Gabriel Fauré.

WORKS
selective list; complete list in SACEM

DRAMATIC
all published in Paris

Madame Tallien, ou Thérésa Cabarrus (pièce historique, 5 [8 tableaux], P. Berthelot and C. Roland), vs (1901)
La belle au bois dormant (féerie illustrée, L. Métivet), vs (1902)
Au bal de Flore (ballet-pantomime, 1, G. de Dubor), vs (1902)
Aladin (féerie chantée, 15 tableaux, Métivet), vs (1904)
Arlette (operetta, 3, Roland and L.Bouvet), Brussels, Théâtre Royal des Galeries St Hubert, 28 Oct 1904, vs (1905)
Sur le pont d'Avignon (fantaisie-opérette, 1, L. de Lahitte), vs (1937)
Piège d'amour (fantaisie-lyrique, 1, de la Vaudère), vs (1905)

OTHER WORKS

Orch, chamber and solo inst: Amoroso, intermezzo, vn, pf/mand, pf; Au coin du feu, vn/vc, pf; Au pays parfumé, 1v/vn, pf; Castillane, waltz, pf/(pf, mand); Chanson du soir, pf/(vn, pf/harp)/(vc, pf/harp); Colombine, air de ballet, pf/(pf, orch); Griserie de caresses, pf/(pf, orch) [also vocal arr.]; Ivresse et parfums, pf/(pf, orch); Lever de l'aurore, vn, pf; Marche des alguazils, pf, mand; Marquise bergers (Chanson Louis XV), pf/(pf, orch); Minuetto, str qt/pf qnt; Morceaux détachés, pf, orch; Nymphes et papillons, pf/(pf, orch); Séduction, pf/(vn, pf); Sérénade d'Aladin, pf/(vn, pf); Tarantelle, (pf, orch)/pf/harp; Valse des merveilleuses, orch/pf; Valse des rousses, pf/(vn, pf); pieces for solo pf
Vocal: Choeur du printemps, women's chorus; Ave Maria, 1v, pf/harp, vc, org ad lib; Chant des faneurs, lv, pf, mand/vn ad lib; Griserie de caresses, 1v [also inst arrs.]; Je vous salue (Salut à vous, Marie), 1v, pf/harp, vc, orch ad lib; O salutaris!, lv, vc/vn, org/pf; Sous la brume, 1v, gui, mand; songs, 1v, pf

BIBLIOGRAPHY

CohenE; *PazdirekH*; *SchmidlD*

JUDY S. TSOU

Vigneron-Ramackers, Josée (Christiane) (*b* Leopoldsburg, 25 Jan 1914). Belgian composer. She studied harmony and counterpoint at the Limburgsche Orgelschool in Hasselt, also receiving prizes there for piano and organ performance. She taught music and singing at the Koninklÿk Atheneum of Eisden and at the Atheneum of Maaseik (1934–69). In 1945 she founded and became director of the Muziekakademie in Eisden (based in Maasmechel from 1973), and a decade later founded a section of Jeugd en Muziek in the same city. She has composed most of her works for small ensembles. Initially influenced by impressionism, her music later became neo-classic in character. Her writings include the monographs *Van kleuterdreun naar notenleer* ('From Children's Songs to Solfeggio'; Eisden, 1967) and *Door volkslied tot notenleer* ('Solfeggio through Folksongs'; Eisden, 1968) as well as textbooks for beginning music theory.

WORKS
selective list

Stage: Het daghet (Y. P. Stasse), chorus, orch, 1938
Orch: Etudes, suite, chamber orch, 1957; Concertino, ob, chamber orch, 1958
Choral: 3 zangen van liefde en dood, 1972
Solo vocal (for 1v, pf unless otherwise stated): Rossignol, es-tu damné? (A. Bernier), 1943; 4 mélodies (Bernier), 1943; 3 mélodies (Bernier), 1v, chamber orch, 1956; Vocalise no.1, 1972; Vocalise no.2, 1981; 8 mélodies, suite, 1982; 10 vocalises, 1984
Chamber and solo inst: Duo rapsodique, cl, pf, 1958; Hommage à Maurice Van Guchte, 8 cl, 1958; Sax Qt, 1959; 3 études de style, ob/sax, 1960; Petit cortège presque chinois, pf, 2 timp, 1965; Ballade des oiseaux captifs, pf, 1967; 6 mini-studi, pf, 1968; Mobiles, suite, 4 cl, perc, str, 1969; 2 préludi, pf, 1971; Alternato, eng hn, pf, 1972; Hautes Fagnes, org, 1972; Variations sur Harbouya, gui, 1972; Sonatina, ob, org, 1984

MARIE CORNAZ

Vito-Delvaux, Berthe di (*b* Angleur, 17 May 1915). Belgian composer. After studying at the Conservatoire Royal de Musique in Liège, she was taught composition by Léon Jongen in Brussels and won the Prix de Rome (1943). She has composed in all musical genres, with a preference for opera and oratorio; although interested in contemporary music, in her own works she remained faithful to her traditional musical upbringing, rejecting serialism and atonality. In 1962 she was awarded the Grétry prize for the corpus of her operatic works.

WORKS
selective list

Stage: La Malibran, op.29 (opéra romantique, 3 acts and 2 scenes, N. de Sart), 1944–6; Les amants de Sestos, op.37 (drame lyrique, 2 acts and 3 scenes, F. Bodson), 1949; Abigail [Acts 1, 3, 4], op.45 (opéra, 3, J. de Sart), 1950–51, [Act 2], op.74, 1956; Le semeur du mal, op.77 (ballet, 2, Lazzini), 1957; Pourquoi, op.85 (ballet, 2, choreog. A. Bourdaloue), 1960; Magda: 'L'ange dans les ténèbres', op.87 (opéra-ballet, 4, J. de Sart), 1961; Le miroir, op.134 (ballet, 4 scenes, after B. Lotigiers: *La 4e dimension*), 1974; Grétry, op.137 (opéra comique, 3, J. Schetter), 1975–6
Orch: Images d'Espagne, op.13, 1941; Improvisation et Finale, op.30, pf, orch, 1944; Ouverture dramat-ique, op.32, 1945; Capriccio, op.43a, vn, chamber orch, 1949; Variations sur 'Te Hasselt langs de baan', op.78, str orch, 1957; 2 hn concs., op.93, 1963, op.100, 1965; Pf Conc., op.120, 1969; Nellovim, op.123, tpt, orch, 1970; Variations sur un vieux cramignon, op.132, 1972;
Chamber and solo inst: Pf Sonata, op.7, 1939; Suite, op.14, cl, pf, 1941; Suite, op.15, bn, pf, 1941; Suite, op.35, str qt, 1947; Va Sonata, op.60, 1953; Cl Sonatina, op.61, 1953; Suite, op.63, pf, 1954; Vn Sonata, op.81, 1959; Suite, op.98, ww qt, 1965; 3 mouvements, op.99, 2 pf, 1965; 3 pf sonatinas, op.102, 1965, op.108, 1966, op.110, 1966; Ww Qnt, op.112, 1966
Choral: L'enfant prodigue, op.10 (cantata, H. Liebrecht), chorus, orch, 1940; Héro et Léandre, op.11 (cantata, Bodson), chorus, orch, 1940; Gethsemani, op.132 (oratorio, S. Berth), T, mixed vv, orch, 1972
Solo vocal (for 1v, pf, unless otherwise stated): 6 mélodies, op.1, 1938; Extases: 6 chants d'amour, op.25 (N. de Sart), 1943; Source enchantée, op.41 (S. Boussa), S, pf, 1949; L'amour vainqueur, op.46 (Bodson), S, pf, 1951; Nuages gris, nuages bleus, op.80 (C. Morraye), 1959; La bien-aimée, op.106 (M. Carême), 1965; 6 mélodies, op.131 (S. Berth), 1972; Carnaval, op.138 (M.-L. Voilier), Mez/Bar, pf, perc, 1978

Principal publishers: Brogneaux (Brussels), CeBeDeM, Schott, Tyssen (Liège)

BIBLIOGRAPHY
CohenE
P. Legrain, ed.: *Dictionnaire des Belges* (Brussels, 1981)
CHRISTINE BALLMAN

Vivado (Orsini), Ida (*b* Tacna, 30 Aug 1908; *d* Santiago, 23 Oct 1989). Chilean composer and pianist. She took her degree in piano performance in 1941, but also studied traditional compositional techniques with Domingo Santa Cruz and dodecaphonic serialism with Frè Focke. Between 1981 and 1987 she was president of the Asociación Nacional de Compositores. She specialized in small-scale compositions with didactic purposes. Her works include *Picaresca* for contralto and orchestra (1977) and, for piano, *Tres preludios y tema con variaciones* (1952), Suite (1955), *Estudios* (1966) and *Ocho trozos* (1974).

BIBLIOGRAPHY
R. Bustos: 'Ida Vivado Orsini', *Revista musical chilena*, nos.142–4 (1978), 106–12
RAQUEL BUSTOS VALDERRAMA

Vizzana [Vizana], **Lucrezia Orsina** (*b* Bologna, 3 July 1590; *d* Bologna, 7 May 1662). Italian composer, singer and organist. About 1598 she entered the Camaldolese convent of S Christina, Bologna, where she probably learnt music from her aunt,

Camilla Bombacci, sometime convent organist, and from Ottavio Vernizzi, unauthorized music master at S Christina from about 1615 to about 1623. By contrast with the lavish, double-choir music by Adriano Banchieri, Gabriele Fattorini, G. B. Cesena (Biondi), and Ercole Porta dedicated to nuns at S Christina and almost certainly performed there, Vizzana's own motets, published in *Componimenti musicali de motetti concertati a 1 e più voci* (Venice, 1623), chiefly solos or duets with continuo, betray the influence of the *stile moderno* in their delicately virtuoso ornamentation for rhetorical effect, frequent insertion of phrases in declamatory style, juxtaposition of chromatic chords a 3rd apart, and, most notably, in expressive leaps from suspended dissonances, a technique Vizzana probably learnt from works by Claudio Monteverdi or Porta. (It is possible, but unlikely, that the four motets by 'Lucio Ursini' in German anthologies – *RISM* 1616^2, 1626^2, 1626^4 and 1627^1 – are in fact by Vizzana, although they do not overlap the 1623 publication.) Some motets were conceived for feast days at the convent; the greatest number are directed to Christ as redeemer or spouse, or as the object of veneration in the sacrament or on the cross; others may reflect the political struggles at S Christina from 1620 onwards. Vizzana's early retirement from music probably resulted from increasing ill health and from the convent's notorious battles with the diocesan curia between 1623 and 1647, partly provoked by music. According to her confessor, Vizzana was so traumatized by these events that she lost her mind.

BIBLIOGRAPHY

FétisB; *GerberL*; *SchillingE*; *SchmidlD*

J. L. A. Roche: *North Italian Church Music in the Age of Monteverdi* (Oxford, 1984), 28

J. Bowers: 'The Emergence of Women Composers in Italy, 1566–1700', *Women Making Music: the Western Art Tradition 1150–1950*, ed. J. Bowers and J. Tick (Urbana and Chicago, 1986), 116ff

C. Monson: 'Disembodied Voices: Music in the Nunneries of Bologna in the Midst of the Counter-Reformation', *The Crannied Wall: Women, Religion, and the Arts in Early Modern Europe* (Ann Arbor, 1992), 191ff

—— : 'La pratica della musica nei monasteri femminili bolognesi', *La cappella musicale nell'Italia della Controriforma*, ed. O. Mischiati and P. Russo (Cento, 1993), 143ff

—— : 'The Making of Lucretia Orsina Vizzana's *Componimenti musicali* (1623)', *Creative Women in Medieval and Early Modern Italy*, ed. E. A. Matter and J. W. Coakley (Philadelphia, forthcoming)

—— : *Disembodied Voices: Music and Culture in an Early Modern Italian Convent* (Berkeley, CA, forthcoming)

CRAIG MONSON

Vlad, Marina Marta (*b* Bucharest, 8 March 1949). Romanian composer and teacher. She graduated in 1973 from the Bucharest Conservatory, where her teachers included Tudor Ciortea, Ştefan Niculescu and Aurel Stroe for composition, and Zeno Vancea and Myriam Marbé for counterpoint. In the same year she was appointed professor of theory at the Conservatory.

Her compositions include *Mişcare simfonică* ('Symphonic Movement', 1979) and the cantata *Pământul ţării* ('Land of the Country', 1986), but specially notable are her chamber works (two string quartets, two string trios, sonatas for piano and for violin), in which atonality, virtuoso passages and subtle timbres are skilfully combined. Her didactic works and writings include *Solfeggii atonale* (Bucharest, 1990), suites for children and *Teoria muzicii* ('Theory of Music', 1990).

BIBLIOGRAPHY

T. Grigoriu: *Muzica şi nimbul poeziei* [The Music and Aura of Poetry] (Bucharest, 1986)

VIOREL COSMA

Vorlová, Sláva [Johnová, Miroslava] (*b* Náchod, 15 March 1894; *d* Prague, 24 Aug 1973). Czech composer. She studied singing for a short time at the Vienna Conservatory and took private lessons with Vítězslav Novák (composition) and Václav Stěpán (piano). She passed the state examinations in 1918, but discontinued composing until 1932; the following year she wrote her op.1 string quartet, which was given its première by the Ondříček Quartet. The success of this work encouraged her to continue her studies with František Maxian (piano) and Jaroslav Řídký (composition). After World War II she graduated from Řídký's class at the Prague Conservatory (1948) with *Symphony JM* op.18, dedicated to Jan Masaryk. Some works written during the war, including the cantata *Malička země* ('Little Country') and the work for women's chorus *Bílá oblaka* ('White Clouds'), contributed to the Czech war resistance; at the same time her chamber works gained recognition in Europe.

After the communist regime took power in the 1950s, Vorlová's artistic opportunities and social position were ruined. To avoid the frustration imposed by doctrinal mass culture, she turned to folksongs and historical themes in her works, as in the operas *Zlaté ptáče* ('The Golden Bird', 1949–50), *Rozmarýnka* (1952–3) and *Náchodská kasace* ('Náchod Cassation', 1955). She also wrote songs and other compositions in jazz style

Kybernetické studie, op.56, 1962; Double Conc., op.59, ob, harp, orch, 1963; Dedikace [Dedication], op.64, 1965; Bhukhar [Feverish Birds], op.67, 1965; Model Kinetic, op.69, ballet, 1966–7; Chamber Conc., op.74, db, str, 1968; Korelace [Correlation], op.75, b cl, pf, str, 1968; Polarizace [Polarization], op.84, harp, wind, perc, 1970; Emergence, op.92, vn, orch, 1973

Vocal: Maličká země [Little Country], op.7 (cantata, Vorlová), solo vv, chorus, orch, 1941–2; Bílá oblaka [White Clouds], op.8 (Vorlová), female chorus, orch, 1942–3; Stesk [Longing], op.13 (O. Scheinpflugová), 1v, pf, 1946; Zpěvy Gondwany [Songs of Gondwana], op.19 (V. H. Roklan), solo vv, chorus, orch, 1948–9; Tango cantabile, op.23 (Roklan), 1v, orch, 1951; My lidé dvacátého století [We People of the 20th Century], op.46 (Roklan), chorus, children's chorus, orch, 1959; Magellan vesmíru [Magellan of the Universe], op.49 ('modern oratorio', Roklan), solo vv, mixed chorus, children's chorus, orch, 1960; other songs and choral works

Chamber and solo inst: Bezkydy Str Qt, op.1, 1933; Str Qt, op.5, 1939; Nonet, op.10, 1944; 5 Bagatelles, op.15, vc, pf, 1947; Str Qt, op.22, 1950; Šarády [Puzzles], op.32, 2 pf, 1953, orchd as op.32b, 1956; Fantazie na české lidové téma [Fantasy on a Czech Folksong], op.33, va, 1953; Pantumy [Pantoumes], op.47, harp, 1959; Miniatury, op.55, b cl, pf, 1962; Serenata desta, op.58, fl, b cl, pf, 1962; Dessins tetraharpes, op.60, 4 harps, 1963; Sonata lirica da tre, op.62, vn, va, gui, 1964; Droleries basclarinettiques, op.63, b cl, 1964; Il fauno danzante, op.66, b cl, 1965; 6 pro 5, op.71, brass qnt, 1967; Colloquii, op.82, 4 fl dolce, 1969; Efemeridy, op.83, cymbalom, 1969; Imanence, op.88, fl, b cl, pf, perc, 1971; other chamber pieces, educational music

Principal publishers: Czech Music Fund, Panton

BIBLIOGRAPHY

CohenE; *ČSHS*; *ČSS*

J. Vacková: 'Maličká země S. Vorlové', *Tempo* [Prague], xx (1948), 133

V. Šefl: 'Rozmarýnka, lidová zpěvohra S. Vorlové' [Rozmarýnka, a Folk Opera by Vorlová], *HRo*, viii (1955), 472

E. Pensdorfová: 'Na památku statečné ženy-skladatelky' [In Memory of a Brave Woman Composer], *HRo*, xxvi (1973), 463–4

V. H. Roklan: 'Konfese Slávy Vorlové', *OM*, v (1973), 155

A. Šerých: *Sláva Vorlová* (Prague, forthcoming)

ANNA ŠERÝCH

Sláva Vorlová

(under the pseudonym Mira Cord) in an attempt to earn money, but these jazz works were never performed. She was the first modern Czech composer to employ the trumpet and bass clarinet as solo instruments in concertos. Her late works employ modernistic techniques without sacrificing sonority and melodic charm; beginning with *Bhukhar* ('Feverish Birds', 1965), Vorlová devised her own numerological method for serial music, producing some of her best works. Some of her compositions have been recorded by Panton and by Supraphon.

WORKS
selective list

Stage: Zlaté ptáče [The Golden Bird], op.27 (fairy-tale opera, prol, 6 scenes, V. H. Roklan), 1949–50; Rozmarýnka, op.30 (folk opera, Roklan, after V. Hálek), 1952–3; Náchodská kasace [Náchod Cassation], op.37 (historical opera, Roklan, after A. Jirásek), 1955; Dva světy [Two Worlds], op.45 (1, Roklan, after B. V. Ron), 1958

Orch: Sym. JM, op.18, 1947–8; Božena Němcová, op.24, suite, 1950–1; Symfonická předehra FOK [Sym. Prelude FOK], op.25, 1951; Pastorální koncert [Pastoral Conc.], Eb, op.28, ob, orch, 1952; 3 české tance, op.29, 1952–3; Tpt Conc., a, op.31, 1953; Slovácký Conc., op.35, va, orch, 1954; Doudlebské tance [Dances from Doudleby], op.36, 1953–4; Cl Conc., d, op.41, 1957; Duryňské tance [Dances from Thuringia], op.44, 1957; Fl Conc., b, op.48, 1959; Conc., op.50, b cl, str, 1961;

Voronina, Tat'yana Alexandrovna (*b* Leningrad [now St Petersburg], 12 Jan 1933). Russian composer and pianist. She studied at the Leningrad Conservatory with Orest Yevlakhov, for composition, and Moisey Khal'fin, for piano, graduating with two diplomas (1957–8); in 1960 she was appointed to teach chamber music there. She has given many concerts, performing not only the classical repertory but also contemporary works, by Leningrad and Lithuanian

composers in particular. In her own compositions, melodic lines are developed according to the principles of monody, while textures are heterophonous. The style is detailed and intense: before the 1970s her desire for detailed elaboration proved an obstacle to the creation of large-scale works, but later compositions show that she has been able to achieve a balance between the demands of larger formal structures and her own particular musical language. Voronina's music is also lyrical and intimate, a kind of ceaseless monologue in which the voice attains special significance and instrumental themes are vocally inspired.

WORKS
selective list

Orch: Suite, 1953; Conc.-Ballade, pf, orch, 1960

Choral: Pamyatnik [Memorial] (A. Lunacharsky), chorus, org, orch, 1967; Tristishch'ye (chamber cantata, Voronina), 1v, chorus, 1974; Tomu nazad odno mgnoven'ye [T'was One Instant Ago] (cantata, M. Lermontov and A. S. Pushkin), chorus, orch, 1987

Other vocal: 5 Russian Folksongs, arr. 1v, pf, 1962; Pesni odinokogo strannika [Songs of a Lonely Wanderer] (M. Basyo), 1v, 3 vn, 1966; Veresk [Heather] (R. Burns), 1v, pf, 1970; Do kontsa [Till the End; poem in memoriam A. D. Sakharov] (N. Rubtzov and B. Chichibabin), 2v, pf, 1991

Chamber and solo inst: Str Qt, 1959; Kontsertnaya fantaziya na temï operï 'Voyna i mir' [Fantasia-Conc. on Themes from Prokofiev's War and Peace], pf, 1962; Str Qt, 1969; 6 Pieces, pf, 1972, orchd A. Knayfel'; Pf Sonata, 1976; Sonata, 2 vn, 1981; Mini-ballet, suite, vn, pf, 1989; Sonata, fl, vn, 1991

BIBLIOGRAPHY

K. Yuzak: 'Kvartet T. Voroninoy' [Voronina's Quartet], *SovM* (1960), no.7, pp.48–9

OLGA MANULKINA

Vuiet, Caroline. *See* WUIET, CAROLINE.

W

Walker, Gwyneth Van Anden (*b* New York, 22 March 1947). American composer. She began composing at the age of two, and developed an interest in folk music and rock and roll before beginning formal music studies. She graduated from Brown University (BA 1968) and from Hartt School of Music, University of Hartford (MM 1970, DMA 1976), where her principal composition teacher was Arnold Franchetti. After teaching at Oberlin (1976–80), she worked part-time at Hartford Conservatory and Hartt School of Music but left teaching in 1982 to pursue composition full-time. On moving to a dairy farm in Vermont she began to take a grass roots approach to composition, writing for local performers of varying skills, from community and school groups to professional orchestras and concert soloists, as well as for national organizations such as the Women's Philharmonic. In her concern for accessibility she has brought familiar aspects of life to the concert platform (in *Three Songs in Celebration of the Family Farm* the chorus imitates the sound of farm machinery and cows, and the conductor uses milking gestures) and has staged performances at such non-traditional sites as a dairy barn. She has even linked compositions with athletics: in *Holding the Towel*, a comic song cycle for Super Bowl Sunday 1992, and, most notably, in *Match Point*, when the tennis player Billie Jean King performed as guest soloist at Lincoln Center, bouncing tennis balls on percussion and performing a mimed rally with the conductor (the composer had been a nationally ranked junior tennis player). Melodic gesture and texture are the prime sources of organization and motion in Walker's compositions. Her harmony is diatonic, often consisting of non-referential triads with some quartal harmonies. Her orchestration features wind, and especially brass, prominently. In 1988 she helped found the Consortium of Vermont Composers, of which she later became director.

WORKS
selective list

Orch: Fanfare for the Washington Festival Orch, 1978; Fanfare, Interlude & Finale, 1980; Essay for Orch, 1985; Match Point, 1985 [also for band]; The Light of 3 Mornings, 1987; Bicentennial Suite, 1990; Open the Door, 1990; Up-Front Conc., hand drums, orch, 1993

Chamber: Fl Sonata, 1978; Raise the Roof!, brass qnt, 1987; Braintree Qnt, ww qnt, opt. chorus/audience, 1988; 3 American Portraits, str qt, 1988; Salem Reel, vn/cl, vc, pf, 1989

Choral: Cheek to Cheek (C. Tucker), mixed chorus, pf, 1978; The Radiant Dawn (R. H. Calkins), mixed chorus, org, vc, 1978; The Troubled Sweet of Her (Amante), mixed chorus, 1978; As the Stars had Told (H. D.), mixed chorus, org, opt. chimes, 1979; White Horses (E. E. Cummings), mixed chorus, pf, 1979; Sounding Joy [updated tune by J. Morgan], mixed chorus, 1985; 3 Songs in Celebration of the Family Farm (M. Holden), mixed chorus, orch/pf, 1988; American Ballads (folksongs), mixed chorus, fl, 1992

Vocal: My love walks in velvet (Walker), medium v/high v/chorus, pf, 1978; Though love be a day (E. E. Cummings), high v, pf, 1979; Fergus Falling (G. Kinnell), spkr, fl, vn, va, vc, 1991; Holding the Towel: Sportsongs (M. Swenson), high v, pf, 1991

Many works for pf and org solo

Principal publisher: ESC

BIBLIOGRAPHY
Anderson2; *WAM*

J. L. Zaimont and K. Famera, eds.: *Contemporary Concert Music by Women* (Westport, CT, 1981), esp. 130–31

J. Rockwell: 'Rondi Charleston Wins Art Song Vocal Competition', *New York Times* (6 May 1990) [review of *Though Love be a Day*]

T. Pfaff: 'Mostly New Music', *San Francisco Examiner* (5 Nov 1990) [review of *Open the Door*]

Gwyneth Walker (Boston, 1991, rev. 1992) [E. C. Schirmer composer brochure]

J. MICHELE EDWARDS

Wallach, Joelle (*b* New York, 29 June 1946). American composer. She spent part of her childhood in Morocco, then returned to New York to attend the Juilliard Preparatory School, where she studied the piano, singing, theory and composition. She obtained degrees in composition at Sarah Lawrence College (BA 1967) and Columbia University (MA 1969), and, as a pupil of John

Corigliano, at the Manhattan School of Music (DMA 1984). She has received several awards, including one from the National Orchestral Association in 1991 for *The Tiger's Tail*; commissions include a work for the New York Choral Society in 1994. Wallach's works are widely performed in the USA and Europe and several have been recorded.

Her sacred works use a post-Wagnerian tonal idiom, while the more experimental orchestral works exhibit a wide range of influences – including Hebrew chant and North African dance traditions – and effects.

WORKS
selective list

Dramatic: The Assent of the Swallow, nar, solo vv, chamber orch, 1985; The King's 12 Moons (chamber opera, 1), 1989

Orch: Glimpses, 1981; Turbulence, Stillness and Saltation, chamber orch, 1983; The Tiger's Tail, 1990; Shadow, Sighs and Songs of Longing, vc, orch, 1991; Where angels may lie down among us, chamber orch, 1992

Other inst: Organal Voices, vib, bn, 1982; Forewords, tpt, hn, 1983; Str Qt, 1986; O llama de amor viva, ww qnt, 1987; Cl Qnt, 1989; Sticky Grimaces, Toothy Grins, perc, pf, 1991; Music for Manda, 2 gui, 1992; Sweet Briar Elegies, sax, 8 vc, 1992

Vocal: On the beach at night alone, solo v, SATB, 1977; 3 Whitman Visions, SATB, 1977; 3 Short Sacred Anthems, Tr chorus, 1980; Of Honey and of Vinegar, Mez, 2 pf, 1982; 5 American Echoes, SATB, 1984; Orison of St Theresa, SATB, (str orch)/(str qt, harp)/(pf), 1985; 3 Spanish Songs, 1v, pf, 1985; Cantares de los Perdis, 1v, tuba, timp, crotales, 1987; 2 Songs, 1v, b cl/heckelphone, 1988; 3 Whitman Songs, Bar, cl, hn, vc, 1989; Love in the Early Morning, S, pf, 1990; Midnight Menageries, children's chorus, pf, 1991; Toward a Time of Renewal, 4 solo vv, chorus, orch, 1993

Principal publisher: ACA

LISA B. ROBINSON

Wandall, Tekla Griebel (*b* Randers, 1866; *d* Copenhagen, 28 June 1940). Danish composer. From the age of six she was taught the piano by her father, Theodor Griebel. In 1885 she decided to become an opera composer and prepared herself for the entrance examination at the Kongelige Danske Musikkonservatorium in Copenhagen, where she studied singing, the piano and music theory (1889–91). In 1896 she studied instrumentation with Felix Draeseke in Dresden. Thereafter her opportunities for composing became fairly restricted: after her mother's death in 1891 she took over the household and when in 1902 she married the aging theologian Frederik Wandall, by whom she had a child, she had to support the

family by giving music lessons. She acquired a benefactor in the music publisher Henrik Hennings, who published some of her music and, in 1894, arranged a performance of her opera Skøn Karen (as Schön Karin) in Breslau (now Wrocław). The opera was given at the Kongelige Teater in Copenhagen in 1899. In all, she composed some 115 works, of which about 20 are published. She wrote on music theory: *En epokegjørende Opfindelse paa Stryge-Musikens Omraade* ('An Epoch-Making Discovery in the String Music Field'; Copenhagen, 1886), *Musikteori i korte Traek: Hjaelpemiddel ved Sangundervisningen* ('Music Theory in Brief: an Aid to Teaching Singing'; Copenhagen, 1900) and *Tonernes Mikrokosmos* (unpublished); she also wrote poems, short stories and *Rigmor Vording* (1915), a quasi-autobiography.

WORKS
selective list

Stage: Don Juan de Marana (opera), 1886; Skøn Karen (opera, E. Christiansen), 1894 [perf. with Ger. text], 1899; I Rosentiden (ballet), 1895

Choral: Fred! (Peace cantata, B. Bjørnson), S, A, SSAA, pf, *c*1899; 2 other cantatas, 1914, *c*1920; Leonore (G. A. Bürger), female chorus, rec, pf

Pf: Folkevise-Album; Dannebrogs-Marsch; Klaver-kompositioner, 2 bks; Musikalsk Børnehave [pf method], 1898

Songs: Den flyvende Hollaender, 1894; 2 Sange, 1894; 3 Lieder, 1894; Bercés par la nuit, 1894; 5 Sange, 1894; Nocturne, 1919; 3 Sange, 1928

BIBLIOGRAPHY

E. Dahlerup: 'Tekla Griebel-Wandall – en biografi', *KIM-NYT: medlemsblad for Kvinder i Musik* (1989), no.17, pp.27–30; no.18, pp.16–19

INGE BRULAND

Wang, Qiang (*b* Yantai, Shandong, People's Republic of China, 23 Jan 1935). Chinese composer. Her desire to forge her own unique style rooted in Chinese tradition is evident in works for orchestra, chorus and many film scores. The early instruction she received after joining an army art troupe at the age of 12 inspired her first interest in musical structure. She later studied Chinese traditional folk music, Western music theory and composition as a prizewinning student of Ding Shande at the Shanghai Conservatory. After graduation (1960), she joined the composition faculty there and was appointed associate professor in 1986. In 1959 she began a 20-year series of travels to Inner Mongolia, Yunnan, Fujian and Hainan Island collecting folksongs, which have inspired many of her compositions. A member of both the Shanghai and the China musicians' associations, she retired from teaching in 1991 to compose full time in Hong Kong. Recent work incorporates the languages of folk music, painting and weaving.

WORKS
selective list

Inst: Soldiers' Dance, chamber orch, ob, cl, hn, tpt, trbn, vn, va, vc, snare drum, accordion, 1951; Ga Da Mei Lin, vc/orch, 1960; Trumpet and Drum, orch, 1979; Songs of Hong Hu, fl, va, harp, 1981; Jiu Jie Bian (Folk Dance), chamber orch, *c*1983; 12 Pieces, 8 vc, 1988; 5 Duets, vc, db, 1990; 12 Pieces, zheng [zither] qt, 1990; Feeling Sad, Selling Dumplings, 2 folksong arrs., fl, zheng, er-hu [bowed lute], 1991; Aspiration, ov., orch, 1992; 2 Chinese Folk Dances, Chin. orch, 1993; Love, fantasy-ov., orch, 1993

Choral: Rivers of Happiness, cantata, chorus, orch, 1958, collab. 3 other composers

Film scores (orch): The Magic Gourd, 1963; Wait till Tomorrow, 1963; Aurora, 1979; Xue Hua and Lizi Qiu, TV film, 1980; The Girls Selling Cokes, TV film, 1982; Song of Life, 1983

Principal publishers: People's Music Publishing House, Beijing; Shanghai Literature and Art Publishing House

BIBLIOGRAPHY

CohenE
Ding Shande, Ni Ruilin and Zhu Jian: 'Biographical Sketches of Modern Chinese Composers', *Music Technology* (Hong Kong, 1985), Aug, 238 [Chin. text]
J. L. Zaimont and others, eds.: *The Musical Woman: an International Perspective*, iii: *1986–90* (Westport, CT, 1991), 177 [discography]

JOYCE LINDORFF

Ward, Amy. See WOODFORDE-FINDEN, AMY.

Warren, Elinor Remick (*b* Los Angeles, 23 Feb 1900; *d* Los Angeles, 27 April 1991). American composer and pianist. Her parents were accomplished amateur musicians. After local study in Los Angeles and a year at Mills College, she went to New York in 1920 for further work with Frank LaForge and Clarence Dickinson; she also attended masterclasses in Los Angeles with Leopold Godowsky and later with Arnold Schoenberg, and undertook private study in Paris with Nadia Boulanger (1959). Her early works came to the attention of Charles Cadman and George Enescu, who encouraged her. By 1922 her compositions were appearing in the catalogues of leading New York music firms. From 1921 to the early 1940s she toured the USA as accompanist and assisting artist with leading singers such as Florence Easton, Lawrence Tibbett, Richard Crooks, Margarete Matzenauer and Lucrezia Bori, who were among the many artists to sing her songs.

Elinor Remick Warren

The New York première (1936) of *The Harp Weaver* brought Warren critical attention as a composer in the larger orchestral forms. The première by Albert Coates and the Los Angeles PO of *The Legend of King Arthur* (1940) established her reputation internationally, and her larger works received performances by important orchestras under such conductors as Pierre Monteux, John Barbirolli, André Kostelanetz, Wilfrid Pelletier and Alfred Wallenstein.

The beauty of nature – particularly the West, where Warren lived and worked most of her life – inspired many compositions, among them *The Crystal Lake* (1946), *Singing Earth* (1950, revised 1978), Suite for Orchestra (1954, revised 1960), and *Along the Western Shore* (1954). Mysticism is also a prominent theme, notably in *The Harp Weaver* (1932), *The Legend of King Arthur* (1939, revised 1974), Requiem (1965) and a large body of smaller works.

A prolific composer, Warren was active into her 90th year; her catalogue contains 200 published compositions, including works for orchestra, chorus and orchestra, chamber ensemble, voice and chorus. She has been described as 'the only woman among the group of prominent American neo-romanticists that includes Howard Hanson, Samuel Barber and Gian Carlo Menotti'

(Ammer). A review of Requiem in the *Los Angeles Herald-Examiner* (4 April 1966) remarks that 'The choral writing . . . lies gratefully for the voice without lapsing into platitudes. Canon and counterpoint are incorporated freely, expertly and unobtrusively', and describes the work as 'a dignified, meditative and distinguished contribution to choral literature'. Her orchestral works have been characterized as 'emotionally intense, dramatic, colorful' (*American Music*, Fall 1991).

Warren's honours include nomination as Woman of the Year in Music by the *Los Angeles Times* (1953); she won the GEDOK competition in Mannheim (1961) for *Abram in Egypt*, given at the Israel Festival (1976), and she was recipient of an NEA Fellowship (1976). She bequeathed her memorabilia, books, manuscripts, scores and recordings to the New York Public Library at Lincoln Center.

WORKS
selective list

CHORAL

The Harp Weaver (E. St V. Millay), Bar, women's chorus, orch/(harp, pf), 1932; Merry-go-round (A. MacLeish), male vv, pf, 1934; The Fountain (S. Teasdale), female vv, pf, 1937; The Legend of King Arthur [orig. The Passing of King Arthur] (A. Tennyson), T, Bar, chorus, orch, 1939, rev. 1974; The Sleeping Beauty (Tennyson), S, Bar, B-bar, chorus, orch, 1941; To my Native Land (H. W. Longfellow), chorus, opt. orch, 1942

Transcontinental (A. M. Sullivan), Bar, chorus, orch/pf, 1958; Abram in Egypt (Dead Sea Scrolls; Bible, *Genesis*), Bar, chorus, orch, 1959; Our Beloved Land (S. Bonner [E. R. Warren]), chorus, orch/pf, 1963; The Night will Never Stay (E. Farjeon), female vv, pf, 1964; Requiem (Lat., Eng. trans. Warren), S, Bar, chorus, orch/chamber orch, 1965 [incl. Sanctus (1965)]; A Joyful Song of Praise (Bible, *Isaiah* xxv), chorus, org, 1966

My heart is ready (Ps cviii), chorus, org, 1967: Hymn of the City (W. C. Bryant), chorus, org/orch, 1970; Little Choral Suite (R. B. Bennett, L. W. Reese), female vv, pf, 1973; Night Rider (R. L. Stevenson), chorus, pf, 1975; Good Morning, America! (C. Sandburg), nar, chorus, orch, 1976; Songs for Young Voices (Stevenson, C. Rossetti, Teasdale), female vv, pf, 1976

White Iris (B. Carman), female vv, pf, 1979; Praises and Prayers (Bk of Common Prayer, J. Byrom and others), (chorus, org, brass insts)/(unacc. chorus), 1981; Time, you Old Gypsy-Man (R. Hodgson), chorus, pf, 1981; Now Welcome, Summer! (G. Chaucer), chorus, chamber orch/pf, 1984; On the Echoing Green (W. Blake), chorus, chamber orch/pf, 1985

SONGS
for 1v and piano, unless otherwise stated

A Song of June (B. Carman), 1918; The Heart of a Rose (A. Noyes), 1922; I have seen dawn (J. Masefield), 1924; Dreams (B. Fenner), 1927; Lady Lo-Fu (M. M. Wood), 1v, fl, cl, pf, 1927; Silent Noon (D. G. Rossetti), 1928; Piano (D. H.

Lawrence), 1932; White Horses of the Sea (H. Henry), 1932; By a Fireside (T. Jones jr), 1934; Sweetgrass Range (E. F. Piper), 1934; Wander Shoes (H. C. Crew), 1936; Snow towards Evening (M. Cane), 1937

The Nights Remember (H. Vinal), 1937; Christmas Candle (K. L. Brown), 1v, fl, cl, pf, 1940; If you have forgotten (S. Teasdale), 1940; King Arthur's Farewell, Bar, pf/orch, 1941 [from The Legend of King Arthur]; Heather (M. Wilkinson), 1942; We Two (W. Whitman), 1946; Singing Earth (C. Sandburg), S, orch/pf, 1950, rev. 1978; Sonnets (E. St V. Millay), S, str orch/str qt, 1954; For you with Love (L. Untermeyer), 1967; many others

INSTRUMENTAL

Orch and chamber: Wind Qnt, *c*1935–6; Scherzo, 1938; The Fountain, 1938; Intermezzo, 1939, rev. 1974 [from The Legend of King Arthur]; The Crystal Lake, 1946; Poem, va, pf, 1948; Along the Western Shore: Dark Hills, Nocturne, Sea Rhapsody, 1954; Suite: Black Cloud Horses, Cloud Peaks, Ballet of the Midsummer Sky, Pageant across the Sky, 1954, rev. 1960; Sym. in 1 Movt, 1970

Pf: Frolic of the Elves, 1924; The Fountain, 1933; Dark Hills, 1946; Poem, 1946; Sea Rhapsody, 1946; The Lake at Evening, 1988

Pf transcrs.: J. S. Bach: Bist du bei mir, 1939; S. Foster: 3 Melodies, 1940

Org: Carillon Theme, 1958; Processional March, 1967

Principal publishers: Ditson, C. Fischer, Flammer, Galaxy, Lawson Gould, H. W. Gray, Presser, E. C. Schirmer, G. Schirmer

BIBLIOGRAPHY

LePageWC, ii

E. Goodland: 'Composer Elinor Remick Warren Brings Musical Honors to the City of her Birth', *Los Angeles Times* (27 Dec 1953)

E. Lerner: *The Music of Selected Contemporary American Women Composers: a Stylistic Analysis* (Amherst, MA, 1978)

C. Ammer: *Unsung: a History of Women in American Music* (Westport, CT, 1980)

S. P. Finger: *Women Composers in Los Angeles: 1918–1939* (diss., U. of California, Los Angeles, 1986)

V. Bortin: *Elinor Remick Warren: her Life and her Music* (Metuchen, NJ, 1987)

—— : *Bio-Bibliographies in Music: Elinor Remick Warren* (Westport, CT, 1992)

VIRGINIA BORTIN

Wartel [née Andrien], **(Atale) Thérèse (Annette)** (*b* Paris, 2 July 1814; *d* Paris, 6 Nov 1865). French pianist, teacher, composer and critic. Educated at the Paris Conservatoire, she studied with Louis Adam and Fromental Halévy, winning prizes in piano and practical harmony in 1830. From 1831 to 1838 she was on the staff of the Conservatoire as an accompanist and teacher of solfège, but was never promoted to the piano department. In 1833 she married the tenor Pierre-François Wartel. After several years based in Vienna she returned to Paris, where she became a central figure in chamber music circles and was renowned particularly as an interpreter of Beethoven. Her last major publication was a series of essays on his piano sonatas: *Leçons écrites sur les sonates pour piano seul de L. van Beethoven* (Paris, 1865). Earlier writings, including a notable review of Louise Farrenc's Nonet (1850), appeared in the *Revue et gazette musicale de Paris*.

Little is known about her activity as a composer before 1847. Two works only, both for piano, were published in Paris: *Six études de salon* op.10 (1850), dedicated to Halévy, and an Andante op.11 (1851), dedicated to Farrenc. These and an unpublished Andante cantabile in F♯ (1847) reveal Wartel as a composer who combined a late Classical sense of harmonic procedure, motivic working and phrase structure with the forms and rich pianistic textures of her time. She was keen to explore techniques of delineating a legato melody from a complex accompaniment, employing Sigismond Thalberg's 'three-handed' technique in two of the *Six études*. As was noted at the time, the power and scale of the sixth *Etude*, which, like the first and the fifth, is based on a single idea, goes beyond the traditional confines of a salon study. The Andante op.11 presents a hymn-like theme with accompaniments of increasing intensity, the whole welded together by a thematically derived middle section. The Andante cantabile of 1847 is a salon miniature of a mere 25 bars.

WORKS
all for piano

Andante cantabile, F♯, 1847; 6 études de salon, op.10 (Paris, 1850); Andante, op.11 (Paris, 1851); Fantasie (Leipzig, n.d.)

BIBLIOGRAPHY

FétisB; *FétisBS*; *Grove1†* (A. Chitty)

KATHARINE ELLIS

Watson Henderson, Ruth (Louise) (*b* Toronto, 23 Nov 1932). Canadian composer, pianist and organist. She studied the piano at the Toronto Conservatory of Music with Viggo Kihl (1937–42) and Alberto Guerrero (1945–52) and at the Mannes College of Music, New York, with Hans Neumann (1952–4); she also took composition lessons with Oskar Morawetz, Richard Johnston and Samuel Dolin. Her début as a concert pianist was in Toronto in 1952, and she has held posts as organist and choir director in Winnipeg (1957–62) and Kitchener (1962–8), and in Toronto as accompanist to the Festival Singers (1968–79) and the Toronto Children's Chorus (1978–). A large

part of her output consists of well-crafted choral compositions in a predominantly tonal idiom with colourful sonorities, of which the best-known work is the first *Missa brevis* (1976). She was a prizewinner at the GEDOK competition in Mannheim in 1989 and in 1992 her *Voices of Earth* won the national choral award from the Association of Canadian Choral Conductors. Her compositions for young people include a short music drama about Inuit children, *Clear Sky and Thunder* (1983).

WORKS
selective list

Orch and chamber: Ob Sonata, 1976; Suite, vc, pf, 1984; Suite, str orch, 1985

Sacred choral: Pater noster, SATB, 1973; Missa brevis, unacc. chorus, 1976; Sing to the Lord a new song, 1977; Lullaby for the Christ Child, unison vv, 1979; A Sequence of Dreams, choral suite, mixed chorus, pf, 1983; Christ is our cornerstone, SATB, org, 1984; Songs of the Nativity, 1984; The Beatitudes, 1985; Barnyard Carols, 1986; Creation's Praise, 1986; Eternal ruler of the ceaseless round, 1986; The Bloor Street Mass, 1987; Missa brevis no.2, 1989; The Last Straw (christmas cantata, Thury), 1990; Gloria, 1993

Secular choral: 2 Canadian Folksongs, arrs. (G. V. Thompson), 1975: Les Raftsmen, Bar, SATB, Mary Ann, SATB, pf; Musical Animal Tales (Thompson), SA, pf, 1979; The Ballad of St George, S, B, SATB, org, harp, 2 tpt, 1981; Through the Eyes of Children (Thompson), children's vv, pf, 1981; Crazy Times, 1986; Dandelion Parachutes, 5 songs, 1986; Crazy Times, 1989; 5 Ontario Folksongs, arrs., 1990; Voices of the Earth (Lampman, St Francis of Assisi), 1992

Children's drama: Clear Sky and Thunder (music drama, L. Peterson), SSA children's vv, fl, pf, perc, 1983

Kbd: Suite [in memory of Alberto Guerrero], pf, 1978; Chromatic Partita, org, 1989; Two at the Zoo: 4 Duets, pf, 1989

GAYNOR G. JONES

Webenau, Julia von. *See* BARONI-CAVALCABÒ, JULIA.

Weichsell [Weichsel], Elizabeth. *See* BILLINGTON, ELIZABETH.

Weigl, Vally [Valerie] (*b* Vienna, 11 Sept 1889; *d* New York, 25 Dec 1982). American music therapist, composer and teacher, of Austrian birth. She studied the piano in Vienna with Richard Robert and, at Vienna University, musicology with Guido Adler and composition with Karl Weigl, whom she later married. She taught for a period as Robert's assistant and also worked with Karl Weigl at the Musicological Institute of Vienna University. In 1938 she and her husband moved to New York, where she continued to compose and perform and took up teaching appointments at the Institute for Avocational Music and the American Theater Wing. After receiving the Master's degree from Columbia University in 1955, she pursued a lifelong interest in music therapy by becoming chief music therapist at the New York Medical College. She also taught at the New York New School and directed research projects at Mount Sinai Hospital's Psychiatric Division and at a Home for the Aged in New York City. She contributed many papers to music therapy literature and lectured widely in the USA and abroad. In addition she devoted much of her time to the preservation of the considerable musical legacy of Karl Weigl, a portion of whose output, though well-known in Europe, had not yet been introduced to the USA. In 1964 she became chairperson of the Friends' Arts for World Unity Committee, for which she organized international cultural programmes. She was awarded many grants, including ones by the ACA and the Mark Rothko Foundation as well as the 1976 NEA Fellowship grant. Her music has been widely performed and published.

WORKS
selective list

Chamber and inst: Bagatelle, pf 4 hands, 1953; Mood Sketches, ww qnt, 1953–4; New England Suite, cl/fl, vc, pf, 1955; Five Occurrences, ww qnt, 1977; other works and pf pieces for children

Vocal–Chamber: Songs of Remembrance (E. Dickinson), Mez, fl/cl, pf, opt. cl/va, 1952; Songs beyond Time (song cycle, F. Blankner), S/T, vn/fl, pf, 1956; Dear Earth (Blankner), Mez, hn, pf, vn, vc, 1956; Lyrical Suite from 'All my Youth' (Blankner), Mez, fl/cl, pf, vc, 1956; Nature Moods (H. Woodbourne), S/T, fl/cl, vn, 1956; Songs from 'Do not Awake me' (M. Edey), A, fl/vn, pf, 1957; Songs from 'No Boundary' (L. Marshall), Mez, va/cl/vn, pf, 1963; 5 songs from 'Take my Hand' (E. Segal), Mez, fl, cl, b cl/vc, pf, 1975; Revelation, S, str qt, 1982

Choral: Prayer of St Francis of Assisi, women's vv, fl, pf, 1945; The Nightwind (R. L. Stevenson), unacc. mixed vv, 1956; Fear no more (W. Shakespeare), SATB, pf, 1958; Let there be Music, unacc. women's vv, 1960; Let my Country Awake (R. Davidson), S, A, T, B, chorus, pf, 1967; 3 Choral Songs of the South-West (P. Benton), SATB, pf, 1967; Shelter for All (K. Boulding), S, A, T, B, pf, 1967; The People, Yes! (C. Sandburg), S, A, T, B, chorus, tpt, trbn, timp, pf, str qt, 1976

Also numerous solo songs

Principal publishers: BMI, Jelsor Music, Theodore Presser, E. C. Schirmer

ROSARIO MARCIANO

Weir, Judith (*b* Cambridge, 11 May 1954). British composer. During her school years in London she studied composition with John Tavener and played the oboe. At the same time her parents imbued her with a deep and lasting love of the folk music of their native Scotland. After a semester at MIT working on computer music with Barry Vercoe, she entered King's College, Cambridge, where she studied composition with Robin Holloway (1973–6). Her orchestral work *Where the Shining Trumpets Blow* was performed by the Philharmonia Orchestra, and a short time later, under the tutelage of Gunther Schuller at Tanglewood (summer 1975), she wrote the wind quintet *Out of the Air*, her first published work. She was Southern Arts Composer-in-Residence, 1976–9; taught at Glasgow University, 1979–82; spent two years at Cambridge on a creative arts fellowship at Trinity College; and returned to Glasgow as Guinness Composer-in-Residence at the Royal Scottish Academy of Music and Drama, 1988–91. In 1992 she moved to London. She has received commissions from, among others, the BBC, the Boston SO, the St Magnus and Cheltenham festivals and several major opera companies.

Judith Weir

Scene from 'A Night at the Chinese Opera', by Judith Weir, first performed at the Cheltenham Festival in 1987

Weir's themes include an early Icelandic saga, the Bayeux tapestry, Chinese Yuan dramas, Serbian folksongs and the Spanish epic *El Cid*. But if her topics are generally outside her listeners' experience, her presentation of them is not, for her musical language is referential – to folk music, to classical composers, and most often to tonality itself, even in such a modernist study of colouristic fragmentation as *Isti mirant stella*. Mixing the exotic and the familiar, her stock-in-trade is irony. This tone is often conveyed through the satirization of musical convention: in the 11-minute *King Harald's Saga*, a 'grand opera in three acts', the unaccompanied solo soprano sings eight roles and acts as smooth-voiced radio announcer; in *The Art of Touching the Keyboard* the virtuoso pianist displays tactile dexterity *ad absurdum*; and in 'Bonnie James Campbell' (the second song of *Scotch Minstrelsy*), the art of Brittenesque folksong arrangement is subtly mocked as the melody refuses to succumb to its extravagant accompaniment. This ironic humour is often intensified by a deadpan text, written or assembled by the composer herself. Thus, as King Harald sails away to war, the mournful, antiphonal 'Farewell' of his wives – shrill soprano and deep alto – is intoned quite comically by a lone singer (for good measure, as David Wright has observed, the music mischievously quotes from *Götterdämmerung*); and in the opening scene of *The Vanishing Bridegroom* the gasping plea of the dying father, 'Hear my last words', is constantly interrupted by the laments of his distraught sons.

Of Weir's three full-scale operas, *A Night at the Chinese Opera* includes in its second act fragments from an earlier, highly successful music drama, *The Consolations of Scholarship*. The two later operas are based on magical themes: *The Vanishing Bridegroom* on a set of three interlinked Scottish folktales, and *Blond Eckbert* on a fairytale by the early German Romantic writer Ludwig Tieck. Weir generally writes her own librettos and consistently conveys a symbiotic relationship between the text-as-spoken and its musical setting. But the characteristics of speech permeate even her instrumental works; for instance, phrases are clearly delineated, melodies stress a prime referential pitch (the second movement of *I Broke off a Golden Branch* is an extreme example), and rhythmic patterns, elastic or fluid, serve to emulate spontaneity.

Commentators have discerned in Weir's music the influence of, among others, Stravinsky, Janáček, and her British predecessors, Peter Maxwell Davies and Harrison Birtwistle, but her lineage is not so clear. She often seems to turn the concept of bass-generated tonality on its head, creating music from the top downwards. Occasional doubling of the melody in the bass (as in no.1 of *Scotch Minstrelsy*) serves both to acknowledge fleetingly her tonal heritage and to reinforce her iconoclastic approach.

WORKS
most works published in London

Operas: A Night at the Chinese Opera (3, Weir, after Chi Chun-hsiang: *The Chao Family Orphan*, and others), Cheltenham, Everyman Theatre, 8 July 1987; The Vanishing Bridegroom (3, Weir, after

Popular Tales of the West Highlands), Glasgow, Theatre Royal, 17 Oct 1990; Blond Eckbert (2, Weir, after J. L. Tieck), London, Coliseum, 20 April 1994

Other dramatic: Hans the Hedgehog (Weir, after J. L. Grimm and W. C. Grimm), spkr, 2 ob, bn, hpd, 1978; King Harald's Saga ('grand opera in 3 acts', Weir, after Snorri Sturluson), S, 1979; Thread! (Weir), nar, 8 players, 1981; The Black Spider (children's opera, 3, Weir, after J. Gotthelf), 1984; The Consolations of Scholarship (music-drama, 2, Weir, after Chi Chun-hsiang and others), Mez, fl + a fl + pic, ob, cl, bn, hn, vn, vc, pf, perc, 1985; Heaven Ablaze in his Breast (opera-ballet, 1, Weir, after E. T. A. Hoffman: *Der Sandmann*), 2S, A, T, 2B, 2 pf, 8 dancers, 1989; Scipio's Dream (Weir, after P. Metastasio), S, Mez, T/Bar, B, SATB ad lib, chamber ens, 1991 [after Mozart: Il sogno di Scipione]; Combattimento II (A. Vehstedt, after T. Tasso), 12 solo vv, 2 vn, va, vc, db, 1992; The Gift of the Gorgon (incid. music, P. Shaffer), 1992; The Small Moments in Life (happening, with M. Duncan), 1992; The Skriker (incid. music, C. Churchill), 1993

Orch: Where the Shining Trumpets Blow, 1974; Isti mirant stella, chamber orch, 1981; The Ride over Lake Constance, 1984; Variation on 'Summer is icumen in', 1987; Heroische Bogenstriche, 1992; Music Untangled, 1992

Chamber, inst: Out of the Air, fl, ob, cl, bn, hn, 1975; King Harald Sails to Byzantium, fl + pic, cl + b cl, vn, vc, pf, mar + glock, 1979; Several Concertos, fl + pic + a fl, vc, pf, 1980; Music for 247 Strings, vn, pf, 1981; Spij dobrze [Pleasant Dreams], db, tape, 1983; A Serbian Cabaret, vn, va, vc, pf (all also speaking), 1984; Sketches from a Bagpiper's Album, cl, pf, 1984; The Bagpiper's String Trio, vn, va, vc, 1985; Airs from Another Planet, fl + pic, ob, cl, bn, hn, pf, 1986; Gentle Violence, pic, gui, 1987; Sederunt principes, chamber ens, 1987; Mountain Airs, fl, ob, cl, 1988; Distance and Enchantment, vn, va, vc, pf, 1989; Str Qt, 1990; I Broke off a Golden Branch, vn, va, vc, db, pf, 1991

Kbd: An mein Klavier, pf, 1980; Wild Mossy Mountains, org, 1982; The Art of Touching the Keyboard, pf, 1983; Ettrick Banks, org, 1985; Michael's Strathspey, pf, 1985 [also version for org]; Ardnamurchan Point, 2 pf, 1990; Roll off the Ragged Rocks of Sin, pf, 1992; El rey de Francia, vn, va, vc, pf, 1993

Solo vocal: Black Birdsong, Bar, fl, ob, vn, vc, 1977; The Three Ravens, The Twa Corbies; Ballad (Weir), Bar, orch, 1981 [after Wagner: Der fliegende Holländer, Act 2]; Scotch Minstrelsy, T/S, pf, 1982: 1 Bessie Bell and Mary Gray, 2 Bonnie James Campbell, 3 Lady Isobel and the Elf-Knight, 4 The Gipsy Laddie, 5 The Braes of Yarrow; Lovers, Learners and Libations, scenes from 13th-century French life, Mez, T, Bar, rec, rebec, vielle, harp, 1987: 1 Hic enim servus dei, 2 Ad faciendes cordas lire, 3 Cantus al aliquibus; Songs from the Exotic, Mez, pf, 1987: 1 Sevdalino, my Little One, 2 In the Lovely Village of Sevenisje, 3 The Romance of Count Arnaldos, 4 The Song of a Girl Ravished Away by the Fairies in South Uist; A Spanish Liederbooklet, S, pf, 1988: 1 Romance de fonte frida, 2 Romance de rosa fresca, 3 Serranilla de la zarzuela; The Romance of Count Arnaldos, S, chamber ens, 1989 [arr. of A Spanish Liederbooklet

no.3]; Don't Let that Horse (L. Ferlinghetti), S, hn, 1990; Ox Mountain was Covered by Trees (Mencius), S, Ct, Bar, 1990; On Buying a Horse, medium v, pf, 1991; The Alps (E. Dickinson), S, cl, va, 1992; Broken Branches (Weir), S, pf, db, 1992

Choral: Ascending into Heaven (after Hildebert of Lavardin, 11th century), SATB, org, 1983; Illuminare Jerusalem (15th-century Scottish text), SATB, org, 1985; Missa del Cid, SAAATTTBBB, 1988

Principal publishers: Novello/Chester

BIBLIOGRAPHY

CC (B. Morton); *Fuller-LeFanuRM*

J. Weir: *King Harald's Footnotes: an Annotated Guide to King Harald's Saga*, Scottish Music Information Centre (Glasgow, n.d.)

M. Dreyer: 'Judith Weir, Composer: a Talent to Amuse', *MT*, cxxii (1981), 593–6

J. Greenhalgh: 'Oriental Underground', *Classical Music* (4 July 1987)

J. Weir: 'A Note on a Chinese Opera', *MT*, cxxxviii (1987), 373–5

——: 'A Night at the Chinese Opera' Cheltenham, Everyman Theatre, 8 July 1987 [Kent Opera programme book]

Interview, *Judith Weir* [Chester Music composer brochure, Oct 1988]

T. Morgan: 'Judith Weir', *New Music 1988*, ed. M. Finnissy, M. Hayes and R. Wright (Oxford, 1988), 22–50

N. Kenyon: 'An Eye for Music', *The Observer* (20 Nov 1988)

——: 'Sandman Gets into his Stride', *The Observer* (19 Nov 1989)

J. Weir: 'Heaven Ablaze in his Breast', Basildon, Towngate Theatre, 5 Oct 1989 [Second Stride programme booklet]

R. Dawson Scott: 'When Old Scotch Myths Strike a New Chord', *Sunday Times* (14 Oct 1990)

N. Kenyon: 'The Haggis after the Chinese Cracker', *The Observer* (14 Sept 1990)

F. Maddocks: 'Highland Wedding', *Opera Now* (1990), Oct, 32–5

R. Milnes: 'The Vanishing Bridegroom', *Opera*, xli (1990), 1498–500

'Judith Weir', *Sunday Times* (24 Aug 1990)

D. Walters and B. Martin: 'Heroic Notes', *Yamaha Educational Supplement*, no.13 (1992), 8–9 [interview]

D. Wright: 'Weir to Now?', *MT*, cxxxiv (1993), 432–7

C. Jay: *The Vocal Music of Judith Weir* (BA diss., U. of Oxford, 1993)

RHIAN SAMUEL

Weissberg, Julia Lazarevna. *See* VEYSBERG, YULIYA LAZAREVNA.

Weldon [née Thomas, later Treherne], **Georgina** (*b* Clapham, 24 May 1837; *d* Brighton, 11 Jan 1914). English soprano and composer. She married Captain Weldon in 1860, but they had separated before she met Charles Gounod (aged 53) in London in 1871. That year she sang in London at the St James's Hall Popular Concerts, the Crystal

Palace, the Philharmonic Society and elsewhere; Gounod invited her to Paris to take the solo soprano part in his patriotic cantata *Gallia* at Notre Dame, the Opéra-Comique and the Conservatoire. They returned to London in November and took up residence at her home in Tavistock House, Bloomsbury, which also housed the orphan children attending her National Training School of Music. When Gounod suffered a stroke in 1873, leaving him unconscious for extended periods, Weldon experienced visions and claimed to have heard Christ speak to her during her bedside vigils. Gounod recovered and returned to Paris in June 1874. She published *Hints for Pronunciation in Singing: with Proposals for a Self-Supporting Academy* (London, c1875) as well as songs by Gounod and other composers, and memoirs including *La destruction du 'Polyeucte' de Charles Gounod* and *Mon orphelinat et Gounod en Angleterre* (both c1875), apparently in aid of her orphanage. In 1878 *The History of my Orphanage, or The Outpourings of an Alleged Lunatic* appeared.

Weldon's earliest known published song is a setting of Tennyson, *The Brook* (London, 1859). She also composed songs to French texts (which she translated into English) for children, including *The Little Boy and Robin Redbreast's Nest* and *Night Thoughts* (London, 1879), and later – under the name 'Grannie Weldon' – *Cradle Song, Pussie's Christmas Song* and *The Song of the Sparrow* (London, 1908). In 1879 she sang at Jules Rivière's Promenade Concerts with a women's choir which she trained and directed, giving rise to a protracted lawsuit. Her last professional engagement was in 1884.

BIBLIOGRAPHY

FétisBS; *Grove1* (A. Chitty)

JULIE ANNE SADIE

Wennerberg-Reuter, Sara (Margareta Eugenia Euphrosyne) (*b* Otterstad, Skaraborgs län, 11 Feb 1875; *d* Stockholm, 29 March 1959). Swedish composer, niece of the composer, poet and politician Gunnar Wennerberg. She studied the organ and harmony with Elfrida Andrée in Göteborg and then took examinations in organ playing and choral church music at the Stockholm Conservatory (1893–5). She was a pupil of Salomon Jadassohn and Carl Reinecke at the Leipzig Conservatory (1896–8), and studied counterpoint with Max Bruch at the Berlin Hochschule für Musik (1901–2). She was awarded the Litteris et Artibus in 1931, and from the 1930s until her death she was the only woman in the Swedish composer society, Föreningen Svenska Tonsättare. She composed more than a hundred works. The most popular were the cantatas – among them those for the consecration in 1906 of St Sofia, Stockholm (where she was organist from 1918 to 1945), and for the quincentenary of the town of Lidköping (1946) – and also the melodious and lively male-voice quartets and songs.

WORKS
selective list

Orch: Romans, vn, orch; other pieces
Choral: Skogsrået [The Wood-Spirit] (V. Rydberg), solo vv, male chorus, orch, orchd E. Westberg; Skogsrået (G. Wennerberg), solo vv, male chorus, mixed chorus, orch, orchd E. Ellberg; cantatas, hymns, motets, c20 male-voice qts
Vocal: Världens gång [Way of the World] (G. Fröding), lv, orch
Songs (1v, pf): Dina smala, vita händer [Your Sweet White Hands] (A. Gullstrand), En vintervisa [A Winter Song] (Fröding), Gud välsigne dessa hjärtan [God Bless this Heart] (J. O. Wallin), Lillebarn [Little Child] (B. Bergman), Sen uppå fåglarna [Look upon the Birds] (H. Reuter, Bible, *Matthew* vi.27), [2] Sånger (Reuter, Gullstrand), [3] Sånger (P. Bjerre), Stilla komme och välkomna [Come Calmly and be Welcome] (Wallin), Varde ljus [Let there be Light] (I. Wennerberg), Videvisan [The Willow Song] (Z. Topelius), c17 other songs
Inst: Vn Sonata; Angelus, Höststämning [Autumn Mood], I regnet [In the Rain], pf; Högtidsmarsch [Festival March], När löven falla [When the Leaves Fall], org

Principal publisher: Elkan & Schildknecht

BIBLIOGRAPHY

B. Hagman: 'Sara Wennerberg-Reuter', *Svenska män och kvinnor*, viii (Stockholm, 1955), 261

ROLF HAGLUND

Wertheim, Rosy M. (*b* Amsterdam, 19 Feb 1888; *d* Laren, 27 May 1949). Dutch composer. After gaining a piano teaching certificate from the Nederlandse Toonkunstenaarvereeniging, she studied harmony and counterpoint with Bernard Zweers and Sem Dresden. She taught the piano and solfège at the Amsterdam Muzieklyceum and was a conductor of women's and children's choirs. As a composer, she began her career by writing choral works. Soon, however, she became attracted to the music of Debussy, Ravel and Stravinsky, and in 1929 moved to Paris; there she studied briefly with Louis Aubert. Until 1935 her home in Paris was a meeting-place for many composers, including Elsa Barraine, Arthur Honegger, Jacques Ibert and André Jolivet. She spent a year in Vienna, then went to the USA, where some of her works were performed by the

Composers' Forum Laboratory in New York. In 1937 she returned to Amsterdam but was forced to go into hiding during World War II. Her musical style is typified by many impressionist elements.

WORKS
selective list

Ov., orch, 1919: La chanson déchirante, Mez, fl, pf, 1926; Str Qt, 1933; Divertimento, chamber orch, 1934; 3 morceaux, fl, pf, 1939; Pf Conc., 1940; Miserere, domine miserere, A, pf, 1941

Principal publishers: Broekmans & Van Poppel, Donemus

HELEN METZELAAR

Westenholz [née Fritscher], **(Eleonore) Sophia Maria** (*b* Neubrandenburg, 10 July 1759; *d* Ludwigslust, 4 Oct 1838). German composer, singer and pianist. The daughter of Fritscher (organist at Neubrandenburg and later Schwerin), she studied the piano and singing from 1769 (at the instigation of Prince Ludwig) with the Schwerin court composer J. W. Hertel. At 16, she was already employed as a singer in the Mecklenburg-Schwerin Hofkapelle at Ludwigslust. She became the second wife of the Kapellmeister Carl August Friedrich Westenholz in the summer of 1777; they had eight children. Both as a singer and as a piano virtuoso, she had enormous success in Berlin, Leipzig, Ludwigslust and Rostock. Her admirers included the Weimar court composer E. W. Wolf (who dedicated six piano sonatas to her in 1783) and C. F. Cramer. J. F. Reichardt called her 'one of the leading musicians of Europe'. Contemporaries also praised her playing on the glass harmonica. She retired in 1821. She was piano teacher to the princesses and was much in favour at court, but also worked as a composer, performing her own music in concerts at the court. As a composer, she is most noteworthy for her songs. Influenced at first by J. A. P. Schulz and J. F. Reichardt, she later wrote in the fashionable sentimental song style of F. H. Himmel, Vincenzo Righini and Ignace Pleyel. She composed both strophic songs in folksong style and through-composed bravura works (e.g. *Der Bund*). A manuscript chronicle of the Westenholz family, letters and other documents are held at the Wissenschaftlichen Allgemeinbibliothek (formerly Mecklenburgischen Landesbibliothek) in Schwerin.

WORKS

Vocal: 12 deutsche Lieder, op.4 (Berlin, 1806), 2 ed. B. G. Jackson in *Lieder by Women Composers of the Classic Era*, i (Fayetteville, AR, 1987); Gesänge aus

'Wilhelm Tell' (Leipzig, 1807); Liebe, nur Liebe, lied, 1811, *D-SWl*; Der Bund (F. von Matthisson), S, 2 vn, va, b, *B-Bc*; 2 arias with orch, *Bc*; other lieder, songs and choruses, *c*1800, all *Bc*

Kbd: Rondo, op.1 (Berlin, 1806); Thème avec 10 variations, op.2 (Berlin, 1806); Sonata, 4 hands, op.3 (Berlin, 1806); 2 sonatas, *Bc*; Sonata, *D-SWl*

BIBLIOGRAPHY

FétisB

'Beiträge zur mecklenburgischen Kunst- und Künstlergeschichte', *Mecklenburgisches Journal* (1806)

Obituary, *Freimaurer-Abendblatt*, no.1041 (1838)

O. Kade: *Die Musikalien-Sammlung des Grossherzoglich Mecklenburg-Schweriner Fürstenhauses aus den letzten zwei Jahrhunderten* (Wismar, 1893)

M. Friedlaender: *Das deutsche Lied im 18. Jahrhundert*, ii (Stuttgart and Berlin, 1902)

C. Meyer: *Geschichte der Mecklenburg-Schweriner Hofkapelle* (Schwerin, 1913)

H. Rentzow: *Die mecklenburgischen Liederkomponisten des 18. Jahrhunderts* (Hanover, 1938)

Schwerin und die Musik (Schwerin, 1955)

DIETER HÄRTWIG

Westerkamp, Hildegard (*b* Osnabrück, 8 April 1946). Canadian composer, teacher and soundscape researcher, of German origin. She emigrated to Canada in 1968 and settled in Vancouver. She studied at the University of British Columbia (BMus 1972) and at the Department of Communication, Simon Fraser University, Vancouver (MA 1988), where in 1982 she began to give courses in acoustic communication. In 1972 she married the Canadian poet and playwright Norbert Ruebsaat; they have collaborated on a number of artistic projects. Very important to her creative work was her contact (*c*1969) with the Canadian composer and author R. Murray Schafer, who in 1969 founded the World Soundscape Project (WSP), a research group dedicated to exploring the sonic landscape, at Simon Fraser University. Westerkamp joined the WSP as a research assistant in 1973. In 1991 she began the *Soundscape Newsletter*, which was later adopted as the official publication of the World Forum for Acoustic Ecology, an international, interdisciplinary organization formed in 1993. As a composer she works primarily with the medium of tape (sometimes in conjunction with live instruments or voices), employing environmental sounds which are combined, manipulated and/or processed in ingenious ways. The result is a body of work which possesses a high degree of artistic integrity and which often reflects the WSP's sociological message: the need to listen critically to our acoustic environment. She divides her output into compositions, sound documents (the audio equivalent of a film documentary, but without narration), and composed environments; the last as a genre lies somewhere between the other two categories. Westerkamp's writings include *ssh . . . Noise Handbook* (Vancouver, 1974) and *Listening and Soundmaking: a Study of Music-as-Environment* (MA thesis).

WORKS

COMPOSITIONS

Whisper Study, 2-track tape, 1975; Familie mit Pfiff, 2-track tape, 1976; Fantasie for Horns I, 4-track tape, 1978, II, hn, 4-track tape, 1979; Streetmusic, any portable inst, 2-track tape, 1981; A Walk through the City (N. Ruebsaat), spkr, 2-track tape, 1981; Windmusic, any wind inst, 2-track tape, 1981; Cool Drool, spkr, 2-track tape, 1983; His Master's Voice, 2-track tape, 1985

Harbour Symphony, boat sirens, 1986 [*c*100 sirens, Vancouver harbour, Expo '86; 6 sirens, St John's harbour, Newfoundland, 1988]; Cricket Voice, 2-track tape, 1987; Moments of Laughter, female v, 2-track tape, 1988; Music from the Zone of Silence: 1 Desertwind, 2 Meditation, 3 The Truth is Acoustic, 1–4 spkrs, 2-track tape, 1988; The Deep Blue Sea (B. Shein), spkr, 2-track tape, 1989, collab. Ruebsaat

Kits Beach Soundwalk, spkr, 2-track tape, 1989; Breathing Room, 2 track-tape, 1990; Breathing Room 2, 2-track tape, bottles, audience, 1990; Ecole polytechnique, 8 church bells, mixed choir, b cl, tpt, perc, 2-track tape, 1990; Breathing Room 3 – a Self Portrait, 2-track tape, 1991; My Horse and I (S. Thesen), 2-track tape, 1991; Beneath the Forest Floor, 2-track tape, 1992

COMPOSED ENVIRONMENTS

Cordillera (Ruebsaat), 4-track tape, 1980; Zone of Silence Story, 2-track tape, 1985, collab. Ruebsaat; Coon Bay (Canadian west coast), 2-track tape, 1988; Tueren der Wahrnehmung, 1989 [for Ars Electronica '89, Linz]

SOUND DOCUMENTS

Under the Flightpath [life near an airport], 1981; Streetmusic [Vancouver street musicians], 1982; Voices for Wilderness [environmental festival, Stein Valley wilderness, BC], 1985, collab. Ruebsaat; Women Voicing [women's music], 1985, in *Musicworks* no.31 (1985); Convergence [Canadian Electroacoustic Community symposium, Banff, Alberta, 1989], 1990; One Visitor's Portrait of Banff [soundscape of Banff], 1992

Soundtracks for film

BIBLIOGRAPHY

EMC 2 (K. Bazzana)

D. Zapf: 'Inside the Soundscape: the Compositions of Hildegard Westerkamp', *Musicworks*, no.15 (1981)

G. Young: 'Composing with Environmental Sound', *Musicworks*, no.26 (1984)

R. Chatelin: 'Hildegard Westerkamp: Wake-up and Hear the Crickets', *Music Scene*, no.360 (1988)

KIRK MACKENZIE

White, Maude Valérie (*b* Dieppe, 23 June 1855; *d* London, 2 Nov 1937). English composer and writer. She studied harmony

Maude Valérie White

and composition with W. S. Rockstro in Torquay and Oliver May in London, and from 1876 to 1879 with G. A. Macfarren at the RAM. In 1879 she was the first woman to win the Mendelssohn Scholarship, but was forced to resign this two years later because of ill-health. After a brief period in South America, she completed her music education in winter 1883 with Robert Fuchs in Vienna. Recurrent illness caused her to travel widely in Europe and elsewhere in search of suitable climates and she became a proficient linguist, translating many of her own song texts and a number of books, among them Froelich-Bum's study of J. A. D. Ingres. White is remembered chiefly as a gifted songwriter. She wrote some 200 songs, most of which fall into the category of the Victorian drawing-room ballad, a genre that she cultivated with distinction in such songs as *The Devout Lover*, and with something approaching greatness in her setting of Byron's *So we'll go no more a roving*. The style of her piano accompaniments, particularly in the German settings, owed much to the example of Robert Schumann. There are also several

French songs, among which the *Trois chansons tziganes* are particularly striking for their bold, declamatory passages and their adventurous harmony. Her greatest asset, however, was an appealing if at times sentimental lyricism; her occasional essays in extended instrumental forms are on the whole undistinguished. She published the autobiographical volumes *Friends and Memories* (London, 1914) and *My Indian Summer* (London, 1932).

WORKS
selective list

Vocal: Agnus Dei, chorus, orch, 1879, unpubd; 4 Songs from Tennyson's In memoriam (London, 1885); 16 German Songs (H. Heine, J. W. von Goethe, F. Bodenstedt, K. Siebel, J. Sturm, J. Kerner, E. Tegner, R. Burns) (London, 1885); 6 Volkslieder (London, 1893); 3 chansons tziganes (Russ., trans.) (London, 1913); Du bist wie eine Blume (Heine), 5vv, n.d.; many other songs, several vocal duets

Inst: Rondo scherzando, pf (London, 1879); 8 South American Airs, pf duet (London, 1882); Scherzetto, pf/(vn, pf)/pf duet (London, 1883); 4 Sketches, pf (London, 1886); Danse fantastique (Milan, 1888); Pictures from Abroad, pf (London, 1892); Naissance d'amour, vc, pf (London, 1893); Barcarolle, pf (London, 1893); Waltz and Gavotte (Little Pictures of School Life), pf (London, 1899); La fanfaluca, pf (London, 1916)

Stage: The Enchanted Heart, ballet, 1912–13; incid. music

Principal publishers: Boosey, Chappell, S. Lucas, Ricordi, Weber

BIBLIOGRAPHY
SchmidlD

MALCOLM BOYD

White, Ruth (S.) (*b* Pittsburgh, 1 Sept 1925). American composer, pianist and educator. She received a classical training in piano and briefly studied a variety of other instruments (violin, cello, harp, clarinet and horn), which laid a foundation for her later writing for orchestra. She completed her first composition at the age of eight and since she was 15 she has produced a steady stream of works for diverse media in a variety of styles and genres. White began formal composition studies with Nikolai Lopatnikoff at the Carnegie Institute of Technology (later Carnegie Mellon University: BFA 1948, piano and composition; MFA 1949, composition). She continued her training with John Vincent at UCLA (1950–54); during this time she met George Antheil and became, from 1951 to 1954, one of only three students he ever accepted. White credits Antheil with making her fully aware of the principles of classical sonata form, which provided 'the key to writing larger works that were logical and structurally sound'.

White's involvement in electronic music was precipitated by a belief that all the experiments in traditional media, from impressionism to atonality, polytonality and the like, were closed paths – that 'this medium, with its fundamental key relationships, had been exhausted, had reached its zenith by the end of the nineteenth century, and, since then, its basic principles were being systematically destroyed'. She also found much early electronic music 'chaotic and senseless', eventually concluding that those 'unshaped and arbitrary sounds being made were noise and just that'. After building her own electronic music studio (1964–70; now on display at the Kenneth G. Fiske Museum of Musical Instruments), she developed her own brand of electronic music, which explored new timbral and harmonic resources without renouncing the order and logic instilled by her classical training. *Short Circuits*, among her best-known compositions, consists of electronically orchestrated versions of familiar pieces by composers from Couperin and Scarlatti to Shostakovich. Other electronic works, such as *Pinions*, *Seven Trumps from the Tarot Cards* and *Flowers of Evil*, are notable for their inventiveness, power of communication and (somewhat rare in contemporary music) melodic appeal and memorability.

Her career has followed many paths, sometimes simultaneously, sometimes sequentially. She has stated: 'I never do the same thing twice. Some composers get bogged down on repetition and slight changes in the name of perfection. I do something, as well as I can do it, then go on to do something else'. Throughout her career she has been involved in creating materials that teach children through music, producing teacher-training films, dance recordings and other resources intended to both educate and entertain. She also has been on the cutting edge of new technologies, such as 'analog animation' (the manipulation of visual sound waves) and other video and electronic music combinations. One of her art pieces, *Steel*, animated to an original score, received an Atlanta Film Festival award (1971), and she has received other recognition for her varied endeavours. Among White's recent projects is an opera-musical theatre trilogy, for which she is writing both text and score; using acoustic and electronic music, as well as a variety of special effects, this work represents a convergence of different paths in her career, a reopening of past doors through which new vistas can now be seen. Many of her works have been recorded (chiefly by Rhythm Productions and Limelight/ Mercury Records).

WORKS
selective list

Stage: The Owl and the Pussycat (children's ballet, after E. Lear), nar, fl, cl, bn, 2 pf, perc, 1965

Orch: Suite, 1949; Shofar Sym., 1965

Vocal: Songs from the Japanese Poets (trad. haiku), 1v, pf, 1947; Palestinian Song Cycle (anon.), S, bn, pf, perc, 1950; Settings for Lullabies from 'Round the World' (trad.), T, S, pf, vc, ob, eng hn, 1955; A Certain Slant of Light (E. Dickinson), S, pf, 1955

Chamber and solo inst: Pf Sonata, 1948; Tpt Sonata, 1952–3; Music for Dance, 1962–8, incl. Study no.1, hn, tpt, pf, perc; Study no.2, 2 pf; Perc Patterns, elec; Kaleidoscope I, elec; Divertissement in F, hn, tpt, pf, perc; Dance Suite, hpd; Archetonics, pf; Pentatonics, hpd; Little Suite, fl, cl, pf; Synthesonics nos.1–2, elec; Contrasts, altered insts

Elec: Pinions, ballet, 1966; 7 Trumps from the Tarot Cards, 1967, staged as a ballet, 1970; Flowers of Evil (C. P. Baudelaire), 1969; Short Circuits, 1970

Music videos, mixed media and educational materials: Butterflies, 1971 [elec realization of Grieg's *Schmetterling*, op.43 no.1, with animated graphics], 1971; Steel, 1971 [with animated graphics]; A Child's Garden of Delights, mixed media, 1972–3; 6 Fantasies for Children: The Adventures of Mr Windbag, 1973–4; c60 albums with songs, lyrics, stories, etc. for children (1955–)

Film scores; music for television commercials

BIBLIOGRAPHY

R. Nusser: 'Toward a New Consciousness: Ruth White and the Electronic Tarot', *After Dark* (1968), Nov

K. Monson: 'Intellectual Mystic Composer', *Los Angeles Herald Examiner* (21 Sept 1969)

—— : 'Ruth White and the Electronic Tarot', *Coast FM & Fine Arts* (1970), Feb

M. Peterson: 'Electronic Music Composer Ruth White', *Los Angeles Times* (14 Feb 1971)

ALLAN B. HO

Whitehead, Gillian (*b* Whangarei, 23 April 1941). New Zealand composer and teacher. One eighth Maori, she was born into a musical family. During her childhood she absorbed the natural world of sea, hills and trees about her, especially its Maori associations. She began composing at an early age, always attracted to themes with literary associations. After attending the University of Auckland (1959–62), where she worked under Ronald Tremain, and Victoria University, Wellington (BMus 1964), she studied composition with Peter Sculthorpe at the University of Sydney (MMus 1966). Peter Maxwell Davies's lectures on analysis and composition in Adelaide (1966) stimulated her to continue studying with him in England the follow-

ing year. She was composer-in-residence at Northern Arts, Newcastle upon Tyne, 1978–80, before joining the staff at the Sydney Conservatorium of Music in 1981; she later became Head of Composition there, taking leave every second year to concentrate on her own work.

As a first-year student she wrote that she wanted to compose music that was Debussyan in harmony, Webernian in orchestration and Dufay-like in structure, and to some extent she has adhered to those aims. A series of works on Maori themes, such as *Pakuru* (1967) and *Whakatau-ki* (1970), which described in vivid imagery the seasonal cycle, was succeeded by string and piano compositions. In 1978 the success of her first chamber opera, *Tristan and Iseult* (composed 1975), opened up new possibilities. With the poet Fleur Adcock, she wrote a number of larger-scale vocal works, such as *Inner Harbour* (1979), *Hotspur* (1980), a north-country dramatic saga for soprano and chamber ensemble, and the opera *The King of the Other Country* (1984). Whitehead makes constant but not exclusive use of her own version of the 'magic square' (a number grid, much used as a pre-compositional device by Maxwell Davies), projecting this into pitches and rhythms; she feels music is a totality of form, rhythm and melody with the quality of wholeness. Her works can glow with colour and warmth besides having at times a sinewy steely quality, redolent with the influence of natural sounds – 'of birds, the sound of wind from nothing, the sound of rain and the great sense of space and the changing light'.

WORKS
selective list

Stage: Tristan and Iseult (chamber opera, M. Crowthers, M. Hill), 1975; The Tinker's Curse (children's opera, J. Aiken), 1979; Requiem, Mez, org, dancers, 1981; The King of the Other Country (chamber opera, F. Adcock), 1984; The Pirate Moon (chamber opera, A. M. dell'Oso), 1986; Bride of Fortune (chamber opera, dell'Oso), 1988; Angels Born at the Speed of Light (C. McQueen), 1992, choreog. B. Judge

Orch: Te tangi a Apakura, str, 1975; Tirea, ob, vn, vc, hpd, str, 1978; Hoata, chamber orch, 1979; Resurgences, 1989

Choral: Missa brevis, SATB, 1963; The Inner Harbour (F. Adcock), SATB, chamber orch, perc, 1979; Low Tide: Aramoana (C. McQueen), Mez, SATB, 3 tpt, 2 trbn, timp, 1982; The Virgin and the Nightingale (5 songs, Adcock, after medieval lyrics), S, Mez, C, T, Bar/B, chorus/sextet, 1986; Moments, SATB unacc., 1993

Other vocal: Pakuru, S, fl, cl, va, vc, hpd, perc, 1967; Whakatau-ki (Maori proverbs), male v, chamber ens, 1970; Bright Forms Return (K. Raine), Mez, str qt, 1980; Hotspur (F. Adcock), S, ens, 1980; Pao, S, cl, pf, 1981; Eleanor of Aquitaine, Mez, ens, 1982; Out of this Nettle: Danger (Adcock, after K. Mansfield), Mez, ens, 1983; These Isles your Dream (Raine), Mez, va, pf, 1983; Awa Herea, S, pf, 1993

Chamber: Okuru, vn, pf, 1979; Antiphons, 3 tpt, 2 hn, 3 trbn, tuba, 1980; Ahotu (o matenga), ens, 1984; Windstreams, perc, 1985; Napier's Bones, 24 perc, improvised jazz pf, 1989, also arr. 6 perc, improvised jazz pf; Angels Born at the Speed of Light, str qt, 1990; Moon, Tides and Shoreline, str qt, 1990

Pf: Fantasia on 3 Notes, 1966; La cadenza sia corta, 1974; Voices of Tane, 1976; Tamatea Tutahi, 1980; 5 Bagatelles, 1986

BIBLIOGRAPHY

CC (S. Mays); Fuller-LeFanuRM; LePageWC, iii

W. Southgate: 'Tristan and Iseult', Islands, vi/4 (1978), 416–19

E. Kerr: 'Gillian Whitehead Talks to Music in New Zealand', Music in New Zealand, vi/spr. (1989), 11–19

J. M. Thomson: Biographical Dictionary of New Zealand Composers (Wellington, 1990)

J. M. THOMSON

Wichern, Caroline (b Horn, nr Hamburg, 13 Sept 1836; d Horn, 19 March 1906). German teacher and composer. She worked in Hamburg and in Manchester, where Slater's Directory lists her (1887–96) as a teacher of singing, music and harmony; she returned to Hamburg in 1896. Her published music seems to have been primarily teaching material and salon music. It includes Consecrated Melodies, being Favourite Secular Tunes with Sacred Words (London, 1897) – arrangements and adaptations of 41 folk-songs, ten Schubert songs and other pieces. That 25 ein- und zweist. Lieder für kleine und grosse Kinder (Leipzig and London, n.d.) is op.43 illustrates the size of her output. Most of this collection is in Twenty-Two Songs in One and Two Parts for Children Old and Young (translated by Lady Macfarren, Miss Marie Liebert and others; London, 1883). Her success is borne out by Alte und neue Weihnachtslieder für Schule und Haus, published in Hamburg and reprinted 16 times (it was also arranged for piano by Elizabeth Friedericks; Hamburg, n.d.). In spite of Wichern's large number of publications and apparent celebrity in her own lifetime, almost none of her music is preserved, possibly because of its lighthearted nature.

BIBLIOGRAPHY

WCBH

Slater's General and Classified Directory of Manchester and Salford (Manchester, 1887–96)

ELAINE MOOHAN

Wieck, Clara. See SCHUMANN, CLARA.

Wieniawska, Irena Regina. See POLDOWSKI.

Wikström, Inger (b Stockholm, 11 Dec 1939). Swedish pianist, composer and conductor. She studied the piano with Gottfried Boon in Stockholm and with Ilona Kabos in London. In 1959 her débuts in Stockholm and London were so successful that she was named Artist of the Year; her subsequent career as a pianist included world-wide tours. In 1977 she founded the Nordic Music Conservatory at Österskär (north of Stockholm), of which she is principal and senior piano teacher. During the late 1970s she also began to compose and to conduct. Most of her compositions are vocal works; her music is lyrical, but with elements of expressionism and Swedish neo-romanticism, especially in the Rilke songs and the opera Den Fredlöse.

WORKS

Stage: Junker Nils av Eka [Junker Nils of Eka], op.14 (family opera, A. Lindgren), 1982; Den fredlöse [The Outlawed] (opera, after A. Strindberg), 1985; Elddonet [The Tinderbox] (musical, after H. C. Andersen), 1990; Den brottslige modern [The Guilty Mother] (after P.-A. Beaumarchais), 1992; Näktergalen [The Nightingale] (after Andersen), 1993

Vocal (for 1v, pf, unless otherwise stated): 6 Lieder, op.10 (R. M. Rilke), 1982; Orpheus-Euridike-Hermes, op.11 (Rilke), 1982; 3 lieder, op.12 (Rilke), 1983: Liebeslied, An die Musik, Du bist die Zukunft; 3 sånger, op.15, 1983; 4 Kattsånger [4 Cat Songs] (H. Lewin), 1989; 2 Kattsånger [2 Cat Songs] (Lewin), duets, 1990

Inst: Ballad, op.13, pf, 1982; Ballad, op.17, pf, str orch, 1988; 3 duets, op.18, 2 vn, 1988; 7 Preludes, op.19, pf, 1991

Some material in S-Sic

EVA ÖHRSTRÖM

Wilhelmina [Wilhelmine; Sophie Friederike Wilhelmine], Princess of Prussia, later Margräfin of Bayreuth (b Berlin, 3 July 1709; d Bayreuth, 14 Oct 1758). German composer. She was the daughter of Frederick William I and a favourite sister of Frederick the Great, with whom she shared a great interest in music. She lived in Bayreuth after her marriage to Prince Frederick of Bayreuth in 1731 and the 30 years of cultural liveliness that followed there were due to her cheerful and musical personality; she and her husband built the superb Baroque opera house that attracted Wagner to the town a century later. Her compositions include the opera Argenore (1740), six arias for Andrea Bernasconi's L'huomo and a keyboard concerto in G minor. The concerto is scored for strings

Wilhelmina, Princess of Prussia, later Margräfin of Bayreuth: portrait by Anna Dorothea Lisiewska-Therbusch

with obbligato flute and could have been played with either her brother or her husband as the flautist. Her love of the music of J. S. Bach is manifest in the vigorous first movement, while the second and third movements show that she could be equally expressive in the natural simplicity of slow music and the more artful ornamented style of French gavottes.

BIBLIOGRAPHY

CohenE

A. Laurence: *Women of Notes* (New York, 1978)

S. Stern: *Women Composers: a Handbook* (Metuchen, NJ, 1978)

DIANA AMBACHE,
MARTHA FURMAN SCHLEIFER

Wilkins, Margaret Lucy (*b* Kingston-upon-Thames, Surrey, 13 Nov 1939). English composer. She studied music at Trinity College of Music, London, and at the University of Nottingham (1957–60). In 1976 she was appointed as a senior lecturer at the Huddersfield Polytechnic (now University of Huddersfield). She performed with the Scottish Early Music Consort,

1969–76, and became director of the contemporary music group Polyphonia in 1989. In 1970 performances of *Dieux est*, Concerto grosso and *Music for an Exhibition* attracted notable interest, and her compositions have been presented regularly in Britain and abroad since that time. In addition to orchestral and chamber works, she has written multi-media compositions, including *Kanal*, chosen for performance at the ISCM Festival in Poland in 1992. Her music is characterized by its attention to texture and by its keen sense of drama.

WORKS
selective list

Orch: Concerto grosso, 1970; Dance Variations, str orch, hpd, 1973; Hymn to Creation, 1973; Music of the Spheres, 1975; Sym., 1989; Musica angelorum, 12 solo str/str orch, 1991

Brass band: Epistola da San Marco, 1987

Choral: Gitanjali, SATB, 1981; Lest we Forget, SATB, synth, 1982; Revelations of the Seven Angels, S, chorus, orch, 1988

Chamber: Dieux est, S, fl, vn, perc, harp, 1970; The Silver Casket, S, vn, va, vc, harp, 1971; Witch Music, Mez, cl, tpt, db, 1971; Orpheus, vn, pf, 1973; Struwwelpeter, S, 3 cl, pf, perc, 1973; Ave

Maria, Mez, fl, cl, vn, vc, pf, harp, perc, 1974; Circus, fl, cl, b cl, tpt, hn, vn, db, pf, perc, 1975; L'Allegro, Ct, rec, hpd, 1977; The Tree of Life, T, Bar, B, fl, cl, vn, vc, pf, perc, 1978–9; Aspects of Night, rec, gui, 1981; Aries, rec, 1984

Kbd: A Dance to the Music of Time, hpd, 1980; Deus ex machina, org, 1982; Study in Black and White no.1, pf, 1983; A Joyful Noise!, org, 1988; Study in Black and White no.2, pf, 1992

El-ac and multi-media: Music for an Exhibition, musique concrète, 1970; Rêve, Réveil, Révélation, Réverbérations, a fl, cl, b cl, bn, vib, mar, gui, harp, 4 vn, va, vc, db, synth (DX7.2), 1988; The Cello in my Life, vc, pf, live elec, 1989; Kanal, singers, brass, perc, dancers, actors, 2 elec tapes, 1990; Stringsing: an Electro-Acoustic Work for Dance, 1992

Principal publisher: Satanic Mills Press
Some material in GB-Lmic

BIBLIOGRAPHY

Fuller-LeFanuRM (G. Smith and N. Walker-Smith)

V. O'Brien: 'Living British Women Composers', The Musical Woman: an International Perspective, i: 1983, ed. J. L. Zaimont and others (Westport, CT, 1984), 228–30

M. L. Wilkins: 'View from the Industrial North', Contact, no.32 (1988), 54–6

C. Askew: 'Kanal: a Multi-Media Environmental Experience', ILWC Journal (1992), March, 9–10 [also pubd in: Women in Music Newsletter, no.18 (1992)]

P. Adkins Chiti: Donne in musica, ii: 1899–1939 (Novara, forthcoming)

S. Fuller: The Pandora Guide to Women Composers – British and American (London, forthcoming)

MARIE FITZPATRICK

Williams, Grace (Mary) (b Barry, 19 Feb 1906; d Barry, 10 Feb 1977). Welsh composer. She was educated at Barry Grammar School and University College, Cardiff, where she took the degree of BMus in 1926 before continuing her studies with Ralph Vaughan Williams and Gordon Jacob at the RCM, London. Her fellow students there included Dorothy Gow, Imogen Holst and Elizabeth Maconchy, an unusually gifted group of women composers who maintained contact with each other in later years. In 1930 a travelling scholarship took Williams to Vienna, where she completed her studies with Egon Wellesz. On her return to London she taught for several years at Camden School for Girls and at Southlands College of Education. During the 1930s she enjoyed the friendship of Benjamin Britten, but declined an invitation to act as his assistant (the position was later occupied by Imogen Holst). In 1946 Williams returned to Wales, where she worked on educational programmes for the BBC and gradually made her name as a freelance composer. Most of her major works were written in response to commissions from the BBC, the Royal National Eisteddfod and festivals at Llandaff (Cardiff) and Swansea. Her output is mainly for orchestra and for voices with orchestra, and includes two symphonies (the first of which she withdrew), three concertos, a one-act opera and a mass. She also wrote several songs but showed little interest in instrumental chamber music, partly no doubt because of its relatively short tradition in Wales but also because her own musical temperament inclined more towards lyrical and declamatory forms than towards contrapuntal and dialectical ones (the direction 'liricamente' is one frequently encountered in her scores).

The music Williams wrote before about 1955 is to some extent influenced by that of her teacher Vaughan Williams. Edward Elgar is another perceptible influence, and there are passages of chromatic writing reminiscent of Richard Strauss, for example in the last of the Sea Sketches and in the first two movements of the Violin Concerto. Folksong is encountered in vocal settings and in the orchestral Fantasia on Welsh Nursery Tunes, a piece that loosely strings together Welsh tunes. Penillion for Orchestra, written for the National Youth Orchestra of Wales in 1955, inaugurated a period of greater maturity and more pronounced individuality. Many of the later pieces are deeply national in feeling (e.g. Ballads for Orchestra, Carillons, the Missa cambrensis and Castell Caernarfon). Although they include no actual folk melodies they are shaped by the rhythms and cadences of old Welsh poetry and oratory. The so-called Scotch snap applied to a rising tone or semitone is a particularly distinctive fingerprint; another is the juxtaposing, or superimposing, of major and minor 3rds. While the harmony remains basically (though at times shiftingly) tonal, melodies are often cast in a mode that includes both the augmented (Lydian) 4th and the flattened 7th (and sometimes too the flattened 6th). Structures involving quasi-improvisatory variation within a rigid stanzaic repetition are closely related to the oldest traditions of ballad and penillion singing in Wales. The Trumpet Concerto may be seen as the natural outcome of a lyrical, even expressive, approach to this instrument which characterizes most, if not all, of the later orchestral scores.

A more cosmopolitan style is evident in her only opera, The Parlour, to a libretto brilliantly adapted by the composer herself from a story by Guy de Maupassant.

Comparison with Benjamin Britten's Maupassant opera, *Albert Herring*, is inevitable, but Williams's music shows a genuine individuality and inventiveness, allied to a rare sense of stagecraft. Since its Welsh National Opera première in 1966 *The Parlour* has been revived a number of times, and several other choral and orchestral pieces have been recorded. But one of the finest achievements of her later years, the *Missa cambrensis*, a large-scale setting of the mass ordinary with interpolations, has been unaccountably neglected since its first performance in 1971.

WORKS
selective list

Stage: The Parlour (opera, 1, Williams, after G. de Maupassant: *En famille*), 1961, Cardiff, New Theatre, 5 May 1966

Orch: Fantasia on Welsh Nursery Tunes, 1940; Sinfonia concertante, pf, orch, 1941; Sym. no.1, 1943, withdrawn except Scherzo barbaro e segreto; Sea Sketches, str, 1944; The Merry Minstrel (Williams, after J. L. Grimm and W. C. Grimm), nar, orch, 1949; Vn Conc., 1950; Penillion for Orchestra, 1955; Sym. no.2, 1956; Processional, 1962; Tpt Conc., 1963; Carillons, ob, orch, 1965; Ballads, 1968; Castell Caernarfon, 1969

Choral: Hymn of Praise (Gogonedawg Arglwydd) (from the 12th-century Black Book of Carmarthen, trans. Williams), chorus, orch, 1939; The Dancers (H. Belloc, T. Chatterton, M. Sarton, K. Raine), S, female chorus, str, harp/pf, 1951–2; All seasons shall be sweet (S. T. Coleridge, W. Blake, W. Shakespeare, T. Heywood, J. Thomson, R. Southwell), S, female chorus, small orch/pf, 1959; Benedicite, SA/SATB youth chorus, orch, 1964; Missa cambrensis, S, A, T, B, chorus, boys' chorus, orch, 1971; Ye highlands and ye lowlands (anon., R. Burns, W. Scott), male chorus, pf, 1972; Ploratione cygni (9th century), 1972; Ave maris stella (8th century), SATB, 1973; 2 interlinked choruses: Harp Song of the Dane Women (R. Kipling), Mariners' Song (T. L. Beddoes), SATB, 2 hn, harp, 1975

Vocal: The Song of Mary (Magnificat setting), S, chamber orch, 1939; 6 Poems of Gerard Manley Hopkins, A, str sextet, 1959; The Billows of the Sea (W. Scott, A. Tennyson, J. Gay, anon.), A, pf, 1969; Fairest of Stars (J. Milton), S, orch, 1973; My Last Duchess (R. Browning), Bar, pf, 1974; other songs, folksong arrs.

Also film music

Principal publishers: OUP, University of Wales Press

BIBLIOGRAPHY
A. F. L. Thomas: 'Grace Williams', *MT*, xcvii (1956), 240–43
—— : 'The Music of Grace Williams', *Anglo-Welsh Review*, xv (1965), 90–103
G. Williams and A. J. H. Rees: 'Views and Revisions', *Welsh Music*, v/4 (1976–7), 7–18
E. Davies, 'A Pianist's Note on Grace Williams's Sinfonia Concertante', *Welsh Music*, v/9 (1978), 22–9
A. Whittall: 'Grace Williams 1906–1977', *Soundings*, vii (1978), 19–25
M. Boyd: 'Benjamin Britten and Grace Williams: Chronicle of a Friendship', *Welsh Music*, vi/6 (1980–81), 7–38
—— : *Grace Williams* (Cardiff, 1980)
E. Davies: 'Grace Williams and the Piano', *Welsh Music*, vi/4 (1980), 18–25
E. R. Warkov: 'Traditional Features in Grace Williams's "Penillion"', *Welsh Music*, vii/1 (1982), 15–24
'Grace Williams: a Self Portrait', *Welsh Music*, viii/5 (1987), 7–16 [4 radio scripts]
D. Mitchell and P. Reed, eds.: *Letters from a Life: Selected Letters and Diaries of Benjamin Britten* (London, 1991)

MALCOLM BOYD

Williams, Mary Lou [née Scruggs, Mary Elfrieda] (*b* Atlanta, GA, 8 May 1910; *d* Durham, NC, 28 May 1981). African-American jazz pianist, arranger and composer. She also used the last names of her stepfathers: Winn and Burley. A musically gifted child, she was periodically on the road from her early teen years. Her piano solos and arrangements, which combined blues and jump rhythms, brought distinction to the Andy Kirk band (1929–42). She provided arrangements for Benny Goodman, Louis Armstrong, Duke Ellington (including a six-month tour in 1943), Bob Crosby, Cab Calloway, Earl Hines, Tommy Dorsey, Jimmie Lunceford and Dizzy Gillespie. Later she became the spiritual anchor for bebop musicians such as Thelonious Monk and Bud Powell. The original trio version of *Zodiac Suite* emerged over 12 weeks during 1945 on her own radio show (WNEW); a performance with studio players in Town Hall, New York, followed, and an arrangement for herself and the New York PO was given at Carnegie Hall in 1946. In 1954 she abandoned music to devote herself entirely to charity work but resumed her career in 1957 at the Newport Jazz Festival. She remained active throughout the 1960s and 70s, not least of all as a teacher in Pittsburgh schools, at the University of Massachusetts, Amherst (1975–7) and at Duke University (1977 until her death). She established her own publishing company, the Cecilia Publishing Co., and also founded Mary Records, the oldest label owned by a black artist, which issued some of her material.

Among her more than 350 compositions, most of the jazz pieces and arrangements came from the earlier decades of her career. Her playing and arrangements evolved from swing to bebop and on to a more dissonant avant-garde style, yet always remained rooted in blues and boogie-woogie. After her conversion to Roman

Catholicism in 1957, she began to focus on religious expression in her works, combining various styles of black music: jazz, spirituals and gospel. Her most acclaimed composition, *Mary Lou's Mass*, was commissioned by the Vatican, choreographed by Alvin Ailey (1971), and performed world-wide. She frequently revised her religious works, keeping in mind the particular abilities of each performing group.

She received honorary doctorates from a number of American universities and in 1990 became the first woman instrumentalist admitted to the *Down Beat* Hall of Fame. She was much admired by other jazz performers and frequently cited as an influence and inspiration, especially by women jazz pianists, for example Marian McPartland and Betty Hall Jones.

WORKS

selective list; many works originally published by Leeds and Robbins or later by Cecilia Publishing Co., selected recordings given in parentheses

JAZZ

Orig.: Zodiac Suite, jazz trio, 1945 [also perf. larger groups]; In the Land of Oo-bla-dee, fairy-tale bebop piece, mid-1940s [with Milton Orent, for Dizzy Gillespie; recorded by Gillespie's big band]; Waltz Boogie, 1946 (Victor 202025); Perdido, by 1957; I Love Him, 1957; A Fungus Amungus, 1963 (Folkways FJ 32843) [a satire on avant-garde trends she felt threatened the blues/gospel/swing styles of jazz]; Blues for Peter, 1965 [contemplative tribute to Father Peter O'Brien]; Medi I, pf, db, perc, by 1974 (Mary Records M103); Medi II, 2 pf, db, perc, by 1974 (Mary Records M103); Play it Momma, pf, db, perc, by 1974 (Mary Records M103); Praise the Lord, pf, db, perc, by 1974 (Mary Records M103)

Arrs. (some incl. orig. tunes by Williams): Cloudy, 1929 [for A. Kirk]; Corky Stomp, 1929; Froggy Bottom, 1929 [for Kirk]; Messa Stomp, 1929 [for Kirk]; Walkin' and Swingin', 1936 [for Kirk]; Little Joe from Chicago, 1936–8 [for Kirk]; Mary's Idea, 1936–8 [for Kirk]; Roll 'Em, 1937 [for Benny Goodman]; Trumpets No End [version of Blue Skies], 1946 (Skata 502) [for Ellington, who made 1952 live recording]

SACRED

St Martin de Porres (Black Christ of the Andes; Hymn in Honor of St Martin Porres) (A. Woods), SATTBB, pf, 1962 (Saba 15062; Folkways FJ 32843); version for vv, jazz trio, 1965

Mass, chorus, pf, 1963 [in jazz/gospel idiom for Pittsburgh students at Seton High School]

The Devil, chorus, pf, by 1963 (Folkways FJ 32843)

Mary Lou's Mass [orig.: Music for Peace], 1969; rev. version choreog. A. Ailey, 1971; arr. children's chorus, 1975; various other arrs.; (Mary Records 102)

PIANO

Five Piano Solos: A Mellow Bit of Rhythm, Toadie Toddle, Scratchin' in the Gravel, Mary Lou Williams Blues, Walkin' and Swingin', 1941

Six Original Boogie Woogie Piano Solos: Special

Freight, Deuces Wild, Twinklin', Bobo and Doodles, The Duke and the Count, Chili Sauce, 1944

WRITINGS

'My Friends the Kings of Jazz', *Melody Maker*, xxx (3 April–12 June 1954) [sometimes listed under M. Jones: 'Mary Lou Williams: a Life Story']

Hear me Talkin' to ya, ed. N. Shapiro and N. Hentoff (New York, 1955) [short writings on various jazz musicians]

Jazz Women: a Feminist Perspective (Stash ST109, 1977) [record notes]

BIBLIOGRAPHY

SouthernE

S. Pease: *Boogie-Woogie Piano Styles* (Chicago, 1940) [incl. short biography and transcr. of *Overhand*]

M. McPartland: 'Mary Lou', *Down Beat*, xxiv/21 (1957), 12, 41

—— : 'Into the Sun', *Down Beat*, xxxi/24 (1964), 16–17, 36

J. S. Wilson: Interview with Mary Lou Williams, NEA Jazz Oral History Project, Institute of Jazz Studies, Rutgers U., 1973

D. Tudor and N. Tudor: *Jazz* (Littleton, CO, 1979) [incl. discography, esp. for compilations]

D. A. Handy: 'Conversation with Mary Lou Williams: First Lady of the Jazz Keyboard', *BPiM*, viii (1980), 195–214

B. Rowes: 'From Duke Ellington to Duke University, Mary Lou Williams Tells the World: "Jazz is Love" ', *People Weekly* (12 May 1980), 73–4, 77

S. Placksin: *American Women in Jazz* (New York, 1982)

M. Unterbrink: *Jazz Women at the Keyboard* (Jefferson, NC, 1983), esp. 31–51

L. Dahl: *Stormy Weather: the Music and Lives of a Century of Jazzwomen* (New York, 1984)

J. McManus: 'Women Jazz Composers and Arrangers', *The Musical Woman: an International Perspective*, i: *1983*, ed. J. L. Zaimont and others (Westport, CT, 1984), 197–208

J. Leder: *Women in Jazz: a Discography of Instrumentalists, 1913–1968* (Westport, CT, 1985), 272–89, 293–4, 299, 304

J. McDonough: 'Mary Lou Williams', *Down Beat*, lvii/Sept (1990), 21

Music on my Mind, Film & Video Workshop, New York, 1990 [video dir. J. Burke; review by J. Hiett, *Library Journal* (1 June 1991), 210]

M. J. Budds: 'African-American Women in Blues and Jazz', *Women and Music: a History*, ed. K. Pendle (Bloomington, IN, 1991), 282–97, esp. 294–6

H. Walker-Hill: *Piano Music by Black Women Composers: a Catalog of Solo and Ensemble Works* (New York, 1992), 106–9

J. MICHELE EDWARDS

Wolf [née Benda]**, Maria Carolina** (*b* Berlin, 27 Dec 1742; *d* 8 Feb 1820). German singer and composer. The daughter of Franz Benda and his first wife, Franziska Louise, she studied singing and the piano with her father and took a position as a court singer in Weimar in 1761. She married the Weimar Kapellmeister Ernst Wilhelm Wolf in 1770, but continued her career as *Hofsängerin* and performed at the Weimar Liebhabertheater (1775–83), where J. W. von Goethe was director. She composed the songs *Die Rose* and *An die Rose* (published in *Der teutsche Merkur*, 1779) and a setting of *Ich träumte wie um Mitternacht*, which appeared first in her husband's collection *Ein und fünfzig Lieder* (1784) and later in the *Mildheimisches Liederbuch* (1817).

BIBLIOGRAPHY

F. Lorenz: *Die Musikerfamilie Benda: Franz Benda und seine Nachkommen* (Berlin, 1967)

NANCY B. REICH

Wolfe, Julia (*b* Philadelphia, 18 Dec 1958). American composer. She studied music and theatre at the University of Michigan (BA 1980) and composition at Yale University with Martin Breswick (MM 1986). She enrolled in the doctoral programme at Princeton to study the music of Louis Andriessen, whom she acknowledges as a major influence. She has received a Fulbright Fellowship as well as many grants. As co-founder of the Wild Swan Theater in Ann Arbor, her responsibilities included playwriting, directing and acting as well as composing; with David Lang and her husband, Michael Gordon, she is co-director of New York's Bang on a Can Festival, which, since its founding in 1988, has presented hundreds of new and unknown pieces. Music of all types, from late Beethoven to Led Zeppelin, has been influential on her work. She has received commissions from the Huddersfield Festival, UK, and from the Orkest de Volharding, the Netherlands, for *Arsenal of Democracy*. Several of her compositions have been recorded, including *Four Marys* by the Cassatt Quartet.

WORKS

Orch: Amber Waves of Grain, 1988; Window of Vulnerability, 1992

Chamber and solo inst: On Seven-Star-Shoes, ww qnt, 1985; Williamsburg Bridge, fl/pic, ob, cl, s sax, hn, tbn, vn, vc, 1987; The Vermeer Room, chamber ens, 1989; Four Marys, str qt, 1991; Muscle Memory, el gui, 1992; Arsenal of Democracy, 13 brass/ww ens, 1993; Early that Summer, str qt, 1993; My Lips from Speaking, 6 pf, 1993

Choral: Song at Daybreak, SATB, pf, cl, vc, perc, 1986

RHIAN SAMUEL

Woll, Erna (*b* Sankt Ingbert, Saar, 23 March 1917). German composer. She studied church music at the Evangelisches Kirchenmusik-Institut, Heidelberg (1936–8)

with Wolfgang Fortner and others, and school music in Munich (1940–44), where her teachers included Joseph Haas; she then studied in Cologne (1946–8) with Heinrich Lemacher and others; she also studied German and musicology in Heidelberg, Munich and Würzburg. She worked as a church organist and Kantor in Cologne, Munich, Heidelberg and elsewhere in Germany, and between 1948 and 1972 taught at the church music institute in Speyer, the Gymnasium in Weissenhorn and at the University of Augsburg, specializing in music education techniques; her publications on the subject include *Buchprogrammiertes Musiklernen* (Wolfenbüttel, 1970) and *Praxis der programmierten Unterweisung im Musikunterricht* (Frankfurt, 1972). She has won many awards for composition, including the Valentin Becker and Deutscher Allgemeiner Sängerbund prizes. Most of her output is vocal, mainly sacred, music. Between 1957 and 1987 she composed about 50 choral works, including masses (one to a Dutch text, *Eer aan God*, 1967), cantatas and psalm settings. She has also composed songs, including *Lieder der Liebe* (1945), for mezzo and keyboard instrument, and the chamber work *Spielmusik*, for three violins and cello. Her music has been widely published in Germany.

BIBLIOGRAPHY

KompA-Z

B. Sonntag and R. Matthei, eds.: *Annäherungen an sieben Komponistinnen*, i (Kassel, 1986)

A. L. Suder, ed.: *Erna Woll*, Komponisten in Bayern, xii (Tutzing, 1987)

DETLEF GOJOWY

Wood, Mary Knight (*b* Easthampton, MA, 7 April 1857; *d* Florence, Italy, 20 Dec 1944). American composer, pianist and teacher. She studied the piano with B. J. Lang in Boston, performed locally in solo and chamber music recitals, and was active in many of Boston's leading musical organizations. Lang encouraged her to compose, and she continued to study the piano and composition in Boston with Arthur Foote, then in New York, with Henry Huss, Albert Parsons and J. H. Cornell. Her songs, chamber works and sacred vocal music display solid craftsmanship and a conservative, refined style. She married A. B. Mason and lived in Florence for many years.

WORKS

selective list

Chamber: Pf Trio

Sacred vocal: Christmas comes but once a year, mixed chorus (London, n.d.)

Songs (for 1v, pf, and pubd in Boston, unless otherwise stated): Don't Cry (J. W. Riley) (1893); 2 Songs, with vn obbl (1895): Autumn (R. King), A Romance (W. A. Purrington); Dodelinette (1896); 3 Songs (1896): Love blows into the heart (J. Wright), Afterward, thy Name; At Dawn (C. Thaxter), with vc obbl (1897); Love's Missing Bow (A. Warner), with vc obbl (1990); On Land or Sea (C. H. Goldthwaite) (1900); To my Lady (King) (1902); Ashes of Roses (New York, n.d.); Clover Blossoms (New York, n.d.); Meadow Lark (n.p., n.d.); Wailing (n.p., n.d.); c25 others

BIBLIOGRAPHY

R. Hughes: 'The Women Composers', *Contemporary American Composers* (Boston, 1900), 423–41, esp. 440

PAMELA FOX

Woodforde-Finden, Amy (née Ward, Amelia) (*b* Valparaiso, 1860; *d* London, 13 March 1919). British composer. She was one of nine children of an American serving as British Consul in Valparaiso; on his death, her mother took the surviving children to London. She began composing at an early age and was a pupil of Carl Schloesser, Winter and Amy Horrocks. Under the name Amy Ward she published a few songs, including *O Flower of All the World*, which attracted little attention. For some years she lived in India, travelling in Kashmir and marrying Colonel Woodforde-Finden, a medical officer in the Bengal Cavalry, in Bombay in 1893. In 1902 she produced her settings of *Four Indian Love Lyrics* from the recently published *The Garden of Kama* by Laurence Hope, the wife of an army officer with whom Colonel Woodforde-Finden had served in India. Rejected by publishers, the songs were first published privately; they were then taken up by the singer Hamilton Earle, who achieved a striking success with them, especially the *Kashmiri Song* ('Pale hands I loved beside the Shalimar'). As a result, the songs were acquired by Boosey & Co., thereby gaining her a regular publisher and a faithful public. She followed them with *A Lover in Damascus* (Charles Hanson Towne; 1904), *On Jhelum River* (Frederick John Fraser; 1905), *The Pagoda of Flowers* (Fraser; 1907) and other collections, as well as many individual songs. These sometimes drew on the Latin-American world of her childhood, at other times the exoticism of the East, always remaining notable for their fluent, easy-going melody and sound workmanship.

BIBLIOGRAPHY

SchmidlD

M. R. Turner and A. Miall: *The Edwardian Song Book* (London, 1982)

ANDREW LAMB

Woof, Barbara (*b* Sydney, 2 Sept 1958). Australian composer. She graduated in music from the University of Sydney (1981), then studied with Jan van Vlijmen and Jan Boermann at the Royal Conservatory in The Hague. In 1988 she was appointed to a teaching post at the Utrecht School of Arts. Despite being based in the Netherlands, she has continued to maintain musical connections with Australia and returned there in 1992 to take up a year's residency with the ABC, composing for the Sydney SO. Many of her works were written for ensembles based in the Netherlands, including the music-theatre piece *Voyeurs* for the 1993 Holland Festival. Her tape composition *Syzygy* (1984) won the Martin Codex prize in Spain.

WORKS

Music-theatre: Voyeurs, 1993

Orch: Sui morbidi cuscini del tempo, chamber orch, 1984; Canzone, 1989; Banshee's Dances, 1992; Night Crossing, 1993

Other inst: Maldoror, vn, 1983; Schiamachy, 2 gui, 1984; Caoine, a sax, 1985; Star Stream, hpd, perc, 1986; Hymn and Melodies, sax qt, 1987; Tenebrae, b cl, mar, 1990, rev. 1994

Elec: Syzygy, 1984

GRAHAM HAIR, GRETA MARY HAIR

Amy Woodforde-Finden

Woolf, (Sophia) Julia (*b* 1831; *d* Hampstead, 20 Nov 1893). English pianist and composer. She was thrice elected King's Scholar at the RAM, where she was the favourite pupil of Cipriani Potter. She married John Isaacson (*d* 1889). She published about 20 songs, some of which were incorporated into theatrical productions; several of her 20 piano pieces were arranged for orchestra as theatrical entr'actes. Her two-act comic opera *Carina* (libretto by E. L. Blanchard and C. Bridgman; vocal score, London, 1889) was produced at the Opera Comique, London, in September 1888 and at Crystal Palace in November 1888.

BIBLIOGRAPHY

FétisB

JOHN R. GARDNER

Wrighton, Mrs **James**. *See* POWNALL, MARY ANN.

Wuiet [Vuiet], **Caroline** [Auffdiener, Baronne] (*b* 1766; *d* 1835). French author and composer. The daughter of an organist in Rambouillet, she was trained as a pianist and later obtained patronage from Marie-Antoinette. She studied with P.-A. Beaumarchais and J.-B. Greuze, and took composition lessons from A.-E.-M. Grétry. Two of his later letters to her survive (Froidcourt). Her *L'heureuse erreur* (1786) was intended as a sequel to Grétry's and Desforges' *L'épreuve villageoise* (1784) and was rehearsed with orchestra at the Comédie-Italienne, but not voted for public performance. At the Revolution she was arrested, but fled to Holland and then England.

Under the Directory, Wuiet returned to fashionable Paris society. In about 1807 she married one Colonel Auffdiener and lived with him in Lisbon, where he was posted. On the defeat of the French armies they returned to France but lived separately, and Wuiet continued to write both music and fiction. Her literary works include the three-act *opéra Zéphire et Flore* (Brussels, 1784), the *comédies Angélina* (1782) and *Sophie* (1787), and *Esope au bal de l'Opéra, ou Tout Paris en miniature* (Paris, 1802).

WORKS

L'heureuse erreur (opéra comique), rehearsed, Paris, Comédie-Italienne, Feb 1786

L'heureux stratagème, ou Le vol supposé (opéra bouffon, 1, G. Saulnier), Paris, Théâtre des Beaujolais, 19 Aug 1786; ov. arr. for kbd, vn obbl, n.d.

6 romances (Paris, 1798); 6 romances, *F-Pc*; Comme elle était jolie, romance; Moi, j'aime la danse, chansonette; 3 sonatas, kbd, vn, b, op.1 (Paris, 1785);

Pot-pourri, pf, op.2 (Paris, n.d.); arrs. for kbd, vn obbl of ovs. to Sacchini: L'amore soldato (Paris, *c*1779) and Anfossi: Le mari insolent, n.d.

BIBLIOGRAPHY

FétisB

Registres de l'Opéra Comique, cxviii, f.69 (Feb 1786, *F-Po*)

M. Brenet: *Grétry, sa vie et ses oeuvres* (Paris, 1884)

C. D. Brenner: *A Bibliographical List of Plays in the French Language 1700–1789* (Berkeley, 1947, 2/1979)

G. de Froidcourt: *La correspondance générale de Grétry* (Brussels, 1962)

N. Epton: *Josephine, the Empress and her Children* (London, 1975)

DAVID CHARLTON

Wurm [Verne], **Mary** [Marie] **J. A.** (*b* Southampton, 18 May 1860; *d* Munich, 21 Jan 1938). British pianist, conductor and composer of German parentage. She studied the piano and composition at the Stuttgart conservatory and later became a piano pupil of Clara Schumann, Joachim Raff, Franklin Taylor, Józef Wieniawski and others. Her composition teachers in London included Arthur. Sullivan, C. V. Stanford and Frederick Bridge; she won the Mendelssohn Scholarship three times in succession, which enabled her to study composition at Leipzig, with Carl Reinecke, in 1886. She made her début as a pianist at Crystal Palace in 1882, and followed this with engagements in London, Leipzig, Meiningen and Berlin. Germany was her home for most of her life; she became a teacher in Hanover and Berlin, and eventually moved to Munich. In 1898 she established a women's orchestra in Berlin which she conducted and took on tour until 1900. Her sisters, Adela, Alice and Matilde, changed the family name to Verne, and pursued careers as pianists in England.

Wurm's earlier works fall into two distinct stylistic categories, English and German, which merge in later compositions. Her German vocal music is heavily indebted to Robert Schumann's choral style of the late 1840s, but her English vocal pieces simultaneously look backwards to the 18th-century glee tradition and forwards to Ivor Gurney and George Butterworth (the part-song *Under the greenwood tree* anticipates the modality of the post-World War I English folk music revival). Her mature style is English in its quasi-contrapuntal aspects and lightness of touch, and German in its harmonic basis. Her piano music exhibits a fondness for neo-classical pastiche: the Musette from the D minor Gavotte (*Three Pieces*, 1887) is prophetic of Béla Bartók in its high, tinkling treble over a drone bass.

WORKS
*printed works published in London
unless otherwise stated*

Stage: Prinzessin Lisa's Fee (Japanese children's oper-
etta, 2), Lübeck, Stadttheater, Jan 1890; Die
Mitschuldigen (opera, 1, after J. W. von Goethe),
Leipzig, Stadttheater, spr. 1921

Orch and chamber: Lullaby, vn, pf/vc, pf (? Leipzig,
1887), also arr. pf; Meteor-Walzer, str orch, also as
Empire Waltz, pf (Leipzig, 1887); Clotilde Kleeberg
Gavotte, str orch/pf (1889); Str Qt, Bb, op.40, 1894;
Estera Gavotte, str orch/pf (?1898), vn, pf (1898);
Concert Ov., orch; Dalila's Traum, str orch; Pf Conc.,
b; Vc Sonata; Vn Sonata, op.17; other pieces, vn, pf

Pf: Empire Waltz (Leipzig, 1887); Lullaby, op.7 (Leipzig, 1887); Suite, op.8 (1887); Barcarolle, op.22
(1892); Sylph Dance, op.23 (1892); 4 Duets, op.24
(1892); Valse de concert, op.27 (1893); Tanzweisen,
4 hands, op.28 (Leipzig, 1892); Suite, op.40 (1894);
Fairy Music, op.44 (1894); Sonata; other pieces,
some pubd

Partsongs (4 female vv unless otherwise stated): 5
Trios (S. G. Franz), 3 female vv (1890); About the
sweet bag of a bee (R. Herrick) (1892); Einst thät ein
Lied erklingen (F. A. Leo), op.33 no.1 (1892); Gute
Nacht (Leo) (1893); Under the greenwood tree (W.
Shakespeare) (1893); Wo nur dem Leben Lust erb-
lüht (A. Kurs) (1893); One by One (V.E.A.C.),
male vv, op.45 (1894)

Other vocal: Mag auch heiss das Scheiden brennen,
solo vv, women's chorus, str orch/pf, op.39; songs
(1v, pf) incl. O let me bathe my heart (Franz) (1888),
The Scots Guards' Band is playing (Cornwallis
West) (1894), 9 Lieder, op.25, 3 Lieder, op.55

BIBLIOGRAPHY
Baker6; *Grove5* (J. A. Fuller-Maitland); *MEMM*;
PazdirekH; *RiemannL 12*; *SchmidlD*; *WCBH*

O. Thompson, ed.: *The International Cyclopedia of
Music and Musicians* (London, 4/1942)

V. Manferrari: *Dizionario universale delle opere melodrammatiche* (Florence, 1954)

S. Stern: *Women Composers: a Handbook* (Metuchen,
NJ, 1978)

NIGEL BURTON

Wurmbrand-Stuppach [née Vrabely],
Stephanie [Brand-Vrabely, Stephanie] (*b*
Pressburg [now Bratislava], 26 Dec 1849;
d Vienna, 16 Feb 1919). Austrian composer,
pianist and writer of Slovak origin. She used
the pseudonym Stephanie Brand-Vrabely.
She was the daughter of the post office
director in Pressburg. Through her cultured
family circle she became acquainted with
Peter Cornelius, Brahms and Liszt, and with
Carl Tausig, who later became her teacher.
As a pianist she performed a wide range
of Romantic music, sometimes playing
arrangements for four hands with her sister
Seraphine (Tausig's wife). After her marriage
to Count Ernst Wurmbrand-Stuppach she
lived in Vienna, where her compositions
were performed by leading Austrian musicians. Her virtuoso piano music is typical of
the late Romantic period; it includes Die

schöne Melusine op.33 ('musikalische Illustrat-
ionen'), *Phantasiestücke* op.21, *Konzertstück im
ungarischen Stile* (for two pianos), waltzes,
paraphrases and studies. Other works include a violin sonata (op.35) and songs. She
also promoted the first performances of Béla
Bartók's music in Vienna and Manchester.

ALEXANDRA TAUBEROVÁ

Wylie, Ruth Shaw (*b* Cincinnati, 24 June
1916; *d* Estes Park, CO, 20 Jan 1989).
American composer and teacher. She studied
French (AB 1937) and composition (MA
1939) at Wayne State University in Detroit,
concluding her composition studies at the
Eastman School (PhD 1943); her composition
teachers included Bernard Rogers, Howard
Hanson, Arthur Honegger, Samuel Barber
and Aaron Copland. She taught music theory
and composition at the University of Missouri (1943–9) and at Wayne State University
(1949–69), where she founded and directed
the Improvisation Chamber Ensemble.
Among her awards are ASCAP Standard
Awards (1977–88) and an NEA grant for
Views from Beyond (1978). *Psychogram* (1968),
for piano, has been recorded.

WORKS
selective list

Orch: Suite, chamber orch, 1942; 2 syms.: no.1, 1943,
no.2, 1948; Conc. grosso, 1952; Concertino, cl,
orch, 1967; Memories of Birds, 1977; Views from
Beyond, 1978; Shades of the Anasazi, 1984; Conc.,
fl, str, 1986

Ballets: String Madness, pf, 1951; Façades (E.
Sitwell), fl, cl, pf, perc, 1956; Ragged Heart, 1961

Choral: 5 Madrigals (W. Blake), 1950

Chamber: Str Qt no.1, 1941; Str Qt no.2, 1946; Va
Sonata, 1954; Str Qt no.3, 1956; Fl Sonata, 1959; 25
pieces for improvisational ens repertory, 1966–8; 3
Inscapes, fl, va, gui, pf, perc, 1970; Incubus, fl, cl,
perc, vc ens, 1972; Imagi, 6 performers, 1974;
Nova, solo perc (cel, mar, vib), fl, cl, vn, vc, 3 perc,
1975; Toward Sirius, fl, ob, vn, vc, pf, hpd, 1976;
Airs above the Ground, fl, cl, vn, 4/8 vc, 1977;
Terrae incognitae, fl, va, gui, pf, perc, 1979; Music
for Three Sisters, fl, cl, pf, 1981; Str Qt no.4, 1983;
Signs and Portents, fl, vc, pf, 1988

Solo inst: Pf Sonata no.1, 1945; Pf Sonatina, 1947; 5
Preludes, pf, 1949; Pf Sonata no.2, 1953; Soliloquy
for Left Hand, pf, 1966; Psychogram, pf, 1968; The
White Raven, pf, 1983; Flights of Fancy, fl, 1985

Principal publishers: Harold Branch, Columbia
University Press, Cor, Peters

MSS in California State University, Northridge, CA;
some material in AMC

BIBLIOGRAPHY
WAM

K. Kroeger: 'Ruth Shaw Wylie', *Sonneck Society
Bulletin*, xv/2 (1979)

J. L. Zaimont and K. Famera: *Contemporary Concert
Music by Women* (Westport, CT, 1981)

CATHERINE PARSONS SMITH

X · Y

Xiao, Shuxian [Hsiao, Shu-sien] (*b* Tianjin, 9 April 1905; *d* Beijing, 26 Nov 1991). Chinese composer and educator. She was a prizewinning graduate of the Brussels Conservatoire Royale de Musique in 1932. From 1935 to 1954 she was married to the conductor Hermann Scherchen; the composer Tona Scherchen is their daughter. During the 1930s and 40s she spent 14 years in Switzerland, where she worked as a composer and was influential in promoting Chinese culture in Europe through her lectures and writings.

Her *Chinese Children's Suite* (1938; published Zürich, 1946) for voice and piano and the symphonic orchestral suite *Huainian Zuguo* ('A Commemoration of my Homeland') were among the first works by a Chinese composer to become known in the West. Her style combines Chinese folk materials with Western techniques, a concept later developed in her teaching of polyphony. In 1950, motivated by a desire to contribute to her country's development, she returned to China with her three children. From that time until her death she taught composition at the Central Conservatory in Beijing. Her output consists mostly of songs and piano pieces.

Xiao translated into Chinese Ernő Lendvai's publication on Béla Bartók's form and harmony (Beijing, 1979) and Charles Koechlin's *Précis des règles du contrepoint* (Beijing, 1986). Her *Collected Compositions* were published in a special edition of the *Journal of the Central Conservatory of Music* (Beijing, 1992); her *Collected Polyphonic Works* were also published in Beijing in 1992.

BIBLIOGRAPHY

S. Xiao: 'La chanson populaire chinoise', *Sinologica: Zeitschrift für Chinesische Kultur und Wissenschaft*, i/1 (1947), 65–86
P. Duan: 'Qi Xiao Shuxian xian sheng' [Introducing Professor Xiao Shuxian], *Journal of the Central Conservatory of Music*, xi/2 (1983), 51–3
Y. Xiao: 'Wan xia wei bi xun chen xi – Fang Xiao Shuxian jiao shou' [A Cloud at Sunset is as Good as One at Dawn – an interview with Professor Xiao Shuxian], *Renmin Ribao* [Beijing] (6 Jan 1990)
G. Zhou: 'Qun can tu si tao li fen fang – Fang zhu ming yinyao jiao yu jia Xiao Shuxian' [Like the Silkworm, or a Tree that Bears Fruit, a Saint Nourishes Those under her Guidance and Teaching – an Interview with the Famous Educator Xiao Shuxian], *Yinyao Zhoubao* (19 Jan 1990)
P. Duan: 'Hong yang bao gui di feng xian jing shen – Xiao Shuxian jiao shou zuo pin yinyao hui ting hou gan' [Magnified is the Noble Spirit of Dedication – after Attending the Concert of Xiao Shuxian's Compositions], *Journal of the Central Conservatory of Music*, xxxix/2 (1990), 20–22
S. Xiao: 'Zhi you zha gen min zu cai neng zou xiang shi jie' [Only Deeply Rooted in the Nation can we Move toward the World: Placing Hopes in the Young Composers], ibid., 18–19
S. Zhang: 'Hun qian meng ying hua xia' [Thoughts and Dreams are All of China], *Renmin Ribao* [Beijing] (14 Feb 1990) [overseas edn]
F. Liao: 'Dao nian Xiao Shuxian dai jie' [In Memory of Xiao Shuxian], *The Art of Music*, xlix/2 (1992), 64–6
P. Duan: 'Huainian wo guo yinyao jie di qian bei Xiao Shuxian' [In Memory of our Predecessor, Xiao Shuxian], *People's Music*, no.320/5 (1992) 29–30
M. Xiao: 'Feng xian di yi sheng – Huainian wo di muqin Xiao Shuxian' [An Offering Life – in Memory of my Mother, Xiao Shuxian], ibid., 26–8

JOYCE LINDORFF

Xin, Huguang (*b* Shanghai, 16 Oct 1933). Chinese composer. She began her musical activities in her early teens and entered the Beijing Central Conservatory of Music in 1951. Her graduate composition, *Gada Meilin*, a symphonic poem based on the life of the Mongolian hero, is regarded as a successful synthesis of folk music material with Western techniques. Between 1956 and 1980, she lived in the Inner Mongolia Autonomous Region, teaching composition at the Inner Mongolian Arts School; her works from this period were based on Mongolian folk music. In 1981 she moved to Beijing, working as a composer for the Beijing Music and Dance Company. Her music has a strong personal style, with flowing, extended melodies and colourful orchestration.

WORKS
selective list

Orch: Gada Meilin, sym. poem, 1956; Caoyuan zuqü [Suite of Prairie], 1963; Caoyuan yinshi [Tone-

Poem of Prairie], conc., matou qin [morin khuur], 1976
Oratorio: Cao yuan yinxong xiao jiemei [The Heroic Sisters of Prairie], 1964
Chamber: Str Qt, 1980
Film scores: Zuguo a, muqin [O my Mother, my Country], 1977; Saomo sanji [Notes on Desert], 1982

YANDI YANG

Xosroviduxt [Khosrovidukht] (*fl* early 8th century). Armenian hymnographer and poet. Following the abduction of her brother by Muslim Arabs, Xosroviduxt, who was of royal blood, was taken to the fortress of Ani-Kamakh (now Kemah), where she lived in isolation for 20 years. She is reported to have written the *šarakan* (canonical hymn), 'Zarmanali ē inj' ('Wondrous it is to me'), which honours the memory of her brother, killed in 737 for reclaiming his Christian faith. Despite its secular subject, this florid *šarakan* has been sanctioned by the Armenian Church for use during service.

BIBLIOGRAPHY

Ł. Ališan: *Hušikkʻ hayreneacʻ hayocʻ* [Memories from the Land of the Armenians], ii (St Lazar, 2/1921), 136

H. Ačaṙyan: *Hayocʻ anjnanunneri baṙaran* [Dictionary of Armenian Proper Names] (Beirut, 2/1972), 539

D. Der Hovanessian and M. Margossian, trans. and eds.: *Anthology of Armenian Poetry* (New York, 1978), 43–4

G. A. Hakobyan: *Šarakanneri žanrĕ hay mijnadaryan grakanutʻyan mej* [The Genre of *šarakan* in Medieval Armenian Literature] (Erevan, 1980), 167–71

N. Tʻahmizyan, ed.: *Hay ergi goharner: Oskepʻorik* [Treasures of Armenian Song: a Collectarium] (Erevan, 1982), 26–7

ŞAHAN ARZRUNI

Young, Polly. *See* BARTHÉLEMON, MARIA.

Z

Zaimont, Judith Lang (*b* Memphis, 8 Nov 1945). American composer. She studied the piano at the Juilliard School with LeLand Thompson (1958–64) and with Zaven Khachadourian at the Long Island Institute of Music (diploma 1966). Her major teachers in composition were Hugo Weisgall at Queens College, CUNY (BA 1966), and Jack Beeson and Otto Luening at Columbia University (MA 1968); she also took private lessons in orchestration in France with André Jolivet (1971–2). She has been a resident at the MacDowell Colony and has won a number of prizes and awards. She taught at Hunter College, New York (1980–88), and at Adelphi University, Garden City, New York (1989–91), then becoming senior professor of composition at the University of Minnesota in Minneapolis.

Zaimont has received commissions from, among others, the Gregg Smith Singers and Western Wind. She edited a directory, *Contemporary Concert Music by Women* (1981), and is editor-in-chief of a continuing series, *The Musical Woman: an International Perspective* (1984–); vol. iii (1991) won the Pauline Alderman Prize for new scholarship on women in music. She is also the author of a textbook in composition, *Twentieth Century Music: an Analysis and Appreciation* (1980), and other teaching materials.

In her works up to the 1980s, Zaimont concentrated on song cycles with elaborate instrumental accompaniments, selecting texts from a wide range of sources; *From the Great Land* (1982) incorporates unusual instrumental timbres. Her music reveals a rhythmic affinity with French composers (Debussy, Ravel, Messiaen) and Stravinsky. The writing for piano in such works as *Nocturne* (1978) is imaginative; other essentially tonal, neo-romantic pieces are found among her chamber compositions. Subsequent works are mainly instrumental and include four orchestral pieces, of which *Chroma* won first prize in the competition in honour of the Statue of Liberty Centennial.

A symphony was jointly commissioned by three orchestras for 1994.

WORKS

Stage: Goldilocks and the Three Bears (chamber opera, D. Kosloff), S, A, T, B, pf, 1985; Jan 1986

Orch: Pf Conc., 1972; Tarantelle, 1985; Chroma: Northern Lights, 1986; Monarchs, 1988

Chamber and solo inst (except pf): Fl Sonata, 1962; 2 Movts, wind qt, 1967; Grand Tarantella, vn, pf, 1970; Capriccio, fl, 1971; Music for Two, any tr ww/(ww, brass insts), 1971, rev. any 2 b insts, 1985; Valse romantique, fl, 1972; De infinitate caeleste: Of the Celestial Infinite, str qt, 1980; Sky Curtains, fl, cl, bn, va, vc, 1984; Dance/Inner Dance, fl, ob, vc, 1985; Winter Music, brass qnt, 1985; Hidden Heritage: a Dance Symphony, fl/a fl, cl/b cl/t sax, el pf, amp vc, perc, 1986; Dramatic Fanfare, brass nonet, 1987; When Angels Speak, wind qnt, 1987; Trio: Russian Summer, vn, vc, pf, 1989; Doubles, ob, pf, 1993

Pf: Portrait of a City, 1961; Variations, 1965; Toccata, 1968; Scherzo, 1969; Snazzy Sonata, pf 4 hands, 1972; A Calendar Set, 12 preludes, 1972–8; 2 Pf Rags, 1974; Calendar Collection, 1976; Nocturne: la fin de siècle, 1981; Stone, 1981; Black Velvet Waltz, 1983; several other works

Choral: 3 Ayres (W. Shakespeare, B. Jonson, W. Blake), SATB, 1969; Man's Image and his Cry (Jewish book of prayer), A, Bar, SATB, orch, 1970; The Chase (cantata, Zaimont), SSATB, pf, 1972; Sunny Airs and Sober (5 madrigals, Shakespeare, P. B. Shelley, J. Gay, R. Herrick), SSATB, 1974; Sacred Service for the Sabbath Evening (Union Prayer Book), Bar/A, SSATB, orch/pf, 1976; The Tragickal Ballad of Sir Patrick Spens (trad.), SSATB, pf, 1980; Serenade: To Music (W. H. Auden), SSATTB, 1981; Lamentation (Bible), Mez, Bar, double chorus, 1982; Parable: a Tale of Abram and Isaac (Brome Mystery Play, W. Owen), S, T, Bar, SSATTB, (org)/(str, hpd), 1986; The Spirit of the Lord, SSAATTBB, brass qnt, org, 1992

Vocal: 4 Songs (E. E. Cummings), Mez, pf, 1965; The Ages of Love (5 songs, Byron, E. St. V. Millay C. Rossetti), Bar, pf, 1971; Chansons nobles et sentimentales (5 songs, C. P. Baudelaire, A. Rimbaud, P. Verlaine), high v, pf, 1974; Songs of Innocence (W. Blake), S, T, fl, vc, harp, 1974; Greyed Sonnets (Rossetti, S. Teasdale, Millay), S, pf, 1975; The Magic World: Ritual Music for Three (Native American chants), Bar, pf, perc, 1980; Deep Down (spiritual, Zaimont), medium v, pf, 1982; From the Great Land (F. Buske), Mez, cl, pf, drums, 1982; In the Theater of Night: Dream Songs on Poems of Karl Shapiro, high v, pf, 1983; New-

Fashioned Songs (5 Eng. poets), low v, pf, 1984, arr. medium v, pf; Nattens monolog [Night Soliloquy] (D. Hammarskjöld), S, pf, 1985; Will's Words (scena, Shakespeare), Bar, 1990; Vessels, Mez, pf, 1992

Principal publisher: Galaxy

BIBLIOGRAPHY

Anderson 2

L. McNeil: *The Vocal Solo Works of Judith Lang Zaimont: an Annotated Bibliography* (diss., Arizona State U., 1988)

S. L. Baird: *The Choral Music of Judith Lang Zaimont* (diss., Florida State U., 1991)

ELIZABETH WOOD

Zallman, Arlene (*b* Philadelphia, 9 Sept 1934). American composer and pianist. She studied at the Juilliard School (1955–9) and at the University of Pennsylvania (1965–8). She taught at Oberlin Conservatory of Music (1968–71) and at Yale University (1972–3), and later chaired the Music Department at Wellesley College in Massachusetts (1982–5, 1991–3). Her awards include a Fulbright grant for study in Italy with Luigi Dallapiccola (1959–61), as well as grants from the NEA (1973) and Mellon Foundation (1981). Zallman's compositions are written primarily for small instrumental and vocal ensembles. She has explored a broad range of historical styles and idioms, as represented, for example, by the piano variations on 'Alma che fai', based on a 15th-century villanella by Luca Marenzio, the *Songs and Dances from Milton's 'Comus'* and the choral work *Il blues delle cicche* to a text by Cesare Pavese. Nevertheless, she has evolved her own integrated, frequently atonal, harmonic language, and highly personal modes of continuity.

WORKS
selective list

Choral: Emerson Motets, chorus, 1985; And with ah! bright wings, chorus, org, 1986; Canticles pour le Divin Enfant, chorus, chamber ens, 1988; Il blues delle cicche (The Cigarette-Butt Blues) (C. Pavese), female chorus, sax, pf, db, 1991

Solo vocal: Sonnet XVIII, S, pf, 1957; Ballata, T, pf, 1960; Per organo di barberia, S, vc, 1975; 3 Songs from Quasimodo, S, fl, vc, 1976, Sonnet XXXIII 'Injury', Bar, hn, pf, 1979; Sonnet CXXVIII 'The Virginal', Bar, pf, 1980; Nightsongs II, S, fl, a fl, 2 cl, 1988; Sonnet/Sonata (Shakespeare CII), 1v, vn, 1990; Songs and Dances from Milton's 'Comus', Mez, va, hpd, 1993; Vox feminae, S, pf, 1994

Chamber and solo inst: Racconto, pf, 1968; Analogy, fl, 1971; Variations, cl, vn, pf, 1977; Nightsongs I, vn, pf, 1984; Sololoquium, vc, 1986; Sei la terra che aspetta, vc, pf, 1990; A Whimsical Offering, pf, 1990–93; Variations on 'Alma, che fai', pf, 1992

MICHELLE C. SWEET

Zechlin, Ruth (*b* Gross Hartmannsdorf, Saxony, 22 June 1926). German composer,

harpsichordist and organist. She studied music at the Leipzig Hochschule für Musik (1943–9), where her teachers (from 1945) included J. N. David for composition and Karl Straube and Günther Ramin for organ. From 1950 she worked at the Hanns Eisler Hochschule für Musik, East Berlin, first as a teacher of analysis, and from 1969 as a professor of composition; she was made a full professor in 1984, the first woman in Germany to be so appointed, and in 1986 guest professor. In 1970 she became a full member of East Germany's Akademie der Künste, where she was responsible for a master's degree course in composition; she was considered one of the most important composers in that country. In 1990 she was made vice-president of the Berlin Akademie der Künste and became a member of the Deutscher Musikrat. As a performer she has specialized in early English keyboard music, J. S. Bach and contemporary music.

Although Zechlin has written many chamber, vocal and dramatic works, orchestral music has been central to her output. The focus of her compositional orientation has been the music of J. S. Bach, whose influence, together with others, is evident in her works; yet, she has developed an original, personal style. The pieces dating from the 1960s are characterized by the use of 'free tonality', those of the 70s by their unconstrained melodies and rhythms as well as by the introduction of noise elements that show Zechlin's expert handling of sound colours, and those of the 80s by balanced formal structures. Her preoccupation with other artistic media, particularly architecture, has helped her develop a broader conception of form, structure and colour.

WORKS
selective list

Dramatic: Reineke Fuchs (radio play, J. W. von Goethe), 1962, stage version for actors, 1967; Keunergeschichten (B. Brecht), spkr, chamber ens, 1966; Mysterium buffo (incid. music, W. W. Majakowsky), 1967; Egmont (incid. music, Goethe), 1974; An Aphrodite (Sappho, Homer, Anyte), A, Bar, mime artists, 7 musicians, 1977; Adam und Eva (radio play incid. music, P. Hacks), 1979; La vita: Konstellationen (ballet), 1983; Die Salamandrin und die Bildsäule (opera, F. Göhler, after C. M. Weiland), 1990

Orch: Musik, small orch, 1960; Vn Conc., 1963; Syms., no.1, 1965, no.2 1966; Concertino, ob, chamber orch, 1969; Thema mit 5 Veränderungen, 1969; Sym. no.3, 1971; Emotionen, 1971; Pf Conc., 1974; Org concs., no.l, 1974, no.2, 1975; Kristalle, hpd, str, 1975; Dionysos und Apollo, 4 fl, str, perc, 1976; Briefe, 1978; Reflexionen, 14 str, 1979; Musik, 1980; Org Conc. 'Prag', 1980; Situationen, 1980; Metamorphosen, 1982; Musik zu Bach, 1983;

Linien, hpd, orch, 1986; Kristallisation, 1987; Träume, 1987; Linien II, hpd, insts, 1988; Vn Conc. 'Hommage à György Kurtág', 1990

Chamber: Fl Sonatina, 1955; Trio, ob, va, vc, 1957; Str qts, no.1, 1959, no.2, 1965; Amor und Psyche, chamber ens, hpd, 1966; Gedanken über ein Klavierstück von Prokofieff, pf, chamber ens, 1967; Chamber Sym., 1967–8; Str qts, no.3, 1970, no.4, 1971, no.5, 1971; Stationen, ww qnt, kbd insts, 1972; Chamber Sym. no.2, 1973; Begegnungen, chamber orch, 1977; Str Qt no.6, 1977; Harp Trio, 1978; Szenen 'Hommage à Shakespeare', chamber ens, 1978; Aktionen, 4 solo str, 1979; Konstellationen, 10 brass insts, 1985; Konfrontationen, chamber ens, 1986; Portrait, chamber ens, 1986; Prometheus (F. Kafka), spkr, pf, perc, 1986; Bewegungen, trbn qnt, 1990

Solo inst: Toccata und Passacaglia, hpd, 1962; Spektrum, org, 1973; Beschwörungen, perc, 1981; Evolution, org, 1981; Genesis, org, 1981; Da capo, vn, 1982; Traum und Wirklichkeit, org, 1982; Musik, vc, 1983; Fantasie, Interludium und Fuge, spinet, 1986; Im Salon der Rahel Levin, hpd, 1986; 5 Mobiles, harp, 1988

Choral: Lidice, cantata, 1958; Wenn der Wacholder blüht, oratorio, 1960; Aphorismen über die Liebe, unacc. mixed vv, 1970, rev. 1972; Der Sieg von Guernica (P. Eluard), 4vv, 1975; Ave Maria, 4–12vv unacc., 1980; Der Zauberlehrling (Goethe), Bar, 4vv, pf, 1981; Angelus Silesius Sprüche, unacc. mixed vv, 1983

Solo vocal: 4 Lieder, S, pf, 1960; Ode an die Lufte (P. Neruda), Mez, orch, 1962; 7 Borchert-Lieder, C/B, pf, 1964; Canzoni alla notte (S. Quasímodo), Bar, orch, 1974; Das Hohelied (Bible), T, orch, 1979; Kanzone (L. Lechner), Bar, orch, 1983; 4 Lieder (C. Paris), 1v, 6 insts, 1983; 3 Shakespeare Songs, Ct, hpd, 1985; Ein Lied der Liebe (E. Lasker-Schüler), solo A, 1986; Monolog aus 'Romeo und Julia', Ct, chamber ens, 1987; Varianten zu Michelangelo, A/Mez, vc, 1987; Frühe Kafka-Texte, 1v, pf, 1990

Also documentary film scores, incl. Rosa Luxemburg, 1970

Principal publishers: Breitkopf & Härtel, Henschel, Peters, Ries & Erler, Verlag für Musik, Zimmermann

BIBLIOGRAPHY

U. Stürzbecher: 'Ruth Zechlin', Komponisten in der DDR: 17 Gespräche (Hildesheim, 1979), 150–71

M. Daschke: 'Erfahrungen bei der Ausbildung unseres kompositorischen Nachwuchses: aus Gesprächen mit Ruth Zechlin, Günter Kochan und Siegfried Köhler', Musik und Gesellschaft, xxx (1980), 513–18

G. Altmann: 'Ruth Zechlin: ein Komponistenportrait', Musik und Schule, xxxii (1981)

B. Sonntag: 'Gedankenaustausch mit Ruth Zechlin: Briefwechsel im Herbst 1984', Zeitschrift für Musikpädagogik, x/29 (1985), 3–12

H. Mainka and J. Mainka, eds.: Ruth Zechlin – Situationen, Reflexionen: Gespräche, Erfahrungen, Gedanken (Berlin, 1986)

R. Matthei and B. Sonntag, eds.: 'Ruth Zechlin', Annäherungen an sieben Komponistinnen, i (Kassel, n.d.), 57–64

B. Schröder-Nauenberg: 'Ungewöhnliches Ausdrucksbedürfnis', 5 Jahre internationales Festival Komponistinnen gestern–heute und 5th International Congress on Women in Music, ed. R. Sperber and U. Feld (Heidelberg, 1989), 231–7

ROSWITHA SPERBER

Zegers (y Montenegro), Isidora (b Madrid, 1 Jan 1803; d Santiago, 14 July 1869). Spanish singer and composer. She studied singing with Federico Massimino in Paris, where she also took lessons in the piano, the harp, the guitar and composition. In 1822 she left Europe for Chile and played a prominent role in the development of that country's musical culture; in 1827 she and Carlos Drewetcke helped to found the Santiago Philharmonic Society and in 1850 to form the National Conservatory, of which she was made honorary director the following year. With José Zapiola she collaborated in 1852 in founding Seminario musical, a weekly publication to which she was a regular contributor of articles and translations. Some of her compositions are lost, but those piano pieces, including a set of contradanzas, and songs that survive, mostly from her time in Paris, conform to Classical-Romantic style traditions.

WORKS
selective list

Pf: La Camille, 1922; La Mercedes, 1922; other contradanzas and romances

Songs: L'absence, S, pf, 1823; La coquette fixée (Mlle Aurore), S, pf, 1823; Les regrets d'une bergère (A. Gauthier), S, pf, 1823; Canción (J. Arboleda), 1846

BIBLIOGRAPHY

E. Pereira Salas: Los orígines del arte musical en Chile (Santiago, 1941), 94–103

—— : Historia de la música en Chile (1850–1900) (Santiago, 1957)

J. Urrutia Blondel: 'Doña Isidora Zegers', Revista musical chilena, xxv/113–14 (1971), 3–17

RAQUEL BUSTOS VALDERRAMA

Zhubanova, Gaziza Akhmetovna (b Aktyubinsk region, Kazakhstan, 2 Dec 1927). Kazakh composer. She was the daughter of the composer and scholar Akhmet Zhubanov, who was the organizer and conductor of the Kazakh Instruments Orchestra. She studied composition with M. Gnesin and L. Shtreiher at the Gnesin music school, Moscow, and with Yu. A. Shaporin at the Moscow Conservatory, from which she graduated in 1954, continuing with postgraduate work until 1957. Between 1962 and 1968 she was chairwoman of the Kazakh Composers' Union. She taught composition at the Alma-Ata Conservatory from 1967 and was its director from 1975 to 1987.

A significant part of Zhubanova's output consists of large-scale works, in which a blurring of generic boundaries is evident: traits of oratorio appear in her operas, such as *Enlik-Kebek* and *Dvadtsat' vosem'* ('Twenty-Eight'), as do operatic traits in oratorios, including *Pesnya Tat'yani* ('Tat'yana's Song'). She has perpetuated the Eastern tradition of writing dedications; for example her 'Zhiger' Symphony is dedicated to the folk composer Dauletkerei, and the opera *Kurmangazï* to a famous exponent of the Kazakh instrumental genre, the *küi*. In both its meditative and its dynamic forms, the *küi* is often the basis of Zhubanova's music; authentic *küis* act as cultural symbols where they appear in her compositions, but the versions she herself has written, even those that occur, paradoxically, in choral textures, still remain within the nature of the genre.

WORKS
selective list

Stage: Khirosima [Hiroshima] (ballet, 1, A. Mambetov), 1966; Enlik-Kebek (opera, 3, S. Zhiyenbayev, after M. Auezov), 1975; Dvadtsat' vosem' [Twenty-Eight] (opera, 2, Mambetov), 1981; Kurmangazï (opera, 3, H. Yergaliyev), 1987 [completion of A. Zhubanov's opera]; Karagoz (ballet, 2, Mambetov, G. Alexidze, after Auezov), 1990; Burannïy Edigey (Legendï Aytmatova) [Blizzard Edigey (Aytmatov's Legends)] (opera, 3, Mambetov, Zhiyenbayev, after Ch. Aytmatov); incid. music [over 30 scores]

Orch: Vn Conc., 1957; Sym. no.1 'Zhiger' [Energy], 1973; Sym. no.2 'Ysla de las mujeres', 1983; Pf Conc., 1986; Sym. no.3 'Sarozekskiye metaforï' [Sarozek Metaphors], 1989; Vc Conc., 1991

Choral: Danushpan [Genius] (oratorio, K. Murzaliyev), 1969; Kui-poema (H. Yergaliyev), unacc. chorus, 1973; Aral'skaya bïl' [Aral Story] (oratorio, S. Zhiyenbayev), 1978; Pesnya Tat'yanï [Tat'yana's Song] (oratorio, after A. S. Pushkin: *Yevgeny Onegin* and other poems, trans. Abay), 1983; Vozlyubi chelovek cheloveka [Man, Love Man] (oratorio, O. Suleymanov, R. Gamzatov, Yu. Drunina, Aytmatov, I. Bergman), 1988

Chamber and solo inst: Str Qt, 1952; Pf Trio, 1985; Str Qt, 1990; Suite, tpt, pf, cel, perc, 1992; pieces for fl, qobuz, va; pf sonatas, preludes and other pieces

Also songs and film music

BIBLIOGRAPHY

L. Uzkikh: 'Oratoriya G. Zhubanovoy "Zarya nad step'yu"' [Zhubanova's Oratorio 'Dawn over the Steppe'], *Muzïkoznaniye* [Alma-Ata], vii (1975), 121

—— : 'Teoreticheskiye zametki o simfonii G. Zhubanovoi "Zhiger"' [Theoretical Notes on Zhubanova's Symphony 'Zhiger'], *Muzïkoznaniye* [Alma-Ata], viii–ix (1976), 103

L. Izmailova: 'Bïl', stavshaya legendoi' [A True Story Became a Legend], *SovM* (1980), no.4, pp.52–3

Interviews, *SovM* (1985), no.4, pp.21–6

S. Shubina: 'Poysk obshchechelovecheskikh tsennostei' [A Search for Universal Values], *SovM* (1989), no.1, pp.23–9

L. S. Ajazbekova: 'Muzïkal'naya traditsiya etnosa i ego rol' v formirovanii kompozitorskogo mïshleniya (na primere opernogo tvorchestva G. Zhubanovoi)' [Ethnic Musical Tradition and its Role in the Formation of Composers' Thought (Based on the Operatic Works of Zhubanova)] (diss., All-Union Scientific Institute of History of Arts, Moscow, 1990)

OLGA MANULKINA

Zielińska, Lidia (*b* Poznań, 9 Oct 1953). Polish composer. She studied composition with Andrzej Koszewski at the Poznań State Higher School of Music (MA 1978); at the same time she was a violinist in the Poznań PO and in the Agnieszka Duczmal Chamber Orchestra. From 1979 she took part in composers' workshops and seminars in Poland and abroad, and from 1984 lectured at workshops and courses in Belgium, the Netherlands and Switzerland. She was guest composer at an electronic music conference in France in 1985 and has produced her works at the electronic studios in Kraków, in Warsaw (Polish Radio) and at the Instituut voor Psychoakoestik en Elektronische Muziek in Ghent; she has her own private computer studio. Apart from teaching at the Academy of Music and the State Higher School of Visual Arts in Poznań, she cooperates with theatres, including the Eight Day Theatre, is a member of the artistic group Artificial Cult, and organizes contemporary music festivals (as artistic director of the Poznań Musical Spring and repertory committee member of the Warsaw Autumn festivals). For many years she served in the Polish section of the ISCM and has continued to serve on juries of composers' competitions and other enterprises.

Zielińska's musical interests are broad and she is not afraid to free herself from tradition in her search for new techniques and means of expression, particularly in instrumental music, in musical theatre and in multi-media productions. She has won many prizes in Polish and international competitions, including first prize in 1983 for *Farewell Mr Toorop* at the Max Deutsch International Competition in Paris; her *Solfatara*, for mixed choir, received an honourable mention at the GEDOK competition in Mannheim in 1981. Her works have been performed at festivals and broadcast by several European networks.

WORKS
selective list

Dramatic, multi-media: Eh Joe (monodrama, S. Beckett), mime, tape, orch, 1978; Mrs Koch (tragifarce, M. Białoszewski), solo vv, vocal and inst ens, tapes, 1981; Cascando (Beckett), actor, double mixed choir, 1983–91; Artificial Cult (W. Olesiak, after F. Zappa), tape, video, neon signs, visual objects, 1985; Heldenleben, tape, video, shadowgraph, 1986; Kaleidoscope (passacaglia for children), perc, slides, clapping hands, 1987; 8 heures de la vie des femmes (music-theatre), 9 performers, 1988; A Piece about Everything (rondo), perc, children, 1988; The Same (performance), 1988; Sound Museum (live installation for children), 1989; In the Field (mini-spectacle), 1990

Orch: Vn Conc., 1979; 2 Dances, str orch, 1981; Farewell Mr Toorop, 1981; Fiction, 1986; Pleonasmus, ob, vn, str orch, 1987; Little Atrophic Sym., 1988

Vocal: Solfatara, mixed choir, 1981; Concrete Music, choir, orch, 1987

Chamber and solo inst: Litany, str qt, 1979; Minuten-Sonate, 1 opt. inst, 1981; Treatise, ob qt, 1982; Lullaby Gagaku, db, 1984; Mazurko for Tadeusz Wielecki, db, 1985; Sonnet on the Tatras, 4 performers, 1985; Glossa, va/vn, 1986; Str Qt, 1988; Jacquard Loom, 15 performers, 1991; Fago, bn, db, accordion/el kbd, 1992

Elec: Music for Stanisław Wyspiański, 1985; Polish Dances for Tape after Rev. Baka, 1986; Musica Humana or How Symphonies are Born, radio piece, 1989; Short Piece, fl, elec, 1992; see also dramatic and multi-media works

Principal publisher: Brevis

BARBARA ZWOLSKA-STĘSZEWSKA

Zieritz, Grete von (*b* Vienna, 10 March 1899). Austrian composer and pianist. She studied at the Graz conservatory (1912–17) with Hugo Kroemer (piano) and Roderich Mojsisovics (composition). In 1917 she moved to Berlin and continued her studies with Martin Krause (piano) and Rudolf Maria Breithaupt. From 1919 she taught at the Stern Conservatory. She began to attract notice as a composer in 1921 with the first performance of her Japanese songs for soprano and piano. In 1926 she went to the Berlin Hochschule für Musik to continue her composition studies with Franz Schreker, and it was through him that she forged a strongly individual style. In 1928 she was awarded the Mendelssohn Prize for composition as well as the Schubert Grant from the Columbia Phonograph Company. She was the first woman to receive the title of honorary professor from the Austrian president (1958), later honours included the Austrian Ehrenkreuz für Wissenschaft und Kunst (1978) and the Verdienstkreuz am Bande der Bundesrepublik Deutschland (1979). Zieritz toured extensively in Germany and other countries, often performing her own works. In 1988 her *Zigeunerkonzert* was played to celebrate her 89th birthday in a concert given by the Moscow PO. As a composer she was most at home in chamber works, many of which feature wind instruments, but she also

wrote a substantial number of orchestral, choral and solo vocal pieces. She never abandoned tonality. Many of her musical ideas had their genesis in visual images and pictures, and her writing is distinguished by vivid tone painting and clarity of form.

WORKS
selective list

ORCHESTRAL

Kleine Abendmusik, str, 1916; Triple Fugue, str, 1926; Intermezzo diabolico, 1932; Bilder vom Jahrmarkt, fl, orch, 1937; Das Gifthorner Konzert, fl, harp, str, 1940; Triple Conc., fl, cl, bn, orch, 1950; Le violon de la mort (Danses macabres), vn, pf, orch, 1956–7; Divertimento, 12 solo insts, chamber orch, 1962; Sizilianische Rhapsodie, vn, orch, 1965; Conc., 2 tpt, orch, 1975; Org Conc., 1977; Fanfare, 1979; Zigeunerkonzert, vn, orch, 1982

CHAMBER

For 4–9 insts: Str Qt, 1916; 2 Pieces, str qt, 1926; Suite, fl, ob, cl, bn, pf, 1937; Dance Suite, gui/hpd, cl, bn, perc, 1958; Qnt, tpt, trbn, 2 pf, perc, 1959; Serenade, fl, ob, cl, bn, hn, 1964–5; Sextet, bn, str qnt, 1965; Concertino, cl, hn, bn, str qnt, 1982; Kassandra-Rufe, 8 solo insts (vn, va, vc, db, B♭-cl, E♭-cl, b cl, bn), nonet (ob, B♭-cl, bn, tpt, perc, vn, va, vc, db), 1986

For 2–3 insts: Trio, cl, hn, pf, 1955; Die Jagd, cl, hn, pf, 1957; Kaleidoskop, vn, va, 1969; 5 Aphorismen, vn, vc, 1971; Trio, ob, cl, bn, 1971; Josefas Garten, fl, bn, org, 1977; Kapriolen, ob, cl, bn, 1977; Danza, 3 gui, 1979; Ildico und Attila, vn, 5-str db, 1979

For 1 inst, pf: 1914: Phantasie-Sonate, vn, pf, 1917; Bokelberger Suite, fl, pf, 1933; Bilder vom Jahrmarkt, fl, pf, 1936; Va Sonata, 1939; Suite, a fl, pf, 1952; Le violon de la mort, vn, pf, 1952; Variations, hn, pf, 1956; Musik, cl, pf, 1957; Le violon de la mort, va, pf/hpd, 1964; Arabeske und Aria, eng hn, pf, 1976; Folkloristische Fantasie, vn, pf, 1982

Solo inst: 2 Fugues, pf, 1921; Prelude and Fugue, pf, 1924; Pf Sonata, 1928; 6 Dämonentänze, pf, 1948; 5 Pieces, pf, 1963; Autobiographie, vn, 1965; Cascade, tpt, 1975; Suite, va, 1978; Une humoresque diabolique, db, 1980; Triptychon, fl + a fl + pic, 1968; Le roi a fait battre tambour, ob d'amore, 1973; Prelude and Fugue, org, 1977; Der Waldspaziergang, cl, 1983; Triptychon, vn, 1984–6

VOCAL

With orch: Passion im Urwald (Zieritz), S, orch, 1930; Vogellieder, S, fl, orch, 1933; Hymne (Novalis), Bar, orch, 1943; Die Zigeunerin Agriffina, S, orch, 1956; Japanische Lieder, S, chamber orch, 1972

With pf: 10 Japanische Lieder, S, pf, 1919; 9 Lieder des Hafis, Bar, pf, 1924; Fiebergesichte (K. Hamsun), A, pf, 1933; 5 Gesänge (F. Nietzsche), 4 solo vv, pf, 1935; Das ewige Du (von Below), A, pf, 1938; 5 Sonneten (L. Labé), S, pf, 1942; 5 Lieder (R. M. Rilke, H. Hesse), T, pf, 1943; Der letzte Weg (Moslé), A, pf, 1950; Der Sonnengesang von Amarna, men's chorus 4vv, pf, 1976; 3 Lobgesänge (Pol. poems), Mez, pf, 1979

With other insts: 4 geistliche Lieder, Bar, fl, pf, 1926; 6 Gesänge (S. George), Bar, str qt, 1935; 3 Gesänge

(F. Blücher von Wahlstatt), Bar, vc, pf, 1946; Stimmen im Walde, S, fl, 1954; Zigeunermusik, S, fl, vn, pf, 1955; Zlatorog, Bar, cl, hn, pf, 1957–9; Qt, S, ob, cl, harp, 1972; Berliner Psalm (Friedenberg), 1v, cl, pf, 1974; Lieder zum Mond (Lavant), S, fl, ob, cl, bn, 1974

Unacc.: Dem Sonnengott (F. Hölderlin), women's chorus 4vv, 1940; Berglied, mixed vv, 1962; 4 Alt-Aztekische Gesänge, mixed chorus 8vv, 1966; 5 Portugiesisch-Spanische Gesänge, mixed chorus 8vv, 1966; 7 Gesänge (contemporary black poetry), mixed chorus 8vv, 1966; 3 Chöre (T. Fontane), men's chorus 4vv, 1973

Principal publishers: Astoria, Ries & Erler

BIBLIOGRAPHY

MGG (W. Suppan); RiemannL 12
W. Suppan: Steirisches Musiklexikon (Graz, 1962–6)
J. Lansky: 'Grete von Zieritz', Mitteilungen des Steirischen Tonkünstlerbundes, xix–xx (1964), 1–3
U.Werk: Grete von Zieritz (Berlin, 1989)

ROSARIO MARCIANO

Ziffrin, Marilyn J(ane) (b Moline, IL, 7 Aug 1926). American composer, teacher and musicologist. She attended the University of Wisconsin at Madison (BM 1948), Columbia University (MA 1949) and the University of Chicago, and studied composition privately with Karl Ahrendt and Alexander Tcherepnin. She taught in public schools, then at Northeastern Illinois State College (1961–6), New England College in Henniker, New Hampshire (until 1982), and at St Paul's School in Concord, New Hampshire (until 1991). Several times a fellow at the MacDowell Colony, she has also received awards from ISCM (Chicago chapter, 1955), the Delius competition (1971, 1972), the American Council of Learned Societies (1974), and from ASCAP (1981–91). Ziffrin's instrumental music is dissonant, rhythmically complex and vigorous, with elegant and eloquent melodic lines.

Her writings include Carl Ruggles: Composer, Painter and Storyteller (Urbana, IL, 1994). Several of her works have been recorded (chiefly by Crystal, Capra and Opus One).

WORKS
selective list

Orch and band: Waltz, orch, rev. 1957; Ov., band, 1958; Small Suite, str orch, 1963; Orch Piece, 1977; Colors, orch, rev. 1979; Salute to Lexington, ov., band, 1985; Sym. 'Letters' for Neva Pilgrim, 1v, orch, 1988; Movie Music, suite, orch, 1993

Vocal: Jewish Prayer, chorus, 1950; Death of Moses, cantata, chorus, 1954, rev. 1983; 3 Songs, Mez, pf, 1957; Prayer, chorus, 1966; Haiku (song cycle, K. Martin), S, va, hpd, 1971; Trio, S, tuba, xyl, 1974; Chorus [from Alcestis], 1990; 3 Songs of the Trobairitz, S, pf, 1991; Choruses from the Greeks, SATB, 1992

Chamber: The Little Prince, suite, cl, bn, 1953; In the

Beginning, perc ens, 1968; XIII, chamber ens, 1969; Str Qt, 1970; Movements, cl, perc, 1972; Sonata, vc, org, 1973; Trio, vn, vc, pf, 1975; Qnt, ob, str qt, 1976; Conc., va, ww qnt, 1978; Sono, vc, pf, 1980; Yankee Hooray, pf 4 hands, 1984; Conversations, db, hpd, 1986; Tributum, Bb-cl, va, db, 1992

Solo inst: Theme and Variations, pf, 1949; Suite, pf, 1955; Toccata and Fugue, org, 1956; Rhapsody, gui, 1958; 4 Pieces, tuba, 1973; Fantasia, bn, 1986; 3 Movements, gui, 1989; Incantation and Dance, gui, 1989–90

Film score: White Lies, 1984

Principal publishers: Editions Orphee, Music Graphics

BIBLIOGRAPHY

J. L. Zaimont and K. Famera: Contemporary Concert Music by Women (Westport, CT, 1981)

CATHERINE PARSONS SMITH

Zimmermann, Agnes (Marie Jacobina) (b Cologne, 5 July 1847; d London, 14 Nov 1925). German pianist and composer. Her family moved to England when she was very young; from the age of nine she studied at the RAM with Cipriani Potter and Charles Steggall. Later her teachers included Ernst Pauer and G. A. Macfarren. She won the King's Scholarship in 1860 and again in 1862 and her compositions were performed at the RAM students' concerts. Although performing frequently at the RAM she made her public début in 1863 at Crystal Palace, where she performed two movements of Beethoven's 'Emperor' Concerto. Except for a successful tour to Germany in 1864, when she played at the Leipzig Gewandhaus, and two subsequent tours abroad (1879–80 and 1882–3), she remained in England until her death.

She was well known in England as a composer of works in Classical form and style; yet she made her name in London mainly as a pianist, through her performances at the Monday Popular Concerts and at the Hanover Square Rooms. With Clara Schumann she played her own Andante and Variations for two pianos at St James's Hall (19 March 1868). She excelled at performances of Classical music. She also edited the sonatas of Mozart and Beethoven and the piano works of Robert Schumann; her Schumann edition was among the earliest English publications to use 'continental' fingering.

WORKS
selective list

Vocal: solo songs; duets; partsongs, 4vv
Chamber music: Vc sonata, op.17; Pf Trio, op.19; 3 vn sonatas, opp.16, 21, 23

Pf solo: Mazurka, op.11; Presto alla tarantella, op.15; Sonata, op.22; various salon pieces

BIBLIOGRAPHY

FétisB; SchmidlD

J. A. Fuller-Maitland: *English Music in the Nineteenth Century* (London, 1902)

Obituaries: *The Times* (17 Nov, 1925), 16; *MT*, lxvi (1925), 1136

Lady Arbuthnot: 'In Memoriam Agnes Zimmermann: Pianist and Composer, 1847–1925', *MT*, lxvii (1926), 28

P. Scholes: *The Mirror of Music 1844–1944* (London, 1947)

JOHN R. GARDNER, GAYNOR G. JONES

Agnes Zimmermann

Zimmermann, Margrit (*b* Berne, 7 Aug 1927). Swiss composer and teacher. She studied the piano and music theory in Berne, Lausanne and Paris. Her first composition teacher was Arthur Honegger; she later studied composition and conducting at the Milan Conservatory. She has received many commissions and several works have been recorded for radio and on disc. In 1987 she won second prize at the first international competition for women composers at Unna in Germany. Zimmermann describes her style as 'atonal, but traditional', though in her search for new timbres she often employs techniques such as cluster glissandos and quarter-tones that are more commonly associated with a progressive aesthetic.

WORKS
selective list

Stage: Gasel, op.25 (sym.-ballet), 1981; Jason und Medeia, op.28 (ballet), 1982

Orch: Introduzione e Allegro, op.12, sym., 1979; Transcendency, op.55, 12 sym. episodes, 1989; Pianorama, op.59, conc., pf, str orch, 1990; Seidenstrasse, op.63, sym., 1992

Choral: Panta-Rhei, op.39 (N. Bach), S, women's chorus, vn, org, 1987; Spuren innerer Kreise, op.53 (Bach), 16vv, 1988; Wo sich berühren Raum und Zeit, op.60 (M. Kaléko), 9 female vv, 1990; In urbis honorem, op.61 (G. Schaeffner), SATB, orch, 1991

Other vocal: 3 Lieder, op.5 (H. Peyer), high v, pf, 1978; Pensieri, op.31 (3 sonnets, Petrarch), T, gui, fl, 1984; Plis, op.37, sym., 1v, 16 solo insts, 1985; Alle 7 Jahre, op.56 (Kaléko), Mez, pf, 1989

Chamber and solo inst: 3 str qts: no.1, op.7, 1979–82, no.2, op.11, 1980, no.3 'Il gioco', op.16, 1981; Aus Black-Box, op.10, ob, cl, hn, bn, 1982; Sonata, op.33, vn, 1985; Sonata, op.35, cl, 1986; Bianchi-Neri, bk 1, op.36, 6 studies for pf, 1984, bk 2, op.65, 1993; Orphische Tänze, op.43, fl, cl, va, vc, pf, kettophon, 1986; Aus Black-Box, op.47, cl, 1988; Quadriga, op.51, sonata, pf, 1987; Triptychon, op.58, trbn, org, 1989; Serenade, op.62, fl, pf, 1992; Fascination, op.64, trbn, 1992; Suite, op.66, fl, pf, 1992

CHRIS WALTON

Živković, Mirjana (*b* Split, 3 May 1935). Serbian composer. She studied composition with Stanojlo Rajičić at the Belgrade Academy of Music (graduation, 1964) and later studied with Olivier Messiaen and Nadia Boulanger in Paris (1967–8). Her early compositions include neo-Baroque features, though their atonal language is also to some extent expressionist. Later works, such as *Zaboravljeni kontrapunkt* ('Forgotten Counterpoint', 1980), for soprano, alto, tenor and bass, show a greater economy of means and speak more directly. Her output includes *Sinfonia poliphonica* (1964) for orchestra; *Basma* ('Incantations', 1968), for mezzo and four timpani; *Symphonic Metamorphosis* (1974) for piano and orchestra; and *Glasovi* ('Voices', 1979), for harpsichord.

MELITA MILIN

Zubeldia, Emiliana de [Bydwealth, Emily] (*b* Salinas del Oro, Navarra, 6 Dec 1888; *d* Hermosillo, Sonora, 26 May 1987). Mexican composer and pianist of Spanish birth. At the age of eight she entered the Pamplona Academia Municipal de Música, studying the piano with Joaquín Maya, and at 15 the Madrid Real Conservatorio, completing her course there in 1906. After her father's death in 1909, she returned to Pamplona; there she was appointed *profesor auxiliar de piano* at the institution from which she had graduated. Her brother, Nestor, canon archivist of

Pamplona Cathedral, officiated at her marriage in 1919 to Dr Joaquin Fuentes Pascal (1887–1976), from whom she separated three years later. She then moved to Paris, studying at the Schola Cantorum with the Bach specialist Blanche Selva, for piano, and composition with Vincent d'Indy. She undertook many concert tours in the following years; in 1931 she played at Town Hall, New York, being billed as a Basque composer. She gave a further concert at the Roerich Museum, New York, later in the same year, which culminated with her eight Basque Folk Dances for two pianos, choreographed by dancers from the Centro Basco Americano of New York City. In New York she met the prominent Mexican acoustician, Augusto Novaro (1893–1960), inventor of a keyboard instrument with changeable tone-colour. Already a composer of symphonies, piano music and songs, she was profoundly affected by his harmonic theories and her musical language evolved accordingly. Just over a year later, Zubeldia moved to Mexico City, continuing her studies with Novaro and giving her first recital at the Teatro Hidalgo on 18 August 1933. Shortly thereafter she undertook a concert tour of Central America. She took Mexican citizenship in 1942. In 1947, after a decade of teaching in Mexico City, she accepted an invitation to spend a year developing choruses at the University of Hermosillo, but this one year stretched into 40. In August 1956, José Vásquez conducted the orchestra of the Universidad Nacional Autónoma de México in the première of her *Sinfonía elegíaca*, composed in 1940 in memory of her sister Eladia (1887–1939). According to Varela, she wrote 116 works, 42 for voice and piano, 31 for piano, 19 choral, 14 orchestral and 10 chamber. She donated many of her compositions (some published at Pamplona under the name of Emily Bydwealth) to the University of Sonora at Hermosillo.

WORKS
selective list; unless otherwise stated,
dates other than those of publication
are of first performance

Orch: Euzkadi, sym. poem, 1932; Sinfonía elegíaca, comp. 1940; El desierto de los Leones, sym. poem
Chamber and solo inst (except kbd): Trio España, pf trio (Paris, 1927); Capricho basko, gui, 1929; Paisaje basko, gui, ?1931; Paisaje desde el Pirineo, harp, 1934; Vn Sonata, 1957; Vn Sonata, F#; Va Sonata
Kbd (solo pf unless otherwise stated): La petite fleur solitaire (Paris, 1928); 8 danzas vascas, 2 pf, 1931; Sonata en 3 movimientos, 1932; Sonata, 2 pf (Mexico City, 1933); Suite vasca, 2 pf (Mexico City, 1933); Sonata, 1956; Ritmo vasco, 2 pf; 3 pieces: Souvenir de Biarritz, Dans la terrasse, Le printemps

retourne [pubd, n.d., under the pseud. E. Bydwealth]
Choral (all for mixed vv): Canciones populares vascas, 1929; Himno al sul (Quechua text), 1932; Misa de la Asuncíon, 1968; Nuestras vidas son péndulos (R. López Velarde), 1971; Huérfano (López Velarde), 1972; Liñuaren penak (Basque text); Zortiko (Zubeldia)
Songs (1v, pf): Asturiaña, pubd in *ReM*, vii/11 (1925–6), suppl.; 6 melodias populares españolas (Zubeldia) (Paris, 1929); 28 other songs, 3 (A. Mairena) pubd (Mexico City, 1952); When the orange blossom time comes back again (E. McGrath de Galván)

BIBLIOGRAPHY
'Recital of Basque Music', *New York Times* (13 Feb 1931)
T. Iturriaga: 'La música popular vasca y Emiliana de Zubeldia', *Pro arte musical* [Havana] (30 March 1932)
J. L. Vidaurreta: 'Emiliana de Zubeldia', *Diario de la marina* [Havana] (26 April 1936)
E. Pulido: 'Mexico's Women Musicians', *The Musical Woman: an International Perspective*, ii: *1984–5*, ed. J. L. Zaimont and others (Westport, CT, 1987), 313–34
—— : 'Emiliana de Zubeldia', *Heterofonía*, xi/5 (1978), 18
L. T. Varela: *Zubeldia Maestra Maitea* (Hermosillo, 1992) [incl. facsimiles, review by R. Stevenson, *Inter-American Music Review*, xiii/2 (1993), 163]

ROBERT STEVENSON

Zuckermann, Augusta [Gussie]. *See* MANA ZUCCA.

Zumsteeg, Emilie (*b* Stuttgart, 9 Dec 1796; *d* Stuttgart, 1 Aug 1857). German composer, pianist, singer and teacher. She was the youngest of seven children born to the composer Johann Rudolf Zumsteeg (whose compositions included about 200 lieder) and to Luise Andreae. Her father died when she was six, and shortly thereafter her mother opened a music shop, in which young Emilie helped. She studied the piano with Schlick and theory with Wilhelm Sutor. Gifted with a fine alto voice, she was soon singing and performing on the piano (e.g. at the Stuttgart Museumskonzerte). As an adult Zumsteeg was in contact with leading musicians and poets. The literary ties reflected her interest in the lied, her compositional mainstay and the basis of her creative reputation. She also wrote several piano works, such as the early *Trois polonaises*, published in 1821 and favourably reviewed in the *Allgemeine musikalische Zeitung*, and sacred choral music. She occupied a central position in the musical life of Stuttgart as a teacher of singing and the piano and as a leading member of the Verein für Klassische Kirchenmusik.

Zumsteeg's lieder were apparently still known in the late 19th century (Michaelis) but have not remained in the repertory. She composed about 60 songs. The six lieder of her op.6 received a brief but laudatory notice in the *Allgemeine musikalische Zeitung* in 1842. An earlier collection, *Sechs Lieder* op.4 (Mainz, n.d.), includes mainly simple, strophic songs, but occasionally reveals an italianate flair, as in the second song, *Morgenständchen* (in Citron). Zumsteeg's originality further surfaces in *Neun Lieder* (Bonn, n.d.): for example, the hint of fantasy in *Ich denke Dein* and the chamber-like setting of *Des Freundes Wunsch*. A full evaluation of her compositions must await further research into her life and the republication of her music.

BIBLIOGRAPHY

AMZ, xxiii (1821), 479–80; xxiii (1821), 816; xxxi (1829), 747; xxxvi (1834), 484; xliv (1842), 935–6

A. Michaelis: *Frauen als schaffende Tonkünstler: ein biographisches Lexicon* (Leipzig, 1888)

H. J. Moser: *Das deutsche Lied seit Mozart* (Berlin and Zürich, 1937, 2/1968)

K. Haering: 'Emilie Zumsteeg', *Schwäbische Lebensbilder*, ii (Stuttgart, 1941), 537ff

M. J. Citron: 'Women and the Lied, 1775–1850', *Women Making Music: the Western Art Tradition, 1150–1950*, ed. J. Bowers and J. Tick (Urbana and Chicago, 1986), 224–48

MARCIA J. CITRON

Zwilich, Ellen Taaffe (*b* Miami, 30 April 1939). American composer and violinist. She studied with John Boda at Florida State University (BM 1960, MM 1962), then moved to New York to study the violin with Ivan Galamian. As a member of the American SO under Leopold Stokowski, she acquired invaluable training in performance and orchestration. Eventually, she enrolled at the Juilliard School, where she studied with Elliott Carter and Roger Sessions and, in 1975, became the first woman to take the DMA in composition. Meanwhile, performances of her music began occurring with increasing frequency: *Symposium* for orchestra (1973) was conducted by Pierre Boulez, the *String Quartet 1974* was played at the ISCM World Music Days in Boston, and the *Sonata in Three Movements* (1974) was performed by her husband, the violinist Joseph Zwilich. Symphony no.1, first performed in 1982 by the American Composers Orchestra under Gunther Schuller, brought her international renown in 1983, when it was awarded the Pulitzer Prize in music, making Zwilich the first woman to receive that honour.

The publicity engendered by the prize enabled Zwilich to earn a living exclusively from composition. Her music had already begun to change from the jagged melodies,

Ellen Taaffe Zwilich

atonal harmonies and structural complexities of the *Sonata in Three Movements* and the *String Quartet 1974* to a simpler, more accessible vocabulary. That change was partly due to the death of her husband in 1979; afterwards, she became interested in communicating more directly with performer and listener. Although this attitude is evident in the Symphony no.1, its presence accelerated throughout the 1980s and early 90s. Since her earliest mature compositions, Zwilich has been obsessed with the idea of generating an entire work – large-scale structure, melodic and harmonic language, and developmental processes – from its initial motives. However, in her later works, the motivic material itself has become simpler, its development more audible, its melodic treatment more long-breathed, and its harmonic context increasingly tonal.

In later years, Zwilich has employed traditional motivic materials (triads, scales, arpeggios) within classical multi-movement structures, underpinned by recognizable thematic recurrences. Orchestral works like *Symbolon* (1988), Symphony no.2, 'Cello Symphony' (1985), and Symphony no.3 (1992), commissioned by the New York Philharmonic for its 150th anniversary, are characterized by grand gestures, with tonal centres defined by propulsive ostinatos, forceful unisons and lengthy pedal-points.

Her orchestral works, the bulk of her later output, exude a dark-hued intensity reminiscent of Shostakovich and Mahler and possess a directness of utterance that has made Zwilich popular with audiences and performers alike. Concise, economical and clean in texture, Zwilich's music might be classified under the rubric 'neo-classic' were it not for its very 'neo-romantic' expressive force.

Beginning in the late 1980s, Zwilich wrote a series of concertos for the more neglected orchestral instruments, including the trombone (1988), the bass trombone (1989), the flute (1989), the oboe (1990), the bassoon (1992), the horn (1993) and the trumpet (1994); she also wrote a Double Concerto for violin and cello (1991). Numerous repeat performances, a stream of commissions, and her own prolific compositional skills have combined to make Zwilich one of America's most frequently played and genuinely popular living composers.

WORKS

Orch: Symposium, 1973; Sym. no.1 (3 Movts for Orch), 1982; Prologue and Variations, str orch, 1983; Celebration, 1984; Conc. grosso 1985, 1985; Sym. no.2 (Cello Sym.), 1985; Conc., pf, orch, 1986; Images, 2 pf, orch, 1986; Tanzspiel, ballet, 4 scenes, 1987; Ceremonies, band, 1988; Conc., trbn, orch, 1988; Symbolon, 1988; Conc., b trbn, str, timp, cymbals, 1989; Conc., fl, orch, 1989; Conc., ob, orch, 1990; Conc., vn, vc, orch, 1991; Conc., bn, orch, 1992; Sym. no.3, 1992; Conc., hn, str, 1993; Fantasy, 1993; Romance, vn, chamber orch, 1993; Conc., tpt, orch, 1994

Choral: Thanksgiving Songs, chorus, pf, 1986; Immigrant Voices, chorus, brass, timp, str, 1991

Solo vocal: Einsame Nacht (song cycle, H. Hesse), Bar, pf, 1971; Im Nebel (Hesse), A, pf, 1972; Trompeten (G. Trakl, trans. Zwilich), S, pf, 1974; Emlékezet (S. Petöfi), S, pf, 1978; Passages (A. R. Ammons), S, fl + a fl + pic, cl + b cl, vn, va, vc, pf, perc, 1981, orchd 1982

Chamber: Sonata in 3 Movts, vn, pf, 1973–4; Str Qt 1974, 1974; Clarino Qt, 4 tpt/4 cl, 1977; Chamber Sym., fl + pic, cl + b cl, vn, va, vc, pf, 1979; Str Trio, 1982; Divertimento, fl, cl, vn, vc, 1983; Intrada, fl + pic, cl, vn, vc, pf, 1983; Chamber Conc., tpt, fl + pic, b cl + cl, db, pf, perc, 1984; Conc. for Tpt and 5 Players, tpt, fl + pic, cl + b cl, pf, perc, db, 1984; Double Qt, str, 1984; Trio, vn, vc, pf, 1987; Qnt, cl, str, 1990

Kbd: Fantasy, hpd, 1983; Praeludium, org, 1987

BIBLIOGRAPHY

R. Dreier: 'Ellen Taaffe Zwilich', HiFi/MusAm, xxxiii/9 (1983), 4–5, 18

J. Rubinsky: 'Ellen Taaffe Zwilich's Upbeat Road to the Pulitzer', Keynote, viii/9 (1984), 16–19

T. Page: 'The Music of Ellen Zwilich', New York Times Magazine (14 July 1985)

'Conversations with American Composers: Ev Grimes Interviews Ellen Taaffe Zwilich', Music Educators Journal, lxxii/6 (1986), 61–5

H. Waleson: 'Composer Ellen Taaffe Zwilich Living her Dream', Symphony Magazine, xxxvii/2 (1986), 20–23, 67

R. Samuel: 'Ellen Taaffe Zwilich, Concerto for Trumpet and Five Players: Concerto grosso 1985', ML, lxix (1988), 143–4

P. Moor: 'Ellen Taaffe Zwilich', HiFi/MusAm, cix/2 (1989), 16–17

Ellen Taaffe Zwilich (New York, 1988) [BMI composer brochure]

K. ROBERT SCHWARZ

Illustration Acknowledgments

The publishers would like to thank the institutions and individuals listed below who have kindly provided material for use in this book. The following abbreviations are used:

RCM   Royal College of Music (Department of Portraits), London
RM   Richard Macnutt, Withyam, Sussex

Preface (p.x) New York Public Library for the Performing Arts; **Agnesi, Maria Teresa**: Museo Teatrale alla Scala, Milan; **Akiyoshi, Toshiko**: Kendor Music, Delevan, New York; **Allitsen, Frances**: RCM; **Anderson, Laurie**: Redferns, London / photo Leon Morris; **Andrée, Elfrida**: Musikmuseet, Stockholm; **Anna Amalia (ii)**: Stiftung Weimarer Klassik; **Anspach, Elizabeth**: Sotheby's, London; **Archer, Violet**: Canadian Music Centre, Toronto; **Armer, Elinor**: photo Kingmond Young, San Francisco; **Arrieu, Claude**: Gérard Billaudot, Paris / photo Guy Vivien; **Aylward, Florence**: RCM; **Barnes, Ethel**: RCM; **Bauer, Marion Eugénie**: E. P. Dutton, New York, from *Modern Music-Makers* (1952) by Madeleine Goss; **Beach, Amy Marcy**: RCM; **Beauharnais, Hortense Eugénie de**: (p.52) Institut de France, Fondation Dosne-Thiers (Collection F. Masson); (p.53) Private Collection / photo RCM; **Bembo, Antonia**: Bibliothèque Nationale, Paris (Rés Vm¹ 117, f. 78); **Berberian, Cathy**: Peters Edition, London / photo Annette Lederer, Hamburg; **Bertin, Louise**: (p.60) Bibliothèque Marguérite Durand, Paris; (p.61) Bibliothèque et Musée de l'Opéra, Paris / photo Bibliothèque Nationale; **Billington, Elizabeth**: The Beaverbrook Art Gallery (Gift of Lord Beaverbrook), Fredericton, New Brunswick; **Blahetka, Leopoldine**: Österreichische Nationalbibliothek, Vienna; **Bonis, Mélanie**: Private Collection; **Boulanger, Lili**: Roger-Viollet, Paris; **Boulanger, Nadia**: Roger-Viollet, Paris; **Boyd, Anne**: Australian Music Centre, Sydney; **Branscombe, Gena**: photo Bruno, Hollywood; **Brentano, Bettina**: Goethe Museum, Frankfurt; **Brillon de Jouy, Anne Louise Boyvin d'Hardancourt**: American Philosophical Society, Philadelphia (781.508 B 762 Music no.2); **Bruzdowicz, Joanna**: (p.90) photo Susanna Fels; (p.91) photo Juliusz Multarzyński, Warsaw; **Caccini, Francesca**: (p.95) The Musical Quarterly, Oxford University Press, New York; **Candeille, Julie**: Collection Rondel, Paris, from *Enciclopedia dello Spettacolo* (Rome: Casa Editrice Le Maschere, 1954); **Carreño, Teresa**: RCM; **Chaminade, Cécile**: RM; **Clostre, Adrienne**: Editions Choudens, Paris / photo Michel Meunier; **Coccia, Maria Rosa**: Civico Museo Bibliografico, Bologna; **Coleridge-Taylor, Avril**: photo Jane Plotz, Johannesburg; **Crawford, Ruth**: Judith Tick; **Daniels, Mabel Wheeler**: E. P. Dutton, New York, from *Modern Music-Makers* (1952) by Madeleine Goss; **Dickson, Ellen**: Private Collection / photo RCM; **Dlugoszewski, Lucia**: photo Peter Kaplan; **Dring, Madeleine**: Private Collection / photo Michael Boys, London; **Droste-Hülshoff, Annette von**: Archiv für Kunst und Geschichte, Berlin; **Duchambge, Pauline**: Musée de Versailles / photo Bibliothèque Nationale, Paris; **Eckhardt-Gramatté, S.-C.**: Canadian Music Centre, Toronto; **Ellicott, Rosalind Frances**: RCM; **Farrenc, Louise**: (p.164) from *L'illustration* (13 January 1855); (p.165) Bibliothèque Nationale, Paris; **Firsova, Elena**: Boosey & Hawkes, London; **Fowler, Jennifer**: photo Barry Atkinson; **Freer, Eleanor Everest**: RM; **Gardner, Kay**: photo David Walters; **Gipps, Ruth**: Hulton Deutsch Collection, London; **Glanville-Hicks, Peggy**: Australian Music Centre, Sydney; **Gröndahl, Agathe**: RCM; **Gubaydulina, Sofiya Asgatovna**: (p.200) photo Malcolm Crowthers, London; (p.202) © 1991 by Musikverlag Hans Sikorski, Hamburg; **Hardelot, Guy d'**: RCM; **Hays, Sorrel**: photo Ilhan Mimaroglu; **Hildegard of Bingen**: (p.218) Hessische Landesbibliothek, Wiesbaden; (p.219) Benedictine Abbey of St Peter and St Paul, Diest (MS 9, f.159r); **Holmès, Augusta**: (p.223) RCM; (p.224) RM; **Holst, Imogen**: photo Nigel Luckhurst, Cambridge; **Howe, Mary**: photo Doris Ullman; **Isabella Leonarda**: Private Collection; **Jacquet de la Guerre, Elisabeth-Claude**: (p.236) Bibliothèque Nationale, Paris; (p.237) Civico Museo Bibliografico, Bologna; **Jaëll, Marie**: RCM; **Janotha, Natalia**: RCM; **Kaprálová, Vítězslava**: Český Hudebni Fond, Prague; **Kolb, Barbara**: Boosey & Hawkes, London / photo Carlo Carnevali; **Konishi, Nagako**: photo Dorothy Williams; **Kuyper, Elisabeth**: (p.256) New York Public Library for the

Performing Arts; (p.257) Women and Music Foundation, Amsterdam; **La Barbara, Joan**: Wizard Music, Los Angeles, CA / photo Debbie Richardson; **Lang, Margaret Ruthven**: Boston Public Library; **Larsen, Libby**: The Minnesota Orchestral Association; **Lebrun, Franziska**: Art Gallery of South Australia (Gift of Gladys Penfold Hyland in memory of her husband Frank, 1964), Adelaide; **LeFanu, Nicola**: photo David Lumsdaine; **Leginska, Ethel**: RCM; **Lehmann, Liza**: RCM; **Loder, Kate**: RCM; **Lombardini Sirmen, Maddalena Laura**: Civica Raccolta Bertarelli, Milan; **Louie, Alexina**: Canadian Music Centre, Toronto; **Lutyens, Elisabeth**: Schott, London / photo Jane Bown; **Macirone, Clara Angela**: Royal Academy of Music, London / photo RCM; **Maconchy, Elizabeth**: Chester Music, London / photo Suzie Maeder; **Mahler, Alma Maria**: Österreichische Nationalbibliothek, Vienna; **Malibran, Maria**: RM; **Maria Antonia Walpurgis**: Residenzmuseum, Munich / photo Mansell Collection, London; **Martínez, Marianne von**: Haydn Museum, Vienna / photo Museen der Stadt Wien; **Martinez, Odaline de la**: photo Coneyl Jaye; **Mendelssohn, Fanny** (p.323): Kupferstichkabinett, Staatliche Museen / Bildarchiv Preussischer Kultur-besitz, Berlin; (p.324) Mendelssohn Archiv (MS 74), Staatsbibliothek, Berlin; **Milanollo, Teresa**: RCM; **Monk, Meredith**: Houston Grand Opera / photo Jim Caldwell; **Moore, Mary Carr**: Catherine Parsons Smith; **Mori, Junko**: photo J. Michele Edwards; **Mucha, Geraldine**: Margot Leigh Milner; **Musgrave, Thea**: Novello, London; **Pentland, Barbara**: Canadian National Library, Ottawa; **Puget, Loïsa**: RM; **Rainier, Priaulx**: Schott, London / photo Malcolm Crowthers; **Richter, Marga**: Carl Fischer, New York / photo Alan Skelly; **Riego, Teresa Clotilde del**: RCM; **Rimskaya-Korsakova, Nadezhda Nikolayevna**: Muzïka, Moscow, from N. A. Rimsky-Korsakov (1988) by A. Kruchinina and I. Obraztsova; **Rivé-King, Julie**: RCM; **Saariaho, Kaija**: photo Malcolm Crowthers, London; **Sappho**: · Staatliche Antikensammlungen und Glyptothek, Munich; **Schröter, Corona Elisabeth Wilhelmine**: Goethe Museum / Stiftung Weimarer Klassik; **Schumann, Clara**: Robert-Schumann-Haus, Zwickau; **Serova, Valentina Semyonovna**: Society for Cooperation in Russian and Soviet Studies, London; **Smyth, Ethel**: (p.429) Hulton Deutsch Collection, London; (p.430) Museum of London; (p.431) RM; **Strozzi, Barbara**: Staatliche Kunstsammlungen, Dresden; **Stuart-Coolidge, Peggy**: Catherine Parsons Smith; **Sutherland, Margaret**: Australian Music Centre, Sydney / photo J. Albert; **Szymanowska, Maria Aghate**: Polskie Wydawnietwo Muzyczne, Cracow (Sesac, New York), from *Maria Szymanowska, Album* (1953); **Tailleferre, Germaine**: Roger-Viollet, Paris; **Talma, Louise**: Carl Fischer, New York / *Philadelphia Bulletin*, photo Vincent Gonzales; **Temple Hope**: RCM; **Tower, Joan**: G. Schirmer, New York / photo Steve J. Sherman; **Ustvol'skaya, Galina Ivanovna**: Boosey & Hawkes, London; **Viardot, Pauline**: (p.475) Mary Evans Picture Library, London; (p.476) Roget-Viollet, Paris; (p.477) RM; **Vorlová, Sláva**: Český Hudebni Fond, Prague / photo Marśal; **Weir, Judith**: (p.488) photo / Malcolm Crowthers, London; (p.489) photo Catherine Ashmore, London; **White, Maude Valérie**: RCM; **Wilhelmina**: Archiv für Kunst und Geschichte, Berlin; **Woodforde-Finden, Amy**: RCM; **Zimmermann, Agnes**: RCM; **Zwilich, Ellen Taaffe**: MAA Music Associates of America, Englewood, NJ / photo Cori Wells Braun, New York.

List of Contributors

The list below includes the names of all those whose work appears in the dictionary. For living contributors, the name is followed by his/her last known place of work or residence.

Abert, Anna Amalie (Kiel, Germany)
Allroggen, Gerhard (Detmold, Germany)
Ambache, Diana (London, UK)
Ammer, Christine (Lexington, MA, USA)
André, Naomi (Cambridge, MA, USA)
Andrieux, Françoise (Paris, France)
Anthony, James R. (Tucson, AZ, USA)
Antonio, Irati (São Paulo, Brazil)
Aprahamian, Felix (London, UK)
Ard, Jamée (New York, NY, USA)
Arias, Raquel C. de (Buenos Aires, Argentina)
Arzruni, Şahan (New York, NY, USA)

Baldwin, Olive (Brentwood, Essex, UK)
Ballman, Christine (Brussels, Belgium)
Banfield, Stephen (Birmingham, UK)
Barandoni, Stefano (Pisa, Italy)
Béhague, Gerard (Austin, TX, USA)
Beimel, Thomas (Wuppertal, Germany)
Benser, Caroline Cepin (La Crosse, WI, USA)
Bent, Ian D. (New York, NY, USA)
Berdes, Jane L.
Bernstein, Jane A. (Medford, MA, USA)
Blankenburg, Walter
Block, Adrienne Fried (New York, NY, USA)
Blom, Eric
Bonaventura, Sam di (Fairfax, VA, USA)
Borroff, Edith (Durham, NC, USA)
Borthwick, E. Kerr (Edinburgh, UK)
Bortin, Virginia (Los Angeles, CA, USA)
Boucourechliev, André (Paris, France)
Bowers, Jane M. (Madison, WI, USA)
Boyd, Malcolm (Cardiff, UK)
Boydell, Brian (Dublin, Ireland)
Boyer, Horace Clarence (Amherst, MA, USA)
Bradshaw, Susan (London, UK)
Bridges, Thomas W. (Princeton, NJ, USA)
Briscoe, James R. (Indianapolis, IN, USA)
Brito, Dulce (Lisbon, Portugal)
Brooks, William (Urbana, IL, USA)
Brown, Malcolm Hamrick (Bloomington, IN, USA)
Brown, Rae Linda (Redondo Beach, CA, USA)
Bruce, Phyllis (Ann Arbor, MI, USA)
Bruland, Inge (Copenhagen, Denmark)
Burn, Sarah M. (Greystones, Co. Wicklow, Ireland)
Burt, Amanda M. (Fairfax, VI, USA)

Burton, Anthony (East Barnet, Herts., UK)
Burton, Nigel (Reading, UK)

Calam, Toni (Colchester, UK)
Cantero, Alicia Valdés (Habana, Cuba)
Carnegy, Patrick (London, UK)
Carreira, Xoán M. (La Coruña, Spain)
Carter, Stewart (Winston-Salem, NC, USA)
Casares-Alonso, Alicia (Madrid, Spain)
Casares Rodicio, Emilio (Madrid, Spain)
Cascudo, Teresa (La Coruña, Spain)
Cavicchi, Adriano (Ferrara, Italy)
Charlton, David (Norwich, UK)
Chechlińska, Zofia (Warsaw, Poland)
Chisholm, Duncan (London, UK)
Chitty, Alexis
Christie, Margaret (Edinburgh, UK)
Citron, Marcia J. (Houston, TX, USA)
Cohn, Arthur (New York, NY, USA)
Coldwell, Maria V. (Seattle, WA, USA)
Cole, Hugo (London, UK)
Cook, Elisabeth (London, UK)
Cornaz, Marie (Brussels, Belgium)
Cosma, Viorel (Bucharest, Romania)
Cox, David (London, UK)
Craw, Howard Allen (La Sierra, CA, USA)
Cruz, Gabriela (Austin, TX, USA)
Cudworth, Charles
Cusick, Suzanne G. (Charlottesville, VA, USA)

Dahlström, Fabian (Turku, Finland)
Dahm, Cecilie (Trondheim, Norway)
Damiani, Paola (Rome, Italy)
Davies, Hugh (London, UK)
Davies, Rhian (London, UK)
Dawes, Frank
Dean, Winton (Godalming, Surrey, UK)
Deaville, James (Hamilton, Ont., Canada)
Doctor, Jennifer R. (London, UK)
Doyle, John G. (Mansfield, PA, USA)
Dreyfus, Kay (Camberwell, Victoria, Australia)
Đurić-Klajn, Stana

Edwards, J. Michele (St Paul, MN, USA)
Elias, William Y. (Tel-Aviv, Israel)
Elkins-Marlow, Laurine (College Station, TX, USA)
Ellis, Katharine (Charlbury, Oxon., UK)

Fauser, Annegret (Berlin, Germany)
Feldman, Mary Ann (Minneapolis, MN, USA)
Finn, Robert (Lyndhurst, OH, USA)
FitzLyon, April (London, UK)
FitzPatrick, Marie (Sheffield, UK)
Fontijn, Claire A. (Durham, NC, USA)
Forbes, Elizabeth (London, UK)
Foreman, Lewis (Rickmansworth, Herts., UK)
Fox, Pamela (Miami, OH, USA)
Franklin, Peter (Leeds, UK)
Friedland, Bea (New York, NY, USA)
Friedmann, Susana (Bogotá, Colombia)
Fuller, Sophie (London, UK)
Fuller Maitland, J. A.

Gardner, John R. (London, UK)
Geiringer, Karl
Gillett, D. (Honolulu, HI, USA)
Gilson, Philippe (Liège, Belgium)
Girardot, Anne (Paris, France)
Glickman, Sylvia (Wynnewood, PA, USA)
Gojowy, Detlef (Unkel/Rhein, Germany)
Goldberg, Loretta (New York, NY, USA)
Graziano, John (Flushing, NY, USA)
Griffiths, Paul (Lower Heyford, Oxon., UK)
Grinde, Nils (Oslo, Norway)
Grove, George
Gustafson, Bruce (Lancaster, PA, USA)

Haglund, Rolf (Bramhult, Sweden)
Hair, Graham (Glasgow, UK)
Hair, Greta Mary Hair (Glasgow, UK)
Halász, Gábor (Ludwigshafen, Germany)
Hallová, Markéta (Prague, Czech Republic)
Hansell, Sven (Iowa City, IA, USA)
Härtwig, Dieter (Dresden, Germany)
Hayes, Deborah (Boulder, CO, USA)
Heintze, James R. (Washington, DC, USA)
Helm, Eugene (College Park, MD, USA)
Heward Rees, A. J. (Cardiff, UK)
Highwater, J. (New York, NY, USA)
Hinkle-Turner, Elizabeth (Iowa City, IA, USA)
Ho, Allan B. (Edwardsville, IL, USA)
Höft, Brigitte (Mannheim, Germany)
Holcomb, Dorothy Regina (New York, NY, USA)
Hostetter, Elizabeth A. (Mansfield, PA, USA)
Howard, Keith (London, UK)
Hurd, Michael (West Liss, Hants., UK)

Indenbaum, Dorothy (New York, NY, USA)

Jablonski, Edward (New York, NY, USA)
Jackson, Barbara Garvey (Fayetteville, AR, USA)
James, Richard S.
Jepson, Barbara (New York, NY, USA)
Jobin, Sara (San Francisco, CA, USA)
Jones, Gaynor G. (Toronto, Ont., Canada)

Kaizinger, Rita (Budapest, Hungary)
Kasilag, Lucrecia R. (Manila, Philippines)
Kawka, Daniel (Roche la Molière, France)
Kelemen, Éva (Budapest, Hungary)
Kemp, Ian (London, UK)
Kendrick, Robert L. (Cambridge, MA, USA)
Keren, Zvi (Tel-Aviv, Israel)
Kidd, Ronald R. (West Lafayette, IN, USA)
Kirk, Elise K. (Washington, DC, USA)
Klein, Rudolf (Vienna, Austria)
Korhonen, Kimmo (Helsinki, Finland)
Kos, Koraljka (Zagreb, Croatia)
Kovnatskaya, Ludmila (St Petersburg, Russia)
Kuna, Milan (Prague, Czech Republic)

La Pusata, Maria Sabrina (Pisa, Italy)
Laini, Marinella (Venice, Italy)
Lamb, Andrew (Croydon, Surrey, UK)
Laurie-Beckett, J. N. F. (Evesham, Worcs., UK)
Leedy, Douglas (Oceanside, OR, USA)
Leotsakos, George (Athens, Greece)
Lerma, Dominique-René de (Appleton, WI, USA)
Lerner, Ellen D. (New York, NY, USA)
Libby, Cynthia Green (Springfield, MO, USA)
Lindorff, Joyce (Shatin City One, New Territories, Hong Kong)
Locke, Ralph P. (Rochester, NY, USA)
Loosley, Sheila Eastman (Vancouver, BC, Canada)
Louvier, Alain (Boulogne, France)

Mabry, Sharon (Clarksville, TN, USA)
McBurney, Gerard (London, UK)
Macdonald, Hugh (St Louis, MO, USA)
Maceda, José (Manila, Philippines)
Macek, Jiří (Průhonice, Czech Republic)
McGinty, Doris Evans (Washington, DC, USA)
MacKenzie, Kirk (Bellevue, KY, USA)
Magaldi, Cristina (Los Angeles, CA, USA)
Manolova, Magdalena (Sofia, Bulgaria)
Manulkina, Olga (St Petersburg, Russia)
Marciano, Rosario (Vienna, Austria)
Masson, Marie Noëlle (Plerin, France)
Marshall, Ingram D. (Kensha, WI, USA)
Matsushita, Hidemi (Denver, CO, USA)
Meckna, Michael (Fort Worth, TX, USA)
Meisel, Maribel (Pawcanck, CT, USA)
Mell, Albert (Flushing, NY, USA)
Merrill, Sally (Cumberland Center, ME, USA)
Mertens, Corneel
Metzelaar, Helen (Amsterdam, Netherlands)
Metzer, David (Arlington, VA, USA)
Michelsen, Kari (Trondheim, Norway)
Mike, Celia (London, UK)
Milin, Melita (Belgrade, Serbia)
Milner, Margaret Leigh (London, UK)
Milsom, John (Oxford, UK)
Monastra, Margaret (Brooklyn, NY, USA)

Monson, Craig (St Louis, MO, USA)
Montague, Stephen (London, UK)
Moohan, Elaine (Glasgow, UK)
Morgan, John (New Haven, CT, USA)
Morgan, Paula (Princeton, NJ, USA)
Münster, Robert (Munich, Germany)

Nachman, Myrna S. (Rego Park, NY, USA)
Neff, Severine (Cincinnati, OH, USA)
Neuls-Bates, Carol (New York, NY, USA)
Nieminen, Risto (Paris, France)

Öhrström, Eva (Uppsala, Sweden)
Oja, Carol J. (New York, NY, USA)
Olson, Judith E. (Mineola, NY, USA)
Orledge, Robert (Liverpool, UK)
Osborne, William (Granville, OH, USA)
Owens, Margareth (Flossmoor, IL, USA)

Parker, Ian R. (Amsterdam, Netherlands)
Parsons Smith, Catherine (Reno, NV, USA)
Pasler, Jann (San Diego, CA, USA)
Passy, Charles (Long Island City, NY, USA)
Patton, Faye E. (Camberwell, Victoria, Australia)
Payne, Anthony (London, UK)
Perlis, Vivian (New Haven, CT, USA)
Petersen, Barbara A. (New York, NY, USA)
Petteys, M. Leslie (Huntington, WA, USA)
Picoto, José Carlos
Pistolesi, Laura (Florence, Italy)
Pocknell, Pauline (Hamilton, Ont., Canada)
Poniatowska, Irena (Warsaw, Poland)
Poupet, Michel
Preston, Katherine K. (Williamsburg, VA, USA)

Radic, Thérèse (Melbourne, Victoria, Australia)
Rasch, Rudolf A. (Utrecht, Netherlands)
Reich, Nancy B. (Hastings-on-Hudson, NY, USA)
Reinhard, Johnny (New York, NY, USA)
Reissinger, Marianne (Frankfurt am Main, Germany)
Rempel, Ursula M. (Winnipeg, Manitoba, Canada)
Restout, Denise (Lakeville, CT, USA)
Richardson, Cynthia S. (Seattle, WA, USA)
Rieger, Eva (Neu Eichenberg, Germany)
Robinson, J. Bradford (Munich, Germany)
Robinson, Lisa B. (New Haven, CT, USA)
Robinson, Philip (Hatfield, Herts., UK)
Roche, Jerome
Rockwell, John (Paris, France)
Rodriguez, Maria Encina Cortizo (Madrid, Spain)
Rollin, Monique (Paris, France)
Rolnick, Neil B. (Troy, NY, USA)
Root, Deane L. (Pittsburgh, PA, USA)
Rosand, Ellen (New York, NY, USA)
Rosen, Judith (Encino, CA, USA)
Rosenstiel, Léonie (New York, NY, USA)
Ruppenthal, Stephen (Woodside, CA, USA)

Rushton, Julian (Leeds, UK)
Ryker, Harrison (Wassenaar, Netherlands)

Saby, Pierre (Villeurbanne, France)
Sadie, Julie Anne (London, UK)
Sadie, Stanley (London, UK)
Salgado, Susana (Alexandria, VA, USA)
Salter, Lionel (London, UK)
Samuel, Rhian (London, UK)
Sanchez, Ramon Sobrino (Madrid, Spain)
Sanchez-Chiong, Jorge (Vienna, Austria)
Sanders, Linda (New York, NY, USA)
Sandow, Gregory (New York, NY, USA)
Sands, Mollie (London, UK)
Sansone, Matteo (Florence, Italy)
Schechter, John M. (Santa Cruz, CA, USA)
Schleifer, Martha Furman (Bala Cynwyd, PA, USA)
Schmid, Birgitta Maria (Heidelberg, Germany)
Schrader, Barry (North Hollywood, CA, USA)
Schwarz, Boris
Schwarz, K. Robert (New York, NY, USA)
Scott, Derek B. (Twickenham, Middlesex, UK)
Selfridge-Field, Eleanor (Sunnyvale, CA, USA)
Šerých, Anna (Prague, Czech Republic)
Shaljean, Bonnie (Cork, Ireland)
Shere, Charles (Berkeley, CA, USA)
Sica, Francesca Perruccio (Florence, Italy)
Sigurbjörnsson, Þorkell (Kópavogur, Iceland)
Smart, Mary Ann (New York, NY, USA)
Southern, Eileen (St Albans, NY, USA)
Sperber, Roswitha (Heidelberg, Germany)
Spink, Ian (Egham, Surrey, UK)
Spuy, Hubert van der (Pretoria, South Africa)
Starr, Lawrence (Seattle, WA, USA)
Starreveld, Rogier (Amsterdam, Netherlands)
Starreveld-Bartels, Maddie (Amsterdam, Netherlands)
Stevenson, Robert (Los Angeles, CA, USA)
Steyn, Mark (London, UK)
Stone, Kurt
Swed, Mark (New York, NY, USA)
Sweet, Michelle C. (Allston, MA, USA)
Swift, Richard (Davis, CA, USA)
Symons, David (Nedlands, Perth, Australia)
Szerző, Katalin (Budapest, Hungary)

Tauberová, Alexandra (Bratislava, Slovak Republic)
Temperley, Nicholas (Urbana, IL, USA)
Thomas, Adrian (London, UK)
Thomson, J. M. (Wellington, New Zealand)
Tick, Judith (Brookline, MA, USA)
Tinker, Christopher (Sedbergh, Cumbria, UK)
Tischler, Barbara L. (New York, NY, USA)
Touliatos, Diane (St Louis, MO, USA)
Trimble, Lester
Tsou, Judy S. (Berkeley, CA, USA)
Tucker, Mark (New York, NY, USA)
Tyrrell, John R. (Nottingham, UK)

Valderrama, Raquel Bustos (Santiago, Chile)
Vargas, Jorge Luis Acevado (San José, Costa Rica)

Wagstaff, John (Oxford, UK)
Walsh, Stephen (Cardiff, UK)
Walter, Horst (Gladbach, Germany)
Walton, Chris (Zürich, Switzerland)
Warburton, Thomas (Chapel Hill, NC, USA)
Weid, Jean-Noël von der (Paris, France)
Wessely, Helene (Vienna, Austria)
Whenham, John (Birmingham, UK)

Wilson, Thelma (Brentwood, Essex, UK)
Wood, Elizabeth (Staten Island, NY, USA)
Wright, David (New York, NY, USA)
Wright, Lesley A. (Honolulu, HI, USA)

Yampol'sky, I. M.
Yandell, Nigel J. (London, UK)
Yang, Yandi (Shanghai, China)
Yener, Faruk (Istanbul, Turkey)

Zwolska-Stęszewska, Barbara (Warsaw, Poland)

Index

The main text of the dictionary is indexed not by page number but by entry headword. References to the prefatory material are indexed by page number (small roman numerals) and those to the chronology (pp.xx–xxxii) by year.

The use of bold capitals for an entry in the index (e.g. **ANDERSON, BETH**) signifies that there is an entry under that name in the dictionary (only those composers mentioned in the chronology, the prefaces, or in articles other than their own, have been indexed). Capitals are used for *see* references from pseudonyms to entries within the dictionary itself.

Abendroth, Hermann Fromm-Michaels
Abilene [TX]
  Abilene Christian University Reid
  Abilene Philharmonic Orchestra Reid
  Hardin-Simmons University Reid
ABRAMS, HARRIETT 1780, 1791
Ábrányi, Kornél Kuliffay
Absil, Jean Bulterijs; Gorne
Académie Française Bocquet
Academy of St Martin-in-the-Fields *see* London
Accademia Filarmonica *see* Bologna
Accademia Musicale Chigiana *see* Siena
Acconci, Vito Anderson, L.
Acker, Dieter Erding
Adam, Adolphe Puget
Adam, Louis Wartel
ADAYEVSKAYA, ELLA GEORGIYEVNA 1873, 1877, 1881
Adcock, Fleur Whitehead
Adelaide
  Adelaide Festival of Arts Gifford; Glanville-Hicks
  Elder Conservatorium Hyde
Adelphi University [Garden City, NY] Zaimont
Adkins Chiti, Patricia xii
Adler, Guido Müller-Hermann
Adler, Samuel Semegen
AGNESI, MARIA TERESA 1747
Agnew, Roy Holland
Agrupación Nueva Musica [Argentina] Moretto
Aharonian, C. Bofill Levi
AHLEFELDT, MARIA THERESIA 1792
Ahrendt, Karl Ziffrin
Aichi Gakuen University of Fine Arts [Aichi Kenritsu Geijutsu Daigaku] [Japan] Massumoto; Mori
Ailey, Alvin 1969; Williams, M. L.
Alabama – University of Alabama LeBaron
ALAMANDA 12th century
Albani, Emma Lemon; Riego
Albany [NY] – Albany Symphony Orchestra Bond, V.
Alberta – University of Alberta [Edmonton] Archer
Albright, William Hugh Clement; Eiríksdóttir
Aldeburgh Festival of Music and the Arts 1974; Musgrave
Alecsandri, Vasile Athanasiu-Gardeev
ALEOTTI, RAFFAELLA 1593
ALEOTTI, VITTORIA 1593
Alexander I, Tsar of Russia Szymanowska
Alexander II, Tsar of Russia 1877
Alma Ata [Kazakhstan] – Kurmangazy State Conservatory Zhubanova
Alpaerts, Flor Tolkowsky
Alwyn, William Carwithen; Keal; Mucha
AMACHER, MARYANNE 1967
AMALIA CATHARINA, Countess of Erbach 1692
AMALIE, Princess of Saxony 1816
Amherst [MA] – Amherst College Suh
American Academy and Institute of Arts and Letters Jolas
American Composers Alliance (ACA) Fine
American Composers Orchestra *see* New York
American Dance Festival [Durham, NC] Lam Bun-ching
American Guild of Organists Bitgood

American Music Guild 1921; Bauer
American Society of University Composers Ulehla
American Symphony Orchestra *see* New York
American Wind Symphony *see* Pittsburgh
American Women Composers Shatin
Amsterdam
  Amsterdam Exhibition [1894] Jeske-Choińska-Mikorska
  Amsterdam Muzieklyceum Wertheim
  Concertgebouw 1933, 1946; Bosmans; Geertens; Manziarly
  Conservatory Bosmans; Cramer; Henneman
  Stichting Sweelinck Conservatorium Hoenderdos; Marez Oyens; Ore
  Universiteit van Amsterdam Bordewijk-Roepman
Amy, Gilbert Olivero; Urreta
Ancona – S Bartolomeo convent Brizzi Giorgi
Andersen, Hans Christian Hartmann
Anderson, Arthur Olaf Price
ANDERSON, BETH Spiegel
ANDERSON, LAURIE xv; 1983
Anderson, Marian Aldridge; Price
ANDERSON, RUTH 1968
Andreae, Felicity Dring
ANDRÉE, ELFRIDA 1879
Andrès Krzyżanowska
Andriessen, Louis Wolfe
Anger, Humfrey Geddes-Harvey
Angoulême [France] – conservatory Sikora
Ani-Kamakh (now Kemah, Turkey) – fortress Xosroviduxt
ANNA AMALIA, Duchess of Saxe-Weimar 1776, 1778
Ann Arbor [MI] – Wild Swan Theater Wolfe; *see also* Michigan
ANSPACH, ELIZABETH, Margravine of 1781, 1799
Antheil, George Glanville-Hicks; White, R.
Antwerp – Koninklijk Vlaams Conservatorium Bulterijs; Fontyn; Tolkowsky
APPIGNANI, ADELAIDE ORSOLA 1842, 1876
Aquinezer, Manuel Escribano
Arányi, Jelly d' Clarke
ARCHER, VIOLET 1942
Ardévol, José Hernández; Ruiz Lastres
Arel, Bülent Cory; LeBaron; Semegen
Argento, Dominick Larsen
Århus Conservatory [Jydske Musikkonservatorium] Linnet
Arienzo, Nicola d' Gubitosi
ARIZTI, CECILIA 1893
ARKWRIGHT, MARIAN 1907
Armstrong, Louis Williams, M. L.
Arne, Thomas Augustine Abrams; Barthélemon, M.
Arnold, Samuel 1781; Anspach
Arnould, Sophie Beaumesnil
Artaria Auenbrugger; Auernhammer
Artists Foundation [USA] Vercoe
Artôt, Désirée Viardot
Arts Council of Great Britain Bauld
Arts Council of Northern Ireland Trimble
Artusi, Giovanni Maria Aleotti, R.
Artyomov, Vyacheslav Petrovich Gubaydulina
Asachi, Gheorghe Asachi
Ascot, Rosita García Prieto
Ashbery, John Dlugoszewski
Ashley, Robert Anderson, B.; La Barbara; Payne

Asian Composers' League   Kasilag
Asociació de Catalana Compositors [Spain]   Pelegrí i Marimón
Asociación Artístico-Musical de Socorros Mutuos [Spain]
    Bengoecha de Cármena
Asociación Nacional de Compositores [Chile]   Vivado
Aspen Music Festival/School [CO]   Clayton; Giteck; Spiegel
ASSANDRA, CATERINA   1609
Associated Board of the Royal Schools of Music   see London
Association of Canadian Women Composers   1980; Southam
Association pour la Collaboration des Interprètes et des
    Compositeurs [France]   1974; Lachartre
Associazione Alessandro Scarlatti [Naples]   Gubitosi
Atehortúa, Blas Emilio   Nova
Athens
    Athens Conservatory [Odeion Athenon]   Lambiri; Sfakianaki
    Athens Festival   Glanville-Hicks
    Olympic Exhibition [1875]   Dellaporta
    Panellinion Theatre   Lambiri
Atlanta [GA]
    Atlanta Symphony Orchestra   Kolb
    Clark College   Price
Attwood, Thomas   Mounsey
Auber, Daniel-François-Esprit   Duchambge; Farrenc
Aubert, Louis François Marie   Wertheim
Aubin, Tony   Lee, Y.; Saint-Marcoux; Szőnyi
Auckland [New Zealand]
    Auckland Philharmonic Orchestra   1991; Castro-Robinson
    Karlheinz Company   Castro-Robinson
    University of Auckland   Castro-Robinson; Franchi; Frykberg;
        Whitehead
Auenbrugger, Katharina   Auenbrugger
Auenbrugger, Leopold von   Auenbrugger
AUENBRUGGER, MARIANNA VON   x; c1781
AUERNHAMMER, JOSEPHA BARBARA VON   1790
Augér, Arleen   Larsen
Augsburg – Universität Augsburg   Woll
Aulin, Tor   Aulin
AULIN, VALBORG   1884, 1889
Auric, Georges   Tailleferre
Austin, Larry   Anderson, B.
Australian Broadcasting Commission (ABC)   Woof
Australian Opera   Gifford
Ax, Emanuel   Berl
AZALAIS DE PORCAIRAGES   12th century
Azerbaijan Composers' Union   Ali-Zadeh

Babbitt, Milton   Allik; O'Leary; Shatin; Thome
BACEWICZ, GRAŻYNA   xvi; 1949, 1960, 1965
Bach, Carl Philipp Emanuel   Anna Amalia (i); Paradis
Bach, Johann Christian   Billington; Guest; Lombardini Sirmen
Bach, Johann Sebastian   xvii; Anna Amalia (i); Bergh
Backhaus, Wilhelm   Coleman
BADALLA, ROSA GIACINTA   1684
BĄDARZEWSKA-BARANOWSKA, TEKLA   1856
Baden-Baden – Brahmshaus   Rubin
Badings, Henk   Colaço Osorio-Swaab
Bahia – Universidade Federal da Bahia [Salvador]   Nogueira
Bailleux, Antoine   Gail
Baillot, Pierre   Bigot
Baird, Tadeusz   Sikora
Baku – Azerbaijan State Conservatory   Ali-Zadeh
Balakirev, Mily Alexeyevich   Rimskaya-Korsakova
Balanchivadze, Andrey   Eksanishvili; Svanidze
Baldi, Lamberto   Carvalho
BALLOU, ESTHER   1963
Baltimore
    Baltimore Symphony Orchestra   1901; Ivey; Lang, M. R.
    Johns Hopkins University   Ivey
    Peabody Conservatory   1922; Clement; Hernández; Howe; Ivey;
        Oh
    Peabody Electronic Music Studio   Ivey
    Women in Music Grand Concert [1901]   Lang, M. R.
Bal y Gay, Jesús   Prieto
Banff [Alberta] – Banff School of Fine Arts   McIntosh
Banfield, Stephen   xvii
Bangor [Wales]
    Normal College   Elwyn-Edwards
    University College of North Wales   Elwyn-Edwards
Banks, Mervyn   see BRAHE, MAY HANNAH
Barbaud, Pierre   Charbonnier
Barber, Samuel   Wylie

Barbirolli, John   Warren
Barcelona
    Cultura Musical Popular   Freixas
    Laboratorio Phonos   Bofill Levi
    Orquesta Catalana de Conciertos   1893; Casagemas
    Orquesta Ciutat de Barcelona   Romero
    Teatre Principal   Freixas
Bard College [Annandale-on-Hudson, NY]   Tower
Bargiel, Woldemar   Janotha; Schjelderup
Barker, Nathan   Sloman
Barkin, Elaine   xvi
Barlow, Wayne   Franks Williams; Kasilag
Barnard College   see New York
BARNS, ETHEL   1903, 1910
BARONI, LEONORA   Basile
BARRAINE, ELSA   1929; Wertheim
BARREAU, GISÈLE   1977
BARRIÈRE, FRANÇOISE   1970
BARRON, BEBE   xv; 1956, 1985
Barron, Louis   1956; Barron
Barry Grammar School [Barry, Wales]   Williams, G.
BARTHÉLEMON, CECILIA MARIA   1791, 1792, 1795
Barthélemon, François Hippolyte   Barthélemon, M.
BARTHÉLEMON, MARIA   1776; Barthélemon, C. M.
Bartholomew, William   Mounsey
Bartlett, Martin   Smith, L. C.
Bartók, Béla   xv; 1942; Archer; Coulthard; Wurmbrand-Stuppach
Baschet, Bernard and François   Fereyra
Bashō, Matsuo   Pistono
BASILE, ANDREANA   1623; Baroni; Caccini, F.
Basle – Musik-Akademie der Stadt   Baader-Nobs
Bassett, Leslie   Clayton; Clement
Battersby, Christine   xvii, xviii
Bauer, Emilie Frances   Bauer
BAUER, MARION EUGÉNIE   1921, 1923
BAULD, ALISON   1975, 1988
BAWR, SOPHIE, Mme DE   1823
Bax, Arnold   Sutherland
Bayle, François   Sikora
BAYON, MARIE EMMANUELLE   1776
Bayreuth
    Bayreuther Festspiele   Faltis
    Hochschule für Kirchenmusik   Dinescu
BBC   see British Broadcasting Corporation
BEACH, AMY MARCY   xiii; 1890, 1893, 1896, 1907, 1921, 1925,
        1929; Bauer; Hier; Howe
Beach, Sylvia   Jolas
Beatles, The   Velázquez
BEATRIZ DE DIA   12th century
BEAUHARNAIS, HORTENSE EUGÉNIE DE   xi
Beaumarchais, Pierre-Augustin   Wuiet
BEAUMESNIL, HENRIETTE ADÉLAÏDE VILLARD DE
        1781, 1784, 1792
Becker, Albert   Holmsen
Becker, Valentin   Woll
Bedford, Herbert   Lehmann
Beecham, Thomas   1909; Smyth
Beeson, Jack   Carlos; Coates, G.; LeBaron; Zaimont
Beethoven, Ludwig van   Bigot; Brentano; Cibbini-Kozeluch; Oury;
        Szymanowska
BEHREND, JEANNE   1965
Behrens, Jack   Telfer
Behrman, David   Payne
Beijing
    Beijing Film Studio   Huang
    Central Conservatory of Music   Chen Yi; Liu; Xiao; Xin
    Central Philharmonic Society/Orchestra   Chen Yi; Liu; Qü
    Central Song and Dance Ensemble   Qü
    Music and Dance Company   Xin
Bekku, Sadao   Massumoto
Belfast – Queen's University   Farrell
Belgrade
    Academy of Music   Frajt; Marić; Mosusova; Nešić; Stefanović;
        Živković
    Musicological Institute, Serbian Academy of Sciences and
        Arts   Mosusova
    Radio Belgrade [Radiotelevizija Beograd]   Stefanović
    Serbian Academy of Sciences and Arts [Srpska Akademija
        Naukai Umetnosti]   Marić
    Sound Workshop, Radio Belgrade   1985; Stefanović
    Stanković Music School   Marić
Bell Telephone Laboratories [USA]   Spiegel

BENARY, BARBARA   xvi
Benda, Franz   Reichardt, J.; Wolf
Bendix, Max   Lang, M. R.
BENGOECHA DE CÁRMENA, SOLEDAD   1874
Ben Haim, Paul   Ran
Benjamin, Arthur   Coulthard; Glanville-Hicks; Harrison, P.
Bennett, William Sterndale   Marshall; Smith, A. M.
Bennington [VT] – Bennington College   Ballou; Davidson; Fine; Jolas; Phillips; Ptaszyńska; Swadow; Tower
BERBERIAN, CATHY   xv; Steinberg
Berenguer, J. M.   Bofill Levi
Berg, Alban   Hier
Bergen
   Musikkonservatorium (formerly Castbergs Musikakademi)   Bakke; Holmsen
   Storetveitkirk   Bakke
Berger, Arthur   Barkin; Silver
Berger, Wilhelm   Lund, S.
Bergersen, Marie   Borroff
BERGH, GERTRUDE VAN DEN   1830
Bergsma, William   Escot; Richter
Berio, Luciano   xv, xvi; Berberian; Di Lotti; McLeod; Oliveira; Olivero
Berkeley, Lennox   Beamish; Boulanger, N.; Hugh-Jones; Roe
Berkshire Music Center/Festival   see Tanglewood Music Center/Festival
Berlier, Paul   Ferrari, G.
Berlin
   Akademie der Künste der Deutschen Demokratischen Republik   1990; Zechlin
   Berlin Akademie der Künste   Zechlin
   Berlin Contemporary Jazz Orchestra   Bley
   Berlin Philharmonisches Orchester   Havenstein
   Deutsche Staatsbibliothek (formerly Königliche Bibliothek)   Anna Amalia (i)
   Hochschule der Künste   Havenstein
   Hochschule für Musik   1908; Ahrens; Barkin; Fromm-Michaels; Kuyper; Landowska; Samter; Schlonsky; Ticharich; Viðar; Wennerberg-Reuter; Zieritz
   Hochschule für Musik Hanns Eisler   1984; Zechlin
   Jaques-Dalcroze institute   Moberg
   Joachimstalschen Gymnasium   Anna Amalia (i)
   Königliche Oper   Smyth
   Kronprinzliches Palais   1867
   Neue Akademie der Tonkunst   Grøndahl
   Preussische Akademie   Eckhardt-Gramatté
   RIAS Radio   La Barbara
   Salvatorkirche   Ahrens
   Singakademie   1820; Carreño; Mendelssohn
   Städtische Oper   Faltis
   Städtisches Konservatorium   Havenstein
   Sternsches Konservatorium   Fromm-Michaels; Schonthal; Zieritz
   Tonkünstlerinnen-Orchester   Kuyper
Berlioz, Hector   Bertin; Viardot
Bernaola, Carmelo   Malumbres
Bernasconi, Andrea   Della Pietà, A.; Della Pietà, M.; Della Pietà, S.
Berne
   Ensemble Neue Horizonte   Radermacher
   Konservatorium für Musik und Theater   Radermacher
Bernstein, Leonard   Ran
Bertrand des Baux   Tibors
Bettinelli, Bruno   Brusa; Furgeri
Bexhill School of Music [Bexhill-on-Sea, England]   Gipps
BIBBY, GILLIAN   1982
BIDART, LYCIA DE BIASE   1975
Big Bear Lake [CA] – Woodland Theater   Dillon
Bilthoven [Netherlands] – electronic music centre   Lockwood
BINGHAM, JUDITH   1977
Birkedal-Barfod, Ludwig Harbo Gote   Meyer
Birmingham [AL] – Original Gospel Harmonettes   Coates
Birmingham [England]
   Birmingham and Midland Institute   Ewart
   City of Birmingham Choir   Gipps
   Repertory Theatre   1923
   University of Birmingham   Beat; Sekacz
Birtwistle, Harrison   Fox; Paredes
Bispham, David   1911; Bond, C.; Collins; Freer; Moore, M. C.
Bizet, Georges   xvi; Grandval
Blacher, Boris   Ahrens; Barkin; Eckhardt-Gramatté; Klinkova
BLACKWOOD, HELEN   1833; Norton
BLAHETKA, LEOPOLDINE   Cibbini-Kozeluch

Blanchard, E. L.   Woolf
BLANCHE OF CASTILE   13th century
Blanck, Hubert de   Botet Dubois
Bley, Paul   Bley
Blitzstein, Marc   1927; Crawford
Bloch, Ernest   Hier; Leginska
Block, Adrienne Fried   xii
Blockley, John   Norton
Boccherini, Luigi   Brillon de Jouy
Bochsa, Nicholas Charles   Milanollo
BOCK, BERTA   1927
Body, Jack   Bowater
Boëly, Alexandre Pierre François   Montgeroult
Boepple, Paul   Jolas
Bogolyubova, Nadezhda   Elcheva
Bogotá [Colombia]
   Conservatorio Nacional   Nova
   Orquesta Sinfónica   Nova
Böhmer, Karl   Kinkel
Bohrnsted, Wayne   Bitgood
Boieldieu, Adrien   Gail
Boito, Arrigo   Garelli della Morea
Boleyn, Anne   x
Bologna
   Accademia Filarmonica   1773, 1774, 1819; Bottini; Brizzi Giorgi; Coccia; Martínez, M. von
   Arciconfraternità di S Maria della Morte oratory   1696; Moratori Scanabecchi
   Conservatorio Statale di Musica G. B. Martini   Benati; Furgeri
   S Christina convent   Vizzana
   S Filippo Neri oratory   1689; Moratori Scanabecchi
   Teatro Nazionale (formerly Teatro di Via Nosadella)   1876; Appignani
Bolzoni, Giovanni   Garelli della Morea
BOND, CARRIE   1910
BONDS, MARGARET ALLISON   1934, 1972
BONHOMME, ANDRÉE M. C.   1928
BONI, ANNA LUCIA   1756
Bonn
   Maikäferbund, Der   Kinkel
   Musikalische Liebhabergesellschaft   Kinkel
Bonno, Guiseppe   Martínez, M. von
Bordeaux – Grand Théâtre Municipal   1892
Bordewijk, Frans   Bordewijk-Roepman
BORDEWIJK-ROEPMAN, JOHANNA   1940
Bori, Lucrezia   Warren
Born, Georgina   xviii
Borodin, Alexander Porfir'yevich   Rimskaya-Korsakova
Borowski, Felix   Barnett; Branscombe
Borsieri, Girolamo   Sessa
Boscovich, Alexander Uriah   Ran; Thome
BOSMANS, HENRIËTTE HILDA   1946
Boston
   Berklee College of Music   Akiyoshi; Poole
   Boston Conservatory   Pizer
   Boston Philharmonic Orchestra   Leginska
   Boston Pops   Morley; Stuart-Coolidge
   Boston Symphony Orchestra   1896; Beach; Lang, M. R.; Weir
   Boston University   Gideon; Mekeel; Vercoe
   Boston Woman's Symphony Orchestra   Leginska
   Castle Square Opera Company   Roma
   Handel and Haydn Society   Beach
   King's Chapel   Hagan
   New England Conservatory of Music   Anderson, A.; Clayton; Daniels; Escot; Hopekirk; Lomon; Mekeel; Price; Rogers; Roma; Swift
   Simmons College   Daniels
   Women's Music Festival/85   1985; Vercoe
BOTTINI, MARIANNA   1819, 1822
Bottrigari, Ercole   Aleotti, R.
Boucourechliev, André   Barreau; Dianda
BOULANGER, LILI   xiii; 1913, 1918; Boulanger, N.
BOULANGER, NADIA   xvi, xvii; 1908, 1923, 1933; Anderson, R.; Bacewicz; Bauer; Boulanger, L.; Bruzdowicz; Cole; Coulthard; Fereyra; Glanville-Hicks; Howe; Klechniowska; Malmlöf-Forssling; Manziarly; Matuszczak; Mekeel; Moore, B.; Musgrave; Ørbeck; Perry; Ptaszyńska; Rainier; Reisserová; Shlonsky; Szőnyi; Talma; Warren; Živković
Boulez, Pierre   Ancona; Calame; Di Lotti; Dlugoszewski; Kolb; McLeod; Pstrokońska-Nawratil; Zwilich

Boult, Adrian   1938, 1946; Archer; Bosmans; Carwithen; Glanville-Hicks
Bourgain, E.   Aulin
Bourges [France]
   Festival International de Musique Electroacoustique 'Synthèse'   Rampazzi
   Groupe de Musique Expérimentale de Bourges (GMEB) 1970; Barrière
Bourges, Maurice   xii; Farrenc
Bournemouth Municipal Orchestra (later Bournemouth Symphony Orchestra)   1899, 1908, 1928, 1929; Lucas; Scarborough; Swepstone; Tate
Bowers, Jane   xii
Bowles, Paul   Glanville-Hicks
BOYD, ANNE   1991
BOYLE, INA   1920; Maconchy
Braemar [Scotland] – Scottish Festival   Musgrave
Braga, Francisco   Barbosa; Cameu; Jabor; Sodré
Braham, John   Browne, A.
BRAHE, MAY HANNAH   xiii; 1927
Brahms, Johannes   Janotha; Le Beau; Loder; Schumann; Smyth; Viardot; Wurmbrand-Stuppach
Brandeis University [Waltham, MA]   Barkin; Blaustein; Silver
Brandon University [Brandon, Manitoba]   Eckhardt-Gramatté
Brandt, Marianne   Viardot
BRANSCOMBE, GENA   1925; Hier
Brant, Henry   Davidson; Smiley; Swados
Brasília [Brazil] – University of Brasília   Catunda
Bratislava [Slovakia] – conservatory   Bodorová; Janárčeková
BRDLÍKOVÁ, JOSEFINA   1897
Bream, Julian   Musgrave
Bredemers, Henry   Boleyn
Breithaupt, Rudolf Maria   Zieritz
Breitkopf & Härtel   Smyth
Bremen
   Hochschule für Kunst   Kubisch; Pagh-Paan
   Radio Bremen   La Barbara
BRENET, THÉRÈSE   1965
BRENTANO, BETTINA   Kinkel
Brentano, Clemens   Reichardt, L.
Brera [Italy] – S Caterina monastery   Rusca
Brescia – Teatro Sociale   1924
Breswick, Martin   Wolfe
Brewster, Henry   Smyth
Bridge, Frederick   Wurm
Bridgman, Cunningham   Woolf
BRIGHT, DORA   1888
Brighton [England]
   Brighton Festival   1873; Gabriel
   Brighton School of Music   Lomax
BRILLON DE JOUY, ANNE LOUISE BOYVIN D'HARDANCOURT   x; 1777
Brisbane
   Queensland Conservatorium of Music   Beath
   Queensland Symphony Orchestra   Mageau
Briscoe, James R.   xii
Brissac, Jules   see MACFARREN, EMMA MARIA
Bristol
   Royal Theatre   1925
   University of Bristol   Farrell
British Broadcasting Corporation (BBC)   Archer; Bingham; Coleman; Daiken; Firsova; Fowler; Gow; Maconchy; Mucha; Musgrave; Oram; Poston; Rainier; Romero; Scarborough; Swain; Tate; Trimble; Weir; Williams, G.
   BBC National Orchestra of Wales   Samuel
   BBC Northern Ireland Orchestra   Trimble
   BBC Proms   see London, Promenade Concerts
   BBC Radio Orchestra   Morley
   BBC Radiophonic Workshop   xv; Oram
   BBC Singers   Bingham
   BBC Symphony Orchestra   1938; Coleridge-Taylor; Kaprálová
   Children's Hour   Scarborough
British Columbia
   University of British Columbia [Vancouver]   Coulthard; Louie; Pentland; Westerkamp
   World Soundscape Project (WSP), Simon Fraser University   Westerkamp
British Music Movement   1936; Swain
Britten, Benjamin   Bosmans; Holst; Williams, G.
BRIZZI GIORGI, MARIA   1807
Brnčic, Gabriel   Bofill Levi

Brno [Slovakia]
   Conservatory   Kaprálová
   Janáček Academy of Music [Janáčkova Akademie Múzickych Umění] Bodorová; Jiráčková; Petrová, E.
Brock-Smith, Alma   McIntosh
Brodsky, Adolph   Ewart
BRONSART, INGEBORG VON   1867, 1873
Bronsart von Schellendorf, Hans   Bronsart
Bronzini, Cristoforo   Caccini, F.
Brosses, Charles de   Agnesi
Brouwer, Leo   Rodriguez
Brown, Earle   Fereyra; McLeod
BROWNE, HARRIET   Browne, A.
Brown University [Providence, RI]   Carlos; Rodriguez; Walker
Bruch, Max   Kuyper; Wennerberg-Reuter
Brussels
   Conservatoire Royal de Musique   Colin-De Clerck; Diemer; Fontyn; Gorne; Lee, Y.; Poldowski; Uyttenhove; Xiao
   music academy [Anderlecht]   Colin-De Clerck
   Théâtre Royal des Galeries St Hubert   1904; Vieu
BRUZDOWICZ, JOANNA   1969
Bryn Mawr College [Bryn Mawr, PA]   Hoover
BRZEZIŃSKA-SZYMANOWSKA, FILIPINA   1863
BUCHANAN, DOROTHY QUITA   1977
Bucharest
   Academy of Music [Academia de Muzică] (formerly Ciprian Porumbescu Conservatory [Conservatorul de Muzică Ciprian Porumbescu])   Alexandra; Badian; Ciobanu; Dinescu; Donceanu; Hasnas; Hölszky; Marbé; Odăgescu; Petra-Basacopol; Rotaru; Tăutu; Vlad
   George Enescu High School for the Arts [Academia de Arte George Enescu]   Ciobanu; Dinescu
   Institute of Folklore   Tăutu
Buchla, Donald   Ciani
Bucht, Gunnar   Rehnqvist
Buck, Percy   Dring
Buckley, Olivia [DUSSEK]   xii
Bucks County Community College [PA]   Spiegel
Budapest
   Franz Liszt Academy of Music [Liszt Ferenc Zeneművészeti Főiskola] (formerly National Hungarian Royal Academy of Music [Országos Magyar Királi Zeneakadémia])   Hajdú; Kistétényi; Kuliffay; Szönyi; Ticharich
   National Conservatory [Nemzeti Zenede]   Kuliffay; Ticharich
Buenaventura, Antonino   Santos Ocampo
Buenos Aires
   Centro de Investigaciones de la Ciudad   Lambertini
   Collegium Musicum   Milstein
   Conservatorio Nacional de Música   1959; Aretz; Moretto; Paraskevaidis; Terzian; Urteaga
   Instituto del Teatro Colón   Urteaga
   Instituto Torcuato Di Tella   Lockhart; Nova; Paraskevaidis
   Museo de Ciencias Naturales   Aretz
   Universidad Católica Argentina   Lambertini; Luengo
   Universidad de Buenos Aires   Moretto
Buffalo [NY] – Buffalo Philharmonic Orchestra   Bond, V.
Buhlig, Richard   Crawford
Bull, Angela   Dring
Bülow, Hans von   Le Beau
BULTERIJS, NINI   1966
Bumpus, John and Edward   Allitsen
Bunin, Revol Samuilovich   Svanidze
Buonamici, Giuseppe   Galeotti
Buonarroti, Michelangelo   1607, 1610; Caccini, F.; Caccini, S.
Burgess, Anthony   xviii
Burgmüller, Johann August Franz   Bergh
Burney, Charles   x; Abrams; Brillon de Jouy; Lombardini Sirmen; Maria Antonia Walpurgis; Martínez, M. von; Paradis
Burrows, Benjamin   Barrell
Burton, Gary   Bley
Busch, Carl   Price
Bush, Alan   Bingham; Mucha
Busoni, Ferruccio   Ticharich
Bussotti, Sylvano   Berberian; Rampazzi
Butt, Clara   Allitsen; Riego
Byrne, Andrew   Samuel

Caamaño, Roberto   Lambertini
Cabrillo Music Festival   see California
CACCINI, FRANCESCA   x, xii; 1607, 1618, 1622, 1623, 1625; Basile; Caccini, S.

Caccini, Giulio   Caccini, F.; Caccini, S.
CACCINI, SETTIMIA   1610; Caccini, F.
Cadman, Charles Wakefield   Warren
Cage, John   Amacher; Andersøn, B.; Berberian; Dianda; Frykberg; La Barbara; Urreta
Cagliari [Sardinia] – Teatro Civico   1871
Caignet, Felix B.   Lecuona Casado
Calabro, Louis   Davidson; Smiley
Calegari, Cornelia   1659
Calgary [Alberta] – University of Calgary   Archer
California
  Cabrillo Music Festival   Anderson, B.; Oliveros
  California Institute of the Arts [Valencia]   La Barbara; Radigue; Rubin
  California State University, Hayward   Giteck
  California State University, Northridge   Grigsby
  California State University, San Francisco   Armer
  Institute for the Study of Women in Music, California State University [Northridge]   1990
  Schoenberg Institute, University of Southern California [Los Angeles]   Mamlok
  University of California, Berkeley   Armer; Dvorkin; Giteck; Konishi; Ptaszyńska; Irmer
  University of California, Davis   Anderson, B.
  University of California, Los Angeles   Barkin; White, R.
  University of California, San Diego   Galás; Lam Bun-ching; Louie; Oliveros
  University of California, Santa Barbara   Diemer; Ptaszyńska
  University of Southern California [Los Angeles]   Allik; Bond, V.; Bruzdowicz; Grigsby; Jolas
Calloway, Cab   Williams, M. L.
Calvé, Emma   Hardelot
Cambridge [England] – University of Cambridge   Burrell; Firsova; Luff; Milstein; Usher; Weir
Cambridge [MA]
  Harvard University   Amacher; Blaustein; Jolas
  Massachusetts Institute of Technology   Amacher; Bruzdowicz; Weir
  Radcliffe College   Daniels
  Radcliffe Glee Club   Daniels
CAMPANA, FRANCESCA   1629
Campbell-Tipton, Louis   Bauer
Campinas [São Paulo, Brazil] – University   Rosas-Fernandes
Canadian Broadcasting Company (CBC)   Eckhardt-Gramatté; Saint-Marcoux
Canadian Conference of the Arts   1974; Eckhardt-Grammatté
Canadian Music Centre   see Toronto
Canadian Music Council   1986; Louie
Canadian Women Composers   see Association of Canadian Women Composers
CANAL, MARGUERITE   1920
CANALES, MARTA   1929
Canberra
  Australian National University   Clingan
  Canberra School of Music (later Canberra Institue of the Arts)   Clingan
  Gaudeamus   Clingan
CANDEILLE, JULIE   1784, 1792
Canterbury [New Zealand] – University of Canterbury [Christchurch]   Buchanan; Fisher; Frykberg; Lockwood
Canton   see Guangzhou
Cantón, Egardo   Fereyra
Canzona [New Zealand]   Bibby
Cape Town
  South African College of Music   Rainier
  University of Cape Town   Rainier
Cardiff
  New Theatre   1966
  University of Wales, University College   Elwyn-Edwards; Ho Wai-On; Luff; Owen; Tann; Williams, G.
  Welsh National Opera (WNO)   1966; Williams, G.
CARLOS, WENDY   1984
Carlson, Carolyn   Saariaho
Carman, Hayunga   Blomfield Holt
Carmen Sylva [Elisabeth, Queen of Romania]   Adayevskaya
Carnegie Mellon University   see Pittsburgh
Carolina Augusta, Empress of Austria   Cibbini-Kozeluch
Carr, Mrs Walter   xi
Carrie Jacobs-Bond & Son   Bond, C.
Carrillo, Julián   De Blanck Martín
Carroll, Vinette   Grant
Carter, Elliott   Boulanger, N.; Dvorkin; Steiner, G.; Zwilich

CARWITHEN, DOREEN   1947
CASAGEMAS, LUISA   1892, 1893
Casals, Pablo   Adam de Aróstegui; Eckhardt-Gramatté
Casati, Gasparo   Cozzolani; Isabella Leonarda
Casella, Alfredo   1933; Landowska
CASELLA, FELICITA   1849, 1865
CASTELLOZA   13th century
Cash, Johnny   Coates
Castle, J. W.   Steiner, E. R.
CASTRO-ROBINSON, EVE DE   1991
CASULANA, MADDALENA   1568
Catalani, Angelica   Gail
Catán, Daniel   Lara
Catherine II, Empress of Russia   Sinyavina
CATUNDA, EUNICE   1950
Caussade, Georges   Arrieu; Boulanger, L.
Cavalli, Francesco   Bembo; Strozzi
Cavendish, Georgiana, Duchess of Devonshire   Park
CBC   see Canadian Broadcasting Company
CECCONI-BOTELLA, MONIC   1966
Cecilia Publishing Co. [USA]   Williams, M. L.
Celona, John   Smith, L. C.
Centenary College [Shreveport, LA]   Moorman
Cesi, Beniamino   Gubitosi
CESIS, SULPITIA   1619
Chadjiev, Parashkev   Draganova
Chadwick, George Whitefield   Daniels; Hood; Hopekirk; Price
CHAMINADE, CÉCILE   xiii, xvii; 1881, 1882, 1888, 1913
Champagne, Claude   Archer; Saint-Marcoux
Chandler, Theodore   Hernández
Chapelain, Jean   Bocquet
Chapelle Musicale Reine Elisabeth [Argenteuil, Belgium]   Bulterijs; Fontyn
Chapman College [Orange, CA]   Moore, M. C.
Chard Festival of Women in Music   see Women in Music
Chateaubriand, Françoise René de   Duchambge
Chattanooga [TN] – Chattanooga Symphony   Hays
Cheltenham International Festival of Music [UK]   Rainier; Weir
CHEN YI   xvi
Chéron, Elisabeth Sophie   Bembo
Cherubini, Luigi   Bigot; Colbran; Duchambge; La Hye; Szymanowska
Chicago
  Allied Arts Academy   Bonds
  American Conservatory of Music   Barnett; Borroff; Britain; Crawford; Price
  American Opera Society of Chicago   Freer
  Bush Conservatory   Rivé-King
  Century in Progress [world's fair]   1933; Bonds
  Chicago City Opera Company   1935; Leginska
  Chicago Conservatory   Britain
  Chicago Musical College   Barnett; Branscombe; Fine; Price
  Chicago Symphony Orchestra   1934; Bonds; Price; Ran
  Chicago Woman's Symphony Orchestra   Leginska
  De Paul University   Mageau
  Girvin Institute of Music   Britain
  Ravinia Festival, Highland Park   Berl
  University of Chicago   Ran; Ziffrin
  WGN Radio orchestra   Price
  World's Columbian Exposition [1893]   1892, 1893, 1894; Beach; Bonds; Bronsart; Casagemas; Hood; Jeske-Choińska-Mikovska; Lang, M. R.; Steiner, E. R.
Chinese Film Music Society [China]   Liu
Chinese Musicians' Association [China]   1985; Huang; Liu; Qü
Chioggio, Enio   Rampazzi
Chishko, Oles' Semenovych   Elcheva
Chladni, Ernst   x
Chopin, Fryderyk Franciszek   Blahetka; Cibbini-Kozeluch; Szymanowska; Viardot
Choron, Alexandre   x
Chou, Wen-chung   Chance; Chen Yi; Cory; Ekizian; LeBaron; Moore, D. R.; Tower
Chowning, John   Ciani; Ho Wai-On; Sikora
CHUDOVA, TAT'YANA ALEXEYEVNA   1984
Ciamaga, Gustav   Southam
CIBBINI-KOZELUCH, CATHERINA   Blahetka
Cicognini, Jacopo   1622; Caccini, F.
Cilea, Francesco   Baldacci
Cincinnati
  Cincinnati Conservatory   Hier

Cincinnati – *continued*
 Cincinnati Symphony Orchestra   1939; Cole; Hier; León; Mana
  Zucca
 Labunski School of Composition   Abejo
Cinti-Damoreau, Laure   Puget
Ciortea, Tudor   Alexandra; Vlad
Citron, Marcia J.   xvii, xviii
Claghorn, Gene   xii
Clark, Edward   Lutyens
Clarke, Douglas   Archer
CLARKE, REBECCA   xiii, xvii; 1907, 1918, 1919
Clément, Félix   Gail
Clementi, Muzio   Brizzi Giorgi; Cibbini-Kozeluch
CLÉRY, MARIE ELIZABETH   1776, 1785, 1790
Cleveland [OH]
 Cleveland Institute of Music   Ptaszyńska
 Cleveland Museum of Art   Oliveros
 Cleveland Orchestra   Chance; Ptaszyńska
 Cleveland School of Music   Stair
CLOSTRE, ADRIENNE   1949
Clozier, Christian   Barrière
Coates, Albert   Warren
COCCIA, MARIA ROSA   1774
Cocks, Robert   Lindsay
Coenen, Frans   Kuyper
Coffin, Hayden   Allitsen
Cogan, Robert   Escot
Cohen, Aaron I.   ix
COLBRAN, ISABELLA   x, xii
Cole, Nat King   Velázquez
Colegrass, Michael   McIntosh
Coleridge, Samuel Taylor   xviii
COLERIDGE-TAYLOR, AVRIL   1957
Coleridge-Taylor, Samuel   Coleridge-Taylor
Colles, H. C.   xiv
Collingwood, Lawrance   Coleman
Cologne
 Kölner Rundfunk-Sinfonie-Orchester   Galás
 Staatliche Hochschule für Musik (formerly Rheinische
  Musikschule)   Fromm-Michaels; Lockwood; Nogueira
 Westdeutscher Rundfunk   Hays
Coltrane, John   Bond, V.
Columbia Broadcasting System (CBS) [USA]   Crawford
Columbia-Princeton Electronic Music Center (CPEMC)
 see New York
Columbia University   *see* New York
Composers Association of New Zealand   1982; Bibby
Composers Group for International Performance   Steiner
Composers' Guild of Australia   Gifford
Composers' Guild of Great Britain   1959; Gipps; Maconchy; Tate
Composers' Union of Romania [Uniunea Compozitorilor şi
  Muzicologilor din România]   Marbé; Petra-Basacopol; Rotaru
Composers' Union of the USSR [Soyuz Kompozitorov SSSR]
  Levina
Concertgebouw   *see* Amsterdam
Concert Spirituel   *see* Paris
Concord [NH] – St Paul's School   Ziffrin
Coniff, Ray   Velázquez
Connecticut College for Women [New London, CT]   Bitgood
Connolly, Justin   Keal
Conrart, Valentin   Bocquet
Conried, Heinrich   Steiner, E. R.
Constantinescu, Dan   Ciobanu
Converse, Frederick Shepherd   Price
Converse College [Spartanburg, SC]   Strickland
Cook, Will Marion   Bonds; Jessye
Cooke, Frances Judd   Lomon
Coolidge, Elizabeth Sprague   1919; Clarke; Howe
Copenhagen
 Kongelige Danske Musikkonservatorium   Alsted; Hay, D. P.;
  Liebmann, N. M.; Lund, G.; Mazur; Moe; Ozaita; Pade; Sehested;
  Wandall
 Kongelige Teater   1792, 1899, 1914; Ahlefeldt; Sehested; Wandall
 Kvindernes Udstilling [Women's Exhibition, 1895]   Sehested
Copland, Aaron   1927; Beecroft; Boulanger, N.; Coulthard;
  Crawford; Pentland; Wylie
Coppola, Pietro   Malibran
Corbett, Lynn Taylor   Bond, V.
Corder, Frederick   Eggar
Corder, Paul   Parke, D.
Cordero, Roque   Barron
Córdoba [Argentina] – Universidad Nacional   Dianda

Corelli, Arcangelo   Philarmonica
Cork [Ireland] – University College   Patterson
Corghi, Azio   Bo; Brusa
Corigliano, John   Wallach
Cornelius, Peter   Sabinin; Wurmbrand-Stuppach
Cornell, J. H.   Wood
Cornell University [Ithaca, NY]   Archer
Coronaro, Gaetano   Garelli della Morea
Corri-Dussek & Co. [London]   Dussek, S.
Cortot, Alfred   Couper; Leleu
Cotton Plant-Arkadelphia Academy [Arkadelphia, AK]   Price
COUPER, MILDRED   1937
Couperin, François   Ménétou
Courvoisier, Walter   Pejačević
Covent Garden   *see* London
Cowell, Henry   1926, 1937; Barron; Couper; Crawford
Cox, David   xviii
COZZOLANI, CHIARA MARGARITA   1640, 1642
Cravero, Giovanni   Calosso
CRAWFORD, RUTH   xvi, xvii; 1926, 1927, 1928, 1930, 1931;
  Bauer; Davidson; Fine; Hays
Cresswell, Lyell   Milstein
Crete – Moussikos Avgoustos Festival [Iraklion]   Sfakianaki
Crichton, Donald   *see* BRAHE, MAY HANNAH
Crooks, Richard   Warren
Crosby, Bob   Williams, M. L.
Cross, Lowell   Giteck
Crumb, George   Martinez, O. de la
Cui, César   Rimskaya-Korsakova
Cunningham, Allan   Scott
Cunningham, Merce   Amacher; Capdeville; Davidson; Lockwood
Curtis Institute of Music   *see* Philadelphia
Czech Radio [Cesky rozhlas]   Jiráčková; Mucha
Czerny, Carl   Blahetka; Oury

Dahl, Ingolf   Bond, V.; Grigsby
Dahr, Juni   Poole
Daija, Tish   Agolli
DAIKEN, MELANIE RUTH   1971
Dalcroze, Emile Jaques-   *see* Jaques-Dalcroze, Emile
DALBERG, NANCY   1918
Dale, Benjamin   Mucha; Richards
Dallapiccola, Luigi   Perry; Zallman
Dalla Pietà, Candida   Boni
DANIELS, MABEL WHEELER   xiv; 1902; Bauer
Danish Radio [Danmarks Radio]   xv; Pade
D'Annunzio, Gabriele   Garelli Della Morea
Dansk Komponistforening   Liebmann, N. M.
Dansk Koncertforening   Sehested
Dansk Kvindesamfund   Sehested
Dansk Musikpaedagogisk Forening   Liebmann, N. M.
Danzi, Franz   Lebrun, F.; Lebrun, S.
DANZI, MARGARETHE   1801
Dargomïzhsky, Alexander Sergeyevich   Rimskaya-Korsakova
Darke, Harold   Lutyens
Darmstadt
 Institut für Neue Musik und Musikerziehung   Heller
 Internationale Ferienkurse für Neue Musik   Alexandra;
  Ancona; Ciobanu; Coates, G.; Dianda; Escribano; Fereyra;
  Geertens; Heller; Hölszky; LeBaron; Lockwood; Lomon; Marbé;
  Odăgescu; Ozaita; Pentland; Petra-Basacopol; Rampazzi; Rotaru;
  Sato; Schorr; Smith, L. C.; Steinberg
 Königliches Theater   Faltis
Dartington College of Arts [England]   Firsova; Glatz
Dartington Summer School [England]   Brusa; Paredes
Dartmouth College [Hanover, NH]   Fereyra
Davenport, Francis William   Horrocks; Needham
David, Johann Nepomuk   Schorr; Zechlin
Davidovsky, Mario   Beecroft; Chen Yi; Clement; LeBaron; Vázquez
Davies, Peter Maxwell   Erding; Paredes; Whitehead
Davis, Joe   Bonds
Davis, Miles   Mazur
Dawson, William   Price
DE BLANCK MARTÍN, OLGA   Hernández
Debussy, Claude   Bonis; Lehmann; Maddison
Decaux, Abel   Béclard d'Harcourt
De Kresz, Norah   Blomfield Holt
Delalande, F.   Gorne
Delany, Mary   Barthélemon, M.
Delaroche, Nicolas   Candeille
Delius, Frederick   Maddison

DELL'ACQUA, EVA   1890
Della Pietà, Anne Maria   Della Pietà, S.
DELLA PIETÀ, MICHIELINA   1740
DELLAPORTA, SOPHIA   1875
DELLE GRAZIE, GISELLA   1894, 1895
Dello Joio, Norman   Ran
Del Tredici, David   Anderson
DEMARS, HÉLÈNE-LOUISE   c1752
Dempster, Stuart   Oliveros
Dente, Joseph   Munktell
Denza, Luigi   Garelli della Morea
DePauw University [Greencastle, IN]   Santos Ocampo
DERING, MARY   1655
De Sabata, Victor   Recli
Desbordes-Valmore, Marceline   Duchambge
Desforges [P. J. B. Choudard]   1786; Wuiet
DESPORTES, YVONNE   1932
Detroit
    Conservatory of Music   Dlugoszewski
    Improvisation Chamber Ensemble   Wylie
    Wayne State University   Dlugoszewski; Wylie
Deutsch, Max   Fontyn; Shlonsky
Deutscher Musikrat   Zechlin
Díaz-Nieto, Alfredo   Ruiz Lastres
Dickens, Charles   Viardot
Dickinson, Clarence   Warren
Dickinson, Harold   Bonds
Dickson, Stanley   see BRAHE, MAY HANNAH
Diémer, Louis   Adam de Aróstegui
DILLON, FANNIE CHARLES   1918
D'Indy, Vincent   see Indy, Vincent d'
Dionisi, Renato   Bo
Ditlevsen, Tove   Linnet
Dixon, F. A.   Harrison, S. F.
Diyarbakir [Turkey] – Philharmonic Society   Guran
DLUGOSZEWSKI, LUCIA   xv; 1953, 1977
Dodge, Charles   La Barbara
Dolin, Samuel   Southam; Watson Henderson
Donatoni, Franco   Bo; Bodorová; Cecchi; Giraud; Hölszky;
    Kubisch; Luff; Olive; Rampazzi; Steinberg
Donaueschingen Musiktage   Galás
Dondeyne, Désiré   Tailleferre
Donizetti, Gaetano   Malibran
Donovan, Richard Frank   Diemer
Dorazio, Ralph   Dlugoszewski
Doremus, B. W.   Steiner, E. R.
Dorset Philharmonic [England]   Scarborough
Dorsey, Jimmy   Velázquez
Dorsey, Thomas A.   Martin
Dorsey, Tommy   Williams, M. L.
Douglas, Stanton   see BRAHE, MAY HANNAH
Douglas College [New Westminster, BC]   Shatin
Down Beat Hall of Fame [Elmherst, IL]   Williams, M. L.
Draeseke, Felix   Faltis; Moberg; Wandall
Dresden
    Hochschule für Musik (formerly Konservatorium)   Faltis;
        Lucas; Moberg
    Pillnitz castle   Amalie
Drewetcke, Carlos   Zegers
Dreyfus, Laurence   xvii
Dreyschock, Alexander   Adayevskaya
Druckman, Jacob   McTee; Olivero; Shatin; Spiegel
Duarte, Diego   Duarte
Dublin
    Contemporary Music Centre   O'Leary
    Institute of Technology, College of Music   Faltis
    National Concert Hall   O'Leary
    Radio Telefís Eireann (RTE) Orchestra   Bond, V.
    Royal Irish Academy of Music   Farrell; Kelly; Kirkwood;
        Patterson; Trimble
    Royal University of Ireland   Patterson
    University of Dublin, Trinity College   Coghill; Kelly; Trimble
Dubois, Théodore   Ferrari, G.
DUCHAMBGE, PAULINE   Beauharnais; Candeille
Duczmal, Agnieszka   Zielińska
Dudek, Ryszard   Kunkel
Duff, Cloyd   Ptaszyńska
Dufourt, Hugues   Giraud
Duisburg – Universität Duisburg Hochschule   Sonntag
Dukas, Paul   Arrieu; Barraine; Desportes; Gazarossian
Duke University [Durham, NC]   Williams, M. L.
Dun, Finlay   Scott

Dunne, Irene   Swift
Dupré, Marcel   Demessieux; Lalauni
Dupuis, Sylvain   Boorn-Coclet; Thisse-Derouette
Durham [England] – University of Durham   1910; Arkwright;
    Gipps; Smyth
Duruflé, Maurice   Cecconi-Botella
Dushkin, Samuel   Paradis
Dussek, Jan Ladislav   Duchambge; Dussek; Krumpholtz;
    Montgeroult
DUSSEK, KATEŘINA VERONIKA ANNA DUSÍKOVA   xii
DUSSEK, SOPHIA   Krumpholtz
Dutilleux, Henri   Hara
Duval, Alexandre   Kerkado
DUVAL, Mlle   x; 1736
Dvořák, Antonín   Collins; Korn; Smyth
Dyson, George   Holst

Earle, Hamilton   Woodforde-Finden
Ear Magazine [NY]   Anderson, B.; Hays; Spiegel
Eastman School of Music   see Rochester
Easton, Florence   Warren
Ebel, Otto   ix, xi
Eben, Petr   Ahrens
ECKHARDT-GRAMATTÉ, S.-C.   1974
Eddy, Nelson   Mana Zucca
Edinburgh
    Edinburgh International Festival   1971, 1977; Daiken;
        Musgrave; Riseman
    Scottish Chamber Orchestra   Beamish
    University of Edinburgh   Musgrave
Editura Musicală [Bucharest]   Donceanu
Edwards, J. Michele   xviii
Egbert, Gladys   McIntosh
EGEBERG, FREDRIKKE   1849
EGGAR, KATHARINE EMILY   1911
Egger, Frederico   Leite, V. D.
EICHNER, ADELHEID MARIA   1780
Eichner, Ernst   Brillon de Jouy
Einem, Gottfried von   Sonntag
Eisden [Belgium]
    Koninklÿk Atheneum   Vigneron-Ramackers
    Muziekakademie   Vigneron-Ramackers
Eisteddfod   see Wales
EKSANISHVILI, ELEONORA GRIGOR'YEVNA   xvi
ELCHEVA, IRINA MIKHAYLOVNA   xvii
Eleonora, Dowager Empress of the Habsburg Dynasty   1665; Priuli
Elisabeth, Queen of Romania   Adayevskaya
Elkind-Tourre, Rachel   Carlos
ELLICOTT, ROSALIND FRANCES   1889
Ellington, Duke   Williams, M. L.
Elmsly, John   Castro-Robinson
Elson, Arthur   ix
Elwes, Gervase   Riego
Emmanuel, Maurice   Béclard d'Harcourt
Encountros Internacionais de Música Contemporánea
    [Argentina]   1978; Terzian
Enescu, George   Warren
English National Opera   see London
English Opera Group   Musgrave
Englund, Einar   Hannikainen
Enríquez, Manuel   Urreta
Erb, Donald   Ptaszyńska
Erb, Lawrence   Bitgood
Erevan Komitas State Conservatory   Čebotaryan
Erickson, Robert   Lam Bun-ching; Louie; Oliveros
Erjin, Den   Liu
Erkel, Gyula   Kuliffay
Ertel, John Paul   Bauer
ESCOT, POZZI   1975, 1991
Espadero, Nicolás Ruiz   Arizti
Essen – Folkwang-Hochschule   Ahrens
Essenga, Salvatore   Massarenghi
Etude, The [Philadelphia, PA]   Korn; Parkhurst
European Women's Orchestra   see London
Evangelisti, Franco   Di Lotti
Evans, Gil   Mazur
EWART, FLORENCE MAUD   xvi; 1907
Ewing, Alexander   Smyth

Fabre d'Eglantine, Philippe-François-Nazaire   Candeille
Faccio, Franco   Garelli della Morea

Fachiri, Adila Clarke
Fainlight, Ruth Fox
Faith, Percy Velázquez
Faltin, Friedrich Richard Moberg
Faminstïn, Alexander Sergeyevich Adayevskaya
Farinelli Coccia
Farjeon, Harry Tate
Farnese, Odoardo (Cardinal Farnese) Caccini, S.
Farnham Festival [Surrey] Poston
Farquhar, David McLeod
FARRENC, LOUISE 1839, 1840, 1849; Wartel
Farwell, Arthur Newlin
Fassbinder, R. W. xv
Faulkner, Eric see BRAHE, MAY HANNAH
Fauré, Gabriel Boulanger, N.; Maddison; Viardot; Vieu
Fax, Mark Moore, D. R.
Fayolle, François x
Fedeli, Aurelia Bembo
Federation for Asian Cultural Promotion Kasilag
Federation of Women Composers [Japan] Kolb; Konishi; Mori
Feeney Trust [UK] Musgrave
Feldman, Morton Barreau; La Barbara; Smith, L. C.
FENGER, JOHANNE AMALIE 1866
FEREYRA, BEATRIZ 1963
Fernández, Oscar Lorenzo see Lorenzo Fernández, Oscar
Ferneyhough, Brian Arho; Cecchi; Giraud; Pagh-Paan; Rehnqvist;
    Saariaho; Steinberg
Ferrandini, Giovanni Battista Maria Antonia Walpurgis
Ferrara – S Vito convent Aleotti, R.; Aleotti, V.
FERRARI, CARLOTTA 1857, 1866, 1871
FERRARI, GABRIELLE 1909
Ferrari, Giorgio Di Lotti
Festival Hispano-Mexicano do Música Contemporánea Urreta
Festival of Music from Around the World Telfer
Fétis, François-Joseph x, xi; Bertin; Bigot; Farrenc; Gail; Grandval;
    La Hye; Quinault
Fetler, Paul Larsen
Fialkowska, Janina Larsen; Lauber
Fibich, Zdeněk Emingerová
Field, Henry Loder
Field, John Szymanowska
Fields, Dorothy Swift
Fillipeschi, Domenico Grimani
Fine, Irving Barkin
FINE, VIVIAN Davidson; Smiley
Finnish National Ballet see Helsinki
Finnish Radio [Oy Yleisradio Ab] Saariaho
Fioravanti, Valentino Appignani
Fischer, Edwin Eckhardt-Gramatté
Fischer, Irwin Borroff
Fisher, Arthur E. Geddes-Harvey
Fisher, Edward Geddes-Harvey
Fiske Museum of Musical Instruments [Claremont, CA] White, R.
Fitchburg State College [MA] McLean
Fitelberg, Grzegorz Bacewicz
Flagello, Nicolas Ekizian
Fleming, Austin see LEMON, LAURA G.
Flipse, Eduard 1940; Bordewijk-Roepman
Florence
    Conservatorio di Musica Luigi Cherubini (formerly Istituto
        Musicale) Baldacci; Capuis
    international exhibition [1890] Ruta
    Teatro della Pergola Uccelli
    Villa Poggio Imperiale Caccini, F.
Florida
    Florida Conservatory of Music and Art Roma
    Florida State University [Tallahassee] Van de Vate; Zwilich
    University of South Florida [Tampa] Oliviera
Florimo, Francesco Ruta
Flotow, Friedrich Grandval
Focke, Frè Alexander; Vivado
Foerster, Josef Bohuslav Müller-Hermann; Reisserová
Foggia [Italy] – conservatory Procaccini
FOLVILLE, EUGÉNIE-EMILIE JULIETTE 1892
Fonds Alex de Vries [Belgium] Tolkowsky
Fontainebleau [France] – American Conservatory Moore, D. R.
Fontei, Nicolò Strozzi
FONTYN, JACQUELINE 1959, 1964, 1976
Foote, Arthur Wood
Föreningen Svenska Tonsättare (FST) [Society of Swedish
    Composers] 1970; Malmlöf-Forssling; Rehnqvist; Wennerberg-
    Reuter

Fortunatov, Yuri Svanidze
Forzano, Giovacchino Rosselli-Nissim
Foss, Lukas Beecroft; Galás; Kolb; Polin
Foster, Stephen Collins Parkhurst; Sloman
FOWLER, JENNIFER xv; 1971
FOX, ERIKA 1991
Fox, Wilbur B. see BRAHE, MAY HANNAH
Françaix, Jean Boulanger, N.
Franceschini, Furio Catunda
Franchetti, Arnold Kolb; Walker
FRANCHI, DOROTHEA ANNE 1950
Franchomme, Auguste Haenel de Cronenthall
Franck, Antonio Barradas
Franck, César Bonis; Holmès; Jaëll
Frankfurt
    Dr Hochs Konservatorium Leginska; Schumann; Senfter
    Oper Frankfurt 1962; Talma
Franklin, Benjamin 1777; Brillon de Jouy
Fraser-Enoch Publications Fraser
Frauenmusik [Switzerland] Capuis
Frau und Musik, Internationaler Arbeitskreis [Germany] 1979;
    Alexandra; Heller
Frederick, Prince of Wales 1748
Frederick II (Frederick the Great), King of Prussia Anna Amalia (i);
    Anna Amalia (ii); Boni; Maria Antonia Walpurgis
Freiburg
    Institut für Neue Musik Paraskevaidis
    Staatliche Hochschule für Musik Lee, H. A. K.; Olive; Pagh-
        Paan; Rodriguez; Saariaho; Steinberg
French radio see Office de Radiodiffusion-Télévision Française;
    Radio France
Frenn, Franz Kralik von Mayerswalden
Freschl, Marion Szekely La Barbara
Fresno, Saturnino del Prieto
Freudenberg, Wilhelm Lehmann
Freyer, August Niewiarowska-Brzozowska
Friars, Percy Gerrish-Jones
Fribourg Cathedral Coleman
Fricker, Peter Racine Carr-Boyd; Freed; Lockwood
Frieberth, Karl Paradis
Friedericks, Elizabeth Wichern
Friedrich Wilhelm II, King of Prussia Eichner
Friends' Arts for World Unity Committee [USA] Weigl
Frye, Theodore R. Martin
Fuchs, Robert Faltis; White, M. V.
Fuente, Francisco Arizti
Fulgonio, Fulvio Mariani Campolieti
Furtwängler, Wilhelm Fromm-Michaels

GABRIEL, MARY ANN VIRGINIA 1867, 1873
Gade, Niels Andrée; Aulin; Liebmann, N. M.
Gadsby, Henry Aylward
Gadski, Johanna Mana Zucca
Gagliano, Giovanni Battista da 1622; Caccini, F.
Gail, Jean François Gail
GAIL, SOPHIE x; 1813, 1814, 1818; Bawr
Gál, Hans Musgrave
Galeotti, Vincenzo Ahlefeldt
Galindo Dimas, Blas Sanz
Galli-Curci, Amelita Mana Zucca
Gallon, Jean Desportes
Gallon, Noël Arrieu; Barberis; Demessieux; Desportes; Lee, Y.
Galway, James Alotin
GAMBARINI, ELISABETTA DE 1748
Gandini, Gerardo Lambertini
Ganz, Rudolf Barnett
Garant, Serge Lauber
García Lorca, Federico xv
Gardano, Angelo Casulana
GARELLI DELLA MOREA, VINCENZA 1915, 1916, 1924
Garrick, David Abrams
GARSENDA, Countess of Provence 13th century
Gasparini, Francesco Della Pietà, M.
Gasparini, Quirino Lombardini Sirmen
Gauthiez, Cécile 1929; Pentland
Gebauer, Johan Christian Liebmann, N. M.
Gédalge, André Bauer; Poldowski
GEDDES-HARVEY, ROBERTA 1903
GEDOK see Mannheim, Gemeinschaft Deutscher Organizationen
    von Künstlerinnen und Kunstfreundinnen
Geminiani, Francesco Gambarini

Genée, Adeline   Bright
Geneva – Ecole Supérieure d'Art Visuel   Calame
Genlis, Stéphanie-Félicité du Crest de Saint-Aubin   Bayon; Candeille; Demars
Genoa – Conservatorio Statale di Musica N. Paganini   Cecchi
Genzmer, Harald   Heller; Martins
George, Prince of Wales [later George IV]   Paradis
George III, King of England   Paradis
Georgia Council for the Arts [Tucker, GA]   Hays
Gerber, Ernst Ludwig   x; Gambarini
Germani, Fernando   Procaccini
Gershwin, George   Jessye; Swift
Gesellschaft der Musikfreunde   see Vienna
Gevaert, François-Auguste   Poldowski
Ghana – University of Ghana [Accra]   Daiken
Ghedini, Giorgio Federico   Furgeri; Giuranna
Ghent, Emmanuel   Spiegel
Ghent – Instituut voor Psychoakoestik en Elektronische Muziek   Zielińska
Gherardini, Arcangelo   1585; Massarenghi
Ghiglia, Oscar   Benati; Spiegel
Ghirlinzoni, Alberto   Ricci
Gianneo, Luis   Lambertini
Giannetti, Giovanni   Bidart
Giannini, Vittorio   Claman; Franks Williams; Mamlok; Ulehla; Viðar
Giarda, Luigi Stefano   Canales
GIDEON, MIRIAM   xvi, xvii; 1974; Bauer
Giessen [Germany] – Justus-Liebig-Universität   Sonntag
GIFFORD, HELEN   xvi
Gillespie, Dizzy   Williams, M. L.
Ginastera, Alberto   Terzian
Giordani, Tommaso   1781; Anspach; Lombardini Sirmen
Girardin, Mme Emile de   Duchambge
Giuffre, Jimmy   Bley
GIURANNA, BARBARA   1936, 1967, 1983; Pistono
GLANVILLE-HICKS, PEGGY   xvi; 1931, 1938, 1950, 1952, 1954
Glasgow
  Royal Scottish Academy of Music and Drama   Beat; Liddell; Weir
  Scottish Ballet (formerly Scottish Theatre Ballet)   Musgrave
  Scottish Early Music Consort   Wilkins
  Scottish National Orchestra (later Royal Scottish National Orchestra)   Musgrave
  Scottish Opera   1977, 1990, 1992; Musgrave
  Theatre Royal   1990
  University of Glasgow   Milstein; Weir
Glass, Philip   Ciani; La Barbara
Glastonbury Festival [Glastonbury, England]   Maddison
Glazunov, Alexander Konstantinovich   Rimskaya-Korsakova; Veysberg
Glier, Reyngol'd Moritsevich   Levina
Glinka, Mikhail Ivanovich   Adayevskaya
Globokar, Vinko   Galás
Gluck, Alma   Hodges
Gluck, Christoph Willibald   Anna Amalia (i); Beaumesnil; Viardot
Gnatt, Poul   Franchi
Gnazzo, Anthony J.   Giteck
Gnesin, Mikhail Fabianovich   Zhubanova
Godard, Benjamin   Aulin; Chaminade; Freer; Munktell
Godfrey, Dan   1899, 1908; Scarborough; Swepstone
Godowsky, Leopold   Warren
Goehr, Alexander   1971; Beat; Carr-Boyd; Chen Yi; Daiken; Milstein; Semegen
Goethe, Johann Wolfgang von   Anna Amalia (ii); Brentano; Eichner; Schröter; Szymanowska; Wolf
Goetschius, Percy   Cole; Fuchs; Hier; Jessye; Strickland; Swift
Gojowy, Detlef   xv
Goldman, Richard Franko   Landowska
Goldmark, Rubin   Cole; Dillon
Golisciani, Enrico   Rosselli-Nissim
Golubev, Yevgeny   Nikolayeva
Gomez, Jill   Mucha
Gómez, Julio   Romero
GONZAGA, CHIQUINHA   1912
Gonzaga, Ferdinando   Caccini, S.
González, Hilario   Hernández
González-Zuleta, Fabio   Nova
Goodman, Benny   Williams, M. L.
Goodrich, Alfred John   Strickland
Goossen, Frederic   LeBaron
Gordon, Michael   Wolfe

Goss, John   Marshall
Gossett, Walter   Bonds
Göteborg [Sweden] – Labour Concerts   Andrée
Gottschalk, Louis Moreau   Carreño
Gounod, Charles   xii; Ferrari, G.; Grandval; Viardot; Weldon
GOW, DOROTHY   Maconchy; Williams, G.
Gozzano, Guido   Pistono
Gradova, Gitta   Crawford
Graham, Martha   Davidson; Fine
Grainger, Percy   Simons
Gramatges, Harold   Ruiz Lastres
Gramatté, Walter   Eckhardt-Gramatté
Granados, Enrique   Freixas
Grandi, Cesare Augusto   Benati
GRANDVAL, MARIE   1859, 1863, 1864, 1868, 1869, 1880, 1892
Grannie Weldon   see WELDON, GEORGINA
Graun, Carl Heinrich   Anna Amalia (i)
Graz – Steiermärkische Musikverein conservatory   Kubisch; Pagh-Paan; Zieritz
GRAZIANINI, CATERINA BENEDICTA   1705; Raschenau
Green, M. D.   xii
Grétry, André-Ernest-Modeste   1786; Bawr; Grétry; Wuiet
GRÉTRY, LUCILE   xii; 1786
Greussay, Patrick   Bokanowski
Grieg, Edvard   Smyth
Grignon, Ricardo Lamote de   Romero
GRIMANI, MARIA MARGHERITA   1713; Raschenau
Grobe, Charles   Sloman; Sullivan
GRØNDAHL, AGATHE   Egeberg; Holmsen; Schjelderup
Gropius, Walter   Mahler
Groupe de Recherches Musicales   see Paris
Grove, George   xi
Gruenberg, Louis   James
Grunn, Homer   Cole
Guangzhou [Guangdong, China] – Beijing Opera Troupe   Chen Yi
Guarini, Giovanni Battista   1611; Aleotti, V.; Quinciani; Ricci
Guarnieri, Camargo   Campos; Catunda; Silva
GUBAYDULINA, SOFIYA ASGATOVNA   1986
Guelph [Ontario]
  Royal Opera House   Geddes-Harvey
  St George's Anglican Church   Geddes-Harvey
GUERIN, Mlle   1755
Guerrero, Alberto   Watson Henderson
Guerrero Díaz, Félix   Ruiz Lastres
GUEST, JANE MARY   x; 1783
Guézec, Jean-Pierre   Jolas
Guggenheim, Peggy   Hays
Guggenheim Fellowship   1930; Blaustein; Clayton; Clement; Crawford; Dlugoszewski; Ekizian; Fine; Glanville-Hicks; Kolb; LeBaron; Martinez, O. de la; Perry; Ran; Talma; Tower
Guildhall School of Music and Drama (GSM)   see London
Guillén, Nicolás   Hernández
Guilmant, Alexander   Boulanger, N.
Guinjoán, Juan   Bofill Levi
Guinovart, Carles   Pelegrí i Marimón
Guiraud, Ernest   Aulin; Bonis; Chrétien; Krzyżanowska
Guyonnet, Jacques   Calame

Hába, Alois   Jiráčková; Marić; Snížková
Haden, Charlie   Bley
Hadjiev, Parashkev   Klinkova
Hague, The
  Haghe Sanghers, Die   Appeldoorn
  Konklijk Conservatorium   Woof
  National Exhibition on Women's Work   1898; Oosterzee
  women's symphony orchestra   Kuyper
Halévy, Fromental   Wartel
Halffter, Ernesto   Hannikainen
Halffter, Rodolfo   Escribano; Prieto; Sanz; Schonthal; Urreta
Halifax [Nova Scotia]
  Atlantic Symphony Orchestra   Raum
  St Mary's University   Ran
HALL, PAULINE   1938
Hambourg, Michael   Poldowski
Hamburg
  Singverein   Reichardt, L.
  Staatliche Hochschule für Musik   Birnstein; Escot; Fromm-Michaels; Kubisch
Hamma, Fridolin   Jaëll
Handel, George Frideric   Gambarini
Hanover – Staatliche Hochschule für Musik   Kats

Hanslick, Eduard   Le Beau
Hanson, Howard   Diemer; James; Wylie
Harper, Emerson   Bonds
Harraden, Beatrice   Harraden
HARRADEN, R. ETHEL   1891, 1895
Harris, Roy   Bonds; Boulanger, N.; Santos Ocampo; Thome
Harris, Victor   Lang, M. R.
HARRISON, ANNIE FORTESCUE   1876
Harrison, Lou   Glanville-Hicks
Hart, Fritz   Glanville-Hicks; Sutherland
Hartford [CT]
    conservatory   Walker
    Hartt School/College of Music   Kolb; Smith, J.; Walker
    University of Hartford   Walker
Hartmann, Johan Peter Emilius   Liebmann, N. M.
Hartmann, Per   Leite, V. D.
Harvard University   see Cambridge [MA]
Harvey, Jonathan   Anderson, A.; Tann
Hasegawa, Yoshio   Shiomi
Hasse, Johann Adolph   Hodges; Maria Antonia Walpurgis;
    Martínez, M. von
Hasselt [Belgium] - Limburgsche Orgelschool   Vigneron-
    Ramackers
Haubenstock-Ramati, Roman   Franks Williams; Olive
HAULTETERRE, ELISABETH DE   1740, 1744
Haüy, Valentin   Paradis
Havana
    Bach conservatory   Hernández
    Choral de la Habana   Hernández
    Conservatorio Amadeo Roldán (formerly Conservatorio
        Municipal)   Botet-Dubois; Hernández; Ruiz Lastres
    Conservatorio de Música y Declamación   Arizti; Delfin; León
    Conservatorio Hubert de Blanck   Botet-Dubois; De Blanck
        Martín; Hernández
    Grupo de Renovación Musical   1942; Hernández
    Instituto Nacional de Cultùra   Hernández
    Instituto Superior Pedagógico   Ruiz Lastres
    Museo de la Música   De Blanck Martín
    Orquesta Feminina de Concierto   1937; Lecuona Casado
    Orquesta Sinfónica de La Habana   Adam de Aróstegui
Hawaii - University of Hawaii   McLean
Hawkins, John   ix
Haydn, Joseph   1792; Abrams; Auenbrugger; Barthélemon, C. M.;
    Bigot; Brizzi Giorgi; Dussek, S.; Krumpholtz; Martínez, M. von;
    Paradis; Parke, M. F.
HAYS, SORREL   xv; 1981, 1993
Heard, Alan   Telfer
Hecker, Wilhelm   Bibby
Heerlen [Netherlands] - music school   Bonhomme
Heffley, Eugene   Bauer
Heidelberg
    Evangelisches Kirchenmusik-Institut   Woll
    Hochschule für Kirchenmusik   Dinescu
Heiden, Bernhard   Santos Ocampo
Heidt, Horace   Grever
Heimler, Hans   Riseman
Heinze, Bernard   Glanville-Hicks
Helsinki
    Finnish National Ballet [Suomen Kansallisbaletti]   Saariaho
    Helsinki Festival [Helsingin Juhlaviikot]   Saariaho
    orchestral school   Moberg
    Sibelius Academy [Sibelius-Akatemia] (formerly Helsinki Music
        Institute)   Arho; Hannikainen; Leiviskä; Moberg; Saariaho
Hemans, Felicia   Browne, H. M.
Hemingway, Ernest   Jolas
Henkemans, Hans   Marez Oyens
Hennesse, Don   xii
Hennings, Henrik   Wandall
Henry, Pierre   Gorne; Radigue
Henry VIII, King of England   Boleyn
Henselt, Adolf   Adayevskaya; Bronsart
Henze, Hans Werner   Berberian; Scherchen
Hereford Festival   Smith, A. M.
Hermans, Henri   Bonhomme
Hermosillo [Mexico] - Universidad de Sonora   Zubeldia
Hernandez Medrano, Humberto   Lara
Hervig, Richard   Hays; McTee
Herz, Henri   Jaëll
Herzogenberg, Heinrich   Smyth
Hewitt, James   Pownall
Hewson, George   Boyle
HIER, ETHEL GLENN   1918, 1925, 1939

High Fidelity/Musical America [Great Barrington, MA]   La Barbara
HILDEGARD OF BINGEN   1151
Hill, Alfred   Holland
Hiller, Johann Adam   Anna Amalia (ii); Schröter
Hiller, Lejaren   Nogueira; Oliveira
Hilversum   see Radio Hilversum
Hindemith, Paul   Archer; Diemer
Hines, Earl   Williams, M. L.
Hirst, Linda   Fowler
Hitzacker [Germany] - Sommerliche Musiktage Hitzacker
    Havenstein
Hixon, Don   xii
Hlobil, Emil   Jiráčková; Loudová; Obrovská; Petkova
Hobart [Tasmania] - Festival of Contemporary Opera and Music
    Sutherland
Hoddinott, Alun   Tann
Hoff-Barthelson Music School [Scarsdale, NY]   Ulehla
Höffer, Paul   Guran; Ørbeck
Hoffman, Gerda Wismer   Gerrish-Jones
Hohlfeld, Ernst   Reisserová
Hol, Richard   Rennes
Holland Festival   Woof
Holloway, Robin   Weir
Holm, Hanya   Fine
Holmboe, Vagn   Hay
HOLMÈS, AUGUSTA   1881, 1889
Holmes, William Henry   Barnard
Holon [Israel] - Conservatory of Music   Feigin
Holst, Gustav   Holst
HOLST, IMOGEN   1928, 1930, 1931; Williams, G.
HÖLSZKY, ADRIANA   xv
Holter, Iver   Lund, S.
Holzbauer, Ignaz   Lebrun, F.
Honegger, Arthur   Tailleferre; Wertheim; Wylie; Zimmermann, M.
Hong Kong
    Chinese University of Hong Kong   Ho Wai-On; Lam Bun-ching
    Hong Kong Chinese Orchestra   Chen Yi
    University of Hong Kong   Boyd
Honolulu - Kawaiaha'o church   Lili'uokalani
Hood College [Frederick, MD]   Ballou
HOOVER, KATHERINE   xvi
Hope, Laurence   Woodforde-Finden
HOPEKIRK, HELEN   xiv
Hopkins, Gerard Manley   xviii
Hopkins, James   Allik
Horn, Camillo   Frank-Autheried
HORROCKS, AMY ELSIE   1889, 1899; Woodforde-Finden
Houston
    Houston Grand Opera   1991; Monk
    Houston Symphony   Bond, V.
    University of Houston   Oliveros
Hovhaness, Alan   Van Appledorn
HOWE, MARY   1922, 1925, 1933; Bauer; Hier
HOWELL, DOROTHY   1919, 1921; Kirkwood
Howells, Herbert   Dring; Elwyn-Edwards; Fraser; Lucas; Trimble
Huber, Klaus   Arho; Olive; Pagh-Paan; Saariaho
Huddersfield [England]
    Contemporary Music Festival   Wolfe
    Huddersfield Polytechnic (later University of Huddersfield)
        Wilkins
Hughes, R.   xii
Hugo, Victor   Bertin
Hullah, John   Mounsey
Hultberg, Cortland   Louie
Hummel, Johann Nepomuk   Beauharnais; Szymanowska
Humperdinck, Engelbert   Branscombe; Veysberg
Humphrey, Doris   Fine
Huneker, James Gibbons   Rivé-King
Hungarian Broadcasting Authority [Magyar Radio és Televizie]
    Hajdú
Hungarian Women's Art and Education Association   Kuliffay
Huss, Henry Holden   Bauer; Wood
Hutchens, Frank   Beath
Huygens, Constantijn   Duarte

Iaşi [Romania]
    Conservatory [Conservatorul de Musică]   Asachi; Barberis;
        Chefaliady-Taban
    Humpel Girls' Institute   Chefaliady-Taban
Ibert, Jacques   Wertheim
Ibuse, Masuji   Miyake

Iceland Symphony Orchestra see Reykjavík
Ikenouchi, Tomojirō Hara; Konishi; Mori
Iliff, James Graham; Ho Wai-On
Illinois
  Northeastern Illinois State College [Chicago] Ziffrin
  University of Illinois Grant; Moretto; Payne
Imbrie, Andrew Welsh Konishi
Indiana University McLean; Ptaszyńska; Santos Ocampo
Indy, Vincent d' Adam de Aróstegui; Barberis; Béclard d'Harcourt;
  Hagan; Munktell; Poldowski; Zubeldia
Inner Mongolian Arts School [Ulan Bator, Mongolia] Xin
Institut de France Farrenc; Leleu
International Congress on Women in Music 1977, 1980, 1981,
  1982, 1984, 1986, 1988, 1990, 1991, 1992, 1993; Beath; Hays
International Institute for the Study of Women in Music
  see California
International League of Women Composers 1975, 1990; Beath;
  Hays; O'Leary; Pizer; Tann; Van de Vate; Vercoe
International Leonard Bernstein Academy Giuranna
International Music Council see UNESCO
International Panama-Pacific Exposition [1915] see San
  Francisco
International Rostrum of Composers see UNESCO
International Society for Contemporary Music (ISCM) 1928,
  1933, 1938, 1950; Catunda; Clarke; Crawford; Eckhardt-Gramatté;
  Gentile; Gifford; Glanville-Hicks; Ivey; Kaprálová; Lam Bun-ching;
  Lara; Louie; Maconchy; Manziarly; Matuszczak; Ore; Pentland;
  Wilkins; Zielińska; Ziffrin; Zwilich
International Society of Hildegard von Bingen Studies [USA]
  1991; Escot
International Society of Music Educators (ISME) Martins
International Women's Music Sound Archive [Three Mile Bay, NY]
  Pizer
Iowa - University of Iowa Hays; McTee; Radigue
Ireland, John Holland
Irino, Yoshirō Massumoto; Sato
Irish Music Festival [Feis Ceoil] Needham; Patterson
Irish radio see Radio Eireann
Isaacs, Leonard McIntosh
ISABELLA LEONARDA 1665, 1693; Cozzolani
ISCM see International Society for Contemporary Music
Ishiketa, Mareo Hori
Israel
  Israel Broadcasting Authority Franks Williams
  Israel Festival Riseman; Warren
  Israeli Defense Forces Riseman
  Israel Philharmonic Orchestra see Tel-Aviv
Istanbul - conservatory Karamanuk

Jackson, Mahalia Akers; Coates, D. L.
Jacksonville [IL] - conservatory Stocker
Jacob, Gordon Coleridge-Taylor; Coulthard; Dring; Gipps; Glatz;
  Harrison, P.; Holst; Williams, G.
Jacobi, Frederick Pentland
Jacobs, W. W. Smyth
Jacobson, Maurice Lucas
Jacobs Pillow Dance Festival [Lee, MA] Bond, V.
JACQUET DE LA GUERRE, ELISABETH-CLAUDE ix, xiii;
  1685, 1687, 1694, c1695, 1707, 1708, 1715, 1721
Jadassohn, Salomon Hopekirk; Smyth; Wennerberg-Reuter
JAËLL, MARIE 1877, 1879
James, Paul Swift
Janáček Academy of Music see Brno
Janos see TATE, PHYLLIS
Jaques-Dalcroze, Emile Harrison, P.; see also Berlin,
  Jaques-Dalcroze institute
Jarnach, Philipp Escot
Jarrett, Keith Bley
Jazz Composers Guild Orchestra see New York
Jelinek, Hanns Ørbeck; Sønstevold
Jerome, William Nugent
Jerusalem - Hebrew Union College Fleischer
Jeugd en Muziek België Vigneron-Ramackers
Jiménez, Manuel Berroa
Jirák, K. B. Maconchy
Jiránek, Josef Mallá
Joachim, Joseph 1903; Barns; Ewart; Farrenc; Lehmann; Schumann
John, David Scarborough
Johnson, Robert Boleyn
Johnston, Ben Payne
Johnston, Richard Watson Henderson

Johnstone, A. E. Swift
JOLAS, BETSY 1974, 1984, 1990; Barreau; Blaustein; Sikora
Jolivet, André Lachartre; Lejet; Loudová; Wertheim; Zaimont
Jolivet, Louis Koptagel
Jones, Betty Hall Williams, M. L.
Jones, Charles Giteck
Jones, David Poston
Jongen, Joseph Vellère
Jongen, Léon Vito-Delvaux
Jora, Mihail Donceanu; Marbé; Petra-Basacopol
Joseph I, Holy Roman Emperor of the Habsburg Dynasty 1707; Rossi
Josif, Enrico Nešić; Stefanović
Joubert, Célestin Bonis
Joyce, James Jolas
Juilliard School see New York
Jung, Carl Gustav xviii
Juon, Paul Sodré

Kàan, Jindřich z Albestů Brdlíková
Kabalevsky, Dmitry Borisovich Levina
Kabeláč, Miloslav Loudová
Kagel, Mauricio Bibby; Escribano; Henderson, M.; LeBaron;
  Nogueira; Odǎgescu; Suh
Kalkbrenner, Frédéric Blahetka
Kammermusikforeningen [Denmark] Sehested
Kansas State University [Manhattan, KS] Abejo
Kapr, Jan Petrová, E.
KAPRÁLOVÁ, VÍTĚZSLAVA xviii; 1938; Mucha
Karastoyanov, Assen Karastoyanova
Karayev, Kara Ali-Zadeh
Karkoschka, Erhard Hölszky; Silver
Karlsruhe – Staatliche Hochschule für Musik Pagh-Paan
Karr, Gary Lauber
KASILAG, LUCRECIA ROCES 1956
KASSIA 9th century
Katowice [Poland] – Academy of Music [Akademia Muzyczna]
  Moyseowicz
Kaufmann, Dieter Skouen
Kaun, Hugo Barnett; Dillon; Hier
Kazakh Composers' Union 1962; Zhubanova
Kazan' – State Conservatory Gubaydulina
KEAL, MINNA 1989
Keele [England] – University of Keele Firsova
Kelemen, Milko Erding; Hölszky
Keller, Hans Bauld; Bingham; Brusa
Kelley, Edgar Hier
Kelly, Michael Martínez, M. von
Kenneth G. Fiske Museum of Musical Instruments [Claremont, CA]
  White, R.
Kentucky - University of Kentucky [Lexington] Anderson, B.
KERKADO, LE SÉNÉCHAL DE 1805
KERN, FRIDA 1927
Kestenberg, Leo Alotin
Ketten, Henri Ferrari, G.
KEW ensemble [Poland] Sikora
Khrennikov, Tikhon Nikolayevich Chudova
Kihl, Viggo Watson Henderson
King, Billie Jean Walker
King, Gilbert see HARRISON, SUSIE FRANCES
Kirchner, Leon Armer
Kiriac-Georgescu, Dumitru Athanasiu-Gardeev
Kirk, Andy Williams, M. L.
Kirk, Elise xvii
Kirnberger, Johann Philipp Anna Amalia (i)
Kitson, Charles Herbert Boyle
Klein, Bruno Korn; Stocker
Klein, Lothar Allik
Klepper, Leon Marbé; Petra-Basacopol
Kloeppel, Louise Ballou
Klosé, Hyacinthe Eléonore Holmès
Knittel, Krzysztof Sikora
Knorr, Iwan Senfter
Knowlton, Kenneth Spiegel
Knussen, Oliver Keal
Kodály, Zoltán Hajdú; Szőnyi
Koeberg, Frits Ehrhardt Adrian Appeldoorn; Beijerman-Walraven
Koechlin, Charles xvii; Urner
Koellreutter, Hans Joachim Catunda; Scliar
Koenig, Gottfried Michael Lockwood; Marez Oyens
Koepke, Paul Oliveros
Kohn, Karl Blaustein

Kohoutek, Ctirad   Bodorová; Jiráčková
Kokoschka, Oskar   Mahler
KOLB, BARBARA   1969, 1987
Kolerus, Birgitte   Alsted
Kolesovsky, Zikmund   Brdlíková
Kollwitz, Käthe   Ticharich
Komadina   Nešić
Komorous, Rudolf   Smith, L. C.
Konta, Robert   Lalauni
Kontarsky, Aloys   Bibby
Koprowski, Peter Paul   Telfer
Korean Society of Women Composers   Suh
Körner, Thomas   xv
Korte, Karl   Reid
Kostelanetz, André   Warren
Kosugi, Takehisa   Shiomi
Koszewski, Andrzej   Zielińska
Kotoński, Włodzimierz   Lara; Semegen
Kovach, Andras   Lauber
Kovnatskaya, Ludmila   xvii
Kozeluch, Leopold   Auernhammer; Brizzi Giorgi; Cibbini-
   Kozeluch; Paradis
Kozłowski, Józef   Likoshin
KPFA Pacifica Radio [CA]   Giteck
Kraków
   Academy of Music [Akademia Muzyczna] (formerly
      Conservatory; State Higher School of Music)   Dziewulska;
      McTee; Moszumańska-Nazar; Moyseowicz
   electronic music studio   Zielińska
   Music Institute   Klechniowska
Kraus, Karl   Pejačević
Krebs, Johann Ludwig   Gottsched
Krehl, Stephan   Klechniowska
Kremer, Gidon   Gubaydulina
Krenek, Ernst   Grigsby; James; Nordenstrom
Krieger, Armando   Nova
Krieger, Edino   Scliar
Kristjánsson, Arni   Viðar
Kronos Quartet   Coates, G.; Saariaho
KRUMPHOLTZ, ANNE-MARIE   Pittar
Kufferath, Hubert-Ferdinand   Milanollo
KUNKEL, RENATA   1991
Kupferman, Meyer   Cory
Kurowski, Andrew   xvii
Kurtz, Eugene   Clayton
Kuryokhin, Sergei   Miyake
K'ušnaryan, K'.   Čebotaryan
KUYPER, ELISABETH   1905, 1908, 1910, 1922
Kvinder i Musik [Women in Music] [Denmark]   Alsted; Hay
Kyoto – Doshisha University   Hara

LA BARBARA, JOAN   xv
Laboratorio Phonos   see Barcelona
La Borde, Jean-Benjamin de   ix
Lacerda, Oswaldo   Rosas-Fernandes
LACHARTRE, NICOLE   1974
Lachenmann, Helmut Friedrich   Kats; Odăgescu
La Chevardière, Louis Balthazard de   Gail
Lacombe, Louis   Casella
Lacour, Marcelle de   Coleman
Ladurner, Ignace Antoine   Montgeroult
LaForge, Frank   Warren
LA HYE, LOUISE-GENEVIÈVE DE   1830, 1835
Lamartine, Alphonse de   Duchambge
Lambert, Alexander   Mana Zucca
Lambert, Constant   Glanville-Hicks
Lambert, John   Anderson, A.
Lambiris, Georgios   Lambiri
LAM BUN-CHING   1991
LANDOWSKA, WANDA   Coleman
Lang, Benjamin   Lang, M. R.; Salter; Sullivan; Wood
Lang, David   Wolfe
Lang, Henry Albert   Heckscher
LANG, JOSEPHINE   1882
LANG, MARGARET RUTHVEN   1887, 1893, 1901
Lange, Daniël de   Kuyper
Lange, Gustav   Schjelderup
Lango, Achille   Procaccini
Langston University [Langston, OK]   Jessye
Lanier, Nicholas   Duarte
La Plata [Argentina] – university   Milstein

LARSEN, LIBBY   1973, 1983
LAUBER, ANNE   1987
Laurence, A.   xii
Lausanne – Conservatoire de Lausanne   Lauber
Lauska, Franz   Liebmann, H.
Lavagnino, Angelo Francesco   Heller
Lavignac, Albert   Leonardo
LaViolette, Wesley   Price
Lavista, Mario   Agudela; Lara; Urreta
Lawes, Henry   1655; Dering
Laxenburg [Austria] – Schlosstheater   1791
Lazzarini, Scipione   Nascinbeni
League of Composers   see New York
League of Composers–ISCM [USA]   Ivey
League of Filipino Composers   1956; Kasilag
LE BEAU, LUISE ADOLPHA   1877, 1887, 1894
Leborne, François   Ferrari, G.
LEBRUN, FRANZISKA   1780; Lebrun, S.
Leclair, Jean-Marie   Haulteterre
Le Couppey, Félix   Chaminade
LECUONA CASADO, ERNESTINA   1937
Lee, Young-Ja   xvi
Leeuw, Ton de   Hoenderdos; Ore; Rubin
LEFANU, NICOLA   xv, xvii; 1973, 1987, 1993; Maconchy
Lefort, Bernard   Tailleferre
Le Gallienne, Dorian   Gifford
LEGINSKA, ETHEL   1935
Lehár, Franz   Grever
Lehmann, Amelia   Lehmann
LEHMANN, LIZA   xiii; 1896, 1911
Leibowitz, René   Alexander
Leimer, Kurt   Di Lotti
Leipzig
   Conservatory (Hochschule für Musik)   Ewart; Ferrari;
      Hopekirk; Klechniowska; Lambiri; Rogers; Smyth; Wennerberg-
      Reuter; Zechlin
   Gewandhaus   Sainton-Dolby; Schumann; Zimmerman, A.
   Neuestheater   1906
   Stadttheater   1910; Maddison
Leite, Luiz Felipe   Casella
LEJET, EDITH   1968
LELEU, JEANNE   xv
Leman, Albert Semyonovich   Gubaydulina
Lemare, Iris   1931; Lutyens
Lemoine, Gustave   Puget
Leningrad   see St Petersburg
León, Argeliers   Hernández
LEONARDO, LUÍSA   1877
Leoni, Leone   Trissina
LePage, Jane Weiner   xii
Leschetizky, Theodor   Leginska
Leseman, Frederick   Allik
Leu-la-Forêt [France] – Ecole de Musique Ancienne   Landowska
Levasseur, Rosalie   Beaumesnil
Levi, Hermann   Smyth
Levy, Heniot   Barnett
Lévy, Lazare   Karamanuk
Lewis, C. S.   Poston
Lewis, Matthew Gregory ('Monk')   Abrams; Bland
Lewis, Ruth   Owen
LeWitt, Sol   Anderson, L.
Licette, Miriam   Hardelot
Liebig, Karl   Mayer
Liège – Conservatoire Royal de Musique de Liège   Blaustein;
   Boorn-Coclet; Demessieux; Folville; Gorne; Thisse-Derouette; Vito-
   Delvaux
Ligeti, György   Birnstein; Escribano; Fereyra; LeBaron; Odăgescu;
   Scherchen; Silver
Lilburn, Douglas   Bibby; Freed; McLeod
LILI'UOKALANI, Queen of Hawaii   xvi; 1869
Lima [Peru]
   Sas-Rosay academy of music   Escot
   Universidad Nacional Mayor de San Marcos   Escot
Limón, José   Ballou
Lincoln, Abraham   Carreño
Lind, Jenny   Aldridge
Lindegren, Johan   Munktell
Lindeman, Ludvig Mathias   Grøndahl
Lindner, Edwin   Pejačević
LINDSAY, MARIA   Dickson
Linley, Elizabeth Ann   Blackwood; Norton
Linn, Robert   Grigsby

Lips, Fridrikh Robertovich Gubaydulina
Lisbon
  Colecviva Capdeville
  Conservatório Nacional Capdeville; Martins
  Escola Superior de Música Capdeville
  Teatro Dona Maria 1849; Casella
  Universidade Nova de Lisboa Capdeville
Liszt, Franz Bronsart; Carreño; Freer; Grøndahl; Jaëll; Le Beau;
  Menter; Rivé-King; Ruta; Sabinin; Szymanowska; Tyrrell; Viardot;
  Wurmbrand-Stuppach
Litinsky, Genrik Eksanishvili
Litta, Archbishop Alfonso Calegari; Cozzolani
Live Music Now [Belgium] Tolkowsky
Ljubljana [Slovenia] – Ljubljana University [Univerza v Ljubljani]
  Mosusova
Loa College [Kaneshe, HI] Van de Vate
LOCKWOOD, ANNEA xv; 1970
LODER, KATE 1846
Lodi [Italy] – Teatro Sociale 1868
Łodź [Poland] – Institute for Popular Music Klechniowska
Loeffler, Charles Martin Swift
Loewe, Carl Mayer
LOMAX, LOUISA EMILY 1918
LOMBARDINI SIRMEN, MADDALENA LAURA x, xi; 1768,
  1771
LOMON, RUTH xvi
London
  Academy of St Martin-in-the-Fields Beamish
  All Saint's, Poplar Stirling
  Associated Board of the Royal Schools of Music Furze
  Barnet Choral Society Tate
  Boyd Neel Orchestra 1938; Lucas
  Brandenburg House Anspach
  Camden School for Girls Williams, G.
  Chanticleer Orchestra Gipps
  City of London School Swepstone
  Contemporary Chamber Orchestra see London, London
    Chamber Symphony
  Covent Garden 1771, 1799, 1902, 1974, 1984; Anspach;
    Gambarini; Lombardini Sirmen; Musgrave; Paredes; Smyth
  Crosby Hall Mounsey
  Crystal Palace 1890; Barns; Bright; Macirone; Smyth; Weldon;
    Woolf; Wurm; Zimmermann, A.
  Donmar Warehouse Theatre Bauld
  Drury Lane (Theatre Royal, Drury Lane) Anspach
  Electronic Music Studios, Putney Lockwood
  English Chamber Orchestra Musgrave
  English Ensemble Clarke
  English National Opera (ENO) 1994; Sekacz
  European Women's Orchestra Alberga; Martinez, O. de la
  Exeter Hall Macirone
  Furzedown College Carwithen
  Gaiety Theatre 1891; Harrison, A. F.
  Gallery of Illustration 1867; Gabriel; Harrison, A. F.
  Garden Venture, The 1991; Fox; Paredes
  German Reed Company Gabriel
  Goldmith's College Burrell
  Great Room, Dean Street Gambarini
  Guildhall School of Music and Drama (GSM) Allitsen;
    Aylward; Coleridge-Taylor; Kelly; Lehmann; Paredes; Swepstone
  Hampstead Music Club Tate
  Handel Commemoration concerts Parke, M. F.
  Hanover Square Rooms 1843; Delaval; Orger; Zimmermann, A.
  Haymarket Theatre 1781; Anspach
  Hickford's Rooms Davis
  His/Her Majesty's Theatre (King's Theatre) 1771, 1908;
    Lebrun, F.; Lombardini Sirmen; Malibran; Oury; Smyth
  Holloway Prison 1912; Smyth
  Inter-Artes Ho Wai-On
  King's College see London, University of London
  Laban Centre Bauld
  Ladies' Concerts 1791; Abrams
  London Academy of Music and Dramatic Art Roe
  London Ballad Concerts Aylward
  London Chamber Symphony (formerly Contemporary
    Chamber Orchestra) Martinez, O. de la
  London Coliseum 1994
  London Contemporary Dance Theatre Alberga
  London Contemporary Music Centre Tate
  London International Opera Festival 1988; Bauld
  London Musical Society Smith, A. M.
  London Philharmonic Orchestra (LPO) Carwithen; Hyde

London – continued
  London Repertoire Orchestra Gipps
  London Sinfonietta Beamish
  London Symphony Orchestra (LSO) Coleridge-Taylor; Hyde;
    Musgrave; Smyth
  London Women's Symphony Orchestra 1922; Kuyper
  Lontano Alberga; Beamish; Fowler; Martinez, O. de la
  Macnaghten-Lemare Concerts 1931; Lutyens; Maconchy; Tate
  Morley College Daiken; LeFanu
  Music and Gender Conference 1991
  Music Theatre Ensemble 1971; Daiken
  National Gallery Concerts Harrison, P.
  National Training School for Music Ewart; Weldon
  Norah Clench Quartet Clark
  Opera Comique Harrison, A. F.; Woolf
  Philharmonia Orchestra Weir
  Philharmonic Society see London, Royal Philharmonic Society
  Professional Concerts Guest
  Promenade Concerts (Queen's Hall Promenade Concerts;
    BBC Proms) 1910, 1912, 1919, 1930, 1962, 1973, 1989;
    Barns; Burrell; Gipps; Howell; Keal; LeFanu; Lucas; Maconchy;
    Musgrave; Poldowski
  Queen's Concert Rooms, Hanover Square Linwood
  Queen's Hall 1910, 1912, 1925; Barns; Swain; Swepstone
  Royal Academy of Music (RAM) 1879, 1888, 1889, 1918,
    1920, 1921, 1945, 1947; Alberga; Bailey; Barns; Bingham;
    Bright; Carmichael; Carwithen; Clarke; Daiken; Eggar; Ellicott;
    Furze; Graham; Horrocks; Ho Wai-On; Howell; Keal; Last;
    Lemon; Loder; Lomax; Macirone; Marshall; Martinez, O. de la;
    Mucha; Needham; Owen; Parke, D.; Poston; Prescott; Rainier;
    Roe; Sainton-Dolby; Scarborough; Smith, A. M.; Tate;
    Uyttenhove; White, M. V.; Woolf; Zimmermann, A.
  Royal Albert Hall Coleridge-Taylor
  Royal College of Music (RCM) 1907, 1928, 1930, 1931, 1940,
    1950; Aldridge; Anderson, A.; Clarke; Coulthard; Dring;
    Elwyn-Edwards; Fox; Franchi; Fraser; Gipps; Glanville-Hicks;
    Glatz; Gow; Grigsby; Harrison, P.; Holland; Holst; Hyde; LeFanu;
    Liddell; Lockwood; Lutyens; Maconchy; Nelson; Swain; Trimble;
    Williams, G.
  Royal Opera House see London, Covent Garden
  Royal Philharmonic Orchestra (RPO) Musgrave
  Royal Philharmonic Society (formerly Philharmonic Society)
    1867, 1883; Boulanger, N.; Bright; Howell; Marshall; Menter;
    Milanollo; Mounsey; Musgrave; Sainton-Dolby; Smith, A. M.;
    Weldon
  Sadler's Wells Theatre Musgrave
  St Andrew's Undershaft Stirlin
  St James's Hall 1868; Lehmann; Weldon; Zimmermann, A.
  St James's Theatre A'Beckett
  St Martin's Hall 1855; Mounsey
  St Paul's School for Girls LeFanu
  Salomon concerts Delaval; Dussek; Krumpholtz; Parke, M. F.
  Savoy Theatre Harrison, A. F.; Temple
  Sounds Positive Anderson, A.
  Surrey Gardens theatre A'Beckett
  Tobias Matthay Pianoforte School Richards
  Trafalgar Square Theatre 1895
  Trinity College of Music Coleridge-Taylor; Olive; Wilkins
  Turner Grand Opera Roma
  Unicorn Theatre for Children Sekacz
  University of London, Extra-mural Musgrave
  University of London, Goldsmiths College Daiken
  University of London, King's College 1991, 1993; LeFanu;
    Milstein
  University of London, University College Richards
  West Central College of Music Riego
  Willis's Rooms Guest
Londonderry – Victoria College Needham
Long, Kathleen Coulthard
Long, Marguerite Arrieu; Leleu
Long Island Institute of Music [NY] Zaimont
Long Island University [Greenvle, NY] Tautu
Longton, Michael Smith, L. C.
Lontano see London
Lopatnikoff, Nikolai White, R.
López, Anselmo 1893
López, Martín Barradas
Lord, Roger Dring
Lorel, Antoinette Chaminade
Lorenzo Fernândez, Oscar Cameu
Loriod, Yvonne Daiken
LORRAINE, Duchess of 13th century

Los Angeles
   Hollywood Bowl   Leginska
   Inner City Repertory Theater   Bonds
   Los Angeles Chamber Orchestra   Musgrave
   Los Angeles City College   Louie
   Los Angeles Music Center Opera   1992; Musgrave
   Los Angeles Philharmonic Orchestra   1972; Bonds; Saariaho;
      Warren
   Los Angeles Symphony Orchestra   1919; Mana Zucca
   Metro-Media film studios   Bond, V.
   Occidental College   Tucker
   Olga Steeb Piano School   Moore, M. C.
   Olympic Arts Festival   La Barbara
   Universal Pictures   Bond, V.
   see also California
Lothar, Mark   Ørbeck
Louegk, Günter   Hölszky
Louel, Jean   Bulterijs
LOUIE, ALEXINA   xvi; 1986
Louisiana State University [Baton Rouge]   Coates, G.
Louisville Orchestra [KY]   1954; Dlugoszewski; Glanville-Hicks
Louis XIV, King of France   Ménétou
Lourdes College [Cagayon de Oro City, Philippines]   Abejo
Louvain [Belgium] – Institut Interdiocésan de Musique d'Eglise
   (Lemmens Institute)   Bulterijs
Lovell, Henry   Brahe
Lozano, Maria Antonieta   Rodriguez
Lübeck – Hochschule für Musik   Birnstein
Lucas, Charles   Loder
LUCAS, MARY   1928, 1929, 1938
Lucca – Istituto Musicale   Cecchi
Lücheng, Zheng   Huang
Lucier, Alvin   La Barbara; Payne
Ludwigslust – Mecklenburg-Schwerin Hofkapelle   Westenholz
Luening, Otto   Ballou; Carlos; Chance; Coates, G.; Dvorkin; Shatin;
   Tower; Zaimont
LUFF, ENID   Usher
Lully, Jean-Baptiste   ix
Lunceford, Jimmie   Williams, M. L.
LUND, SIGNE   1917
Lutosławski, Witold   Lomon; Semegen; Van de Vate
LUTYENS, ELISABETH   xvi; 1931, 1939, 1969; Bauld; Freed;
   Gow; Graham; Luff
Lu Xun Academy of Arts [Yanan, Shaanxi, China]   Huang
L'viv/Lwów (formerly Lemberg) - Conservatory   Klechniowska;
   Szajna-Lewandowska
Lyons - Concerts des Pauvres   Milanollo

Maas, Louis   Smyth
Maaseik [Belgium] – Atheneum   Vigneron-Ramackers
Maastricht [Netherlands]
   city orchestra   1928; Bonhomme
   Jan van Eyck Akademie   Kubisch
Maatschappij tot Bevordering der Toonkunst [Association for the
   Promotion of Music] [Netherlands]   1830; Bergh; Oosterzee
Mabarak, Jiménez   De Blanck Martín; Sanz
McBurney, Mona   Brahe
McClary, Susan   xviii
McCombie, Bruce   McTee
MacCunn, Hamish   Lehmann
Macdonald, Ian   see LEMON, LAURA
Macdonald, M. I.   Steiner, E. R.
MacDonald, Margaret   Steiner, E. R.
MacDowell, Edward   Hopekirk
MacDowell Colony [Peterborough, NH]   1918, 1921; Anderson, R.;
   Barreau; Bauer; Beach; Britain; Brusa; Chance; Clement; Crawford;
   Daniels; Dillon; Escot; Hier; Howe; James; Kolb; Pentland; Semegen;
   Talma; Zaimont; Ziffrin
Macek, Jiří   xvii
McEwen, John   Howell
Macfarren, George   Macfarren; Macirone; Marshall; Prescott; Smith,
   A. M.; Stirling; White, M. V.; Zimmermann, A.
McGee, David   Frykberg
McGill University   see Montreal
McINTOSH, DIANA   1977; Southam
MACIRONE, CLARA ANGELA   1878
Maciunas, George   Shiomi
Mackenzie, Alexander   Hopekirk
McLean, Barton   McLean
Macnaghten, Anne   Lutyens
Macnaghten-Lemare Concerts   see London

MACONCHY, ELIZABETH   xvi; 1930, 1953, 1959, 1976, 1977,
   1987; LeFanu; Williams, G.
McPartland, Marian   Williams, M. L.
McPhee, Colin   Glanville-Hicks
MADDISON, ADELA   1910
Maderna, Bruno   Ancona; Beecroft; Berberian; Rampazzi
Madrid
   Biblioteca Nacional   Freixas
   Casa Velasquez   Reverdy
   Conservatory   Adam de Aróstegui; Prieto; Rodrigo; Zubeldia
   Sociedad de Conciertos   Bengoecha de Cármena
   Teatro de la Zarzuela   1915
   Teatro Jovellanos   1874; Bengoecha de Cármena
Maegaard, Jan   Pade
Maeterlinck, Maurice   Boulanger, L.
Maganza, Giambattista   Casulana
MAHLER, ALMA MARIA   1910
Mahler, Gustav   xvi; Mahler
MAIER, KATERINA   c1795
Maksymiuk, Jerzy   Coates, G.
Malec, Ivo   Canat de Chizy
MALIBRAN, MARIA   1836; Viardot
Malipiero, Gian Francesco   Dianda; Hier
Malling, Jørgen   Meyer
MALMLÖF-FORSSLING, CARIN   1970
Malvern Girls' College [Malvern, England]   Hugh-Jones
MAMLOK, URSULA   León
MANA ZUCCA   1919
Manchester – Royal Northern College of Music   Luff
Manchester Union Leader [Manchester, NH]   Schuyler
Mandl, Richard   Hopekirk
Mandyczewski, Eusebius   Faltis
Manhattan School of Music   see New York
Manila
   Centro Escolar University   Santos Ocampo
   Cultural Centre of the Philippines   Kasilag
   Philippine Women's University   Abejo; Kasilag
   St Paul College   Santos Ocampo
   St Scholastica's College   Abejo
   Stella Maris College   Santos Ocampo
Manitoba – University of Manitoba   McIntosh; Pentland
Manna, Gennaro   Maria Antonia Walpurgis
Mannes College of Music   see New York
Mannheim
   Gemeinschaft Deutscher Organizationen von Künstlerinnen
      und Kunstfreundinnen (GEDOK)   Alexandra; Ciobanu;
      Donceanu; Fowler; Furgeri; Hölszky; Krzanowska; Kunkel;
      Loudová; Marbé; Moszumańska-Nazar; O'Leary; Petrová, E.;
      Pstrokońska-Nawratil; Schorr; Sikora; Szajna-Lewandowska;
      Warren; Watson Henderson; Zielińska
   Gesellschaft für Neue Musik   Nordenstrom
   Hochschule für Musik   Heller
Manns, August   Bright; Smyth
Mantler, Mike   Bley
Mantovani   Velázquez
Mantzaros, Nikolaos   Nerantzi
MANZIARLY, MARCELLE DE   1933
Mara, Gertrud Elisabeth   Maria Antonia Walpurgis
MARBÉ, MYRIAM LUCIA   Ciobanu; Dinescu; Vlad
Marcello, Benedetto   x
MARCELLO, ROSANNA SCALFI   x
Marcesso, B.   1655; Strozzi
Marchant, Stanley   Poston
Marclay, Christian   Miyake
Marcus, Adele   McIntosh
Maretzek, Max   Rogers
MARGOT, Dame   13th century
Maria Anna Carolina Pia, Empress of Austria   Cibbini-Kozeluch
MARIA ANTONIA WALPURGIS, Electress of Saxony   1754,
   1760
MARÍA BARBARA, Queen of Spain   1750
MARIA DE VENTADORN   12th century
Maria Theresa, Empress of Austria   Agnesi; Paradis
Marié, Irma   Puget
Marie, Jean-Étienne   Ancona
Marino, Giam Battista   Caccini, F.; Quinciani
Mariscal, León   Urreta
Mark, Peter   Musgrave
Marlboro Music Festival [VT]   Kolb
Marmontel, Antoine François   Chaminade; Leonardo; Tanco
   Cordovez de Herrera
MAROIE, Dame   13th century

MAROIE DE DREGNAU DE LILLE   13th century
Marriner, Neville   Larsen
Marsh, Audrey   Monk
MARSHALL, FLORENCE ASHTON   xi
Martens, Heinrich   Samter
Martín, Edgardo   Hernández
MARTÍNEZ, MARIANNE VON   1773
Martini, Giovanni Battista (Padre Martini)   Coccia; María
   Barbara
Martinů, Bohuslav   xvii; Kaprálová
Martirano, Salvatore   Payne
Martucci, Giuseppe   Galeotti; Gubitosi
Marx, Adolf Bernhard   Mayer
Marx, Burle   De Blanck Martín
Marx, Joseph   Bach
Maryland – University of Maryland   Diemer
Mary Records [NY]   Williams, M. L.
Masetti, Enzo   Procaccini
Mason, William   Rivé-King; Runcie
Massachusetts
   University of Massachusetts, Amherst   Williams, M. L.
   University of Massachusetts, Lowell   McLean
   Massachusetts Institute of Technology   see Cambridge [MA]
MASSARENGHI, PAOLA   1585
Massé, Victor   Grandval
Massenet, Jules   Adam de Aróstegui; Aulin; Landowska; Schjelderup;
   Viardot
MASSON, ELIZABETH   1839
Mathews, Max   Ciani; Spiegel
Matisse, Henri   Jolas
Matsumura, Teizō   Mori
Matzenauer, Margaret   Warren
Maugars, André   Baroni
Maurel, Victor   Hardelot
Maury, Renaud   Hardelot
May, Oliver   White, M. V.
MAYER, EMILIE   1852, 1885
Mayerl, Billy   Sønstevold
Mazzucato, Alberto   Ferrari, C.
Meares, Richard   Philarmonica
Medici, Isabella de'   Casulana
Mehta, Zubin   1972; Bonds; Ran
Melartin, Erkki   Leiviskä
Melba, Nellie   Hardelot; Riego
Melbourne
   Australian Exhibition of Women's Works   1907; Arkwright;
      Ewart
   Marshall Hall Conservatorium   Sutherland
   Melba Memorial Conservatorium   Glanville-Hicks
   Melbourne Theatre Company   Gifford
   Sacre-Coeur convent   Henderson
   University of Melbourne, Conservatorium   Gifford; Sutherland
Mellers, Wilfrid   Boyd
Memphis State University [Memphis, TN]   Van de Vate
Mendelsohn, Alfred   Odăgescu
MENDELSSOHN, FANNY   xi; 1819, 1820, 1831, 1846, 1847;
   Kinkel; Schauroth
Mendelssohn, Felix   xi; Bigot; Kinkel; Lang, J.; Mendelssohn;
   Mounsey; Sainton-Dolby; Schauroth; Schumann
MÉNÉTOU, FRANÇOISE-CHARLOTTE DE SENNETERRE,
   Mlle DE   1691
Menichetti, Giuseppe   Rosselli-Nissim
Mennin, Peter   Polin
MENTER, SOPHIE   1883; Athanasiu-Gardeev; Faltis
Menuhin, Yehudi   Glanville-Hicks; Rainier
Mercadante, Saverio   Gabriel; Malibran
Mesmer, Anton   Paradis
Messager, André   Temple
Messiaen, Olivier   xvi; 1984; Ahrens; Alexander; Ancona; Barreau;
   Bruzdowicz; Clostre; Daiken; Eckhardt-Gramatté; Giteck; Jolas;
   Loudová; McLeod; Pstrokońska-Nawratil; Reverdy; Sato; Scherchen;
   Schorr; Szőnyi; Živković
Mester, Jorge   Samuel
Metastasio, Pietro   Coccia; Maria Antonia Walpurgis; Martínez,
   M. von
Metropolitan Opera House   see New York
Metz [France] – Centre Européen pour la Recherche Musicale
   Renard
Mexico City
   Academia de Danza Mexicana   Sanz
   Camerata de México   Urreta
   Carlos Chávez workshop   Guraieb

Mexico City – continued
   CENEDIM (Carlos Chávez National Centre for Musical
      Research, Documentation and Information)   Lara
   Centro Universitario de Teatro   Sanz
   congress of women composers [1993]   Sanz
   Conservatorio Nacional de Música   Agudela; Lara; Sanz;
      Urreta; Vázquez
   Escuela de Arte Dramático   Sanz
   Escuela Nacional de Música   Velázquez
   Instituto Politécnico Nacional   Urreta
   Mexican society for new music   Lara
   Orquesta Sinfónica Nacional   Urreta
   Teatro Hidalgo   Zubeldia
   Universidad Nacional Autónoma de México   Agudela; Barron;
      Zubeldia
   XEQ radio   Velázquez
Meyerbeer, Giacomo   Szymanowska; Viardot
Mezangère, Mme la Marquise de la   x
MGM Records [CA]   Richter
Michelangelo   see Buonarroti, Michelangelo
Michigan
   Eastern Michigan University [Ypsilanti]   James
   Michigan State University [East Lansing]   Newlin
   University of Michigan [Ann Arbor]   Borroff; Clayton; Clement;
      Eiríksdóttir; Gardner; Maddison; Stocker; Vercoe; Wolfe
Michniewski, Wojciech   Sikora
Middleschulte, Wilhelm   Barnett
Milan
   Conservatorio di Musica G. Verdi (formerly Conservatorio)
      Berberian; Bo; Browne; Castegnaro; Ferrari, C.; Ferrari, G.;
      Kubisch; Rampazzi; Zimmermann, M.
   Regio Ducal Teatro   1747; Agnesi
   S Agata convent, Lomello   Assandra
   S Margarita convent   Calegari
   S Maria Annunciata   Sessa
   S Radegonda monastery   Badalla; Cozzolani
   Studio di Fonologia Musicale, RAI   Dianda
   Teatro alla Scala   Lebrun, F.; Malibran; Respighi
   Teatro di S Radegonda   1857
Miles, Percy   xvii
Milhaud, Darius   Ahrens; Anderson, R.; Armer; Bonhomme; Clayton;
   Clostre; Coulthard; Giteck; Jolas; Lachartre; Lauber; Prieto; Thome
Milleville, Alessandro   Aleotti, R.; Aleotti, V.
Milliet, Paul   Ferrari, G.
Mills, Sebastian Bach   Rivé-King
Mills College [Oakland, CA]   Anderson, B.; Armer; Ballou; Giteck;
   Jolas; Kolb; Payne; Prieto; Urner; Warren
Mills Tape Music Centre   see San Francisco
Milojević, Miloje   Frajt
Milošević, Predrag   Mosusova
Minerva Society [New Harmony, IN]   1839; Runcie
Mingotti, Regina   Maria Antonia Walpurgis
Minneapolis [MN]
   Minnesota Composers Forum   1983; Larsen
   Minnesota Orchestra   1973; Larsen
   Walker Art Center   Oliveros
Minnesota – University of Minnesota, Minneapolis   Barron;
   Larsen; Nordenstrom; Zaimont
Mississauga [Ontario] – International Music Conservatory   Lee,
   H. A. K.
Missouri – University of   Wylie
MIYAKE, HARUNA   xvi
Mizuno, Shūkō   Shiomi
MOBERG, IDA GEORGINA   1906
Modena – S Agostino convent   Cesis
Moers [Germany] – International New Jazz Festival Moers   Galás
Mojica, José   Grever
Mojsisovics, Roderich   Zieritz
Molina, Antonio   Kasilag; Santos Ocampo
Molique, Bernhard   Gabriel
Möller, Hans-Dieter   Ahrens
Moncada, Hernández   Urreta
MONK, MEREDITH   1969
Monk, Thelonious   Williams, M. L.
Mons [Belgium] – Conservatoire Royal de Musique   Gorne
Montepulciano [Tuscany] – Cantiere Internazionale d'Arte
   [festival]   Coates, G.
Monteux, Pierre   Warren
Monteverdi, Claudio   Basile; Caccini, S.
Montevideo [Uruguay]
   Comedia Nacional   Pereyra-Lizaso
   Conservatorio Musical La Lira   Barradas

Montevideo [Uruguay] – *continued*
  Instituto de Enseñanza Musical Pereyra-Lizaso
  Kolischer conservatory Pereyra-Lizaso
  Normal Institute Barradas
MONTGEROULT, HÉLÈNE DE NERVO DE *c*1795; Candeille
Montreal
  Concordia University Coulthard; Lauber
  Conservatoire de Musique Lomon; Saint-Marcoux
  Ecole Vincent d'Indy [Outremont] Saint-Marcoux
  McGill University Archer; Lee, H. A. K.; Lomon
  Montreal Symphony Orchestra Saint-Marcoux
  Montreal Women's Symphony Orchestra Archer
  Université de Montréal Bruzdowicz; Lauber
Moog, Robert Carlos
MOORE, DOROTHY RUDD 1968
MOORE, MARY CARR 1909, 1911, 1912
Moore, Thomas Browne, A.
Morandi, Giorgio Smith, L. C.
MORATORI SCANABECCHI, ANGIOLA TERESA 1689,
  1694, 1696
Morawetz, Oskar Allik; Watson Henderson
Morelle, Max *see* TATE, PHYLLIS
Moretti Baldacci
Mori, Francis Milanollo
Moroi, Makoto Konishi
Morris, Gareth Lucas
Morris, Richard Claman
Morris, R. O. Coulthard; Gipps; Lucas
Mortari, Virgilio Procaccini
Mortensen, Finn Skouen
Moscheles, Ignaz Blahetka; Cibbini-Kozeluch; Jaëll; Rogers
Moscow
  Bol'shoy Theatre 1885
  Central Music School [Tsentral'naya Detskaya Muzïkal'naya
    Shkola] Chudova; Nikolayeva
  Gnesin State Pedagogical Institute [Muzïkal'no-pedagogicheskiy
    Institut imeni Gnesinïkh] Zhubanova
  Moscow Conservatory [Moskovskaya Konservatoriya] (later
    Moscow State Tchaikovsky Conservatory [Gosudarstvennaya
    Moskovskaya Konservatoriya imeni P. I. Chaykovskogo])
    Chudova; Eksanishvili; Firsova; Gubaydulina; Krasteva; Levina;
    Nikolayeva; Pakhmutova; Sanz; Svanidze; Zhubanova
  Moscow Experimental Electronic Studio Gubaydulina
  Moscow Philharmonic Orchestra [Moskovskiy Filarmonicheskiy
    Orkestr] Zieritz
  Moscow Private Russian Opera Company [Moskovskaya
    Chastnaya Russkaya Opera] Serova
  Solodovnikov Theatre 1899
Moszkowski, Moritz Couper; Hood; Manning
MOSZUMAŃSKA-NAZAR, KRYSTYNA 1962; McTee
Moten, Etta Price
Motherwell, Robert Dlugoszewski
Motte, Diether de la Birnstein
Mottl, Felix Smyth
MOUNSEY, ANN 1855
Mounsey, Elizabeth Mounsey
Mozart, Franz Xaver Wolfgang Baroni-Cavalcabò; Szymanowska
Mozart, Leopold Auenbrugger; Danzi; Mozart
Mozart, Wolfgang Amadeus Auernhammer; Liebmann, H.;
  Martínez, M. von; Mozart; Paradis
Mucha, Jiří Mucha
Muck, Carl Hopekirk
Mujeres en la Música [Spain] 1992; Ozaita
Muklé, May Clarke
Mumma, Gordon Payne
Munich
  Deutsches Theater Dianda
  Hochschule für Musik 1902; Daniels; Hays; Heller
  Königliche Vokalkapelle Lang, J.
  Philharmonic Society 1885; Mayer
MUNKTELL, HELENA 1889
Münster
  Kunstakademie Kubisch
  Pädagogische Hochschule Sonntag
Murail, Tristan Giraud
Murphy, Howard Bitgood
MUSGRAVE, THEA 1962, 1974, 1976, 1977, 1979, 1984, 1992;
  Boulanger, N.
Music Educators National Conference [USA] Beach
Music Teachers National Association [USA] Beach
Musorgsky, Modest Petrovich Rimskaya-Korsakova
Myaskovsky, Nikolay Yakovlevich Levina; Nikolayeva

Nairne, Carolina Scott
Naples
  Conservatorio di Musica S Pietro a Majella Ferrari, G.;
    Giuranna; Gubitosi; Ravinale; Ruta
  Teatro S Carlo Colbran
Nashville [TN]
  Fisk University Moore, U. S.
  George Peabody College for Teachers, Vanderbilt University
    Hagan
Natanson, Tadeusz Krzanowska; Pstrokońska-Nawratil
National Association for American Composers and Conductors
  Ulehla
National Broadcasting Company (NBC) [USA] Delfin
National Federation of Music Clubs [USA] Korn; Smith, J.
National Gallery Concerts *see* London
National Institute of Arts and Letters [USA] 1974; Gideon;
  Talma
National Intercollegiate Bands [USA] Van Appledorn
National Peace Federation Convention [USA] Collins
National Symphony Orchestra *see* Washington, DC
Naumann, Johann Gottlieb Maria Antonia Walpurgis
Navrátil, Karel Hopekirk
Nedbal, Oskar Pejačević
Nederlandse Toonkunstenaarvereeniging [Dutch Musicians'
  Society] Wertheim
Negri, Marc'Antonio 1611; Quinciani
Nelson [New Zealand] – School of Music Bowater
Nemo, Pierre Thys
NEMO Concerts [England] Swain
Nenov, Dimiter Baeva
Nepomuceno, Alberto Cameu; Faria; Sodré
Neukomm, Sigismund Gail
Neuls-Bates, Carol xii
Neumann, Hans Watson Henderson
Newcastle upon Tyne [England] – Northern Arts Whitehead
New England College [Henniker, NH] Ziffrin
New England Conservatory of Music *see* Boston
New Haven Symphony Orchestra [CT] Archer; Hagan
NEWLIN, DIKA Pentland
New Music America/New Music Alliance Davidson; Lockwood
New Music Edition [San Francisco] 1937; Couper
New Orleans [LA] – Tulane University of Louisiana Martinez,
  O. de la
Newport Jazz Festival [USA] Coates, D. L.; Williams, M. L.
New South Wales State Conservatorium of Music *see* Sydney
New York [city]
  Aeolian Hall Heckscher
  Alice Tully Hall Bond, V.
  American Composers Orchestra 1983; Dlugoszewski; León;
    Zwilich
  American Symphony Orchestra Mana Zucca; Moorman;
    Zwilich
  American Theater Wing Weigl
  American Women's Symphony Orchestra 1922; Kuyper
  Artists' Company Glanville-Hicks
  Bang on a Can Festival Wolfe
  Bank Street College of Education Vázquez
  Barnard College Anderson, L.; Dvorkin
  Beethoven Society 1918; Dillon
  Bel Canto Opera Bond, V.
  Branscombe Choral Branscombe
  Bronx Community College Moore, D. R.
  Brooklyn Academy of Music 1983; Anderson, L.
  Brooklyn College, CUNY Gideon; Kolb; León; Spiegel; Steiner
  Brooklyn Philharmonic Orchestra Chen Yi; Galás; León
  Carnegie Hall 1918; Clarke; Delfin; Williams, M. L.
  Cathedral of St John the Divine Galás
  Centro Basco Americano Zubeldia
  Chamber Music Society of Lincoln Center Berl; Bley;
    Dlugoszewski
  Chickering Hall 1894; Steiner, E. R.
  City College, CUNY Gideon; Kaminsky; Vázquez
  City University of New York (CUNY) Anderson, R.; Berl;
    Gideon; Spiegel; Zaimont
  Columbia Phonograph Co. 1928; Zieritz
  Columbia-Princeton Electronic Music Center (CPEMC) (later
    Electronic Music Center of Columbia University)
    Anderson, R.; Beecroft; Semegen; Smiley
  Columbia University Anderson, L.; Anderson, R.; Berberian;
    Bitgood; Carlos; Chance; Chen Yi; Clement; Coates, G.; Cory;
    Dvorkin; Ekizian; Gideon; LeBaron; Newlin; Semegen; Talma;
    Tower; Vázquez; Wallach; Weigl; Zaimont; Ziffrin

New York [city] – *continued*
Columbia University Teacher's College   Moore, U. S.
Composers' Forum   1950; Glanville-Hicks; León; Richter;
  Wertheim
Composers Group for International Performance   1968;
  Steiner, G.
Cooper Union for the Advancement of Science and Art
  Spiegel
Da Capo Chamber Players   1969; Chance; León; Tower
Dance Theatre of Harlem   León
Diller-Quaile Music School   Vázquez
Erick Hawkins Dance Company   Dlugoszewski
First Presbyterian Church, Brooklyn   Browne
Florilegium Chamber Choir   Chance
Fluxus   Shiomi
Gregg Smith Singers   Zaimont
Guggenheim Museum   *see* New York, Solomon R. Guggenheim
  Museum
Guild Theatre   Grever
Harlem School of the Arts   Moore, D. R.
Hunter College, CUNY   1968; Anderson, R.; Lockwood; Talma;
  Zaimont
Inner City Institute   Bonds
Institute for Avocational Music   Weigl
Institute of Musical Art   *see* New York, Juilliard School
Jazz Composers Guild Orchestra (later Jazz Composer's
  Orchestra)   Bley
Jewish Theological Seminary of America   Gideon
Juilliard Graduate School   Bonds; Cole; Smith, J.
Juilliard Preparatory School   Wallach
Juilliard School (formerly Institute of Musical Art)   1975;
  Ballou; Bauer; Bond, V.; Claman; Escot; Fine; Fuchs; Hier;
  La Barbara; Miyake; Moore, U. S.; Moorman; Parker; Pentland;
  Perry; Polin; Richter; Shatin; Spiegel; Steinberg; Steiner, G.;
  Strickland; Swift; Viðar; Zaimont; Zallman; Zwilich
Kaufmann Concert Hall   Berl
Kingsborough Community College   Mamlok
League of Composers   1927; Crawford; Glanville-Hicks
La Mama Experimental Theater Company   Swados
Lincoln Center for the Performing Arts   Berl; Bley;
  Dlugoszewski; Walker
Lincoln Center Repertory Theater   Smiley
Little Theatre   Grever
Lycée Français   Jolas
Lyceum School of Acting   Collins
Manhattan School of Music   1970; Cory; Ekizian; Franks
  Williams; Fuchs; Gideon; Hoover; Lee, Y.; Mamlok; Moore, U. S.;
  Steinberg; Ulehla; Wallach
Mannes College of Music (formerly David Mannes School)
  Berl; Couper; Dlugoszewski; Fuchs; Mamlok; Ran; Watson
  Henderson
Manuscript Society   Freer; Korn
Merkin Concert Hall   Giteck; Mamlock
Metropolitan Museum of Art   Glanville-Hicks
Metropolitan Opera House   1902, 1920; Recli; Smyth; Steiner,
  E. R.
Morosco Theater   Steiner, E. R.
Mount Calvary Baptist Church, Harlem   Bonds
Museum of Modern Art   1952; Glanville-Hicks
Museum of Natural History   Steiner, E. R.
Musicians' Accord   Kaminsky
Music New to New York   Kolb
National Conservatory of Music in America   Korn
New Amsterdam Symphony Orchestra   Bond, V.
New Music Orchestral Project   Samuel
New Music Theatre   León
New School for Social Research   Cory; Crawford; Oliveira;
  Weigl
New Wilderness Preservation Band   La Barbara
New York Avant Garde Festival   Moorman
New York Choral Society   Wallach
New York City Opera   1974, 1977; Musgrave
New York Philharmonic Orchestra   1975; Dlugoszewski; Escot; Kolb;
  León; Mana Zucca; Ran; Schuyler; Williams, M. L.; Zwilich
New York Philharmonic Society   1938; Lucas
New York Shakespeare Festival   Benary
New York State Council on the Arts   Kaminsky
New York Symphony Orchestra   Leginska
New York University   Bauer; Berberian; Fine; Fleischer; La Barbara;
  León; Mamlok; Moore, D. R.; Radigue; Simons; Smith, J.;
  Spiegel; Talma
92nd Street Y Chorale   Kaminsky

New York [city] – *continued*
Old City Concerts   Hagen
Original Dixie Jubilee Singers   Jessye
Orchestrette Classique of New York   Smith, J.
Park Theatre   Malibran
Queens College, CUNY   Barkin; Berl; Cory; Hays; Zaimont
Quintet of the Americas   Chance
Roerich Museum   Zubeldia
St Bartholomew's Protestant Episcopal Church   Beach
St Cecilia Chorus   Lang, M. R.
Solomon R. Guggenheim Museum   1969; Monk
Symphony Society   Beach
3rd Street Music School   Kolb
Town Hall   Delfin; Kaminsky; Williams, M. L.; Zubeldia
Trinity Church   Hodges
Union Theological Seminary   Bitgood
Western Wind   Zaimont
WNET Experimental Television Laboratory   1976; Spiegel
WNEW radio   Williams, M. L.
Women's Interart Center festivals   Hoover
Women's Philharmonic Society   Korn
New York [state]
State University of New York (SUNY), Binghamton   Borroff;
  Thome
SUNY, Buffalo   Barreau; Nogueira
SUNY, Stony Brook   Gardner; LeBaron; Semegen; Smith, L. C.
New Zealand Ballet Company   Franchi
Nice
Festival Musiques Actuelles   Escot
Théâtre Impérial   1865; Casella
Nichols, Caroline B.   Steiner, E. R.
Nichols, Robert   Coleman
Niculescu, Ştefan   Hölszky; Vlad
Nielsen, Carl   1918; Dalberg
Nielsen, Tage   Linnet
Nietzsche, Friedrich   xviii
Nikisch, Arthur   1893; Fromm-Michaels; Lang, M. R.; Smyth
Nikolayev, Alexander Alexandrovich   Sergeyeva
Nilsson, Erika   Lund, S.
Nin, Joaquín   Botet Dubois
Noble, Thomas Tertius   Bitgood
Noelte, Albert   Britain
Nogueira, Teodoro   Leite, C.
Nono, Luigi   Bofill Levi
Norfolk [VA] – Virginia Opera   1979, 1984; Musgrave
Norfolk and Norwich Triennial Musical Festival [England]
  1872; Smith, A. M.
Nørgård, Per   Linnet
Norman, Ludvig   Andrée; Aulin; Munktell
North Adams State College [North Adams, MA]   Beach
North Texas State College   *see* Texas
Northwestern University [Evanston, IL]   Bonds; Payne
Norton [MA] – Wheaton College   Escot
NORTON, CAROLINE ELIZABETH SARAH   1833, 1853;
  Blackwood
Norwegian Association of Composers [Norsk Komponistforening]
  1917; Lund, S.
Norwegian Broadcasting Organization [Norsk Rikskringkasting
  (NRK)]   Skouen; Søstevold
Noskowski, Zygmunt   Jeske-Choińska-Mikorska
Nottingham [England] – University of Nottingham   Wilkins
Novák, Vítězslav   Emingerová; Kaprálová; Mallá; Vorlová
Novara [Italy]
cathedral   Isabella Leonarda
Collegio di S Orsola   Isabella Leonarda
Novaro, Augusto   Zubeldia
Nowak, Lionel   Davidson
NUGENT, MAUDE   1896
Nuove Proposte Sonore [Italy]   Rampazzi
Nuremberg
Fachakademie für Musik   Olive
Stadttheater   Faltis
Ny Musikk [Norwegian branch of the ISCM]   1938; Hall

Oberlin [OH] – Oberlin College, Conservatory of Music   Borroff;
  Kaminsky; Walker; Zallman
Odessa [Ukraine] – State Conservatory [Gosudarstvennaya
  Konservatoriya imeni A. V. Nezhdanovoy]   Levina
Office de Radiodiffusion-Télévision Française (ORTF) (formerly
  Radiodiffusion-Télévision Française (RTF))   Arrieu; Barrière;
  Jolas; Szőnyi

Ohain [Belgium]
  Métamorphoses d'Orphée   Gorne
  Musiques et Recherches   Gorne
Okanogan Music Festival [Canada]   Krzanowska
Oklahoma – University of Oklahoma   Archer
Olah, Tiberiu   Alexandra; Badian; Odăgescu; Rotaru
OLIVE, VIVIENNE   1978
OLIVEROS, PAULINE   1977, 1985; Hays; Lam Bun-ching; Louie; Rubin
Oller, R. Nogueras   Freixas
Omaha [NE] – **Trans-Mississippi Exposition** [1898]   Beach
Ondříček Quartet   Vorlová
Ono, Yoko   Moorman
Ontario – University of Western Ontario [London, Ont.]   Allik; Louie; Telfer
OOSTERZEE, CORNÉLIE VAN   1897, 1898
Operto [Portugal] – **conservatory**   Sousa
Oppens, Ursula   Bley
ORAM, DAPHNE   xv; 1958
Ordem dos Músicos do Brasil   Jabor; Leite, V. D.
ORE, CECILIE   1988
Orgeni, Aglaja   Viardot
ORGER, CAROLINE   1843
Orton, Richard   Usher
Osaka
  Kansai University   Tann
  Osaka University [Osaka Geijutsu Daigaku]   Hara
Oslo (formerly **Christiania**)
  Dagbladet   Hall
  Norges Musikkhogskøle (formerly **Musik-Konservatoriet**)   Ore; Schjelderup; Skouen
  University of Oslo   Bakke; Sønstevold
Österreichischer Tonkünstlerverein   Kralik von Mayaerswalden
Otago [Dunedin, New Zealand] – **University of Otago**   Bibby; Bowater
Oxford – University of Oxford   1926; LeFanu; Smyth; Spiegel; Stirling

Pablo, Aurora   Barradas
Pablo, Luis de   Di Lotti
Pablo, Vicente   Barradas
Paccagnini, Angelo   Kubisch
Pacific Lutheran University [Tacoma, WA]   McTee
Pacini, Giovanni   Malibran
PADE, ELSE MARIE   xv
Padua
  Centro di Sonologia Computazionale, University of Padua   Rampazzi
  Conservatorio di Musica C. Pollini   Rampazzi
  Nuove Proposte Sonore   1965; Rampazzi
  Teatro Garibaldi   1915
Paganini, Nicolò   Oury; Sloman
Page, Frederick   Freed
PAGH-PAAN, YOUNGHI   xvi; 1980
Pagin, André-Noël   Brillon de Jouy
Paik, Nam June   Moorman; Shiomi
Paisiello, Giovanni   Brizzi Giorgi; Sinyavina
PAKHMUTOVA, ALEXANDRA NIKOLAYEVNA   xvi
Palma, Athos   Aretz
Palma, Federico   Freixas
Palmer, Frederick   see HARTMANN, EMMA SOPHIE AMALIA
Pamplona [Spain] – **Academia Municipal de Música**   Zubeldia
Pankhurst, Emmeline   Smyth
Papaioannou, Yannis Andreou   Sfakianaki
Paradies, Domenico   Paradis
PARADIS, MARIA THERESIA VON   x; 1786, 1791, 1792, 1797, 1800
Paraíba [Brazil] – **Universidade Federal da Paraíba**   Nogueira
Parepa, Euphrosyne   Barnard
Parepa-Rosa Grand English Opera   Rogers
Paris
  Académie de France   Krzyżanowska
  Académie des Beaux-Arts   Marbé
  Académie Française   Bocquet
  Académie Royale de Musique   1694; Duval; Jacquet de la Guerre; see also Paris, Opéra
  Apsone-Cabasse studio   Radigue
  Association Marie Jaëll   Jaëll
  Centre d'Etudes de Mathématique et Automates Musicales   Bofill Levi

Paris – continued
  Centre Pompidou   Saariaho; see also Paris, Institut de Recherche et de Coordination Acoustique/Musique
  Cité Internationale des Arts   Vercoe
  Comédie Française   Candeille; Quinault
  Comédie-Italienne   1786; Wuiet
  Comité Franco-Américain du Conservatoire National   Boulanger, L.
  Concerts Lamoureux   Leleu
  Concert Spirituel   1768, 1784; Beaumesnil; Candeille; Cléry; Duval; Haulteterre; Krumpholtz; Lebrun, F.; Lombardini Sirmen; Paradis; Ravissa
  Conservatoire (Conservatoire National Supérieur de Musique)   c1795, 1830, 1880, 1908; Ahrens; Ancona; Arrieu; Barraine; Barreau; Barrière; Bonis; Boulanger, L.; Boulanger, N.; Brenet; Canal; Canat de Chizy; Cecconi-Botella; Charbonnier; Chrétien; Clostre; Daiken; Demessieux; Desportes; Eckhardt-Gramatté; Farrenc; Finzi; Gazarossian; Giraud; Giteck; Gorne; Grandval; Haenel de Cronenthall; Hardelot; Jaëll; Jeske-Choińska-Mikorska; Jolas; Krzyżanowska; Lachartre; La Hye; Lee, Y.; Lejet; Leleu; Leonardo; McLeod; Montgeroult; Renard; Reverdy; Sato; Scherchen; Szőnyi; Tailleferre; Tanco Cordovez de Herrera; Vieu; Wartel; Weldon; see also Prix de Rome
  court theatre   Guédon de Presles
  Ecole Normale de Musique   Lutyens; Reisserová
  Ecole Pratique des Hautes Etudes   Barrière
  Exposition [1867]   Haenel de Cronenthal
  Exposition [1889]   Lang, M. R.
  Groupe de Musique Algorithmique   Charbonnier
  Groupe de Recherches Musicales [of the ORTF]   1963; Barreau; Bokanowski; Dianda; Fereyra; Loudová; Saint-Marcoux; Sikora
  Groupe International de Musique Electro-Acoustique   1969; Bruzdowicz; Saint-Marcoux
  Hôtel de Ville   1835; La Hye
  Institut de Recherche et de Coordination Acoustique/Musique (IRCAM)   1984; Jolas; Kolb; Renard; Saariaho; Sikora
  Institut National de l'Audiovisuel   Renard
  International Music Council   see UNESCO
  International Rostrum of Composers   see UNESCO
  Notre-Dame de Paris, cathedral   Weldon
  Nouveaux Jeunes   Tailleferre
  Opéra (Académie Royale de Musique)   1736, 1784; Beaumesnil; Bertin; Candeille; Duval; Holmès; Quinault; Viardot
  Opéra Bastille   1990; Jolas
  Opéra-Comique   1805, 1813, 1836, 1868; Bertin; Gail; Kerkado; Puget; Weldon
  Palais de Glace   Canal
  Pasdeloup orchestra   1877; Leonardo
  Saint-Esprit church   Demessieux
  Salle Favart   1868; Candeille
  Salle Herz   Beauharnais; Leonardo
  Salle Pleyel   1889; Coleman; Munktell; Tanco Cordovez de Herrera; Urner
  Schola Cantorum   Ancona; Béclard d'Harcourt; Hagan; Koptagel; Poldowski; Schapira; Urreta; Zubeldia
  Société Musicale Indépendante   Urner
  Sorbonne   see Paris, Université de Paris, Sorbonne
  Studio d'Essai   Radigue
  Théâtre de la Foire   Jacquet de la Guerre
  Théâtre de la Reine   Guédon de Presles
  Théâtre de la République   Candeille
  Théâtre de l'Athénée   Thys
  Théâtre de l'Egalité   Candeille
  Théâtre des Beaujolais   1786
  Théâtre des Bouffes-Parisiens   1859; Grandval; Thys
  Théâtre du Champs-Elysées   Haenel de Cronenthall
  Théâtre du Gymnase   1869; Puget
  Théâtre du Vaudeville   Thys
  Théâtre Feydeau   1813, 1814, 1818; Gail
  Théâtre Français   1792; Candeille
  Théâtre Impérial du Cirque   Thys
  Théâtre Italien   1776, 1869; Bayon
  Théâtre Lyrique   1863; Thys
  Théâtre Montansier   1792; Beaumesnil
  Union Chrétienne des Dames de St Chaumont   Bembo
  United Nations Educational, Scientific and Cultural Organization   see UNESCO
  Université de Paris, Sorbonne   Canat de Chizy; Lee, Y.; Petra-Basacopol; Reverdy; Stocker
  Université de Paris, Vincennes   Bokanowski
Parisotti, Alessandro   Contini Anselmi

PARK, MARIA HESTER   1785, *c*1795, 1811
PARKE, MARIA F.   1799; Park
Parke, William Thomas   Abrams; Guest; Parke, M. F.
PARKER, ALICE   1948
Parker, Charlie   Bond, V.
Parker, Horatio   Hagan; Korn
PARKHURST, SUSAN MCFARLAND   1864, 1866
Parra, Benito García de la   Prieto
Parry, Hubert   Ellicott
Parsons, Albert   Wood
Partos, Oedoen   Alotin
Pasadena [CA] – Pasadena City College   Louie
Pasdeloup, Jules Etienne   Grandval
Pasquini, Ercole   Aleotti, R.; Aleotti, V.
Patras [Greece] – conservatory   Lambiri
Patterson, Paul   Martinez, O. de la
Pauer, Ernst   Zimmermann, A.
Pauk, Alex   Louie
Paulus, Stephen   1973; Larsen
Payer, Hieronymus   Blahetka
Payne, Anthony   Luff
Paz, Juan Carlos   Moretto
Peabody Conservatory; Peabody Electronic Music Studio
   see Baltimore
Pears, Peter   Bosmans; Musgrave
Pedrell, Felipe   Freixas
Pedrollo, Arrigo   Rampazzi
Pedrotti, Carlo   Garelli della Morea; Mariani Campolieti
PEJAČEVIĆ, DORA   1918
Pekarsky, Mark Il'ich   Gubaydulina
Peking   *see* Beijing
Pelletier, Wilfrid   Warren
Pellisson, Paul   Bocquet
Penderecki, Krzysztof   McTee; Van de Vate
Pendle, Karen   xii
Pennisi, Francesco   Cecchi
Pennsylvania
   Pennsylvania State University [University Park]   San Ocampo
   University of Pennsylvania [Philadelphia]   Amacher; Thome;
      Zallman
PENTLAND, BARBARA   xvi; 1929, 1956
Pépin, Clermont   Saint-Marcoux
Percussive Arts Society [Lawton, OK]   Ptaszyńska
Perdizes [Brazil] – Faculdade Santa Marcelina   Setti
Performing Right Society (PRS) [UK]   Tate
Peri, Jacopo   Caccini, F.
Perle, George   Berl
Perne, François-Louis   Gail
Perolé String Quartet   Fuchs
Perrin, Jean   Lauber
Persichetti, Vincent   Bond, V.; Miyake; Polin; Richter; Steiner, G.
Perspectives of New Music [USA]   Barkin
Perugia – Sagra Musicale Umbra [festival]   Alotin
Perugia, Noëmie   Bosmans
Peruzzi, Elio   Rampazzi
Petersfield [England]
   Petersfield Musical Festival   Bailey
   Petersfield Orchestra   Bailey
Petrassi, Goffredo   Beecroft; Di Lotti; Gentile; Ravinale
Petrželka, Vilém   Kaprálová
Peyko, Nicolay Ivanovich   Gubaydulina; Svanidze
Pfitzner, Hans   Fromm-Michaels
Pfohl, Ferdinand   Beach
Philadelphia
   Curtis Institute of Music   Behrend
   Free Library   Behrend
   Orchestra Society of Philadelphia   Davidson
   Pennsylvania Ballet   Bond, V.
   Philadelphia College of the Performing Arts   Behrend
   Philadelphia Conservatory of Music   Polin
   Philadelphia Festival of Western Hemisphere Music   Behrend
   Philadelphia New Orchestral Project   Davidson
   Philadelphia Operatic Society   Heckscher
   Philadelphia Orchestra   1976, 1991; Chance; Musgrave; Ran
   Temple University   Kolb
PHILARMONICA, Mrs   1715
Philippine Foundation of Performing Arts in America   Abejo
Philippine Women's University   *see* Manila
Phillipps, Adelaide   Hodges
Phillips, Burrill   Semegen
Phillips, S.   Prescott
Piacenza – conservatory   Bo

Piazza, A.   Malibran
Pierné, Gabriel   Bonis
Pijper, Willem   Bosmans
Pillnitz castle   *see* Dresden
PINEL, JULIE   1736
Piños, Alois   Jiráčková
Pinza, Ezio   Edwards
Pirumov, Alexander   Firsova
Pisk, Paul A.   Samuel
Piston, Walter   Boulanger, N.
Pitt, Percy   Poldowski
PITTAR, FANNY   Krumpholtz
Pitton, Edda   Rampazzi
Pittsburgh
   American Wind Symphony   Stuart-Coolidge
   Carnegie Mellon University (formerly Carnegie Institute of
      Technology)   Grigsby; White, R.
   Pittsburgh Symphony Orchestra   Bond, V.
   Pittsburgh Youth Orchestra   Bond, V.
Pittsfield Festival [Pittsville, MA]   Clarke
Pizzetti, Ildebrando   Recli
Plançon, Pol   Hardelot
Plé-Caussade, Simone   Jolas
Pointer, George   Brahe
POLDOWSKI   1912
Pomona College [Claremont, CA]   Blaustein; Dillon; Rubin
Ponce, Manuel   Prieto; Schonthal
Ponchard, Louis-Antoine-Eléonore   Puget
POOL, JEANNIE   1977
Poradowski, Stefan Bolesław   Pstrokońska-Nawratil; Szajna-
   Lewandowska
Porpora, Nicola   Della Pietà, M.; Della Pietà, S.; Maria Antonia
   Walpurgis; Martínez, M. von
Porta, Giovanni   Della Pietà, A.; Della Pietà, M.; Della Pietà, S.;
   Maria Antonia Walpurgis
Porter, Quincy   Stuart-Coolidge
Porto Alegre [Brazil] – Associação Juvenil Musical   Scliar
Potter, Cipriani   Loder; Woolf; Zimmermann, A.
Pougin, Arthur   x
Pousseur, Henri   Ancona; Berberian; Blaustein; Calame; Dianda;
   McLeod
Powell, Bud   Williams, M. L.
Powell, Jane   Grever
Powell, Mel   Rubin
POWNALL, MARY ANN   1794
Poznań
   Academy of Music [Akademia Muzyczna im. Ignacego J.
      Paderewskiego] (formerly State Higher School of Music)
      Matuszczak; Ptaszyńska; Zielińska
   Poznań Philharmonia [Państwowa Filharmonia w Poznaniu]
      Zielińska
   Poznań Spring Music Festival [Poznań Wiosna Muzyczna –
      Festival Polskiej Muzyki Współczesnej] Krzanowska; Zielińska
   State Higher School of Fine Arts [Państwowa Wyższa Szkola
      Szłuk Plasłucznych]   Zielińska
Pradère, L.-B.   Montgeroult
Prado, José de Almeida   Rosas-Fernandes
Prague
   Academy of Musical Arts [Akademie Múzíckych Umění]
      Bodorová; Emingerová; Janárčeková; Loudová; Petkova
   Charles University [Univerzita Karlova]   Petrová, E.
   Conservatory   Jiráčková; Kaprálová; Loudová; Mallá; Marić;
      Obrovská; Snížková; Vorlová
   Estates Theatre   1797
   Mozart society   Snížková
Pratt, J. H.   Moore, M. C.
Pressler, Menahem   Richter
Prévost, André   Lauber
Price, Curtis   xvii
PRICE, FLORENCE BEA   xvi; 1932, 1934; Bonds
Price, Leontyne   Bonds; Price
Primavera [London]   Luff; Usher
Princeton [NJ]
   Princeton University   1973; Allik; Anderson, R.; O'Leary; Ran;
      Shatin; Tann; Thome
   Westminster Choir College   Perry
PRIULI, MARIETA MOROSINA   1665
Prix de Rome [France]   1908, 1913, 1920, 1929, 1943, 1949, 1959,
   1965, 1966, 1968, 1969, 1984, 1991; Barraine; Boulanger, L.;
   Boulanger, N.; Brenet; Canal; Cecconi-Botella; Desportes;
   Ekizian; Fontyn; Kolb; Lam Bun-ching; Lejet; Leleu; Sato; Silver;
   Thisse-Derouette

Prix de Rome [Belgium]   1943; Bulterijs; Vito-Delvaux
Pró, Serafín   Hernández
PROCACCINI, TERESA   1956
Promenade Concerts   see London
Pro Musica Society [USA]   Crawford
Prout, Ebenezer   Barns; Bright; Carmichael; Needham
PTASZYŃKA, MARTA   1986
Puccini, Giacomo   xvi
PUGET, LOÏSA   1836, 1869
Pugno, Raoul   Bauer; Boulanger, N.
Puig, Michel   Bokanowski
Pujol, Juan B.   Freixas
Pulitzer Prize in Music [USA]   1983, 1991; Ran; Zwilich
Puteanus, Erycius   Sessa

QÜ, XIXIAN   1985
Quebec
  Conservatoire de Musique de Québec   Lomon
  Orchestre Symphonique de Québec   Lauber
  Société de Musique Contemporaine du Québec (SMCQ)
    Saint-Marcoux
  Université du Québec, Montréal   Lauber
  Université du Québec, Trois-Rivières   Lauber
Queensland – University of Queensland [Brisbane]   Henderson;
  see also Brisbane
Queen's University [Kingston, Ont.]   Allik
Quevedo, Maria Muñoz de   Hernández
Quilmes [Argentina] – Unversidad Nacional de Quilmes   Luengo
QUINCIANI, LUCIA   1611
Quinet, Marcel   Fontyn; Lee, Y.
Quintanar, Héctor   Agudela; Urreta
Quito [Ecuador] – Ecuador opera   Vercoe

Radecke, Rudolf   Oosterzee
Radio Eireann (later Radio Telefís Eireann)   Coghill
Radio France   Sikora
Radio Hilversum [Netherlands]   Gifford
Radiotelevizinnea Romana   Hasnaş
Radoux, Jean-Théodore   Boorn-Coclet; Folville
Ragazzoni, Ernesto   Calosso
Raichev, Alexander   Petkova
Raimbaut de Vaqeiras (Raimbaut d'Orange)   Beatriz de Dia;
  Tibors
RAINIER, PRIAULX   xvi; 1920, 1983
Rajičić, Stanojlo   Živković
Ramnefalk, Marie Louise   Eiríksdóttir
RAMPAZZI, TERESA   1965
RAN, SHULAMIT   1991
Randall, James K.   Tann
Rands, Bernard   Boyd; Lam Bun-ching; Olive; Steinberg
Ránki, György   Hajdú
RASCHENAU, MARIA ANNA DE   1703
Rattenbach, Agosto   Erding
Raunkilde   Lehmann
Rauzzini, Venanzio   Abrams
Ravel, Maurice   xv
RAVINALE, IRMA   1966, 1989; Gentile; Pistono
Ravinia Festival   see Chicago
RAVISSA, Mme   1778
Razaf, Andy   Bonds
Re, Benedetto   Assandra
Read, Gardner   Diemer; Vercoe
Reading [England] – University of Reading   Samuel
Rebottaro, Alica   Brahe
Redlands [CA] – University of Redlands   Bakke; Lam Bun-ching
Reger, Max   Fromm-Michaels; Lambiri; Senfter; Veysberg
Regina [Saskatchewan]
  Contemporary Directions   Raum
  Regina Symphony Orchestra   Raum
  University of Regina   Raum
Reibel, Guy   Canat de Chizy; Gorne
Reich, Steve   Birnstein; La Barbara
Reicha, Antoine   Farrenc; Viardot
Reichardt, Johann Friedrich   x; 1805
REICHARDT, JULIANE   x; Reichardt, L.
REICHARDT, LOUISE   x; 1800, 1805, 1811, 1819; Reichardt, J.
Reinecke, Carl   1888; Bright; Holmsen; Hopekirk; Rivé-King;
  Smyth; Wennerberg-Reuter; Wurm
Reinhardt, Ad   Dlugoszewski
Remacha, Fernando   Malumbres; Ozaita

Rennes [France] – conservatory   Krzyżanowska
RENNES, CATHARINA VAN   1898
Renosto, Paolo   Benati
RESPIGHI, ELSA   xii
Respighi, Ottorino   Ewart; Respighi
Reus, Eduard   Faltis
Révész, André   xviii
Rey, Cemal Reşit   Koptagel
Reykjavík
  Iceland Symphony Orchestra [Sinfoníuhljómsveit Íslands]
    Beamish
  Reykjavík College of Music [Tónlistarskólinn í Reykjavík]
    Eiríksdóttir; Viðar
Reynolds, Roger   Lam Bun-ching
Rheinberger, Joseph   Le Beau
Ricci, Francesco Pasquale   Boetzelaer
Rice, Edward Everett   Steiner, E. R.
RICHARDS, KATHLEEN   1944
Richardson, Alan   Beamish
Richmond [VA]
  Virginia Commonwealth University   Newlin
  Virginia Union University   Moore, U. S.
Richter, Georg Friedrich   Auernhammer
RICHTER, MARGA   Hays
Ridgway, James   Billington
Řídky, Jaroslav   Obrovská; Vorlová
Riedinger, Johann   Paradis
Rieger, Eva   xii
Riegger, Wallingford   Ballou; Barron
Ries, Ferdinand   Liebmann, H.
Ries, Franz   Kinkel
Riga – Latvian Academy of Music   Feigin
Rigel, Henri-Joseph   Brillon de Jouy
Righini, Vincenzo   Paradis
Riley, Peter   see COLERIDGE-TAYLOR, AVRIL
Riley, Terry   Anderson, B.
Rimmer, John   Castro-Robinson
RIMSKAYA-KORSAKOVA, NADEZHDA NIKOLAYEVNA   xvii
Rimsky-Korsakov, Nikolay Andreyevich   Rimskaya-Korsakova
Ring, Montague   see ALDRIDGE, AMANDA IRA
Rio de Janeiro
  Academia Brasileira de Música   Cameu; Carvalho; Leite, V. D.
  Associação Juvenil Musical   Scliar
  Conservatório Brasileiro de Música   Cameu; Catunda; Rosas-
    Fernandes
  Escola Nacional de Música (formerly Instituto Nacional de
    Música)   Barbosa; Cameu; Faria; Jabor; Leite, V. D.; Sodré
  Escola Popular de Educação Musical   Barbosa
  Instituto Villa-Lobos   Barbosa; Scliar
  Pró-Arte music school   Barbosa
  Superintendência de Educação Musical e Artística (SEMA)
    Barbosa
  Teatro Príncipe Imperial   Gonzaga
Rippl-Rónai, József   Ticharich
Ritzler, Otto   Tyrrell
Rivard, Achille   Swain
Rivier, Jean   Cecconi-Botella; Clostre; Lachartre
Roanoke [VA] – Opera Roanoke   Bond, V.
Robbins, David   McTee
Robert Shaw Chorale   1948; Parker
Robeson, Paul   Aldridge
Robinson, Raymond   Stuart-Coolidge
Rocha [Uruguay] – Conservatorio Teresiano   Pereyra-Lizaso
Rochberg, George   Amacher
Rochester [NY]
  Eastman School of Music   1939; Abejo; Diemer; Franks
    Williams; Hier; Hoover; Ivey; Kasilag; Kolb; Moore, U. S.; Raum;
    Semegen; Thome; Van Appledorn; Wylie
  Rochester Philharmonic Orchestra   Cole
Rockstro, William   White, M. V.
Rodrigo, Joaquín   Koptagel
RODRIGO, MARIA   1915
Rogalski, Theodor   Marbé
Roger-Ducasse, Jean   Arrieu; Karamanuk
Rogers, Bernard   Diemer; Van Appledorn; Wylie
Roguski, Gustaw   Jeske-Choińska-Mikorska
Roldán, Amadeo   De Blanck Martín
Rolland, Paul   Nelson
Romani, Felice   Casella
Romanian Union of Composers   Donceanu; Rotaru
Rome
  Accademia Arcadia   Maria Antonia Walpurgis

Rome – *continued*
  Accademia di S Cecilia/Conservatorio di Musica S Cecilia
    1774, 1842, 1966, 1989; Appignani; Coccia; Contini Anselmi;
    Gentile; Giuranna; Picconi; Pistono; Procaccini; Ravinale;
    Respighi
  Accademia Filarmonica Appignani
  American Academy Kolb
  Conservatorio di Musica S Cecilia *see* Rome, Accademia di
    S Cecilia
  Goffredo Petrassi Chamber Orchestra Gentile
  Istituto Nazionale di Musica Respighi
  Nuovi Spazi Musicali Gentile
  Vatican 1971; Williams, M. L.
  Villa Medici Barreau; Boulanger, L.; Canal; Giraud; Renard;
    Schapira
Ronnenfeld, Sputz Escribano
Roosevelt, Theodore Bond, C.
Roots, Olav Nova
Rose, Leonard Moorman
Rosenhoff, Orla Sehested
ROSSI, CAMILLA DE 1707, 1708; Raschenau
Rossi, Gaetano Uccelli
Rossini, Gioachino Carreño; Colbran; Szymanowska
Rössler, Almut Ahrens
Roth, Sandor Urreta
Rothschild Foundation Fine
Rothwell, Walter Henry Bauer
Rotoli, Augusto Garelli della Morea
Rotterdam – Rotterdams Philharmonisch Orkest 1940;
  Appeldoorn; Bordewijk-Roepman
Roubakine, Boris McIntosh
Roussel, Albert Reisserová
Rowley, Alec Coleridge-Taylor
Royal Academy of Music *see* London
Royal College of Music *see* London
Royal Northern College of Music *see* Manchester
Royal Philharmonic Orchestra *see* London
Royal Scottish Academy of Music and Drama *see* Glasgow
Royal Scottish National Orchestra *see* Glasgow
Royal Shakespeare Company [England] Sekacz
Royal Society of Female Musicians [UK] 1839; Masson
Roze, Nicolas Bawr
Rubenson, Albert Aulin
Rubini, Nicolò Athanasiu-Gardeev
Rubinstein, Anton Adayevskaya; Athanasiu-Gardeev; Leonardo
Rudhyar, Dane Crawford
Rudorff, Ernst Janotha
Rudziński, Witold Lara
Rudziński, Zbigniew Sikora
Ruebsaat, Norbert Westerkamp
Ruggles, Carl Crawford
RUNCIE, CONSTANCE FAUNT LE ROY 1859
RUSCA, CLAUDIA 1630
Ruskin, John xviii
Russell, George Bley
Rutgers University [New Brunswick, NJ] Benary; Polin
Ryazanov, A. Eksanishvili
Rzewski, Frederic Bley; Miyake

SAARIAHO, KAIJA 1988
Sabine, Wallace C. Gerrish-Jones
SABININ, MARTHA VON 1868
Sacerdote, Edoardo Lambiri
Sadai, Yizhak Olivero
SAHAKDUXT 8th century
Sainsbury, John H. x
Saint-Amans, Léon *see* LA HYE, LOUISE-GENEVIÉVE DE
St Louis [MO]
  St Louis Conservatory of Music Samuel
  Saint Louis Symphony Orchestra Chance; Samuel; Tower
  Washington University Oliveira; Samuel
St Magnus Festival [Orkney Islands, Scotland] Weir
SAINT-MARCOUX, MICHELINE COULOMBE 1969
St Mary's College [Notre Dame, IN] McLean
SAINTON-DOLBY, CHARLOTTE 1843, 1876; Barnard; Orger
St Paul [MN]
  Hamline University Nordenstrom
  Saint Paul Chamber Orchestra Musgrave
St Petersburg (Leningrad; Petrograd)
  Imperial Chapel Choir Adayevskaya
  Mariinsky Theatre Serova

Musorgsky College [Uchilishche imeni M. P. Musorgskogo]
  Elcheva
**St Petersburg Conservatory (Leningrad N. A. Rimsky-
  Korsakov State Conservatory** [Gosudarstvennaya
  Konservatoriya imeni N. A. Rimskogo-Korsakova]) Adayevskaya;
  Č'ebotaryan; Elcheva; Menter; Metallidi; Moberg; Rimskaya-
  Korsakova; Serova; Ustvol'skaya; Veysberg; Voronina
St Petersburg Philharmonic Society 1844
Young Workers' Conservatory Veysberg
Saint-Saëns, Camille Bonis; Grandval; Holmès; Jaëll; Viardot
Salas, Juan Orrego Santos Ocampo
Salazar, Adolfo Prieto
Salieri, Antonio Auenbrugger; Bigot; Paradis
Salle, Marquis de La Beaumesnil
Salomon, Johann Peter Abrams; Krumpholtz
Salomon concerts *see* London
Salvat, Ricard Bofill Levi
Salzburg
  International Sommer-Akademie, Mozarteum Di Lotti;
    Hölszky; Oh
  Mozarteum Scherchen
  Orff Institute Martins
Salzer, Felix Dlugoszewski
Saminsky, Lazare Gideon
Sánchez Gavañach, Francisco Casagemas
Sand, George Athanasiu-Gardeev; Viardot
San Diego [CA]
  San Diego Civic Symphony Orchestra Barnett
  San Diego Historical Society Barnett
  San Diego Opera Guild Barnett
  San Diego Symphony Orchestra Galás; Musgrave
San Fernando Valley State College [Northridge, CA] Dianda
San Francisco
  Bay Area Women's Philharmonic *see* San Francisco Women's
    Philharmonic
  Chamber Music Society Beach
  Exploratorium Payne
  Mills Tape Music Center (formerly **San Francisco Tape Music
    Center**) Oliveros
  New Music Society 1926; Crawford
  Panama–Pacific Exposition [1915] Beach
  Port Costa Players Giteck
  San Francisco Conservatory of Music Armer
  San Francisco Opera Glanville-Hicks
  San Francisco Sound Institute Payne
  San Francisco Spring Opera Musgrave
  San Francisco State College Oliveros
  San Francisco Symphony Orchestra Fine; Giteck; Mamlok;
    Musgrave
  San Francisco Women's Philharmonic (formerly the **Bay Area
    Women's Philharmonic**) Berl; Bond, V.; Shatin; Urner
  Tivoli Opera House Roma
San José [CA] – **San José State University** Pizer
San José [Costa Rica]
  Conservatorio Nacional de Música Sanz
  Orquesta Sinfónica Nacional Castegnaro
San Juan, Pedro De Blanck Martín
San Pedro, Lucio Santos Ocampo
Santa Barbara [CA] – **Santa Barbara Symphony Orchestra**
  Diemer
Santa Cruz, Domingo Vivado
Santiago [Chile]
  Conservatorio Nacional de Música Zegers
  Sociedad Filarmónica Zegers
Santoro, Cláudio Oliveira; Scliar
São Paulo [Brazil]
  Conservatório Dramático e Musical Carvalho; Leite, C.;
    Setti
  Escola Superior de Musica Santa Marcelina Rosas-Fernandes
  Museu do Folclore Silva
  Orquesta Feminina Carvalho
  Universidade de São Paulo Setti
SAPPHO ix; 7th century BC
Saracinelli, Ferdinando 1607; Caccini, F.
Sarah Lawrence College [Bronxville, NY] Benary; Cory; Monk;
  Wallach
Sarajevo Music Academy [Muzička Akademija u Sarajevu]
  Ludwig-Pečar
Sarazin, Jean-François Bocquet
Sardi, Gasparo Aleotti, R.
Sas, Andrés Escot
Satie, Erik Tailleferre

SATO, KIMI   xvi; 1984
Sauret, Emile   Barns; Carreño
SAVAGE, JANE   1783, 1790
Savard, Marie-Gabriel-Augustin   Chaminade
Savasta, Antonio   Giuranna
Sayn, Elena de   Beach
Scabia, U. A.   Capuis
Scalero, Rosario   Behrend
SCARBOROUGH, ETHEL   1908
Scarlatti, Domenico   María Barbara
Schaeffer, Myron   Beecroft
Schaeffer, Pierre   1963; Arrieu; Bokanowski; Bruzdowicz; Fereyra; Gorne; Pade; Radigue; Saint-Marcoux; Sikora
Schafer, R. Murray   Westerkamp
Scharwenka, Xaver   Hood
SCHAUROTH, DELPHINE VON   xi
Scherchen, Hermann   Catunda; Dianda; Scherchen; Scliar; Xiao
SCHERCHEN, TONA   xvii; 1979; Xiao
Schidlowsky, Leon   Olivero
Schiller, Friedrich von   Schröter
Schilling, Gustav   xi
Schiske, Karl   Sønstevold
Schloesser, Carl   Woodforde-Finden
Schmidl, Carlo   xi
Schmidt, Franz   Kern
Schmit, Camille   Fontyn
Schmitt, Florent   xv
Schnabel, Helen   Jolas
Schneider, Urs Peter   Radermacher
Schobert, Johann   Brillon de Jouy
Schoenberg, Arnold   xv; Coulthard; Fromm-Michaels; Mahler; Newlin; Warren
Schoenberg Institute   see California
Schönbach, Dieter   Dianda
SCHONTHAL, RUTH   xv
Schopenauer, Arthur   xviii
Schreker, Franz   Ticharich; Zieritz
Schröder, Regina von   Siegling
SCHRÖTER, CORONA ELISABETH WILHELMINE   x; 1786
Schubert, Franz   Beauharnais; Blahetka
Schubert, Franz Anton   Amalie
Schulhoff, Ervín   Maconchy
Schulhoff, Julius   Athanasiu-Gardeev
Schuller, Gunther   1983; Kolb; Shatin; Steiner, G.; Weir; Zwilich
Schultz, Svend S.   Lund, G.
SCHUMANN, CLARA   x, xi, xii; 1831, 1837, 1844, 1846, 1868, 1870; Bergh; Janotha; Le Beau; Lehmann; Sabinin; Smyth; Szymanowska; Wurm; Zimmermann, A.
Schumann, Robert   Baroni-Cavalcabò; Cibbini-Kozeluch; Droste-Hülshoff; Farrenc; Kinkel; Lang, J.; Sabinin; Schauroth; Schumann; Szymanowska; Viardot
Schumann-Heink, Ernestine   Lang, M. R.; Salter
Schuster, Joseph   Amalie
Schütz, Heinrich   Sophie Elisabeth
Schweitzer, Albert   Jaëll
Schweitzer, Anton   Anna Amalia (ii)
SCLIAR, ESTHER   Leite, V. D.
SCOTT, ALICIA ANN   1838
Scott, Derek B.   xvii, xviii
Scott, Walter   Adam de Aróstegui
Scottish Ballet   see Glasgow
Scottish Chamber Orchestra   see Edinburgh
Scottish National Orchestra   see Glasgow
Scottish Opera   see Glasgow
Scottish Society of Composers   Beat
Scribe, Eugène   Bertin; Puget
Scudéry, Mlle de   Bocquet
Sculthorpe, Peter   Boyd; Whitehead
Searle, Humphrey   Anderson, A.
Seattle [WA]
   American Music Center   1909; Moore, M. C.
   Century 21 Exposition [1962]   Swift
   Cornish College of the Arts   Giteck; Lam Bun-ching
Sechter, Simon   Blahetka
Seeger, Charles   Crawford
Segal, Naomi   xvii
SEHESTED, HILDA   1914
Seiber, Mátyás   Morley
Selva, Blanche   Hagan
SEMEGEN, DARIA   LeBaron
Sender, Ramon   Oliveros
SENFTER, JOHANNA   1910

Seoul
   Ewha Woman's University   Lee, Y.
   Hanyang University   Suh
   Kyung Hee University   Oh
   National University of Seoul   Lee, Y.; Pagh-Paan; Suh
   Yonsei University   Lee, C.
Serao, Matilde   Garelli della Morea
Serkin, Peter   Berl
SEROVA, VALENTINA SEMYONOVNA   1885, 1899
Serrano, Emilio   Rodrigo
Serrao, Paolo   Ferrari, G.
Šerých, Anna   xvii
SESSA, CLAUDIA   1613
Sessions, Roger   Bond, V.; Diemer; Dvorkin; Fine; Gideon; Mamlok; Newlin; Polin; Zwilich
Settacciole, Giacomo   Ewart
Seville – Latin-American Exhibition   1929; Canales
Sgambati, Giovanni   Contini Anselmi; Couper; Garelli della Morea; Respighi
Shalyapin, Fyodor Ivanovich   Coleman
Shande, Ding   Liu; Wang
Shanghai
   Academy/Conservatory of Music   Boyd; Liu; Qü; Wang
   Shanghai Film Studio   Huang
Shapero, Harold   Barkin; Silver
Shapey, Ralph   Franks Williams; Mamlok; Ran; Riseman
Shaporin, Yury Alexandrovich   Chudova; Zhubanova
Shawn, Allen   Smith, L. C.
Shea, George Beverly   Akers
Shebalin, Vissarion Yakovlevich   Eksanishvili; Gubaydulina; Pakhmutova
Sheridan, Elizabeth   Blackwood; Norton
Sheridan, Richard Brinsley   Blackwood; Norton
Sherlaw Johnson, Robert   Usher
Sherwood, Percy   Pejačević
Shibata, Minao   Massumoto; Shiomi
Shifrin, Seymour   Blaustein; Silver
Shimer College [Mt Carroll, IL]   Spiegel
SHIOMI, MIEKO   1961
SHLONSKY, VERDINA   1931
Shorter, Wayne   Mazur; Miyake
Shorter College [Little Rock, AR]   Price
Shostakovich, Dmitry   Ustvol'skaya
Shtreiher, L.   Zhubanova
Sibelius, Jean   Moberg
Sibelius Academy   see Helsinki
Siccardi, Honorio   Dianda
Siegl, Otto   Sonntag
Siegling Music House [Charleston, SC]   Siegling
Siena – Accademia Musicale Chigiana   Bodorová; Capuis; Cecchi; Di Lotti; Heller; Hölszky; Procaccini; Steinberg
Sikorski, Kazimierz   Bacewicz; Bruzdowicz; Matuszczak
Silver, Lucas   Owen
SILVER, SHEILA   xvi
Simonetti, Signor   Agnesi; Gubitosi
Simon Fraser University [Burnaby, BC]   Westerkamp
Sindacato Musicisti Italiani   Recli
Sivori, Camillo   Athanasiu-Gardeev
Six, Les   1920; Tailleferre
Škerjanc, Lucijan Marija   Ludvig-Pečar
SKOUEN, SYNNE   1983
Slavenski, Josip   Frajt; Marić
Sloper, Lindsay   Prescott
Smart, George   Linwood
SMITH, ALICE MARY   1861, 1863, 1867, 1872, 1882, 1884
Smith, Bessie   Hays
Smith, Carleton Sprague   Glanville-Hicks
Smith, Edgar   Steiner, E. R.
SMITH, JULIA   xii
Smith, Matthew   Ticharich
Smith, Mrs Gerrit   Lang, M. R.
Smith Brindle, Reginald   Martinez, O. de la
Smith College [Northampton, MA]   Parker
SMYTH, ETHEL   xiii, xiv, xv, xvii, xviii; 1880, 1890, 1891, 1902, 1906, 1909, 1910, 1911, 1912, 1913, 1919, 1922, 1923, 1925, 1926, 1944; Hays; Holmès; Richards
Sociedade Brasileira de Musicologia [Brazil]   Setti
Society for Electro-Acoustic Music [USA]   1985; Barron
Society for New Music [Mexico]   Lara
Society for the Promotion of New Music (SPNM) [UK]   1976; LeFanu; Maconchy

Society for the Promotion of New Music in the Three Americas Terzian
Society of American Women Composers 1925; Bauer; Beach; Hier; Howe
Society of Black Composers [USA] 1968; Moore, D. R.
Society of British Musicians Loder; Orger
Society of Swedish Composers see Föreningen Svenska Tonsättare
Society of Women Composers [Korea] Suh
Society of Women Musicians [UK] 1911; Eggar; Lehmann; Poston; Richards
Sodré, Francisco Gonzaga
Sofia
    Institute for Music and Choreography Petrova, M.
    Open Society Foundation Baeva
    Philip Konter Folksong and Dance Company Klinkova
    Radio Sofia Baeva
    Sofia State School of Choreography Karastoyanova
    State Academy of Music Baeva; Cenova; Draganova; Karastoyanova; Klinkova; Krasteva; Petkova; Petrova, M.
Solenière, Eugénie de xii
Soler, José Pelegrí i Marimón
Solesmes [France] – abbey Grigsby
Somer, Hilde Hays
Sonus: Journal of Investigation into Global Musical Possibilities [Cambridge, MA] Escot
SOPHIE ELISABETH, Duchess of Brunswick-Lüneburg 1651, 1667
Sorbonne see Paris, Université de Paris, Sorbonne
SOUTHAM, ANN 1977, 1980; McIntosh
Southampton [England]
    Institute of Sound and Vibration Research, University of Southampton Lockwood
    Southampton Concert Orchestra Bailey
    University of Southampton Tann
Southern, Ann Grever
SPIEGEL, LAURIE 1976, 1977
Špiler, Miroslav Ludvig-Pečar
Spohr, Louis Mounsey
Stachowski, Marek McTee
Stade, Frederica von Berl
Stagg, Katherine Steiner, E. R.
Stamaty, Camille Haenel de Cronenthall
Stanford [CA]
    Stanford Computer Center for Research in Music and Acoustics Sikora
    Stanford University Grigsby; Ho Wai-On
Stanford, Charles Villiers 1907; Clarke; Swain; Wurm
Starer, Robert Bonds
STEFANOVIĆ, IVANA 1985
Steggall, Charles Zimmermann, A.
Stein, Leonard Rubin
Steinbach, Fritz Fromm-Michaels
STEINER, EMMA ROBERTO 1894, 1920
STEINER, GITTA 1968
Stenhammar, Fredrika Andrée
Štěpán, Václav Vorlová
Sterling, Antoinette Viardot
Stern, Susan xii
Steuermann, Edward Mamlok
Stevens, Bernard Fox
Stewart, Humphrey J. Gerrish-Jones
Stichting Vrouw en Muziek [Women in Music Foundation] [Netherlands] 1991
Still, William Grant Price
Stock, Frederick Eckhardt-Gramatté; Price
Stockhausen, Karlheinz Amacher; Ancona; Bibby; Capdeville; McLeod; Martins; Odăgescu; Urreta
Stockholm
    International Rostrum for Electroacoustic Music 1988; Ore
    Kungliga Musikaliska Akademien [Royal Academy of Music] 1879; Andreé; Aulin; Malmlöf-Forssling; Munktell; Netzel; Schonthal; Wennerberg-Reuter
    Kungliga Musikhögskolan Rehnqvist
    Nordiskt Musikkonservatorium [Österskär] Wikström
    St Sofia church Wennerberg-Reuter
Stöhr, Richard Frank-Autheried
Stokes, Eric Larsen
Stokowski, Leopold 1952; Eckhardt-Gramatté; Glanville-Hicks; Zwilich
Storace, Stephen Bland
Stoyanov, Veselin Draganova; Petrova, M.
Strang, Gerald Grigsby
Strasbourg – Conservatoire National de Région Giraud

Strassburg, Robert Thome
Strauss, Johann Milanollo
Strauss, Richard Lalauni
Stravinsky, Igor Berberian; Capdeville; Oliveira; Prieto
Streicher, Johann Andreas Oury
STRICKLAND, LILY xvi
Stringham, Edwin Bitgood
Stroe, Aurel Hasnaş; Vlad
STROZZI, BARBARA ix; 1644, 1651, 1655, 1657, 1664
Strozzi, Giulio Strozzi
Strube, Gustav Hernández; Howe
STUART-COOLIDGE, PEGGY 1970
Stuttgart
    Staatliche Akademie der Bildenden Künste Kubisch
    Staatliche Hochschule für Musik und Darstellende Kunst (formerly Konservatorium für Musik) Erding; Hölsky; Schorr; Wurm
    Universität Stuttgart Erding
    Verein für Klassische Kirchenmusik Zumsteeg
Subotnick, Morton Giteck; La Barbara; Oliveros; Rubin
Suggia, Guilhermina Clarke
Suk, Josef Marić
Sullivan, Arthur Wurm
SUNY see New York [state]
Surrey [England] – University of Surrey [Guildford] Martinez, O. de la
Suslin, Viktor Yevseyevich Gubaydulina
Sussex [England] – University of Sussex [Falmer, Brighton] Anderson, A.; Boyd
Suter, Robert Baader-Nobs
Svendsen, Johan Dalberg
Sverdlovsk (now Yekaterinburg) – Conservatory [Gosudarstvennaya Konservatoriya imeni M. P. Musorgskogo] Lyadova
SWAIN, FREDA 1925, 1936
SWEPSTONE, EDITH 1899
Świejkowski, H. Krzyżanowska
Swift, Richard Anderson, B.
Swift, Samuel Swift
Switten, Henry Perry
Sydney
    National Institute of Dramatic Art Bauld
    New South Wales State Conservatorium of Music Bauld; Beath; Boyd; Hill; Holland; Kats; LeFanu; Sutherland; Whitehead
    New South Wales State Orchestra Sutherland
    Sydney Mandolins Carr-Boyd
    Sydney Symphony Orchestra Cole; Woof
    University of Sydney 1991; Bauld; Boyd; Carr-Boyd; Whitehead; Woof
Syracuse [NY] – Syracuse University La Barbara; Liu
Szabó, Ferenc Kistétényi
Szalonek, Witold Havenstein
Szeligowski, Tadeusz Matuszczak; Szajna-Lewandowska
Szell, George Mamlok
SZYMANOWSKA, MARIA AGHATE 1816, 1820; Brzezińska-Szymanowska

Tagliaferro, Magda Demessieux
TAILLEFERRE, GERMAINE xv, xvi; 1920
Takahashi, Yuji Miyake
Taku, Koji Shiomi
TALMA, LOUISE xvi, xvii; 1962, 1974
Tanevey String Quartet Ran
Tanglewood Music Center/Festival (formerly Berkshire Music Center/Festival) [MA] Beecroft; Brusa; Clement; Diemer; Kolb; La Barbara; Olivero; Pentland; Polin; Ran; Weir
Tannenbaum, Ed Payne
Tariot, A.-J.-D. Haenel de Cronenthall
Tartini, Giuseppe Lombardini Sirmen
Tastu, Mme Amable Duchambge
Tausig, Carl Menter; Wurmbrand-Stuppach
Tavener, John Weir
Taylor, Helen Brahe
Tbilisi [Georgia]
    conservatory Eksanishvili; Svanidze
    First Musical College Eksanishvili
    Paliashvili Central Music School Eksanishvili
Tchaikovsky, Pyotr Il'yich Korn; Rimskaya-Korsakova; Smyth
Tcherepnin, Alexander Coates, G.; Hara; Ziffrin
TEGNÉR, ALICE 1892
Teitelbaum, Richard Miyake

Tel-Aviv
  Academy of Music Shlonsky
  Bar-Ilan University Alotin; Fleischer
  Israel Philharmonic Orchestra Ran
  Music Teachers' College Alotin; Fleischer
  Rubin Academy of Music (formerly **Israel Academy of Music, University of Tel-Aviv**) Alotin; Fleischer; Olivero; Riseman
  Telma Yalin Music High School Riseman
Temple University *see* Philadelphia
Tennessee – University of Tennessee [Chattanooga] Hays
Teplov, A. G. Maier
TERZIAN, ALICIA 1959, 1978
Terziani, Eugenio Picconi
Teyber, Anton Asachi
Teyte, Maggie Riego
Texas
  North Texas State College/University [Denton] Archer; McTee; Simon
  Texas Lutheran College [Seguin] Bakke
  Texas Tech University [Lubbock] Van Appledorn
  University of Texas, Austin Moorman; Reid
Thebom, Blanche Price
Thomas, Dylan Poston
Thomas, John Charles Leginska; Mana Zucca
Thomas, Theodore Lang, M. R.; Rivé-King; Salter; Steiner, E. R.
THOME, DIANE 1973
Thomson, Virgil Crawford; Dlugoszewski; Glanville-Hicks; Jessye
Three Choirs Festival [England] 1882, 1889; Ellicott
Thuille, Ludwig 1902
Thybo, Leif Ozaita
Tibbett, Lawrence Mana Zucca; Warren
TIBORS 12th century
Tick, Judith xii
Tieck, Ludwig Weir
Tiensuu, Jukka Arho
Tilburg [Netherlands] – **conservatory** Henneman
Tiller, Terence Poston
Time [New York] Cole
Tirana [Albania]
  conservatory Agolli
  Higher Institute of Fine Arts [Instituti i Lartë i Arteve] Agolli
  Jordan Misja Art Lyceum Agolli
Titon du Tillet, Evrard Jacquet de la Guerre
Toch, Ernst Diemer
Togni, Camillo Rampazzi
Tokyo
  Group-Ongaku 1961; Fluxus; Shiomi
  spring festival Leite, C.
  Tōhō Gakuen School of Music [Tōhō Gakuen Daigaku] Hori; Massumoto; Sato
  Tokyo National University of Fine Arts and Music [Tokyo Geijutsu Daigaku] Hara; Hori; Konishi; Massumoto; Mori; Shiomi
Tong, Sang Liu
Tonkha, Vladimir Konstantinovich Gubaydulina
Toronto
  Canadian Music Center 1987; Lauber
  Mercer Union Gallery Smith, L. C.
  New Music Concerts Beecroft
  Royal Conservatory of Music (formerly **Toronto Conservatory of Music**) Beecroft; Blomfield Holt; Harrison, S. F.; Louie; McIntosh; Southam; Watson Henderson
  Toronto Dance Theatre (later **New Dance Group of Canada**) Southam
  Toronto Symphony Orchestra Lauber; Louie
  Trinity College Geddes-Harvey
  University of Toronto Allik; Beecroft; Ivey; Lee, H.; Southam
Torres, Dolores Ruiz Lastres
Tosatti, Vieri Pistono
Tosti, Paolo Garelli della Morea
Tovey, Donald Smyth
TOWER, JOAN 1969, 1988; La Barbara
Towers, John xii
Trambitsky, Viktor Nikolayevich Lyadova
Trapp, Max Eckhardt-Gramatté
Tremain, Ronald Whitehead
Tremblay, Gilles Saint-Marcoux
Trieste – Teatro Filodrammatico 1895; Delle Grazie
TRIMBLE, JOAN 1940
Trimble, Valerie Trimble
Trinidad [Cuba]
  San Francisco de Asís Berroa
  Santísima Trinidad Berroa

Trinity College *see* Dublin; Toronto; Washington, DC
Trinity College of Music *see* London
TRISSINA, ALBA 1622
Troubadours Alamanda; Azalais de Porcairages; Beatriz de Dia; Castelloza; Garsenda; Maria de Ventadorn; Tibors; *see also* Trouvères
Trouvères Blanche of Castile; Lorraine; Margot and Maroie; Maroie de Dregnau de Lille; *see also* Troubadours
Tulane University of Louisiana *see* New Orleans
Turc de Mairona Castelloza
Turgenev, Ivan Sergeyevich Viardot
Turin
  Conservatorio Statale di Musica Giuseppe Verdi Capuis; Di Lotti
  international exhibition [1911] Rosselli-Nissim
  Orchestra Sinfonica di Torino, RAI Ravinale
  Teatro Alfieri 1916
  Teatro Balbo 1894; Delle Grazie
Turina, Joaquin Romero
Tussenbroek, Hendrika van Rennes
Twain, Mark Sloman; Sullivan

UCCELLI, CAROLINA 1830
Uchida, Hyakken Miyake
Uhl, Alfred Gary-Schaffhauser; Skouen; Sommer
ULEHLA, LUDMILA 1970; Steinberg
UNESCO (United Nations Educational, Scientific and Cultural Organization)
  International Music Council Kasilag; Terzian
  International Music Fund Glanville-Hicks
  International Rostrum of Composers 1960, 1980, 1984, 1986; Bacewicz; Castro-Robinson; Clayton; Davidson; Fleischer; Lam Bun-ching; Mamlok; Pagh-Paan; Pstrokońska-Nawratil; Ptaszyńska
Union College [Schenectady, NY] Tann
Upton, George Putnam ix
Urban, Heinrich Dillon; Landowska
URNER, CATHERINE MURPHY xvi, xvii
USHER, JULIA Luff
Ussachevsky, Vladimir Carlos; Chance; Franks Williams; Semegen; Smiley
USSR Union of Composers 1970; Stuart-Coolidge
USTVOL'SKAYA, GALINA IVANOVNA xvii; Metallidi
Utrecht
  city orchestra Appeldoorn
  Institute of Sonology Ore;.Rampazzi
  Utrecht School of the Arts Woof
  Utrecht University Fowler

Vacaresco, Hélène Ferrari, G.
Vaccai, Nicola Malibran
Vacchi, Fabio Cecchi
VALENTINE, ANN 1798
Valera, Roberto Ruiz Lastres
Valette, Pierre *see* VIEU, JANE
Vancouver
  Expo '86 World Festival Louie
  Simon Fraser University Frykberg
VAN DE VATE, NANCY 1975
Varela, Lopez Romero
Varèse, Edgard Dlugoszewski; Jolas; Shlonsky
Vassar College [Poughkeepsie, NY] Lockwood; O'Leary
Vaughan Williams, Ralph 1931; Boyle; Coulthard; Dring; Gipps; Glanville-Hicks; Glatz; Gow; Maconchy; Poston; Trimble; Williams, G.
Vecchi, Orazio Massarenghi
VELÁZQUEZ, CONSUELO xiii
VELKIERS, ESTHER ELIZABETH ix
Venice
  Accademia degli Unisoni Strozzi
  Biennale di Venezia, Festival Internazionale di Musica Contemporanea 1936; Giuranna
  Fondo Respighi Respighi
  Ospedale dei Mendicanti Lombardini Sirmen
  Ospedale della Pietà 1740; Boni; Da Ponte; Della Pietà, A.; Della Pietà, M.; Della Pietà, S.
  S Salvatore Marcello
Ventura, Grigore Athanasiu-Gardeev
Verband Deutscher Musikerzieher und Konzertierender Künstler [Germany] Samter
Vercoe, Barry Weir
VERCOE, ELIZABETH xv
Verdi, Giuseppe xvi; Freer

Vergniaud, Pierre-Victorin   Candeille
Vermont – Consortium of Vermont Composers   Walker
Versailles [France] – Conservatoire National de Région
    Barrière
Viadana, Lodovico   Assandra
Viardot, Louise Héritte   Viardot
Viardot, Paul   Viardot
VIARDOT, PAULINE   xi; 1904; Malibran; Schumann
Vicenza
    Accademia Olimpica   Casulana
    Araceli monastery   Trissina
Victoria [British Columbia] – University of Victoria   Allik;
    Smith, L. C.
Victoria, Queen of Great Britain   1878; Chaminade; Lemon;
    Macirone
Victoria University of Wellington   see Wellington
Vidal, Paul Antonin   Boulanger, L.; Boulanger, N.
VIÐAR, JÓRUNN   xvi
Vienna
    court chapel   Rossi
    court theatre   Grimani
    Gesellschaft der Musikfreunde   Schumann
    Hochschule für Musik und Darstellende Kunst (formerly
        Conservatorium der Gesellschaft der Musikfreunde;
        Akademie für Musik und Darstellende Kunst)   1927;
        Chefaliady-Taban; Faltis; Frank-Authered; Gary-Schaffhauser;
        Gyring; Halácsy; Kern; Klechniowska; Kralik von Mayerswalden;
        Lalauni; Pessiak-Schmerling; Skouen; Sommer; Sønstevold; Tyrrell;
        Vorlová
    Hofoper   Mahler
    Hotel zum Römischen Kaiser   Blahetka
    Marinellitheater   1792
    Neues Konservatorium der Stadt Wien   Müller-Hermann
    Universität Wien   Gary-Schaffhauser; Kern; Weigl
    Vienna Bach society   Kralik von Mayerswalden
    women's choral society   Kralik von Mayerswalden
Vierne, Louis   Boulanger, N.
VIEU, JANE   1904
Vieu, Maurice and Jane [Paris publishers]   Vieu
Vigny, Alfred de   Duchambge
Villa-Lobos, Heitor   Barbosa; Behrend
Villa Medici   see Rome
Vincent, John   White, R.
Vindolin, Alvise   Rampazzi
Virginia
    Black Music Center, Virginia State College [Petersburg]
        Moore, U. S.
    Virginia Center for Computer Music, University of Virginia
        [Charlottesville]   Shatin
    Virginia State College [Petersburg]   Moore, U. S.
Virginia Opera   see Norfolk
Viski, János   Kistétényi
VITO-DELVAUX, BERTHE DI   1943
Vivanco, Ana Luisa   Berroa
VIZZANA, LUCREZIA ORSINA   1623
Vladigerov, Pancho   Cenova
Vogler, Georg Joseph   Paradis
Vogt, Hans   Heller
Vogt, William G.   Korn
Volfenson, Sergey   Elcheva
Voříšek, J. V.   Cibbini-Kozeluch
VORLOVÁ, SLÁVA   Jiráčková
Vries, Klaas de   Geertens
Vrouw en Muziek   see Stichting Vrouw en Muziek

Wagenaar, Bernard   Ballou; Claman; Coulthard; Pentland
Wagenaar, Johan   Appeldoorn
Wagner, Johanna   Sabinin
Wagner, Richard   Bronsart; Viardot
Wagner-Régeny, Rudolf   Klinkova
Wales – Royal National Eisteddfod   Williams, G.
Wallenstein, Alfred   Warren
Walsworth, Ivor   Oram
Walter, Bruno   Mahler
Walther, Johann Gottfried   ix, x
WANDALL, TEKLA GRIEBEL   1899
WANG, QIANG   xvi
Ward, Clara   Coates
Warlock, Peter   Poston
Warren, Raymond   Farrell

Warsaw
    Academy of Music [Akademia Muzyczna im. Fryderyka Chopin]
        (formerly Conservatory; State Higher School of Music)
        Bacewicz; Bruzdowicz; Dziewulska; Klechniowska; Kunkel; Lara;
        Ptaszyńska; Sikora
    Polish Chamber Orchestra [Sinfonia Varsovia]   Coates, G.
    Polish Radio electronic music studios   Zielińska
    Polish Radio Orchestra   Bacewicz
    Radio Warsaw   Rampazzi
    University of Warsaw   Bacewicz
    Warsaw Autumn, International Festival of Contemporary
        Music [Warszawska Jesień, Międzynarodowy Festiwal Muzyki
        Współczesnej]   Bulterijs; Coates, G.; Zielińska
Washington [state]
    University of Washington [Seattle]   Anderson, R.; Thome
    Washington State University [Pullman]   Bakke
Washington, DC
    American University   Ballou
    Archive of American Folk Song, Library of Congress
        Crawford
    Catholic University of America   Abejo; Lee, C.
    Chamber Music Society of Washington   Howe
    Festival of American Women Composers   1925; Hier
    Howard University   Moore, D. R.
    John F. Kennedy Center for the Performing Arts   1985
    Lincoln Concert Hall   Lang, M. R.
    National Symphony Orchestra   Howe
    Opera America   Hays
    Smithsonian Institute   Martin
    Trinity College   Ivey
    White House   1963; Ballou
Washington, Dinah   Grever
Washington University   see St Louis
Waters, Horace   1864; Parkhurst
Way, Brenda   Larsen
Weber, Carl Maria von   Amalie
Webern, Anton   xvi
Weidig, Adolf   Barnett; Crawford; Fine; James
Weidman, Charles   Fine
Weigl, Karl   Weigl
Weimar
    court at   Anna Amalia (ii)
    Hoftheater   Smyth
    Liebhabertheater   Wolf
    Noble Girls' Institute   Sabinin
Weinberg, Henry   Berl
Weiner, Richard   Ptaszyńska
Weininger, Otto   xviii
Weinrich, Carl   Jolas
Weinzweig, John   Allik; Beecroft
WEIR, JUDITH   xvii; 1990; Milstein
Weisgall, Hugo   Berl; Zaimont
Weissenhorn [Germany] – Gymnasium   Woll
Weissweiler, Eva   xii
Weldon, Fay   Sekacz
WELDON, GEORGINA   xii
Wellesley College [Wellesley, MA]   Salter; Stocker; Vercoe; Zallman
Wellesz, Egon   1930; Glanville-Hicks; Gow; Hier; LeFanu; Williams, G.
Wellington
    New Zealand Ballet Company   Franchi
    Victoria University of Wellington   Bibby; Bowater; Fisher;
        Freed; McLeod; Whitehead
Welsh National Opera   see Cardiff
Werfel, Franz   Mahler
Wesley, Samuel   Mounsey
Wesleyan University [Middletown, CT]   Benary
WESTENHOLZ, SOPHIA MARIA   1806
Western Australia – University of Western Australia [Nedlands]
    Fowler
Western University [Quindaro, KS]   Jessye
White, Donald   Santos Ocampo
WHITE, MAUDE VALÉRIE   xiii; 1879; Lehmann
WHITE, RUTH   xv
WHITEHEAD, GILLIAN   xvi
Whitney, Myron W.   1887; Lang, M. R.
Whittaker, William G.   Glatz
Widmer, Ernst   Nogueira
Widor, Charles-Marie   Boulanger, N.; Leleu; Netzel
Wiechowicz, Stanisław   Moszumańska-Nazar
Wieland, Christoph Martin   Anna Amalia (ii)
Wieniawski, Henryk   Poldowski
Wieprecht, Wilhelm   Mayer

Wiesbaden – Internationale Maifestspiele   Matuszczak
Wildberger, Jacques   Baader-Nobs
Wilhartitz, Adolph   ix
WILHELMINA, Princess of Prussia   1740
Wilhelmina, Queen of the Netherlands   1898; Rennes
Wilks, Norman   Blomfield Holt
Willan, Healey   Blomfield Holt; James
Williams, Burley   see WILLIAMS, MARY LOU
WILLIAMS, GRACE   1930, 1966; Maconchy
WILLIAMS, MARY LOU   1969, 1990
Williams, Winn   see WILLIAMS, MARY LOU
Williamsburg [VA] – College of William and Mary   Bley
Willner, Arthur   Leiviskä
Wilson, George Balch   Clayton; Clement
Wilson, James   Kelly
Wilson, Robert Barclay   Kelly
Winchester [England] – Winchester Art College   Anderson, A.
Windsor [Ont.] – University of Windsor   Archer
Winge, Per   Lund, S.
Wingham, Thomas   Ellicott
Winkel Holm, Mogens   Lund, G.
Winneba [Ghana] – National Academy of Music   Kaminsky
Winnipeg [Manitoba] – Music Inter Alia   1977; Southam
Winter-Hjelm, Otto   Holmsen
Winterthur [Switzerland] – Musikschule und Conservatorium   Irman
Wisconsin – University of Wisconsin [Madison]   Hays; Ziffrin
Władisław, Prince of Poland   1625; Caccini, F.
Wolf, Ernst Wilhelm   Anna Amalia (ii); Westenholtz
WOLF, MARIA CAROLINA   Reichardt, J.
Wolff, Christian   Payne
Wolpe, Stefan   Franks Williams; Mamlok; Simons
Women Band Directors National Association [USA]   Van Appledorn
Women in Music [Denmark]   see Kvinder i Musik
Women in Music [UK]   1988; LeFanu; Martinez, O. de la
   Chard Festival of Women in Music   Alberga; Martinez, O. de la
Women's Music Festival/85   see Boston
Women's Philharmonic Society [USA]   Korn; Walker
Women's Social and Political Union (WSPU) [UK]   1911; Smyth
Wood, Charles   Boyle; Maconchy
Wood, Henry J.   1919; Clarke; Gipps; Howell
Woolf, Virginia   xvii
Workers' Educational Association [UK]   Richards
World Council of Churches   Telfer
World's Columbian Exposition   see Chicago
World Soundscape Project   see British Columbia
Wormser, André   Temple
Worshipful Company of Musicians [UK]   1983; Rainier

Wrocław – Academy of Music [Akademia Muzyczna im. Karola Lipińskiego we Wrocławiu] (formerly State High School of Music)   Krzanowska; Pstrokońska-Nawratil; Szajna-Lewandowska
Wuensch, Gerhard   Telfer
WUIET, CAROLINE   1786
Wuorinen, Charles   Clayton; Cory; Farrell
WURM, MARY J. A.   1898
Wykes, Robert   Oliveira; Samuel
Wyner, Yehudi   Berl

Xenakis, Iannis   Bofill Levi; Frykberg; Galás; McLean; Odăgescu; Oliveira
XIAO, SHUXIAN   Scherchen
Xiaolin, Tan   Qü
XOSROVIDUXT   8th century

Yale University [New Haven, CT]   Archer; Blaustein; Bruzdowicz; Cory; Diemer; Guraieb; Hagan; Hoover; Jacobs; McTee; Mekeel; Nogueira; Olivero; Payne; Schonthal; Semegen; Wolfe; Zallman
Yashiro, Akio   Konishi; Massumoto; Mori
Yellow Springs Institute [OH]   Benary
Yevlakhov, Orest Alexandrovich   Metallidi; Voronina
York [England] – University of York   1993; Bauld; Boyd; LeFanu; Olive; Usher
York University [North York, Ont.]   Louie

Zagreb – Croatian Music Institute [Hrvatski Glazbeni Zavod]   Pejačević
Zapiola, José   Zegers
Zaremba, Nikolay Ivanovich   Adayevskaya
Zawirski, M.   Jeske-Choińska-Mikorska
ZECHLIN, RUTH   1984, 1990
Zelenka, Karl   xii
Zelter, Carl Friedrich   Mendelssohn
Zemlinsky, Alexander   Mahler; Müller-Hermann
ZHUBANOVA, GAZIZA AKHMETOVNA   1962
ZIERITZ, GRETE VON   1928
ZIMMERMANN, AGNES   1868
ZUMSTEEG, EMILIE   1842
Zuqiang, Wu   Chen Yi
Zürich
   Frauenmusik   Capuis
   Konservatorium und Musikschule   Kubisch
ZWILICH, ELLEN TAAFFE   1975, 1983
Zwilich, Joseph   Zwilich
Zwolle [Netherlands] – conservatory   Hoenderdos; Marez Oyens